MW01381014

Fun Ways to Learn the Whole Story of Jesus and His Love

Learning to Love Like Jesus

Life and Lessons of Jesus Series

Creative Bible-Learning Activities for Children Ages 6-12

The buyer of this book may reproduce pages for classroom or home use.
Duplication for any other use is prohibited without written permission from David C. Cook Publishing Co.

Copyright © 1991 by Tracy Leffingwell Harrast. Published by David C. Cook Publishing Co.
Printed in the United States of America.

All puzzles and Bible activities are based on the NIV.

Scripture taken from the Holy Bible, New International Version, Copyright © 1973, 1978, 1984 International Bible Society.
Used by permission of Zondervan Bible Publishers.

Book Design by Tabb Associates
Cover Illustration by Gary Locke
Interior Illustrations by Anne Kennedy

THIS BOOK BELONGS TO:

Life and Lessons of Jesus Series

To My Children and Others Who Read This Book

Jesus loves you more than you can even imagine. He loves you when you're nice; He loves you when you're mean; and He loves you when you're sort of in between. He loves you all the time . . . no matter what. He loves everybody around you that much, too. And that's the way He wants you to feel about them.

Jesus wants you to care about people, forgive them, help them, and tell them how much He loves them. He even wants you to love people who are hard to love (sometimes they're the ones who need love most). Don't be afraid to let the love of Jesus go right through you to others.

—Tracy L. Harrast

Learning to Love Like Jesus

CONTENTS

A New Commandment

In John 13:34, 35, Jesus gave His disciples a new commandment to follow. They were to love each other as He loved them.

Make Heart-stamped Bible Verse Cards About Love

What You Need

- potato
- pencil
- plastic knife
- paintbrush
- red paint
- markers
- at least three index or blank recipe cards

What You Do

1. Cut the potato in half and draw a heart on the potato. Using the knife, carefully carve away the part of the potato around the heart.

2. Brush red paint on the heart and then press it on each card. Decorate the card.

3. Look up these Bible passages about love: Matthew 5:43-46; 22:37-39; and John 13:34-36. Write them on the cards.

Memorize these verses. Ask God to help you follow His commandment to love one another.

Make a Bible Verse Card Stand

What You Need

- clean, empty plastic detergent bottle
- ruler
- permanent marker
- scissors

Make a stand for your Bible Verse Cards. Put your verse cards about love on the stand and place it on your desk or dresser. As you get ready for school, pull a card out of the stand and practice memorizing that verse.

What You Do

1. Soak the bottle in warm water until the label peels off easily.

2. Poke a hole in the bottle about 3 inches from the top. Stick the scissors through the hole and cut off the top of the bottle.

3. Next, measure 4 inches from the bottom of the bottle and draw a line around the bottle. Cut the bottle along that line.

4. Draw slanted lines on the sides of the stand as shown. Draw a notch where the cards will sit, and then draw a straight line across the front. Cut along the lines.

5. Draw hearts on the front of the stand. Store your verse cards in the stand.

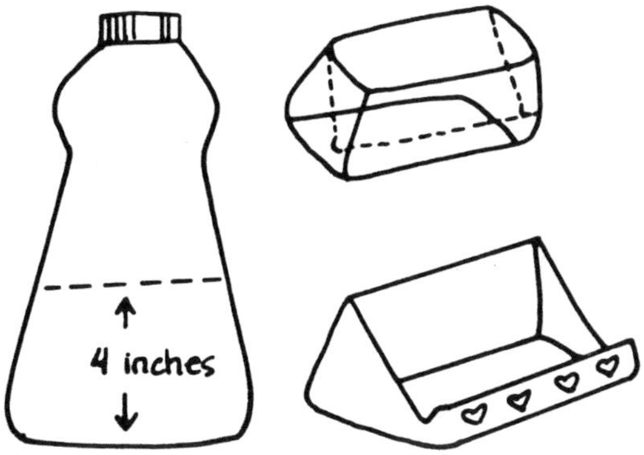

☐ *Draw a star in this box when you've read Matthew 5:43-46; 22:37-39; and John 13:34, 35.*

Make a Tin Punch Pie Plate

Here's another reminder to love one another as Jesus did. Follow these directions to make a tin punch pie plate of Jesus' new commandment.

What You Need

- 9-inch disposable aluminum pie plate
- newspaper
- pattern from this page (you can trace it or make a photocopy)
- masking tape
- a pushpin
- liquid shoe polish, any color
- silver duct tape
- paper clip

What You Do

1. Place the pie plate on a stack of newspapers. Next, tape the pattern from this page into the pie plate.
2. Carefully poke the pushpin through each dot of the pattern. Then remove the pattern and tape.
3. Dab shoe polish on the pie plate to make it look antique.
4. Use duct tape to attach a paper clip to the back for hanging.

The Golden Rule

In Luke 6:31, Jesus said, "Do to others as you would have them do to you." In other words, treat people the way you would want them to treat you. Some people call this the "golden rule." Make a golden ruler and practice treating others the way you would like to be treated.

Make a Golden Ruler

What You Need

- 12-inch ruler
- cardboard box
- gold spray paint, silver spray paint (or another color besides gold)
- alphabet macaroni
- glue
- scissors
- spray lacquer

What You Do

1. Lay the ruler inside the cardboard box. Spray paint the front of the ruler gold and let it dry. When the front is dry, turn the ruler over and spray paint the other side gold.
2. While the ruler is drying, use the macaroni alphabet letters to spell out "Do to others as you would have them do to you." Spray paint the letters silver or another color. Let them dry.
3. When both the ruler and letters are completely dry, place the letters on the ruler to get the correct spacing between words. Then glue each letter to the front of the ruler. Let the glue dry.
4. Copy the message below, cut it out, and glue it to the back of the ruler.
5. Spray both sides of the ruler with lacquer. Let dry.

How to Use Your Golden Ruler

As a family or with a group of friends, agree that for the next couple of days, all of you will treat others as you would like to be treated. To do this, think of how you would like to be treated or think of something that would make you happy, then secretly do it for someone else, and leave the ruler where that person can find it. Within 24 hours that person should do something for someone else. Even when you don't have the golden ruler, keep treating others the way you want to be treated.

☐ *Draw a star in this box when you've read Luke 6:31.*

Practice the Golden Rule

The Golden Rule is easy to remember but a lot harder to practice. Read each of these situations and think about ways to practice treating others as you would want to be treated.

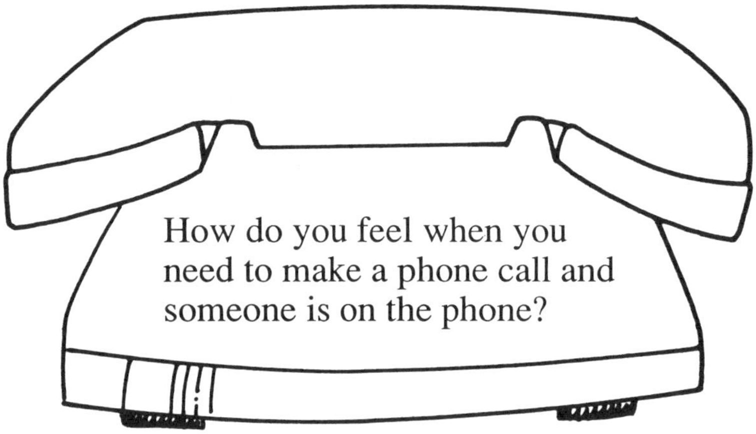

How do you feel when you need to make a phone call and someone is on the phone?

1. How can you practice the golden rule when you're talking on the phone and someone else wants to use it?

If you had a hard day and then got mad at your brother or sister, what would you want him or her to do? Yell at you? Tattle on you? Forgive you?

2. How can you practice the golden rule when someone gets angry at you?

There are two pieces of pie left. Your sister is ready to hand out the last two pieces of pie—one's big and the other's small. Which piece would you like her to offer you?

3. Suppose you're handing out the pieces of pie. According to the golden rule, which should you offer your sister?

How do you feel when your brother or sister borrows your things without asking?

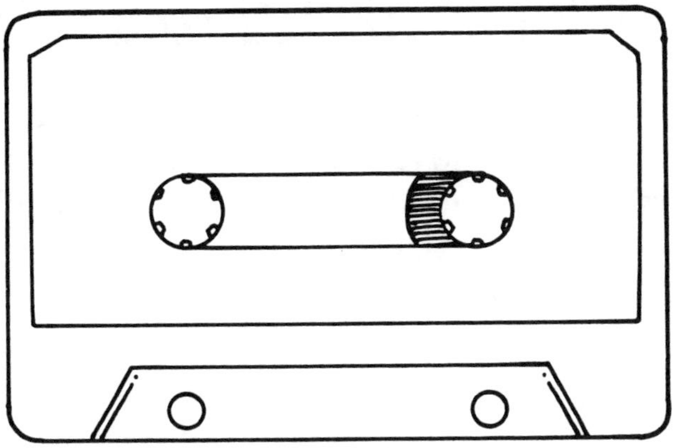

4. If you were practicing the golden rule, what would you do if you wanted to listen to your brother's tapes?

You're watching TV and your brother comes into the room. He's not interested in the show you're watching. What would you want him to do?

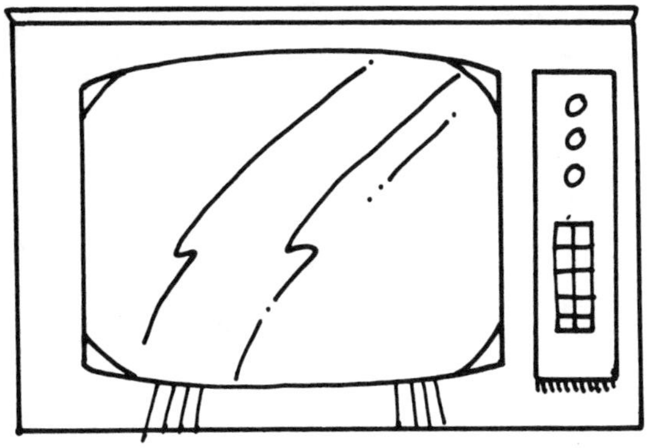

5. How would you practice the golden rule if your brother was watching a TV show you didn't like?

Give Warm Fuzzies

Some people describe a "warm fuzzy" as a feeling of being loved. *Make this "warm fuzzy" critter to give to someone. All you have to do is glue plastic eyes or felt eyes to a fuzzy pom-pom. Look for these materials in a craft store. Send a note along with your "warm fuzzy" that says how much you care for this person and what you like best about him or her.*

The Good Samaritan

In Luke 10:30-37, Jesus told a story in answer to a man's question. The man knew that God's law said to love God wholeheartedly and to love your neighbor as yourself. The man asked Jesus who his neighbor was, and Jesus told the story of the Good Samaritan. *Take the extra letter out of each word to read the story Jesus told.*

At mane woent froom Jerustalem tot Jjericho. Thievers atttacked hime, trore boff hist cloothes, sand lefst shim hoalf dread.

Ar pariest hoappened toe comet theat sway mand wohen dhe staw tehe shurt manx, her pastsed bye thim lon ther mother stide wof them troad.

At Lrevite alsos crame bay, slooked bat ther shurt mant, dand spassed bey pon thex bother stide.

Bute la Sqamaritan (ar manc froom aa sneighboring countlry, whosee speople wered thated byr thes Jewsz) crame swhere thev shurt mani wase, land wahen hev sawd thim, hbe lhad crompassion fort fhim.

Thes Sbamaritan wentl tov himo, clfeaned ande bandoaged mhis wrounds, agnd sput bhim pon lhis sown ranimal. Hew brorught thes sinjured mane tov ran minn, band stook caret lof fhim.

Theb snext dray wahen sthe Slamaritan leeft, hhe grave them binnkeeper wsome mnoney rand staid, "Trake scare cof hirm; kand whatlever moret youv spends, I'lll pray youv whern Id treturn."

Theno Jresus masked at mane, "Whirch lof thez threet wast ar nelighbor tot thew victims?" Thec mant fanswered, "Thew bone whot slhowed mercry tox hime." Jesust staid, "Goe hand dot them samet."

☐ *Draw a star in this box when you've read the story in Luke 10:30-37.*

Tell the Good Samaritan Story with Puppets

Jesus told the story of the Good Samaritan to help people understand that loving your "neighbor" means caring for people no matter who they are. *Make some egg puppets and use the puppets to perform this story.*

What You Need

- seven hard-boiled eggs
- waterproof markers

What You Do

1. *Rinse and dry the cool boiled eggs.*
2. *Use the markers to draw faces on the eggs. See the illustrations for the kinds of faces to draw for the characters in the story.*
3. *Move the eggs around as you tell the story of the Good Samaritan.*

Two Robbers

The Victim

The Levite

The Priest

The Samaritan

The Innkeeper

Love Your Neighbor As Yourself

In Matthew 22:37-39, Jesus said the first and greatest commandment was to love the Lord God with all your heart, soul, and mind. And He said the second is to love your neighbor as you love yourself. Your neighbors aren't just the people who live on your street. A neighbor can be anyone you may meet. Try to make a new friend each day. Make this Buddy-a-Day calendar and have fun making new friends.

Buddy-a-Day Calendar

Number this calendar to match the month that's coming up next. Begin this activity on the first day of the month. Each day try to get to know someone you haven't talked with very much in the past. Write that person's name on the square for that date, or have the person autograph that square. By the end of the month, you'll be pleased to see how many new "neighbors" you've met.

SUNDAY	MONDAY	TUESDAY	WEDNESDAY	THURSDAY	FRIDAY	SATURDAY

☐ *Draw a star in this box when you've read Matthew 22:37-39.*

Include Others

Suppose your mom said you could invite some people over to spend the night. Who would you invite? Your friends, of course—who else is there to invite? In Luke 14:12-14, Jesus said that there are other people to include, people who might not be at all like you. People who belong to the out group and can't ever return the invitation. But that's what loving Jesus is all about—including everyone, no matter what. Here is a fun idea for an "in" party—that's a party in which you **in**clude other people you usually don't hang around with.

Plan a Cookie Pizza Party

First get you parents' permission to have a party. Then plan a cookie pizza party for after school. Invite your friends as well as people who don't usually get invited to parties. Introduce them to your friends.

When each guest arrives, give him or her a fruit to prepare for the pizza. God will bless you for having the courage to reach out to lonely people.

What You Need

- sugar cookie dough (homemade or purchased)
- cream cheese frosting (homemade or purchased)
- different fruit of your choice (at least one kind for each guest)
- knives for slicing fruit
- grown-up help

What You Do

1. Preheat the oven to the temperature in the recipe on the package. Spread the cookie dough onto a lightly buttered pizza pan. Bake until golden (see the recipe or package for the amount of time. Check often).
2. When the dough is done baking, let it cool. Then spread a thin layer of cream cheese frosting on the cookie crust.
3. Let everyone arrange their slices of fruits on it however they wish.
4. Cut the "pizza" into thin slices and enjoy eating.

☐ *Draw a star in this box when you've read Luke 14:12-14.*

The Least of These

In Matthew 25:31-46, Jesus talks about a scene that will take place in the future, after He comes back for His followers. But there's something we can learn from this passage and practice right now, before Jesus comes back. It has to do with our attitude and what we do for people who have needs. *Correct the spacing to read this story. The first line is done for you.*

The|S on|of|God|w ill|sit|o n|a|thro ne|and|sa y|to|so me|o f|the|pe ople|“Co me, youwho areble ssedby MyFa ther, inhe ritak ingdo mth atwas prep aredfo ryouwhe nthewo rldwa screated. Iwashun gryand youga veMesome thingtoe at. Iwa sthir styand youga veMe som ethingtod rink. Iwasas tran gerand youin vitedM ein. Iw asna kedand youclo thed Me. Iwa ssicka ndyo uloo keda fterMe. Iwa sinpri son an dyo uca metoMe.”

The ntho sewho areri ghte ouswi llsay, “Whe ndidwe dotho sethings fo rYou?” TheKi ngwi llan swer, “Whe nyo udid itfo rthe leasto fMy bro thers, yo udidi tfo rMe.”

Je sussa idthe ot her swillbe pun ishe dfor nothelping Himwhe nHe wasin need. They’llsay, “Whe ndi dwe seeYo uin nee dand wedi dn’thel pYou?” He’llsay, “Whe nyoudi dn’the lpthelea stof Mybro thers, youdi dn’thel pMe.” Je sussaid tho sewho didn’thelpHi mwillg otoe ver lasti ngpu nish ment,bu tthose whowe reri ghteous willgot olive wit hGo dfo rever.

☐ *Draw a star in this box when you've read Matthew 25:31-46.*

Help Others and Help Jesus

Jesus said that if you're helping people in need, you're helping Him. There is plenty for you to do even though you're young and even if you don't have a lot of money. Here are some ideas.

- Pray and ask God to show you people who need your help.
- Ask your parents if your family can contribute food to a food pantry or to a church group that feeds the poor. Maybe your family could take a meal to a family in which the parents are out of work. Ask if you can give away clothes you no longer wear or buy some new ones for people who need them.
- Ask your Sunday school teacher or another church leader if your class can plan a project to help people who are poor, sick, or lonely.
- You might plan a short visit to a classmate who has been sick. Or you could send a card to someone in the hospital.

Make a Bed Table for Someone Sick

What You Need

- a strong box that is wider than a person's lap
- scissors or knife
- Con-Tact paper
- goodies for the box
- grown-up help if needed

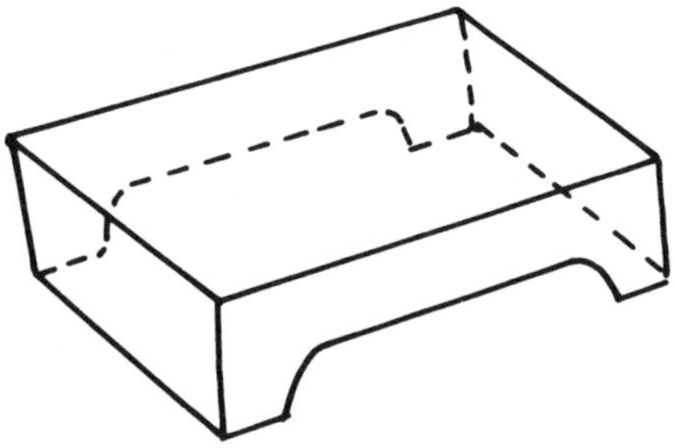

What You Do

1. Using either the scissors or the knife, cut away parts of the sides as shown in the illustration. You want the box to be able to fit over a person's lap. If it is too hard for you to cut the box yourself, ask a grown-up for help.

2. Cover the box with Con-Tact paper.

3. To make the table an extra special surpise, turn it upside down and line it with tissue paper. Then fill it with different get-well goodies. For example, lemons for making hot lemonade, comic books or magazines, puzzle or activity books, homemade stationery, and a homemade get-well card.

Jesus Washed His Disciples' Feet

In John 13:1-17, Jesus set an example of serving others. In Bible times, because the roads were dusty and dirty, servants washed the feet of guests when they entered the host's home. When the disciples came to an upper room for the Passover supper, there was no servant to wash their feet. And certainly none of them would stoop to do a servant's work and wash feet. That's when Jesus began His lesson about serving. *Read each word backward. Then color the picture.*

sA eht revossaP reppus saw gnieb devres, suseJ koot ffo siH retuo sehtolc, depparw a lewot dnuora siH tsiaw, dna deruop retaw ni a egral lwob. nehT eH detrats gnihsaw eht 'selpicsid teef dna gniyrd meht no eht lewot taht saw depparw dnuora miH.

nehW ti saw nomiS s'reteP nrut, eh t'ndid tnaw suseJ ot hsaw sih teef. suseJ dias, "sselnU I hsaw uoy, uoy evah on trap htiw eM." reteP dias, "toN tsuj ym teef tub ym sdnah dna ym daeh sa llew." suseJ dias enoemos ohw sah dah a htab ylno sdeen sih teef dehsaw ot eb yletelpmoc naelc. eH dias, "uoY era naelc, hgouht ton yreve eno fo uoy." eH dias taht esuaceb eH wenk saduJ toiracsI saw gniog ot nrut tsniaga miH dna llet dab elpoep erehw ot dnif miH.

drawretfA, suseJ desserd dna tas nwod niaga. eH deksa, "oD uoy dnatsrednu tahw I evah enod rof uoy? uoY llac eM rehcaeT dna droL, dna ylthgir os rof taht si tahw I ma. woN taht I, ruoy droL dna rehcaeT, evah dehsaw ruoy teef, uoy osla dluohs hsaw eno s'rehtona teef. I evah tes uoy na elpmaxe taht uoy dluohs od sa I evah enod rof uoy. I llet uoy eht hturt, on tnavres si retaerg naht sih retsam, ron si a regnessem retaerg naht eht eno ohw tnes mih. woN taht uoy wonk eseht sgniht, uoy lliw eb desselb fi uoy od meht."

Show that you're willing to serve, and offer to give your mom or dad a foot massage. Rub lotion on the feet. Your parents will enjoy the extra treat, especially after a hard day.

☐ *Draw a star in this box when you've read John 13:1-17.*

Jump at the Chance to Serve God

Jesus had a lot to say about serving others. In Matthew 20:25-28; Mark 9:33-35, and Mark 10:43-45 Jesus gave a different defintion about being great or being first. Jesus said that true greatness comes through serving others. This project will remind you to "hop" right to it when it comes to serving God.

What You Need

- 4 pipe cleaners (chenille wires)
- index cards, cut in half

What You Do

1. Bend the pipe cleaners into a bunny shape as shown in the illustration. Also bend the bunny's paws so they hold the cards.

2. Take time to pray and ask the Lord to show you different ways you can serve others. As you think of some ideas, write them on the cards. When you do serve the Lord in one of the ways, take that card out of the bunny's paws. To keep the bunny's paws full, keep asking God to help you find ways to serve your family, friends, neighbors, and other people you know.

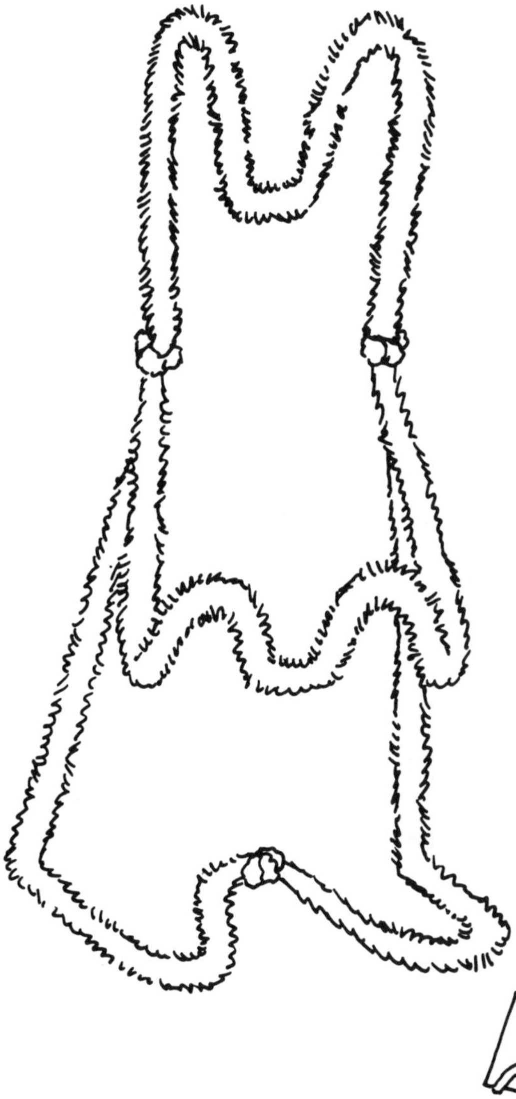

☐ *Draw a star in the box when you've read Matthew 20:25-28; Mark 9:33-35; 10:43-45.*

The Forgiven Servant Who Didn't Forgive

One time Peter came to Jesus and asked Him how many times he should forgive someone. Jesus then told this story about true forgiveness. *To read this story from Matthew 18:22-25, change the letters so E is A and A is E. Change them so O is U and U is O.*

Tha kingdum uf haevan is lika e king whu hed e sarvent thet uwad him milliums of dullers. Tha sarvent cuoldn't pey su tha king wes guing tu heva tha men end his femily suld intu slevary. Ell uf tha men's pussassiuns wara tu ba suld, elsu. Bot tha sarvent baggad tha king tu ba petiant with him end seid ha wuold pey it ell. Tha king falt surry fur tha sarvent, furgeva him, end seid ha didn't heva tu pey.

Whan tha sarvent laft tha king, tha sarvent grebbad e men by tha thruet whu uwad him moch lass then ha hed uwad tha king. Tha sarvent damendad thet tha men pey right than. Tha men baggad tha sarvent just es tha sarvent hed baggad tha king. Bot tha sarvent hed tha men pot in jeil.

Whan tha king haerd ebuot it, ha wes vary engry baceosa ha hed shuwn marcy tu tha sarvent bot tha sarvent hedn't shuwn marcy tu uthars. Tha king sant tha men tu ba turtorad ontil ha hed peid avarything ha hed uwad. Jasos seid this is whet uor haevanly Fethar will du tu os if wa dun't furgiva uor bruthars frum uor haerts.

Unscramble why we should forgive others:

OGD ASH ROFVIGNE SU.

☐ *Draw a star in this box when you've read Matthew 18:22-35.*

Erase Unforgiveness from Your Heart

When you are alone, use a pencil to write inside this heart the names of people you need to forgive. Pray and ask God to get rid of your hurt and anger. When your bad feelings toward each person are gone, erase that person's name off the list until all of the unforgiveness is gone from your heart.

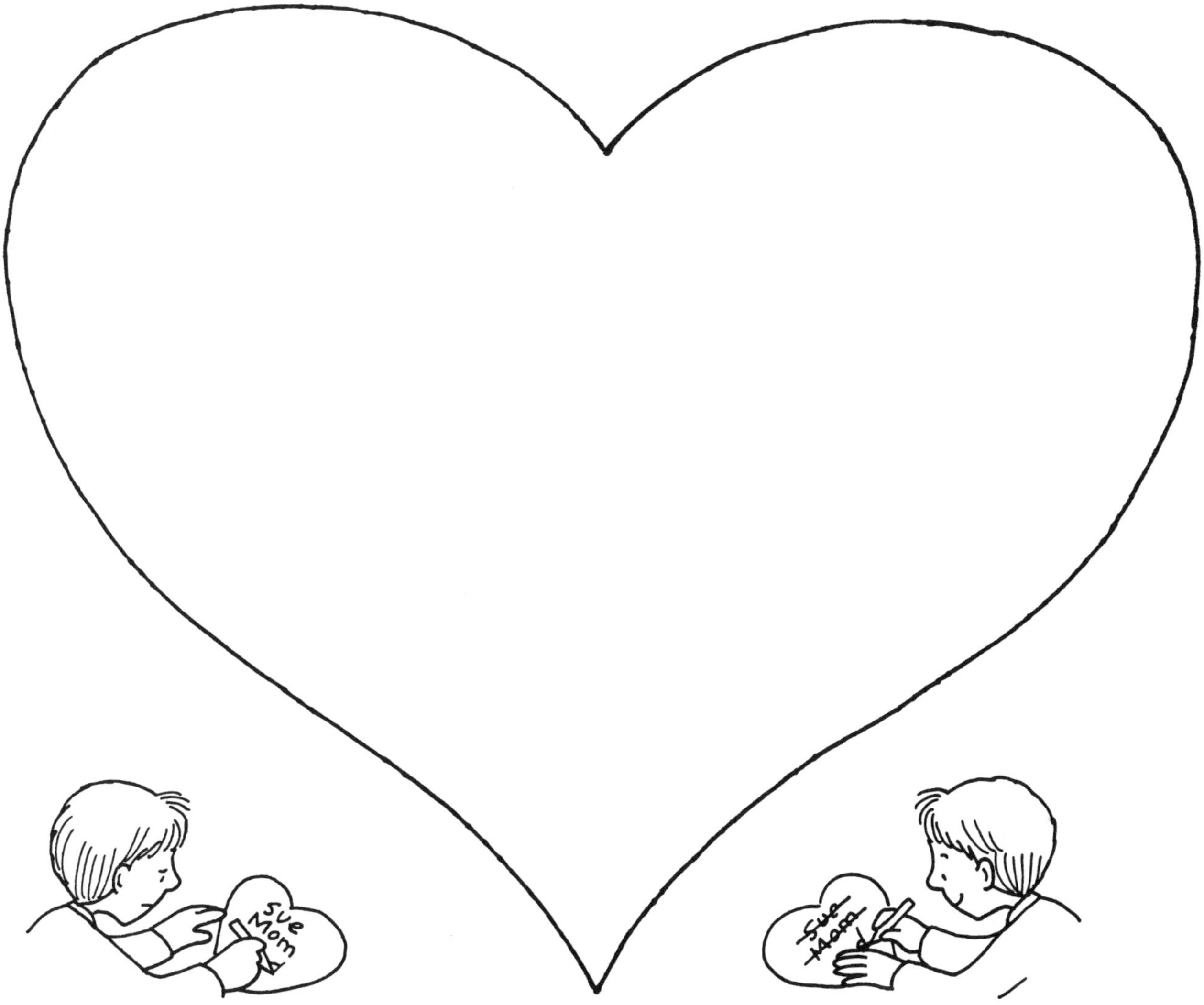

Unlimited Forgiveness

Simon Peter asked Jesus how many times he should forgive his brother who sinned against him. Peter suggested seven times, but Jesus answered seventy times seven. Now, Jesus didn't mean 490 times and that's it—no more forgiveness. He wanted Peter to understand that even if someone keeps doing things that hurt you, God wants you to keep forgiving.

Find the Path to Forgiveness

Lightly draw a line along the path that runs from the angry kids to where they have made up with each other. Vowels along the correct path will help complete the sentences at the bottom of the page. Write the first vowel in the blank of the first sentence and continue until all the sentences are completed.

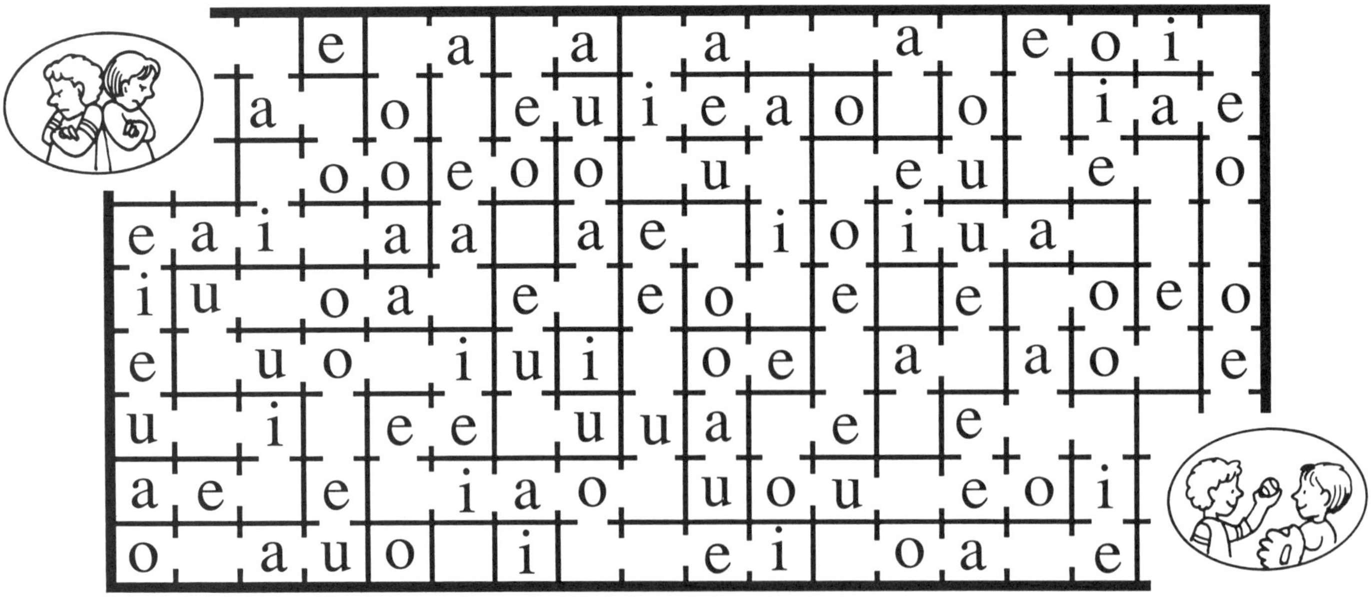

1. Pr__y f__r G__d t__ t__k__ __w__y y__ __r __nf__rg__v__n__ss.

2. Th__nk __b__ __t why th__ p__rs__n d__d wh__t sh__ d__d.

3. T__lk __b__ __t th__ pr__bl__m wh__n y__ __'r__ b__th c__lm.

4. Try t__ l__v__ th__ p__rs__n l__k__ G__d d__ __s.

☐ *Draw a star in this box when you've read Matthew 18:21, 22.*

Make Up Quickly

In Matthew 5:23-26, Jesus said if someone was bringing a gift to God at the altar and remembered that someone was mad at him or her, that person should go and make things right before worshiping God. Jesus said it is important to make things right with someone quickly. Later Paul wrote in Ephesians 4:26 that you shouldn't let the sun go down while you're still angry. Make this setting sun and hang it in your room to remind you to make up quickly with people.

Make a Setting Sun

What You Need

- twine
- scissors
- plastic wrap
- glue
- paper cup
- orange, gold, or red glitter
- paper plate

What You Do

1. Unwind some twine and measure it out according to this picture. You want enough twine to outline the sun and its rays. When you have the correct length, cut the twine.
2. Lay plastic wrap over this page.
3. Pour two or three tablespoons of glue into the cup. Dip the piece of twine in the glue.
4. Pour some glitter on the paper plate, and lay the twine in it. Turn the string over so both sides are coated.
5. Next, carefully place the glitter-covered twine on the plastic, in the shape of the sun.
6. When the twine design is completely dry, carefully lift the plastic and hold it over a trash can. Gently remove the plastic, letting extra glitter fall into the trash can.
7. Use thread and a thumbtack or pushpin to hang your twine design from the ceiling.

☐ *Draw a star in this box when you've read Matthew 5:23-26 and Ephesians 4:26.*

Love Everyone . . .

In Matthew 5:44-47 and Luke 6:32-35, Jesus said to love your enemies, to do good to those who hate you, and to pray for those who are mean to you on purpose. God makes the sun rise on both the evil people and the good. He sends rain on both the just and the unjust. He said you shouldn't just love those who love you; you should love everyone.

Love All of Your Classmates at School

•On the squares below, write the names of all of your classmates under the faces. Next, add hair, glasses, and other details to make the faces look like your classmates.

•Now think about each person and ask yourself, "Does this person know that I like him or her?" If you can honestly answer yes, draw a heart around that person's head.

•Ask the Lord to help you love everyone in your class—even people who are hard to love. Look for things to admire about each person. Be nice to each person.

•As you genuinely learn to like each person and you show it enough that the person knows you like him or her by your actions, draw a heart around each of the other faces.

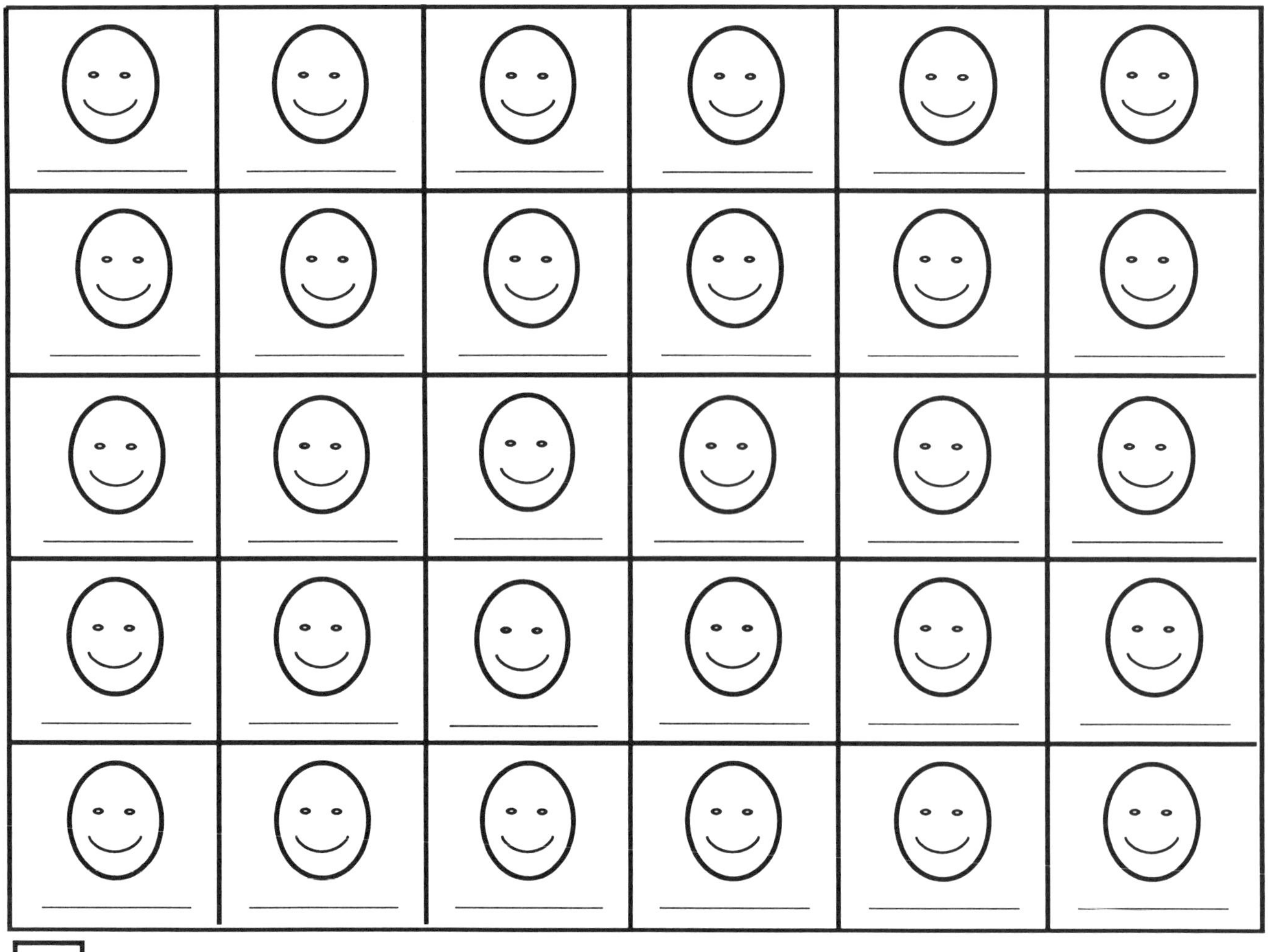

☐ *Draw a star in this box when you've read Matthew 5:44-47; Luke 6:32-35.*

The Good News

It's good news to know that God forgives our sins and we can live with Him because Jesus died for our sins and came back to life. The greatest way to show love for people is to tell them about Jesus.

Before you can tell this good news, there's one important question you have to answer: Have you trusted Jesus to forgive you and allow you to live forever with God? You can trust Jesus by praying a prayer like this:

Dear God,

I've done wrong things, and I'm sorry. Please forgive me. I believe Jesus died for my sins and that He came back to life.

I trust You to forgive my sins. I want to follow You all of my life. Thank You for forgiving me and letting me live with You forever because of Jesus. I love You.

In Jesus' name. Amen.

Now that you believe in Jesus, you have some good news to tell everyone. In Mark 16:15, Jesus told His followers to do the same. Here is one way you can tell a friend about Jesus.

Personalize a Bible for a Friend

What You Need

- paperback Bible
- piece of stationery
- picture of yourself
- pen or pencil
- wrapping paper
- gluestick

What You Do

1. Save your money and buy an inexpensive Bible for your friend.
2. When you have a Bible, cut a piece of stationery to fit inside the front cover.
3. Glue your picture to the piece of stationery and write a letter telling your friend how much you like reading the Bible and learning about Jesus. Also tell your friend that you know Jesus loves him or her and that God will forgive your friend's sins so he or she can go to heaven if your friend trusts Jesus as the only way. Offer to pray with your friend about it.
4. Gift wrap the Bible and give it to your friend.

☐ *Draw a star in this box when you've read Mark 16:15.*

Jesus Ate with Sinners

In Jesus' day, the Pharisees looked down on people they considered "sinners." The Pharisees thought they were better than everyone else because they strictly followed God's laws—and even added some of their own to follow. They would never dream of eating with these so-called sinners. Jesus, however, had a different opinion. In Matthew 9:10-13, Jesus and the disciples were having dinner with these "sinners," when the Pharisees asked why Jesus ate with these kind of people. Jesus said that He didn't come for people who thought they were good enough, but He came to encourage sinners to come to Him.

Jesus doesn't want us to look down our noses at people who don't follow Him or people who are really different from us. He wants us to love them and show them His love, too.

Make a Funny Nose

A reminder that it's silly to to be snooty to people.

What You Need

- 6 slices of white bread
- white school glue
- 1/2 teaspoon dishwashing liquid
- water
- toothpick
- paintbrush and paint
- newspaper
- lacquer
- two 24-inch pieces of twine or ribbon
- scissors
- mirror

What You Do

1. Tear the crusts off the bread and feed them to the birds.
2. Crumble the rest of the bread into tiny pieces in a bowl. Add 6 teaspoons of glue and 1/2 teaspoon dishwashing liquid.
3. Stir with a spoon until mixed. Then mix the dough with your hands until it isn't sticky. If it's too dry, add a few more drops of glue. If it's too sticky, add part of another slice of bread.
4. Shape the dough to fit loosely on your nose (it will shrink a little as it dries). Shape it to make your nose look extra long. Turn it up at the end. Use the toothpick to poke a small hole on each side of the nose for the strings.
5. When your funny nose is finished, paint it with a mixture of 4 tablespoons of glue and 4 tablespoons of water. This will help prevent cracking.
6. When the nose is completely dry, paint it wild colors. Let it dry and spray it with lacquer.
7. Tie a piece of twine or ribbon through each hole. Place the nose on your face and tie the twine or ribbons behind your head. You're ready to show how silly it is to be snooty.

☐ *Draw a star in this box when you've read Matthew 9:10-13.*

The Speck and the Plank

Have you ever noticed that it's very easy to see other people's faults, but it's hard to see our faults and sins even when our faults and sins are much bigger than theirs? In Matthew 7:3-5 and Luke 6:41, 42, Jesus talked about the same thing, comparing a speck of sawdust to a plank. Jesus asked His listeners why they look at a speck of sawdust in another person's eye, but they don't notice the plank in their own eyes. He asked how a person could say, "Brother, let me pull out the speck that's in your eye" when that person can't even see the board that's in his own eye. Jesus called this kind of person a "hypocrite" (someone who pretends to be one thing, but actually is something else). Jesus' message to this kind of person: "First take the plank out of your eye, and then you will see clearly to remove the speck from your brother's eye."

Draw a Cartoon

Draw yourself with a board in your eye trying to help someone with a speck in his eye.

☐ *Draw a star in this box when you've read Matthew 7:3-5; Luke 6:41, 42.*

Don't Judge

In Matthew 7:1, 2 and Luke 6:37, Jesus said not to judge. That means we shouldn't condemn people like a judge in a courtroom might do. Jesus said, "Don't judge, and you won't be judged. Don't condemn, and you won't be condemned. Forgive, and you'll be forgiven." One reason why we can't judge other people very well is that we don't know what's going on. It's hard to see to the heart of the matter. In I Samuel 16:7, God told Samuel that man looks on the outward appearance, but the Lord looks at the heart.

We Can't Judge Because It's Hard to See the Heart

Let's imagine that this kid is "judging" the situations. How do you think she sees each situation? What do you think is going on? *Find the hidden heart on each person this kid is judging. When you're done, look at the bottom of page 27 to see what the real circumstances were.*

1. Find the heart of the pastor entering the liquor store.

2. Find the heart of the man hitting his son.

3. Find the heart of the girl sticking a doll in her purse at the store.

4. Find the hearts of the girls who look like they're gossiping.

The Real Circumstances

1. The pastor's car broke down near the liquor store and he went in to call his wife.
2. The man was helping his son practice a scene from the school play.
3. The girl brought her own doll to the store to see what size clothes to buy for it.
4. The girls were talking about how happy the other girl would be when she found out about the surprise party they were planning for her.

☐ *Draw a star in this box when you've read Matthew 7:1, 2 and Luke 6:37.*

Make a Pointing Finger Mobile

When you point a finger at someone else, what do you have pointing back at you? Three fingers! When we criticize other people, we are sometimes more guilty than they are. Next time you start thinking about what's wrong with someone else, stop and see what *you* need to work on instead.

Make a pointing finger mobile to remind you that three fingers are pointing at you when you point at someone else.

What You Need

- poster board scraps
- markers
- scissors
- glue
- leftover sewing decorations (sequins, gold cord, etc.)
- paper hole punch
- twine or ribbon
- two coat hangers
- grown-up help

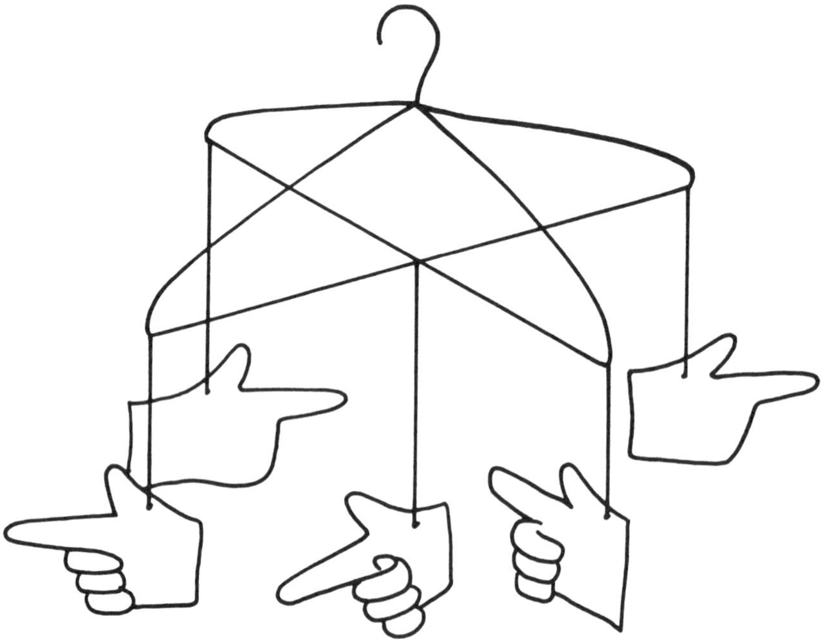

What You Do

***1.** With a marker, trace your hand five times on pieces of poster board. Cut out the handprints, and draw details like fingernails on the hands. If you'd like, glue on the sewing decorations for jewelry.*
***2.** Punch a hole at the bottom of the thumb of each handprint.*
***3.** Make the handprints look like they are pointing by bending the middle finger, ring finger, and little finger where the knuckles would be.*
***4.** Bend two coat hangers into the shape that's shown in the illustration.*
***5.** Tie the handprints so they dangle from the four corners and middle of the mobile.*
***6.** Hang the mobile by tying a thread from the hook at the top of the mobile.*

The Two Men at the Temple

In Luke 18:9-14, Jesus told a story about two men. One was a proud religious leader (called a "Pharisee"); the other was a humble man who knew he was a sinner. As you read this story, think about this: Are you more like the proud, religious leader or the humble man? *To read the story, change each letter to the letter that follows it in the alphabet. Change the letter Z to A.*

Idrtr rzhc svn ldm vdms sn sgd sdlokd sn opzx. Nmf vzr z Ogzqhrdd; sgd nsgdq z szw bnkkdbsnq. Sgd Ogzqhrdd rsnnc zmc oqzxdc zants ghlrdke. Gd rzhc, "Fnc, H sgzmj Xnt sgzs H zl mns khjd nsgdqr—bgdzsdqr zmc duhkcndqr—nq dudm khjd sghr szw bnkkdbsnq. H cn fnnc sghmfr khjd ezrshmf zmc fhuhmf z sdmsg ne dudqxsghmf H nvm sn sgd bgtqbg."

Sgd szw bnkkdbsnq vzr snn zrgzldc ne ghr rhmr sn khes ghr dxdr sn Fnc. Gd ghs ghr bgdrs zmc rzhc, "Fnc, okdzrd enqfhud ld dudm sgntfg H cnm's cdrdqud hs. H'l z rhmmdq."

Idrtr rzhc sgd szw bnkkdbsnq vzr enqfhudm ats sgd Ogzqhrdd vzrm's. Zmxnmd vgn oteer ghlrdke to vhsg oqhcd vhkk ad gtlakdc zmc gd vgn gtlakdr ghlrdke vhkk ad khesdc to sn khud vhsg Fnc.

☐ *Draw a star in this box when you've read Luke 18:9-14.*

Blessed Are the Peacemakers

In Matthew 5:9, Jesus said that peacemakers are blessed because they will be called the children of God. What does it mean to be a peacemaker? A peacemaker is someone who helps others get along. A peacemaker doesn't look for trouble or pick fights. A peacemaker settles arguments fairly and forgives others. Are you a peacemaker? *Unscramble these words to discover more traits of a peacemaker. Circle the ones that describe you.*

1. SOED ONT GHIFT ______________________________
2. HEPLS OTHRES EGT LOAGN ______________________________
3. SPERECTS HTORES ______________________________
4. HOSWS VOLE ______________________________
5. SERAC OHW THOERS EELF ______________________________
6. SKAEPS NIKDYL ______________________________
7. TASYS LACM ______________________________

Stay As "Cool As a Cucumber"

Have you ever heard the expression "cool as a cucumber"? It means that a person doesn't let his or her temper get hot. When you feel yourself getting angry, try to calm down first. Take a deep breath and when you breathe out, ask God to help you be a peacemaker and stay as cool as a cucumber.

Make a Cool Cucumber Man to Eat

What You Need

• cucumber • carrot • potato peeler • raisins • pimento slice or small slice of cheese

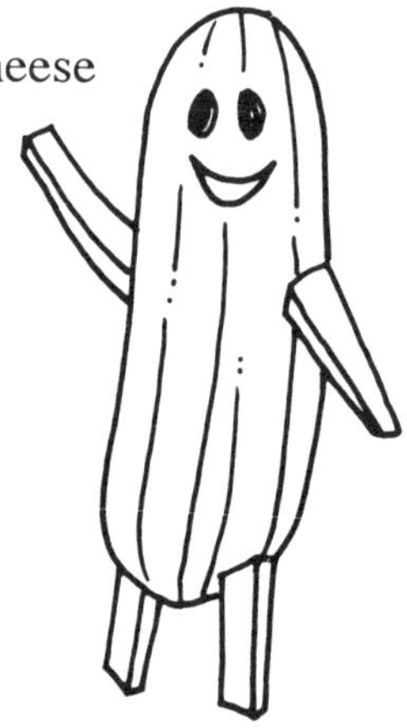

What You Do

1. Using a potato peeler, peel the cucumber and a carrot. Then cut holes in the cucumber for eyes, arms, and legs. Also cut a notch in the cucumber for a mouth

2. Cut the carrot into four sticks. Poke the carrot sticks into the arm and leg holes. Press raisins into the eyeholes. Push a pimento slice or a small piece of sliced cheese into the mouth slit.

☐ *Draw a star in this box when you've read Matthew 5:9.*

Be a Peacemaker for Your Country

A person who is a peacemaker tries to understand people and their situations. A peacemaker accepts others even if they are different. One way to be a peacemaker with people of other countries is to become a pen pal.

For free information about becoming a pen pal, you can write to the Student Letter Exchange at the address on the envelope below. Be sure to include your name, age, whether you're a boy or a girl, and a self-addressed, stamped envelope.

Watch Your Words

Jesus said that on the Judgment Day, we will have to explain every careless word we have said. He doesn't want us to be angry with people or call them names. If we really love Jesus and follow Him, we will love other people. What we say about them and to them shows whether we actually love them.

Make Sweet Words to Eat

Have you ever heard someone say that you may have to "eat your words"? It means that you might have to "swallow" things you've said for one reason or another. If your words are sweet, however, you won't mind eating them.

First, unscramble the letters to discover some good advice. Then follow the recipe to make these letters out of dough. Eat your words and share them with others.

PEKE OURY RDOWS EWSTE

Letter Dough Recipe

What You Need

- 1/2 cup softened margarine
- 1/2 cup peanut butter
- 1/2 cup granulated sugar
- 1/2 cup brown sugar
- 1/2 teaspoon vanilla
- 1 1/4 cups all-purpose sifted flour

What You Do

1. *Mix the ingredients together in a bowl to make a dough. Shape the dough into letters.*

2. *Spell out the good advice and then eat your words, sharing the letters with other people.*

☐ *Draw a star in this box when you've read Matthew 5:21, 22; 12:36, 37.*

Give and Lend

People are much more important than things. When you love people, you care more about them than your belongings. Jesus said we should give to people who ask and not say no to people who want to borrow things. Jesus also said not to ask for things back. When you give, it will be given back to you like a measuring cup that is pressed down, shaken together to make room for more, and running over.

Help Hoarding Horace Give

Horace has much more than he needs. Whenever you see an extra of anything in his room, circle it. Can you find ten extra objects for Horace to give away?

Do you have things you can give away? *Sort through your things to find items you don't need. Ask your parents if you can give these items to others who might like to have them.*

☐ *Draw a star in this box when you've read Matthew 5:40-42; and Luke 6:27-38.*

Go the Extra Mile

In Matthew 5:41, Jesus said that if someone makes you go a mile, you should go two. In other words, do more for that person than he or she asked.

Here's a practical way you can belong to the "extra mile club." *Every time one of your parents gives you a chore, do it right away and do a little more than they asked. Each time you do something they tell you to do, color in a square. If you "go the extra mile," color in another square. How many days will it take you to reach the extra mile club?*

☐ *Draw a star in this box when you've read Matthew 5:41.*

Marriage

Jesus wants you to love everyone, especially the person you marry. When a man and woman marry, God joins them together and they become one. It's not God's plan for people who marry to split up.

Even though you're young, and marriage seems far away, now is a good time to decide that when you grow up and if you get married, you'll always work at loving the person you married.

Make a Colored Rice Picture

One wedding custom is to throw rice at the bride and groom as they leave the church after their wedding. *Glue colored rice onto this heart to decorate it.*

What You Need

- one cup Minute Rice
- four paper cups
- water
- food coloring
- glue
- paper towels

What You Do

1. Pour 1/4 cup of rice into each cup. Add only enough water to dampen the rice. Stir.
2. Stir in two drops of food coloring into each cup.
3. Drain off any extra water. Dry the rice on paper towels.
4. Glue the rice to the heart.

☐ *Draw a star in this box when you've read Matthew 5:31, 32; 19:3-9; and Mark 10:2-12.*

Just for Fun— Pretend You're Married

It's fun to imagine what you'll be like when you grow up. Here is a chance to play using some fun props. As you play, think about how you might solve problems that come up in real families.

Make a Bride's Hair and Veil

What You Need

- medium-size paper bag
- sheer curtain or piece of netting
- scissors
- stapler and staples

What You Do

***1.** Cut a medium-size paper bag as shown in this illustration.*
***2.** Use one blade of a pair of scissors to curl the hair.*
***3.** Staple a piece of a sheer curtain or a piece of netting to the paper bag wig.*

Make Flowers for the Bride's Bouquet and the Groom's Boutonniere

What You Need

- facial tissue
- scissors
- wire or thread

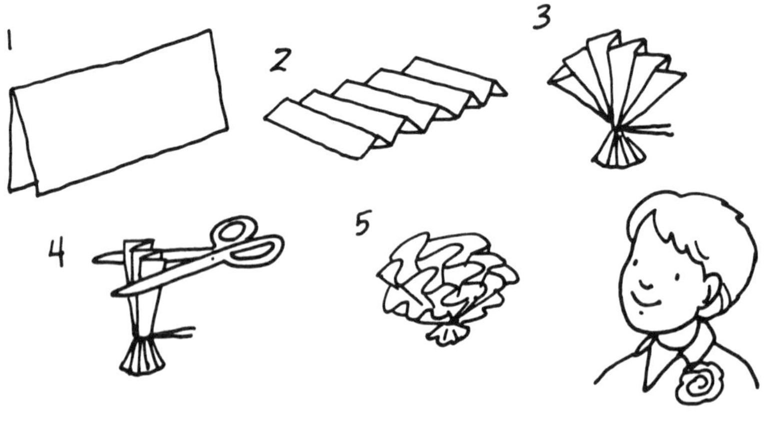

What You Do

***1.** Fold a facial tissue in half the long way. Make 1/2-inch pleats. Cut off the folded edge.*
***2.** Tie the center with wire or thread. Carefully pull apart the tissues.*

Make a Paper Beard

What You Need

- paper bag
- scissors
- string

What You Do

1. Cut a paper bag into a beard as shown in the illustration. Cut the slits to look like hair.
2. Curl the "hair" using one blade of the scissors.
3. Poke a hole on each side of the beard. Tie a string through each hole. Put the beard over your mouth, and use the strings to tie it around your head.

Make Poster Board People Puppets

What You Need

- poster boards
- pencil and markers
- scissors

What You Do

1. Draw a circle slightly bigger than your face. Cut it out.
2. Draw clothes on the poster boards. If you want to, decorate them with colored paper or fabric scraps and sewing decorations.

Jesus Gives You a New Heart

Have you asked Jesus to be your Savior and Lord? Do you know what that means? When you ask Jesus to be your Savior, you are trusting Him to save you from punishment you deserve after you die for the wrong things you've done. You are saying you believe He already took the punishment for you. When you ask Jesus to be your Lord, you're asking Him to lead you and you're promising to try to follow Him. If you haven't asked Jesus to be your Savior and Lord yet, please do it right now.

In Ezekiel 36:26 the Lord promised, "I will remove from you your heart of stone and give you a heart of flesh." A stony heart is cold and unfeeling. It's hard to love with that kind of heart. When you trust Jesus as your Savior and follow Him as your Lord, He gives you a heart filled with love for others.

Make New Heart "Stained-Glass" Cookies

What You Need

- chilled sugar cookie dough (store-bought or homemade)
- red, clear, hard candies or lollipops
- plastic bag
- hammer
- aluminum foil
- cookie sheet
- grown-up help

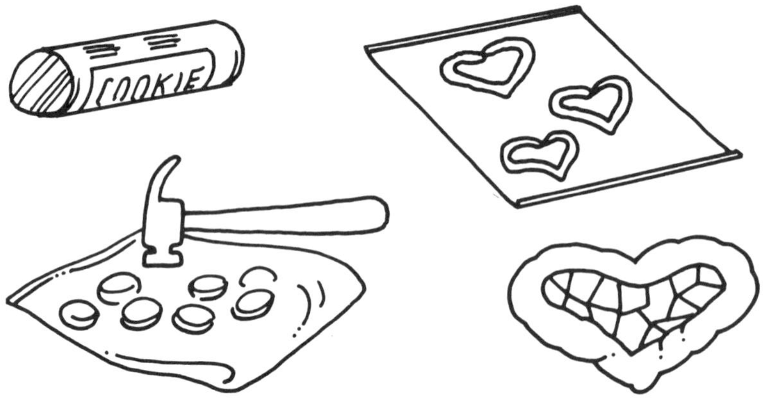

What You Do

1. Preheat oven according to the directions for the cookie dough.
2. Line cookie sheet with foil.
3. Put candies in a plastic bag. Tap them with the hammer gently until they are in small pieces (but not complete crushed into powder). Set aside.
4. Roll cookie dough into long ropes as thin as you can get them (about 1/4" thick). Shape the ropes into hearts on the cookie sheets. Be sure the pieces connect well.
5. Sprinkle the pieces of candy into the centers of the hearts.
6. Bake until the cookies brown slightly and the candies melt. Be careful not to overcook.
7. Remove the pan from the oven. When the cookies are cool, carefully pull the foil off the back of each. As you eat the cookies, thank Jesus for changing your heart.

☐ *Draw a star in the box when you've read Ezekiel 36:26.*

Give Your Heart

Here are some fun ways to show your love for others. Put your heart into making these projects for other people.

Heart Art to Decorate a Kind Note

What You Need

- red stamp pad or plate with red paint
- white construction paper for the note card

Fingerprint Hearts

What You Do

Press your index finger on a red stamp pad or a plate with red paint. Then slant your finger as you press it onto paper to make hearts. Write notes to friends, parents, and teachers, letting them know how much you appreciate them.

Potpourri Heart

What You Need

- clean Styrofoam meat tray
- potpourri
- paper clip
- duct tape
- white construction paper for the note card

What You Do

1. *Cut a heart shape from a clean Styrofoam meat tray. Spread glue on it, and sprinkle it with potpourri.*

2. *Use duct tape to attach a paper clip to the back for hanging the tray. Make a small loop of duct tape to attach the heart to a card. When you give the card to someone you love, mention that the heart can be pulled off and hung on the wall.*

Give Your Heart

Gelatin Hearts

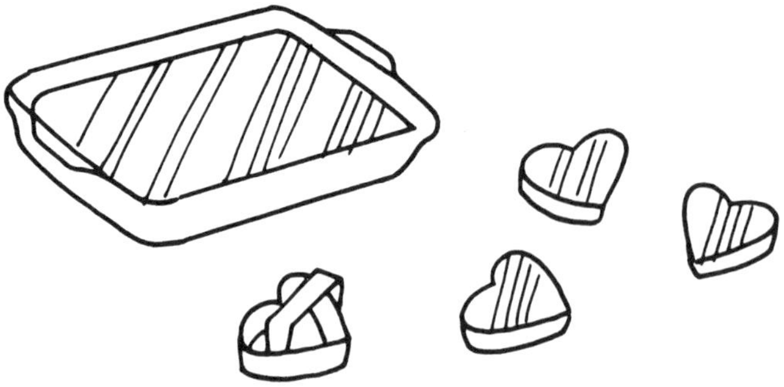

What You Need

- two 3-oz. packages of strawberry or cherry gelatin
- one cup boiling water
- 9-inch square baking dish
- heart-shaped cookie cutter
- spatula

What You Do

1. *Mix two 3-oz. packages of strawberry or cherry gelatin with one cup of boiling water. Stir until dissolved and pour into a square 9-inch baking dish.*
2. *When the gelatin is firm, cut out heart shapes with the cookie cutter. Remove the hearts from the dish with the spatula.*

A "Heart-y" Meal

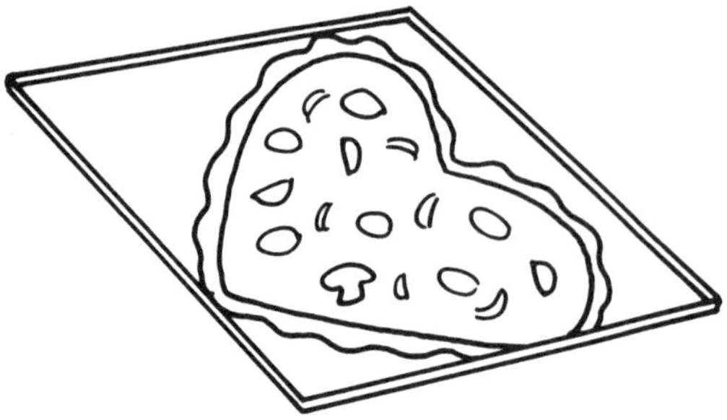

Offer to help your mom make a meal. See if you can find ways to add hearts to whatever she is fixing. You could cut cheese chunks or carrot slices into hearts for a salad. You could cut strawberry or banana slices into hearts. You could shape a pizza or meat loaf into a heart. Be creative.

Painted Cupcakes

Simply dip a clean watercolor brush into one or two drops of food coloring and paint hearts on frosted cupcakes. Give the cupcakes to people you love.

I DID IT!

COMPLETED	DATE
☐ A New Commandment	________
☐ Make a Tin Punch Pie Plate	________
☐ The Golden Rule	________
☐ Practice the Golden Rule	________
☐ The Good Samaritan	________
☐ Tell the Good Samaritan Story with Puppets	________
☐ Love Your Neighbor As Yourself	________
☐ Include Others	________
☐ The Least of These	________
☐ Help Others and Help Jesus	________
☐ Jesus Washed His Disciples' Feet	________
☐ Jump at the Chance to Serve God	________
☐ The Forgiven Servant Who Didn't Forgive	________
☐ Erase Unforgiveness from Your Heart	________

COMPLETED	DATE
☐ Unlimited Forgiveness	________
☐ Make Up Quickly	________
☐ Love Everyone . . .	________
☐ The Good News	________
☐ Jesus Ate with Sinners	________
☐ The Speck and the Plank	________
☐ Don't Judge	________
☐ Make a Pointing Finger Mobile	________
☐ The Two Men at the Temple	________
☐ Blessed Are the Peacemakers	________
☐ Watch Your Words	________
☐ Give and Lend	________
☐ Go the Extra Mile	________
☐ Marriage	________
☐ Give Your Heart	________

ANSWERS

Page 14 The|S on|of|God|w ill|sit|o n|a|thro ne|and|sa y|to|so me|o f|the|pe ople|“Co
me,|you|who|are|ble ssed|by|My|Fa ther,|inhe rit|a|k ingdo m|th at|was|prep
ared|fo r|you|whe n|the|wo rld|wa s|created.|I|was|hun gry|and|you|ga
ve|Me|some thing|to|e at.|I|wa s|thir sty|and|you|ga ve|Me|som ething|to|d
rink.|I|was|a|s tran ger|and|you|in vited|M e|in.|I|w as|na ked|and|you|clo thed
Me.|I|wa s|sick|a nd|yo u|loo ked|a fter|Me.|I|wa s|in|pri son|an d|yo u|ca
me|to|Me.”

The n|tho se|who|are|ri ghte ous|wi ll|say,|“Whe n|did|we|do|tho se|things|
fo r|You?”|The|Ki ng|wi ll|an swer,|“Whe n|yo u|did|it|fo r|the|least|o f|My|
bro thers,|yo u|did|i t|fo r|Me.”

Je sus|sa id|the|ot her s|will|be|pun ishe d|for|not|helping|Him|whe n|He|
was|in|need.|They’ll|say,|“Whe n|di d|we|see|Yo u|in|nee d|and|we|di
dn’t|hel p|You?”|He’ll|say,|“Whe n|you|di dn’t|he lp|the|lea st|of|My|bro
thers,|you|di dn’t|hel p|Me.”|Je sus|said|tho se|who|didn’t|help|Hi m|will|g
o|to|e ver lasti ng|pu nish ment,|bu t|those|who|we re|ri ghteous|will|go|t
o|live|wit h|Go d|fo rever.

Page 18 God has forgiven us.

Page 20

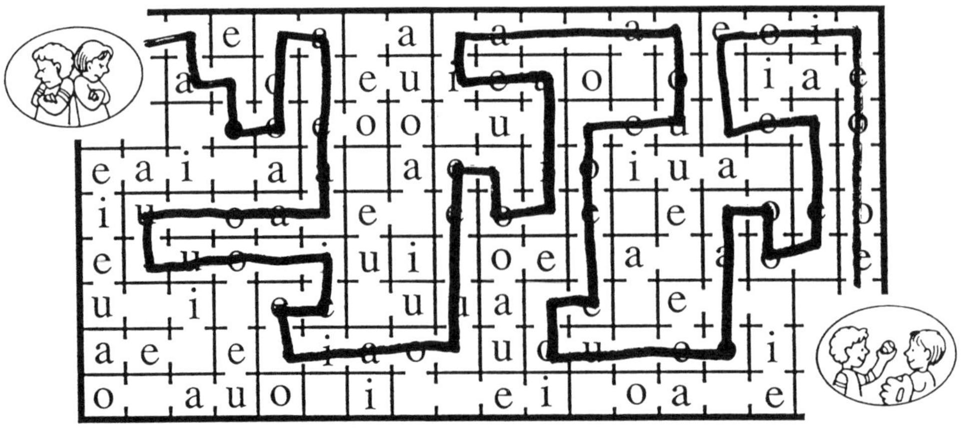

1. Pray for God to take away your unforgiveness.
2. Think about why the person did what she did.
3. Talk about the problem when you’re both calm.
4. Try to love the person like God does.

Page 26
1. Heart is on his shoe
2. Heart is in his hair
3. Heart is on her left-hand sleeve
4. Heart is on button of the girl on the right-hand side

ANSWERS

Page 29 Jesus said two men went to the temple to pray. One was a Pharisee; the other a tax collector. The Pharisee stood and prayed about himself. He said, "God, I thank You that I am not like other men–cheaters and evildoers–or even like this tax collector. I do good things like fasting and giving a tenth of everything I own to the church."

The tax collector was too ashamed of his sins to lift his eyes to God. He hit his chest and said, "God, please forgive me even though I don't deserve it. I'm a sinner."

Jesus said the tax collector was forgiven but the Pharisee wasn't. Anyone who puffs himself up with pride will be humbled and he who humbles himself will be lifted up to God.

Page 30
1. Does not fight
2. Helps others get along
3. Respects others
4. Shows love
5. Cares how others feel
6. Speaks kindly
7. Stays calm

Page 32 keep your words sweet

Page 33 teddy bear, frog, piggy bank, tennis racket, jacket, hat, fishing pole, ball, water gun, baseball bat

Index of *The Life and Lessons of Jesus* Series

BOOKS

1. Jesus Is Born
2. Jesus Grows Up
3. Jesus Prepares to Serve
4. Jesus Works Miracles
5. Jesus Heals
6. Learning to Love Like Jesus
7. Jesus Teaches Me to Pray
8. Following Jesus
9. Jesus Shows God's Love
10. Names of Jesus
11. Jesus' Last Week
12. Jesus Is Alive!

Index of *The Life and Lessons of Jesus* Series

If you would like to write the author, send your letter to:

Your address here

Stamp
here

Tracy L. Harrast
c/o Church Resources Dept.
David C. Cook Publishing Co.
850 N. Grove Avenue
Elgin, IL 60120

MW01380777

Living

SECOND EDITION

Living: AN INTRODUCTION TO BIOLOGY

Melissa Stanley
George Andrykovitch

George Mason University

ADDISON-WESLEY PUBLISHING COMPANY
Reading, Massachusetts
Menlo Park, California
London ▫ Amsterdam ▫ Don Mills, Ontario ▫ Sydney

To all biologists who strive to interpret the living world
and
to their students whose decisions may determine the fate of future generations

This book is in the Addison-Wesley Series in the Life Sciences.

Sponsoring Editor: Nancy J. Kralowetz
Production Manager: Karen Guardino
Production Editor: Margaret Pinette
Text Designer: Catherine Dorin
Illustrators: Intergraphics; John M. and Judith A. Waller; and Sandra McMahon
Copy Editor: Carol Beckwith
Art Development Editor: Arthur Ciccone
Art Coordinator: Dick Morton
Cover Designer: Richard Hannus, Hannus Design Associates
Cover Painting: F. Palizzi, *After the Flood.* Editorial Photocolor Archives, Inc.
Manufacturing Supervisor: Ann DeLacey

Library of Congress Cataloging in Publication Data

Stanley, Melissa.
Living: an introduction to biology.

Includes bibliographies and index.
1. Biology. I. Andrykovitch, George. II. Title.
QH308.2.S7 1984 574 83-15850
ISBN 0-201-16460-4

Reprinted with corrections, June 1984

Copyright © 1984, 1982 by Addison-Wesley Publishing Company, Inc. All rights reserved. No part of this publication may be reproduced, stored in a retrieval system, or transmitted, in any form or by any means, electronic, mechanical, photocopying, recording, or otherwise, without the prior written permission of the publisher. Printed in the United States of America. Published simultaneously in Canada.

CDEFGHIJ-DO-898765

Preface for Instructors

CONCEPTS PRESENTED IN CONTEXT: THE INTERPRETIVE APPROACH

This second edition of *Living* has been written for students in introductory biology courses, who want and deserve more than abstract theories and concepts. To meet their needs we have organized this text around the biologically important aspects of the world—from the inside of the human body to the organisms and organization that constitute the biosphere. Integrated within our discussion of human life and the biological world you will find the molecular and cellular biology, the genetics and evolution, and the botany and zoology you expect in a nonmajors text. In short, we have retained the interpretive approach while responding to your suggestions for making this book a more useful teaching tool.

A NEW SECTION ON EVOLUTIONARY BIOLOGY

New chapters on animal behavior and diversity are part of a section emphasizing both mechanisms of evolution and the history of life.

MANY CHAPTERS REWRITTEN

We reorganized several key chapters including those on chemistry and genetics to bring together topics from other sections. New material such as transposable genetic elements and speciation by punctuated equilibrium was added. But in selection of information we followed our original requirement that facts and concepts must contribute to the understanding of important biological processes.

NEW PHOTOGRAPHS ADDED AND ILLUSTRATIONS REDRAWN

Color photographs illustrate the new diversity chapter and the living ecosystems section. We carefully evaluated each illustration and replaced many to achieve a more uniform technical level. The script used to highlight processes in the first edition drawings has been replaced with easier-to-read type. Many drawings have been relabeled. Color was added to make the illustrations easier to understand. To take better advantage of space some illustrations have been enlarged and others reduced.

LEGENDS SHORTENED

Illustrations are closely tied to the text. The legends stress identification of the subject or process presented.

KEY MATERIAL HIGHLIGHTED

Sentences and phrases presenting important facts and ideas are underlined. We explain the significance of biological observations as you do in lecture and use underlining just as you might write key matter on the blackboard.

CHAPTER-END QUESTIONS ADDED, FURTHER READINGS UPDATED

Ten or more study questions have been added at the end of each chapter. Further readings appear at the end of sections and emphasize recent, relatively nontechnical articles.

THOUGHT AND CONTROVERSY, CROSS-REFERENCES, AND CHAPTER SUMMARIES RETAINED

We were pleased with the positive response to the openended thought and controversy sections. Cross-references to the location of related material on earlier pages have been well-received along with the chapter summaries.

INDEX AND GLOSSARY

Both the index and the glossary have been expanded to make them more effective study aids.

SUPPLEMENTAL MATERIALS

A full package of teaching and learning aids accompanies this textbook. Contact your Addison-Wesley representative for information on the instructor's manual, student study guide, test bank, 35 mm slides, and overhead transparencies.

Revisions, like first editions, depend on the help of many individuals, reviewers, editors, illustrators, and others to whom authors are indebted. We owe special thanks to the fine people at Addison-Wesley and our colleagues at George Mason University, who have worked so hard to help us make this a clear, forceful, and meaningful introduction to life sciences. Although we delight in finding new and better ways to express fundamental concepts, our insight alone is inadequate. We urge you to not only notify us of errors, but to forward suggestions for a third edition.

Fairfax, Virginia
November, 1983

M.M.S.
G.E.A.

To the Student

PERHAPS THIS IS YOUR FIRST SCIENCE COURSE and you are wondering how to study biology. One strategy is to complete all the exercises in the study guide available specifically to accompany this textbook. Another, more general method is to pretend that *you* are teaching this course! Write yourself the kind of notes you would need if you were teaching. In preparing such notes, use the notes you take in lecture, this text, and at least one other text from the library. Follow your notes from lecture as a guide to overall organization and the material to be covered. Use the texts to check each piece of information. Most important of all, use your head to decide exactly what to write.

The process of deciding what to write is the crucial part. Active participation stimulates learning. As you write, don't merely copy; put everything into your own words. To do so, you must understand the matter at hand. Therefore you must read and think.

After you have written your notes, review them. Every time you sit down to write new notes, review those you have written previously. Consider each point and make sure you can explain it to someone else. Before an examination, it is worthwhile to write a condensed outline of your notes. The more time you devote to perfecting your notes, the better you will understand the material for the more you will have thought about it.

When practical, vocalize your notes. Perhaps you can form a study group with classmates and hold informal seminars. All kinds of students can help one another. Those who are well prepared will correct one another. Those who haven't devoted much time to study can provide questions that stimulate others to teach and thus to review the material over and over.

Both the study guide and the make-believe teaching experiences we suggest require that you study actively. When you examine facts and ideas, organize them, and question them, you will find that you learn readily. Learning may be work but active participation makes it fun, too.

We hope you enjoy studying this book as much as we have enjoyed writing it. Despite our best efforts it is imperfect, as you are sure to find. We urge you to write us with corrections and suggestions to make the book a more effective learning tool. Address your comments in care of Addison-Wesley Publishing Company, Reading, Massachusetts 01867.

Fairfax, Virginia M.M.S.
November, 1983 G.E.A.

P.S. To sharpen your graph-reading skills, study Box 1B in Chapter 1.

Abridged Contents

Contents

PART ONE

Perspectives on Living

PART TWO

To Keep Living

10

HOMEOSTASIS CHALLENGED: DISEASE AND DEFENSE 209

PART THREE

Future Living

11

GENETIC LEGACIES: FROM ONE GENERATION TO ANOTHER 238

12

REPRODUCTION: SEX AND PROCREATION 276

13

DEVELOPMENT: FROM THE EGG TO OLD AGE 297

PART FOUR

Diverse Living

PART FIVE

Living Ecosystems

PART SIX

Living in the Biosphere

PART ONE

Perspectives on Living

We are living on the earth as parts of a dynamic complex of organisms and lifeless matter. Surely to continue living is our most fundamental goal. How long we succeed may be influenced by how well we understand ourselves and our environment.

This text provides an introduction to the requirements for human life and to the nature of the world in which we live. We believe it will help you to understand problems that people face today and to make decisions that will promote human life.

There are four major topics to be covered: the biology of humans, reproduction and inheritance, the living and nonliving components of our environment, and management of this environment. Each makes up a major section of the book. Your understanding of these topics will be enhanced by an introduction to biological principles and to the history of human life. Thus the first two chapters are intended to help you interrelate those that follow and to view the living world as a whole.

1

Basic Biology: Principles and Practice

ANY ATTEMPT TO ANALYZE THE NATURE OF HUmans and their relationships with other living things and with their physical environment is an ambitious project. Biological processes are often complicated, and their interactions are extensive and intricate. So let us begin by establishing a groundwork of biological informatio. Consider this chapter an overview of biology. Subsequent chapters will build and expand on the information given here, so you may want to consult this chapter frequently as we examine the living world together. If you return to these pages at the end of your studies, you will surely have a greater appreciation of the chapter's basic themes.

THE UNITY OF LIFE

Is there anyone who does not marvel at the tremendous diversity of life on our planet? Most of us never lose that sense of wonder we experienced when we first visited a zoo or stopped in a beautiful garden or spent a summer at the seashore and found incredible living things among the rocks. On the surface, each kind of organism seems special and unique, but the extraordinary diversity of outward forms is deceptive.

Biologists have long recognized that there is a fundamental unity of life. Organisms share common patterns of chemical composition, structure, and activity. The unity of life is a basic philosophical principle underlying our belief that organisms can be studied systematically and that the knowledge gained may be applicable in widely separated situations.

A Common Chemistry

Some of the chemical constituents of organisms are found in both the living and nonliving worlds. However, certain chemicals are uniquely associated with life. The list includes **proteins, polysaccharides, nucleic acids,** and **lipids**. Each of these substances is important in its own way, but proteins and nucleic acids have special significance. Chromosomes, which carry the genes that determine the characteristics of an organism, are composed of **deoxyribonucleic acid** (DNA). The genetic information in DNA includes directions for making proteins. And although some proteins, such as those of hair, are purely structural in their uses, many others are **enzymes**. Enzymes are substances responsible for initiating most of the chemical activities essential to life.

The chemical activities of organisms are collectively referred to as **metabolism**. Certain metabolic activities are common to all forms of life. Each organism must accumulate raw materials to make the constituents of living matter. At the same time, organisms must generate the energy needed to accomplish these activities along with others, such as movement.

All organisms coordinate and regulate their activities. In fact, life processes occur under conditions of relative **homeostasis**—that is, under con-

FIGURE 1.1 **Obvious Differences between Organisms Hide the Fundamental Unity of Life.** Here, the North American lizard, *Anolis carolinensis*, waits for its next meal amid the lush background of the sea ox-eye daisy.

ditions that remain nearly constant, despite changes in the outside environment. Most metabolic processes proceed in a step-wise fashion, with each step controlled by a particular enzyme. Many organisms exert a more generalized control by means of chemical messengers such as **hormones**. In people, hormones travel in the blood and sometimes act swiftly, far from the gland where they were secreted.

Patterns of Organization

Organisms are not random stews of chemicals thrown casually together. Living material is intricately structured. The **cell** (Fig. 1.2) is the smallest unit of organization that exhibits the full range of interrelated activities that characterize life. Plant and animal cells are themselves composed of cytoplasm and organelles. Cell organelles include specialized structures such as the nucleus that contains the chromosomes.

Although many small organisms consist of only one or a few cells, most familiar plants and animals contain billions of cells. In these complex organisms each cell is **differentiated** (specialized) for a particular function. Groups of cells of the same structure and function form a **tissue** (Fig. 1.3). Usually these cells are woven together to form distinct microscopic or visible structures, such as muscle, bone, or cartilage, but the cells of some tissues are free to move about. Blood is an example of such a tissue.

In animals, tissues are organized into distinct organs that perform more complex functions. The brain, stomach, liver, and heart are key human organs. The heart tissues include muscle, which makes up most of the mass; connective tissues, which bind the muscle together; and nerve fibers, which regulate the heartbeat. Many animals have **organ systems** composed of interacting organs. For example, the mouth, esophagus, stomach, intestine, liver, and pancreas are components of the

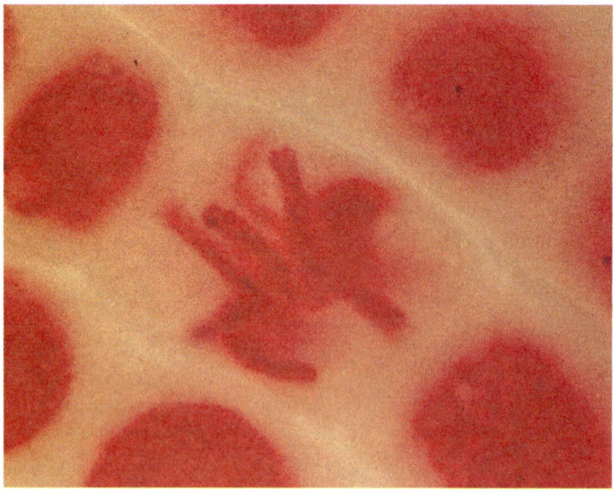

(a)

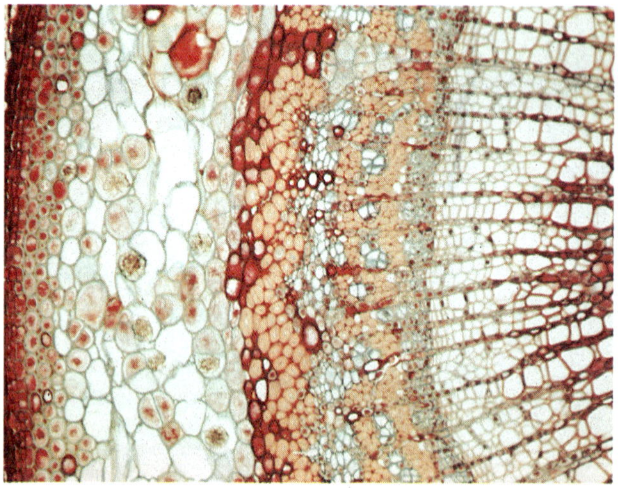

(b)

(c)

(d)

FIGURE 1.2 **Levels of Biological Organization in Plants.** (a) Chromosomes in root cells; (b) tissue layers of a stem; (c) reproductive organs of the red chokeberry; (d) two populations in a community.

human digestive system. Together these organs digest and absorb nutrients. Many plants have organs such as leaves, stems, and roots. Systems of organs aren't usually recognized in plants, although male and female parts (organs) of a flower might be considered a plant organ system.

Although in one sense individual organisms are independent, each is related by origin to other members of its kind, or **species**. Every organism is born into a **population** of its species. Members of a population share many potential interactions—reproduction, for example.

In any area, all the members of every species influence each other in one way or another, however slightly. These interactions take many forms, but the most obvious is the **food chain**. One species eats another and is usually eaten in turn, so that there are long chains of nutritional transfers involving many species. Many effects between species are more subtle, as when large plants provide smaller ones with shelter from sun, wind, or rain. Populations of organisms that live in a particular environment rely on one another so much that they are said to constitute a **community**. The use of the term "community" in this context compares the interactions of the members of a biological community to those in a human social community.

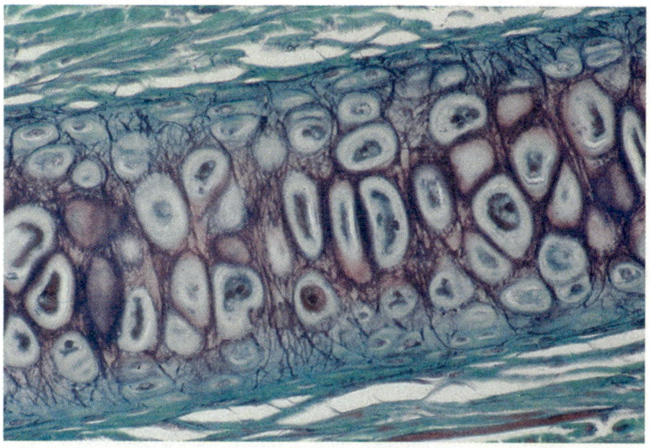

(a)

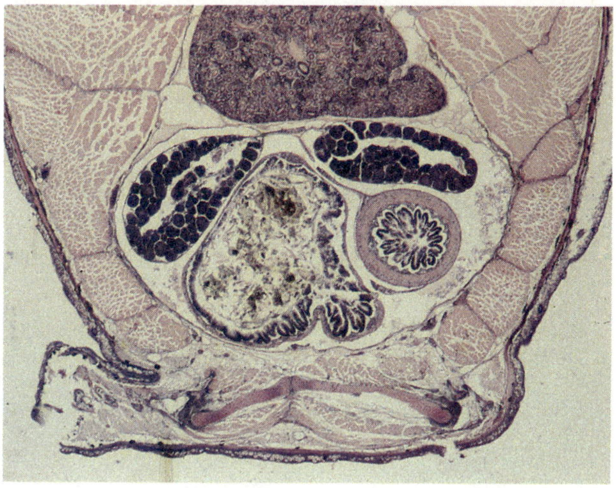

(b)

(c)

(d)

FIGURE 1.3 Levels of Biological Organization in Animals. (a) Cells of connective tissue; (b) organs of a fish; (c) an organism; (d) a population.

Consider how many different ways there are to "make a living" in human society. Overall, the interactions within a biological community far exceed those among people in a simple social community.

Before you read further, examine Fig. 1.4 for a summary of the levels of organization that biologists see in the living world. Reflect on the fact that all organisms share common patterns of structure and organization. Together with biochemical similarities, these patterns indicate a basic unity of life and suggest that all organisms may be expected to be subject to the same general laws. What we learn about one species should give us insight into others.

FIGURE 1.4 Levels of Biological Organization.

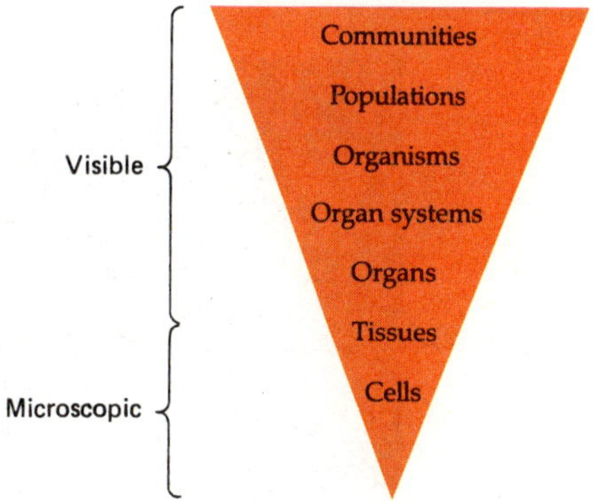

FIGURE 1.5 **Diversity of Life.** (a) Desmids are common aquatic microorganisms. (b) The fleshy-leaved sand verbena is well adapted to its hot, dry environment. (c) A ghost crab feasts on a worm. (d) Orange cup fungi secrete digestive enzymes that literally dissolve wood. (e) Ferns do best in moist, shady habitats because their sperm must swim to the eggs. (f) When the tide comes in the marsh snail climbs up plant stems and avoids predators. (g) Wood ibises use their sensitive beaks to probe for their next meal. (h) Ground-hugging plants and needle-leaved evergreens are able to withstand cold and drying winds. (i) Hartebeests, like so many mammals, are active at dusk and dawn.

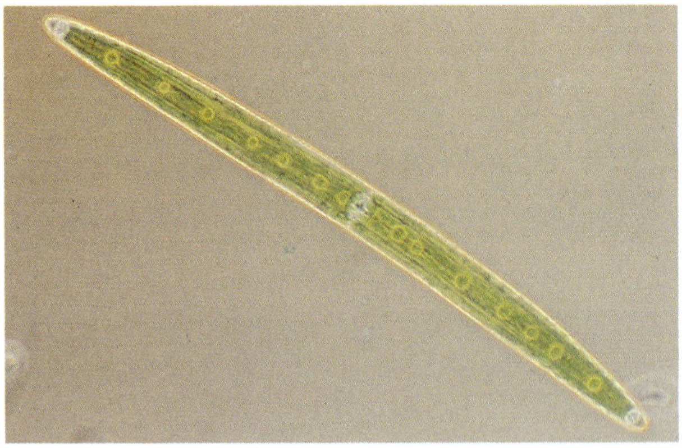

(a)

(b)

(c)

(d)

(e)

(f)

(g)

(h)

(i)

ECOLOGY AND INTERDEPENDENCE

We have already noted that organisms in any area affect one another. But they also affect the environment, just as the environment affects them. Obvious as this may seem to us today, the extent of such interactions has only recently been fully appreciated. This recognition is the basis of the branch of biology called **ecology**.

The Ecosystem Approach to Understanding the Environment

All organisms, even humans, belong to some ecosystem. (In fact, most humans participate in numerous ecosystems.) Each **ecosystem** is composed of a living community of organisms and its nonliving surroundings. Ecosystems are "systems" in that they are self-contained units with smoothly interacting parts.

Individual ecosystems such as lakes and forests never exist in isolation. They continuously exchange both organisms and nonliving materials with nearby areas. One ecosystem interacts with the next, so that all the organisms in the world and all the land, water, and air they inhabit really make up one giant ecosystem. Biologists reserve the term **biosphere** for the worldwide ecosystem.

One process that characterizes each ecosystem and relates one part to another is energy transfer.

FIGURE 1.6 A Community of Interacting Populations. It doesn't take long for a dead tree stump to be colonized by bacteria, fungi, and molds. Worms and insects soon join the feast, some not only eating their way through wood but also excavating passageways for themselves and others. And where there are herbivores, there are sure to be predators.

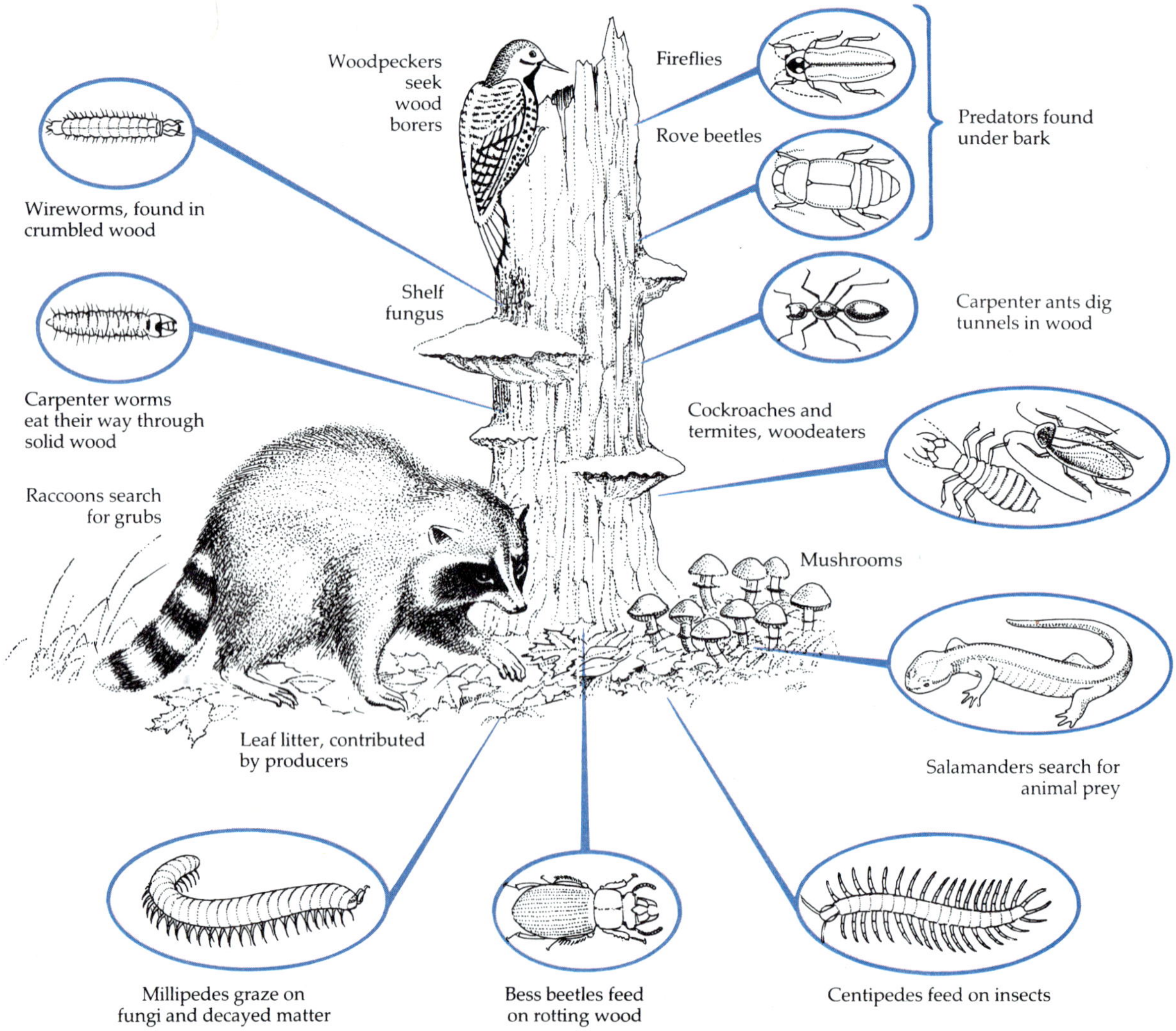

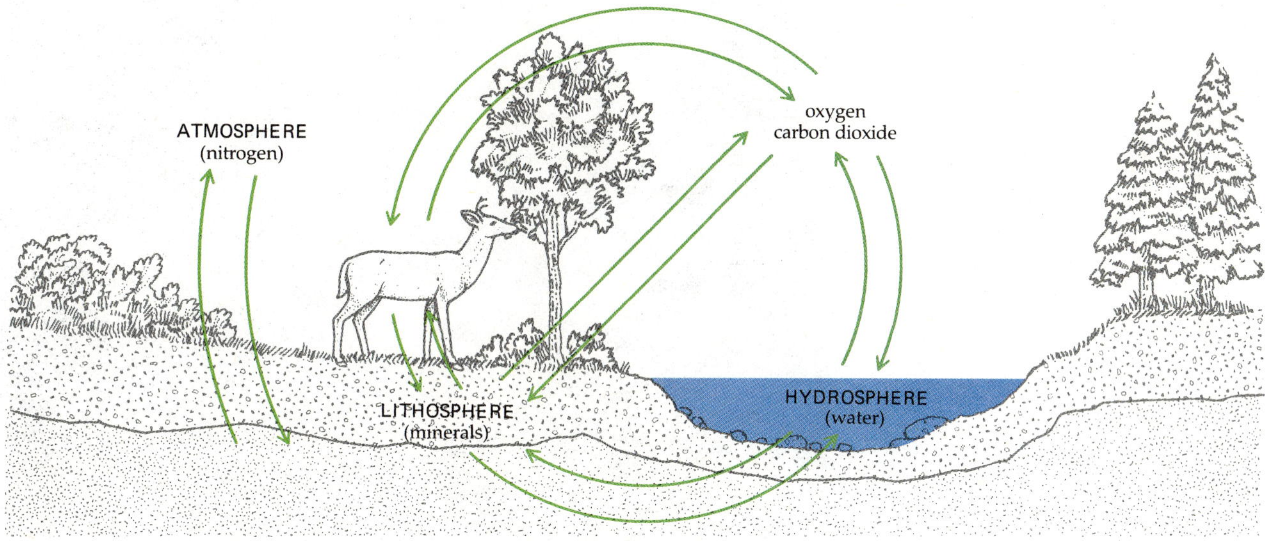

FIGURE 1.7 **Biogeochemical Cycles.** The chemicals necessary for life come from the atmosphere, from water, and from the earth's crust. Organisms accumulate these substances from their nonliving sources, to which they are returned after cycling through the various food chains and food webs of the biosphere.

Energy enters ecosystems as sunlight. Green plants trap light energy and make some of it available to other organisms in the form of food. In this sense, plants are the **producers** of an ecosystem. **Herbivores** are animals that feed on plants, and they, in turn, fall prey to **carnivores** (flesh-eating animals). When plants and animals die, their bodies become the energy source for a multitude of small **decomposers,** decay-causing microorganisms and insects (Fig. 1.6). This sequence of energy transfers in an ecosystem is often called a food chain.

The term **food web** more accurately describes the complex nature of interdependence within natural ecosystems. There are always many kinds of plants and animals in a food web. And almost all animals feed on more than one species. To complicate matters further, many animals are **omnivores**; that is to say, they eat both plants and animals.

Food webs are more than just patterns of energy transfer. They are key elements in the movement of matter between the living and nonliving worlds. The chemicals that compose organisms are extracted by plants from soil, water, and air. Then from plants these chemicals pass to herbivores, carnivores, and omnivores. And as organisms die, their dead bodies decay and their chemical constituents are returned to the physical environment. Thus, in a smoothly operating ecosystem, chemicals cycle between the living and nonliving components. Because life (bio-), earth (geo-), and chemistry are all involved, these are known as **biogeochemical cycles** (Fig. 1.7). It is important to note that although chemicals continuously cycle within ecosystems, there is only a one-way flow of energy. Energy transfers are inherently inefficient. As each member of the food web uses energy, less is available to the next in line. Thus an ecosystem needs a constant supply of outside energy to keep operating.

Implications of Interdependence

All organisms and all other parts of the biosphere are bound together in a chemical sense; however, organisms are also related by inheritance. An unbroken stream of cells links every individual alive today to the origin of life, perhaps as many as three billion years ago. Have you ever wondered how long it will last? Do you particularly question how long our species will endure? Surely there can be no more all-encompassing goal for humans than to preserve their kind. Here we find one aspect of the immortality we all desire. But what are we doing to keep people alive, not just for a few generations but for millions of years?

As living organisms we depend on ecosystems, especially on the biosphere as a whole. If we are to continue to exist, we must maintain an intact

FIGURE 1.8 **Acid Drainage from a Strip Mine Fouled This Stream.**

biosphere. Nevertheless, every society on earth is actively degrading its environment (Fig. 1.8). Our growing numbers are dangerous. If world population continues to grow at its current rate—doubling every 36 years—we will be in deep trouble by the end of the century. In fact we are in trouble now, because we don't know how to stop our population explosion. Human multiplication is causing the food crisis to build like a thunderhead on a hot day. But that is only one of the problems we must solve to make long-term survival possible.

We may get by the impending food shortage only to perish because of a multitude of "little things." In some ways the biosphere can be compared to the economic health of a business or to our personal financial situation. People frequently complain that ever-increasing numbers of small expenses, such as taxes, interest, and similar obligations, are pushing them toward bankruptcy. Each expense by itself may be small, but together they add up and "nickel and dime us to death." The same principle applies to ecosystems. Today the ties that bind the biosphere together are being frayed. Pollution, small alterations of biogeochemical cycles, minor climatic modifications, erosion of soil, and the extinction of species each tend to pull the biosphere apart. Often one change makes another worse. Before we know it, these endless small changes in the biosphere may lead to a major disturbance. But environmental modifications don't just add up and compound one another. Usually one change precipitates another.

The very nature of ecosystems decrees that we can never do only one thing. Any alteration in an ecosystem initiates a chain reaction. Like a falling row of dominos, one effect brings another. One adjustment requires a second. Although minor fluctuations are normal in any ecosystem, major disturbances can potentially interrupt the pattern of movement of energy and essential materials. Because the flexibility of an ecosystem lies in its organisms, and because organisms change only slowly as their species evolve, ecosystems are vulnerable to fundamental change. Even the most vigorous ecosystem can succumb.

EVOLUTION

The theory of evolution is the single most unifying idea within biology. It explains not only the similarities in the chemistry and structure of organisms but also their marked diversity. Although the likenesses are due to a common origin, differences result from the evolution of various species to fit into particular ecosystems. Furthermore, the complex relationships among the species of an ecosystem exist because these species have evolved together.

Evolution Is Change

In the simplest sense "evolution" implies a process of gradual change. The reader must understand that this change occurs *not within individual organisms* but, rather, *only between generations that are parts of populations.* This is true because each organism retains throughout life the same hereditary makeup. In other words, the cells of each organism contain genetic information that, under proper environmental conditions, permits that organism to develop specific structures and to function in certain ways. This genetic legacy, together with the environment, determines the characteristics of the new individual.

Most organisms result from **sexual reproduction**, whereby parents produce young that possess a combination of parental traits. This is one source of variability within a population. Another—and an ultimately more important—source of variation is **mutation**, the sudden appearance of characteristics totally different from those of the parents. Mutations are rare and usually lethal. Occasionally, however, under the prevailing conditions, a mutation can be harmless or even beneficial.

Obviously, the genetic endowment an organism receives must be reasonably compatible with its environment if the new individual is to exist at all. But the better the fit between these two factors, the greater the chance that the organism will survive to reproduce, and the larger the number of its offspring that are likely to survive. Because the environment favors the growth and reproductive success of individuals whose genetic makeup best suits them to the circumstances, certain inherited traits are favored. As a result, these traits are more common in the next generation. Changes in inherited characteristics may be small for any generation, so evolution occurs very slowly. Nevertheless, the role of the environment in determining the reproductive success of individuals lies at the core of the evolutionary process. This role is known as **natural selection**.

Although most of the history of life can be only inferred, sometimes we can observe evolution directly. English moth collectors have documented a tiny but telling example of evolution in the peppered moth (Fig. 1.9). Prior to the industrial revolution, the peppered moth was common in Eng-

(a)

(b)

FIGURE 1.9 Evolution of the Peppered Moth. (a) *Biston betularia* and its black form, *carbonaria*, at rest on a tree trunk in unpolluted countryside; (b) light and dark moths on a soot-covered oak trunk near Birmingham, England.

FIGURE 1.10 **Natural Selection Often Favors Camouflage.** A "dead leaf" can be (a) a mantid waiting for its lunch or (b) a frog that a snake will miss as it searches for dinner. (c) Being told that one looks like a bird dropping is not a compliment, but it can make a caterpillar unlikely to be eaten. (d) Mimicking a thorn reduces the likelihood of being eaten while sucking plant juices. (e) Some mantids mimic green leaves. (f) And some caterpillars can pass as part of a leaf.

(a)

(b)

(c)

(d)

(e)

(f)

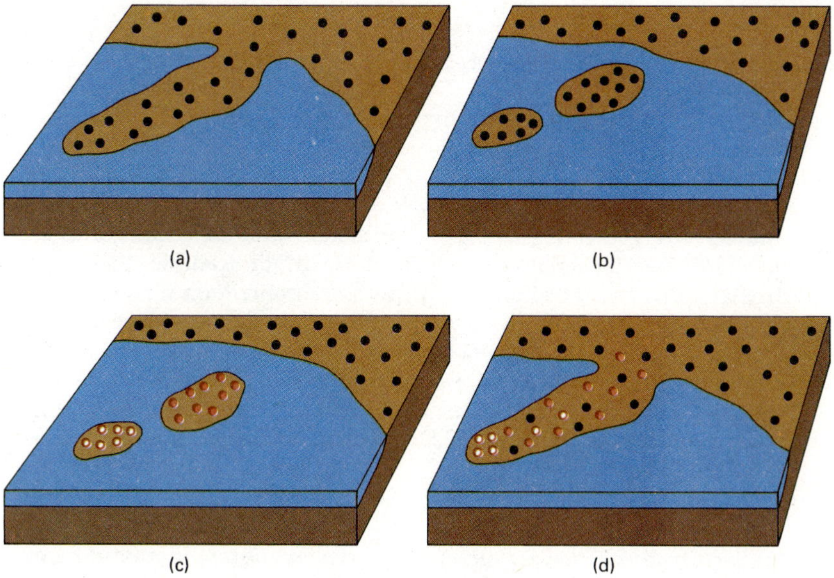

FIGURE 1.11 Isolation and Evolution. Geologic changes can create geographical barriers that divide a single population into separate populations. Consider a hypothetical case (a) where a species exists as a continuous population on a peninsula. Rising water can create islands separated from one another and from the mainland (b). Differing selective pressures acting on the isolated populations can result in evolution of distinct species (c). If a dry period reestablishes contact between the islands and the mainland (d), the new species may intermingle but will remain distinct because they cannot interbreed.

land, where it was characterized by a blotched or "peppery" pigment pattern. This mottled pattern camouflaged the moths as they rested on tree trunks during daylight hours. After the introduction of coal as a major energy source, soot from the smoke of coal fires blackened all the trees and buildings in industrial regions. In the following years, dark moths of the same species, which previously had been found only in small numbers, gradually replaced the once-typical "peppery" ones. Why? Because the original peppery-patterned moths had become more visible to birds or other predators, but uniformly dark moths blended with the sooty surfaces. In some areas, recent reductions in air pollution have been accompanied by an increasing reappearance of the lighter, peppery moths.

Small environmental changes may cause minor evolutionary changes, but marked environmental alterations can lead to widespread **extinction**. This happens because organisms are complex and delicately balanced systems. Hence radical changes are not likely to be compatible with life.

Species Formation

A species maintains its characteristics because its members can breed only with others of their own kind. The separation of one species into two requires some barrier that prevents interbreeding between two populations. For example, a **geographical barrier** may come to separate a species into isolated populations (Fig. 1.11). Because no two environments can be identical, each exerts different selective pressures. **Chance** can also alter the genetic makeup of small populations. One way or another, two initially identical populations can become quite different. After a long period of time, enough changes accumulate in isolated populations to preclude interbreeding even if the opportunity should occur. Thus two populations of one species can evolve into two separate species.

We will return to the subject of species formation later, when we discuss evolution in terms of specific genetic mechanisms. For now we ask you to remember that a **species** is a group of organisms that can interbreed (and produce fertile offspring) only among themselves.

The web of interdependence within an ecosystem causes change to sweep through like a wave. People sometimes view the world as stable, but this view is taken only because humans live for such a short while. In the long run we are all part of an ever-changing biosphere. With this change can come extinction as well as new species. The less the biosphere changes, the longer our kind is likely to endure.

BIOLOGY: SCIENCE AND METHOD

Biologists seek to explain natural phenomena. In this effort they use insight, intuition, logic, deduction, and testing. Philosophers speak of the **sci-**

BOX 1A

WHAT'S IN A NAME?

Each species has a unique scientific name that positively identifies it. The system avoids the difficulties with common names that can vary from place to place and language to language. The words in scientific names are either Latin or latinized.

Each species is given two names, one for the species itself and the other for the genus (plural genera), the group of related species to which the organism belongs. Both terms are italicized, and the genus name is capitalized. For example, the wolf is *Canis lupus*, and the domestic dog is *Canis familiaris*. A close relationship between these two species is shown by placing both in the genus *Canis*. Sometimes a genus consists of only one species. Thus the only present-day member of the genus *Homo* is our species, *Homo sapiens*. Once a species has been fully identified in a discussion, the generic term may be abbreviated—for example, *H. sapiens*.

This system is part of a larger scheme for classifying organisms. The scheme traces to a Swedish botanist, Carolus Linnaeus, who based his classification on what he thought were levels of complexity in the order of nature. To Linnaeus, in 1756, these levels seemed part of the Creator's master plan. But most present-day biologists believe that the similarities Linnaeus recognized reflect evolutionary relationships rather than preordained levels of complexity. In other words, similar organisms are closely related to each other, and they share a relatively recent common ancestor.

Although some of Linnaeus's basic assumptions are no longer accepted, his scheme of organization remains useful. The present-day classification system, based on the Linnaean scheme, is composed of large groups, each of which is subdivided again and again into smaller units of increasing similarities. Consider the classification of humans.

Kingdom: Animalia (all animals, including jellyfish and oysters)

Phylum: Chordata (includes mammals, fish, birds, frogs, and many more)

Class: Mammalia (rats, elephants, cows, and primates, too)

Order: Primates (monkeys, bush babies, and others in addition to humans)

Family: Hominidae

Genus: *Homo*

Species: *Homo sapiens*

Except for species, biologists recognize that these categories are arbitrary. For example, there are no absolute criteria for lumping species into a genus. One authority can legitimately divide ten related species into seven genera, whereas another authority on the same group places the ten species in only two genera. Both are making their decisions on degrees of similarities. But because each species is unique, there can be no rule to determine exactly how similar species must be to be placed in the same genus. Thus genera and higher categories are only convenient ways to catalog the tremendous number of species and to reflect what is believed to be their evolutionary history.

In contrast, species have a biological reality. Members of a species will interbreed in nature only with members of the same species. Every species consists of members with characteristics unique to that species.

entific method as if it were a single ritualistic procedure. It is not. Science is fundamentally a creative endeavor. And as such, there is no sure recipe for success.

To some extent every scientist employs his or her own scientific method, which varies from day to day. No one can explain just *how* an idea came to mind. Ideas happen. We can't list six easy ways to stimulate creativity. But creativity is largely what science is about. In this way the scientist is as much an artist as the painter, sculptor, composer, or writer. And with these other artists the scientist shares a need for training. It is true that "destiny favors the prepared mind."

Along with other serious artists and craftspeople, scientists must develop discipline. Creative scientists may daydream, but they must confine their work to questions and ideas that can be tested. In every true scientist, the ability to formulate a question that can be answered must be combined with the insight to design the experiment that can provide the answer. Someone has described this combination as "being able to ask the right question at the right time." Always the question must have an answer within the grasp of available technology. Often the challenge comes in applying old techniques in new ways.

Biologists at Work

Typically, when a biologist ponders a problem, the question "Why?" or "How?" arises. Both these questions are understood in terms of mechanisms and immediate causes, rather than in terms of metaphysical principles. For example, a physiologist who devoutly believes in God will nonetheless seek an explanation in terms of chemical laws rather than attribute the observation to "manifestations of God's will." Even though the physiologist may *believe* this to be the ultimate cause, such belief is untestable; hence it is beyond the realm of science.

A creative biologist develops a possible explanation for the question at hand. In all likelihood, the explanation is based on some prior knowledge or experience. What it is, though, is a hunch. In formal language, this informed, scientific hunch is

FIGURE 1.12 Scientists Make Careful Observations. Tools as simple as a ruler or as refined as an automatic data recorder help scientists make accurate measurements.

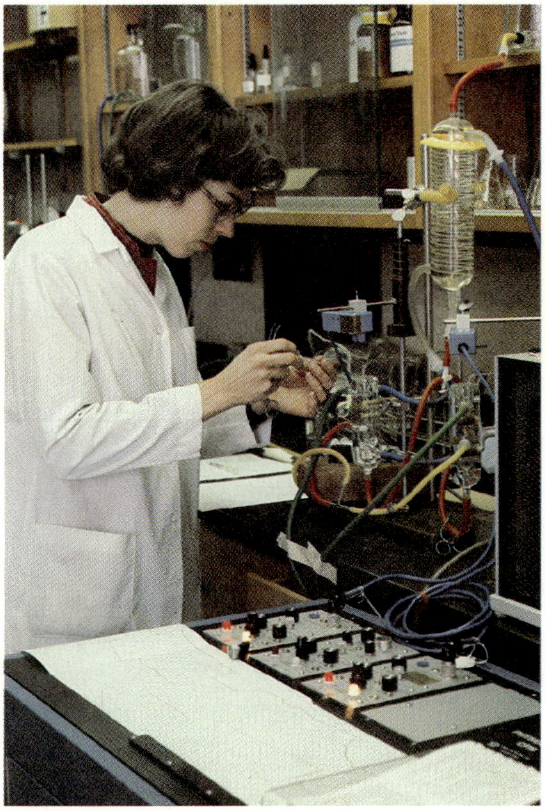

BOX 1B

SOME IMPORTANT CONTRIBUTIONS TO THE ADVANCE OF BIOLOGY

Histories of biology are usually thick volumes. Which observations, experiments, and controversies are the most important is a controversial topic in itself. Other authors might select a list that is quite different from the one given here.

c. 300 B.C. Aristotle, Greek philosopher

Recognized unity of life. First to attempt a systematic classification of organisms.

c. 70 B.C. Lucretius, Roman philosopher

Recognized organisms as composed of the same basic materials as the nonliving world and realized that life need not be explained by mystical concepts.

1648 Jan Van Helmont, Belgian physician

Careful weighing of a willow sapling in a tub of dirt over a five-year period demonstrated that plant growth occurred mainly at the expense of air and water.

1674 Antoni van Leeuwenhoek, Dutch merchant

Perfected one-lens microscope, with which he observed bacteria, protozoa, and sperm.

1665 Robert Hooke, English engineer

Was the first to describe cells, actually the cell walls of dead plant cells.

1735 Carolus Linnaeus, Swedish botanist

Established present system for naming and classifying plants and animals.

1828 Friedrich Wöhler, German chemist

By synthesizing urea, demonstrated that organic compounds can form outside organisms. This furthered the view that life processes can be explained in physical and chemical terms.

1839 M.G. Schleiden and T. Schwann, German botanists

Established cells as universal unit of life.

1847 Alexander von Humboldt, German botanist

Laid the foundations of ecological plant geography.

1850s J.B. Boussingault, French chemist

Showed that plants absorb nitrates from the soil and carbon dioxide from the air.

1859 Charles Darwin and A.R. Wallace, English naturalists

Developed a theory of evolution through natural selection of inherited traits.

1855 Claude Bernard, French physiologist

Discovered role of pancreas and liver and from this developed concept of a constant internal environment essential to life.

1866 Gregor Mendel, Czechoslovakian monk

Discovered basic laws of inheritance.

1860s Louis Pasteur, French chemist

Demonstrated that microorganisms cause spoilage and that microorganisms come from others of their kind, just as do larger organisms.

1876 Robert Koch, German physician

In study of anthrax in cattle, first showed that microorganisms cause disease in vertebrates. Developed techniques to isolate microorganisms in pure culture.

1887 Sergius Winogradsky, Russian microbiologist

Proved that bacteria convert dead matter into nitrates of soil.

1899 Jacques Loeb, German zoologist

By experimentally stimulating development of frog eggs (without participation of sperm), furthered belief that life processes can be explained in physical terms.

1902 Walter S. Sutton, American biologist

Theorized that chromosomes carried genes and thus determined heredity.

1907 R.G. Harrison, American biologist

Demonstrated that cells could be grown outside the organism in "tissue culture."

1913 A.H. Sturtevant, American biologist

Designed experiments that permitted determination of gene location on chromosomes.

1921 F.G. Banting and C.H. Best, Canadian biologists

Isolated insulin and identified its physiological activity.

1926 J.B. Sumner, American biologist

First to isolate an enzyme.

1928 Frederic Clements, American botanist

Established concept of succession in plant communities.

1929 Alexander Fleming, British microbiologist

Extracted the antibiotic penicillin from the mold that secretes it.

1931 Barbara McClintock and Harriet Creighton, American biologists

In studies of corn, showed how chromosomes exchange hereditary information and thus increase genetic variety.

1935 C.F. Cori and Gerty Cori, American biochemists

Discovered how cells metabolize glucose.

1957 E.W. Sutherland, American physiologist

Demonstrated that cyclic AMP is a "second messenger" released inside cells when certain hormones act.

1959 Macfarlane Burnet, Australian immunologist

Proposed theory to explain how the body discriminates against foreign substances while recognizing its own components.

1961 Francois Jacob and Jacques Monod, French microbiologists

Proposed that genes act through messenger RNA and developed a model to explain regulation of gene activity in bacteria.

1961 M.W. Nirenburg and J.H. Matthaei, American biochemists

Broke the genetic code and explained how nucleic acid structure specifies protein structure

1963 Ruth Sager, American biologist

Discovered that not all genes exist on chromosomes.

1970 David Baltimore and H.M. Temin, American biologists

Demonstrated how cancer-causing viruses transform the DNA of infected cells.

a **hypothesis**. As we have implied, a hypothesis is useful only if it can be tested. A testable hypothesis leads to predictions or deductions that can be compared with observations or otherwise tested. If the predictions and the results agree, then the hypothesis is supported. If several predictions or deductions support a hypothesis, then it may be considered correct with some degree of confidence. The more evidence there is in favor of a hypothesis, the greater confidence you should have in it.

Design of experiments always requires careful consideration. When one is looking for cause and effect, there must be a **control** group for comparison. To determine, for example, whether some chemical causes cancer, two groups of animals must be tested. The control group must be treated in exactly the same way as the experimental group, except that the control group does not receive the test chemical. Both groups must be of the same age, sex, and size, and they must be housed identically and receive the same diet. If the chemical is injected into the experimental animals, then the controls must receive injections, too. However, the controls receive only the liquid in which the test chemical is ordinarily dissolved. For example, if the chemical is injected in water, then the controls receive an injection of water only.

There are many types of experiments, each with its special requirements. When it is not possible to manipulate the subject (as, for example, with human inheritance), "experiments of nature" can sometimes be used. The geneticist may predict that certain observations can be made—e.g., that one parent of children affected with a certain disease will always show the disease, too. If examination of many randomly selected cases shows this observation to be true, then the results have the same value as those of other kinds of experiments. One way or another, a hypothesis must be tested. It may then be rejected or, if it passes the test, expanded and further tested.

Certainty and Uncertainty

Eventually a hypothesis may become a generalized explanation. If widely accepted because of overwhelming evidence in its favor, the hypothesis is technically termed a **theory**. In everyday language, "theory" is used broadly to cover many ideas that would more rightly be called hypotheses.

As you might guess, the scientist who propounds a theory is not necessarily the one who

HOW TO READ A GRAPH

It is often useful to present scientific data in the form of a graph. Most graphs have one horizontal and one vertical axis (Graph A). The point of intersection of the two axes is called the origin. It is from the origin that numbers progress from left to right (horizontal axis) and from bottom to top (vertical axis), corresponding to the data. As you can see in Graph B, the numbers increase with distance from the origin. Here the horizontal axis is numbered in days and the vertical axis in gram weight of lovebirds.

Graph C illustrates how data are used to plot a graph. Note that lovebird weights of 7.5 grams at 5 days and 14 grams at 10 days have already been entered. The dashed lines show how a weight of 30 grams at 15 days would be plotted. At 20 days the weight of lovebirds was found to be 45 grams. Plot this data point and note that if each point in Graph C is connected, the shape of the curve drawn in Graph B begins to emerge.

A graph shows the relationship between two conditions or the effect of one condition on another. Ordinarily one reads the horizontal axis and then the vertical axis. Thus Graph B shows the effect of time on the weight of lovebirds. In other words, it illustrates lovebird growth. Starting with the origin and following the curve to the right, we see that the rise in the curve corresponds to an increase in lovebird weight with time. Beginning at 30 days, the curve starts to level off, indicating a slowing of growth as the birds reached their maximum size.

Often graphs are greatly simplified and used only to illustrate a general trend. Even when data numbers are omitted, however, the implication is that the data values increase as one moves farther from the origin. With that in mind, what story does Graph D tell about lovebird growth? Can you see that lovebird growth stopped for a short time before resuming?

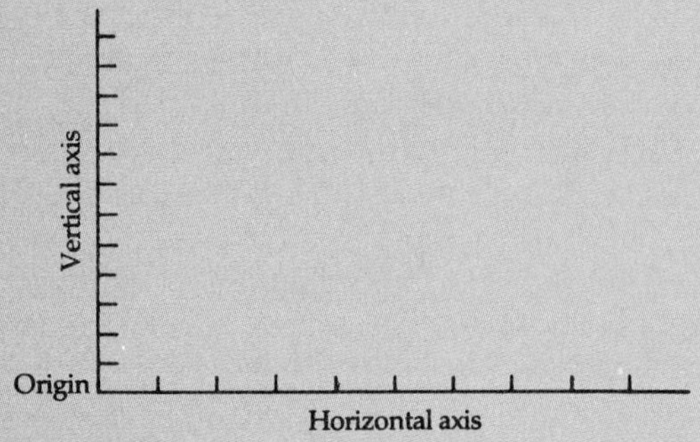

A

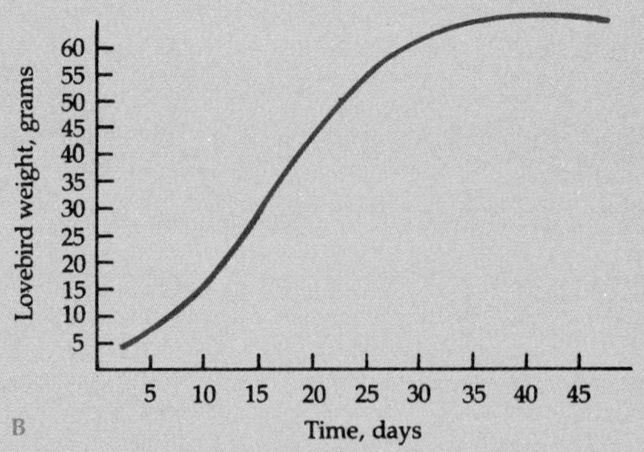

B

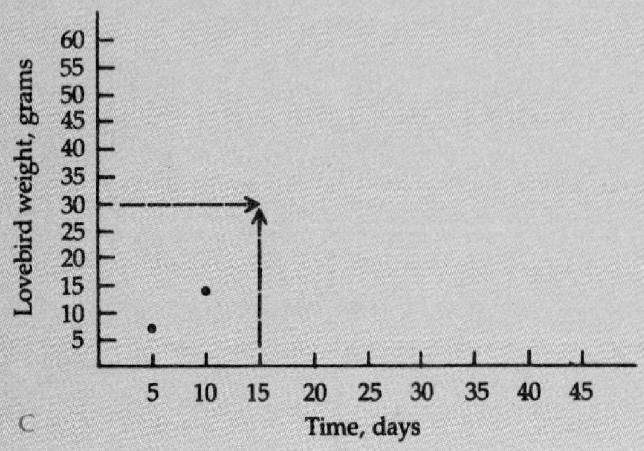

C

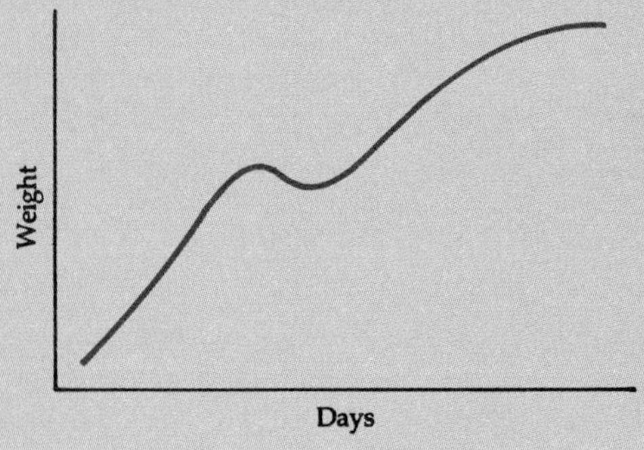

D

formulated the parent hypothesis. Some general theories develop from very old ideas. More specific theories are usually derived from suggestions put forth in recent publications that describe related research. In fact, the importance of publication in scientific journals (periodicals) lies largely in providing a body of data and hypotheses for future retesting and interpretation. Before scientific articles are accepted for publication, they are normally reviewed by several scientists who evaluate the methods and conclusions. These articles must demonstrate the significance of the work, but only infrequently do they proclaim a theory outright.

That theories have withstood the test of time doesn't guarantee them as absolutely correct. Even if a theory becomes "law," it can be dismissed when new ideas or new techniques lead to experiments that contradict the "law." More often scientific "laws" and theories are modified, just a bit, to take account of new evidence.

You may now be wondering if you can believe anything scientists say. Well, you can have the same confidence in their direct observations that you can have in your own senses. Of course, we have all been fooled occasionally by illusions or other sensory "tricks." Perhaps more profound reservations are in order for scientific speculations. Strictly speaking, hypotheses are not facts. They are only the most probable explanations available at present. On the other hand, theories, such as the theory of evolution, ought to be more reliable than hypotheses are. In fact, in order to be widely accepted, theories must be supported by a variety of evidence. This requirement is certainly met by the theory of evolution.

The chemical and organizational similarity of organisms is more understandable if the organisms evolved from some common ancestor. Furthermore, since all organisms live under the same general conditions of the biosphere, they may be expected to cope with living in similar ways. Yet one can see how selective forces resulting from interactions within ecosystems could mold new species in the process of evolution. And of course, by accepting this evolutionary process, we have an explanation for why the species of an ecosystem interact so smoothly. Thus, to a biologist at least, the theories of the unity of life, of evolution by natural selection, and of ecosystem interaction appear to be "true." Are they not as "true" as any other truths based on human experience? If you disagree, you may have a definition of truth that is different from ours. To what test do you put the "truths" in which you believe?

Scientists and Authors: Professional Students

Individuals interested in a particular area of biology probably read as much of the current and relevant scientific literature as they can. Most biologists (especially those who write textbooks) also try to keep abreast of divergent topics, not only by reading review articles and books in which information has been compiled, interpreted, and criticized but also by attending meetings of various scientific societies. The volume and complexity of these contributions, even though condensed and organized, are nevertheless staggering.

So many scientists have made significant contributions to the advance of biological knowledge that it would be impossible to credit each of them in a general textbook. Nor is it possible to present their work in any detail. Some authors describe a handful of experiments that may lead the reader to deduce basic principles or to relive the history of a theory. We have chosen instead to emphasize a coherent interpretation of the biological world in terms of current knowledge. Although we do not mention the men and women responsible for specific material, they are the real authorities. What you read are observations, hypotheses, and theories we have selected and organized into a "big picture." It is as accurate as we could make it, but it is a static picture of a dynamic science. And, of necessity, it is drawn in bold strokes.

Summary

1. Organisms have a common chemical composition. Proteins, polysaccharides, nucleic acids, and lipids are examples of chemicals that are unique to living things. Of these, proteins (because they include enzymes) and nucleic acids (because they carry genetic information) are the most important.

2. Organisms share similar patterns of organization. All organisms are composed of cells. In multicellular organisms, cells may become differentiated and organized into distinctive tissues, organs, and organ systems. All organisms of the same kind belong to the same species. The members of a species in any one area constitute a population. Communities are made up of the populations of many species.

3. The biosphere consists of recognizable ecosystems in which living and nonliving components are linked by the patterns of energy transfer inherent in food webs and by the operation of biogeochemical cycles.

4. Evolution is the slow genetic change that can occur in populations of organisms over time. Changing environments select organisms best suited to the new conditions. Geographical isolation encourages evolution of species by preventing interbreeding of populations.

5. Scientists make direct observations or perform experiments and use the information obtained to try to explain natural phenomena. Scientific explanations may be first stated as hypotheses and later expanded into theories or laws, which are nevertheless subject to change as knowledge accumulates.

Thought and Controversy

1. Although all organisms share fundamental similarities, each species differs from all others because each is adapted to a particular way of life. Some plants attract specific pollinators with characteristic odors or color patterns. In a few orchids the blooms resemble certain female insects and thus draw the attention of male insects of that species. Similarly, animals are adapted to every factor affecting life and reproduction. For example, several species of warblers may nest in the same woods because they eat different insects and don't compete for resources. Of course, all adaptations trace to differences in biochemistry. Life is as diverse as it is unified.

2. When we try to establish evolutionary relations and identify long-extinct ancestors, we must remember that every species, whenever it originated, evolved in response to its environment. The environment selected individuals with characteristics that permitted them to live and reproduce under existing conditions. No species ever evolved to be the ancestor of another species! When we envision life millions of years ago, we must imagine variety, specialization, and diversity. This conclusion is supported by what we find in the preserved bones and other fossil remains from the past.

3. The people listed in Box 1B made major contributions to biology. What comments can you make about the general versus specialized nature of the occupations of those at the beginning of the list as compared with those at the end of the list? About the general versus specialized nature of their contributions? Can you suggest any explanations? For insight into why women scientists appear so late on the list, read Margaret W. Rositer's *Women Scientists in America* (Johns Hopkins University Press, 1982).

Questions

1. What chemicals and chemical processes are common to all forms of life?

2. Define the following terms; order them numerically from the smallest to the largest level of organization.

community	population
organism	tissue
cell	organ

3. What is the critical difference between the way *chemicals* move through food webs and the way *energy* moves through them?

4. Why do biologists consider ecosystems to be fragile biological units?

5. Can an individual organism evolve? Why?

6. What is meant by natural selection? Give an example that illustrates the phenomenon.

7. What is the difference between a hypothesis and a theory?

8. List the hierarchical groups of the Linnaean system of classification in descending order. Which of these groups is easiest to define? Why?

2

The Road to Here: Our Animal Nature and Biological History

WE BELIEVE THAT LIVING IS A CONTINUOUS, DYNAMIC process. Threads of the great web of life connect us to other living organisms and trace back ultimately to the origin of life. All people belong to a single species, have common ancestors, and share the same basic biological characteristics. Humans must bow to the same physical and biological laws that govern other organisms.

Only by seeing ourselves as part of nature can we appreciate our interdependence with other organisms. We must recognize that humans are forever subject to the selective forces that mold species and drive them to extinction. This remains true, although we are living at a time when medical advances and agricultural technology have temporarily lifted some of the traditional selective pressures. The resulting unparalleled growth of human populations has led some people to assume that we control the earth. Nevertheless, humans remain part and product of an infinitely complex system.

To learn the details of this important concept, we begin our tour of the world of life with a brief look backward. Our goal is to examine the ever-changing earth as well as our own biological history.

THE MOST DISTANT PAST

Astronomers place the origin of the universe at a time 15 to 20 billion years ago. Little is known about this ancient event, but the most common hypothesis is often referred to as "the Big Bang." Light from the most distant stars reveals that the universe is continuously expanding. This observation suggests that at one time all matter was associated together and is today in the late stage of a giant explosion. Such an explosion must surely have released tremendous radiation. Remnants of this radiation are found in radio waves that travel in all directions through space. The attraction of matter for matter that we know as gravity accounts for the condensation of bits and particles that chanced near one another. The heat generated by pressure and nuclear reactions provided energy for other explosions as the universe continued to change. Eventually, swirling masses of gas contracted into billions of stars. One of these, our sun, appeared some five billion years ago. About one-half billion years later, remaining bits of matter condensed to form the planet earth.

The Unresting Earth

Never has the earth been still. The contraction of matter that formed our planet produced heat so intense that in its early years the earth was a churning mass of molten matter. Water vapor and other gases bubbled to the surface as the mass cooled, and a thin outer crust formed. Violent eruptions, tremors, and meteor impacts created a constant state of chaos. As time passed, temperatures dropped sufficiently to permit the condensation of great volumes of water on the planet's surface. Once water vapor and other gases had formed an atmosphere there were winds and dramatic weather patterns. And as the crust developed over time, it cracked into numerous plates that floated on the semi-molten rock below. At least we know that this is the case today and has been for hundreds of millions of years.

Drifting Continents and Changing Oceans. The earth's crust is thin, thinner proportionately than the skin on an apple. The **crustal plates** that make up this skin do not correspond exactly with familiar geographic boundaries. All the ocean floor is broken into plates, but only some of these plates bear continental masses. Like ice cubes floating in water, adjacent plates rub together and slide past or over one another as they are pushed apart by upheavals of molten rock from below. Although volcanoes reveal the molten state of matter not far from the surface, most crustal activity occurs beneath the floor of the ocean, hidden from easy observation. The most obvious clue is evident in the complementary shapes of certain continental coastlines (Fig. 2.1). Two hundred and forty million years ago the continents were joined together; the present oceans formed when the continents drifted apart. This explains not only why the continents fit together like pieces of a jigsaw puzzle, but also why rocks found on ocean bottoms are among the youngest rocks

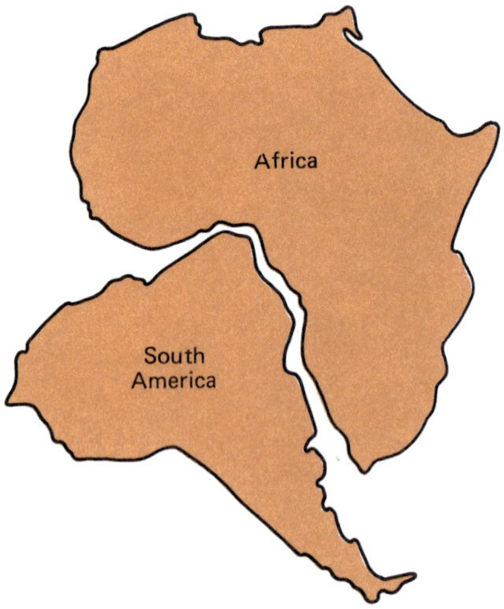

FIGURE 2.1 **Continental Fit.** Continental drift explains the fact that some continents fit into others.

FIGURE 2.2 **Crustal Movements.** Molten material flows to the surface at mid-oceanic ridges and solidifies as new crust. Because crust is added to the plates on both sides of the ridge, the older parts of the two plates are pushed apart. Where one plate is forced against another, the oceanic crust is drawn down and melted. This drawing down creates deep oceanic trenches.

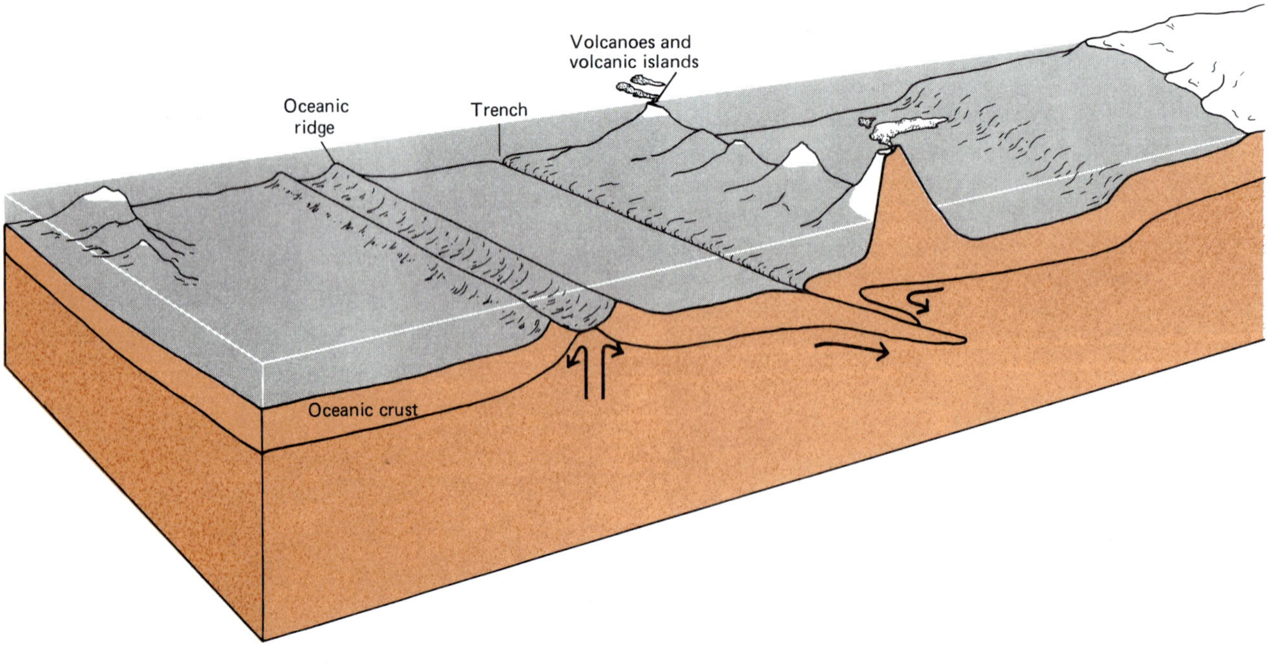

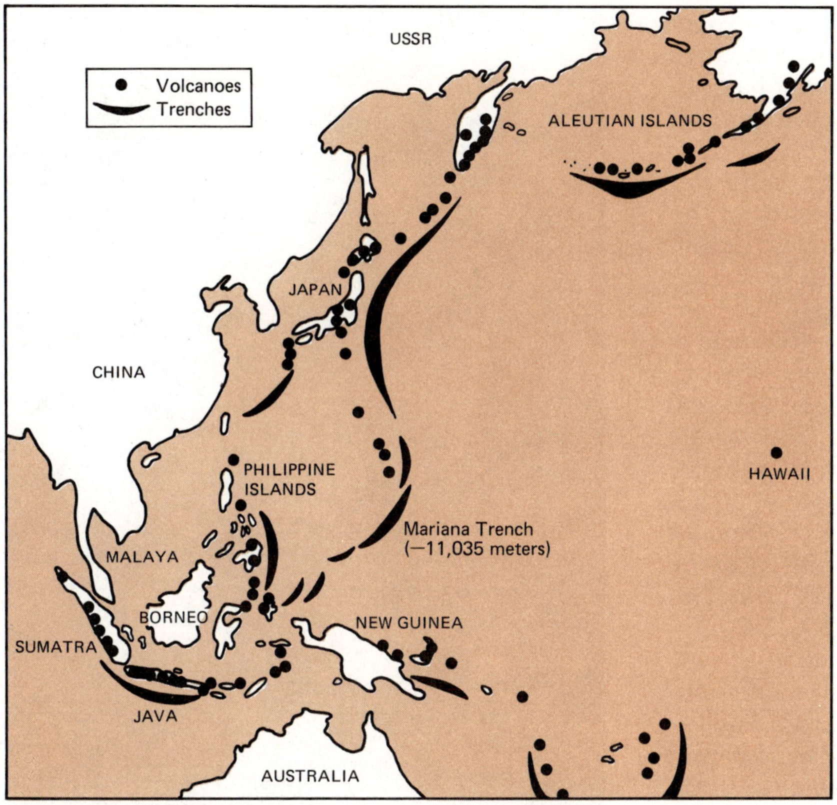

FIGURE 2.3 **Volcanoes and Trenches.** The island arcs of the western Pacific result from volcanic activity associated with submarine trenches.

on earth. Cores drilled from the Atlantic Ocean floor reveal that the oldest rocks that make up this ocean basin are in fact much younger than most rocks found on the continental surface. The presence of these young rocks indicates that new crust is forming here.

The North and South American plates were once continuous with those of Europe and Africa. The plates were spread apart by the formation of new crust at what is now a mid-oceanic ridge (Fig. 2.2). At such ridges, new crustal material seeps from fissures and forms additional sea floor. As the floor grows, it pushes the continents apart. Such activity is occurring today in several places but, since the earth is not expanding in circumference, old parts of the crust must be undergoing destruction. This destruction happens at **ocean trenches**, where one plate is forced under the other. Some trenches, such as those in the eastern Pacific, are more than six miles deep.

Volcanoes are particularly common along ocean ridges where plates are growing. Such volcanoes form mountains beneath the water's surface; sometimes they protrude as islands. The area we know as Iceland was formed by volcanoes along the mid-Atlantic ridge. Volcanoes appear also near trenches where one crustal plate slips over another. Along these trenches, strings of volcanoes may create island arcs. The Aleutian Islands and the Japanese Islands result from such processes (Fig. 2.3). Not surprisingly, earthquake zones are associated with these island arcs as well as other plate margins.

Collisions between plates create **folded mountains**. The union of India (once an island continent on a crustal plate) with Asia crumpled the rocky plates and formed the Himalayan Mountains. Plates sliding past one another may leave isolated fragments or exchange bits of their masses. Bermuda, the Falklands, and the Canary Islands are examples of abandoned fragments. There is evidence that Florida was transferred to the North American plate from Africa, Newfoundland from Europe, and parts of the Far West from Asia. The concept of movement of large blocks of the earth's crust was first known as **continental drift**. Because it involves the activity of crustal plates, this explanation of the origin of major earth features is also known as the **theory of plate tectonics**.

Uplift, Erosion, and Sedimentation. The earth's crust moves not only as parts of plates but also in much smaller units propelled by wind or water.

As the young earth's temperature fell, water vapor condensed in the primordial atmosphere and fell as rain. From that time forward, water has dissolved minerals and streams have moved particles varying in size from specks to boulders.

Wherever land protrudes above the surface of the oceans, rock and soil are slowly destroyed and carried away by water and wind. This destruction, known as **erosion**, is only one aspect of a giant cycle. The dust, sand, gravel, and dissolved minerals move downhill and come to rest as **sediments**. Sediments can accumulate in thick layers with sufficient weight that the lower layers are fused into new rock. These **sedimentary rocks** form mainly along the edges of continents, on the ocean floor, and at the bottom of lakes and other quiet bodies of water. We find such sedimentary rocks exposed after they have been lifted up as the result of the folding of the crustal plates. Once raised, these and all other rocks are subject to erosion (Fig. 2.4). Erosion, deposition of sediments, formation of new rocks, and uplift through crustal movements continuously modify the surface of the earth. Life appeared and evolved in this ever-changing environment. Indeed, it is change in the physical environment that provides the major driving force of evolution. New environments select organisms with different inherited traits.

FIGURE 2.4 **Eroded Sediments.** Erosion in Bryce Canyon reveals the many layers of sediments that make up the earth's surface in this area. The curious shapes result from the fact that some layers are softer than others and therefore wash away faster.

Time, Fossils, and Sediments. The sediments that accumulate from erosion provide the burial grounds for those evidences of past life that we term **fossils**. How fossils form and how they can be used to trace the history of life are described in Box 2A.

Both the great age of the earth and the length of time that life has existed are important to our understanding of the past. Only with the vast expanse of time could so many diverse forms of life evolve. Although nineteenth-century scientists, such as Charles Darwin, recognized that the numerous species had originated by natural selection, they lacked firm evidence of the length of time life has existed. Accurate dates of rock formation have confirmed the passage of sufficient time for so many diverse species to evolve. The basis of these age determinations is explained in Chapter 3. For now, we need remember only the immense age of our ever-changing earth.

Animal Origins

Humans share a biological history with other animals and, as suggested by the unity of life, with all other species as well. The origin of life is unknown. Many scientists believe life arose spontaneously, but this hypothesis must not be confused with the theory of evolution, which deals with the formation of new species from existing ones.

The oldest firmly identified fossils are simple microscopic organisms thought to be bacteria. Such fossils appear in rocks that are over three billion years old. The earliest evidence we have of animals is about 700 million years old. By 600 million years ago animals were abundant and included most of the major types we know today. Soon afterward we find the earliest fish. These and all other fish are vertebrates, just as we are. Vertebrates are distinguished by brains enclosed in skull cases and bodies supported by a series of backbones known as vertebrae. Fish evolved many diverse groups that followed numerous ways of life. Some breathed air, a distinct advantage where water was silty from erosion or fouled by rotting plants.

Certain of these air-breathing fish, equipped with elongate fins, crawled out on land. Some such fish population was ancestral to **amphibians**, and in turn to reptiles, birds, and mammals. But these air-breathing fish were not the first organisms to live on land nor were they the first land animals. Much earlier, plants had colonized the land near waterways, and ancestors of the millipedes and scorpions had long since moved ashore.

Unlike amphibians, **reptiles** lay shelled eggs in which they provide their young with a moist environment independent of lakes and streams. This freedom from the aquatic environment was one factor in the evolutionary success of reptiles. The dinosaurs represent only two of more than a dozen now-extinct reptilian groups. Although both birds and mammals evolved from reptilian ancestors, reptiles remained the dominant land animals for more than a hundred thousand years after mammals appeared.

It was their constantly warm body temperatures that allowed early **mammals** to survive in a largely reptilian world. Mammals can be active in cold weather and on cool nights when reptiles are dormant. This **nocturnal behavior** explains the fact that most mammals rely on **olfaction** (the sense of smell) much more than they rely on vision. There is insufficient light for good vision during the hours when typical mammals are out and about. Mammals also have the advantage of **hair** that serves as insulation. And all mammals nurse their young, thereby ensuring them a supply of energy-rich food.

During the 200 million years that mammals have existed many changes have occurred in the crust of the earth as well as in climate. After a time of widespread deserts, there followed a long warm and wet period. Beginning about 2.5 million years ago and ending only recently, temperature fluctuations produced the Ice Age. During this time, known as the **Pleistocene** (PLY-stuh-seen) many mammalian species disappeared. As we will see, our ancestors were Pleistocene hunters and may have had a hand in this extinction.

HUMANS AS PRIMATES

Human beings and the animals most similar to humans are known as **primates**. The choice of this term isn't surprising, for it means "first rank." Among the primates we find humans, apes, monkeys, and some lesser-known animals, including the lemurs and bushbabies (Fig. 2.5).

FIGURE 2.5 **Lesser-Known Primates.** Unlike most primates, bushbabies (a) feed at night. This fact explains their large eyes and ears. The ring-tailed lemur (b) represents an unusual group of primates that has evolved on the Island of Madagascar, where many common kinds of mammals are missing.

(a) (b)

BOX 2A

HOW FOSSILS COME TO BE

Any evidence of a once-living organism, including invisible substances recognizable only by chemical methods, can be termed a fossil. Even tracks and tunnels can fossilize if they become filled with sand or mud that differs from the surrounding material. However, most animal fossils are hard parts. These include bones, teeth, shells, and exoskeletons (outside skeletons, such as those of crabs and insects). Likewise, in the case of plants, only the most resistant parts fossilize.

A knowledge of the process of fossilization helps explain why the fossil record is always incomplete. Such an understanding also explains why we have better fossil evidence of some organisms than of others. Optimal conditions for fossilization include protection from mechanical and chemical disturbances. Burial in mud, silt, or sand beneath quiet water is ideal. The fine sediments seal the remains from oxygen that would otherwise support decay and spontaneous chemical disintegration. In quiet water there is no mechanical churning that might break up the body. If more and more sediments accumulate, the deeply buried sediments may turn to rock that will encase the remains and protect the fossil. Therefore organisms that fall into lake-bottom muds have a good chance of becoming fossils.

On the other hand, the remains of animals that die in a warm, moist forest are likely to be torn apart and consumed by insects and other scavengers. If bones should be trampled into the earth intact, acid soil waters will soon dissolve bone minerals. Since most primates live in warm, moist forests, it isn't surprising that primate fossils are rare compared with those of clams, for example. Clams nearly always leave their shells in the accumulating sediments of lakes or ocean shores.

But just because an organism fossilizes, there is no guarantee—nor is it even probable—that the fossil will end up in a museum. The longer a fossil remains in the earth, the deeper it is likely to be buried and the more apt it is to be deformed by heat, pressure, or the folding of surrounding rock. Furthermore, people find only those fossils that are revealed through erosion or by mining and other rock-moving operations. Most fossils lie buried where human eyes will never see them. And when rare fossils are ex-

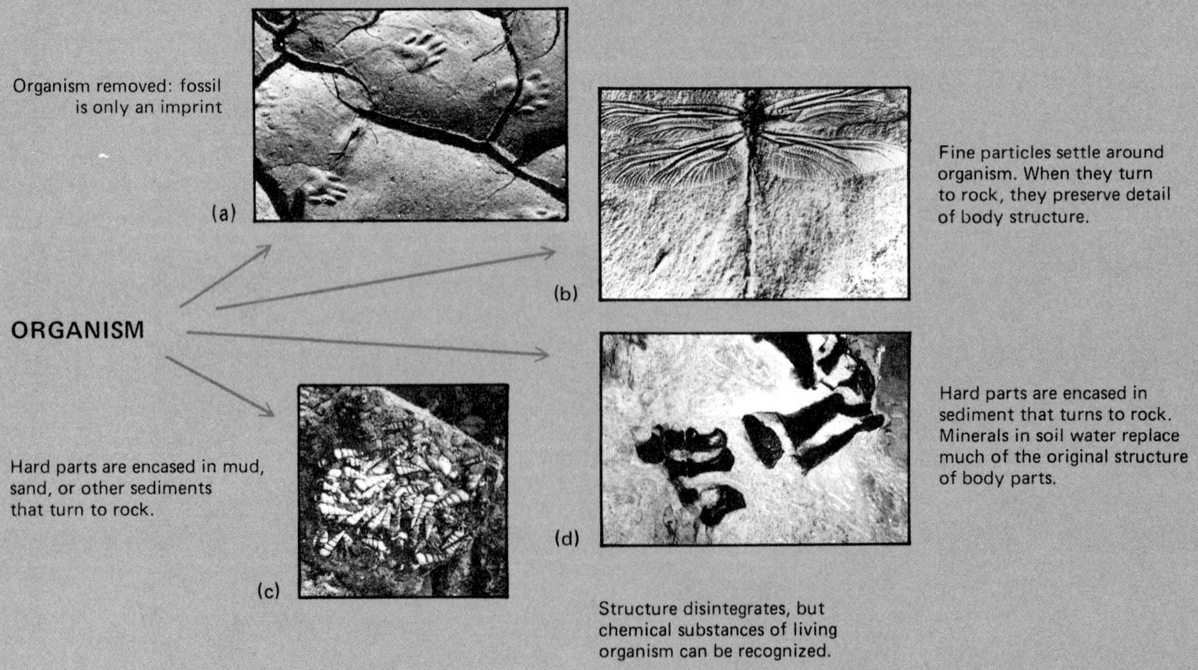
Organism removed: fossil is only an imprint
(a)
Fine particles settle around organism. When they turn to rock, they preserve detail of body structure.
(b)
ORGANISM
Hard parts are encased in sediment that turns to rock. Minerals in soil water replace much of the original structure of body parts.
Hard parts are encased in mud, sand, or other sediments that turn to rock.
(d)
(c)
Structure disintegrates, but chemical substances of living organism can be recognized.

posed by erosion, they often go unrecognized and unpreserved.

FROM FOSSILS TO THEORIES

The fruitful study of primate fossils requires teams of scientists with many skills. After the location of a fossil find is marked precisely, geologists examine the rock structure and determine the age of the fossil or of the layer in which it lay. The site is then carefully excavated and precise records are made of the location of any other objects. All animal or plant fossils must be identified, for they may provide clues about the habitat. Bits of garbage can reveal which animals were hunted or bear marks showing the use of tools or fire. Discovery of domestic varieties of plants or animals can establish the existence of agriculture. In addition to fossils, humans leave artifacts, objects they have modified intentionally. Stone tools are the most common artifacts at older sites. Such tools are classified as both fossils and artifacts.

Discovering and excavating a fossil site is only the beginning. Interpretation of primate fossils demands additional work. The assembly of fossil fragments requires extensive knowledge and experience. Minute details can provide clues concerning the proper placement of a fragment within the skeleton. The shape of a bone can indicate posture or suggest patterns of movement. Even when it is possible to reconstruct a nearly complete skull or skeleton, much work remains to be done. Specimens must be examined and compared repeatedly to determine their significance. Despite careful work, conclusions are tentative and must be reconsidered as further data become available.

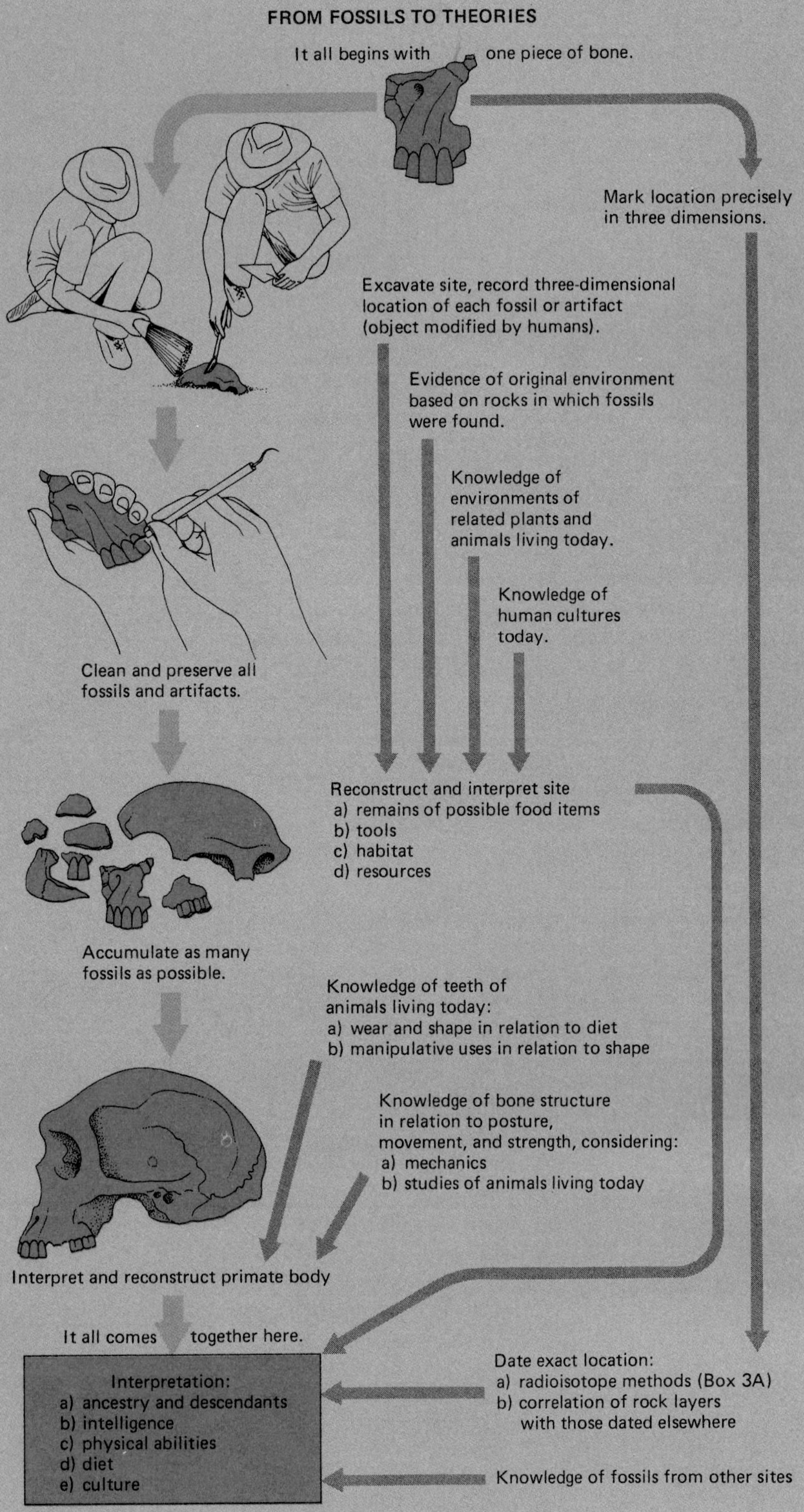

Life in the Trees

Most present-day primates live in tropical forests, and all of them can climb trees, at least at some time in their lives. The arboreal ("in the trees") habitat appears basic to primates, although we must note that a few species (baboons, for example) live almost exclusively on the ground and use trees only to escape from predators. Mammals generally do not live in trees; consequently, we might expect primates to exhibit special characteristics that favor the arboreal life. To begin the list, primates rely mainly on vision (sight) instead of smell, which is the primary sense of most mammals. This difference is most certainly related to tree-dwelling.

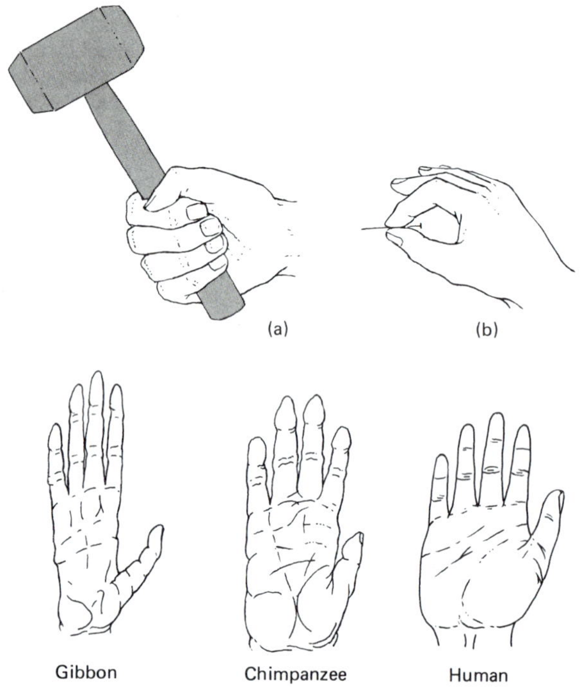

FIGURE 2.6 **All in the Thumb.** Any ape can make a power grip (a), but only humans are capable of the precision grip (b). This requires that the thumb rotate at its base and that it be of proper length compared with the fingers. Note that neither the gibbon nor the chimpanzee has a thumb long enough to reach the tip of its cupped fingers.

Switching Primary Senses. As we pointed out earlier, typical mammals are nocturnal. Most either burrow in the ground or keep close to the surface where odors linger. Under these circumstances, the sense of smell is more useful than vision. In contrast, most primates are active during daylight hours, and all have good vision.

Of course, good vision is useful to animals that must move through swaying trees searching for edible tidbits. Unlike most mammals, primates have **binocular vision**; i.e., they can see objects with both eyes at the same time. Binocular vision makes effective depth perception possible, because each eye views objects from a slightly different point and hence from a slightly different angle. The farther away an object is, the more closely the views of the two eyes coincide. Primates also have **color vision**. As we will see later, color vision requires bright light; consequently it is most useful in diurnal animals.

Because the breezes of treetops dilute and mingle scents, a good sense of smell is of little value there. Consequently the olfactory structures that account for large noses are reduced. Although some primates, such as lemurs, retain a distinct muzzle, the faces of others are nearly flat. Over the course of evolution, reduction in the muzzle has permitted reorganization of muscles of the face and upper lip of many primates. This has allowed use of facial expression in short-range communication between individuals. In humans these muscles contribute not only to facial expression but also to speech.

Generalized Hands and Feet. Vision is essential for moving through treetops, but so is agility. Any fall is dangerous, and even one broken bone can make it impossible for an individual to keep up with the band, where there is safety in numbers.

In such a complex environment it is advantageous to be able to jump, cling, walk, and hang in every conceivable position and from surfaces of all shapes and sizes. The range of movements possible with general-purpose appendages exceeds those in limbs highly specialized for one kind of action. Thus it isn't surprising that primates retain relatively general arms and legs. Though the hands and feet of primates show considerable modification compared with those of ancestral vertebrates, primates are less specialized than many other mammals. To see this, compare the range of movement in a cat's paw or a horse's hoof with that of your hand. Even without our specialized thumb (Fig. 2.6), our forelimbs would be much more versatile than either a paw or a hoof.

In nearly all primates, **nails** have replaced the claws of ancestral mammals. The need for precise knowledge about limb surfaces increases reliance on fingertip information. Flattened nails provide firm, even support for fingertip sense organs. The skin ripples that are responsible for fingerprints also have a special function in the trees. These **friction ridges** make it easier to hang on to smooth limbs.

Generalized Food and Teeth. Food available high in the forest consists mostly of seeds, leaves, and fruit. But in addition to plant materials, there are many insects, as well as a variety of bird eggs and nestlings, lizards, frogs, and even smaller primates. Although each species has its food preferences, the overwhelming majority of primates are **omnivorous** (eating a variety of foods, including both plants and animals). However, all primates rely more on plant foods than on animal foods. The importance of vegetation in the diet is reflected by the broad cheek teeth, which are necessary for grinding rough plant tissues. Primates of all sizes have forefeet they use for manipulation. With these they carry out activities that most other mammals perform with their teeth.

Complex Environment Favors Complex Brain. Animals are best able to make quick, coordinated maneuvers and cope with unpredictable food supplies if they have a complex nervous system. The many threats and problems primates face cannot be met with simple formulas. Thus inherited behavioral patterns are too rigid to be much used in a tree habitat. The behavior of mammals in general tends to be more flexible than that of other vertebrates, but primate behavior has an especially large learned component. It is probable that the primate way of life has favored the survival and reproduction of those with the ability to meet new problems in new ways. It can be argued that life in the trees favored evolution of **reasoning** and **problem solving**. Whatever their origin, these distinctive mental abilities are best developed in the higher primates. The flaw in this argument is that many of these species—for example, the chimpanzee, the gorilla, and various baboons—are largely terrestrial.

Correlated with learned behavior is enlargement of the anterior part of the skull. It is here we find the **forebrain**, the seat of reasoning and learning. This relationship is important, because attempts to trace human ancestry rely in part on changes in skull shape and size.

And Young Born Singly. Life in trees is precarious for young animals. The complex nervous system needed there requires a long time for development. And since food in tropical forests is widely scattered, the primate troop must be always on the move, and the mother must carry her young. Under these circumstances, several young born at once would impose an impossible burden. In fact, only a few primates have twins; single births are typical. The room available in the uterus to a single young allows it to remain inside the mother until quite large. This, in turn, permits the fetus sufficient time to form a large and intricate nervous system.

The true relationship between a complex nervous system, tree dwelling, and long uterine development is difficult to untangle. Without doubt, a complex nervous system is valuable in the treetops. But the extent to which it evolved among tree dwellers remains uncertain. Whether typical small primates are smarter than similar-sized terrestrial mammals is an unanswered question. Many carnivores, such as the African hunting dog, may compare favorably to most primates. Some of the brightest primates, such as the chimpanzee and the gorilla, are largely terrestrial.

We can also question whether the advantage of a single infant born at an advanced stage was the pressure that lengthened uterine development and permitted increased brain complexity. Maybe the primary advantage was a complex nervous system. The increased uterine development necessary for a larger nervous system could have favored single births.

At best we are left with the impression that tree dwelling was important in the evolution of traits associated with primates. It was upon these basic primate traits that other selective forces built the human species. But our way of life was never an arboreal one nor were our immediate ancestors arboreal.

Our Closest Kin

Humans exhibit each of the primate characteristics we have discussed: reliance on vision instead of olfaction, binocular vision, color vision, generalized limbs, omnivorous diet, well-developed forebrain, and young born singly. Comparison of the human skeleton with that of another primate (Fig. 2.7) reveals many additional similarities. The evidence is convincing that if we are related to other animals at all, we must be primates. But which

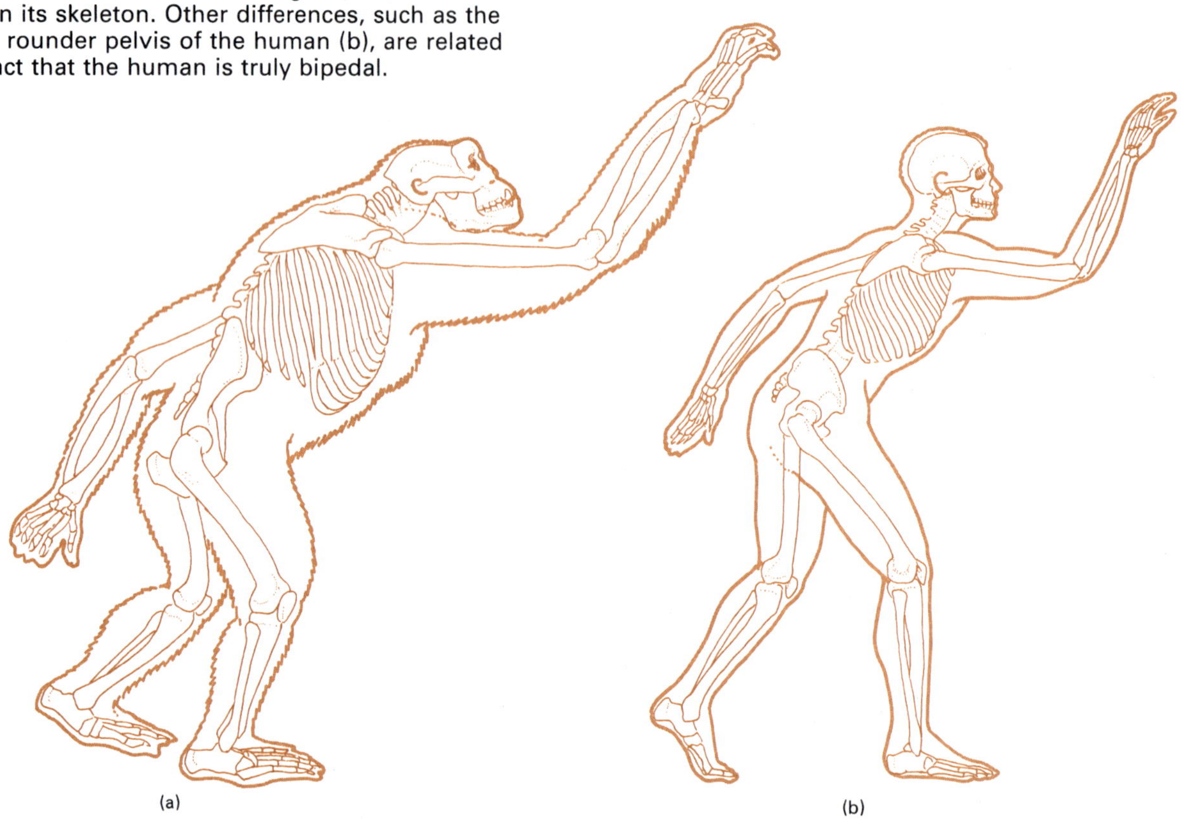

FIGURE 2.7 **Gorilla and Human Skeletons.** The longer arms and heavier muscles of the gorilla (a) are reflected in its skeleton. Other differences, such as the smaller, rounder pelvis of the human (b), are related to the fact that the human is truly bipedal.

primates are our closest relatives? With which other primates do we share close ancestors? The evidence indicates that our nearest living nonhuman relatives are apes.

Characteristics that link humans to **apes** include lack of an external tail, a large brain relative to body size, and the possession of the same number of each kind of tooth (incisors, canines, premolars, and molars). Tooth shapes are also similar.

If it is true that our nearest nonhuman relatives are apes, how can that knowledge help us understand the origin of our species? In approaching this question, we must consider how humans are different from apes. Apes show structural specializations for **brachiation**, i.e., hanging from tree limbs and moving along hand over hand (Fig. 2.8). This is true of all four ape groups: the gorillas, the chimpanzees, the orangutans, and the gibbons and their relatives, the siamangs. Yet only the orangutans, gibbons, and siamangs spend most of their time in trees. Nevertheless, the gorillas and chimps, both largely terrestrial, have the long arms that are the mark of brachiators. They also have long fingers with short thumbs that make good limb clasps. And they have highly muscular arms and chest. The most likely explanation for the presence of brachiation adaptations in these terrestrial apes is that they are derived rather directly from tree dwellers.

It has been argued that humans show brachiation characteristics to some degree, but our body build is quite different. In humans it is not the arms but the legs that are long relative to the trunk. Furthermore, the human foot is a unique structure, fully adapted to walking. In contrast, the ape foot seems best adapted to catching hold of limbs. The evidence suggests that humans have a long line of terrestrial ancestors. And since our closest affinities seem to lie with the apes, we should look to the terrestrial apes for evidence of kinship.

Chimpanzees quickly solve simple problems, such as how to use boxes and sticks to obtain a bunch of bananas hung out of reach. Several chimps have learned the rudiments of language, and they communicate either with plastic symbols or in sign language. Chimps also make and use simple tools. These traits are, of course, important human characteristics, but there are large differences between development of such traits in chimps and in us.

Their cheerful dispositions and fascinating facial expressions have brought a lot of attention to chimpanzees. However, we know less about gorillas. Both species walk on the knuckles of their hands (Fig. 2.9) much of the time. Neither assumes the fully upright posture of humans. Anatomically, gorillas resemble humans a little less than do chimps. One factor is the large difference in size between male and female gorillas. This difference is much greater than in chimps or humans. On the other hand, attempts to teach young gorillas human language promise to be at least as successful as related work with chimpanzees.

FIGURE 2.8 **Brachiation.** Apes cling to overhead vegetation and move hand over hand.

FIGURE 2.9 **Knuckle Walking.** When traveling on all four limbs, apes walk on the knuckles of their hands. This habit, combined with their long arms, gives apes a partially upright posture.

Biochemical studies demonstrate greater similarities between chimpanzees and humans than between gorillas and humans. The chemical patterns of chimps and humans correspond so well that they provide little basis for separating the two species. Considering the anatomical differences, these similarities can be used as evidence that chemical evolution and structural evolution proceed at different rates. But the mere fact that we can't see the chemical similarities makes them no less real.

Returning to the question of what is our nearest living relative, we see that evidence points to the chimpanzee. If we seek our nearest nonhuman ancestor, we must look for an animal more like a chimpanzee than anything else now alive. Of course, this ancestral species lived in an environment different from that of the chimpanzee and differed both structurally and behaviorally from the chimpanzee.

BOX 2B

CHIMPS AREN'T CHUMPS

How similar are the mental abilities of chimpanzees to those of people?

Several human couples have raised baby chimpanzees in their homes. In general, the little chimps act much like human babies and quickly gain the affection of their foster parents. Other than the fact that mental development in apes soon lags behind, the most obvious difference between young chimps and human children is that the chimps don't learn to speak. With careful coaching the chimps can utter a few words, at best. Due to anatomical differences (see drawing), human sounds are difficult for chimpanzees to mimic.

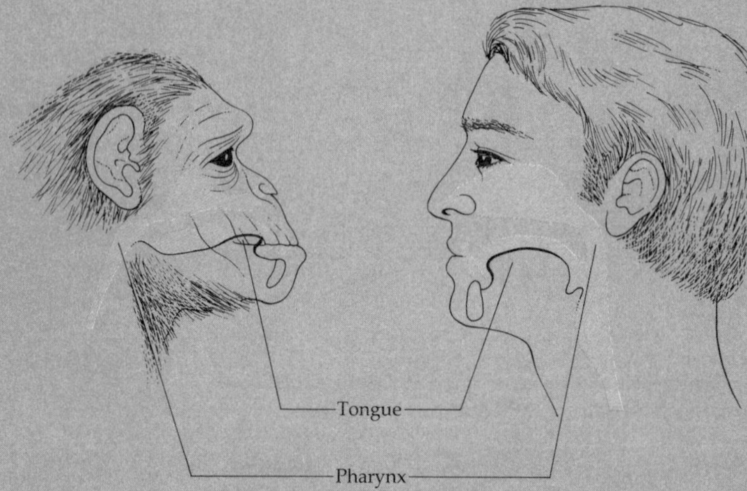

To circumvent this problem, Allan and Beatrice Gardner of the University of Nevada taught the sign language of the deaf to their baby chimp, Washoe. This sign system relies mainly on arbitrary symbols but includes some finger spelling. The Gardners' choice of sign language was based on firm knowledge of chimpanzee behavior. These animals are keen observers of facial expression and other close-range visual signals. An opportunity to learn sign language was a good test of Washoe's mental capacities, which proved to be substantial. Within 51 months of training, she had acquired a vocabulary of 132 signs. (She used 85 signs within the first 36 months of training.) Washoe generalized both correctly and incorrectly, as would a human child. For example, when she wanted a bottle of soda pop uncapped, Washoe spontaneously used the sign for "open" that she learned in connection with doors. But when she first saw a human navel, she signed "hurt" as she had learned to do for the small injuries she sustained while playing.

Ann and David Premack of the University of California at Santa Barbara tried a different technique with their chimp, Sarah. They used pieces of plastic in various shapes and colors to represent specific nouns, verbs, adjectives, and concepts. Not only did Sarah learn concepts such as "sameness" and "if–then," but she mastered complicated sentences. Although Sarah never asked questions, she learned to answer them. Certainly Sarah's performance is as impressive as that of most two-year-old children.

These and numerous subsequent studies provide what seems to be good evidence that chimpanzees can grasp some elements of language. Nevertheless, some scientists challenge the significance of these findings and consider them no more significant than the fact that you can train a dog by rewarding desirable behavior.

Although chimps do not use speech in nature, they do use tools. In this context, we define a tool as "any object intentionally modified for use in an action impossible with the unaided body." During her years of observing wild bands of chimpanzees in Tanzania, Jane Goodall saw them remove projections from twigs, moisten the twigs in their mouths, and then poke the wet twigs into termite nests. After a few moments the chimps withdrew the twigs, which were now covered with termites, and licked the termites off the stick. Goodall also observed chimps chewing leaves into soft masses and then

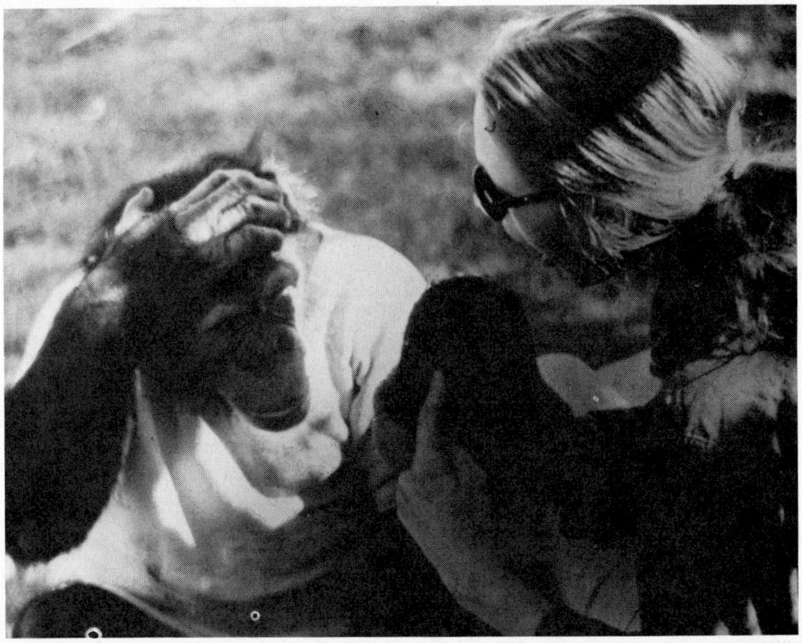

using them to sponge up water from tiny crevices. By sucking the wet-leaf masses, they could get water they couldn't drink directly. The young chimps learned to make these simple tools by watching their elders, just as children learn by watching older humans.

Not only do chimps make tools, but they also go hunting. Their prey seems limited only by availability and size. In the Tanzania study area, chimps prey on young bushbucks, bush-pigs, immature baboons, and three species of monkeys. At times one or more males cooperate in chasing or stalking a single animal. The chimpanzees kill by biting the neck, twisting the head, or grabbing the animal by the hind legs and smashing the skull against the ground.

Simple hunger seems an unlikely motive for hunting by chimpanzees. Meat accounts for less than one percent of their diet. Furthermore, attacks most often occur when the chimps are already stuffed with fruit or vegetation. It may be that the chimps have protein hunger. A diet consisting largely of fruit and leaves can be poor in protein. The fact that the chimps eat every bit of the kill supports this view.

In comparing chimpanzees with people, we see many of the same qualities and a pattern of similar behavior. Where the limits lie we can't say. And we may never know, because wild chimps are threatened by expanding human populations, as are other primates around the world. Important as laboratory studies are, we can never take the full measure of a species in captivity.

THE RECORD

Now that we have established the nature of our nearest nonhuman ancestor, we are ready to survey the fossil record in search of this animal. To learn about fossils and the ways that scientists interpret them, see Box 2A.

The oldest fossil evidence of apes was found in Egypt in rocks formed about 29 million years B.P. (before the present). This early ape shows distinct similarities to *Dryopithecus* (dry-o-PITH-e-kus), a group of apes that lived several million years later. ("Pithekos" is a Greek root meaning "ape"; you'll find that it occurs repeatedly in the names of apes and apelike humans. For a further explanation of scientific names, see Box 1A.)

Remnants of *Dryopithecus* are widespread from Spain to China and south to Uganda. These fossils are from a large group of generalized apes that varied in size but all of which had limbs somewhat specialized for brachiation. Their molar teeth, used for chewing, resembled those of chimps and humans. *Dryopithecus* is so similar to present-day chimpanzees that one fossil was named *Proconsul*, in honor of a well-known chimp, Consul, in the London Zoo.

Closely related to *Dryopithecus* is a series of 9- to 14-million-year-old fossils classified as *Ramapithecus* (rah-ma-PITH-e-kus). These differ in minor ways from dryopithecine apes. Interestingly, these differences are in the direction of human characteristics. Perhaps a population of *Ramapithecus* was ancestral to humans but not to chimps or other present-day apes. On the other hand, recent studies have accumulated extensive evidence of biochemical similarities between apes and humans. These similarities are much greater than expected.
4 Due to the minimal differences in DNA (Fig. 2.10) and blood proteins among humans, chimps, and gorillas, some scientists hypothesize that the ape and human lines separated only about five million years ago.

Early Humans

The fossil record reveals that early **hominids**, animals having basic human characteristics but not necessarily fully human, were living four million years ago. This was before the beginning of the Ice Age (Pleistocene). All the older hominid fossils are from Africa, making it likely that hominids originated there.

FIGURE 2.10 **DNA Comparisons Show Humans Similar to Chimps.** The distances in this diagram represent differences in DNA patterns. This similarity of the genetic material is greater than might be expected from external appearances.

Controversy surrounds these early fossils. Evolutionary relationships remain uncertain. Most authorities divide all known hominid fossils into two genera. Some of the oldest hominid fossils have been assigned to the genus *Australopithecus* (aw-stray-loh-PITH-e-kus). One distinctive characteristic of this genus is a small brain case. Reconstructions indicate that the *Australopithecus* brain case did not exceed 600 cubic centimeters (cc), or little more than a pint. Interpretation of this fact is difficult. Although there is some correlation between brain size and intelligence, living humans of normal intelligence have brain cases ranging from 1000 to more than 2000 cc (0.95 to 1.9 qt). On the other hand, gorillas have brain cases of about 500 cc (0.53 qt). Body size is a factor affecting such comparisons. Large male gorillas weigh 225 kg (nearly a quarter ton) compared with an estimated 22–44 kg (50–100 lb) for australopithecines. Surely larger animals require larger brains than smaller animals merely to control the same body activities. Thus the small brains of *Australopithecus* can be misleading, especially since we have so few complete skeletons from which to estimate body size. What evidence we have suggests that some of the australopithecines were much smaller than most present-day humans.

The type and quality of tools produced are another measure of mental ability. Although durable rock tools have been found in the vicinity of australopithecine remains, it is possible that the tools were manufactured by other hominids, who preyed on the australopithecines. Just as we cannot be certain that the rock tools were made by australopithecines, other fiber or wooden tools they may have made would have decayed long ago.

Skeletal evidence and foot tracks in 3.5-million-year-old volcanic ash deposits indicate that some australopithecines walked erect. This may not have been true of all species, but it seems likely that they all had hands free to carry and use tools. The australopithecine face protruded as is characteristic of animals that use their mouths for manipulation. Nevertheless, australopithecines lacked the greatly enlarged canine teeth apes use for holding and tearing.

The relationship between the several species of *Australopithecus* and *Homo* is a matter of contention. Some authorities identify fossils more than two million years old as *Homo*. Many scientists believe that *Australopithecus* and *Homo* existed side by side. There is little doubt that these two groups share a common ancestor (Fig. 2.11).

Although their immediate ancestry is uncertain, there is no doubt that humans much like ourselves walked the earth a million and a half years ago. Remains from Asia, Africa, and Europe show that these people were fully erect and quite similar to humans today. Their estimated cranial capacity averages slightly less than the brain cases of modern people and somewhat greater than those of australopithecines. A large lower jaw, heavy brow

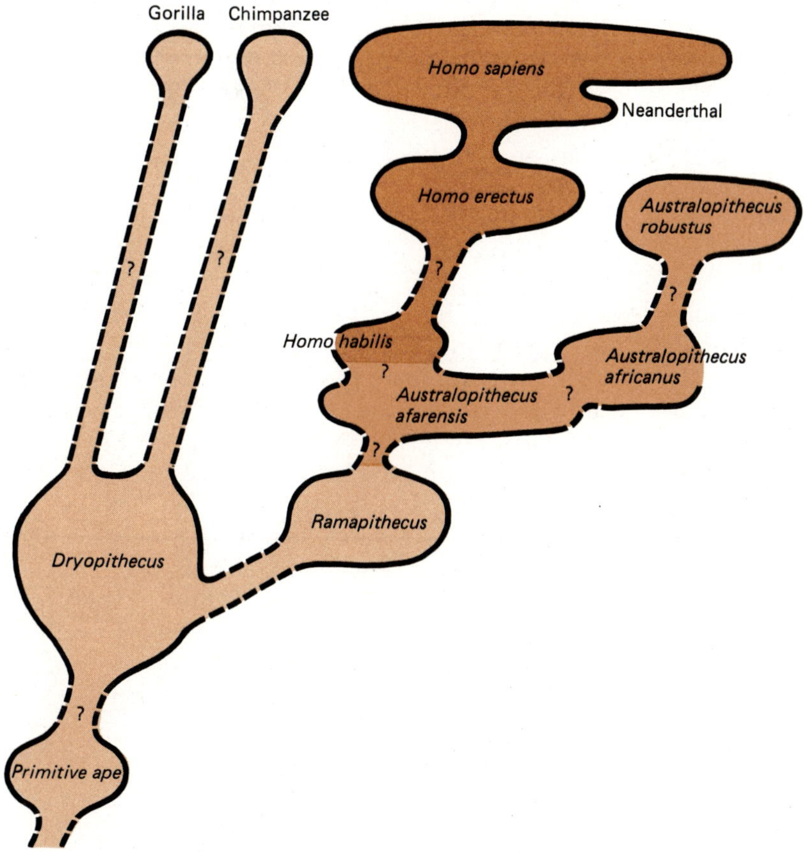

FIGURE 2.11 The Family Tree? The relationships among fossil and living apes and humans are still open to speculation. Here is one possible scheme. It shows *Australopithecus afarensis* as ancestral to all humans. *A. afarensis* includes a relatively complete female skeleton nicknamed "Lucy" and numerous skulls found at Afar in Ethiopia. *Homo habilis* has smaller teeth and a larger brain case. Specimens are from Olduvai Gorge in Tanzania.

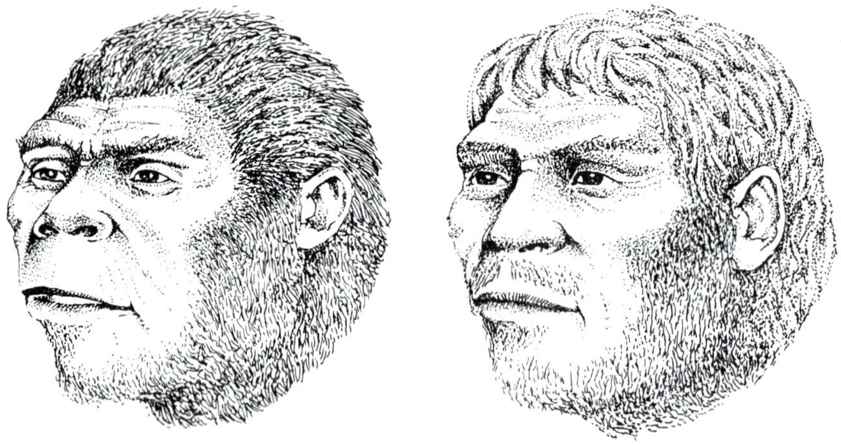

(a) Homo erectus

(b) Homo sapiens Neanderthalensis

FIGURE 2.12 **Putting Flesh on Fossils.** These are artist's conceptions of the appearances of humans known only from fossil bones. If you could meet these individuals in street clothes, do you think you would be able to distinguish them from other living humans? What traits would you use?

ridges, and the absence of a well-developed chin distinguish these fossils from present-day humans. These early humans may be classified as another species, *Homo erectus*, or more simply, as early members of *Homo sapiens*. Most authorities prefer to use the designation *H. erectus*.

Recent Humans

The inadequacies of the fossil record and, perhaps, a gradual evolution of the human line make it difficult to decide exactly when modern people appeared. A few of the oldest fossils identified as *Homo sapiens* may be nearly one-half million years old, but some much like *H. erectus* are considerably younger. Perhaps not all fossils represent populations ancestral to people today. On the other hand, there is no evidence that our species traces to a single isolated group. The full story remains untold. It may be far more complicated than we have suggested.

Most of the older *Homo sapiens* were stocky people with distinct brow ridges, heavy teeth, and lacking the chin characteristic of people today. These are the **Neanderthals** (nee-AN-der-thawlz), whose cultural accomplishments have gone largely unrecognized.

It Takes Skill to Live in a Tundra. During the last great Ice Age many Neanderthals lived on the edge of tundra or nearby, where the cold steppe merged with forests north of the Black Sea. Life in such a climate is impossible for humans without significant cultural adaptation. Clothing is essential. The abundance of discarded skin scrapers left here by Neanderthals suggests that they wore animal skins. The many distinctive shapes of the stone tools show skill in tool-making. The animal bones in the garbage heaps suggest that the Neanderthals were expert hunters. They took woolly mammoth, woolly rhinoceros, bison, moose, brown bear, cave bear, and wild boar as well as an array of smaller animals.

The Neanderthals are the first people we know to have buried their dead. The very act of burial suggests a sense of bereavement or belief in life after death. So do the red pigments found with some remains. Perhaps these were used to paint the body or to create special grave goods. Or maybe the pigment itself was so treasured that it was buried with other cherished possessions. Engraving on bone tools may reflect magic rites, record keeping, or perhaps an aesthetic sense. Detailed examination of one burial site in Iraq revealed high concentrations of fossil pollen, all from plants known for their medicinal qualities. Whether the grave flowers were picked for their curative powers or merely because they were available, no one knows. However, all we do know about the Neanderthals points to a highly developed culture.

Body Features. Finally, we must evaluate the physical features of the Neanderthal. One of the most complete early discoveries was the skeleton of an arthritic old man. Because the effect of disease on this skeleton wasn't recognized immediately, there were exaggerated reports of the coarseness of features and stoop-shouldered posture. Nevertheless, Neanderthals' facial bones were heavier than ours. Indeed, their entire skeletons were heavier in proportion to their height. Among species living today, stout bones reflect heavy muscles. Hence it seems that the Neanderthals sported muscles we would consider massive. But why did their way of life favor stronger muscles than have been needed by later peoples?

Although the Neanderthals had a hitherto unparalleled kit of stone tools, perhaps they employed their bodies in novel ways. After all, they wrung an existence from a particularly harsh environment. For example, they may have softened animal hides by chewing them. The advantage conferred by tremendous jaw muscles might have been sufficient to select humans with especially strong facial muscles and coarse facial bones.

The short, stocky body form may have been advantageous in cold weather. Because a compact body has less surface area for heat loss, chunky people retain heat better than slender ones.

Cro-Magnon: Usurper or Descendant? Humans whose skeletons are indistinguishable from our own lived at least 35,000 years ago. Those humans are represented by the **Cro-Magnon** skulls from sites in France. Priceless cave drawings are associated with such human remains. Presumably the pictures were drawn for religious rites or record keeping rather than for aesthetic reasons, since they sometimes overlap each other. Many drawings line narrow crevices, where they are unlikely to be seen.

Popular prehistory has emphasized the abrupt replacement of the Neanderthals by the Cro-Magnon people. Perhaps this question has received more attention than it deserves. Natural selection may have molded a lighter-framed population from neanderthoid stock, or migration may have brought another group into the area.

Interpretation of the fossil record involves so much speculation that only the broad outlines are certain. We have ignored as many details as possible to focus on the general scheme of human evolution from a generalized ape. Our inheritance is so clear that some biologists insist that humans *are* apes. Others stress that our culture makes us very different. But no matter how much we change the world, our bodies obey the laws of the biosphere.

THE CHANGING WAYS OF HUMANS

As far as we know, early people had little effect on their environment. There were few of them, and they were hunters and gatherers. We can speculate that these people had about as much impact on their environment as does a baboon or a lion. But as human culture advanced, people began to alter the world significantly.

Where Did All the Animals Go?

The fossil record shows that several species of large mammals that are now extinct were present in the northern hemisphere a few million years ago. Eight species are now missing from temperate Eurasia, and more than two dozen species have disappeared from North America. Among them are mammoths, mastodons, ground sloths, horses, and camels. Undoubtedly the warming climates that followed the Ice Ages reduced the habitat of some cold-adapted species, such as the mammoth, woolly rhinoceros, and musk-ox. But it seems equally likely that increasingly efficient human hunters played a part.

The devastating effects of relatively unsophisticated humans on animal populations is well documented. Island animals that evolved in the absence of humans seem particularly vulnerable. The dodo is only one of many. The first people who reached New Zealand 900 years ago found there another group of large flightless birds, the moas. These birds were an ever-ready food supply that knew no fear and could be clubbed to death. By the time European explorers arrived in New Zealand, all evidence of the moas was gone except a few giant eggshells. Much the same thing happened when Madagascar was settled about 800 years ago. A species of pygmy hippopotamus, two groups of terrestrial lemurs, and *Aepyornis*—yet another giant flightless bird—all quickly disappeared. Half the bird species present on the Hawaiian Islands when the Polynesians arrived around 1500 B.P. were gone at the beginning of the European occupation 300 years ago.

Fire: Harnessed Energy Modified the Landscape

Primitive people use fire to manipulate their environment to an extent seldom appreciated today. Many drive game by setting fires. In addition, fire can be used to create habitats for desirable plants

BOX 2C

WALKING, HUNTING, AND GATHERING

Studies of the !Kung San* who live in the Kalahari Desert of Botswana give insight into the lifestyle fundamental to our species. The !Kung have no agriculture at all and almost no exchange with other people. Nevertheless they eat well, enjoy abundant leisure, and are generally comfortable and healthy.

The !Kung recognize some 85 plant and 54 animal species as edible, but they have distinct preferences and normally eat only a few of them. Their staple is the mongongo nut, which supplies about one-third of their diet. Adults eat an average of 210 grams (just under half a pound) of mongongo nutmeats every day. Wart hog, antelope, and other animal flesh supply a slightly larger portion of the diet (just over half a pound of meat a day). An assortment of plant foods make up the remainder.

Not only do !Kung eat well, but the average adult works only about 2.5 days a week in hunting or gathering. They spend the other 4.5 days in camp or visiting neighboring groups. Leisure is sufficient to permit endless rounds of socializing. !Kung love to argue and compare notes on weather, animal movements, and plant growth. There is also plenty of time to repair the grass huts and make tools, pipes, and simple musical instruments. Not the lack of time or skill but their seminomadic life prevents the !Kung from accumulating extensive material goods.

Game is so scarce that when hunters leave camp in the morning, they spread out singly or in pairs and may walk 15 miles looking for some trace of an animal. Their poisoned arrows kill slowly; a hunter often shoots his prey one day and then returns the next day with friends to help carry the carcass. After tracking the animal to where it died, the !Kung sometimes must scare off lions or hyenas that have found the carcass first.

Extensive walking is as necessary for plant gathering as for hunting. A !Kung woman walks up to 12 miles a day, usually carrying a young child. On the homeward journey she has an additional 15 kg (33 lb) of mongongo nuts. It is easy to suppose that regular exercise contributes to the good health of the !Kung. But much of what we have recounted here is to emphasize the importance of walking to hunter-gatherers.

Apes would never walk so far, so often, on two feet. When they travel on the ground, they

* The symbol ! is employed to indicate the clicking sound produced when the tongue is drawn quickly away from the roof of the mouth. Languages of the San (the larger group, of which the !Kung are a part) are rich in clicking sounds unused in European tongues.

put their knuckles down and go on all fours. Of course this position makes carrying tools or food almost impossible. Only humans have a foot structure that permits the smooth, balanced stride necessary to cover many miles with their arms full. Instead of the wide-spread big toes that apes have, ours lie beside the other toes and extend directly forward. And in contrast to the bent-knee shuffle of an ape, a human strides with the leg nearly straight as the heel strikes the ground. Weight is transferred from the heel to the side of the foot, then to the ball, and finally, at the push-off, to the big toe. The stride and long legs permit people to take larger steps than apes can take.

These big steps contribute to efficiency. So does the leg swing from the hip. In addition, our double-curved spine and pelvic structure place our center of gravity just behind the hip joints. Only a little energy from the calf muscles keeps us upright. In contrast, the C-shaped spine and bent posture of apes place their center of gravity high and far forward. Only constant contraction of heavy muscles keeps apes from falling on their faces. Altogether, walking on two legs is much easier for humans than for apes. This ease has permitted hunting with specialized weapons and gathering food to be shared at a central shelter. Perhaps our lower extremities and trunk structure are as central to a human way of life as are our hands or our brains.

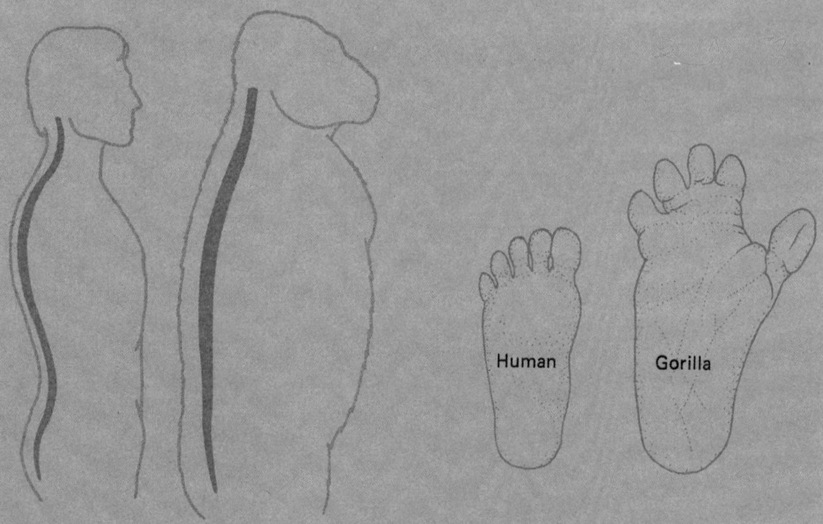

FIGURE 2.13 Ever More Rapid Cultural Change. Our cultural evolution occurs at an ever-increasing rate.

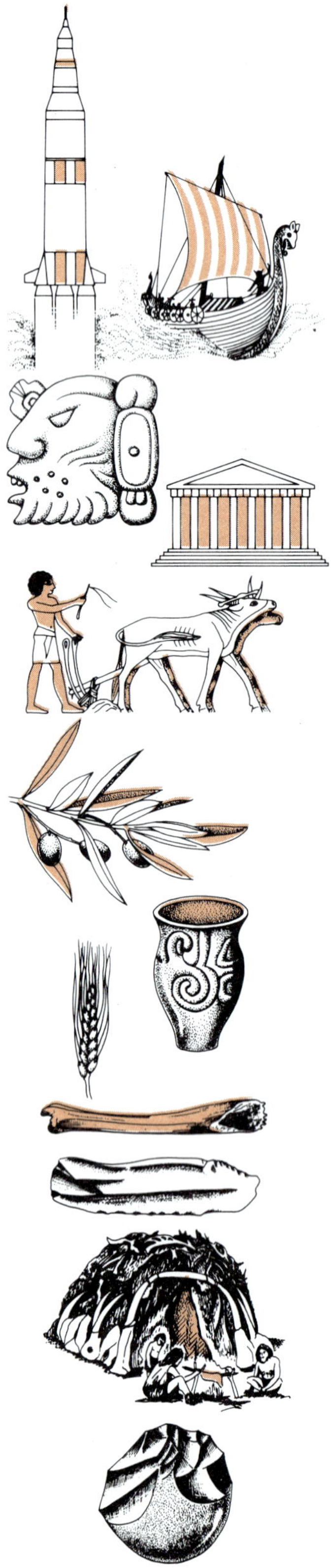

Thousands of years before the present	
0	Nuclear energy; humans travel to the moon.
1	Norse discover America; Aztec and Inca civilizations.
2	Roman Empire; Mayan civilization in Mexico.
3	Development of Greek civilization.
4	Mass production of copper from ore in Turkey and eastern Mediterranean countries; iron extraction (temperatures over 1500°C [2732°F]).
5	Beginnings of agriculture in northwestern Europe; rice cultivated in Thailand; Egyptians plow with cattle.
6	Olives cultivated in Palestine; irrigation-based civilizations in the Near East.
7	Barley and wheat support village life in western Asia.
8	Copper casting (requires 1083°C [1976°F]).
10	First sea voyages.
11	Native copper worked.
12	Pottery made in the Near East and Japan.
14	Humans in Peru.
18	Seminomads plant dates and wheat in Egypt.
20	Baked clay figures made in Czechoslovakia; edge-ground tools used in southern Asia.
28	Bone tools with engravings used in the Yukon of North America.
35	Narrow flint blades and end scrapers used in Europe.
60	Inhabitants of the Ukraine use mammoth bones to support shelters heated with fire. They wear furs and make chipped stone tools including points, notches, and side scrapers.
2500	Stone tools manufactured in Africa.

or animals. Deer and rabbits thrive on the low, leafy vegetation that appears after a temperate forest burns. The grass seeds thus produced feed many birds, and the berries attract both bears and humans.

Lost: The Forests and the Soil

Early farmers relied on digging sticks or hoes to bury seeds, but grassland sods defied these poor tools. Before the iron plowshare was invented, only the soft soils of flood plains, sandy semideserts, or burnt-over forest lands could be planted. In much of the world, forest burning became a standard method to obtain agricultural land. In many places it still is.

We can sample the effect of humans on the earth by examining the history of the lands north of the Mediterranean and eastward into Southwest Asia. Seven thousand years ago evergreen oaks and pines stood in open forests across the lowlands from Spain eastward. Cedar, pine, and juniper flourished on Middle-Eastern mountainsides. Even the arid plains or steppes supported mile after mile of widely spaced pistachio trees.

The writings of Homer and other early Greeks help us understand what happened to the forests that once surrounded the Mediterranean Sea. Wood was used to build cities and to make wine casks; it was also used as fuel. In addition, shipbuilding made persistent demands on Mediterranean forests. And there, as elsewhere, the ever-present goat cropped young tree seedlings back to the earth. Probably goats were primarily responsible for preventing the reestablishment of forests in burned or lumbered woodlands. Furthermore, sheep by the millions were herded up the mountains every summer and back to the lowlands each fall. Like swarms of lawnmowers, they clipped everything in sight. Grasses that might have replaced the lost forests could not withstand the heavy grazing.

Permanent destruction of the forests changed both the soil and the fate of water that fell on the soil. As long as the hills bore trees, the soil was shaded and litter-covered. It remained cool and even moist. Deforested, the soil quickly dried. In the absence of leaf litter, the once-spongy soil packed solidly. Water from the occasional rains raced downhill instead of sinking into the soil where it could be taken up by plant roots or released gradually to springs, wells, and streams. One result was the reduced availability of water between rains. In addition, the rainwater rushing over the surface to the sea washed away the fertile topsoil.

According to Plato, deforestation was complete and the soils around Athens were ruined by 2111 B.P. Then, as now, the hills carried only patches of scrub brush, aromatic shrubs such as thyme, and a few dwarf evergreens.

Is the End in Sight?

Of all animals, humans have by far the greatest impact on the earth. All other species change only through the slow process of biological evolution. Although people originated through the same evolutionary process and continue to be subject to natural selection and other biological processes, much of our influence on the earth results from cultural evolution. Most species cannot evolve biologically rapidly enough to respond to changes that human cultural evolution brings. As a result, we literally dominate the earth. Humans have displaced other species wholesale. We presently consume much of the
10 photosynthetic product of most ecosystems.□
This increased nutrient base has permitted a thousandfold increase in the human population. It is clear that there were once fewer people on earth. Some three million people lived on earth as hunters and gatherers; now there are four billion people here. All other factors aside, the human population today may be greater than the
biosphere□ can support permanently. In any 10
case, controlling our numbers is the most pressing worldwide problem today.

Our present use of world ecosystems is largely destructive. We are altering biogeochemical cycles□ and simplifying communities by dis- 11
placing other species. Most organisms are unable to evolve rapidly enough to adjust to human influences. As a result, the net of interactions that supports the world of life is breaking down. Unless we quickly establish different and wiser poli-

cies worldwide, catastrophe lies in sight. The cultural evolution that permitted us to have our way in the world can be our undoing.

Homo sapiens, the animal species, is the theme of this book. We will return many times to our role in the biosphere. But to understand how people can continue to live in the biological world, we must first know the internal functions of the human animal and its physical requirements. That is the topic of Part Two of this book.

Summary

1. Humans share many traits with other mammals but have more in common with primates than with any other group. Primates can be characterized as having traits valuable for an arboreal way of life. Unlike other mammals, primates rely more on sight than on the sense of smell. The complex and unpredictable nature of arboreal environments has selected for unusual problem-solving ability in the primates.

2. Humans are more similar to chimpanzees, gorillas, and other apes than to the other primates. Traits common to humans and apes include lack of a tail, a large brain relative to body size, and certain tooth characteristics. Apes have long arms and trunk modifications for brachiation. These characteristics are only slightly evident in humans. Instead, the human pelvis, legs, and feet are specialized for long strides that permit people to walk across many miles of ground in a day.

3. Fossils form only when remains of organisms are protected from decay and from chemical and physical breakdown. Because primates seldom die in situations where fossilization is likely, we have only a scant record of primate evolution.

4. Careful examination of key bones can reveal posture as well as mode of locomotion. To gain as much information from primate fossils as possible, a team of scientists must make extensive observations, not only of the fossil but of the site where it was found.

5. The fossil record contains representatives of many groups of hominoids. They include members of the genus *Australopithecus* and the genus *Homo*. The exact relationship among the various extinct populations remains to be determined. Our species, *H. sapiens*, has as its ancestors early members of the genus *Homo* usually identified as *Homo erectus*.

6. It seems likely that humans share with *Australopithecus* a common ancestor, perhaps *Ramapithecus*. *Australopithecus*, *Homo*, and chimpanzees may share a yet more-distant common ancestor that we describe as an ape. This ape is not a chimpanzee but probably a dryopithecine ape.

7. Neanderthals, the earliest members of our species, were people of substantial cultural achievement. They lived in harsh climates, made specialized tools, hunted giant mammals, and buried their dead.

8. Studies of the last remaining human populations living as hunters and gatherers reveal complex cultural adaptations and general good health.

9. Human culture has drastically altered the biosphere. Hunters and gatherers began this change in prehistoric times. Because cultural advances accumulate from generation to generation through learning, human culture evolves much faster than biological evolution can alter the character of species.

10. The biological classification system is an attempt to describe evolutionary relationships. It is useful for conveying information, but except for the species level, it is a matter of opinion.

Thought and Controversy

1. How many points does it take to make a line? Ever since Darwin dared to hint that humans share a common origin with other animals, people have spoken of the "missing links." How much fossil evidence is necessary to establish a line of ancestry? Is it possible to prove relationships through the use of fossils? (Can science prove anything?)

2. The discovery that a number of Neanderthal skulls appear to have been opened in a regular fashion has given rise to a new hypothesis that might explain the sudden disappearance of the Neanderthals. Until a few years ago, the Fore people of New Guinea believed it was right and proper to eat the brains from the bodies of their dead relatives. Apparently this practice permitted **kuru**, a viral disease that causes a slow degeneration of the nervous system, to be transmitted in a peculiar familial pattern. Some say that kuru disappeared when the government insisted that the Fore cease to cannibalize their dead. Perhaps the Neanderthals adopted the practice of eating the brains of their dead. If a disease similar to kuru was introduced (acquired by eating the brain of an infected animal), the stage would have been set for disaster. The more people who died from the disease, the more who would become infected.

3. If humans are physically apes by inheritance, can our emotional and social patterns best be understood if viewed in the same light? Some years ago a spate of books (D. Morris, *The Naked Ape*, McGraw-Hill, 1968; R. Ardrey, *The Territorial Imperative*, Atheneum Press, 1966; K. Lorenz, *On Aggression*, Harcourt, Brace & World, 1966; and A. Storr, *Human Aggression*, Atheneum Press, 1968) discussed aggression as part of the biological nature of humans. Although some biologists accept this interpretation, many do not. Skeptics point out that superficial similarities between a human activity and an activity of another species is not sufficient reason to assume that the basic process is the same. In addition, there is a wide range of behavior patterns among different animals, including the apes.

4. Was life hard for our ancestral hunters and gatherers? For that matter, is life difficult for present-day hunters and gatherers such as the !Kung San? During the southern winter there are freezing nights in the Kalahari Desert. Most North Americans, if suddenly introduced to this area and clad only in the animal skins the !Kung wear, would be miserable. In much the same vein, many Westerners would consider a 12-mile hike carrying a baby—even without the addition of a 30-pound load of nuts on the return trip—difficult, if not impossible. But there is no reason to think that people acclimatized to the weather and conditioned by exercise find this life unpleasant. Physiological adaptation is a fact of life. For example, Europeans who enter the tropics initially feel that the humid heat is unbearable. But after a few years in the tropics, the same people are uncomfortable if the temperature drops below 80°F. And even many middle-aged people who undertake exercise programs are eventually able to run five or ten miles without distress. The psychological stress and physical activity that characterize discomfort are useful when they cause people to improve their situation. But unremitting discomfort wastes energy and produces fatigue. It seems inconceivable for the !Kung to be particularly uncomfortable in a life that permits so many to reach old age and that maintains a stable population. Of course, we wouldn't deny that they may be miserable sometimes; so are we.

Questions

1. Describe the processes that produce change in the physical aspects of our environment.

2. What are the major characteristics of primates? Relate these to the arboreal environment. In which of these characteristics do primates differ from most other mammals?

3. What is a fossil? Describe some of the ways fossils can form. Primate fossils are much rarer than whale fossils. Explain this in terms of the habitats of the two groups.

4. How is the great length of time since the origin of life and the antiquity of such recent species as *Australopithecus afarensis* important to an understanding of evolution?

5. What is the evidence used to argue that the immediate ancestors of humans were terrestrial, not arboreal, animals?

6. Discuss the key fossil primates suggested to be ancestral to humans; comment on their relationships.

7. What were the cultural advances of the Neanderthal? Can you suggest some reasons why these advances were largely ignored until recently?

8. Numerous species are now on the endangered list due partly to destruction of their normal environment, partly to human hunting, and partly to the introduction of organisms (such as dogs) previously absent from their habitat. Have earlier human activities posed similar threats that led to the extinction of species? Give examples.

9. Compare the rates at which biological and cultural evolution occur. What is the significance of these differences?

10. Briefly summarize the differences between humans and apes—e.g., the chimpanzee.

Further Reading for Part One

Hay, Richard L., and Mary D. Leakey, 1982. The fossil footprints of Laetoli. *Scientific American* 246(2):50–57 (February).

Johnson, Donald C., and Maitland A. Edy, 1981. *Lucy: The Beginnings of Mankind.* Simon & Schuster, Inc., New York.

Lovejoy, C. Owen, 1981. The origin of man. *Science* 211(4480):341–350.

Mayr, Ernst, 1982. *The Growth of Biological Thought: Diversity, Evolution, and Inheritance.* Belknap/Harvard, Cambridge, Mass.

Monod, J., 1971. *Chance and Necessity: An Essay on the Natural Philosophy of Modern Biology.* Knopf, New York.

Rayburn, Paul, 1983. An uncommon chimp. *Science 83* 4(4):40–48 (June).

Rukang, Wu, and Lin Saeglong, 1983. Peking man. *Scientific American* 248(6):86–94 (June).

Singer, C., 1962. *A History of Biology to about the Year 1900.* Abelard-Schuman, New York.

Thomas, L., 1979. *The Medusa and the Snail: More Notes of a Biology Watcher.* Viking, New York.

Zihlman, Adrienne L., 1982. *The Human Evolution Coloring Book.* Barnes and Noble Books, Harper & Row, New York.

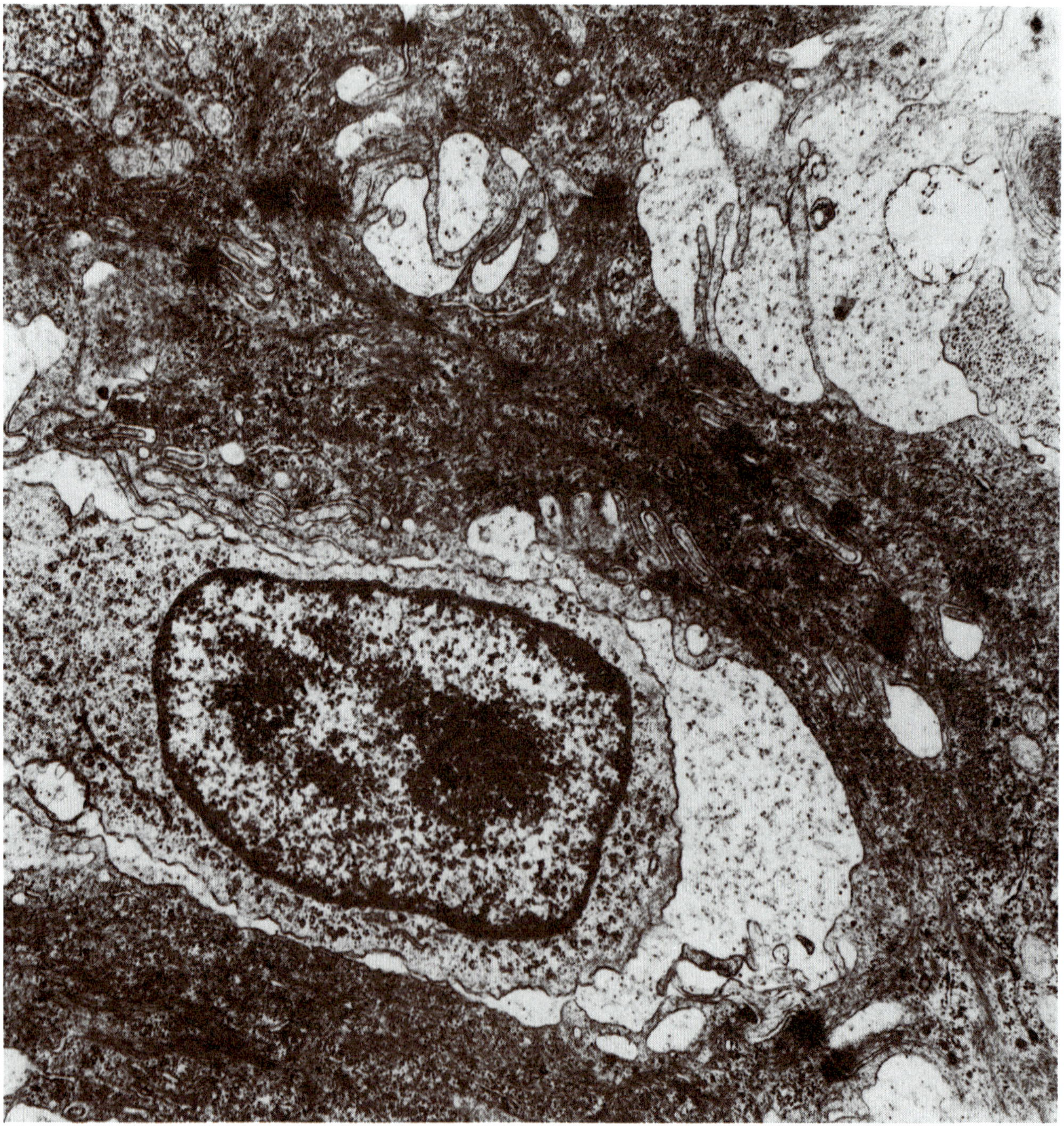

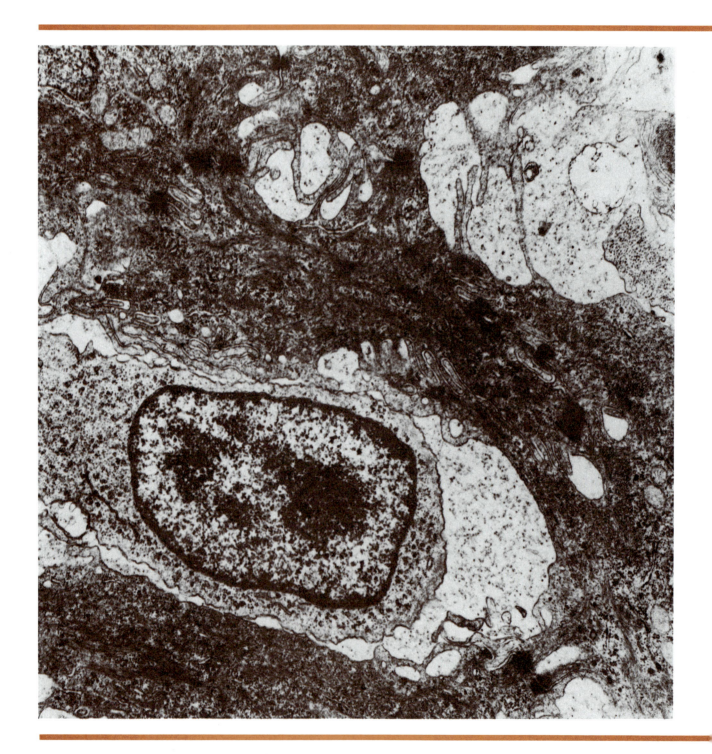

PART TWO

To Keep Living

Living isn't easy.

Each organism is an unlikely organization—unlikely in the sense that the physical world tends to randomness and to be living means to be organized. Both the concentration and the arrangement of substances within organisms are different from those in nonliving matter. Thus to keep living we must have a supply of specific materials from our environment and sufficient energy to organize these materials and to keep them organized.

In the following chapters you will learn how humans meet their physical needs, how they maintain a constant internal environment, how they respond to their external environment, and how they defend themselves against foreign organisms. We hope you will consider these processes in terms of their contribution to the unusual organization that is human life. All of these processes are essential if we are to continue living.

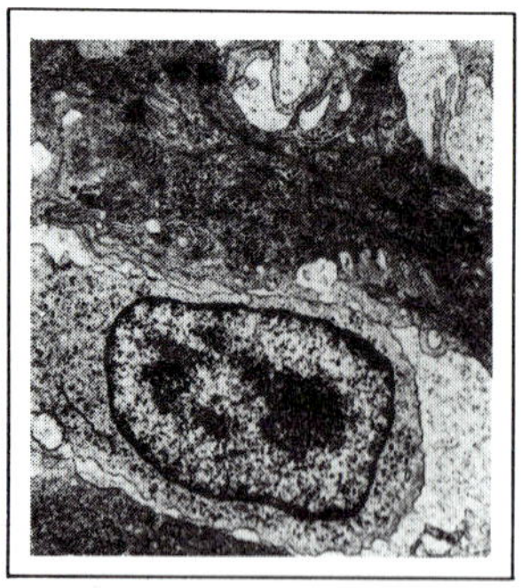

3

Starting from Scratch: Matter and Energy

THE TERMS MATTER AND ENERGY ARE SO FAMILiar that they almost seem to define themselves. Simply stated, matter is the physical substance of which all objects, including organisms, are composed. We can see and feel matter; matter has shape, and it takes up space. These things are not so in the case of that much more elusive quantity, energy. But though we can't see or touch energy, we can measure it, at least indirectly. Since energy is what must be "put in" in order to "put out," a common definition for energy is the capacity to perform work—that is, to do things or cause change.

Simple operational definitions such as these are useful in their way, but they mask the many mysteries that surround the fundamental natures of matter and energy. And ultimately our understanding of the biological world is limited by our knowledge of these phenomena.

Before we search into the less obvious properties of matter and energy, let us remember some basic ideas that will channel our inquiries into a biological perspective: The energy for life comes from the sun. Solar energy is harvested by green plants and used to convert the nonliving chemical substances of soil, water, and air into living plant matter. Other organisms rely either directly or indirectly on plant products both for energy and for the raw materials of life. It isn't surprising, then, that all organisms have basically the same chemical compositions.

SOME BASIC FACTS ABOUT MATTER: ELEMENTS AND ATOMS

All matter, living or otherwise, is composed of **elements**, substances that cannot be broken down into simpler forms by chemical means. But of the more than 100 existing elements, only about 25 percent are common in living matter. Even more striking, just six elements—**hydrogen, oxygen, carbon, nitrogen, phosphorus,** and **sulfur**—account for more than 90 percent of the weight of most organisms (Table 3.1).

Atomic Structure and the States of Matter

The smallest amount of an element that can exist is an **atom**. Atoms are so small that it is hard to imagine the number of them in even the smallest bit of matter. To illustrate, the period at the end of this sentence probably contains as many as three or four *billion* atoms.

In a **solid**, atoms are stacked together in a very orderly way. Although atoms are in constant motion except at extremely low temperatures, such movements are restricted and hard to detect in a solid. But when energy in the form of heat is added, the energized atoms begin bouncing about rather more freely, until the formerly ordered arrangement of the solid is slowly destroyed. We call this process *melting*, and the result is the formation of a **liquid**.

TABLE 3.1 Abundance of the Major Elements in the Earth's Crust and in the Human Body

ELEMENT	SYMBOL	APPROXIMATE % OF EARTH'S CRUST	APPROXIMATE % OF HUMAN BODY
Oxygen	0	46.6	65
Silicon	Si	27.7	trace
Aluminum	Al	8.1	trace
Iron	Fe	5.0	trace
Calcium	Ca	3.6	1.5
Sodium	Na	2.8	0.2
Potassium	K	2.6	0.4
Magnesium	Mg	2.1	0.1
Hydrogen	**H**	**0.1**	**9.5**
Manganese	Mn	0.1	trace
Phosphorus	**P**	**0.1**	**1.0**
Sulfur	**S**	**0.05**	**0.3**
Chlorine	Cl	0.05	trace
Carbon	**C**	**0.03**	**18.5**
Fluorine	F	0.03	trace
Copper	Cu	0.01	trace
Boron	Bo	trace	trace
Nitrogen	**N**	**trace**	**3.3**
Cobalt	Co	trace	trace
Zinc	Zn	trace	trace
Molybdenum	Mo	trace	trace
Iodine	I	trace	trace

As more heat is applied to a liquid, its atoms become increasingly turbulent and eventually reach a state so energetic that some of them pop free from the surface of the fluid. This **boiling** turns the liquid into a **gas**.

Under proper conditions, any substance can be converted from one physical state to another (Fig. 3.1). Some substances require extreme, unearthly conditions if they are to undergo change, but water is one example of a common substance that exists in all three states (ice, liquid water, and water vapor) in our "ordinary" environment.

Substances that consist of a single element are unusual. The rarity of gold (gold atoms) and diamonds (carbon atoms) serves to illustrate the point quite well. Most substances are **compounds**, formed by chemical reactions between different elements. When substances, either elements or compounds, do not chemically react but merely physically intermingle, **mixtures** are formed. A rock run through by a vein of gold is a heterogeneous mixture (Fig. 3.2). However, seawater is a **solution**—a homogeneous mixture of compounds, including water, salt, and many more.

Compounds, as we have said, are the result of chemical change. Changes of this type are brought about by chemical reactions whereby the atoms in substances (the reactants) undergo rearrangement to form entirely new substances (products). Since such chemical change underlies all biological processes, our immediate goal is to understand its basis. We will find that chemical reactivity depends on atomic structure, specifically on the number and arrangement of subatomic particles within an atom.

Of the many subatomic particles that scientists have postulated or identified, only three concern us here. **Electrons** are particles bearing a negative charge; **protons** possess a positive charge; and **neutrons** have no charge at all. Many properties of atoms are a reflection of the electrical properties of their subatomic particles, since particles with similar electrical charges repel one another and those with opposite electrical charges attract one another.

FIGURE 3.1 Liquid and Solid Water. At low temperatures the hydrogen bonds between water molecules become stabilized and snowflakes and icicles are formed.

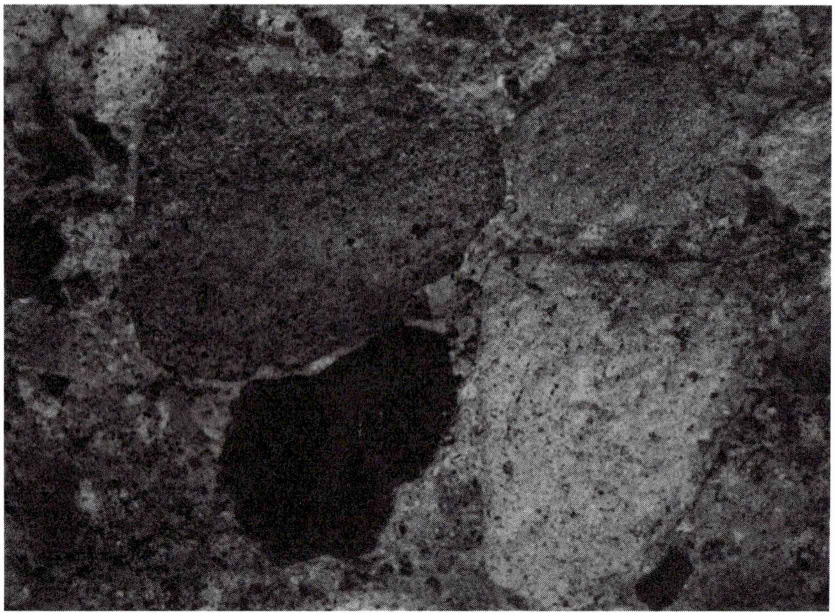

FIGURE 3.2 Conglomerate Rock—A Heterogeneous Mixture.

Protons and neutrons are always found in the central portion, or **nucleus**, of an atom, while the electrons spin around the nucleus within defined orbital **shells** (Fig. 3.3). In an electrically neutral atom, the number of electrons must be equal to the number of protons. The electrons are maintained in orbit because the positively charged nucleus attracts the negatively charged electrons.

The ordinary hydrogen atom, with one proton and one electron, is the smallest and simplest atom.

FIGURE 3.3 The Structure of an Atom.

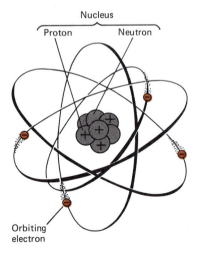

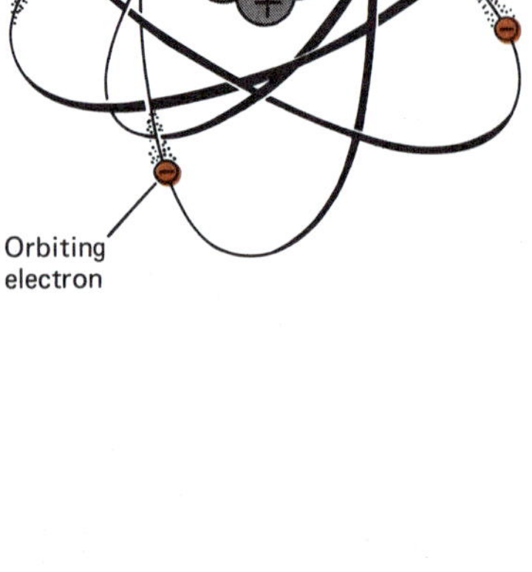

All other atoms contain more protons and electrons plus some neutrons. In the naturally occurring elements, the number of electrons per atom ranges from one in hydrogen to 92 in uranium. Figure 3.4 shows the atomic structures of the six biologically most important atoms.

The Atomic Nucleus. Protons and neutrons are the largest and heaviest of the subatomic particles. Just how the uncharged neutrons and the positively charged protons are organized within the nucleus is a matter of conjecture. What is certain is that a powerfully attractive strong force must operate between the protons and neutrons of the nucleus. Otherwise the nucleus would blow apart because the similarly charged protons should push away from one another. The true nature of this strong force is still somewhat mysterious; we do know that it must be tightly internalized, since it does not affect the attraction of protons for electrons. The strength of the strong nuclear force is seen when a small portion is tapped in the release of **atomic energy** (Chapter 22).

The number of protons in an atom of a single element is a constant characteristic and is given as the **atomic number**. The **atomic weight** is essentially equal to the number of protons plus the number of neutrons in the atomic nucleus. It is not the real weight of an atom, but its relative weight as compared with other atoms.

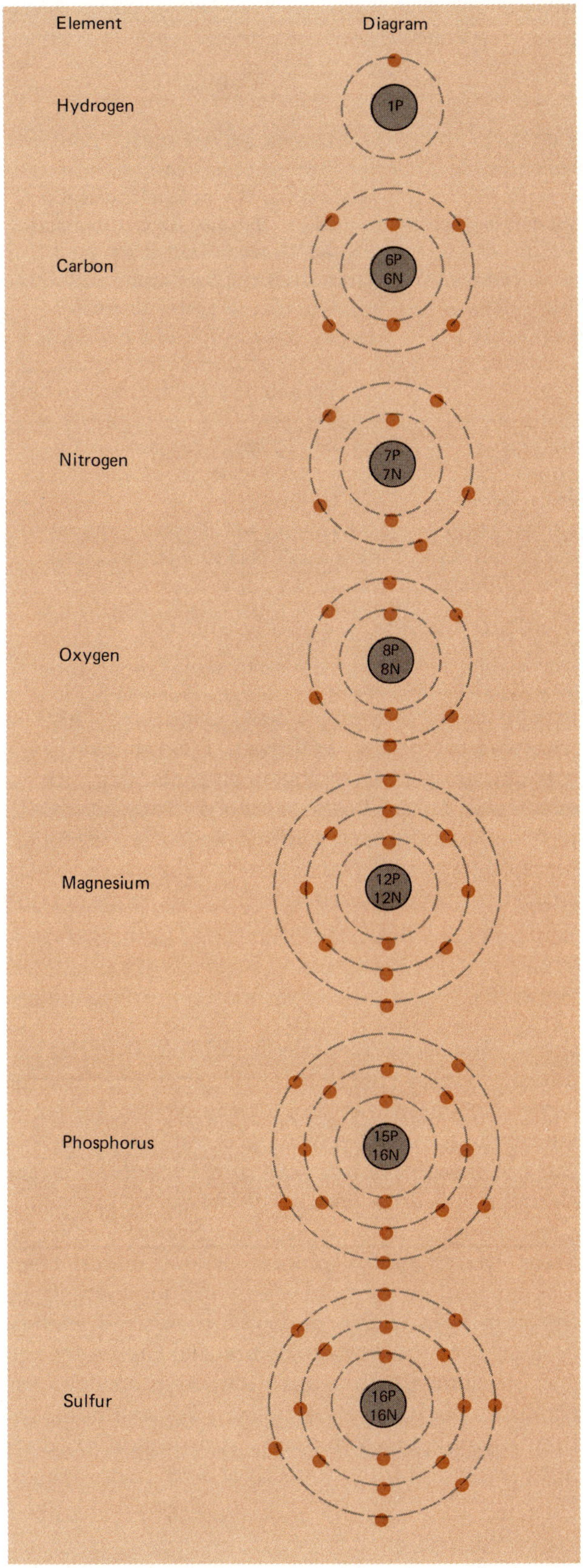

Although the number of protons in an atom of a single element is constant, the number of neutrons may vary slightly. Atoms with the same number of protons but different numbers of neutrons are **isotopes** of the same element. In nature, one isotopic form of an element usually predominates, and the others are found only in minute amounts. Not all elements have isotopic forms, yet some have many.

The presence or absence of a few neutrons does not affect the nature of an atom, so isotopes of an element have the same chemical properties. When it is useful, we can distinguish among isotopes by noting the variation in their atomic weights, as when we refer to carbon-12 and carbon-14.

You are probably aware that some isotopes are radioactive. The reason **radioactive isotopes** are radioactive is that they are atoms with too few or too many neutrons. As might be expected, this irregular condition in an atom sometimes causes the nucleus to be unstable. When the nucleus is unstable, it eventually disintegrates and releases radiation in the form of particles or energy or both. Perhaps the most widely recognized radioactive isotope is the unstable atom carbon-14. Not all isotopes are radioactive, however. For example, neither of the two heavy isotopes of oxygen is unstable.

The Arrangement of Electrons in an Atom. Even if we had a microscope powerful enough to enable us to see an atom, it is unlikely that we would actually see an individual negatively charged particle. Electrons are clouds of matter that ripple around the nucleus in their orbital shells. Pinpointing an electron at any given moment would be like trying to follow a lone spoke of a spinning bicycle wheel. What we might see instead is a blur, or what physicists call an electron cloud. But regardless of this fact, it is often convenient to illustrate electrons as discrete particles; we do so in this book.

For reasons of simplicity we are also going to ignore the fact that not all electron shells are completely circular. Some of them are elongated into an ellipse or swing back and forth in the shape of a figure 8. If you are worried that electrons may smash into one another as they scoot around the nucleus, it will be helpful to know that the orbital shells are tilted at various angles.

FIGURE 3.4 **Some Biologically Important Elements.**

BOX 3A

RADIOACTIVE CLOCKS

Radioactive isotopes that decay, or break down very slowly, and that are likely to be found in living organisms, are useful for dating fossils and rocks. Both carbon-12 and its radioactive isotope, carbon-14 are found in all plant and animal tissues. Atoms of these two isotopes behave almost identically in living organisms, but carbon-14 disintegrates spontaneously and at a constant rate to form nitrogen-14:

$$\text{carbon-14} \xrightarrow{\text{time}} \text{nitrogen-14} + \text{electron (beta radiation)}$$

Radioactive decay is measured in half-lives, or the length of time required for half the number of atoms in a population to decay. Carbon-14 has a half-life of 5586 years; consequently, it takes 5586 years for half the carbon-14 originally present in a substance to disintegrate. But this doesn't mean that all the radioactive isotopes will be gone after 11,172 years. The second 5586 years permits the disappearance of only one-half of the first half! In theory, all the radioactivity will never disappear, but eventually only an infinitesimal amount will remain.

Because animals obtain their carbon from plants that earlier obtained it from carbon dioxide in the air, the proportion of carbon-14 in living organisms is the same as the proportion of carbon-14 in atmospheric carbon dioxide. When an organism dies, the ratio of carbon-14 to carbon-12 in its tissues decreases slowly as the carbon-14 decays and is not replaced. Hence the relative amounts of carbon-14 become a radioactive clock that measures the time since the organism died.

Fossils over 70,000 years old have so little carbon-14 left that accurate measurement isn't possible. But all organisms contain potassium, so the potassium/argon method is used to date older materials. This method takes its name from the fact that potassium-40 disintegrates to form argon-40. Potassium-40 has a half-life of 1.3 billion years. Potassium/argon and other isotopes can also be used to determine when crystals in rocks formed. In this way, rock layers as well as fossils can be dated.

By using radioactive isotopes to date earth rocks, scientists have established that the earth is at least 3.8 billion years old. If the moon was formed at the same time the earth was formed, then the date must be pushed back to 4.5 billion years, for that is the age of the oldest moon rocks. Dating of fossil-containing rock shows that multicellular animals were on earth more than 700 million years ago.

It also helps if you know (and this was illustrated in Fig. 3.1) that electrons travel at different distances from the nucleus. And notice by examining Fig. 3.4 that crowding is further controlled because each shell has a maximum population of electrons. None of the atoms shown there has more than two electrons in the first (innermost) shell. Note too, that once the second shell is filled with eight electrons, a third shell must be formed to accommodate additional electrons. Although it's not illustrated here, a fourth shell is required once the third shell contains eight electrons.

The most accurate way to describe electron shells is in terms of energy levels. Shells close to the nucleus are of a lower energy level than are shells located farther away. This is because the closer an electron is to the nucleus, the more strongly it is attracted to the oppositely charged protons located there. Thus a close-in, tightly held electron has less energy than one located farther from the nucleus. Since the outermost-shell electrons are higher in energy than other electrons, it is not surprising that the outermost electrons are most involved in the chemical reactions that occur between atoms.

From Atoms to Molecules. The chemical characteristics of an element are determined largely by the number of electrons in the outermost shell of its atoms. Studies of the chemically **inert**—that is, stable—elements has shown that the atoms of these elements have full outer shells. For example, helium, with just two electrons in its only shell, does not react with other atoms. Nor does neon, which, with ten electrons, has two electron shells and a full complement of eight electrons in the second shell.

When an atom has an outer electron shell that is only partially filled, it tends to be chemically active. Return again to Fig. 3.4 and see that the biologically important atoms shown there are all chemically reactive, since they all have unfilled outermost shells. Chemically reactive elements have atoms that tend to gain, lose, or share electrons with other atoms in order to achieve a more stable state. This results in the formation of compounds in which the participating atoms have filled outermost shells.

Chemical Bonds: Ties that Bind Atoms into Compounds

Chemical bonds are attractive forces that bind atoms together into compounds. Some chemical bonds are very strong, and breaking them requires large amounts of energy. Other chemical bonds are considered weak because they are so easily broken. As we shall see in the following discussion, the strength of chemical bonds is dependent on the nature of their environment.

Covalent Bonds. The six biologically most important elements (C, H, O, N, S, P) can mimic the stable electronic configurations of inert elements by sharing electrons with one another. This sharing of electrons creates **covalent bonds**. Covalent bonds result when partially filled electron shells of two atoms overlap as they approach each other in order to share a pair of electrons. For instance, two atoms of hydrogen join with one atom of oxygen to form a water molecule, as pictured in Fig. 3.5. The term **molecule** is frequently used to refer specifically to those compounds formed by the sharing of electrons.

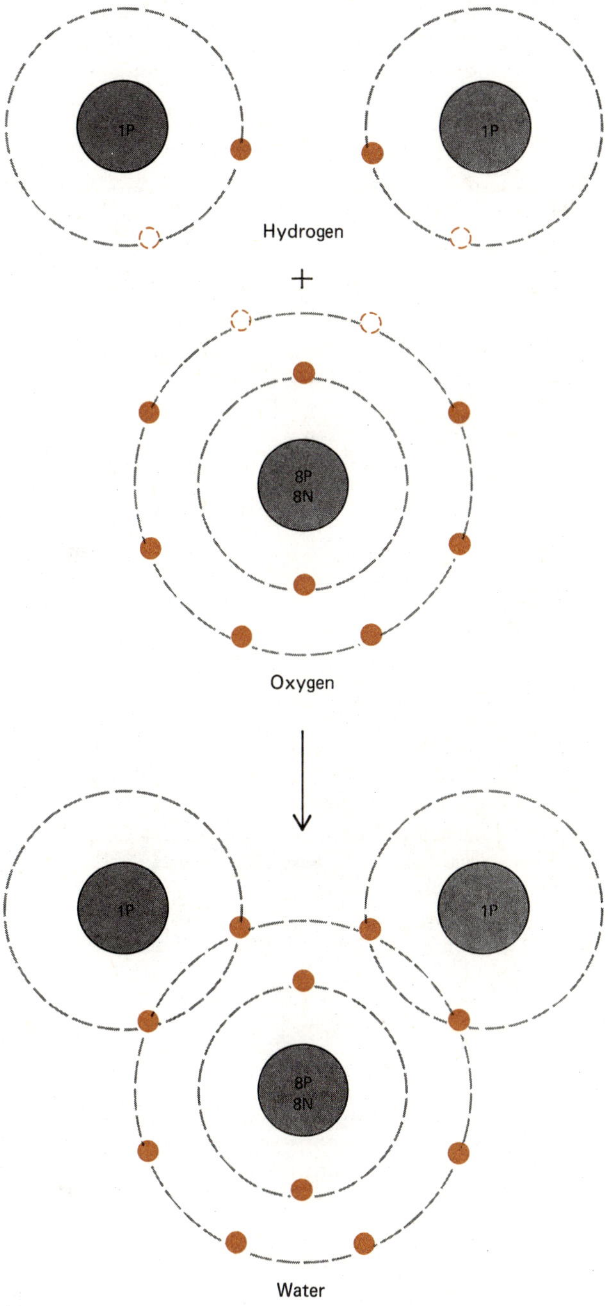

FIGURE 3.5 **Covalent Bonding.**

Ionic Bonds. Not all atoms share electrons to achieve stability. Atoms lacking one or two electrons to fill their outer shells sometimes pull electrons away from other atoms. Donor atoms usually have only one or two electrons in their outer shells, so the loss of these electrons increases their stability, too. Because such transfer of electrons does not alter the number of protons in the nucleus of either atom, each becomes electrically charged. The atom gaining the electrons becomes negatively charged, because it has more negative electrons than positive protons. The atom donating the electrons becomes positively charged, because it has more positive protons than negative electrons. Negatively or positively charged atoms or groups of atoms are known as **ions**.

Because of their opposite charges, negative and positive ions attract one another and may, in fact, be bound together by the affinity of unlike charges. Such **ionic bonds** are important in the formation of many mineral compounds. Ordinary table salt,

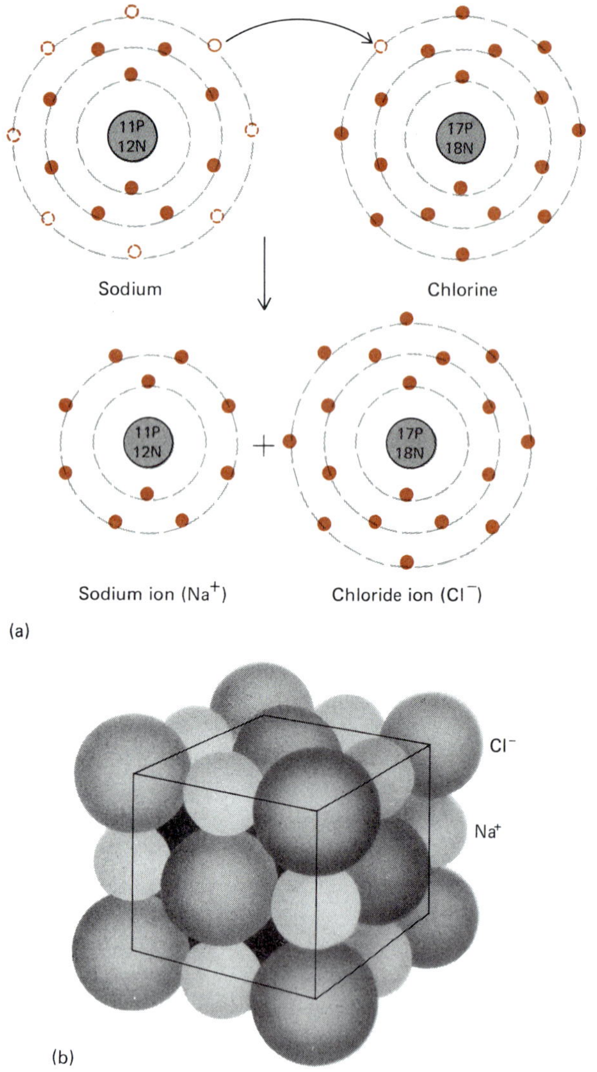

FIGURE 3.6 **Ionic Bonding.** The electrostatic attraction of sodium and chloride ions explains the formation of crystalline sodium chloride as shown here.

known as sodium chloride, provides a good example (Fig. 3.6). A salt crystal consists of a repeating pattern of sodium and chlorine ions.

Hydrogen Bonds. Much weaker than either covalent or ionic bonds are **hydrogen bonds**. These are formed when a hydrogen atom already attached to a weakly negative atom is attracted to another weakly negative atom of the same molecule or of a molecule nearby. One of the best examples of this type of attraction occurs between water molecules.

If you check Fig. 3.5, you can see that the larger oxygen atom of water has eight positively charged protons, while each tiny hydrogen atom has only one proton. Thus the larger oxygen nucleus pulls the hydrogen's electrons more strongly than does either small hydrogen nucleus. As a consequence, a water molecule has a vaguely triangular shape with a slightly negative oxygen end and a slightly positive hydrogen end.

Molecules such as those of water, in which there is an unequal distribution of charges, are said to be **polar molecules**. Because of their polarity, water molecules are attracted to one another. In liquid water the molecules orient themselves end-to-end, forming a loose network (Fig. 3.7) with hydrogen bonds holding the positive end of one molecule to the negative end of a nearby molecule.

Hydrogen bonds are not limited to water. Because they are weak (with only about 5 percent of the strength of a covalent bond) and easily broken, hydrogen bonds are often involved in temporary linkages between atoms and molecules.

Chemistry of Life: Inorganic versus Organic

Chemical compounds are broadly classified as either inorganic or organic. Both types are found in organisms, but organic compounds occur almost exclusively in living organisms or their remains. Chemically, the two are distinguished this way: **organic compounds** always contain both carbon and hydrogen, whereas **inorganic compounds** almost never contain both carbon and hydrogen.

Although a variety of inorganic and organic compounds are vital to life, organisms contain five main chemical constituents: water, lipids, carbohydrates, proteins, and nucleic acids (Table 3.2). You may find the brevity of this list somewhat surprising, considering the complexity ordinarily associated with the living world. Perhaps even more unexpected is the fact that the most common constituent by far is also the simplest—namely, *water*.

The Importance of Water to Life. On the average, organisms are about 70 percent water. The exact percentage varies from tissue to tissue and from organism to organism. For example, the unusually active nerve cells are about 85 percent water, whereas the typical human body cell content is only 60 percent. And, as humans get older, there is a progressive decrease in the water content of body cells.

Jellyfish are obvious examples of unusually watery organisms. They are about 95 percent water.

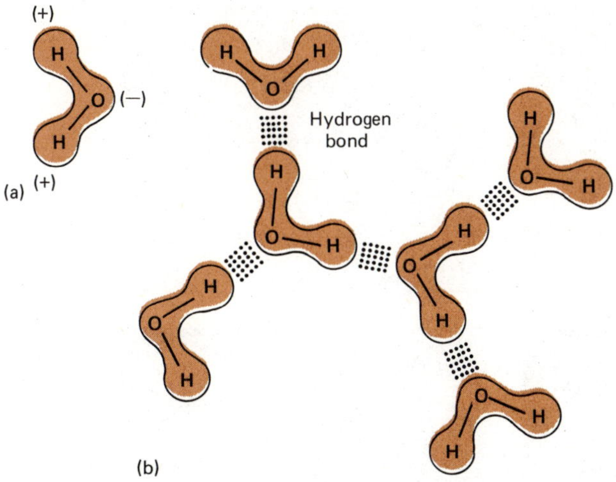

FIGURE 3.7 **Polarity of Water.** (a) A water molecule has a positive and a negative end. (b) Water molecules tend to become oriented with respect to one another because of hydrogen bonding.

TABLE 3.2 **Components of Muscle Tissue**

COMPONENT	APPROXIMATE %	MAJOR ELEMENTS REPRESENTED
Inorganic Substances		
Water	75	hydrogen, oxygen
Minerals, mainly ions	1.5	sodium, magnesium, phosphorus, sulfur, chlorine, potassium, calcium
Organic Substances		
Lipids	10	carbon, hydrogen, oxygen, phosphorus
Carbohydrates	4	carbon, hydrogen, oxygen
Proteins	7	carbon, hydrogen, oxygen, nitrogen, sulfur
Nucleic acids	1.5	carbon, hydrogen, oxygen, nitrogen, phosphorus

On the other hand, some resting stages, such as seeds, contain as little as 5 percent water. The inactivity of dry seeds reflects the near absence of water and hints at the qualities that water imparts to life.

Much of the biological importance of water derives from its exceptional capacity as a solvent. Not everything dissolves in water, but so many substances do that it is sometimes called the "universal solvent." Water-soluble molecules are conveniently transported within and between cells by the movement of water. And because dissolved substances are more reactive than solid substances, water facilitates many metabolic reactions just by being present. Water itself is often a reactant or a product of metabolism. For instance, water is used to split food molecules during digestion. It is also the source of hydrogen and oxygen atoms for the manufacture of many other molecules.

Water also acts as a lubricant and as an insulator for the body. Being slow both to absorb and to release heat makes it an excellent temperature stabilizer for organisms and for the environment as well. The tremendous cooling effect of the evaporation of just a little water from the skin demonstrates water's ability to absorb large quantities of heat.

The hydrogen bonding capacity of water explains many of its important properties. The temperature of a substance is related to the vibratory motion of its atoms or molecules: the more movement, the higher the temperature. Because water molecules are mutually attracted by hydrogen bonds, they resist increased molecular movement and thus temperature change.

Hydrogen bonding also explains water's remarkable capacity as a solvent. To some extent, water dissolves anything that carries an electrical charge. It may be a strong charge, such as ions possess, or one that is weak because of unequal sharing of electrons, as in water itself. Water dissolves substances by establishing a positive-negative interaction with them.

Since water is strongly attracted to other polar molecules, it is a determining factor in the organization of many biological molecules (Fig. 3.9). In the watery environment of cells, chemical components orient themselves according to solubility. Water-soluble, or **hydrophilic**, portions of biological structures are attracted to water, whereas water-insoluble, or **hydrophobic**, parts recoil from water.

Because of the solubility of various parts of other molecules in water, these molecules bend

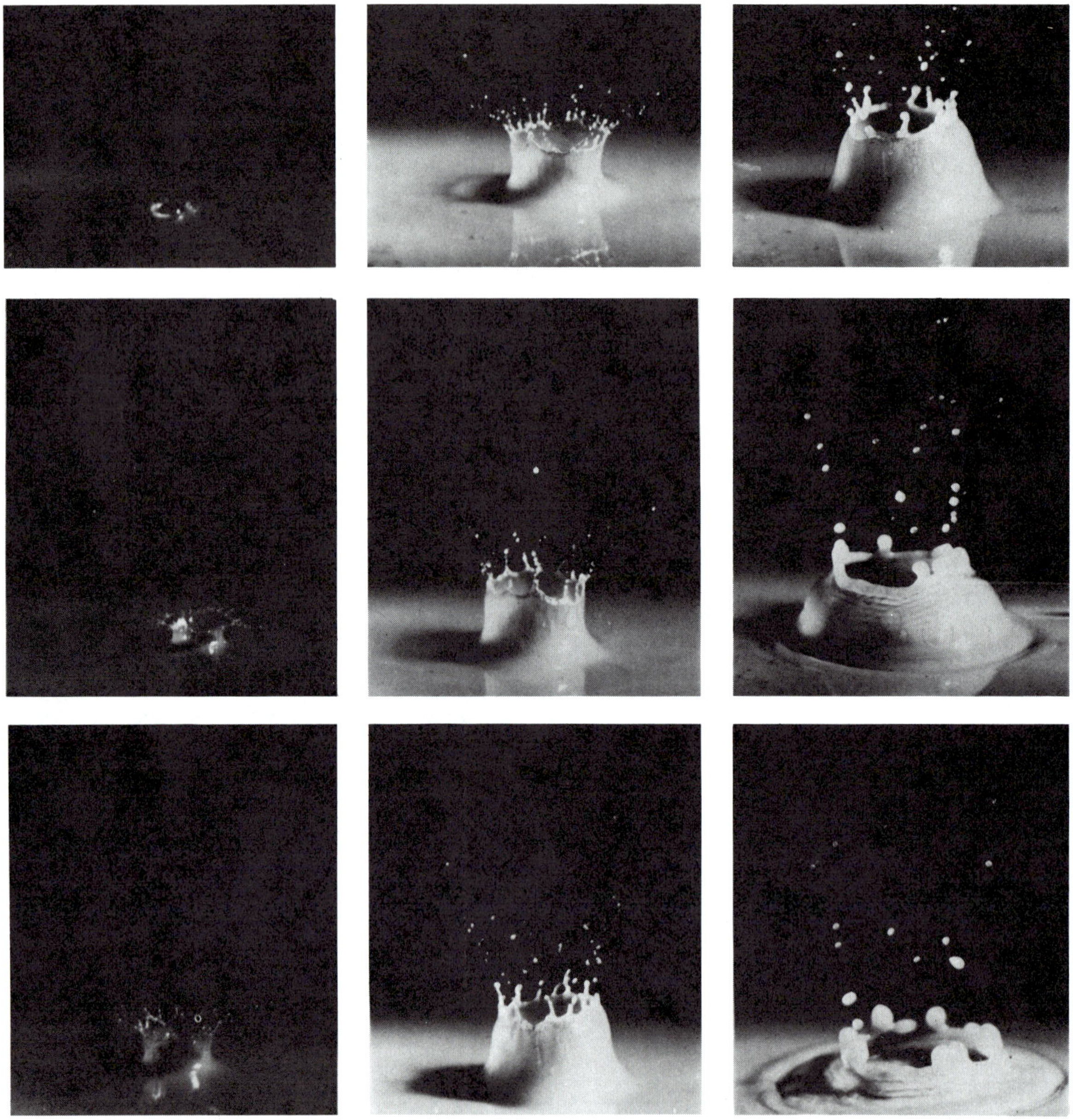

FIGURE 3.8 A Raindrop Falling on Water Demonstrates the Cohesiveness of Water Molecules.

and turn or fold and loop as they adjust to the water in their midst. The end result is that water-soluble parts of the molecules lie exposed to water, and hydrophobic parts are protected in the interior of the molecule. In this way water forces many biologically important molecules to assume specific shapes and contribute to the ultimate form of many biological structures.

Compounds that are completely soluble in water are dissolved as water seeps in and around their molecules or ions, forcing and keeping them apart. This is what happens when ionic compounds such as sodium chloride are dissolved in water (Fig. 3.10), and the salt dissociates into sodium and chloride ions. Sodium chloride and other salts are invariably ionized when found in living systems. Many other substances, including acids and bases, undergo ionization in water.

Acids, Bases, and pH. Acids are substances that dissociate in water to yield hydrogen ions (H^+). The stronger the acid, the larger the quantity of

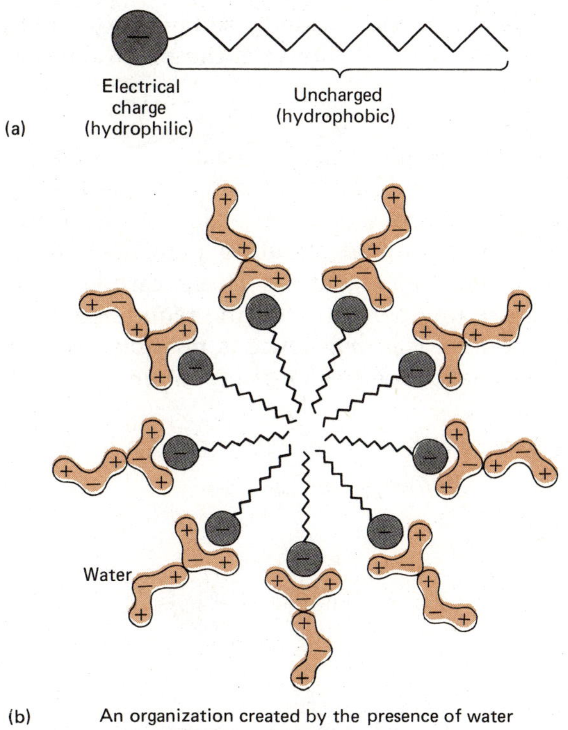

FIGURE 3.9 Hydrophobic Bonds and Organization. (a) Many biologically important molecules have polar (electrically charged) and nonpolar (uncharged) parts. (b) When placed in water, such molecules orient themselves so that their hydrophilic portions are in contact with water and their hydrophobic portions turned away from water.

H^+ ions set free at a given acid concentration. Hydrochloric acid (HCl) is a strong acid. Its dissociation can be written as follows:

$$HCl \rightarrow H^+ + Cl^-$$

Hydrochloric acid is an inorganic or mineral acid. Other inorganic acids include nitric (HNO_3) and sulfuric (H_2SO_4). Acetic acid (CH_3COOH), the principal ingredient of vinegar, is an example of an organic acid. Acetic acid and other organic acids are relatively weak; they exist mainly in the undissociated form and release few hydrogen ions. The sour taste of lemon and grapefruit juices, "sour" milk, and sauerkraut is attributed to the presence of weak acids.

Bases, or alkalis, have a slimy or soapy feel and a bitter taste. These compounds yield hydroxyl (OH^-) ions in solution; for example:

$$NaOH \rightarrow Na^+ + OH^-$$

As with acids, strong bases ionize to a greater degree than weak bases. Sodium hydroxide (NaOH), commonly called lye, and calcium hydroxide [$Ca(OH)_2$], known as slaked lime, are widely used to neutralize acids. When an acid and a base combine, they form a salt and water:

$$HCl + NaOH \rightarrow NaCl + H_2O$$

Strong acids are known for their corrosive, burning properties, but even weak acids, though much slower in action, are highly reactive chemicals. The reactivity of acids is due largely to the hydrogen ions they release. A hydrogen ion is a hydrogen atom without its electron. In other words, it is a free proton, and as such it is an extremely small, fast-moving, reactive particle.

Weak acids have a variety of functions in biological systems, not the least of which is to provide protons that are needed for various metabolic reactions. But it is important to keep the number of hydrogen ions under the strictest control, since an excess can lead to cell damage. A variety of compounds in both plants and animals will loosely bind hydrogen ions when they are abundant and then release them as needed. These **buffers** serve to control acidity.

A common buffer in biological systems is the bicarbonate ion (HCO_3^-). It is also a common in-

FIGURE 3.10 Sodium Chloride Dissolves in Water. Water's polar charges tug and pull at sodium and chloride ions and break them away from the crystalline lattice of solid sodium chloride.

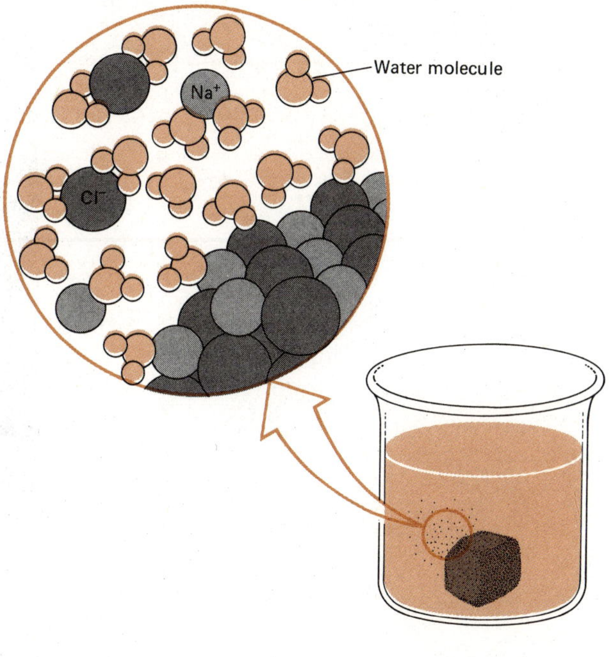

gredient in tablets taken to relieve acid indigestion. Hydrogen ions are absorbed by the bicarbonate and the much weaker carbonic acid is produced:

$$H^+ + HCO_3^- \rightarrow H_2CO_3 \rightarrow H_2O + CO_2$$

Carbonic acid slowly decomposes to water and carbon dioxide gas. (Anyone who has ever taken an antacid containing bicarbonate knows that gas is formed soon after.)

Because internal and external hydrogen-ion concentration is so important to life processes, it is often necessary to measure the acidity or alkalinity of a system. The most widely used index of acidity (and its opposite, alkalinity) is the **pH scale** (Fig. 3.11).

Carbon and Carbon Compounds. In spite of water's great importance, carbon compounds are the real backbone molecules of life. Remove the water from cells, and about 95 percent of what remains is organic matter. These carbon compounds are uniquely fitted to the requirements of life processes. Their existence is possible because of the special properties of carbon atoms.

FIGURE 3.11 **The pH Scale.** A difference of one pH unit is equivalent to a tenfold change in hydrogen-ion concentration. Thus there are a thousand times more hydrogen ions in a solution at pH 1 than there are in a solution at pH 3.

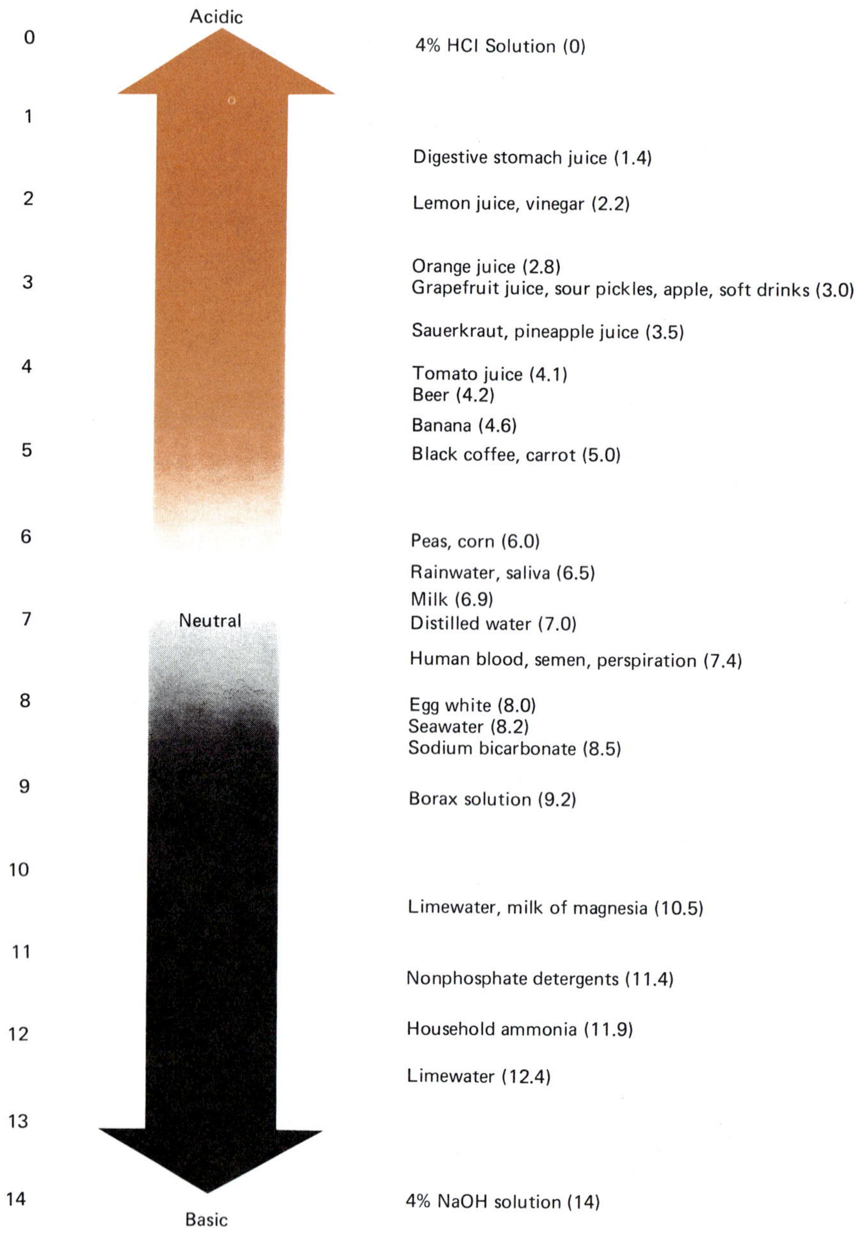

Of all elements, carbon has the most versatile properties for combining with other atoms. First and foremost, carbon has a marked tendency to couple repeatedly with other carbon atoms to form chains and rings of various sizes (Fig. 3.12). Second, every carbon atom can form four covalent bonds. Third, carbon atoms will share electrons with atoms of many other elements—most notably hydrogen, oxygen, and nitrogen. The result is an almost infinite number of compounds that contain carbon. Over one million natural and synthetic carbon compounds are known.

The simplest organic compounds are combinations of carbon and hydrogen known as **hydrocarbons**. Of these, methane (CH_4) is the simplest. Few hydrocarbons are found in biological systems. Most biologically important organic molecules contain elements other than carbon and hydrogen alone. Nevertheless, the structure of methane serves to illustrate why all organic molecules have a three-dimensional shape.

The covalent bonds that hold methane together are formed at specific angles so that the carbon atom is at the center of a triangular pyramid. The hydrogen atoms are evenly distributed around the carbon atom, and they form the points of the pyramid (Fig. 3.13). This is the most stable position in which four atoms can share electrons with one carbon. The tendency for bonds to be at specific angles ensures that *all carbon compounds are geometrical molecules* (Fig. 3.14). But since we have already mentioned the importance of water to the organization of biological molecules, it is clear that the shape of these molecules is determined by a variety of forces besides bond angles.

Many biologically significant organic compounds are relatively small molecules; sugars, amino acids, and vitamins, for example, are composed of only a few dozen atoms. On the other hand, some of the most important biological molecules contain thousands or even millions of atoms. Such **macromolecules** include polysaccharides, nucleic acids, and proteins, all of which can have very complex shapes. In Chapter 4, we will consider these com-

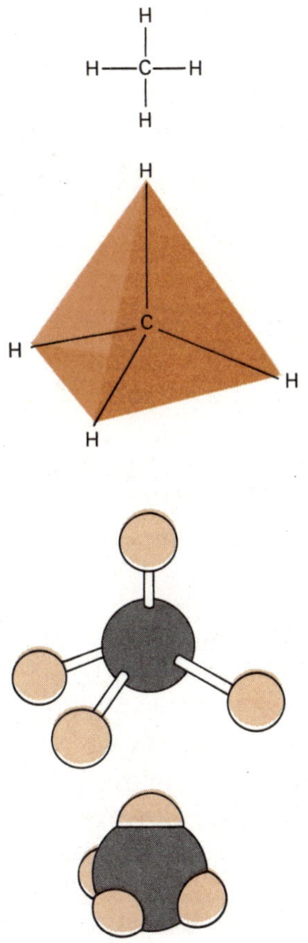

(a) A diagramatic depiction of methane; dashes symbolize the covalent bonds between atoms.

(b)The tetrahedron shape of methane, indicating the relative geometrical positions of the atoms. Note the bond angles.

(c) A ball-and-stick model of methane, showing the relative positions of the carbon and hydrogen atoms.

(d) A more realistic model that shows how the methane molecule actually occupies space.

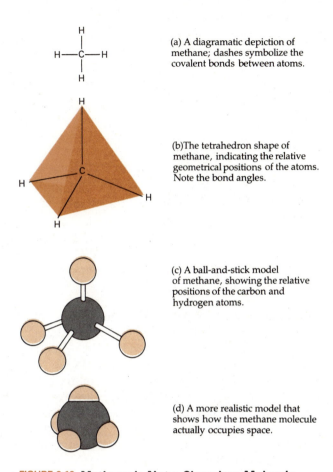

FIGURE 3.13 Methane Is Not a Shapeless Molecule.

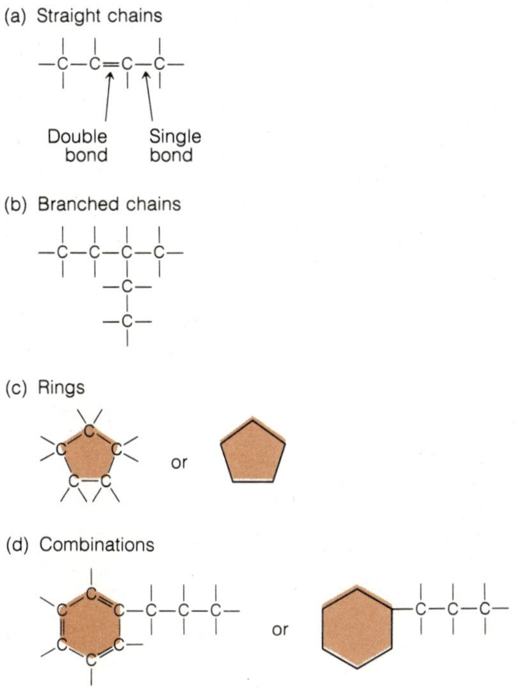

FIGURE 3.12 Carbon Atoms Bond Together to Form Chains and Rings.

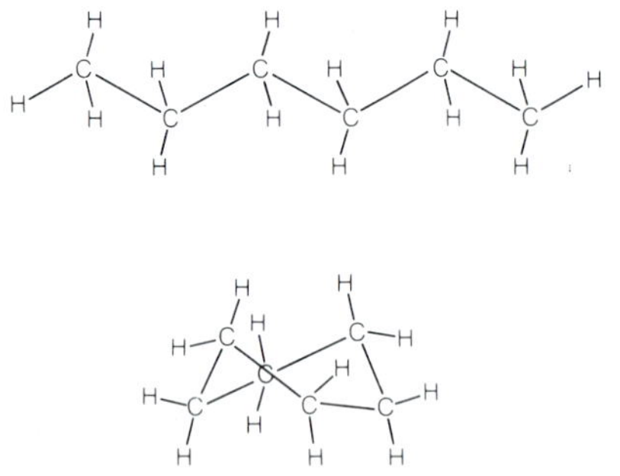

FIGURE 3.14 **All Organic Molecules Are Three-Dimensional.**

pounds further and also address the importance of their shapes to their functions.

Sources of Carbon for Life. All organisms must have a continuous supply of carbon, hydrogen, oxygen, nitrogen, and all the other elements necessary to produce organic molecules. As we have already indicated, water is a primary source of hydrogen and oxygen for organisms. However, organisms are divided into two major categories depending on the nature of their carbon sources. **Autotrophs** can produce their organic structures using carbon dioxide of the air or water as the sole carbon source.

The term *autotroph* means "self-feeder" and refers to the fact that autotrophs have no need for an external source of organic molecules. That is to say, they require no real "food."

Green plants and some bacteria are autotrophs. They carry on photosynthesis, a process whereby the energy of sunlight is used to construct all necessary organic compounds from carbon dioxide, water, and minerals (Fig. 3.15). Photosynthesis, the major source of organic compounds on earth, produces organic compounds "from scratch." Most autotrophs obtain nitrogen for their production of proteins and other organic nitrogen compounds from nitrogen-containing minerals.

We are **heterotrophs**, which means "other feeders." Organisms like ourselves cannot manufacture organic compounds using carbon dioxide as the sole carbon source. We must consume food that contains presynthesized organic compounds. In other words, we must consume other organisms or their products. The ultimate source of the organic food molecules required by heterotrophs is, of course, photosynthesis (Fig. 3.16).

ENERGY AND LIFE

Potential energy is pent-up energy, energy that is not being expended. The energy in a pressurized container, such as a bottle of soda pop, is a good

FIGURE 3.15 **Photosynthesis Produces Food.**

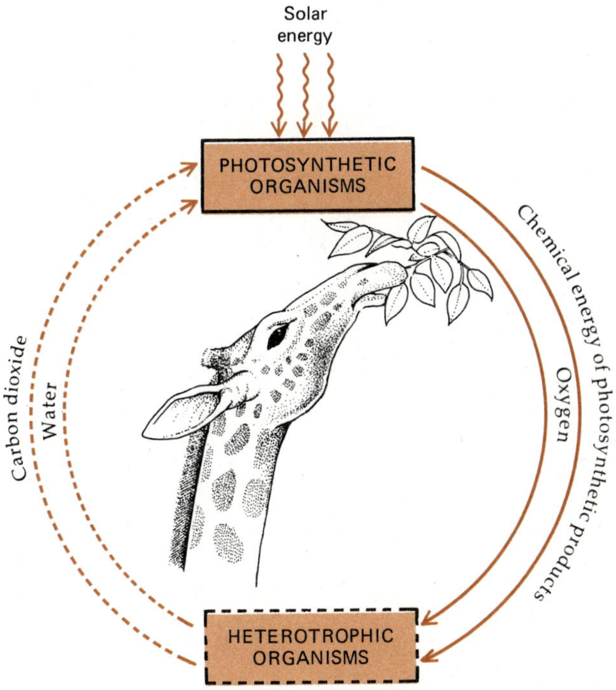

FIGURE 3.16 **What Makes the Biological World Go 'Round.** Energy enters the biosphere from the sun. It is transformed into chemical energy by plants. Animals consume plant products and one another. The waste materials of animal metabolism are the raw materials of photosynthesis.

example of potential energy. **Kinetic energy** is active energy (Fig. 3.17). Think of the energy released when a soda pop bottle is opened and gas bubbles rise to the top and sometimes gush out. All familiar forms of energy, including mechanical, electrical, chemical, heat, and solar energy, exist in potential and kinetic states.

Energy in Biological Systems

Photosynthesis converts solar energy into the potential energy of chemical bonds. Therefore, although radiant energy of sunlight is the ultimate source of energy for biological systems, almost all energy inside organisms is chemical energy. Photosynthesis as an energy-conversion process is discussed in Chapter 17.

Chemical Energy. That chemicals contain energy is certainly not news. The cost of gasoline, oil, and natural gas and the search for alternative energy sources have made chemical energy a topic of everyday conversation. All chemical compounds are characterized by a certain energy content; some are high in energy, others low. This energy comes from the bonding forces that hold the atoms of a molecule together. Thus the exact amount of potential energy in a compound depends on the kinds—and thus the configurations—of the chem-

FIGURE 3.17 **Kinetic Energy.** Movements of the earth's crust permit rock, gases, and ash to escape to the surface during a volcanic eruption.

BOX 3B

RADIATION: ENERGY ON THE MOVE

Radiations are energy emissions. They are said to radiate because they stream through space, away from their source. When radiations strike material bodies, they may be absorbed or reflected.

The major source of natural radiations is the sun. Solar energy is discharged by thermonuclear fusions, powerful changes in matter that occur on the sun's surface. This energy consists of pulsating waves with electric and magnetic properties. Electromagnetic radiations include infrared light, visible light, ultraviolet light, x-rays, and gamma rays. Each is known by its characteristic wavelength and energy content. In the accompanying diagram, the numbers are wavelengths given in nanometers (nm). One nanometer is equal to 1/1,000,000,000 of a meter (1 m = 39 in.). Notice that high energy is associated with short wavelength.

Other forms of radiations include cosmic rays, which drift to the earth from the depths of space, and radiations that are produced by the disintegration of radioactive elements. Radioactive emissions, such as those thrown off when uranium ore disintegrates into lead, include alpha, beta, and gamma rays.

The excitation of molecules by absorbed radiation can be biologically useful. For example, when human eye pigments become excited by certain wavelengths of visible light, they initiate a sequence of chemical events that culminates in vision. High-energy radiations, such as x-rays and gamma rays, can be quite dangerous, however, because they stimulate chemical changes that may lead to inactivation or disintegration of biological molecules.

The spectrum of electromagnetic radiations

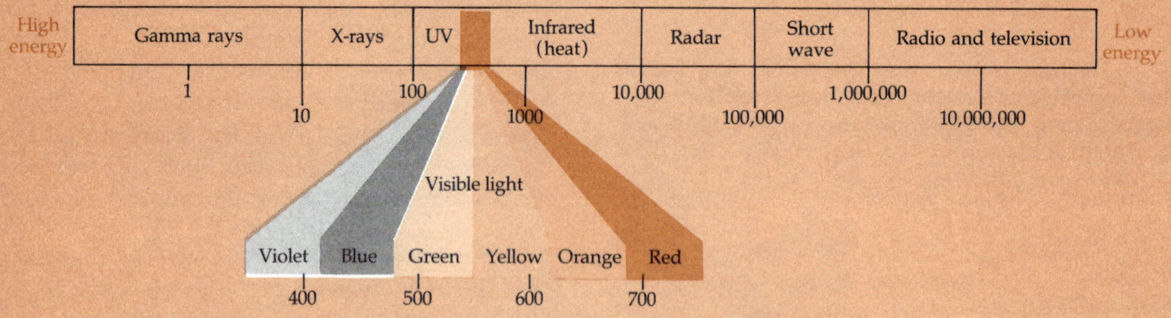

ical bonds within the molecules. For this reason, we speak of chemical energy being "in" chemical bonds.

The energy in biologically important chemicals is usually measured in terms of **calories**. A calorie is the amount of heat required to raise the temperature of one gram of water one degree Celsius. Since all other forms of energy can be converted into heat, any kind of energy can be measured as heat energy.

Dieticians use a different unit to measure the energy content of food. Their Calorie (written with a capital C) is really a kilocalorie or 1000 ordinary calories.

The caloric value of a compound—sugar, for example—is determined by placing it in a combustion chamber surrounded by water and enclosed in an insulated container (Fig. 3.18). The change in temperature of the water during burning of the compound is then measured.

Chemical Reactions and Energy Changes. Just as different atoms react to achieve greater stability, so do different molecules. It is relatively easy to detect the disappearance of the original ingredients (reactants) of a chemical reaction and the appearance of the products. What is not so easy to appreciate about chemical reactions are the changes in energy associated with them. We will describe two general types of chemical reactions on the basis of their energy relationships.

Exergonic reactions are those that always proceed to the eventual release of energy. An example of such an occurrence is the violent explosion that

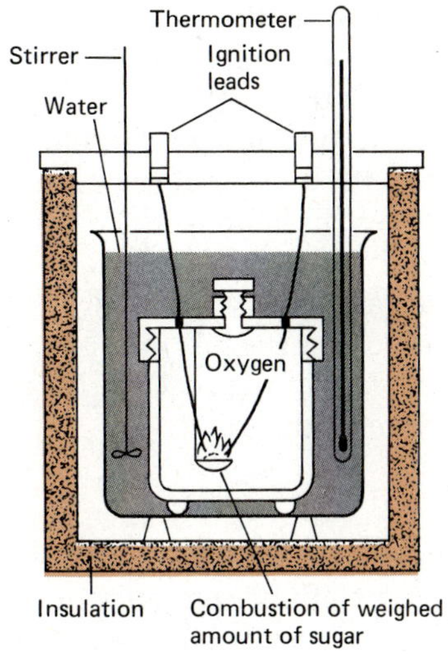

FIGURE 3.18 **A Calorimeter.** An electric spark ignites material placed on a pan in the combustion chamber of a calorimeter. The heat produced by the burning of the material raises the temperature of the water surrounding the chamber. With this information, one can calculate the number of calories released during combustion.

accompanies the addition of an electric spark to a mixture of hydrogen and oxygen gases:

$$H_2 + O_2 \rightarrow H_2O + \text{ENERGY (Exergonic)}$$

Endergonic reactions never release energy; they require it. Consider, for example, the reverse of the reaction written above. Water cannot be converted back into hydrogen and oxygen gases without an energy input at least equal to the amount produced by the explosion that created the water in the first place:

$$H_2O \not\rightarrow H_2 + O_2 \text{ (Endergonic)}$$

An important generalization can be obtained from the examples we've just described. Synthetic (building) reactions are endergonic and require energy, whereas degradation (breakdown) reactions release energy. Both kinds of reactions occur in biological systems all the time. As a matter of fact, the energy released in degradation reactions is used to drive synthetic reactions. This is the reason why energy-yielding and energy-requiring metabolic reactions are said to be **coupled**. Coupling occurs, for instance, when food is digested to provide the energy for growing hair. Degradation reactions provide biologically useful energy to drive the long series of chemical reactions that produce hair from something as far removed as apple pie. To learn more about this phenomenon, read on!

Biological Oxidation Reactions. Oxidation reactions such as the burning (combustion) of wood, coal, and oil are familiar everyday sources of energy. Although the relationship may seem obscure, the energy in food molecules is also released via oxidations.

Exactly what *is* an oxidation reaction? Technically, **oxidation** occurs when one or more electrons are removed from a molecule. In biological oxidations these electrons are often those of hydrogen, so we sometimes speak of oxidation as a loss of hydrogens, or as a dehydrogenation. Note that oxidations do not necessarily involve oxygen.

Oxidation reactions are, of necessity, accompanied by reduction reactions. A **reduction** occurs when a molecule accepts one or more electrons lost by another. Thus oxidation-reduction reactions are interdependent.

Most biological oxidations are carried out in a cellular process called **respiration**. Cellular respiration is an exergonic process. When sugars fuel cellular respiration, it can be summarized as follows:

$$\underset{\text{sugar}}{C_6H_{12}O_6} + \underset{\text{oxygen}}{O_2} \rightarrow \underset{\text{carbon dioxide}}{6CO_2} + \underset{\text{water}}{12H_2O} + \underset{\text{energy}}{\text{ENERGY}}$$

Note that while glucose loses hydrogens and is oxidized to carbon dioxide, oxygen is reduced to form water.

The energy released by the oxidation of sugars is the chemical bond energy captured in the photosynthesis of sugars by plants (Chapter 17). Thus photosynthesis is an endergonic process. It is, in fact, the reverse of cellular respiration:

$$6CO_2 + 12H_2O + \text{ENERGY} \rightarrow C_6H_{12}O_6 + O_2$$

Here, carbon dioxide is reduced and incorporates energy as it is photosynthesized into sugar. And water, the source of hydrogens for the reduction, is oxidized and split with the release of oxygen.

Unlike oxidation by combustion, the cellular respiration of sugars and other nutrients provided by plants is a carefully controlled process. In cells, only a few electrons at a time are removed from fuel molecules. And, although a small portion escapes as heat, most of the released energy is captured. This requires packaging of the energy into **energy-carrier molecules**.

The primary energy carrier molecule of cells is ATP. ATP stands for *adenosine triphosphate*, which is formed by the addition of a phosphate group to adenosine diphosphate (ADP), incorporating the energy made available by oxidation steps of cellular

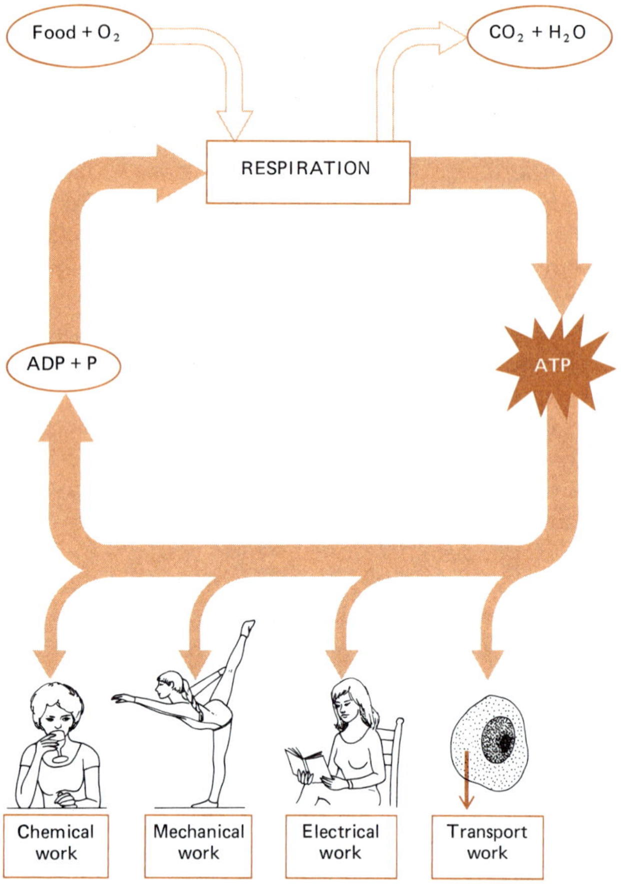

FIGURE 3.19 Transfer of Energy Through ATP. Both plants and animals carry on respiration to produce ATP, which provides energy for all types of biological work. Plants can also make ATP in photosynthesis.

respiration. Once formed, ATP serves as a source of energy to drive cellular endergonic reactions such as the synthesis of hair from apple pie (Fig. 3.19). Cellular respiration and ATP are discussed further in Chapter 5.

Thermodynamics and Bioenergetics

Thermodynamics is the study of energy changes. The name comes from the fact that thermodynamic principles were first determined by studying heat (thermal) energy. Although the laws of thermodynamics were formulated by studying such mechanical systems as the steam engine, these laws govern energy changes in other systems, including living organisms. Bioenergetics is a convenient term for the study of energy changes in living systems.

The **first law of thermodynamics** recognizes that energy can be converted from one form into another, but that the total amount of energy never changes. The **second law of thermodynamics** recognizes that with every energy conversion, some energy becomes dissipated into a form that is unable to cause change; that is, some energy becomes useless. The fact that some energy becomes unavailable with change is just another way of saying that every process in the real world tends to move in the direction of disorder.

Useless Energy. Physicists have coined the term **entropy** to describe disorder. Experience tells us that there is a natural tendency for a system to achieve its lowest energy state. If you drop a handful of carefully arranged matches to the floor, they land in complete disarray. You would not expect matches to fall into the same neat pile you purposefully created in your hand. We can generalize from this that everything tends to break down, wear out, and become randomized. Or as we started out by saying, all things have a tendency to reach their lowest energy state. Our example also points out another fact: energy is required to create order. Think of the work involved when you arranged the matches so they made a neat fistful.

Entropy Spells Doom. Living things are highly organized systems of atoms aggregated into cells, tissues, and organs. Living is a constant uphill battle to hold together, to maintain order, and to replace parts. Life requires a constant input of energy. Every single creature loses the battle in the end. Bodies wear out and die.

Entropy is constantly increasing. Animal life is sustained and the natural increase in entropy that accompanies death is postponed by consumption of energy in the form of food. Nevertheless, food production ultimately depends on the continued energy output of the sun. But the sun must be increasing in entropy, too! Although we can't know the exact future of the sun, thermodynamic laws tell us that it is ever so slowly burning out. Someday it will emit its last ray of usable energy. Then our little corner of the universe will be dead—finally dead.

Does this mean that all heavenly bodies will cease to shine someday and there will be no usable energy anywhere? Perhaps, if the law of entropy applies to the entire universe. But that is something we don't know. Laws that seem to apply to our world may not hold universally.

Energy and Evolution: The Origin of Life

The energy crisis is not new; in fact, it is old as life itself. Living is a continuous struggle to obtain energy for continued existence. The endless energy crisis has been a continued stimulus to evolution. The diversity of life on our planet is a tribute to the variety of solutions to the age-old problem of getting energy.

There seems little doubt that the first organisms were not photosynthesizers, as you might have guessed, but heterotrophs that evolved in the chemical soup that existed on the primordial earth. The ancient earth was a cauldron in which chemical reactions, triggered by intense heat, electrical storms, and other forces, turned simple elements into increasingly complex chemical compounds. According to the theory of chemical evolution, these complex compounds grew ever more organized until they became life itself. The early organisms grew and reproduced at the expense of the chemicals in the surrounding "soup." Then came the first energy crisis.

Chemical energy became limiting as the population increased and the conditions on earth mellowed, so that spontaneous formation of organic compounds stopped. This was the selective force that resulted in the evolution of photosynthesizers, organisms capable of utilizing an alternative energy source, that of the sun. The original heterotrophs probably died out, but new ones, including ourselves, arose to take advantage of the photosynthesizers.

The early photosynthesizers not only renewed the organic compounds used up by the first heterotrophs, but from water they produced the oxygen that made cellular respiration as we know it today possible. Before plants evolved, the earth's atmosphere contained little, if any, oxygen. In fact, the organic compounds that grew into cells could never have formed spontaneously in an oxygen-rich environment. Oxygen gas is just too potent an oxidizing agent. If it had been present in the atmosphere of the early earth, organic compounds could not have lasted long enough for life to evolve.

Summary

1. Matter is composed of elements, the most biologically important of which are carbon, hydrogen, oxygen, nitrogen, sulfur, and phosphorus. Each element is a unique chemical substance composed of only one kind of atom. Most substances are compounds or mixtures of several different elements.

2. Atoms consist of a centrally located nucleus containing positively charged protons and uncharged neutrons. The atomic nucleus is surrounded by orbiting electrons, which carry a negative charge.

3. Electrons are precisely distributed about the atomic nucleus in concentric shells. Electrons in shells closest to the nucleus are lower in energy than those located farther away. Atoms whose outermost electron shells are unfilled are chemically reactive. They tend to combine with other atoms in ways that achieve the stability of a filled outer shell.

4. When two or more atoms react with one another they form chemical bonds. Sharing of electrons produces covalent bonds of molecules. Transfer of electrons between atoms results in ionic bonds.

5. Molecules are described as organic if they contain carbon and hydrogen, inorganic if they do not. The most abundant inorganic molecule of biological systems is water. The unique contributions of water to the chemistry of life depend largely on its capacity for hydrogen bonding.

6. Acids are highly reactive substances that release hydrogen ions. The degree of acidity is measured on a pH scale. Buffers are substances that control acidity by resisting pH changes.

7. The unique capacity of carbon atoms to form covalent bonds results in the formation of a tremendous number of organic compounds of diverse size and shape. Hydrogen and other weak secondary bonds are responsible for maintaining the shape of many biologically important organic compounds. Although some biologically important organic molecules are small, most biological structures are composed of macromolecules.

8. Autotrophs such as green plants can synthesize all their organic components from carbon dioxide and water via photosynthesis. Heterotrophs such as ourselves need organic raw materials to synthesize their organic components. These raw materials ultimately come from green-plant photosynthesis.

9. During biological oxidations such as those that occur in cellular respiration, food molecules lose electrons and energy and ATP is produced. ATP is a universal energy carrier, supplying energy to cellular endergonic reactions. As with physical systems, biological energy conversions are inefficient. Thus organisms need a constant input of energy in order to maintain themselves.

Thought and Controversy

1. Why is life built around carbon compounds instead of silicon compounds? Silicon is more abundant in the environment than carbon is; yet it is found in only trace amounts in living matter—in spite of the fact that silicon, like carbon, achieves stability by forming four covalent bonds. The difference is that the silicon atom is larger than the carbon atom. This fact makes silicon-silicon bonds weaker than carbon-carbon bonds. As a consequence, macromolecules produced from silicon are unstable in aqueous environments. Furthermore, silicon reacts with oxygen to form insoluble silicates and quartz. Thus in air silicon becomes unavailable for biological processes.

2. The structure and properties of liquid water change substantially when substances are dissolved in it. When table salt (NaCl) is dissolved in water, the ions separate as a "shell" of water forms around them. Because of the strong charge of the ions, the water shell is very stable and tough. In effect, the molecules of the water shell are less attracted to other water molecules than they would be in the absence of ions. Thus the normal structure of liquid water is disrupted in the presence of solutes. This explains why salt water freezes at a lower temperature and boils at a higher temperature than pure water. How do you think organisms are affected by these facts?

3. Are microwaves safe? Microwaves are a form of electromagnetic radiation that fall into the radio frequency band. They are used to treat sore muscles, run burglar-alarm systems, and relay radio and television programs. They have many industrial uses as well, but their most common use is to cook food. These low-energy radiations bounce back and forth inside an oven, agitating the water molecules in food and thereby increasing its temperature. Since 1971 all microwave ovens have been covered by a radiation safety standard that permits emission of no more than five milliwatts per square centimeter during their lifetime. Some studies have shown that animals try to get away from microwaves, also that microwaves cause changes in DNA and reduce resistance to disease. Yet when it was learned that Russian surveillance equipment had subjected the U.S. Embassy in Moscow to microwaves for twenty years, studies showed no significant increase in death or disease rates among the embassy employees. Because of such contradictory observations, many scientists agree that more research is needed to determine the effects of microwaves on humans.

4. In a bygone era popular songs often referred to romantic love as the result of "chemistry." This tongue-in-cheek explanation for a very human condition nevertheless recognizes the importance of chemical events to life.

Does studying molecules seem far removed from studying living, breathing creatures? If it does, consider the fact that the molecular approach has been particularly valuable in cancer research, because cancer cells have a unique chemistry. Molecular biology, the modern name given to the study of life at the chemical or molecular level, has resulted in much other practical knowledge. In subsequent chapters, you will find many chemical explanations for biological phenomena. Some investigators even feel that certain aspects of life can be understood only at the submolecular level.

Questions

1. What accounts for the differences in the physical states of solids, liquids, and gases?

2. What is the relationship between an element and an atom? Between a compound and a molecule?

3. Name the six most important elements found in organisms. For each element, identify a biological compound that contains that element. Are the compounds organic or inorganic?

4. Define the following: electron, proton, neutron, shell, isotope.

5. Describe how ionic and covalent bonds are formed in terms of the atomic structure.

6. What range of pH would you expect for an acid? A base? A salt? In chemical terms, what does the pH of a solution indicate?

7. How do exergonic and endergonic reactions differ? What is meant when it is said that such reactions are "coupled?"

8. Explain the effect of the thermodynamic laws, especially entropy, on life processes.

9. How does the hydrogen bonding capacity of water explain its unusual properties, such as its action as a solvent?

10. Define the term *oxidation*. Compare ordinary oxidations with cellular respiration. Include in your answer a discussion of the role of ATP.

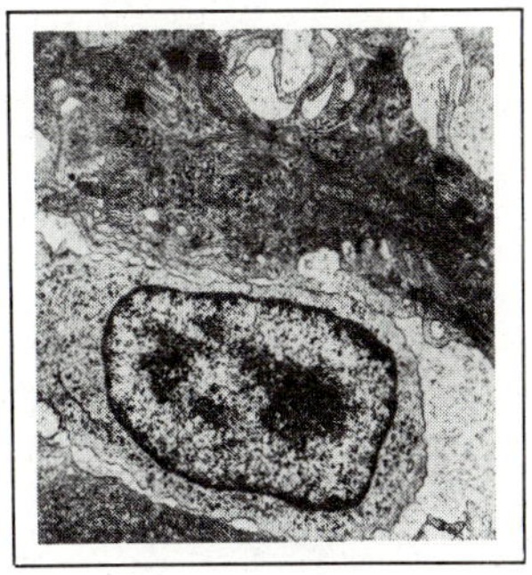

4

Cellular Organization: Chemicals and Organelles

LIKE ALL ANIMALS—AND PLANTS, TOO—OUR bodies are composed of cells and substances accumulated and organized by cells. In fact, there are a hundred trillion cells in each one of us. Everything we are or can do can be traced to the structure and action of cells.

Although cellular architecture can be examined with a microscope, cellular function can be understood only if observation is accompanied by chemical analysis of cell parts. Such analysis reveals that most cell structures are assembled from proteins in conjunction with polysaccharides, nucleic acids, or lipids.

COMPLEX CHEMICALS OF CELLS

Proteins, polysaccharides, and nucleic acids are large
59 macromolecules.□ Sometimes they are called **polymers**, meaning that they are made of many subunits. A common feature of macromolecules is that they are constructed of hundreds or even thousands of repeating building-block subunits that are linked together in long chains. Proteins are composed of amino acid units, polysaccharides are composed of sugar units, and nucleic acids are composed of nucleotides.

Macromolecular chains tend to fold, twist, and loop, partly in response to their watery environment. In doing so, they assume specific shapes. In turn, cellular structures are produced by specific associations of macromolecules and other biological molecules, such as lipids, to form larger and larger complexes (Fig. 4.1).

Lipids aren't really big enough to qualify as macromolecules; but just like macromolecules, they are built up from molecules that are smaller still.

Proteins

Although many plant and animal structures are composed of protein, the importance of protein to cells extends far beyond its structural use. All enzymes are proteins, and as we noted in Chapter 1, enzymes regulate the chemical activities of cells.

Most proteins are macromolecules composed
of tens of thousands of atoms.□ In addition to car- 48
bon and hydrogen, elements found in all organic compounds, proteins contain oxygen and nitrogen. Frequently there is some sulfur present as well. The tremendous versatility of proteins is owed to the way these five kinds of atoms are strung together.

Amino Acids. The basic building blocks of proteins are **amino acids**. There are 20 different amino acids, each with the distinctive nitrogen-containing amino group (Fig. 4.2). From 50 to 500 amino acids are linked together by **peptide bonds** to produce long polypeptide chains. A seemingly endless variety of polypeptide chains can be constructed simply by altering the order and number of amino acids used.

Every polypeptide chain has its unique *three-dimensional configuration*. Polypeptides fold and bend
or twist, partially in response to water,□ but also 55
because amino acids at different places along a chain can react with one another (Fig. 4.3). A **protein** can

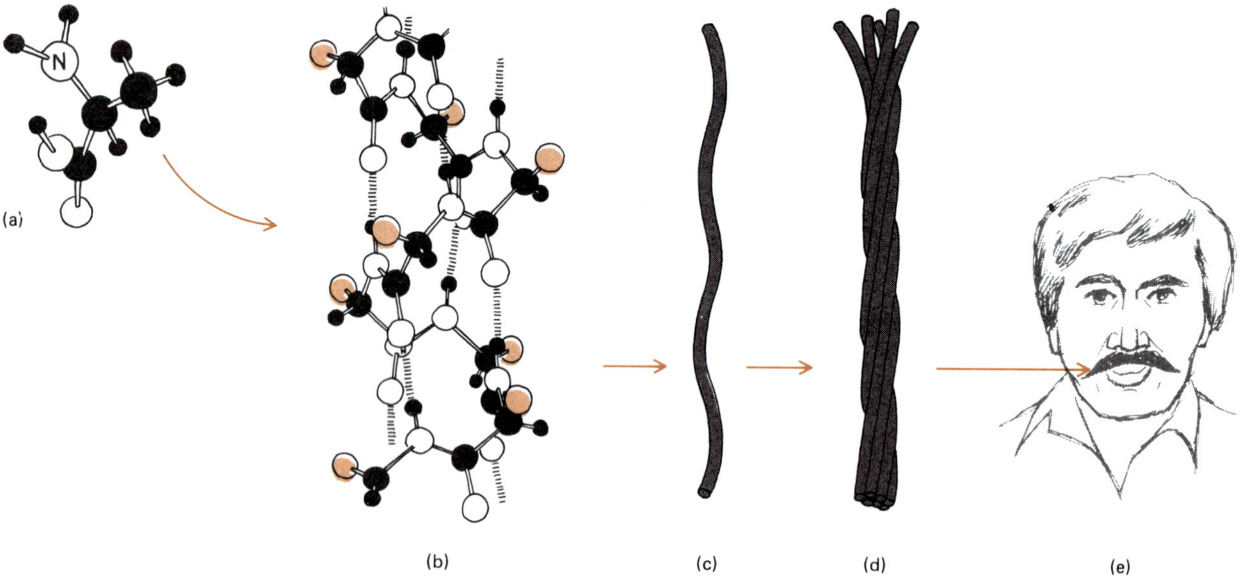

FIGURE 4.1 Macromolecules Assemble into Biological Structures. Amino acid building blocks (a) are fitted together to produce a helical macromolecular chain (b). The completed chain (c) intertwines with similar molecules to produce a protein (d). We observe the process in the growth of cells that make a hair (e). Most biological structures are a mixture of molecules.

FIGURE 4.2 From Amino Acids to Proteins. (a) Every amino acid has an amino group and an acid group bonded to the same carbon atom. (b) Four amino acids with different side groups. (c) Amino acids join together by the removal of water between the acid group of one amino acid and the amino group of another amino acid. (d) Polypeptides are polymers of many amino acids linked by peptide bonds.

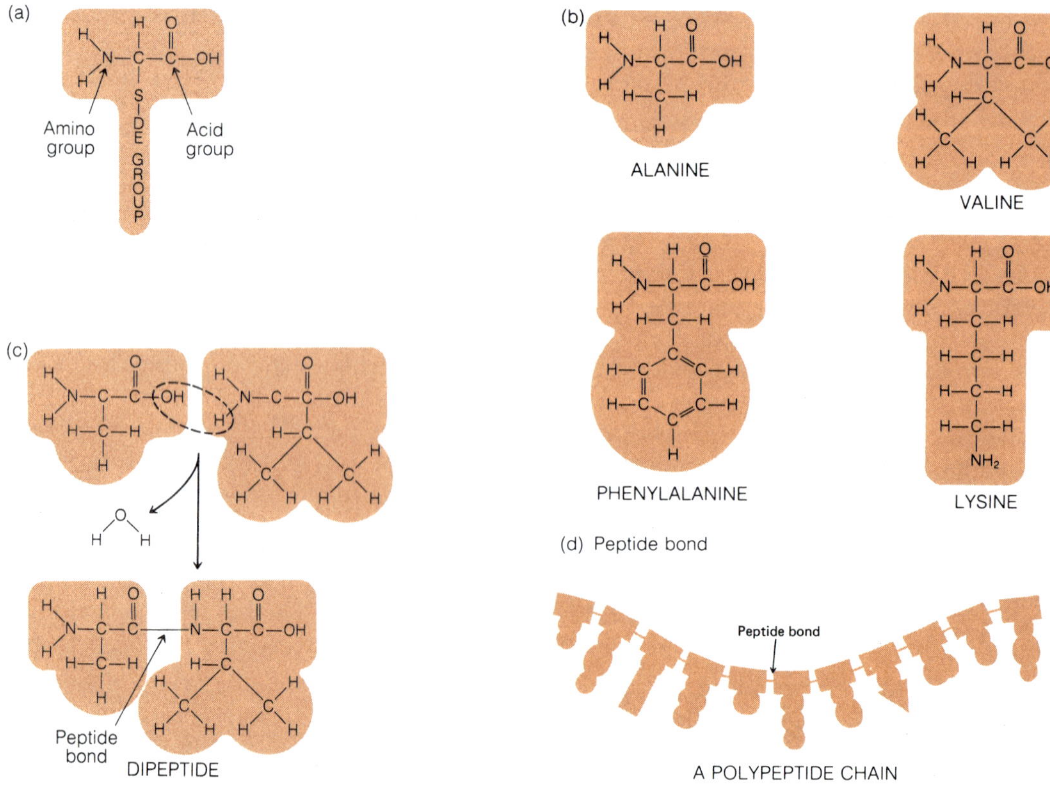

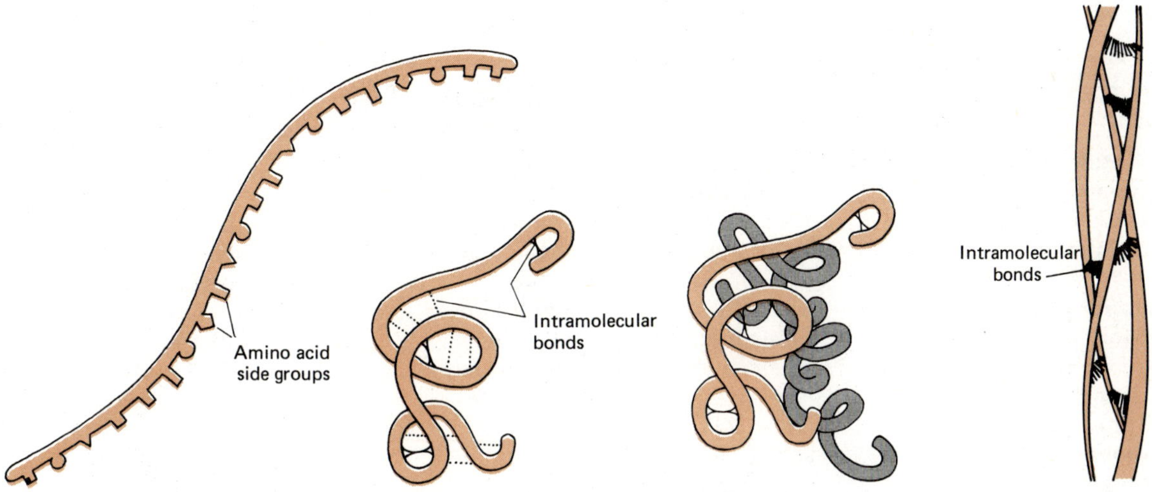

(a) A stretched-out polypeptide chain showing its full length

(b) The same polypeptide chain when permitted to naturally coil and fold and thus achieve a globular shape

(c) The same polypeptide chain after reacting with another polypeptide chain to give a larger globular protein having a more complex shape

(d) Most fibrous proteins have a regular orientation. Here three polypeptide chains are twisted into a ropelike triple helix

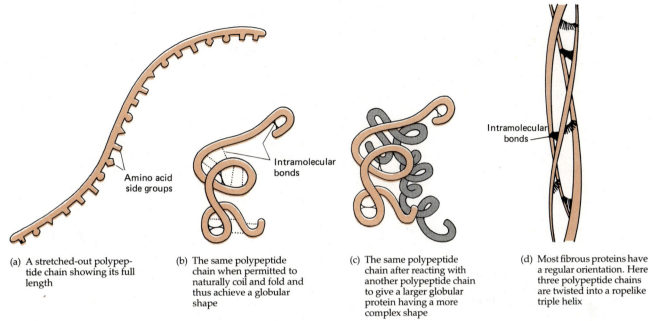

FIGURE 4.3 **Globular and Fibrous Proteins.**

be a single polypeptide chain, or it may consist of several. For example, insulin consists of one polypeptide chain, but hemoglobin contains four.

Denaturation. Heat, caustic chemicals, or physical stress can alter or **denature** proteins. A denatured protein cannot function, because its natural shape has been destroyed (Fig. 4.4). The damage done to cells by high temperatures, acids, and drying is mostly the result of denaturation of cellular proteins.

Denaturation can be observed during the cooking of protein foods—meat, for example. The red color of raw meat is not due to blood, which is drained from animals at the time of slaughter, but to myoglobin, a red protein found in muscle cells. Denatured myoglobin has the grayish-brown color associated with well-done meat.

Cooking tenderizes meat largely by the denaturation of **collagen**, a tough, fibrous protein that binds muscles together. By causing the ropelike collagen molecules to unwind, heat converts collagen into a more tender protein, **gelatin**. Commercially, gelatin is extracted from animal carcasses by prolonged boiling. Incidentally, the effect of water on macromolecules is illustrated in the process of making a gelatin dessert. With the addition of hot water, packaged gelatin granules swell into a pliable "gel," which has properties far different from either pure water or dried gelatin.

Polysaccharides and Other Carbohydrates

When plants trap solar energy, they store much of it by manufacturing carbohydrates. Plant-produced carbohydrates are the chief source of energy for most cells, whether plant or animal. Carbohydrates include sugars, starches, and numerous other substances built from sugar subunits.

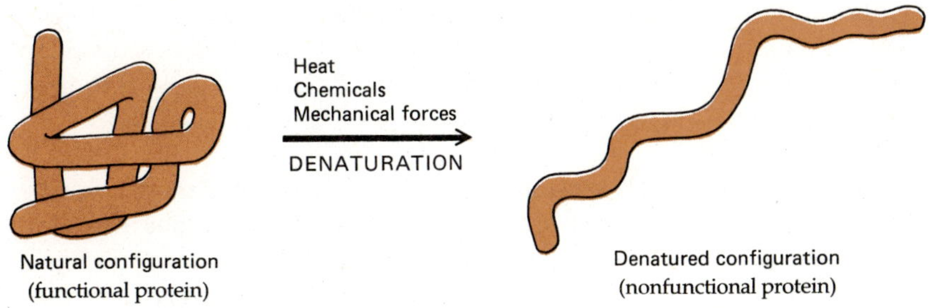

FIGURE 4.4 **Protein Denaturation.**

BOX 4A

THE THREE-DIMENSIONAL STRUCTURE OF PROTEINS

In a polypeptide chain the amino acid side groups hang loose and so are free to react with one another. Such intramolecular reactions result in bonds that cause the polypeptide chain to twist, bend, and fold into a particular shape. For example, disulfide bonds (a) may form between sulfur-containing amino acids, and hydrogen bonds (b) can occur where hydrogen and oxygen atoms of different amino acid side groups come into close proximity. Because proteins exist in a watery environment, hydrophobic bonds (c) between amino acids with hydrocarbon-like side chains have a major influence on the configuration of many proteins. Although covalent disulfide bonds are stronger than hydrogen or hydrophobic bonds, they are less important in establishing the overall shape of a protein. For every disulfide bond there may be thousands of weaker bonds. Disulfide bonds are like anchors—or, to use another analogy, like the few pins that hold cloth in place while a hem is being sewn. The differences in shape of globular and fibrous proteins are based in amino acid sequence. Fibrous proteins, such as those in hair cells, tend to have simple, repetitive amino acid sequences. As a result, fibrous proteins form regular coils that twist into ropelike aggregations (see Figs. 4.1 and 4.2) or flat, pleated structures. Globular proteins such as hemoglobin and enzymes have a more variable amino acid content. Therefore they have irregular patterns and more complex shapes, as pictured here.

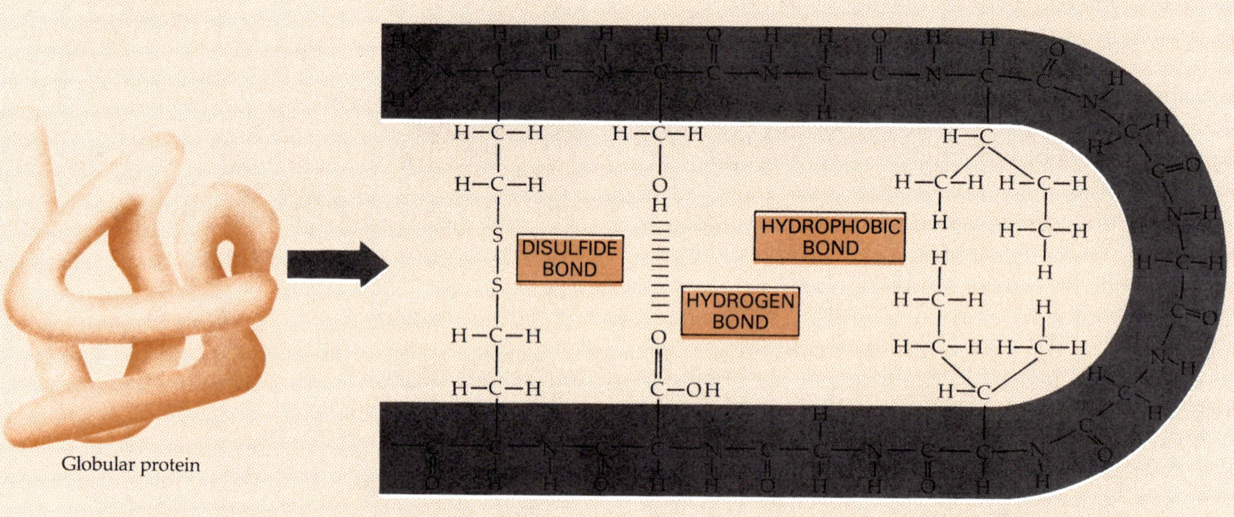

Sugars. **Monosaccharides** are the simplest sugars. Among the most important is **glucose**, also known as *dextrose* or *blood sugar*, because it is the chief circulating nutrient of the body. However, few people eat pure glucose. Plants rapidly convert the glucose they manufacture into starch or other carbohydrates, and for this reason concentrated glucose is rarely available as a food. One exception is honey. It contains both glucose and **fructose**, a closely related monosaccharide.

When monosaccharides are combined by twos, double sugars—or **disaccharides**—are produced (Fig. 4.5). Many plants combine glucose and fructose to make **sucrose**. This is the sugar extracted from sugar cane, sugar beets, and sugar maple. Not all sugars are particularly sweet, as shown by the fact that **lactose**, another disaccharide, is present in milk. Lactose makes up five percent of cow's milk and slightly more of human milk. Calves and babies digest lactose to glucose and the monosaccharide **galactose**.

Polysaccharides. A **polysaccharide** is made up of a large number of sugars linked together into a long chain (Fig. 4.6). Plant cells tie glucose into long, branched starch chains and then twist them into

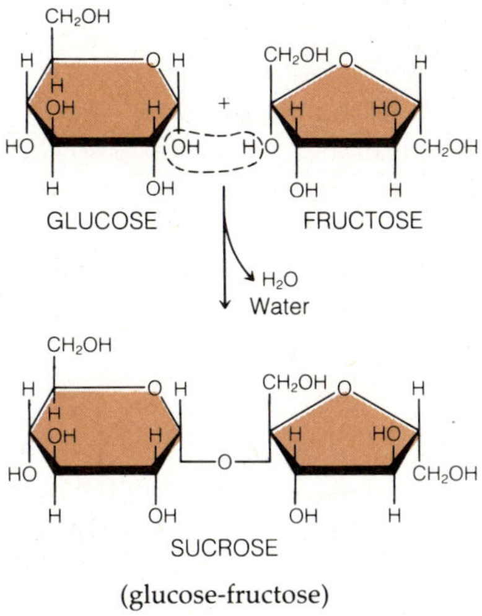

FIGURE 4.5 Two Monosaccharides Join to Form a Disaccharide. Sucrose is produced by the removal of water between glucose and fructose.

starch grains. In our bodies, starch is digested into the disaccharide **maltose** and then into glucose molecules we can absorb and use for energy. If we have excess glucose, it can be converted to **glycogen**, an animal starch.

Plants make **cellulose** from much of the glucose they manufacture. The thick walls that surround and support plant cells are composed largely of cellulose. In fact, cellulose is the primary structural material of plants. Lumber, cotton, and paper are examples of plant products consisting almost entirely of cellulose. Fruits and vegetables have a high cellulose content, too. Humans cannot digest cellulose, although some bacteria and other microorganisms do. For humans, cellulose is merely roughage.

Amino acids, sugars, and other small biological molecules are often joined together, not with others of their kind to make proteins or starches, but with distinctly different sorts of compounds. Some of the resulting substances are of extraordinary significance. The occurrence of sugars in nucleic acids is a prime example.

Nucleic Acids

Deoxyribonucleic acid (DNA) and **ribonucleic acid** (RNA) make up only a small part of a cell, but they possess genetic blueprints that determine all cell activities. Nucleic acids consist of **polynucleotides**—that is, chains of nucleotide subunits.

A **nucleotide** is a complex of one to three **phosphate** groups, a **sugar** (either deoxyribose or ribose), and a **nitrogenous base**. There are five major nitrogenous bases: adenine, guanine, cytosine, thymine, and uracil. The presence of a particular nitrogenous base largely determines the character of the nucleotide.

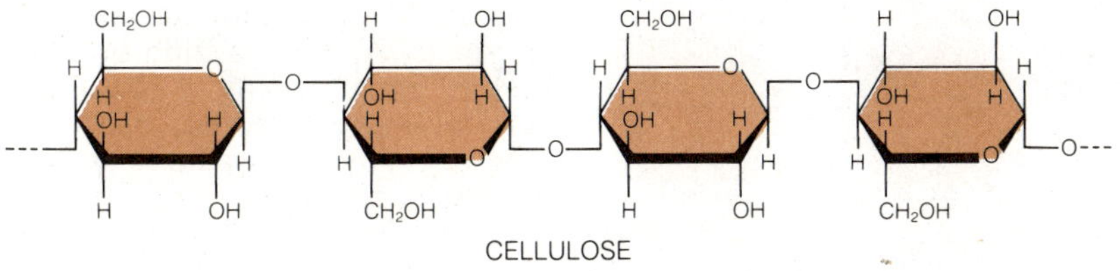

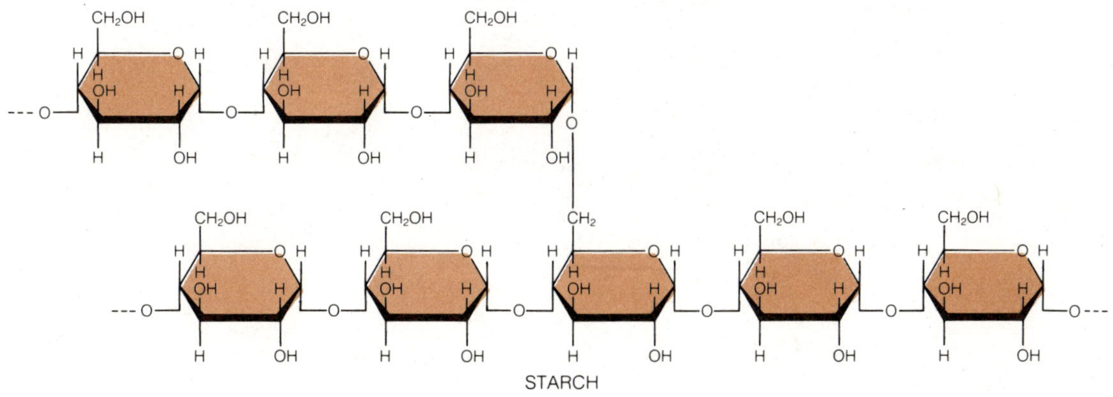

FIGURE 4.6 Polysaccharides. Both starch and cellulose are long chains of glucose subunits. Their different properties are due to the way the subunits are joined together. In cellulose every other glucose is upside down.

DNA is a narrow, long macromolecule consisting of two polynucleotide chains twisted into a **helix**. Within a cell, a DNA double helix is greatly compacted. Cellular RNA, by way of comparison, is a single-stranded polynucleotide. Several forms of cellular RNA exist, all of them much smaller than DNA. Some RNAs are so minute as to be soluble; others are insoluble particles.

People digest the nucleic acids present in foods, but these substances are not major nutrients because they occur in very small amounts. As we have noted, DNA and RNA are carriers and interpreters of hereditary information. The structure and function of nucleic acids will be considered further in Chapter 11.

Lipids

Fats, oils, waxes, and cholesterol are among the substances collectively called **lipids**. Although different in many ways, all lipids share one important characteristic: they are more or less insoluble in water, but they are soluble in one another. Many cell structures contain lipids. In addition, most cells store some lipids as an energy reserve. Fat-tissue cells store such a quantity of lipids that they resemble fat-filled balloons. Spread out just under the skin and packed around internal organs, the blubbery fat tissue makes an excellent insulation and acts as a shock absorber.

Fats. Figure 4.7 illustrates the structure of a simple fat. As you can see, a fat consists of a short backbone of **glycerol** to which **fatty acids** are attached. Fatty acids are most often 16 to 18 carbons in length. They may be either **saturated**, containing only single bonds between the carbons, or **unsaturated**, having double bonds as well. In general, animal fats have a higher proportion of saturated fatty acids than do plant fats. Polyunsaturated fats (fats with many double bonds) are liquids at room

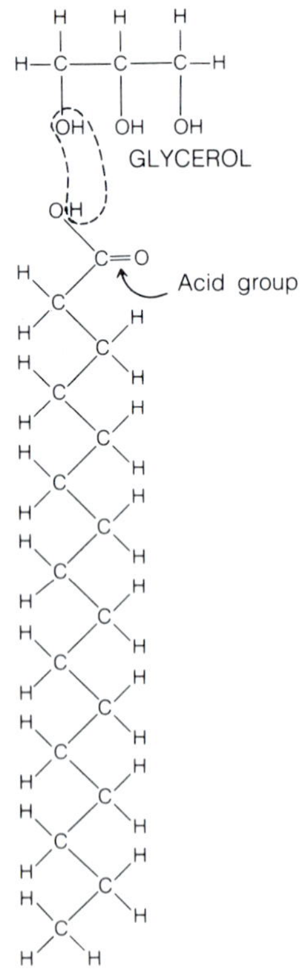

(a) FATTY ACID

(palmitic acid)

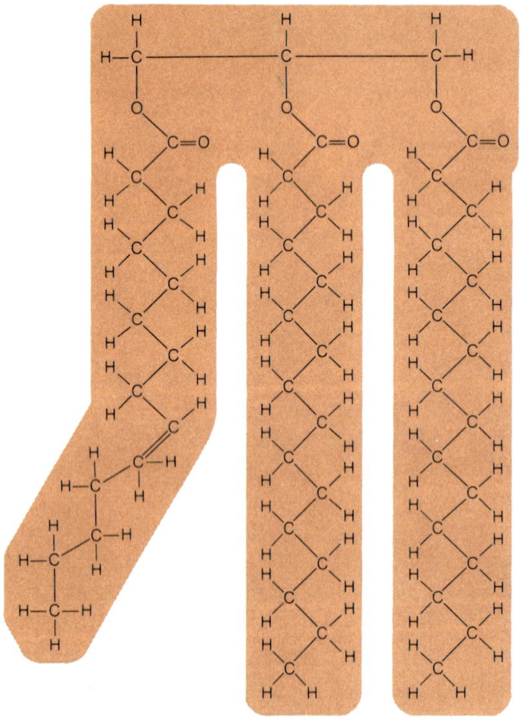

(b) TRIGLYCERIDE

FIGURE 4.7 **Simple Fats and Fatty Acids.** (a) Fatty acids are added to glycerol by the removal of water between the two substances, as shown by the dashed lines. (b) Most fats are triglycerides, meaning that they contain three fatty acids. The one illustrated here contains one unsaturated and two saturated fatty acids. (c) A fat consisting of only saturated fatty acids is a solid at ordinary temperatures. (d) The presence of unsaturated fatty acid chains is disruptive and imparts fluidity to the mixture.

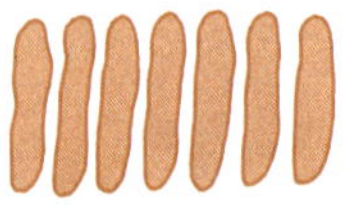

(c) Tightly packed saturated fatty acid chains

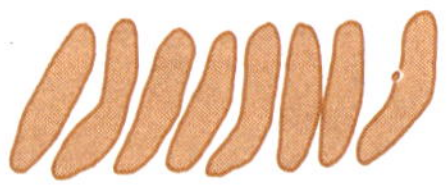

(d) Looser aggregation of saturated and unsaturated fatty acids

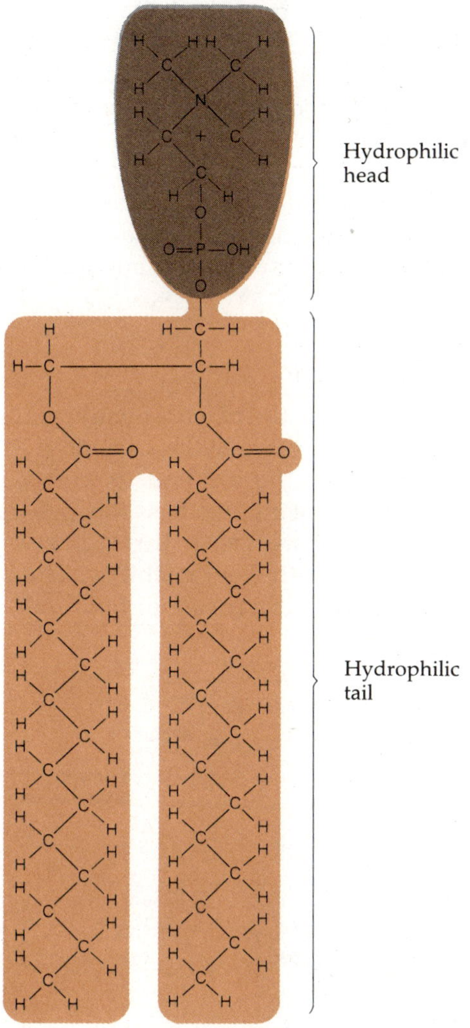

LECITHIN

FIGURE 4.8 **Phospholipids.** The electrically charged head of a phospholipid is hydrophilic, but its fatty acid tail is hydrophobic.

temperature. Olive oil, linseed oil, corn oil, and many other vegetable oils belong to this category.

The distinction between saturated and unsaturated fats is of dietary significance, since unsaturated fats are easier to digest. The nature of cellular structures composed of lipids is influenced by the proportion of unsaturated fatty acids found in them. The presence of a greater number of unsaturated fatty acids makes the structure more fluid and hence more pliable.

Phospholipids and Steroids. Fats and **phospholipids** are structurally similar. The main difference is that in phospholipids one of the fatty acids has been replaced by a phosphate-containing compound (Fig. 4.8). This composition gives phospholipids unusual but useful properties. Phospholipids are partly polar. One end of a phospholipid molecule is water-insoluble like an ordinary fat, but the other end (the one bearing the phosphate) is electrically charged and thus soluble in polar substances such as water.

The presence of both water-soluble and water-
insoluble parts□ makes phospholipids natural 57
emulsifiers (Fig. 4.9). **Lecithin**, a phospholipid abundant in egg yolk, is used extensively in commercially processed foods as an emulsifier to prevent separation of oil and water components. Likewise, the emulsifying ability of phospholipids finds many uses in the largely aqueous cell environment.

Steroids are complex waxy lipids that have a four-ringed structure often combined with fatty acids (Fig. 4.10). The best known steroid is **cholesterol**, but many hormones and vitamins share the steroid structure.

FIGURE 4.9 **Emulsification by Phospholipids.** (a) The hydrocarbon tails of phospholipids always orient themselves away from water. (b) When mixed together with oil and water, phospholipids prevent the separation of oil and water phases.

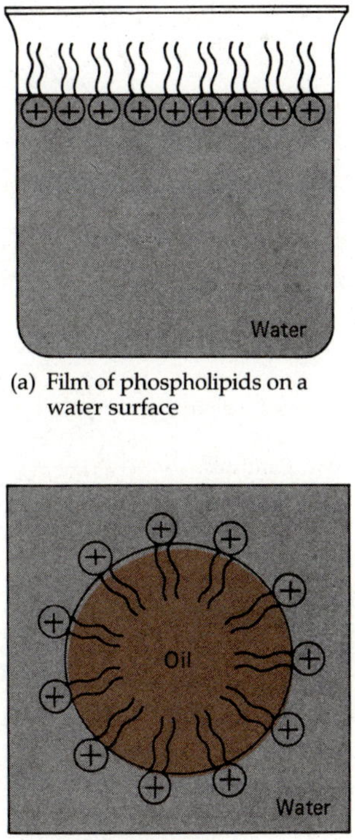

(a) Film of phospholipids on a water surface

(b) Emulsification of oil by phospholipids

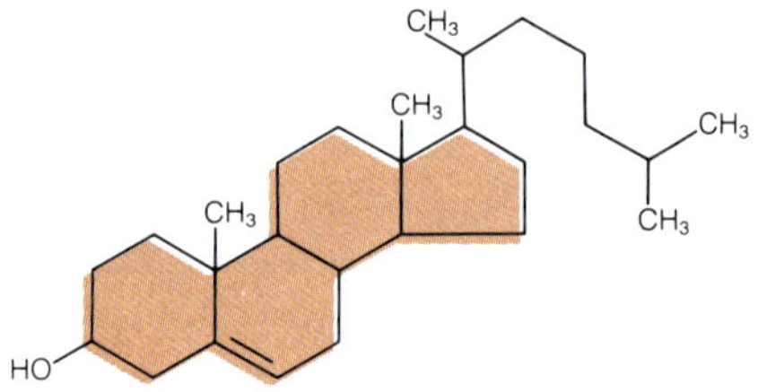

FIGURE 4.10 **Cholesterol.** All steroids have the basic four-interlocking-ring structure shown here for cholesterol. They vary in the nature of the side groups attached to the rings.

CELLS MAKE THE (WO)MAN

Although we can analyze cells to determine their chemical nature, mixing the right chemicals together does not create life. As far as we know, all life comes from preexisting life—at least at the present time. Cells conceive cells. Only they have the ability to arrange macromolecules, lipids, and other chemicals into an organization capable of growth, reproduction, and adaptation to environmental conditions—in other words, into a living arrangement.

Human cells come in various shapes and sizes, but all share certain features (Fig. 4.11). These features are found in the cells of other animals and of plants, as well. But this is not surprising, of course, when we consider that all cells face similar problems and thus have similar needs and requirements.

Getting Things In and Out of Cells

An ultrathin sheath, the **plasma membrane**, covers the entire surface of a cell. This membrane is the boundary between the cell and its environment, allowing some substances to pass through but barring others. Biologists refer to this property of discrimination as **selective permeability**. The plasma membrane governs the intake of nutrients from a

FIGURE 4.11 **A Generalized Animal Cell.**

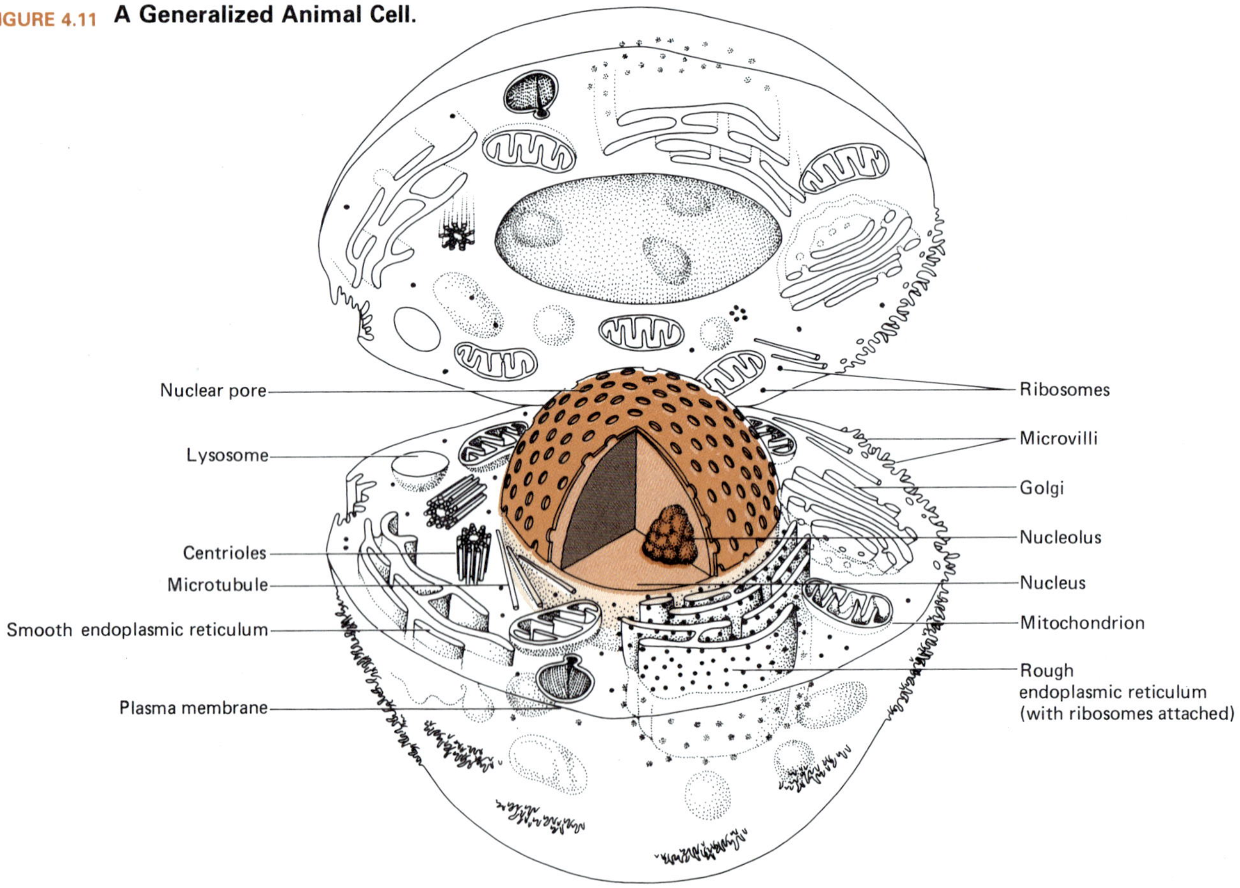

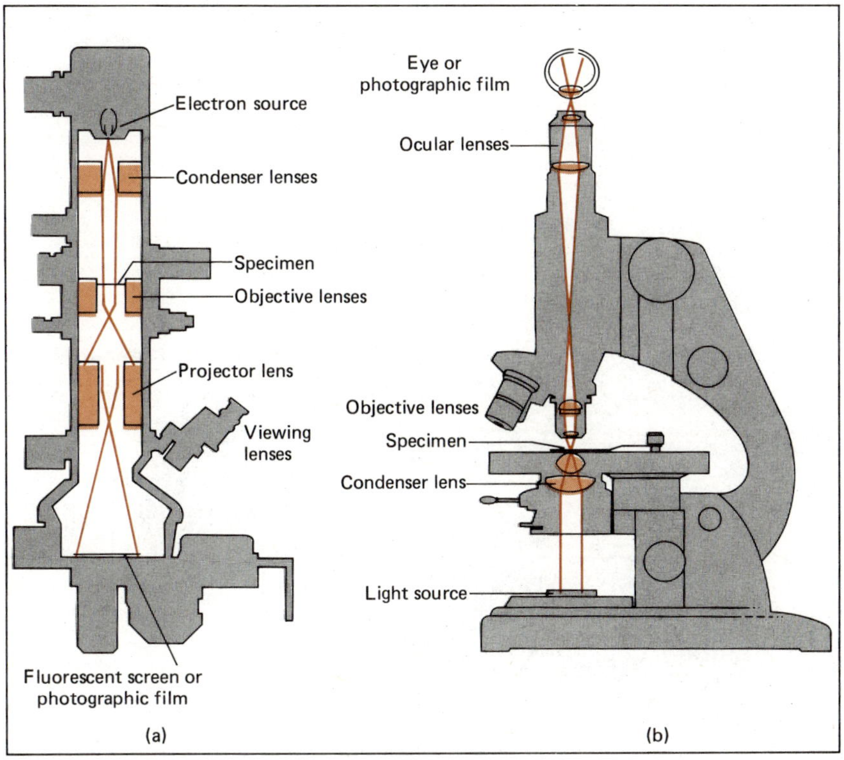

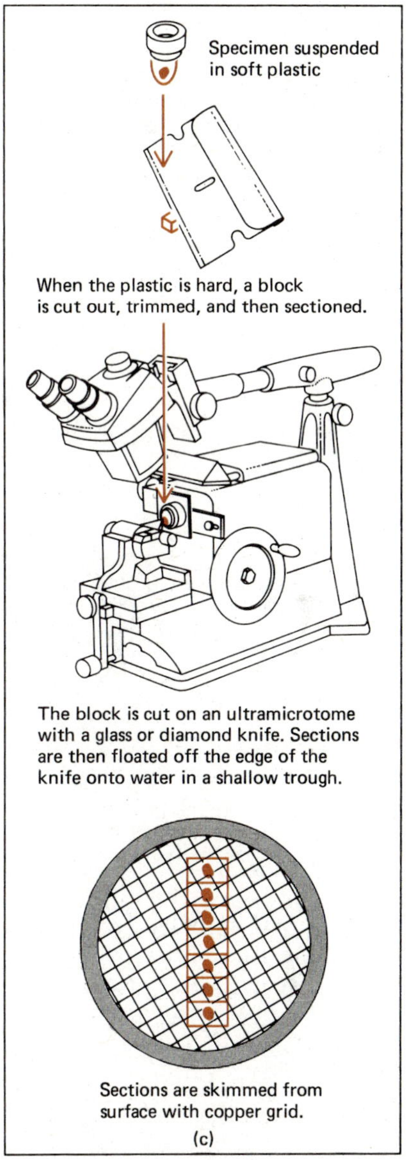

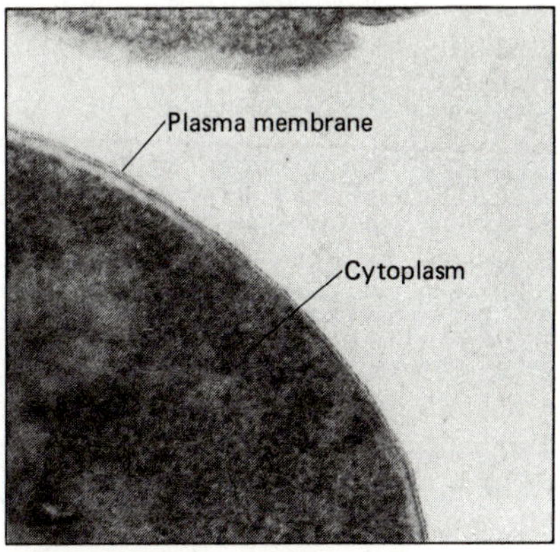

(d)

FIGURE 4.12 Electromicrographs. In principle, the operation of an electron microscope (a) is similar to that of a light microscope (b). Instead of using light waves to create an image, an electron microscope uses electrons. There are several different ways of preparing specimens for electron microscope examination. Thin sections are prepared by embedding cells or tissue in a plastic material (c). The resulting block can be sliced into thin sections, which are then placed on a tiny grid for viewing. As electrons bombard the specimen, some pass through and others are held back by the material, depending on its nature. Electrons that pass through the specimen hit the fluorescent viewing screen, causing it to emit light. Electron-dense areas of the specimen appear as gray or dark areas on the screen. The overall effect is to produce an image of the specimen. If photographic film is placed in front of the viewing screen, a black-and-white photograph, or micrograph, can be obtained. The specimen shown in this electron micrograph (d) was stained to show the dark–light–dark banding pattern of the plasma membrane. Stains used in electron microscopy are not colored compounds but substances that create a better picture by subtly altering the electron density of a specimen.

cell's surroundings, the secretion of cell products, and the excretion of waste materials.

Membrane Structure and Permeability. When cut through and viewed on edge with an electron microscope, the plasma membrane resembles a railroad track (Fig. 4.12). There is a light middle layer

FIGURE 4.13 The Fluid Mosaic Membrane Model. The plasma membrane consists of two layers of lipid. Globular membrane proteins are embedded on one or the other side, or they extend through the bilayer. Short carbohydrate "antennae" extend outward.

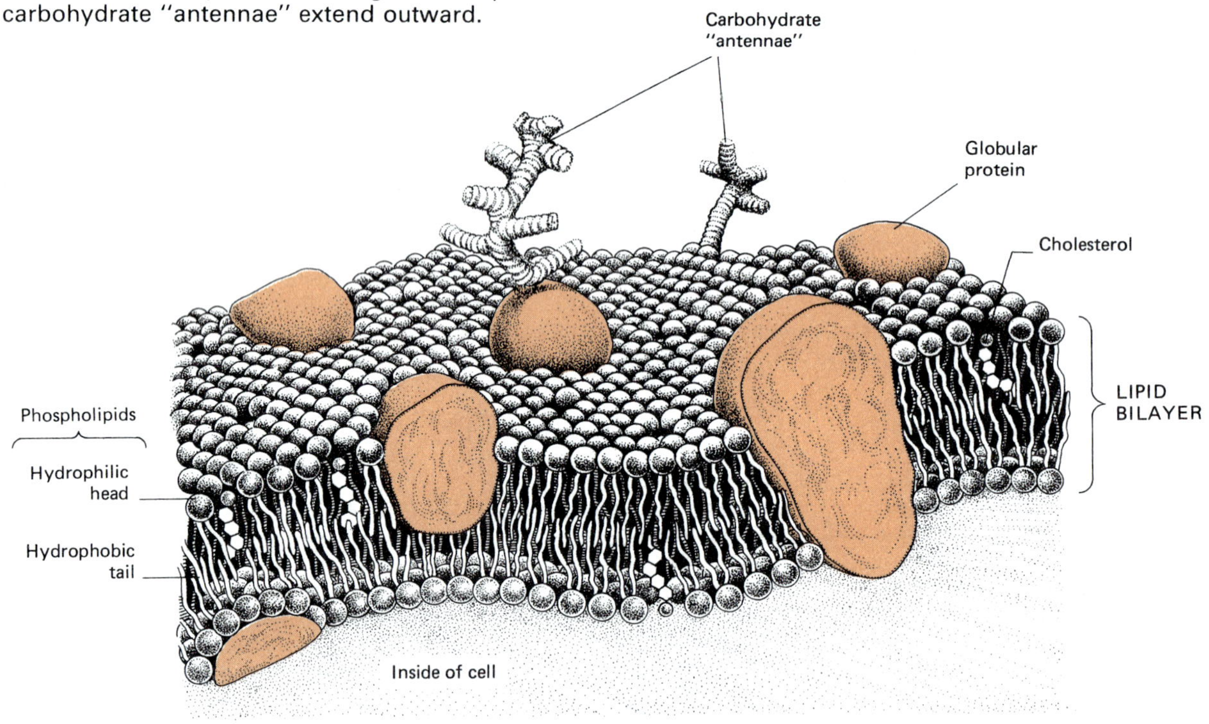

sandwiched between two dark outer layers. For a long time this pattern was interpreted as a rigid lipid bilayer coated on two sides by protein. We now know that the plasma membrane is plastic, not rigid, and that a small number of carbohydrates are present in addition to lipids and proteins.

Although attitudes about the plasma membrane are being reevaluated constantly, there is no quarrel with the old idea that its basic architecture is established by lipids. However, recent studies indicate that these substances are more fluid than was previously supposed.

Two neat layers of lollipoplike lipids create the backbone of the plasma membrane. The electrically charged phospholipid heads are directed toward the inside and the outside of the cell, where water is plentiful. Necessarily, the hydrophobic phospholipid tails are directed toward one another, away from water, in the middle of the membrane structure. Unsaturated fatty acid tails and scattered steroids, including cholesterol, keep the bilayer
73 fluid□ and pliable (Fig. 4.13).

Evidence has been accumulating that membrane proteins conform to no simple pattern. Proteins may be inside or outside the phospholipid bilayer, or they may extend all the way from one side to the other. In a manner of speaking, the protein components of a plasma membrane float and bob in an oily sea.

Analysis shows that membrane molecules are constantly replaced and altered. Hence the modern view is that the plasma membrane is a highly variable, dynamic structure, keenly attuned to changing cellular needs.

The permeability of the plasma membrane reflects its lipid content. In general, those substances that are soluble in lipids pass through the membrane readily. And as might be expected, the membrane is a barrier to the passage of water-soluble substances. However, there is a contradiction here, because many biologically important molecules are soluble in water and, like water itself, move through the plasma membrane with unexpected ease.

It has been proposed that water and other seemingly antagonistic substances flow through protein-lined pores in the plasma membrane. If that proposal is true, those substances would thus avoid a confrontation with membrane lipids. But convenient as membrane pores may seem, they have never been observed. In any case, pores do not explain the special kind of selectivity shown by plasma membranes; they do not explain how water-soluble substances of similar size and shape enter cells at vastly different rates of speed. It seems that water itself can freely **diffuse** through the plasma membrane, but the passage of other substances is assisted in one way or another. This type of movement is known as **facilitated diffusion**. Still other materials are pumped through the membrane by **active transport**. The importance of these processes requires that we look at each in some detail.

Diffusion: Movement along a Concentration Gradient. Common experiences tell us that vapors and dissolved substances eventually distribute themselves evenly throughout all available space. This happens because all molecules, ions, and free atoms are in constant random motion. These movements are imperceptible in a solid, but they are substantial in a gas or liquid. One needs only to open a bottle of ammonia in the corner of a room to prove the movement of molecules.

Diffusion is the movement of substances from a region of high concentration to one of lower concentration—that is, along a **concentration gradient** (Fig. 4.14). The force that drives this kind of intermingling is the energy of the random motion of particles. Just as you can smell ammonia when you open the bottle and it diffuses through the air to your nose, you can see diffusion by adding a bit of food coloring to a glass of water. Even if you do not stir the solution, the dye will slowly spread throughout the container.

In the same way that a fence is a barrier to the free movement of dogs, a plasma membrane is a barrier to the free diffusion of molecules. This barrier function has its positive aspects. It would be undesirable if the cellular molecules retained by the plasma membrane could simply wander off someplace else! Instead, the plasma membrane keeps in what must be kept in. And it also keeps some substances out. Simply stated, the plasma membrane is **selectively permeable.**

As we have said, a plasma membrane is not a barrier to the movement of water. A special term, **osmosis**, is used to describe the diffusion of water through a selectively permeable membrane, such as the plasma membrane. The free permeability of cells to water by osmosis can be demonstrated by placing some red blood cells in distilled water. The water outside will diffuse into the cells because cells contain dissolved substances and consequently less water. So much water will enter that the ensuing buildup of internal pressure eventually causes the cells to explode like an overblown bal-

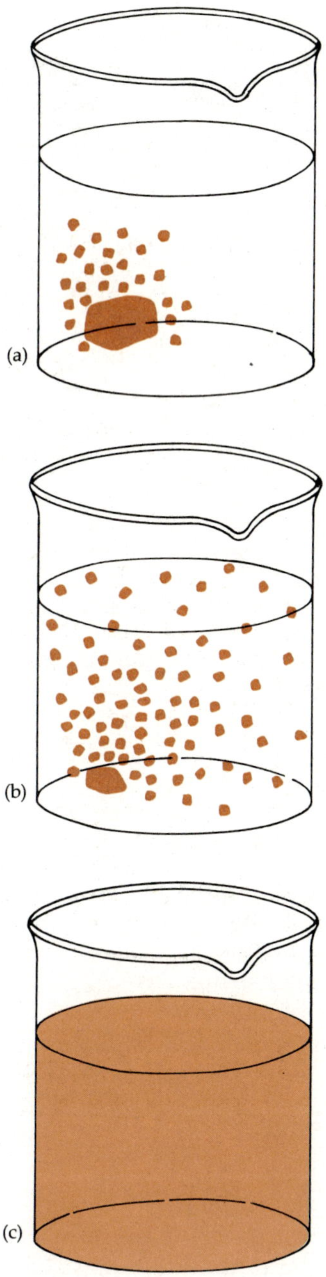

FIGURE 4.14 **Diffusion.** In this example, dissolving molecules move from a region of higher concentration (a) to areas of lower concentration (b) until the molecules are evenly distributed (c).

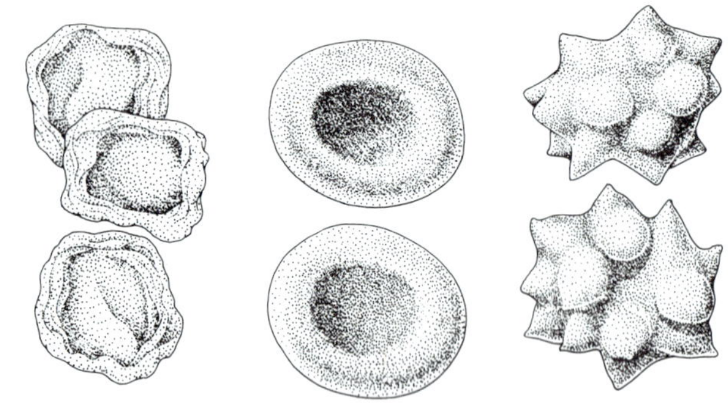
(a) Hypoosmotic medium
(b) Isoosmotic medium
(c) Hyperosmotic medium

FIGURE 4.15 Osmotic Relationships of Cells. A cell in an isoosmotic medium (one with the same concentration of dissolved substances as found in the cell) does not gain or lose water. In a hyperosmotic medium (one with more dissolved substances than are found inside the cell), water is lost by diffusion and the cell shrinks. In a hypoosmotic solution (one with fewer dissolved substances than are found inside the cell), a cell gains water and may eventually burst.

loon (Fig. 4.15). On the other hand, placing red blood cells in a solution containing more salt than is present in the cells causes the cells to shrivel up as water is lost to the exterior. In the body, of course, the external environment of red blood cells must be kept fairly constant to prevent such radical events from occurring.

Besides water, such small molecules as carbon dioxide and oxygen and fatlike molecules can diffuse through the plasma membrane. To them, the membrane is hardly more than a sieve. Perhaps, as we have already suggested, these substances move through pores or between the atoms of membrane molecules. Or instead, some of them may melt into the membrane by dissolving in its lipid components and then diffusing to the other side.

It has become increasingly clear that a variety of substances diffuse across the plasma membrane only with the assistance of specific carriers. In essence, here is what happens when **facilitated diffusion** takes place: Molecules are attracted to membrane carrier proteins, which pick them up, float them through the lipid barrier, and then release them on the other side (Fig. 4.16). This sequence occurs only while the transported molecule is in greater concentration on one side of the membrane than on the other side. The diffusion is facilitated, but it is still diffusion and dependent on the existence of a concentration gradient.

The specificity of membrane carriers for facilitated diffusion explains some of the selectivity of the plasma membrane. Unless there is a carrier to facilitate their passage, many substances that are insoluble in lipids encounter an insurmountable barrier when they approach the plasma membrane.

Active Transport—Extra Energy Makes a Difference. If diffusion were the only means whereby substances could enter or exit cells, we would expect to find the concentration of permeable substances to be the same on both sides of the plasma membrane. Since simple and facilitated diffusion operate only when there is a concentration gradient to drive them, net movement stops once a substance is evenly distributed. And yet we know that cells can accumulate large quantities of desirable substances.

A particularly striking example of such a situation is the unequal distribution of various inor-

FIGURE 4.16 Steps Involved in Carrier-Mediated Membrane Transport.

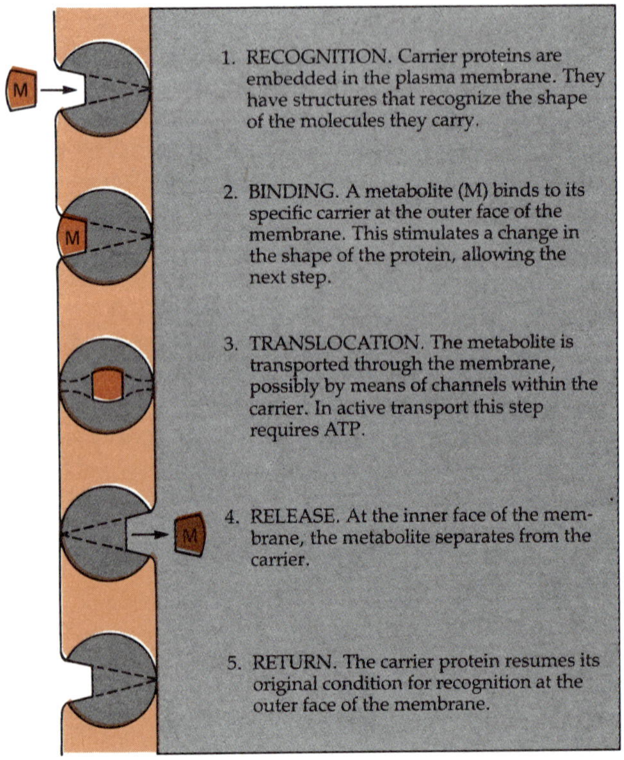
M
1. RECOGNITION. Carrier proteins are embedded in the plasma membrane. They have structures that recognize the shape of the molecules they carry.
M
2. BINDING. A metabolite (M) binds to its specific carrier at the outer face of the membrane. This stimulates a change in the shape of the protein, allowing the next step.
3. TRANSLOCATION. The metabolite is transported through the membrane, possibly by means of channels within the carrier. In active transport this step requires ATP.
M
4. RELEASE. At the inner face of the membrane, the metabolite separates from the carrier.
5. RETURN. The carrier protein resumes its original condition for recognition at the outer face of the membrane.

TABLE 4.1 Concentration of Some Important Ions in Red Blood Cells and the Surrounding Blood Plasma

	(MILLIEQUIVALENTS/LITER)*			
	K^+	Na^+	Cl^-	Ca^{2+}
Red blood cell	150	26	74	70.1
Blood plasma	5	144	111	3.2

*The units given here are not important. Note only that the concentrations of potassium and calcium are much higher inside than outside red blood cells, and that the opposite is true of sodium and chloride. A similar situation exists for other cell types. Our conclusion is that some process must be countering the equalization that would be effected by simple diffusion.

ganic ions inside cells and in surrounding fluids (Table 4.1). Obviously cells can force some substances to move against a concentration gradient. Active transport can move substances against a concentration gradient, but the effort requires work and the expenditure of substantial amounts of energy by cells. Much of the ATP produced in cellular
63 respiration□ is used to drive active transport.

Some membrane carriers are active-transport pumps, which pull certain substances into a cell and push other substances out. Using energy from nutrients, they make it possible for cells to accumulate critical materials even when these materials are in very low concentration in surrounding fluids.

Consider, for example, the fact that the blood nourishes all our cells, but that it has nearly the same composition throughout the body. However, the needs of various cells differ. During a late afternoon ball game, muscle cells of the players may be contracting and nerve cells may be sending messages, while stomach cells are relatively inactive. Active transport permits cells to acquire nutrients or discharge wastes and other substances according to their individual needs.

Active transport and facilitated diffusion share many attributes since both involve membrane carrier proteins (Fig. 4.16). Both involve recognition of the substance to be transported, binding of that substance to the carrier protein, translocation of the substance through the membrane barrier, release at the opposite side of the membrane, and—finally—return of the carrier protein to its original condition, ready to begin the process again. But active transport uses ATP to translocate substances against a concentration gradient. Facilitated diffusion does not use ATP; it functions only to move substances from a region of higher concentration to one of lower concentration.

Phagocytosis and Pinocytosis. Although diffusion, facilitated diffusion, and active transport appear to be the chief means for the exchange of substances with the environment, a few kinds of cells simply "eat" matter too large to pass through the membrane (Fig. 4.17). In **phagocytosis**, solid substances are engulfed into little pockets of the plasma membrane. Gradually the pocket pinches off, enclosing the ingested material within a membranous sac trapped inside the cell. The process can even be reversed to expel secretion products and wastes. The most important phagocytes (phagocytic cells) of the human body are white blood cells.

Although the process is similar to phagocytosis, the ingestion of liquids by cells is given a special name, **pinocytosis**. Researchers have observed pinocytosis in egg cells of the human ovary as they are "nursed" by surrounding nutrient-secreting cells.

Cell Recognition, Adhesion, and Communication. In keeping with its role as barrier between the cell and its outer environment, the plasma membrane has special surface structures whose existence permits communication between cells, recognition of other cells and such cell products as hormones, and in some cases adhesion of one cell to another (Fig. 4.18).

Modified sugars coat the outer surface of animal cell membranes. These surface carbohydrates are anchored to proteins or lipids of the membrane, but they project away from the membrane itself. Apparently patches of the sticky sugar coating differ from one kind of cell to another. Therefore similar cells recognize one another. Indeed, the chemical nature of the cell coat causes cells of a tissue to literally stick together.

On the other hand, it is the lack of proper recognition sites on transplanted cells that permits the body to reject them as foreigners. Recognition sites are also involved in disease. Viruses and disease-causing bacteria identify cells they are capable of infecting by the nature of the carbohydrate coat. A virus can invade the cell only if the surface of the virus can react with the surface of the cell.

The membranes of adjacent cells are also involved in cell adhesion. Adjacent membranes are

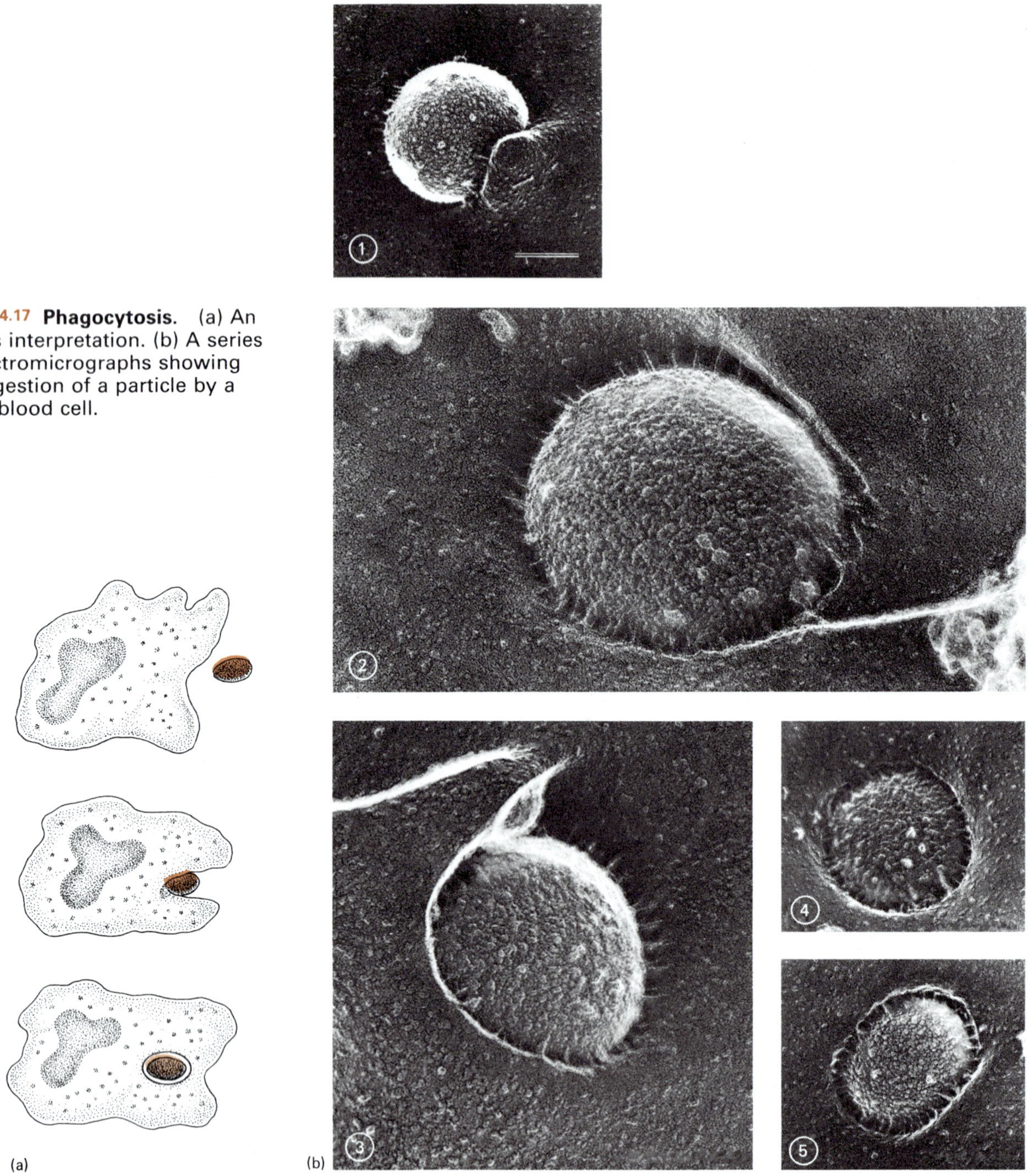

FIGURE 4.17 Phagocytosis. (a) An artist's interpretation. (b) A series of electromicrographs showing the ingestion of a particle by a white blood cell.

sometimes modified to form **desmosomes** that bind cells firmly together (Fig. 4.19). In other cases, the outer leaflets of the membranes of adjacent cells are fused. Such **tight junctions** create barriers to the movement of materials between cells. Since substances cannot move between cells at places where tight junctions exist, they must pass through the cells themselves. Thus their migration can be regulated by direct cellular action.

Of special interest are membrane structures called **gap junctions**. These are channels that provide continuity between the contents of one cell and that of the next. Although the function of gap junctions is still under investigation, we know that

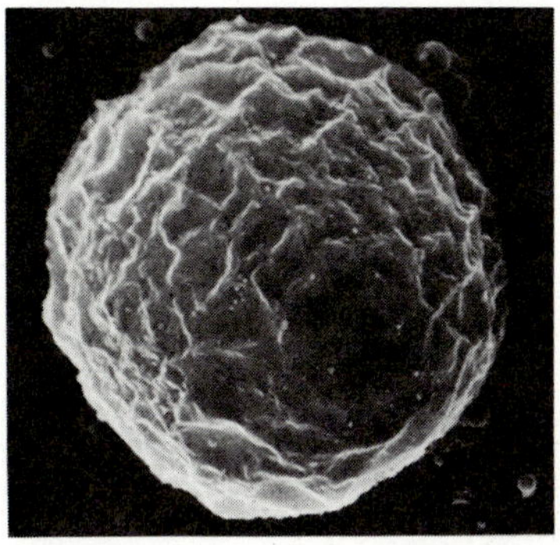

(a)

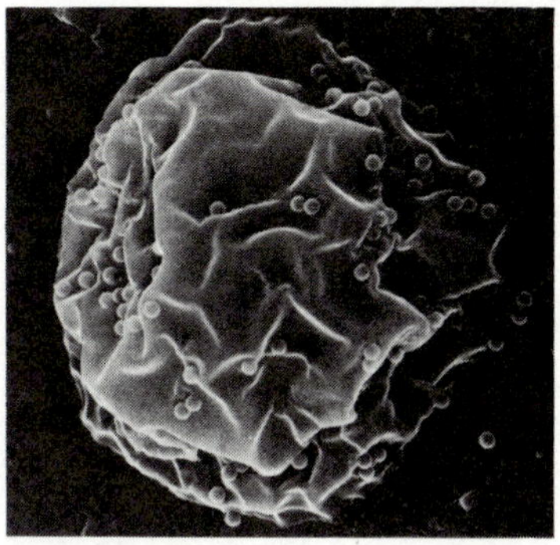

(b)

FIGURE 4.18 Binding Sites. Insulin binding sites on fat cells can be identified by using insulin-coated plastic beads as markers. (a) An ordinary fat cell. (b) Fat cell with beads bound to surface receptors.

ions and small molecules can flow from cell to cell through these channels. Communication between the cells of a tissue is essential, and in this process gap junctions certainly play a crucial part.

Beneath the Surface

Roughly speaking, the material inside the plasma membrane is divided into two principal regions: the **nucleus**, usually a spherical, central body, and the surrounding **cytoplasm**. Cytoplasm consists mainly of membranes and membranous organelles (Fig. 4.20). Between the organelles and membranes there is the **cytosol**, which consists of more fluid components.

Although relatively unstructured in some places, the cytosol is laced with an assortment of fibers, called **microfilaments** and **microtubules**. These threadlike or tubelike structures are organized into a kind of cellular skeleton that supports the cell and determines its shape (Fig. 4.21). Microtubules, as we will soon discover, are major components of centrioles, basal bodies, cilia, and flagella.

The membranous structures of a cell are also sites of much metabolic activity. Perhaps most cellular processes occur in conjunction with membranes—if not *in* membranes, then on the surface of membranes. At the very least, they occur *near* membranes. Inside a cell nothing is very far away from a membranous structure.

To the best of our knowledge, internal cell membranes are selectively permeable structures similar to the plasma membrane. It seems reasonable to assume that intracellular membranes gov-

FIGURE 4.19 Desmosomes. (a) Electron micrograph of intestinal mucosa cells showing numerous desmosomes. (b) An interpretation of desmosome structure.

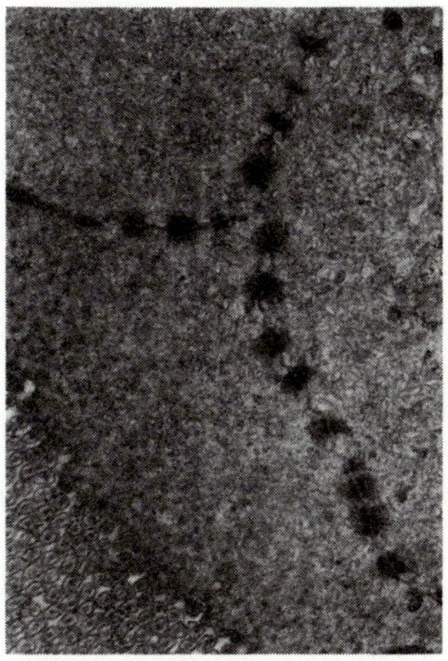

(a)

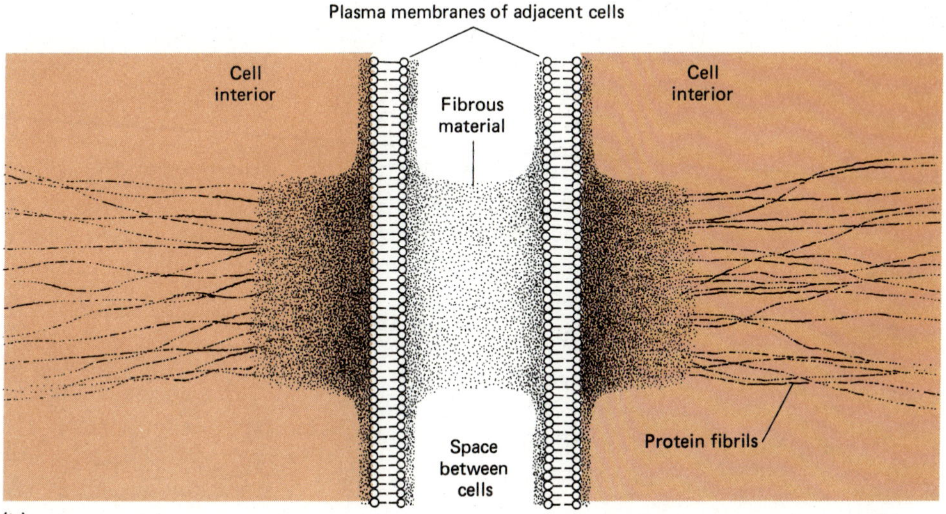

(b)

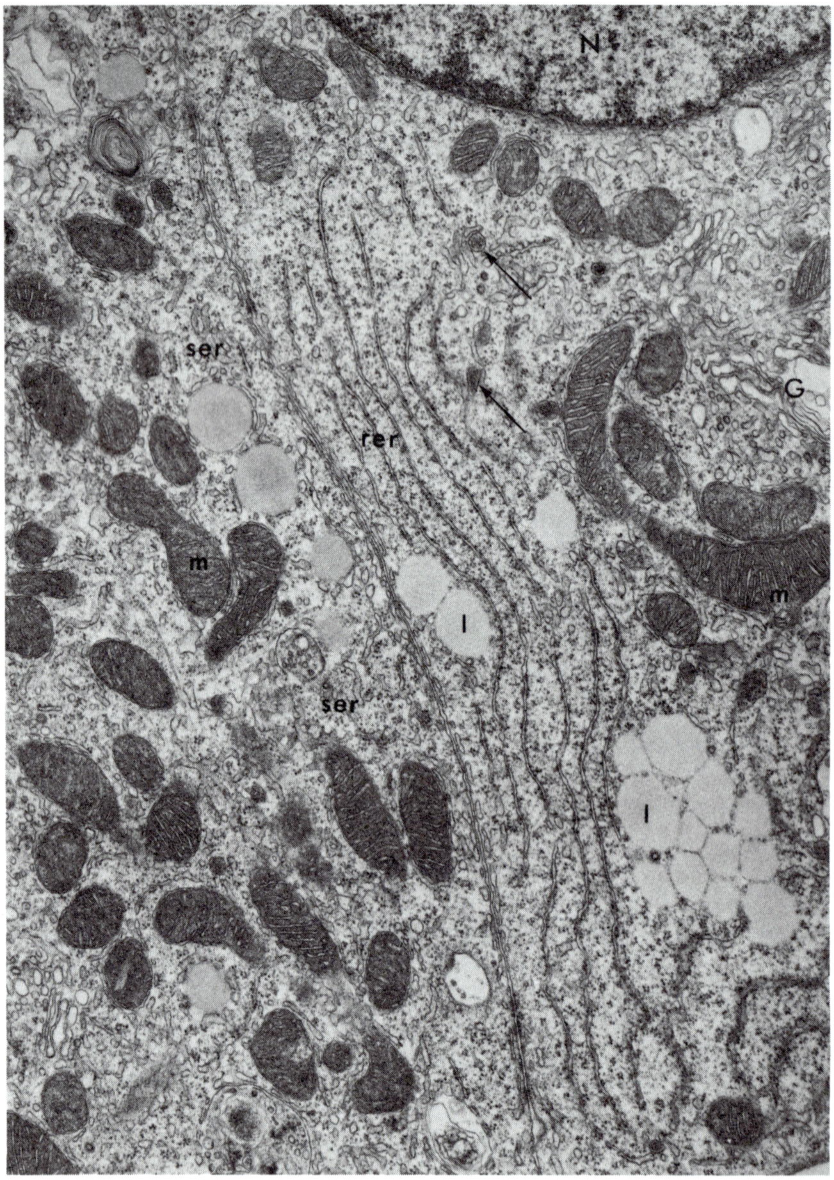

FIGURE 4.20 **Cytoplasmic Organelles and Membranes.** G = Golgi, l = lipid, m = mitochondrion, N = nucleus, rer = rough endoplasmic reticulum, ser = smooth endoplasmic reticulum.

ern the movement of materials within a cell. They certainly divide the cytoplasm into compartments where different activities can occur without interfering with one another. For example, the cytoplasm and the nucleus are separated by a nuclear membrane.

Nucleus—the Control Center. Just looking at the nucleus, one would hardly guess what a busy place it is. Ordinarily the only clearly defined internal feature is a dense-appearing **nucleolus** (Fig. 4.22). Nevertheless, the nucleus is constantly receiving information about the environment and about happenings within the cytoplasm. Moreover, directions for making enzymes and other cell proteins are regularly sent out from the nucleus. In fact, it is by directing the synthesis of particular enzymes that the nucleus controls cell activities.

Information for making proteins is contained in the **genes**, nearly all of which are found in the nucleus as parts of **chromosomes**. Since genes are made of DNA, so are chromosomes. But chromosomes also contain **histones**, proteins bound to the DNA. Normally chromosomes work invisibly within

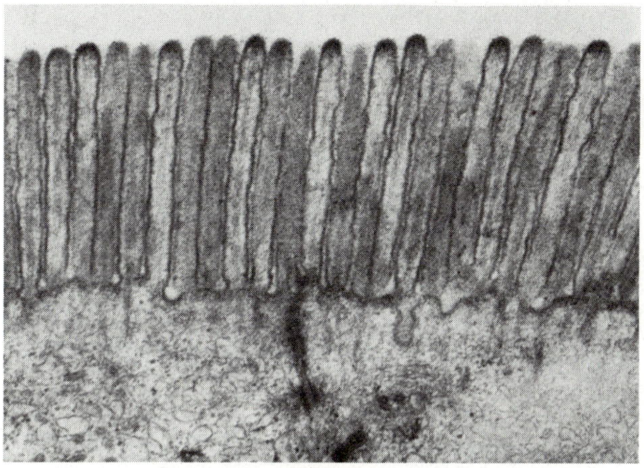

(a)

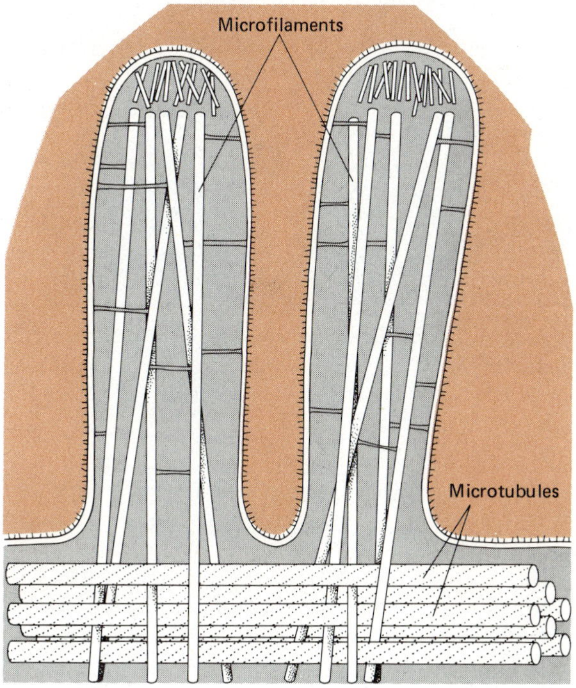

(b)

FIGURE 4.21 Microtubules and Microfilaments. (a) Look closely at the fingerlike projections (microvilli) of the intestinal cells pictured here. The fuzzy surface is due to the slimy carbohydrates that project from the surface of the plasma membrane. (b) Organization of microfilaments and microtubules of intestinal cell cytoplasm.

the nucleus. Their shapes become evident only when a cell is about to divide. We will learn more about genes and chromosomes in Chapter 11.

The **nuclear membrane** that surrounds the nucleus is really two membranes separated by a narrow space. Its outer surface looks pock-marked, somewhat like a golf ball. These "pocks" are really pores formed where the two membranes have fused together. Undoubtedly these nuclear pores regulate the movement of materials in and out of the nucleus.

Centrioles—the Organizers. Near the nucleus, just outside the nuclear membrane, there are two hollow cylindrical **centrioles**. These bodies normally lie at right angles to each other. Each centriole is composed of nine microtubule triplets (Fig. 4.23). During cell division, the centrioles help organize the **spindle fibers**. These fibers, which consist of microtubules, are responsible for the separation of duplicated chromosomes into daughter cells during cell division.

Endoplasmic Reticulum—the Manufacturing Maze. It is believed that the nuclear membrane

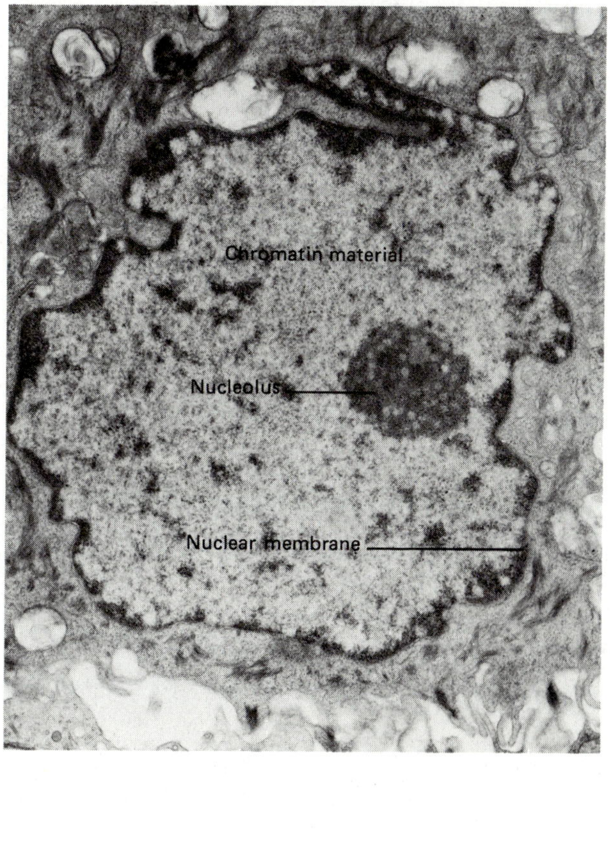

FIGURE 4.22 Electron Micrograph of a Nucleus. Note the granular, unevenly stained appearance of the chromatin material.

BOX 4B

MOTILITY: CELLULAR MOTION

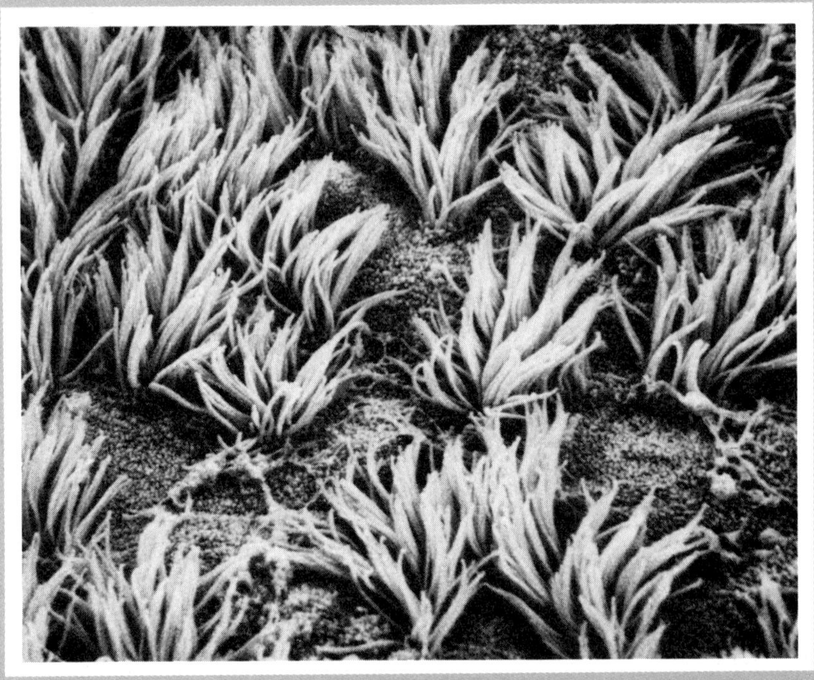

Motility is not a common property of human cells, but two obvious exceptions come to mind. Sperm cells and white blood cells are both capable of independent movement, although by entirely different means. Sperm (male sex cells) are propelled by long tails called flagella. Microtubules are the basic units of flagellar structure. Inside flagella, nine pairs of microtubules are arranged in a circle around two central microtubules. The beating of flagella is thought to occur through a mechanism similar to muscle contraction (Chapter 9). The process involves the sliding of the microtubules past one another so that the individual flagellum is drawn back and forth.

Flagella are wrapped in an extension of the plasma membrane. They are anchored in the cytoplasm by basal bodies. These cylindrical bodies are identical in structure to centrioles and, in fact, are believed to be derived from them.

Cilia are shorter versions of flagella. Whereas flagellated cells generally have no more than one or two flagella, ciliated cells are always covered with numerous cilia. A variety of one-celled animals are propelled by the rowing-oar action of beating cilia. In humans, ciliated cells do not move, even though their cilia beat continuously. Instead, they propel substances past themselves. Such cells are found lining the lungs. The coordinated beating of their cilia sweeps mucus-entangled foreign particles up and out of the lungs.

White blood cells creep from one place to another by what is called amoeboid movement.

Amoebas are free-form, free-living, single-celled animals. They move by extension of pseudopodia (false feet). The process is poorly understood, but it seems to involve the contraction of muscle-like cytoplasmic filaments, coupled with localized changes in the consistency of cytoplasm. As a pseudopodium is extended, cytoplasm streams into it because the tip of the pseudopodium is less contracted and less viscous, whereas the rear is more contracted and more viscous. The cell creeps along because the cytoplasm takes the path of least resistance.

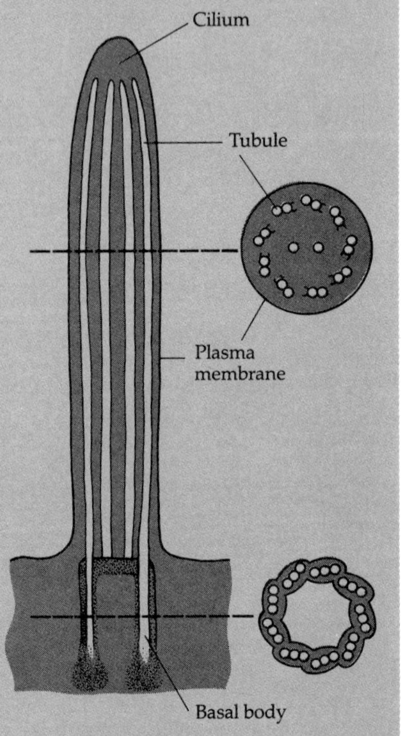

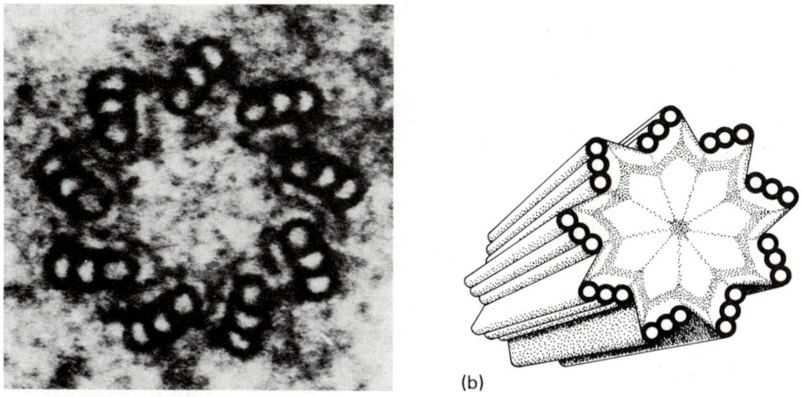

FIGURE 4.23 **Centriole Structure.** The cartwheel organization of the triplet microtubules of centrioles is evident in this electron micrograph (a). (b) The nine triplet tubules form a hollow cylindrical body.

is continuous with the **endoplasmic reticulum** (ER), an elaborate system of tubes and channels that winds through the cytoplasm (Fig. 4.24). If this is true, then one function of the ER may be as a nuclear-cytoplasmic communication network. There is no doubt, however, that many new molecules are manufactured within the endoplasmic reticulum.

In some places the ER is smooth, but more often it is studded with oval **ribosomes**. Whether free in the cytoplasm, as some of them are, or attached to the endoplasmic reticulum, ribosomes are assembly points for proteins. Ribosomes themselves are assembled, at least in part, from RNA particles that originate in the nucleolus (Fig. 4.25).

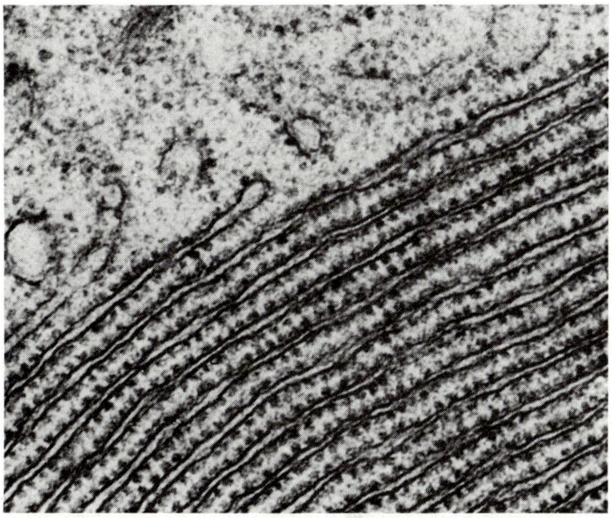

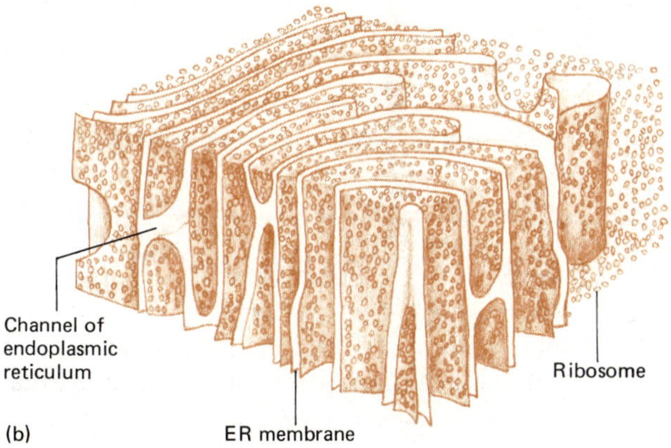

FIGURE 4.24 **Endoplasmic Reticulum.** (a) An electron micrograph showing rough endoplasmic reticulum coated with granular ribosomes. (b) A drawing showing the three-dimensional structure of the rough ER.

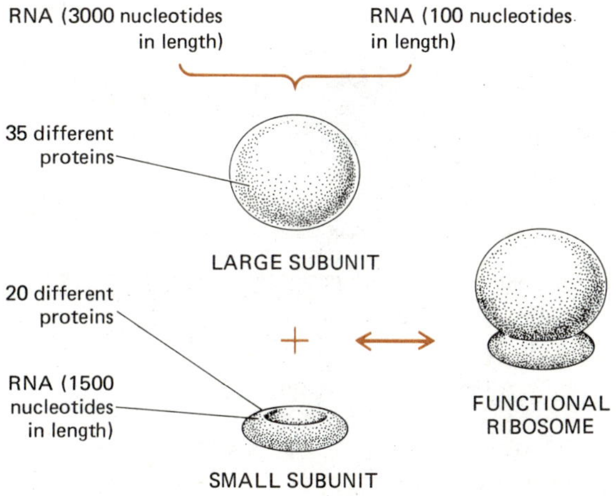

FIGURE 4.25 **A Ribosome Has Two Subunits.** Ribosomes consist of several different RNAs and more than 50 different proteins. The large and small subunits join together to carry out protein synthesis and then fall apart immediately after the job is done.

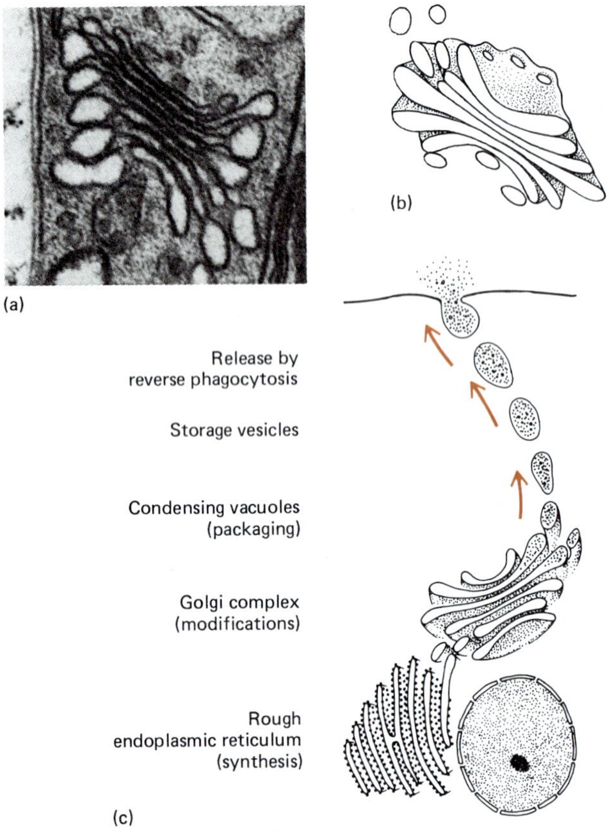

FIGURE 4.26 **The Golgi Body.** (a) Stacked Golgi membranes, seen in a lengthwise section. (b) A diagrammatic view that emphasizes the swollen ends of the Golgi, and packaging of Golgi contents by pinching off of sacs (vesicles). (c) A summary view of the process of secretion.

The ER functions in the production, transport, and storage of a multitude of cell products. After assembly on ribosomes along the outer surface of the ER, enzymes, hormones, and other proteins slip inside the membranous channels and slide through them to their destinations. Products to be secreted by the cell are caught in the fingerlike ends of the ER tubes. These ends pinch off, holding their contents in membranous sacs. Some sacs move directly to the cell surface, where they spew their contents from the cell by reverse phagocytosis. The ER also functions to replace and extend cellular membranes. As a cell grows, the plasma membrane is expanded by the incorporation of ER sac membranes at the cell surface.

Packaging secretions is a particular function of the **Golgi body** (Fig. 4.26), a stack of flattened membranes closely allied to the endoplasmic reticulum. Often enzymes of the Golgi convert secretory products into their final form before they are released. One such substance is **mucus**, made in Golgi bodies by linking a sugar to a particular protein. In addition to their other roles, Golgi bodies may give rise to **lysosomes**.

Lysosomes—the Digestion Bags. Lysosomes are membranous bags filled with digestive enzymes. Almost any worn-out cellular component can be attacked by lysosomal enzymes. There are lysosomes in all cells, but they are especially abundant in phagocytes. Lysosomes fuse with phagocytized material and digest it. In most cells, it is the function of lysosomes to dispose of old or obsolete cell parts (Fig. 4.27). Bits and pieces of other cell organelles are regularly seen inside lysosomes. Veteran lysosomes contain large quantities of wastes from their digestive activities.

When a cell is seriously injured, diseased, or aged, it may self-destruct because damage to the lysosomal membranes unleashes digestive juices. Decomposition of a dead body is partially the result of such lysosomal action.

A number of rare degenerative diseases have been attributed to enzyme-deficient lysosomes. Undigestible substances, mostly complex lipids and carbohydrates, accumulate in cells with abnormal lysosomes. Because nerve cells are especially sen-

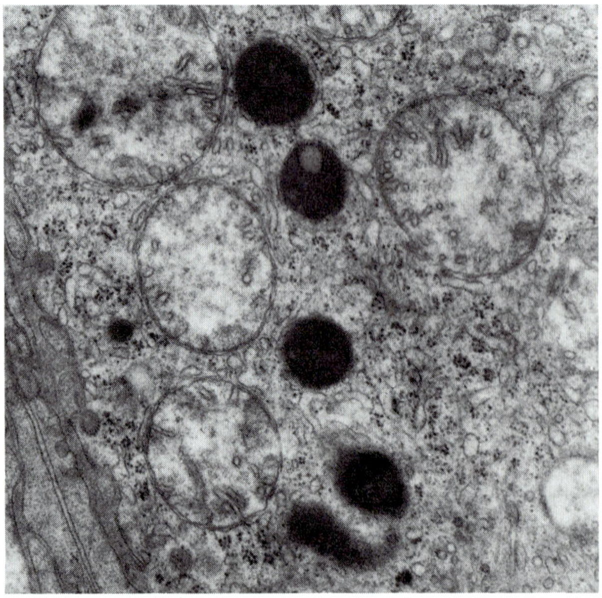

FIGURE 4.27 **Lysosome Digestion.** The dark, roughly spherical bodies in this kidney cell are lysosomes. Presumably the grayish, splotchy material inside the lysosomes is partially digested waste.

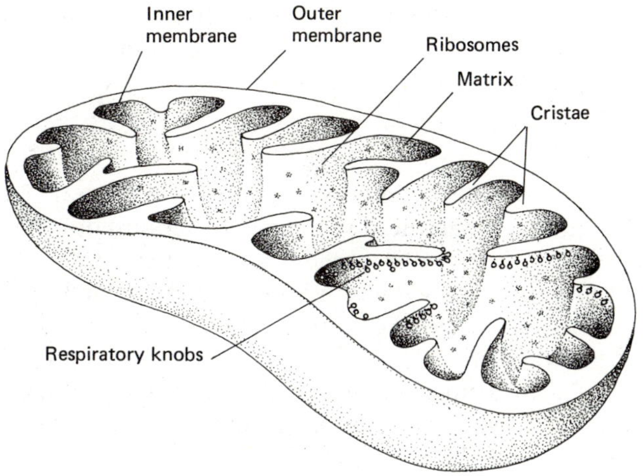

FIGURE 4.28 **A Mitochondrion.** The cristae of some mitochondria have mushroomlike projections or knobs that contain certain respiratory enzymes involved in ATP synthesis. Can you now recognize the mitochondria in the electron micrograph in Fig. 4.27? Although they have been cut differently and so have a different shape, you can identify them by the folded inner membrane.

sitive to these compounds, mental retardation frequently accompanies "lysosomal disease."

Perhaps you have heard of **Tay-Sachs disease**. About six months after birth, formerly healthy infants begin to show telltale signs of paralysis, mental retardation, and blindness. There is no cure for this tragic disease, which has high incidence among Jews of East European descent. In all likelihood, Tay-Sachs disease is the result of the absence of a single lysosomal enzyme. Lysosomes that lack this crucial enzyme allow a lethal accumulation of certain lipids around the nucleus of nerve cells.

Mitochondria—the Cellular Dynamos. Masses of mitochondria dot a cell's cytoplasm. Mitochondria are often kidney-shaped bodies (Fig. 4.28), but they are just as likely to be round or rod- or Y-shaped. In any event, all mitochondria have an outer and inner membrane. The outer membrane is smooth, but the inner one is folded and covered with knobs.

Mitochondria have their own ribosomes for manufacturing special mitochondrial proteins. They even have some genes of their own. In some respects, therefore, mitochondria behave independently of the cytoplasm and nucleus. In a sense, they are tenants. Mitochondria live and work in the cytoplasm, which supplies them with nourishment and oxygen from the environment. When a cell divides, some of its mitochondria go to each of the two new cells. As the daughter cells mature, their inherited mitochondria do, too. Eventually the old mitochondria develop buds that break off and become new mitochondria.

As cytoplasmic tenants, mitochondria pay a substantial rent. A cell depends on its mitochondrial enzymes to harvest a major portion of the energy available in nutrients. Mitochondria are the main sites of the oxidations of cellular respiration that produce most of the ATP needed for cell activities. Not surprisingly, liver, muscle, and other extremely active cells may have a thousand or more of these little dynamos. In the next chapter, you will be confronted with the fact that mitochondria are practically the sole sites of oxygen utilization by cells. You may indeed conclude that mitochondria are the real reasons we breathe!

WHY CELLS?

Why are cells the basic units of life? Part of the answer lies in history. We should see cell structure as evidence of the unity of life and of a common origin. Beyond this, cells also seem to be the only way to form large organisms. The small size of cells is of fundamental importance.

A Typical Cell Is Small

To get a feeling for the size of a cell, take a good look at the period that ends this sentence. Laid side by side, fifty of your white blood cells would be no wider than that period. Yet white blood cells are rather ordinary-sized cells. About the only cells that are enormously larger are the eggs of birds, reptiles, and sharks. In eggs, what we call the yolk is the egg cell. Most of it is stored food. Remove this material and the cell would be transformed into one that is more typical in size.

It seems likely that the small size of cells is a great advantage in obtaining nutrients and getting rid of wastes. First, there is a tremendous surface area on a small cell compared with its volume. This is often expressed as the **surface:volume ratio**.

Smaller cells have a much greater surface: volume ratio than do larger cells (Table 4.2). This means that in proportion to the volume of cytoplasm, the area for exchange between the cell and its environment is greater in small cells than in larger cells. In addition, the interior of a small cell is closer to the cell surface than the interior of a large cell is to its surface.

TABLE 4.2 Relative Increases in Surface Area and Volume of a Cube

Length each side (meters)	1	2	4	8	16
Surface area (square meters)	6	24	96	384	1536
Volume (cubic meters)	1	8	64	512	4096
Surface:volume ratio	6	3	1.5	0.75	0.375

As the size of a cube grows, its volume increases much faster than does the surface. In fact, doubling the length of each side reduces the surface:volume ratio by half. The unit chosen for this table (meters) is of no significance. The surface:volume ratios would have been the same if we had used a small unit (micrometer) nearer the actual size of cells.

The small size of cells clearly favors efficiency of exchange with the environment, but it also favors efficient internal communication. The short distances molecules must travel within cells apparently makes unnecessary any elaborate system for communication between opposite ends of the cytoplasm or between nucleus and cytoplasm. But there is another kind of efficiency inherent in cells, the efficiency resulting from compartmentalization.

Compartmentalization: A Way of Life

Many biological reactions involve substances present in scant supply. In order to interact, these substances must be brought together and concentrated so that they can contact one another. It is the selective nature of biological membranes that makes this concentration possible. Furthermore, the tiny membrane-bound compartments inside cells provide ideal areas for concentration of different substances.

Although it is the plasma membrane that principally determines what will enter or leave a cell, the endoplasmic reticulum and other membranous organelles have the same ability on a smaller scale. In addition, they provide a multitude of vesicles and other individual structures where substances can be concentrated and chemical reactions can occur. Many of these reactions involve enzymes that are part of the membrane structures. Concentrated substances may be processed along the membrane, much as manufactured goods are processed along an industrial assembly line.

In addition to the efficiency resulting from cell structure, there are other factors that help explain the cellular nature of organisms. These relate to the advantage of cellularity in differentiation.

Self-Sufficiency versus Multicellularity

Each body cell is, in effect, a miniature animal. To defend this statement, we need only point out that human cells have the same basic structure and carry out many of the same activities as single-celled **protozoa** (Fig. 4.29). Hundreds of these microscopic creatures can be found in just one drop of pond water. In a number of respects, the life protozoa live is not so very different from the life your cells lead in your body.

Like protozoa, human cells live in an aquatic environment. Our blood is mostly water, and our cells are continuously bathed in a fluid derived from it. Both human cells and protozoa obtain oxygen and nutrients from their watery habitat. Water and oxygen are used by human and protozoal cells alike
to release energy from nutrients□ and to transform 64
them into living substance. But, unlike human cells, protozoa live totally free and independent lives. They fend for themselves. Each must find its own food, get rid of its own wastes, and carry out all the other activities necessary to continued life. Such unicellular structure is the rule for all very small organisms, whether they are animals, bacteria, or plants such as green algae.

The Ultimate in Self-Sufficiency—Photosynthetic Plant Cells. Plant cells differ from animal cells in a number of ways, as illustrated in Fig. 4.30. Out-

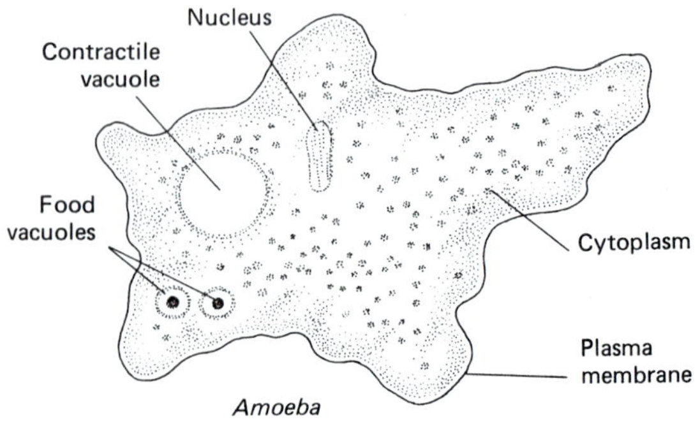

FIGURE 4.29 An Amoeba. This free-living protozoan has most of the structures found in human cells plus others adapted for a solitary life. Contractile vacuoles squirt waste water to the outside. Amoebas move by the same mechanism that permits them to send out cellular extensions to engulf food.

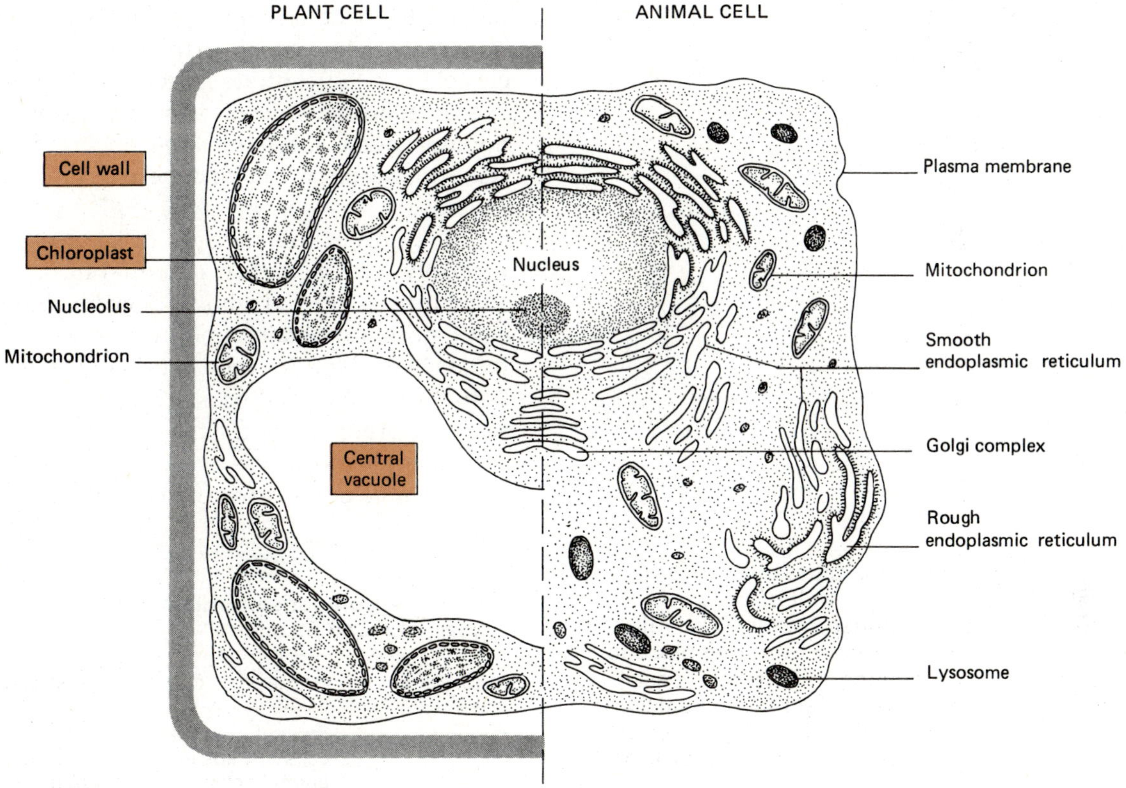

FIGURE 4.30 **Plant and Animal Cells Compared.** Those structures peculiar to plants are indicated by colored labels.

side its plasma membrane, a plant cell has a thick **cell wall** composed chiefly of cellulose and other carbohydrates. The cell wall gives plant cells a more rigid shape as compared with animal cells. All photosynthetic plant cells also have **chloroplasts**. These complex membranous organelles are the sites of photosynthetic metabolism. Chloroplasts contain a number of pigments, including the green pigment **chlorophyll**. These pigments absorb the light used in photosynthesis. Having chloroplasts makes plants self-sufficient, since these organelles contain the light-propelled machinery to manufacture organic molecules from carbon dioxide and water.

Many plant cells have a large **central vacuole**, which is a membrane-enclosed sac. Vacuoles are found in many kinds of cells, but the central vacuole is unique to plants. It is quite large, often taking up 80–90 percent of the mature cell volume. The central vacuole is filled with fluid known as *cell sap*. We will learn more about the central vacuole and plant cells in general when we get to Chapter 17.

The simplest of all photosynthetic plants are the **algae**. They include familiar single-celled forms that often collect as pond and aquarium scums. Other algae are multicellular.

Living Together. Seaweeds are algae, but superficially they bear little resemblance to single-celled algae. Although multicellular, seaweeds are still "lower" plants. They are distinguished from "higher" plants, such as grass and trees, because they have no real roots or stems and little cell specialization. Seaweed leaves are nothing more than layers of similar cells.

Some simple multicellular organisms show a degree of cooperativeness. The molds are a case in point. Their cells grow into masses because they usually stick together after they divide. **Molds** are filamentous organisms related to mushrooms. Both have cell walls but lack chloroplasts. Not having chloroplasts means that mold cells have nutritional needs similar to those of protozoal cells. But because cell division leaves the nonmotile mold

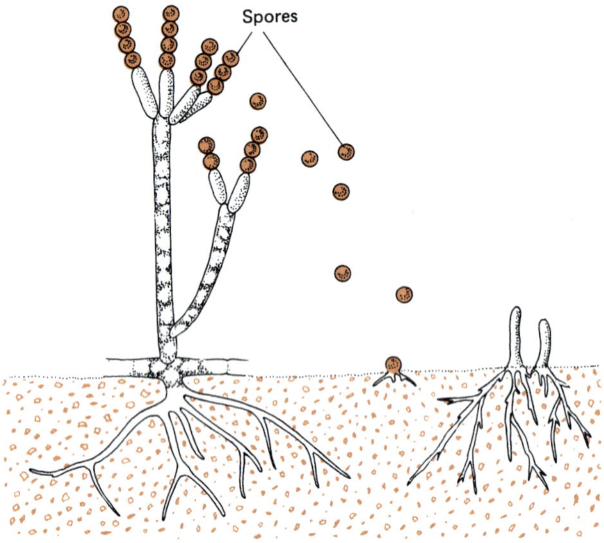

FIGURE 4.31 **Penicillium.** This blue-green mold is commonly found growing on fruit or bread. At maturity, aerial filaments produce spores. Dissemination of spores spreads the mold from one place to another. Although considered a household pest, *Penicillium* is the source of the antibiotic penicillin, which it secretes to inhibit the growth of other organisms that would compete with the mold for food sources.

cells massed together, only some can feed directly. Nevertheless, all the mold cells need food, which they get by a division of labor. Some of the cells of bread mold, for example, grow down into the bread and anchor there. These and other mold cells secrete juices to digest the bread into liquid morsels. Then those cells closest to the bread pass a portion on to those farther away. This permits some of the mold cells to grow into tall stalks that support fuzzy spores (Fig. 4.31). When the spores break off and are carried away by the air, they can grow into new molds somewhere else.

The cells of larger organisms are even more cooperative. The greater division of labor is evident from the more varied appearance of the cells. They are **differentiated**, that is, specialized for a particular job. Moreover, cells of the same structure and function are generally grouped into working units, or **tissues**. This is true in higher plants as well as in higher animals, ranging from tapeworms to beetles and from earthworms to people.

The distinct division of labor among the different cells is extremely useful. By being specialized and depending on others for most essential services, a cell can carry on one major function. Not having to make any special efforts to obtain food or oxygen or to respond to their environment, muscle cells can concentrate largely on contraction, for example, and gland cells can concentrate on secretion. Of course, these functions must serve the other cells of the organism and be coordinated appropriately.

Not only is this division of labor efficient, but probably it is absolutely essential in organisms of substantial size. Cells lying deep in the organism can't possibly obtain food, water, or oxygen for themselves. Nor can they get rid of wastes without help from their neighbors. Thus cell specialization seems a prerequisite for the development of large organisms. And it was certainly necessary for the evolution of organisms that can take advantage of

TABLE 4.3 **A Comparison of Eucaryotic and Procaryotic Cell Structure**

FEATURE	EUCARYOTIC CELLS	PROCARYOTIC CELLS
Cell wall	Present in plant cells but absent in animal cells	Almost always present but chemically distinct from plant cell walls
Plasma membrane	Present	Present
Nuclear membrane	Present	Absent
Chromosomes	Multiple	Single, free in cytoplasm
Endoplasmic reticulum	Present	Absent
Ribosomes	Present	Present
Mitochondria	Present	Absent; some functions carried out in plasma membrane
Photosynthetic apparatus	In membrane-bound chloroplasts of plant cells, lacking in animal cells	When present, not found in chloroplasts; often found in plasma membrane
Golgi	Present	Absent
Lysosomes	Usually present	Absent
Flagella	When present, contain microtubules	When present, do not contain microtubules

certain kinds of resources. The way of life available to a tree or a sparrow or a cat could never be exploited by cells of only one kind.

But to return to our original question, "Why is cell structure fundamental to life?" We have seen that a division of labor based on specialization is necessary for organisms of any size. Why has this occurred on the cellular level? Since all organisms show cellularity, it must be that the first organisms were single cells. And either life is so conservative that a substitute for cellularity has never been found, or there is no other equally efficient organization.

The Other End of the Scale

Cells are categorized as being either **eucaryotic** or **procaryotic**. All the cells we have described up to this point have been eucaryotic cells. Such organisms as molds, yeast, protozoa, most algae, and all higher plants and animals are thus designated **eucaryotes**. They are so named because their cells have a well-defined nucleus—in other words, a nucleus surrounded by a nuclear membrane. The term *eucaryotic* means "having a true nucleus." In addition to having a true nucleus, all eucaryotic organisms have mitochondria and other complex membranous organelles (Table 4.3).

Procaryotes. **Bacteria**—including the cyanobacteria, or blue-green algae—are procaryotes, that is, prenuclear. As their name implies, they are simple organisms (Figs. 4.32 and 4.33). Procaryotes lack a true nucleus. Their single chromosome is not separated from the cytoplasm by a nuclear membrane. Compartmentalization is somewhat limited in procaryotes, but there are mesosomes, which are infoldings of the plasma membrane (Fig. 4.32). These can be quite extensive in some species. Although there are numerous ribosomes, the cytoplasm contains none of the membrane-bound organelles that populate eucaryotic cytoplasm.

FIGURE 4.32 **A Bacterial Cell.**

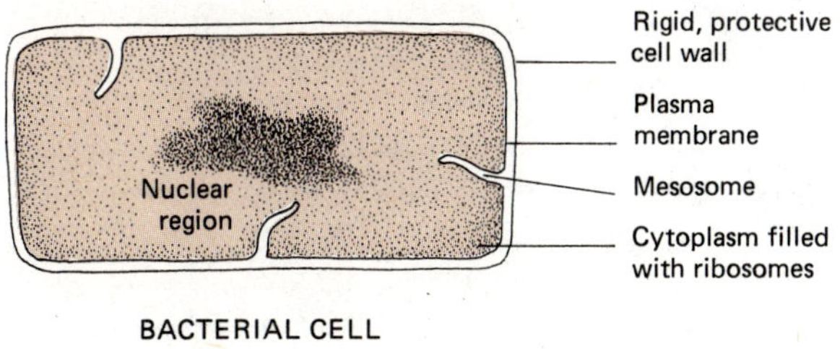

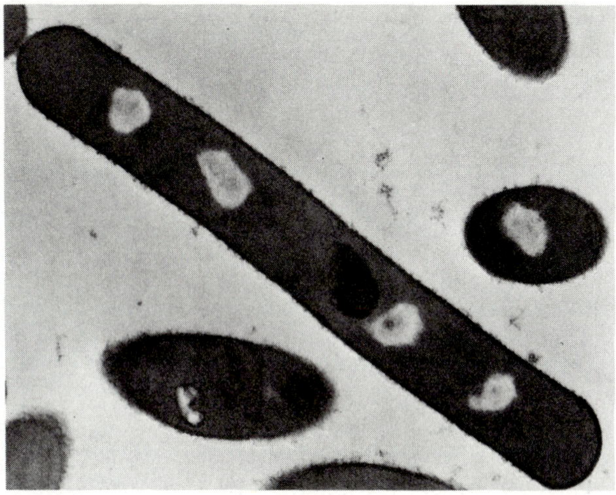

(a)

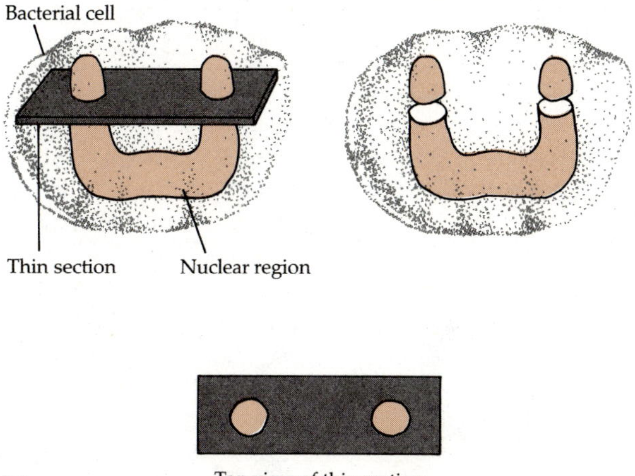

(b)

FIGURE 4.33 **The Beginning of a Bacterial Chain.** (a) A wall is beginning to form across the middle of this long rod-shaped bacterial cell. The dark whorl of membranes connected to the emergent cross wall is a mesosome. Involvement in cell division is just one of many functions of mesosomes. They are actively involved in formation of new nuclear material, too. The light spots you see are nuclear regions. Each cell half appears to have two nuclear regions (remember that there is no nuclear membrane and thus no true nucleus in bacteria), but that isn't necessarily so. Analyzing electron micrographs of thin sections requires ingenuity and perception. While you might be tempted to believe that this electron micrograph shows both rod-shaped bacteria and nearly round ones, it is likely that all the cells shown are similar. The difference in appearance may reflect the way the cells were cut. Similarly, you might presume that the dividing cell contains four nuclear regions. (b) This diagram illustrates how a thin section of a cell with a single U-shaped nuclear region can appear to show two nuclear regions.

BOX 4C

CELLS FORM TISSUE

Although the human body contains many different kinds of tissues, there are four fundamental types: nervous tissue, muscle tissue, epithelial tissue, and connective tissue. As we will see in Chapter 8, nervous tissue occurs primarily in the central nervous system. Muscle tissue (Chapter 9) is found mainly in skeletal muscles, the heart, and the walls of body passages. Epithelial tissues and connective tissues are more widespread. Because these tissues are major components of most organs, they are discussed here rather than with specific organs.

Epithelial tissues form the boundary between the body and the nonliving world. Indeed, all body surfaces, cavities, and passageways have somewhat similar covering layers. The cells of epithelial tissues are bound tightly together. In places, the membranes of adjacent cells fuse as tight junctions. This close association between epithelial cells permits them to regulate the movement of substances into and out of organs or into or out of the body itself.

In contrast to epithelial tissues, connective tissues are rich in nonliving materials produced and maintained by the connective tissue cells. Some of these cell products are protein fibers, such as collagen. Other cell products are formless substances that hold cells and tissues together. Yet others are the minerals that give bone its hardness. Together these nonliving materials provide strength and support that living cells cannot provide directly. Because of these cell products, connective tissues are able to support the body, to hold the components together, and to provide anchorage necessary for movement. Bone and cartilage form distinct structures, but much of the connective tissue lies inside the various organs, where it binds epithelial, muscle, and nervous tissues together.

With the notable exception of nervous tissue, minor damage to body tissues can result in repair by regeneration. Regeneration implies nearly perfect repair by proliferation of tissue exactly like that which was lost. Usually, however, tissue damage is repaired by the growth of nonfunctional scar tissue. Damaged cells are replaced by proliferating connective tissue heavily infiltrated with collagen fibers.

Plants are also organized of characteristic cell types specialized for particular functions. Plant tissue structure is discussed in Chapter 17.

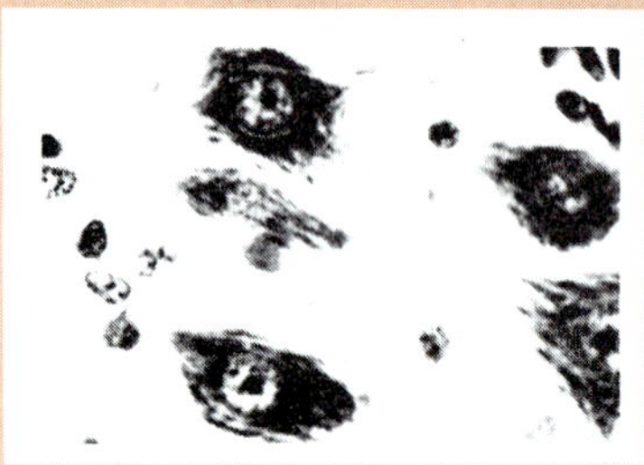

(a) Nervous tissue

(b) Muscle tissue

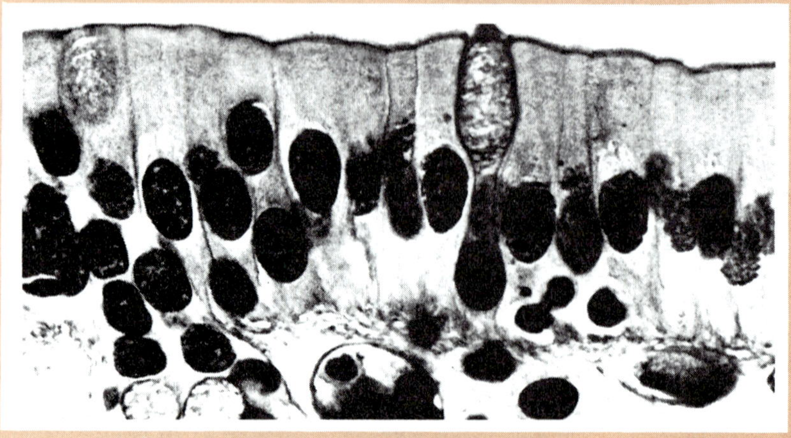

(c) Epithelial tissue

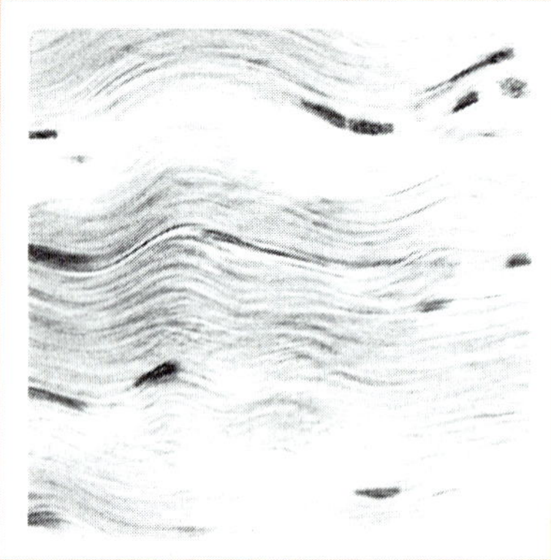

(d) Connective tissue

Almost all procaryotic cells are protected by a rigid cell wall. Underneath the cell wall is a thin plasma membrane that encloses the cytoplasm. Some procaryotes are single-celled bacteria, and others form chains, filaments, or other kinds of groupings (Fig. 4.33). Although they are microscopic organisms, a sufficient number of cells may accumulate to produce a visible **colony** or cluster. Nevertheless, whether bacterial cells are grouped in chains, filaments, or colonies, each one is an independent unit. There is no real tissue organization or cooperation between the individual members of a group.

Even though procaryotes are primitive, they carry out all the basic life functions. The fact that they are structurally simple limits their abilities somewhat, but at the same time they have advantages. For instance, they multiply very rapidly. It just doesn't take as long to reproduce something simple as it does to reproduce something complex. Simple as they are, however, procaryotes are not the simplest biological forms. That distinction belongs to the viruses.

Viruses—a Group Apart. Since they are totally devoid of cellular characteristics, **viruses** defy description as organisms. A virus particle is merely a package of genes with a hard protein coat that protects the core of genetic material from damage (Fig. 4.34). The virus genes carry the genetic blueprints for making more virus particles.

Isolated virus particles can perform no activity on their own. They are inert, and therefore many scientists do not consider viruses truly alive. Although viruses possess genetic information for their own reproduction, they lack the machinery for putting this information to use.

Viruses "come to life" only when they enter cells of plants, animals, or microorganisms. Cells contain the raw materials and machinery needed

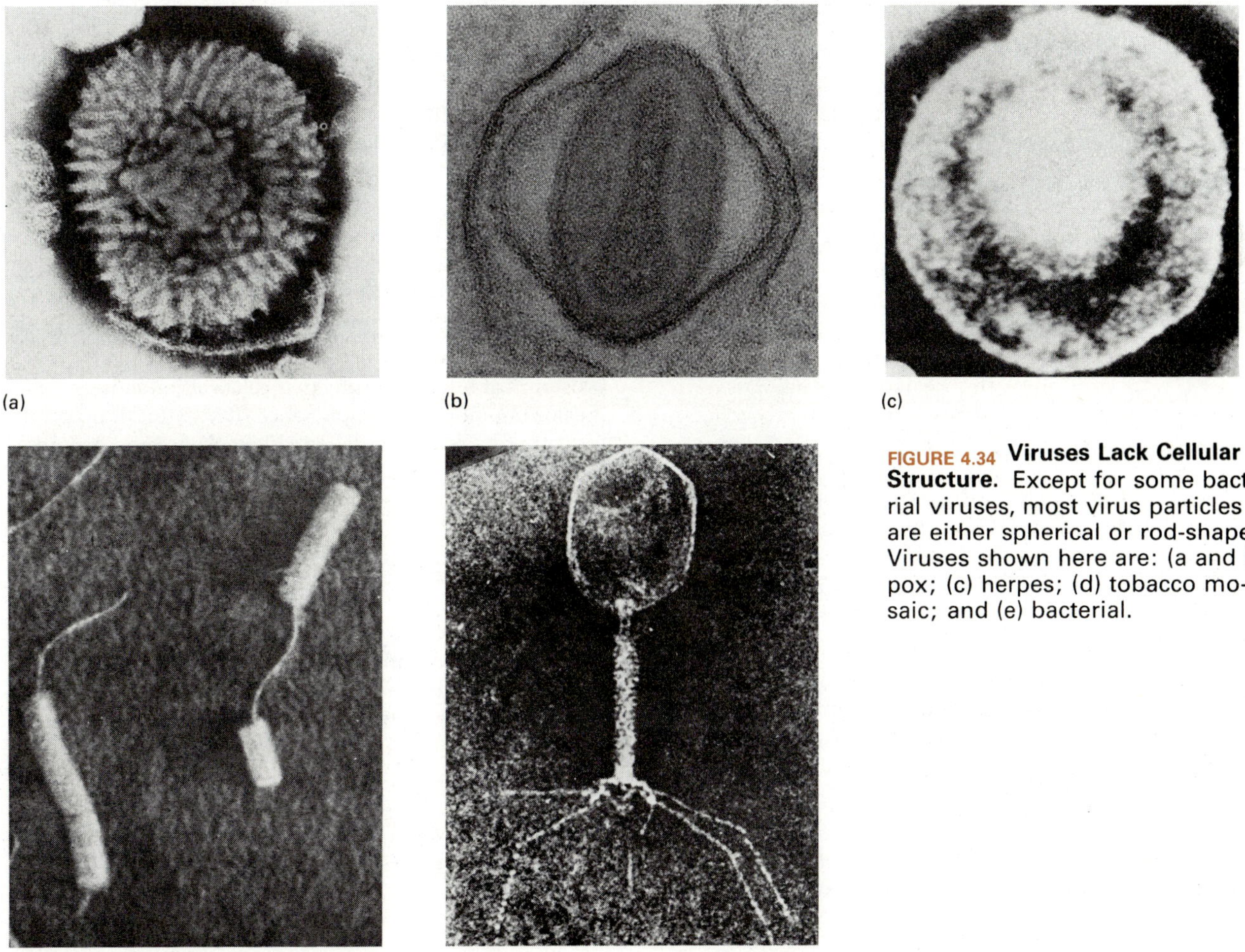

(a) (b) (c) (d) (e)

FIGURE 4.34 **Viruses Lack Cellular Structure.** Except for some bacterial viruses, most virus particles are either spherical or rod-shaped. Viruses shown here are: (a and b) pox; (c) herpes; (d) tobacco mosaic; and (e) bacterial.

for viral reproduction. Once a cell has been infected, viral genes commandeer the cells' enzymes,
63 ribosomes, and ATP and force the cell to manufacture more virus particles. We will learn more about this process in Chapter 11, but even without knowing the exact details of how viruses operate, you can probably see why viruses can be considered quite sophisticated biological forms, at least in one sense. Viruses have done away with the need for cellular structure and organization. They just use somebody else's.

Thousands of virus particles can be produced by an infected cell. Although viral particles may be assembled and released over a long period of time, the strain on the cell is often so great that the cell dies. Of course, not all virus infections have such serious consequences. Some cells recover from virus infections and resume their normal existence.

Organization: The Key to Life

However we look at life, we find not a random distribution of components but distinctive organization. Chemical structure is basic to this organization. We see organization in the repeating units of macromolecules such as proteins, nucleic acids, and polysaccharides. Even water participates in organization as it helps to mold the shape of giant protein molecules. Differences in solubility are crucial to the structure of membranes and to their ability to separate cells from the outside. This is equally true for the membranes that create tiny compartments within cells. Here substances can be concentrated and special environments organized.

Thus chemical and cellular organization merge. Meanwhile the cells of multicellular organisms both cooperate and specialize. All this organization requires raw materials and energy. In the next chapter, we examine how these needs are met.

Summary

1. Most cell structures are constructed from lipids and/or macromolecules. The macromolecules are made of small building-block subunits; proteins from amino acids, polysaccharides from sugars, and nucleic acids from nucleotides. Lipids include fats, oils, phospholipids, and steroids.

2. Proteins are important structural elements of all cells. In addition, all enzymes are proteins. Polysaccharides and lipids are used for both structure and energy storage. Nucleic acids are involved in heredity.

3. All cells are surrounded by a selectively permeable plasma membrane made of lipids and proteins. The membrane's function is to control which materials can enter and leave the cell. Passage through the plasma membrane is usually accomplished by simple diffusion, facilitated diffusion, or active transport. Some cells engulf particulate matter by phagocytosis.

4. The living matter within the plasma membrane is divided into compartments by membranous channels and organelles. The major cell organelle is the nucleus, which has the capacity to control most aspects of cell life by its control of protein synthesis. The material outside the nuclear membrane is the cytoplasm.

5. Membranous channels known as the endoplasmic reticulum (ER) wind through the cytoplasm. Ribosomes, the sites of protein synthesis, are found free in the cytoplasm, or they coat some parts of the ER. The endoplasmic reticulum functions in secretion and the synthesis of membranes and organelles, as does the Golgi body, a highly specialized collection of membranous channels.

6. Cytoplasmic organelles include lysosomes, which contain many different digestive enzymes, and mitochondria, which are the sites of cellular respiration. Both organelles are membrane-bound.

7. Typical plant cells differ from animal cells by the presence of a tough protective cell wall outside the plasma membrane, the presence of membranous photosynthetic organelles called chloroplasts, and a fluid-filled membranous sac, the central vacuole.

8. Organisms exist as single-celled individuals or as multicellular aggregations. In the most sophisticated multicellular organisms the cells become differentiated and grouped into working units called tissues.

9. Bacteria are extremely simple cells because there is no nuclear membrane to separate the nucleus from the cytoplasm. Such cells are called procaryotic cells, and they are further distinguished from eucaryotic cells, which have a nuclear membrane, by the absence of such membranous organelles as mitochondria. Viruses are even simpler biological structures. Having no cellular organization at all, they are merely packages of protein-coated genes that are functional only when a cell is parasitized.

Thought and Controversy

1. Pioneer women made soap by soaking wood ashes in water and then boiling animal fats in the water. The extract from the ashes contained lye, which broke the fats into fatty acids and glycerol. Commercial soap manufacture follows the same principles.

Soaps are modified fatty acids, which are good cleaning agents because one end of the fatty acid molecule is soluble in water and the other end in lipids. Ordinarily, lipids such as greases repel water, but the fatty acids bind the water and lipids together. This permits water to lift the greasy lipids and wash them away. Perhaps you remember threats to wash out children's mouths with soap as punishments for using dirty words. Since some fatty acids taste and smell terrible, that punishment was more than symbolic. And given this property of fatty acids, it is no surprise that perfumes are traditionally added to toilet soaps.

Synthetic detergents work in a manner similar to that of soaps and have replaced them for many uses. Some are employed as antibacterial agents; it is common practice to wash simple wounds with soap or detergents. Can you see how these substances could destroy the cells of bacteria or other organisms? And do you know why the extensive use of soaps or detergents may cause "dishpan hands" or other minor skin damage?

2. Biologists delight in unusual organisms that permit them to delve into life's secrets. *Acetabularia*, a giant one-celled marine plant, is such an organism. There are several species of *Acetabularia*, each more than an inch long and each having a stalk and cap. Thus they resemble delicate mushrooms, but there are differences from species to species in the shape of their caps. The nucleus of *Acetabularia* always lies in the base of the stalk, and it is simple to cut members of different species in parts and make grafts from one to another. Any large piece containing a nucleus is capable of regenerating into a complete organism. Many times pieces from one species have been grafted onto the nucleus-containing base of a member of a different species. But no matter what the arrangement, regeneration always yields a cap characteristic of the species to which the nucleus belongs. Is this what you would expect in light of the role of the nucleus in the cell?

3. If you are distressed to learn that single cells, such as those that constitute *Acetabularia*, can be inches long, here is a partial explanation. These and other plant cells contain large water vacuoles, so most of the volume is not living cytoplasm. Thus some single plant cells can be unusually large.

4. What do you suppose a description of cells written 50 years ago would be like? Before World War II, nucleic acids were known, but it seemed likely that the genetic material was a protein. Without the electron microscope we knew nothing of membrane structure or of the extensive membrane systems inside cells. Mitochondria were only tiny particles, sometimes recognized because they used oxygen and changed the color of certain dyes. Biologists argued whether or not the Golgi body really existed, and no one had ever heard of a ribosome. These details and volumes more have been pieced together by people working on grants and contracts funded by the National Institutes of Health, the National Science Foundation, military agencies, drug companies, foreign governments, and many other organizations. Scientists seeking money for basic research—that is, research not directly related to practical problems—are facing increasing pressure. Why spend money merely to increase knowledge? What good will it do? But is there any knowledge that has no practical value? How could we hope to manipulate organisms without knowing their fundamental structure? Can you think of other reasons to do basic research? Do you find any personal satisfaction in sharing such new information as the elements of cell structure?

Questions

1. How does the amino acid sequence of a polypeptide chain determine its shape? Consider both globular and fibrous proteins.

2. Describe the difference between a simple fat and a phospholipid. Are both kinds of lipids good emulsifiers? Why?

3. Why is the structure of the plasma membrane described as a fluid mosaic?

4. How are diffusion and facilitated diffusion similar? How are they different? Answer the same questions with regard to facilitated diffusion and active transport.

5. Make two lists. In one list name all the cell structures that are composed of membranes or are bounded by membranes. In the second list name all the nonmembranous cell structures. Give the function of each structure you have listed.

6. What advantage does a large surface:volume ratio give to cells?

7. What cell structures are unique to plant cells?

8. Define each of these terms:

denaturation	deoxyribonucleic acid
differentiation	desmosome
disaccharide	

9. How do procaryotic cells differ from eucaryotic cells? What is the common name for procaryotic organisms?

10. Why are viruses not considered to be organisms? Is it because they are composed of different chemicals?

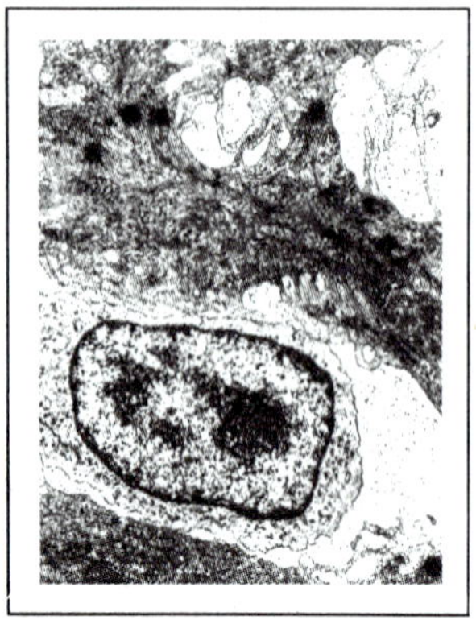

5

Metabolism and Nutrition: How Foods Fit into the Cell Picture

IN ORDER TO LIVE, CELLS MUST METABOLIZE. THAT is to say, cells must transform nutrients into energy and into their own characteristic components. Cells need energy to move, to conduct bioelectric impulses, to accumulate nutrients, and to perform many other functions. Living is a dynamic process of continuous chemical activity. Healthy cells ceaselessly adjust, repair, and replace themselves. Of course, doing these things means making new molecules, and that requires energy, too.

When we consider all this, it becomes clear that cellular metabolism has two distinct aspects; we refer to them as **degradation** (breaking down) and **synthesis** (building up). One drives the other. *Degradation* of nutrients provides energy and raw materials for *synthetic* reactions.

Some nutrients must be made available in bulk amounts to supply the vast energy and raw material requirements of cells. Other nutrients are needed in much smaller quantities. These are equally essential, however, as they cannot be synthesized from the major nutrients. For this reason, no single nutrient can sustain all the metabolic reactions of cells. In the next few pages, we will explore the topic of cellular metabolism in some detail. Then we will put this information to practical use when we discuss human nutrition in the latter part of the chapter.

EXTRACTING ENERGY FROM NUTRIENTS

In Chapter 3, we discussed oxidation-reduction reactions as the chief way in which cells obtain energy from chemicals. Most cells oxidize glucose to obtain energy. The overall reaction is as follows: 60

$$\underset{\text{glucose}}{C_6H_{12}O_6} + \underset{\text{oxygen}}{6O_2} \rightarrow \underset{\text{carbon dioxide}}{6CO_2} + \underset{\text{water}}{6H_2O} + \text{Energy}$$

This single-step reaction is what would occur if glucose were burned in air. As with other combustion reactions—exploding gasoline, for example—a great deal of heat energy is released all at once. Within cells, glucose is degraded differently. High temperatures and sudden release of large amounts of energy are not compatible with life.

Cellular oxidation-reduction reactions occur in a piecemeal fashion so that energy is released slowly and in small, controllable amounts. In fact, cellular metabolism, whether degradative or synthetic, occurs by a progression of carefully controlled enzymatic steps.

Enzymes and Metabolic Control

If you have ever built a wood fire, you know that it is not a simple job. The logs must be arranged just so. And there must be kindling to produce sufficient heat to ignite the larger pieces of wood. Similarly, an electric spark is necessary to release energy from the gasoline in an automobile engine.

In a way, enzymes act as kindling for metabolic reactions. But instead of supplying energy, as kindling does, enzymes reduce the **activation energy**□ needed for a reaction. 60

A substance that increases the rate of a reaction by lowering the activation energy barrier is called a **catalyst**. Chemists have discovered a variety of catalysts that can speed their test-tube reactions. Enzymes are biological catalysts (Fig. 5.1). They speed up cell reactions that would otherwise occur only slowly—too slowly to support living systems at temperatures that permit life. Just like kindling, enzymes are effective in small doses. Unlike kindling, however, enzymes are not consumed in the reactions they promote. They can be used over and over again.

How Enzymes Work. Enzymes are proteins, consisting of one or more long chains of amino acids. As with other proteins, multitudes of weak bonds between amino acids at different points cause the chains to fold and twist very precisely, so each enzyme has a unique structure. Most important, the structure of an enzyme provides a surface where catalytic activity is centered.

Part of the surface of every enzyme is shaped into an **active site**. This place is where **substrates** (substances to be changed) bind to the enzyme. The active site conforms to the shape of substrate molecules (Fig. 5.2). Although enzyme and substrate combine, the union is only temporary. Soon the substrate is converted into the **product**, which separates from the enzyme. This leaves the enzyme free to catalyze the reaction of still more substrate molecules.

A chemist might try to accelerate a test-tube reaction by heating the contents of the tube. This may do the job, because at elevated temperatures molecules move about more rapidly and are much more likely to bump into one another and react. Just as important, fast-moving molecules frequently collide with sufficient force to cause chemical bonds to rupture or rearrange. Of course, not all collisions, not even all forceful ones, result in reactions. Reactions, as we learned in Chapter 3, occur only when they are energetically favor-
62 able.□ Nevertheless, even energetically favorable reactions will not occur unless the chemically reactive portions of reactant molecules come into contact.

There is probably no single explanation for how all enzymes work. As with ordinary chemical reactions, enzymatic ones usually involve more than one substance. Where there is more than one substrate, the affinity of the enzyme for the substrates effectively increases collisions between the reactants. In a cell, therefore, an enzyme sorts out its substrates from the mixture of substances found

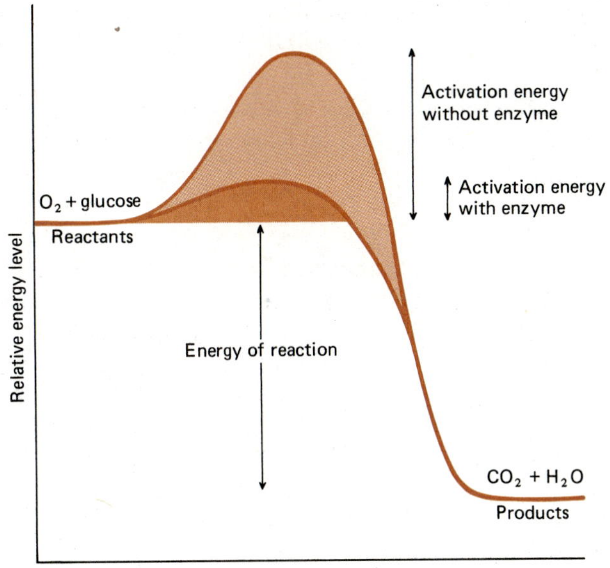

FIGURE 5.1 Enzymes and Activation Energy. Reactants must be pushed over a small energy "hill" before they react. Enzymes lower the activation energy hill.

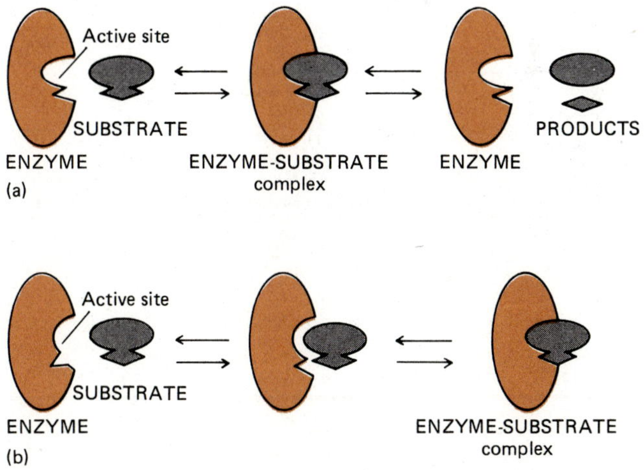

FIGURE 5.2 Interaction of Enzyme and Substrate. (a) The specificity of an enzyme for certain substrates is explained by the precise "fit" of enzyme and substrate. The active site of an enzyme conforms to the shape of its substrate much as a lock conforms to the shape of its key. (b) Not all enzymes have perfectly shaped active sites. In some cases the enzyme is induced to mold itself to its substrate as the two come into contact.

there. Furthermore, the active site is a perfect meeting place, because it permits the enzyme to hold the substrate molecules in positions that favor reaction between them.

Careful study of a few enzymes indicates that the binding of substrate to enzyme induces the enzyme to mold itself more closely to the substrate. Apparently the enzyme then proceeds to squeeze and strain the substrate molecule and weaken its bonds. Is it any wonder, then, that substrates are more reactive in the presence of their enzymes?

Considering how enzymes operate, we can now appreciate the importance of the numerous, though
70 individually weak, bonds that shape an enzyme.□ If an enzyme were held in some rigid configuration by strong bonds, it would be immobilized. Effective enzyme action requires pliability. Because an enzyme is rather loosely shaped, it can easily mold itself to substrates.

The requirement that enzymes fit their substrates explains the specific nature of enzymes. There is no all-purpose enzyme. We have a specific enzyme for almost every metabolic reaction.

Enzyme Sensitivity. Because enzymes can be used over and over again, cells require only a limited number of each kind. Still, just like all tools, enzymes wear out and must eventually be replaced. When enzymes lose their unique shape and consequently their active site, they are said to be
69 **denatured**.□ Denaturation may result from ordinary wear and tear or from various forms of environmental damage (Fig. 5.3).

Easy susceptibility to denaturation is the price proteins pay for their exceptional structural characteristics. The weak bonds so easily rearranged in the course of enzyme activity can be permanently disrupted by high temperatures. It is true, however, that a few enzymes are particularly resistant to heat, at least for short periods. Some examples are the enzymes that are obtained from cells and used as cleansing agents or as meat tenderizers.

To a great extent, the heat sensitivity of essential enzymes determines the maximum temperature an organism can tolerate. We take advantage of this fact when we use heat to destroy harmful "germs" in food or water. The temperature sensitivity of enzymes also explains why a high fever is so dangerous. Some human cells die quickly at temperatures above 42.2°C (108°F) because their enzymes "cook" or denature. Normal body temperature is 37°C (98.6°F).

Enzyme structure and function are also affected by acidity or alkalinity. □Many enzymes seem 56
to work best in a neutral environment—one that is neither acid nor alkaline. Others can function in stomach acid of about pH 2, strong enough to burn a hole in this page.

For the most part, digestive enzymes are extracellular enzymes, secreted by cells to the outside. Inside a cell, numerous membranous compartments provide mini-environments with conditions appropriate for the function of the enzymes located there.

Many poisons are chemicals that react with enzymes and denature them. This explains the deadly effects of cyanide, the heavy metals lead and mercury, and certain other chemicals (Fig. 5.4). When a poison such as mercury is taken by mouth, a common antidote is egg white. It must be administered shortly after the poison is ingested, however. In the stomach the poison reacts with the egg-white protein much as it would react with enzyme protein. In so doing, the poison becomes trapped

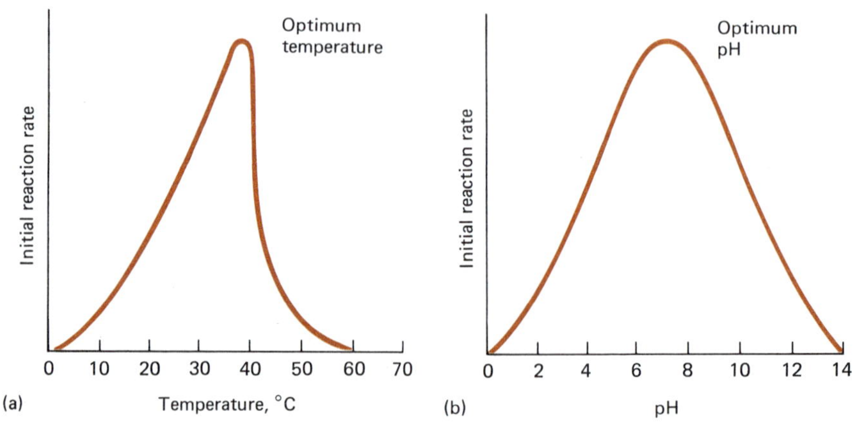

FIGURE 5.3 **Effect of Temperature and pH on Enzymes.** At low temperatures, molecular movement is so slow that even enzyme-catalyzed reactions are slow (a). As temperatures increase, movement increases. Eventually, however, the heat causes enzyme denaturation, and the reaction rate falls. Many enzymes work best at neutrality, as seen in (b). On either side of pH 7, the acid or alkaline conditions reduce enzyme effectiveness. At either extreme, denaturation follows.

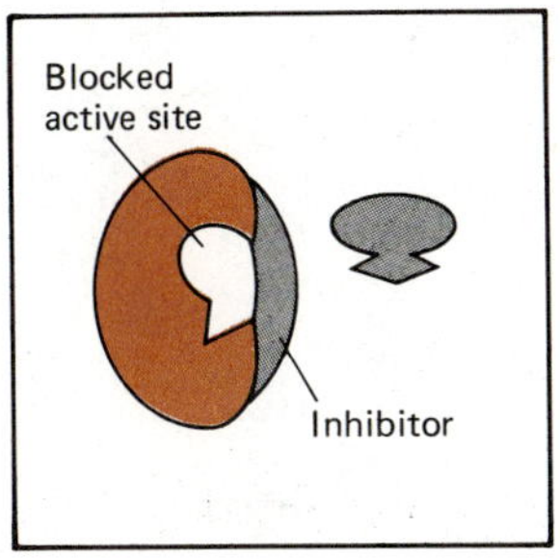

FIGURE 5.4 **Enzyme Poisons.** Some poisons are inhibitors of enzyme activity. These reactive molecules may alter enzyme structure so that an enzyme-substrate complex cannot be formed.

in the precipitated, denatured egg white. Following the administration of this antidote, however, a stomach pump must be used to remove the precipitate, or something must be given to cause vomiting. Otherwise the denatured egg white will eventually be digested and the poison released back into the system.

Inhibition Can Be Useful. Although we generally think of inhibition as undesirable, it is one means through which cells regulate their metabolism. Intracellular metabolism can be manipulated by subtle changes of pH. For instance, acid production in a cellular compartment may inhibit some enzymes but activate others. A more dramatic kind of control, perhaps, is the phenomenon of **feedback regulation**. In feedback regulation, accumulation of the end product of an enzymatic sequence inhibits one or more key enzymes involved in its production (Fig. 5.5).

Feedback regulation involves alteration in the shape of the affected enzyme. An enzyme under feedback control is called an **allosteric enzyme**. Such enzymes have a control (allosteric) site as well as an active site. When the end product of the reaction sequence begins to accumulate, it binds to the control site of the enzyme. This distorts the enzyme's shape, so the substrate can no longer gain access to the active site. As a consequence, the enzyme cannot work and the whole reaction sequence grinds to a halt.

So long as there is a need for the end product, it does not accumulate and the reaction sequence that produces it proceeds normally. But when the supply of product exceeds the demand, the sequence begins to slow down. Usually enzymes are stopped by feedback regulation fairly early in the reaction sequence. This is an efficient means of control, since it prevents the wasteful accumulation of intermediates that would occur if the sequence of events was halted at a later point.

Eventually, as it is used up by other metabolic reactions, the backlog of end product will begin to disappear. At some point, demand for the end product becomes so great that even those molecules bound to inhibited enzymes will be released. This permits the enzymes to function, thus turning on the reaction sequence once more.

Feedback regulation permits a cell to turn on or turn off selected chemical reactions. It now becomes clear that enzymes not only *catalyze* the chemical reactions of life, but *regulate* them as well!

Enzymes and Energy Capture

At the beginning of this chapter, we stressed the important difference between combustion, in which energy is released "at a single blow," and biological oxidation, which is gradual. While we were on this

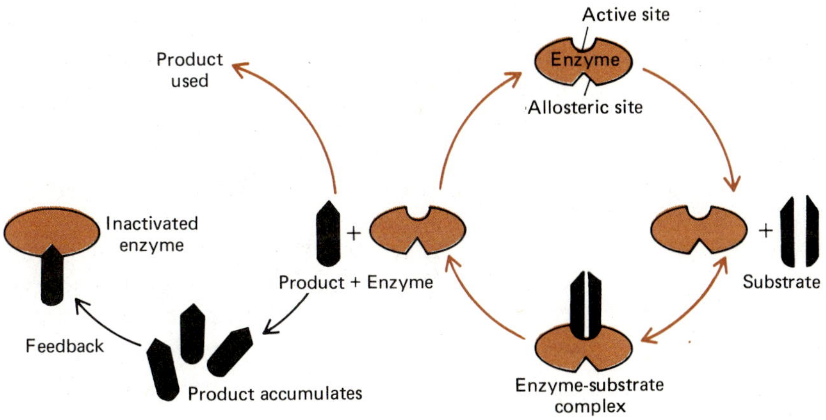

FIGURE 5.5 **How Allosteric Enzymes Are Controlled by Feedback.** When the end product combines with the allosteric site, the shape of the enzyme is changed so that the substrate can no longer bind.

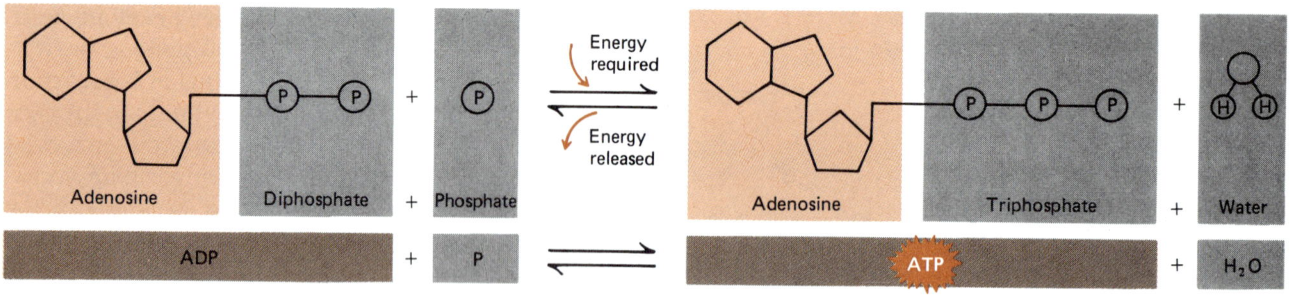

FIGURE 5.6 ATP Formation. Like so many important biological reactions, the addition of the third phosphate to ADP is a dehydration synthesis, in which water is removed when two chemical units are joined together. And as in other synthetic reactions, energy is required to make the new bond. This energy is released when the bond is subsequently broken and the reverse reaction occurs.

topic, we might also have mentioned that biological oxidations are not as slow as other kinds of oxidations—for example, the rusting of metal. Enzymes cause biological oxidations to occur one step at a time, at just the right rate of speed, and in such a way that when energy is released, it can be captured and used to perform cellular work.

Coupled Reactions. Earlier we mentioned that cells capture energy released in biological oxidations by making **adenosine triphosphate** (ATP). Since ATP formation requires energy, we say that the synthesis of ATP is coupled with biological oxidations,
63 such as dehydrogenations.□ Enzymes accomplish the coupling. Energy lost when the bonds of nutrient molecules are broken is used to make the bonds of ATP, which is produced from adenosine diphosphate (ADP) and inorganic phosphate (Fig. 5.6). Often such reactions are simplified by writing them as follows:

$$AH_2 + B \xrightarrow[\text{ADP} \;\curvearrowright\; \text{ATP}]{} A + BH_2$$

How ATP Is Used. We don't expect the furnace that heats our home to supply the energy to run all the electrical appliances and mow the lawn. On the other hand, this would not be an unreasonable expectation if the furnace powered an electric generator. Conversion of heat energy into electrical energy facilitates the performance of a greater variety of tasks. A cell may be compared with a modern power plant that produces electricity from coal, gas, or oil. Cells similarly convert energy from many chemically different nutrients into a single useful form, but instead of producing electricity, they generate ATP.

The principal **energy-transfer compound** of cells, ATP has been called an "energy currency." A cell can pay the energy price for its many operations by using ATP as a general power source. When ATP powers a cellular function, the ATP loses one of its phosphates and becomes ADP. ATP is later regenerated when food molecules are oxidized. The energy that is released from food is used to add phosphate to ADP.

The ADP-ATP cycle operates much like a rechargeable battery that provides a constant supply of electricity. However, not all the energy released by biological oxidations is harnessed in the form of ATP. Because all energy conversions are inefficient, some energy is always lost as heat. Part of this heat energy is used to maintain the body temperature.

Before going further, let us stop to consider an important point about ATP. It is *not* an energy storage compound. Cells do not manufacture piles of ATP for later use. The chemical nature of ATP is such that it is extremely reactive. An ATP molecule is poised like a spring, ready to give up its energy at the slightest provocation. It just wouldn't be safe for an organism to store energy in such a volatile form. All could be lost through "spontaneous combustion." Instead, cells make ATP continuously and use it immediately. Energy is stored by converting excess nutrients into such relatively stable substances as fats.

Every body cell makes the ATP it needs by oxidizing nutrient molecules. These energy-rich substances are systematically degraded into smaller and smaller pieces, and the energy is transferred to ATP. Not every metabolic step is an oxidation step. Some reactions are preparatory steps that make the capture of energy more efficient in the end. Eventually, however, only energy-poor waste products are left. Although all major types of food molecules can be oxidized, carbohydrates are especially important energy sources.

Generating ATP from Carbohydrates

Before we can get energy from the food we eat, the food must be digested. Digestion does not actually release any biologically useful energy; it is merely the process by which food is converted into a form that can be absorbed into the body. Humans
69 eat and digest a variety of carbohydrates, but most individual body cells are served only **glucose**. In Chapter 6, you will discover how the body converts other carbohydrates into this simple sugar. For now, let us consider only how cells obtain energy from the glucose that's made available to them.

Cellular breakdown of glucose to carbon dioxide and water requires something like two dozen different enzymatic steps. The process is often referred to as **cellular respiration**, because it involves the consumption of oxygen and the evolution of carbon dioxide. However, oxygen is not needed for the first ten reactions. Accordingly, cellular respiration can be divided into two stages. The first, **glycolysis**, is *anaerobic*—that is, it does not require oxygen. Only the second stage of glucose metabolism is *aerobic*, or oxygen dependent.

Stage 1. Glycolysis occurs in the cytoplasm of a cell. In summary what happens is this:

$$\text{glucose} + 2\text{ADP} + 2\text{ phosphate} + 2\text{NAD} \rightarrow 2\text{ pyruvic acid} + 2\text{ATP} + 2\text{NADH}_2$$

Figure 5.7 tells the full story. As you can see, the first few glycolytic reactions involve subtle changes in the glucose molecule. Note that two of the early steps are priming reactions that utilize ATP energy. These reactions prepare the glucose for the more drastic steps that lie ahead. They make ATP synthesis possible.

Eventually, the six-carbon sugar is cleaved into two pieces. Then each of the three-carbon fragments is partially oxidized. Here is an example of a biological oxidation that does not involve
63 oxygen. The two three-carbon fragments are oxidized by being stripped of some of their hydrogens. These hydrogens carry with them a portion of the energy that was locked into the original glucose molecule. The enzyme that removes the hydrogens deposits them with a **hydrogen carrier** named NAD, a substance that is derived from the vitamin niacin. The reaction occurs as follows:

$$\text{NAD} + 2\text{H} \rightarrow \text{NADH}_2$$

The oxidized sugar fragments have unstable structures. They quickly degenerate, giving up some of their energy by reacting with ADP to produce ATP. In the end, each of the three-carbon fragments has been converted into **pyruvic acid**. Note that again no oxygen has been utilized, and no carbon dioxide has been produced.

Stage 2. When there is an adequate supply of oxygen, the pyruvic acid produced in glycolysis can be oxidized to carbon dioxide and water. The overall result can be summarized as follows:

$$2\text{ pyruvic acid} + 36\text{ADP} + 36\text{ phosphate} + 6\text{O}_2 \rightarrow 6\text{CO}_2 + 6\text{H}_2\text{O} + 36\text{ATP}$$

The process begins with the movement of pyruvic acid into the mitochondria.

The reactions that occur within the mitochondria are complicated but extremely efficient in extracting chemical energy from pyruvic acid. Almost 20 times more ATP is generated in the mitochondria than through glycolysis, which occurs in the surrounding cytoplasm.

The Krebs Cycle. As soon as pyruvic acid arrives at the interior of a mitochondrion, it is attacked by enzymes that first split off a carbon dioxide and then remove some energy-rich hydrogen atoms, passing them to waiting hydrogen carriers. The two-carbon acetic acid that remains is activated by addition to coenzyme A (CoA), a derivative of the vitamin, pantothenic acid. The acetyl-CoA formed is fed into the Krebs cycle (Fig. 5.8). This enzymatic sequence is a busy oxidation factory. It is a metabolic mill that degrades acetic acid into carbon dioxide and thus releases more hydrogens.

Acetyl-CoA is drawn into the cycle by its reaction with a special acceptor found in the mitochondrion. As this complex is acted on by one and then another Krebs cycle enzyme, more and more hydrogens are detached. Some of the hydrogens are passed to NAD, and others combine with a different hydrogen carrier, FP, which is a derivative

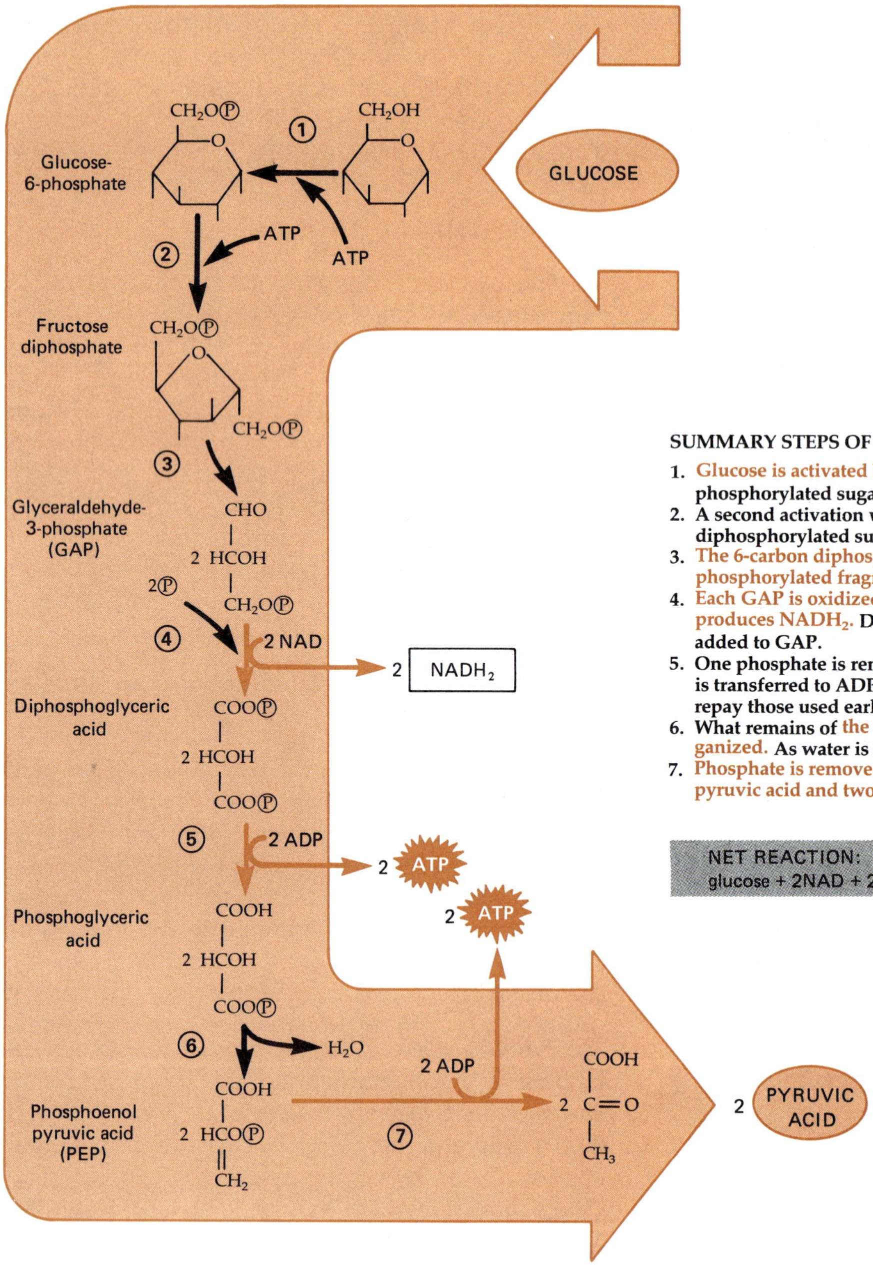

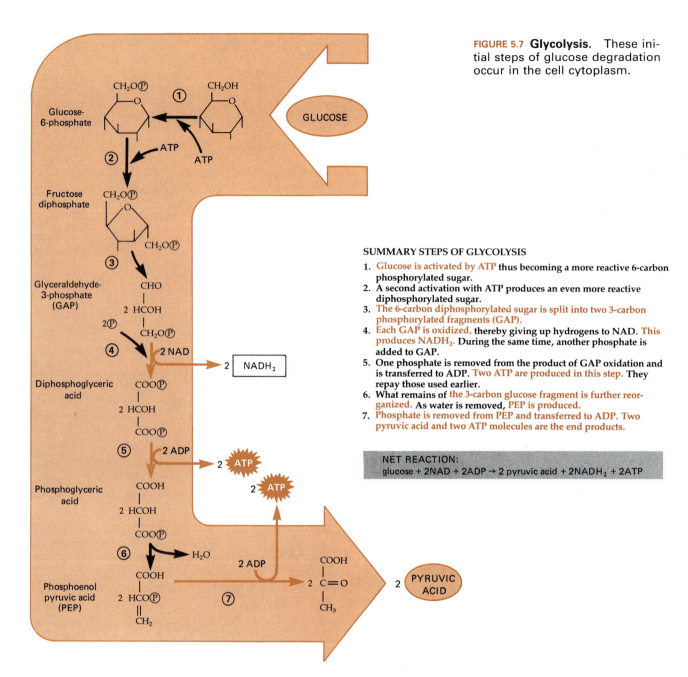

FIGURE 5.7 **Glycolysis.** These initial steps of glucose degradation occur in the cell cytoplasm.

SUMMARY STEPS OF GLYCOLYSIS

1. Glucose is activated by ATP thus becoming a more reactive 6-carbon phosphorylated sugar.
2. A second activation with ATP produces an even more reactive diphosphorylated sugar.
3. The 6-carbon diphosphorylated sugar is split into two 3-carbon phosphorylated fragments (GAP).
4. Each GAP is oxidized, thereby giving up hydrogens to NAD. This produces $NADH_2$. During the same time, another phosphate is added to GAP.
5. One phosphate is removed from the product of GAP oxidation and is transferred to ADP. Two ATP are produced in this step. They repay those used earlier.
6. What remains of the 3-carbon glucose fragment is further reorganized. As water is removed, PEP is produced.
7. Phosphate is removed from PEP and transferred to ADP. Two pyruvic acid and two ATP molecules are the end products.

NET REACTION:
glucose + 2NAD + 2ADP → 2 pyruvic acid + $2NADH_2$ + 2ATP

of the vitamin riboflavin. In time, each of the two dehydrogenated acetic acid carbons is released as carbon dioxide. And at one point during the degradations, enough energy is released to convert ADP to ATP.

In the course of subsequent reactions, the acetyl-CoA acceptor is regenerated, thus closing the cycle. The cycle recommences when the rejuvenated carrier picks up a new acetic acid fragment. Upon completion of each "turn" of the metabolic mill, one three-carbon pyruvic acid is oxidized to three molecules of carbon dioxide.

The Respiratory Chain and Oxidative Phosphorylation. As you have probably noticed, oxygen is not directly involved in the oxidations of the Krebs cycle. Nevertheless, oxygen must be present for the mill to operate. Oxygen acts as the **final acceptor** of the hydrogens that were only temporarily deposited with the hydrogen carriers. If these carriers are not relieved of their load in this way, soon the limited number of carrier molecules in a cell are all filled up, and energy-yielding oxidations abruptly cease. By passing their hydrogens to oxygen, the carriers are again free to pick up more

FIGURE 5.8 The Krebs Cycle. Mitochondrial enzymes oxidize pyruvic acid to carbon dioxide, yielding a few ATP but plentiful $NADH_2$. Two turns of the Krebs cycle are required to degrade the two pyruvic acids provided by one glucose molecule.

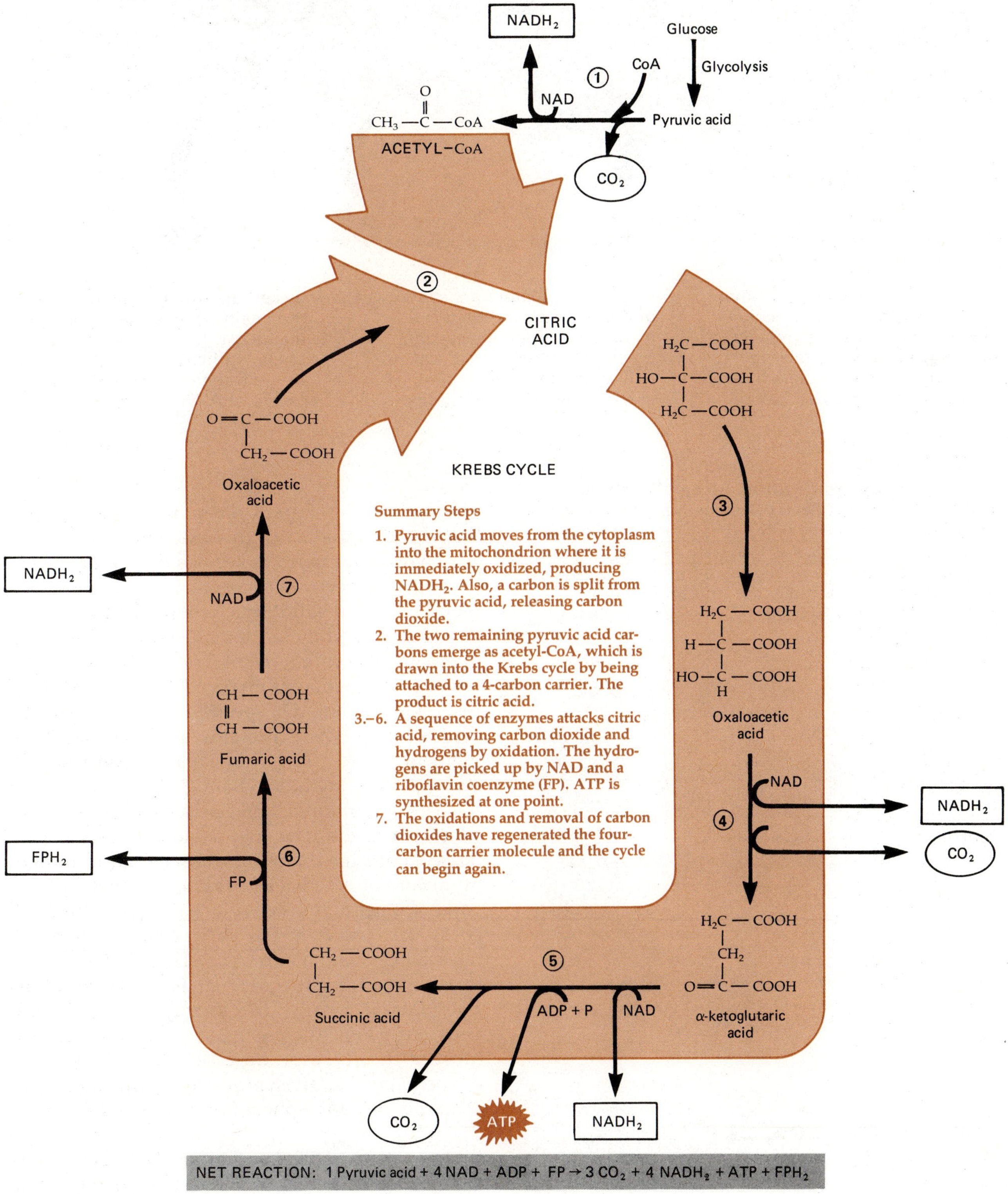

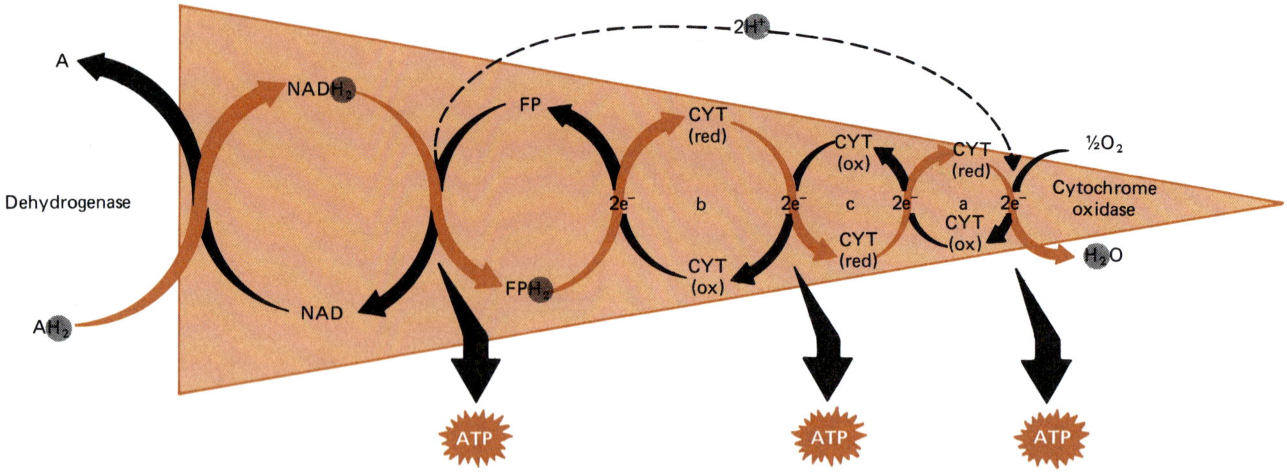

FIGURE 5.9 The Respiratory Chain. $NADH_2$, produced by oxidation of substances such as pyruvic acid (represented here by the symbol AH_2), transfers its hydrogens to other members of the respiratory chain. Each step of the respiratory chain is an oxidation-reduction reaction. Since the cytochromes transfer only electrons, the protons (H^+) are simply released and then picked up again at the end of the chain when water is produced. At three steps in the chain, sufficient energy is lost in the transfer to permit synthesis of ATP.

FIGURE 5.10 Cytochrome Structure and Function. (a) All cytochromes have the same basic structure of an iron-containing (Fe) heme unit attached to a protein. Their name indicates that they are colored compounds. Each has a slightly different hue. (b) It is the heme unit—actually the iron of the heme unit—that carries electrons. The reaction is illustrated here.

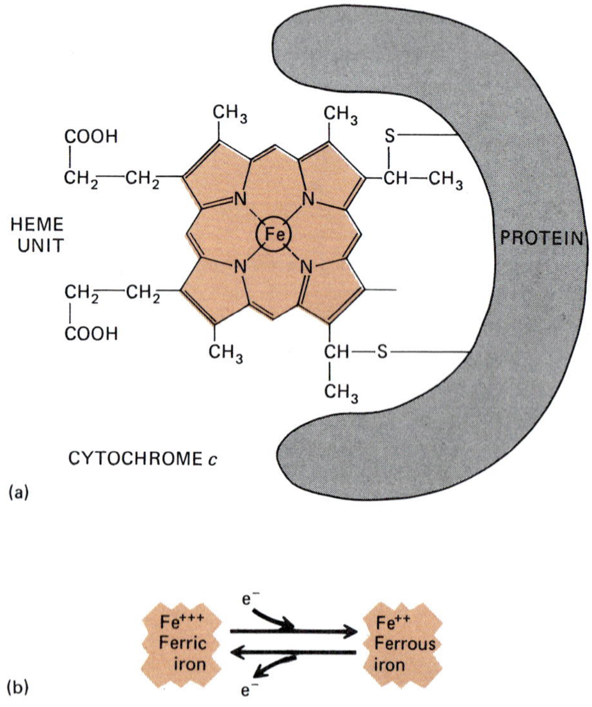

hydrogens and thereby keep respiration going. Water is the product of this reaction.

Hydrogen carrier molecules do not pass their hydrogens directly to oxygen. Instead, they feed them into the **respiratory chain** (Fig. 5.9), a group of closely linked molecules packed into the neatly folded mitochondrial membranes. At least five different components are involved in the action of the respiratory chain. Of special importance are the **cytochromes**. These proteins are iron-containing pigments (Fig. 5.10). They catalyze the last four steps of the respiratory chain.

The respiratory chain operates something like a bucket brigade. The energy-laden hydrogens are passed along the chain from one enzyme to another by means of a series of oxidation-reduction reactions. With each transfer, a little energy is "spilled." At several points in the chain enough energy is released to manufacture ATP. The technical name for this manufacture of ATP is **oxidative phosphorylation**. Finally, the energy-drained hydrogens are given to oxygen, and water is formed. Most of the ATPs produced in the complete oxidation of glucose are synthesized in the respiratory chain via oxidative phosphorylation (Table 5.1).

Chemiosmotic ATP Synthesis. For many years biologists have been puzzled as to exactly how the

TABLE 5.1 ATP Yield from Glucose

STAGE OF RESPIRATION	NUMBER OF ATP
Glycolysis	2
Mitochondrial oxidations	
Krebs metabolic mill	2
Respiratory chain	34
Total (per glucose molecule)	38

energy "spilled" during mitochondrial oxidation-reduction reactions is captured to make ATP. Currently popular is the **chemiosmotic theory**, which proposes that ATP synthesis is driven by a proton gradient created through the operation of the respiratory chain.

A crucial property of many components of the respiratory chain is that they can carry electrons
49 but not protons. You recall that biological oxidations usually involve removal of hydrogen atoms, and that hydrogen atoms consist of one electron and one proton. So, although hydrogens from glucose are fed into the respiratory chain, only electrons can travel the full length of the chain; their companion protons are scuttled along the way.

The mystery of the scuttled protons has always been heightened by the knowledge that they must finally be regained to make water. After all, water consists of two complete hydrogen atoms and one oxygen atom. The question has been: What are the protons doing in between? To answer that question, we need to know a little more about the structure of mitochondria.

Mitochondria have two membranes, but only
74 the inner membrane is selectively permeable. And it is the inner membrane that contains the apparatus for making ATP (Fig. 5.11). The inner membrane is constructed so as to create a proton gradient. Hydrogen carriers pass hydrogen atoms to the first member of the respiratory chain. This component then expels the protons outside the membrane and gives only the electrons to the next member of the chain.

Because the mitochondrial membrane is selectively permeable, the scuttled protons are segregated from the mitochondrial matrix. Thus the actions of the respiratory chain create a proton gradient in which protons are accumulated on one side of the membrane. As the number of protons outside the inner membrane grows—that is, as the gradient grows—certain patches on the outer surface of the membrane become sensitized to the high level of protons. These regions are associated with the **respiratory knobs** that line the mitochondrial cristae. At critical concentrations, the crowded pro-

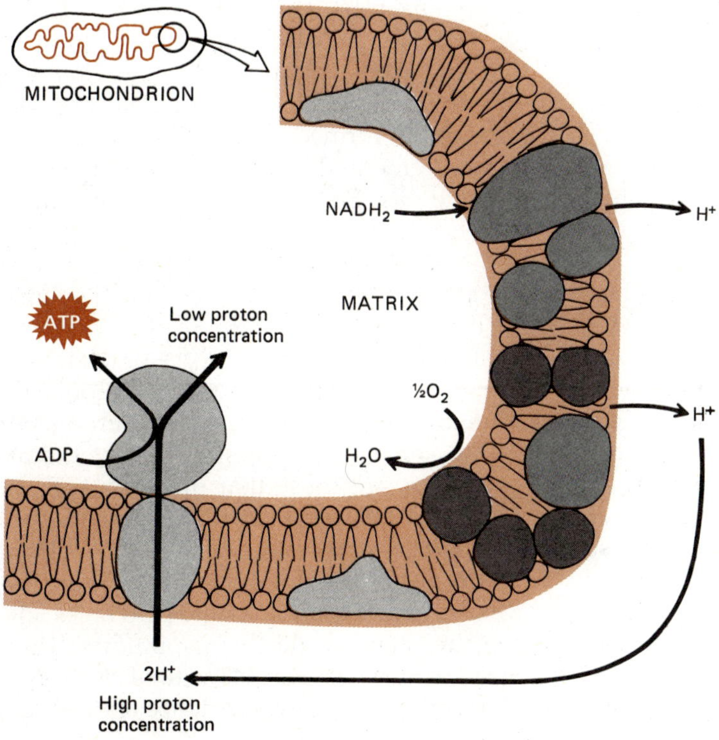

FIGURE 5.11 Chemiosmotic ATP Synthesis. The respiratory chain components are part of the inner mitochondrial membrane structure. As electrons are passed from $NADH_2$ to one and then another respiratory chain component (the shaded structures at the far right), protons (H^+) are pumped out of the mitochondrial matrix, creating a proton gradient. The flow of protons back into the mitochondrial matrix provides the rush of energy to generate ATP from ADP.

tons force their way back through the membrane, much as a rush of water flows through a crack in a dike. The energy of this sudden surge of protons is what drives ATP synthesis.

Nearly all the oxygen taken up by a cell is consumed by mitochondrial respiratory-chain oxidations. Red blood cells and other cells that lack mitochondria cannot use oxygen at all. Such cells are obliged to function anaerobically. The same is true of cells that are deprived of oxygen.

When There Isn't Enough Oxygen to Go Around

In the absence of oxygen—that is, under anaerobic conditions—mitochondria cannot generate ATP, because there is no final electron acceptor. Without oxygen, most body cells are deprived of their primary source of usable energy. Some cells, brain cells in particular, suffer serious damage if there is even a brief scarcity of oxygen. Others cope, at least for a while.

In humans, oxygen shortages occur during heavy exertion, such as running, when the circulation is not adequate to meet the oxygen demands of the muscles. Under these circumstances the pyruvic acid that cannot be oxidized by the mitochondria is transformed into **lactic acid**.

Under anaerobic conditions even glycolysis will grind to a halt unless some hydrogen acceptor is present to unload hydrogens from $NADH_2$. If the $NADH_2$ molecules were allowed to remain "filled up" because of the anaerobic condition, eventually there would be no NAD available to receive hydrogens, and glucose oxidation would come to an end. This is prevented when the hydrogens of $NADH_2$ are unloaded into pyruvic acid, which is turned into lactic acid. Lactic acid is formed because pyruvic acid acts as a hydrogen acceptor in the absence of oxygen, and NAD molecules are then free to load up again.

As it happens, lactic acid is somewhat toxic. Humans can tolerate only a limited amount of lactic acid before discomfort requires a reduction in energy consumption. We become fatigued. The lactic acid dilates surface blood vessels, accounting in part for the flushed face that accompanies heavy exertion. Eventually exertion must cease because the body can tolerate no more lactic acid. The body can go into **oxygen debt** only so far.

When oxygen again becomes available, the lactic acid is converted into harmless compounds. The liver transforms most of the lactic acid into glycogen. The remainder of the pyruvic acid is immediately respired through the metabolic mill. The oxidation of so much pyruvic acid clearly produces a large amount of ATP. In addition, a great deal of heat is released, accounting for the surge of warmth we feel *after* the exertion is over.

How Other Organisms Get ATP

Bacteria, yeasts, molds, and other microorganisms are noted for their metabolic diversity (Chapter 10). Although many microbes produce ATP from glucose as do human cells, others can oxidize unusual compounds ranging from jet fuel to aspirin.

Fermentation and Anaerobic Respiration. Unlike humans, some organisms are capable of indefinite existence in the total absence of oxygen. In certain of these organisms, glucose degradation is restricted to glycolysis. The pyruvic acid produced from glucose becomes the final hydrogen acceptor and is thereby converted into lactic acid. The souring of milk and certain other foods results from lactic acid produced by bacteria growing in the absence of oxygen. This process is called **fermentation** (Fig. 5.12), but essentially it is no different from what occurs in muscle tissue that lacks oxygen.

A more familiar fermentation is the production of alcohol by yeast cells growing on grain or fruit under anaerobic conditions. Instead of forming lactic acid from pyruvic acid, yeasts split pyruvic acid into two parts, adding hydrogens from $NADH_2$ to one of them. Ultimately, ethyl alcohol and carbon dioxide are formed. The bubbles we associate with many fermented beverages are bubbles of carbon dioxide gas. So are the bubbles that make bread rise.

Not all microorganisms ferment sugars; some are able to utilize amino acids and even nucleotides to make ATP. Anyone who has smelled rotting flesh is familiar with the work of these decomposers. It is no mystery why fermentations that yield foul-smelling wastes are called **putrefactions**.

In some ways the strangest of the anaerobic organisms are those that produce ATP via **anaerobic respiration**. This process should not be confused with glycolysis, which is an anaerobic stage of ordinary (ultimately aerobic) respiration. Anaerobic respiration of sugars involves glycolysis, the Krebs cycle, and the respiratory chain; but instead of using oxygen as the final electron acceptor, some other inorganic substance is substituted. Cer-

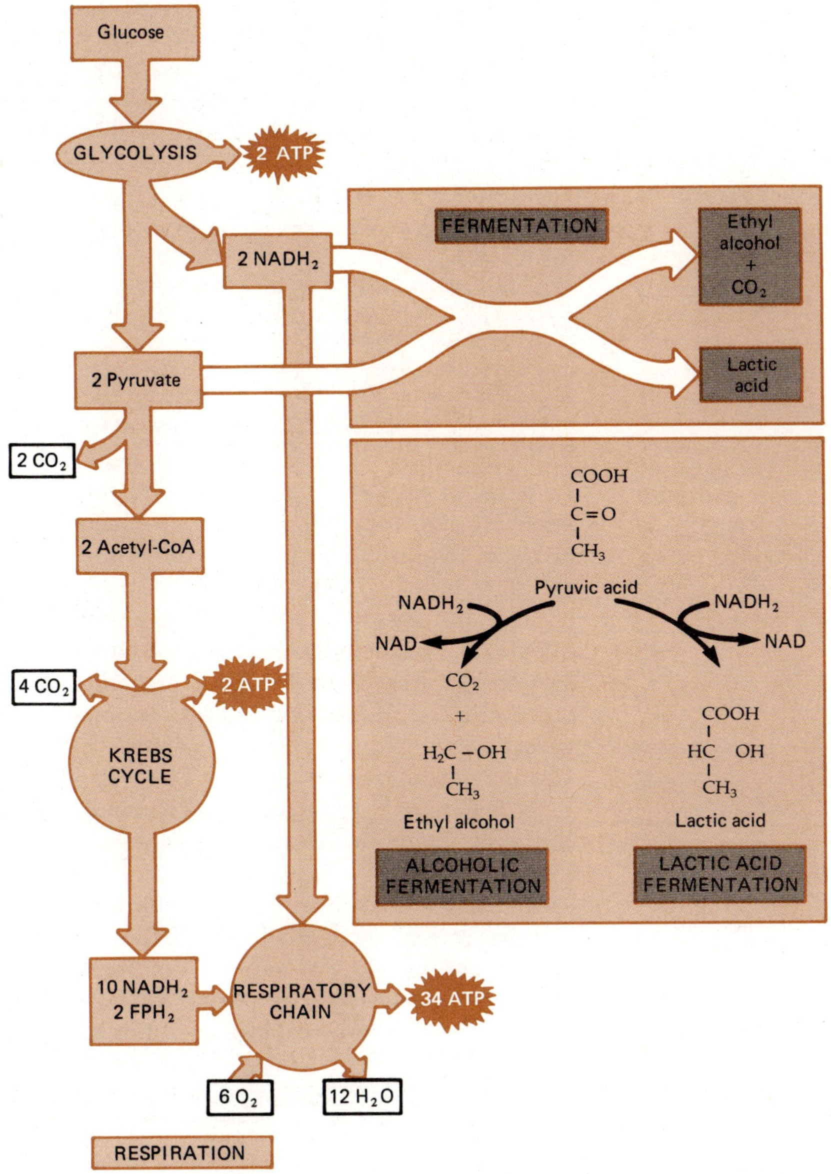

FIGURE 5.12 **A Comparison of Cellular Respiration and Fermentation.** Note that glycolysis is a part of both forms of metabolism. Note, too, that only two ATP can be produced via fermentation of glucose; this is because pyruvic acid must act as a final electron acceptor to regenerate NAD. Respiration permits complete oxidation of glucose and produces more ATP.

tain soil bacteria, for example, can use nitrate as a final electron acceptor. Apparently, anaerobic respiration is not limited to microorganisms; there is evidence that certain primitive mud-dwelling worms also obtain ATP this way.

Stranger still are the **methane bacteria** of swamps and other anaerobic places that abound in carbon dioxide and hydrogen gas produced by resident fermenters. Methane bacteria can oxidize hydrogen gas, and through a special respiratory chain they pass the released electrons to carbon dioxide. The valuable product of this form of anaerobic respiration is methane (natural gas). We will discuss methane bacteria again in Chapters 10 and 16.

Photosynthesis and Chemosynthesis. Earlier in the text, we pointed to photosynthesis by autotrophs as the ultimate source of organic food molecules for heterotrophs. However, contrary to what you might think, not all autotrophs are photosynthesizers. Although the topic of light as a source of energy for ATP synthesis will be explored further in a later chapter (Chapter 17), it seems appropriate to mention here those exceptional autotrophs that do not depend on light but on chemicals to provide energy. **Chemosynthetic autotrophs** use carbon dioxide as their sole carbon source, but obtain ATP by oxidizing inorganic compounds such as ammonia or hydrogen sulfide. These bacteria

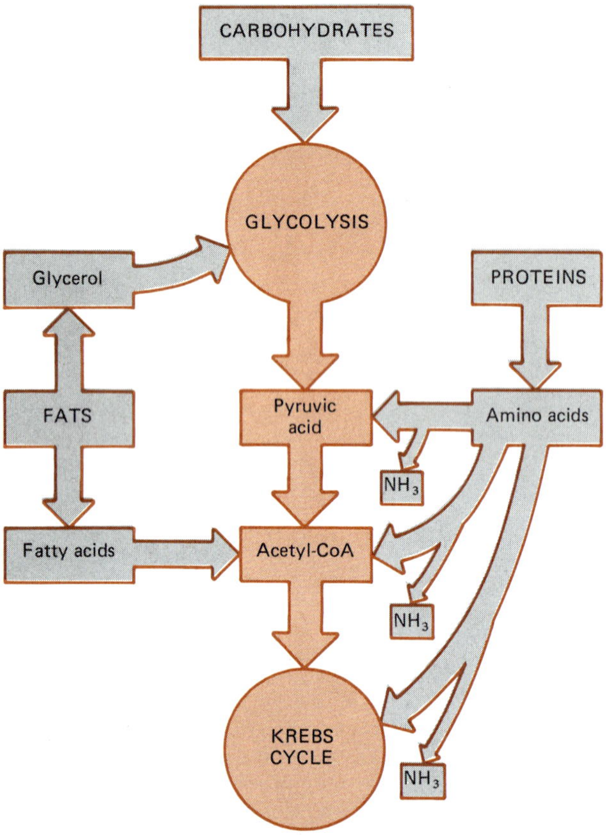

FIGURE 5.13 **All Roads Lead to the Metabolic Mill.** The Krebs cycle is the "hub" of metabolism in the sense that every major kind of food molecule is at least partially degraded in the mill.

are crucial to the operation of the biogeochemical cycles of nitrogen and sulfur and are responsible for maintaining soil fertility (Chapters 17 and 22).

Generating ATP from Fats and Proteins

Because it is such a versatile oxidation factory, the Krebs cycle is sometimes called a *metabolic mill*. Not only carbohydrates, but also most digestion products from proteins or fatty foods enter the mill at one point or another and are oxidized. To illustrate, let us consider the use of fats, which the body
72 digests into glycerol and fatty acids. Glycerol is a three-carbon compound that is readily converted into pyruvic acid and respired. The long fatty acid chains (16–18 carbons) are fragmented into acetyl-CoA, which is also processed by the metabolic mill.

Getting energy from proteins is more complicated, because the digestion of proteins yields 20
67 different kinds of amino acids. However, each amino acid is ultimately broken down to smaller pieces that can be oxidized by the enzymes of the metabolic mill. Because the amino portion of every amino acid contains nitrogen, complete oxidation of proteins produces ammonia (NH_3) in addition to carbon dioxide and water.

Sugars other than glucose are metabolized also. Thus all the major categories of human foods contain energy, and all can be oxidized to release it (Fig. 5.13).

NUTRITION, DIET, AND HEALTH

Earlier we mentioned that from the standpoint of
nutrition, humans are classified as heterotrophs. 60
Organisms as diverse as yeasts and termites are heterotrophs, too, but we cannot survive indefinitely on the same diets that yeasts and termites eat. The food we eat must be in forms that our bodies can use and must include the proper quantities of particular nutrients. Although we can obtain energy from carbohydrates, proteins, or fats, our diet must supply amino acids for protein synthesis and small amounts of vitamins, minerals, and certain fatty acids.

Good health depends on a balanced diet that contains adequate amounts of specific nutrients. Excesses, as well as deficiencies, can lead to disease. In fact, diet-related diseases are among the leading causes of death in the United States. In later chapters, we will explain how diets high in sugar, fat, cholesterol, and salt and low in dietary fiber contribute to heart disease, high blood pressure, tooth decay, and certain forms of cancer. But first, let us explore the basics of nutrition.

Major Dietary Constituents: Form and Function

The bulk of the human diet is oxidized to obtain energy. In the United States today, carbohydrates provide 45 percent of an average individual's energy needs; another 40 percent comes from fats, and the remainder comes from protein. Apparently it makes no difference which nutrients supply energy so long as the use of proteins for energy does not rob the body of its supply of amino acids.

Human energy needs vary with activity. Even at rest a minimum amount of energy is required to maintain the body. This includes energy for internal muscular movements (for example, contraction of the heart), energy for operation of the nervous system, and energy for the synthesis of molecules to replace those that wear out.

By means of the instrument described in Fig. 3.18, the caloric values of many foods have been
62 determined.□ Of all the major food constituents, fats have been shown to have the highest caloric content: 9300 cal/gram. This may be compared with 4100 cal/gram for both carbohydrates and proteins. Keep in mind, however, that although energy is measured as heat, organisms do not use heat to perform most biological work. The heat produced when food is burned in a combustion chamber is only a reflection of the amount of ATP energy that an organism would obtain from the food if it were eaten, digested, absorbed, and metabolized.

The amount of energy needed to satisfy the basal or resting requirements of a human depends on the age, sex, and size of the individual. The average daily requirement for simple maintenance is 1500–2000 kilocalories. Anywhere from 500 to 4000 more may be needed for physical activity and for maintenance of body temperature in a cold environment. A person doing heavy labor may need more than twice as much energy as a sedentary business executive.

Common Denominators. Just as carbohydrates, fats, and proteins can all serve as energy sources, so are they to some extent interconvertible. This is possible because the Krebs cycle is reversible. Not only do substances enter the cycle to be oxidized, but also the Krebs cycle and other metabolic pathways can be reversed to allow the manufacture of cellular building blocks (Fig. 5.13). Thus glucose and proteins can be converted into fat. Similarly, fats and proteins can be used to synthesize glucose. Conversion of glucose or fat into certain amino acids is possible, but only if there is an adequate supply of amino groups. Normally we acquire these by eating protein and transferring amino groups from the constituent amino acids to metabolic mill components to synthesize other amino acids. Some important amino acids cannot be synthesized and must be eaten in the diet.

Building Blocks for Growth and Repair. Although proteins can serve as an energy source, they are much more important as raw material for growth and repair of body tissues. Human proteins contain 20 different amino acids, of which we can synthesize only 10. Those that we cannot synthesize are the **essential amino acids** and must be present in our diet. Consequently, we must eat enough protein to supply us with these amino acids.

A strictly protein diet must provide enough protein to meet all energy needs and the need for essential amino acids as well. On the other hand, if we eat only enough protein for normal growth and repair but insufficient carbohydrate or fat to supply energy, some of the precious protein will be oxidized for that purpose. The resulting shortage of amino acids will result in protein deficiencies that impair health.

Because various proteins differ in their content of essential amino acids, not all foods are adequate sources of raw material for synthesis of human proteins. Meat and such animal products as milk and eggs contain almost the same ratio of essential amino acids as do human tissue. Unfortunately, the same is not true of plant proteins.

Some plant foods are markedly deficient in one or more essential amino acids. For example, grains, such as wheat, rye, barley, oats, rice, and corn contain little lysine, isoleucine, and tryptophan. However, most legumes, including beans and soybeans, have large amounts of these amino acids, but are low in methionine and cystine. Leafy green vegetables have a good balance of all the essential amino acids except methionine.

People who rely mainly on plants as a source of protein can receive an adequate assortment of amino acids only by combining proteins from several plant sources. Mexicans, for whom beans and corn or beans and rice are dietary staples, are among the many peoples who have evolved nutritionally sound mixtures of complementary foods.

There is convincing evidence to indicate that humans cannot synthesize certain unsaturated fatty acids needed to form some body structures. Fortunately, these **essential fatty acids** are present in nearly all foods and the amounts needed are so minute that deficiencies seldom occur.

Vitamins: Essential in Small Quantities

In comparison with their need for carbohydrates, fats, and proteins, our cells require only tiny amounts of vitamins. The term *vitamin* stresses their "vital" or essential nature. Vitamins are small organic molecules that ordinarily cannot be synthesized in sufficient quantities to meet body needs. Therefore they must be provided in the diet. Vitamins do not serve as building blocks, nor are they energy sources. Each has a highly specialized function. A number are the principal ingredients for the enzyme helpers we call **coenzymes**. Coenzymes usually act as

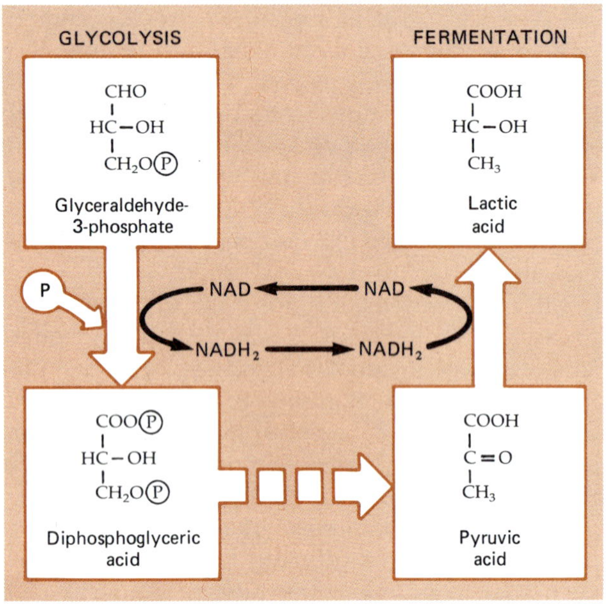

FIGURE 5.14 Action of Coenzymes. NAD is a carrier molecule, shuttling hydrogens between different enzymes according to their needs.

carrier molecules; they pick up chemical groups from one enzyme and pass them on to another (Fig. 5.14).

Although the biochemical roles of many vitamins are established, there is still controversy over the functions of others and over the amounts essential for optimal health. Some highlights concerning well-known vitamins appear in the next paragraphs. Table 5.2 is a more comprehensive list of vitamins important for human health.

Scurvy, Colds, and Vitamin C. In the seventeenth century it was discovered that an ounce or so of lime juice daily would prevent the symptoms of scurvy among seamen; this led to the nickname "limey" for British sailors. The active ingredient in citrus juice turned out to be **ascorbic acid**, also known as **vitamin C**. Just 10 mg/day will alleviate the poor healing of wounds, tender gums, and bleeding that characterize scurvy.

There is still much to be learned about the biological importance of ascorbic acid. It is thought

TABLE 5.2 Vitamins

VITAMIN	NAME	SOME DEFICIENCY SYMPTOMS	SOME SOURCES
A	carotene	dry, flaky skin; night blindness	green or yellow vegetables, fruits, egg yolk, fish-liver oil
B-complex	thiamine (B_1)	beri-beri, paralysis, heart failure, mental confusion	yeast, liver, pork, nuts, whole grains
	riboflavin (B_2)	cataracts, cracked lips and tongue, poor growth	dairy products, yeast, eggs, whole grains
	niacin (B_3)	pellagra, irritability, skin lesions, abdominal pain	meat, yeast, whole grains
	pyridoxine (B_6)	inflamed skin, convulsions	fish, meat, whole grains, fresh vegetables
	cyanocobalamin (B_{12})	anemia	brain, kidney, liver, other meats
	biotin	inflamed skin and eyes, hair loss	liver, eggs, fresh vegetables
	folic acid	anemia	leafy vegetables, liver
	pantothenic acid	numbness of hands and feet, depressed resistance to infection	almost all food
C	ascorbic acid	scurvy, inability to form connective tissues	citrus fruits, tomatoes, brussels sprouts, mustard greens
D	calciferol and other compounds	rickets, defective bone	dairy products, eggs, fish oils

BOX 5A

WHAT WE DON'T KNOW ABOUT HUMAN NUTRITION AND WHY

Nutrition is sometimes treated like an unwanted stepchild of medical science. Part of the problem is historical. Medicine became wedded to science at the beginning of the twentieth century, soon after it was first obvious that many terrible diseases were caused by bacteria or other microorganisms. That discovery revolutionized medicine and made nutrition seem ordinary and uninteresting. Only recently have medical schools again begun to emphasize nutrition in their curricula. Still, people who stress nutrition in medicine are sometimes dismissed as "quacks."

Another part of the problem is the difficulty faced by those who attempt to demonstrate human nutritional needs. Experimentation, especially on children, is hard to justify. Nevertheless, variation among species makes conclusions based solely on laboratory animals open to question.

Furthermore, optimal health is hard to establish, both because it is tough to recognize and because it results from the interaction of many factors. Surely it is tempting to maintain that people able to go about their daily tasks are, by definition, optimally nourished.

Finally, there is no reason to assume that the needs of two individuals of the same age, sex, and activity are identical. Just as there are inherited differences in our external appearances, there are likely to be inherited differences in our biochemistry.

In the face of all these problems, it isn't surprising that people argue about our food requirements. Or that a Nobel prize–winning chemist could find himself in conflict with medical authorities over human nutrition. That is what happened to Linus Pauling a few years ago when he published scientific and popular articles maintaining that optimal health requires larger amounts of vitamin C than has been generally accepted.

Although Pauling acknowledges that only small amounts of vitamin C are necessary to prevent scurvy, he maintains that much larger quantities are essential for optimal human health. According to Pauling, the fruit-eating ancestral primates consumed such large amounts of vitamin C in their diet that the biochemical machinery for making vitamin C became excess baggage that was eliminated through natural selection. His hypothesis is consistent with the observation that all animals except other primates, a few fruit-eating birds, a fruit-eating bat, and the common guinea pig, synthesize vitamin C within their bodies and thus have no need to eat it.

The dependence of humans and certain other species on dietary vitamin C very likely does result from the evolutionary loss of synthetic abilities. It is easy to understand how such a loss might have occurred in an ancestral primate that could rely on fruit for this important vitamin.

Pauling has taken this line of reasoning one step further and calculated the average daily intake of vitamin C from a 2500 calorie diet composed solely of fruit. Depending on the kind of fruit, he obtained values as high as 10 grams a day (a thousand times more than the 10 mg/day necessary to prevent scurvy). Pauling recognizes that 10 grams is many times the average daily amount available to the ancestral primate, but he uses it to emphasize that large dietary supplies were necessary to make obsolete the biosynthetic pathways that manufacture vitamin C.

For this reason Pauling maintains that the daily human requirement is several times greater than the 50–60 mg/day recommended by the U.S. Food and Nutrition Board. As further support, Pauling notes that animals whose diets contain vitamin C at the level recommended retain the ability to synthesize it. Thus the extra vitamin C they make must be of value.

to be involved in oxidation reactions in cells, but the exact role is unclear. More specifically, vitamin C is required for the formation of collagen, the fibrous protein that holds tissues together. Scurvy symptoms result, at least in part, from loosening of the tissue in the absence of this vitamin.

There is some evidence, all of it controversial, that vitamin C can affect heart disease, colds, and even cancer. Ascorbic acid may be involved in cholesterol metabolism and thus in heart disease. (The relationship between cholesterol and heart attacks will be discussed in Chapter 6.) Although some studies indicate that ascorbic acid cannot prevent colds, other data suggest that sufficient vitamin C may shorten the duration of a cold and lessen the symptoms. And although vitamin C may speed processes that rid the body of some cancer-causing chemicals, it may slow the removal of others.

Because so many foods contain little or no vitamin C, we note its presence in substantial quantities in brussels sprouts, mustard greens, and other members of the cabbage family. Probably these were important antiscurvy food for northerners before trade brought oranges, tomatoes, and peppers, all rich in vitamin C. Vitamin C breaks down spontaneously under some conditions. Consequently, stored or cooked products may contain less vitamin C than fresh foods do. This is just one example of how manipulation of foods can reduce their nutritional value.

Thiamine (Vitamin B_1)—a Coenzyme Discarded in Milling. Minor thiamine deficiencies cause loss of appetite and weight. If prolonged, thiamine deficiency leads to degeneration of nerves and, in the extreme, to heart failure. **Beri-beri**, as this condition is called, was once a serious affliction in the Orient, where rice is the staple food. The problem is that when rice is polished, the tough seed coats that contain thiamine are removed. A diet high in polished rice can lead to beri-beri unless the rice is enriched with vitamin B_1. A similar problem involves wheat flour.

A few generations ago, all wheat bread was made with whole flour. Then the development of milling techniques led to the introduction of white flour. Unfortunately, 90 percent of the thiamine is discarded in the milling. Federal law requires that flour and bread be "enriched" by addition of vitamins to at least partially replace those lost in milling. But it is ironic that the additional labor, energy, and expense required to produce refined, enriched flour result in a nutritionally poorer product than our great-grandparents ate.

Thiamine is so widespread in foods that deficiencies occur most often in individuals who rely on highly refined foods or on a very limited variety of nutrients. Some alcoholics fall into the latter category. They may satisfy most of their energy requirements with alcohol and eat very little food containing vitamins. Not surprisingly, many of the physical symptoms associated with severe alcoholism accompanied by malnutrition are relieved by thiamine therapy.

Our bodies use thiamine to make one of the coenzymes involved in the oxidation of pyruvic acid during cellular respiration. Without thiamine, glucose oxidation cannot be completed, and pyruvic and lactic acids accumulate. The poisonous effect of these acids and the decreased energy production because of incomplete glucose oxidation cause the symptoms of thiamine-deficiency disease.

Pellagra, Poverty, and Niacin. Thiamine isn't the only vitamin that acts as a coenzyme in energy metabolism. Niacin, another member of the B complex, forms part of NAD, the hydrogen carrier used in glycolysis and the metabolic mill. This important role of niacin is indicated by the dire symptoms of **pellagra**, a condition that develops in its absence. Mild deficiencies produce inflammation of the skin and the digestive tract, but in its severest form pellagra involves mental aberrations and causes death. Remarkably, the nervousness, insomnia, irritability, suspiciousness, hallucinations, and depression that characterize a severe case of pellagra disappear after only two *days* of niacin therapy.

Like several other vitamins, niacin is widespread in organisms, and deficiencies develop only from unusual diets. Often pellagra can be traced to a diet of corn supplemented with little else. Until the 1930s, pellagra was common among the poor of the American South, for whom cornbread was the staple and who could not afford meat, vegetables, or other cereals. Ordinarily the body absorbs some of the niacin that intestinal bacteria make from the amino acid tryptophan. But corn contains limited tryptophan, as well as little niacin. This situation points out the importance of a balanced diet containing a variety of foods.

Vitamin-A Conversions. The human body not only converts vitamins into key molecules, but also makes some vitamins from other substances. In fact, the definition of certain vitamins is somewhat hazy. Vitamin A is a good example. Although it is available in some animal products, such as liver, milk, and egg yolks, we need not eat vitamin A as such. Instead the body can convert **carotenes**, a widespread group of plant pigments, into vitamin A. Carotenes are abundant in green vegetables, including members of the cabbage family. It is the presence of carotenes that give color to yellow and red fruits and vegetables such as carrots, sweet potatoes, tomatoes, apricots, and beets. This is one reason for the nutritional rule about eating one yellow (or red) vegetable in addition to a green vegetable every day.

Vitamin A apparently has a variety of functions. One use is as a constituent of **rhodopsin**, an eye pigment necessary for vision in dim light. With inadequate vitamin A there is inadequate rhodopsin, and the eye becomes unresponsive to small amounts of light. This symptom of vitamin-A deficiency is sometimes called "night blindness."

Severe shortages of vitamin A lead to increased formation of **keratin**, a fibrous protein normally present in the skin. When vitamin-A deficiency causes keratin to form in the delicate coverings of the eyeball and in the tear gland, these tissues become dry and hard, and blindness can result. Keratinization of the lining of the lungs predisposes people to pneumonia and other respiratory infections. In some developing countries vitamin-A deficiency is a major cause of childhood blindness and death.

Vitamin D—the Sunshine Vitamin. Sunlight transforms certain plant and animal molecules into
62 vitamin D. In fact, the ultraviolet light of sunshine converts a cholesterol-like substance of the skin into vitamin D. Dietary sources of this vitamin include butter, milk, egg yolks, and fish oils. (Cod-liver oil was once a standard dietary supplement.) In addition, many natural foods are fortified with vitamin D. Often such foods carry the label "irradiated ergosterol added." Ergosterol is a cholesterol derivative extracted from yeast. It is added to food, and the food is then exposed to ultraviolet rays, which convert ergosterol to vitamin D. Milk contains a substance similar to ergosterol; as a result, irradiation of milk serves to enrich its vitamin-D content.

People who live in tropical or subtropical areas rarely suffer from inadequate vitamin D. In places where sunlight is limited, some vitamin D must be consumed. In fact, there is a possibility that the very light skin of Eskimos and Scandinavians is an adaptation to take advantage of the available ultraviolet radiations of the far north. Light skin would filter out a minimum of the valuable rays that produce vitamin D.

Vitamin D regulates the use of calcium and phosphorus by the body. It does so by stimulating intestinal cells to absorb these minerals from the food we eat. Vitamin D also controls the deposition of calcium and phosphorus by bone cells. Lack of vitamin D may cause **rickets**, a disease characterized by malformation of growing bones. Although adults need less vitamin D than children do, chronic deficiencies may lead to localized softening of bone even in adults.

Too much vitamin D can be harmful. One effect is calcification or hardening of normally soft tissues. For example, excess vitamin D can cause minerals to accumulate in the kidney, impairing its function. It is quite likely that the dark skin of some races evolved as protection against excessive vitamin-D production. Dark skin is also a protection against skin cancer, which may be caused by overexposure to ultraviolet radiation.

Minerals: Inorganic Nutrients

People seem less obsessed with mineral nutrition than they are with vitamins. Nevertheless, minerals are as essential as vitamins to good health. 79
Mineral imbalance is associated with many chronic diseases, including anemia, infertility, and irregular heart rhythms.

How Cells Use Minerals. Just as vitamins serve as coenzymes, minerals sometimes act as enzyme helpers (Table 5.3). Many enzymes can function

TABLE 5.3 Some Elements Important in Mineral Nutrition

ELEMENT	CHEMICAL SYMBOL	USE IN THE BODY
**Calcium*	Ca	bone structure, enzyme function
**Chlorine*	Cl	nerve and muscle function
Chromium	Cr	insulin function
Cobalt	Co	enzyme function
Copper	Cu	essential for some oxidative enzymes
Fluorine	F	strength of teeth and bone
Iodine	I	thyroid hormone structure
Iron	Fe	hemoglobin and cytochrome structure
**Magnesium*	Mg	enzyme function, bone structure
Manganese	Mn	enzyme function
**Phosphorus*	P	bone structure; found in many organic molecules, including ATP and nucleic acids
**Potassium*	K	nerve and muscle function
Selenium	Se	liver function
**Sodium*	Na	nerve and muscle function, absorption of nutrients
Zinc	Zn	enzyme function

*Major nutrients required in large amounts

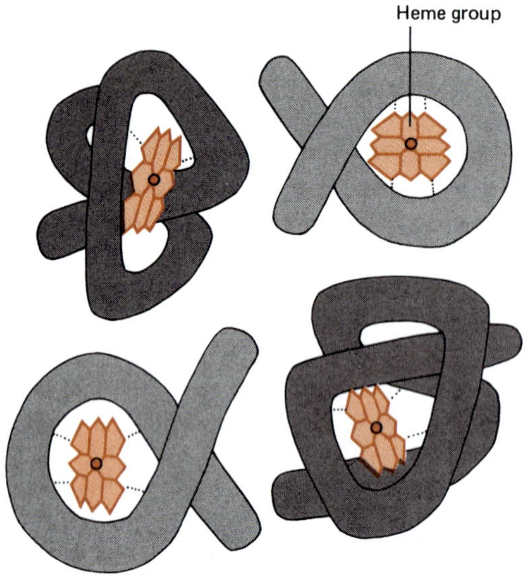

FIGURE 5.15 **Hemoglobin and Iron.** The globin, or protein, part of a hemoglobin molecule consists of an association of two alpha (α) and two beta (β) polypeptide chains as shown schematically here. An iron-containing structure, or *heme*, is bound to the center of each chain. The four heme units bind four molecules of oxygen.

only in a specific ionic environment. For example, **calcium** ions are necessary for a crucial step in blood clotting. Minerals also serve to activate various processes. Inside muscle cells, calcium is concentrated in membranous compartments and released as the final step in a chain of messages that lead to contraction.

Many mineral elements become parts of organic molecules. Probably most readers know that **iron** is necessary for healthy blood. The reason is that hemoglobin, the molecule that carries oxygen in red blood cells, contains iron (Fig. 5.15). And recall (Fig. 5.10) that iron is a component of the cytochromes of the mitochondrial respiratory chain. **Phosphorus** is another element needed to manufacture organic molecules. As we have seen, ADP becomes highly charged with energy when it adds a third phosphate to form ATP.

The thyroid gland in the neck incorporates **iodine** into a hormone it secretes. Through secretion of this hormone, the thyroid gland is able to regulate cellular respiration. Iodine deficiencies result in lower levels of the thyroid hormone and thus lowered metabolism and even mental dulling. Severe deficiencies during pregnancy result in drastic mental retardation in the offspring. These children, known as **cretins**, are hopelessly handicapped intellectually.

Other symptoms of iodine deficiency include abnormal growth of the thyroid itself. Through a feedback mechanism, inadequate hormone production stimulates increased size of the gland, which in turn increases hormone production if iodine is present. But in the absence of iodine the growth is futile and results only in an enlarged thyroid, which protrudes in the front of the neck as a **goiter**.

Bone as a Special Mineral Store. Cells deposit calcium and phosphorus around themselves in the course of bone development. This process makes bone hard, of course, but it provides more than skeletal support. Bone serves as a reservoir of calcium and phosphorus from which the living cells extract and circulate these minerals as they are needed elsewhere in the body. This dynamic equilibrium between bone and the rest of the body ensures adequate calcium and phosphorus when there are temporary shortages in the diet. Problems develop when prolonged dietary deficiencies weaken bone by draining away the minerals. Teeth contain similar mineral deposits and also participate in this exchange.

Because of the need of calcium and phosphorus to form bones and teeth, infants need tremendous amounts of these minerals if they are to grow normally. Usually the need is met by the high mineral content of milk. However, milk production makes a large demand on the mother's body. Nursing mothers must eat well in order to maintain their own health, because they are obliged to supply calcium and phosphorus, even at the expense of withdrawing materials from their own teeth and bones. This drain begins while the baby is growing in the uterus.

As important as calcium and phosphorus are to teeth and bones, the crystals there should also contain traces of other minerals, particularly **fluorine**. The incorporation of fluorine into the calcium phosphate crystal dramatically increases the strength of the crystal. As a matter of fact, individuals living in areas where this trace element is present in the water have fewer dental cavities than do those living in areas where the fluoride level is extremely low.

Mineral Sources. All cells, whether from plants or animals, have similar mineral requirements. And most organisms use them in about the same proportions. Thus a diet adequate in other respects is likely to supply all the minerals we ordinarily need. Most mineral deficiencies involve elements that are usable only in specific forms or elements that we absorb poorly. Important examples are calcium and iron.

We have already mentioned the importance of vitamin D to proper absorption and utilization of calcium and phosphorus. Although the cause is uncertain, calcium absorption varies with the kind of food eaten. For instance, despite the fact that cow's milk contains four times more calcium than human milk does, children do not absorb calcium as readily from cow's milk as they do from human milk. Therefore infants drinking cow's milk have greater needs for vitamin D.

The form of iron we eat makes a large difference in whether or not it is absorbed. The environment of the digestive tract is also important. Inorganic **ferrous iron**, which carries two positive charges, is the easiest to absorb. Acid in the stomach helps convert iron into the ferrous form. On the other hand, a high concentration of calcium or phosphorus in the diet reduces iron absorption. Some foods contain organic molecules that tend to combine with inorganic iron and make it less absorbable.

Of course, iron deficiencies are not due totally to poor absorption. Some diets are inherently low in iron. Milk contains little iron, and babies who are maintained too long on an unsupplemented milk diet will suffer from **anemia**—that is, low hemoglobin. In the United States, alone, iron-deficiency anemias occur at a rate as high as one in every three children between the ages of 4 and 24 months.

Menstrual blood loss and inadequate iron intake explain why iron-deficiency anemias are distressingly common among women of reproductive age. Persistent dieting can further aggravate this problem by reducing the amount of iron consumed.

Distribution of Trace Elements. Some elements are needed in quite small amounts by organisms. These **trace elements** are often rare or scattered unevenly through the biosphere. We have already mentioned that local deficiencies of fluorine have adverse effects on tooth structure.

The fluorine content of water ordinarily reflects the amount of this trace element in the surrounding soil and rock. Some communities now add minute amounts of sodium fluoride to their water supplies to ensure better tooth development and reduce cavities. Controversy surrounds this practice, partly because larger doses of fluorine are poisonous, and even small excesses cause defective bone crystals. Another reason is that some people object to having no personal control over the supplementation.

Although **iodine** is rare on land (Fig. 5.16), it is abundant in the ocean. Soil iodine comes almost entirely from particles thrown into the air by ocean

FIGURE 5.16 Distribution of Iodine. A deficiency of iodine in food and water supplies in certain parts of the world (darkened areas) can make goiters a common disease unless iodized salt is used. What parts of the United States are likely regions of iodine deficiency?

spray and carried worldwide by the wind. The iodine falls out of the air, but of course, coastal areas receive more than do inland regions. Although it plays no known role in plants, iodine is absorbed by roots and distributed throughout the plant. Then iodine is carried through the food chain by animals that eat the plants. Naturally, sea foods contain more iodine than do foods grown on the land. Likewise foods grown in coastal regions have higher iodine concentrations than those grown in inland areas. Fortunately the use of iodized table salt ensures adequate amounts of iodine with no apparent risk.

Many other trace elements are similarly absorbed and distributed by plants.

HUNGER AND MALNUTRITION

According to some estimates, as much as one-half to two-thirds of the world's population is poorly nourished. Malnutrition is not just a problem of getting *enough* to eat. There are a variety of causes, including some you may not have considered. For example, malnutrition can come from *over*nutrition. In the United States and elsewhere, many people suffer from diabetes, hypertension, obesity, and other ill effects of rich diets. Yet even as they grow fat from overindulgence, these people may suffer from deficiency diseases because one or more essential nutrients are missing from their meals. The sad fact is that while some people are eating too well and others are eating foolishly, many more are facing a severe food shortage.

More Mouths than Food

Agricultural production is seriously deficient in many countries of Latin America, Asia, and Africa. And these countries have very little money to buy what surplus food may be available in world markets. Four hundred million people are said to exist on near-starvation diets. Worse yet, according to the World Health Organization, 12,000 people starve to death every day of the year!

Without doubt, one of the most pressing human problems in the world today is human hunger. It is a predicament of ever-increasing proportions because of spiraling population growth. An astounding million and a half new mouths must be fed each week. And although chronic hunger is debilitating in young and old alike, it is the children that are most harmed by malnutrition.

Suffering Little Children

The causes of infant and childhood malnutrition are complex. Some cases result from ignorance or ingrained cultural patterns. Others directly reflect food shortages. But whatever the cause, malnutrition in childhood hampers normal physical and mental development. Children who are inadequately nourished can be handicapped as adults.

A Poor Start in Life. Normally a mother's milk meets the needs of her newborn child, but within a few months the quantity of her milk becomes insufficient, and the child requires substances such as iron that aren't present in milk. In most of the developing countries, the supplements provided during the first year or two of life are inadequate. Many cultures make little or no effort to prepare foods specifically for the young child. Infants merely receive occasional bits of the adult fare, apparently more to accustom them to the taste and consistency than to nourish them. In the event that special foods are provided for babies, they usually consist of gruels of high-carbohydrate and low-protein substances, such as bananas, yams, or sugar cane. Nutritious portions of the adult diet are commonly forbidden to young children in the mistaken belief that they are harmful. Thus the children more often than not receive a nutritionally poor start in life, even when food supplies are adequate. The harm can be dramatic and permanent.

Kwashiorkor—a Belly Full of Empty Calories. Children can get plenty to eat but still be badly nourished. This happens when the diet contains too little protein. Indeed, protein deficiency accompanied by considerable caloric intake is in some ways *worse* than total starvation. The child may appear plump, though small, but can be seriously ill with **kwashiorkor**. The name derives from the Ghan language and means "the sickness the older child gets when the next child is born." In other words, it is a disease of weaning.

If the diet contains calories but little protein, any amino acids that are available must be used to synthesize the enzymes needed to digest and use the calorie-containing food. This function takes first priority for amino acids; none may be left for building proteins for cell growth. Eventually, there may not even be enough amino acids to supply the digestive system, and the organs degenerate.

Kwashiorkor victims typically have badly bloated bellies, because their tissues become filled with water. The blood of kwashiorkor victims contains so little protein that the circulation is hampered. Fluids stagnate in the tissues, and the body swells.

Empty Stomachs. It is bad enough not to get necessary vitamins and minerals or enough protein, but a diet that is low in calories as well means true starvation. Children with extreme protein-calorie deficiencies are emaciated and dwarfed. The condition is known as **marasmus**. With less severe starvation, growth is slow. Poorly fed children are always small for their age.

The effect of childhood nutrition on adult stature and weight can be seen from observations of Japanese-American children. Early Japanese immigrants were small people, much shorter and lighter than Americans of other backgrounds. Over the past three generations the living standards of these people have improved, and so have the growth rates of their children. Unlike their grandparents, the young Japanese-Americans of today are not much smaller than U.S. citizens of other ethnic extraction. Something similar has happened in Japan itself. Recent years have been prosperous ones for the Japanese—so prosperous, in fact, that the present generation of young people are markedly taller and heavier than their forebears. What were once thought to be genetically determined differences of height and weight were largely reflections of early childhood diet.

With malnutrition comes increased susceptibility to childhood diseases and illnesses. Early death may come not from starvation itself but from sickness. Sadly, those who survive marasmus are usually mentally dull or even retarded.

Experiments with dogs show that severe amino acid deficiencies in the diet of the pregnant mother or the newborn result in drastic disorders of the nervous system. Because the human brain completes most of its growth by six months after birth, it is little wonder that the absence of adequate building materials early in life results in mental retardation. The end result of inadequate nutrition is inadequate bodies and stunted minds.

You Are What You Eat

Our food, like ourselves, consists mostly of water, minerals, and organic compounds. Only inorganic compounds are abundant in the physical environment. Organic molecules are rarely found in the world outside cells or cell products. Green plants photosynthesize organic molecules from inorganic raw materials. They are thus the primary source of organic compounds for most other forms of life. They are the basis of every
11 food chain.□

Humans and other heterotrophs can make organic constituents only when organic raw materials are available. Since cells are the only
61 sources of such organic matter, heterotrophs□ can obtain it only by feeding on others. And because cells contain water and minerals, too, they can supply these inorganic constituents. Heterotrophs consume plant and animal cells or cell products, break them down, use some parts outright, and rebuild others into forms suitable for their own existence. You might say that people and other heterotrophs are reconstructionists.

Our specifically human nutritional needs are determined by the metabolic machinery of our bodies. Human cells lack the enzymes needed to manufacture certain molecules that are necessary to life. These molecules, in addition to water, minerals, and energy sources, must be present in the food we eat if our cells are to survive. But basically all cells have the same nutritional needs: water and sources of carbon, energy, nitrogen, minerals, and sometimes growth factors such as vitamins. Not surprisingly, then, most cells—at least, most heterotrophic cells—have a similar metabolism.

Glycolysis and respiration occur in yeast cells as well as in muscle cells. The metabolic mill is a crossroad of degradative and synthetic metabolic routes in nearly every organism. And since many aspects of metabolism are widely shared, many enzymes are found in all cells. Other enzymes are unique, giving cells that have them distinctive metabolic characteristics. Different metabolic capabilities account for the specialization of cells in different tissues, as well as for the differences among organisms.

Summary

1. The chemical reactions that take place in cells are collectively called metabolism. The two major aspects of metabolism, degradation and synthesis, proceed in a stepwise fashion, each step controlled by an enzyme.

2. Enzymes are specific protein catalysts that promote metabolic reactions by reducing the activation energy necessary for a reaction to occur. Binding of substrate to the enzyme's active site hastens the formation of product molecules. Enzyme structure and function are sensitive to heat and to a variety of chemical agents that cause denaturation.

3. Among the most important enzymatic reactions are dehydrogenations, biological oxidations that yield energy that can be captured to make ATP. An energy-transfer compound, ATP can donate its energy to metabolic reactions, such as synthetic reactions, that require energy.

4. Most cells obtain ATP from the oxidation of glucose in the process of cellular respiration. The first stage of respiration, called glycolysis, occurs in the cytoplasm. Glycolysis is an anaerobic process that degrades glucose to pyruvic acid but produces very little ATP. In the second stage of respiration, which occurs in the mitochondria, pyruvic acid is completely oxidized to carbon dioxide via the Krebs cycle. At the same time, large amounts of ATP are produced in the respiratory chain.

5. The oxidation of pyruvic acid in mitochondria requires oxygen. In muscle cells, lack of oxygen may result in the conversion of pyruvic acid to lactic acid, a slightly toxic substance that inhibits muscular contraction when it accumulates. The formation of alcohol from sugar by yeast is a similar incomplete oxidation, or fermentation.

6. Although carbohydrates, fats, and proteins can all serve as energy sources, proteins are more important as the source of amino-acid building blocks for the growth and repair of tissues. A balanced diet is important, because it must supply substances the body cannot synthesize. These include 10 of the 20 amino acids, certain fatty acids, vitamins, and minerals. No one food can supply all these needs.

7. Vitamins play an essential role in metabolism. However, none are needed in large amounts, although their absence in the diet can lead to severe deficiency diseases. Vitamins are neither building blocks nor energy sources. Several—niacin and thiamine, for example—are coenzymes necessary to the function of particular enzymes.

8. Minerals are inorganic nutrients also needed in very small amounts. A number of minerals act as metabolic activators. Some enzymes require specific minerals in order to function.

9. Malnutrition is one of the most important problems of the world today and is likely to continue to be so because of the population explosion and the limitations of agriculture. Among the most serious consequences of poor nutrition is the hampered physical and mental development of children who suffer from kwashiorkor and marasmus.

Thought and Controversy

1. Frances Moore Lappé, in her popular book *Diet for a Small Planet,* points out U.S. Department of Agriculture data indicating that many Americans eat much more protein than they need. Furthermore, it is mostly animal protein. The cattle, chicken, sheep, and hogs that supply our meat consume even greater quantities of plant protein. Lappé suggests that we might better eat the plant protein ourselves, and she offers tables and recipes to aid in planning nonmeat menus providing adequate amounts and properly balanced ratios of amino acids. Is this suggestion sound nutritionally? Ecologically? Would the adoption of such a diet by large portions of the population be more or less expensive than the present high-meat diet? Lappé also notes that the United States imports both meat and animal food from other countries, including those whose own citizens are often extremely poorly nourished. If this trade were reduced, how might it affect the economies of those countries?

2. Not many years ago "reverence for life" was a popular ethic that well-educated American parents sought to instill in their children. Partly as a result, young adults of today show considerable interest in vegetarian diets and often remonstrate against the killing of animals for classroom study or research. Can a meaningful distinction be drawn between the life we are permitted to destroy and the life we ought not to destroy? How many wheat embryos are ground and cooked to make a loaf of bread? Is it ethically sounder to eat many organisms lower on the food chain or to eat fewer ones of higher rank? Is the human omnivore charged with responsibilities different from those of a hawk or a bass or a bear? Can we base our decision on the original way of life of our species? Is our present way any less natural than the earlier one? Is the use of higher animals for food defensible, whereas the killing of animals for teaching or research is not? Why do so many people who readily squash a fly or a cockroach feel revulsion at the killing of higher vertebrates? Is the common hesitance about killing animals biologically determined or simply learned? Is it hard for humans to learn to kill other humans, or must they be taught *not* to harm other people? Is it possible for humans both to revere life and to destroy other animals? Although you may not have answers to these questions now, ponder them from time to time as you continue your study.

3. It seems clear that the mental symptoms associated with pellagra arise from the absence of sufficient niacin in the microenvironment of certain brain cells. Furthermore, there is good evidence that protein or iodine deficiencies either before or after birth can cause mental retardation. As we shall see later, a wide variety of genetic and environmental disturbances during development produce mental defects, probably because normal development and function of the nervous system require many complex series of interactions. Consequently, mental health can be sabotaged at innumerable points. One is left to wonder how many other mental diseases or conditions have their roots in nutritional inadequacies.

4. A famous socialite once said, "You can never be too rich or too thin." In our culture thinness is equated with youth, good looks, and a healthy athleticism. But you can be too thin. You can make yourself sick trying to be thinner than is healthy for your height and bone structure. Distorted perceptions of appearance and low self-esteem have led some young women into a psychological quagmire of eating disorders. Bulimia is a binge-purge phenomenon in which eating huge amounts of food is followed by self-induced vomiting and excessive use of laxatives. Anorexia nervosa is more serious. This compulsive self-starvation continues even though the victim is visibly starving to death. And without medical help that is exactly what happens. Apparently for cultural reasons, bulimia and anorexia primarily afflict young women. Some authorities have suggested that the male equivalent of anorexia is exhibited by runners who are particularly compulsive about their exercise regimen.

Questions

1. Use the terms *active site* and *activation energy* to explain why enzymes are good catalysts.

2. Of what value is feedback regulation to cells?

3. Why is the term *energy currency* an apt description for ATP?

4. How are glycolysis and cellular respiration similar? Different?

5. Explain the role of coenzymes such as NAD in cellular respiration. How do the Krebs cycle and the respiratory chain contribute to an NAD–$NADH_2$ cycle?

6. In which cellular compartments do glycolysis, the Krebs cycle, and the respiratory chain occur? Which of these metabolic pathways produces the most ATP?

7. Why is the Krebs cycle sometimes called the metabolic mill?

8. What substances must be included in a balanced diet? Identify those dietary components that supply carbon building blocks, energy, and nitrogen.

9. Give several examples that distinguish between the roles of vitamins and minerals in human nutrition.

10. What forms of childhood malnutrition have the most serious consequences? Why?

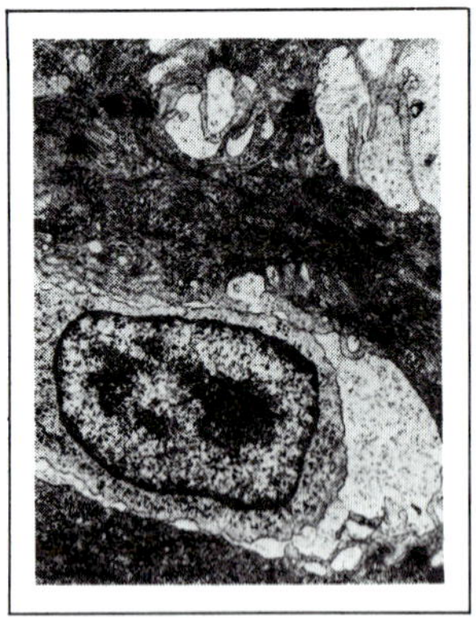

6

Circulation and Gas Exchange: Contributions to a Constant Internal Environment

TO PRIMITIVE ONE-CELLED CREATURES, TRANSport means getting things in and out and around and about inside themselves. Human cells have similar transport functions, but their lives are complicated by our multicellular form. Consider just one example: Few of our cells live close enough to the outside of our bodies to get oxygen and nutrients directly. Simple diffusion is not enough for moving nutrients through multiple cell layers. Our cells depend on transport systems. The circulatory system, with the help of the lymphatic system, provides them with these essentials of life—and, as we shall see, with much more.

FIGURE 6.1 **Plasma and Serum.** Plasma is the liquid part of blood. Serum is the liquid left after blood has clotted. It has a composition similar to plasma, except that the proteins that enable the blood to clot are missing.

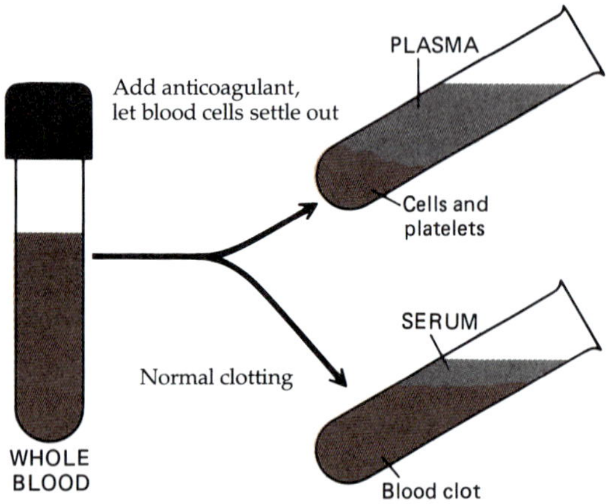

BLOOD AND CIRCULATION

The chief function of the circulatory system is to carry substances from place to place within the body. In so doing, it helps maintain a stable, healthy environment for our cells. This it does, in part, by keeping them supplied with food, oxygen, and water, and by carrying away the wastes of cellular metabolism. Furthermore, the circulatory routes make excellent communication channels. Among the substances distributed by the circulation are hormones, which coordinate cellular functions, and antibodies and other agents, which help fight off infections. Basically the circulatory system consists of a transporting fluid, **blood**; a network of **vessels**, through which blood flows; and a **heart**, a pump that keeps the blood moving.

Blood

A simple pinprick proves that we are well supplied with blood. The average person has five or six liters (that's 10–12 pints). From a biological standpoint,
blood is tissue—a liquid tissue whose red and white 92
cells float in a yellowish fluid called **plasma** (Fig. 6.1).

Plasma. Plasma is the blood minus the blood cells. This liquid makes up slightly more than half the total volume of the blood. Like other body fluids, plasma consists mostly of **water**. The remainder consists of **proteins, salts, nutrients,** and **waste products** dissolved in water.

Although plasma is more than 90 percent water, the presence of proteins gives it a much thicker consistency than it would otherwise have. Plasma proteins are not nutrients. Instead, they are important in maintaining blood flow and in blood clotting. In addition, some of the plasma proteins are antibodies, whose function is to fight infection.

The chief nutrient carried in blood plasma is **glucose**, or blood sugar. Normally the blood-sugar level is about 0.1 percent. Other useful substances transported by the plasma include fats, cholesterol, amino acids, vitamins, and hormones. There are wastes, too—among them, urea. The liver synthesizes urea from carbon dioxide and ammonia, a noxious substance released when amino acids are broken down for energy.

53 A wide variety of mineral ions□ gives blood its slightly salty taste. Of special importance are chloride, carbonate, phosphate, and sulfate, frequently found in combination with sodium, calcium, potassium, and magnesium. Beyond satisfying the mineral requirements of cells, some of the salt ions
57 act as buffers□ to prevent undesirable chemical changes in the blood. Carbonates, for instance, neutralize potentially harmful acidic waste products.

The amount of dissolved substances in the plasma counterbalances the amount of dissolved substances found inside the blood cells. This must be so if the cells are to remain intact. For example, if blood is diluted with plain water, the water
77 diffuses□ into the slightly salty cell interior. The cells gradually swell to bursting. Just the opposite happens when cells are placed in a very concentrated salt solution. The blood cells shrivel up, because they lose their own water to the environment. Physiological saline is a salt solution that contains the same amounts and kinds of salts as are normally present in blood plasma. When blood is lost but the loss is not too severe, such saline may be used as a replacement fluid if whole blood or plasma is not available.

In a healthy person the chemical composition of the blood plasma stays relatively constant. Although nutrients are always being used, they are also being continuously replenished from the food stores of the body. At the same time, the levels of hormones and of some other substances change intermittently according to body activities.

Blood Cells. Blood is red because most of the cells in the plasma are filled with **hemoglobin**, an iron-containing red pigment. The oxygen-carrying function of **red blood cells** (Fig. 6.2) is due to the oxygen-carrying capacity of hemoglobin. In fact, the normal mature red blood cell contains little else but hemoglobin. It is devoid of a nucleus, mitochondria, and most other standard cell organelles. Although the extra space makes red blood cells very efficient transport vehicles, it contributes to their short life span. The average red blood cell lives barely over 120 days.

FIGURE 6.2 **Blood Cells.** Red blood cells (rbc); several white blood cells, including a lymphocyte (l), a monocyte (m), and a neutrophil (n); and many small disc-shaped platelets (p) can be seen in this preparation.

In the last chapter, we observed that anemia occurs when there is insufficient hemoglobin to carry the oxygen needed by the body. This condition can result from nutritional imbalances, decreased red blood cell production, or abnormal destruction of red blood cells.

Although ingestion of lead inhibits hemoglobin synthesis, the subnormal amounts of hemoglobin found in **dietary anemia** arise from inadequate iron and vitamin B_{12} consumption. People with **pernicious anemia** suffer from an insufficiency of a gastric secretion that promotes the absorption of vitamin B_{12} and folic acid into the blood.

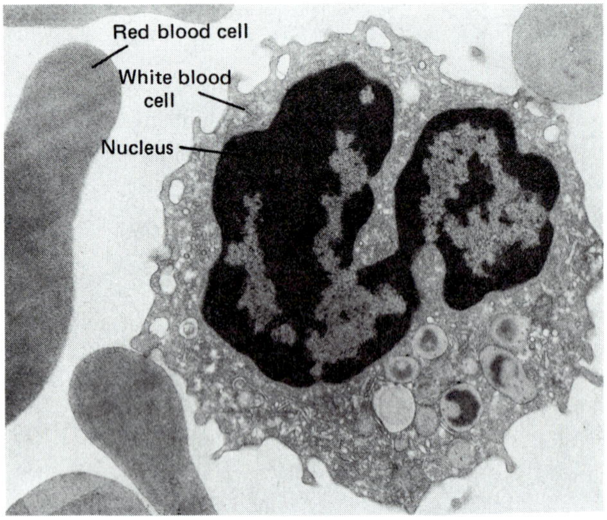

FIGURE 6.3 **Internal Structure of Blood Cells.** Note the absence of organelles in red blood cells.

In treatment of pernicious anemia, normal red blood cell production is stimulated by injections of vitamin B_{12} and folic acid.

Rupture of red blood cells characterizes **hemolytic anemia**. Many factors, including drug use and infection, can contribute to increased fragility of red blood cell membranes. The source of **jaundice**, a yellowish discoloration of the skin and whites of the eyes that accompanies hemolytic anemia, is described in Chapter 7.

Most often, people suffering from anemia have a pale appearance and experience endless fatigue. A half-liter (pint) of normal blood contains about 2500 billion (2,500,000,000,000) red blood cells, but only 3.5 billion (3,500,000,000) **white blood cells**. White blood cells are usually about twice as large as red blood cells. Furthermore, they are complete cells, containing all the organelles absent from their red counterparts (Fig. 6.3). The function of white blood cells is indicated by the fact that their numbers increase dramatically in the event of an infection. Most, if not all, of the five kinds of white blood cells are involved in defending the body against infection or foreign matter.

The protective function of white blood cells is accomplished in two ways. Many white blood cells are phagocytes, which destroy bacteria, cell debris, and other unwanted particles by engulfing and digesting them (Fig. 6.4). Other white blood cells are lymphocytes, which produce antibodies and have other related protective functions. These will be examined in Chapter 10.

Neutrophils are the main blood phagocytes. Any out-of-the-ordinary increase in the number of neutrophils in the blood is an indication of a serious infection. Neutrophils and other blood phagocytes can circulate in the bloodstream, or, when neces-

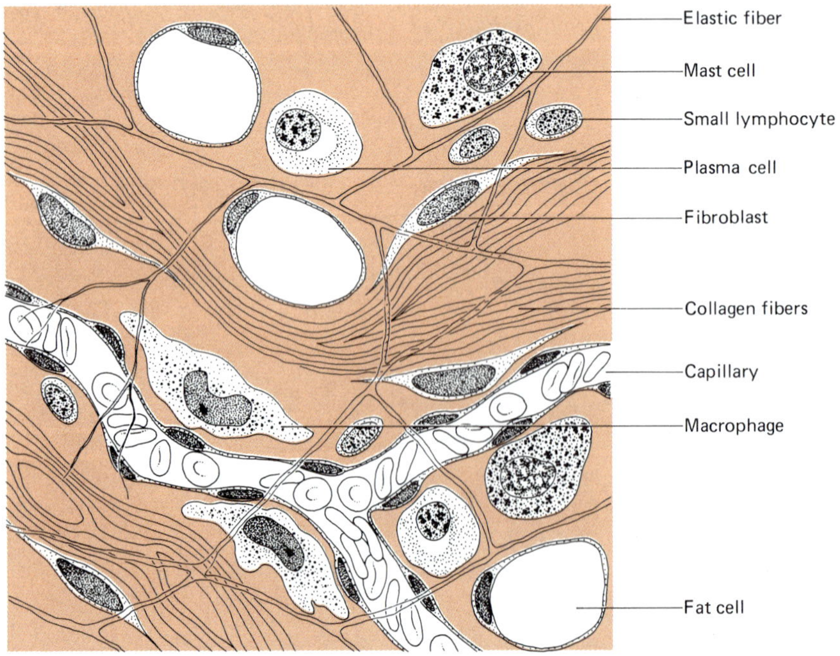

FIGURE 6.4 **White Blood Cells Are Not Restricted to the Blood.** Examination of connective tissue reveals many migrating white blood cells among the regular residents, some of whom are white blood cells permanently stationed there.

sary, they can squeeze through the narrow spaces between the cells of small blood vessels to reach their prey. Neutrophils rapidly accumulate at the site of an infection.

Because red and white blood cells age so rapidly, they must be constantly replaced. This renewal process continues throughout our lifetime. Most blood cells originate in the **bone marrow**. The rapidly dividing progenitor cells there are easily poisoned. Industrial pollutants such as benzene and arsenic can depress or destroy these bone-marrow cells. So can numerous drugs, including antihistamines and antibiotics. This is one reason why labels on many over-the-counter drugs caution against prolonged use except under the scrutiny of a physician. Drugs with high risk of this side effect are available only on prescription. Cancer of the bone-marrow tissue that produces white blood cells is known as **leukemia**. The blood becomes clogged with useless, immature white blood cells and production of red blood cells is suppressed. Thus, in leukemia the fatal blow is often the severe anemia that results.

Platelets are disk-shaped cell fragments produced by fragmentation of giant bone marrow progenitor cells. They initiate the blood-clotting process.

How Blood Clots. When a small blood vessel is damaged, its muscular walls constrict rapidly. Whereas platelets show no tendency to stick to the normally smooth lining of blood vessels, they do adhere to rough, damaged tissue. As the platelets aggregate, they form a plug; this plug may be sufficient to stop the flow of blood out of the smallest vessels.

The temporary platelet plug is then bound by threads of **fibrin**, a protein precipitated out of plasma. Formation of a fibrin clot involves a complex cascade of reactions whereby a soluble plasm protein, **fibrinogen**, is converted into a dense network of fibrin strands. The resulting blood clot consists of a network of yellowish fibrin molecules and trapped blood cells (Fig. 6.5).

The entire sequence of events that leads to the clotting of blood is triggered initially by the release of **thromboplastin** from damaged cells. Acted upon by a secretion of plugged platelets, thromboplastin, in the presence of calcium, gives rise to **thrombin**, an enzyme that converts fibrinogen to fibrin.

Table 6.1 summarizes the steps involved in blood clotting. These steps must be interrupted if blood is to be collected and saved for transfusions. **Citrate**, an anticoagulant, binds calcium and thus prevents the cascade of clotting reactions when added to collected blood samples. Natural anticoagulants of the circulatory system help protect the body against accidental triggering of the clotting mechanism, but unfortunately they cannot always prevent the development of potentially harmful blood clots.

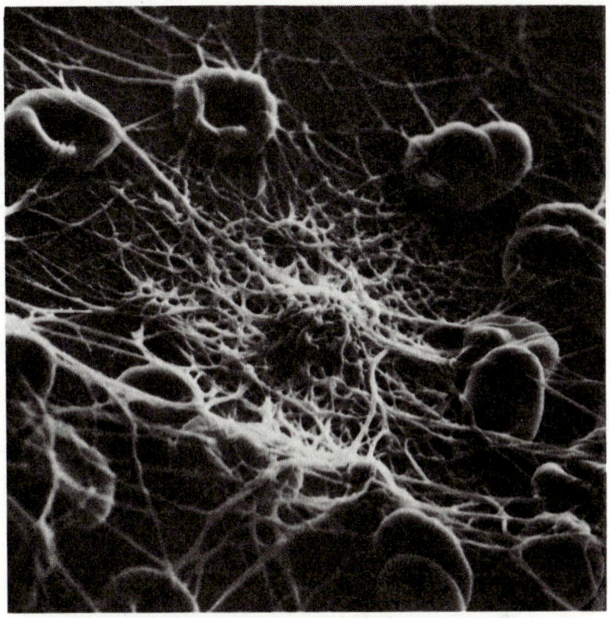

FIGURE 6.5 **A Blood Clot.** Red blood cells become entangled in masses of fibrin threads.

Blood Vessels

There are three kinds of blood vessels. Blood is carried away from the heart by **arteries**. The main arteries divide into smaller and smaller branches,

TABLE 6.1 **The Cascade of Reactions that Cause Blood Clotting**

1. Platelets adhere to collagen fibers of damaged tissue.
2. Cells of damaged tissue release thromboplastin.
3. An activator secreted by platelets combines with thromboplastin.
4. In the presence of calcium, thromboplastin catalyzes the formation of the enzyme *thrombin*.
5. Thrombin converts the soluble fibrinogen of plasma into an insoluble network of fibrin strands.
6. The web-like fibrin clot, which may catch red blood cells, contracts and pulls the ruptured blood-vessel walls together.

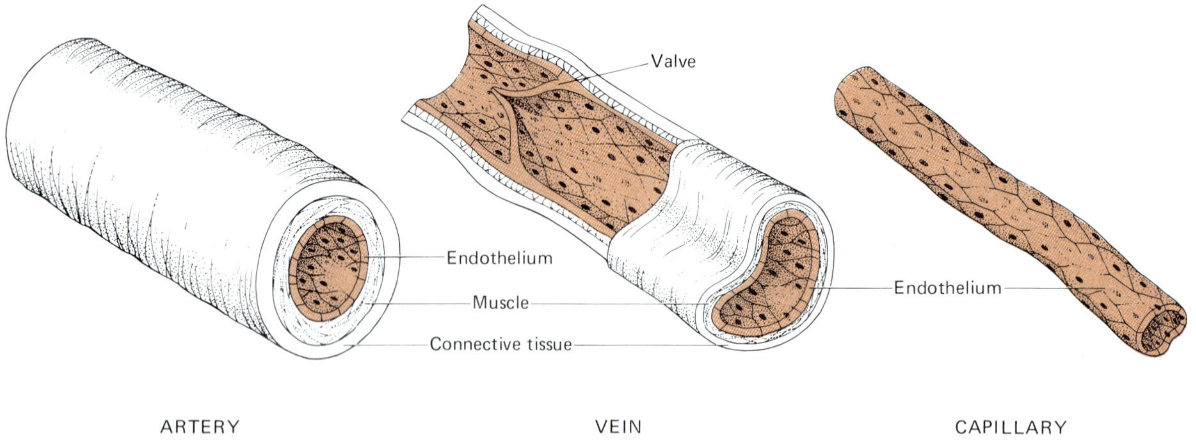

FIGURE 6.6 **Arteries, Veins, and Capillaries.**

eventually ending in fine **capillaries**. Blood flows through capillaries into tiny **veins**, which lead to larger veins and back to the heart.

Arteries and Veins. Both arteries and veins are lined on the inside by a single layer of flattened cells, the **endothelium** (Fig. 6.6). Surrounding the endothelium is a layer of muscle, which is itself covered by a fibrous supporting tissue. In general, arteries have much thicker, stronger, and more elastic walls than do veins. Arteries are built to be resilient. They can "give" in response to surges of blood, and they can expand or contract to help control the flow of blood.

Unlike arteries, thin-walled veins collapse when they are empty. Veins are equipped with valves that open toward the heart, and thus they channel blood only in that direction. When these valves become weakened, blood tends to stagnate in the veins. This may cause swollen or **varicose veins**, which can be extremely painful.

Phlebitis, or inflammation of a vein, may result in sufficient damage to stimulate formation of a blood clot. Death can result if a clot in a vein breaks loose and is carried to the lung, where it can block an artery.

Capillaries. Arteries and veins are merely tubes that carry blood to and from the capillaries, where the real work of the circulatory system takes place. Nutrients, oxygen, carbon dioxide, and other substances are exchanged between the bloodstream and the tissues across the walls of capillaries. Exchanges are facilitated because capillary walls consist of only a single layer of endothelium.

Every organ and most tissues of the body contain an extensive bed of capillaries. As a matter of fact, capillaries are so numerous that few body cells are far away from flowing blood. Even the walls of arteries and veins are served by their own capillaries. Most capillaries are very narrow, just wide enough to permit the passage of red blood cells.

The flow of blood into a capillary bed is controlled by a miniature muscular ring, or sphincter, at the place where a small artery branches into capillaries. All the capillary beds of the body are not open all the time. For example, relatively few capillaries are open in the digestive tract except after a meal. And more capillaries are open in a working muscle than in a relaxed one.

Circulatory Pathways. The blood circulation of humans and of other mammals essentially involves two pathways (Fig. 6.7). In the **pulmonary pathway**, arteries transport dark red blood, poor in oxygen, from the heart to the lungs. There the blood is rejuvenated with oxygen as it courses through the capillaries of the lungs. From the lungs, bright red blood is returned to the heart via the pulmonary veins. Thus the pulmonary arteries carry *deoxygenated* blood, and the pulmonary veins carry *oxygenated* blood.

In the **systemic pathway**, the heart pumps oxygenated blood to the tissues. Blood leaves the heart through the **aorta**, a large artery that sends its many branches to all parts of the body. Systemic veins return deoxygenated blood to the heart (Fig. 6.8).

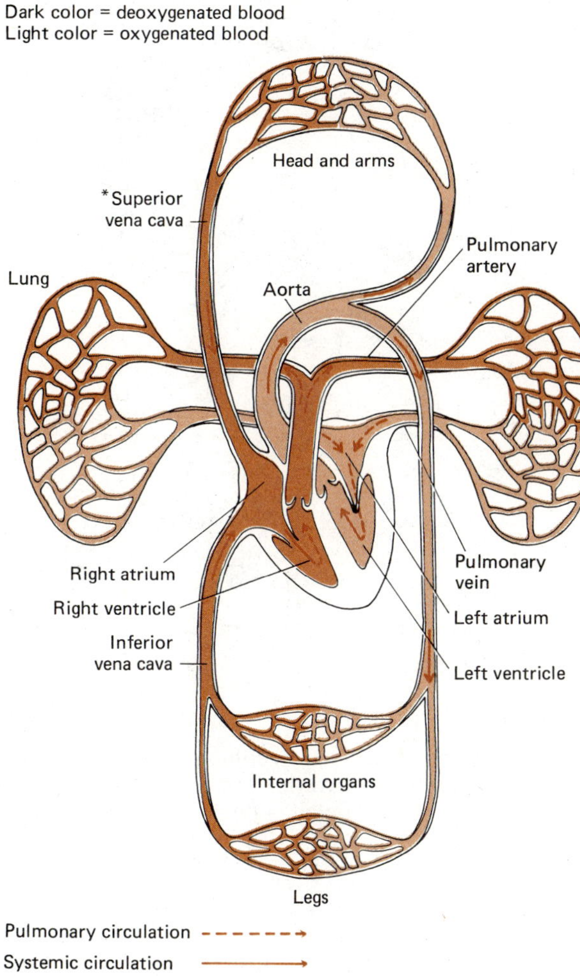

FIGURE 6.7 Pulmonary and Systemic Circulation. Place your finger on the superior vena cava (*), and follow the flow of deoxygenated blood into the right-hand side of the heart, which pumps the blood into the pulmonary artery, which in turn carries the blood to the lungs, where it is oxygenated. As your finger continues to traverse the pulmonary loop, you will see that the pathway leads back to the heart, this time the left-hand side. From here the freshly oxygenated blood is pumped into the aorta and is carried to the body tissues. The systemic loop is completed as the now deoxygenated blood returns to the vena cava to repeat the cycle.

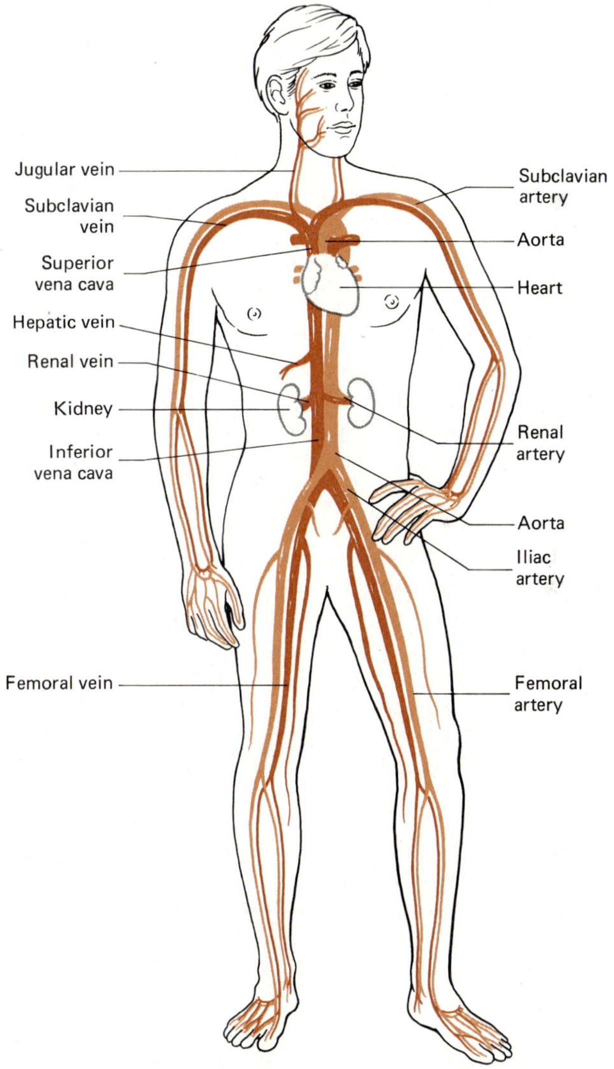

FIGURE 6.8 Major Blood Vessels. Arteries are shown in light color and veins in dark color. Branches of the aorta carry blood from the heart to all sections of the body, including the digestive organs and glands as well as the kidneys, which are shown. Veins from these same areas lead to the vena cava, which returns the blood to the heart.

The Heart

To accommodate both pulmonary and systemic circulation, the heart has two pumping channels, right and left (Fig. 6.9). The right-hand side pumps blood to the lungs, the left-hand side pumps blood to the rest of the body. Each channel has strong muscular walls with valves to direct the flow of blood. Furthermore, each channel consists of two chambers. The upper chamber is called the **atrium**, the lower one the **ventricle**. Atria are thin-walled receiving chambers that collect blood from the veins. The thick-walled, muscular ventricles pump blood into the arteries.

Blood coming from the body tissues via the systemic pathway enters the right atrium of the heart. The chamber expands as it fills with blood. Then the atrium contracts and squeezes its contents into the relaxed right ventricle. The filled ventricle immediately contracts, and blood pulses up into

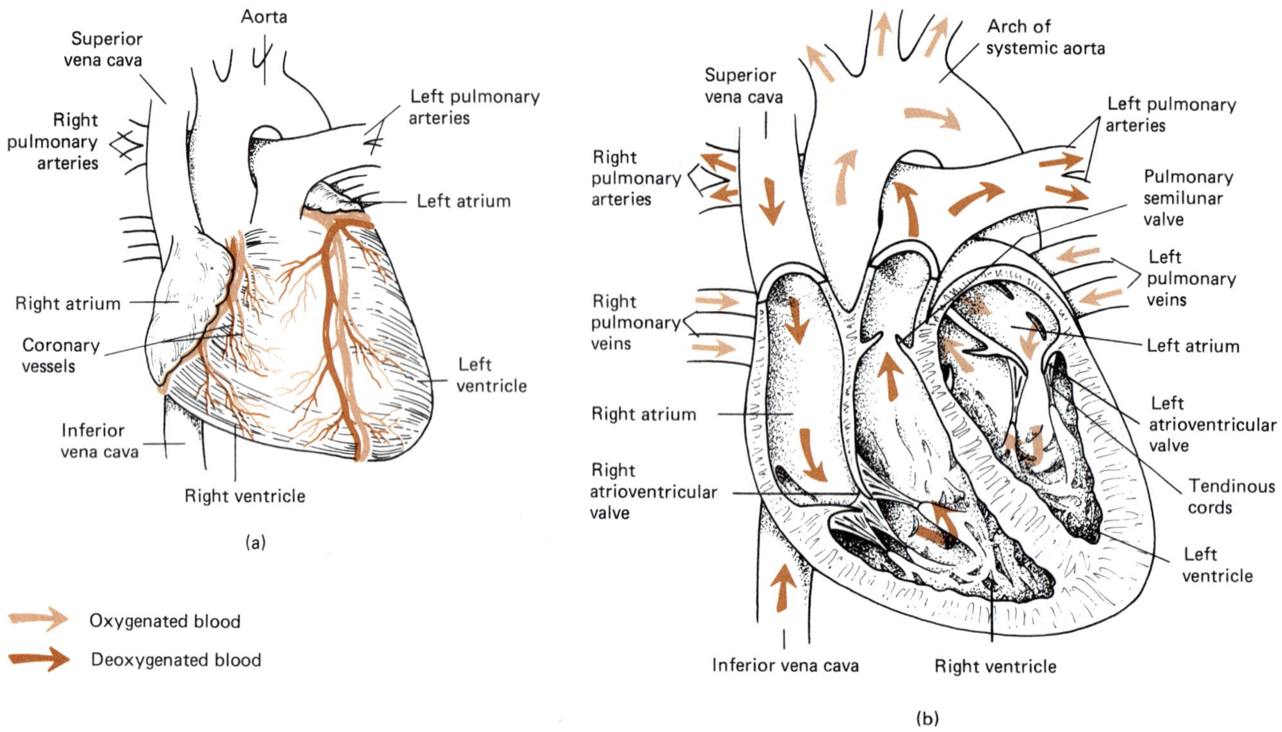

FIGURE 6.9 Two Views of the Heart. (a) The external appearance of the heart. (b) A look inside the heart to help you see how blood flows through the organ. Trace the flow of blood by following the arrows, beginning with the entrance of deoxygenated blood via the superior and inferior vena cava. Note the location of the pulmonary arteries. Where do they lead? Note also that the heart wall is thicker and more muscular on the left. Why do you think this is so? Does one side of the heart work harder than the other?

the pulmonary artery and flows to the lungs. From the lungs, freshly oxygenated blood runs through the pulmonary veins to the left atrium. Contraction of the left atrium sends blood surging into the empty left ventricle. Now the left ventricle pumps the blood into the aorta and to the body capillaries. The cycle is completed when veins return blood to the right atrium.

Valves. Backflow of blood in the heart is prevented by heart *valves*. When the ventricles contract, the **atrio-ventricular valves** block off the atria so that blood can leave only through the arteries. Similarly, delicate **semilunar valves** at the base of the pulmonary artery and of the systemic aorta close after the ventricles contract (Fig. 6.9). This ensures that blood, once it is in the arteries, cannot run backward into the heart.

During the course of a routine examination, the physician listens to your heart with a stethoscope to determine whether the valves are operating properly. The doctor hears the normal heartbeat as a double sound, something like "lubb-dupp." These sounds are created by the turbulence of moving blood and the action of the heart valves. The "dupp" sound signals the closing of the semilunar valves. If the heart valves are defective, the flaps vibrate abnormally or the blood rushes loudly. Unusual sounds may result from blood being forced through narrow, rigid valves or leaking backward through valves that close improperly. Out-of-the-ordinary heart sounds are known as **heart murmurs**.

Valve defects can be congenital—that is, inborn—or they can be caused by scars left by infection. Childhood rheumatic fever was once a common culprit. Individuals with slight murmurs may suffer no noticeable disability. However, major valve defects markedly reduce the efficiency of blood circulation. Fortunately, faulty heart valves can be replaced with artificial ones in many cases.

How the Heart Beats. Although the heart is a double pump, with the right-hand side pumping blood to the lungs and the left-hand side pumping blood to the remainder of the body, the two halves beat almost in unison. The heartbeat is synchronized by a mass of specialized muscle tissue, the **pacemaker**, in the wall of the right atrium. Long before birth, the pacemaker begins to generate impulses that set the rhythm of the heartbeat.

Periodically, and without outside stimulation, the pacemaker triggers changes in other specialized muscle cells that behave much like nerves. These specialized cells carry messages that cause first the aorta and then the ventricles to contract. Although the heart contracts spontaneously, its action is monitored continuously by control centers in the brain. As we will learn in Chapter 8, the pacemaker is stimulated or inhibited by the nervous system, according to body needs.

Heart Vessels and Arterial Disease

Just like other organs, the heart has its own supply of blood vessels to provide it with oxygen and nutrients. This may seem strange, since the blood flows through the heart. However, the walls of the heart are much too thick to be nourished by substances from the heart chambers. Moreover, the right-hand side of the heart contains only low-oxygen blood on its way back to the lungs.

Blood travels to heart tissue via **coronary arteries**, which arise from the systemic aorta just above the semilunar valve. **Coronary veins** collect blood from the heart capillaries and drain into the right atrium.

Heart Attacks. Because heart muscle is continuously active and uses large amounts of nutrients and oxygen, it is especially vulnerable to any interruption of its blood supply. Such interruptions cause "heart attacks," or coronaries. Attacks can result from spasms in the wall of a coronary artery or from blockage of flow in the vessel. A **coronary thrombosis** occurs when an internal blood clot, or **thrombus** forms in a damaged coronary artery.

Whenever a region of heart muscle is deprived of its blood supply for even a short time, that region dies. Even if the individual survives, the heart is usually permanently damaged, because the dead muscle is replaced only by scar tissue.

Fatty Degeneration. Most heart attacks result from **atherosclerosis**. In this condition, regions of the arterial walls become infiltrated with cholesterol
73 and transformed into mushy lumps or plaques of cholesterol,□ cells, and debris. Sometimes there is so much cholesterol that when arteries are severed during an autopsy, a granular yellow mass of almost pure cholesterol leaks out.

Although arteries anywhere in the body can be affected by atherosclerosis, the coronary arteries are particularly susceptible. Because they are early branches of the aorta, the coronary arteries are subjected to the full force of the blood surging from the heart. The turbulence of the blood as it gushes into the coronary arteries can tear into the endothelial lining. Injuries such as these may stimulate development of **atherosclerotic plaques** (Fig. 6.10).

There is always some cholesterol circulating in the blood; it may be derived from nutrients or manufactured by the liver to satisfy normal body needs. One theory is that cholesterol becomes lodged in the rough regions around injuries to the coronary lining. A plaque begins to grow as passing cells, scar tissue, and debris—as well as cholesterol—accumulate in the area. The wall becomes weakened and the blood passageway narrowed. Often blood clots form around the plaque. Bits of a plaque or small clots can wash away only to plug smaller arteries farther along.

Atherosclerosis is a serious medical problem, and much research has gone into finding ways to prevent it. One approach has been to look for ways to reduce high blood pressure and thus reduce the chance of blood-vessel injuries that might encourage plaque development. Researchers are also trying to establish more clearly the role of cholesterol.

Some experts believe that low-cholesterol diets may reduce the risk of atherosclerosis. But the situation is complicated by the fact that cholesterol is synthesized within the body, regardless of what we eat. This waxy lipid is an important constituent of all cell membranes and so is naturally found throughout the body. There is some evidence that eating highly saturated fats, such as are found in butter and eggs, increases cholesterol levels.

But cholesterol provides no simple key to understanding atherosclerosis. Comparative studies of different populations suggest that other dietary factors, lack of exercise, stress, and heredity may also be involved. It is known that cigarette smokers are more likely to suffer atherosclerosis than are nonsmokers.

Brain Damage. Although atherosclerosis can be responsible for ruptured arteries or clots anywhere, such accidents are particularly damaging when they occur in vessels of the brain. In seconds or minutes or hours they can strike a person down. Often these

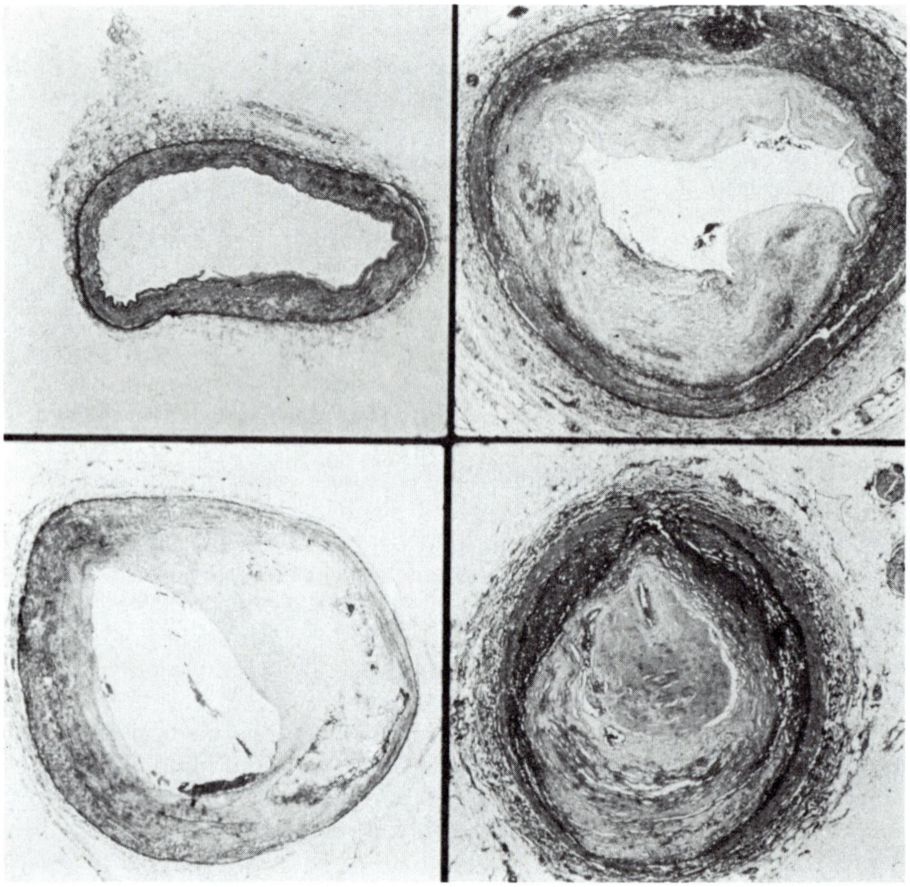

FIGURE 6.10 Atherosclerosis Gradually Leads to the Complete Obstruction of an Artery.

strokes, as they are called, involve plugged arteries that deprive the brain of oxygen. But the fact that the brain is encased in the bony skull makes it particularly vulnerable to damage from hemorrhages. When a weakened artery there ruptures, blood that seeps out will create pressure within the skull. Thus brain damage may result from pressure on the tissue, as well as from interruption of the blood supply. The aftereffects of a stroke depend on the extent of tissue damage and the area involved.

Blood Pressure

Because the heart pumps by cycles of contraction and relaxation, blood enters the arteries in periodic spurts that we count as the **pulse**. Each heartbeat sends a surge of blood under high pressure into the arteries. Since the walls of arteries are elastic, they expand to accommodate the blood flow and thereby dampen the pulse wave. As the volume of blood in an artery decreases, the wall springs back to its original size. Thus the elasticity of the arteries helps to maintain some pressure on the blood even between heartbeats.

Measurements. Since arterial pressure increases with each pulse and decreases between pulses, blood pressure is expressed as two values. The higher **systolic pressure** reflects contraction of the heart, whereas the lower **diastolic pressure** marks ventricular relaxation. Although "normal" blood pressure is usually given as 120/80, there is a considerable range among healthy young adults. Increasing blood pressure often accompanies middle age. Absolute standards have not been established, but a diastolic pressure consistently above 100 is usually considered evidence of disease.

Blood pressure is ordinarily measured in the arteries of the upper arm, because the blood vessels there are accessible and close to the heart. Naturally, the blood pressure is greatest in the aorta, and it decreases steadily with the distance from the heart. By the time the blood reaches the capillaries, the blood pressure is relatively low.

Blood entering veins from capillaries is under very little pressure. The pressure is so low that massage from contracting skeletal muscles is necessary to squeeze venous blood from the lower part of the body to the heart. Because the valves along the veins open in only one direction, back-flow of blood is prevented, and it moves steadily toward the heart. Standing motionless causes swelling of the extremities due to stagnation of blood. Under these conditions fainting may occur, because so little blood is returned to the heart that the supply to the brain is drastically reduced.

Regulation. In order for the circulatory system to function normally, the blood pressure must be constantly gauged and regulated. Blood pressure is basically determined by three factors: alterations in heart rate or in the strength of contraction; changes in the size of the blood-vessel system (as can happen when vessel elasticity is altered or when muscular contractions reduce the diameter of blood vessels); and changes in the blood volume (severe bleeding can cause blood pressure to drop dangerously). The **vasomotor center** of the brain controls the blood pressure by sending out nerve impulses that regulate the diameters of blood vessels. An illustration of how such adjustments are made can be found in Fig. 6.11. Another mechanism for controlling blood pressure involves endocrine secretions from the kidney. This control is related to the fact that kidney function depends on carefully regulated blood pressure.

Apparently these regulatory mechanisms can go awry, for many people suffer from **essential hypertension**. This type of high blood pressure is not due to any obvious factor, such as disease of the arterial walls. Often the circulatory system is simply constricted. Sometimes people with high blood pressure are put on low-salt diets because salt promotes water retention by the tissues, and can lead to constriction of blood vessels and to higher blood pressure.

Regardless of the cause, hypertension places an extraordinary burden on the heart because it must pump harder to force the blood through the vessels. Not surprisingly, then, hypertension is a principal cause of heart trouble.

Capillary Exchange

The exchange of materials between capillaries and tissue fluids occurs as fluids leave the arterial ends of capillaries and return to the venous ends. This flow both distributes nutrients and collects wastes.

Blood pressure is one factor in determining the direction of fluid movement. On the arterial end, the blood pressure of a capillary averages about 35 mm of mercury. (This is the height to which a standard column of mercury will rise when subjected to this pressure.) On the venous end, the blood

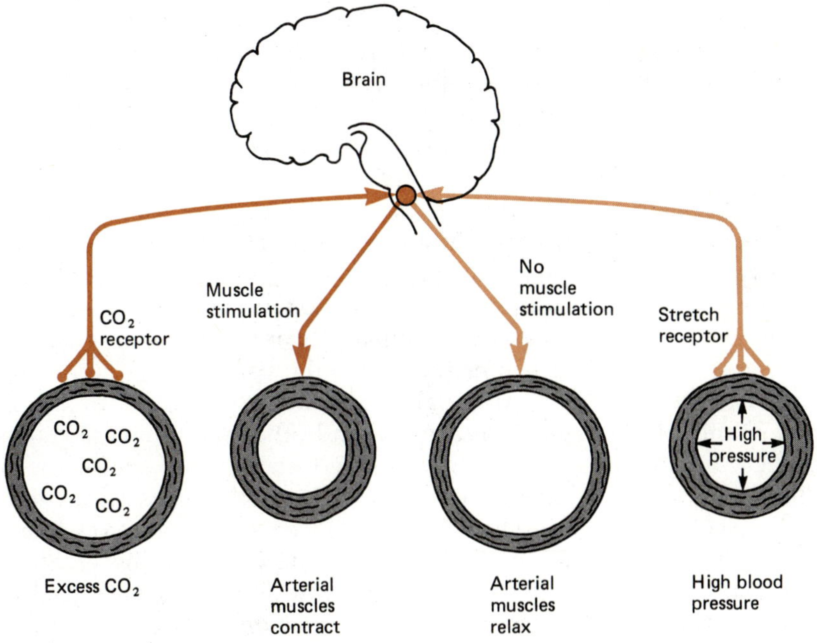

FIGURE 6.11 **Nervous Control of Blood Pressure.** Impulses from carbon-dioxide-detecting receptors of certain blood vessels cause contraction of arteries. This increases blood pressure, and therefore oxygenation of the blood. Impulses from stretch receptors of blood vessels inhibit the vasoconstrictor center, which permits arterial muscles to relax. The result is reduced blood pressure.

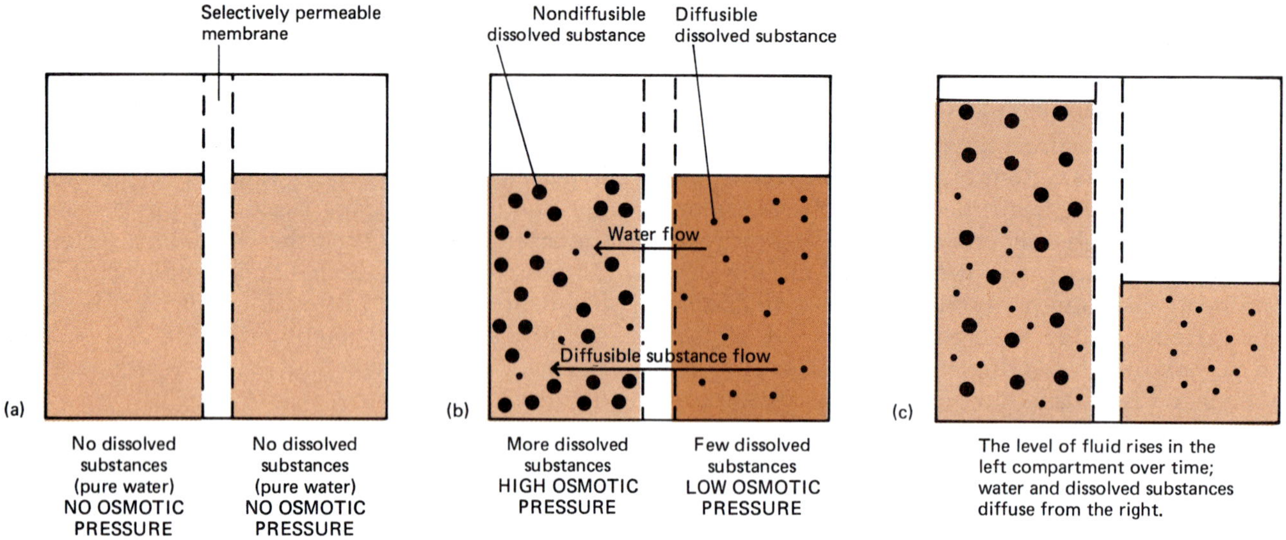

FIGURE 6.12 **Osmotic Pressure.** If pure water is separated into two compartments by a membrane—even one that is permeable to it—there is no net flow of water (a). There is no osmotic pressure, because osmotic pressure is a property that is dependent on the presence of dissolved substances in water. The higher the concentration of dissolved substances, the higher the osmotic pressure a solution will exert with respect to a more dilute solution on the other side of a membrane. Water diffuses from the solution with low osmotic pressure into the solution of high osmotic pressure (b). If a nondiffusible soluble substance is trapped inside a membrane-bound compartment, a permanently high osmotic pressure is created (c). The level of water will rise until the hydrostatic pressure of the column of water equals the osmotic pressure. At that point, net movement stops.

pressure is about 15 mm. These facts explain why fluids leave the arterial end of capillaries, but more information is necessary to understand why fluids reenter the venous end. It is osmotic pressure that draws water back into the capillaries.

In Chapter 4, we used the term **osmosis** to describe the diffusion of water through a selectively
74 permeable membrane.□ **Osmotic pressure**, then, is the pressure created as water diffuses from a solution where water concentration is high (and concentration of dissolved substances correspondingly low), through a selectively permeable membrane, into a solution where the water concentration is low (and concentration of dissolved substances correspondingly high). The phenomenon is not so difficult to understand as it sounds. Figure 6.12 will help.

Properties of the capillary wall are critical to the development of osmotic pressure within the capillaries. Water diffuses readily through the capillary wall, but blood proteins penetrate the wall poorly. Hence the capillary wall is a selectively permeable membrane. Remember that capillary walls consist of one layer of endothelium. Therefore substances moving in and out of capillaries must actually pass through the plasma membrane on one side of an endothelial cell, then through the endothelial cytoplasm, and finally through the plasma membrane on the other side.

Because of the presence of proteins, blood plasma contains a lower concentration of water than does **interstitial fluid**, the watery fluid surrounding tissue cells. As a result, water tends to diffuse into the capillary. Proteins, though concentrated in the plasma, are trapped by the capillary wall and cannot diffuse outward. Whereas interstitial fluids are more than 99 percent water, blood plasma is less than 93 percent water. The osmotic pressure (or pull) into the capillary is about 25 mm of mercury. Although this difference does not prevent blood pressure from forcing fluids from the arterial end of the capillary, it is sufficient to ensure the return of water into the venous end (Fig. 6.13).

Although observations indicate that water, gases, nutrients, and other small molecules easily diffuse through the thin capillary walls, the passage is not simple because the walls are composed of cells. Some substances seem to get from one side to the other by passing between the endothelial cells of the capillary walls. Other substances are apparently picked up on one side by a process like phagocytosis, and they are then ferried across the

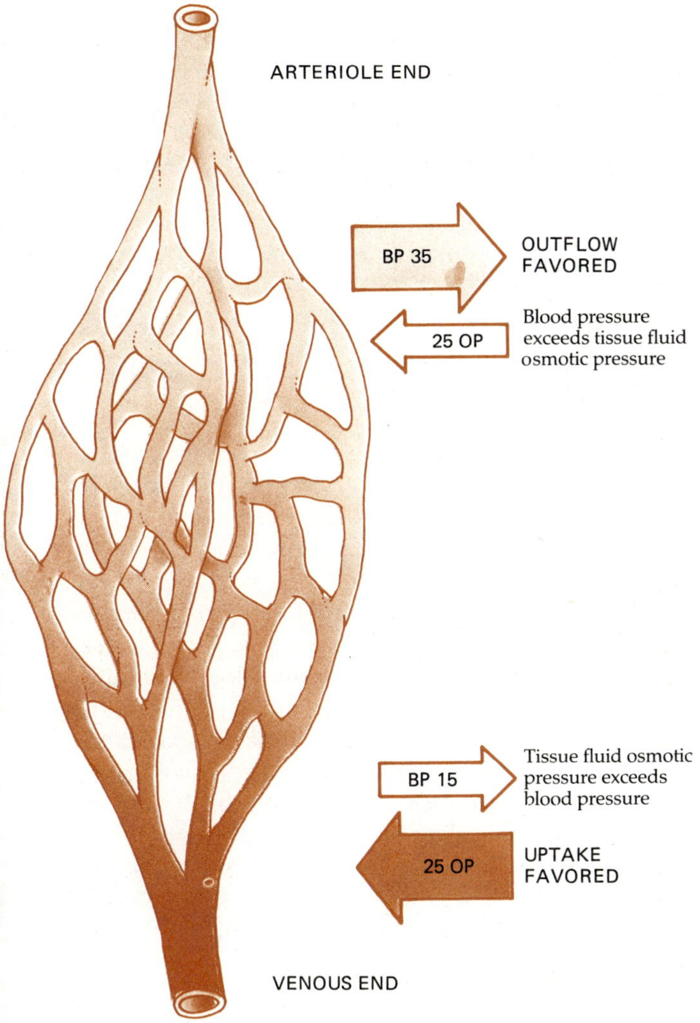

FIGURE 6.13 **Capillary Function.** The combined effects of blood pressure and osmotic pressure permit the exchange of materials across selectively permeable capillary walls.

cytoplasm to the other side, where they are dropped off by the reverse procedure.

At any rate, oxygen and dissolved nutrients move out of the capillaries and diffuse into the tissues where they are needed. And wastes such as carbon dioxide, which are released by the tissue cells, diffuse into the bloodstream and are carried away.

As we have already mentioned, blood flow into a capillary bed is controlled by muscular bands, or sphincters. Stimuli that cause arteries to contract or relax also affect capillary sphincters. Thus, for example, increased carbon dioxide in the blood opens the sphincters, and as a result, more oxygen and nutrients can reach the tissues. Even local metabolic changes can cause appropriate sphincters to open and close as necessary.

The Lymphatic System

Any excess tissue fluid not returned to the blood capillaries directly is collected by an auxiliary circulatory pathway, the **lymphatic system** (Fig. 6.14). Lymphatic capillaries with extremely porous walls originate in all body tissues. The watery fluid from around body cells oozes into the lymphatic capillaries, where it is called **lymph**. The lymph flows from lymph capillaries into progressively larger vessels. In the neck, large lymphatic ducts empty into veins that return the fluids to the blood circulation.

Lymphatic Organs. At strategic points, notably the throat, armpits, and groin, lymphatic vessels converge to enter **lymph nodes**. Cells in these nodes phagocytize debris and any foreign organisms that may be present in the lymph. In this manner many disease-causing microorganisms, dead cells, and

FIGURE 6.14 **The Lymphatic System.** Most of the body's lymphatic vessels drain into the thoracic duct, which then empties into the bloodstream near the heart.

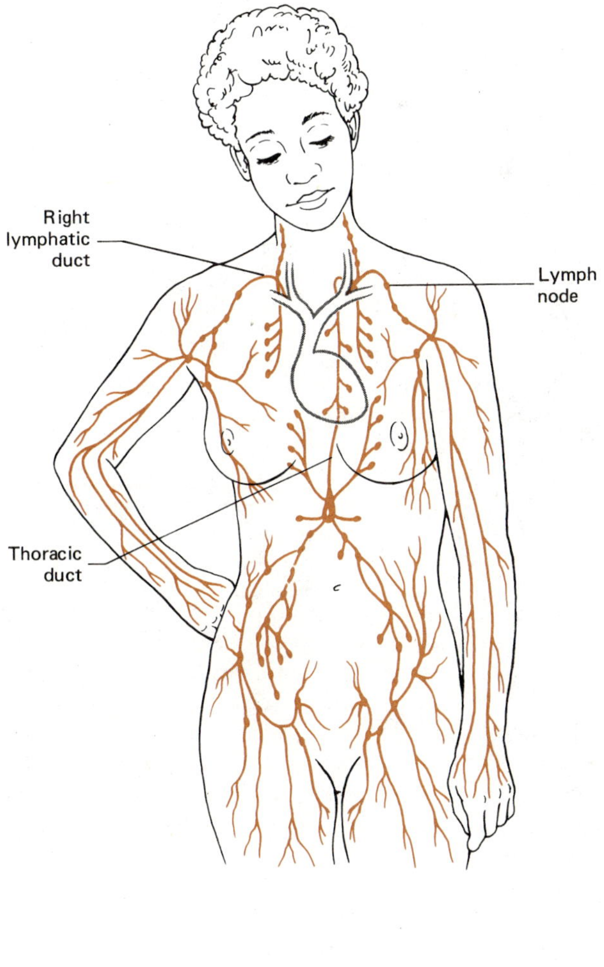

other particulate matter are prevented from entering the bloodstream. Sometimes organisms from infected tissue settle and multiply in the nodes and cause them to be sore and inflamed. For this reason swollen, tender lymph nodes (a condition commonly called "swollen glands") are considered signs of infection. Migrating cancer cells are also caught in lymph nodes, which must often be removed during cancer surgery.

The lymph nodes function as body defense organs in still another way. Certain lymphocytes within the nodes secrete **antibodies**. These plasma proteins combine with disease-producing agents and destroy them. This is one aspect of specific immune responses, which we'll discuss further in Chapter 10.

The adenoids, tonsils, and spleen all contain spongy lymphatic tissue similar to that of the lymph nodes. Although the full story has yet to be revealed, each of these organs is involved in resistance to infection, and all are sites of antibody formation.

The **spleen**, which is 12–15 centimeters (five to six inches) long and about 10 centimeters (four inches) wide, is the largest lymphatic organ in the body. It lies on the left side, a little behind the stomach. Although the spleen is a filter, as are the lymph nodes, it filters blood rather than lymph. Its principal responsibility is to remove worn out blood cells and platelets from the circulation. The spleen is useful but not essential for human life. If it is removed, damaged blood cells are scavenged by phagocytes in the liver.

The **thymus**, a lymphatic mass at the base of the neck, has puzzled biologists for a long time. Unlike other lymphatic organs, it is large at birth and shrinks with maturity. Probably the thymus is involved in establishment of the immune functions of other lymphatic organs.

Edema. Normally there is a balanced flow of fluids into and out of body tissues. Any accumulation of water around the body cells causes swelling, a condition known as **edema**. Sometimes edema results from severe blows, crushing injuries, or burns. These can damage capillary walls and destroy the barrier that ordinarily permits osmotic pressure to pull water into the circulatory system. Low blood protein, whether from inadequate food intake or from kidney disease, also lowers the osmotic pressure and can similarly produce edema. For this reason, children suffering from kwashiorkor are bloated.

Elephantiasis is an especially grotesque, localized edema. It occurs when the body is infected with microscopic worms that plug lymph vessels. This prevents return of tissue fluids to the blood

BOX 6A

SHOCK

Physical injuries, fright, hemorrhage, disease, and even certain drugs can impair the function of the circulatory system sufficiently to cause a person to go into "shock." The victim becomes pale and has a weak pulse and very low blood pressure. There may also be profuse sweating.

The symptoms of shock occur whenever there is insufficient blood to fill the circulatory system. As a result, many or all body tissues fail to receive an adequate blood supply. If brain function is impaired, the victim may lose consciousness.

After severe injuries, hemorrhage can reduce blood volume enough to induce shock. But crushing injuries that produce edema often result in decreased blood volume and shock, too. In fact, any massive stimulation of the nervous system can cause dilation (expansion) of the blood vessels and thus diminish the flow of blood in the body.

Prolonged shock leads to serious organ damage. The low blood pressure and slow movement of blood favors the formation of many clots that obstruct blood vessels. Oxygen and nutrient starvation gradually take their toll on the heart, the brain, and other vital tissues.

Shock is the most common immediate cause of death from accidents and warfare. First-aid courses always stress the importance of stopping hemorrhages and keeping the victim flat to facilitate circulation. So long as the brain and heart receive plenty of blood, there is a good chance for recovery. Emergency medical aid also often involves transfusion with fluids to restore blood volume.

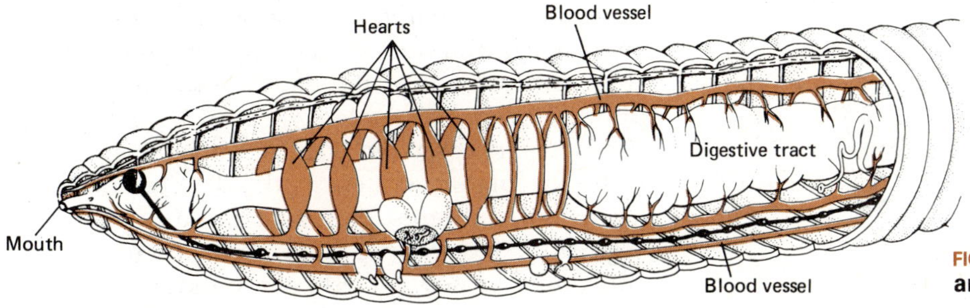

FIGURE 6.15 **The Many Hearts of an Earthworm.**

and results in severe swelling of the affected body region.

Other Ways of Circulation

Like many other animals, humans have what is called a **closed circulatory system**. Our blood never leaves the heart or the blood vessels—although blood-derived fluids do.

One of the simplest closed circulatory systems is that of the earthworm. It is simple in spite of the fact that an earthworm has five pairs of "hearts"! These so-called hearts are not chambered organs such as our own, however. They are merely more muscular, specialized parts of certain circulatory vessels (Fig. 6.15).

Open Circulation. In snails, clams, and insects (to name but a few) the heart merely pumps blood into spaces, or **sinuses**, within the body tissues. Such **open circulatory systems** are naturally rather sluggish. Body movements tend to distribute the blood so that it is eventually drawn back into the heart (Fig. 6.16).

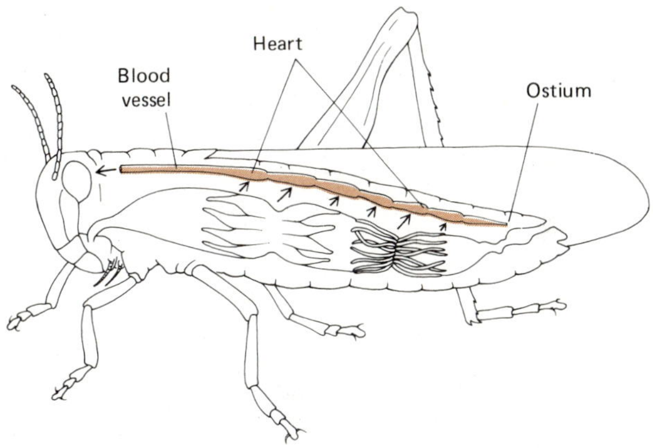

FIGURE 6.16 **Open Circulation in the Grasshopper.** A grasshopper has six hearts but only one short blood vessel. Blood is pumped forward and out the open end of the short blood vessel. From the head region, the blood oozes slowly toward the abdomen, where it is sucked into holes of the multiple hearts.

Fish, Amphibians, and Reptiles. Sharks and other fish have only one atrium and one ventricle. Blood is pumped to the gills for oxygen uptake; then, without returning to the heart, it flows to the tissue capillaries. From the tissues, the blood flows back to the heart. Thus the blood of fish is not pumped directly into the tissues, and systemic circulation is rather slow.

Amphibians such as frogs have a more efficient arrangement. It involves a three-chambered heart with two atria. One atrium receives deoxygenated blood from the tissues, and the other receives oxygenated blood from the lungs. Since both atria empty into a single ventricle, oxygenated blood is mixed with deoxygenated blood. Unlike fish circulation, amphibians' blood is pumped into the tissues directly, but it is only partially oxygenated. Figure 6.17 compares the circulatory systems of a fish, an amphibian, a reptile, and a mammal.

Circulation: At the Core

Our discussion of circulation has occurred at the beginning of our investigation of body function, because the circulatory system is so intimately involved in the operation of other systems. Already we have found it necessary to mention the immune functions of the blood and to bring up the lymphatic organs. But the circulatory system has many more interrelationships. The value of the circulation as a means of communication will become especially evident when we consider the extent of the endocrine glands and the importance of their

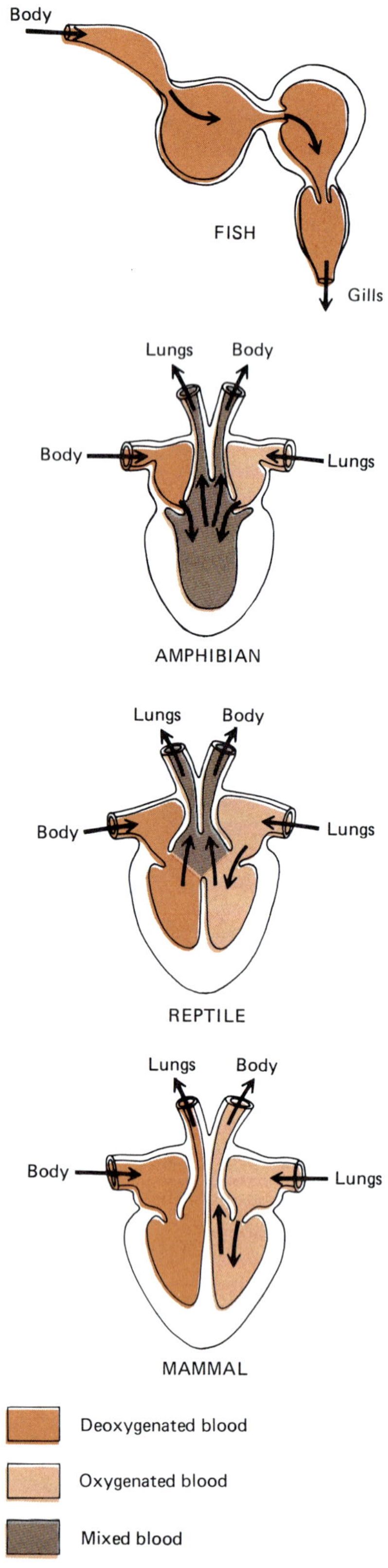

FIGURE 6.17 **Vertebrate Heart Evolution.**

hormones. Similarly, finding out how the kidney regulates the amount of body water will reveal further involvement of the circulation, both directly and as a transport system.

But perhaps what is most obvious is the role of the circulatory system in the distribution of oxygen and nutrients. Some of these details must wait until we explore food absorption and liver function. For now we will concentrate on the crucial transport of gases, a function shared between the circulatory system and the respiratory system.

GAS EXCHANGE

Breathing is but one step in the sophisticated process that provides our cells with oxygen and removes the carbon dioxide the cells produce. Gas exchange may begin in the nose or mouth, but it extends into the deepest regions of the body. The upper respiratory passages, lungs, blood vessels, and red blood cells are all involved.

The Respiratory System

Normally we breathe through our noses, and as the air winds through the nasal passages, suspended dust and microorganisms become trapped in sticky secretions of mucus. If the inhaled air is dry or cold, the moist, warm nasal linings add water or heat it up. From the nose, air enters the **pharynx**, an upper part of the throat. Then it flows through the **larynx** into the **trachea**, or windpipe, which extends almost to the lungs (Fig. 6.18).

If you run your hand along the front of your throat, you can detect the larynx just under your chin. Its common name, the "voice box," is quite apt, for the larynx has a boxlike shape. The vocal cords are stretched across the sides of the larynx. When air is forced over the vocal cords, they vibrate. This vibration initiates the sounds of the human voice, but these sounds are modified as they pass through the pharynx and mouth. Laryngitis is an inflammation of the vocal cords that may cause you to lose your voice because the inflamed vocal cords cannot vibrate freely.

The trachea itself is supported by C-shaped cartilage bands that you can feel in your lower neck. Further down, the trachea branches into **bronchi**. These tubes branch again and again within the lungs to form smaller and smaller **bronchioles**. The trachea, bronchi, and bronchioles are all lined with mucus-secreting and ciliated cells. Beating of the

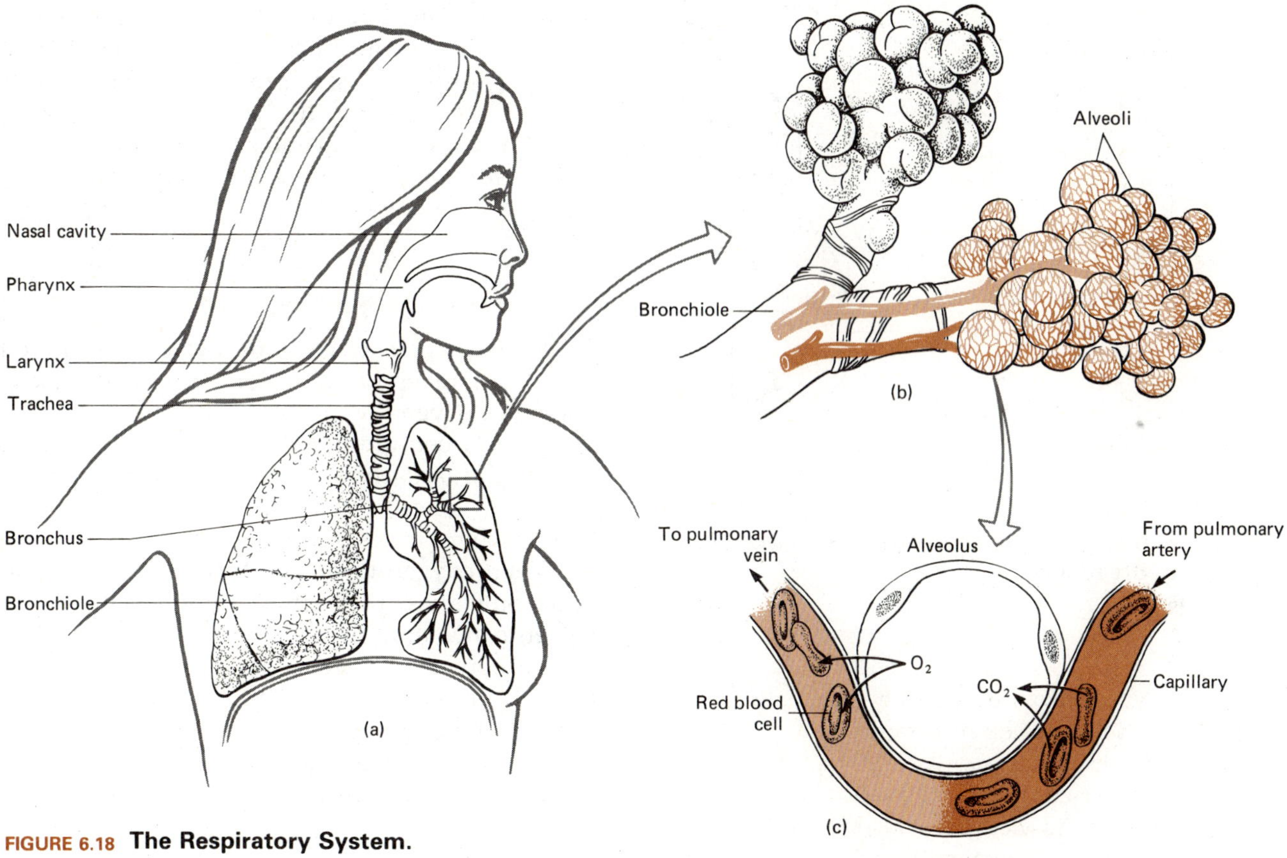

FIGURE 6.18 The Respiratory System.

cilia constantly moves mucus and any particles caught in the sticky stuff upward, away from the lungs.

The smallest bronchioles terminate in berry-shaped clusters of air sacs, called **alveoli**. The thin, delicate alveolar walls are embedded with an extensive capillary network. Here the blood exchanges carbon dioxide for oxygen from the air.

The exquisite design of the lungs cannot be overemphasized. Because these fragile gas-exchange surfaces are deep within the body, they are well protected. But despite their hidden location, the lung surface area is 40 times greater than that of the skin.

Respiration and Its Control

Breathing is accomplished by means of changes in the volume of the **thoracic cavity**, in which the lungs are located (Fig. 6.18). A thin lubricated membrane, the **pleura**, lines this cavity. A similar moist membrane covers each lung, so they can move easily within the chest.

Ribs encircle the thoracic cavity. At its bottom is the **diaphragm**, a muscle that separates the thoracic cavity from the abdominal cavity. During inspiration, contraction of the diaphragm and the muscles between the ribs enlarges the chest cavity. Because this results in a decrease in internal pressure, air is sucked into the lungs. Expiration involves the relaxation of these muscles. This relaxation and the natural elasticity of the tissues reduce the volume of the chest cavity so that air is squeezed out of the lungs. However, all the air is never expelled. Some always remains in the lungs, even when expiration is forced by contraction of the muscles of the abdominal wall (Fig. 6.19).

Because every body cell needs an uninterrupted supply of oxygen, respiration is a vital activity. The rate and depth of respiration are correlated to body needs, just as are heart rate and blood pressure. If you try to hold your breath for

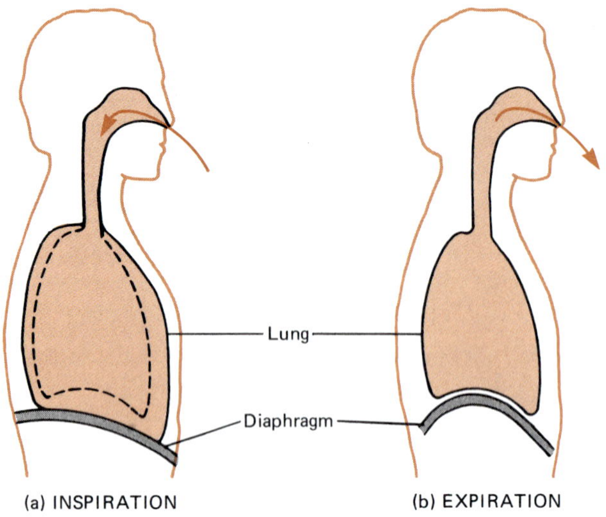

FIGURE 6.19 Changes in the Volume of the Thoracic Cavity During Breathing.

very long, you will discover that breathing becomes totally involuntary. The respiratory control center in the brain produces impulses that stimulate the rhythmic contraction and relaxation of the diaphragm and rib muscles. Overdoses of barbiturates (commonly called "downers") can numb the respiratory control center and lead to death.

Our respiratory requirements are monitored by special sense organs. Cells within major vessels measure the amount of carbon dioxide and oxygen in the blood and signal the brain accordingly. Whenever the carbon dioxide concentration increases even slightly, the respiratory center responds by stimulating deeper and more rapid breathing to remove the excess carbon dioxide.

Emphysema

An increasing number of older people in industrialized nations suffer from **emphysema**. This degenerative disease frequently results from exposure to cigarette smoke and other air pollutants. Such substances stimulate excessive secretion of mucus, edema of the bronchial epithelia, and increased susceptibility to infection. In response to this irritation, the muscles in the air passages contract. Aggravation of this **chronic bronchitis** causes the respiratory passages to become even narrower and more used air is retained in the lung. Thus with every new breath, more air must be inhaled to give the same amount of oxygen. Under these conditions a person must breathe harder. Forced breathing puts excessive pressure on the delicate alveoli. After a while, the alveolar walls stretch, and eventually many disintegrate. The disease can be fatal if enough of the gas exchange surface of the lung is destroyed (Fig. 6.20).

Gas Exchange at the Cellular Level

Oxygen exchange between the alveolar air and red blood cells relies on diffusion and on the loose binding of oxygen by hemoglobin. So does the exchange between red blood cells and body tissues. Oxygen diffuses from the alveoli, where it is present in high concentration, into the pulmonary capillaries, where there is less oxygen.

When oxygen-laden red blood cells flow into tissue capillaries, they enter regions of decreased oxygen concentration. In this situation, the loose linkage between oxygen and hemoglobin breaks down. Naturally, the freed oxygen diffuses into the tissues, where its concentration is much lower.

Diffusion also accounts for much of the exchange of carbon dioxide as it enters the blood in

FIGURE 6.20 Emphysema. Compare these two photographs: (a) shows the smooth appearance of healthy normal lung tissue and (b) shows the widespread destruction of lung tissue in a case of emphysema. Do you still want to smoke? Are you glad you don't?

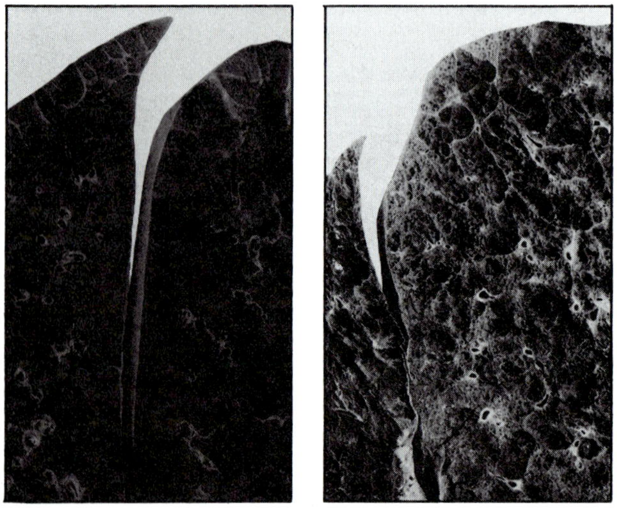

(a) Normal (b) Emphysema

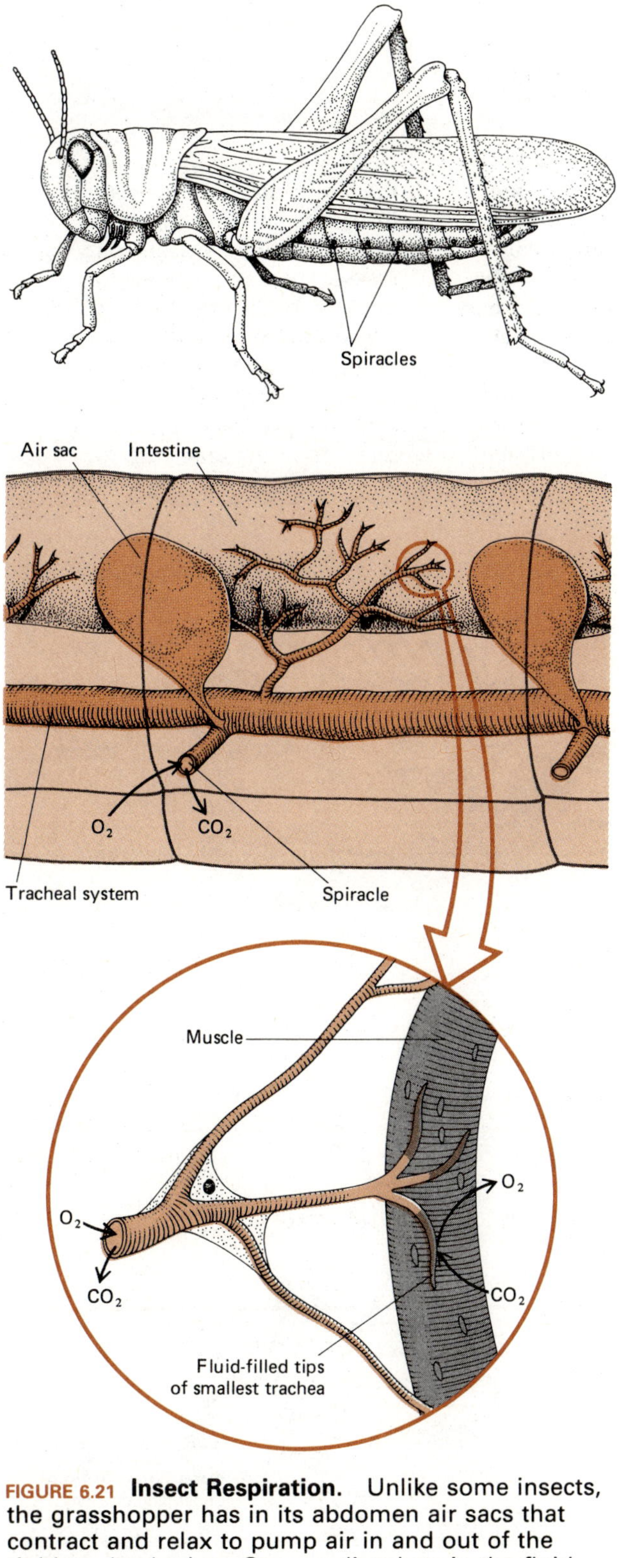

FIGURE 6.21 Insect Respiration. Unlike some insects, the grasshopper has in its abdomen air sacs that contract and relax to pump air in and out of the rigid tracheal tubes. Oxygen dissolves in the fluid within the smallest tracheoles before actually reaching body cells.

the systematic capillaries and leaves the blood in the pulmonary capillaries. In the tissues, carbon dioxide diffuses into the capillaries. Some dissolves in the plasma. Most carbon dioxide, however, passes into the red blood cells. Here part combines with hemoglobin, but the majority is carried as bicarbonate. **Carbonic anhydrase**, an enzyme of red blood cells, facilitates the normally slow formation of bicarbonate from water and carbon dioxide via an intermediate compound, carbonic acid.

$$CO_2 + H_2O \rightleftharpoons \underset{\text{carbonic acid}}{H_2CO_3} \rightleftharpoons \underset{\text{bicarbonate}}{HCO_3^-} + H^+$$

In the lungs the reaction is reversed, as carbonic acid dissociates to form carbon dioxide and water. This carbon dioxide and that small amount carried by hemoglobin diffuses out of the red blood cells and into the alveoli. Then the cycle of gas exchange is ready to begin again.

Tracheae and Gills

Insects and some of their close relatives breathe air by a system completely different from our own. These organisms have a system of branched tubes termed **tracheae** that are connected to the outside by openings called **spiracles** (Fig. 6.21). The tracheae form a network that reaches throughout the body to pipe oxygen to the tissues.

In some insects, body movements cause the opening and closing of spiracles and create currents that move air through the tracheae. This type of gas-exchange system, which does not involve the circulatory system, keeps insects small. The giant insects of science fiction could not exist as tracheal breathers. Tracheal systems simply could not supply the oxygen needs of large animals.

Tracheae—and lungs, too—are internal respiratory surfaces. Found mainly in land animals, they are an adaptation that ensures that the respiratory surfaces can remain moist, because they are internal.

Fish **gills** (Fig. 6.22) are respiratory structures that are essentially outgrowths of the body surface. They are thin filamentous flaps of tissue that provide an extensive surface area for gas exchange. Gills have a rich supply of blood just as do the alveoli of the lungs. Often there is some mechanism for forcing water over or through the gills, so oxygen can be removed and carbon dioxide can be given up to the water.

BOX 6B

TOBACCO, CIRCULATION, AND CILIA

Tobacco smoke is a foul, irritating vapor containing many poisonous chemicals. Among them are carbon monoxide, hydrocyanic acid, nitrosamines, benzopyrene, even ammonia, and—of course—nicotine. It is this last substance that is responsible for both the stimulating and the soothing qualities of tobacco. In fact, nicotine effectively "soothes" insects to death. It is one of the most potent insecticides available from plant sources. Plants commonly produce noxious alkaloid compounds, such as nicotine, to discourage animals from eating them. Unfortunately, human smokers are not easily discouraged.

Most people quickly develop a deceptive tolerance to nicotine. Any dizziness or nausea disappears after a few days of smoking. Still, nicotine increases the heart rate and blood pressure, constricts blood vessels, and decreases intestinal movements. Luckily, within the body nicotine is eventually converted into a harmless compound that is excreted. Nevertheless, tobacco smoking can have serious consequences in the long run. Many

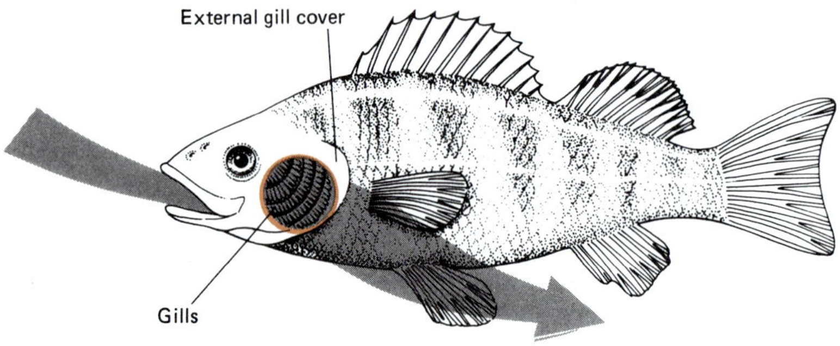

FIGURE 6.22 **Fish Gills.** "Breathing" is accomplished by closing the external gill cover against the body as the gill arches bulge forward and the mouth opens. Water enters, the mouth is closed, and the gill cover opens, causing the water to flow over the gills and out of the body.

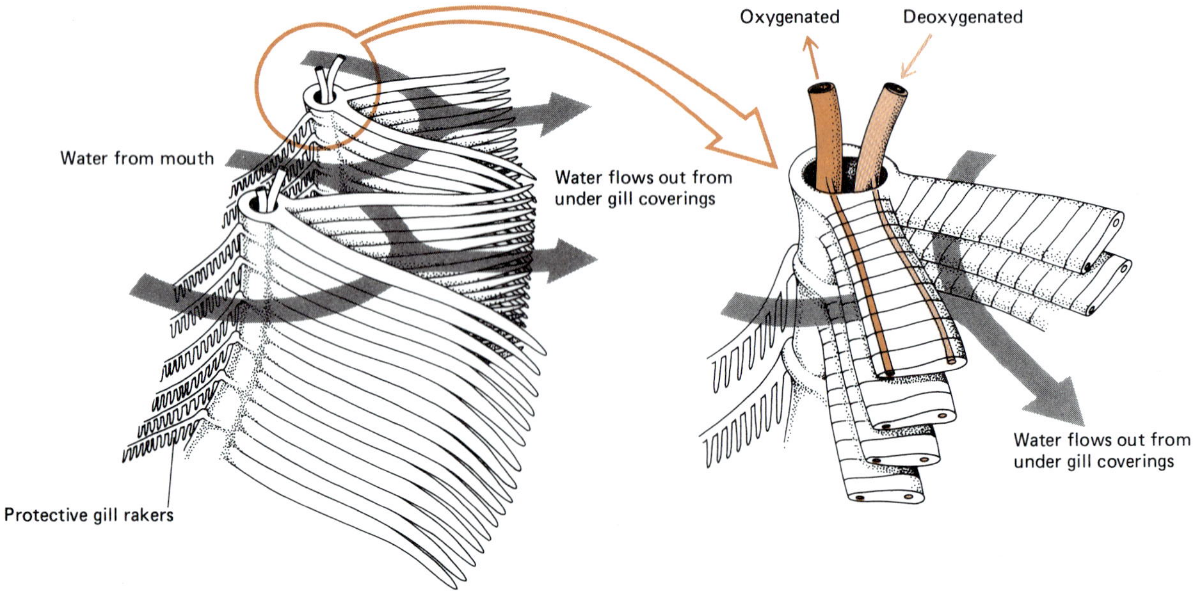

people recognize that chain-smoking causes cold, tingling fingers. In some cases, circulation in the extremities is so drastically affected that cells there die from lack of oxygen, and gangrene develops. But a greater danger to chronic smokers is heart disease. For some reason, cigarette smokers suffer nearly twice as many heart attacks as nonsmokers.

Nicotine is also known to damage the lining of the bronchial passages of the lungs. The bronchi of heavy smokers have fewer mucous cells and fewer ciliated cells. And the cilia that remain are much shorter. Moreover, nicotine paralyzes ciliary action. It is not unlikely that the loss of the cleansing effect of cilia-propelled mucus is important in the development of lung cancer and emphysema. Benzopyrene, nitrosamines, and other cancer-causing substances from tobacco smoke probably remain in contact with the tissues longer and have greater opportunities to affect cells under these conditions. So do the irritants, like ammonia, that constrict the bronchioles and lead to emphysema.

Homeostasis: A Constant Internal Environment

Most of us eat only three meals a day. Yet the cells of our body are working all the time, and they need continuous nourishment. You can rest assured that our cells do not starve between meals. If we determine the concentration of nutrients in the blood at different times of the day, we find that the amounts are fairly stable. The food we digest isn't used or discarded according to momentary needs. Some of it is stored and then parceled out later to ensure a steady supply of nutrients for all the cells of the body.

Our cells exist in a relatively constant environment. This stable condition is called **homeostasis**. The roots of this word mean "the same" (*homeo*) and "to stay" (*stasis*). The word itself is a convenient distillation of a major principle: all organisms must maintain a more or less constant internal state. And this they must do while coping with a fluctuating environment.

Later it will become evident that homeostasis requires the coordinated function of all parts of the body. However, we can list many of these activities now. Homeostasis involves acquiring and processing nutrients, having the appropriate concentration of gases, excreting wastes, responding to changes in the environment, preventing fluctuations in salt and water concentration, dealing with competition from other organisms, and numerous other chores. The movement of nutrients, collection of wastes, gas exchange, distribution of regulatory substances, resistance to infections, and the numerous other functions of the circulatory system, the lymphatic system, and the respiratory system are all necessary for homeostasis. But these are only some of our homeostatic devices.

Keep the concept of homeostasis in mind as we move on to the digestive and excretory systems. For the function of these systems, too, is best understood in terms of their contribution to a stable internal environment.

Summary

1. The circulatory system consists of blood, blood vessels, and the heart. The fluid part of blood is called plasma. Glucose, or blood sugar, is dissolved in the blood plasma. Blood also contains blood cells. The red blood cells contain hemoglobin, a pigment that carries oxygen. White blood cells function to protect the body against invasion by foreign matter.

2. The blood vessels include arteries, veins, and capillaries. Arteries and veins carry blood to and from the heart, respectively. Capillaries are thin-walled vessels that permit the exchange of gases and nutrients between the blood and tissues. The heart is a muscular double pump, the right and left sides each consisting of an atrium and a ventricle. One-way valves control the movement of blood through the heart.

3. Deoxygenated blood from the body tissues flows via veins to the right atrium, passes to the right ventricle, and then flows to the lungs by means of the pulmonary arteries. In the lungs blood gives up carbon dioxide and takes up oxygen. The newly oxygenated blood then travels back to the heart through the pulmonary veins. It enters the left atrium and then passes into the left ventricle, which contracts with sufficient force to propel the blood into the aorta, the artery that distributes oxygenated blood to body tissues.

4. The heart pumps by cycles of contraction and relaxation. The cycles are controlled by the pacemaker, which is itself under the control of the nervous system. The strength and rate of the heartbeat can thus be altered to suit body needs.

5. The lymphatic system serves to recycle excess fluid not returned to the bloodstream in the course of capillary exchange. Furthermore, lymphatic tissues filter and destroy foreign material.

6. The circulatory system plays a role in the operation of many body functions. For example, the exchange of gases is accomplished through the cooperation of the circulatory system and the respiratory system.

7. The human circulatory system is characterized as a closed system. Snails, clams, and insects are examples of organisms with an open circulatory system in which blood bathes the tissues directly.

8. The respiratory system consists of the lungs, the passageways leading from the nose to the lungs, and the diaphragm and rib muscles. The rate and depth of breathing are correlated to body needs by specific brain centers.

9. Oxygen exchange depends on the properties of hemoglobin. In the lung alveoli, where oxygen concentrations are high, oxygen diffuses into the red blood cells, where it combines with hemoglobin. In the tissues, where metabolism has reduced the oxygen concentration, hemoglobin has a lower affinity for oxygen and gives it up to the tissue cells.

10. Carbon dioxide exchange also occurs by diffusion; however, carbon dioxide diffuses into the blood from the tissues and is released in the lungs. Some carbon dioxide is carried by hemoglobin, but mostly it is carried as bicarbonate in the plasma or in red blood cell cytoplasm.

11. Insects carry out gas exchange by means of branched tubes called tracheae, which pipe oxygen from the outside environment to the tissues. Many aquatic organisms have thin, filamentous gills, which provide an extensive gas exchange surface.

Thought and Controversy

1. Emphysema victims often die of congestive heart failure. These deaths reflect a breakdown of essential homeostatic mechanisms involving the whole body. Although all the blood must pass through the lungs after each trip in the systematic circulation, blood pressure in the lungs is ordinarily low, because the capillary bed there is large and short, so blood moves easily. In emphysema the destruction of numerous alveoli is necessarily accompanied by loss of the capillaries through the alveolar walls. As a result, the same amount of blood must use fewer capillaries. Furthermore, lack of oxygen decreases the size of pulmonary vessels. Much greater force is thus necessary to push the same amount of blood through the lungs at the same rate. This increases pulmonary blood pressure and strains the right-hand side of the heart. Although the heart naturally adjusts so that each contraction empties the ventricles completely, eventually the right-hand ventricle reaches its maximum work level and gradually falls behind. As blood accumulates, the ventricle is stretched and strained even more. Sometimes overexpansion prevents complete closure of the valves and lets blood leak backward, only to make matters worse. As the right-hand ventricle fails, blood accumulates in the right atrium and in the systematic veins. The liver and other vital organs become congested with blood, and the work load of the left-hand side of the heart is increased, too. Drugs such as digitalis, which strengthen heart contractions, help for a while. But in time the heart may simply fail to move sufficient blood to maintain life. If the direct threat of suffocation from emphysema isn't enough to discourage smokers, will the prospect of congestive heart failure have any effect?

2. Even without the dramatic tragedy of a stroke, a gradual reduction in oxygen available to the brain often accompanies progressive atherosclerosis. The process is insidious and may affect aged leaders for years before becoming sufficiently evident to force their retirement. How often has the course of history been altered by decisions influenced by this disease?

3. Sometimes apparently healthy babies unexplainably die in their cribs. The shock devastates parents, who fear they are at fault. Autopsies have shown many of the infants to have increased muscle in small pulmonary arteries. This increase suggests a chronic oxygen shortage in the lungs, for pulmonary arteries contract when oxygen is insufficient and such continued contraction promotes muscle growth. Production of red blood cells in the livers of sudden-death-syndrome infants is further evidence of oxygen lack. So is the lag observed in their growth after birth. The problem may lie in the carbon-dioxide sensors in the blood vessels or in the respiratory control centers in the brain. But neither the defect nor the primary cause has been established. Surveys indicate a number of factors to be related to sudden death syndrome. Infant blood type, maternal use of cigarettes or barbiturates, anemia of the mother, uterine infections during pregnancy, and crowded family housing conditions all show correlation with the disease. The importance of these factors and how they relate to infant defects presents a considerable challenge. Researchers must determine if more than one factor is involved and must face the fact that the correlations could all be coincidental. The problem is compounded by the fact that infants likely to suffer sudden crib death are difficult to identify in advance.

4. Can it be that heart attacks result from an unusual kind of cancer? Some scientists believe that the plaques of atherosclerosis represent tumorous growths, and that the frequency of this disease is related to exposure to cancer-stimulating chemicals. It is known that such substances are present in cigarette smoke and some foods. Furthermore, a rare form of cholesterol has an unusual chemical structure found in certain chemicals that cause cancer. A tiny proportion of cholesterol in the body is always in this form. There is also a positive correlation between atherosclerosis-related heart attacks and deaths from cancer of the colon.

Questions

1. Compare and contrast the structure and function of red and white blood cells.

2. Outline the steps involved in formation of a blood clot.

3. Draw a simple diagram of the heart, its chambers, and the major blood vessels involved in pulmonary and systemic circulation. Use arrows to indicate blood flow. Shade those areas that carry deoxygenated blood.

4. What is the relationship between blood, plasma, and lymph?

5. Describe how the combined effects of blood pressure and osmotic pressure permit capillary exchange.

6. Describe the location and operation of the heart pacemaker.

7. What determines blood pressure?

8. Give the basis of the following conditions: anemia, heart murmurs, strokes, elephantiasis, and emphysema.

9. What is the relationship between cellular respiration and lung respiration?

10. Indicate the respiratory role played by each of the following: alveoli, diaphragm, hemoglobin, carbonic anhydrase.

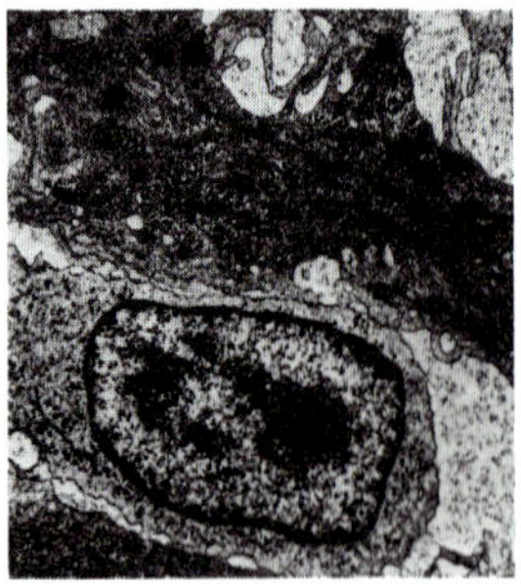

7

In and Out: Digestion and Excretion

DIGESTION AND EXCRETION ARE ABSOLUTELY ESsential to homeostasis. The food we eat to supply building blocks for the synthesis of new cellular material and to supply energy for carrying out cellular functions largely consists of the tissues of other organisms. Before it can provide nourishment, food must be digested—that is, broken down into small molecules that can pass through the plasma membranes that surround body cells. Food comes in large pieces that must be digested before entering body cells. The process of excretion is equally important, because it regulates our salt and water composition and rids our bodies of excess substances and chemical wastes.

But fundamental as digestion and excretion are, they would be futile or impossible without the circulatory system. Digestion depends on the fact that some of the oxygen-laden blood of the aorta is shunted through the digestive system, where it picks up nutrients. And the excretory system functions only because another portion of aortic blood enters the kidneys, where the concentration of useful components can be adjusted and wastes removed. Of course, blood draining from the digestive and excretory systems eventually mixes in the veins, so the whole body benefits. The entire sequence occurs quickly: one complete cycle of blood flow through the systemic circulation takes only about 90 seconds.

We mention the circulatory system here not just to point out the interdependence of body parts, but also to show that in the final analysis the digestive and excretory systems keep the blood chemically balanced. Only in this way can they service all our tissues.

PROCESSING AND USING NUTRIENTS

Very little food can be absorbed in the form in which it is eaten. First it must be **digested** through a complex series of physical and chemical changes. These changes gradually reduce the food to small particles dissolved or suspended in water; this enables them to make intimate contact with the cells that line the intestine. Equally important, most large molecules are divided into smaller units that the tissues can absorb.

The Digestive Tract, or "Down the Little Red Lane"

Basically, the digestive tract is a long tube that runs through the body from the mouth to the anus (Fig. 7.1). Along its entire length the tube consists of an epithelial lining overlaid with muscle and connective tissue, but different regions are specialized for specific functions. It is, in fact, an impressive digestion factory, but it requires the cooperation of several closely associated digestive glands. The salivary glands, the liver, and the pancreas are located outside the digestive tube itself, but some digestive glands are microscopic and hidden within the walls of the gut. This situation will be explained further as we follow a mouthful of food "down the little red lane."

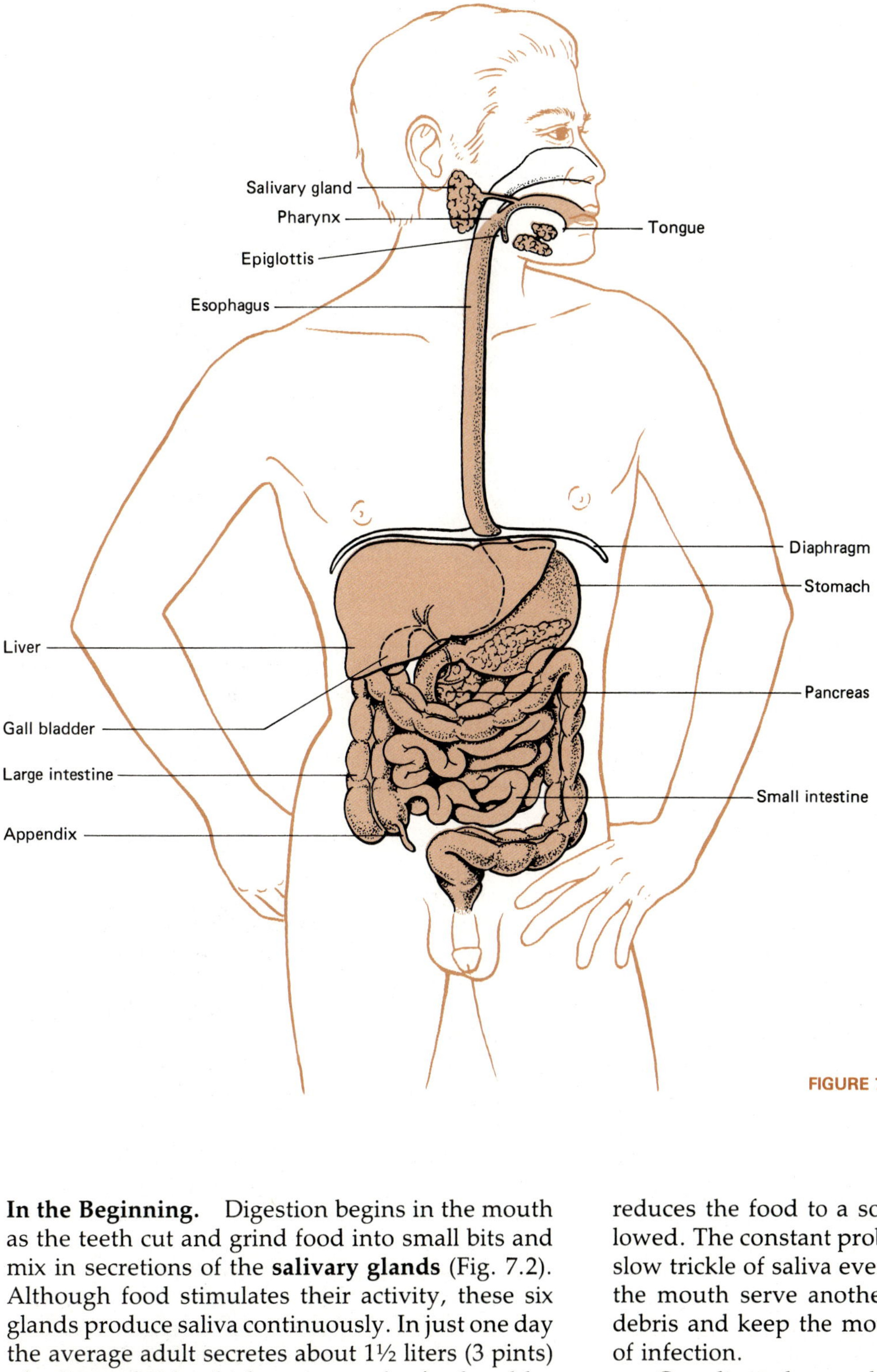

FIGURE 7.1 **The Digestive Tract.**

In the Beginning. Digestion begins in the mouth as the teeth cut and grind food into small bits and mix in secretions of the **salivary glands** (Fig. 7.2). Although food stimulates their activity, these six glands produce saliva continuously. In just one day the average adult secretes about 1½ liters (3 pints) of salivary fluid, which moistens the food and lubricates its passage.

The tongue and lips manipulate food as we chew; they turn it again and again and force it between the teeth. Gradually this physical activity reduces the food to a soft mass that can be swallowed. The constant probing of the tongue and the slow trickle of saliva even when there isn't food in the mouth serve another purpose: they dislodge debris and keep the mouth surfaces soft and free of infection.

Coordinated muscular contractions thrust food from the mouth, through the pharynx, and into the **esophagus**. This simple tube lies behind the trachea and leads to the stomach. Since the respiratory and digestive pathways cross in the pharynx

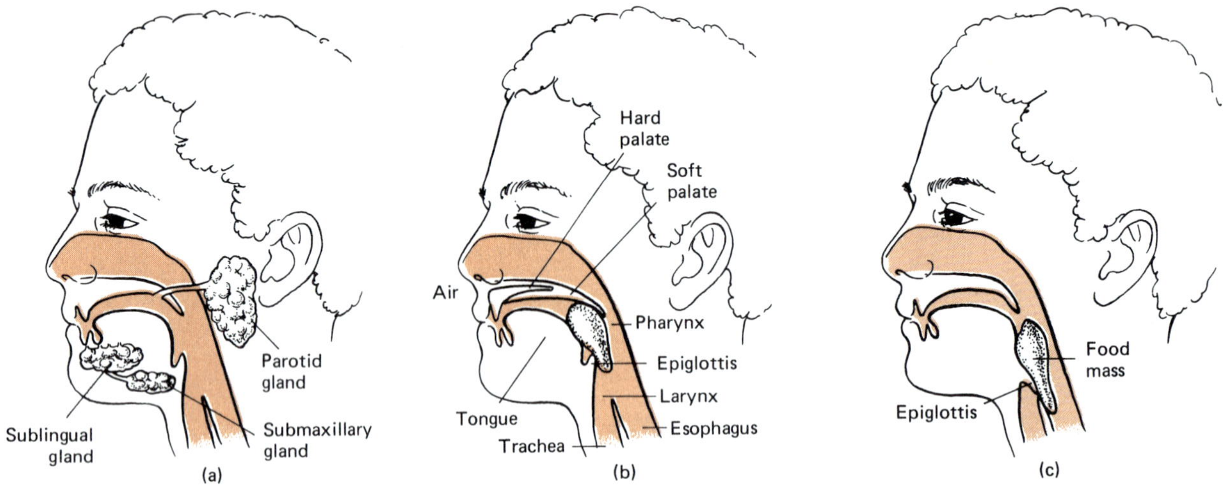

FIGURE 7.2 **The Mouth and Pharynx.** (a) Three sets of glands secrete saliva. (b) The trachea is normally open for the passage of air to the lungs. (c) Swallowing food forces the epiglottis to cover the opening to the respiratory pathway.

(Fig. 7.2), there is a great potential for choking on food particles. A surprising number of people choke to death, frequently after alcohol has whetted their appetite and dulled their coordination. Victims are often thought to be suffering from a heart attack. Suspect strangulation when someone stops eating, shows great distress, but makes no sound. Emergency measures are shown in Fig. 7.3.

When we begin to swallow, certain muscles pull the larynx upward and partially under the **epiglottis**. In this position the flap-like epiglottis will ordinarily shield the opening to the windpipe and prevent food from going the wrong way.

The voluntary action of swallowing forces food about one-third of the way down the esophagus. From there the automatic rhythmic contractions of muscles, referred to as **peristalsis**, push the food along to the stomach (Fig. 7.4). Cats, dogs, and many other animals must gulp down their food because their esophageal muscles, unlike those of humans, are completely voluntary and under conscious control.

The Stomach—Mainly a Holding Bag. The stomach is a distensible bag whose principal function is to hold food until it can be processed by other parts of the digestive system. The few digestive enzymes and acids secreted by the stomach are so unimportant that digestion is unaffected by surgical removal of the organ. The only handicap is the necessity of eating smaller and more frequent meals.

While waiting in the stomach, food is churned by strong peristaltic contractions of the stomach's muscular walls. At the same time, the food is mixed with **gastric juice** secreted by stomach glands under control of the nervous system. Hydrochloric acid,□ one of the main ingredients of gastric juice, 57
helps the churning stomach turn food into a semifluid mush, called **chyme**. Stomach acid is very corrosive, so a mucous coating□ protects the walls 86
of the organ. Sometimes stomach secretions work back up into the esophagus. We call the resulting irritation "heartburn."

Occasionally, either acid secretion increases or the mucous barrier breaks down. When either happens, open sores develop in the stomach lining. These **peptic ulcers** are continuously irritated by the stomach secretions. There is some evidence that stress can trigger ulcer formation, perhaps by altering the nature of stomach secretions. Actually, ulcers are more frequent in the part of the intestine that lies just next to the stomach.

Although food may be churned for three or four hours in the stomach, very little absorption occurs there. Only water, salts, simple sugars such as glucose, and some drugs, including alcohol, are readily absorbed. One reason alcohol affects people so quickly is that much of it is absorbed early in the digestive process.

The Small Intestine—Where the Action Is. The real work of digestion and absorption, which many people associate with the stomach, actually occurs in the **small intestine**. The fluid chyme squirts into the small intestine from the stomach through a small opening, the **pyloric sphincter**, which is a ring of muscle that closes in response to the hormone **enterogasterone**. Whenever a certain amount of food is present in the small intestine, the walls there secrete enterogasterone into the bloodstream. When some of this chemical messenger reaches the sphincter, it closes. Stretching of the intestine also stimulates closure of the pyloric sphincter. And if acidic stomach contents enter too rapidly, they irritate the intestinal lining, and the sphincter closes. Each of these mechanisms ensures that whenever the small intestine is filled with food, the entrance of more material is prevented.

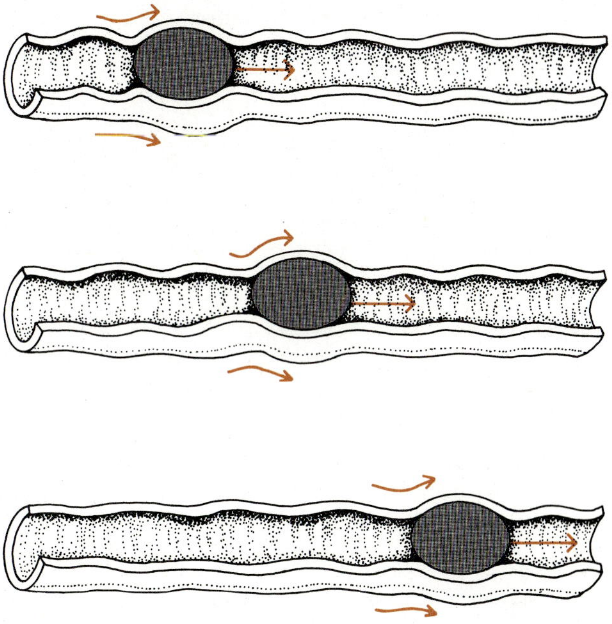

FIGURE 7.4 **Peristalsis.** Successive waves of contraction squeeze food through the digestive system. The mechanism can be likened to squeezing the last bit of toothpaste to the top of a tube.

FIGURE 7.3 **The Heimlich Maneuver.** Three ways to dislodge food that is blocking the trachea.

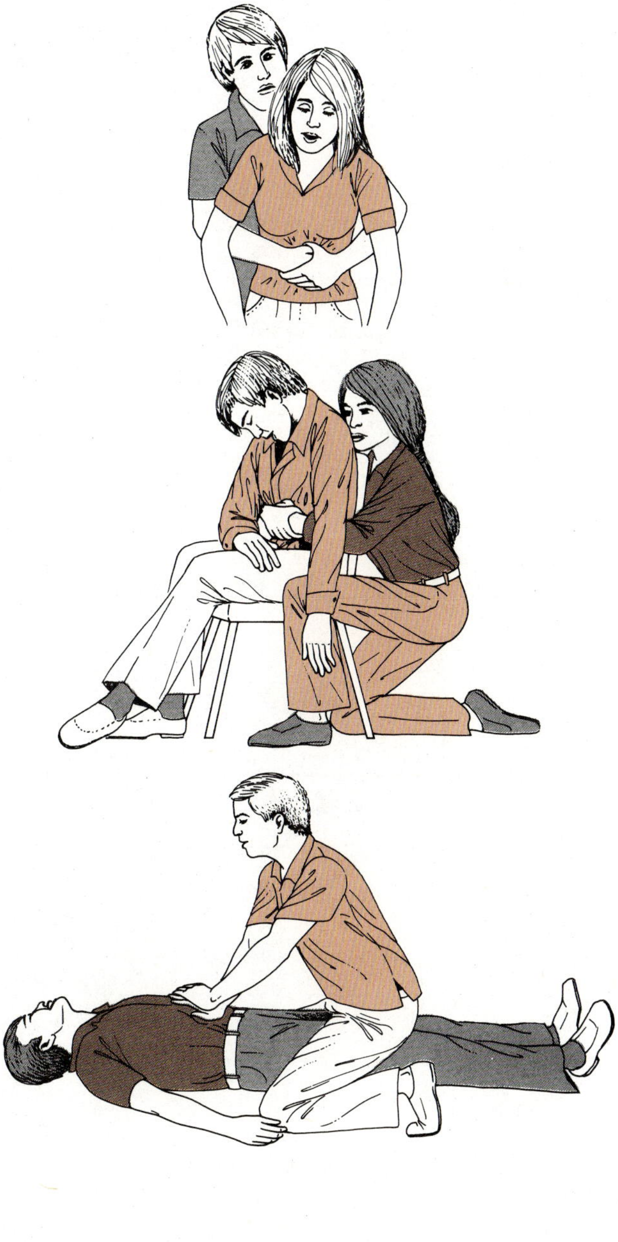

Food moves through the small intestine by peristaltic contractions of its muscular walls. These and other localized involuntary contractions also mix the food with digestive juices. Enzymes released by cells sloughed off the intestinal lining, pancreatic juice secreted by the pancreas, and bile from the liver together account for the breakdown of all the major classes of food molecules in the small intestine (Table 7.1).

The **pancreas**, the largest and most important digestive gland, is nestled in the first curve of the small intestine. The presence of food in the small intestine causes it to produce the hormone **secretin**. Secretin stimulates the pancreas to release **pancreatic juice**, which flows to the small intestine via the pancreatic duct (Fig. 7.5). Pancreatic juice contains a wide variety of digestive enzymes plus alkaline salts that help neutralize stomach acids that reach the small intestine.

The **gallbladder** stores bile produced by the liver. An intestinal hormone stimulates the gallbladder to empty its contents into the bile duct, which joins the pancreatic duct just before it enters the small intestine. **Bile** is a greenish liquid that

TABLE 7.1 **Agents of Human Digestion**

SOURCE	AGENT	SUBSTRATE	PRODUCT	SITE OF ACTION
Salivary glands	Salivary amylase	Starches	Maltose	Mouth
Stomach (gastric) glands	Pepsin	Proteins	Peptides	Stomach
	Renin	Milk protein	Clotted protein	Stomach
	Hydrochloric acid	Many foods	Smaller units	Stomach
Pancreas	Pancreatic amylase	Starches	Maltose	Small intestine
	Lipase	Fats	Fatty acids, glycerol	Small intestine
	Trypsin	Proteins	Peptides	Small intestine
	Chymotrypsin	Proteins	Peptides	Small intestine
	Carboxypeptidase	Proteins	Peptides	Small intestine
	Nucleases	DNA and RNA	Nucleotides	Small intestine
Small intestine	Maltase	Maltose	Glucose	Small intestine
	Lactase	Lactose	Glucose, galactose	Small intestine
	Sucrase	Sucrose	Glucose, fructose	Small intestine
	Aminopeptidase	Peptides	Amino acids	Small intestine
	Dipeptidase	Dipeptides	Amino acids	Small intestine
	Phosphatase	Nucleotides	Smaller units	Small intestine
Liver	Bile	Large fat droplets	Emulsified fats	Small intestine

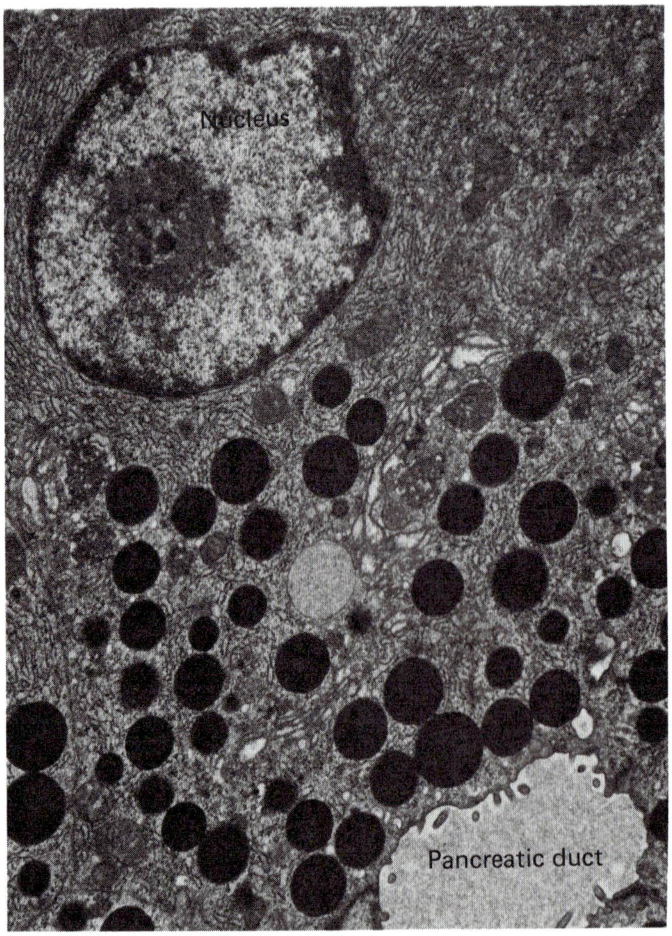

FIGURE 7.5 **Digestive Glands.** (a) The dark bodies in this pancreatic cell are enzyme storage granules about to eject their contents into the pancreatic duct. (b) Ducts from the liver, gallbladder, and pancreas join near the point where their contents empty into the small intestine.

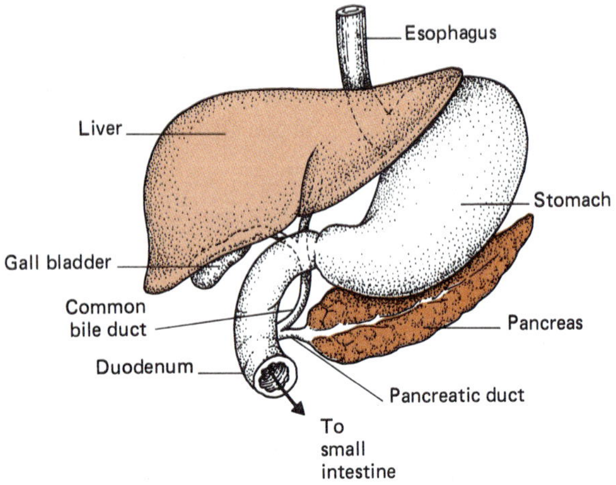

contains, among other things, **bile salts**. These substances are excellent emulsifiers. That is, by a kind of detergent action, bile salts break fats into microscopic droplets, making them more accessible to digestive enzymes.

73 Bile also contains some cholesterol. If the gallbladder concentrates bile too much, the cholesterol precipitates to form **gallstones**. Small stones can pass down the gall duct—accompanied by considerable pain—but larger ones block the passageway. When blockage occurs, bile pigments build up in the bloodstream, causing **obstructive jaundice**, a condition characterized by a yellowing of the whites of the eyes and, in some cases, of the skin. This is one of several forms of jaundice. Diseases of the liver, which produces bile pigments by processing breakdown products of hemoglobin from worn-out blood cells, account for certain others.

The small intestine has an extensive surface area for absorption. Not only is it long—usually from 20 to 25 feet—but its interior is arranged in numerous folds. Moreover, the entire lining is covered with microscopic, fingerlike projections called **villi** (Fig. 7.6). Each cell of the intestinal lining has a brush border of **microvilli**. Thus the villi have villi, making the total absorptive surface area immense. At their cores the villi contain blood and lymph capillaries to carry away absorbed foods.

The Colon and Absorption of Water. The **large intestine** is often called the **colon**. It is a wide tube only about one-tenth as long as the small intestine. The material that enters the large intestine is a watery mixture of undigested food, bile, and digestive juices. One of the chief functions of the large intestine is to recover water and minerals from this material. Absorption of water helps transform the intestinal contents into solid **feces**. Mucus produced by cells of the intestinal wall holds the fecal matter together and acts as a lubricant during its passage from the body.

The contents of the large intestine support the growth of tremendous numbers of microorganisms. In fact, at least half the dry weight of feces is dead or living microorganisms. Intestinal microbes digest cellulose and other residual organic matter present in the colon. Their metabolism is fermentative, producing large quantities of carbon dioxide and foul-smelling gases and other wastes. These microbial substances contribute to the odor of feces and intestinal **flatus** (gas).

The microbes that ordinarily inhabit the human colon are harmless; some of them are thought to

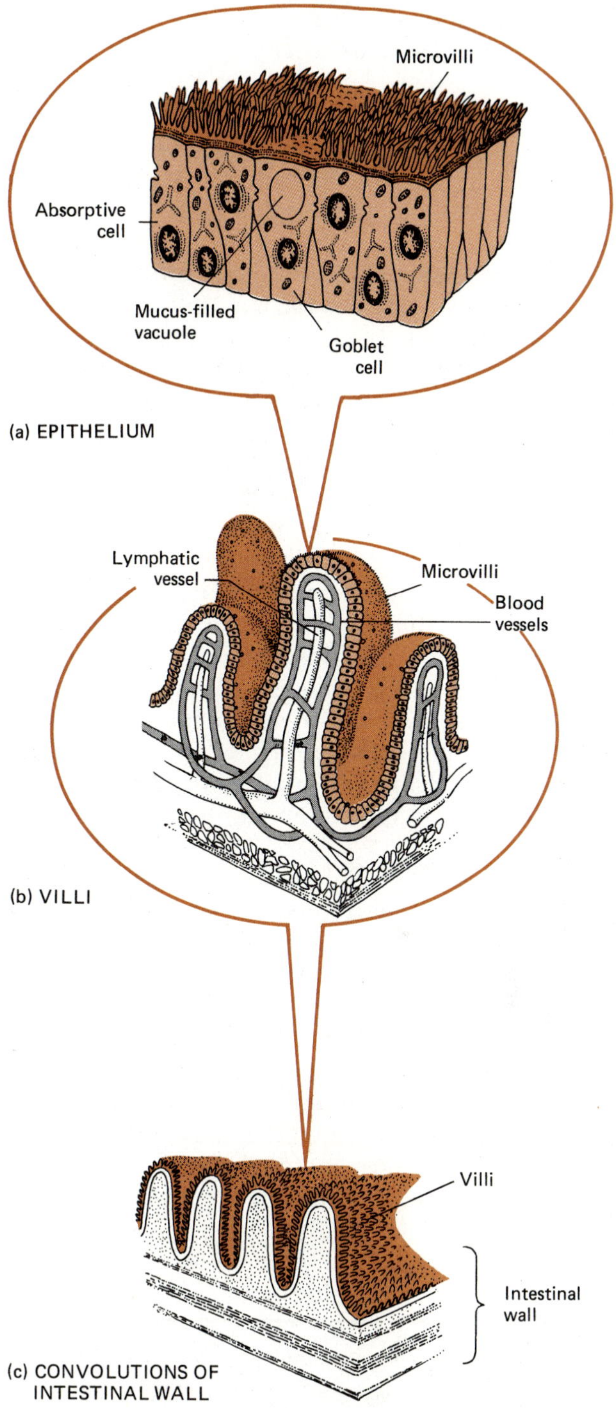

FIGURE 7.6 Inside the Small Intestine. Three structural features enhance the absorptive function of the small intestine by increasing its surface area: (a) fuzzy microvilli bordering epithelial cells of the lining of the intestine; (b) fingerlike villi projecting from the intestinal wall; and (c) convolutions or folds of the intestinal wall. The goblet cells scattered in the intestinal epithelium secrete mucus, which may protect the other cells from damage by digestive enzymes.

produce vitamins that are then absorbed by the intestine. **Vitamin K**, a substance necessary for blood clotting, as well as some B vitamins, may be supplied in this way.

The **appendix** is a worm-shaped offshoot of the colon on the right-hand side of the body near where the small intestine and large intestine join. It is a narrow sac, no larger than your little finger. The appendix has no apparent digestive function, but food residues and bacteria may lodge there and cause trouble. As the food rots and bacteria grow, the little sac becomes swollen and sore. A diseased appendix must be removed. If it ruptures, the infection can spread into the body cavity and lead to **peritonitis**, a very serious condition.

Elimination. Distension of the rectum by fecal matter initiates muscular contractions that propel the stool out through the anus. Normally the **rectum**, which is the terminal section of the large intestine, is empty until just before defecation (the act of elimination). Entrance of the stool causes the smooth muscle of the **internal anal sphincter** to relax. Elimination is accomplished by the conscious opening of the **external anal sphincter**. Pressure from contraction of abdominal muscles aids elimination.

The dark color of feces comes from excreted bile pigments. Odd-colored feces usually indicate nothing more than a change in the diet, but occasionally they mean something more serious. Light stools can indicate reduced bile secretion due to liver disease or an obstruction of the bile duct. Extremely dark stools may be caused by the presence of digested blood from internal bleeding.

Diarrhea occurs when the large intestine fails to reabsorb the normal amount of water. Failure may be due to bacterial infections, poisons, vitamin deficiencies, or stress. Often these causes increase motility and reduce the time material remains in the intestine. **Constipation** occurs when feces move through the intestine so slowly that too much water is removed, leaving a hard, dry stool. A diet high in "roughage" foods, such as fruit, vegetables, and whole grains, stimulates intestinal movements and prevents constipation. The fibers and other tough materials found in natural (unprocessed) foods are a normal part of every human diet. Such roughage provides no nutrients, since it is indigestible, but it helps retain the moisture necessary for a soft stool. There is reason to believe that the continual strain of eliminating hard stools promotes **diverticulitis**. Diverticula are pouches that develop where the intestinal wall becomes thin and weak. Diverticulitis occurs when these pouches trap fecal material and become infected. **Hemorrhoids** (piles) are varicose veins that develop if straining puts unusual pressure on veins of the rectal lining.

In developed countries, many foods are processed for various reasons, often merely to improve their "aesthetic" qualities or texture. Usually the processing results in the elimination of important nutrients and, in some foods, roughage. The best 112
example is the milling of wheat to make white flour. Alterations of traditional human foods may explain the high incidence of intestinal cancer today. Some researchers have suggested that slow-moving, hard stools, which are typical with low-roughage diets, contain greater than usual numbers of intestinal bacteria that produce cancer-causing chemicals. It has been suggested that prolonged presence of stools in the intestine would also favor absorption of cancer-stimulating substances, either from the diet or from bacterial activity.

Chemistry of Digestion

Although saliva contains enzymes that can start digestion of carbohydrates, for all practical purposes chemical digestion begins in the stomach. Here hydrochloric acid, aided by constant churning of the stomach walls, helps liquefy solid foods. You can demonstrate the action of hydrochloric acid in the laboratory by dropping a piece of meat into a beaker of hydrochloric acid and then watch the chunk of muscle gradually dissolve. When this happens in the stomach, it releases nutrients hidden in the interior of solid food and makes them more accessible to digestive enzymes of the small intestine.

Vitamins and minerals released during disintegration of large pieces of food can be absorbed without further digestion. So can simple sugars and amino acids. Most food, however, consists of large molecules that cannot be absorbed directly but must first be degraded to their fundamental subunits. Carbohydrates are absorbed only as simple sugars, proteins as amino acids, and ordinary fats usually as fatty acids and glycerol.

Enzymatic digestion involves hydrolysis (*hydro* means water; *lysis* means release). To put it another way, the breakdown of the large molecules requires water, which is incorporated into the smaller molecules that are released (Fig. 7.7). This is true in

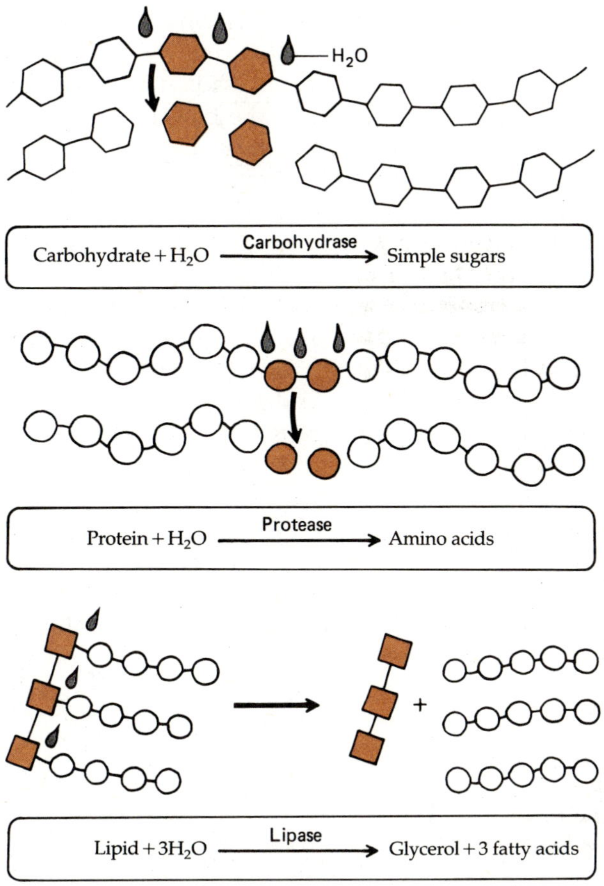

FIGURE 7.7 **Enzymatic Hydrolysis.** Digestive enzymes degrade food by hydrolysis. In the process, chemical bonds that hold the subunits of large molecules together are broken by the addition of water. The small digestion products are easier to absorb.

the digestion of carbohydrates and proteins as well as fats. Note that these hydrolytic reactions are just the reverse of the reactions by which the large molecules were synthesized in the plant or animal that provided the food. Before reading further, you may find it useful to review the chemistry of food mol-
67 ecules, as described in Chapter 4.□

Proteins. The digestion of giant protein molecules is a tremendous task that requires the concerted action of several enzymes. The long protein chains are first broken into shorter chains by **pepsin** in the stomach and **trypsin** and **chymotrypsin** enzymes secreted into the small intestine by the pancreas. Each enzyme is quite specific and can attack protein chains only at certain points, but together the four enzymes quickly degrade any protein into shorter peptide chains.

Digestive enzymes are secreted in an inactive form and become activated only within the digestive cavity. Thus digestive enzymes can be stored in digestive glands without threat of self-digestion. Hydrochloric acid in the stomach activates pepsin. As partly digested food passes from the stomach to the intestine, it carries with it small amounts of a stomach enzyme whose sole function is the activation of trypsin in the intestine. Once activated, trypsin can activate more trypsin, as well as chymotrypsin and elastase. The risk of spontaneous activation of trypsin is so great that the pancreas contains special blocking factors that combine with the active sites on the enzymes it secretes.

Peptides must be further digested before absorption can occur. The intestine secretes **peptidases** that nibble away at the short peptide chains, removing one amino acid at a time from each end. In this way all proteins are broken down into their component amino acids.

Carbohydrates. Common food carbohydrates include **polysaccharides**, particularly starch and glycogen (animal starch). As you know, polysaccharides are long, branched chains of sugars. They are digested by enzymes secreted by the pancreas and small intestine. First the long chains are cleaved into two-sugar units, or **disaccharides**, by pancreatic amylase. **Maltose** is the disaccharide released from glycogen and starch.

Specific enzymes called **disaccharidases** divide the double sugars into their component simple sugars, which can be absorbed. Maltose digestion releases two glucoses. **Sucrose**, ordinary table sugar, is a disaccharide digested to glucose and fructose. Digestion of **lactose**, the disaccharide found in milk, produces glucose and galactose. Failure of some adults to secrete the enzyme lactase makes them unable to digest lactose. The undigested lactose cannot be absorbed by the intestine and so must be excreted. In fact, the high concentration of lactose in the gut causes large amounts of water to diffuse out of the intestinal cells, making the feces watery. The result is intestinal distress and, of course, diarrhea whenever milk is consumed.

Up to about the age of four, children secrete lactase, since milk is an important part of their diet. In fact, most adults continue to secrete the enzyme. In some countries, however, very few adults retain the ability to digest lactose. The evolution of this trait is related to the availability of milk as a food for adults. In some parts of Africa, for instance,

there is no source of milk other than mother's milk. Adults from these regions do not synthesize lactase, and they get sick when they drink milk. However, they have no problem with such dairy products as cheese or yogurt. During the fermenta-
106 tion of milk to produce these products, the lactose is converted to lactic acid.

Fats. Unlike the digestion of carbohydrates and proteins, fat digestion is a relatively nonspecific process. Fatty foods are first prepared for digestion by emulsification into tiny droplets by bile salts. Then, **lipases** secreted by the pancreas and intestine degrade the fats to fatty acids and glycerol in a single step. For a step-by-step summary of digestion, see Table 7.1.

Absorption of Nutrients

Absorption is a poorly understood process. Some substances simply diffuse from the gut into the bloodstream, where they are present in much lower concentration. However, other digestion products, including glucose and amino acids, are present in relatively large amounts in the blood at all times. As a result, these materials must be absorbed into the circulation by active transport pumps that require the expenditure of metabolic energy. 78

It is known that bile salts greatly enhance the diffusion of fatty acids into intestinal cells. For some reason, much of the absorbed fatty acid and glycerol is resynthesized into fats once it enters the intestinal cells. However, much of the fat is never digested chemically, and directly after emulsification it enters intestinal cells (Fig. 7.8). Most of the fats in the intestine do not reach the bloodstream immediately; instead, they pour into lymph capillaries and travel through the lymphatic system to the veins.

Fatty materials that enter the bloodstream from the lymphatic system are transported to fat-storage areas or are degraded by a lipase in the blood. By

FIGURE 7.8 Absorption of Fats. (a) Resting intestinal epithelial cells. (b) Similar cells of an animal fed a high fat meal. Note the fat droplets.

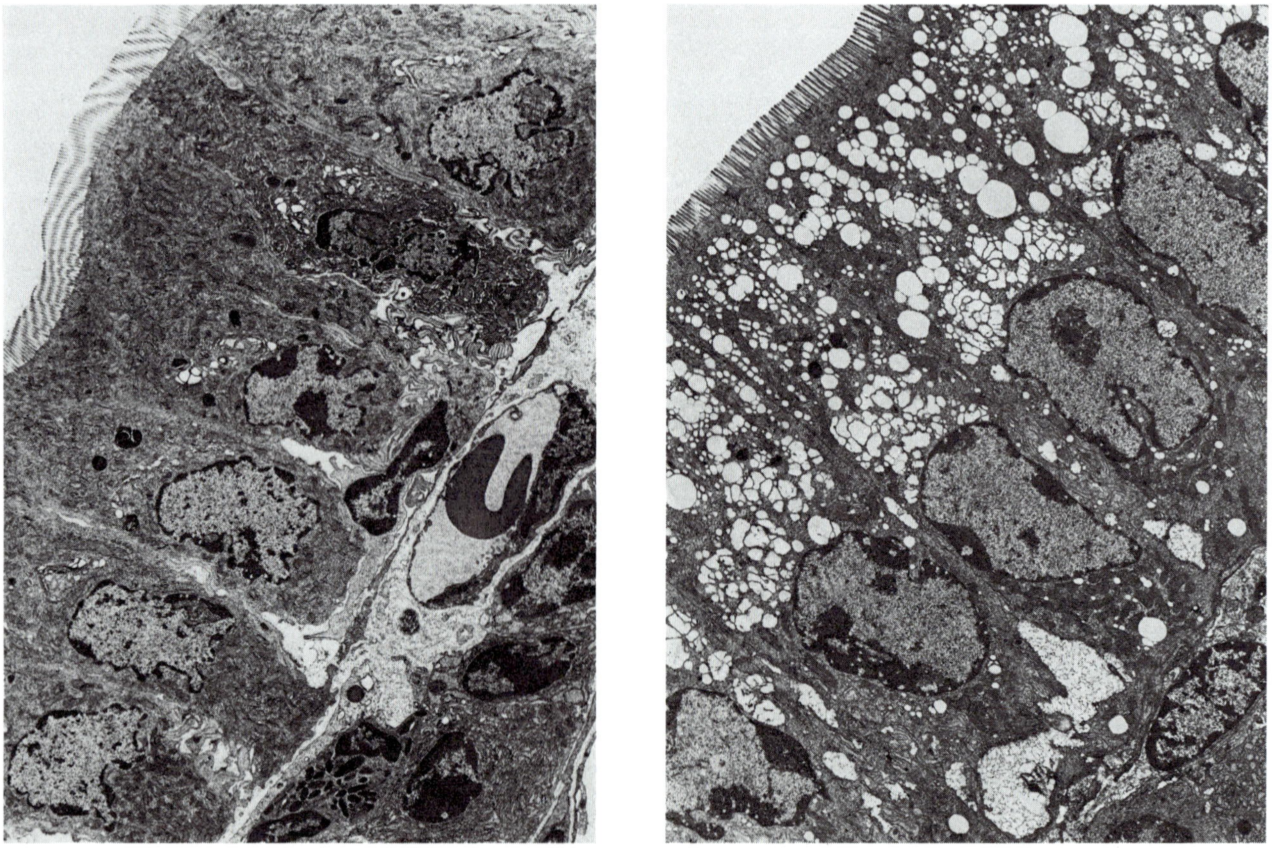

(a) (b)

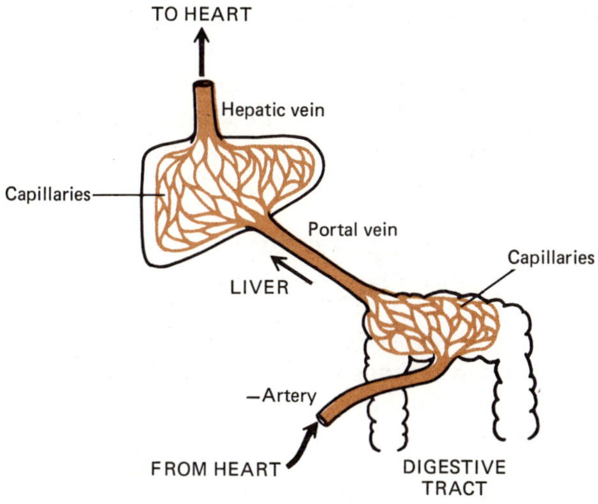

FIGURE 7.9 **Hepatic-Portal Circulation.** Arteries bring blood to the digestive tract, where nutrients are absorbed. Blood from intestinal capillaries then flows to the liver through the portal vein. In the liver excess nutrients are removed. Blood from the liver is collected by the hepatic vein and returned to the heart.

this means, fatty acids and glycerol are made available for cellular use directly. However, the simple sugars, amino acids, and the few fatty materials that enter the blood capillaries of the intestine are not transported to the body tissues immediately. They go to the liver first.

The Liver and Nutrient Utilization

Most of the nutrients absorbed from the intestinal tract are sent directly to the liver. The **hepatic portal vein** carries the blood from the intestinal capillaries directly to the liver. This is an unusual circulatory pathway, because the blood travels from one capillary network to another without passing through the heart (Fig. 7.9).

The liver carries out a number of activities that promote homeostasis and control body function. Besides secreting bile salts, the liver stores certain vitamins and iron. It is even involved in removing old red blood cells from circulation. The liver is also responsible for the detoxification of many poisons. Another protective function is provided by phagocytic cells that line the liver blood passages to destroy stray microorganisms. But perhaps the most important function of the liver is to regulate the composition of the blood. The liver manufactures many of the blood plasma proteins. In addition, the liver regulates the level of sugar, amino acids, and fat in the blood.

Glucose Metabolism. In cooperation with the pancreas and other organs, the liver ensures that each body cell is provided with nutrients for synthesis and for energy (Fig. 7.10). Since the primary source of energy for most body cells is glucose, the cells must have a constant supply. After a meal, the blood entering the liver from the gut is rich in glucose and other simple sugars. Unless they are needed for other purposes, the liver converts all sugars to glucose. But only enough glucose is allowed to flow into the general circulation to maintain the normal blood-sugar concentration. The excess glucose is converted into the storage polysaccharide, glycogen.

The liver has a limited capacity to store glycogen. Therefore, if the carbohydrate supply is excessive, extra glucose is converted to fat. Then the fat is transported in the blood to fat storage areas of the body. Between meals, or at times when there is an inadequate intake of sugar, the liver releases glucose from its glycogen stores to maintain the blood-sugar level.

The blood-sugar level is monitored by the pancreas. When glucose concentration in the blood increases, as can happen immediately after a meal, the pancreas secretes **insulin**. This hormone stimulates the liver to remove excess glucose and synthesize it into glycogen. Insulin also increases

FIGURE 7.10 **Liver Metabolism.** The central role of the liver is to process, apportion, and appropriately convert incoming sugars, amino acids, and lipids. Of course, the liver does this for all the cells of the body, not just for muscle cells.

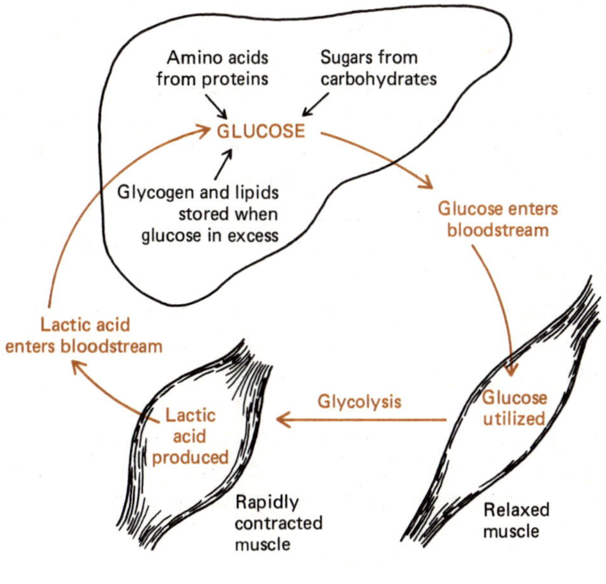

permeability to glucose of many kinds of body cells, so that glucose is rapidly utilized. This helps the blood-sugar level fall back to normal. **Glucagon**, a second pancreatic hormone, is secreted when the blood-glucose concentration reaches an unacceptably low level. Glucagon stimulates the liver to degrade its stored glycogen and release glucose into the blood.

Hypoglycemia is a condition characterized by low blood sugar and excessive insulin levels. Individuals affected by this disorder may experience dramatic feelings of nervousness and faintness a few hours after eating candy or other readily absorbable forms of sugar. Those who suffer from **diabetes** experience negative symptoms from eating the same types of foods, but for a different reason: their inadequate levels of insulin result in an excessively high concentration of sugar in the blood. Because hypoglycemic and diabetic people cannot maintain a normal blood-glucose concentration after a sugary meal, they are said to be glucose intolerant.

The nervous system is particularly sensitive to glucose concentration. If the supply of glucose in the blood vessels serving the brain falls by only a fraction, there is a feeling of dizziness and nausea. When we are hungry, the brain stimulates the production of epinephrine by the adrenal gland, causing the liver to release glucose into the blood. Similarly, under conditions of stress or fear, the nervous system can cause a massive outpouring of glucose to cope with the emergency energy requirements.

Amino Acid and Fat Metabolism. The liver also regulates the flow of amino acids to the tissues of the body. Although amino acids can be used by many cells as a source of energy, they are not preferentially used for this purpose. Instead, they are assembled into the proteins that are needed for the growth and repair of tissues. Small quantities of excess amino acids can be stored in the liver, to be gradually released as required for metabolic use by the body. Some of the amino acids arriving in the liver from the intestine are used for the liver's own synthetic activities—for example, the formation of blood proteins. Excess amino acids are converted to glucose or fats, which are stored either in the liver or elsewhere.

The first step in the conversion of amino acids to glucose involves the removal of the nitrogen-containing portion of the amino acid. This process is called **deamination**, and it produces a toxic nitrogenous waste, ammonia. The liver combines ammonia with carbon dioxide to form a relatively harmless nitrogenous waste material, **urea**. The urea passes by way of blood to the kidneys, where it it excreted. A small amount of urea and other nitrogenous wastes are excreted via the sweat glands (Fig. 7.11).

Most body organs can use glycerol and fatty acids as energy sources. However, so long as the carbohydrate supply is sufficient, the body uses glucose and stores fat. The liver uses some fatty acids for the synthesis of certain lipids, including cholesterol. In the presence of a sustained glucose shortage, the brain sometimes adapts to the use of fatty acids. During times of starvation this permits the conservation of muscle and other body proteins, which would otherwise have to be degraded to amino acids for conversion into glucose to supply the brain with energy.

Diabetes. In diabetes mellitus, or "sugar diabetes," many of the delicate mechanisms that control nutrient utilization are upset. At least part of the problem is insufficient insulin. Without insulin the liver does not remove excess glucose from the blood. Despite the high blood sugar, most body cells are starved for glucose, because insulin, you see, promotes absorption of glucose by body cells. For this reason, glucose accumulates in the blood of diabetics and must be excreted in the urine. The additional water necessary to carry glucose out of the kidneys depletes the body of water. This explains the excessive thirst and frequent urination that are classic symptoms of diabetes.

Because the tissues cannot take in enough glucose, diabetics must rely more heavily on amino acids, glycerol, and fatty acids for their energy. This abnormal metabolism produces poisonous wastes. In addition, the body cells react by converting their own proteins into glucose. And as a result, the tissues simply waste away.

Actually, two major forms of diabetes are recognized. One begins abruptly, usually in children or young adults. The symptoms are severe; treatment almost always requires injections of insulin. A milder diabetes appears often in older people. Usually this form can be managed with diet or oral drugs that stimulate the pancreas to secrete adequate insulin. Many otherwise normal people show a predisposition to the disease. A **prediabetic condition** can be diagnosed by determining how quickly the blood glucose falls after an oral dose of sugar.

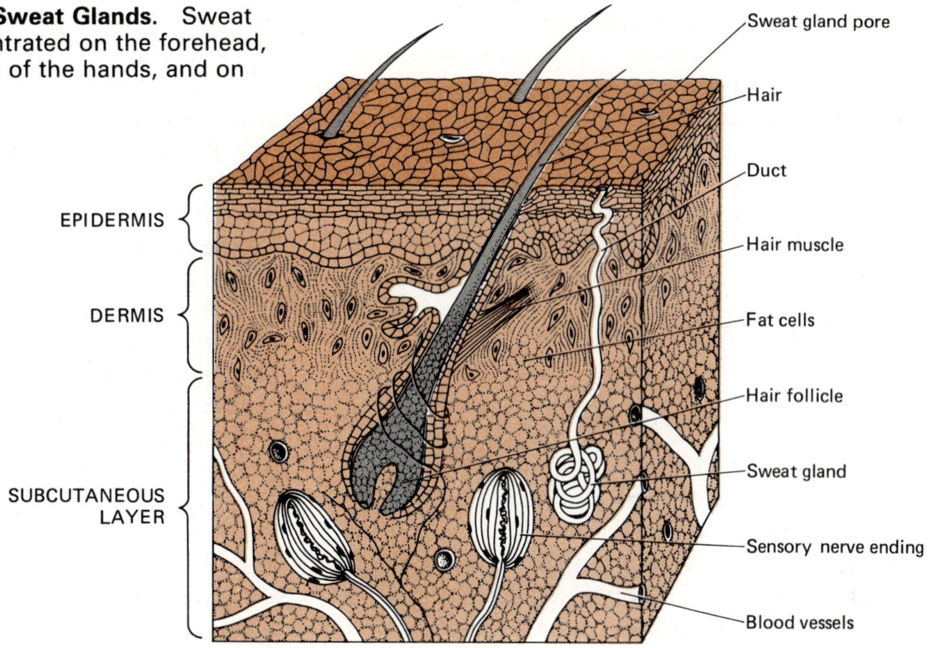

FIGURE 7.11 Skin Layers and Sweat Glands. Sweat glands are especially concentrated on the forehead, in the armpits, on the palms of the hands, and on the soles of the feet.

Prediabetic individuals almost always develop diabetic symptoms later in life.

Unfortunately, although diabetes is treatable, success with insulin therapy has been neither uniform nor complete. Slight overdoses lower the blood sugar drastically. The brain is rapidly affected; the confusion and staggering that result are sometimes mistaken for drunkenness. Coma and death may follow. Diabetics often carry hard candy to eat at the first sign of insulin "shock."

The prevalence of long-term diabetic complications confirms the conclusion that many cases are never completely arrested. Cataracts, impaired nerves, kidney damage, and atherosclerosis have always been common among those afflicted with the disease. Some scientists believe that the complications result from imperfect regulation of insulin dosages—a frequent occurrence since insulin requirements vary with food intake and activity. Others insist that there is more to diabetes than a simple defect in insulin secretion.

More than likely, there is some truth to both assertions. The aberrant glucose metabolism that accompanies fluctuating insulin levels causes unusual metabolic products to accumulate within cells. When there are such accumulations in the lens of the eye, the altered cell fluids precipitate cell proteins. The cells become opaque and a cataract forms. Similar changes presumably account for damage to nerve, kidney, and other cells. Mounting evidence indicates that there is indeed more to diabetes than insulin deficiency. Researchers have found that increased amounts of a second pancreatic hormone, glucagon, are produced by diabetics. It seems that treatment of diabetes should include suppression of glucagon as well as administration of insulin.

Many of the metabolic defects characteristic of diabetes are puzzling. High blood sugar is enhanced by the conversion of amino acids to glucose. The condition is further aggravated because very little glucose is converted to fat, as might be expected when there is excess sugar available.

The complications created by diabetes illustrate the complexities of providing the body with a constant supply of nutrients. This is just one more aspect of maintaining the internal environment. Another is the removal of the wastes of cellular metabolism. We have already learned how carbon dioxide is disposed of through the lungs. Now let us see how the body contends with other waste products.

EXCRETION AND HOMEOSTASIS

Some byproducts of body activities are not only useless but actually harmful in large quantities. To maintain life, they must be removed from the body routinely.

The kidneys are the organs responsible for the excretion of body wastes. Their smooth surface shows nothing of the sophisticated internal organization that allows kidneys to filter the blood to remove wastes but to reabsorb such potentially useful substances as sugar, water, and salts. Overall, the kidneys are major homeostatic organs. In addition to filtration and reabsorption, their functions include regulation of blood-water volume, adjustment of blood pressure, and control of blood pH and ion levels.

Kidney Structure and Function

Although some excretion can occur through the sweat glands and intestinal walls, the **kidneys** are our main excretory organs. Each fist-sized human kidney (Fig. 7.12) contains about a million individual excretory units, or **nephrons**. Each nephron consists of a **nephric tubule** entangled with blood vessels. Several nephric tubules drain into a single collecting tubule. A branch of the renal artery leads to the **glomerulus**, a distinctive knob of capillaries within the cupped end of the nephric tubule. From the glomerulus the blood enters a second arteriole. This small artery leads to an extensive capillary network that surrounds the remainder of the nephric tubule. Figure 7.12 provides a diagrammatic view of these kidney structures.

Filtration, Reabsorption, and Secretion. Because they flow into a narrow, elastic arteriole rather than into thin-walled, flaccid veins (as do most capillaries), there is a substantial blood pressure within the glomerulus capillaries. This high **filtration pressure** indiscriminately forces water and most other small molecules from the glomerular capillaries into the nephric tubule. Only blood cells, proteins, and fat globules are retained by the capillaries. As you can see, a high filtration pressure in the glomerulus is absolutely essential to kidney function. In fact, it is so important that the kidneys themselves help regulate blood pressure.

A human makes about 180 liters (190 quarts) of glomerular filtrate every day. No organisms could afford the extravagance of permitting the valuable substances in this material to be excreted. Therefore much of the work of the kidney is to salvage the useful substances from the filtrate. All but a liter to perhaps a liter and one-half of liquid is returned to the bloodstream. This is accomplished by **selective reabsorption**.

Water, glucose, amino acids, vitamins, hormones, and minerals are among the substances that

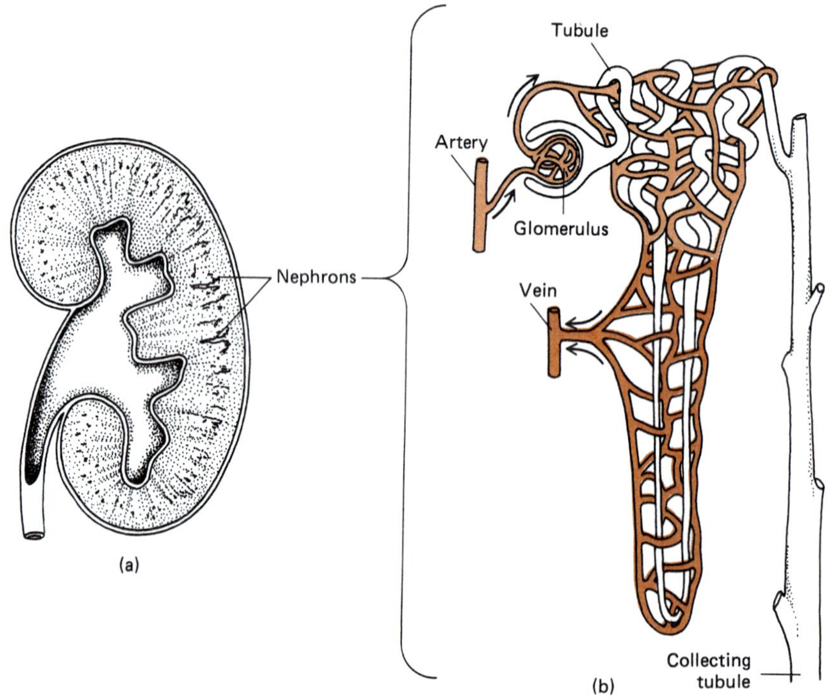

FIGURE 7.12 Structure of the Kidney. (a) A diagrammatic view of a section through a kidney. (b) Nephrons are the functional units of the kidney. There are thousands of them.

are reabsorbed into the capillaries that entangle each nephric tubule. Except for water, most of the substances are recovered by active transport. Reclaimed molecules are pumped out of the nephric tubules into the surrounding tissues, from which they reenter the circulatory system through nearby capillaries. Little is known about the exact steps involved.

No substance present in the blood in excessive amounts is ever fully reabsorbed from the kidney filtrate. For example, when blood sugar is abnormally high, glucose is retained in the tubules and excreted in the urine. However, a word of caution about the meaning of sugar in urine is necessary. It can indicate faulty utilization, but it can also mean excessive sugar consumption. Even for normal individuals, eating a box of candy can produce the transient appearance of glucose in the urine.

As we said earlier, it is part of the job of the kidneys to maintain the normal, nearly neutral pH of the blood. This is not accomplished simply by excretion of excess acid and base, because acids and bases are already neutralized by blood buffers. The role of the kidney is to return the buffers to the blood, thus restoring its buffering capacity while eliminating the acids and bases.

Although urine is formed primarily by glomerular filtration and selective tubular reabsorption, a few substances are added to urine by **tubular secretion**. Through this auxiliary mechanism, tubule cells actively remove substances from the blood in the surrounding capillaries directly into the interior of the tubules. Tubular secretion is responsible for the elimination of some excess potassium and a number of relatively minor metabolic wastes, but perhaps a more important function is its role in the excretion of abnormal blood constituents such as penicillin and certain other drugs.

Kidney function is controlled by complex feedback mechanisms. In one series of reactions, reduced pressure in renal arteries causes the kidney to release an enzyme, **renin**, into the bloodstream. Renin, in turn, stimulates production of **aldosterone**, and this hormone promotes reabsorption of water from kidney tubules. This increases the fluid volume of the blood and thus increases blood pressure. As normal blood pressure returns, the kidney's renin production slacks off.

Water, Fluid Volume, and Blood Pressure. Reabsorption of water from the nephric tubules determines the water content of the blood and of the body generally. Water moves out of the kidney tubules back into the blood purely by diffusion. This passive reabsorption occurs because the selective absorption of glucose and other valuable substances, especially sodium ions, creates a favorables concentration gradient. As the tubular filtrate becomes more dilute, the water concentration becomes greater inside the tubules than in the surrounding tissues and blood. The result is that water diffuses out of the nephric tubules. What remains is a relatively concentrated substance that is urine.

Reabsorption is so precisely regulated that the water content of body tissues is nearly constant. When the body is short of water, only enough is excreted to keep urinary wastes in solution. If the blood is diluted just a bit, increased secretion of **antidiuretic hormone** (ADH) by the pituitary gland promotes reabsorption of water. Secretions of the adrenal cortex also lead to a more concentrated urine. These secretions increase active transport of sodium into the blood and thus increase the osmotic pull there. As a result, more water is drawn from the renal tubules.

Of course, these hormonal controls can be upset. Large amounts of glucose in the nephric tubules reduce the concentration of water there and oppose its reabsorption. This is the reason for the large volume of urine produced in untreated diabetes. Alcoholic beverages stimulate urine production by depressing the secretion of ADH. This effect is compounded by the large volume of water consumed in beverages, especially beer. Caffeine is another **diuretic**—that is, a substance that increases urine production. The caffeine of coffee, tea, and cola beverages probably causes diuresis by dilating blood vessels in the kidney.

Urine. Most of the organic wastes in urine are substances produced to detoxify products of the metabolism of nitrogen-containing compounds. **Urea**, a colorless tasteless chemical, is the chief nitrogenous waste. As we have said, it is synthesized from carbon dioxide and the ammonia released by deamination of amino acids. **Uric acid** is another nitrogenous waste found in urine. Humans produce only a little uric acid, mostly from the degradation of nucleic acids. Uric acid is poorly soluble in water. Occasionally people suffer from **gout**, an arthritis-like disease arising from excessive uric-acid formation. Crystallization of the uric acid in the joints causes pain and swelling.

The yellow color of urine comes from a compound that results from the breakdown of bile pigments. Normally urine is slightly acid—except after meals, when acid is needed for digestion. Unless a person is suffering from an infection, there are no bacteria in fresh, clean-collected urine. It is salty, however, because some mineral salts are always excreted.

A physician can learn much about a patient's general health by examining the urine. An ordinary **urinalysis** includes a series of simple tests. Urine samples are checked for the presence of sugar, protein, and other substances not supposed to be there, including bacteria, pus, and blood cells. Abnormalities of the urine can indicate metabolic disorder, kidney damage, or infection.

FIGURE 7.13 **The Urinary System.**

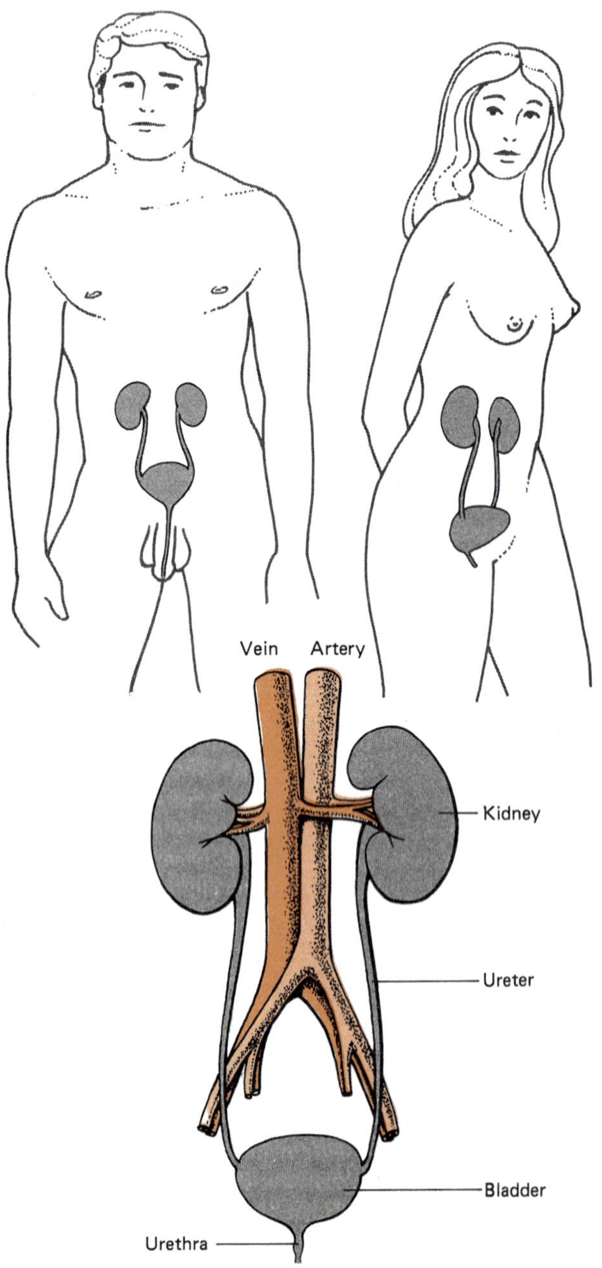

Urine Disposal

Thousands of tiny collecting tubules gather the urine produced by the nephrons. The collecting tubules themselves drain into a large central cavity known as the pelvis of the kidney. This space lies near the indentation of each bean-shaped kidney. Urine flows from the pelvis of each kidney into its **ureter**, which extends to the urinary bladder (Fig. 7.13). Normally the slit-like entrances of the ureters into the bladder are closed. Intermittent contractions of the muscular walls of the ureters propel the urine downward into the bladder, where it is stored.

The **bladder** is a thin muscular bag, collapsed when empty, but easily capable of expanding to hold a half liter (about a pint) or more of urine. From the bladder, urine travels to the outside via another tube, the **urethra**. The urethra has a double function in males. As it passes through the penis, the urethra is joined by ducts associated with the male reproductive system. In females, however, the urethra serves only as an excretory duct. It has no reproductive function.

When the bladder becomes distended by urine, the pressure initiates a nervous-system response that causes the bladder to contract. Expulsion of urine is limited by a circular muscular sphincter that surrounds the junction between the urethra and the bladder. The sphincter opens reflexively when the bladder is distended with urine. We can consciously hold back the flow of urine by contraction of the skeletal muscles that compress the urethra.

Infection and Failure of the Urinary System

Such infections of the lower part of the urinary tract as **cystitis** (bladder infection) and **urethritis** (urethra infection) can lead to kidney infections. Urethritis can involve serious diseases, such as gonorrhea, or infections usually found only on the skin (Chapter 10). Many women experience urethritis when they first become sexually active. Because of anatomical differences, men are less likely than women to suffer infections caused by accidental introduction of fecal bacteria into the urethra.

Nephritis, a bacterial infection, is an inflammation of the glomeruli. Failure of diseased glo-

meruli to filter the blood permits poisonous wastes
132 to build up in the body. Edema also develops, particularly around the ankles, and examination of the urine will reveal that proteins have escaped from the blood. Both low blood protein and poor water elimination contribute to the edema.

A seriously infected kidney may have to be removed surgically to protect the other kidney from becoming infected as well. But so long as one kidney remains healthy, there is enough capacity to allow the individual to pursue a normal, active life.

Besides infection, a number of conditions can lead to progressive kidney failure; these include hypertension, diabetes, and certain congenital disorders.

The final stage of renal failure is **uremia**. Although this name derives from the fact that urea is retained by the body, the ill effects of severe uremia result more immediately from the imbalance of sodium, potassium, and hydrogen ions rather than from urea retention. Elevated blood potassium, for example, inhibits the contraction of heart muscle and can lead to heart failure.

A kidney machine can maintain life when both kidneys fail. The user's blood is circulated through the apparatus. Within the machine, the blood flows past a thin membrane that separates it from a bathing fluid with a composition similar to that of normal plasma. Urea and other wastes diffuse through the membrane into the bath solution.

In some situations amino acids or mineral salts such as calcium phosphate precipitate from the urine to form **kidney stones**. The stones become lodged in the urinary ducts, where they impede the flow of urine. This turn of events is not only serious but quite painful as well. However, kidney stones often can be dissolved with medication; and if this treatment fails, their surgical removal is a common medical procedure.

DIFFERENT DIGESTIVE AND EXCRETORY SYSTEMS

Digestion and excretion are processes that must be accomplished by all animals. The structural details differ in various animals, just as their modes of life differ. On the other hand, the differences are not always so great as might be imagined.

Some invertebrates—**coelenterates** such as jellyfish, for example—have simple sac-like bodies wherein foods and wastes pass through a single opening (Chapter 16). But even the lowly earthworm has a complete digestive tract with a mouth and an anus.

Earthworm Adaptations

Earthworms literally eat their way through the soil. Dirt, decayed leaves, and other bits of organic matter are consumed by the combined action of fleshy lips, which grasp soil particles, and a muscular **pharynx**, which gulps them into the **esophagus** (Fig. 7.14). Ingested material is stored in the **crop** before it enters the **gizzard**, where violent

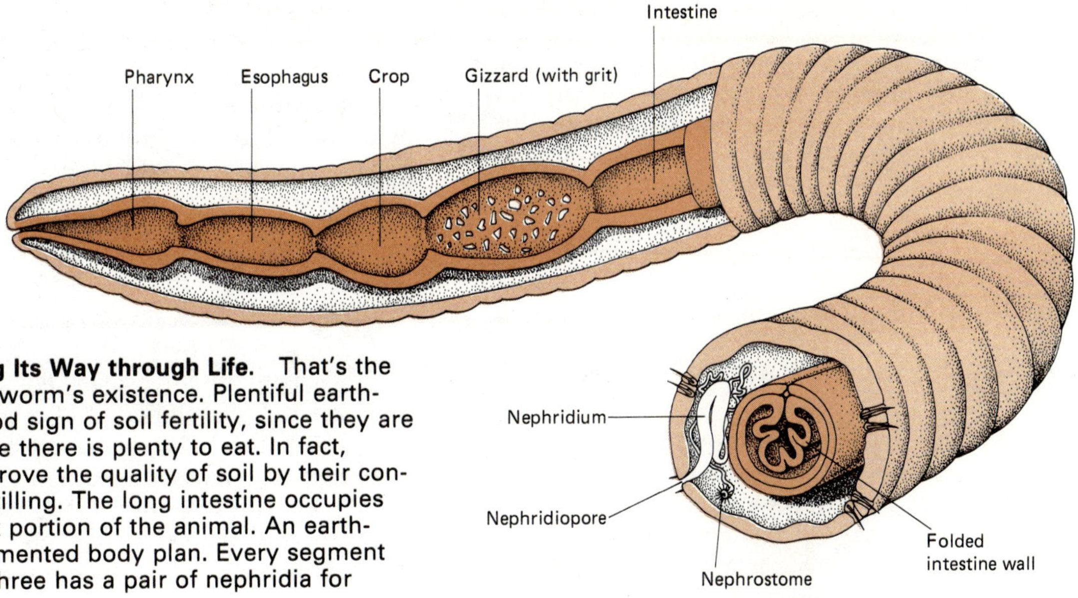

FIGURE 7.14 Eating Its Way through Life. That's the story of an earthworm's existence. Plentiful earthworms are a good sign of soil fertility, since they are found only where there is plenty to eat. In fact, earthworms improve the quality of soil by their constant, ravenous tilling. The long intestine occupies most of the back portion of the animal. An earthworm has a segmented body plan. Every segment except the first three has a pair of nephridia for excretion.

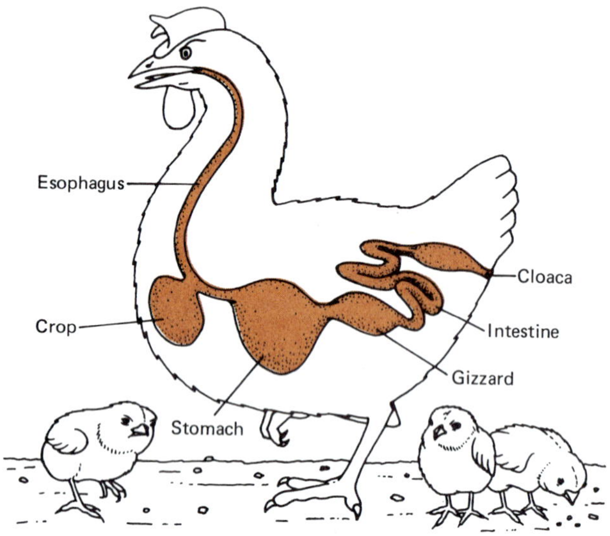

FIGURE 7.15 **Chicken Guts.** The crop is an extension of the esophagus. The gizzard is a muscular sac in which grit grinds grain to a pulp. The cloaca is the common exit for feces, urinary wastes, and eggs.

muscular contractions grind the food against soil particles. From the gizzard, food is pushed into a long **intestine,** where enzymatic digestion and absorption occur, Undigested matter is eliminated through the anus.

Each ring, or body segment, of an earthworm contains a pair of tubular excretory organs known as **nephridia**. At its inner end each nephridium has a ciliated funnel, the **nephrostome**, which drains wastes from the body cavity. Other wastes are removed from a capillary network coiled around the nephridia. Useful substances are returned to the blood, much as in the human kidney. The nephridium terminates externally as a small **nephridiopore**.

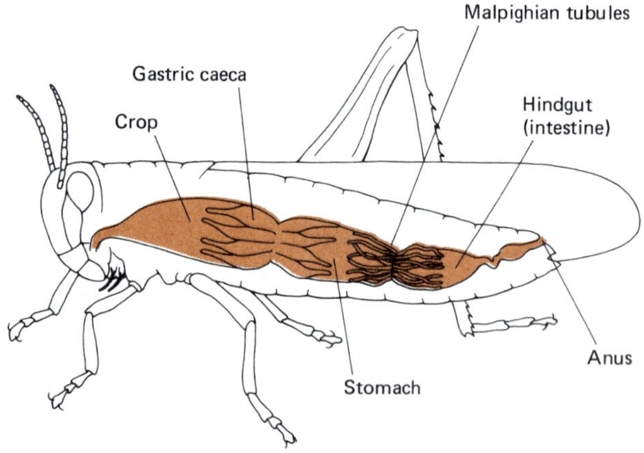

FIGURE 7.16 **Digestive and Excretory Organs of the Grasshopper.** Two sets of fingerlike projections are joined to the digestive tract. The fatter ones are gastric caeca, which secrete digestive enzymes into the stomach. The threadlike Malpighian tubules are excretory organs that discharge wastes into the intestine.

Excretion in birds is typical of many animals that have no bladder. In reptiles, as well as in birds, the ureters discharge into the **cloaca** (Fig. 7.15), a cavity that serves both the urinary and digestive tracts. **Uric acid** is the chief nitrogenous waste of these animals. It is usually excreted as white crystals mixed with the feces in the cloaca. Excretion of dry "urine" is a form of water conservation for these animals.

Nearly dry uric acid is also excreted by insects. Typically, insect excretion is by means of **Malpighian tubules** (Fig. 7.16). These threadlike tubes are attached to the hindgut of insects. They extract waste materials from the blood and discharge them into the intestine.

Bits and Pieces: Parts of the Whole

Looking back over this chapter, you will find that digestion and excretion are more than simply "in and out" as the chapter title suggests. The overall job of the digestive system is to supply energy and raw materials, both necessary ingredients for maintenance. And excretion of potentially dangerous wastes is equally fundamental to well-being. Digestion and excretion, quite obviously, contribute to homeostasis in all animals. We have studied the human systems in considerable detail. We have seen that sphincters regulate food passage, that foods trigger enzyme secretion, that the liver controls blood sugar, and that the kidney separates wastes from valuables. Each of these processes is a significant addition to the growing story of our human homeostatic machinery.

Summary

1. In order for nutrients to be absorbed, large food particles must be digested into smaller units. This process takes place in the digestive system, a muscular tube that receives the secretions of the digestive glands.

2. Digestion begins in the mouth, where food is converted into a soft mass before being swallowed. Peristalsis propels the food mass toward the stomach and from there through the remainder of the digestive tract.

3. Gastric juices and muscular churning convert a food mass into a semifluid chyme in the stomach, where it is held until it is ready to be received by the small intestine.

4. In the small intestine, enzymes of intestinal juice and pancreatic juice, together with liver bile, act to digest carbohydrates, fats, and proteins. Most digestion products are absorbed into the bloodstream. However, fats are absorbed into lymphatic capillaries from the small intestine.

5. The function of the large intestine is to remove water and minerals from the mixture of undigested food, bile, and digestive juices that enter from the small intestine. The material that remains when digestion is completed is called feces.

6. Most of the nutrients absorbed from the digestive tract are processed in the liver. In addition to maintaining the normal blood-sugar level, the liver stores glycogen, synthesizes lipids and amino acids, produces blood proteins, secretes bile, and detoxifies many poisons.

7. The kidneys are major homeostatic organs. Metabolic wastes are eliminated from the body primarily through the action of the kidneys. Urine is formed by the filtration of blood through the kidney nephrons. Glucose and other useful substances are reabsorbed from the kidney filtrate before elimination.

8. Coelenterates have a digestive cavity, but their wastes merely pass out through the single body opening. Earthworms have a tubular one-way digestive system and excretory tubules resembling nephrons. Birds, reptiles, and insects secrete solid nitrogenous waste material.

Thought and Controversy

1. Alexis St. Martin, a French Canadian trapper accidentally shot with a musket, lived to provide nineteenth-century medicine true insight into the stomach. The curious could literally "look in"! A few minutes after the accident, William Beaumont, a U.S. Army surgeon, examined St. Martin and found the man's breakfast pouring through the musket wound. Beaumont bandaged St. Martin and took care of him; after many months St. Martin recovered, but the wound never healed properly. Instead, the stomach attached itself to the body wall, so a hole in the body wall led directly into the stomach. Only a tight bandage kept food in St. Martin's stomach. But otherwise he seemed all right. Beaumont couldn't resist experimenting with his unusual patient. One day in 1825, Beaumont strung pieces of beef, salt pork, bread, and shredded cabbage on a string and shoved them through the opening in St. Martin's stomach. An hour later Beaumont pulled out the string and found the cabbage half gone but the meat little changed. Undaunted, Beaumont returned the food-laden string to St. Martin for further digestion. Although his initial conclusions were of limited value, Beaumont continued his studies with St. Martin for eight years; the work led to the discovery of pepsin. We are left to wonder at both men.

2. How do we justify medical costs? How much is a human life worth? If resources are limited, whose life should be prolonged and who should be sacrificed? As inhumane as these questions seem, they can be real. The use of kidney machines and kidney transplants are prime examples. Individuals who require kidney machines to stay alive need treatment every few days. Done in a hospital on an outpatient basis, the expense can be $20,000 or more a year. If the patient and family members are capable of carrying out the process at home, the initial equipment requires an investment of more than $5000, and supplies can cost thousands of dollars a year. Kidney transplants are possible only when someone, usually a relative, is willing to accept the risk involved in donating one healthy kidney; occasionally it is possible to obtain a kidney from an accident victim quickly enough to transplant it before the tissue dies. But transplants aren't always successful, and the demand for kidney transplants usually exceeds the supply of donated kidneys. How do we decide who receives a transplant? Does anyone who needs a kidney have the right to expect that one will be provided somehow?

3. Why do we have an appendix? We often hear that the appendix is useless, and people sometimes wonder why the appendix hasn't been eliminated through natural selection, since it is so often the site of serious infection. But is the appendix really useless? The walls are packed so completely with lymphatic tissue that on microscopic examination the appendix resembles a tonsil. It seems plausible that a role in immunity, particularly to organisms that can invade from the intestine, will someday explain the retention of this controversial organ.

4. As a body waste, urine is sometimes regarded as dirty. But is it? Not in the sense of containing bacteria or other disease-producing organisms. Normally the urogenital tract is sterile; infections are serious matters. And the wastes are harmless except in very high concentrations. True, freshly voided urine has a distinctive odor, but this traces to dietary substances. However, urea and other components of urine will support bacterial growth, so urine spoils unless it is kept free of microorganisms. Ammonia released from the urea is smelly, and bacteria multiply in it so quickly that the urine will turn milky in a few days. But fresh urine should be as clean as our blood, at least in the male, whose urine can be released without undue contamination from body surfaces. If a male rinses the opening to his urinary system with a spurt of urine, the remainder is ordinarily so clean that some military authorities teach medics to use it to wash battle wounds in emergencies where clean water or other more appropriate solutions are unavailable.

Questions

1. You have just eaten a roast-beef sandwich. List in order the digestive organs that the sandwich would encounter until only undigestible materials remain. Make a separate list of accessory organs necessary to digestive function but not physically encountered by foods.

2. Presume that the sandwich is composed of starch (bread) protein and fat (meat), cellulose (lettuce), and water (everything). Describe how, or whether, each substance is digested and absorbed.

3. Do body cells obtain energy from digestion? Hint: What is the relationship between digestion and cellular respiration?

4. What is the value of the intestinal villi? of peristalsis?

5. To confirm the liver's essential role in homeostasis, compile a list of liver functions.

6. Why, in the absence of insulin, does the body excrete sugar when the body cells are starved for this compound?

7. The hepatic-portal and kidney-nephron circulatory pathways are different from most other body circulatory pathways. How does this relate to their functions?

9. Define the following terms:
glomerular filtration
tubular reabsorption
tubular secretion

10. Besides excretion, what are the other functions of the kidneys? Explain.

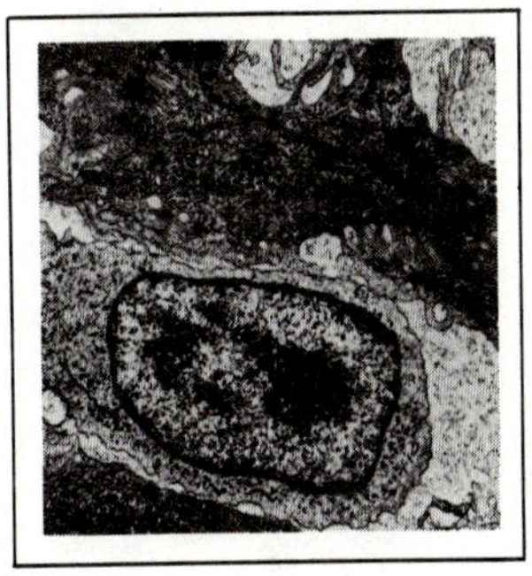

8

Coordinators: Nerves and Hormones

TO MAINTAIN HOMEOSTASIS, MOST ANIMALS DEpend on two interrelated systems. The **nervous system** integrates information about internal and external conditions and coordinates responses through cell-to-cell stimulation. The **endocrine system** also responds to internal conditions and coordinates responses, but through cell secretions that are carried in body fluids. In animals such as ourselves most of these messengers are carried in the blood; we
145 151 152 153 155 call them **hormones.** Hormones are so important that we have mentioned several in earlier discussions of body activities.□ Later in this chapter, we will emphasize the similarities between endocrine cells and nerve cells and show that the endocrine system is controlled largely by the nervous system.

NEURAL COORDINATION

The nervous system of vertebrates is tremendously complex. It extends throughout the body and is composed of billions of cells. Many of these cells are **neurons** (nerve cells). Other cells of the nervous system support and nourish neurons and, perhaps, have other yet-to-be-explained duties.

Because the nervous system fans so widely through the body and is so intricate, any classification of the parts must be an oversimplification. But for convenience, we speak of the brain and spinal cord as the **central nervous system.** The brain, of course, is a massive structure within the skull cavity. The spinal cord extends from the skull and passes through channels in the vertebral column (backbones). Nerves and associated structures that extend from the brain or spinal cord into the remainder of the body constitute the **peripheral nervous system.** But the central and peripheral nervous systems are no more separate than are your heart and blood vessels. In fact, many neurons extend within both "systems" (Fig. 8.1).

Neurons and Neural Organization

Nerve cells are highly specialized. Each consists of a large cell body and one or more nerve fibers. The **cell body** of a neuron contains the nucleus and the usual cytoplasmic structures. The **nerve fibers** are extensions, often extremely long, of the cytoplasm (Fig. 8.2). In humans some of the longest nerve fibers extend from the spinal cord at shoulder level clear to the tips of the fingers. Others reach from the lower back to the toes. Most neurons bear some nerve fibers that are **dendrites.** These are highly branched and often knobby. Dendrites receive incoming signals and transmit them toward the cell body. Usually one fiber, the **axon,** carries messages away from the cell body. At a **synapse,** the region where two neurons meet, it is the axon of one neuron that passes the message to a dendrite of the second neuron. Axons are of uniform diameter throughout and usually branch only toward the end.

Long nerve fibers are generally covered with **myelin sheaths,** which are actually portions of sur-

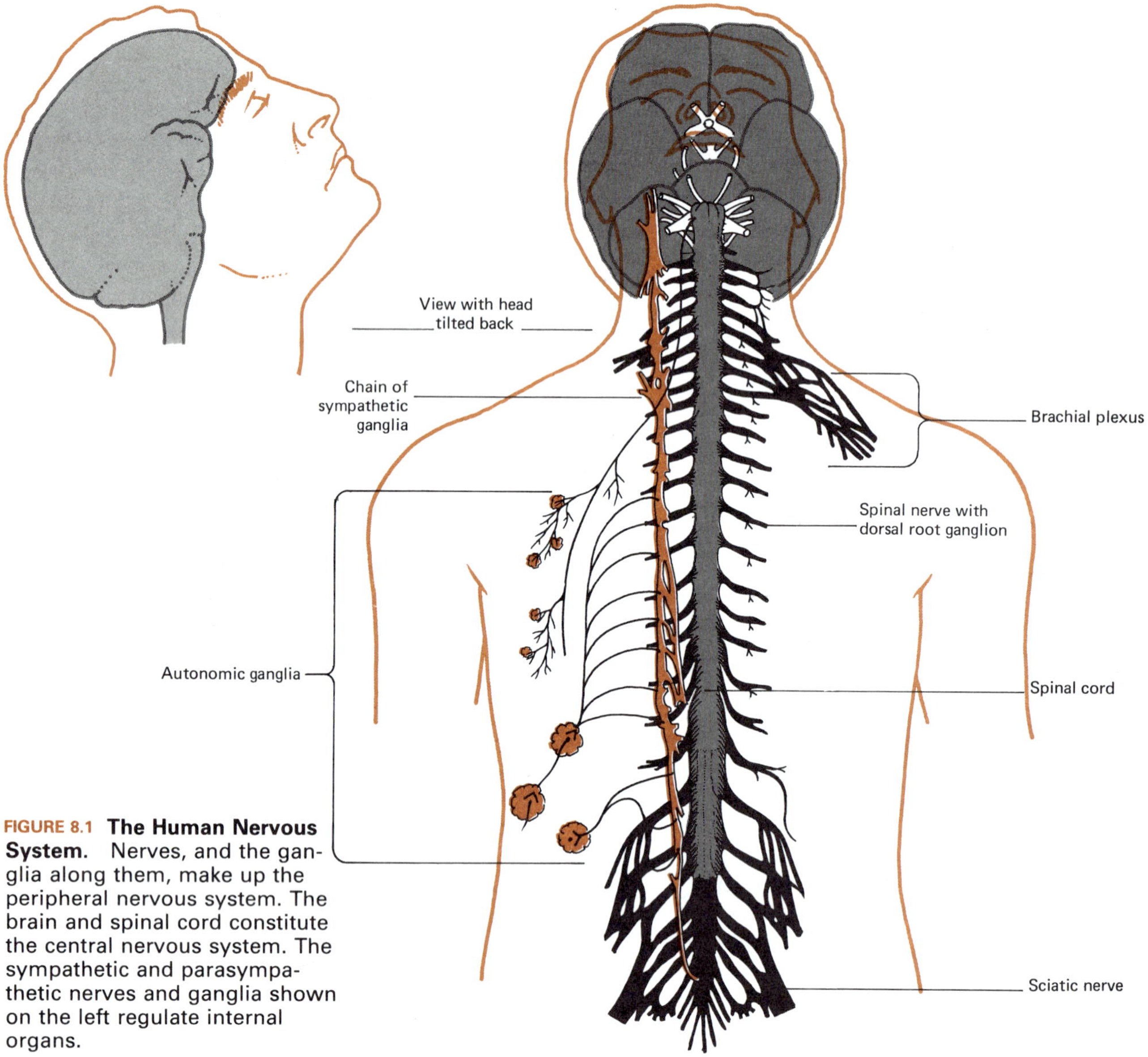

FIGURE 8.1 The Human Nervous System. Nerves, and the ganglia along them, make up the peripheral nervous system. The brain and spinal cord constitute the central nervous system. The sympathetic and parasympathetic nerves and ganglia shown on the left regulate internal organs.

rounding cells wrapped around the nerve fiber. The sheath cells are drawn so thin and wrapped so tightly that the myelin sheath is little more than the plasma membranes of the sheathing cells (Fig. 8.3). The high lipid content of these cell membranes gives myelin sheaths a whitish, greasy appearance. Myelinated fibers transmit messages faster than those lacking such a sheath.

Not only are many neurons fantastically long and structurally specialized; they are also unusually active metabolically. Neurons use a great deal of energy and are extremely busy at protein synthesis. These expenditures maintain highly organized structural and chemical systems that permit the neuron to transmit impulses.

Neurons are classified according to their functions. **Sensory neurons** are those of the peripheral nervous system that transmit impulses from sense organs to the central nervous system. **Motor neurons** deliver messages from the brain or spinal cord through the peripheral nervous system to individual muscles and glands. Actually these activities are only a tiny part of the work of neurons. Most neurons are involved in storage of information, cor-

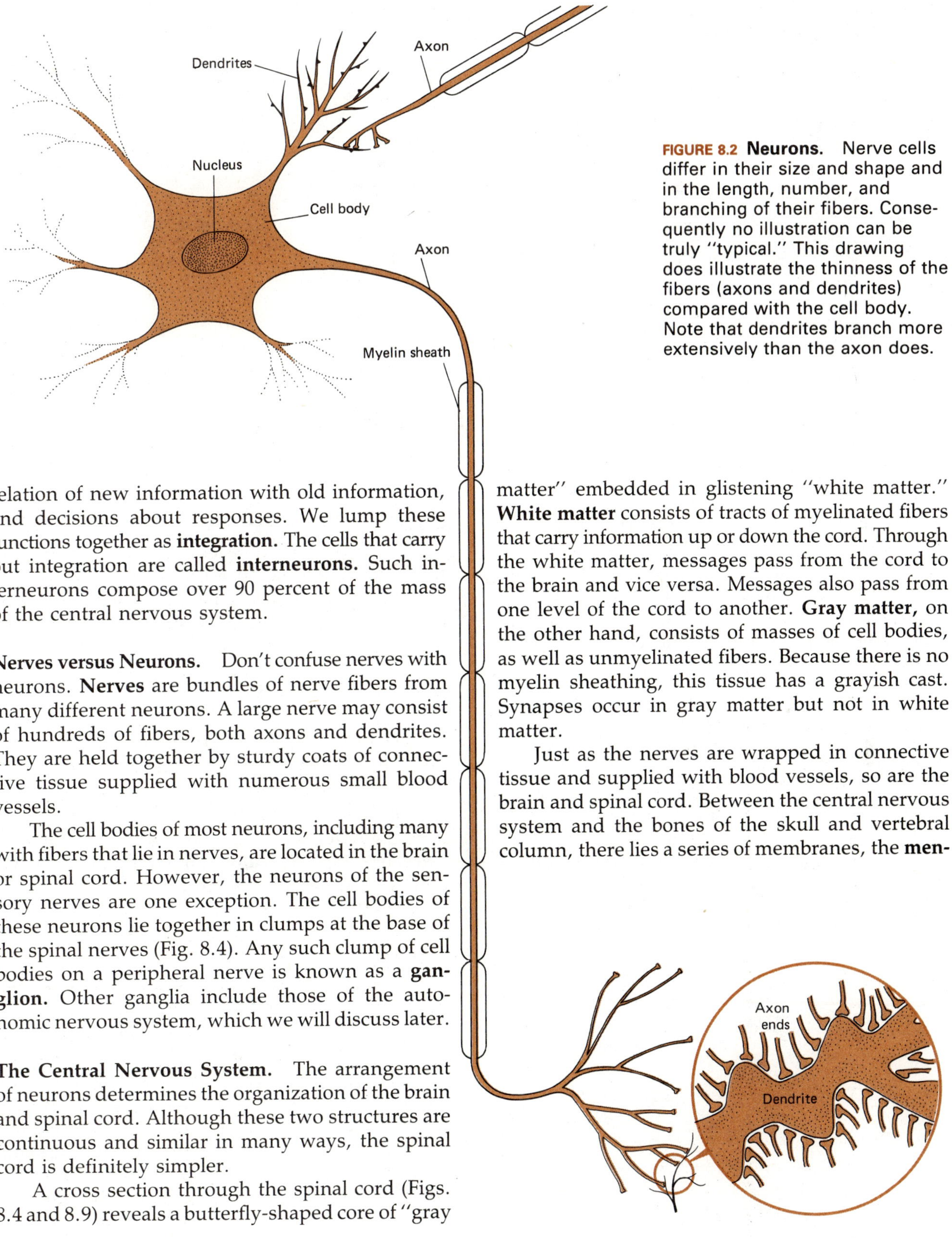

FIGURE 8.2 **Neurons.** Nerve cells differ in their size and shape and in the length, number, and branching of their fibers. Consequently no illustration can be truly "typical." This drawing does illustrate the thinness of the fibers (axons and dendrites) compared with the cell body. Note that dendrites branch more extensively than the axon does.

relation of new information with old information, and decisions about responses. We lump these functions together as **integration.** The cells that carry out integration are called **interneurons.** Such interneurons compose over 90 percent of the mass of the central nervous system.

Nerves versus Neurons. Don't confuse nerves with neurons. **Nerves** are bundles of nerve fibers from many different neurons. A large nerve may consist of hundreds of fibers, both axons and dendrites. They are held together by sturdy coats of connective tissue supplied with numerous small blood vessels.

The cell bodies of most neurons, including many with fibers that lie in nerves, are located in the brain or spinal cord. However, the neurons of the sensory nerves are one exception. The cell bodies of these neurons lie together in clumps at the base of the spinal nerves (Fig. 8.4). Any such clump of cell bodies on a peripheral nerve is known as a **ganglion.** Other ganglia include those of the autonomic nervous system, which we will discuss later.

The Central Nervous System. The arrangement of neurons determines the organization of the brain and spinal cord. Although these two structures are continuous and similar in many ways, the spinal cord is definitely simpler.

A cross section through the spinal cord (Figs. 8.4 and 8.9) reveals a butterfly-shaped core of "gray matter" embedded in glistening "white matter." **White matter** consists of tracts of myelinated fibers that carry information up or down the cord. Through the white matter, messages pass from the cord to the brain and vice versa. Messages also pass from one level of the cord to another. **Gray matter,** on the other hand, consists of masses of cell bodies, as well as unmyelinated fibers. Because there is no myelin sheathing, this tissue has a grayish cast. Synapses occur in gray matter but not in white matter.

Just as the nerves are wrapped in connective tissue and supplied with blood vessels, so are the brain and spinal cord. Between the central nervous system and the bones of the skull and vertebral column, there lies a series of membranes, the **men-**

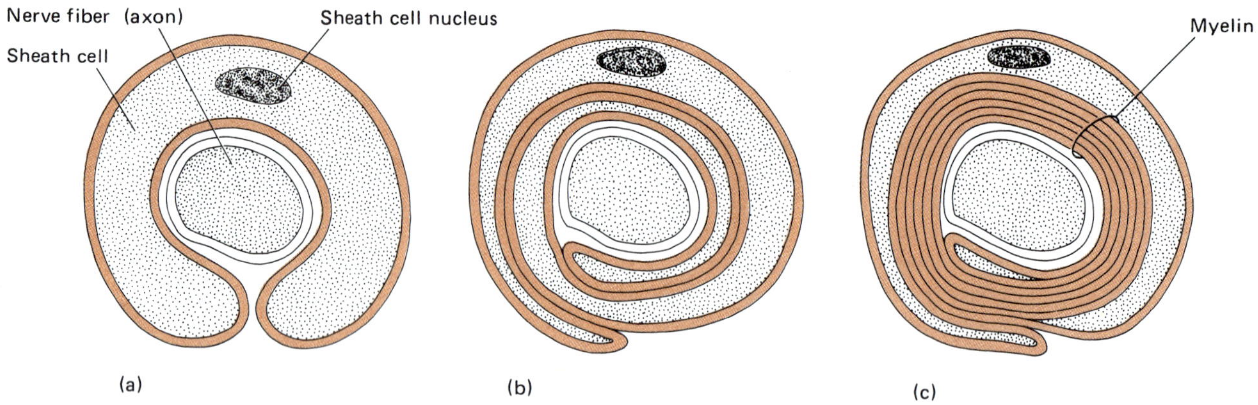

FIGURE 8.3 **Formation of the Myelin Sheath.** The sheath that covers most long nerve fibers consists largely of many layers of plasma membranes belonging to sheath cells. Formation of this myelin sheath begins when sheath cells wrap themselves around the nerve fiber (a). The sheath cells draw themselves thin as they wind around the fiber (b). Accumulations of these membrane-rich sheets constitute myelin (c).

inges (Fig. 8.4). The outer layer is especially tough. The inner two layers are separated by a lymphlike fluid that cushions the nervous system against physical blows. Because this **cerebrospinal fluid** originates within the brain and is in communication with brain tissues, its composition can provide clues to conditions deep inside. Infections, hemorrhages, and many diseases alter the cerebrospinal fluid. Liquid for diagnosis can be withdrawn harmlessly. Physicians use a long needle to tap a reservoir of cerebrospinal fluid in the meninges near the base of the spinal cord.

FIGURE 8.4 **The Spinal Cord.** Three connective-tissue layers known as the meninges enclose the spinal cord. The cord is further protected by the vertebrae through which it passes.

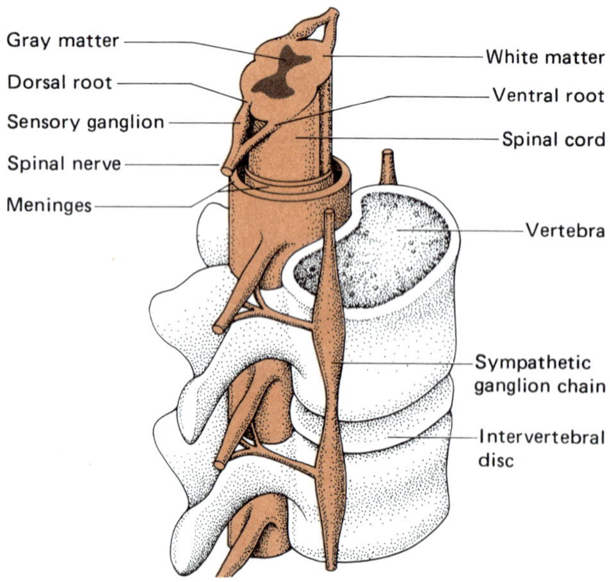

Nerve Impulses

The characteristic activity of neurons is the transmission of messages, or **impulses,** as they are called, from one to another. The ability of cells to transmit impulses arises from the unequal distribution of ions□ on either side of the plasma membrane. And 74
since ions are electrically charged, the unequal disbution produces an electrical potential across the membrane. One can measure it by placing a tiny electrode inside a neuron and another outside, then connecting the two through a voltmeter (Fig. 8.5). The **resting potential** of a neuron (that is, the potential of one not sending an impulse) is about -70 millivolts, or $-70/1000$ of a volt. The inside of the neuron is negative with respect to the outside. Chemically, the positive ions are mainly sodium and potassium, whereas the negative ions that are concentrated on the inside include large organic substances, such as amino acids, proteins, and nucleic acids.

There is a high concentration of sodium ions (Na^+) outside the cell and a substantial concentra-

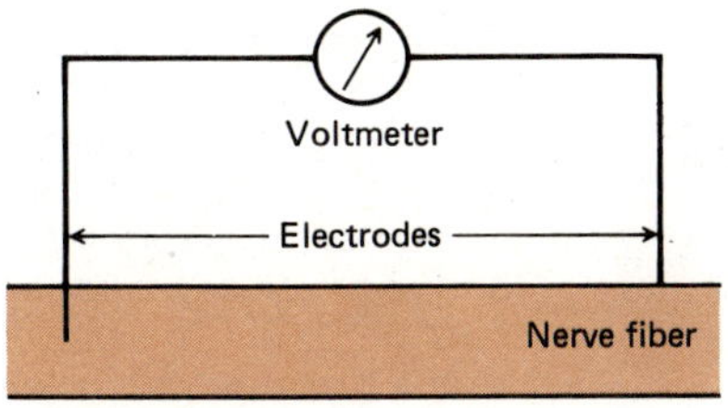

FIGURE 8.5 **Apparatus for Measurement of Electrical Potential in Nerve Fibers.** One electrode is placed inside the nerve fiber and one just outside. If there is a difference in electrical charge between the outside and the inside, a current will pass through the voltmeter.

tion of potassium (K^+) inside. This unequal distribution is maintained by a **sodium-potassium pump,** an active-transport system that pumps sodium out of cells and potassium into cells. In this process energy is used to collect sodium ions from inside the cell, where they are scarce, and move them to the outside, where sodium is more abundant. At the same time that the pump is exchanging sodium ions for potassium ions and thereby concentrating potassium inside the cell, the small size of potassium ions permits them to leak out. This outward diffusion of positively charged potassium ions and the fact that large negatively charged organic ions are trapped inside the membrane results in more negative ions inside than outside. The resulting difference in electrical charges is the source of the resting potential (Fig. 8.6).

A Nerve Impulse Involves Depolarization of the Membrane. Neurons respond to a variety of stimuli that temporarily inactivate the sodium-potassium pump. Such stimulation alters the distribution of sodium and potassium ions. When the pump is inactivated, sodium ions flood into the nerve cell. As more and more positively charged sodiums diffuse into the neuron, its electrical potential begins to drop, and the cell membrane becomes depolarized. At this point there is no charge difference between the inside and the outside. Then, for a fraction of a second as sodium ions continue to flood into the neuron, the inside of the cell actually becomes positive, relative to the outside (Fig. 8.7). This **action potential** persists for only a few milliseconds before the membrane recovers and restores the resting potential.

Depolarization does not occur over the entire neural membrane at once. Instead, a wave of de-

FIGURE 8.6 **Resting Potential.** Normally the surface of a neuron is positively charged relative to the inside. This difference in electrical potential results from several factors. The sodium-potassium pump trades sodium ions (Na^+) for potassium ions (K^+), moving sodium to the outside and potassium to the inside. There is a tendency for potassium to diffuse from its high concentration inside the membrane to the area outside, where it is in lower concentration. Sodium would diffuse inward, but the membrane is essentially impermeable to sodium except through the sodium-potassium pump mechanism. Thus the diffusion of potassium leaves more positive charges on the outside than on the inside. The negatively charged organic ions (Oi^-) would follow the potassium ions outward because of attraction of opposite charges. However, these organic ions are much too large to pass through the plasma membrane. As a result, there remain more positive ions on the outside and more negative ions on the inside. Note that there are negative and positive ions both inside and outside the membrane. The electrical potential is a reflection of the fact that there are more positive ions outside and more negative ions inside. The symbol Cl^- represents the chloride ion.

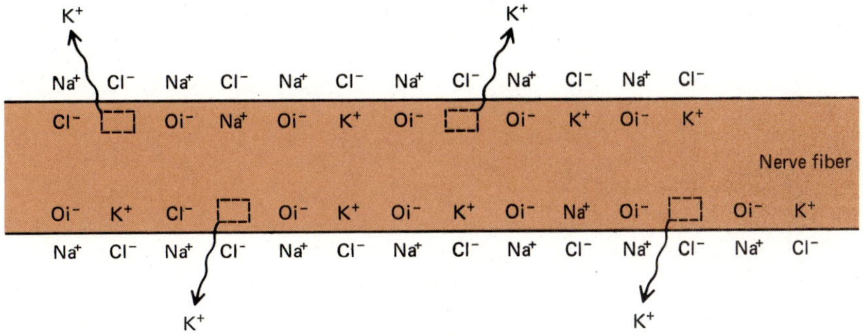

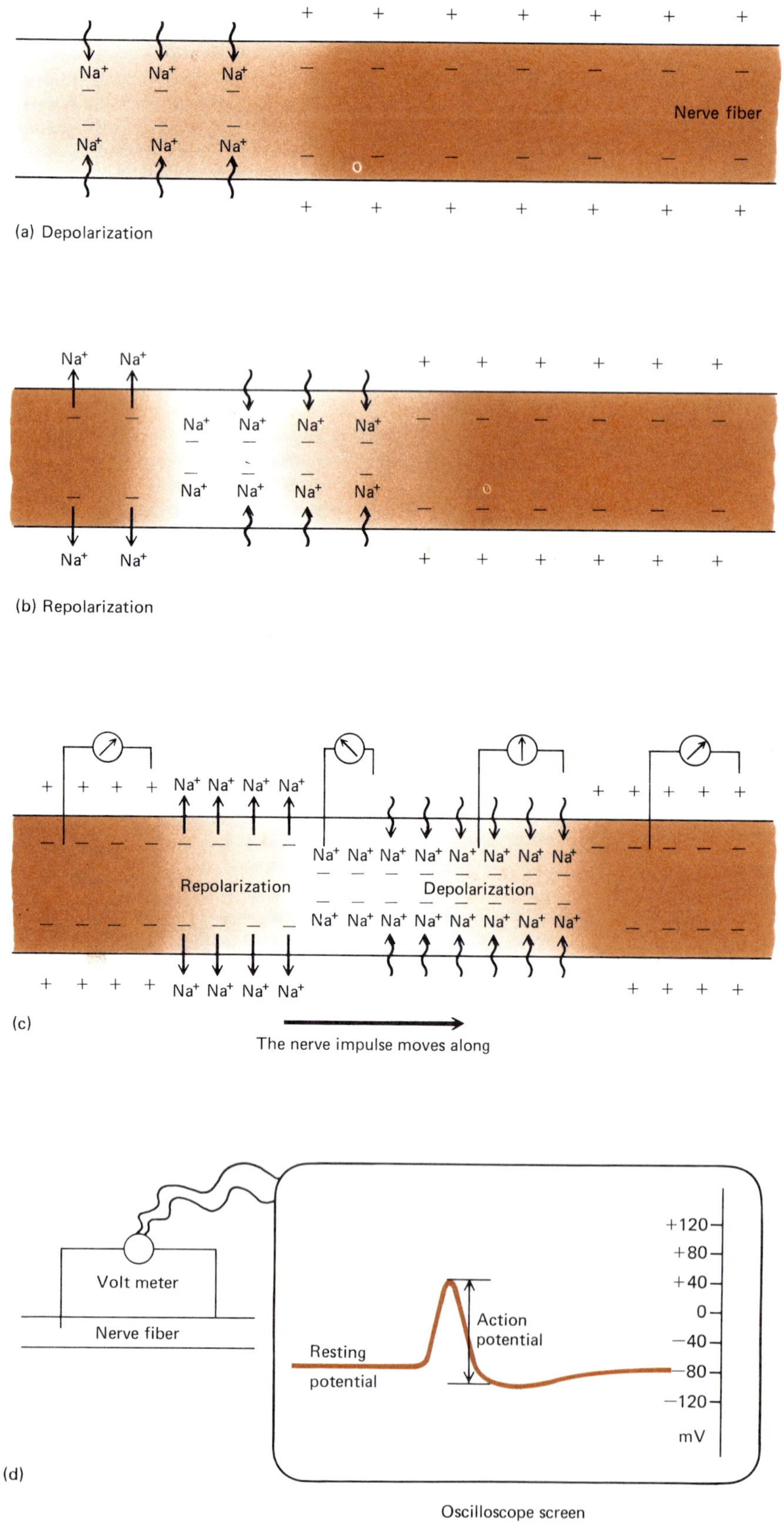

FIGURE 8.7 The Nerve Impulse as the Action Potential. As the result of the sodium-potassium pump, the resting neuron has more negative ions on the inside and more positive ions on the outside of the membrane. Most of the positive ions are sodium. A nerve impulse consists of a wave of temporary depolarization of the membrane that occurs when the sodium-potassium pump stops momentarily. Sodium diffuses inside (wavy arrows) and depolarizes the plasma membrane (a). Repolarization (b) swiftly follows depolarization as the sodium pump again functions and by active transport (straight arrows) forces sodium back out of the cell. Depolarization at one point leads to depolarization in the adjacent area of the membrane, so the impulse moves along the fiber, with repolarization following in its wake (c). Changes in polarization constitute the action potential that can be measured by voltmeter readings as the nerve impulse passes. Note the changes in the voltmeters. (d) Nerve impulses can be visualized on an oscilloscope screen (much like a TV screen). The straight line of the resting potential is interrupted by the upward spike that represents the action potential. Afterward, polarization drops below the previous resting level for a brief time before the resting potential becomes stabilized again.

polarization sweeps over the neuron from the point of stimulation. Depolarization at one point triggers the depolarization of adjacent regions of the membrane. In other words, depolarization is self-propagating. The process spreads along the entire length of the neuron, constituting a **nerve impulse.** After experiencing one wave of depolarization, a neuron cannot respond to a second stimulation until the sodium-potassium pump reestablishes the original distribution of ions.

A Nerve Impulse Is an All-or-None Matter. Just as the trigger must receive a certain degree of pressure before a gun will fire, a neuron will not send an impulse in response to just any stimulus. Only stimuli of a certain minimum strength, the **threshold** value, can effect an impulse. A minor stimulus may produce a partial depolarization of the membrane, but such a depolarization will spread only a short distance and then die out. However, once a depolarization of sufficient magnitude is established, a nerve impulse is inevitable. Its speed and effect are independent of any further influence, just as the force and speed of a bullet are independent of the trigger finger that sent it.

Not a Current. Although we have discussed nerve impulses in electrical terms, it would be a grave mistake to assume that the nerve impulse that passes along a fiber is an electrical current. Two observations may help you remember this critical distinction. First, a nerve impulse is due to the movement of ions, not electrons, as in electricity. This movement of ions occurs *across* the membrane depolarizing it. The impulse that moves along the fiber is a movement in the location where depolarization is occurring at any given moment. Second, an electric current such as operates an electric toaster, for example, moves three million times faster than does a nerve impulse. Electricity travels at the speed of light (299,800 kilometers or 186,000 miles per second). Messages from your brain to your toe move no more than 100 meters (325 feet) per second.

From One Neuron to Another

Usually a nerve impulse must move from one neuron to another in order to reach its final destination. Neurons form distinct patterns; the axonic end of one neuron branches and abuts on the dendritic ends of several other neurons. But adjacent nerve fibers never actually touch. There is a very narrow gap at each **synapse,** or junction. The manner in which nerve impulses bridge the synaptic gap has important consequences.

Once initiated, a nerve impulse is transmitted along the surface of a neuron in all directions from the site of stimulus. But the impulse does not pass randomly to all connecting neurons. If it did, any stimulus would provoke a generalized response throughout the body. Instead, nerve impulses can be transmitted across a synapse in only one direction. For this reason, our responses to stimuli can be highly specific actions. The one-way nature of synapses results from differences in the two sides of the synapse.

Nerve impulses can pass only from the axon of one neuron to receptors on the next. Close inspection reveals that the tips of axons are swollen (Fig. 8.8). These bulbous ends of axons contain membrane-bound sacs of neurotransmitters. **Neurotransmitters** are chemicals that can alter the permeability of the plasma membrane and thus either cause or prevent an impulse in a second neuron. When a nerve impulse reaches the tip of an axon, it causes tiny sacs of neurotransmitters to move to the synaptic surface. Here the sacs burst and release their contents into the gap between the axon and the dendrite.

At synapses neurotransmitters released by axons combine with specific sites on other neurons. Usually these sites are on dendrites. Since there are several kinds of neurotransmitters, there are also several kinds of receptors. It is important to recognize that *neurotransmitters are secreted* by axons. Thus there is a fundamental similarity between functions of neurons and of the endocrine tissues that produce hormones. Both secrete chemicals that have specific effects on other cells and that are effective in tiny quantities.

Since neurotransmitters alter dendrite membranes, it is essential that the transmitters be removed so that the dendrite can recover and be ready to respond to subsequent signals. Different neurotransmitters are removed in different ways, but the best-known transmitter, **acetylcholine,** is destroyed by an enzyme. This enzyme, **cholinesterase,** is normally present in the synapse. Inhibitors of cholinesterase cause havoc in the nervous system. Nerve gases developed for biological warfare include cholinesterase inhibitors. So do the organophosphate insecticides. Some neurotrans-

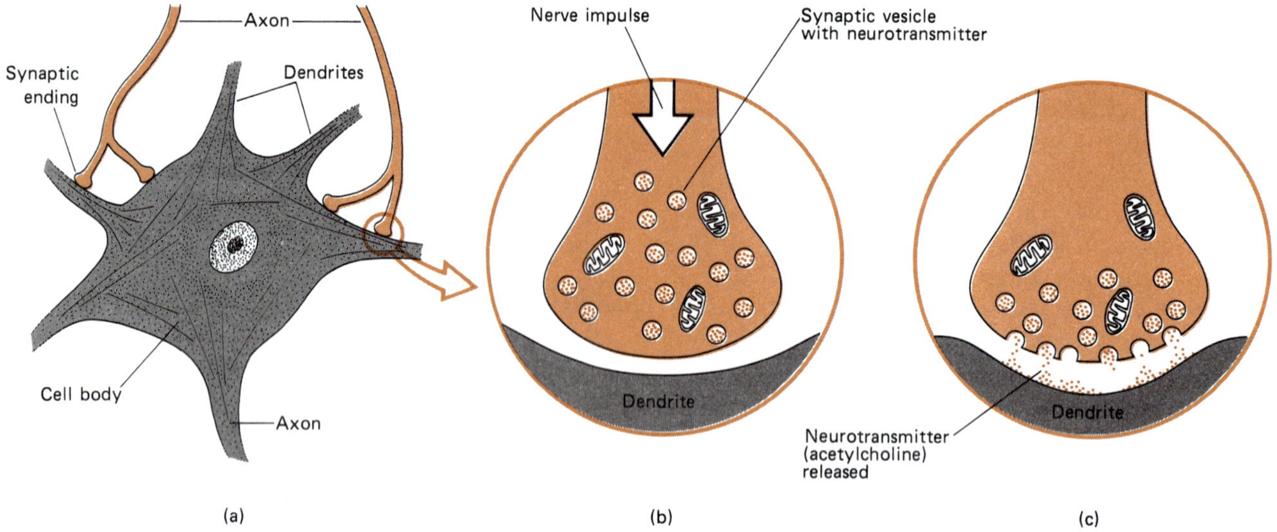

FIGURE 8.8 A Synapse. When a nerve impulse reaches the bulbous ends of an axon (a), the sacs of neurotransmitter there move to the plasma membrane adjacent to the dendrite. Fusion of the membrane of the sac with that covering the cell releases neurotransmitter into the gap that separates the axon from the dendrite (b). The neurotransmitter—acetylcholine, for example—diffuses across the gap and alters the membrane of the dendrite.

mitters, such as **norepinephrine,** are recycled from the synapse back into the axon.

A variety of substances act as neurotransmitters. Some rather ordinary chemicals—the amino acids glycine and histamine, for instance—have been shown to be neurotransmitters. Perhaps it isn't unusual for neurotransmitters to have other functions. Serotonin, for example, is both a neurotransmitter and a factor in blood clotting. It seems likely that many neurotransmitters are yet to be discovered.

Neurotransmitter defects are responsible for much mental illness. **Alzheimer's disease,** a common form of senility, involves acetylcholine deficiency. The shaking and muscle rigidity that characterize **Parkinson's disease** result from a defect of dopamine-secreting neurons involved in motor coordination. Although the exact nature of the problem remains to be discovered, many people suffering from Parkinson's disease are helped by L-dopa, a substance that cells use to make dopamine. Some depressed people, including many who attempt suicide, produce inadequate serotonin, a neurotransmitter involved in arousal and consciousness. In some instances depression is relieved by drugs that inhibit the enzymes that destroy norepinephrine and dopamine. Drugs that affect the nervous system usually do so by altering neurotransmitter action. Mechanisms include:

- mimicry (binding to the same site with the same effect);
- blocking the site (binding with no effect);
- abnormal destruction of the neurotransmitter; and
- interfering with normal destruction, or recycling.

For examples, see Box 8A.

Reflexes: Small-Scale Examples of Neural Function

To comprehend how the nervous system works we need to understand how neurons interact. The examples provided by reflexes are easy to analyze and may illustrate processes at work in more complex activity.

A **reflex** is a behavior pattern that is

- adaptive,
- predictable, and
- automatic.

BOX 8A

DRUGS—WHAT THEY ARE AND WHAT THEY DO

The definition of the term drug varies. In the broad sense all medicines are drugs. But to many people "drugs" have come to mean substances used mainly for their effect on the mind—and that effect is understood to be unhealthy or inappropriate or otherwise undesirable. Drug use seems linked with evil and hence with the forbidden. The roots of these attitudes probably extend to the nearly universal use of mind-affecting plant extracts in primitive religious ceremonies. Wherever possible, the early Christian church suppressed other beliefs as pagan and marked their rituals as consortiums with the devil. The mind-affecting drugs used in these forbidden ceremonies received the same stamp. And, of course, most of these drugs are poisonous, especially in large quantities.

Although mind-altering drugs can be readily classified by their effects, the mechanisms underlying most of these effects are obscure. Perhaps ether, chloroform, and the many solvents used in glues and paint thinners exert their effects because they dissolve lipids. Modifications of lipids in the neuronal membrane may inhibit nerve impulses. Of the other mind-altering drugs that are understood at all, most interfere with neurotransmitters.

Members of the potato family, including deadly nightshade, mandrake, and Jimson weed, are well known for their poisonous or mind-altering effects. The action of Jimson weed results from the presence of atropine, scopolamine, and hyoscyamine, all compounds that block acetylcholine receptors on the dendritic surface. In the presence of these drugs, acetylcholine is rendered ineffective. Use of these drugs has long been associated with witchcraft ceremonies.

Many synthetic drugs also affect neurotransmitters. Among the best known is the tranquilizer chlorpromazine (Thorazine®), which blocks dopamine receptors. Soon after its commercial introduction, chlorpromazine made possible the release of many long-term inmates of mental institutions. Although chlorpromazine has proved beneficial to both schizophrenics and those who suffer from manic-depressive conditions, there is no reason to think that the drug gets to the root of their problems. Rather, chlorpromazine reduces symptoms, just as aspirin relieves the pain of a toothache without affecting the decayed tooth.

Other substances known to interfere with neurotransmitters include:

Nicotine	Mimics acetylcholine.
Tofranil® (imipramine)	Reduces rate of reuptake of norepinephrine and thus is an antidepressant.
Parnate® (tranyl-cypromine)	Inhibits enzyme that breaks down norepinephrine, dopamine, and serotonin.
Valium® (diazepam)	Mimics gamma amino butyric acid.
Amphetamines (Dexedrine® and speed)	Mimic dopamine and norepinephrine.
LSD; mescaline	Block serotonin receptors and thus act as hallucinogens.

Obviously this is only a partial list. Failure to include marijuana is not an oversight. The cellular effects of this and many other substances is yet to be established.

Consider the reflex that occurs when you're walking barefoot and step on a tack. Invariably, the stimulus of the tack causes you to quickly withdraw the injured foot and the same time extend the opposite leg. The adaptive value of these actions is clear. Withdrawing the damaged foot prevents further injury, contraction of muscles on both sides of the opposite leg locks the leg straight and makes it a stable support for the body. Reflexes such as this occur without conscious decision and are therefore automatic.

Reflexes involve series of components that form reflex arcs. At a minimum, a **reflex arc** includes a sense organ, a sensory neuron, a motor neuron, and an effector, such as a muscle (Fig. 8.9). The **sense organ** receives the stimulus and initiates depolarization of the **sensory neuron,** which passes from the sense organ into the central nervous sys-

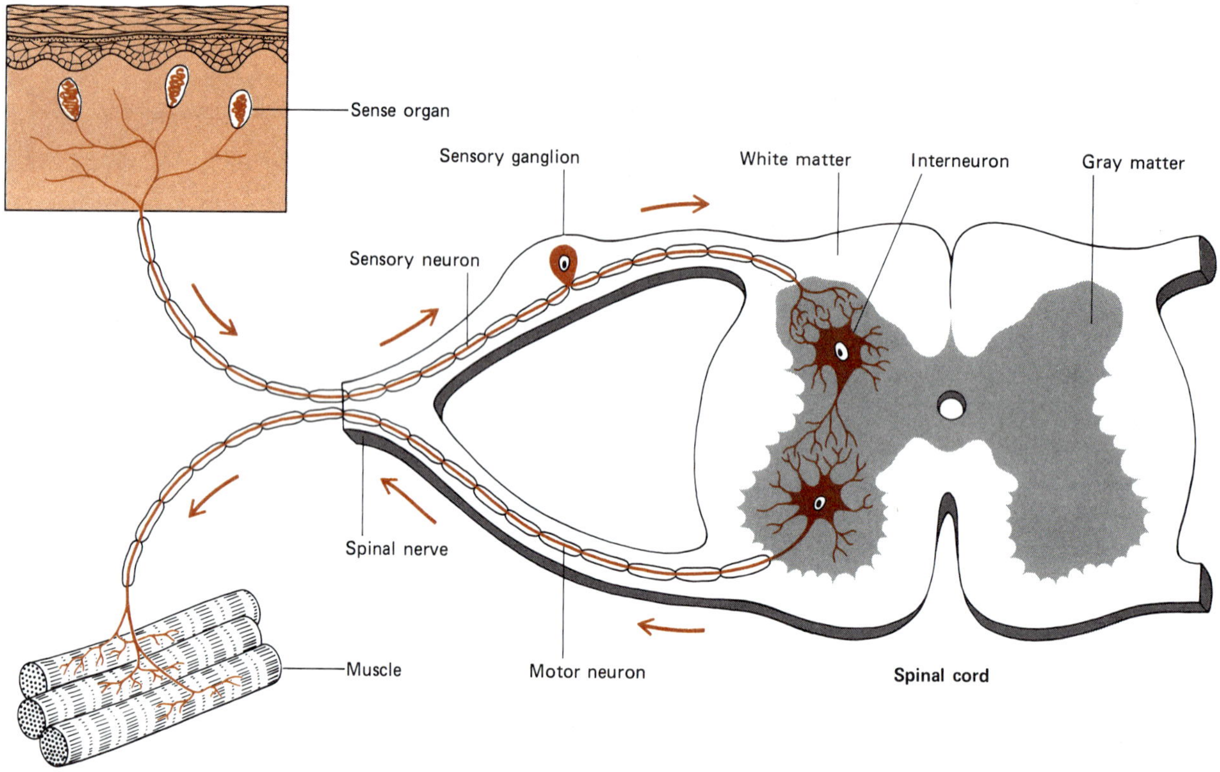

FIGURE 8.9 Reflex Arc. Stimulation of a sense organ initiates an impulse in sensory neurons. These impulses are transmitted to motor neurons and from there to particular muscles.

tem. Within the central nervous system the sensory neuron either synapses directly with a **motor neuron,** or indirectly through one or more **interneurons.** The axons of the motor neurons extend to the **muscle** or **gland** that produces the response.

When you step on a tack, impulses pass from sensory neurons through interneurons to motor neurons that cause the affected leg to bend. Interneurons also carry impulses that cause the opposite leg to be extended. Still other neurons transmit impulses to the brain and permit you to be aware of the tack.

Inhibition. The components outlined above may seem to explain responses to stepping on a tack, but in truth, there is more to the story. These reflexes involve neurons that *inhibit,* as well as those that stimulate. Normally when you stand, the muscles on both the front and back of your legs are partially contracted. Such contraction results from balance reflexes. If you start to fall forward, the muscles in the back of the leg are stimulated to contract. If you start to fall backward, the muscles in the front of the leg are stimulated to contract. These reflexes are finely tuned so that both sets of muscles contract gently and continuously as you keep your balance.

But consider the effect on these balance reflexes when you step on a tack and another reflex initiates powerful contractions of muscles on the back of the leg. Clearly, the balance reflex would cause the opposing muscles on the front of the leg to contract and prevent the leg from bending. Withdrawal from the painful tack is possible only if passage of motor impulses to the front muscles is inhibited. Such inhibition is a necessary part of almost all neural activity.

Inhibition occurs at synapses. The dendrites of neurons receive axons from numerous other neurons. Certain axons release neurotransmitters that make depolarization of the dendritic membrane more difficult. The process may involve increased polarization or other mechanisms. Odd as it may seem, one neurotransmitter can be inhibitory to some cells and stimulatory to others. Well-known inhibitory neurotransmitters include glycine and gamma amino butyric acid.

Facilitation: Making It Easier. Reflexes also provide examples of situations in which passage of the neural message across the synapse occurs more easily at some times than at others. Probably you recognize that your reflexes are especially sensitive at certain times. When we respond dramatically to minor stimuli, we say that we are "nervous" or "jumpy" or "edgy." On other occasions we are depressed—and so are our reflexes. Such changes in how we feel and behave reflect differences in the ease with which neurons are depolarized. Stimulation of a neuron by certain axons will **facilitate** (make easier) the passage of a nerve impulse from other axons to that neuron. Perhaps the neurotransmitter substances released by several neurons add together to produce sufficient depolarization to create an action potential. Inhibition and facilitation are major factors in the integration of the nervous system. They are involved in far more than simple reflexes.

The Brain: Its Regions and Their Work

It would be convenient if we could assign a different function to each brain part (Fig. 8.10), but the truth is that most brain activities require the coordinated action of several regions. The following description is far from complete. We omit many regions and volumes of details concerning functions.

FIGURE 8.10 **The Brain.** This is a view of one side of a brain that has been split into right and left halves.

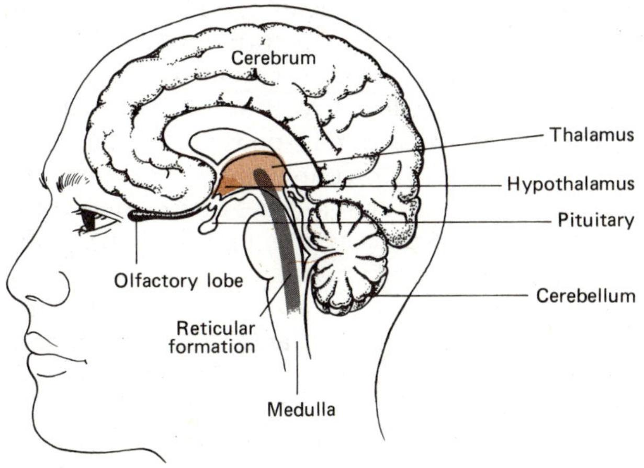

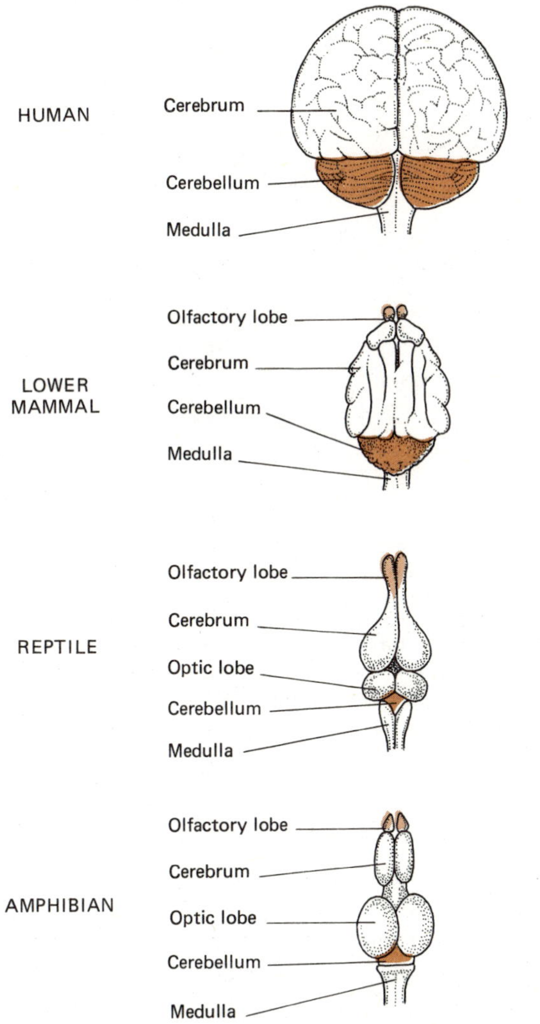

FIGURE 8.11 **Relative Proportions in Vertebrate Brains.** This dorsal view of various vertebrate brains reveals important differences in the size of specific regions. The tiny olfactory lobes of the human lie hidden under the cerebrum.

The Most Human Part. The convoluted outer **cortex** of the **cerebrum** consists of gray matter containing billions of interneurons. These interneurons are involved in reasoning, will power, and other "higher" attributes, as well as control of conscious movement and awareness of sensation. The cerebral cortex is the part of the brain that has changed most during the evolution of mammals. Indeed, the dominant role of the cerebrum is one of the distinguishing features of humans and other primates (Fig. 8.11).

Stimulation of specific areas in the motor region of the cerebral cortex results in movement of

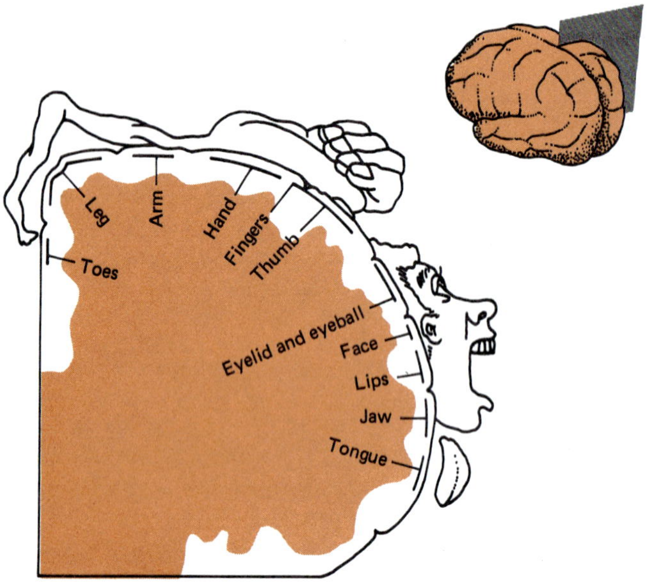

FIGURE 8.12 **Map of the Motor Area.** Some regions of the cortex have clear-cut functions. The motor cortex is one such region. Note that muscles used in complex or delicate manipulations cover proportionally greater areas than those used in larger-scale movements.

particular body parts. This has been known for years, and the motor cortex is thoroughly mapped (Fig. 8.12). From this illustration it is evident that those body regions possessing the greatest dexterity (such as the lips and fingers) are controlled by areas of the cortex larger than those governing regions engaged in less delicate movements (e.g., the elbows and thighs). Whether or not specific cortical neurons control specific muscles remains uncertain. It is puzzling that mild stimulation of particular regions causes contraction of certain muscles, but that stronger stimulation of other areas causes these same muscles to respond. Furthermore, complete loss of a given portion of the motor cortex does not always result in permanent paralysis of a body region.

Touch, pressure, temperature, and pain in skin, muscles, and other body parts are reflected in specific sensory areas. So are vision and hearing. There are even special color-vision areas. This regularity of organization extends to the cellular level. Stimulation of adjacent regions of the skin results in electrical potentials in adjacent groups of neurons. This regionalization of the cerebral cortex is evident when tumors, strokes, or injuries to particular areas produce predictable loss of body functions.

A deep furrow separates the cerebrum into right and left hemispheres, and both halves contain many similar areas. Neural pathways from the motor cortex cross from one side of the brain to the other before entering the spinal cord. This is why interruption of the blood supply on one side of the cerebrum (as may happen during a stroke) paralyzes the opposite side of the body.

One-Sided Specialization. Some functions must be localized in only one side of the cortex even if they involve actions of both sides of the body. For example, at any one time there can be only one speech pattern and one will. If any meaning is to be expressed, the two sides of the brain can't act independently. One side must dominate. Normally the two sides complement each other but both have the potential for independent action.

The two halves of the cerebrum are sometimes separated surgically as a treatment for severe epilepsy. After such an operation, the patient can call out the name of an object felt with the right hand only but not the names of those felt with the left hand only. (Remember that the left-hand side of the brain connects to the right-hand side of the body and vice versa.) Nevertheless, these individuals do recognize objects touched only with the left hand. When given number-shaped objects, split-brain humans can indicate that they recognize the number by holding up the appropriate number of fingers. These and other observations indicate that analytical ability, speech, and writing are usually localized in the left cerebrum. Spatial interpretation, mental images, and musical ability reside primarily in the right cerebrum.

Motor Coordination. Observations on reflexes of normal infants provide evidence that the cerebral cortex dominates motor activities. Newborn babies will reflexively grasp a finger thrust onto their palms and hang on, even while being lifted into the air. Another infant reflex is rotation of the head and opening of the mouth in response to a light tap on the cheek or chin. Of course, this reflex helps the baby find a nipple. Both reflexes occur whether the newborn is awake or asleep, and both disappear as the child's cerebrum matures. Nevertheless, these reflexes sometimes reappear in adults with damaged cerebrums. The fact that infants born without a cerebrum exhibit these reflexes and retain them indicates that the reflexes arise from centers in the lower parts of the brain. Such reflexes are normally suppressed by the mature cerebral cortex.

The cerebellum integrates detailed sensory data concerning contraction of muscles and body position with motor commands from the cerebrum. Activities of the cerebellum permit smooth, coordinated movements. When the cerebellum is damaged, actions disintegrate into their exaggerated components. For example, a normal walk is reduced to a stumbling gait.

Control Centers for Fundamental Activities. The **hypothalamus,** which lies deep under the cerebrum, controls certain basic behaviors. This control can be demonstrated by electrical stimulation of the hypothalamus. Mild shocks from electrodes in one place will evoke behavior recognized as evidence of hunger. Animals stimulated in other regions will show thirst, rage, or sexual arousal. In addition to drives that result in overt activity, the hypothalamus is the center for regulation of internal body functions through autonomic responses. For example, the temperature control center lies in the hypothalamus. The fundamental role of the hypothalamus is underscored by the fact that it links the nervous system to the endocrine glands.

The **medulla,** the region of the brain joining the spinal cord, controls such essential life functions as breathing and heart action. For this reason, serious injuries to the medulla result in death. Reflex centers for vomiting, coughing, hiccupping, and swallowing also lie in the medulla.

In addition to life-sustaining reflexes, the medulla is a throughway for traffic between the spinal cord and higher centers. Some of the neurons here are part of the **reticular formation** that screens sensory data and determines which messages will be transmitted to the cerebrum.

Pleasure and Pain. A series of newly discovered compounds have effects surprisingly similar to heroin, morphine, and other opium drugs. Several years ago it was found that the chemical naxolone blocks the effects of heroin and related drugs by binding to receptor sites on neurons. This discovery lead to questions concerning the normal function of these receptor sites. We now know that the opiate-binding sites are the targets of a special class of neurotransmitters. These "opiate transmitters" are the **enkephalins,** and **endorphins,** and the **dynorphins.** One function of such compounds is pain relief. Minute quantities of endorphins injected into the cerebral spinal fluid can dull the pain of cancer just as effectively as morphine and without the morphine side effects. Action of the opiate transmitters is thought to involve inhibition of impulses that would otherwise reach the consciousness as pain.

Knowledge of our resident opiates is far from complete. These compounds aren't limited to the brain. They also occur in the adrenal and the anterior pituitary. Nor is pain relief their only likely role. Just as heroin injections produce a rush of pleasurable sensations, these opiate transmitters may further our sense of well-being. Increased endorphin levels are found in the blood after strenuous exercise. It isn't surprising that so many people report they feel "really good" after jogging or playing racquetball.

Learning and Memory. Human experience shows that there are at least two kinds of memory. One is quite short-term. It permits us to remember a fact only briefly—for instance, a phone number long enough to dial or punch it. Other experiences may be remembered over a hundred years of life. The distinction between long-term and short-term memory is readily evidenced by those senior citizens who can remember vivid details of their childhood but can't quite recall what they did yesterday.

It has been suggested that short-term learning may result from the initiation of nerve impulses that then reverberate through the "learned" neural circuits. Experimentation with cerebrocortical neurons shows that they exhibit continued electrical activity long after stimulation has ceased. Whether or not continuous activity is involved in short-term memory, it seems unlikely that such a mechanism could account for the long-term memory that can survive anesthesia, electric shock treatments, and other physical assaults that temporarily interrupt higher brain functions.

To explain long-term memory, many scientists have turned to molecular theories. One popular explanation involves the production of chemicals in which information is coded in much the same manner as genetic information is known to be stored in the DNA of chromosomes (see Chapter 11). Protein synthesis has been shown to occur with learning, and there is considerable interest in the association of learning and enzyme activation. Some explanations of long-term memory involve alterations in the properties of synapses or even the establishment of new synapses. Despite much study, no widely accepted explanation has emerged.

Memory seems to be a function of the cerebral cortex in general. Surgical removal of various regions of the cortex from experimental animals grad-

BOX 8B

HUNGER AND OBESITY

Weight control is the most serious health problem many people face. Both present and past nutritional states are involved. It was long believed that fat cells do not increase in number after birth. Weight gain was thought to result from growth in the size of fat cells. Laboratory studies of rats, however, have established that certain fatty tissues increase in cell number during adult life. Furthermore, surgical removal of skin fat from three-week-old rats is followed by cell multiplication when nutrition is adequate. On the other hand, older rats that have been surgically deprived of much of their body fat eat less of a fat-rich diet and gain less than control rats. Nevertheless, fat-cell size in the two groups remains identical. Research workers have interpreted these observations to indicate that fat-cell size is fixed and regulates appetite. Or they may indicate that fat-cell size and appetite are regulated by a common mechanism. Tempting as it is to generalize these animal studies to humans, caution is in order. Not only can we expect differences between species, but all human fat cells do not behave uniformly, even within one individual.

Women with fat tissue concentrated in the upper body find it easier to lose weight than do women with fat tissue concentrated below the waist. When women with lower-body obesity do lose weight, they also lose fat cells. In contrast, weight loss in upper-body-obese women is a matter of reduced cell size.

Mechanisms of appetite regulation are far from understood. For years, biologists and physicians have accepted the hypothesis that low blood sugar initiates sensations of hunger and that the availability of glucose satisfies that hunger. This makes good sense and corresponds to much of our everyday experience. Nevertheless, many people report that high-carbohydrate diets promote hunger. Animal studies, too, show that access to sugar results in increased food consumption. Recent experiments indicate that it may be the rate of sugar intake that influences the satisfaction of hunger. Glucose sent directly by tube to the small intestine results in decreased hunger if administered slowly, but stimulates hunger if given rapidly. This is interesting, as natural carbohydrates are mainly starch and related large molecules that take time to digest.

The hypothalamus has long been thought to be the site of our appetite regulation. Thus it was no surprise to learn that releasing glucose in the intestine increased norepinephrine in the hypothalamus. Nor was the resulting depression of hunger unexpected. Cholecystokinin, an intestinal hormone released in response to large fatty meals, also depresses hunger. This depression may involve norepinephrine. Glucose release in the intestine is thought to stimulate special glucose sense organs that promote norepinephrine secretion in the hypothalamus. The obese mouse strain is characterized by an unlimited appetite and by reduced brain cholecystokinin.

Common explanations for obesity have been poor eating habits or inherited tendencies. Until recently, few people thought of obesity as an infectious disease. However, about a quarter of the mice surviving an acute infection of canine distemper (a viral disease) developed dramatic weight gains. Both fat-cell number and fat-cell size increased. Decreased norepinephrine and dopamine levels were found in the forebrains of these mice, but levels in the hypothalamus were not unusual.

Weight control, like so many body functions, is complex and vulnerable to many kinds of disturbances.

ually decreases learning, but no specific areas have proved crucial. However, stimulation with electrodes implanted in the human cerebral cortex sometimes evokes vivid memories.

The Autonomic Nervous System

We have left the autonomic "nervous system" for last, partly because it isn't a simple anatomical part but, instead, involves many different regions. Nevertheless, the autonomic system controls actions independent of our consciousness and crucial for homeostasis. Through motor nerves to the intestine, heart, blood vessels, and other internal organs, the autonomic nervous system regulates activities we could not consciously monitor every minute of the day and night. As noted earlier, autonomic centers lie in the hypothalamus.

A unique characteristic of the autonomic nervous system is its pattern of dual innervation. Nearly all organs that receive autonomic fibers have two kinds of fibers. One stimulates activity, and the other inhibits the organ. Thus the autonomic nervous system provides mechanisms to either speed up or slow down nearly every internal function. Nevertheless, it is incorrect to characterize either of the two parts of the autonomic system (sympathetic or parasympathetic) as being stimulatory or inhibitory. Instead, each division adjusts the body for a particular sort of situation.

The Sympathetic Division. In general, sympathetic stimulation primes the body for crises. Any sudden scare brings on a sympathetic "fight-or-flight" response. The heart pounds, blood pressure rises, and the bronchioles of the lungs expand as we gasp deeply for air. At the same time, the blood sugar rises, blood vessels in skeletal muscles dilate, and digestive functions are depressed. The body is poised for action.

Most terminal axons of the sympathetic system secrete **norepinephrine.** The **adrenal medulla,** usually included as one of the endocrine glands, also produces norepinephrine along with a similar compound, **epinephrine,** also known as adrenalin. Secretion of closely related chemicals by sympathetic neurons and by the adrenal medulla is a reflection of their common embryonic origin. Furthermore, the adrenal medulla secretes in response to sympathetic stimulation. These facts support the argument that neural and endocrine mechanisms are fundamentally similar.

The Parasympathetic Division. As noted, sympathetic stimulation predominates under stressful circumstances. Parasympathetic stimulation produces the opposite effect. The heartbeat is retarded, breathing is slowed, and digestive juices flow readily. If the sympathetic system is to be remembered for the "fight or flight" response, then we should think of the parasympathetic system in terms of a "contented cow" adjustment.

Many basic differences underlie the contrast between the sympathetic and parasympathetic portions of the autonomic nervous system. As we have already mentioned, the sympathetic neurons exert their action through secretion of norepinephrine. In contrast, parasympathetic neurons secrete **acetylcholine.** Another difference is that sympathetic fibers arise from spinal nerves along the middle of the cord, but parasympathetic nerves come from the brain or from the lower end of the spinal cord. As an example of autonomic activity, we will examine control of heart rate.

Autonomic Control of Heart Rate: An Example of Homeostasis. As pointed out earlier, heart muscle contracts even if all nerves to it are severed. However, the rate of contraction is normally regulated by the autonomic nervous system. One function of this regulation is to control blood pressure. The amount of blood the heart pumps per second is a factor in determining blood pressure. When blood pressure falls, heart rate must be increased. If pressure becomes excessive, the heart rate must be slowed. These adjustments are achieved through autonomic reflexes. Sympathetic and parasympathetic nerves from centers in the medulla constitute the motor portions of the reflexes. The sensory neurons originate in pressure sense organs in the walls of large arteries. Rising pressure in these arteries stimulates sensory neurons and thereby increases activity of parasympathetic neurons arising in the medulla. These neurons secrete more acetylcholine in the heart, and consequently slow its contractions. The same sensory nerves that stimulate the parasympathetic neurons also inhibit sympathetic neurons. This lessens epinephrine (adrenalin) secretion and also slows the heart. When arterial blood pressure falls, the actions are reversed and the heart beats faster.

Repair in the Nervous System

Once nerve cells develop their specialized characteristics, they lose the ability to divide. There are no reserve cells that can replace the old nerve cells. Unlike most other tissues, the nerve cells must last a life-time. And last they do, unless subjected to unusual damage. When there is injury to the nervous system, recovery is sometimes possible.

Because peripheral nerves contain nerve fibers but not cell bodies, a severed nerve may repair itself. The neuronal fibers degenerate, often as far back as the cell bodies. Then, after a period of recuperation, the damaged cells sprout new fibers in the direction of the original connection. Meanwhile, the myelin sheath has degenerated but surviving cells have multiplied and formed a cord of cells along the old nerve pathway. The tips of the new fibers probe as they grow along this old pathway. Extending 1–2 mm per day, the new fibers sometimes reestablish the original connections. Surgical techniques that bring the cut ends of a nerve together increase the likelihood that the fibers will find their way and restore feeling and motor control. Still, regeneration is seldom complete. Sometimes scar tissue gets in the way of emerging fibers and they tangle up. Sensory fibers that fail to reach their sense organ may twist into painful lumps. Recovery from peripheral nerve damage can involve more than regeneration of fibers. For example, muscle cells deprived of motor neurons are sometimes reinnervated by branches of neurons that originally served other muscle cells.

Unfortunately for those who suffer neck or back injuries, spinal-cord fibers that are torn never heal. Studies with laboratory animals show that injured fibers in the central nervous system sprout anew but do not establish connections. Perhap scar tissue blocks the fibers from reaching the proper point. Despite lack of replacement of destroyed fibers, the paralysis and other handicaps resulting from brain and spinal cord injury are sometimes temporary. In many cases, neurons are injured by the pressure of swollen tissues or suffer from decreased blood supply. If the neurons survive until the swelling subsides or blood flow becomes normal, neural function may be restored. It has also been demonstrated that uninjured fibers branch and replace some of the synapses of lost fibers in the brain. One way or another, many stroke victims learn to walk and talk after losing these abilities. Viral infections also can make neurons temporarily sick without destroying them. During the polio epidemics of the 1940s, many people suffered paralysis due to virus in the motor neurons necessary for respiration. Only the use of a crude "iron lung," which supplied continuous artificial respiration, kept these people alive. But many recovered and lead normal lives today.

Similarities and Differences in Nervous Systems

Irritability is a basic property of life. This ability to respond to stimuli is found in green plants and fungi and likewise in microorganisms. Consider the example of bacteria that swim toward an oxygen source despite the absence of structures to coordinate their actions.

Among animals, similarities of the nervous system provide striking evidence of the unity of life. Except for the sponges, all animals have neurons. Most animals have a clearly definable central nervous system with an anterior brain and peripheral nerves (Fig. 8.13). Though certainly complex, the nervous systems of animals such as mollusks and worms offer scientists relatively simple systems for exploration of neural mechanisms. Much of our fundamental knowledge about neurons was obtained with such animals as the squid. Because the rate of impulse transmission is related to diameter of the axon, the neurons used in the stereotyped escape reactions of lower animals are giant ones (Fig. 8.14). These **giant neurons** are so large that they could be penetrated by the crude electrodes first used to record electrical potentials from the inside of cells. Except for the fact that some synapses resemble gap junctions and allow ions to flow directly from one neuron to another, there are few fundamental differences between the neurons

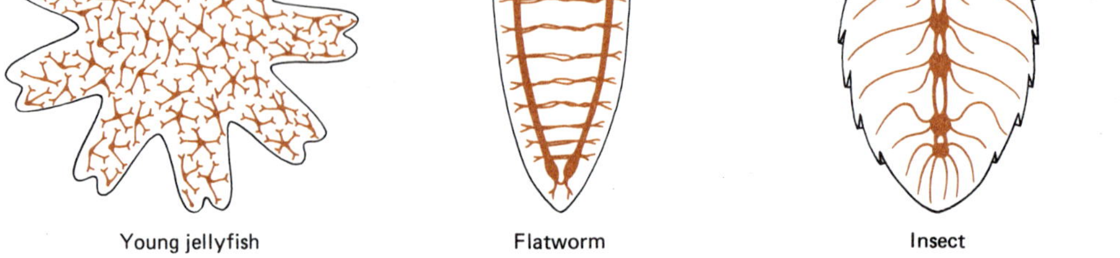

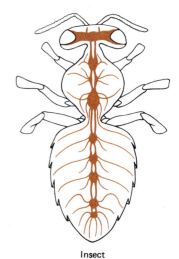

FIGURE 8.13 **Heads and Brains.** Nearly all animals have a brain located in the front end and a nerve cord. Exceptions include the jellyfish, a headless animal that has a nerve net which lacks significant central control.

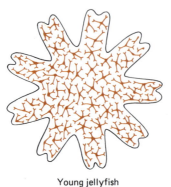

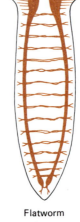

of these animals and those of mammals. Most synapses involve release of neurotransmitters from the axons; some of the same chemicals serve as neurotransmitters. Only jellyfish (Fig. 8.13), hydra, and their relatives have dramatically different neurons. These animals have no head, no body part that consistently meets the environment first, and consequently, no brain. Because stimuli are received by different body parts at different times, it is advantageous to have a **nerve net** along which messages can travel in any direction. In such animals most synapses between neurons can transmit in both directions. These **two-way synapses** are unknown in higher animals.

HORMONES: CHEMICAL MESSENGERS

As we have seen, nerve action relies on the neurons' secretion of chemical messengers. However, neurotransmitters carry information only a short distance, specifically across the synaptic gap between axon and dendrite. Other chemical messengers of the body usually work at a distance from their point of origin. These are the **hormones** secreted by **endocrine tissues** (Table 8.1).

It is customary to speak of an **endocrine system,** but this system is not comparable to the digestive or nervous system in that it is not structurally united. Instead, the components of the endocrine system are scattered about the body. They constitute a "system" only in that they share some modes of operation and are responsible for important aspects of homeostatic regulation. Many endocrine tissues occur as large masses of glandular tissue named as distinct organs. Other endocrine cells are hidden in organs better known for other functions. Examples include intestinal cells that produce the digestive hormones secretin and enterogastrone (see Table 8.1 for their functions). But no matter what the exact organization of endocrine tissues is, their secretions enter the blood. Because the blood distributes hormones throughout the body, there

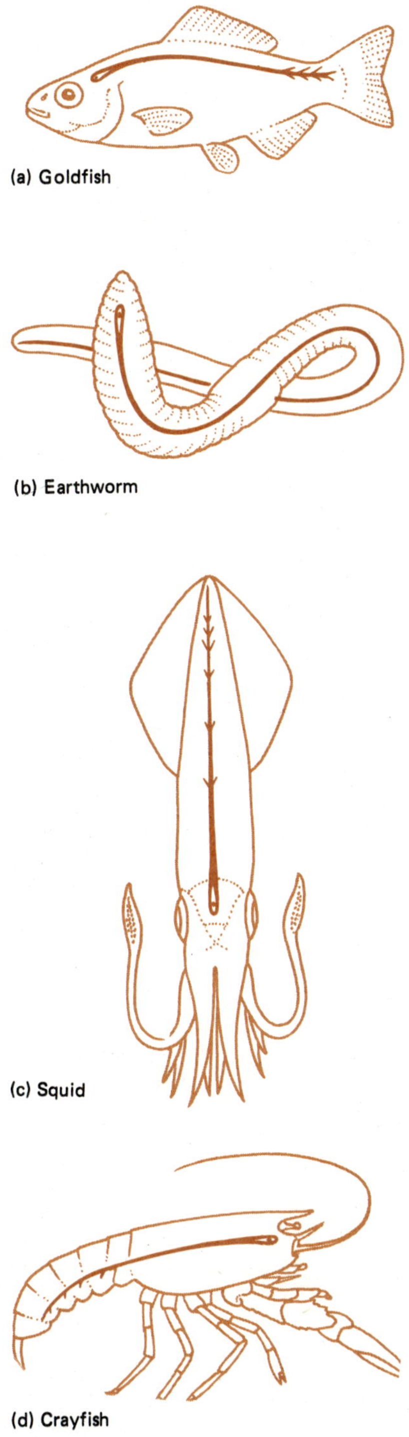

FIGURE 8.14 Giant Neurons. Both large diameter and the absence of the synapses, which separate a series of small neurons, make giant neurons ideal for escape responses. One giant neuron extends from each side of the fish's brain to its tail. Arrangements of inhibitory neurons ensure that the two giant neurons fire alternately. As a result muscles on one side contract first, followed by those on the other side. Three giant neurons carry impulses that cause a startled earthworm to snap back into its burrow. In squid, giant neurons conduct impulses that allow the squid to squirt out a jet of water and propel itself to safety. The tail flip of crayfish also depends on giant neurons. These neurons innervate muscles that pull the tail under the abdomen, drawing the animal back into deeper water.

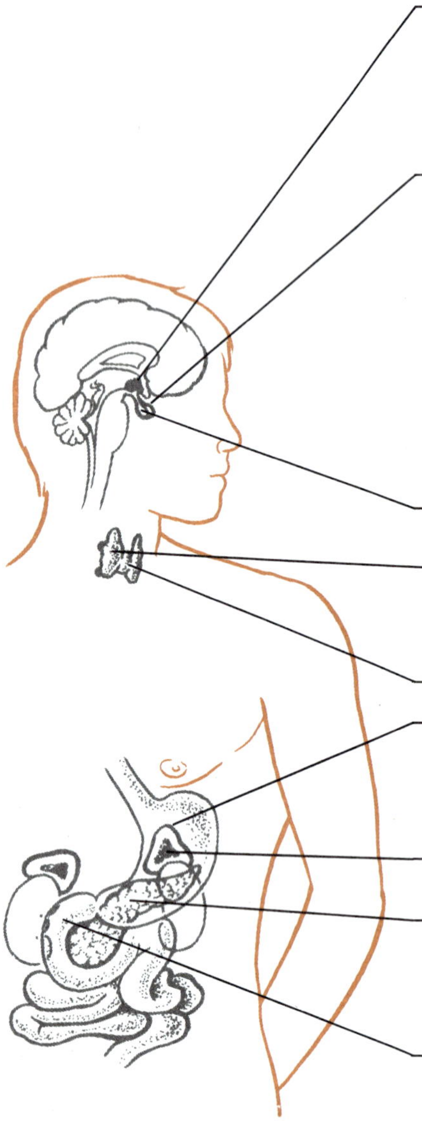

TABLE 8.1 **Some Major Hormones**

SOURCE	HORMONE	REGULATES
Hypothalamus	**ACTH RELEASING FACTOR (RF)**	Secretion of **ACTH**
	FSHRF	Secretion of **FSH**
	LHRF	Secretion of **LH**
	GHRF	Secretion of **GH**
	Prolactin RF	Secretion of prolactin
	TSHRF	Secretion of **TSH**
Ant. Pituitary	**ADRENAL CORTICOTROPIC HORMONE (ACTH)**	Cortisol secretion
	FOLLICLE STIMULATING HORMONE (FSH)	Ovarian follicles and female secondary sex characteristics
	Growth hormone (GH)	Growth, especially skeletal
	Prolactin	Milk secretion
	THYROID STIMULATING HORMONE (TSH)	Thyroxin secretion
	Luteinizing Hormone (LH)	Ovulation, dev. of corpus luteum, female; testosterone secretion, male
Post. Pituitary	**ANTIDIURETIC HORMONE**	Water resorption in kidney
	Oxytocin	Birth; milk release
Thyroid	Calcitonin	Lowers blood calcium
	THYROXIN	Increases energy metabolism and protein synthesis
Parathyroid	Parathyroid hormone	Raises blood calcium
Adrenal Cortex	***ALDOSTERONE**	Sodium resorption from kidney filtrate
	*Cortisol	Glucose synthesis; suppresses inflammation
Adrenal Medulla	**EPINEPHRINE**	Mimics sympathetic stimulation
Pancreas	Glucagon	Glucose synthesis from glucogen
	INSULIN	Glycogen synthesis from glucose; entrance of glucose into cells
Digestive Tract	Enterogasterone	Pyloric sphincter
	Choleocystokinin	Gall bladder dumping
	Gastrin	Secretion intestinal enzymes
	Secretin	Bicarbonate secretion
Ovary	***ESTROGEN**	Uterine muscle, lining; secondary sex characteristics female; mammary glands
	***PROGESTERONE**	Uterine lining; breast development
Placenta	**CHORIONIC GONADOTROPIN**	Replaces LH in support of placenta
Testis	***TESTOSTERONE**	Sperm production and male secondary sex characteristics

*Steroid Hormones. Others are proteins, short chains of amino acids, or modified amino acids.

is no need for endocrine glands to have ducts. Unlike glands that secrete lubricating fluids or digestive enzymes, endocrine glands are ductless (Fig. 8.15). Although all the organs of the body come into contact with most hormones, in many cases only one or a few kinds of **target cells** actually respond to a particular hormone.

Hormones generally control characteristic life patterns and make relatively slow, gradual adjustments. Thus hormones regulate growth, sexual development and activity, the water content of the body, the metabolic rate, and some aspects of digestion. By way of contrast, nerves are mainly responsible for more rapid changes. Our nervous system permits us to respond to our environment and manipulate it. Nerves are largely responsible for regulating muscles, both the skeletal muscles that move our bones and internal muscles like those of the heart and blood vessels. Any attempt to divide neural and hormonal activities blurs, of course, as we have already seen in our discussion of the effect of adrenal hormones on the heart muscle.□ 175
But the complex relationship between the nervous system and the endocrine system doesn't end here. Ultimately, the nervous system controls most endocrine glands.

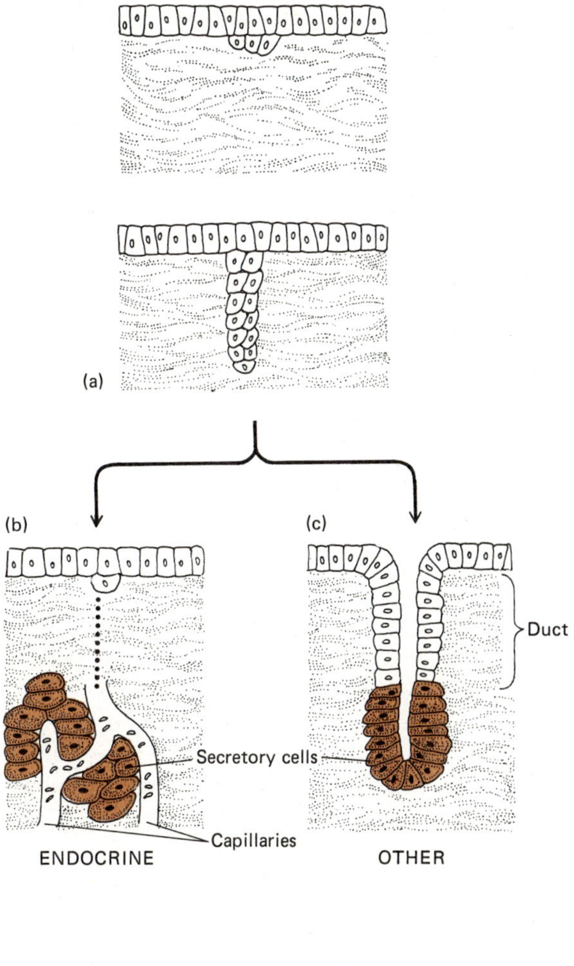

FIGURE 8.15 How Endocrine Glands Develop without Ducts. All glands arise from cords of epithelial cells that grow down into the underlying connective tissue (a). In endocrine glands the cells at the tip of the cord differentiate to secrete hormones, and the remainder of the cord degenerates (b). The secretory cells are left buried, and they can then secrete only into capillaries. Other glands, such as those that produce mucus, sweat, saliva, or digestive enzymes, retain the cells between the secretory cells and the surface. These cells become a hollow duct that carries secretions to the surface (c).

The Hypothalamic-Pituitary Axis

The **pituitary,** a pea-sized gland, lies at the base of the brain just below the hypothalamus. Here it is protected in a bony pocket of the skull. The pituitary consists of distinct anterior and posterior lobes.

The posterior lobe of the pituitary is attached by a stalk to the hypothalamus and is really part of the brain. In fact, hormones released by the **posterior pituitary** (antidiuretic hormone□ is one) are 155
synthesized in the cell bodies of neurons within the hypothalamus. These hormones pass along axons of the hypothalamic cells into the posterior pituitary, where they are stored for later release.

The posterior pituitary is merely a projection of the brain itself, but the **anterior pituitary** is distinctly different. The cells of the anterior pituitary lack neuronal characteristics, and this gland originates from the roof of the mouth and is connected to the brain only by blood vessels. It is the anterior pituitary that is sometimes called the "master gland" of the body. Through hormone secretion, the anterior pituitary controls the activities of the thyroid, adrenals, and sex glands. Furthermore, an anterior pituitary hormone controls growth. Nevertheless, the hypothalamus determines to a large extent the activity of the anterior pituitary.

Although the hormones of the anterior pituitary are secreted within the gland itself, these hormones are released only when the anterior pituitary is stimulated by **releasing factors** produced by the hypothalamus. A special network of blood vessels carries blood from the hypothalamus directly to the anterior pituitary. Through these vessels the releasing factors reach the anterior pituitary.

Perhaps dependence of the endocrine system on the nervous system should be expected. After all, it is the nervous system that receives stimuli from outside the body and hence is in a position to determine the proper level of activities of other internal organs.

Feedback Control

Do you recall the discussion of feedback control of
99 enzymes in Chapter 5?[□] It turns out that the production of many hormones is regulated by a similar but somewhat more complex arrangement in which the hypothalamus plays a key role. Here is the usual pattern.

The hypothalamus secretes a specific releasing factor that stimulates the anterior pituitary to produce a particular hormone. The target organ for this pituitary hormone is another endocrine gland that responds by secreting its characteristic hormone, which produces a useful physiological effect. An increase in the blood concentration of this final hormone beyond a critical level inhibits secretion of the releasing factor by the hypothalamus. This, in turn, slows secretion of that particular pituitary hormone. This explanation is illustrated by the relationship between the hypothalamus, pituitary, and thyroid.

FIGURE 8.16 Negative-Feedback Regulation of Thyroid Activity. Thyroid-stimulating hormone releasing factor (TSHRF) secreted by the hypothalamus stimulates release of thyroid-stimulating hormone (TSH) by the anterior pituitary. TSH stimulates secretion of thyroxin from the thyroid. Thyroxin, in turn, inhibits production of TSHRF. Thus decreased thyroxin leads to an increase in its secretion, and increased thyroxin leads to a decrease in its secretion.

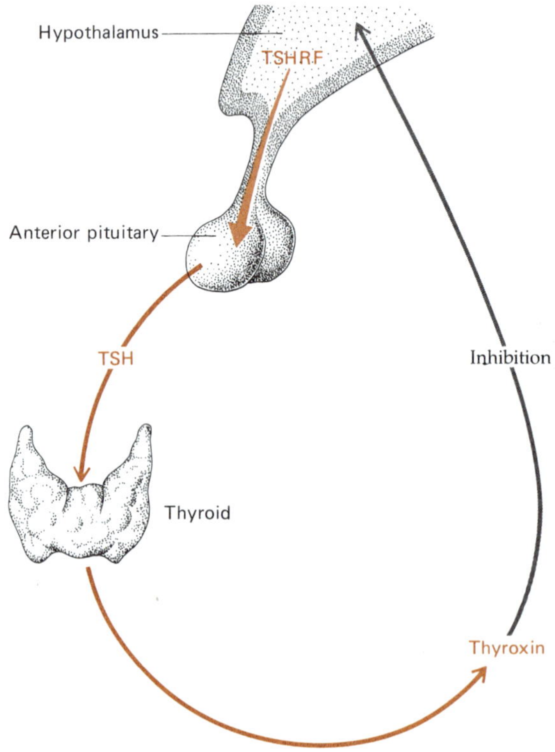

Thyroid-stimulating hormone releasing factor (TSHRF) from the hypothalamus causes the anterior pituitary to secrete **thyroid-stimulating hormone** (TSH), which causes the thyroid to produce **thyroxin.** The presence of thyroxin in the blood of the hypothalamus inhibits production of TSHRF and thus limits secretion of thyroxin (Fig. 8.16).

Because thyroxin regulates cellular respiration and hence the heat available to maintain our body temperature, this system must be adjusted to meet long-term fluctuations in environmental temperatures. We receive the first cool breezes of fall as if they were wintery blasts, partly because our metabolism is still set for summer conditions. But after a few weeks the hypothalamus responds to decreased environmental temperatures by secreting more TSHRF. As a result, thyroxin production increases, cellular respiration is accelerated, and we are comfortable at temperatures several degrees cooler than we could accept previously. Feedback control involving the hypothalamus, anterior pituitary, and reproductive hormones will be discussed in Chapter 12.

How Hormones Work

As diverse as hormones are, most seem to exert their action on particular target cells by one or the other of two methods. Hormones that are
steroids[□] (mainly secretions of the adrenal cortex, 73
ovary, and testis; see Table 8.1) penetrate the plasma membrane and bind to nuclear components. It seems likely that the activity of these hormones involves a somewhat direct regulation of the action of genes.

The nonsteroid hormones are proteins or related smaller compounds made up of amino acids or modified amino acids. These hormone messengers bind to specific receptors on the plasma membrane. The binding activates an enzyme located in the membrane and causes the enzyme to manufacture an internal or second messenger. One such messenger is **cAMP** (cyclic adenosine monophos-

BOX 8C

PROSTAGLANDINS: THE NOT-SO-NEW BODY REGULATORS

Within the last decade, a whole new class of biological compounds has attracted the attention of the medical world. These compounds are the prostaglandins, fatty acids that affect the diameter of respiratory passages, constriction of blood vessels, blood clotting, secretion of stomach mucus, joint inflammation, and numerous other functions.

Discovery of the importance of prostaglandins explains the necessity for tiny amounts of certain unsaturated fatty acids in the diet. These fatty acids are modified to make prostaglandins.

Prostaglandins differ from the familiar hormones in that prostaglandins are neither steroids nor amino-acid based compounds. And although prostaglandins can be widely distributed in the body, their action is usually local and they are short-lived. Exactly how prostaglandins work remains unknown, but there is evidence that they may be intermediaries in cyclic AMP systems (Fig. 8.17).

Among the best-known prostaglandins are prostacyclin and thromboxane. Prostacyclin is produced by cells lining the blood vessels; it acts to relax muscle of the vessel walls. Thromboxane has the opposite effect: it promotes muscle contraction in the vessel walls. Thromboxane also increases stickiness of blood platelets and stimulates blood clotting. Normally, prostacyclin and thromboxane production are balanced, but when blood vessels are injured, prostacyclin production can decrease. The excess thromboxane leads to constriction of the vessels and clot formation

Aspirin inactivates a key enzyme that synthesizes prostaglandins. This recent discovery explains how aspirin conquers certain kinds of pain and also accounts for some aspirin side effects. By reducing prostaglandin levels, aspirin relieves much of the inflammation of arthritis. At the same time, suppression of prostaglandins in the stomach leads to decreased mucus secretion. This is why heavy and prolonged use of aspirin to control arthritis results in stomach bleeding. With less mucus to protect the stomach wall from the acidic contents, the acid attacks the living tissues.

Prostaglandins were first discovered some fifty years ago when gynecologists reported that some component of semen stimulated contraction of uterine muscle. This component was traced to secretions of the prostate gland, which explains the name "prostaglandins." The uterine contractions resulting from prostaglandins move semen up the female tract and thus carry sperm toward the egg. Probably prostaglandins also promote contractions during childbirth. Menstrual cramps, too, result from such uterine contractions. We now understand why aspirin is so effective in relieving menstrual discomfort.

phate), which is produced from ATP. Increased cAMP stimulates cell activity. Exactly which activity increases, however, depends on the nature of the cell. For example, cAMP causes pancreatic cells to secrete glucagon, but it stimulates thyroid cells to produce thyroxin and liver cells to convert glycogen into glucose. Thus cAMP is a **second messenger,** which serves as a relay between the hormone that stops at the plasma membrane and the metabolic activity within the cell (Fig. 8.17).

Hormones and the Unity of Life

So far we have treated hormones as though each is the secretion of a particular gland or tissue. In reality it's not quite that simple. For example, insulin comes from the pancreas—but it is also made in the brain. Perhaps more surprising, insulin can be isolated from such organisms as flies, protozoa, fungi, and bacteria. The association of hormones with certain organs is a case of "you find what you look for." Only recently have biologists thought to look for the synthesis of a hormone in more than one organ or in diverse organisms. The wide distribution of hormones suggests that they are molecules fundamental to life.

Our specific division of glands into endocrine (ductless) ones that secrete into the blood, and others that have ducts to the outside, may be just as artificial as our assumption that insulin was a prod-

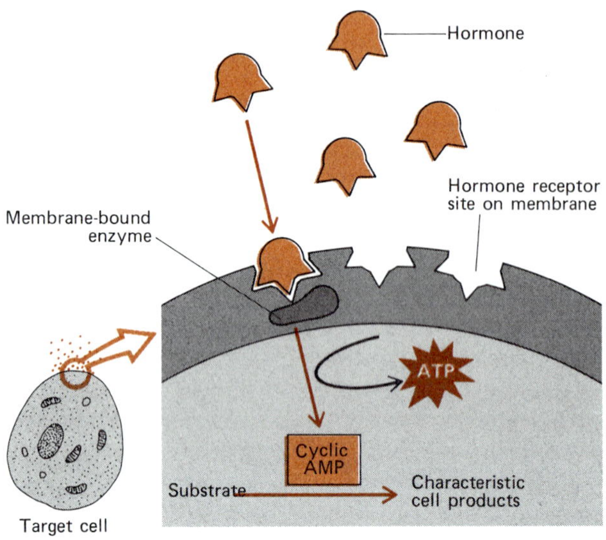

FIGURE 8.17 Cyclic AMP as a Second Messenger. According to current thinking, many hormones act through increased production of cAMP within their target cells. Such a hormone is the first messenger, and it attaches to appropriate receptor sites on the target plasma membrane, thus stimulating production of cAMP inside the cell. The cyclic AMP is a second messenger, which in turn stimulates reactions that yield products characteristic of that particular target cell.

uct only of the pancreas. A number of hormones, such as gastrin, luteinizing hormone, and the prostaglandins, occur in milk, semen, saliva, and other products released from glands with ducts.

If hormones are fundamental substances produced in a variety of organs, then it isn't too surprising that some hormones have multiple functions. For example, antidiuretic hormone both promotes absorption of water by the kidney tubules and constricts blood vessels. In addition, it serves as a neurotransmitter in the hypothalamus.

Finally, many hormones are chemically related. The sequence of amino acids that constitute glucagon and secretin are quite similar. Antidiuretic hormone and oxytocin differ by only two amino acids. Such similarities are thought to arise when an organism has genes permitting it to make more than one form of a hormone. If the hormone has multiple functions, natural selection may favor evolutionary change so that the two forms become separate hormones with separate functions. The result is greater flexibility in regulation. Perhaps such evolution is reflected in the structure and function of antidiuretic hormone and oxytocin. In nonmammalian vertebrates the functions of these two hormones are served by a single substance, vasotocin.

A Look at the Whole

Important as they are, neurons and endocrine cells can't regulate our internal environment by themselves. You will recall that reflex control of heart rate requires sense organs that measure pressure in the arteries. Similarly, the hypothalamus-pituitary-thyroid system for regulating metabolism responds to input from temperature sensors. It seems obvious that mechanisms for maintaining a constant internal environment require information about both internal and external conditions. In addition, many adjustments of our external environment rely on skeletal muscles. Similarly, adjustments of our internal environment may involve muscle of the intestines or other internal organs. In reality, sense organs and muscles are both components of our homeostatic apparatus. These are topics for the next chapter.

Summary

1. Although the nervous system consists of one physically continuous and interfunctioning unit, the brain and spinal cord are often designated as the central nervous system and the nerves and ganglia as the peripheral nervous system.

2. Neurons are the nerve-impulse-transmitting cell type. Neurons bear cytoplasmic extensions (fibers) known as axons and dendrites. The region where an axon of one neuron passes an impulse to the dendrite of a second neuron is known as a synapse.

3. Individual nerve fibers may be sheathed in myelin, a wrapping of membranes from cells that accompany the neurons. Myelinated fibers make up the "white matter" of the central nervous system. Nonmyelinated fibers and cell bodies are "gray matter." Peripheral nerves consist of many nerve fibers bundled in connective tissue. The meninges, three connective-tissue layers, surround the central nervous system. A cushion of cerebrospinal fluid lies between the inner two meningeal layers.

4. Through expenditure of energy, neurons maintain an electric potential across their cell membranes. A nerve impulse consists of a wave of temporary depolarization that passes from point to point along the cell membrane. Passage of impulses across a synapse involves secretion of neurotransmitters from the ends of axons. These chemicals, of which acetylcholine is the best known, act by altering polarization of the dendritic membrane. Many drugs that affect the nervous system do so by interfering with neurotransmitters.

5. The simplest unit of neural response is a reflex. In reflex actions, a specific stimulus causes sensory neurons to send impulses to particular motor neurons (usually by way of interneurons). The motor neurons stimulate a certain muscle or gland to produce a predictable response that is adaptive to the organism.

6. Coordinated activity requires both facilitation (processes that increase the ease of passage of impulses across synapses) and inhibition of synaptic transmission.

7. Although observation of the effects of electrical stimulation and of brain damage makes it possible to assign functions to particular brain regions, there is no simple division of labor within the central nervous system. Most activities require coordinated participation of several regions interconnected by neural fibers. Generally, the cerebral cortex dominates sensory and motor activities on a conscious level. Regulation of internal organs is mainly a function of the hypothalamus and the medulla.

8. The autonomic nervous system, centered in the hypothalamus, provides automatic regulation of many functions not under conscious control. Regulated organs, such as the heart, generally receive both sympathetic and parasympathetic fibers. A balance between stimulation of these two kinds of motor fibers adjusts activity in accord with demands. Sympathetic stimulation predominates in "fight-or-flight" crises, and parasympathetic stimulation is dominant when the body is at rest.

9. Although differentiated neurons cannot divide, fibers in peripheral nerves can regenerate.

10. All organisms show irritability. In most animals this is a property of a nervous system that includes an anterior brain. Neural functions are generally similar except that some lower animals have synapses much like gap junctions.

11. All animals, including humans, exhibit inherited behavioral patterns. Learning also requires inherited biological mechanisms.

12. The nervous system is not the only body regulator. The endocrine system also regulates body activities. Endocrine tissues, usually in distinct glands, secrete hormones that are carried by blood or other tissue fluid to target cells sensitive to the hormones. Small amounts of a hormone can cause marked adjustments in the activities of its target cells. The endocrine system exerts sustained control and usually makes gradual adjustments over body activities. In contrast, the nervous system generally achieves rapid and specific responses to external stimuli. Nevertheless, there is considerable overlap between these two systems. Note that both pass messages through secretion of chemicals. Functions of the two systems are coordinated through hypothalamic control of the anterior pituitary, which, in turn, dominates many other endocrine organs.

13. Steroid hormones penetrate the cell membrane and exert control on the nucleus. Hormones consisting of amino acid units bind to the cell membrane and activate production of a second messenger, such as cAMP, within the cell.

14. Many hormones are chemically similar; many are produced by several organs; many have multiple functions, including service as neurotransmitters; and many occur in diverse organisms.

Thought and Controversy

1. All pleasure is temporary. We feel good sensations only when we can compare them with their absence. Drugs that produce euphoria affect neurotransmitters. There seem to be physiological mechanisms that always compensate for these alterations. As a result, our perception of euphoria or depression is adjusted to a baseline against which change can be compared. Such adjustments explain the tolerance that develops to LSD, barbiturates, and amphetamines and the requirement of increasing doses to obtain a "high." Perhaps puritanical attitudes have some basis in the realization that pleasure can be sensed but briefly, and to be enjoyed it must be interspersed with mundane or even unpleasant stimuli.

2. The human brain averages 1450 grams. The dolphin brain weighs 1700 grams, but the brain of the finback whale weighs between 6 and 7 *kilograms.* Both these aquatic mammals have complex echo-location devices that enable them to sense other objects in the water, and both demonstrate marvelous motor coordination. But are these functions sufficient to explain the greater relative brain volume (and presumably the larger number of neurons) than humans possess? Or does their large brain size indicate other neural functions that are as sophisticated as ours—or more so?

3. Evaluation of all drugs is influenced by the placebo effect. A placebo is a supposedly inactive substance given in the guise of a drug or medicine. It is often said that when patients demand medication they don't need, doctors will prescribe "little sugar pills" or tablets of starch or some other harmless substance. And the patients report that "the pills really helped . . .," or so the story goes. Indeed, it has been shown repeatedly that mentally healthy people experience effects from placebos. Sometimes placebos relieve symptoms; at other times they produce unpleasant side effects. The phenomenon is so general that medical drug testing usually involves a placebo control. Some individuals receive the test substance and others receive the placebo, but none in either group are told which they are taking. Nor do the physicians administering the drugs know who is getting what, for their expectations could be transmitted subconsciously to the patients.

Placebos relieve pain of many kinds, along with the misery of colds, hay fever, and seasickness. Although biologists, psychologists, and physicians all recognize the placebo effect, the way it works remains unknown.

4. Many nutrients can affect release of neurotransmitters. For example serotonin, a neutrotransmitter involved in numerous activities including sleep, is made in the body from the essential amino acid tryptophane. Large doses of tryptophane may aid people to fall asleep at night. However, because proteins are made up of all 20 amino acids, most contain only a small percentage of tryptophane. Eight of these amino acids compete with tryptophane for transport to brain cells. Consequently a high-protein meal may result in less—not more—tryptophane for serotonin synthesis. Despite popular beliefs that sugar promotes hyperactivity, there is evidence that a high-carbohydrate meal can aid serotonin synthesis and make you sleepy. Without competition from high concentrations of other amino acids, tryptophane transport is more efficient. This assumes, of course, that some tryptophane is available. One study showed less activity in boys after they consumed a sugar-rich drink than after they drank sugarless beverages. It's interesting to note that boys classified as psychiatrically disturbed slowed down an hour after the sugar drink, while the others were not affected for three hours.

Questions

1. Describe the structure of a neuron. Why do neurons differ so much that it is not possible to draw one that is truly typical?

2. Draw a cross section of the spinal cord and then add the components of a simple reflex arc.

3. Contrast a resting potential with an action potential. Describe the factors leading to each.

4. Why do drugs that interrupt energy metabolism (e.g., cyanide) act most quickly on neurons?

5. Give examples of how facilitation and inhibition add to the complexity of function in the nervous system.

6. Discuss the cerebral cortex, including its sensory and motor functions and the division of labor between the two halves.

7. Use control of heart rate to illustrate (a) the function of the autonomic nervous system, and (b) visceral reflexes.

8. Give arguments to support the proposition that the nervous system and endocrine system are not separate but in fact make up a single system that integrates body activities.

9. Compare the manner in which steroid hormones and amino-acid-based hormones affect cell functions.

10. Explain negative-feedback control of hormone levels, using the thyroid–hypothalamus–anterior-pituitary system as an example.

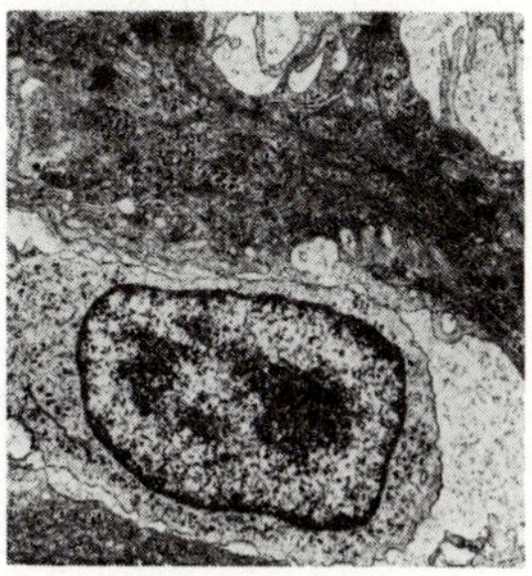

9

Meeting Our Environment: Sensors and Effectors

IMAGINE A NERVOUS SYSTEM WITHOUT SENSE organs or muscles. What a tethered giant it would be! So many messages come from the outside that without sensory input, the nervous system would never develop its full potential. And we learn not only by receiving but by doing and sensing the results. Action involves muscles, bones, and glands, or the **effectors,** as they are called. Input and output are as essential as the functions of the brain itself. We begin with input—sense receptors and sensory nerves.

SENSES AND SENSATIONS

Most sensory nerves originate in **receptors,** each of which responds mainly to one kind of stimulus. These receptors are biological **transducers;** that is, they convert one form of energy into another. We are all familiar with physical transducers. For example, a stereo speaker converts electrical energy into the energy of sound waves. In our bodies each sense organ transduces a particular kind of energy into a nerve impulse. Special areas of the brain are devoted to interpretation of sensory impulses. Thus it is in the brain, not in the receptors, that sensations are perceived.

How Many Senses?

Traditionally, humans have been credited with five senses: sight, hearing, touch, taste, and smell. However, it is clear to biologists that the number of human senses is really much larger. The traditional senses are just the most obvious ones. Yet even the obvious senses are not necessarily easy to localize or to understand.

Everyone knows that sight and hearing rely on the eyes and ears, but the location of receptors for other senses is more obscure. Consider taste and smell, the two categories of chemical sensation. Your usual experiences may lead you to place the **chemoreceptors** for taste in the mouth and those for smell in the nose. But in fact, taste buds on the tongue respond only to salt, sweet, sour, and bitter. All other taste sensations are detected by olfactory receptors in the nasal passages. This helps explain why food seems tasteless when the nasal passages are congested by a head cold. Perhaps you're unaware that acceleration (the sensation you get from jackrabbit auto starts) and your sense of gravity both depend on ear receptors that lie deep in the skull bones. The identity of some sense organs in the skin is unclear even to scientists working in this specialty.

There are still other sense receptors hidden within our internal organs. Many send messages that never reach our consciousness. Earlier we mentioned an example, the blood-pressure receptors within the walls of large arteries.□ 175

Pacinian Corpuscles: Pressure Transducers

In only a few instances can we describe how sense organs respond to stimulation and transduce that stimulation into a nerve impulse. Perhaps the best-understood sense receptors are the Pacinian cor-

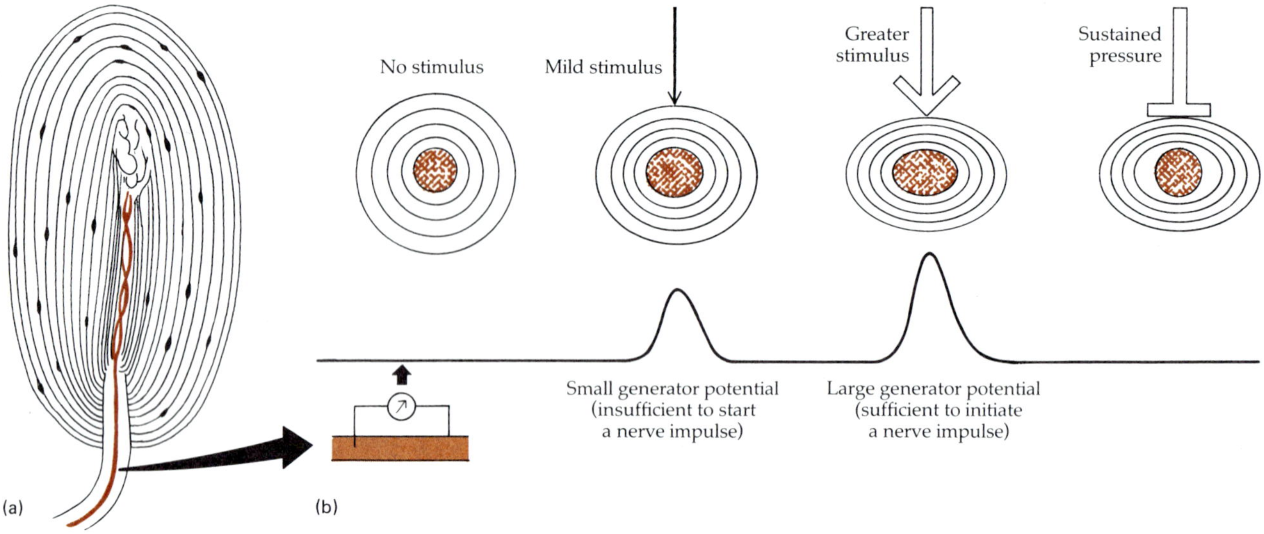

FIGURE 9.1 Pacinian Corpuscle, a Pressure-Sensitive Organ. A longitudinal section through a Pacinian corpuscle (a) shows that it is composed of concentric layers of cells with fluid filling the spaces between the layers and distending them. A sensory neuron lies at the center. Cross sections of Pacinian corpuscles (b) show how pressure initiates impulses in the sensory neuron. The hatched area in the middle is the nerve fiber. Distortion of the nerve fiber causes depolarization of its plasma membrane. A mild stimulus (thin arrow) deforms the fiber only a little and produces a partial depolarization that is insufficient to initiate a nerve impulse. A greater stimulus (heavy arrow) will create a sufficiently large generator potential to start a nerve impulse that is carried into the central nervous system. Sustained pressure (flat marker) permits the corpuscle to adapt. Adaptation occurs because adjustments in the fluid-filled capsule allow the neuron to return to its original shape.

puscles, through which pressure mechanically stimulates sensory neurons.

A **Pacinian corpuscle** consists of thousands of cells that form many fluid-filled layers around a core of fibers belonging to a sensory neuron (Fig. 9.1). Pressure on the corpuscle distorts the nerve fiber and initiates depolarization of the membrane. If this depolarization or **generator potential** is sufficiently large, it will result in one or more nerve impulses.

At this point we must explain that sensory responses are usually superimposed on a background of apparently spontaneous activity. In other words, sense organs initiate occasional nerve impulses without any detectable stimulation. Any stimulus merely changes the frequency of the nerve impulses. A strong stimulus usually produces numerous impulses, but a weak one yields only a few.

Prolonged pressure on a Pacinian corpuscle results in adaptation or **habituation** to the stimulus. That is, a long-continued stimulus, such as that which results from carrying a shoulder bag, produces gradually decreasing effects. Eventually the nerve fires no more frequently than if there were no pressure at all on the corpuscle. Adaptation of the Pacinian corpuscle occurs because the cell layers in the fluid-filled capsule slowly adjust to pressure by changing their position. As a result, the nerve regains its original shape, and it is protected from further stimulation.

Although various mechanisms are involved, all sense receptors undergo either complete or partial habituation to stimuli. This adaptation causes our senses to give us a relative, rather than an absolute, measure of our environment.

The Eye: Our Photoelectric Transducer

Compared with the Pacinian corpuscle, the eye is a hundred times more complex. Not only does the eye transduce light energy into nerve impulses, but it permits us to recognize colors and their sources and intensities over a wide area. As a result, we perceive pattern in our surroundings.

The Outside. Although they are the most obvious of our sense organs, the eyes are still somewhat hidden. They rest within bony sockets of the skull, where they are cushioned with fat pads. Six

FIGURE 9.2 Eye. In a cross section of the head, the right eye might appear as shown here.

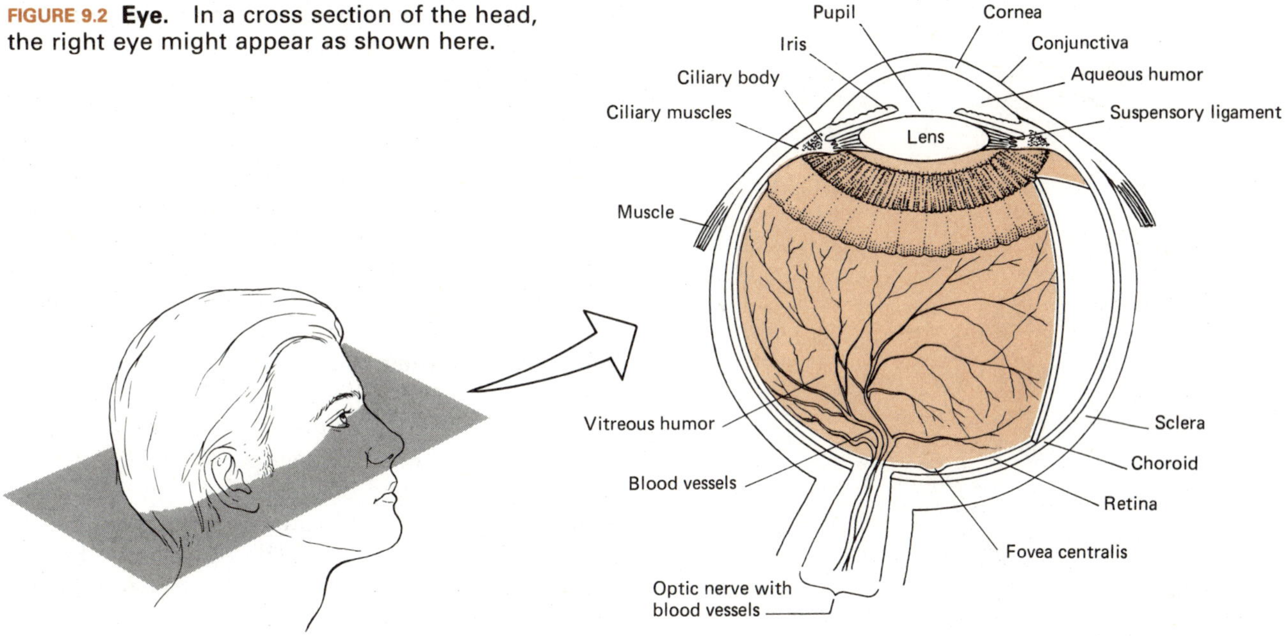

muscles on the outside of each eyeball hold it in place. Contractions of these muscles turn our eyes to follow our interests. So little of the eyeball is exposed that you may not realize that it is nearly an inch in diameter. The structure of the eye is shown in Fig. 9.2.

The **sclera,** or white outer coat, supports the eye. Since it is really a leathery sac, the sclera keeps its shape only because it is distended by the vitreous and aqueous humors inside. Anteriorly the sclera is converted into the clear, bulging **cornea,** which allows light to enter the eye. Over the cornea and exposed portions of the sclera lies the **conjunctiva.** This clear moist membrane also extends over the inside of the eyelids, forming a lubricated sac that allows the eye and eyelids to move past each other without damage. Equally important, the conjunctiva creates on the cornea a fine optical surface; the curved cornea is thus part of our light-focusing apparatus. The **lacrimal glands** secrete tears, the fluid necessary to keep the conjunctiva wet and transparent. These tear glands, as we ordinarily call them, are situated above the eye. A duct drains lacrimal secretions from the conjunctival sac into the nasal cavity. In addition to their other functions, the salty lacrimal secretions are rich in antibacterial substances that protect the eye against infections.

A colored layer, the **choroid,** lines the interior of the sclera. Extensive capillary networks and pigment cells both contribute color to the choroid. Although the choroid doesn't extend onto the cornea, it is visible in the front of the eye as the **iris.** The iris contains muscles that regulate the size of the **pupil,** a hole that permits light to penetrate to the receptor cells. A close examination of the iris will reveal fine circular and radial lines that result from muscles in the iris. In bright light the circular muscles contract reflexively and reduce the pupil to pinhead size. But adaptation to dim light causes these circular muscles to relax, and the radial muscles then pull the iris open wide.

The Basis of Vision. A flattened sphere of cells, the **lens,** is suspended behind the pupil. The cornea provides a fixed focusing device, but the lens shape changes as we change our gaze. Together they permit us to see objects as nearby as a few inches and as far away as the stars. Whatever we see must be focused on the **retina.** This delicate inner layer of the eyeball contains both sense receptors and neurons that transmit visual information to the brain.

In the retina there are two kinds of receptor cells: **rods** and **cones.** The rod-shaped receptors (Fig. 9.3) respond to a wide range of wavelengths or colors in the same way. Hence rod cells do not distinguish between colors. Because rods are extremely sensitive to dim light, they are the only retinal sensors used at night, in poorly lit rooms,

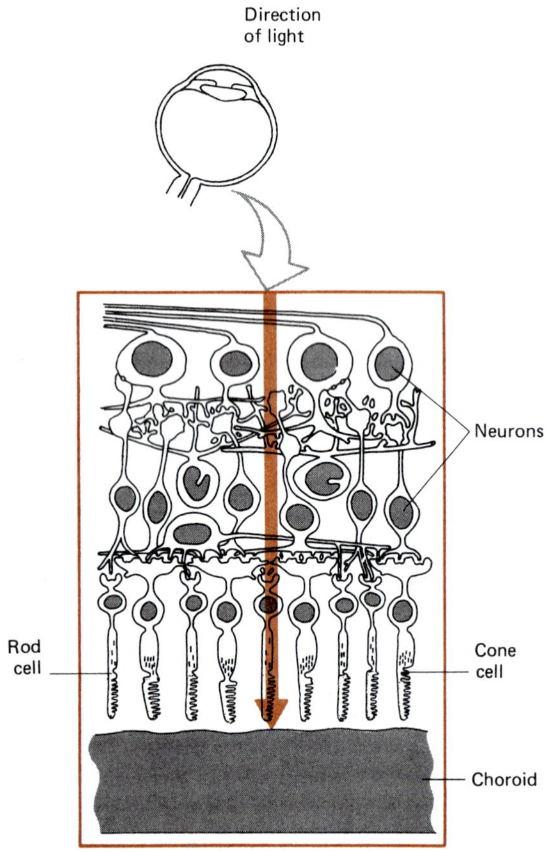

FIGURE 9.3 The Retina of the Eye. The retina originates as part of the brain and as such contains a layer of neurons with complex connections. The rod and cone cells that detect light are not neurons; instead, they are related to the cells that line the fluid-filled cavities of the brain. Absorption of light by pigment associated with complexly folded membranes of the rods and cones initiates depolarization of associated neurons. Note that light passes through the neuron layer of the retina before it reaches a rod or cone.

and at dusk. In such situations we see no color and usually little detail. There are only sensations of black, white, and shades of gray.

Rods contain a light-sensitive, pigmented protein called **rhodopsin.** You may recall that the colored part of this compund is related to vitamin A 112 and other carotenes. In Chapter 5,▫ we related vitamin A deficiency to "night blindness" or the inability to see in poor light.

When rhodopsin absorbs light, the energy of the radiation alters the shape of the molecule. This leads to bleaching of the pigmented rhodopsin molecule and dissociation to yield **retinal** and a protein, **opsin.** This process alters the rod cell so that it generates a nerve impulse in the associated sensory neuron.

Although an enzyme present in the rod cell can recombine opsin and retinal, so much rhodopsin is bleached by bright light that it takes a while to adapt to sudden darkness. Therefore it is hard to see when you enter a darkened movie theater at midday. On the other hand, dark-adapted eyes are so sensitized to light that bright illumination produces a washed-out image when you emerge from a movie theater into the daylight. The reflex that constricts the pupils in bright light is another aspect of our ability to adapt or adjust our eyes for different levels of illumination. There are additional adaptive mechanisms present in the extensive neuronal layers of the retina (Fig. 9.3). Note that light must pass through these layers before reaching rods and cones. The optic nerve begins on the inside of the eyeball; its pathway leaves a **blind spot** in the retina.

Color and Central Vision. As we have indicated, rod cells are responsible for black and white sight, even in the dimmest light. Cone cells provide detailed color vision in bright light. It seems there are three different kinds of cone cells, each containing a different pigment. Although there are pigments that absorb red, green, or blue light, color vision is more complex than individual cones responding positively to a particular wavelength of light. As is true of rod vision, the impulses carried to the brain are determined in large part by interactions of neurons in the retina.

Cone cells are concentrated in the **fovea centralis,** a tiny depression in the retina. The center of our visual field focuses on the fovea. Because cones are closely packed here, this region gives the sharpest vision in good light. Surely you have noticed that only objects you look at directly give a distinct image. Surrounding objects are less clear until you turn your eyes to look at them. Then they become sharp, because they are focused on the fovea. Peripheral vision is normally indistinct, because receptor cells are widely scattered except in the fovea.

Although cone cells are concentrated in the fovea, rod cells are absent from this portion of the retina. To take advantage of the extreme light sensitivity of rod cells, it is necessary that the image not focus on the fovea. To see in dim light we must look at things "out of the corner" of our eyes. Have you ever awakened suddenly in a dark room, aware of a mysterious, frightening shadow—only to find

BOX 9A

CLOCKS AND LIGHT

Life is rhythmic. Some rhythms are daily, some are seasonal, and some reflect other patterns. Both daily and seasonal rhythms can be influenced by patterns of light and darkness.

Daily rhythms are said to be circadian ("circa" means "approximate" and "dies" means "day"). Such daily rhythms are seen in functions ranging from water consumption and body temperature to hormone secretion. The circadian rhythm in adrenal cortical secretion continues after the organ has been removed from the body and cultured in a glass container. Hence it is independent of the brain. Secretion of some other endocrine organs—the anterior pituitary, for example—is dependent on the nervous system.

Circadian rhythms are entrained (set) by the environment. That is, environmental cues set our biological clocks. In a constant environment our clocks gradually run off-time just as mechanical clocks do when they aren't set regularly. Light and temperature may be key factors in keeping body clocks synchronized with the days and nights. When these environmental factors change, so do our internal cycles; and these cycles, in turn, alter how we feel.

Drastic changes in our environments require the resetting of many internal patterns, some of which respond more quickly than others. In the meantime, body activities are out of synchronization. This is the cause of jet lag, the out-of-sorts feeling many people experience after traveling east or west across several time zones. With their days moved forward or backward, their rhythms are disturbed. Only after several days in the new location do the rhythms return to normal.

In some animals daily rhythms are the key to seasonal activities. Examples include the spring breeding of many birds and mammals. The mechanism underlying this response depends on an ever-present circadian rhythm of light sensitivity. Exposure to light during the sensitive portion of the daily cycle triggers reproduction.

The light sensitivity of spring-breeding animals is greatest at night. When the days are short, the animal is not exposed to light during the sensitive period. But with increasing day length during the spring, the animal is exposed to light during its circadian sensitive period, stimulating the reproductive organs to enlarge and begin to function.

In some animals the response to day length involves secretions of the pineal, an endocrine gland that is part of the roof of the forebrain. In certain thin-skulled birds, the pineal senses light directly. Odd as this may seem, light sensitivity of the pineal is consistent with other facts. In a few reptiles the pineal extends through the skull as a light-sensitive third "eye." Furthermore, the retinas of the usually paired eyes of all vertebrates develop from the neural tube that also forms the brain and thus the pineal. (In fact, rods and cones are equivalent to specialized brain cells.) Of course, the pineal of heavy-skulled animals cannot respond directly to light. Instead, day length is detected by the eyes and relayed first to the hypothalamus, and eventually to the pineal by sympathetic nerves.

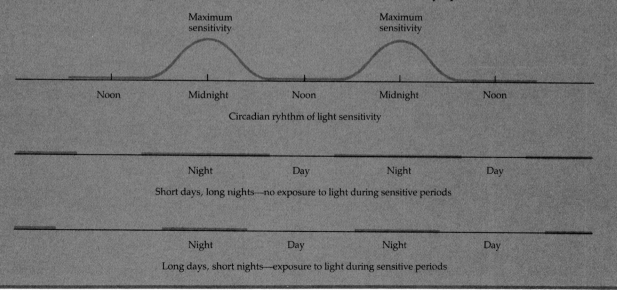

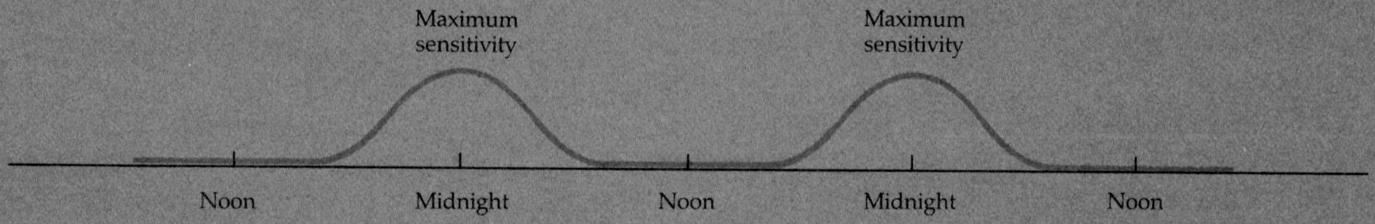

Circadian ryhthm of light sensitivity

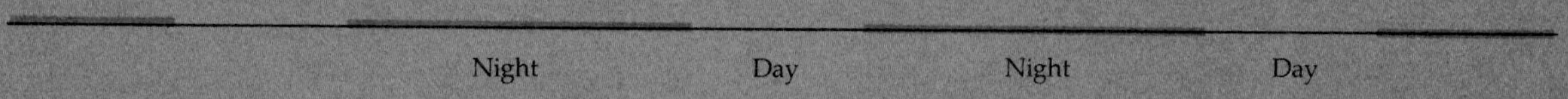

Short days, long nights—no exposure to light during sensitive periods

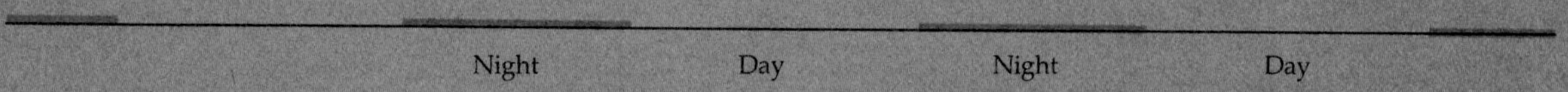

Long days, short nights—exposure to light during sensitive periods

the shadow transformed into a familiar object once you ceased to stare at it? Or on a clear moonless night, have you seen a faint star out of the corner of your eye and then lost it when you tried to look at it directly? Such experiences demonstrate the presence of rods toward the periphery of the retina and their absence from the fovea centralis.

Pathway of Light. We see objects in our field of vision because they reflect light rays onto the cornea of our eyes. From there the rays must penetrate the aqueous humor, the lens, and the vitreous humor before reaching the retina. Obviously, this inch-long pathway must be transparent and not distort the light. Since the **aqueous humor** is largely water and the **vitreous humor** a gelled water similar to plain gelatin, it isn't surprising that both are transparent. But it may seem miraculous that living cells of the cornea and lens are also transparent. We must remember, though, that cells are ordinarily colorless and composed largely of water. It is mainly special pigments in skin, hair, blood, and muscle that make the body opaque. If cells are unpigmented and if they are organized in such a way that their various membranes don't diffract light (as soap bubbles do), then cells tend to be transparent.

The vitreous humor, which forms during development of the eye, is irreplaceable. On the other hand, the aqueous humor is continuously secreted and absorbed. Decreased absorption allows aqueous humor to build up and produce pressure, a condition known as **glaucoma.** If glaucoma goes untreated, pressure on the optic nerve and consequent damage to the retina eventually lead to blindness. The cause of the decreased absorption that leads to glaucoma is largely unknown. Some cases can be traced to thickening of the lens, inflammation, or other physical factors that compress or plug the resorption passageway. Causes of other cases remain mysteries.

To Focus. Although the cornea bends light rays a great deal, it is through changes in the lens that we vary the focus for far or near objects. This **accommodation** involves muscles in the **ciliary body,** a portion of the choroid. Delicate fibers from the ciliary body hold the lens in place behind the pupil. At rest, the eye is focused for distance. Contraction of muscles in the ciliary body draws the ciliary body forward and reduces tension on the lens (Fig. 9.4). This action permits the ordinarily elastic lens to assume its natural rounded state and produces the focus necessary to see near objects clearly. Because relaxation of the ciliary body muscles allows the ciliary body to stretch backward, the lens becomes flatter. This change focuses distant objects on the retina.

Obviously the lens has a limited range of accommodation. In some individuals the eyeball is either so short or so long that the lens cannot focus light exactly on the retina. **Myopic** persons are near-

FIGURE 9.4 How the Eye Focuses on Objects at Different Distances.

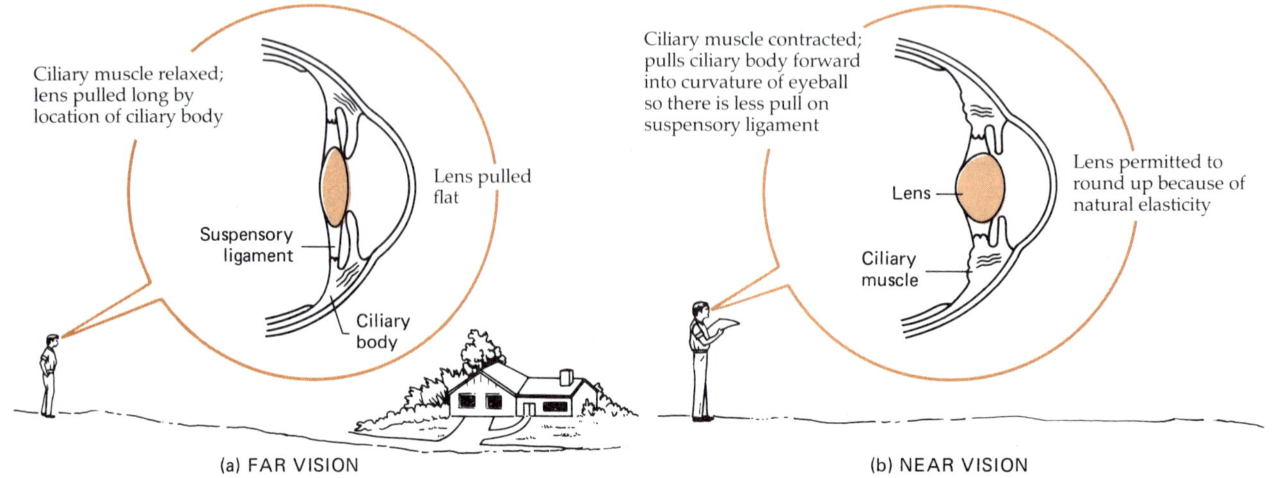

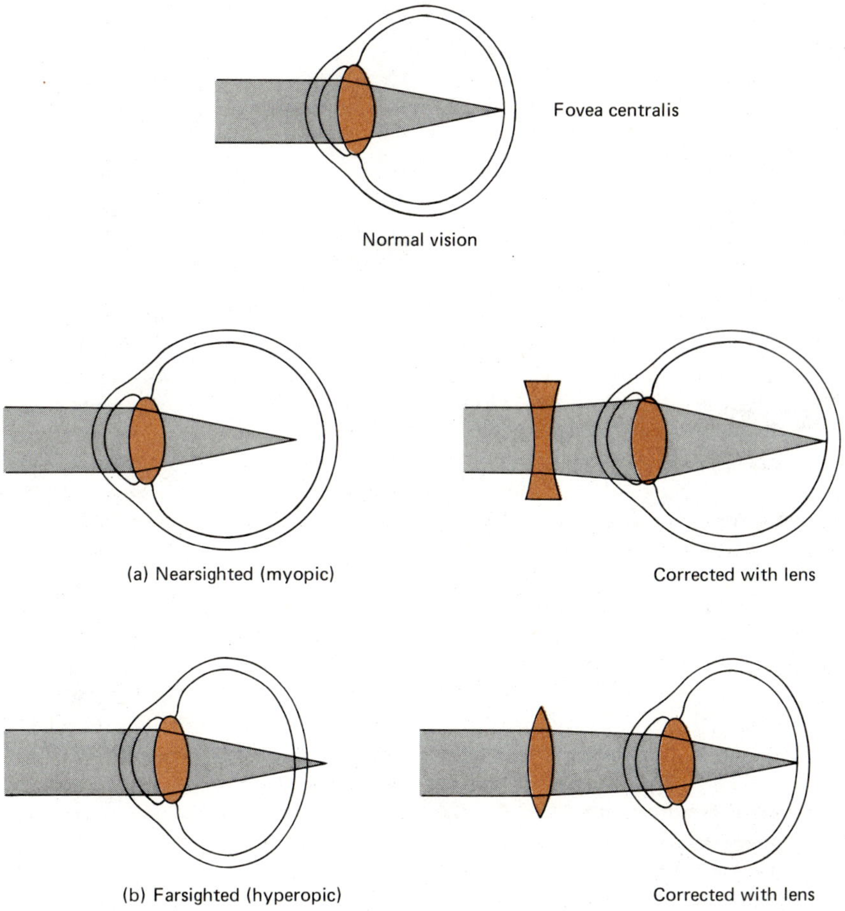

FIGURE 9.5 How Lenses Correct Vision Defects.

sighted, because they have long eyeballs (or too-flat lenses). The eyeballs of **hyperopic** (farsighted) persons are too short (or their lenses will not flatten sufficiently). These conditions can be corrected through the use of properly shaped contact or eyeglass lenses (Fig. 9.5). Irregularities on the surface of either the eye lens or the cornea make it impossible for the entire visual field to be in perfect focus at the same time. Such defects interfere with vision and are known as **astigmatism.** These problems can be corrected by grinding compensating irregularities into eyeglasses. Contact lenses correct for corneal astigmatism by drawing the cornea against the lens.

As we age, our eye lenses lose their elasticity. After about the age of 45, the lens is quite rigid, and the **near point of accommodation** (the closest point you can focus on) recedes so much that reading and other close work become difficult without corrective lenses. See Table 9.1 for a summary of eye structures and their functions.

TABLE 9.1 Functions of Eye Parts

Function	Eye parts
Supports so light can be focused precisely on retina	Sclera Cornea Aqueous humor Vitreous humor
Provides transparent path for light	Conjunctiva Aqueous humor Lens Vitreous humor
Focuses light	Cornea Lens
Regulates amount of light entering eye	Iris
Focuses lens	Ciliary body muscles
Transduces light into nerve impulses	Rods and cones of retina

BOX 9B

TEMPERATURE REGULATION—THE ULTIMATE IN HOMEOSTASIS

Our internal temperature is closely regulated, even when we are subjected to environmental extremes. This homeostatic function may involve more parts of the body than any other activity. It requires participation of numerous heat and cold receptors in the skin and deeper organs, sense receptors in the brain, brain centers, nerves, muscles, the thyroid gland, sweat glands, and the entire circulatory system. In fact, every body cell has a role whenever heat regulation requires changes in the rate of metabolism.

One aspect of temperature regulation is ability to sense temperature changes. Sensory receptors for heat and cold are especially abundant in the skin and other body surfaces. Although physicists tell us that cold is only the absence of heat, we all know the two sensations are different. This difference in sensation reflects the fact that cold receptors are separate from heat receptors. These hot and cold receptors permit us to compare two temperatures, but they give us no absolute measurement. (Have you come indoors on a cold day and felt you were scalding your hands by washing them in lukewarm water?) The receptors are therefore not thermometers but indicators of temperature change. But as such they aid temperature regulation, because they often compel us to change our behavior. We adjust our clothing, seek shelter, or rest from heat-producing exertion.

The hypothalamus serves as the body's thermostat. Receptors there continuously monitor the temperature of blood flowing through the brain. In response to stimulation of these receptors, the hypothalamus directs changes that regulate body temperature.

Humans lose body heat in many ways, but disposal of excess heat occurs largely through evaporation of sweat. When the body temperature rises, stimulation of the hypothalamus causes surface blood vessels to dilate. As a result, more warm blood is carried to the skin. At the same time, the sweat glands begin to secrete profusely. Heat from the warm blood evaporates the perspiration (sweat). In this way excess heat is discharged. Often sweat evaporates as quickly as it is secreted, and we are unaware that we are sweating. Any perspiration that fails to evaporate has little cooling effect. When we drip sweat, we waste water, but that's about all.

The first adjustment in response to cold may be constriction of surface blood vessels. Heat loss from the skin is reduced almost immediately, and the next step is an acceleration of heat production. One way to increase heat production is to raise the metabolic rate. During cellular respiration only a portion of the energy released from foodstuffs is converted into the chemical energy of ATP; the remainder is set free as heat. Thus the greater the rate of cellular respiration, the more heat is produced within the body. Exposure to cold causes the thyroid gland, which is under hypothalamic control, to

The Ear and Its Mechanical Receptors

The **hair cell** serves as the ear's transducer. In different parts of the ear, hair cells detect movements that give us the sense of:

- hearing,
- acceleration/deceleration, and
- gravity.

Strange as it may seem, the same kind of receptor is stimulated by turning a somersault or by listening to a symphony. These experiences do not affect the same hair cell, of course. Hair cells can be used to detect these diverse experiences because the stimuli all involve movement. Each hair cell detects movement in one direction (or movement that has a component in that direction). Here is how they work.

All except one of the "hairs" on each cell are microvilli. The one exception is a cilium. The hairs of each cell are arranged precisely in a bundle (Fig. 9.6). The microvilli increase in size in one direction, and the cilium lies adjacent to the longest microvilli. This specific organization is reflected in the ability of the cell to respond to pressure. If the bundle is moved along the axis of increasing microvillus length, the cell membrane is depolarized. A sufficient depolarization causes the hair cell to release neurotransmitters that initiate a nerve impulse in the associated sensory neuron. However, secrete more hormone. This, in turn, increases the metabolic rate throughout the body.

Heat production is also increased by muscle spasms characterized as shivering. In this case all the energy expended is converted into heat. The skin bumps (or "goose flesh") that usually accompany shivering result from contraction of tiny skin muscles that pull body hairs upright. Although this reaction has little apparent value in humans, in many mammals the hair is thick, and when erect it traps a substantial layer of air. The air acts as insulation against loss of body heat.

If the heat-regulatory center in the hypothalamus cools below 35°C (94°F), it may cease to function. Then the body continues to cool until death intervenes at about 24°C (75°F). A few people have survived body temperatures of 20°C (68°F) but only because they were warmed under careful medical supervision. Hypothermia (low body temperature) is the usual cause of deaths attributed to "exposure." Humans are in danger whenever activity is necessary to maintain body temperature. If fatigue prevents continued exercise, they are doomed. People who hike, climb, sail, or undertake other outdoor activities in cold or even cool weather should be constantly alert to this danger. Many deaths occur at temperatures well above freezing.

Humans are much better adapted to warm than to cold climates. We would find winters in temperate areas intolerable without certain cultural adaptations, including clothing and shelter. On the other hand, a naked human is comfortable in tropical climates and can survive surprisingly high temperatures. This is evidence that our species evolved in a tropical area.

Of course, if temperature regulation fails and either internal or external heat drives the body temperature upward, at some point death becomes inevitable. A temperature of 44°C (111°F) damages vital brain centers, including the hypothalamus. Such deaths may be described as resulting from heat stroke. Usually the cause is failure of evaporative cooling.

On the other hand, the ordinary fever that comes with so many diseases is probably an adaptive response. Macromolecules associated with many microorganisms stimulate a slight increase in body temperature, which can destroy disease-causing organisms without doing harm to body structures.

Under fever conditions, heat-regulatory mechanisms still function, but the "thermostat" is set higher than usual. During the initial period the body reduces heat loss by decreasing peripheral circulation, and it also increases heat production through shivering. The skin is cold, and the individual experiences a "chill." Once the higher temperature is reached, it is kept fairly constant until the fever stimulus disappears. Then the thermostat is reset to the normal temperature, and excess heat is dissipated. What follows is a feeling of great warmth that is supported by the appearance of profuse sweating.

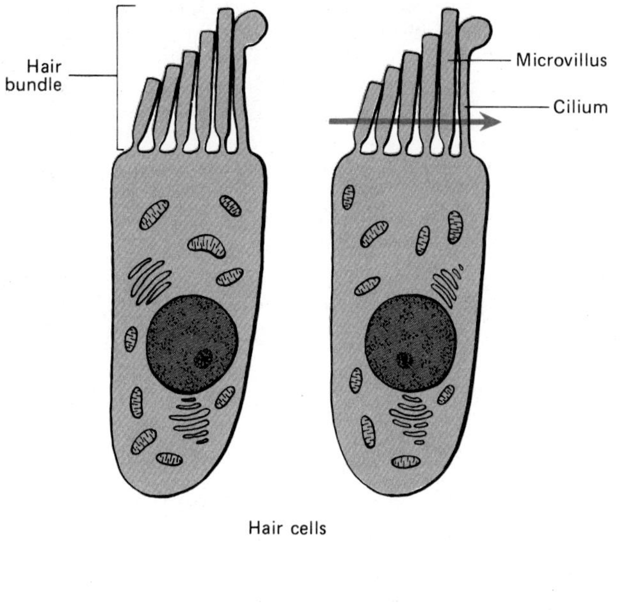

if the hair bundle is moved in the opposite direction, the membrane is not depolarized, but hyperpolarized. And if the bundle is moved at right angles to the axis, there is no effect at all. Thus each hair bundle responds to movement in one direction. However, the hair-cell organs require sensitivity in many directions. This is achieved by

FIGURE 9.6 **Hair Cell Mechanoreceptors.** The sensory cells associated with the ear respond to movement of their hair bundles along a particular axis indicated by the arrow. This directional response is related to the precise arrangement of microvilli of increasing lengths and of the single cilium.

participation of numerous cells, each oriented differently. Figure 9.7 shows how hair cells can respond to different stimuli depending on the organ in which they lie.

The Nature of Sound. Sound consists of vibrations or waves of pressure. The sound we detect is usually conveyed through air. Here it consists of waves of compression, where the air molecules are closer together than they are between the waves (Fig. 9.8a). How close together the waves are determines the **pitch** of a sound. The human voice ranges in frequency from a low of 300 to a high of 3000 waves per second (the frequency at the top of the piano scale is close to 4000 waves per second). But few sounds are pure—that is, of only one frequency. Properly struck, a middle-C tuning fork will vibrate only 256 times a second. The distinct differences between this sound and that of middle C on the piano, violin, and other instruments result from accessory vibrations known as overtones. Loudness, or **volume,** is a reflection of the strength of the sound waves.

Transducing Sound. The **pinna** (external ear) funnels sound waves toward the **tympanic membrane** (eardrum), which they set into motion. These minute vibrations of the tympanic membrane are magnified by the bones of the **middle ear** (Fig. 9.8b). One of these little bones fits into the oval window, a movable portion of the wall of the inner ear. Thus vibrations of the middle-ear bones are transmitted to the inner ear.

The outer and middle ear are air-filled chambers, but the inner ear contains a fluid much like lymph. Vibrations carried from the tympanic membrane by the middle-ear bones create waves of the same frequency in the fluid of the inner ear. In this way, vibrations or waves in the air become vibrations or waves in liquid. It is these vibrations that hair cells respond to and that the brain interprets as sound.

The fluid behind the oval window of the inner ear extends into the spiral **cochlea.** If the cochlea could be unwound, as drawn in Fig. 9.8c, we would see that it contains two large canals that are joined to form a single U-shaped tube. The **oval window**

FIGURE 9.7 **How Hair Cells Are Stimulated.** Sound-detecting hair cells (a) are attached to two membranes, one beneath them and one in which the hair bundles are embedded. Movement of the bottom membrane in response to sound waves bends the hair cells in a particular direction. The hair cells in turn depolarize associated sensory neurons, with the result that we "hear." Quick movements cause hair cells in the semicircular canals to move relative to the canal fluid. This displacement catches masses in which the hair bundles are embedded (b) and pulls on the bundles. Again, sensory neurons are depolarized, but this time we recognize a change in rate of movement, such as a rapid descent in an elevator.

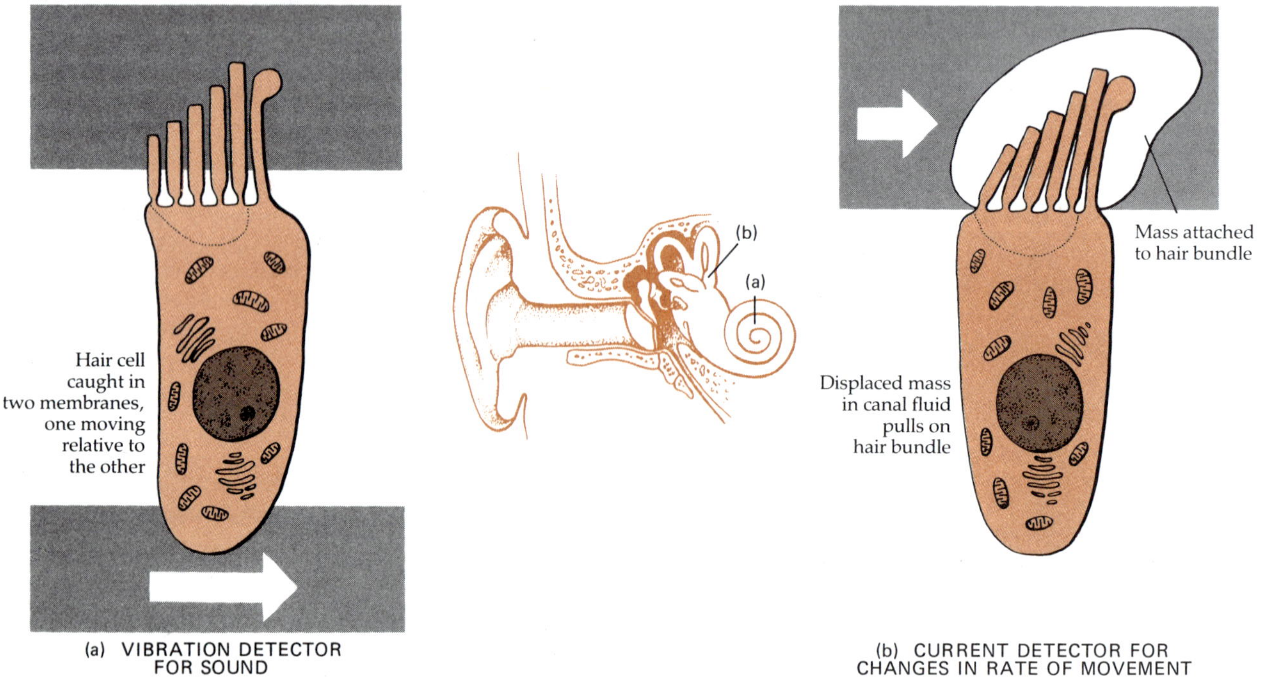

(a) VIBRATION DETECTOR FOR SOUND

(b) CURRENT DETECTOR FOR CHANGES IN RATE OF MOVEMENT

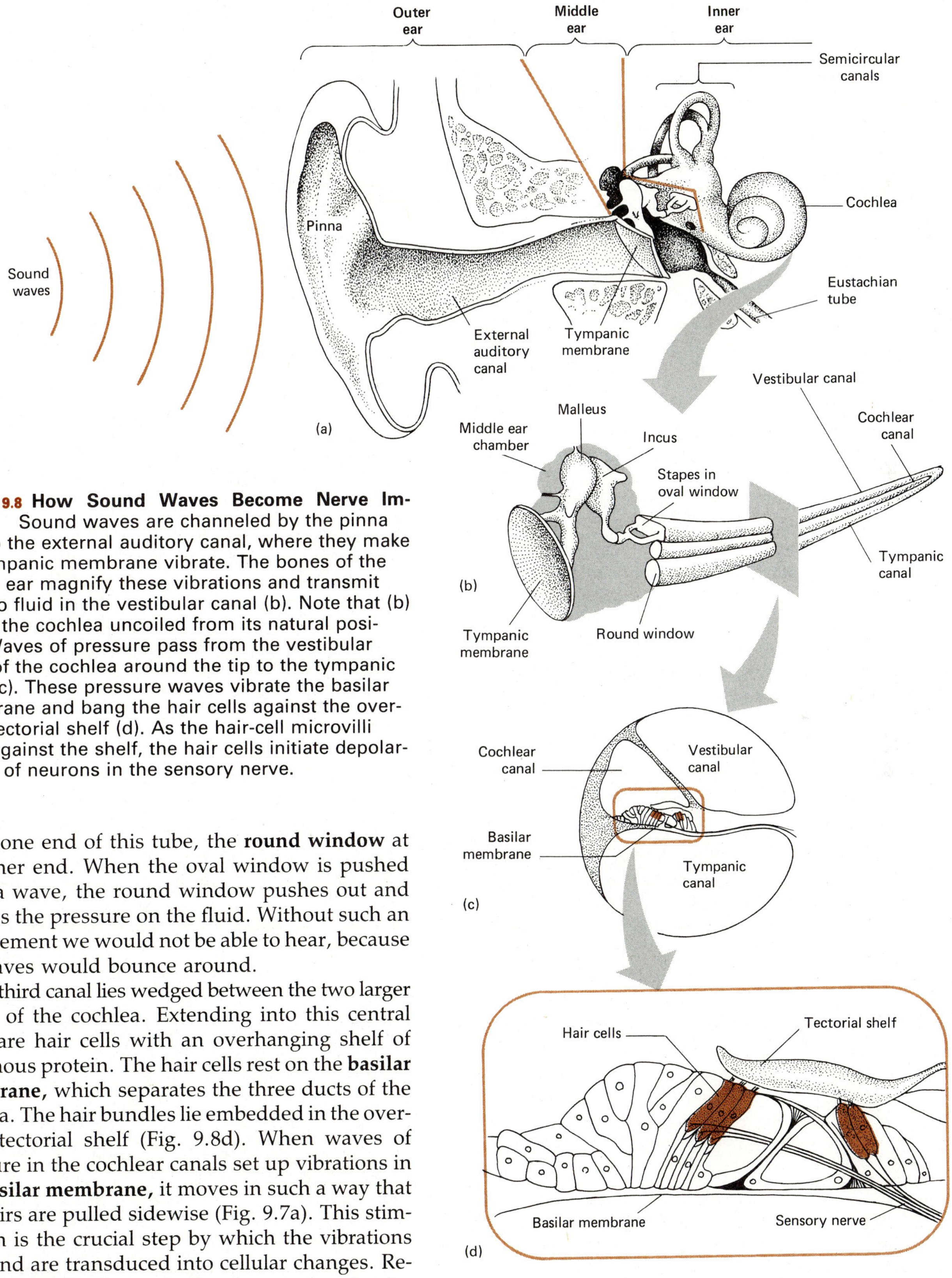

FIGURE 9.8 How Sound Waves Become Nerve Impulses. Sound waves are channeled by the pinna (a) into the external auditory canal, where they make the tympanic membrane vibrate. The bones of the middle ear magnify these vibrations and transmit them to fluid in the vestibular canal (b). Note that (b) shows the cochlea uncoiled from its natural position. Waves of pressure pass from the vestibular canal of the cochlea around the tip to the tympanic canal (c). These pressure waves vibrate the basilar membrane and bang the hair cells against the overlying tectorial shelf (d). As the hair-cell microvilli bend against the shelf, the hair cells initiate depolarization of neurons in the sensory nerve.

lies at one end of this tube, the **round window** at the other end. When the oval window is pushed in by a wave, the round window pushes out and relieves the pressure on the fluid. Without such an arrangement we would not be able to hear, because the waves would bounce around.

A third canal lies wedged between the two larger canals of the cochlea. Extending into this central canal are hair cells with an overhanging shelf of gelatinous protein. The hair cells rest on the **basilar membrane,** which separates the three ducts of the cochlea. The hair bundles lie embedded in the overlying tectorial shelf (Fig. 9.8d). When waves of pressure in the cochlear canals set up vibrations in the **basilar membrane,** it moves in such a way that the hairs are pulled sidewise (Fig. 9.7a). This stimulation is the crucial step by which the vibrations of sound are transduced into cellular changes. Review the path of sound vibrations in hearing by studying Table 9.2.

TABLE 9.2 Path of Sound Vibrations in Hearing

Air collected by pinna (external ear)
Air in external auditory canal
Tympanic membrane
Middle-ear bones
Oval window
Vestibular canal fluid
Tympanic canal fluid
Basilar membrane
Hair cells

Although the sequence described above explains how the ear detects sound, it doesn't tell how the ear discriminates between different frequencies (pitches) of sound. Apparently sound waves of certain frequencies cause particular parts of the basilar membrane to vibrate, thus stimulating specific hair cells. This interpretation is supported by the fact that people who have lost hearing because of loud noises of particular frequencies show damage to specific areas of the cochlea. Such deafness is an occupational hazard for many military and industrial personnel. It has also been reported in people exposed to excessively amplified music.

Impaired Hearing. As noted, exposure to exceedingly loud noises seems to damage selected hair cells, but general kinds of **nerve deafness** trace to infections, chemicals, pressure from tumors, and other physical damage to the sensory cells or to the neurons in the auditory pathway. Other kinds of deafness involve other parts of the ear.

Although the actual transduction of sound waves into nerve impulses occurs in the inner ear, the mechanical work of the middle ear is equally essential to ordinary hearing. Increased air pressure on either side of the eardrum will stretch it and reduce its response to sound waves. Because external air pressure varies with the weather and decreases with altitude, some method of equalizing pressure on both sides of the tympanic membrane is necessary. This function is performed by the **Eustachian tube,** which connects the middle ear to the throat. Ordinarily this soft-walled tube opens occasionally—for example, when we swallow. However, the swelling and inflammation that accompany a cold or sore throat may close the tube for days on end. Frequently this results in sensations of pressure in the ear, as well as reduced hearing. Cabins of commercial airplanes are pressurized, but pressure aloft remains lower than that at ground level. Perhaps you have been aware of your Eustachian tubes "popping open" during an airline flight. Opening the tubes can give a distinct sensation of relief from pressure and improve hearing. Because jaw motion promotes momentary opening of the Eustachian tubes, experienced travelers often chew gum while in flight.

Middle-ear infections, bone disease, or any other process that reduces mobility of the middle-ear bones or of the eardrum can cause deafness. In some cases "frozen" bones can be loosened surgically. Since all the bones around the ear conduct sound waves to some extent, there are other possible pathways to send sound to the inner ear. For example, deafness due to defects in middle-ear transmission can be overcome by hearing aids that amplify sound received by the skull bones.

Knowing Ourselves. So far, we have stressed sense organs that keep us informed about the outside world. We did mention briefly a second class of receptors, including those that measure blood pressure. Such receptors are part of reflexes, but they don't report to our conscious mind. Receptors of a third class describe our bodies but concern matters we control consciously. Good examples of these are the ear components that measure acceleration and determine our position relative to gravity.

Part of the familiar sensations of merry-go-rounds, fast elevators, and tire-screeching auto rides arise from acceleration and deceleration. Hair cells of the **semicircular canals** are the receptors. The three canals of each ear are interconnected (Fig. 9.8a) and arranged at right angles to one another, like the surfaces coming together at the corner of a box. At one end of each canal lies a mass of hair cells with their microvilli embedded in a gelatinous knob that is disturbed by any current in the fluid (Fig. 9.7b). Abrupt starts or stops cause the walls of the canals to move faster than the fluid inside. You can easily demonstrate such inertia of a fluid in a solid container by turning a glass of ice water. Surely you have rotated a glass and seen that the water and ice lagged behind. The same thing happens in the semicircular canals when we move our heads. The fluid moves relative to the container. Because of the position of the three canals, any movement creates a current in at least one canal; most movements disturb the fluid in more than one canal. The resulting stimulation of hair cells associated with one or more canals leads to depolarization of sensory neurons and knowledge that the head is moving in a particular direction. The fluid gradually catches up with the walls, of course, and the stimulation ends. This is why, after the initial moments, a smooth auto ride creates no further sensations.

The hair cells that respond to gravity are much like those in the semicircular canals and in the cochlea. But in this case the microvilli attach to a gummy mass with stonelike inclusions. Because of the weight of the inclusions, turning the head to one side pulls on some microvilli but not on others (Fig. 9.9). By interpreting the pattern of stimulation, we learn the position of the head relative to gravity.

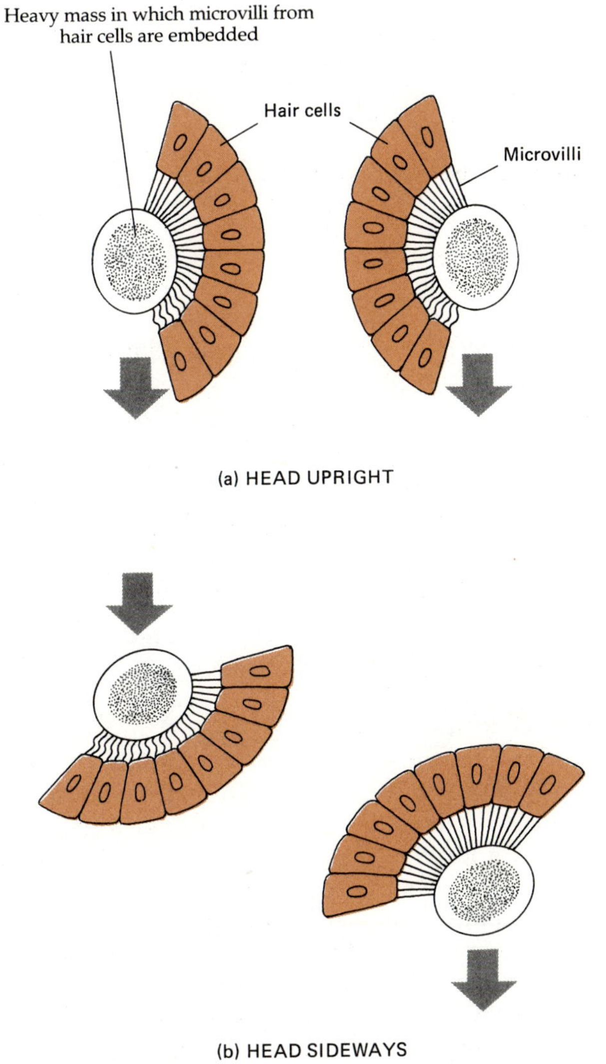

FIGURE 9.9 **Gravity Detectors.** Consciousness of head position results from pull on particular hair cells of the gravity detectors found in the middle ear between the semicircular canals and the cochlea. Microvilli of these hair cells lie embedded within gummy masses that contain heavy mineral deposits. In particular positions, various hair cells are stimulated.

The semicircular canals and the gravity receptors are often considered together as balance organs—and quite properly so. Although we are conscious of the sensory input from these receptors, the information they provide also supplies reflexes that help us keep our balance.

To See the World as Others See It

Each species inhabits a unique sensory world. Even though the sense organs are similar, their sensitivity can differ. Consider, for example, the ability of a bloodhound to trail a fugitive by detecting odors left hours before. No human has an olfactory sense sufficiently acute to duplicate that feat. On the other hand, dogs distinguish colors poorly. At least that is the conclusion drawn from attempts to train dogs with colored and gray papers of varying intensities. Of course, we never know exactly what a dog perceives, any more than we know for certain what another human perceives. In both cases we judge perception by responses.

In animals beyond those that are most familiar to us, we find an even greater diversity in sense organs. For example, the location of chemoreceptors varies widely. Houseflies use chemoreceptors on their feet to taste your hamburger or any other moist surface they land on. Catfish have chemoreceptors over much of their bodies, the better to locate food, living or dead.

Despite the diverse uses of sense organs, there are many instances of underlying unity in their basic structure. Light detection invariably involves pigments associated with membranes (Fig. 9.10). Usually the membranes are densely folded to concentrate the pigment and increase the likelihood of intercepting the smallest amount of light.

Within the vertebrates, basic types of sense receptors have evolved to transduce diverse stimuli. As mentioned earlier, hair-cell organs are used widely to detect sound, changes in acceleration, and gravity. In fish, similar receptors serve additional functions. Hair cells lie in a system of canals that extend over the head and along the side of the fish (Fig. 9.11). In places, this **lateral line system** is open to the outside. Thus displacements of water around the fish or pressure waves in the water are transmitted into the canals. Because the microvilli of the hair cells are buried in gummy masses, like those shown in Fig. 9.7b, pressure or current in the water stimulates the hair cells. Presumably the

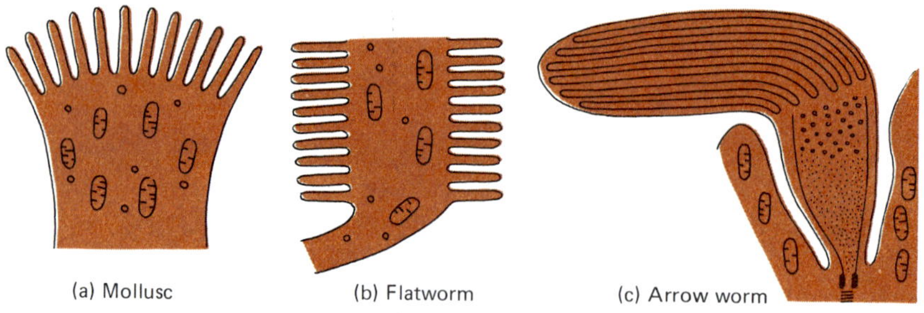

FIGURE 9.10 Light-Sensitive Cells. The light receptors of all animals contain pigments in extensively folded membrane. Compare these cells of lower animals with that of humans in Fig. 9.3.

result is a "distant-touch" sense that permits the fish to detect an object it approaches or other organisms that swim nearby.

In some fish, modified hair cells detect weak electrical fields. These fish emit continuous electrical discharges from modified muscle tissue and thereby produce an electrical field around themselves. Any movement within this field is recorded by the electro-receptors. Since all fish possessing these organs live in muddy waters, perhaps this mechanism is another form of "distant-touch" sense.

EFFECTORS: SKELETON AND MUSCLES

Although our responses to stimuli can involve secretion, such as that of sweat glands, bones and muscles are our major organs for effecting responses. These organs interact in many ways; neither can really function without the other. We may think of support as the work of the skeleton, but it is the muscles that hold the skeleton in place. Yet movement requires more than muscle contractions. If the muscles are not attached to something, their contraction is without effect. Among vertebrates, connective tissue of the muscles usually grows into the bones. The arrangement of muscles relative to the skeleton is crucial, because walking, running, and other movements require that muscles bend the joints between bones.

FIGURE 9.11 Lateral Line System. Fish have variously open and partially closed canals on their heads and along the sides of their bodies. Hair cells lying in these canals are stimulated by movements in the water and thereby give the fish some indication of objects it is swimming past and of the movements of other animals.

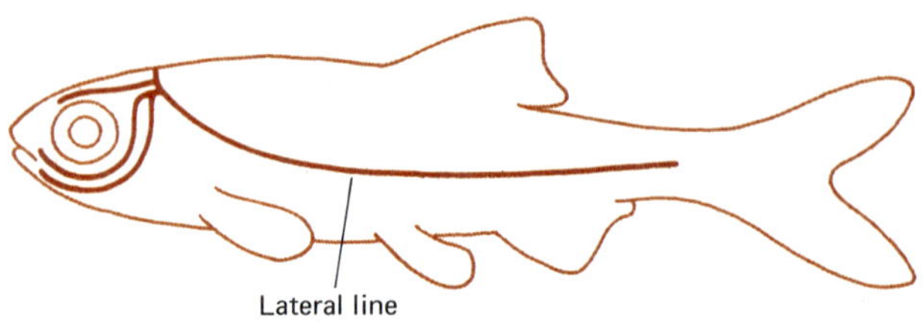

Skeletal Tissue: Hard but Living

Most of the skeleton is **bone.** Despite its rigid, nonliving appearance, bone is an intricately structured, cellular tissue. Of course, the bone cells are embedded in minerals and other nonliving matter. In fact, bone consists of about two-thirds mineral matter, mainly calcium phosphate, plus collagen, a tough fibrous protein. The minerals give bone its hardness, and the collagen fibers provide resiliency and reduce brittleness. The bone also serves as a reserve from which calcium and phosphate are continuously withdrawn and replaced. Both calcium phosphate crystals and collagen are formed through activities of the bone cells.

As bone cells grow, they accumulate minerals and collagen around themselves and become trapped in tiny fluid-filled lakes. Nevertheless, the bone cells are not totally isolated. Threadlike extensions stretch from one cell to another within narrow tubes through the solid matrix (Fig. 9.12). In this way, bone cells maintain contact with one another and with the extensive network of blood vessels that penetrate all bone.

Although bones appear solid on the outside, much of the interior is spongy or sometimes hollow. A soft **marrow** fills any spaces within the bones. Large cavities are usually packed with a fatty **yellow marrow,** and the spongy bone regions often contain **red marrow.** It is in the red marrow that all red blood cells and most white blood cells develop.

A fibrous membrane rich in blood vessels and nerves adheres to the outside of bones except over the joint surfaces. This outer layer, the **periosteum,** is exquisitely sensitive as is evident when we bang our shins. Nerves also course through bones along

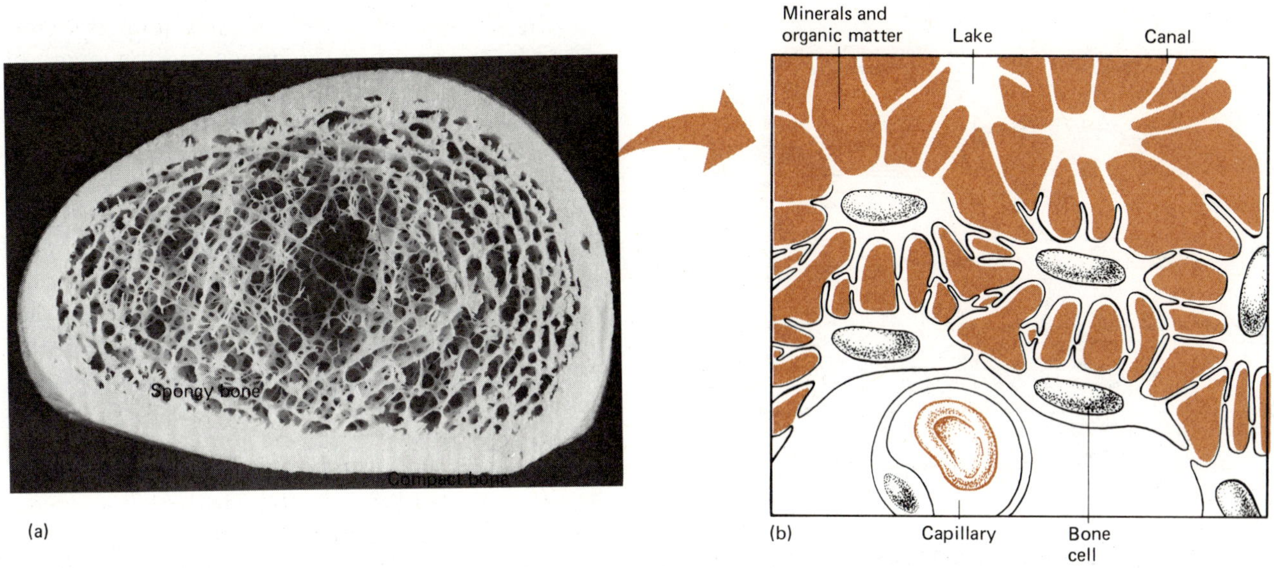

FIGURE 9.12 Bone. The outer surface of a bone is always compact (solid) but interior regions are either hollow, forming a marrow cavity, or consist of spongy tissue (a). In both, the cells lie surrounded by tissue fluid in lake-like cavities (b). Cytoplasmic extensions reach out through the canals that connect adjacent lakes. Tissue fluids bathe the capillaries, as well as filling the canals and lakes. It is through this fluid that bone cells obtain nutrients and rid themselves of wastes. The tinted background areas that define the lakes and canals in the drawing represent the solid matter of bone.

with the blood vessels. Damage to such nerves accounts for part of the pain associated with a broken bone.

Cartilage, another skeletal tissue, resembles bone in that it consists of cells scattered within a solidified mass of cell products. But in cartilage the nonliving materials are limited to gelled organic compounds and collagen fibers. And unlike bone cells, those of cartilage are completely isolated, either individually or in groups of two or three. No tubules connect the little "lakes" that bathe cartilage cells. Furthermore, cartilage lacks an internal blood supply. Consequently, cartilage cells must rely on diffusion of nutrients and wastes over long distances. This difference in efficiency of exchange explains the very different rates of healing of cartilage as compared with bone. A damaged cartilage often requires years to heal, but fractured (broken) bones of young people "knit" well within two months.

The rapid healing of bone is related to the continuous replacement that is occurring in bone at all times. Bone is constantly being reworked, with old bone being absorbed and new bone laid down. Thus bone can change in response to stress as well as to genetically determined growth patterns. The good supply of blood, the ability to reabsorb minerals, and the potential for cell division all contribute to the healing of fractures.

Initially the line of a **fracture** is marked by blood clots. Interruption of the blood supply soon results in a border of dead bone. But if the two broken ends are near each other, a network of new bone quickly bridges the gap, both on the outside of the bone and in the marrow cavity (Fig. 9.13). Usually a ring of cartilage forms around the outside of the break. Gradually the dead bone and debris along the fracture line are removed, and new bone is formed in their place. Eventually bone also replaces the cartilage on the outside, and the only remaining evidence of the fracture is a rough, thickened band around the bone. In time, the excess bone may be reabsorbed and the surface made smooth again.

Joints for Movement and Support

Joints are necessary for movement, and they are equally important in support. Although any point at which two bones come together is considered a joint, we pay most attention to those that allow movement. The many movable joints have similar components, despite their different appearances.

These movable joints are surrounded by fibrous capsules. **Ligaments,** tough collagenous bands

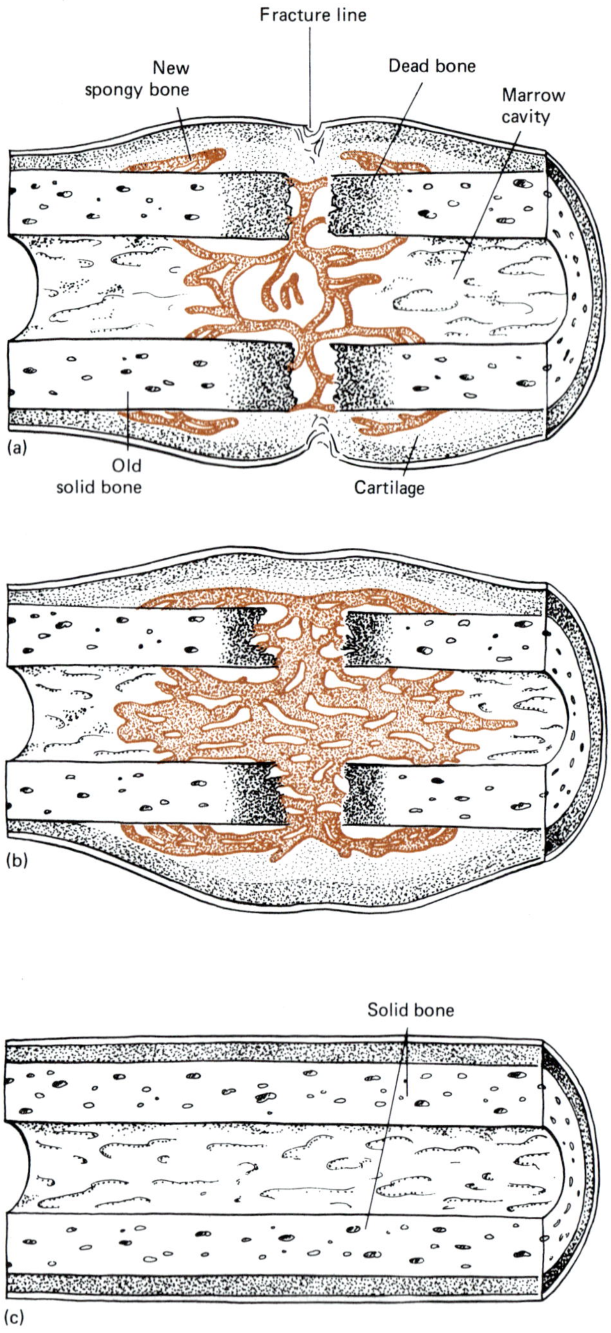

FIGURE 9.13 How Broken Bones Heal.

that hold bones together either make up part of the capsule or pass through it. Between the two bones lies a **joint cavity** (Fig. 9.14) containing a few drops of lubricant. The moving surfaces of the bones are covered with a glassy cartilage that forms part of the joint cavity lining. Because of these smooth cartilage surfaces and the lubricant, joint movements are almost friction-free.

The movement permitted at a joint is determined by the shape of the bones and the length of the ligaments. Joints with cavities are classified on the basis of the movement permitted. The general classes are hinge, sliding, and rotary (Table 9.3). Actual movement at any time depends on the tension in the muscles that span the joint. Such muscles can either hold the joint rigid or bend it. Collagen-rich connective tissues known as **tendons** unite muscles with bones. Frequently tendons and ligaments are alike in structure. In many instances the muscles that control a joint lie some distance away and exert their force through tendons that extend across the joint. Some joints, such as those of the knees, contain **fat pads** that act as shock absorbers. In addition to the cartilage that covers joint surfaces, some joints contain additional cartilage masses that help support the joint and define the limits of motion. The knee joint involves such cartilages. These cartilages are notoriously vulnerable and frequently damaged.

The **vertebral discs** that allow limited motion between vertebra are part of a special class of joints. The strength of the vertebral joints comes partly from the back muscles and partly from the exten-

FIGURE 9.14 Knee Joint. This is an example of a movable joint. The joint cavity is hardly more than a potential space except when inflammation causes excess fluid production and the joint swells and stiffens. In addition to the usual cartilage that covers the moving ends of all bones, the knee has additional cartilages that support the joint and define the movement.

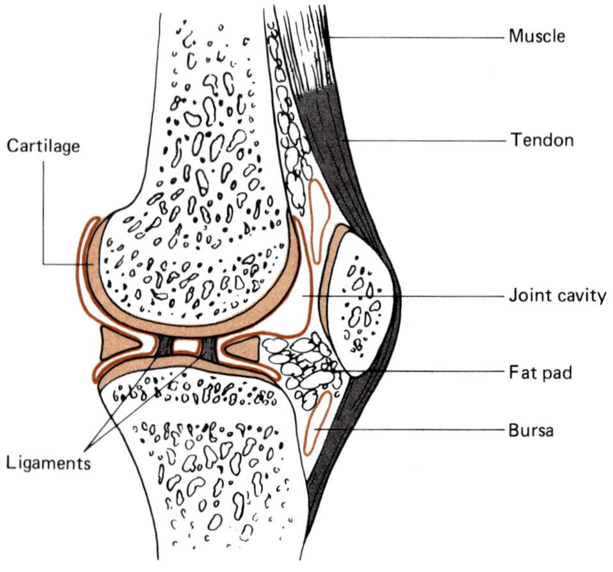

TABLE 9.3 Kinds of Joints

Movable joints (contain lubricated cavities)	
	Hinge (example: elbow)
	Rotary (example: shoulder)
	Sliding (example: wrist)
Limited motion joints	
	Vertebral joints (have discs)
	Pubic symphysis
	Skull sutures

sive collagen fibers that extend from the cartilage of the discs into the bone of adjacent vertebrae. Discs are sac-like; their flexibility and compressibility is due to a spongy central region. Sometimes this soft central tissue bulges through the cartilage, distorting the disc and creating pressure on a spinal nerve. This painful condition is often misnamed a "slipped disc." A better term for it is **herniated**

FIGURE 9.15 The Human Skeleton.

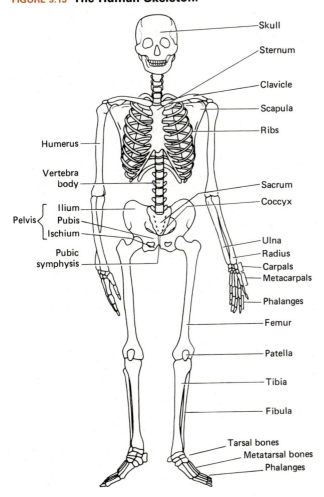

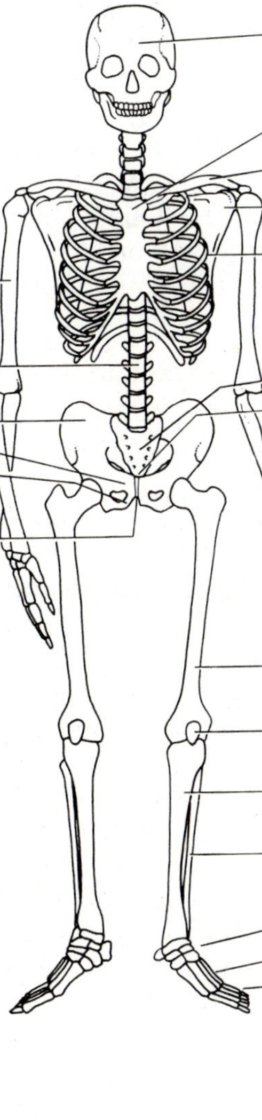

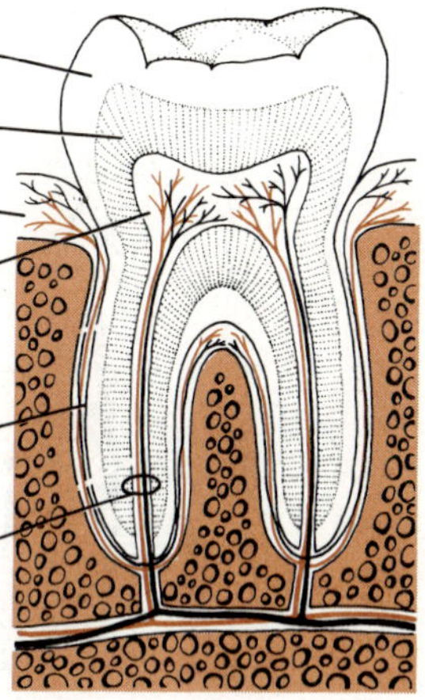

FIGURE 9.16 Teeth. The dentin that makes up most of the tooth is living tissue much like bone except that the dentin cells lie along the inside of the pulp cavity rather than in lakes. But like bone cells, dentin cells send cytoplasmic extensions into the cell products they produce and maintain. The exposed part of the tooth is covered with enamel, the hardest material in the body. Enamel is also a cell product, but in this case the cells die as the enamel-covered tooth erupts from the gums.

disc. The **pubic symphysis** that joins the two halves of the pelvis anteriorly (Fig. 9.15) is somewhat similar to the vertebral joint but lacks a hollow disc. Another type of joint that allows only limited movement is the **suture** that joins adjacent skull bones.

At certain friction points where tendons or muscles pass over bones there are small sacs of fluid called **bursa.** When joints are abused, they become inflamed, a condition known as **bursitis.** Tennis elbow is an example. Excessive pulling that harms tendons and muscle components produces **strains.** Strains should not be confused with **sprains,** which result from violent wrenching or twisting of a joint, with damage to ligaments or the joint capsule.

Teeth can be considered part of the effector system. Dentine (Fig. 9.16) is structurally similar to bone. Biting and chewing are possible only in conjunction with the bones and muscles.

Muscles and Movement

Because a muscle can do work only when shortening, other muscles are necessary to cause movement in the opposite direction. Thus muscles occur in antagonistic groups. For example, the *biceps* flexes the elbow joint and the *triceps* extends the elbow. Naturally the triceps must be relaxed so that it can

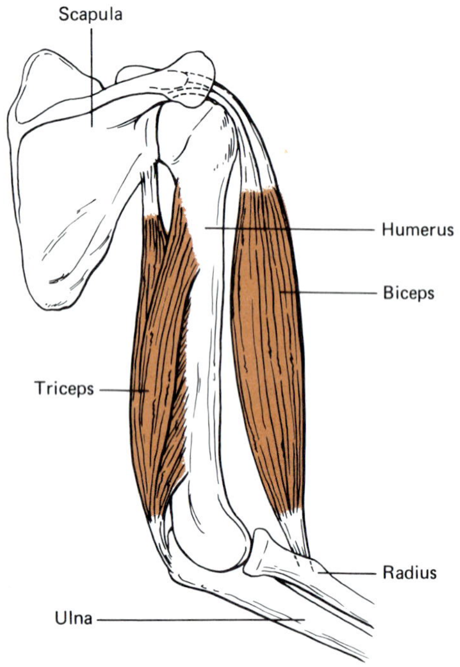

FIGURE 9.17 **Muscle Interaction.** The biceps can bend the elbow joint only as the triceps relaxes. Likewise, for the triceps to straighten the elbow, the biceps must relax. Thus these two muscles are said to be antagonistic toward each other. Note that the biceps attaches on one side of the radius. This attachment permits contraction of the biceps to roll the radius. This action, in cooperation with other muscles, turns the lower arm so that the palm of the hand is upward. The fact that the biceps has two actions is not unusual. Nor is the fact that it cooperates with other muscles.

stretch when the biceps contracts to bend the elbow. On the other hand, a moderate contraction of the triceps can hold the elbow joint in place so that contraction of the biceps only turns the lower arm, bringing the palm of the hand upward. To see how this happens, consult Fig. 9.17.

Although this explanation of arm movements is useful, it is greatly oversimplified. In truth, most movements involve the action of numerous muscles. Consider walking, for example. Muscles of the legs and feet are obviously involved. But in addition, many muscles of the trunk are also used. Just standing erect requires the partial contraction of muscle groups throughout the body.

The Process of Contraction. Skeletal muscles are composed of long, multinucleate **fibers.** The fact that these fibers arise from the fusion of many small cells explains their many nuclei. Bundles of contractile **myofibrils** stretch from one end of a muscle fiber to the other. In between myofibrils, hundreds of mitochondria lie packed. Owing to the alternate dark and light bands of myofibrils, **skeletal muscle** is sometimes called **striated muscle**.

The striations on myofibrils are the visible evidence of their intricate structure (Fig. 9.18d,e). Each myofibril is built from subunits that are themselves made up of precisely arranged thin and thick filaments. The overlapping thin and thick filaments telescope together when a muscle contracts (Fig. 9.18f). **Myosin,** molecules that make up the thicker of the two kinds of filaments, have projections that attach to the thin **actin** filaments. Change in molecular shape causes myosin to pull on actin. As the thin filaments are drawn past the thick ones, the myofibrils shorten and the muscle contracts. When the myosin molecules return to their original shape, they dissociate from actin, and the muscle relaxes. Calcium ions and ATP are necessary for attachment of myosin, but the ATP is broken down and its energy released when the myosin returns to its original shape. If ATP is unavailable, as in the development of **rigor mortis** after death, the muscle remains contracted.

Energetics. While at rest, muscle cells are busily manufacturing ATP by means of cellular respiration.□ Much of this ATP is used immediately 101–105
to make **creatine phosphate,** an energy-storage compound that can be tapped to regenerate ATP when a muscle needs to contract. The reaction is as follows:

Creatine + ATP ↔ Creatine phosphate + ADP.

As you can see, the reaction is a reversible one. But in resting cells it occurs in the direction of creatine-phosphate synthesis.

Of course, even contracting muscles carry out cellular respiration, at least so long as they get enough oxygen. Muscle cells build up stores of **glycogen,**□ so a ready source of glucose is always 71
at hand. And the liver helps out during times of stress by increasing the blood glucose concentration. Still, having creatine phosphate on hand makes sense.

Muscles are often required to contract rapidly or remain contracted for long periods of time. It is impossible to supply enough ATP from ongoing cellular respiration to support extended contraction. The chief limitation is the oxygen supply. This is true despite the fact that heavy exertion diverts most arterial blood to the muscles. The heart can

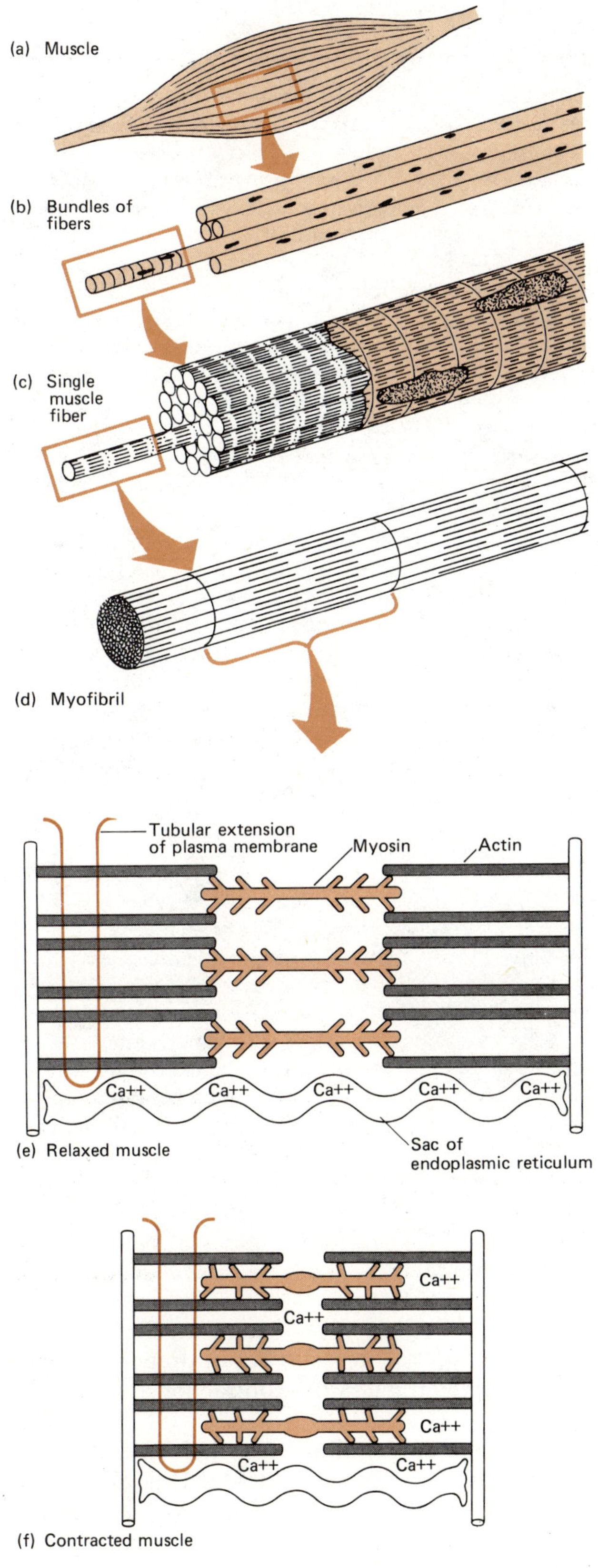

pump just so much blood only so fast. Muscle can store a limited amount of oxygen associated with **myoglobin,** a molecule similar to hemoglobin. Like hemoglobin, myoglobin is red. In sufficient quantities, myoglobin lends a red color to muscle.

Even when a person engages in moderate physical activity, some muscle cells must convert to anaerobic metabolism. Earlier we used the term **oxygen debt** to refer to the condition brought on when muscle cells resort to anaerobic metabolism.□ Lack of oxygen prevents cells from completely oxidizing glucose. Instead of converting glucose and oxygen immediately into carbon dioxide and water, muscle cells can follow an anaerobic process that has lactic acid as its end product. 106

The **lactic acid** must eventually be oxidized, though this can be postponed until later, when the body is at rest and a surplus of oxygen is available. In the meantime, the lactic acid that accumulates represents a debt that must later be paid off through use of oxygen. The size of the oxygen debt a person can incur depends on the ability of the blood to accept lactic acid. Too much lactic acid will change the pH of the blood and affect body tissues. This point is demonstrated by the development of muscular aches and fatigue. Clearly, how soon we tire depends on the efficiency of our respiration and circulation. And these depend on how much exercise we take (see Box 9C).

Muscles and Nerves

The axons of motor neurons terminate at **motor end plates** (Fig. 9.19), where they synapse with muscle cells. These neuron-to-muscle synapses resemble neuron-neuron synapses. A nerve impulse in the axon causes release of a chemical transmitter.

FIGURE 9.18 **Skeletal Muscle.** Skeletal muscle (a) consists of bundles of fibers (b). Each fiber is a multinucleate cell (c) and some are large enough to see with the naked eye. The fibers are tightly packed with cell components, especially myofibrils (d), by which contraction occurs. The myofibrils of a fiber are aligned so that their precisely arranged components, actin and myosin, lie in distinct rows across the fiber. Therefore each fiber appears striated. Contraction of a myofibril involves changes in shape of finger-like projections on the myosin (e). In the process of contraction the myosin "fingers" extend toward the thin actin filaments and hook into the actin. Once attached to the actin, the "fingers" bend and pull the actin filaments inward, thus shortening the myofibril (f).

BOX 9C

THE BENEFITS FROM REGULAR EXERCISE

Too often we ignore the benefits of better health and reduced fatigue that regular exercise can bring. We have forgotten that our bodies were designed by natural selection to live the life of hunters and gatherers,[40] not to drive autos and sit for hours before a TV set. Here are some of the results of exercise.

Regular exercise strengthens the heart and lungs, thereby increasing the body's capacity to deliver oxygen to the muscles. In fact, many experts consider maximum aerobic capacity (the maximal oxygen intake) to be the best measure of cardiorespiratory fitness. But even the most intensive training program will increase the aerobic capacity of an average person no more than 10–20 percent. Probably this limit is set largely by the lungs. Exercise will increase the capillary bed of the lungs, but growth potential here is otherwise limited. We can only use more thoroughly the gas exchange surface already present. One way to do so is through strengthening the respiratory muscles that suck air into the lungs. By fully expanding the lungs, we use them to maximum capacity.

Exercise has much greater effects on the heart. In a poorly conditioned person the amount of blood pumped by the heart is increased during periods of exercise, mainly through stepped-up heart rate. Conditioning reflects an increase in the amount of blood the heart pumps in one contraction. Although there is some evidence that certain athletes have slightly larger hearts than nonathletes, greater size is not the main reason for increased pumping capacity. Instead, the trained heart becomes more efficient in expelling blood. Because of this increased efficiency, the heart rate of athletes is usually lower than that of peopeople who fail to exercise vigorously.

Confusion between the slightly enlarged hearts of some athletes and the over-stretched hearts of individuals suffering from certain heart diseases led to the myth that athletes are predisposed to heart trouble. There is no evidence to support this belief, however.

Conditioning also increases the capillary beds of both skeletal and heart muscle. In fact, the entire circulation of the heart is enhanced. Branches of the coronary arteries increase in size. If a clot develops in the system, increased artery size can be lifesaving. Even though one artery is plugged, blood may reach all the capillary network through other arteries that otherwise wouldn't be large enough to support the entire heart muscle. Physicians often advise heart-attack-prone patients, even those of advanced age, to literally "run for their lives." Of course, such running must be done under careful supervision so as not to overtax previously damaged heart muscle. In fact, it is wise for anyone who undertakes an exercise program to have a physical examination first.

Exercising skeletal muscles does more than increase blood vessels. The muscle itself also increases in size and strength. Additional myofibrils account for part of this growth, and the muscle also synthesizes more myoglobin. This hemoglobin-like protein stores oxygen for aerobic respiration. In the course of short sprints it postpones fatigue that results when anaerobic glycolysis leads to lactic acid accumulation. Exercise also promotes an increase in the mitochondrial enzymes that support aerobic respiration in muscle cells. Finally, any activity that strengthens muscles also thickens the connective tissue that anchors the muscles to the skeleton.

Too often, the role of exercise in weight control is misunderstood. The popular belief that exercise merely increases the appetite is erroneous. Exercise leads to the loss of excess fatty tissue from the muscles and burns up calories as well. In addition, exercise increases muscle tone. Weight loss achieved through a combination of substantial exercise and moderate dietary limitation results in a healthier and trimmer body than that obtained through dieting alone.

If a sufficient amount of transmitter enters the synaptic gap, a wave of depolarization sweeps over the muscle plasma membrane. This wave of depolarization travels along little fingers of plasma membrane that project into the interior. Here the depolarization stimulates release of calcium ions from storage sacs suspended near the myofibrils. The increased calcium ion concentration around the myofibrils triggers the contraction.

Strength of Contraction. A single motor axon usually has many, many branches. Thus each axon innervates numerous muscle fibers. The neuron and the muscle fibers it innervates constitute a sin-

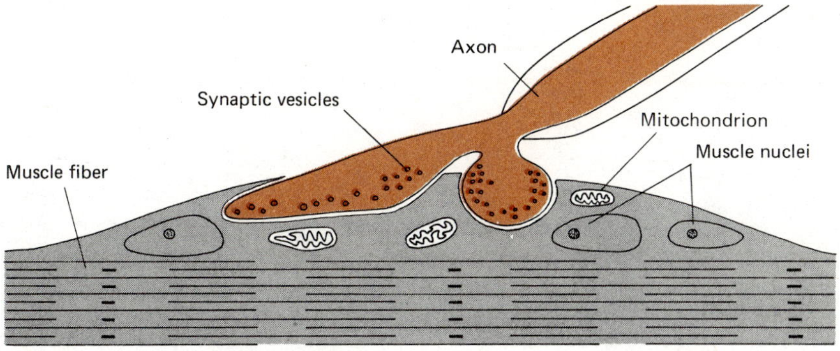

FIGURE 9.19 Motor End Plate. The axons of motor nerves end on muscle fibers. Synaptic vesicles from the axons release acetylcholine, which crosses the gap between the axon and the fiber. The acetylcholine depolarizes the membrane of the muscle fiber and initiates contraction of the myofibrils of the muscle fiber.

gle **motor unit.** The muscle fibers of a motor unit respond together in the same all-or-none fashion that characterizes nerve impulses. The strength of a muscle contraction is generally correlated to the number of such motor units that are working. Because the cells of a given unit are scattered throughout a muscle, the action of a single unit appears as a mild contraction of the entire muscle.

Although each muscle fiber contracts to its maximum when stimulated, this "maximum" is a function of temperature. Warmth increases the efficiency of muscle contractions, because the enzymes involved have temperature optima slightly above the usual body temperature. Consequently, a warm fiber contracts more than the same fiber does when it is cooler. The value of **warm-up exercises** is due partly to the warmth that increased blood flow brings and partly to the heat generated by the muscle contraction.

Muscles Reflect Our Minds. When we are conscious, most of our muscles exhibit **tone.** This state of sustained partial contraction results from the action of scattered motor units. Certain motor neurons fire occasionally and cause their muscle cells to contract. As a result of muscle tone, we respond much faster when action is required. Good muscle tone is one aspect of good physical condition. And since normal posture is dependent on tone, good physical condition is usually accompanied by good posture, and vice versa.

Variation in muscle tone with mental states makes it possible to detect how people feel by observing how they stand. The "chin-up" posture that identifies cheerful people results in part from changes in muscle tone. On the other hand, sagging posture suggests mental depression. Because tone is initiated by the brain, it almost disappears when we fall asleep.

Involuntary Muscles

Except during reflex actions, we consciously control our skeletal muscles. In contrast, the muscles of our internal organs usually disregard our will. Nevertheless, some people have learned to control their involuntary muscles through yoga or related techniques. **Biofeedback** equipment, which monitors the heart rate or other action to be controlled and makes results immediately available, has helped some people learn to control involuntary muscles. Although no one can concentrate on their internal organs continuously, these techniques are helpful in some illnesses.

Heart Muscle. Heart muscle, or **cardiac muscle,** is striated and capable of rapid contractions. In these characteristics it resembles skeletal muscle. But cardiac cells are smaller than skeletal muscle cells, and each contains only one nucleus (Fig. 9.20a). Gap junctions□ between individual cells of cardiac mus- 80
cle allow depolarization in the membrane of one cell to pass directly to another cell. Thus the wave of impulses initiated by the pacemaker sweeps over the entire heart without involving nerves.□ First the 107
atria contract and then the ventricles. Some portions of the ventricular muscles are specialized for conduction. These cells pass impulses rapidly to distant points and ensure coordinated contractions that push the blood toward the arteries.

Heart muscle also differs from skeletal muscle in its resistance to fatigue. Heart muscle relaxes between contractions, but a healthy heart needs no other rest throughout a lifetime.

Smooth Muscle. Muscle cells of the intestine, uterus, and other internal organs (except the heart) are small and spindle-shaped (Fig. 9.20b). These are known as smooth muscle because they lack the

FIGURE 9.20 **Muscle within Internal Organs.**

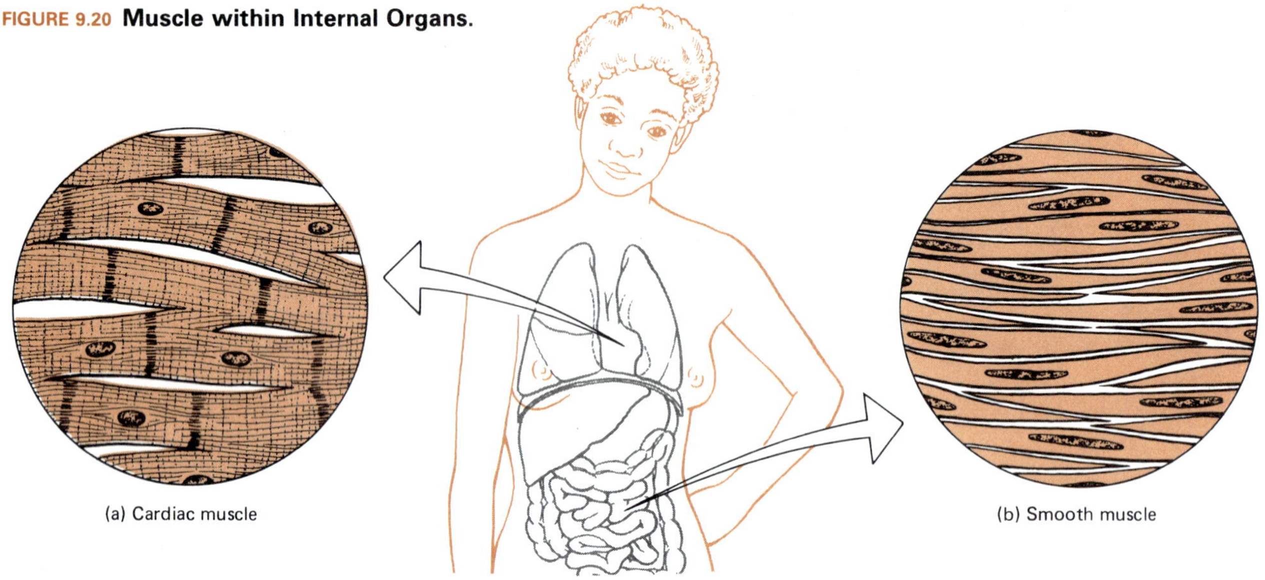

striations found in skeletal and cardiac muscle. The fact that the actin and myosin filaments of smooth muscle are in less orderly arrangements than in other muscle accounts for the lack of visible striations. Contractions of smooth muscle are slow and prolonged in comparison with contractions of other muscle. However, stretching smooth muscle can sometimes initiate contractions directly without participation of the nerves. This happens when stretching alters the plasma membrane and causes depolarization. Thus a single smooth muscle cell can act as both a sensor and an effector. A wave of depolarization can also pass from one smooth muscle cell to another through gap junctions, as in heart muscle. If this blurring of distinctions between neurons and muscles seems disturbing, remember that we are describing cell properties. Although motor neurons and striated muscle cells are highly differentiated for specific functions, smooth muscle is able to combine properties of nerve and muscle within a single cell.

Muscles and Body Structure

As we have pointed out, muscles are only as effective as their attachments. Because the connective tissues of tendons grow so that they are continuous with bone, muscle attachments are evident as rough areas on the surface of skeletons and even on fossil bones. The size, shape, and location of such areas on fossils allow scientists to reconstruct the muscles and determine how the animal moved.

Attachment of muscles is as important in other animals as it is in vertebrates. Whereas vertebrates have an internal skeleton, many organisms—for example, the insects—are surrounded by a rigid coat of cell products termed an **exoskeleton** (Fig. 9.21). In such cases the muscles attach to the inside of the skeleton, but still they must span joints. The anchorage of locomotor devices extends to the smallest scale. The cilia of our respiratory-passage linings are embedded in a mat of filaments and microtubules known as the **cytoskeloton.**□ 81

Movement and Body Function

Movement is so much a part of animal life that we tend to ignore its effect on other activities. Al-

FIGURE 9.21 **Skeleton Outside and Muscle Inside.** Insects, crabs, spiders, and other related animals that have exoskeletons must have their muscles inside. Nevertheless, the muscles will span the joints just as they do in humans, where the skeleton is within and the muscles without.

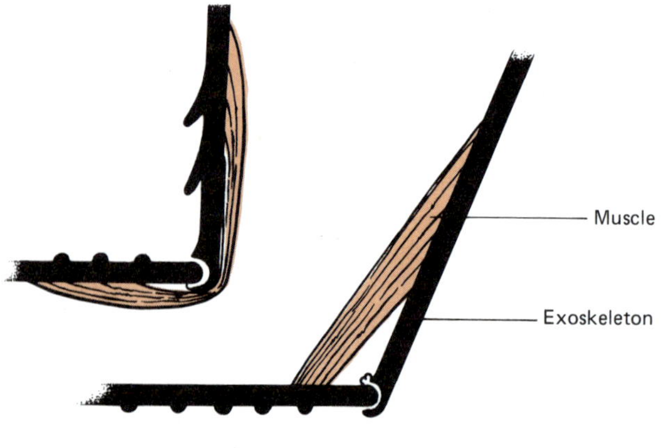

though it is obvious that motion increases demands for energy and oxygen, it is easy to overlook the coordination required to meet these demands. In fact, mammals synchronize breathing with running. At top speeds most mammals breathe once per footfall cycle. For example, jackrabbits breathe once for each bound. At a fast gallop, horses inhale when the load is least on the chest area—that is, when their feet are nearly or totally off the ground. Then they exhale after they come down and their weight is transferred to the chest. Breathing in time with gait isn't inevitable in humans, presumably because our weight isn't transmitted through the chest to the running legs. However, experienced runners couple breathing with gait. The most common pattern is one breath per two stride cycles.

Looking at Both Ends

In this chapter, we have examined mechanistic arrangements that explain the function of certain sense organs as well as the function of effectors. It is our assumption that similarly mechanistic explanations will someday unravel the action of the entire sense-organ–nervous-system–effector complex. But at present, scientists must admit that interpretation in the brain of nerve impulses initiated by sense organs is a puzzle. So are brain processes that use this information to direct the effectors. Since most activities of the brain are not understood, we have—at best— an incomplete understanding of ourselves.

To make matters worse, our sense organs adapt to stimuli. The strength of a stimulus as we perceive it is determined not by its absolute strength but by the length of time the receptor has been exposed to that strength of stimulus. Thus all sensory information is relative. That simple fact forbids us to be absolutely certain of any measurement. Information from our sense organs is usually consistent, so we believe it and say "we know." We know—and yet the philosopher in each of us should remain skeptical of data gathered by our sense organs.

Summary

1. Sense organs convert other forms of energy into the chemical energy of impulses in sensory nerves. The structure of each sense organ allows it to respond to a particular kind of stimulus. Strength of stimulus determines frequency of impulses in the sensory neurons. The brain interprets impulses from particular sensory neurons as particular sensations. Sense receptors adapt to continued stimulation.

2. There are many sense organs, including structures suggested to be receptors, to which no sensation can be assigned. Species other than ours have sense organs that differ from ours in sensitivity, location, and function.

3. The Pacinian corpuscle is a good example of a simple sense organ. Pressure on the corpuscle distorts the membrane of its sensory neuron, thereby producing a generator potential in the neuron. If this potential is sufficiently large, the neuron will fire. If pressed for long, the fluid in the corpuscle will shift so that the neuron is no longer stimulated.

4. The eye is a complex organ. The cornea and lens focus light on the retina, which contains the rod and cone cells. Cones, the color receptors, are concentrated in the fovea centralis, where the center of our visual field is focused. Peripheral areas of the retina contain highly sensitive rods, which respond to a wide range of wavelengths that we perceive as white or shades of gray. The lens is naturally round and elastic, but attachments of the ciliary body permit it to round up only when muscles in the ciliary body are contracted. Conversely, relaxation of these muscles alters the shape of the ciliary body, which then pulls the lens flat. The vitreous and aqueous humors distend the leathery sclera and thereby keep the retina a precise distance from the lens. The iris regulates the amount of light entering the lens.

5. Hair cells, receptors bearing many microvilli and one cilium, are used to sense sound, acceleration, and gravity in the human ear. The same type of receptor in the lateral line system of fish responds to displacement of water. Modified hair cells also permit some fish to detect electrical fields.

6. The pressure waves that constitute sound set the tympanic membrane in motion. These vibrations are magnified by the bones of the middle ear and transmitted to fluid in the vestibular canal of the cochlea. The basilar membrane of the cochlea bears hair cells, which are stimulated as the membrane vibrates. Because certain frequencies cause vibration of only certain portions of the basilar membrane, specific hair cells respond to particular pitches.

7. The skeleton and associated muscles interact to support and move the body. These and glands make up our effectors.

8. Minerals and collagen combine to make bone both hard and strong. Bone contains an extensive blood and nerve supply. Bone cells constantly resorb and lay down new bone, processes that are readily diverted to healing fractures. At joints the bones are held together by ligaments and other connective tissues, as well as by muscles that span the joints. Most movable joints contain a cavity where fluid lubricates the smooth cartilages that cover the ends of bones.

9. Skeletal muscles consist of multinuclear fibers. Cardiac (heart) muscle and smooth muscle of other internal organs are composed of cells with single nuclei. Muscle contraction involves the telescoping of actin and myosin filaments and thereby the shortening of myofibrils found in all muscle cells. Energy for this process is stored as glycogen and creatine phosphate, but the immediate source is ATP.

10. Motor neurons stimulate muscle by release at a motor end plate of a transmitter that depolarizes the membrane of the muscle cell.

11. Heat and cold receptors, the hypothalamus, the circulatory system, sweat glands, the thyroid gland, and other organs together regulate body temperature.

12. Regular exercise increases circulation to the heart and skeletal muscles. Skeletal muscle increases in size, strength, and ability to store oxygen.

Thought and Controversy

1. Not surprisingly, special glasses that invert light reaching the cornea give their wearer the impression that the world is upside down. But after a week of looking only through such glasses, everything appears right side up. Then, if the inverting glasses are discarded, the world again appears upside down for a time. These observations suggest that what we "see" is due in large part to interpretation by the brain. How does this relate to the hypothesis that our sense organs give us absolute information about the world?

2. An individual's signature is the result of learning, practice, and sometimes conscious decision. On first thought it seems that learning to write may be much like learning to figure skate—largely a matter of motor coordination. Once learned, your signature is similar each time and often sufficiently distinct to serve as identification. But consider the fact that when a much different set of nerves and muscles are used to write with chalk and blackboard, the same characteristic signature appears.

3. "Tender loving care" is more than a sentimental motto. It is a real need of all infants. Fondling, affection, and play are as important for normal mental and physical development as is good nutrition. Emotionally distressed parents sometimes reject their babies psychologically, although they tend adequately to the babies' physical needs. Such children grow poorly, have excessive digestive upsets, show little muscle tone, and are listless and depressed. Similar symptoms occur when infants are ill and their parents hesitate to cuddle them for fear of doing harm. Long-term stays in hospitals or orphanages can produce mental and physical retardation or even death unless those responsible for the infants are warm and loving and have the time to give the babies the attention they need. How physical affection promotes normal growth remains uncertain, but the short stature, delayed skeletal development, and low weight of affected children suggest insufficient secretion of pituitary hormones. Since such secretions are under control of the hypothalamus, there is a ready mechanism to translate the stimulus of physical affection into normal development. It seems that sense organs serve for more than simply reporting the outside world. Certain stimuli are necessary for normal health and development.

Questions

1. Explain how the strength of a stimulus is carried in a sensory neuron, remembering that neurons fire in an "all-or-none" manner.

2. What property of sense receptors prevents them from reporting on the absolute state of our environment? How is this property useful?

3. List the structures along the pathway of light in the eye, and explain the function of each.

4. Explain why distant vision is restful to the eyes despite the fact that the lens is pulled flatter in this state.

5. Discuss the distribution of rods and cones in the retina. Relate the distribution to the function of the fovea centralis, the importance of night vision, and the origin of the optic nerve.

6. Explain how hair cells can respond to different stimuli such as sound and gravity.

7. Compare the structure and properties of cartilage and bone. Explain why bone heals faster than cartilage.

8. Compare the stimulation of a skeletal muscle at the motor end plate with a neuron-to-neuron synapse. Then describe how depolarization of the membrane leads to contraction.

9. Explain how smooth muscle may act as both a sense organ and an effector.

10. Discuss the attachments of muscles and explain their importance.

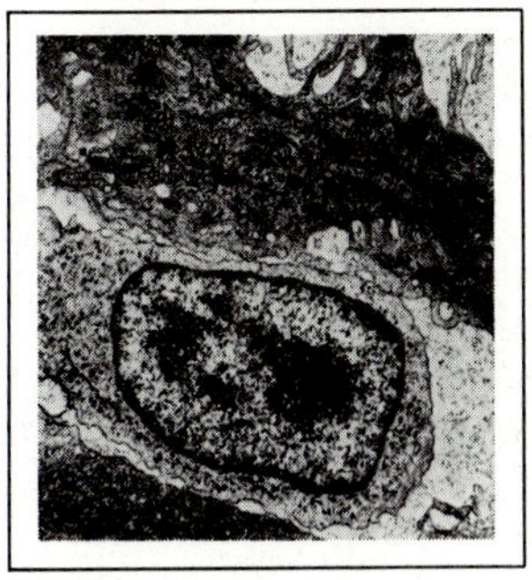

10

Homeostasis Challenged: Disease and Defense

HUMAN DEFENSES AGAINST DISEASE ARE AN INtegral part of homeostasis. Disease, in fact, can be defined as a disruption of that state. You have already learned how some of these disruptions happen. You know, for example, that improper nutrition can make people sick, as can impaired body functions brought on by aging or injuries. In some cases, disease is the result of inherited conditions, or it can be caused by poisoning by pollutants or other chemical agents. And as you are probably aware, psychological factors are known to affect physical health as well as mental health. The central topic of this chapter, however, is disease that occurs when the body is invaded by parasites.

A **parasite** can be defined as any organism that lives on or in the human body and is entirely dependent on its human **host** for nourishment and sustenance. Human parasites include both small animals and microorganisms. Among the most troublesome animal parasites are the bloodsucking arthropods—mosquitoes, lice, ticks, and fleas—and creatures like mites, which burrow under and digest the skin. Unless they carry the germs of more harmful disease, these so-called **external parasites** cause nothing more serious than annoying itching symptoms.

Animal parasites that grow *inside* the body are another matter. Tapeworms (Fig. 10.1) and hookworms, for example, can cause debilitating sickness. Nevertheless, the vast majority of serious parasitic infections of humans are caused not by animal parasites but by **microorganisms.**

THE MICROBIAL WORLD

Microorganisms are everywhere. Some inhabit the soil; others live in rivers, lakes, or the oceans. They can be found in the air we breathe, the food we eat, and the water we drink. Few of the thousands of different kinds of microorganisms actually cause disease, however, and many types are beneficial.

Most people think immediately of "germs," or bacteria (Fig. 10.2) when microbes (another name for microorganisms) are mentioned. Nevertheless, molds are such common household nuisances, that they are probably the most readily distinguishable microorganisms. Yeasts, which are close relatives of molds, are also widely familiar. In addition to bacteria, molds, and yeasts, protozoa and many algae□ also qualify as microbes. 89

The Silent Majority

Microorganisms are distinguished by their diversity of shape, size, and structure, but especially by their diversity of metabolism. Algae and a few bacteria are photosynthetic. Protozoa live primarily by consuming other, smaller microbes. Most other microorganisms are agents of decay. However, these "good guys" rarely receive the attention that the far less numerous disease-causing microorganisms do.

Decay is carried out largely by bacteria, yeasts, and molds. These **decomposers**□ break down dead 11
bodies, plant litter, and other wastes. As a result

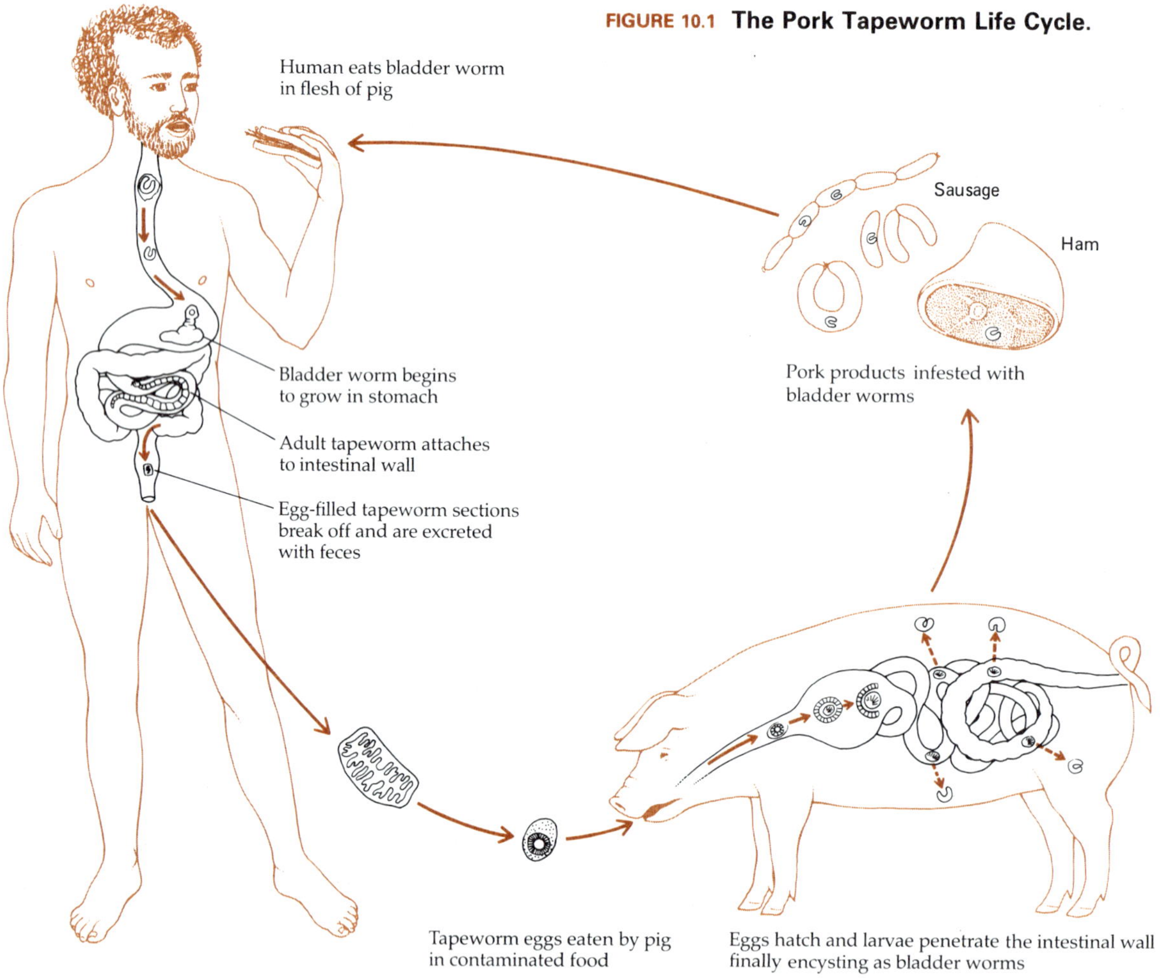

FIGURE 10.1 The Pork Tapeworm Life Cycle.

of their efforts, the chemical elements in such substances are turned over and recycled. It would be difficult to overstate the importance of this process. Decomposition converts dead matter into inorganic plant nutrients that maintain soil fertility. Without decay, the soil would become barren, and plant life would be choked off for lack of nutrients. And of course, without plants as a source of food, all other life would eventually perish.

Some kind of microbe can decompose almost any substance. In fact, the ability of microorganisms to decompose a wide range of organic material is put to use in sewage treatment plants (Fig. 10.3). Among the valuable microorganisms that grow
107 in sewage are the methane bacteria.□ These bacteria may produce enough methane (natural gas) to supply the sewage treatment plant with most of its energy needs. Besides helping us dispose of sewage, microorganisms make many other valuable contributions to human life.

For centuries, linen has been made from fibers liberated from flax by controlled bacterial decomposition. In Chapter 5,□ we learned that yeast fer- 106
mentations make bread and alcoholic beverages possible. Bacterial cultures likewise aid in the manufacture of sour cream, yogurt, butter, and cheese. Similarly, sauerkraut, ripe olives, and pickles come from bacterial fermentations of cabbage, fresh olives, and cucumbers.

Industry is constantly learning new ways to take advantage of microbial metabolism. Microorganisms are the source of vitamins, antibiotics, and a variety of industrial chemicals. But there are other microorganisms that benefit us much more directly.

Our Normal Flora

In a world filled with microbes, it would be surprising indeed if we did not find some of them on the human body. Of course, only those organisms

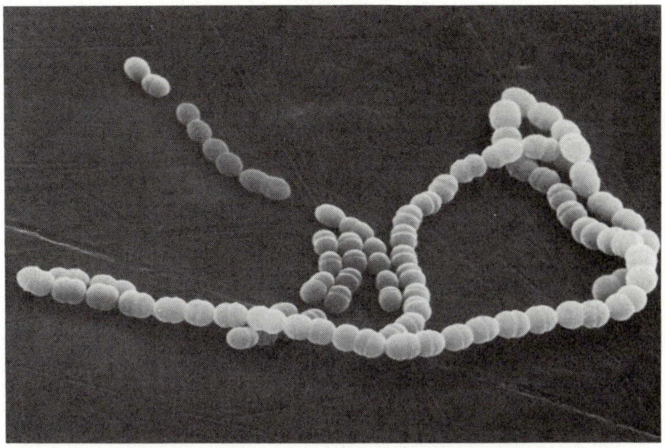

(a)

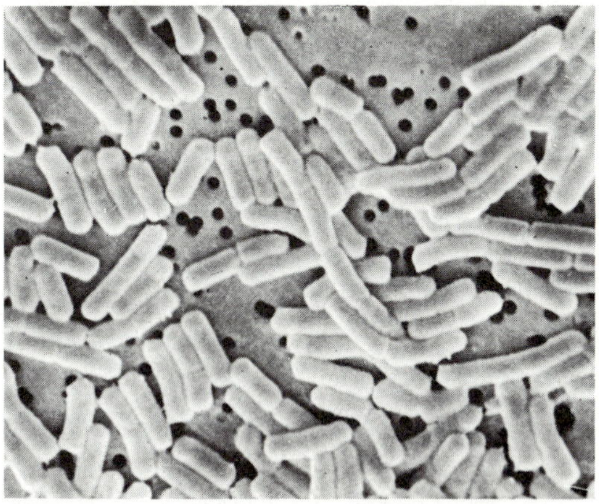

(b)

(c)

FIGURE 10.2 Bacteria Come in Three Basic Shapes. Individual bacterial cells are generally either (a) spherical, (b) rod-shaped, or (c) spiral. It is not unusual for bacterial cells to remain together after cell division. Thus the spherical bacteria (streptococci) shown in the first illustration form chains.

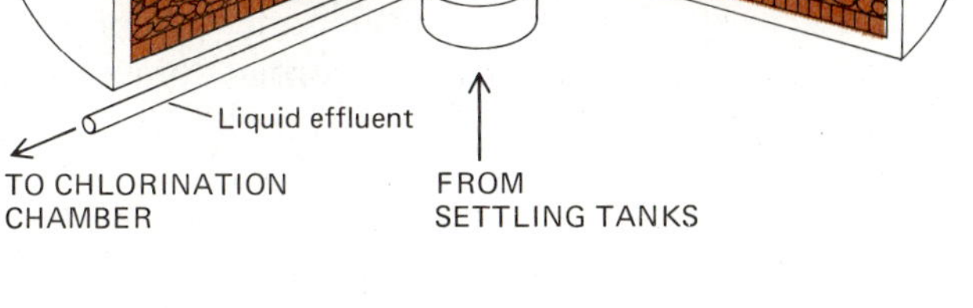

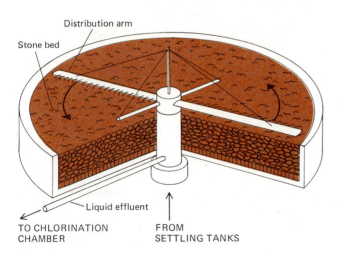

FIGURE 10.3 Sewage Treatment. Once upon a time it was sufficient to dispose of sewage by releasing it into a nearby body of water. There, microorganisms digested the offensive waste material even as it was diluted and carried off. Modern societies produce so much sewage that the old-fashioned way no longer works. Nevertheless, microorganisms are still involved in sewage treatment. After bulk wastes and suspended solids have been allowed to settle out, the remaining fluid is subjected to microbial digestion. One method makes use of the trickle filter illustrated here. Sewage is sprayed over a bed of stone or gravel by a rotating distribution arm. Slimy growths of microorganisms that coat the stone or gravel oxidize the organic wastes in the sewage as it trickles down through the bed. The filtered water is generally chlorinated to ensure disinfection before being discharged.

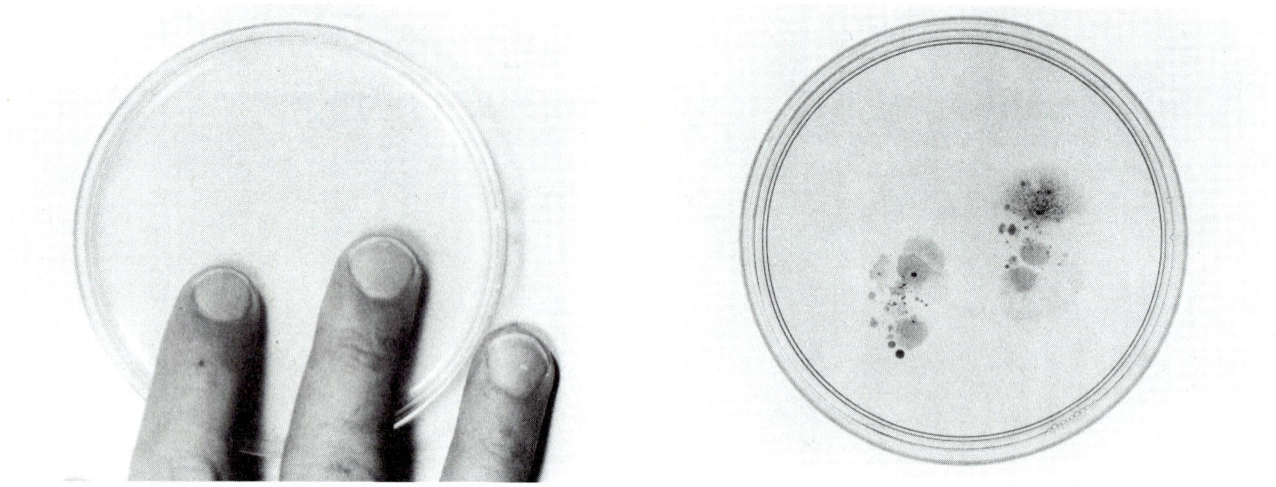

FIGURE 10.4 **Normal Flora of the Skin.** By pressing his unwashed fingers on a nutrient medium, one of the authors (GEA) reveals his normal flora. Bacteria transferred from the fingertips have produced visible colonies (masses of cells) on the growth medium.

that are suited for growth will actually multiply there.

The term **normal flora** has been coined for the microbes we expect to find growing on people (Fig. 10.4). All the exposed parts of the body—skin, mouth, and parts of the respiratory, intestinal, and genital tracts—have continuous resident microbial populations. Since different parts of the body offer unique environments, different groups of microorganisms colonize each body surface. And they are tenacious. No amount of washing can totally remove all the microorganisms that grow on humans.

Although the normal flora are generally considered harmless, this is not always true. Skin-inhabiting bacteria can, for example, incite or contribute to the condition known as **acne.** And nearly everyone suffers to some degree from the activities of the fermentative bacteria that proliferate in between and on the surfaces of teeth. **Dental plaque** is a film of anaerobic bacteria that sticks to tooth surfaces by means of mucoid secretions. Some of these bacteria ferment sugars in food particles, thus
106 producing lactic acid. The acid causes decalcification of the hard dental tissue. Once the hard tissue has softened, other bacteria further the decay
201 by attacking the proteins of the tooth enamel.

Perhaps the most beneficial of the normal flora microorganisms are those that are found in the intestine. These microbes are thought to produce vitamins and even enzymes and other products 147
that aid in digestion. Overall, however, the most useful aspect of our normal flora is the protection they provide—just by being there. These organisms are well adapted to their human environment and therefore so highly competitive that they leave little room for the development of potentially dangerous intruders. Needless to say, however, there are occasions when invaders do gain the upper hand.

Pathogens

Microoganisms that cause disease are called **pathogens.** Of course, there are different degrees of pathogenicity. Especially serious pathogens are said to possess a high degree of **virulence.** If you think about it, you will agree that natural selection must favor a parasite that does little harm to its host over one that is virulent. The reasoning is simple. A pathogen that kills its host is likely to find itself without a food source. Pathogens of low virulence are probably the most successful. In all likelihood, these types have long shared a relationship with the same host species. Using this same line of reasoning, we might guess that our normal flora began their human association as weak pathogens that became better and better adapted.

A weakly virulent pathogen is often one that can invade its host only if body resistance is lowered. Such pathogens are described as **opportunists,** and the "opportunities" depend on the pathogen. Some can attack if a person is already sick. Others can't invade the body except through a cut or other skin injury. A few normal flora organisms fall into this category. Skin inhabitants, for example, frequently cause wound infections.

PEOPLE VERSUS PATHOGENS

The extent to which we can avoid or overcome infectious disease depends on body functions that restrict microbial growth, as well as mechanisms that destroy disease agents within the body. General defenses are directed against almost any form of attack, and specific immune responses provide protection from particular disease agents. Both forms of body defense contribute to the maintenance of homeostasis.

General Defenses of the Body

All of the body's defenses are not equally effective against all invaders. Resistance to infection is a cooperative effort involving an interplay among numerous factors. Although our general defenses usually come into action first, they are aided by specific responses whenever possible. The net result differs among individuals and from time to time in a given person.

Our First Line of Defense. Healthy, intact skin can stop most disease agents. The **epidermis,**□ or outer part of the skin, is composed of many layers of cells. Cells of the bottom layer divide and are pushed toward the outside, where they slowly wear away. As the epidermal cells move outward, they become flattened into scalelike structures composed almost entirely of the tough and somewhat waterproof protein, **keratin** (Fig. 10.5). 153

Few microbes can penetrate the intact epidermis. Even so, skin oils and sweat-gland secretions inhibit the development of microorganisms at the surface. Moist areas, such as the armpits or between the toes, are most vulnerable to colonization. Not surprisingly, skin infections are most common in humid, tropical climates.

Earlier□ we learned that the respiratory tract is well protected against the possibility of infection. Mucus-secreting glands and beating cilia move a 134

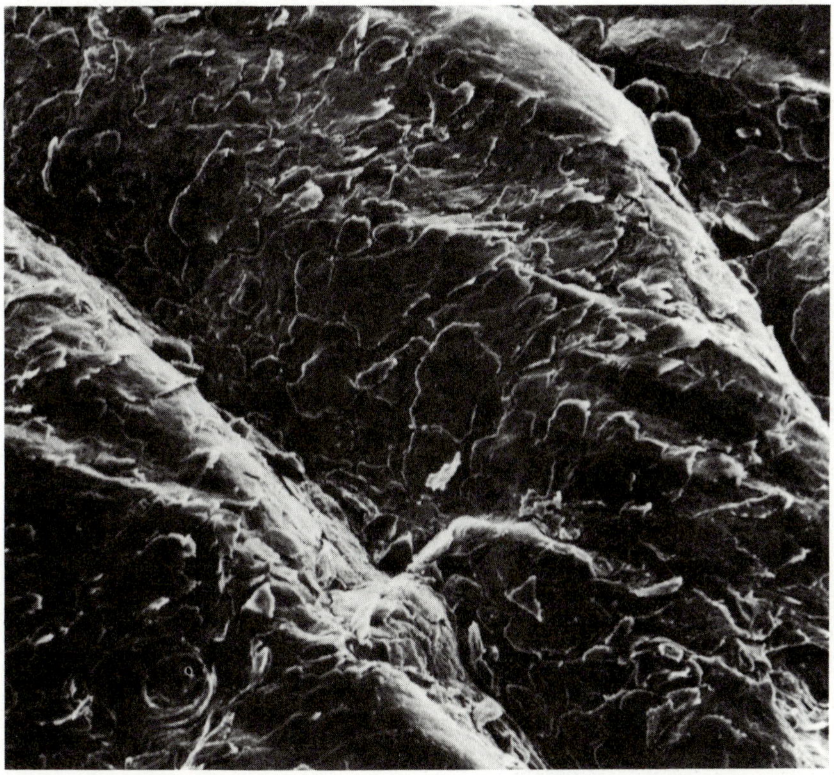

FIGURE 10.5 The Keratinized Surface of Human Skin.

constant stream of mucus upward and away from the lungs. Microorganisms inhaled in the air usually come into contact with the moist lining of the upper respiratory tract. Here they are trapped in mucus and expelled by cough or sneeze reflexes.

Tears and saliva also flush microorganisms from the body. In addition, these fluids contain **lysozyme,** a protein that destroys many bacteria. Many potential pathogens in our food succumb to 144 stomach acids.□ Others flourish in our intestines, and some of them penetrate the linings. These invaders, along with those that penetrate the skin, meet other lines of defense.

Phagocytosis and Inflammation. Aggressively protective phagocytic cells are found in the tissues as well as in the circulatory system. These include **neutrophils** and **monocytes,** which normally circulate in the blood, and **macrophages** (noted for their large appetite), which police the liver, spleen, lungs, and lymph nodes and range widely through connective tissues (Fig. 10.6). White blood cells and macrophages prey on microorganisms that have penetrated the outer defenses.

Phagocytosis often occurs in conjunction with another general defense of the body, **inflammation.** The localized redness, warmth, swelling, and pain of inflammation is a normal body response to infection or any other tissue irritation. Release of **histamine** and **serotonin** from injured cells initiates the inflammatory response. These chemicals stimulate dilation of nearby blood vessels and thus increase blood flow to the affected area. The increased blood accounts for the **redness** and **warmth.**

The increased blood supply that accompanies inflammation is of critical importance, because cell damage quickly occurs if tissue injuries restrict supplies of oxygen and nutrients. In addition, as small veins enlarge, they become more porous, making it easier for phagocytes to migrate from the blood into surrounding tissues. Blood fluids also leak out. The accumulation of these fluids contributes to the **swelling**, and the pressure it puts on nerve endings is a source of **pain**. Plasma clots, which soon form in the injured tissue, help to entrap the offending material and promote its phagocytosis (Fig. 10.6).

Neutrophils are usually the first white blood cells to squeeze through blood-vessel walls and migrate to an inflamed site. As an inflammatory response increases, monocytes follow neutrophils into the area. There they turn into more effective macrophages. Ravenous macrophages not only attack infectious agents, but also help in eventual cleanup operations by engulfing damaged tissue and dead white blood cells of all kinds.

If a local infection is not eradicated quickly, plasma clots will wall off the inflamed area and produce an **abscess** or **boil.** The **pus** that accompanies this condition is a mixture of tissue fluid and dead phagocytes.

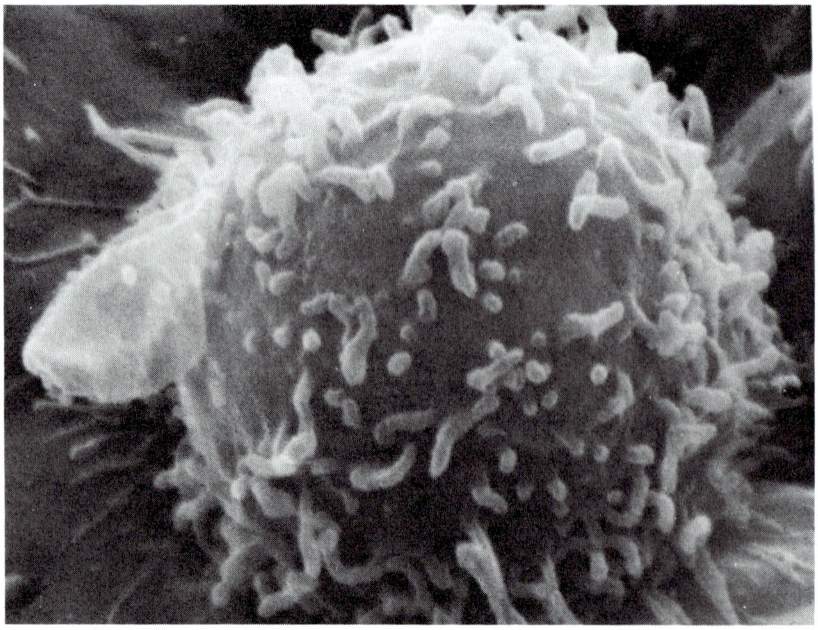

FIGURE 10.6 **An Alveolar Macrophage.**

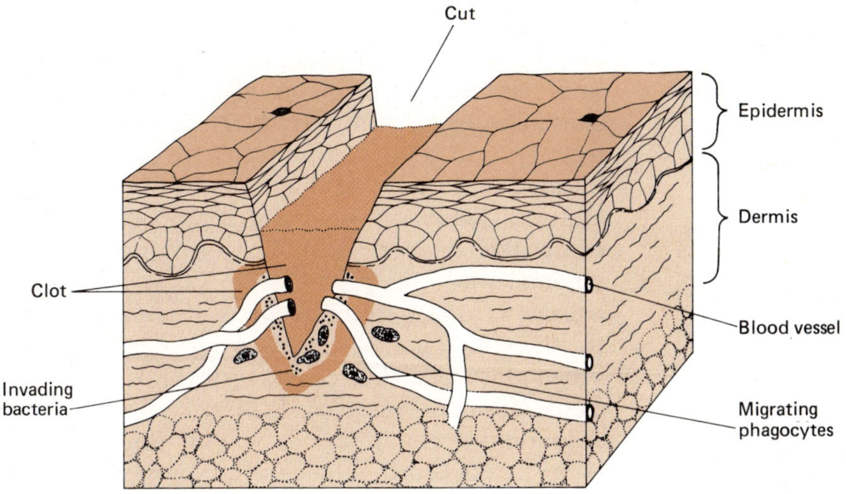

FIGURE 10.7 **Inflammation.** An injury to the body, such as a cut, attracts phagocytes and stimulates blood flow into the damaged area. At the same time, blood vessels become more permeable, and plasma begins to leak out into the surrounding tissue. Clotted plasma may eventually form a sac that helps to prevent the infection from spreading to other areas. Such a closed region, filled with pus, is called an abscess.

Fever frequently accompanies infections. It can be traced to substances released by phagocytes. As
192 we noted in Box 9B,▫ the elevated temperature may destroy microorganisms. Although phagocytosis, inflammation, and fever are crucial to our survival, by themselves they are often insufficient to handle infectious assaults. In fact, body defense is a cooperative effort involving many warriors with plentiful ammunition.

Antimicrobial Substances in Tissues. Interferon and various plasma proteins make important contributions to general body defense. Virus-infected cells secrete **interferon,** which seeps into surrounding tissues and the bloodstream and protects healthy cells from viral infection. Interferon appears also to help regulate some of the immune functions that we will be discussing shortly.

Transferrins are plasma proteins that bind iron in plasma. The iron remains available to human cells but not to microorganisms. This restricts the growth of pathogens in the body. **Complement** is a group of plasma proteins that attach to foreign cells and either cause them to rupture or assist in their phagocytosis. The name complement is derived from the knowledge that these proteins also enhance certain specific immune responses.

Specific Immune Responses

Anyone who recovers from an infectious disease is usually immune to recurrence of that disease for a period of time, sometimes for life. Such specific immune responses are mediated either by antibodies produced by differentiated B cells or by activated T cells.

Antigens and Antibodies. An **antibody** is a protein produced by the body in response to the presence of a foreign substance called an **antigen.** Most antigens are proteins, but polysaccharides and other macromolecules are also sometimes antigenic.

An antigen may be a free chemical, such as a bacterial toxin (poison) or snake venom. But many other antigens are components of larger structures—for example, pollen grains, bacteria, viruses, animal hairs, or even transfused red blood cells of the wrong type. Because such complex objects as bacteria and pollen grains are composed of many different antigenic substances, the body responds by making a different antibody for each different kind of antigen.

The protective effect of an antibody results from the very specific reaction that occurs when the antibody comes into contact with the antigen that stimulated its production. This **specificity** explains why having one disease does not confer immunity to another disease. As shown in Fig. 10.8, antigen and antibody molecules are complementary in shape. One fits into the other to form an **antigen-antibody complex.** The reaction should remind you of an enzyme-substrate reaction.▫ 97

The result of formation of an antigen-antibody complex depends on the exact nature of the interacting antigen and antibody. If the antigen is part of a bacterial cell, the reaction may cause the cell to disintegrate. Sometimes the attachment of an antibody to the surface of a bacterial cell increases

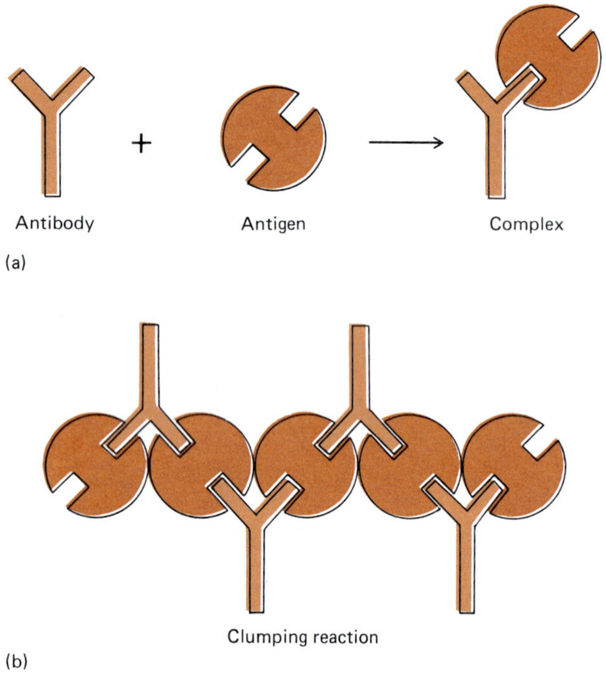

FIGURE 10.8 **The Antigen-Antibody Reaction.** (a) Although antigens and antibodies don't look exactly like these diagrammatic interpretations, both are macromolecules with complex shapes. In fact, an antigen and its specific antibody have complementary shapes, so they fit together precisely (b) to form an antigen-antibody complex, just as enzymes and their substrates fit together.

the cell's attractiveness to phagocytes. On the other hand, poisonous antigens can be neutralized by their antibodies. Often the antigenic surfaces of virus particles become coated with antibody. This interferes with the adsorption of the virus onto potential host cells, a step that is essential to viral infection of animal cells.

Self and Not Self. Usually no substance native to an individual can serve as an antigen in that same individual. Since the proteins and other macromolecules that make up our bodies are antigenic when injected into another person, there must be a normal body mechanism for distinguishing between what is "self" and what is "not self." Details of the development of this immune response are obscure, but it appears that the mechanism becomes operational before birth. All the body chemicals present at that time are considered "self" and are nonantigenic, but everything subsequently encountered becomes "not self," is antigenic, and consequently stimulates an immune response.

A person who produces antibodies against his or her own body components suffers from an **autoimmune disease.** Autoimmunity generally leads to slow self-destruction. Hereditary defects, virus infections, and generalized stress have each been implicated as a cause of this potentially debilitating ailment. Many autoimmune diseases strike the connective tissues,▫ resulting in chronic inflam- 92 mation and a progressive degeneration of collagen▫ throughout the body. 69 **Rheumatoid arthritis,** which first affects the joints, and **lupus erythematosus,** which causes skin and kidney lesions, are two examples. **Multiple sclerosis** is an autoimmune condition of a slightly different sort. Here, loss of coordination and paralysis result from deterioration of myelin sheaths▫ and the conse- 161 quent distortion of nerve impulses.

B cells and Antibody Production. Antibodies belong to a group of proteins called globulins. Until recently they were classed as **gamma globulins** but are now most often called **immunoglobulins.** Some immunoglobulins circulate freely in the blood and tissue fluids. Others are found in tears, saliva, milk, and nasal drippings.

Immunoglobulins, or antibodies if you prefer, are secreted by **plasma cells.** These cells are abundant in the tonsils, lymph nodes, and spleen, as well as scattered in lymphatic tissues,▫ but they 131 originate in the bone marrow.

Plasma cells are highly differentiated forms of **B cells,** lymphocytes that arise from stem cells of the **bone marrow.**▫ After formation, B cells spread 198 throughout the body, colonizing various tissues. B cell colonies serve as a kind of immune surveillance system. Many subpopulations of B cells exist. Each can recognize a different antigen (Fig. 10.9).

Because B cells are always coated with a small amount of antibody, they can identify specific antigens. Binding of antigen to its surface stimulates a B cell to divide. Repeated divisions produce a large population of plasma cells and B-memory cells. The **plasma cells** secrete antibody into the blood and other body fluids. **B memory cells** later develop into and replace the short-lived plasma cells.

Although all the evidence is not yet in, it appears that B cells must have the assistance of macrophages and T cells in order to produce antibody. Macrophages apparently scoop up antigen molecules and present them to appropriate B cells. T cells (a lymphocyte group that we'll soon learn more

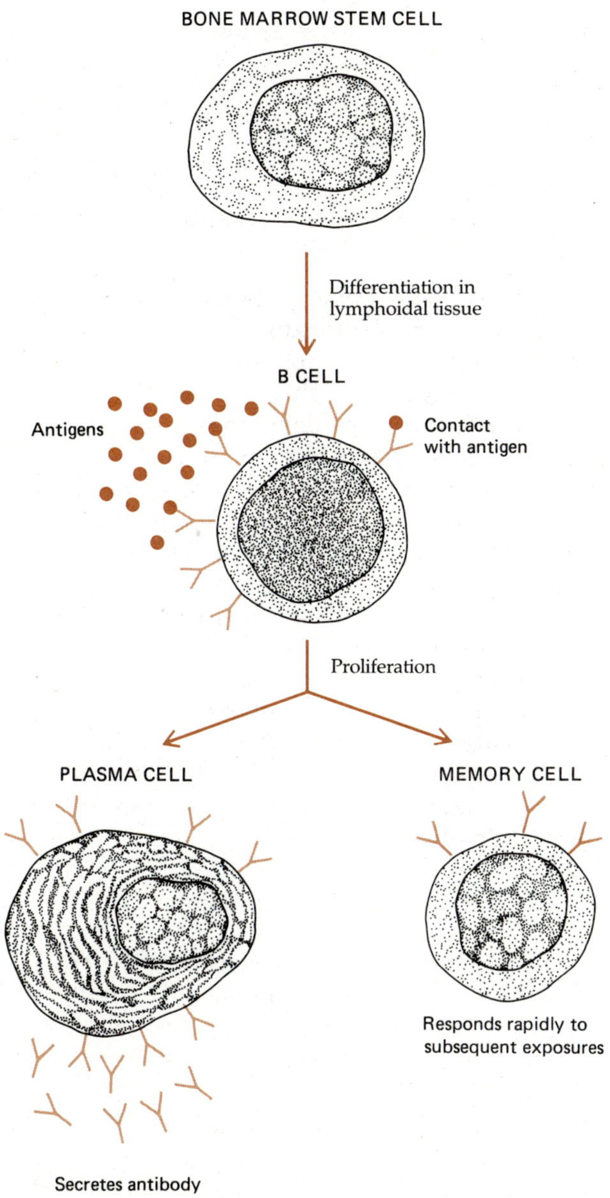

FIGURE 10.9 Antigens Stimulate B Cells to Become Antibody-Secreting Plasma Cells.

about) help by secreting chemicals that encourage plasma cells to secrete antibody.

In any case, subsequent exposures to the same antigen result in a much more rapid immune response than did the initial exposure (Fig. 10.10). Because of the presence of B memory cells, plasma cells appear much sooner. And antibody levels are higher and more persistent. This is the basis of the "booster" shots given in artificial immunization procedures.

Immunization Procedures. Immunity may be acquired either naturally or artificially. One form of natural immunity results from actually having a disease. The common medical practice of vaccination is an artificial immunization procedure.

Vaccines are preparations of viruses, microorganisms, or toxins (poisons) that have been treated (or neutralized) so that they can no longer cause sickness. Despite changes that render these substances harmless, they retain their ability to act as antigens and to stimulate antibody production when they are injected or consumed. Booster doses of vaccines maintain immunological memory and sustain a high level of antibody.

Sometimes a person becomes severely ill from a disease that he or she has not been immunized against and is so sick that it would be dangerous to wait for the infectious agent to stimulate antibody production. It is then necessary to administer antibody that has been produced by another organism. A person protected by antibodies produced by another is said to have **passive immunity.**

Some antibodies are made commercially by the injection of appropriate antigens into large animals, such as horses (Fig. 10.11). After repeated injections and the passage of sufficient time to allow for the production of a large quantity of antibody, the animal is bled and the blood **serum**□ (liq- 120
uid remaining after clotting) is collected. Because the serum contains antibodies produced by the animal, it is appropriately known as **antiserum.** Antisera prepared against toxins (poisonous compounds) are called **antitoxins.**

To produce large amounts of antiserum there must be a major source of antigenic material. This

FIGURE 10.10 An Anamnestic Response. A rapid increase in antibody follows a second exposure to antigenic material. Such an increase is called an anamnestic (memory) response.

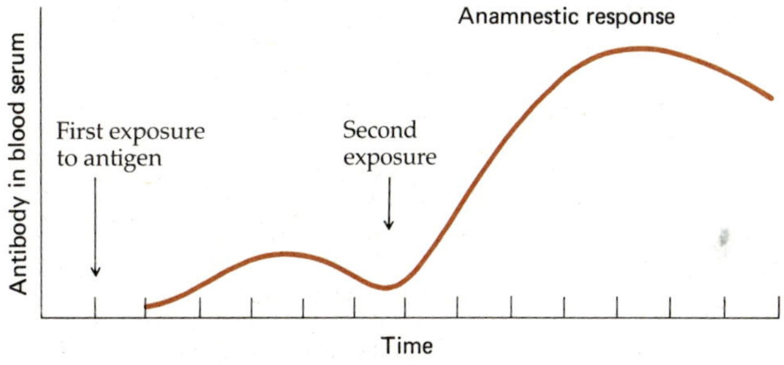

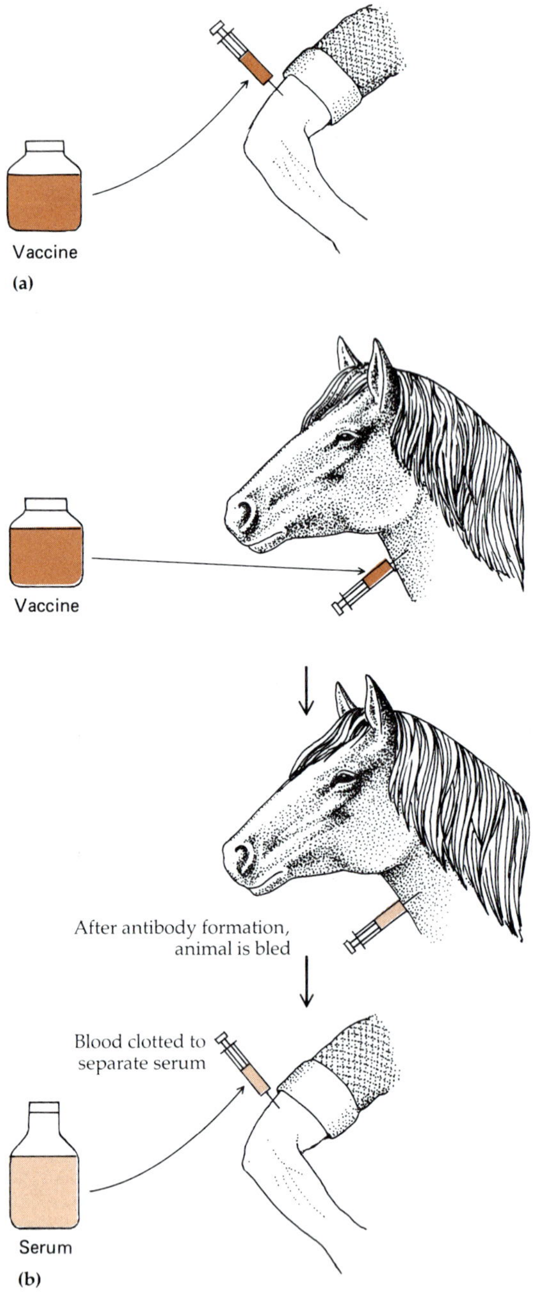

FIGURE 10.11 Vaccine versus Serum. (a) A vaccine is an antigen preparation that is injected directly into a person to stimulate antibody formation. This type of protection is relatively long-lived. (b) An antiserum is serum containing antibodies produced by another animal. Although it offers immediate antibody protection, the protection is short-lived, because the added antibody is gradually used up.

material is usually obtained by growing pathogens in the laboratory. Unfortunately, it is not yet possible to grow many important pathogens, especially certain viruses. This is the reason that no antisera exist for some dangerous diseases, for example, infectious hepatitis. In these cases the only alternative is to administer concentrated human immunoglobulins separated from pooled whole blood. The rationale is that pooled blood from numerous donors will contain antibodies against a wide spectrum of organisms, perhaps including the one of immediate concern.

Newborn babies enjoy passive immunity, which results from antibodies that diffuse through the placenta from the mother's blood to the baby's blood. Other antibodies are secreted in the first milk and enter the newborn when it nurses. As a result of these antibody transfers, a baby shares its mother's immunities for about six months, during which time the baby develops its own immune system.

T cells and Killer Lymphocytes. Certain types of antigens stimulate the development of **T cells,** lymphocytes that arise in the bone marrow and differentiate in the **thymus**, an organ in the neck region. From the thymus, T cells migrate to various other lymphatic tissues or circulate in the blood. When stimulated by specific antigens, T cells proliferate into **activated T cells** and **T memory cells.**

Some activated T cells are helper cells that participate in the development of plasma cells. Others secrete macrophage attractants and thus cause antigens to be phagocytized. Killer lymphocytes are activated T cells that emit molecules that destroy antigens and trigger inflammatory responses (Fig. 10.12). Like B memory cells, T memory cells permit a rapid response to later exposures to antigens.

Transplant Rejection. T cells are responsible for the rejection of organ transplants. Their killer instinct is stimulated by the foreign surface antigens of transplanted tissue. The success or failure of an organ transplant depends largely on **histocompatibility antigens.** Transplants are less likely to be rejected if the donor and recipient are genetically

TABLE 10.1 Common Immunization Procedures for Infants and Children

AGE	IMMUNIZATION
2, 4, and 6 months	Diphtheria, pertussis, tetanus (DPT) Oral polio (OP)
15 to 16 months	Mumps, measles, rubella (MMR)
18 months	DPT booster; OP booster
3 to 4 years or on school entry	DPT booster; OP booster

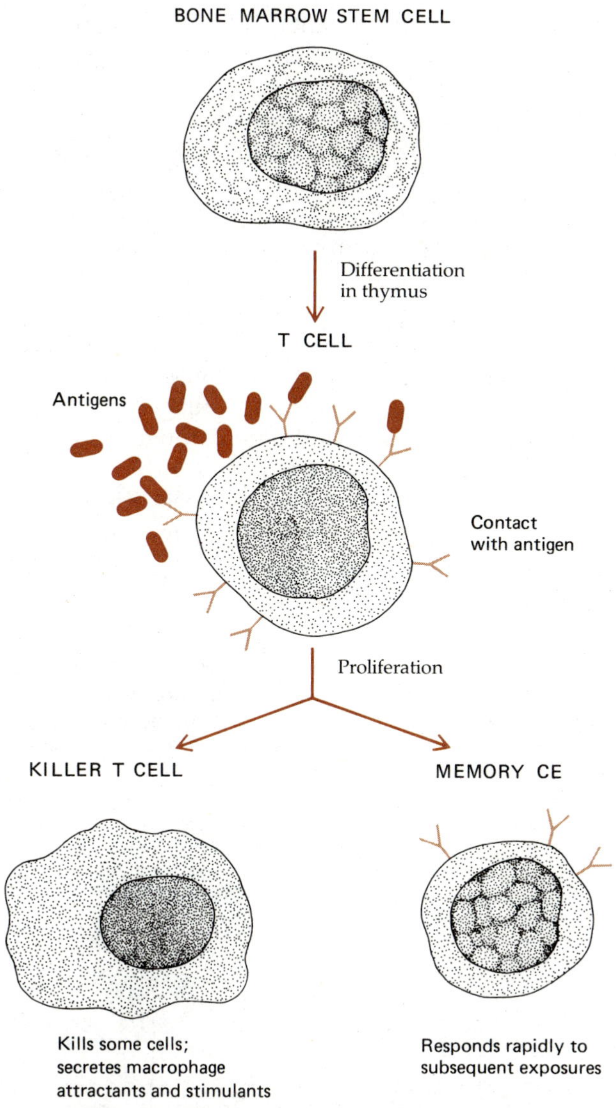

FIGURE 10.12 T-Cell Differentiation.

similar and therefore have similar histocompatibility antigens. For this reason grafts from one part of the body to another or between identical twins are quite often successful. Techniques have been developed to identify the various histocompatibility antigens, enabling to some degree the matching of donor tissue to recipient tissue.

Because a human life hangs in the balance, transplants of skin, heart, liver, and kidney are sometimes attempted even when histocompatibility is not perfect. In an attempt to overcome the rejection phenomenon, physicians treat these patients with **immunosuppressant drugs,** such as **corticosteroids,** which inhibit phagocytosis. Unfortunately, this treatment also reduces the overall resistance of the transplant patient, who may succumb to some infectious disease that cannot be combated effectively with antibiotics.

Interestingly enough, certain tissues of the body can be grafted from one person to another without *any* danger of rejection. The cornea of the eye is such a tissue. Since the cornea is located in a region without any blood or lymphatic vessels, there is no way that a corneal transplant can stimulate the immune surveillance systems of the body.

Allergies: Immunity Gone Wrong. Sometimes our immune responses can harm body tissues or even cause death. Some people become extremely sensitive, actually **hypersensitive,** to contact with certain antigens. Subsequent exposure elicits dramatic **allergic reactions.** Often the **allergens** (antigens that stimulate allergies) are innocuous substances that do not trigger immune responses in the majority of people.

Allergic reactions can involve either antibodies or killer lymphocytes. When an allergen stimulates antibody production, these antibodies attach to cells of certain tissues, most often those of the skin or respiratory tract. Upon subsequent exposure, allergen molecules react with the cell-bound antibody triggering the release of **histamine** and other substances that induce inflammation.

Many of the symptoms we associate with common allergies (rash, runny nose, stuffy feeling) are manifestations of inflammatory responses to tissue damage. Often these symptoms can be relieved by antihistamines, drugs that destroy the biological activity of histamine. The severest allergic reaction, **anaphylactic shock,** results from massive inflammation of vital organs. When this occurs in the lungs, there is difficulty in breathing; when it occurs in the heart, heart failure can result.

Chronically allergic individuals sometimes can be treated effectively through **desensitization.** Although the biological mechanism is not fully understood, it seems that a progressive immunization with larger and larger doses of the damaging antigen causes the production of large amounts of a **blocking antibody.** Such antibodies do not become fixed to tissues but remain free in the body fluids. When the desensitized individual is naturally exposed to the antigen, blocking antibodies intercept the antigen before it can react with the fixed antibody and cause tissue damage (Fig. 10.13).

Poison-ivy rashes and several other so-called contact allergies (Fig. 10.14) result not from antibody production but from the activities of T cells.

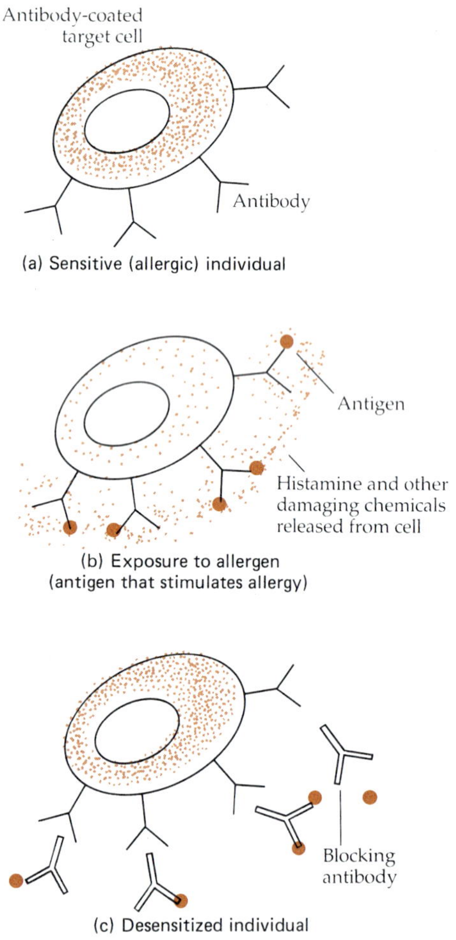

FIGURE 10.13 **Desensitization.** (a) An allergic individual has cells that bind special antibodies produced against irritating substances. The first exposure to the so-called allergen merely sensitizes the individual. (b) Later exposure to the allergen causes tissue damage when the antibody-coated target cells react with the allergen and release damaging chemicals that stimulate inflammation. (c) Desensitization procedures cause the development of circulating antibodies, which react with allergen molecules, thus blocking access to target cells and preventing allergic symptoms from developing.

Because the redness and other symptoms are due to the aggressive nature of T cells and not to the release of histamine, treatment with antihistamines has no effect. However, cortisone and similar immunosuppressants give some relief.

PATHOGENS VERSUS PEOPLE

It is not always easy to say how a particular pathogen makes people sick. Certainly large numbers of microorganisms growing in the blood or some other tissue will use up nutrients and otherwise interfere with normal host functions. Some pathogens secrete toxins that poison body cells. Much damage can also result from allergic or inflammatory responses. Usually, however, the virulence of an organism cannot be attributed to any single factor. As infectious agents invade and then multiply within our bodies, they harm us in many ways.

Spreading and Survival

The ability of some organisms to cause disease seems related to their ability to avoid phagocytosis or to kill phagocytes outright. Some pathogenic bacteria bear a slimy outer covering that either prevents ingestion by phagocytes or protects the bacteria from digestion when they are phagocytized. Tuberculosis bacteria actually multiply inside white

FIGURE 10.14 **The Three-Leaflet Structure of Poison Ivy Is Easy to Identify.** An alcoholic secretion protects poison ivy from herbivores and causes a persistent rash on human skin.

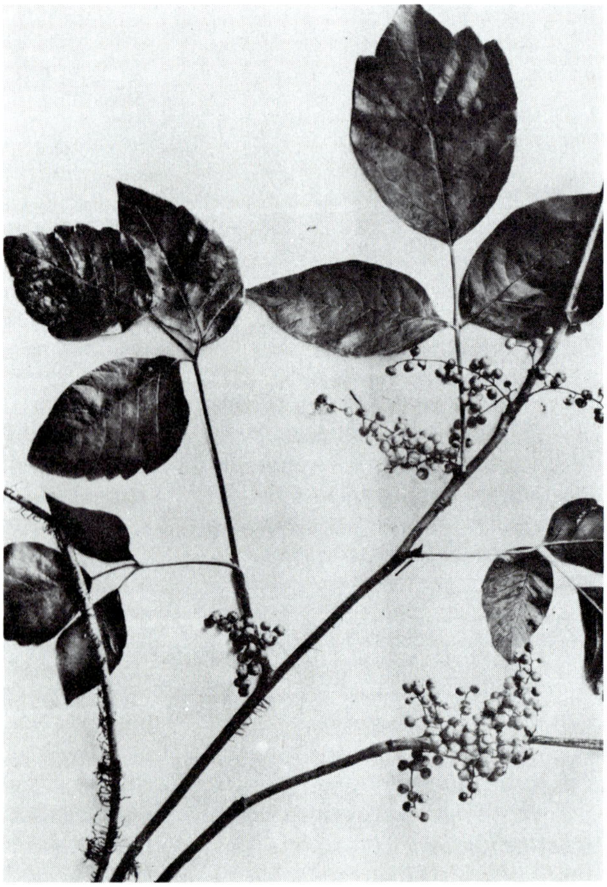

BOX 10A

NEW DISEASES: EPIDEMIOLOGICAL PROBLEMS AND PUZZLES

If you didn't know any better, you might conclude after a walk in the woods that there were no animals living there. Of course, if you had turned over a rock or a rotting stump, or if you had returned at night when most mammals are active, you would have drawn a different conclusion. In other words, you see what you look for.

The same thing is true of "invisible" microorganisms. Often, the first hint of the existence of a previously unrecognized pathogen is some startling occurrence that stimulates intensive scientific snooping. The mysterious, dramatic outbreak of illness at the 1976 American Legion Convention in Philadephia is an example.

Legionellosis is an atypical form of pneumonia. Older people who smoke are the most vulnerable. Epidemiologists were at first quite puzzled by the disease. Eventually they were able to show that the causative agent was a bacterium, which was later named *Legionella pneumonophila*. This microorganism grows naturally in rivers and lakes, but recently it has found a favorable new habitat: the cooling towers of air-conditioning systems.

A special set of circumstances—a large group of older individuals congregating in air-conditioned hotel suites in muggy summer weather—led to the identification of this particular pneumonia-like sickness that is spread by water droplets. Scattered deaths following illness with similar symptoms previously had been reported worldwide, but never in such concentration that they were attributed to a particular "new" cause.

Recently, a potentially more threatening disease has come under intensive investigation by public health agencies. By some standards, acquired immune deficiency syndrome (AIDS) has reached epidemic proportions. Approximately 75 percent of those cases originally diagnosed as AIDS have resulted in death. This disease results from a mysteriously crippled immune system. A common discrepancy seems to be the greater activity of certain T cells known as suppressors. These cells inhibit antibody formation and thus seriously reduce resistance to a number of otherwise rare ailments.

The first indication of illness is months of flu-type symptoms. A patient eventually may succumb to one of a number of ravaging diseases, but most victims die of an uncommon cancer of the skin and internal organs. Researchers tend to believe that no one can survive AIDS.

AIDS was first recognized in young male homosexuals and for a brief time was thought to be limited to them. But soon the syndrome was identified in others: users of intravenously injected drugs and their sex partners, for example, as well as Haitians, hemophiliacs, and some children. The disease appears to be transmitted primarily by sexual contact, because both male and female sex partners of men with AIDS have contracted the disease. Involvement of drug users and hemophiliacs, who regularly receive transfusions of pooled blood products, points to an infectious agent carried in the blood. However, no causative agent has been isolated at this writing. Also, whether or not everyone is equally susceptible to AIDS is an unanswered question.

blood cells, eventually killing them. In the meantime, the wandering phagocytes have spread the infection to a new location.

Certain bacterial strains protect themselves by secreting the enzyme **coagulase.** This enzyme clots blood plasma that leaks out of injured capillaries. Even if the bacteria themselves are not the cause of the injury, a clot forms around them. Thus the bacteria are walled off and protected from meandering phagocytes. Other microorganisms defend themselves by secreting **leukocidins,** substances that kill white blood cells on contact.

Many pathogens secrete **spreading factors,** enzymes that cause tissue damage and thereby aid in the spread of an infection. **Collagenase,** one such substance, digests the collagen fibers of connective tissue. A number of pathogens secrete **hyaluronidase,** which breaks down hyaluronic acid, a polysaccharide that binds connective tissue together.

Spreading factors are not limited to microbial pathogens. Some snake venom contains hyaluronidase. Because hyaluronidase disrupts tissue structure, the venom can penetrate more deeply into the body.

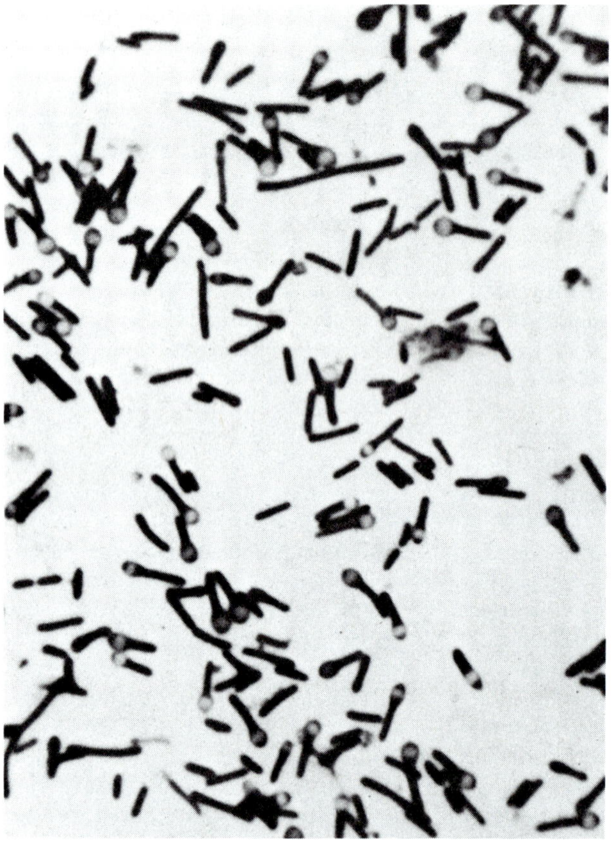

FIGURE 10.15 ***Clostridium tetani*, a Dangerous Endospore Former.** An indication of the resistance of bacterial endospores to damage can be seen in this photograph of *Clostridium tetani,* the causative agent of tetanus, also known as lockjaw. The mother cell quickly takes up the color of biological stains, but the swollen endospore resists coloration and remains clear.

Toxin Production

A number of disease-causing microorganisms produce dangerous **toxins** that cause chemical injury to particular cells and tissues. Diphtheria, tetanus, gas gangrene, food poisoning, whooping cough, cholera, and scarlet fever all involve bacteria that produce toxins.

Members of the genus *Clostridium* produce the most potent toxins. Most of these organisms are strict anaerobes; that is, they can grow and multiply only in the absence of oxygen. When conditions are unfavorable, clostridia enter a dormant state by forming thick-walled endospores (Fig. 10.15). These endospores are resistant to high temperatures, disinfectants, and other factors that would kill ordinary cells. These three characteristics—toxin production, anaerobic metabolism, and endospore production—make a deadly combination.

A Deadly Pain in the Neck. *Clostridium tetani* causes **tetanus**. An organism of decay, like all the other clostridia, it is abundant in many soils.

Because oxygen prevents the growth of clostridia, these organisms cannot multiply in healthy tissue, where there is always a good oxygen supply. However, damaged tissues with interrupted blood flow make excellent conditions for clostridia. Thus when they are introduced into a deep or mangled wound, conditions are perfect for proliferation of the bacteria. Eventually the parasites secrete a toxin that diffuses out of the infected region and kills the entire organism.

The tetanus toxin is a **neurotoxin.** It exerts its effect within the central nervous system and causes spasmodic conflict between muscle groups. Because the muscles of the head and neck are often the first affected, the disease has come to be known as **lock-jaw.** Unless the victim receives tetanus antitoxin quickly, death comes from exhaustion and respiratory paralysis.

Wisdom dictates that tetanus be prevented, not treated. Anyone likely to contract it—and that includes almost everyone, but especially certain occupational groups, such as farmers and soldiers—should be immunized with the **toxoid** (an inactivated toxin). All dirty wounds must be cleaned out surgically to remove the dead tissue in which clostridia can multiply. At this time the physician often administers a booster shot of toxoid vaccine to stimulate rapid antibody production.

Poison in the Can. A fatal food poisoning results from another anaerobic spore-forming soil bacterium, *Clostridium botulinum*. Spores of this organism in improperly canned foods may germinate and thrive in the airtight jar or can. The toxin produced there can kill you by interfering with release of acetylcholine from neurons.□ A creeping paralysis 167
leads to failure of the respiratory muscles, and death.

To ensure a safe product, many foods should be canned with steam under pressure, the only practical way to guarantee the destruction of botulinum spores. Simple boiling will not kill the endospores. Although commercial canneries occasionally fail to maintain proper controls and market products that lead to outbreaks of botulism, home-canned foods are more likely to be inadequately processed. Foods canned in heavy sugar syrups and those that are acid, such as tomatoes, are not conducive to the growth of *C. botulinum*. All others should be canned in a pressure cooker, which produces the high temperatures (121°C) that can kill endospores. The foods most likely to harbor botulism toxin are meats and such vegetables as beans, corn, peas, spinach, asparagus, and mushrooms.

Botulism toxin imparts no strange flavor to food. Although the presence of gas bubbles in a food jar or the bulging of the cap due to gas pressure indicates spoilage, these conditions are not always present, even though the food is contaminated. Boiling food for 15 minutes will inactivate the toxin, but unfortunately canned foods are frequently eaten without being boiled that long.

Picnics for Bacteria. The diarrhea and vomiting of common, nonfatal **food poisoning** is usually due to a toxin from *Staphylococcus aureus*. This spherical bacterium is frequently found in the nose and throat of healthy individuals, as well as in pimples, boils, and abscesses. Food can easily become contaminated with "staph" if people who handle food do not maintain strict hygienic standards. This toxin has its primary effect on cells lining the digestive tract and is most likely to form in foods rich in starch or protein. Potato salad, ham, and desserts with cream fillings are frequently involved in this type of poisoning. Outbreaks commonly occur after picnics, community suppers, and other gatherings at which prepared foods are held for hours without refrigeration.

Just as staphylococci can have a picnic in your potato salad, so they can in your body. A cut or splinter may introduce these bacteria and start an infection. Once through the skin, staphylococci can be highly invasive. Like many other pathogens, "staph" produce an array of enzymatic secretions that help them expand their beachhead. Some highly invasive strains secrete collagenase, leukocidin, and hyaluronidase (Fig. 10.16).

Allergies of Infection

Not infrequently, the symptoms of an infectious disease can be traced to allergies induced by the pathogen. Apparently, humans are as sensitive to the antigenic components of some parasites as they are to poison ivy. Slow-growing pathogens are most likely to stimulate an allergic reaction in their host. Symptoms of many fungal and protozoal infections, of parasitic-worm infestations, and of such

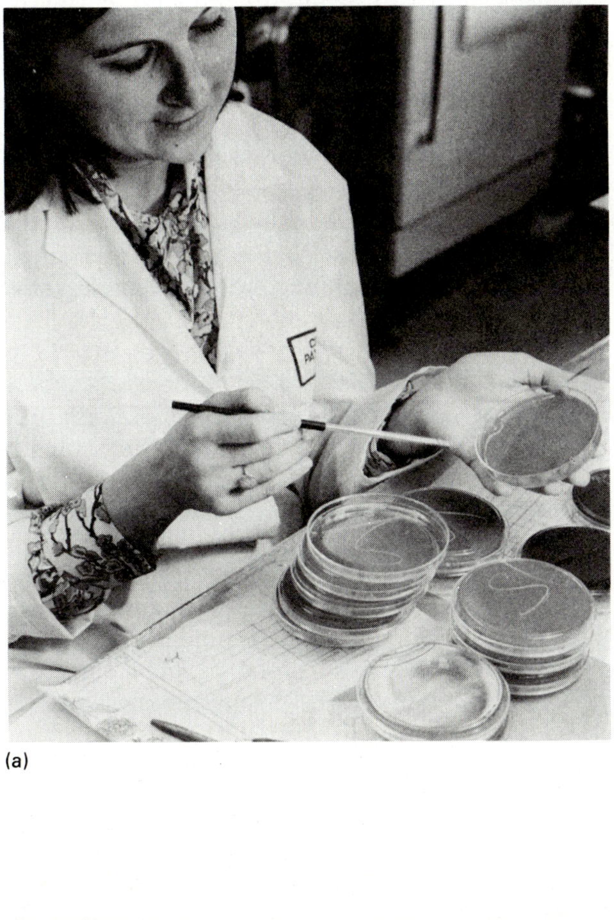

(a)

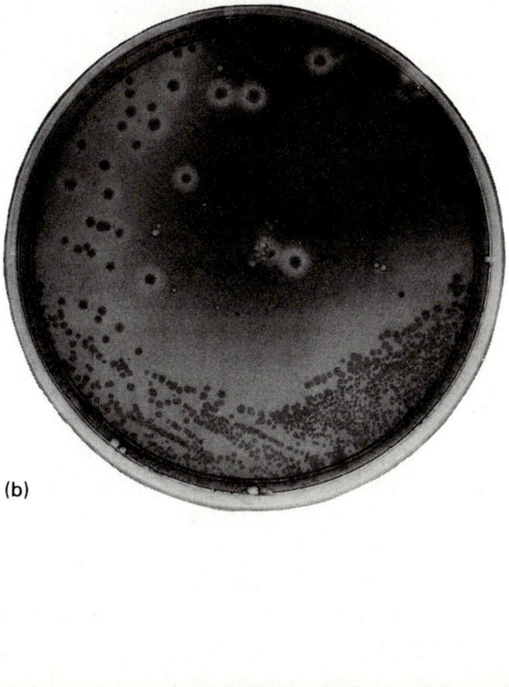

(b)

FIGURE 10.16 **Testing for Virulence.** (a) A bacterial sample is streaked across the surface of a culture medium containing whole blood. The culture is then incubated to allow development of colonies of bacteria. (b) The colonies of *Staphylococcus aureus* growing on the blood-containing culture medium are surrounded by a clear zone that indicates destruction of red blood cells. Such hemolysis is one evidence of virulence.

diseases as leprosy, syphilis, and tuberculosis can be at least partially attributed to an allergic reaction to the infectious agent.

The **tuberculin test** is a diagnostic test that relies on the allergy of infection associated with TB. Small amounts of tuberculin, an antigenic extract of the tuberculosis bacillus, are injected into the skin. Inflammation of the treated area in 48 hours indicates hypersensitivity to tuberculin and usually means that a person has TB or has been exposed to it.

Inflammation Can Be Harmful

Just as immune responses such as allergies can result in disease, inflammation can impair functions of the host. Bacterial pneumonia is a case in point. *Streptococcus pneumoniae,* the causative agent, has very little direct effect on humans, but it stimulates a tremendous inflammatory reaction. During the course of this "host defense mechanism," large amounts of fluid pour out of inflamed cells in the lungs. As the alveoli fill with fluid, respiratory function becomes seriously impaired. Symptoms of other diseases can similarly be traced to the effects of inflammation.

ROUTES AND SOURCES OF INFECTION

Many otherwise harmless microbes can cause disease if artificially injected into the body. Such organisms do not ordinarily cause disease, because they cannot be transmitted naturally. For a disease to become widespread, there must be a means through which the offending organism can escape from one host and enter the body of another.

Escape routes are normally associated with the site of infection. For example, intestinal pathogens are likely to be shed in the feces. Respiratory infections can be spread by droplets discharged into the air. Saliva, mucus secretions, pus, and urine are avenues of escape for other parasites. Pathogens that inhabit the bloodstream are often found to be transmitted by blood-sucking insects.

Some pathogens cause disease only when they enter the body through a specific route. The proper portal of entry depends on which host tissues are susceptible to that organism. Thus pathogens that cause respiratory or urogenital disease usually must gain access through related body openings.

The time between escape and entry is often critical to transmission. Pathogens that are especially sensitive to environmental extremes or that can multiply only within the human body are usually spread by physical contact between people. Less sensitive pathogens can be transmitted by less direct routes. Sneezing and coughing are examples. In some cases, objects or food handled by infected individuals become contaminated. The infectious agent may then be transmitted to persons who later use the items (Fig. 10.17).

Direct Contact: From One to Another

Many diseases spread either only (or largely) through direct contact. Respiratory infections like the common cold are good examples. So are venereal diseases. Agents transmitted by contact do well in large host populations, where chances are good for continuous spread from one nonimmune individual to another. Control of contact diseases in a world such as ours requires either rigid limitations on human-to-human contact or use of immunization.

The Little Pox. Smallpox virus particles introduced into the air by an infected individual can invade the upper respiratory tract of another person. Once there, they multiply and enter lymphatic vessels. From lymphatics the viruses pass into the bloodstream, and they are then distributed to the remainder of the body.

During the initial period of viral multiplication, the human host suffers severe fever, headache, and prostration. These symptoms abate about the time viruses reach the skin. There a rash develops into pimple-like vesicles packed with new virus particles. As the patient gradually recovers, these vesicles form deep lesions that heal into permanent scars. Material oozing from skin and throat sores releases viruses that can infect other people.

Evolution of Smallpox. Smallpox is probably a relative newcomer to the human scene. Perhaps it has existed for less than 10,000 years. The virulence of smallpox argues that the relationship between this virus and its human host is a young one. Natural selection always favors both naturally resistant hosts and less virulent disease organisms. Given time, the host species evolves natural resistance, and the parasite evolves to become less virulent.

The absence of smallpox in pre-Columbian people of the New World is another piece of evidence that it is a new virus. Otherwise smallpox

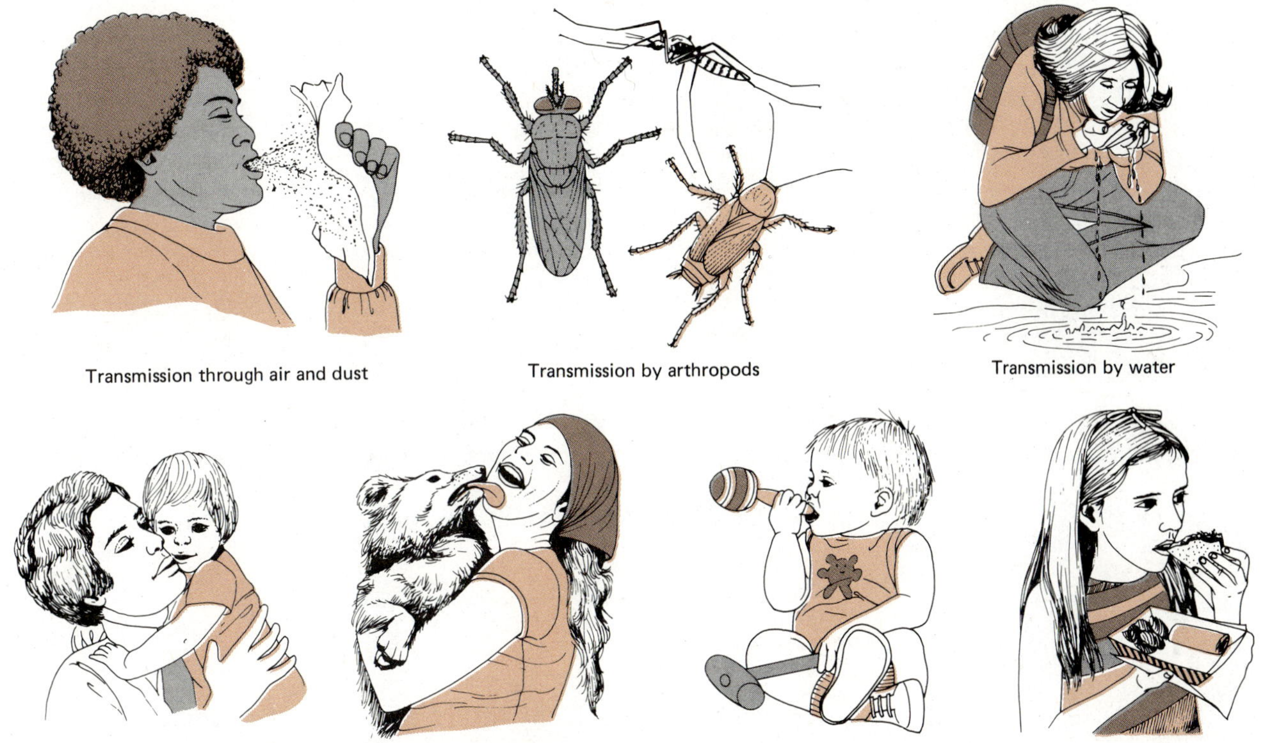

Transmission through air and dust — Transmission by arthropods — Transmission by water

Transmission by direct contact — Transmission of animal disease to human — Transmission by objects — Transmission by food

FIGURE 10.17 Mechanisms of Disease Transmission.

would have come with these people when they migrated from the Old World some 10 to 50 thousand years ago.

If smallpox is a recent disease, where did it come from? We can't be certain, but it seems likely that smallpox evolved from cowpox or some related disease of mammals. Cowpox infections, which are mild, leave humans who contract them from cows immune to smallpox. This antigenic similarity suggests a close relationship between the substances of the two viruses. Once human populations reached substantial size, a chance mutation of cowpox might have created a new virus with a new host and a new virulent way of life. Tradition suggests that smallpox originated in India. If so, the protection against smallpox given by cowpox infection might explain the veneration of cattle by the Hindus. Domestication of cattle in the Middle East some 9000 years ago is consistent with the appearance of smallpox there.

Eradication of Smallpox. The simplest approach to controlling a direct-contact disease such as smallpox is to immunize all susceptible hosts. Without such hosts the disease organism must soon disappear.

The present procedure for smallpox immunization dates to 1798, when an English physician, Edward Jenner, noticed that infection with cowpox results in a mild disease that produces immunity to smallpox. Intentional infection with cowpox to prevent smallpox came to be known as vaccination, because the Latin word for cow is *vacca*. Ordinary cowpox virus is no longer used in vaccination of humans. A harmless laboratory strain called *vaccinia* is employed instead.

Extensive vaccination has virtually eradicated smallpox from the earth. Therefore smallpox immunization, once required of children before they were admitted to school, is no longer necessary.

Smallpox is an example of an acute infection of relatively short duration. The patient soon recovers or dies. Other direct-contact diseases, like syphilis, are chronic conditions that can linger for years.

Syphilis: the Great Pox. Known as the great imitator, the silent killer, the disease of a thousand

BOX 10B

CHEMOTHERAPEUTIC AGENTS

Chemical substances used to treat disease are known as chemotherapeutic agents. They include laboratory creations, such as sulfa drugs, and antibiotics, which are of biological origin. Most antibiotics are microbial products.

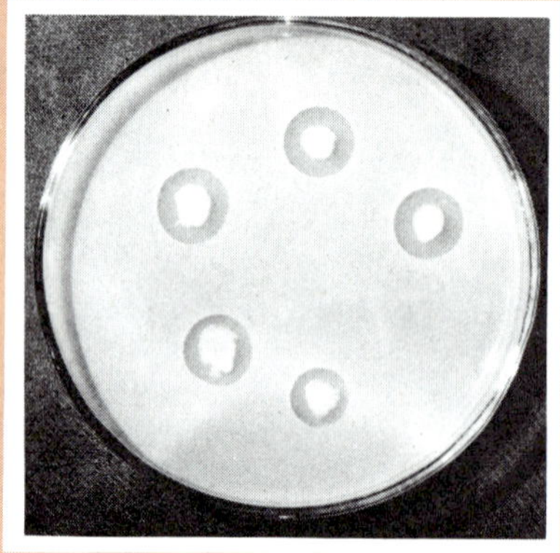

The ability of some microorganisms to produce antibiotics is detected in the following way. Pathogenic bacteria are spread evenly over the surface of a growth medium. Afterwards, strains of suspected antibiotic producers are dabbed on the surface of the medium at different places. The culture is then incubated, and the organisms are allowed to grow. The accompanying picture shows the result of such a test. The white growth that covers most of the medium is due to the pathogenic bacteria that were spread evenly over the surface. The clear rings show how the growth of these bacteria was prevented in the area around the spots where suspected antibiotic producers were dabbed. These microorganisms clearly produce and secrete an antibiotic.

To be medically useful, chemotherapeutic agents must be selectively toxic. That is, they must kill parasites without seriously affecting human cells. Or in the case of cancer, they must kill cancerous cells but not normal cells. Chemotherapeutic agents are generally metabolic poisons. Their selective toxicity depends on some special characteristics of the disease agent. For example, penicillin kills certain kinds of bacteria by interfering with cell-wall synthesis. Sensitive bacteria literally explode in the presence of penicillin. And since human cells do not have cell walls, there is no similar effect on human cells.

Because of the basic similarity in the metabolism of all cells, it is difficult to find compounds that affect one organism but not another. Thus chemotherapeutic agents vary tremendously in their selective action. For example, some can be used externally but not internally. Proper dosage is always important to prevent undesirable side effects. Some individuals develop allergies to chemotherapeutic agents. Even effectiveness is variable. An antibiotic may be toxic only to a single species of pathogens and harmless to others. Broad-spectrum antibiotics are those whose effectiveness covers a wide range of pathogens, but there are no cure-alls.

Because viruses have no metabolism, and, indeed, are not even cells, they are not affected by antibiotics. The millions of antibiotic prescriptions physicians have written for people with colds and other viral infections have been useless except when the antibiotics have deterred bacteria that would otherwise invade a body weakened by a viral infection.

A few antiviral drugs are now available with limited applicability. Although somewhat toxic, it is hoped that they are the first in a long line of medicinals that will bring virus diseases under control in the same way that antibiotics have brought many microbial diseases under control.

names, syphilis spreads only by direct contact. Because the syphilis bacterium is very sensitive to both cold and drying, its transmission results only from intimate physical contact, almost always a sexual contact.

Syphilis passes through three stages. At sometime between ten days and three months after the initial exposure, the first symptom appears. It is a painless white ulcer or **chancre** located wherever the organisms enter the body. The chancre is usually on the genitals but may be in the mouth, in the anus, or at any other place where there has been prolonged contact with the infectious sores of another. This primary lesion heals without treatment, and no further symptoms appear for perhaps two to six months. Then secondary lesions occur, either as a skin rash or as sores on mucous membranes. It is these eruptions that account for syphilis having been called "pox" or "the great pox." (*Pox* is merely an old name for any repulsive rash.)

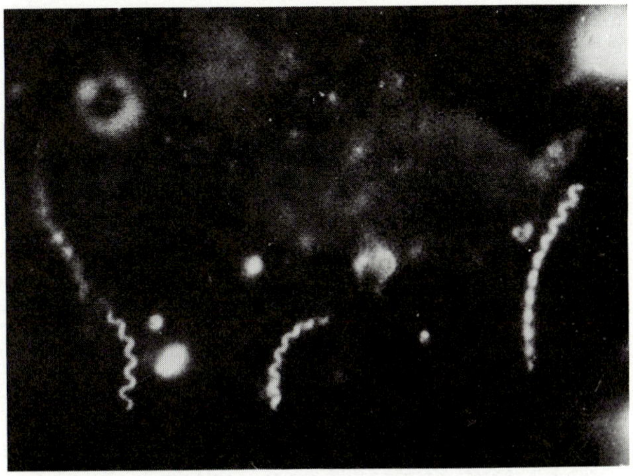

FIGURE 10.18 **Syphilis.** Clinical examination of primary and secondary syphilitic lesions reveals the corkscrewlike appearance of *Treponema pallidum,* the causative agent of syphilis.

Both primary and secondary lesions are full of spiral syphilis bacteria (Fig. 10.18). The disease is usually acquired by touching one of these sores. Secondary lesions also disappear spontaneously, but the organisms are now distributed throughout the body. Years later they may attack other organs, most often the brain, nerves, or blood vessels. Paralysis of any kind can occur. Sometimes the aorta balloons out at a weak spot and then suddenly ruptures. Such tragic deaths may happen 20 years or more after the initial infection. Once the secondary lesions heal, the infected individual is unlikely to transmit the disease to others. For some reason, more than two-thirds of those who are infected apparently recover spontaneously. They have no symptoms beyond the secondary lesions.

A simple course of penicillin injections will arrest syphilis at any time before the nervous system is involved. Later treatment is ineffective, because the antibiotic penetrates the central nervous system poorly. Circulating syphilis antibodies are easily detected. This detection is one purpose of the common "blood test" that many governments require before issuing a marriage license and as a part of the medical care of pregnant women. Most hospitals perform the test routinely on all patients admitted.

An unborn baby can acquire syphilis from its infected mother. **Congenital syphilis** often causes spontaneous abortions. If the baby survives, it may suffer serious abnormalities, including deafness and deformities of the nose or teeth. Infected mothers treated with antibiotics early in pregnancy avoid the risk of congenital syphilis in their children.

Although immunization may seem the obvious answer to permanent control of syphilis, it has not turned out to be. So far, the difficulty of culturing this delicate bacterium has hampered development of a vaccine. Where sexual contacts with more than one person are common, detection and treatment offer the only hope of control.

Gonorrhea. As the result of easy identification routine testing, and effective treatment, the incidence of syphilis is on the decline. In the past 20 years, however, there has been an alarming increase in another veneral disease, **gonorrhea,** sometimes called "clap." This infection is caused by small spherical bacteria known as gonococci (Fig. 10.19). Like the syphilis bacteria, they are extremely sensitive to cold and drying. Therefore gonorrhea is rarely acquired by any means other than direct sexual contact.

Gonorrhea can occur in the mouth or rectum, but it usually begins in the reproductive organs. In males, gonococci initially infect the urethra. In fe-

FIGURE 10.19 **Gonococci.** *Neisseria gonorrhoeae* cocci typically grow in pairs. These organisms are difficult to grow in the laboratory. Like *Staphylococcus aureus,* they prefer to grow on media enriched with blood.

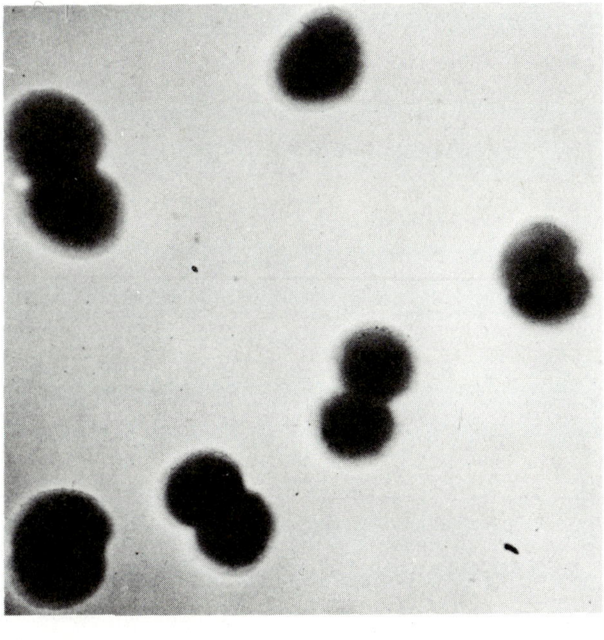

males, not only the urethra but often the vagina and cervix are involved. Gonococci stimulate an inflammatory response that produces a thick, white discharge. Men almost always know that they have a problem, because they experience difficulty urinating and can easily see a urethral discharge. The mild symptoms most women experience permit many to go untreated. They become the unknowing "carriers" of the disease.

Penicillin is often used to treat gonorrhea. Unfortunately, the development of penicillin-resistant gonococcal strains has made it necessary to use ever-increasing dosages. If untreated, gonococcal infections can scar the reproductive passages and cause sterility. They may also spread to other body regions. Inflammation and scarring of the heart valves can lead to rheumatic heart disease. Or inflammation of the joints can produce a type of arthritis. The common gonococcus is no respecter of age. It can enter the eyes of babies as they are born. Because gonorrheal eye infections may cause blindness, silver nitrate or antibiotics are routinely applied to the eyes of all newborn infants.

Herpes and Other Venereal Diseases. A number of sexually transmitted diseases are more common in tropical than temperate regions. **Granuloma inguinale, lymphogranuloma venereum,** and **chancroid,** a mild infection that produces a local sore similar to the chancre of syphilis, are examples.

Genital herpes is now a widespread disease in the United States. The causative agent is *Herpes simplex virus type 2*. It is related to the common cold-sore virus. The disease is characterized by infectious blisters that follow a painful rash on the skin or inner membranes of the vagina, penis, or anus. A first infection may be accompanied by fever and inflammation of the meninges of the brain and spinal cord. The disease may disappear after a few weeks, or it may enter a latent stage and reappear at times of stress or hormonal change.

Some virus diseases can be prevented by vaccines but few of them can be treated with antibiotics (see Box 10 B) or drugs. Limited success has been achieved in treating a number of other herpes infections with drugs, so there is some hope that genital herpes will eventually be treatable.

Some women carry *Trichomonas,* a protozoan that causes severe itching of the vagina and that may be transmitted to males. A common yeast is among the normal flora of the vagina, but some strains produce severe irritation. The yeast can be passed through sexual intercourse.

Diagnosis of infections of the reproductive organs is seldom simple. Special tests are necessary to rule out syphilis and gonorrhea. A sore, itching,

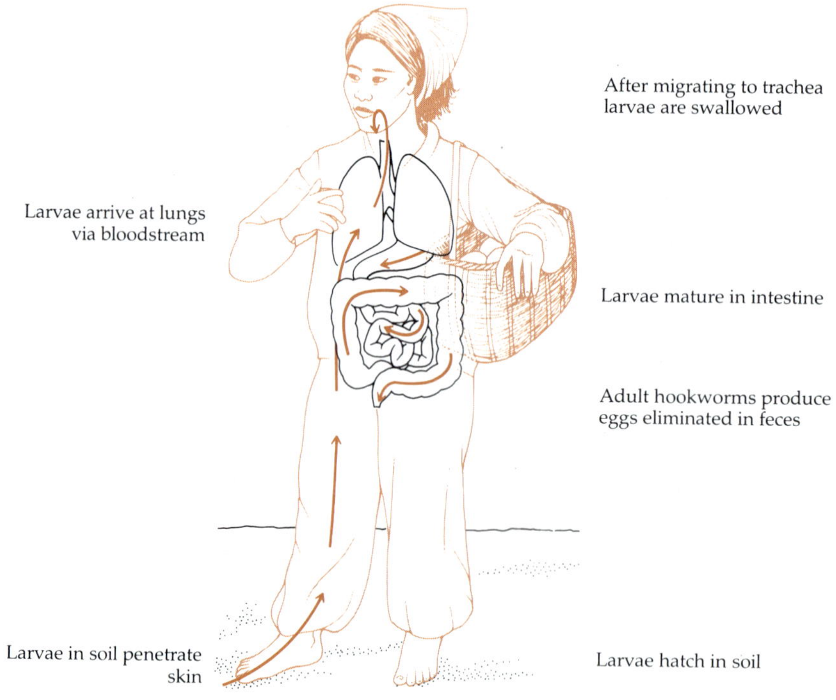

FIGURE 10.20 **Path of the Hookworm in the Body.** This disease is a special problem in those parts of the world where human feces are used as fertilizer.

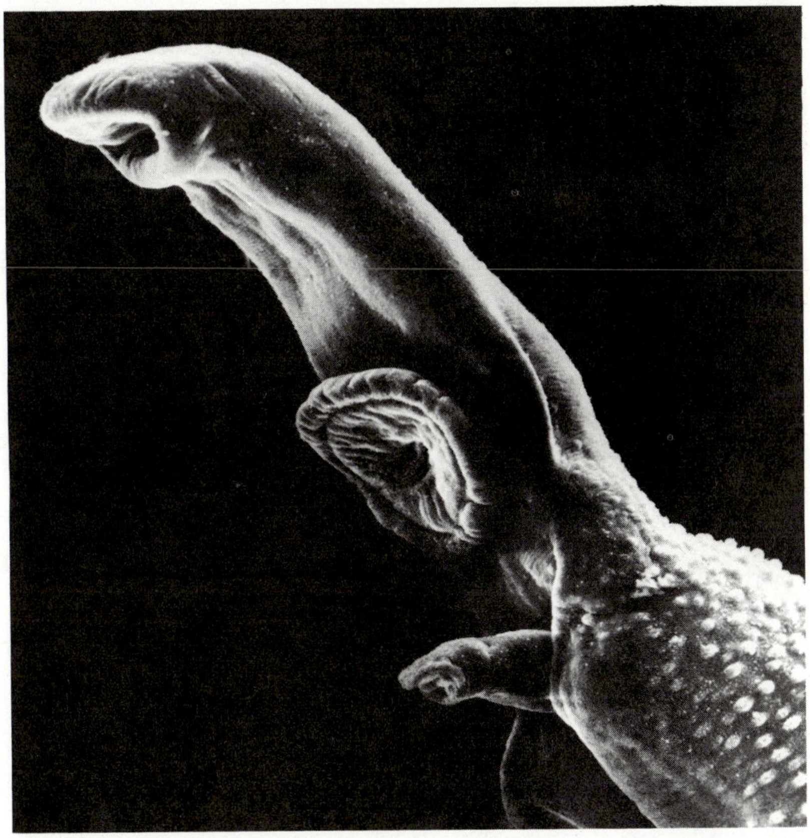

FIGURE 10.21 **A Blood Fluke.**

pain or unusual discharge associated with the reproductive organs is more than sufficient reason for consulting a physician.

Indirect Contact: Disease Caught from Objects

Many pathogenic organisms are never transmitted directly from person to person. Instead, they pass from one human to another through contaminated water, food, or soil. It seems—in principle, at least—that these diseases should be relatively easy to control, and sometimes they are. All that is necessary is to prevent the contamination of water, food, or soil. Yet this often proves to be a nearly unachievable goal.

Wearing Shoes Can Prevent Hookworm. Hookworm is acquired through contact with contaminated soil. The eggs are discharged in the feces of infected persons. Soon the eggs hatch into larvae, which can burrow into bare feet or through any other skin they may touch. The larvae enter blood or lymph vessels, and they are carried by the circulation to the lungs (Fig. 10.20). From there they migrate up the trachea, only to be swallowed down the esophagus. When they reach the intestine, the larvae mature and produce more eggs. Because infection usually occurs through the soles of the feet, one can prevent hookworm by wearing shoes. Simple though that solution seems, it often proves impractical advice for the poor. In any case, the total solution requires that everyone use sanitary sewage-disposal facilities.

Because hookworms ingest blood, humans suffering from the disease are severely anemic. It has been estimated that one-quarter of the world's population is infected with hookworm. The disease is still common in poorer regions of the southern United States.

Flukes and Snails. Blood flukes, or **schistosomes** (Fig. 10.21) also have a complex life cycle. The adult blood flukes live in the veins of either the intestine or the pelvis. The spiny eggs work their way from these veins into the inside of the intestine or bladder, and they are shed in the feces or urine (Fig. 10.22).

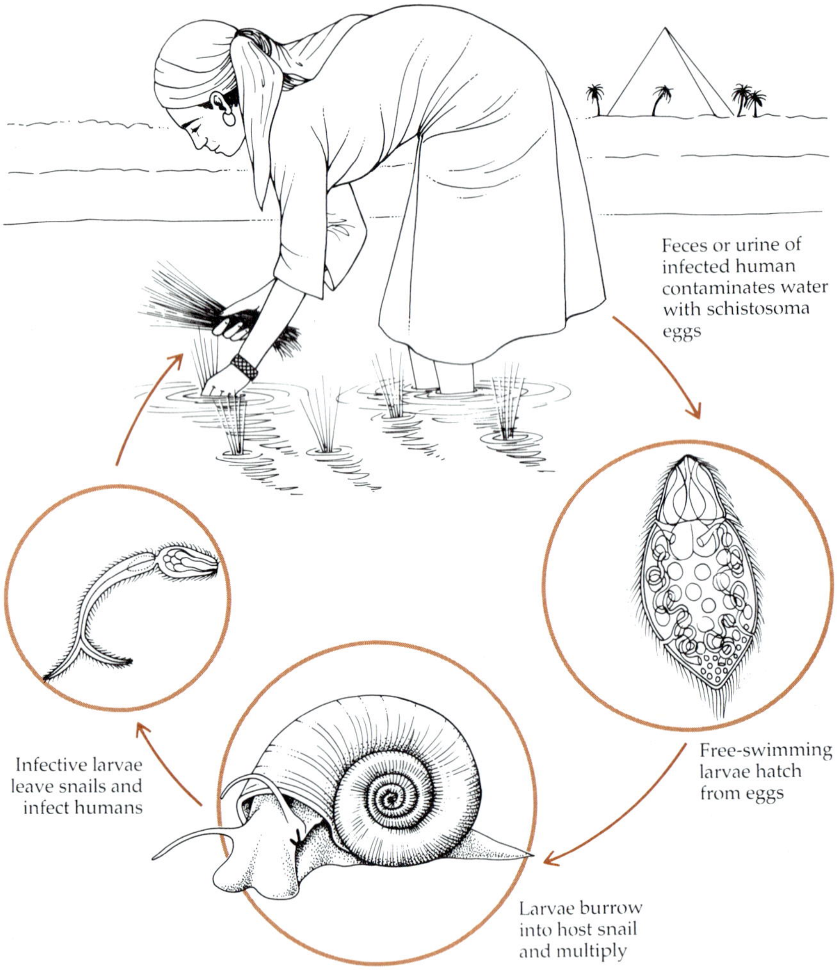

FIGURE 10.22 Schistosomiasis. Perpetuation of the blood flukes that cause schistosomiasis requires two hosts: humans and snails.

When contaminated excrement is diluted with water, the blood-fluke eggs hatch and ciliated larvae emerge. To survive, the larvae must immediately enter one of several species of freshwater snails. Once inside the snail, the larvae undergo two phases of asexual reproduction. One larva can produce as many as 200,000 offspring. These actively swimming, immature flukes leave the snail and within a few days must burrow into the skin of a suitable host, such as a human, or they will die. The juvenile flukes use hyaluronidase and other secretions to penetrate host tissues.

Inside humans, juvenile flukes enter the bloodstream, which carries them to the liver, where they mature. The adults migrate to other parts of the body. The symptoms of **schistosomiasis,** as a blood-fluke infection is called, follow damage to the liver by the adult flukes and injuries caused as the eggs penetrate the intestinal and bladder walls. Masses of eggs lodged in other organs, such as the brain, are walled off by body tissues. As a result distinct nodules form.

In almost all warm countries, people frequent snail-ridden waters for fishing, bathing, laundry, irrigation, and rice culture. Sewage is seldom treated, and workers often urinate or defecate directly into the water. The habitat is perfect for blood flukes. Around the world, perhaps as many as 200 million people are infested. The number increases with every new dam or fishpond. The necessary snails are ever-present. These species are **hermaphroditic** (functioning as both males and females) and can self-fertilize. Thus a single snail carried into a new pond can start a snail population there.

Elimination of schistosomiasis depends on breaking the life cycle of the blood fluke, because drugs that kill the flukes are neither safe nor reliable. It seems obvious that sanitary sewage disposal is the best control for these parasites. Unfortunately, uniform use of sanitary facilities is a difficult goal in overpopulated and underdeveloped countries. Attempts to break the life cycle of the blood fluke by destroying the snails have yet to prove successful. Chemicals that are toxic to snails cannot be used, because they are also harmful to other organisms.

Contaminated Water and Food. Typhoid fever develops from *Salmonella typhosa,* a bacterium sometimes found in food or water contaminated with human excrement. Upon entering the digestive system, the typhoid organisms multiply and invade the blood. After an incubation period of as long as three weeks, the infected person becomes ill from products released by dying bacteria. These substances cause tiny hemorrhages and blood clots. Although initial intestinal symptoms are few, later ulceration of lymphatic tissue in the intestinal wall produces severe discomfort. Bacteria are continuously eliminated in the feces and often in the urine. Hence sewage will be contaminated.

Because oysters and clams feed by straining microscopic particles from water, they can concentrate pathogenic bacteria such as salmonella that may be found there. The oyster or clam remains healthy, but woe to the human who favors raw seafood.

Bacterial dysentery, amoebic dysentery, cholera, and infectious hepatitis are other serious diseases transmitted by fecal contamination of food and water. Standard water treatment procedures destroy most of these pathogens. An exception is the virus that causes infectious hepatitis, a liver disease widely known as yellow jaundice. ▫ 147

Making Water Fit to Drink. Water purification plants ensure that drinking water is free from harmful microorganisms, as well as undesirable or poisonous chemicals (Fig. 10.23). The major operations of such plants are sedimentation, filtration, and chlorination. Sedimentation is carried out in large reservoirs where large particles settle out. Chemicals such as alum (aluminum sulfate) may be added to cause coagulation of the finer contaminating particles. Most microorganisms are removed from the liquid by filtration through sand filters. Finally, the water is disinfected by addition of chlorine. Special techniques are usually needed to remove chemical pollutants.

Laboratory analysis to determine whether or not water is potable (safe to drink) or suitable for recreational use centers on identification of nonpathogenic fecal microorganisms, particularly *Escherichia coli,* in water samples. Although these bacteria themselves do not cause disease their prevalence in feces makes them a valuable detection device. The presumption is that if any fecal microbes are present in water, pathogens may also be present; thus the water is considered unsafe.

Arthropod-borne Diseases: Vectors and Victims

Many devastating diseases pass from one person to another in or on the body of another animal.

FIGURE 10.23 Steps in Water Treatment.

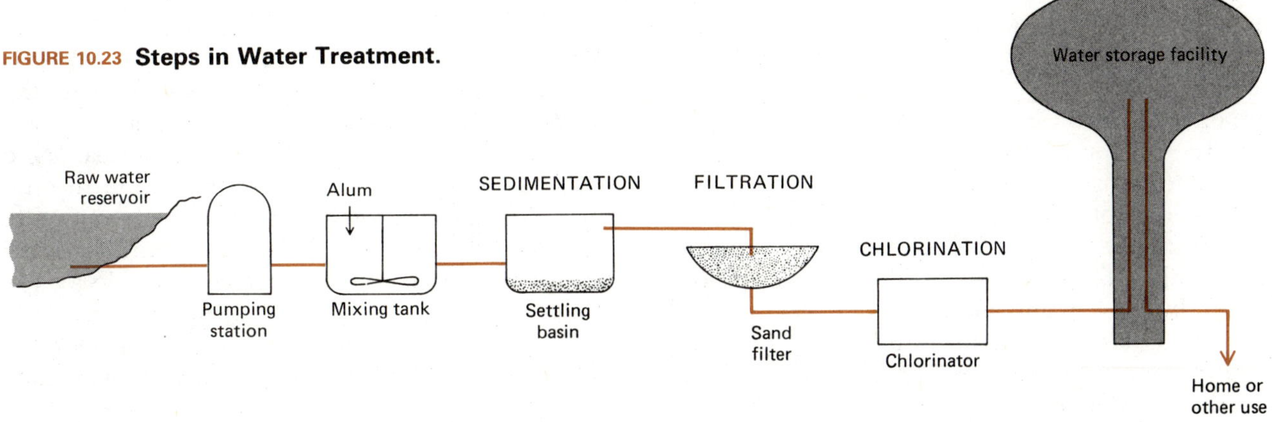

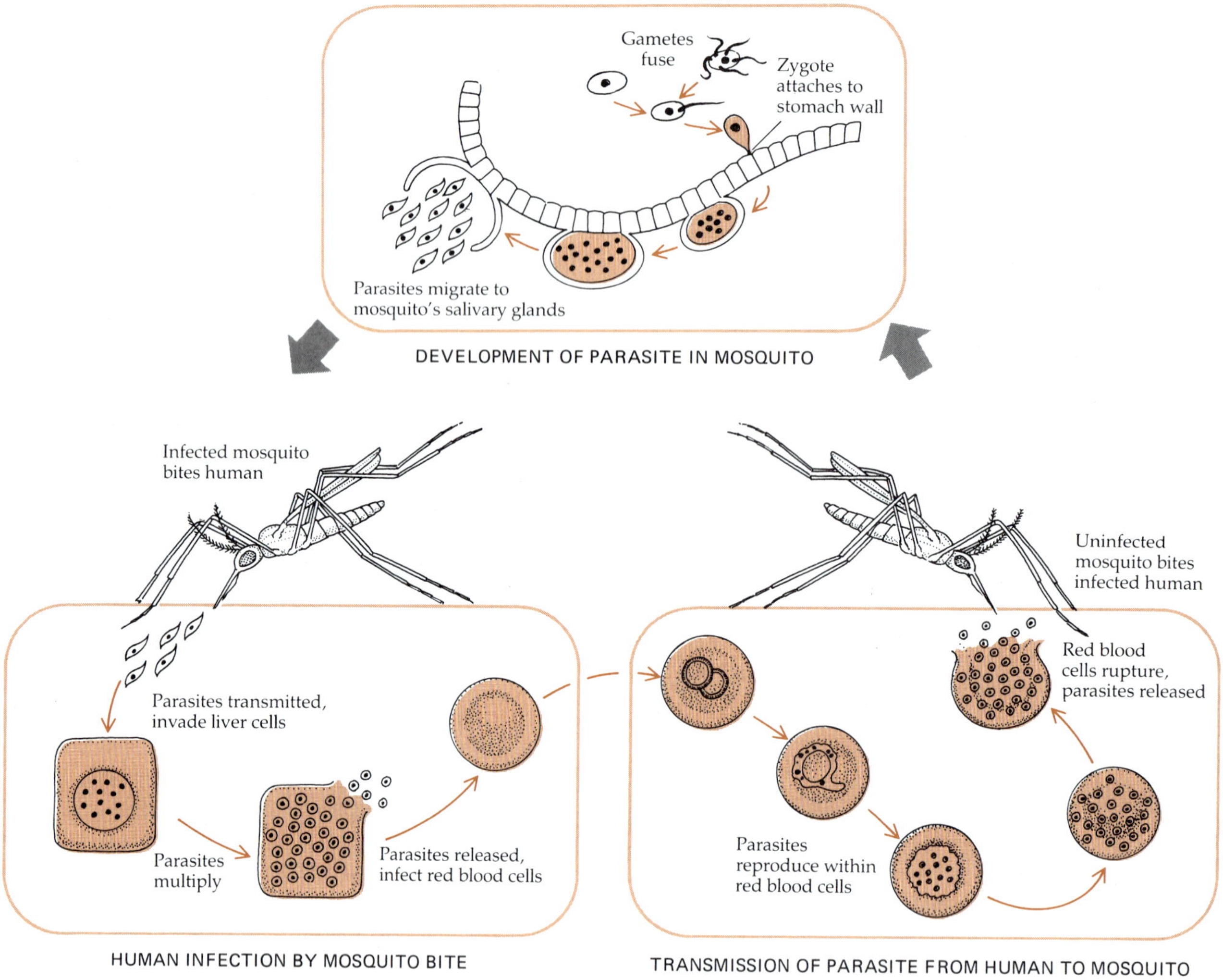

FIGURE 10.24 **How Malaria Is Transmitted.**

Most of these disease transmitters—or **vectors,** as they are called—are insects: lice, fleas, flies, and mosquitoes. A few are ticks and mites. All the pests named are **arthropods,** members of the great horde of species with tough outer skeletons and jointed appendages (see Chapter 16).

The habits of each arthropod vector affect its ability to transmit disease and sometimes provide a means of control of the vector. In mosquitoes, it is the practice of taking blood from another animal that makes them vectors. Although mosquitoes generally suck plant juices, the females of most species require a blood meal to provide sufficient protein for egg production. The fact that eggs must hatch in water often explains the distribution of mosquitoes and can provide a method for limiting these vectors.

Malaria. The protozoan responsible for malaria is an intracellular parasite. Once inside a human, the malarial organisms invade the liver cells and undergo repeated divisions that produce new protozoa. These enter red blood cells, multiply there, and rupture the cells. Released protozoa then infect even more red blood cells. The flood of parasites and materials from damaged blood cells are responsible for the chills and fever characteristic of malaria.

A few of the parasites in the blood develop the potential for sexual reproduction. However, they can mate only in the stomach of an *Anopheles* mosquito. If male and female protozoa are taken up by this insect as it feeds on blood, the protozoa fuse in the mosquito's gut and form a cyst. Repeated cell divisions within the cyst produce thousands of new protozoa. The cyst eventually ruptures, and the protozoa migrate to the mosquito's salivary gland. There they are in position to start a new infection when the mosquito takes its next blood meal (Fig. 10.24).

Malaria is a chronic disease that rarely kills immediately but is devastating nonetheless. There may be not only recurrent bouts of chills and fever but also complications including anemia, convulsions, heart disease, coma, and damage to the liver and spleen.

Breaking the Malaria Cycle. Control of malaria depends either on eradication of the disease by curing all infected humans or on destruction of all vectors. Neither approach has been entirely successful.

Long before the cause of malaria was recognized, quinine water, or "tonic," was used to relieve the symptoms. Today several more effective antimalarial drugs are available. But even these may not destroy the parasites hidden within the liver; relapses occur frequently. For this reason people known to have had malaria are unacceptable as blood donors.

Some antimalarial drugs can be used as **prophylactics,** that is, as agents that prevent the establishment of any parasites entering the body. But control through prophylactics requires that everyone take the drug regularly. The vast number of people that this would involve makes total compliance unlikely.

Insecticides have proved disappointing. Although DDT once promised to eliminate the *Anopheles* mosquito, insects in many areas are now resistant. The selection of resistant insects is a bit of human-induced evolution, which we will explore in later chapters. For now it is sufficient to note that spray programs are more likely to *alter* mosquito populations than to destroy them.

93 **Arboviruses.** So many viruses are transmitted by insect or tick vectors that the term *arbovirus* (meaning arthropod-borne) is used to designate them as a special group. Best known and historically the most important is the yellow-fever virus.

Yellow fever is primarily a disease of monkeys in tropical forests. Usually humans become infected when bitten by *Aedes aegypti,* a tropical mosquito that feeds on both monkeys and humans. During the eighteenth and nineteenth centuries, infected mosquitoes spread yellow fever from person to person in epidemics that plagued cities in the Caribbean and Central America. New Orleans, Philadelphia, Boston, and other northern cities also suffered epidemics when *A. aegypti* was introduced on ships. This insect favors human habitations and breeds readily in less water than would fill a teacup. It thrives in northern summers and multiplies until frost.

Extensive mosquito-eradication programs eventually eliminated yellow fever from cities in the New World, but the disease persists in tropical rain forests of South America and Africa. Yellow fever is still widespread in the tropics, but fortunately the fatality rate is low among people who live in these areas, and individuals who survive are permanently immune. Persons traveling to areas where yellow fever persists should be vaccinated, and every effort must be made to contain *A. aegypti.*

Other Plagues. The **black death,** or bubonic plague, is another disease transmitted by insect bite. Rat fleas spread the plague bacteria from rat to rat as well as from rat to human. Considering the crowded, vermin-infested nature of medieval cities, it is easy to understand the plague epidemics during that time. In the fourteenth century, one-quarter of the people in Europe were killed by this disease. Before humans die of the plague, the bacteria produce a pneumonia, and the disease can then spread by direct contact.

Flea-borne typhus is another disease of rats and rat fleas that appears in rat-infested cities. A second form of typhus is spread by human lice. This disease appears only in places where humans are crowded tightly together and lack even rudimentary facilities for bathing or laundry. In concentration camps, cities under siege, and similar wartime situations, this louse-borne typhus is often the main cause of death.

Another arthropod-carried disease is trypanosomiasis, the **sleeping sickness** of Africa, which is spread by tsetse flies, and thus limited essentially to the moist forests and savannahs that harbor the tsetse. **Rocky Mountain spotted fever** is a tick-borne disease found throughout much of the United States.

The Lesson We've Learned

"An ounce of prevention is worth a pound of cure." Nowhere does that old saying hold truer than in regard to communicable and parasitic diseases. Although physicians have an arsenal of antibiotics and other chemicals that destroy pathogens, these treatments don't always work as intended. The few drug-resistant forms that may naturally exist in a population of pathogens would ordinarily have no advantage over drug-sensitive types and would therefore remain a small proportion of the total population. But when drug treatment kills off the sensitive types, the resistant forms multiply without restraint, since they have no competitors and are drug-resistant. Thus drug therapy encourages the "development" of resistant strains.

In many cases, pathogens are best controlled by interfering with transmission. Public sanitation breaks the cycle of such organisms as hookworms, blood flukes, and typhoid bacteria. Merely a reasonable degree of cleanliness can prevent louse-borne typhus epidemics. For mosquito-carried diseases like malaria and yellow fever, elimination of breeding sites is probably the best way to prevent transmission.

As is shown by the fact that we have a "normal" flora, microbial companionship is a natural part of human life. Since contact with other organisms is inevitable, our health depends on resistance to invaders. The general defenses of a strong body are important. So is specific immunity. Perhaps immunization programs that both protect the individual and deny parasites an opportunity to maintain themselves are the ultimate in techniques that stop transmission.

Summary

1. There is no single cause of disease. Parasitic diseases of humans result sometimes from infection by small animals but more frequently from infection by microorganisms. Most microbes do not cause disease, however. The majority of them are decomposers.

2. All healthy people have a well-developed normal flora of microorganisms that reside in or on the body. Unlike pathogens, normal flora microorganisms do not cause disease. They may even be beneficial.

3. General body defenses against attack by pathogens include the healthy, intact skin, cilia along respiratory passages, tears and other body secretions, phagocytosis, and inflammation. Such defenses are directed against almost any form of attack.

4. B cells and T cells are responsible for specific immune responses. Both kinds of lymphocytes are stimulated by the presence of specific antigens, usually foreign cells or cell products, such as toxins. B cells develop into antibody-secreting plasma cells, while T cells become activated and secrete molecules that stimulate phagocytosis and inflammation.

5. Immunity comes from having a disease, or it can be artificially stimulated by administration of vaccines. An antiserum provides preformed antibodies and thus only temporary protection from infection. Allergic reactions occur when usually innocuous substances stimulate B cell or T cell immune responses.

6. Although the virulence of an organism cannot usually be attributed to any single factor, pathogens can cause harm by competing for nutrients, killing phagocytes, secreting toxins, or stimulating allergic or inflammatory responses. The ability to produce spores as well as toxins is an especially deadly combination.

7. Diseases are commonly transmitted by direct contact, as with smallpox and venereal diseases; by indirect contact, usually through contaminated water, food, or soil; or by the bite of an anthropod vector that carries the disease agent.

8. Since antibiotics vary in effectiveness, and immunization procedures are available for only a limited number of diseases, interference with transmission is the most logical way to control many pathogens.

Thought and Controversy

1. Would it be easier to eradicate syphilis in populations where sexual promiscuity is condoned or where it is forbidden? Consider the reluctance to seek treatment for venereal disease in societies where promiscuity is condemned.

2. Does the role of wild species in disease transmission justify the intentional or casual extinction of any species by humans?

3. The red blood cells of RH-positive individuals contain certain proteins; those who are Rh-negative lack these proteins. Thus an individual who is Rh-negative may make antibodies to the Rh protein if there should be contact with it. Such contact may occur as the result of transfusion of the RH-negative individual with Rh-positive blood or by passage of blood cells from an Rh-positive fetus through the placenta into the tissues of an Rh-negative mother. Although the placenta is supposedly a complete barrier between the circulatory systems of mother and child, it is seldom perfect. After one or more pregnancies with Rh-positive fetuses, an Rh-negative mother has usually developed a significant amount of Rh antibody. This antibody can in turn diffuse across the placenta into the child, where it reacts with the child's blood cells, agglutinating and rupturing them. The hemoglobin loss renders the child anemic, and the accumulated hemoglobin breakdown products may reach sufficient levels of "jaundice" (the products are yellow) to cause brain damage. Such babies should be exchange-transfused as soon as possible to remove most of their blood with the offending maternal antibodies and replace it with normal blood of their own type. Why do such infants not produce anti-Rh antibodies themselves? It is now possible to prevent this condition by administering anti-Rh antibody (formed by using Rh antibody as an antigen) to the mother early in pregnancy. By what mechanism would such therapy work?

Questions

1. Describe the general defenses that a pathogen encounters when it first comes in contact with the body.

2. What is the role of phagocytes in inflammation?

3. Why are redness, heat, pain, and swelling seen in inflammation?

4. What are the differences between the immunity brought on by B cells and that brought on by T cells?

5. Define the following terms: *normal flora, pathogen, interferon, autoimmunity, vaccine.*

6. Distinguish between immunity caused by antibodies and immunity caused by killer lymphocytes.

7. Explain how spreading factors, toxins, allergies, and inflammation each contribute to the virulence of microorganisms.

8. Describe and give examples of the main ways in which infectious diseases are transmitted.

9. How can infectious diseases best be controlled?

10. List and explain the steps involved in water treatment, including those tests that determine its safety.

Further Reading for Part Two

Abraham, E.P., 1981. The beta-lactam antibiotics. *Scientific American* 244(6):76–86. (June)

Benditt, Earl P., 1977. The origin of arteriosclerosis. *Scientific American* 236(2):74–85. (February)

Bloom, Elliott D., and G.J. Feldman, 1982. Quarkonium. *Scientific American* 246(5):66–77. (May)

Creager, Joan G., 1983. *Human Anatomy and Physiology.* Wadsworth, Bellmont, California.

DeBakey, M., and A. Gotto., 1977. *The Living Heart.* McKay, New York.

Dickerson, Richard E., 1980. Cytochrome C and the evolution of energy metabolism. *Scientific American* 242(3):136–153. (March)

Fenton, M. Brock, and James H. Fallard, 1981. Moth hearing and feeding strategies in bats. *American Scientist* 69(3):266–275. (March)

Frieden, E., 1972. The chemical elements of life. *Scientific American 227*(1):52–64. (January)

Hanawalt, Philip C. (ed.), 1981. *Molecules to Living Cells: Readings from Scientific American.* Freeman, San Francisco.

Hinckle, Peter C., and Richard E. McCarty, 1978. How cells make ATP. *Scientific American* 238(3):104–123. (March)

Hubel, David H., and Thorsten N. Wiesel, 1979. Brain mechanisms of vision. *Scientific American* 241(3):150–162. (September)

Hudspeth, A.J., 1983. The hair cells of the inner ear. *Scientific American* 248(1):54–64. (January)

Iversen, Leslie L., 1979. The chemistry of the brain. *Scientific American* 241(3):134–149. (September)

Koffler, David, 1980. Systematic lupus erythematosus. *Scientific American* 243(1):52–61. (July)

Lambert, J.B., 1970. The shape of organic molecules. *Scientific American:* 222(1):58–70. (January)

Lehninger, Albert L., 1971. *Bioenergetics.* W.A. Benjamin, Menlo Park, CA.

Nauta, Walle J.H., and Michael Feirtag, 1979. The organization of the brain. *Scientific American* 241(3):88–111. (September)

Newman, Eric A., and Peter H. Hartline, 1982. The infrared "vision" of snakes. *Scientific American* 246(3):116–127. (March)

Nilsson, Lennart, *et al.*, 1973. *Behold Man: A Photographic Journey of Discovery Inside the Body.* Little, Brown, Boston.

Notkins, Abner Louis, 1980. The causes of diabetes. *Scientific American* 241(5):62–73. (November)

Rose, N.R., 1981. Autoimmune diseases. *Scientific American* 244(3):80–103. (February)

Schaumberg, Gene D., 1974. *Concerning Chemistry.* Wiley, New York.

Scrimshaw, Nevin S., and Lance Taylor, 1980. Food. *Scientific American* 243(3):78–88. (September)

Scrimshaw, Nevin S., and Vernon R. Young, 1976. The requirements of human nutrition. *Scientific American* 235(3):51–64. (September)

Shodell, Michael., 1983. The prostaglandin connection. *Science 83* 4(2):78–81. (March)

Stroud, Robert M., 1974. A family of protein-cutting proteins. *Scientific American* 231(1):74–88. (July)

Thomas, L., 1974. *Lives of a Cell: Notes of a Biology Watcher,* Viking Press, New York.

Vander, A.,J. Sherman, and D. Luciano, 1980. *Human Physiology: The Mechanisms of Body Function,* third ed. McGraw-Hill, New York.

West, Susan, 1983. One step behind a killer. *Science 83* 4(2):36–45. (March)

Wolfe, S., 1981. *Biology of the Cell,* second ed. Wadsworth, Bellmont, California.

Wurtman, Richard J., 1983. Nutrients that modify brain function. *Scientific American* 246(4):50–59. (April)

PART THREE

Future Living

Two characteristics beyond all others distinguish living organisms. First, they use energy to maintain a level of organization that is uncommon in the physical world. All the homeostatic mechanisms that we have discussed in earlier chapters are devoted to this end. Second, organisms reproduce themselves.

But reproduction ensures more than the continuation of the species. And sex is more than a drive to reproduce. The shuffling of genetic information that results from sexual reproduction is a major source of the variability that underlies evolutionary change. Reproduction is crucial to evolution in another way, too. Successful reproduction is all that counts in the struggle of natural selection. Organisms that successfully perpetuate themselves and their genetic patterns are the winners.

Thus when we look at reproduction and development, we should think of more than a fertilized egg that can give rise to organized tissues and functional organ systems. We should also remember that the whole organism must fit into its surroundings. The young that are best adapted to the existing environment are those most likely to survive long enough to leave more offspring. That is the crux of evolution.

So it is that the existence of life in the future, as well as the characteristics of that life, depend on several interacting processes. Their story awaits you in the following chapters.

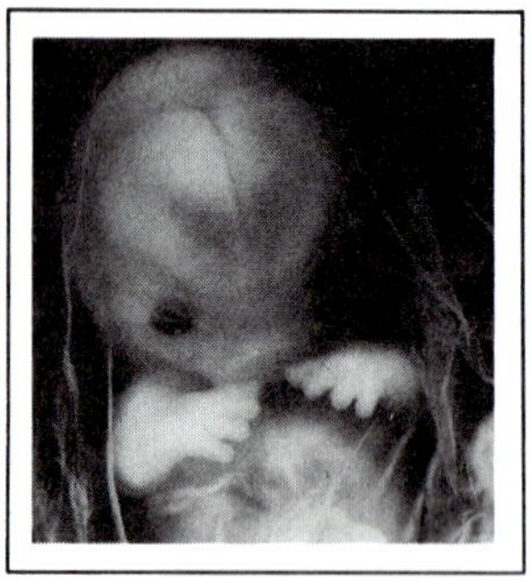

11

Genetic Legacies: From One Generation to Another

CHILDREN USUALLY RESEMBLE THEIR PARENTS. Nevertheless, there are always fascinating differences. Each of us is an extraordinary creature! Parental traits—not only physical features, but also characteristics of personality, temperament, and mental ability—appear in unique combinations in each child, along with other traits evident in neither mother nor father. These are not haphazard events. Hereditary traits appear, disappear, and reappear from generation to generation as the result of precise processes.

Biologists are still a long way from understanding all the laws that govern inheritance, but they have unraveled some of the fundamental rules and gained insight into a few of the underlying mechanisms. The focus of the present chapter is on human genetics and the processes that connect us with past generations, determine our present nature and capabilities, and establish our potential for future change.

THE CELLULAR BASIS OF HEREDITY

Because such physical characteristics as height, hair and eye color, and the shape of the nose are among the hereditary traits most obvious to us, we may fail to see that heredity is a property of cells. Perhaps the truth of this statement is more evident when you consider that we start life as a single cell—a fertilized egg produced by the union of an egg from our mother and a sperm from our father (Chapter 12). What we have become was determined in large part by the genetic legacy imparted to that fertilized egg.

A fertilized egg receives half its hereditary information from each of the sex cells that produced it. As it grows, the fertilized egg duplicates its genetic material so that when it divides, it produces new cells that are genetically identical. Of course, the millions and millions of cells that eventually make up the body come to differ from one another in many ways.

Variations among body cells can be attributed to numerous factors, including cell interactions that cause differential expression of hereditary traits. And, although cell division produces daughter cells that have the same genetic information, they may differ in subtle ways. For example, cells may differ in the amount of cytoplasm they receive.

Every newly formed cell must have not only a complete set of hereditary instructions, but also the machinery for interpreting those instructions. This includes mitochondria, ribosomes, and especially enzymes to catalyze metabolic processes. Production of these constituents is a major cell activity. Look at Fig. 11.1 and you will see that much of the **cell cycle** is devoted to duplication of genetic material. Note that only a relatively short time is required for actual cell division, or **mitosis.**

Mitosis

Mitosis is a form of cell division that guarantees that daughter cells are genetically identical to their mother cells. It involves four phases: prophase, metaphase, anaphase, and telophase. **Interphase** is that part of the cell cycle when mitosis is not occurring and during which a cell grows by synthesizing biological molecules.

Because interphase is the longest part of the cell cycle, most cells we observe microscopically are interphase cells. The nucleus of such "resting" (only in the sense that they are not dividing!) cells contains a dense nucleolus surrounded by a more diffuse material called **chromatin.** This material has a pronounced affinity for certain dyes, but it stains with varying degrees of intensity, giving the interphase nucleus a grainy appearance. The beginning of mitosis and the end of interphase is signaled by the condensation of chromatin into the thick, deep-staining threads that we call **chromosomes.**

Mitosis was first described in the nineteenth century, long before scientists understood the nature of heredity. But the fact that daughter cells receive exactly the same number and kind of chromosomes as the result of mitosis, was not lost on the early observers. Even then it seemed clear that chromosomes had something essential to do with heredity. Of course, we now know that the chromosomes carry genes, the units of heredity.

Prophase. In the first phase of mitosis (Fig. 11.2) the gradually thickening chromosomes can be seen to be already doubled. The two strands, or **chromatids,** of the doubled chromosome are genetically identical. Each pair of chromatids is held together at a constricted region called the **centromere.** Also during prophase, the nuclear membrane begins to disintegrate and the nucleolus usually disappears

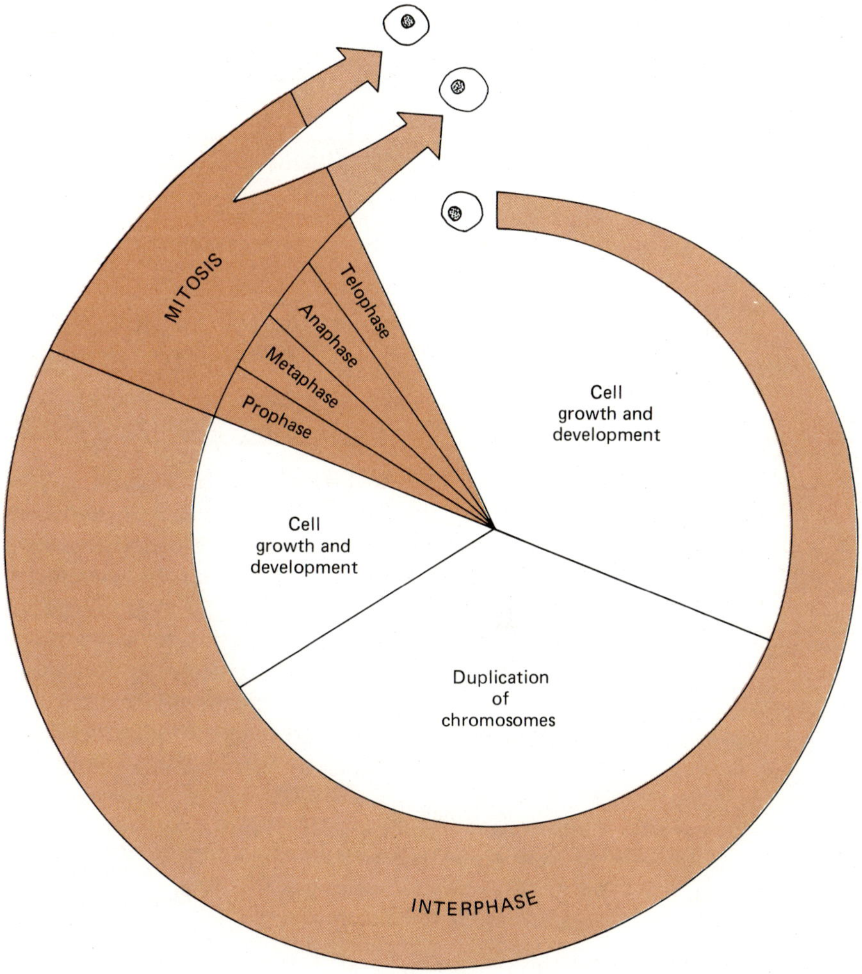

FIGURE 11.1 **The Cell Cycle.**

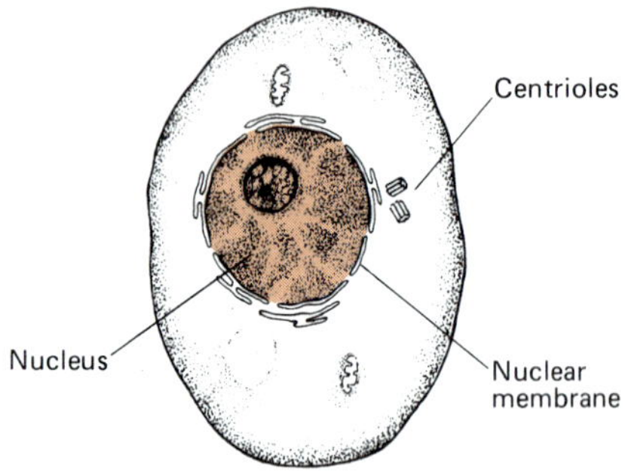

INTERPHASE

The interphase nucleus is easily recognized because no chromosomes are visible, although a dark body, the nucleolus, may be evident.

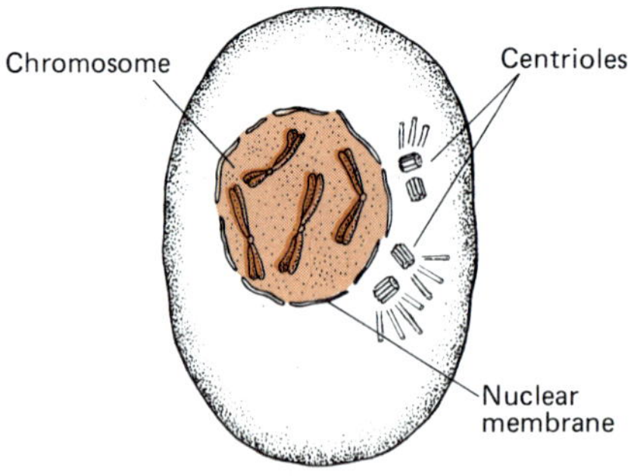

PROPHASE

At the onset of mitosis, the nuclear membrane disintegrates and the chromosomes begin to shorten and thicken. Toward the latter part of prophase each chromosome can be seen to consist of a pair of chromatids joined at the centromere. Spindle fibers begin to form as well.

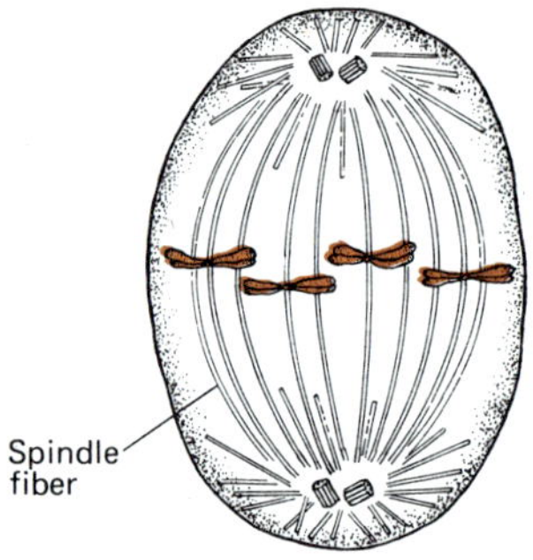

METAPHASE

The centromere of each chromosome is attached to a spindle fiber that extends from pole to pole. Each chromosome is drawn to the cell equator by its spindle fiber.

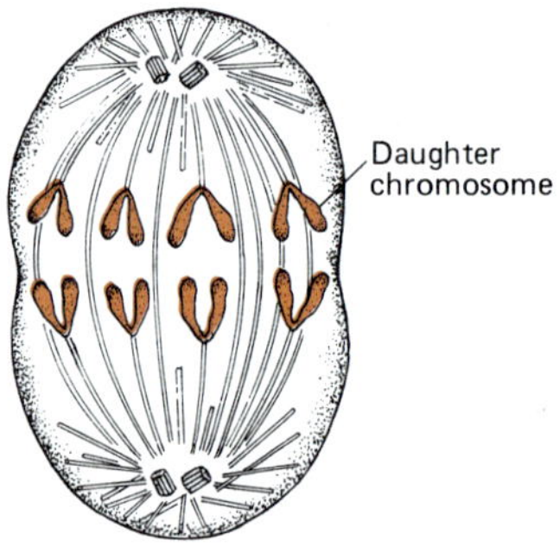

ANAPHASE

As the centromere of each chromosome splits, the daughter chromosomes move to opposite ends of the cell.

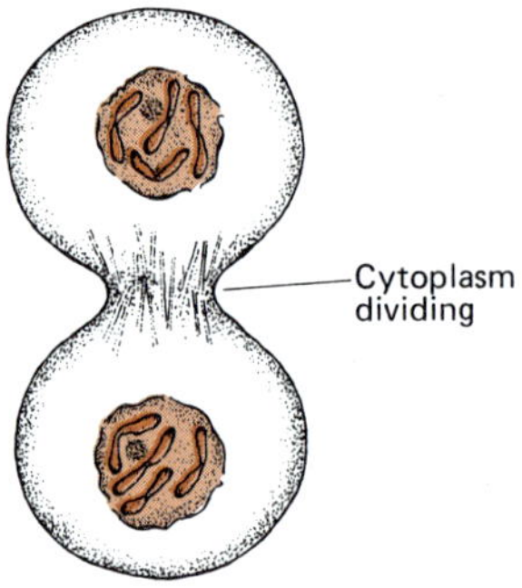

TELOPHASE

Once chromosomes arrive at opposite poles, they begin to become less distinct. About this time, also, a new nuclear membrane is formed and the cytoplasm begins to divide.

FIGURE 11.2 **Mitosis.**

as well. At about the same time, the **mitotic spin**
81 **dle,** composed of long microtubules,□ develops between two pairs of centrioles located opposite one another. Each centromere of the doubled chromosomes is attached to a spindle microtubule. The spindle "fibers" are involved in the movement of chromosomes. As prophase comes to a close, the doubled chromosomes have begun to move toward the middle of the mitotic spindle and line up at right angles to the long axis of the spindle.

Metaphase. When the chromosomes have arrived at the equatorial plane, the cell is clearly in metaphase. Metaphase is very short, lasting only a few minutes at most. At the end of metaphase, the centromeres split so that each chromatid has one.

Anaphase. The start of anaphase is evidenced by the separation of the chromosomes. Pair members move in opposite directions away from the midline of the cell. At this time each chromatid can correctly be called a chromosome. From electron micrographs (Fig. 11.3) we conclude that the attachment of spindle fiber to chromosome is essential to its movement. Although the mechanism is not known, the spindle fiber seems to be pulling the centromere with the chromosome arms trailing behind.

Telophase. Anaphase is completed when the chromosomes arrive at opposite poles. Almost immediately they begin to fade from sight, resuming their interphase condition. During this time the nuclear membrane and nucleolus are restored. Meanwhile, a ring of tiny fibrils forms just under the plasma membrane at the equator of the cell. The fibrils contract, and gradually the cytoplasm is pinched into two parts. Thus two new cells, each with a nucleus identical to that of the parent cell, are produced.

Mitosis follows the same basic pattern in all
91 eucaryotes, although division of the cytoplasm and a few other details vary, especially among plants. Note that the division of the cytoplasm is simply a separation into two parts with no provision for the contents of the parts to be equal. Some cytoplasmic structures, such as mitochondria, can duplicate themselves or be made from other cytoplasmic structures. Thus their number may be adjusted to meet needs of the cell. As we have already suggested, in many cases an unequal division of the cytoplasm is the first step in the process of cell *differentiation* (formation of different kinds of cells).

Chromosomes Are Paired

As we study mitosis, two features of chromosomes become evident. First, every organism has a characteristic number of chromosomes in its cells. Human body cells generally contain 46 chromosomes. Second, when such characteristics as length and centromere placement are compared, chromo-

FIGURE 11.3 Anaphase Chromosome Attached to Spindle Fibers.

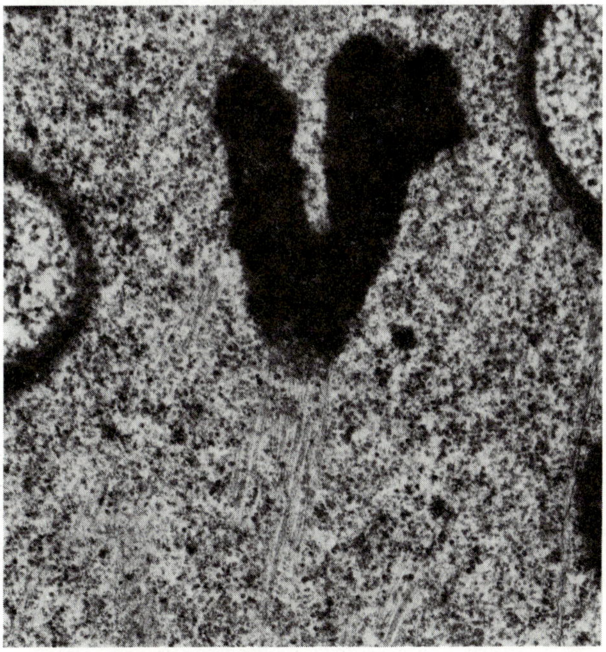

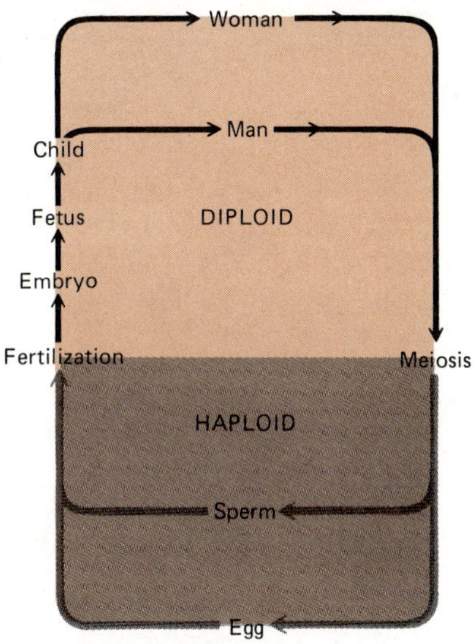

FIGURE 11.4 The Human Life Cycle. The only haploid human cells are gametes produced by meiosis. All other human cells arise from mitosis and are diploid.

somes appear to be paired. Human body cells, like those of other animals, are **diploid;** that is, they contain two of each kind of chromosome. Thus the 46 human chromosomes are divided into 23 pairs. The chromosomes of a pair are **homologous,** meaning they are not only physically similar, but also similar in genetic content. One chromosome of each pair is inherited from the mother; the other is inherited from the father.

Meiosis and Sexual Reproduction

Mitosis assures that daughter cells receive the same number of chromosomes as their mother cell. The only body cells that are not produced this way are eggs and sperm. The sex cells cannot have a diploid number of chromosomes; if they did, their union would yield a fertilized egg with *four* copies of every chromosome. Each egg and each sperm contains a **haploid** number of chromosomes—that is, one-half the number of chromosomes found in ordinary body cells, or 23.

The halving of the chromosome number, an essential step in the production of human sex cells, involves a unique type of division termed **meiosis.** The behavior of chromosomes during meiosis determines the pattern of inheritance of genes on these chromosomes. Therefore an understanding of meiosis is basic to the study of inheritance. Figure 11.4 shows the role of meiosis and fertilization in

FIGURE 11.5 **Meiosis.**

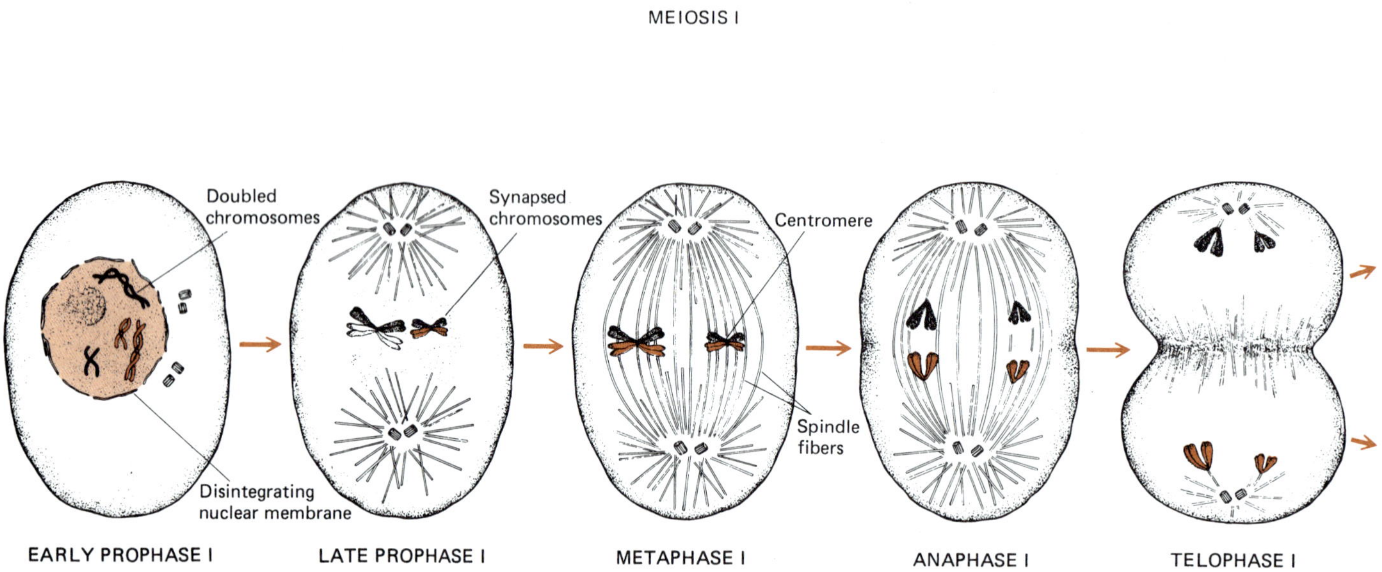

In early prophase the chromosomes first appear and can soon be seen to be doubled except at the centromere (each half of a doubled chromosome is termed a chromatid.) As the chromosomes appear, the nuclear membrane begins to disintegrate and the centrioles of animal cells duplicate so that there are two pairs. Soon microtubules begin to form the spindle fibers. In late prophase I, homologous chromosomes move together in synapsis. Note that each pair consists of four chromatids.

In metaphase I the centromeres of the synapsed chromosomes attach to spindle fibers independently.

The members of a pair separate in anaphase I with one of each pair moving to each pole.

Meiosis I ends as the cytoplasm divides in telophase I.

the human life cycle. Because the significance of meiosis lies in the separation of the two chromosomes of a homologous pair, we must be able to distinguish between the chromosomes of a pair. The one fundamental difference is based on their origin. Therefore we name one member of a pair the *maternal* chromosome and the other the *paternal* chromosome. Of course, both chromosomes are present in the diploid cells of an organism, whether that organism is male or female. Thus spermatogenesis (sperm formation) in men involves both maternal and paternal chromosomes; so does oogenesis (egg formation) in women.

Each meiotic process requires two cell divisions. A single cell entering meiosis divides, and then the daughter cells divide again. These two divisions are quite different from each other; only together do they constitute the complete process of meiosis. Therefore we speak of meiosis I and meiosis II.

Meiosis I

Prophase I. The cytoplasmic events during prophase I resemble those in mitosis; the nuclear membrane disappears, and the centrioles organize a

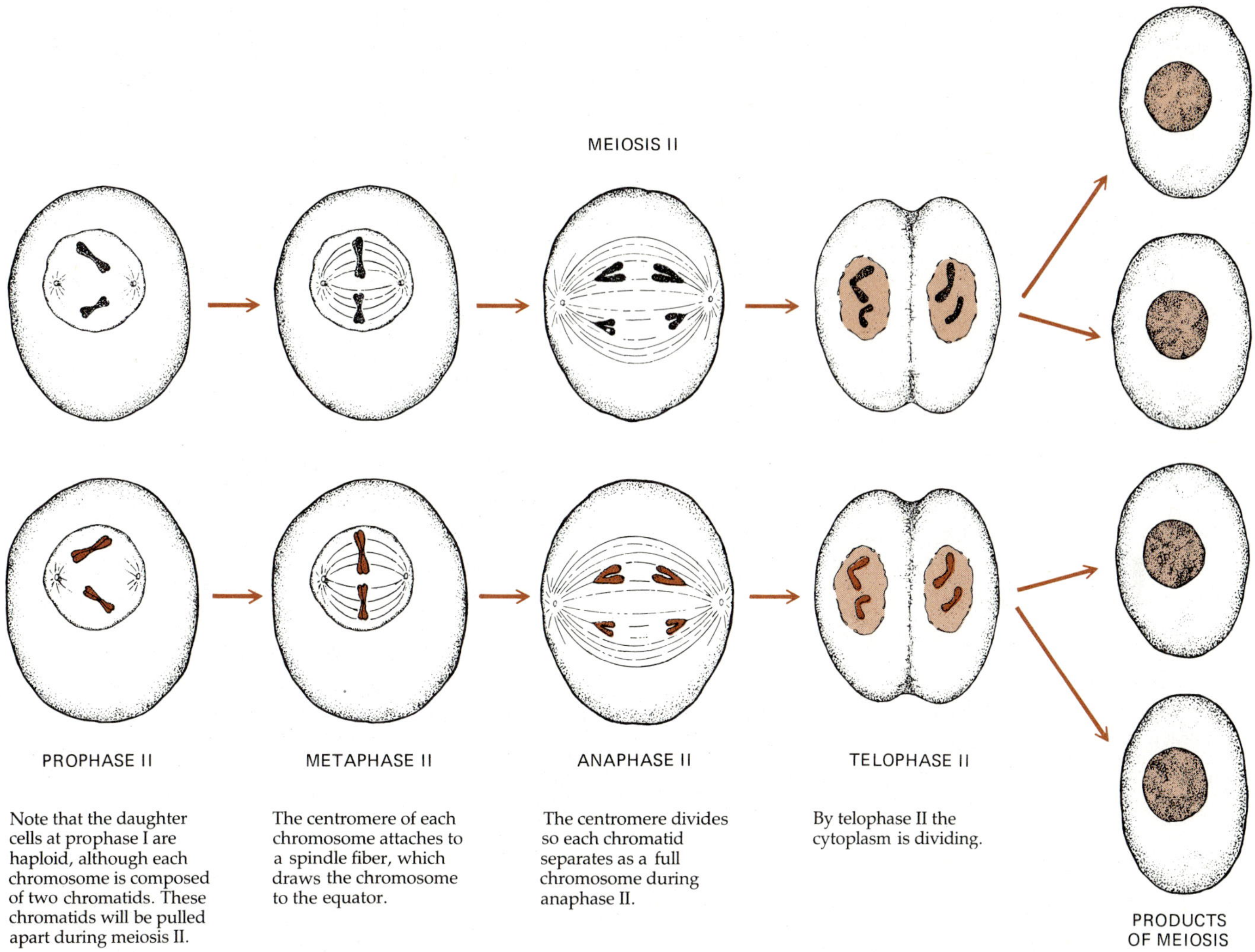

PROPHASE II — Note that the daughter cells at prophase I are haploid, although each chromosome is composed of two chromatids. These chromatids will be pulled apart during meiosis II.

METAPHASE II — The centromere of each chromosome attaches to a spindle fiber, which draws the chromosome to the equator.

ANAPHASE II — The centromere divides so each chromatid separates as a full chromosome during anaphase II.

TELOPHASE II — By telophase II the cytoplasm is dividing.

PRODUCTS OF MEIOSIS — At the end, four haploid cells are present.

spindle. DNA synthesis is already complete early in prophase when the doubled chromosomes appear. But unlike the behavior of mitotic chromosomes, in meiosis the two chromosomes of each pair come to lie together in a very specific gene-for-gene manner (Fig. 11.5).

Because each chromosome of a pair is doubled, or consists of two chromatids, each pair contains four sets of genetic material, two maternal and two paternal. Such a chromosome pair forms a **tetrad.** During this time of close physical pairing, or **synapsis,** adjacent chromatids intertwine and often break and recombine. Exchanges resulting from such **crossovers** create opportunity for genetic variability. This is an important factor in evolution, a topic we will pursue in Chapter 14.

Late in prophase I the paired (synapsed) chromosomes move to the middle of the cell spindle.

Metaphase I. The exact arrangement of the tetrads at metaphase I is the key to the assortment of chromosomes in the cells that result from meiosis. The position of each tetrad is determined randomly. The maternal chromosome of any one tetrad lies toward one pole of the spindle. The paternal chromosome lies toward the other pole. But because the positions of individual tetrads are determined only by chance, seldom will all the maternal chromosomes of a cell lie on the same side of the spindle. At this time it is quite easy to see that the single centromere of each doubled chromosome is attached to an individual spindle fiber.

Anaphase I. In anaphase the two chromosomes of a tetrad separate; one member of the pair migrates toward one pole, the other to the opposite pole. Note that the centromeres do not split in meiosis I, in contrast to their behavior in mitosis. Instead, one doubled chromosome of each pair migrates to one pole of the spindle, the other doubled chromosome to the other pole.

Telophase I. By telophase I the chromosomes have reached their respective poles. The cytoplasm now divides, producing two daughter cells. Meiosis I is over.

Meiosis II

The period of time between telophase I and prophase II is very brief and little of consequence happens. The chromosomes of the two daughter cells need not duplicate, because each is already double. In prophase II each daughter cell forms another spindle, and at metaphase II the doubled chromosomes are arranged on the spindles. This stage differs from metaphase of mitosis in that now there is only one of each pair of chromosomes in each cell, although each chromosome contains two chromatids. The centromeres of these chromosomes soon split, and the new daughter chromosomes migrate to the poles. At telophase II the cytoplasm divides, and the usual interphase nuclear structures reappear. Each of the four new cells that result from meiosis are haploid gametes.

Spermatogenesis and Oogenesis

In the testes, the reproductive organs of males, cells called spermatogonia divide by mitosis to produce primary **spermatocytes.** These cells undergo the first meiotic division, each producing two secondary spermatocytes of approximately equal size. These secondary spermatocytes then undergo the second meiotic division. In this way, each secondary spermatocyte gives rise to four equal-sized **spermatids,** which develop into sperm.

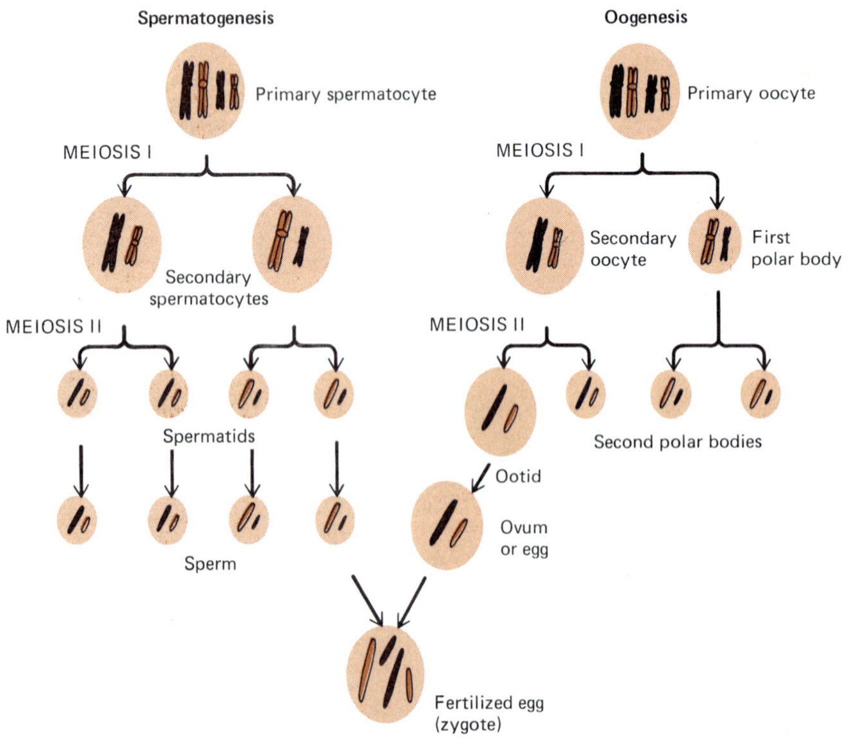

FIGURE 11.6 **Formation of Gametes.** Note the similarity between spermatogenesis and oogenesis. In each case, for every cell that begins gametogenesis, four potential gametes are produced. In oogenesis, however, only one of the four actually matures into an egg.

The situation is somewhat different in the ovaries of females (Fig. 11.6). There, primary **oocytes** divide unequally at the first meiotic division. Each primary oocyte produces one large secondary oocyte and a much smaller cell called a **polar body.** This first polar body and the secondary oocyte undergo the second meiotic division. Again, the oocyte divides unequally. A single large **ootid** and another polar body are produced. Thus one primary oocyte gives rise to three polar bodies (which disintegrate in time) and one ootid, which develops into a single ovum (egg). This unequal division results in a large egg with a disproportionate amount of food and other materials needed to sustain life after fertilization.

Although spermatogenesis in humans begins at puberty and continues into old age, oogenesis is timed differently. The primary oocytes are produced before birth and are arrested in prophase I until puberty. Every month thereafter, certain primary oocytes are stimulated to resume meiosis. The second meiotic division occurs only up to metaphase and then stops unless the egg is fertilized. If that happens, meiosis continues to completion.

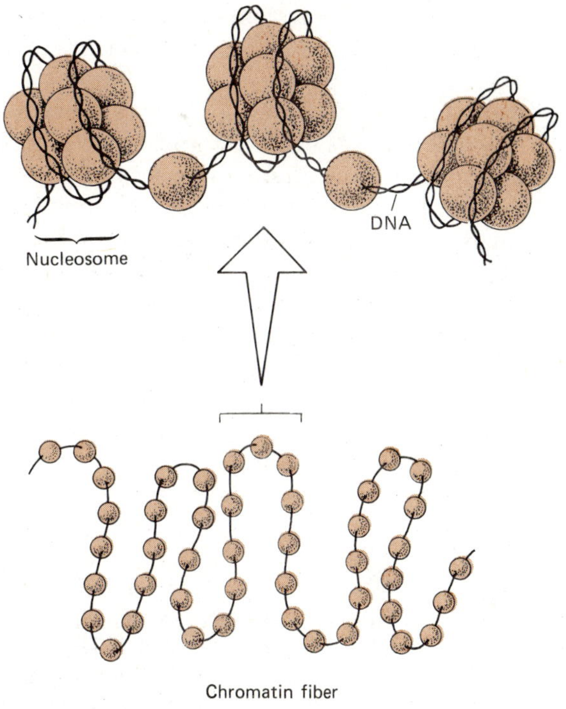

FIGURE 11.7 **Nucleosomes.**

THE MOLECULAR BASIS OF INHERITANCE

Chromosomes exist as distinct bodies only at times of mitosis or meiosis. In that form, the genes they carry can be transmitted between generations in an orderly and reproducible fashion. All other chromosomal functions are carried out during interphase, when the chromosomes have lost their visible identities and exist as parts of chromatin. The physical changes in chromosomes that accompany the cell cycle probably result from the coiling and uncoiling of long fibers that compose chromatin.

Chromatin, and thus a chromosome, is composed primarily of DNA complexed with proteins. This material is sometimes called **nucleoprotein.** Most of the proteins are classified as **histones.** These positively charged proteins make up almost half the weight of the chromatin material. Evidence indicates that the thin strands of DNA are wrapped discontinuously around globular histone masses, resulting in bead-like structures called **nucleosomes** (Fig. 11.7.).

Whereas histones are thought to provide structural support for the nucleic acid, it has been suggested that the nonhistone proteins may help to regulate DNA activity. There is little specific knowledge about the role of proteins in chromosomal function, but there is no doubt that it is DNA that carries the genetic information.

The Chemistry of DNA

Chemical analysis reveals that DNA macromolecules consist of four different **nucleotides.** However, as shown in Fig. 11.8, each nucleotide itself is made up of three subunits: a **deoxyribose sugar,** a **phosphate group,** and a **nitrogenous base.** Note that the four nucleotides differ only in the "base" that is present. Each contains either **adenine** (A), **guanine** (G), **cytosine** (C), or **thymine** (T). In DNA the individual nucleotides are linked together to form a long strand. The sugars and phosphate are the backbone of the strand, and the bases extend out from the sugars.

A complete DNA molecule is actually double-stranded. It consists of two polynucleotide chains coiled around each other to produce a stringlike double helix (Fig. 11.9). The nitrogenous bases of one strand face those of the other strand so that at the center of the helix the bases are stacked in pairs. Because of the shapes of the bases, the pairing is very specific. An A in one strand always pairs with a T in the other. Similarly, G in one strand pairs

only with C in the other. Neither T nor A may pair
54 with G or C. Hydrogen bonds□ between the base pairs hold strands together.

The nature of DNA base-pairing is such that the sequence of bases in one strand of the double helix determines the sequence of bases in the other strand. For example, if one strand is known to have the sequence ATTCG, then the opposite strand must have the sequence TAAGC. The two DNA strands are said to be **complementary,** because they fit together so exactly by **base-pairing.**

Duplication of DNA

Complementary base-pairing provides a built-in method for the accurate duplication of each DNA molecule. Every time a cell divides, the two daughter cells must receive an exact copy of the genetic material. When we observe the process under a microscope, we see the duplication of chromosomes. What occurs behind the scenes is DNA duplication. Here is how it happens.

Several different enzymes are involved in the duplication of DNA. Enzymes known as **unwinding factors** begin the process by causing the two strands of the double helix to separate at many different sites over the length of the molecule. As the weak hydrogen bonds that hold the base pairs together are broken, the helix unwinds in both directions from each initiation site. Then, new polynucleotide partners for the separated strands are laid down.

FIGURE 11.8 **From Nucleotides to Polynucleotides.** The subunits of a polynucleotide are nucleotides such as the one illustrated in (a). When nucleotides are joined together to form polynucleotides, the sugar of one nucleotide binds to the phosphate of the next (b), producing a long chain. The schematic representation (c) may help you see that polynucleotide chains have a sugar-phosphate backbone.

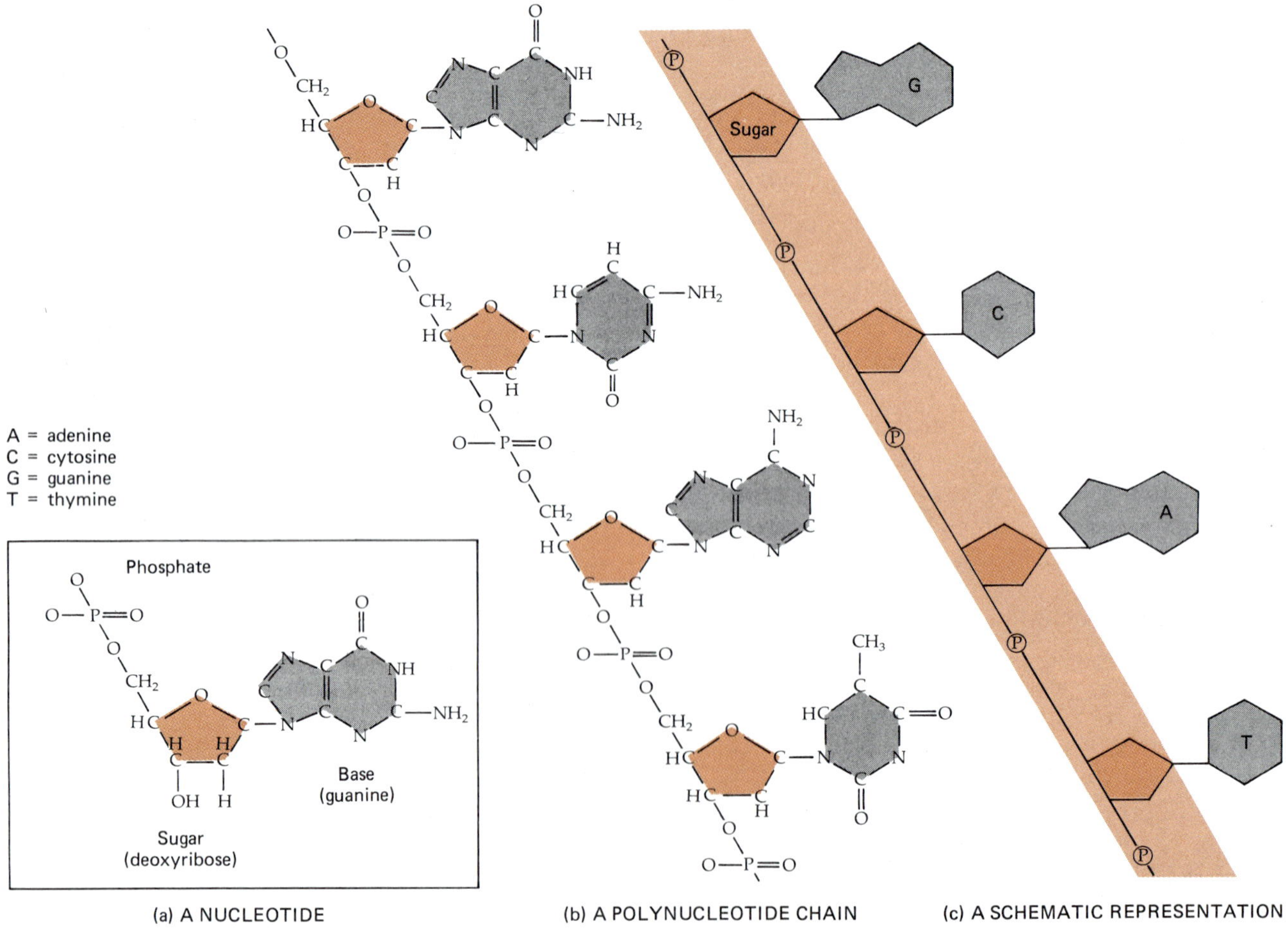

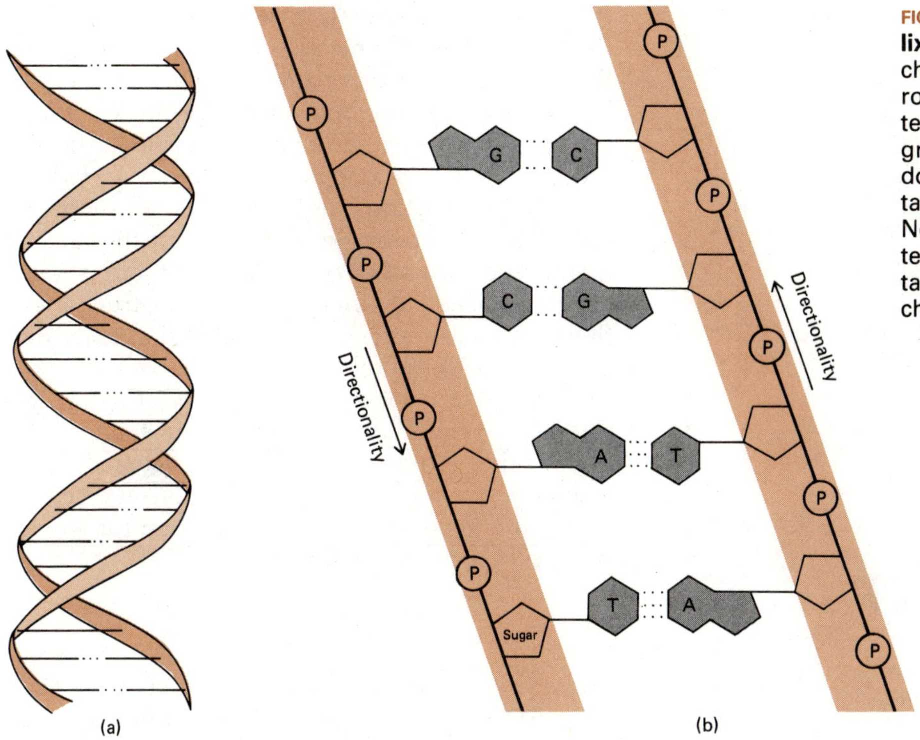

FIGURE 11.9 The DNA Double Helix. In DNA, two polynucleotide chains are twisted into a long, ropelike macromolecule (a). Alternating sugar and phosphate groups form the edges of the double helix, and the center contains the nitrogenous bases (b). Note that hydrogen bonds (dotted lines) between complementary base pairs hold the two chains together.

Figure 11.10 illustrates how each of the parental DNA strands acts as a template for making a new complementary polynucleotide. Previously synthesized nucleotide building blocks move into the **replication fork** (the space where the DNA helix has unwound) and align themselves against each of the template strands. Because of the attraction between complementary bases, A's align themselves next to T's of the template strands, G's align themselves to C's and so forth. Then the properly paired bases are joined together into polynucleotide strands by the enzyme **DNA polymerase.** Each time, the parental DNA opens a little more, and the scenario is repeated. When the unraveling is complete, two identical DNA molecules, each composed of one old and one new strand, will have been produced. And, because of the specific nature of A–T and G–C base pairing, newly synthesized DNA molecules are faithful duplicates of the parent helix.

DNA as an Informational Macromolecule

You are probably wondering how a molecule can contain genetic information. We might try to explain how DNA carries information for making a nose, but the construction of a nose is an enormously complicated enterprise. It would be better to look at something a little simpler. Let us consider a single cell (one *in* your nose if you like). How does DNA determine the nature of a cell—what it is and what it can do?

The answer to that question is "By providing information for making the proper proteins." In addition to having a structure that allows it to duplicate itself, DNA carries instructions for the synthesis of proteins. We have already learned that cellular activities are dependent on and subject to the direct control of enzymes.□ We also know that 96
all enzymes are proteins. Thus it should be obvious that if DNA determines the structure of proteins, it determines the enzymes produced within the cell and thereby can control all other biochemical events as well. In other words, by controlling production of proteins, DNA also controls production of all other cellular substances. Now we are ready to look at how the structure of DNA is translated into the structure of proteins.

The sequence of bases in different segments of DNA codes for the sequence of amino acids in different proteins. (You will recall that the sequence amino acids of a protein determines the shape of

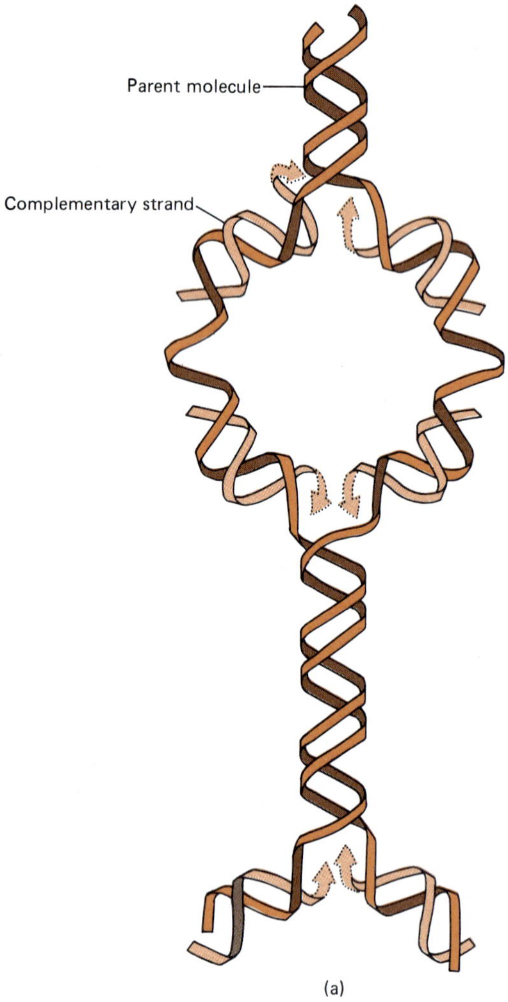

the protein and therefore its function.▫) But, although DNA occurs mainly in chromosomes within the nucleus and, except during cell division, is segregated from the cytoplasm by the nuclear membrane, protein synthesis occurs on the surface of the ribosomes, situated primarily in the cytoplasm. Thus the instructions for making proteins must be conveyed out of the nucleus through the nuclear membrane. We must conclude that there is some sort of intermediate that records the instructions of the nucleus and then moves out of that body into the cytoplasm to the ribosomes. 70

This essential intermediate is RNA (ribonucleic acid. The genetic information in the sequence of nucleotides of a segment of DNA is copied into a sequence of nucleotides of certain RNA molecules, which thereby contain the information for assembling proteins on ribosomes (Fig. 11.11).

What Is a Gene?

There is no absolutely satisfactory definition for a gene. We hear the word used commonly: "He has

FIGURE 11.10 **Duplication of DNA.** The double helix opens at hundreds of sites along its length. Formation of complementary strands proceeds in both directions as the parent molecule unwinds. As the complementary strands grow toward each other, they are joined together into long chains (a). As shown in (b), each of the parental DNA strands acts as a template for making a new complementary strand. When replication is complete, two identical daughter molecules, each composed of one old and one new strand, have been produced.

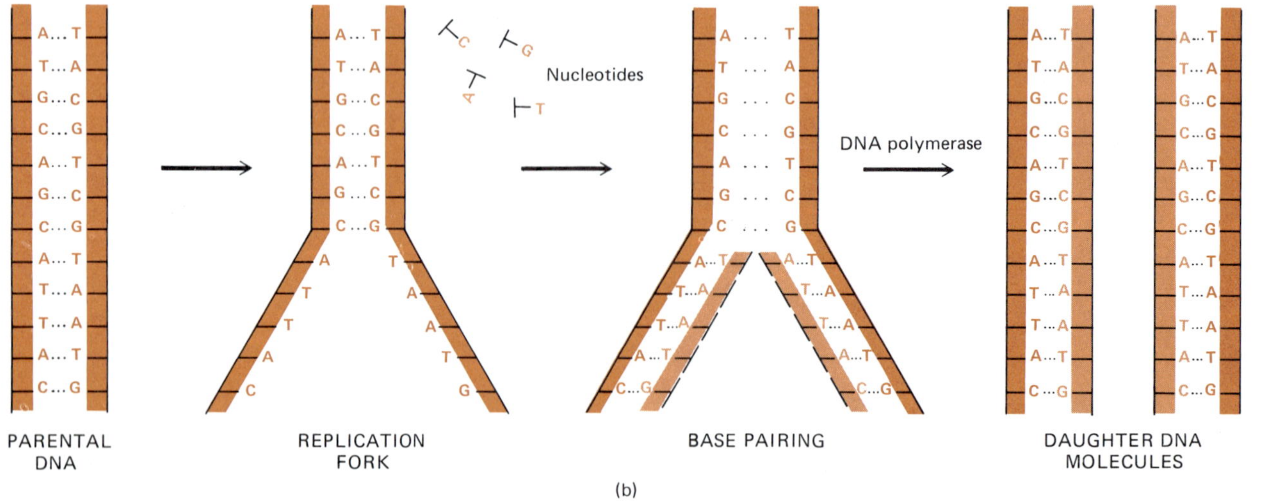

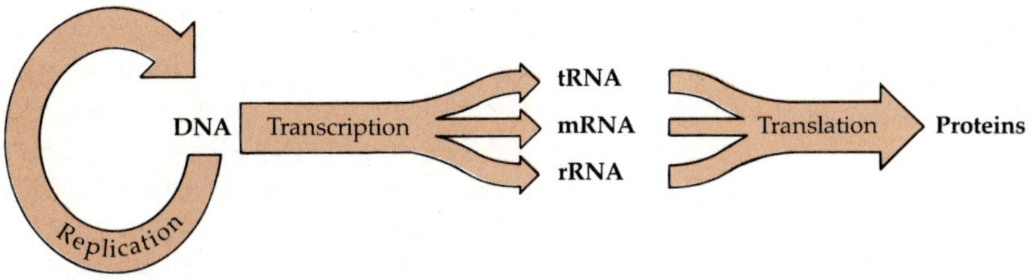

FIGURE 11.11 The Central Dogma of Information Transfer. Biological information is stored in DNA. The double helix contains information for its own duplication and for the regulation of all cellular activities. This information, found in the DNA nucleotide sequence, is transcribed to RNA molecules, which cooperate to sequence amino acids into proteins. Some of these proteins are structural components, but others are enzymes, the biological catalysts that make life possible.

the gene for hemophilia," or even, "Musical talent is in her genes." The implication is that a gene is a genetic factor responsible for the production of a specific trait. But what is the connection between DNA and genes?

Chemically, since they transmit genetic information, genes must consist of portions of the DNA of chromosomes (Fig. 11.12). Considering what we have just learned, genes might be defined as segments of DNA that contain information for synthesizing different proteins. These proteins could be enzymes, but they could also be blood proteins, membrane proteins, or any of the various other body proteins. This **one-gene one-protein** concept is useful for many purposes. However, it is at odds with our first definition, because hereditary traits are generally the result of activities of many enzymes and therefore several "genes."

The definition of a gene is further complicated by the fact that some DNA segments are only *indirectly* involved in protein synthesis. Later in the chapter we will consider the importance of control genes that regulate the action of other genes. Moreover, because three different forms of RNA are required for the synthesis of a single protein, we are obliged to conclude that some genes are units of information for making RNA.

Transcription of RNA from DNA

Each RNA molecule is a complementary copy of a gene located on one of the strands of a DNA mol-

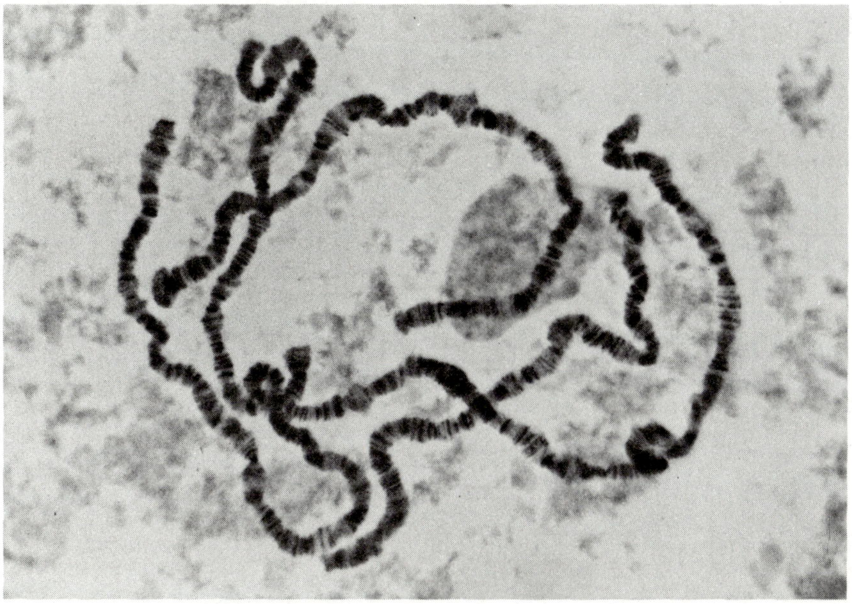

FIGURE 11.12 Fruit-Fly Salivary Gland Chromosome. The salivary gland cells of the ordinary fruit fly are unusually large, and so are their chromosomes. These giant chromosomes are nearly 100 times larger than ordinary chromosomes and so have been the object of considerable investigation. When stained, as these have been, giant chromosomes exhibit a distinctive light-dark banding pattern. The presence, absence, or alteration of these chromosome bands has been correlated with certain genetic changes in fruit flies. Thus it has been possible in some cases to equate bands and genes.

ecule. Thus RNA is in many ways similar to DNA. RNA is also a macromolecular chain composed of four kinds of nucleotides. As is true for DNA, RNA has a sugar-phosphate backbone with bases sticking out from the sugars. But in RNA the sugar is **ribose** instead of deoxyribose. One of the nitrogenous bases of RNA is also different. In RNA, **uracil** (U) replaces thymine of DNA. And whereas DNA is usually double-stranded, cellular RNA is single-stranded.

DNA directs the synthesis, or **transcription**, of RNA in much the same manner as it accomplishes its own duplication. Those segments of DNA that are to be transcribed are designated by unique sequences of bases that act as start-and-stop signals for the enzyme **RNA polymerase.** These signals are segments of control genes that regulate transcription. RNA polymerase binds to the start-signal region of the DNA molecule and stimulates the opening of the helix at that point (Fig. 11.13).

Only one of the DNA strands is transcribed, although the selection method is a mystery. RNA nucleotides line up next to complementary bases on the DNA. That is, C will be opposite G, G opposite C, A opposite T, and U opposite A. (Remember that uracil replaces thymine, so U replaces T.)

As the RNA nucleotides line up, they are linked together by RNA polymerase, which moves along the opening in the DNA template. The double helix continues to open in front of the moving enzyme and then closes behind it. At the stop signal, the RNA polymerase drops off the DNA molecule and the freshly synthesized RNA molecule is freed (Fig. 11.14).

Thus the process of complementary base-pairing ensures the accuracy of transcription. Shortly we will learn exactly how the transcribed sequence of bases is translated into protein structure. And, since proteins are synthesized in the cytoplasm, the RNA transcripts involved must leave the nucleus. Presumably they pass through pores in the nuclear membrane.

The Three Kinds of RNA. Some genes of DNA determine the structure of **ribosomal RNA (rRNA)**,

FIGURE 11.13 **Transcription of RNA from a DNA Template.**

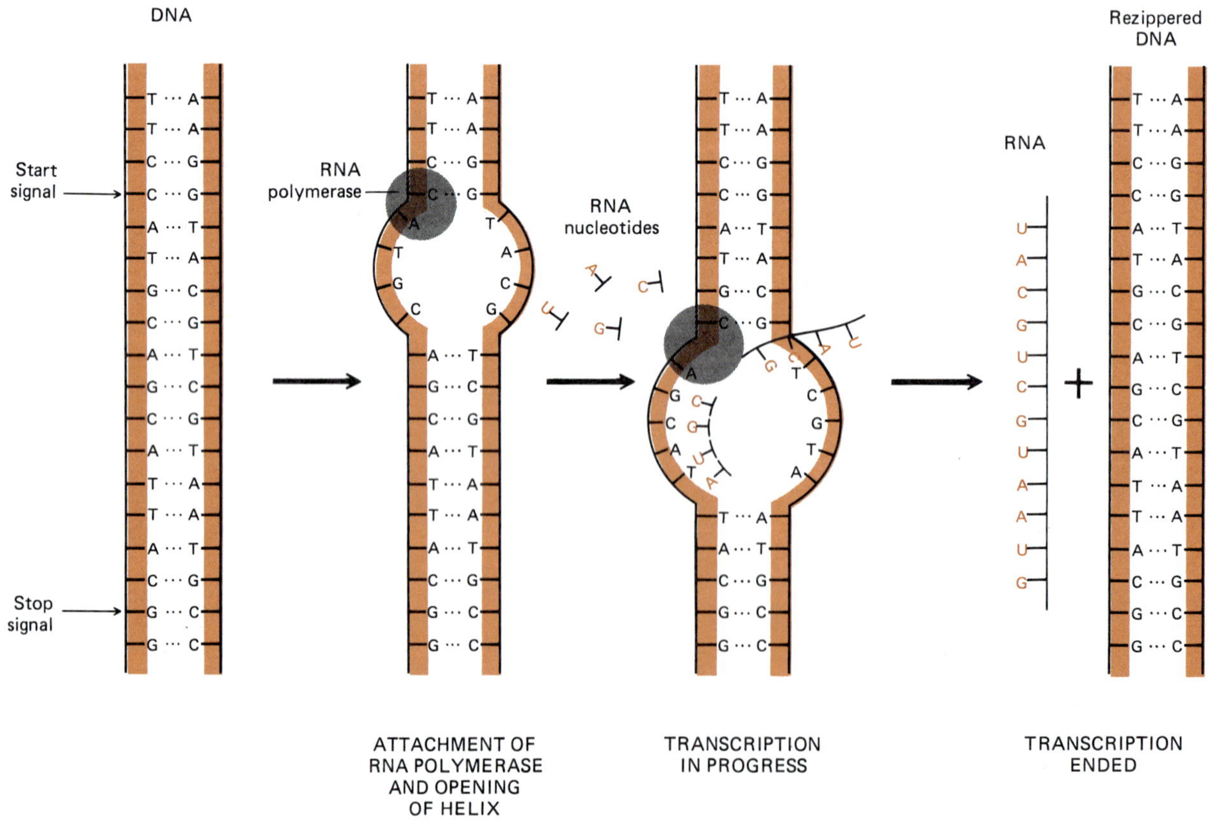

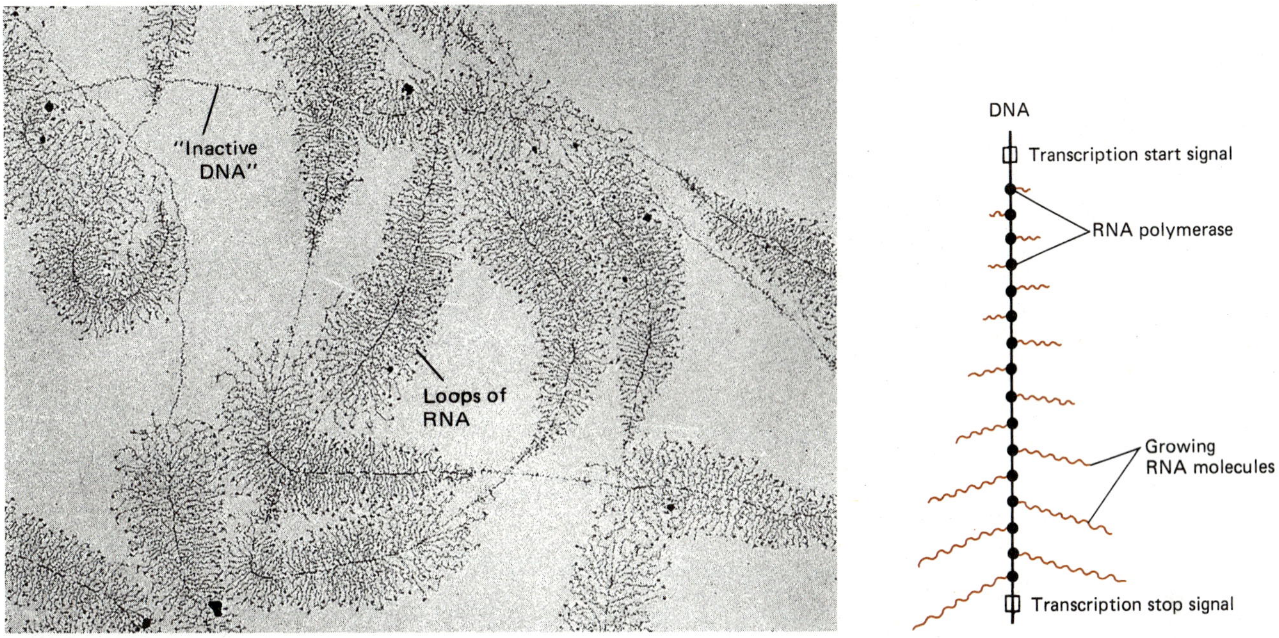

FIGURE 11.14 **Caught in the Act!** The electromicrograph shows genes from an amphibian oocyte undergoing transcription. The feathery chains extending away from the long DNA molecules are lengths of RNA in various stages of completion.

which associates with already synthesized proteins
85 to form ribosomes,☐ organelles that are the sites of protein synthesis. But while rRNA is absolutely essential for synthesis of proteins, it does not possess the instructions for the actual assembly of proteins from amino acids.

The synthesis of a protein requires that its constituent amino acids be put together in the proper
67 sequence.☐ Information for sequencing the amino acids of proteins is found in those genes transcribed into **messenger RNA (mRNA)**. Transcription also produces **transfer RNA (tRNA)**, which transports amino acids to the ribosomes where they are assembled into proteins according to the message supplied by mRNA. Because of its small size, more is known about the structure of tRNA than about any other kind of RNA. Transfer RNAs are composed of only 75 or 80 nucleotides; by comparison, mRNA may contain as many as 10,000 (Fig. 11.15).

Although it is single-stranded like other RNAs, tRNA has a complex shape. It is folded back on itself to form several loops, giving the molecule a vaguely cloverleaf configuration. This shape is stabilized by hydrogen bonds between complementary bases. Each amino acid is carried by its own tRNA. Attachment of an amino acid to its respective tRNA requires a special enzyme and energy supplied by ATP.

To ensure adequate amounts of their products, the genes that determine rRNA and tRNA are repeated many times within various chromosomes, forming what is called **multiple-copy DNA.** However, most genes that produce mRNA, and therefore most cellular proteins, occur as single copies. There is, of course, a unique gene for every different protein.

RNA Processing and Split Genes. After transcription, RNA molecules must sometimes be altered before they can function fully. RNA processing includes addition or removal of sections before the final form is achieved. In various genes, the sequence of nucleotides that stipulates an amino acid sequence is interrupted by a stretch of 50 or so nucleotides that must be clipped out. Such interruptions are called **introns.** They are found within **split genes** whose messages are divided into two parts pieced together after the introns are excised enzymatically.

The function of split genes is uncertain. It is theorized that introns and lengths of apparently

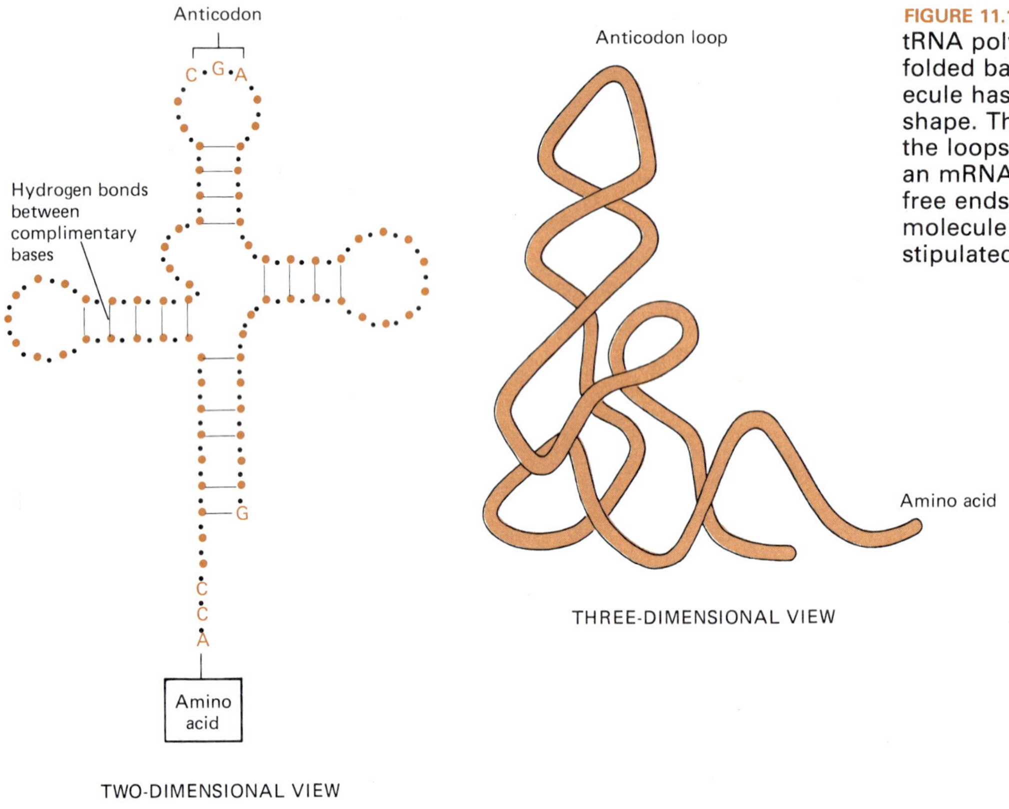

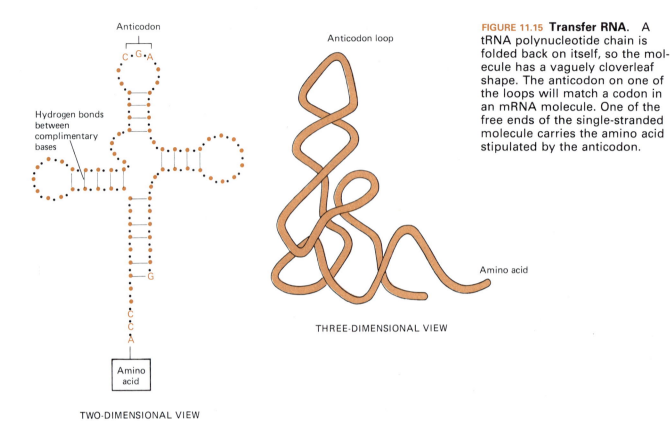

FIGURE 11.15 **Transfer RNA.** A tRNA polynucleotide chain is folded back on itself, so the molecule has a vaguely cloverleaf shape. The anticodon on one of the loops will match a codon in an mRNA molecule. One of the free ends of the single-stranded molecule carries the amino acid stipulated by the anticodon.

TABLE 11.1 **The Genetic Code***

FIRST BASE IN THE CODON	SECOND BASE IN THE CODON *U*	*C*	*A*	*G*	THIRD BASE IN THE CODON
U	Phenylalanine	Serine	Tyrosine	Cysteine	U
	Phenylalanine	Serine	Tyrosine	Cysteine	C
	Leucine	Serine	Stop†	Stop†	A
	Leucine	Serine	Stop†	Tryptophan	G
C	Leucine	Proline	Histidine	Arginine	U
	Leucine	Proline	Histidine	Arginine	C
	Leucine	Proline	Glutamine	Arginine	A
	Leucine	Proline	Glutamine	Arginine	G
A	Isoleucine	Threonine	Asparagine	Serine	U
	Isoleucine	Threonine	Asparagine	Serine	C
	Isoleucine	Threonine	Lysine	Arginine	A
	Methionine††	Threonine	Lysine	Arginine	G
G	Valine	Alanine	Aspartic acid	Glycine	U
	Valine	Alanine	Aspartic acid	Glycine	C
	Valine	Alanine	Glutamic acid	Glycine	A
	Valine	Alanine	Glutamic acid	Glycine	G

*The amino acid appears under the second letter of its codon. For example, CCU codes for the amino acid proline.
†UAA, UAG, and UGA are termination (stop) codons.
††AUG is also the initiation codon.

nontranscribed **spacer DNA** located throughout chromosomes may have a regulatory function, or they may have been accumulated as the result of evolutionary processes.

The Genetic Code

Somehow, the sequence of bases transcribed to mRNA must be translated into the sequence of amino acids in a protein. But because there are only four different nucleotides in RNA and twenty different amino acids in most proteins, the translation of mRNA cannot be direct—that is, one nucleotide for one amino acid. Instead, the nucleotides function three at a time as genetic ''words,'' or **codons.** There are 64 possible triplet codons, composed of combinations of the four different nucleotides taken three at a time in any order, with any nucleotide used once, twice, or three times within a given codon. For some unknown reason, some amino acids are specified by more than one codon. In other words, there are synonyms in the genetic code (Table 11.1).

Each genetic message sent to the ribosomes in the form of mRNA is a sentence composed of codon words. Some codons are initiators, which mean ''begin an amino acid chain here.'' Others are terminators, which mean ''end of this amino acid chain.'' Between the initiator and the terminator are codon ''words'' of a long sentence. The codons do not have spaces between them like the words in a sentence, but each codon contains exactly three bases that designate a particular amino acid.

Just as a sentence in Morse Code can be translated into an English sentence, a mRNA sentence can be translated. However, **translation** of a mRNA sentence results in synthesis of a protein. The entire ''sentence'' of codons specifies a sequence of amino acids that constitutes either a whole protein or a specific part of a protein.

Translation: Protein Synthesis

When not involved in the synthesis of proteins, ribosomes exist as separate large and small subunits. Translation begins when, in the presence of mRNA and initiator tRNA carrying the first amino acid coded in the message, the subunits join to produce a functional ribosomal complex.

Figure 11.16 shows how the mRNA is bound to the small ribosomal subunit so that its initiation

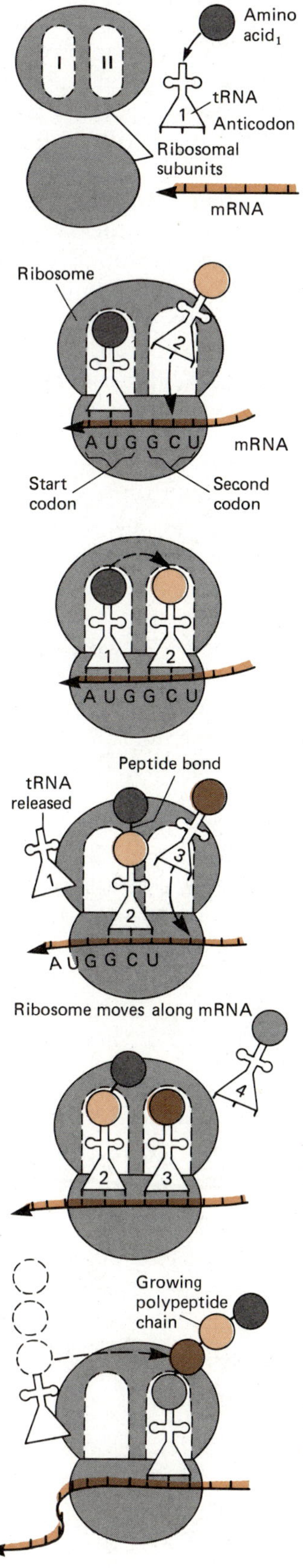

The five components necessary to start protein synthesis. Note that the large ribosomal subunit contains two binding sites.

Once mRNA is bound to the ribosome so that the initiation codon is in reading position, tRNAs begin to translate the message.

The first amino acid is joined to the second amino acid by a peptide bond.

As the first tRNA is released, the second tRNA prepares to occupy the site just vacated. A third tRNA is about to "read" its codon.

The third tRNA is now bound to the ribosome. A new peptide bond will be formed between the dipeptide of the second tRNA and the amino acid carried by the third tRNA.

This process continues, and the polypeptide chain grows until the last codon of the mRNA appears.

FIGURE 11.16 Protein Synthesis: Translation of mRNA.

codon is aligned with the first of two tRNA binding sites on the large ribosomal subunit. As will become clear, this alignment establishes the proper "reading" frame for the translation of all subsequent codons. Note that the second codon is positioned so that it is aligned to the second binding site of the large subunit.

Each codon of mRNA is "read" or recognized only by the kind of tRNA bearing the correct amino acid. The tRNAs recognize the proper mRNA codons because each tRNA possesses a three-nucleotide **anticodon** that is complementary to only one mRNA codon. Attraction between the anticodon of the tRNAs and mRNA codons results from base-pairing. The affinity of complementary codons and anticodons assures that the tRNAs will line up in the proper order at the ribosome.

Thus the initiator tRNA reads the first codon of mRNA and occupies the first site on the large subunit. Soon after, the tRNA bearing the second amino acid reads the second codon and occupies the second ribosomal binding site. At this point, a peptide bond□ is formed between the two amino acids and, simultaneously, the bond holding the first amino acid to its tRNA is broken. The uncoupled tRNA then falls away from the ribosome. This leaves both amino acids attached to the second tRNA.

Next, the tRNA carrying the just-formed dipeptide moves from the second site to the first site and pulls the mRNA over a notch. This brings the third mRNA codon into alignment with the second binding site; now this codon is read by the tRNA carrying the third amino acid, and the steps are repeated.

As each tRNA is attached to the ribosome in its proper turn, the amino acid it carries is hooked to the end of the growing chain. The termination codon at the end of the message stops the synthesis. Then the fully assembled protein is released from the ribosome.

Usually a number of ribosomes "read" an mRNA at the same time. Ribosomes always attach to the front end of an mRNA. After the first ribosome has "read" at the same time. Thus a number of ribo-ribosome can attach to the mRNA and begin to "read" at the same time. Thus a number of ribosomes, one following the other, may be attached to a single mRNA, forming a combination known as a **polyribosome** (Fig. 11.17).

Regulation of Gene Expression

Perhaps you already realize that genes are not transcribed continuously. In fact, some cells may never transcribe certain genes. Since every cell of the body has the same genetic legacy, every cell "knows how" to make any protein of the body. Yet only pancreatic cells make insulin, and stomach cells never make hemoglobin. Controls are surely at work to turn genes on and off as the need arises.

The earliest studies of the regulation of gene expression were done on bacteria. In procaryotes **structural genes,** which produce mRNA, are regulated by one or more **control genes.** Some control genes produce **repressor molecules,** which bind to

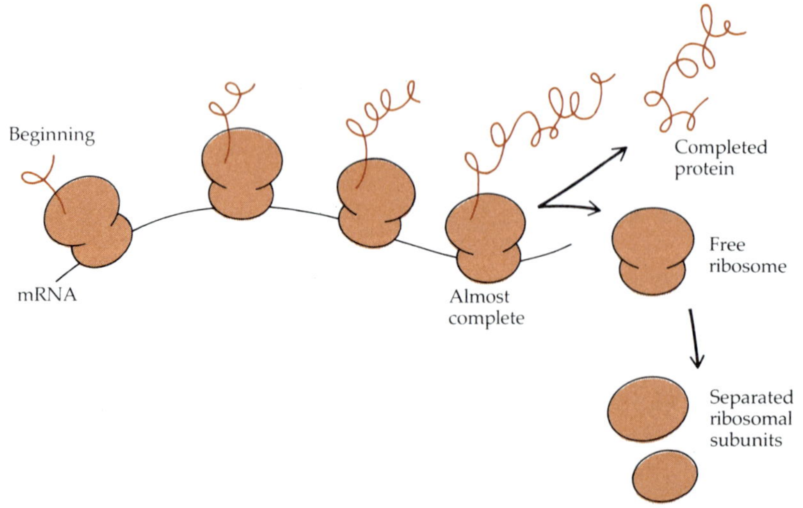

FIGURE 11.17 A Polyribosome. Often several ribosomes, each operating independently, read a single mRNA. Those closest to the front of the mRNA have the shortest polypeptide chains.

BOX 11A

VIRUSES HAVE INFLUENTIAL GENES

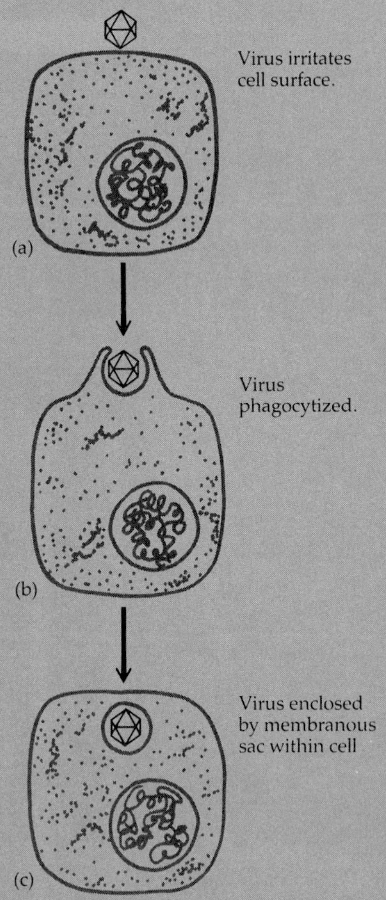

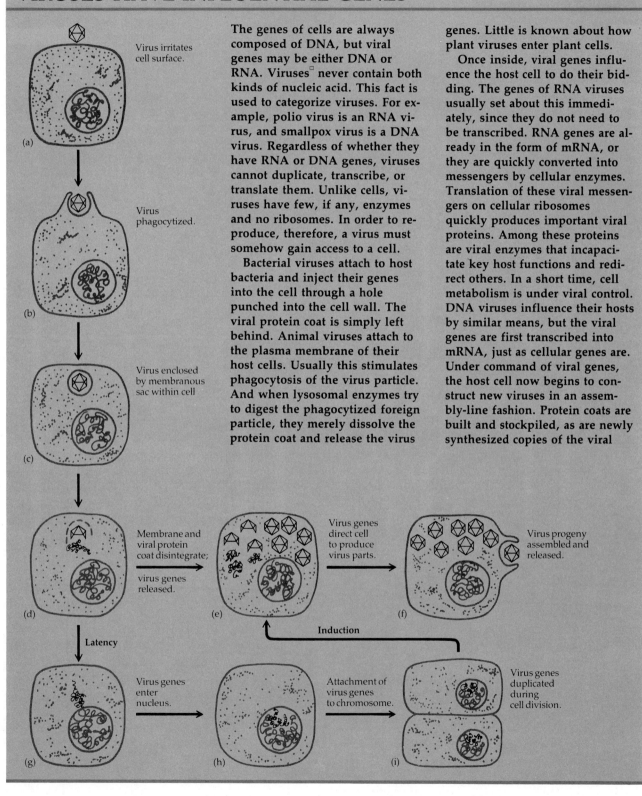

The genes of cells are always composed of DNA, but viral genes may be either DNA or RNA. Viruses never contain both kinds of nucleic acid. This fact is used to categorize viruses. For example, polio virus is an RNA virus, and smallpox virus is a DNA virus. Regardless of whether they have RNA or DNA genes, viruses cannot duplicate, transcribe, or translate them. Unlike cells, viruses have few, if any, enzymes and no ribosomes. In order to reproduce, therefore, a virus must somehow gain access to a cell.

Bacterial viruses attach to host bacteria and inject their genes into the cell through a hole punched into the cell wall. The viral protein coat is simply left behind. Animal viruses attach to the plasma membrane of their host cells. Usually this stimulates phagocytosis of the virus particle. And when lysosomal enzymes try to digest the phagocytized foreign particle, they merely dissolve the protein coat and release the virus genes. Little is known about how plant viruses enter plant cells.

Once inside, viral genes influence the host cell to do their bidding. The genes of RNA viruses usually set about this immediately, since they do not need to be transcribed. RNA genes are already in the form of mRNA, or they are quickly converted into messengers by cellular enzymes. Translation of these viral messengers on cellular ribosomes quickly produces important viral proteins. Among these proteins are viral enzymes that incapacitate key host functions and redirect others. In a short time, cell metabolism is under viral control. DNA viruses influence their hosts by similar means, but the viral genes are first transcribed into mRNA, just as cellular genes are. Under command of viral genes, the host cell now begins to construct new viruses in an assembly-line fashion. Protein coats are built and stockpiled, as are newly synthesized copies of the viral

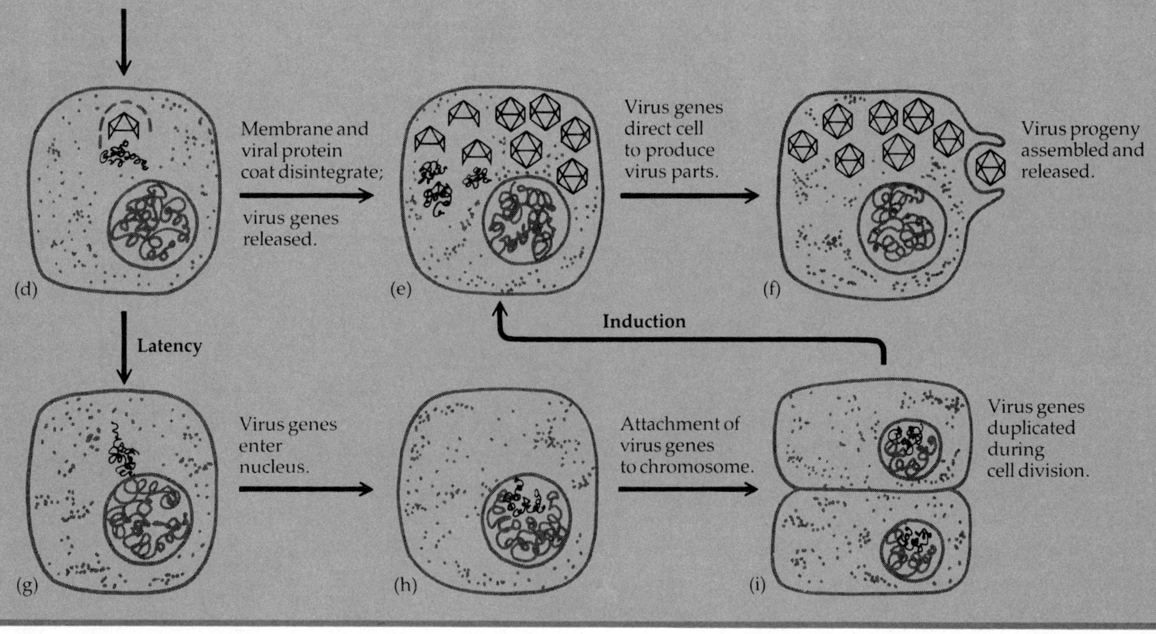

BOX 11A continued

genes. Then, with all parts in readiness, the virus particles are assembled.

Some viruses have a different pattern of infection. Instead of causing virus multiplication, the viral gene attaches itself to a chromosome of the host cell, becoming a provirus. Thus incorporated into a host chromosome, the viral gene is duplicated, along with the genes of the chromosome to which it is attached. Under these conditions, no new virus particles are produced. As a matter of fact, the cell usually shows no obvious signs of being parasitized.

Certain conditions can provoke a provirus to detach from its host chromosome and begin a cycle of viral reproduction. Herpes simplex, type I, the virus responsible for cold sores and fever blisters, is thought to act in this manner. Infected individuals show no evidence of the virus until some form of stress—a fever, sunburn, or perhaps emotional strain—induces the viral genes to initiate production of new virus particles in the ordinary way. Another form of Herpes is similarly responsible for recurrent venereal lesions.□ 228

Bacterial viruses that are capable of becoming proviruses are important tools of genetics research. It has been found that detachment of provirus genes is sometimes defective. For example, neighboring chromosomal genes may be excised along with existing genes. Thus, when new viruses are assembled, they carry bacterial genes.

Viruses that habitually detach incorrectly can be used as "surgical instruments" to remove particular genes from a bacterial chromosome. Afterwards, the virus particles can be broken open, and the genes can be analyzed. Or the virus can be used to infect other cells. Since the virus carries genes from its previous host, such infections transfer genes from one cell to another. Many useful hybrid bacterial strains have been produced in this manner.

the transcription start signals of DNA. This prevents RNA polymerase from initiating transcription. Thus the gene adjacent to the start signal is turned off. Repressor proteins are sensitive to environmental conditions and under some circumstances detach from the DNA sites. This "turns on" the genes so that transcription can take place.

Such adaptive regulatory systems work well to control the synthesis of bacterial enzymes that may not be needed continuously. For example, unlike human cells that have a liver to keep them constantly supplied with glucose, bacterial cells must be able to adapt to a variety of different energy sources. In the absence of a particular sugar, repressors prevent transcription of genes that code for enzymes to degrade that sugar. But, when the sugar becomes available, it enters the cell and reacts with the repressor. This reaction removes the repressor from the transcription start signal and turns on the required gene (Fig. 11.18).

Similar adaptive regulatory processes have been demonstrated in other organisms. There is some evidence to indicate that hormones may function by activation of genes. The female sex hormone estrogen, for example, is known to combine with chromatin after entering target cells. Overall, however, little is known about gene regulation in humans and other eucaryotes. Among the many theories is the suggestion that nonhistone proteins may control gene expression by changing locations and physically blocking transcriptions, thus "turning off" appropriate genes.

Several recent discoveries indicate that many of our ideas concerning genes and their regulation may be altered in coming years. Although most genes are normally located at permanent positions on particular chromosomes, a wide variety of organisms have been shown to possess **transposable controlling elements.** These genes or groups of genes are specialized to move into and out of different chromosomes, inserting themselves at different positions to determine the activity of genes located nearby. Transposable genetic elements may play a significant role in the variable gene expression that must accompany differentiation (Chapter 13).

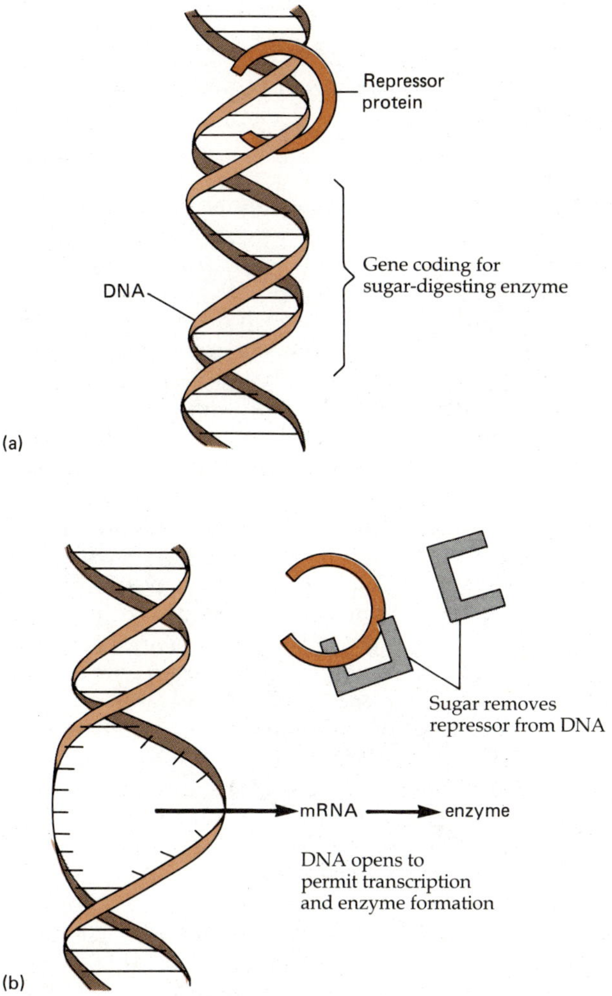

FIGURE 11.18 **How Repressors Work.** Repressors bind to DNA and prevent transcription of adjacent genes. In (a) the gene for an enzyme involved in sugar breakdown is turned off. When the sugar enters cell (b), it reacts with the repressor to permit transcription.

PATTERNS OF INHERITANCE

There are no simple rules to explain all aspects of inheritance. Our knowledge is limited to the inheritance of traits that follow relatively simple and predictable rules. Those genetic laws we understand best have been determined through studies of heredity in microorganisms and by the experimental breeding of various plants and animals. With these organisms, experimenters can limit matings to individuals with traits they wish to investigate. And because such matings produce multiple offspring, patterns of inheritance are easier to predict.

Obviously, similar experimentation cannot be carried out with humans. Our knowledge of human heredity must be obtained largely by interpretation of family pedigrees. Often these records of family inheritance patterns are limited to traits associated with medical problems. Nevertheless, it has been possible to obtain information about the inheritance of a variety of human traits. In fact, we have accumulated sufficient evidence to know that human heredity follows the same basic rules as does the heredity of other organisms.

Dominance/Recessiveness

Each chromosome contains many genes. And since each chromosome is paired, the genes residing on homologous chromosomes are also paired. One gene of each pair is inherited from each parent. Normally, each member of a gene pair occupies the same locus or position on the homologous chromosome.

Although each member of a gene pair affects the same trait, the two genes are not always identical. When the genes of a pair differ from each other in such a way that they affect the same trait in different ways, they are said to be **alleles** of each other. Most genes we recognize come in at least two and sometimes three or more alternative alleles. Of course, normal individuals never possess more than two alleles of any given gene, because they have only two of each kind of chromosome. An individual is said to be **homozygous** for a particular trait if the determining gene pair consists of identical genes. If the genes of a pair are different alleles, the individual is said to be **heterozygous** for that trait.

Often one allele of a gene masks the expression of another allele of that gene. This is the phenomenon of **dominance.** The gene that is expressed is said to be dominant to the other **recessive** allele. If one gene (in each cell) results in the production of enough enzyme to make sufficient product, it matters little whether the allele on the other chromosome codes for this functional enzyme or for a useless protein. At least in some instances, recessive genes are simply DNA sequences that code for a protein lacking the structure to serve as an enzyme for the usual reaction. In other cases, recessive genes produce clearly useful proteins.

Geneticists use letters to represent genes when describing the **genotype** or genetic makeup of an individual. Two letters must be used to describe

BOX 11B

PLASMIDS, RECOMBINANT DNA, AND GENETIC ENGINEERING

The technique of manufacturing and then introducing new genetic material into cells is called genetic engineering. Until recently, genetic engineering seemed only a remote possibility. Now new developments make it potentially possible to create organisms with desired genotypes.

At present, research is centered on the bacterium *Escherichia coli,* the common inhabitant of the human colon. *E. coli* is one of the fastest-growing organisms known (it can divide every 20 minutes) and so has long been a favorite organism for biological studies. Indeed, more is known about the genetics, metabolism, and biochemistry of *E. coli* than of any other organism.

It was in *E. coli* that plasmids were first discovered. Plasmids are genetic elements found in the cytoplasm of bacterial cells. They are tiny bits of DNA, much smaller than chromosomal DNA and independent of it. Plasmids carry genes that are nonessential for the life of the bacterium. As a result, they may be gained or lost without significant damage to the organism. Some plasmids carry unusual traits (that's how they were discovered in the first place), traits such as antibiotic resistance and "maleness" (the ability to reproduce sexually by conjugation with a plasmidless "female" bacterium).

It is possible to isolate plasmids from bacterial cells, cut them open at very specific places, insert pieces of DNA from another source, and then reseal the plasmids. The hybrid DNA thus produced is referred to as recombinant DNA, because it combines genetic material from two different sources. The plasmid is now a carrier of new genetic material, which can be inserted into appropriate receptor cells by mixing the cells with the plasmid DNA under appropriate conditions. The plasmid DNA "infects" the recipient cells in much the same way as a virus might. The newly introduced genes are expressed just as the recipient cell's own genes are expressed.

The ability to produce recombinant DNA is largely the result of the discovery of enzymes (in *E. coli* again) that can be used to manipulate DNA. Of these the most important are the DNA ligases, which ordinarily mend breaks in DNA molecules, and DNA-restriction endonucleases, whose normal function is to break down and thus restrict virus DNA when it enters cells lucky enough to have such protective devices. In the laboratory these enzymes allow scientists not only to open up the plasmids but to obtain small pieces of foreign DNA, insert them into the plasmids, and then reseal them.

What good is this new technology? It may be used to program bacteria to produce useful biological molecules. For example, injection of human genes for insulin into *E. coli* has resulted in bacteria that secrete insulin. Such insulin may prove both cheaper and more effective than the cow or pig insulin now in use. Someday it may be possible to use plasmids inserted into viruses to carry genes into particular cells and cure such diseases as PKU or sickle-cell anemia. Recombinant DNA research may also lead to important advances in agriculture—specifically, the production of cheaper and better food crops.

Scientists who are doing recombinant DNA research recognize both the enormous potential of their efforts and the possible dangers. What if plasmids containing antibiotic-resistant genes were inserted into a pathogen and a new disease-causing organism resistant to antibiotics were created? What will happen if genes of higher organisms are introduced into bacterial cells? Will they be expressed in a different, perhaps harmful, way?

Concern over many of these questions led prominent scientists involved in recombinant DNA research to voluntarily place a temporary moratorium on their studies in 1974. Then in 1976, the National Institutes of Health established guidelines that have allowed research to resume. Some experiments were banned completely. In this category were those involving especially dangerous microorganisms. Certain high-risk experiments require containment facilities that ensure that the newly created organisms cannot escape and reach the general public. And for some experiments, defective *E. coli* strains that can survive only in the laboratory must be used.

each trait. A capital letter indicates a dominant gene, while a lower case letter indicates a recessive allele. **Phenotype** refers to the outward appearance of an individual—that is, to the perceived hereditary characteristics. Analysis of the results of a simple mating (cross) in which the inheritance of only one characteristic is followed will illustrate the use of these genetic conventions.

A Monohybrid Cross

When parental genotypes are known, it is possible to predict the distribution of inherited characteristics among offspring. A simple example will show how this type of genetic analysis is accomplished. Suppose that an individual has one dominant allele for normal body coloring and another allele that blocks the production of melanin, the body pigment, and causes the albino condition. If a heterozygous male of this genotype had children by a woman homozygous for the dominant gene, what would be the genetic makeup of their children?

We can represent the mating as follows:

Aa × *AA*

Where *A* = normal and *a* = albinism.

According to what we have learned about metaphase I of meiosis, one-half the sperm produced by the *Aa* male would contain a chromosome bearing the *A* gene, and the other half would contain a chromosome bearing the *a* allele. Naturally, the eggs of the *AA* woman would each contain one *A* gene.

Using a simple diagram known as a *Punnett square,* we can visually determine the nature of the offspring and their proportions. A Punnett square is a rectangle with the horizontal side representing the total population of sperm the male can produce and the vertical side representing the total population of eggs the female can produce. The area of the rectangle represents the population of possible offspring.

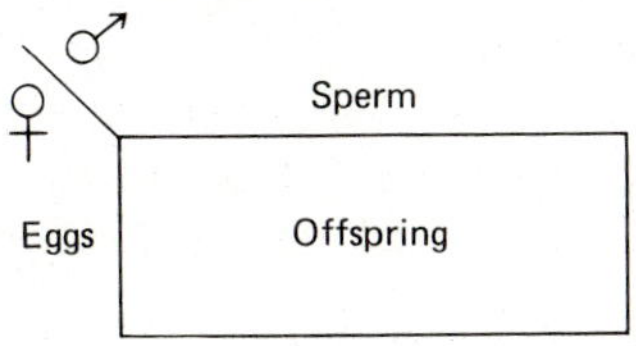

In the present example 50 percent of the sperm are *A* and 50 percent are *a;* thus the side representing the types of sperm should be divided into two equal portions. Since there is only one type of egg, the entire other side represents A eggs. Because fertilization is random, we find that half the area of the rectangle is composed of *AA* individuals and half of *Aa* individuals.

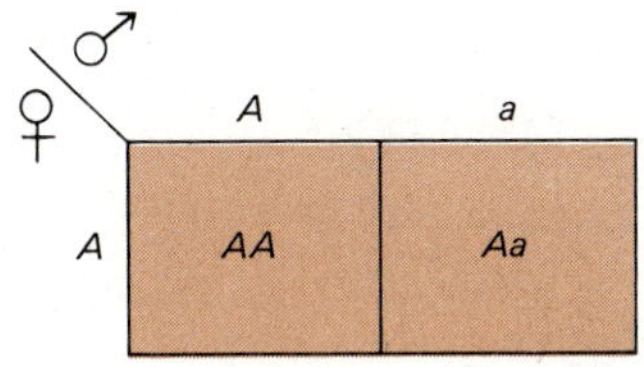

In other words, homozygous dominant and heterozygous individuals would be expected in equal proportions. Because the gene for the production of melanin is dominant to the allele for albinism, all these individuals would exhibit the same phenotype. Obviously any given couple can have only a limited number of children. By chance all of them may be *AA* or all *Aa* or most of them of either type. Because the production of gametes and the fertilization of eggs are both random and independent events, the genotype of the first child has no effect on that of the second or later children.

Using this same kind of reasoning, we can easily determine the expected children of two heterozygous individuals:

Aa × *Aa*

Both parents will produce *A* and *a* gametes in equal proportions, so:

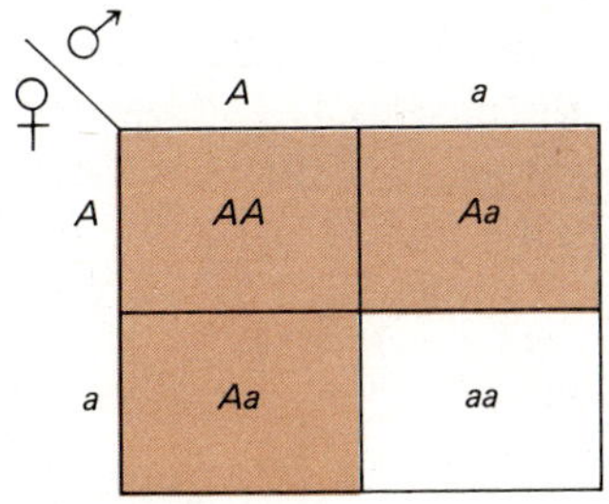

The four quarters of the population of expected children would consist of two quarters that were different from all others (*AA* and *aa*) and two that are identical to each other (*Aa*). Thus the ratio of genotypes, or the **genotypic ratio,** for the offspring of this mating would be 1:2:1. However, the *AA* and *Aa* individuals would be indistinguishable from one another in their appearance, so any classification by visible characteristics, or phenotypes, would lump these two genotypes together. Therefore, the **phenotypic ratio** would be three normally colored individuals to one albino. Similarly *Aa* × *aa* would yield:

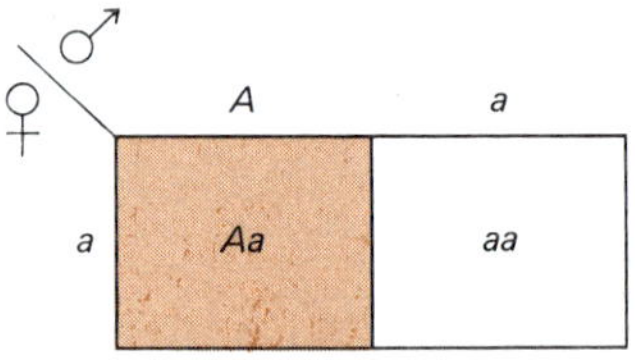

The expected offspring here would appear in a 1:1 ratio of genotypes and, because the genotypes would be reflected directly in their appearance, in a 1:1 ratio of phenotypes.

Probability. Our knowledge of genetic laws provides the opportunity to predict the outcome of conceptions between certain individuals. Genetics thus allows them to decide whether or not they wish to risk bearing defective children. Such predictions are seldom a certainty; they almost always deal in probabilities. For example, in the cross *Aa* × *Aa*, the probability that any given individual will be *aa* is one in four (from a 3:1 ratio). In other words, there is a 25-percent chance that a given child will be *aa*. Probability is stated in decimals, with 1.0 representing certainty of occurrence and 0.00 as certainty of nonoccurrence. If the chance of *aa* is one in four, the probability is 0.25. Similarly, the probability that an individual from a mating between *Aa* and *aa* individuals will be *Aa* is one in two or 0.5. One of the laws of probability states that the probability of two independent events' occurring together is the product of their separate probabilities. For example, assume that the sex ratio is 1:1. The probability that a child from a mating between two *Aa* individuals will be a boy of *aa* genotype is 0.5 × 0.25 = 0.125, or one in eight.

The Test Cross. It should be apparent that the phenotype of an individual does not indicate whether a person is homozygous dominant or heterozygous. In the example we considered above, both *AA* and *Aa* individuals show normal pigmentation. With laboratory animals and plants, it is possible to perform a test cross to determine the genotype of individuals showing the dominant trait. Although we cannot perform such experiments with humans, these findings nevertheless reveal an important aspect of genetic analysis.

In a test cross, an organism of unknown genotype is mated with a homozygous recessive individual. Because the genotype of homozygous recessives is always obvious, the results of a test cross will reveal the nature of the other parent. For example, the test cross *AA* × *aa* would yield only normally pigmented offspring:

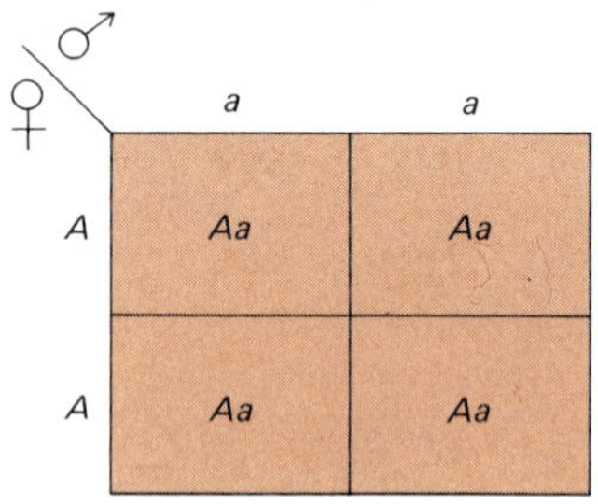

On the other hand, if the questionable individual is heterozygous, the test cross mating *Aa* × *aa* yields a phenotypic ratio of 1:1. The offspring are half normally pigmented and half albino:

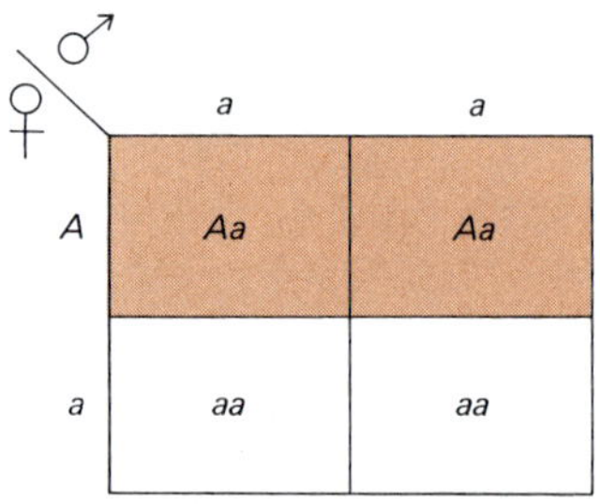

Incomplete Dominance. In many instances individuals with two different alleles will exhibit a phenotype intermediate between those shown by people who are homozygous. For example, sickle-cell anemia results from a defect in the protein portion of the hemoglobin molecule. Some of the hemoglobin molecules in those heterozygous for sickle-cell anemia contain normal proteins; other hemoglobin molecules in these people are abnormal. Individuals homozygous for the sickling allele bear only abnormal molecules. In contrast, the cells of heterozygous individuals sickle rarely. Because a single sickle-cell gene causes a minor form of the trait, this gene is said to show **incomplete dominance.** Situations like this in which the heterozygotes have phenotypes intermediate between those of the homozygotes are also called **intermediate inheritance.**

Polygenic Inheritance

Although some hereditary traits seem to result from the action of only a single pair of genes, most other

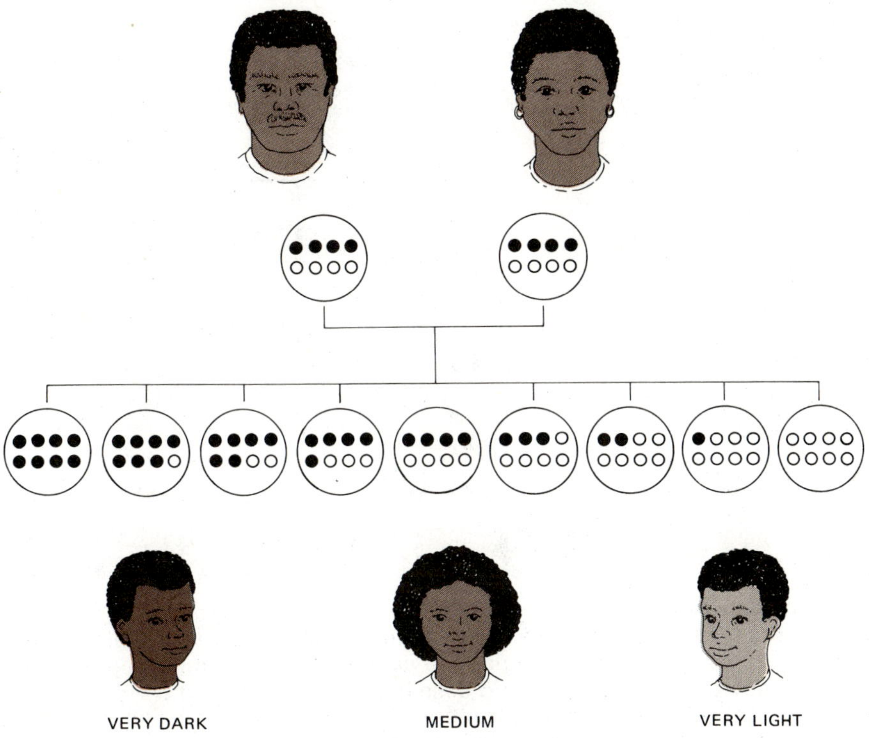

FIGURE 11.19 **Inheritance of Skin Color.** If a couple with medium coloration each have four melanin-producing and four neutral genes, their children may have anywhere from zero to eight melanin-producing genes. Thus moderately pigmented parents may have children who are very dark, very light, or any of seven shades in between.

human characteristics are assumed to be controlled by several pairs of genes. Evidently the expression of any one gene is influenced to some degree by other genes, each exerting a subtle effect on an inherited trait. Such **polygenic inheritance,** though difficult to analyze, is apparent from the continuous variation of certain traits in populations.

Take height, for example. Most humans are neither giants nor dwarfs. Although a few people are very tall or very short, most individuals are intermediates. A tall person's height is not merely the result of receiving a gene for tallness from his or her parents. Human height depends on genetic differences in hormone production, skeletal formation, and many other factors. Moreover, height also depends on environmental differences, such as diet. Other "genetic" traits are at least similarly complex.

Human skin color is not always the result of the inheritance of just one pair of genes, as our earlier examples may have implied. Current theory suggests that at least four different genes are directly involved in determining the broad range of human skin color (Fig. 11.19). Numerous other genes probably exert subtle, indirect effects.

Multitrait Inheritance

When we consider the inheritance of more than one trait, we must be aware of where the genes for the given traits are located. That is, are they on the same chromosome or on different chromosomes? Genes located on the same chromosome are said to be **linked genes.** Those found on different chromosomes are called **nonlinked genes.** Linked genes tend to be inherited together, whereas nonlinked genes are inherited independently. This last fact is of special importance, because it means that all possible combinations of non-linked genes may occur in gametes.

Independent Assortment of Chromosomes

Let us return to metaphase I and review carefully the crucial pattern of chromosome arrangement. The alignment of each tetrad is random; hence the arrangement of the tetrads of several pairs of chromosomes is also random. In other words, the chromosomes arrange themselves independently of each other. If there are two pairs of chromosomes, there are two possible arrangements (Fig. 11.20a). Each

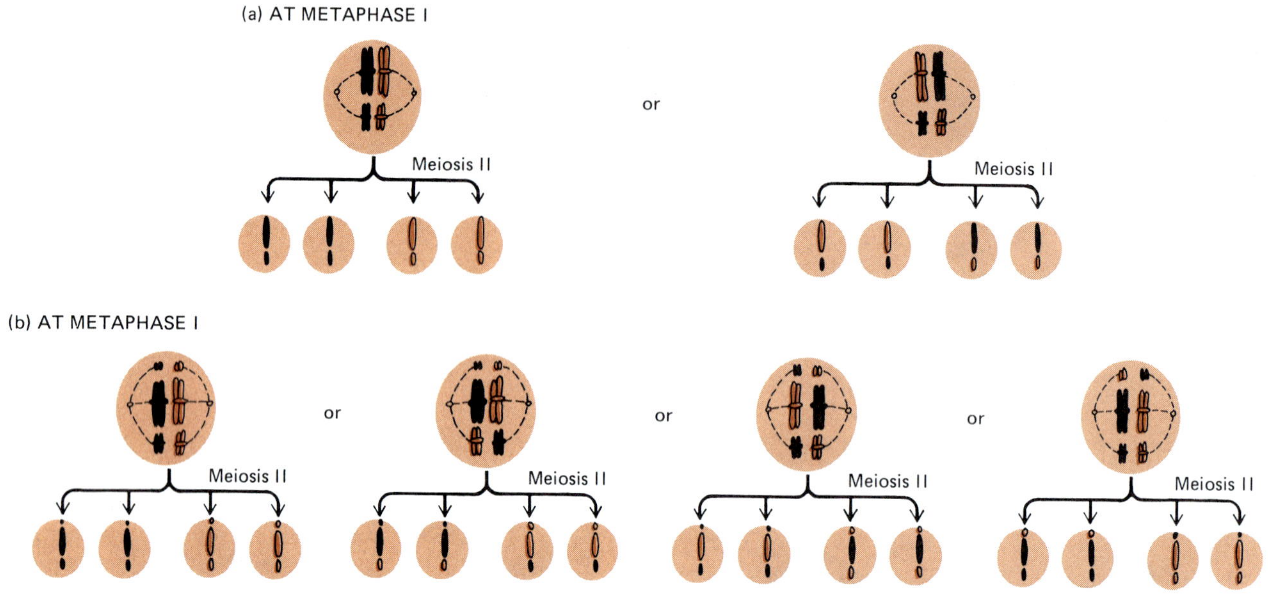

FIGURE 11.20 How Independent Assortment Ensures Variety. The dark chromosomes were inherited from one parent, the light chromosomes from the other parent. As indicated, there is no tendency of the chromosomes from one parent to stay together during meiosis. When the diploid number is four, as in (a), two possible arrangements may occur at metaphase I. Independent assortment thus yields four kinds of haploid cells in this case. In (b), eight different haploid cells have been produced by independent assortment of chromosomes in a cell whose diploid number is six.

is equally likely to occur. Any one cell has chromosomes in one arrangement or the other. Within a large population of cells, both arrangements occur with equal frequency. Because each of the two possible arrangements produces two types of daughter cells, a population of such cells undergoing meiosis will result in four different kinds of daughter cells.

With three pairs of chromosomes there are four possible arrangements, which can result in eight different types of daughter cells (Fig. 11.20b). If there are four pairs of chromosomes, eight arrangements are possible, producing sixteen different types of daughter cells. Thus the number of kinds of daughter cells doubles with each additional pair of chromosomes. Stated another way, the number of types of daughter cells is 2^n, where n equals the number of pairs of chromosomes. Since humans have 23 pairs of chromosomes, the number of kinds of daughter cells produced by meiotic assortment in us is 2^{23} (2 multiplied by itself 23 times). This is a very important source of genetic variability in sexually produced offspring. The effect on inheritance of independent assortment can be seen by consideration of a dihybrid cross.

Dihybrid Crosses. Crosses in which two nonlinked traits are studied are called **dihybrid crosses.** As an example of a dihybrid cross, consider the children to be expected from two individuals both heterozygous for hairline shape and both heterozygous for cystinuria, a predisposition to kidney stones.

A V-shaped hairline is dominant (V) over a smooth hairline (v). Individuals with cystinuria have a defect of the kidneys that prevents the normal reabsorption of four amino acids: cystine, ornithine, arginine, and lysine. Thus these four substances are present in high concentration in the urine. The cystine is only very slightly soluble and precipitates, forming kidney stones. There are other causes of kidney stones and more than one genetic defect that can cause cystinuria. We will consider the most common form, in which heterozygous individuals ($C'C$) have mild cystinuria and individuals homozygous ($C'C$) for this cystinuria excrete large quantities of cystine and are very apt to have kidney stones. Apparently one gene results in the production of a significant amount of the enzyme involved in the reabsorption of these amino acids, but not enough to prevent some loss of amino acids

BOX 11C

OF MONKS AND PEAS AND SCIENCE AND FAME

Gregor Mendel, a nineteenth-century Czechoslovakian monk, formulated the fundamental principles of genetics. His genetic "laws" were conceived in the course of breeding experiments with the ordinary garden pea. Mendel observed patterns of inheritance that proved the existence of independent hereditary factors—what we today call genes.

If you have studied earlier parts of this chapter, you are already aware of the concepts inherent in Mendel's laws. We will not give them in quite the way he did. (In the first place, Mendel didn't call them Mendel's laws.) In essence, Mendel's first law is that hereditary characteristics are controlled by genes, and that these genes occur in pairs. Furthermore, the two alleles of a gene pair can exist together without blending or otherwise contaminating each other. During the formation of sex cells, the members of a gene pair separate. As a result, sex cells contain only one gene of each pair.

Mendel's second law is simply stated. Genes for different traits are inherited independently of one another. Because you know that different pairs of chromosomes are distributed independently of one another at meiosis, these "laws" of Mendel may seem less than earthshaking. That is the way great discoveries usually seem, once they become part of the familiar.

Mendel's findings, based on careful studies of inheritance in garden peas, were ignored in his own lifetime. Surely Mendel was disappointed, for he had been an aspiring scientist and had taken holy orders largely to secure the financial independence he required to support his interest in

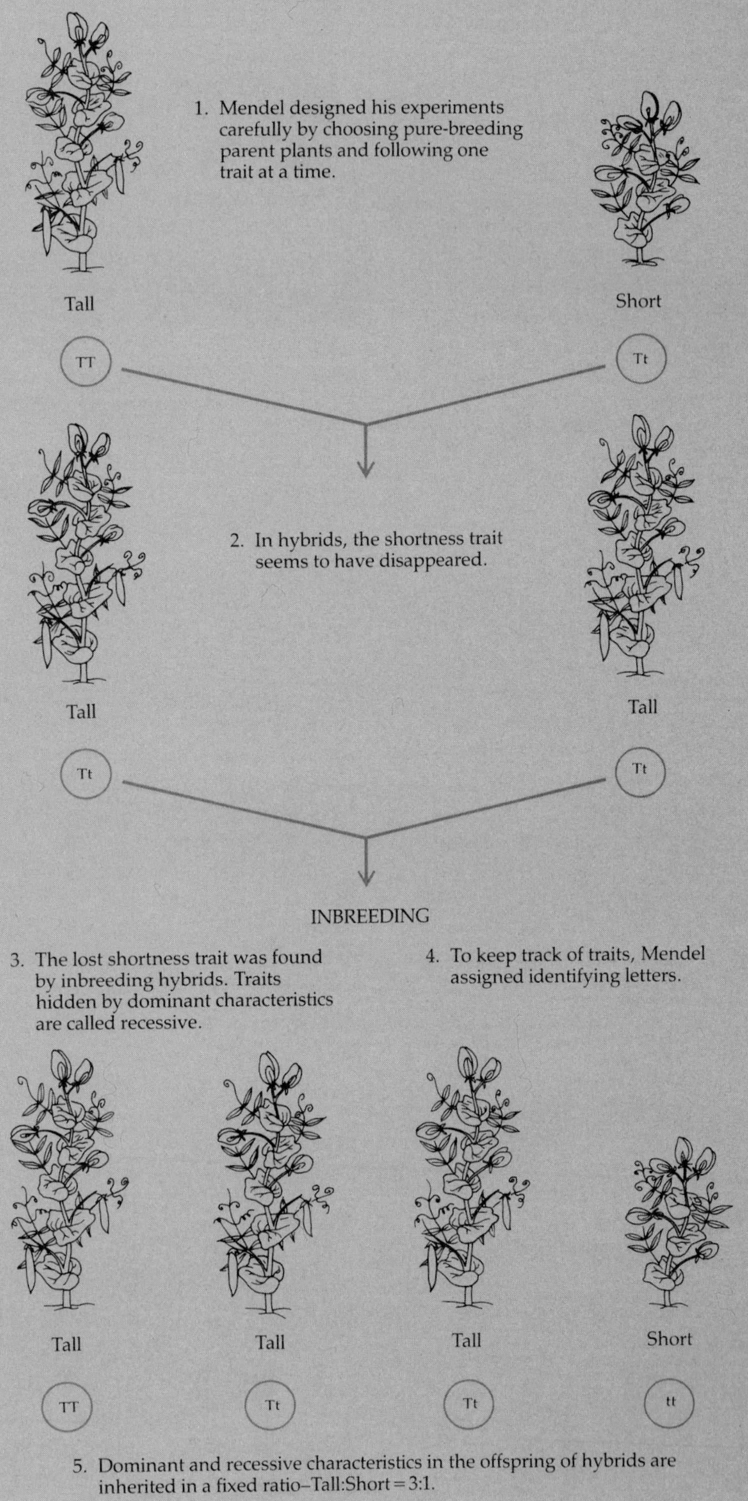

1. Mendel designed his experiments carefully by choosing pure-breeding parent plants and following one trait at a time.
Tall
Short
TT
Tt
2. In hybrids, the shortness trait seems to have disappeared.
Tall
Tall
Tt
Tt
INBREEDING
3. The lost shortness trait was found by inbreeding hybrids. Traits hidden by dominant characteristics are called recessive.
4. To keep track of traits, Mendel assigned identifying letters.
Tall
Tall
Tall
Short
TT
Tt
Tt
tt
5. Dominant and recessive characteristics in the offspring of hybrids are inherited in a fixed ratio–Tall:Short = 3:1.

BOX 11C continued

natural history. He was a successful high school teacher, but his attempts to publish the results of eight years of meticulous experiments were disappointing. Why? After all, he had carefully planned experiments to explore his earlier observations of some regular pattern of inheritance in plants. He had chosen peas because their flower structure favors self-pollination and because so much variation was available in cultivated varieties. And before starting his experiments, Mendel spent several seasons selecting pure breeding strains. For example, he obtained lines that always produced short plants and others that were always tall. He found other strains that produced only yellow seed and some that had only green seed. Once he began his experiments, Mendel devoted untold hours to keeping detailed records. Finally, Mendel analyzed his data, recognized distinct ratios, and proposed reasonable explanations for these ratios.

Though all his hard work and careful planning eventually bore fruit, Mendel was never to know fame. He published his report in 1866 in an obscure journal, and he faithfully distributed copies among European scientists. But no one was impressed.

As so often happens, the importance of Mendel's conclusions were lost on even those who might use them best. When Darwin published his *On the Origin of Species* in 1859, his theory of evolution was incomplete on some points. It was obvious that for natural selection to be effective in creating new species, the hereditary material would have to be passed from one individual to another. And it was equally evident that variability in the genetic material was necessary. Darwin himself suggested that each cell produced little structures that reflected its unique characteristics. These structures were supposedly sent to the eggs or sperm and were thus transmitted to the next generation. Being aware that some traits appeared in children and in their grandparents but not in their parents, Darwin supposed that not all the little structures were used up in making the new organism. Some were left over for the grandchildren!

Lack of exposure wasn't the only bar to recognition of Mendel's work. Although there is evidence that Darwin heard of Mendel's theories, the real reason for disregarding them was the state of science at that time. Generally biologists, and Darwin among them, were unaccustomed to mathematical treatments. The inherent value of quantitative measurements was poorly recognized. Perhaps another reason was that Mendel offered no physical basis for the processes he described.

At about the turn of the century, Mendel's laws began to make sense. By then microscopists had discovered chromosomes, mitosis, and meiosis. In 1900 three different people who were searching the literature for suggestions of how chromosomes are related to inheritance rediscovered Mendel's laws almost simultaneously and interpreted them to the scientific world.

As so often happens, valid conclusions had been long rejected because they failed to meet the mental set of the time. Mendel supplied both the facts and the interpretations, but neither were clearly perceived. Only when the intellectual climate changed was this knowledge accepted.

So much for the idea that science is merely the cataloging of facts or that scientists are purely rational students of the real world.

in the urine. Thus cystinuria can be considered an example of **incomplete dominance,** or **intermediate inheritance.**

A cross between two individuals homozygous for these traits may be written:

$$VvCC' \times VvCC',$$

where v = smooth hairline, V = V-shaped hairline, C' = gene not coding for enzyme necessary for reabsorption of cystine, and C = gene coding for enzyme necessary for reabsorption of cystine.

In order to complete the Punnett square, we must determine the genetic makeup of the eggs and sperm produced by these individuals. *Assuming that the genes for these traits are on different pairs of chromosomes,* we must only recall the pattern of assortment of chromosomes at meiosis I. Because the members of the two pairs behave indepen-

TABLE 11.2 Probable Progeny of the Dihybrid Cross *VvCC′* × *VvCC′*

GENOTYPES	RATIO	PHENOTYPES (RATIO = 9:3:3:1)	ALTERNATIVE EXPRESSION OF PHENOTYPES (RATIO = 3:6:3:1:2:1)
VVCC	1/16	9/16 V-shaped hairline; no tendency toward kidney stones	3/16 V-shaped hairline; no cystinuria
VvCC	2/16		
VVCC′	2/16		6/16 V-shaped hairline; mild cystinuria
VvCC′	4/16		
VVC′C′	1/16	3/16 V-shaped hairline; tendency toward kidney stones	3/16 V-shaped hairline; severe cystinuria
VvC′C′	2/16		
vvCC	1/16	3/16 smooth hairline; no tendency toward kidney stones	1/16 smooth hairline; no cystinuria
vvCC′	2/16		2/16 smooth hairline; mild cystinuria
vvC′C′	1/16	1/16 smooth hairline; tendency toward kidney stones	1/16 smooth hairline; severe cystinuria

dently, it is equally likely that sperm or eggs receiving the *V* gene will receive the *C* or *C′* gene. Thus each parent produces four possible types of gametes: *VC*, *VC′*, *vC*, *vC′*. The Punnett square for the mating is as follows:

♀ \ ♂	*VC*	*VC′*	*vC*	*vC′*
VC	*VVCC*	*VVCC′*	*VvCC*	*VvCC′*
VC′	*VVCC′*	*VVC′C′*	*VvCC′*	*VvC′C′*
vC	*VvCC*	*VvCC′*	*vvCC*	*vvCC′*
vC′	*VvCC′*	*VvC′C′*	*vvCC′*	*vvC′C′*

Tabulating the results, we find that the 16 individual squares that represent the population of possible offspring fall into the groups shown in Table 11.2.

Thus if we record the presence or absence of melanin and only the tendency toward kidney stones associated with severe cystinuria, the result is a 9:3:3:1 ratio. On the other hand, an analysis of the urine of the individuals involved permits us to distinguish between those that have severe cystinuria (the class having kidney stones), those with mild cystinuria, and those with no cystine excretion. This results in a ratio of 3:6:3:1:2:1.

It is possible to use the same principles to determine the offspring from crosses involving three or more traits resulting from genes on as many chromosomes. When we use terms such as monohybrid, dihybrid, or trihybrid, we refer to the number of differences being studied and not to all the differences that actually exist. Paying attention to only one or a few traits at a time is the key to successful genetic analysis. Organisms have so many traits that if we try to follow them all at once, we become hopelessly confused. Interaction among genes adds further complexity to inheritance, as does the fact that many genes are on the same chromosome and thus are inherited together. Remember that when describing the inheritance of albinism and cystinuria, we assumed that the genes involved lie on different chromosome pairs. The predictable ratios we have described depend on the fact that the genes are on different chromosome pairs.

Gene Mutation

New alleles of a gene appear by **mutation** of that gene—that is, by alteration in the structure of the segment of DNA that encompasses that gene. A mutation can involve a change as small as the substitution of one base for another. Such **point mutations,** as well as more substantial changes, can arise spontaneously or may be induced.

TABLE 11.3 A Short List of Chemicals Known to be Mutagenic under Some Conditions

Acridine (coal-tar) dyes
Bromouracil
Carbamates (found in some pesticides)
Cresol (found in disinfectants)
Cyclamate (artificial sweetener)
Formaldehyde (present in some shampoos)
Hydrogen peroxide (traditionally used to bleach hair)
Hydroxylamine
Mercury compounds (found in some pesticides)
Morphine
Mustard gas (employed in World War I)
Nitrates and nitrites (used to preserve some foods)
Nitrosamines
Nitrous acid

Spontaneous mutations have no obvious cause. They may result from cosmic radiation or random errors that occur during duplication of DNA. Whatever the cause, a mutation in one or more bases of DNA alters the codons in a genetic message. Translation of the message may be impossible, in which case no protein will be produced, or it may result in a protein with an altered amino acid sequence. If the change involves only one amino acid, the protein may still be able to function. This new protein may be more efficient or less efficient than the original protein. Thus the new allele may be dominant or recessive to the original allele.

The rate of spontaneous mutation is very low, on the order of 0.5 to 140 mutations per million egg or sperm produced. We quote the mutation rate for gametes because, although mutations can occur within any cell, only those in reproductive tissues can be transmitted to the next generation by gametes. Mutations in nonreproductive tissues are known as **somatic mutations.** Usually somatic mutations are transmitted to only a few cells, but those in embryos can affect a large part of the organism. It may be that somatic mutations are one factor in the appearance of cancer.

Certain chemical and physical agents called **mutagens** can increase the natural rate of mutation dramatically. These mutagens probably cause alterations in DNA similar to those that occur spontaneously.

The Chemical Basis of Mutation

A wide variety of chemicals, some common in our everyday environment, are mutagenic (Table 11.3). Although they may cause mutations in several ways, many of these agents act by chemically changing

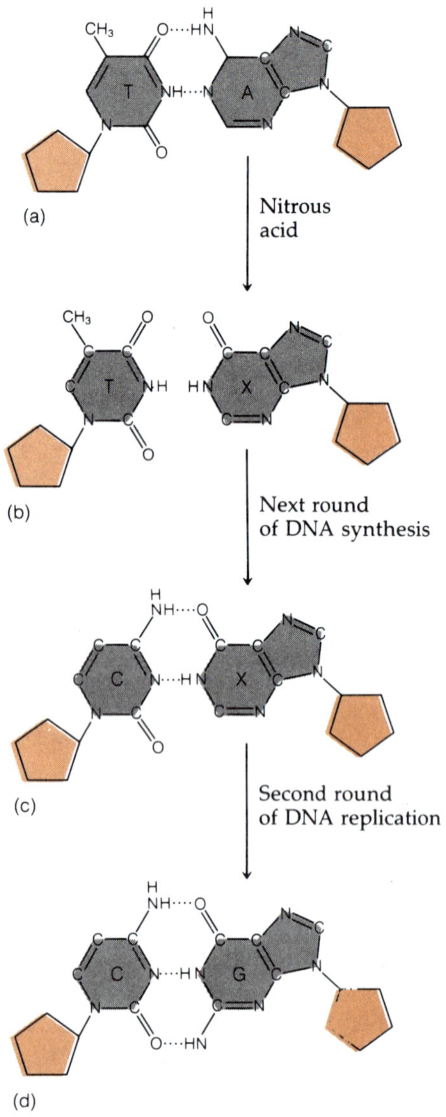

FIGURE 11.21 Chemical Mutagens Can Alter Base Pairing. Chemical reactions that alter the parts of the molecules involved in the hydrogen bonding can permit pairing with the wrong bases and thereby lead to mutations. For example, nitrous acid can react with adenine and convert it to hypoxanthine (X), as shown in (b). As is evident, the structure of hypoxanthine does not allow it to pair with thymine. However, hypoxanthine can pair with cytosine. Thus the next round of DNA synthesis results in a cytosine-hypoxanthine pairing. Then in the following round of synthesis, cytosine will pair with guanine, its normal partner. Thus nitrous acid can cause the substitution of cytosine and guanine in the place of thymine and adenine in the DNA helix.

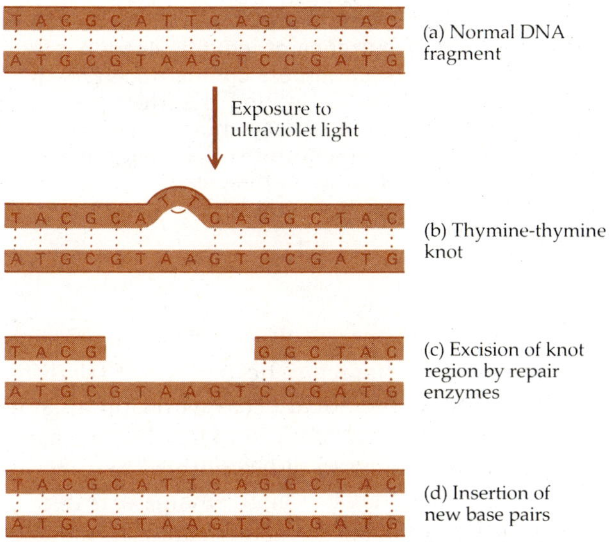

FIGURE 11.22 Repair of Ultraviolet Light-Damaged DNA.

DNA bases. A good example is nitrous acid, a substance that forms from nitrite (a common meat preservative) under acidic conditions (such as in the stomach). In order to understand how nitrous acid works, it is necessary to remember that the two chains of the DNA helix are held together by specific base-pairing. Normally adenine fits only with thymine, and cytosine fits only with guanine. Nitrous acid acts by converting adenine into hypoxanthine, a base that can pair with cytosine. The result is that an adenine-thymine pair is converted to a cytosine-guanine pair during DNA replication (Fig. 11.21).

Radiation-induced mutations also arise by chemical changes in DNA. Of the various forms of radiation, the mechanism of action of ultraviolet light is best understood. Ultraviolet light causes a reaction between adjacent thymines in one strand of DNA. This chemical reaction links the thymines together to form a tight knot that distorts the shape of the DNA molecule and interferes with DNA duplication.

Cells have specific **repair enzymes** for undoing mutations that arise by exposure to mutagens or by accidents that occur during DNA replication. There are enzymes that can fuse breaks that may occur within DNA strands. Others accomplish repair by "cut-and-patch" techniques. For example, thymine knots can be cut out and replaced by the normal thymine nucleotides (Fig. 11.22).

Multiple Alleles

When more than two alleles of a gene exist in a population, the alleles are called **multiple alleles.** The ABO blood group system provides an interesting example of such a situation. Three allelic genes, designated I^A, I^B, and i, are responsible for the four human blood types. The relationship between genotype and phenotype is shown in Table 11.4.

An individual of blood type A may be either homozygous (I^AI^A) or heterozygous (I^Ai). Thus the I^A allele is dominant to the i allele. Similarly, type-B individuals are either I^BI^B or I^Bi. Obviously both the I^A and the I^B alleles are dominant to the i allele. Type-O blood results if the individual is homozygous for the recessive i allele (ii). But how do the two dominant alleles relate to each other? In this case each simply carries out its normal function, so the individual exhibits both A and B substances. Blood type AB is another example of the fact that two alleles need not participate in a dominant-recessive relationship.

Errors in Chromosome Numbers

Accidents during meiosis can increase or decrease the number of chromosomes present in individuals conceived by abnormal gametes. This can happen if homologous chromosomes fail to separate at meiosis I (Fig. 11.23). Such accidents are one cause of **Down's syndrome,** once termed "mongolism" because it produces eye folds suggesting those of Oriental peoples. Down's syndrome results from an extra copy of the small chromosome number 21. The extra but otherwise apparently normal genetic material causes severe mental retardation, a small brain within a peculiarly flattened skull, a high narrow palate, irregular teeth, and short stature. The usual deformities also include short, broad hands with crooked little fingers. The ridges on the palms

TABLE 11.4 Inheritance of Human ABO Blood Types

BLOOD TYPE (PHENOTYPE)	GENETIC MAKEUP (GENOTYPE)	SPECIAL PROTEINS ON RED BLOOD CELL SURFACES
A	$I^A I^A$ or $I^A i$	A
B	$I^B I^B$ or $I^B i$	B
AB	$I^A I^B$	A and B
O	ii	none

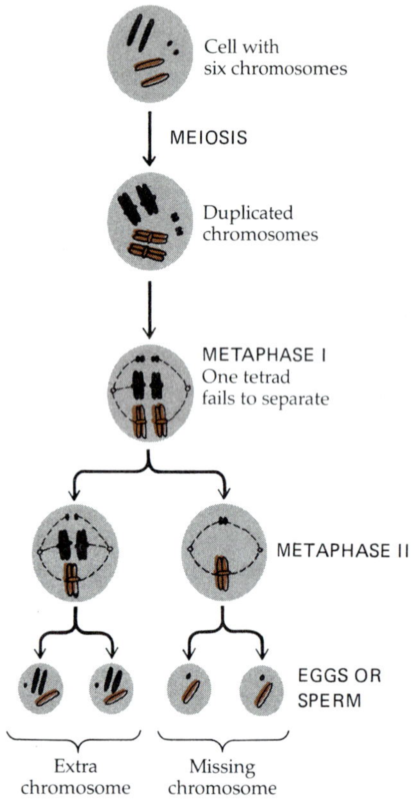

FIGURE 11.23 **When Homologous Chromosomes Fail to Separate.** The occurrence of individuals with abnormal chromosome numbers can be traced to an abnormal egg or sperm. Nothing is perfect. Meiosis of a cell with six chromosomes should yield gametes containing three chromosomes, but failure of chromosomes to separate at meiosis I, for example, can result in gametes with two or four chromosomes instead.

and soles form characteristic patterns that differ from those of people not affected with Down's syndrome. The higher incidence of Down's syndrome among children born to older mothers may be related to the fact that the egg remains arrested in prophase I of meiosis from the time a human female is born until she ovulates the egg as a mature woman.

A baby born when its mother is 46 comes from an egg that has remained in this stage for three times as long as one fertilized when the mother is 15. Perhaps chromosomal damage during this period prevents the normal separation of chromosomes or **nondisjunction** and results in an egg with

FIGURE 11.24 **Chromosome Typing.** Chromosomes are particularly easy to see in metaphase, when each chromosome consists of two chromatids joined at their centromeres. Colchicine, a chemical extracted from the autumn crocus, stops mitosis at metaphase, and it is therefore quite useful for studying chromosomes. Isolated chromosomes can be photographed and then systematically arranged into what is called a karyotype. One can detect hereditary defects caused by

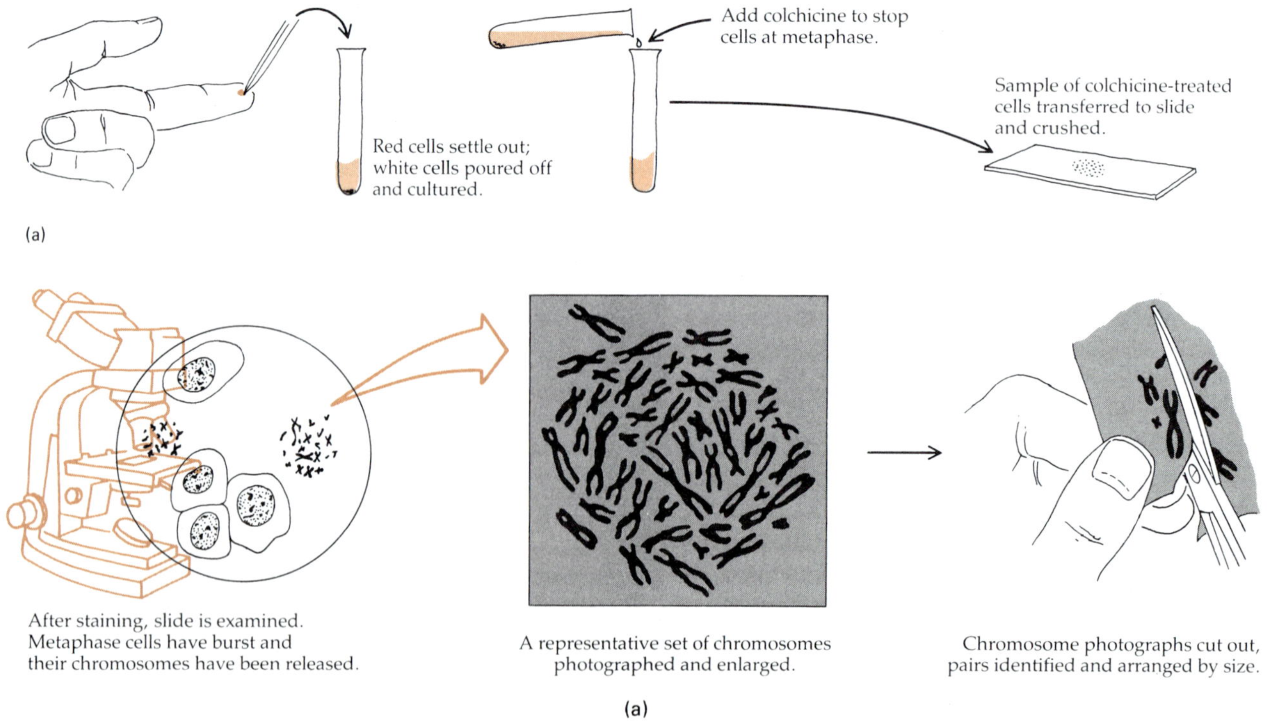

an extra chromosome. If such accidents add an extra chromosome to some eggs, they cause just as many eggs to lack a chromosome. Few of these eggs result in defective babies, however, because the absence of a chromosome is usually lethal. Extra chromosomes of other pairs also produce distinctive malformations.

SEX AND THE CHROMOSOMES

In humans, sex is determined by members of a pair of chromosomes known as the **sex chromosomes,** to distinguish them from the other chromosomes, called **autosomes.** Unlike autosomes, the sex chromosomes differ greatly in size and in the genetic factors they contain. For purposes of identification, one is known as the X chromosome, the other as the Y chromosome. The usual male phenotype results from the presence of one of each of these chromosomes, or XY. In contrast, females bear two X chromosomes and no Y chromosomes. Females are therefore XX.

As suggested by these genotypes, it is the sperm that determines the sex of the child. Normal eggs bear one X chromosome. Half the sperm contain an X chromosome and half a Y chromosome. Eggs fertilized by Y-bearing sperm become males (Fig. 11.25). Thus it is evident that half the babies born should be males and half females.

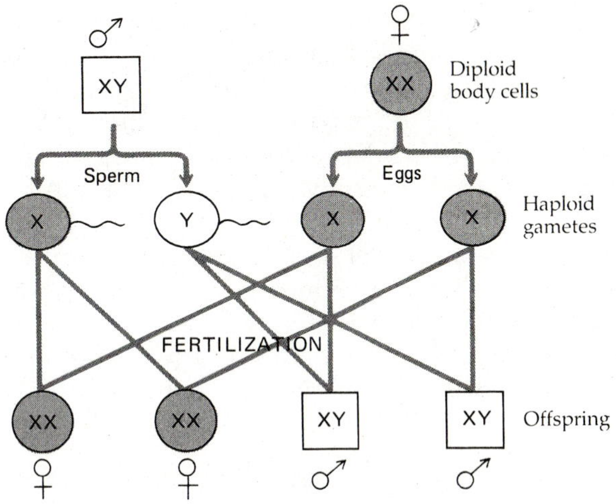

FIGURE 11.25 Determination of Sex. Every cell of a woman's body has two X chromosomes, but men have one X and one Y chromosome. Thus, following meiosis, every egg carries an X chromosome, but sperm have either an X or a Y. And so fertilization of an egg by an X sperm produces a girl, but fertilization by a Y sperm produces a boy.

Surprisingly, there has been considerable controversy over the human sex ratio. At birth the ratio is about 1.06 males to 1.00 female, but some studies of aborted fetuses suggest that the initial ratio may be nearly 1.5 males to 1.0 female. Nevertheless, the ratio at conception is difficult to determine, because many spontaneous abortions occur so early that the embryos are too small to be recovered. And observations of the apparent sex of those recovered is somewhat unreliable, because the external genitals of males and females are almost identical for some time. Recent investigations of the sex of aborted fetuses using chromosome examination techniques indicate that the ratio at conception may approach 1:1.

Marked differences in the genetic content of the X and Y chromosomes and the characteristic distribution of these two chromosomes between males and females result in unusual patterns of inheritance for traits on these chromosomes. Only a small portion, if any at all, of the two members of this pair are homologous in the sense that they contain the same genes or their alleles.

The strikingly larger X chromosome bears numerous genetic factors essential for normal devel-

missing or malformed chromosomes by examining a karyotype. A karyotype can be created manually (a), or the photographed chromosomes can be scanned by computer (b) and arranged automatically (c).

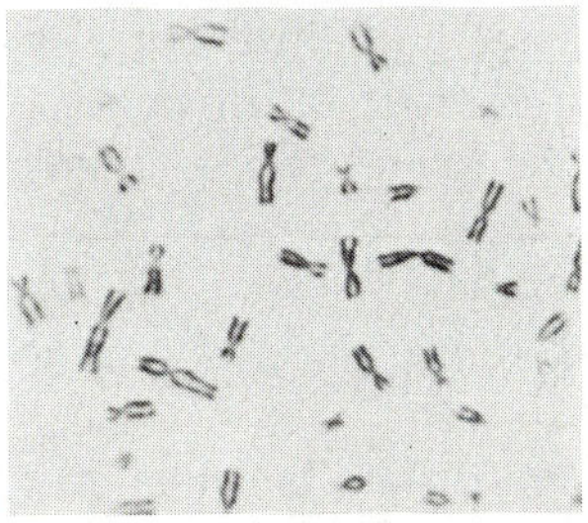
(b)

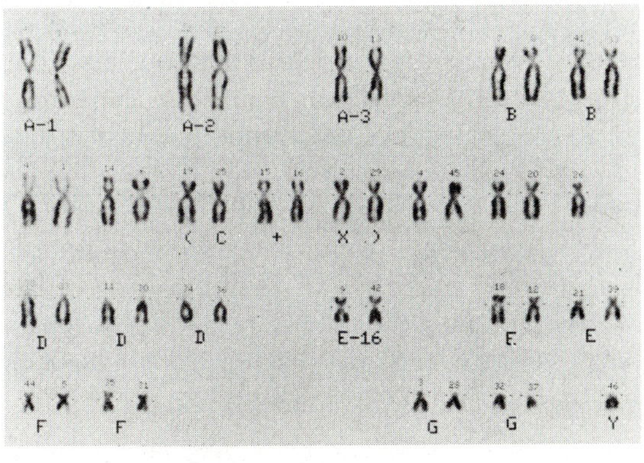

(c)

opment of all individuals. In contrast, the Y chromosome contains only a small number of factors of importance in determining the typical male phenotype and perhaps a very few not directly concerned with maleness. In fact, only one such gene has been reasonably well documented. A rare allele of this gene may result in the "hairy ears" trait. If this is true, all sons of men with hairy ears must have hairy ears. Similarly, all men with hairy ears must have fathers with hairy ears. These conclusions are inevitable, because each male receives his one Y chromosome from his father.

The Role of the Y Chromosome

We can attempt to understand the specific role of the Y chromosome in human males by considering individuals who have abnormal combinations of X and Y chromosomes. The most instructive cases are those in which only one X is present and the Y is absent. Such XO individuals exhibit a set of characteristics termed **Turner's syndrome.** Clearly female, XO women have poorly developed secondary sex characteristics, usually fail to menstruate, and are almost always sterile. Other common traits include being quite short, often under five feet, and possessing a peculiar widening of the neck at its junction with the back.

In contrast to Turner's syndrome is a condition in which men have an extra X chromosome. These XXY individuals are said to show **Klinefelter's syndrome.** Although obviously male, they have poorly developed testes that fail to produce sperm. And they have some feminine traits, such as enlarged breasts, high-pitched voice, and broad pelvis. Also, the pubic hair is limited to a triangle instead of extending upward toward the navel in a diamond as in most males. Long arms and legs, large hands and feet, and knock-knees contribute to a characteristic appearance, but these as well as other traits are quite variable. In a significant number of cases, mental retardation is evident.

The fact that an extra X chromosome accompanied by a Y yields a male (even if somewhat abnormal), and that either one or two X chromosomes not accompanied by a Y produces a female, establishes the Y chromosome as the fundamental cause of maleness, presumably through the genes it bears. Thus individuals lacking a Y become females; those with a Y become males. This correlates with the fact that the fundamental mammalian phenotype is female. If a male is castrated early in development, the absence of secretions of the embryonic testis will result in a phenotypically female individual, although the estrogen levels are inadequate to support full development of the female secondary sex characteristics. Individuals with atypical complements of sex chromosomes are usually reared within their limitations as ordinary males or females, and they behave accordingly. There is no apparent relationship between homosexuality and sex-chromosome abnormalities.

The XYY Genotype

A few years ago, attention was focused on men who have an extra Y chromosome. Because the XYY condition had been observed in some criminals, the hypothesis was offered that XYY men are excessively aggressive and likely to exhibit antisocial behavior. The matter has yet to be satisfactorily resolved.

There is only limited information on the incidence of the XYY trait in the general population. The only trait common to these men is their height, which is often over six feet. Accordingly, some authors have attributed the seemingly high incidence of XYY males in a few correctional institutions (about 2 per 100) to the social effects of increased height. Perhaps a tall boy, encouraged by his advantage, is more prone to be a bully. Or perhaps the attention of police approaching a group of unruly teenagers is most apt to fall on the tallest, whom they presume to be the oldest and the ringleader.

XYY men are fertile males and, interestingly, produce normal sons. The compensating mechanism that results in only X- or Y-bearing sperm remains unknown.

Inheritance of Genes on the X Chromosome

Some genes are said to be **sex-linked** because they are expressed more often in males. These sex-linked genes are recessive alleles that are expressed in females only when they are homozygous for that allele. Because a male has only one X chromosome, each gene on his X chromosome is always expressed. In a heterozygous female a recessive X-linked gene can be masked by a dominant allele.

An affected male receives the gene in question from his mother, because she is the source of his only X chromosome. From his father he inherits the Y chromosome that causes him to develop as a male. And since only females normally receive

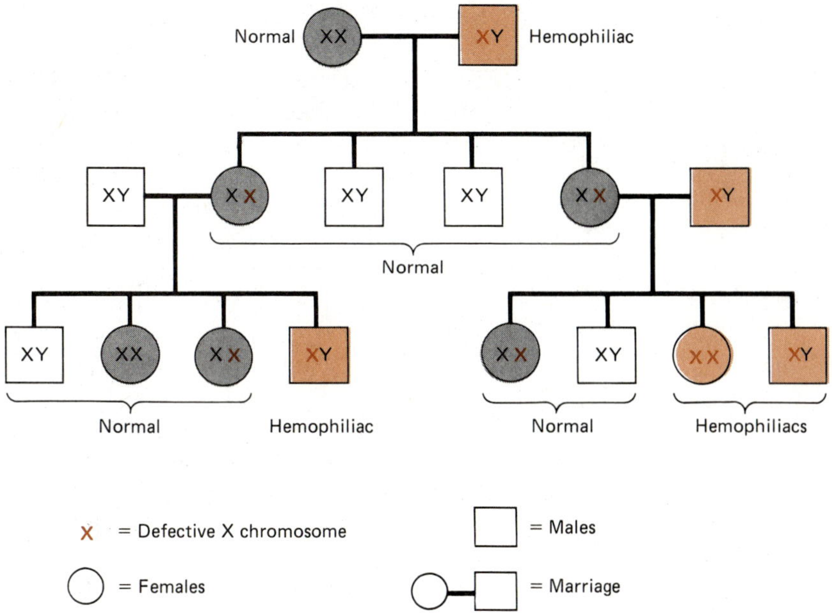

FIGURE 11.26 Pedigree Illustrating Inheritance of an X-Linked Characteristic. If a normal woman marries a man who is a hemophiliac, their children will be normal. The boys will get their single X chromosome from their mother, and so they will be free of the hemophilia trait, but all the girls will inherit their father's defective X chromosome and will be carriers. Therefore the daughters of this marriage, though unaffected themselves, will transmit hemophilia to some of their sons. Ordinarily females do not suffer from X-linked diseases. However, if a carrier marries a man who suffers from such a condition, as illustrated on the right, a daughter may inherit defective X chromosomes from both parents and thus suffer from the disease.

their fathers' X chromosome, all the daughters and none of the sons of affected men carry their fathers' recessive sex-linked genes. Women seldom bear identical recessive genes on both their X chromosomes and thus seldom exhibit these traits. For this reason **pedigrees** (diagrams showing family relationships and the presence or absence of certain traits) usually show the trait skipping generations.

Examine the pedigree in Fig. 11.26. Note not only that the trait skips generations but also that carrier females receive from their fathers a recessive gene they don't exhibit, and they transmit it to their sons, who do exhibit it. Carrier mothers can also transmit recessive X-linked genes to their daughters, who then become carriers.

The genes for hemophilia, or bleeder's disease, are on the X chromosome. Actually, there are two X-linked forms of this disease, caused by two different mutant genes at two different points on the X chromosome. Classical hemophilia, or type A, was at one time the scourge of some European royal families. It appears that individuals lacking the normal dominant allele fail to synthesize factor VIII, which is necessary for one step in the clotting of blood. Such individuals risk internal hemorrhage from the slightest damage to blood vessels. Many become permanently crippled as a result of hemorrhages into the knee joint when tiny vessels are ruptured during childhood jumping and running. Hemophilia B, or Christmas disease (named for the family in which it was discovered), is due to the absence of factor IX, another blood component that is also necessary for clotting.

Other sex-linked traits include several forms of partial color blindness, a common but medically unimportant blood group known as X_g, and **ichthyosis,** a condition in which the skin is so dry and scaly that it suggests fish skin.

Women as Mosaics!

The fact that there are two doses of all X-linked genes in normal females and only one dose in normal males seems surprising in light of the fact that autosomal genes are present in two doses in both sexes, and that any alteration, such as the addition of an extra autosomal chromosome, produces an abnormal individual. Why is the relative number of doses of autosomal genes so important and that of X-linked genes apparently unimportant? The best explanation is that both are important and that some mechanism compensates for the extra X-linked gene in females.

It has been established for some time that a dense region of chromatin, the **Barr body** (Fig. 11.27), appears in most if not all cells of female mammals but is absent in males. Apparently, during early development of a female, one randomly selected

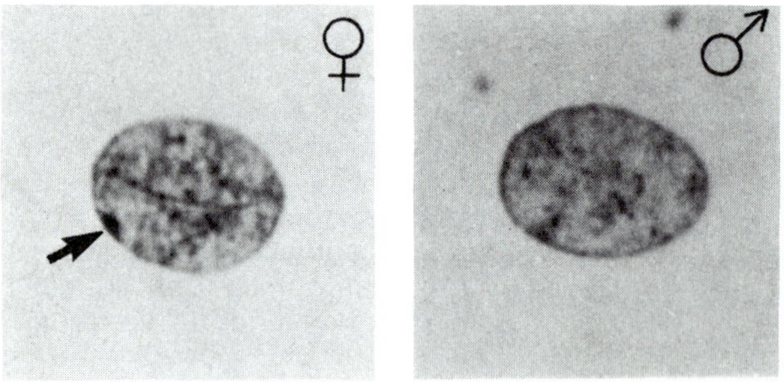

FIGURE 11.27 **The Barr Body.** This bit of dark-stained chromatin material is clearly visible at the periphery of the nucleus of an interphase cheek cell.

X chromosome in each cell is inactivated, and this inactivated X chromosome becomes the Barr body. A logical consequence of this random inactivation of X chromosomes in that each female mammal constitutes a mosaic for all X-linked traits for which she is heterozygous. In other words, all cells bear only one functional X chromosome and exhibit traits due to the genes on this chromosome, but in different body cells opposite X chromosomes may be functional.

Strange as this sounds, it explains many otherwise puzzling observations. Best known of these is the "tortoiseshell" cat. In the domestic cat, yellow and black alleles of a coat-color gene are on the X chromosome. Therefore males are either yellow or black, depending on which allele they carry. Homozygous females are either black or yellow, but heterozygous ones are mottled yellow and black in the familiar tortoiseshell pattern (Fig. 11.28). A similar patchiness has been demonstrated in the skin of women heterozygous for the X-linked trait causing absence of sweat glands in the skin. Thus in each cell of a woman, one—and only one—X chromosome functions. Effectively, each cell contains not two X chromosomes but one.

This random inactivation of X chromosomes evidently occurs when the embryo consists of 3000 to 4000 cells, for this is when Barr bodies appear. The real nature of this inactivation is poorly understood, but it never extends to those cells that will form the reproductive cells. It is obvious that inactivation of one of the X chromosomes in cells that were to form eggs would result in half the eggs bearing inactive X chromosomes.

Further evidence that the formation of the Barr body is a method of compensating for extra X chromosomes is provided by the absence of the Barr body in XO Turner's syndrome individuals. Not surprisingly, XXY men possess the Barr body, just as normal females do.

Because among individuals with the normal number of 46 chromosomes all females exhibit Barr bodies and all males lack Barr bodies, this structure is frequently used as an indicator of genetic sex. It is easily demonstrated in many cells, including those that can be scraped from the lining of the mouth.

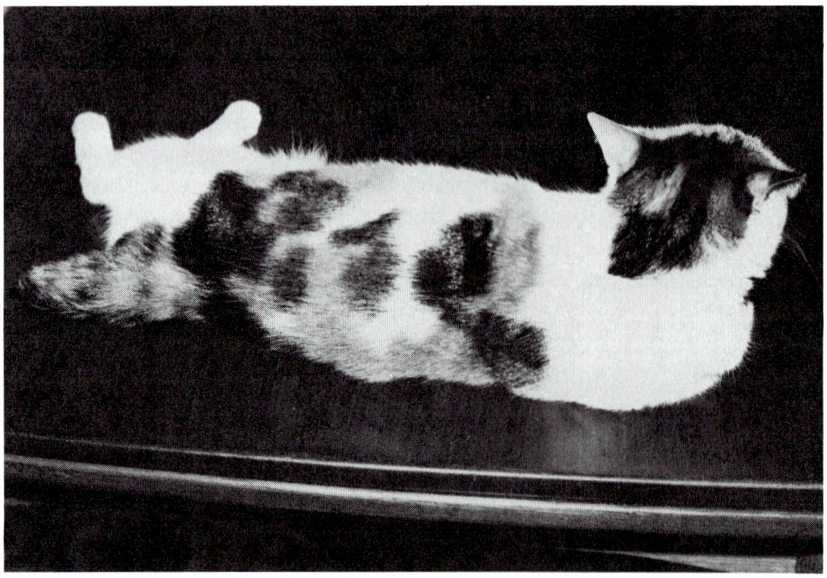

FIGURE 11.28 **A Tortoiseshell Cat.** The patches of black and orange-yellow fur on this female cat's coat result from the fact that one of the X chromosomes of her cells carries a gene for black hair, and the other X chromosome carries a gene for orange-yellow hair. In some hair-producing cells the gene for black fur is inactive, and in others the gene for orange-yellow fur is inactive. Hence the mosaic appearance of her coat.

What We Know and Don't Know

Although many questions remain unanswered, the outline of what genes are, how they work, and how they are passed from one generation to the next seems quite clear. Genes are part of DNA molecules carried within chromosomes. The distribution of chromosomes at meiosis and fertilization determines which genes a given individual receives. Genes control metabolism by acting as patterns for the synthesis of mRNA, which in turn determines the pattern of amino acids in a particular protein. Because cell structure and function are regulated by specific enzymes, control of protein synthesis defines what an organism can do.

In cases of disorders such as hemophilia and sickle-cell anemia, we can relate a genetic defect or a whole series of defects to a single aberrant protein. These problems result from one gene that produces a faulty protein. But we are a long way from understanding all the interactions of genes and gene products that produce a nose, whether it is a pug nose or an Elizabethan nose.

As the reader knows, we have emphasized human heredity and used examples from our species. Much but not quite all we have said is applicable to other organisms as well. In fact, the basic molecular genetics and the role of DNA, RNA, and proteins were determined in bacteria. Now we know that their functions are the same in all biological systems, except for some viruses that substitute RNA for DNA. There are minor differences in the timing of some genetic processes in plants as compared with animals. In most plants, meiosis occurs sometime before appearance of eggs and sperm. Thus plants have haploid cells that divide by mitosis to form sex cells. Nevertheless, the same genetic principles apply.

An understanding of genetics contributes to our view of the unity of life, but it is even more valuable for the insight it provides into evolution. Genetic mechanisms lie at the origin of the innumerable species on earth today, and they account for those already extinct, as well. We will explore this topic in a later chapter.

Summary

1. Mitosis is the usual process of cell multiplication in eucaryotes. In mitosis two daughter cells are produced from one parent cell. The genetic patterns in the daughter cells are identical to those of the parent cell. For this reason all cells of an animal (except eggs and sperm) have the same genetic capabilities. Gametogenesis involves meiosis, a process that reduces the chromosome number from diploid to haploid.

2. The DNA of chromosomes is the carrier of genetic information. This molecule, which is basic to all forms of life, is composed of nucleotide subunits. A nucleotide is made up of deoxyribose, phosphate, and a nitrogenous base.

3. In DNA, nucleotides are joined together through sugar-phosphate linkages to form a double-stranded helix. The two strands are held together by hydrogen bonds between paired nitrogenous bases. Adenine is always paired with thymine, and guanine is always paired with cytosine.

4. The complementarity of DNA bases explains the mechanism of DNA duplication. The two strands separate, and free nucleotides attach themselves to each strand by base-pairing. Polymerization is completed by enzyme action.

5. The genetic information in DNA is found in the sequence of nucleotides, which codes for the sequence of amino acids in proteins. A segment of DNA with the information specifying the structure of a particular protein is a gene. DNA does not participate in protein synthesis directly but directs the synthesis of RNA, which directs the synthesis of proteins.

6. RNA differs from DNA in that it is single-stranded, its nucleotides contain ribose, and uracil is found instead of thymine. RNA is produced from DNA in the nucleus, but it performs its function in the cytoplasm.

7. Messenger RNA carries the genetic code for sequencing amino acids to the ribosomes, where protein synthesis occurs. The code consists of triplet nucleotide codons, whose order stipulates the placement of amino acids. Specific transfer RNAs bring each amino acid to the ribosomes in an orderly manner by reading the codons as they arrive on the synthetic sites of the ribosomal particles.

8. Gene expression is regulated by a variety of processes. Control genes produce repressors that prevent transcription, and hormones and histone proteins of chromosomes may have similar effects. Transposable genetic elements may move from one chromosome to another to control gene action.

9. Nuclei of diploid organisms contain two of each kind of chromosome. This means that genes are also paired. Each member of a gene pair is called an allele. If one allele masks the expression of the other, the first is said to be the dominant allele. Partial or incomplete dominance results in intermediate inheritance. Most inherited traits result from polygenic inheritance.

10. During formation of eggs and sperm, each allelic pair behaves independently of the others, producing an independent assortment of the members of each gene pair in the next generation.

11. Mutations are inherited changes in the genetic material. They may be due to alteration of DNA structure or to gross rearrangements within chromosomes. Mutations occur in both reproductive and somatic tissues.

12. Deviations in the number of chromosomes can have a harmful effect on the development of an individual. Aberrations in chromosome number occur because an individual was conceived by abnormal gametes that resulted from mistakes during meiosis.

13. Females have two X chromosomes, and males have one X chromosome and one Y chromosome. The larger X chromosome contains genes essential for development. The much smaller Y chromosome contains only a few genetic factors, mostly related to maleness.

14. Traits carried on X chromosomes are said to be sex-linked. Since males have only one X chromosome, recessive genes carried on that chromosome are always expressed. They are transmitted from mother to son, because males receive their X chromosome from their mother.

Thought and Controversy: Genetics Problems

1. Interpret the pedigree below, and decide the most probable mode of inheritance of the trait indicated by shading and the noted genotypes of each individual.

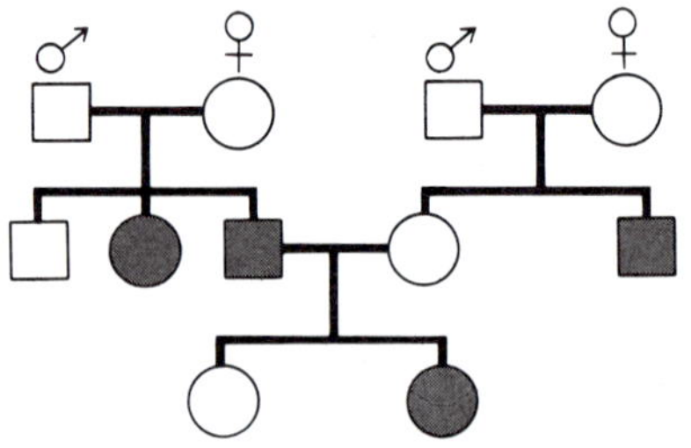

2. Some genes show a peculiar sex-related but not X-linked inheritance. Pattern baldness is a well-known example in which the gene appears dominant in men and recessive in women. If men castrated early in life (eunuchs) carry the single gene, they do not become bald unless they are given testosterone. Draw a possible pedigree showing the expected relationships among individuals exhibiting pattern baldness, which causes balding in as many as 40 percent of male Caucasians.

3. If the first-born child of normal parents is a daughter with phenylketonuria (an autosomal recessive), what is the probability that

a) the next child will be affected?

b) the next child will be a normal son?

c) the next child will be an unaffected person who will carry the gene and have the potential of passing it on to grandchildren?

d) if the second child is an affected daughter, the third will be a normal son?

4. Well-established modes of inheritance have been accepted as legal evidence in cases of disputed paternity. Blood groups are often used. In addition to the usual ABO group, the MN group, which is of no known medical significance, has also been employed. An individual may be MM, NN, or MN. These genes show no dominance. A woman of blood types AB and M with a baby of types A and MN has charged a certain man with unacknowledged fatherhood. Which blood type(s) would establish that the man could not be the father? Is it possible to use blood types to *prove* paternity?

5. Assume that in a given plant, red flower color is known to be dominant over white flower color. Design a test cross to determine the genotype of a red-flowered plant. How would you explain inheritance of flower color in another plant species where purebred red- and white-flowered parents produce pink-flowered offspring?

6. Although eye color is often given in elementary texts as an example of a single gene effect, with brown dominant over blue, a glance around any classroom will indicate that this is a gross oversimplification. Given the following information, can you suggest what kind of inheritance must be involved in determining eye color?

The color of the iris of the eye is due primarily to the presence of melanin, the same brown pigment present in the skin. Individuals have varying amounts of melanin in their eyes and hence different eye colors. Blue-eyed individuals have very little melanin, and their eye color is due to the scattering of light by iris cells against the black background of the eye cavity, much as the scattering of light by the atmosphere gives a blue sky against what is really very dark outer space. A little pigment thinly dispersed gives a yellowish color that overrides the blue effect to produce a hazel color. With increasing melanin, the eye becomes brown and eventually black.

Questions

1. What is accomplished by mitosis? Describe the important features of the four main stages of mitosis.

2. How does meiosis differ from mitosis? What is the relationship between meiosis and gametogenesis?

3. Define the following terms: *interphase, chromatin, chromatid, centromere, homologous chromosome, nucleoprotein.*

4. Describe the arrangement in DNA of sugars, phosphate, and nitrogenous bases. Include a discussion of the importance of complementary base-pairing in DNA structure.

5. How does RNA structure differ from DNA structure? Name the three major forms of RNA and give the function of each.

6. Compare and contrast DNA duplication and transcription.

7. Explain the term *genetic code.* How is the genetic code translated?

8. How do mutations occur? How does a mutation affect the genetic code? Transcription? Translation? Can mutations be repaired?

9. Explain how an individual can have an extra chromosome. Why is the lack of a chromosome usually lethal?

10. Why are females said to be "mosaics"?

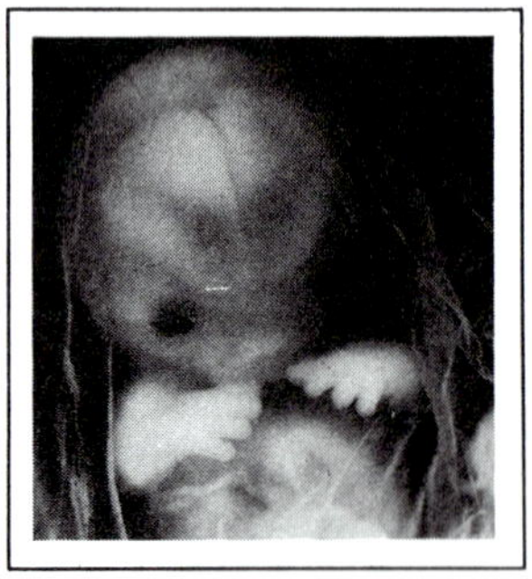

12

Reproduction: Sex and Procreation

DEATH BY ACCIDENT, DISEASE, OR AGING AWAITS all organisms. If a population is to continue, those that die must be replaced. Reproductive mechanisms are as diverse as species, but even though we usually associate reproduction and sex, some species can reproduce asexually.

In **asexual reproduction**, a single parent produces offspring with characteristics identical to itself. This method has important advantages. One is its lack of dependence on the presence of other individuals. One organism can start a whole new population. Furthermore, asexual reproduction may be simpler and more efficient (Fig. 12.1). By comparison, sexual reproduction seems needlessly complicated.

SEX: WHAT AND WHY

Sexual reproduction involves fusion of cells from two individuals. For most species these individuals and their sex cells differ. **Males** produce small, actively motile cells called **sperm.** In contrast, the **female** egg, or **ovum,** is a large cell rich in food reserves and cytoplasmic structures. It cannot move actively; it can only drift or be carried by action of surrounding cells. To form a new individual, the sperm and egg must meet. Elaborate structures and complex behavior can be necessary to bring about this union. The midnight brawls of cats, the spring chorus of frogs, the nesting-season music of song birds, and myriad courtship displays all contribute to bringing sperm and eggs together.

For humans the interest, emotion, and drive that surround sex serve the same purpose: to ensure that sperm reach eggs. The love of children and the desire to have them are powerful forces in many human lives. Nevertheless, what people often seek in sex is personal gratification, companionship, love, or maybe just escape. In our culture the psychological and social consequences of sex blur its biological significance. But in the bargain we conceive and beget children.

Compared with asexual reproduction, sexual reproduction may seem cumbersome. Nevertheless, the vast majority of organisms reproduce by sexual means—and for good reason. Sexual reproduction does not merely preserve the old patterns. Union of hereditary material in the egg and sperm produces young that are different from either parent. Thus every new generation of a sexually reproducing species contains new combinations of characteristics. This increases the chance that the species can survive any environmental changes. For this reason, species that usually reproduce asexually almost always are capable of sexual reproduction as well. Sometimes both asexual and sexual reproduction are part of one life cycle. Other species, including all mammals, are strictly sexual 27
creatures.

MAN: SPECIALIZATION FOR TRANSFER OF GENETIC MATERIAL

The reproductive system of human males consists of an extensive complex of glands and tubes, together with the **external genitals,** the penis and scrotum (Fig. 12.2). The tube system begins in the testes, where it is the site of sperm production, and extends to the penis. Along the way, five glands secrete fluids that contribute to the semen.

The Testes

The testes are the male **gonads,** that is, the source of the sperm. In men these sperm-producing organs lie within the **scrotum,** a pouch of skin that hangs behind the penis. The scrotum is normally quite loose, but when a man is cold or frightened, muscle in the skin contracts and tightens the scrotum, pulling it closer to the body.

To reach the scrotum, the testes migrate from their point of origin near the kidneys, usually during the last two months before birth. As the testes descend into the scrotum, they pass through the **inguinal canals,** openings in the abdominal wall. Blood vessels and nerves serving each testis and its sperm duct (vas deferens) follow the descending testis and lie in the canals thereafter. These canals between muscles of the abdominal wall are weak spots that can be opened by pressure. Lifting or straining may rupture the wall and force a loop of intestine into a canal, producing an **inguinal hernia.**

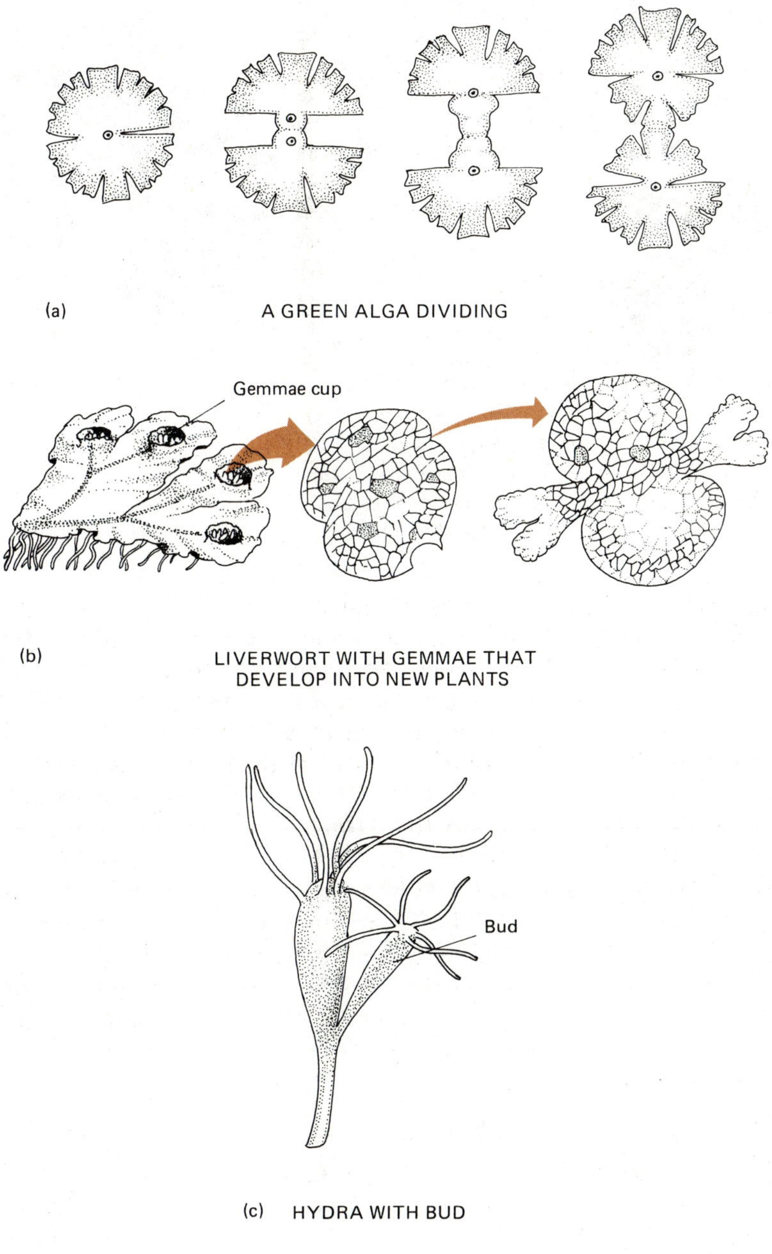

FIGURE 12.1 **Asexual Reproduction.** Reproduction by other than sexual means occurs in a wide range of plants and animals. (a) This microscopic aquatic plant simply divides in two, and each new daughter regenerates missing parts until it resembles the original parent. (b) Liverworts have specialized structures for asexual reproduction. Each mass of cells in the gemmae cups can differentiate into a plant like the parent liverwort. (c) A hydra, a freshwater animal related to coral and jellyfish, forms new members of its kind by budding.

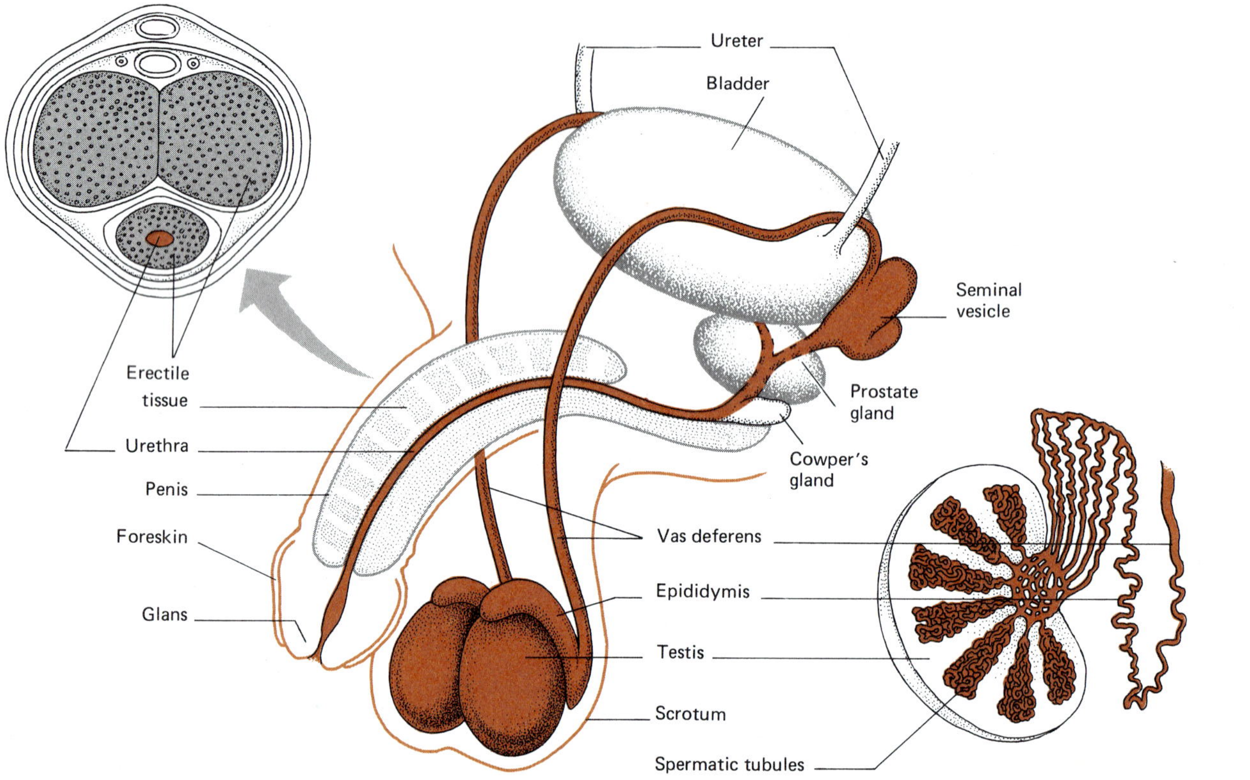

FIGURE 12.2 Male Reproductive System. Trace the sperm pathway from the testis to the penis. The loop you see results from the fact that the testis descends through the abdominal wall above the pubic bone.

The normal location of the testes in the scrotum, rather than deep in the body cavity, seems related to heat sensitivity of the sperm-producing tissue. If the testes remain in the body cavity, the heat there will destroy the germinal tissue. Although testes often fail to descend properly, sterility can be prevented through a simple operation on the newborn baby. The testes are drawn from the abdominal cavity to the scrotum, where they belong.

The testes have two main functions: formation of sperm and production of the male sex hormone, **testosterone.** Sperm develop in long, coiled **spermatic tubules** (Fig. 12.2). Among the tubules lie **interstitial cells,** which synthesize testosterone. Production of sperm and testosterone are continuous in the male, in contrast to the more cyclic nature of female reproductive events.

Testosterone is necessary for full development of the spermatic tubules and for **libido** (sex drive). It is also responsible for the **secondary sexual characteristics** of males, including a low voice, heavy facial hair, a muscular body, and distinctive skeletal build. These and other hormonal aspects of sexual differences will be explored when we compare men and women later in this chapter.

Activity of the testis is regulated by pituitary hormones (Fig. 12.3). **Interstitial-cell-stimulating hormone (ICSH)** from the anterior pituitary is necessary for secretion of testosterone by the interstitial cells. **Follicle-stimulating hormone or FSH** (so named for its function in the female) supports normal development of spermatic tubules. Through a negative-feedback mechanism involving the hypothalamus, testosterone reduces secretion of ICSH and FSH.

Sperm

Sperm formation begins with meiosis. These divisions and their role in the patterns of inheritance were discussed in Chapter 11. Here we will examine only the maturation that converts rather ordinary-appearing cells□, spermatids, into specialized carriers of genetic information. In this process the nucleus condenses to form the dense sperm **head.** At the tip of the head, the **acrosome,** a sac of enzymes develops. Later, these enzymes aid in penetration of the egg. Eventually the scattered mitochondria of the developing sperm become closely packed into a spiral behind the head (Fig. 12.4). This **mitochondrial spiral** is twisted around the root of the flagellum that makes up the long tail. Arranged this way, the mitochondria require little space but are strategically located to supply energy to the flagellum that propels the sperm. During sperm maturation, much of the original cytoplasm is discarded. The fully developed sperm consists only of a densely packed genetic "payload" and the structures necessary to carry this material to the egg.

Sperm are shed from the spermatic tubules into the **epididymis,** an extensively coiled tube that connects with the **vas deferens** (plural, **vasa deferentia**), which translates literally to mean "the vessel that carries away." The vas deferens extends up into the abdominal cavity, where it joins the urethra. Thus the sperm leave the body via the urethra, as does the urine.□ 156

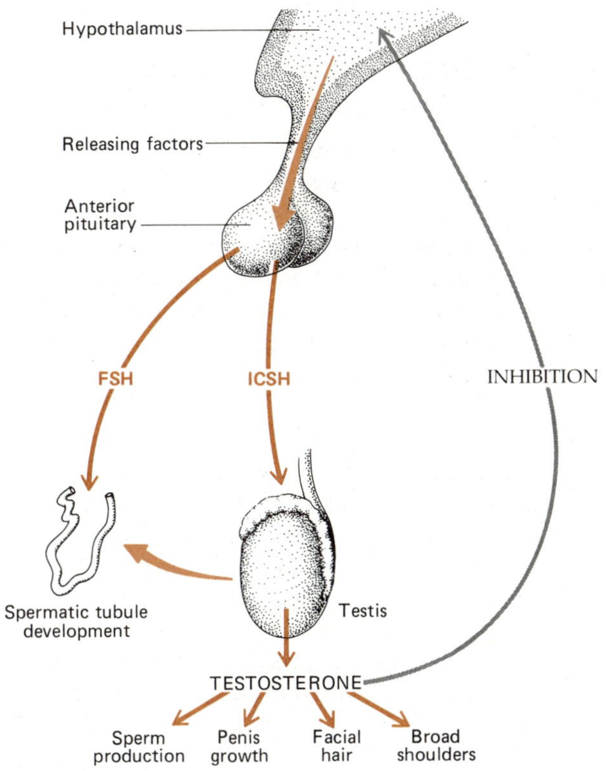

FIGURE 12.3 **Hormones in the Male.**

FIGURE 12.4 **Compare a Sperm with an "Ordinary" Body Cell.** Note that each part of the sperm originates from some organelle found in less structurally specialized cells. (a) Loss of much of its cytoplasm contributes to making a sperm (b) dense with precisely packed organelles.

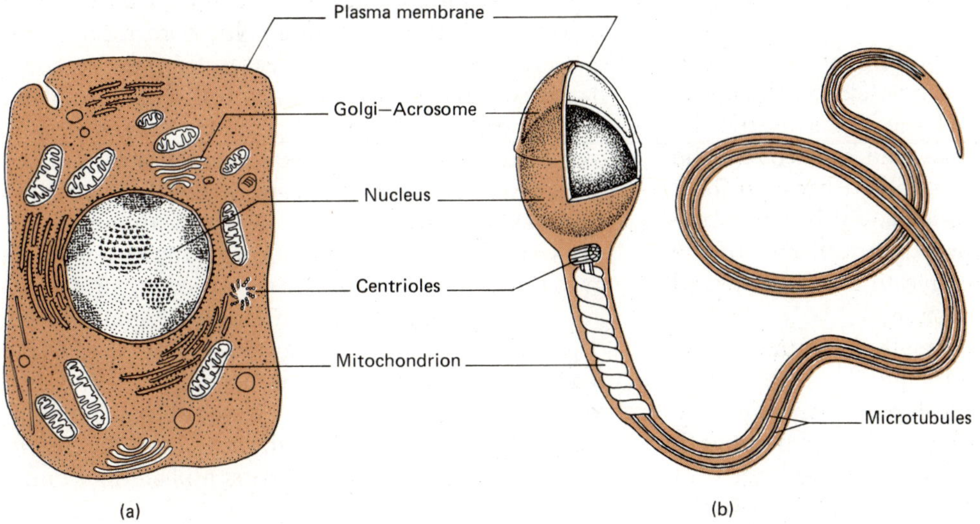

Sperm accumulate in the epididymis and must remain there for at least three weeks before they are completely mature. Although resorption of sperm occurs if the vas deferens is severed surgically, sperm are ordinarily released at intercourse or masturbation or during nocturnal emissions (wet dreams). When sperm leave the male tract, they are fully motile. However, a further change, triggered by female secretions, is necessary before a sperm can fertilize an egg.

Semen

Before they leave the body, sperm are suspended in glandular secretions. These liquids come mainly from the **seminal vesicles,** the **prostate,** and the **Cowper's glands** (Fig. 12.2). Together these fluids and the suspended sperm make up the milky **semen,** the fluid that is ejaculated from a man's body when he experiences orgasm.

Of the three sets of accessory glands that contribute to the semen, the prostate is the largest. The location of the prostate can prove to be a treacherous arrangement in older men. It surrounds the junction of the vas deferens and the urethra. In many aging males the prostatic tissue recommences growth. Usually—but not always—these growths are noncancerous. Nevertheless, even a simple enlargement of the prostate causes problems. The new growth compresses the urethra, making urination difficult or impossible. If this condition remains untreated, urine can back up into the kidneys, and the resulting pressure can destroy them.

The Penis

The penis provides a conduit for the **urethra,** which carries urine and semen to the outside of the body. A vertical slit at the tip of the penis marks the opening of the urethra. The skin that covers the outside of the penis shaft is folded back on itself at the tip to form the **foreskin,** which covers the glans. The **glans** is the large, smooth end of the penis. It is especially sensitive to stimulation and enlarges greatly during erection.

Unlike many other mammals, the human male has no cartilage or bone in the penis, which is normally soft and flaccid. But within the penis lie three masses of erectile tissue. These tissues expand with blood during sexual excitement and enlarge and stiffen the penis. One of the bodies of **erectile tissue** surrounds the urethra and expands at the tip to fill the glans.

WOMAN: CYCLIC CHANGES PERMIT MULTIPLE TASKS

In contrast to the meandering tubes and multiple glands of the male reproductive tract, the female organs appear deceptively simple (Fig. 12.5). They consist of a pair of **ovaries** (female gonads), two **Fallopian tubes** (oviducts) that lead to the **uterus** (womb), the **vagina,** and the external genitals. Some of these organs, especially the ovaries and uterus, undergo marked cyclic changes. These changes occur as each ovum matures and either degenerates or is fertilized and develops into a baby.

Sperm deposited in the vagina make their way through a tiny opening in the **cervix,** or "neck," at the lower end of the uterus (Fig. 12.5). Fertilization most often occurs in the Fallopian tubes. The fertilized egg soon begins to divide. Now referred to as an **embryo,** it passes to the uterus—a journey of a few days—and remains there until birth. Thus the female structures must produce the egg, receive the sperm, permit fertilization, nurture the new individual as it grows to as much as 10 percent of the mother's body weight, and then expel it alive. Once a month the female reproductive tract begins a cycle of dramatic activities that prepare it for these multiple tasks. These activities are regulated by the interactions of a number of hormones.

Ovarian Cycles

A newborn female has hundreds of thousands of partially developed eggs in her ovaries. The ova are in a resting stage; in fact, almost all of them will eventually degenerate. No more than about 400 ova ever ripen to be released from the ovaries. In a sexually mature woman, **follicle-stimulating hormone (FSH)** from the pituitary causes several ova to resume development each month. As the ova grow, they increase in size without the obvious changes in form seen in sperm development.

Growth of an ovum is accompanied by an ever-greater number of **follicle** (nurse) **cells,** surrounding the egg (Fig. 12.6). Although several follicles begin to develop each month, usually only one reaches maturity; the others degenerate. And as a follicle enlarges, it pushes away any smaller follicles that lie between it and the surface of the ovary. Soon the growing follicle forms a blisterlike bulge on the ovary.

FIGURE 12.5 Female Reproductive System. (a) Front view; (b) side view.

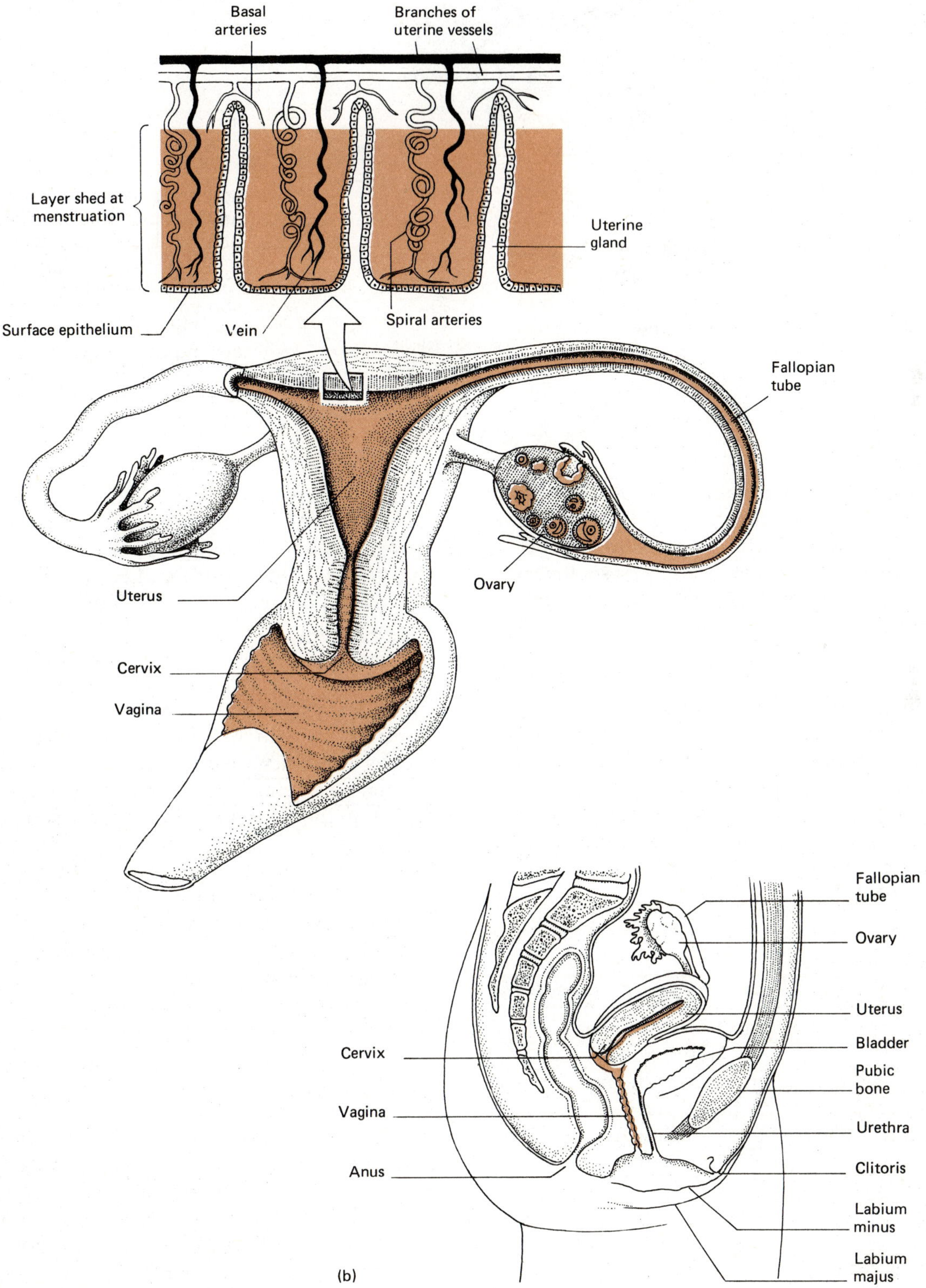

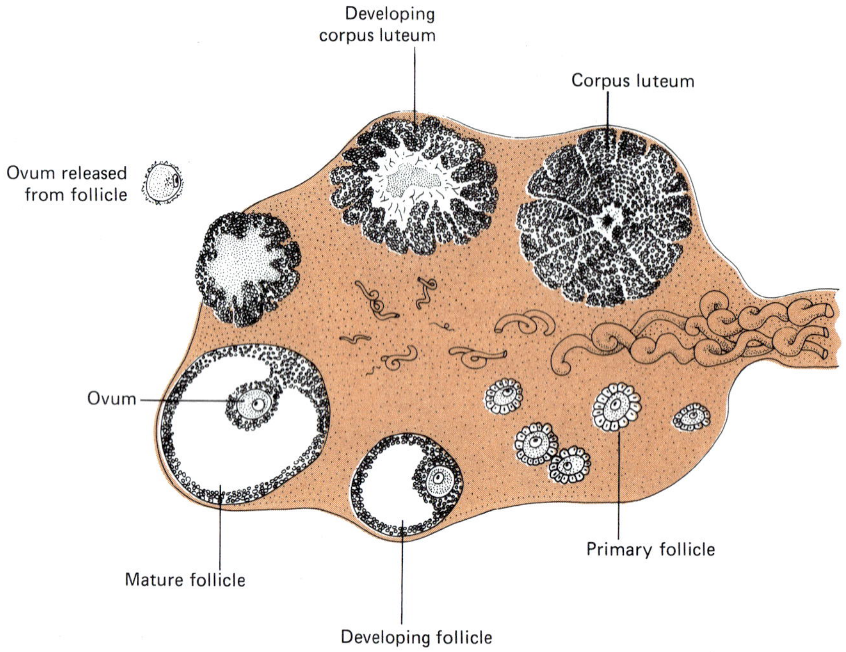

FIGURE 12.6 Diagram of the Life of an Ovarian Follicle. This diagram differs from a real ovary in that the various stages of a follicle and its corpus luteum are shown in counterclockwise order. Follicles do not migrate around the ovary as they mature. Different stages are found scattered about in no particular order.

In addition to stimulating the growth of follicles, FSH spurs the nurse cells of the developing follicles to secrete the hormone **estrogen.** But as follicles grow and estrogen levels increase, the larger amounts of estrogen inhibit the activity of the pituitary, so release of FSH declines (Fig. 12.7). In the absence of sufficient FSH, secretion of estrogen levels off, allowing another surge of FSH. At the same time, the pituitary secretes increasing quantities of **luteinizing hormone,** or **LH.** Together the high concentrations of LH and FSH cause the follicle to rupture and release the egg. This process is **ovulation.** Usually only one follicle matures each cycle. Although numerous follicles begin to enlarge at the start of the cycle, most degenerate before the ova are ready to be released.

After Ovulation

The open mouth of the Fallopian tube extends like a bonnet partway around the ovary. Contractions of the oviduct may draw the finger-like edges of the open mouth of the tube over the ovary surface and gather the egg into the oviduct. Once within the oviduct, the egg is moved toward the uterus by cilia lining the walls and by contractions of muscles within the walls.

After the egg has left the ovary, LH causes the cells of the old empty follicle to transform into a **corpus luteum.** The corpus luteum is endocrine tissue; it secretes both estrogen and a second female hormone, **progesterone.** Progesterone inhibits its secretion of LH, which is necessary to maintain the corpus luteum. Without LH the corpus luteum dies unless pregnancy occurs. If it does, a placental hormone that replaces LH is secreted.

Death of the corpus luteum, followed by elimination of progesterone and estrogen through the urine, leaves the body with little of either ovarian hormone. As you may have recognized, these hormones exert negative-feedback control□ over the 180
pituitary secretions that regulate the ovary (Fig. 12.7a). In their absence, the pituitary soon recovers its activity and again begins to secrete FSH. Actually FSH and LH are produced by the anterior pituitary in response to substances released by the hypothalamus. The inhibitory action of estrogen and progesterone works indirectly through the hypothalamus. Excitement, fear, and other strong emotions frequently alter the normal course of events by their effect on the hypothalamus.

Uterine Cycles

Associated with the cyclic changes in hormones are cyclic changes in the uterus. These changes show themselves as the **menstrual,** or monthly, **cycle.** Estrogen from the growing follicles makes the lining of the uterus thicken. Glands there grow deeper, and blood vessels proliferate. After ovulation, progesterone causes further thickening and enrichment of the uterine tissues. The glands branch out, and the lining becomes plump with blood. All is ready for a fertilized egg if one appears.

In the absence of pregnancy, however, the corpus luteum dies and both estrogen and progesterone levels drop. The uterine lining loses tissue fluids and shrinks. Shrinkage compresses and interrupts blood flow in the spiral arteries that supply the outer layer of the lining (Fig. 12.5). The walls of the capillaries and veins supplied by these arteries soon die. So do the surrounding tissues. Eventually the outer layer of the uterine lining sloughs off, releasing small amounts of stagnant blood. Normally the arteries heal over before the dead layer falls away. Therefore fresh blood is usually not released. The cells lining the depth of the glands remain when the surface layer is lost. These gland cells divide to supply additional cells that grow over the raw surface left by menstruation.

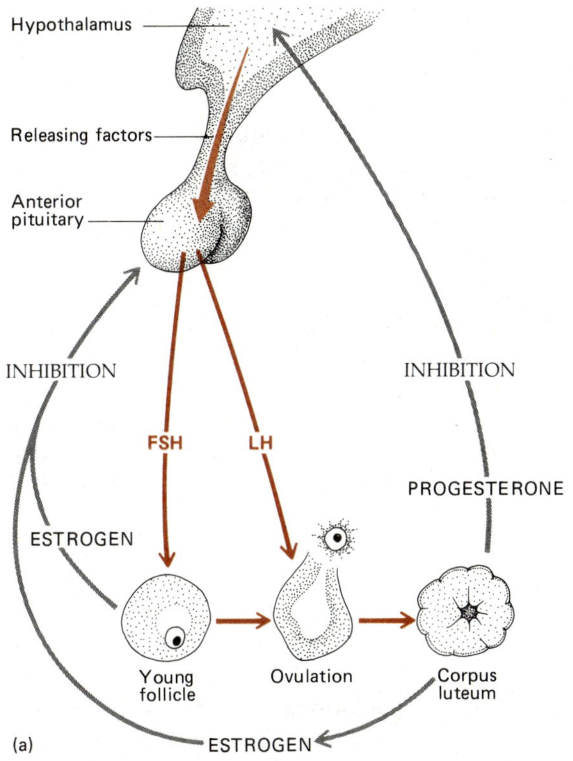

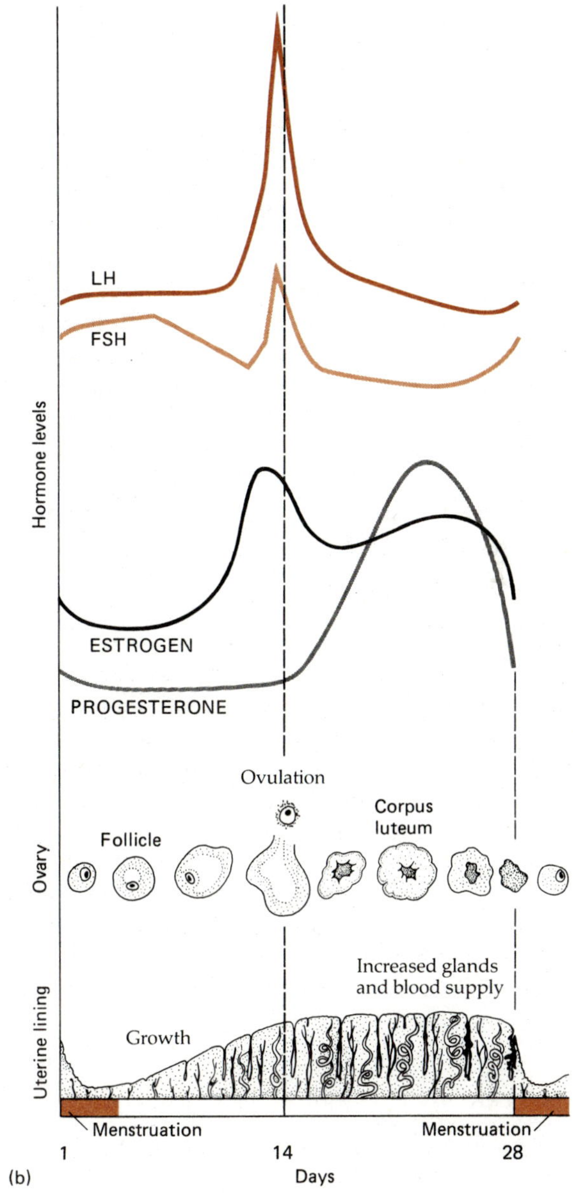

FIGURE 12.7 Hormone-Controlled Female Cycles. Both the ovary and the uterus undergo cyclic changes. One or more releasing factors (RF) secreted by the hypothalamus (a) stimulate the secretion of FSH and LH from the anterior pituitary. The FSH promotes development of ovarian follicles containing the ova (eggs). LH promotes ovulation and development of the follicular remains into a corpus luteum. Estrogen from developing follicles, together with progesterone and estrogen from the corpus luteum, restricts hypothalamic stimulation of the anterior pituitary as well as promoting development of the uterine lining. (b) The negative influence of ovarian hormones on secretion of FSH and LH brings each cycle to a close. Withdrawal of ovarian hormones causes shedding of the uterine lining (menstruation), as well as permitting the hypothalamus to again stimulate the anterior pituitary.

Before continuing further, study Fig. 12.7 carefully. Correlate the changes in pituitary and ovarian hormones, the changes in the ovary, and those in the uterus during the entire menstrual cycle.

Most women suffer some degree of discomfort during menstruation. This discomfort is associated with exaggerated uterine contractions, now [181] believed due to excess prostaglandins.□ Withdrawal of progesterones permits prostaglandins to stimulate uterine contractions. Women who suffer menstrual cramps have excessive prostaglandins in the menstrual discharge. The pain comes from hard contractions that deprive the working muscle of adequate oxygen. Nausea, headache, and other menstrual symptoms may stem from increased contraction of blood-vessel muscles that rob the stomach and brain of adequate blood supply.

The Embryo Supports Itself

During pregnancy, the developing embryo produces a hormone that mimics the effects of LH by keeping the corpus luteum in good health. This hormone is named **chorionic gonadotropin** because it is produced by the embryonic membrane known as the chorion and because it affects the ovary (gonad). So long as estrogen is secreted, FSH production is repressed and no further eggs can develop. Later in pregnancy the placenta secretes massive amounts of both estrogen and progesterone.

Menopause

The cyclic oscillations of pituitary and ovarian hormones occur from puberty (sexual maturity) to menopause. At that point, usually late in the fifth decade, hormonal cycles and menstruation cease. The woman's reproductive life, but not her sexual life, is brought to a close.

Menopause results from exhaustion of the ovary, not of the pituitary. In fact, the level of FSH is sometimes elevated during menopause, because estrogen decreases as the number of developing follicles slowly dwindles. Many of the later cycles produce no ova.

LOVEMAKING

Lovemaking, **coitus,** the sex act, sexual relations, intercourse, and numerous slang terms are synonyms for the process biologists usually refer to as **copulation,** or mating. As humans we are interested not only in the anatomical details of this process but also in the physiological bases of the sexual climax known as **orgasm.**

Sexual experiences have both physiological and psychological components. Until recent years, prudishness—or perhaps awe—prevented scientific study of the phenomena.

What Happens

As everyone knows, people are different from one another. Probably no two sexual experiences are exactly alike, even for the same individual. But basically a sexual experience involves a gradual and then an explosive increase in tension followed by relaxation. The tension arises from the swelling of tissue with blood and from muscle contractions.

Blood-vessel changes occur in many organs, not only those obviously associated with sex. One can direct these changes consciously only by concentrating on sexual stimuli or by rejecting them. Muscle tension is also widespread, but much of this aspect of sexual experience can be controlled consciously as the individual literally works to reach peaks of sensation.

For convenience we divide discussion of the sex act into four phases: excitement, plateau, orgasm, and resolution.

Excitement. Initial sexual excitement can occur in response to any of a variety of stimuli. Sometimes a word, a gesture, a single caress, a picture, or even an odor is sufficient. In men, erection of the penis provides an obvious signal of excitement. The immediate cause of erection is relaxation of the muscular walls of arteries that supply blood spaces in erectile tissue of the penis. The large, thin-walled vessels that make up **erectile tissue** give it a spongy texture and permit it to enlarge. As blood pours in from the enlarged arteries, the erectile tissue expands against a sheath of tough, inelastic connective tissue. Blood leaving the erectile tissue must pass into veins situated just inside the sheath. When blood is entering the erectile tissue fast enough to expand it against the sheath, these veins become compressed. This compression, of course, obstructs the outflow of blood. With more blood entering than leaving, the erectile tissue becomes engorged and rigid, just as a balloon does when it is filled with water.

In women, increased blood flow to the sex organs usually occurs less dramatically. Often the first evidence of excitement is relaxation, enlargement, and moistening of the vagina. The vagina lengthens, partly due to the elevation of the uterus. These changes create a welcome reception for the fully erect penis, even though insertion is possible when a woman isn't aroused.

Plateau. Numerous sensory nerve endings, particularly those within the bulblike glans, are stimulated as the penis is introduced into the vagina and rhythmically rubbed against the walls. Sensation and excitement vary during this **plateau** phase, which precedes orgasm. Engorged blood vessels in the outer part of the vagina may constrict the opening around the base of the penis. Similar congestion of blood vessels enlarges both the **labia minora** and the **labia majora,** fleshy folds of skin that surround the vaginal opening. During this time both men and women experience a relaxation of surface blood vessels that produces a blush beginning at the base of the sternum and spreading upward over the face.

Erotic sensitivity is widespread in both sexes, extending to the breasts, buttocks, lips, anus, thighs, and often over the entire body. The **clitoris** of the female shares with the penis a common developmental history and basic structure. A mass of erectile tissue within the clitoris engorges and flattens and elevates the clitoris.

The role of the clitoris is difficult to explain. It serves as a center of sexual focus for women, and it is exquisitely sensitive to touch. Nevertheless, direct stimulation of the clitoris never occurs in any of the numerous positions of sexual intercourse. As sexual tensions increase, the clitoris withdraws under a clitoral hood. Although manual stimulation of the clitoris can help increase sexual tensions, it can be effective through the hood, as well as when directed along the shaft of the clitoris.

There are as many fallacies associated with the size of the clitoris as with that of the penis. In neither is variation of size or position important. The vagina relaxes to accommodate any penis and can later close snugly against the shaft, no matter what its diameter. Likewise, the sensual functions of the clitoris are the same regardless of its size. And since the clitoris is stimulated only indirectly during coitus, the slight variations in location are inconsequential.

Climax. The sensations of **orgasm** (sexual climax) can be traced to rhythmic contractions of specific muscles. In the male, stimulation of the glans or of the tip of the urethra initiates a reflex. This reflex causes contractions in the walls of the vasa deferentia and the seminal vesicles, contractions that expel both sperm and glandular secretions. Other motor nerve impulses produce spasms in skeletal muscles lying just outside the urethra between the prostate and the penis (Fig. 12.8). The spasms massage the urethra and, when the sphincter around the urethra relaxes, help ejaculate the semen.

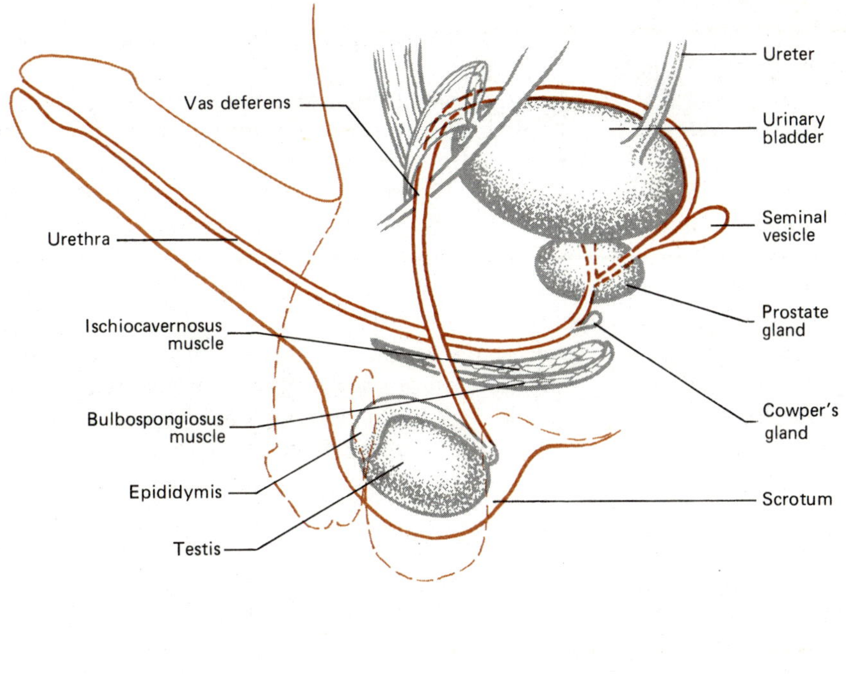

FIGURE 12.8 Ejaculation. Emission of semen results from spasmodic muscle contractions. Initially these are contractions of smooth muscle in the walls of the epididymis, vas deferens, and prostate. The semen entering the urethra is propelled from the body by contractions of the urethral wall and of surrounding skeletal muscle, such as the bulbospongiosus muscle. The skeletal muscle contributes to ejaculation by squeezing the urethra.

Similar reflexes occur in women. The clitoris and urethra are the most sensitive to stimulation. The skeletal muscles around the vaginal opening contract at orgasm. These muscles of the female are essentially the same as those of the male that massage the urethra and contribute to ejaculation. During orgasm the uterus and vaginal walls contract rhythmically 4–10 times at intervals of about 0.8 seconds. Probably such contractions aid the ascent of sperm toward the Fallopian tubes. Whatever assistance these contractions may have, they are not essential for fertilization. Pregnancy can occur whether or not the woman experiences orgasm.

Relaxation and Repetition. After orgasm, the muscle tension and increased blood in the various sexual organs gradually lessen. This is the period of **resolution.** Few males are capable of initiating another coital cycle immediately. Young men at the height of their sexual potency require about twenty minutes to recover. For others the time may be much longer. After an initial orgasm some women can immediately oscillate through several cycles of resolution and repeated orgasms.

Desire without Limit

The natural patterns of human sexual activity lie masked under many layers of cultural rules and expectations. Now that our society is more open to discussion of sexual habits, the pervasive nature of human sexuality has become evident.

No Respecter of Age. Healthy humans often continue sexual relations well into old age. Many couples cease having coitus only when one partner suffers a severe illness. Perhaps the oft-heard tale that old age is sexless can be traced to the Victorian era. During that time the idea that no decent woman enjoyed sex may have led wives to terminate intimacies as early as possible. But today menopause alters neither sex drive nor orgasmic ability in any predictable pattern. Reduced estrogen sometimes causes dryness and tenderness of the vagina and external female organs. Although the sexual appetite of males dwindles with age, many men are **potent** (able to maintain an erection) throughout life. Sperm production also continues. Men in their eighties have fathered children.

Health and Sexuality. Physical disabilities do not necessarily bar sexual activity. For example, there seems to be no more likelihood that sexual exertion will precipitate a heart attack than that any other aspect of ordinary life will do so. Those who survive coronary attacks are generally advised to resume an ordinary sex life when they return to other everyday activities.

Special problems face individuals with broken necks or spines. Because sensation involves centers in the brain, sex in the usual sense is impossible for these people. However, the spinal cord may remain alive, permitting men who are paralyzed by damage high in the cord to continue to respond to local stimulation of the penis. They can ejaculate but without the usual sensations of orgasm.

People with severe damage to the nervous system can offer the rest of us important insights into the real nature of love. Although handicapped in some ways, these people often establish deep intimacies and find a full measure of love and sexuality in physical contact even without coitus. In fact, those whose daily activities are limited by severe physical handicaps may find their most important roles in love relationships. Such people often have more time and energy to expend on others than do those whose faculties are intact.

Nevertheless, it would be a grave mistake to suggest that most disabled people are incapable of an ordinary sex life. Injuries and disease that limit motion but leave sensation intact need have no important effect on coitus or orgasm. Families and friends should expect the newly handicapped to be as loving and sexual as ever. Sometimes sexual positions and techniques must be modified, but the emotions and sensations usually remain the same.

SEX WITHOUT REPRODUCTION

As everyone knows, sexual relations do not always result in pregnancy. Coitus is a means to reproduction, but that is not the only desirable outcome. Although some groups believe it unnatural and morally wrong to use sexual abilities in ways that preclude reproduction, the majority seem not to subscribe to this view. Instead, they find the expression of love, the personal gratification, and the release from the tensions of life adequate justification for sexual activity. For this reason many people seek to uncouple sex and reproduction. And so they have done through the ages.

Contraception

Until recently the leaders of most nations considered large, growing populations in their best in-

BOX 12A

IN THE NAME OF SOCIETY

Operations on the external sex organs are social customs. Circumcision of males has a long tradition as a rite of membership for males in many cultures. Not only Jews, but also Muslims, Australian Aborigines, and many other groups require this surgery on their sons.

Circumcision of a male removes the foreskin, a fold of skin that covers the glans at the tip of the penis. Regardless of religious affiliation or cultural background, most U.S. families today have their baby boys circumcised immediately after birth. The usual justification is that the operation makes it easier to keep the tip of the penis clean. Nevertheless, it is a simple matter to pull back the foreskin and wash beneath it. Another argument for circumcision is that the operation increases sexual sensations. But with erection, the foreskin tends to pull back from the expanding glans. Thus a normal foreskin is no barrier to direct contact of the glans with the partner's body. Furthermore, it has been argued that absence of the foreskin permits so much routine stimulation of the glans that it may become less sensitive to sexual contacts.

Other less well-known penile operations are customary in Pacific cultures. Instead of performing circumcision, Polynesians slit the foreskin on its upper surface. Some Australian aboriginal societies add subincision to circumcision. In subincision the penis is slit lengthwise on the lower side, so the urethra opens there rather than on the tip. And in Borneo, young men may perforate the glans so that they can insert objects said to "tickle" the sexual fancies of their women.

Female circumcision and its even more gruesome companion, infibulation, are techniques to control female sexuality. Female circumcision is really removal of the clitoris. East African tribes sometimes circumcise their daughters on the theory that reduced opportunity for sexual pleasure will keep the girls virgins until marriage or keep them faithful in marriage.

Infibulation is a drastic attempt to create a chastity belt from living tissue. Not only is the clitoris mutilated, but the labia majora (major lips) are scraped raw and sewn with wire or thorns, so they heal together. Scarring and constriction of the lips make intercourse thereafter a painful matter. Some students of African customs speculate that infibulation contributes to a high birth rate. Wives may reject contraceptives because pregnancy relieves them for many months of any obligation to have intercourse with their husbands.

It may be easy to label these operations as the work of primitives, but you should know that either mutilation or removal of the clitoris was a treatment commonly prescribed in the Victorian era for girls caught masturbating. Circumcision of males was similarly thought to lessen the likelihood of masturbation.

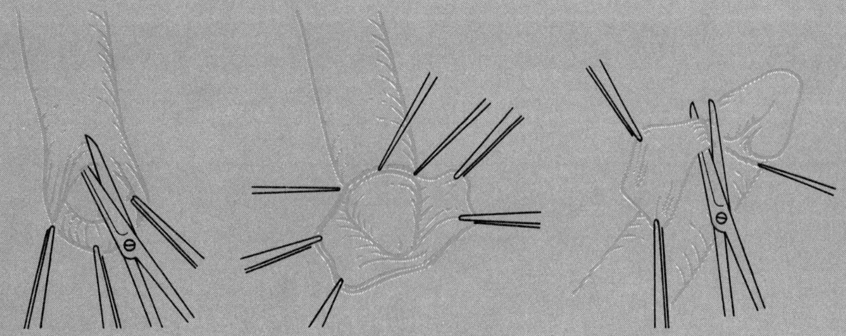

terests. (Unfortunately, some still do.) As a result, legal and religious pressures have been used to deter those who seek sex without reproduction. In the absence of **contraception** (techniques that oppose conception), people's sexual inclinations ensured population growth. Because of this pro-birth attitude, little effort has been directed toward learning how to manipulate human fertility. Consequently, the technology of contraception lags far behind what it might be.

Coitus Interruptus. Even without technology, thoughtful people have tried to control fertility. Perhaps the earliest and surely the most widespread practice is **coitus interruptus.** It was used in biblical times and is known almost everywhere today. Some people call this technique simply "being careful." It is probably the basis for the remark, "If you can't be good, be careful."

As the name implies, coitus interruptus requires termination of the sexual union before it is complete. Withdrawal must occur before the man ejaculates. Use of this technique for birth control is based on the fact that there can be no fertilization if no sperm enter the female tract. However, many men emit some sperm prior to orgasm. Furthermore, ejaculation onto body surfaces near the vaginal opening can permit semen to seep into the vagina. But because large concentrations of sperm are usually required for conception, the greatest risk is that the man will fail to withdraw in time.

Since coitus interruptus relies on attention and self-control, success depends in part on the man's motivation. Another problem is that sperm are left in the urethra after ejaculation, so reinsertion of the penis into the vagina carries a risk of pregnancy. To avoid this risk, lovemaking is often interrupted before the woman reaches orgasm. Altogether, coitus interruptus is not the best contraceptive technique. Nevertheless, the failure rate is no higher than some for other methods (Fig. 12.9), and it has the advantage of always being available.

Condoms. Condoms are sheaths, usually of rubber. They are also known as "prophylactics," because they were long sold as preventives for venereal diseases in states where contraceptives were illegal. The condom is rolled onto the erect penis to catch the semen at ejaculation. Condom failure is possible. If an air pocket is not left at the tip, for example, semen can easily leak out around the base of the penis. Occasionally a condom is lost in the vagina when the penis is withdrawn. Sheaths do rupture, though rarely. Used with care, the condom is an effective contraceptive device.

The Diaphragm. Until development of "the pill," diaphragms were the favorite contraceptives of well-educated Western women. A diaphragm consists of a rubber cap mounted on a circular spring. The spring holds the cap in place over the cervix. Used with a liberal amount of spermicidal (sperm-killing) jelly, a diaphragm prevents passage of sperm from the vagina into the uterus.

The fact that a diaphragm should be inserted no more than two hours before intercourse and left in place for six hours afterwards creates inconvenience. As with all contraceptive techniques, most diaphragm failures can be traced to human failure

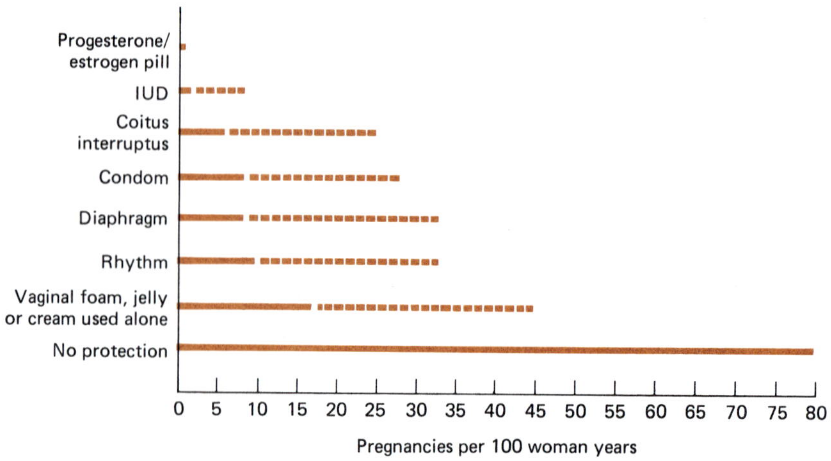

FIGURE 12.9 **Reliability of Contraceptives.** Estimates of the reliability of contraceptive techniques vary widely. The solid lines indicate the minimum number of pregnancies that may be expected among one hundred sexually active women of reproductive age who rely on that method. The dashed extension shows the maximum number of pregnancies that may occur.

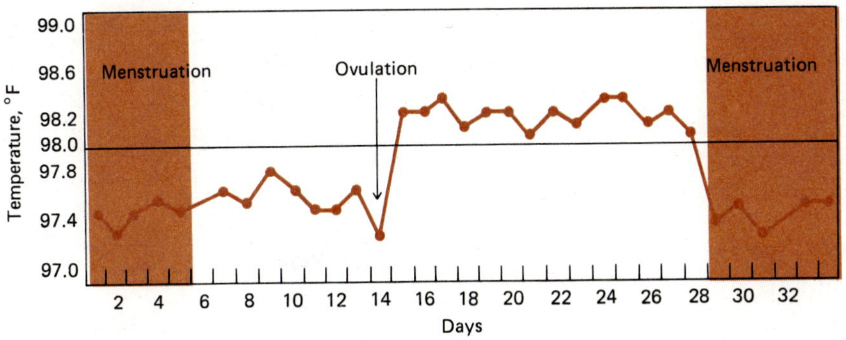

FIGURE 12.10 Body Temperature as an Indicator of Ovulation. Body temperature determined immediately upon waking can be used to detect ovulation. Note that the temperature is depressed slightly on the day of ovulation and elevated about one degree for several days after ovulation.

to use the method consistently rather than to flaws inherent in the technique. Since a diaphragm must be of the correct size, it must be fitted by a trained person.

Vaginal Chemical Preparations. There are numerous contraceptive foams, creams, jellies, and suppositories that contain sperm-killing chemicals. These **spermacides** should be used with a diaphragm, but they are better than nothing by themselves.

Rhythm. The rhythm method relies on the fact that a woman is fertile for only a day or so each month. Because ova usually remain viable for about a day and sperm for about three days, the monthly interval when coitus is likely to result in conception lasts only four days on the average. Unfortunately, it is very difficult to determine when a woman will ovulate. As a general rule, ovulation occurs 14 days before the onset of menstruation. But just try to predict an event 14 days before another uncertain event. Additional days of abstinence to allow a margin for error reduce the number of "safe" days to a precious few.

Women can use their body temperature pattern to determine when ovulation has occurred. Ovulation depresses the body temperature, but in the latter part of the cycle, temperature is elevated about 0.6°F over that prior to the ovulatory dip (Fig. 12.10). Because of an inherent daily cycle in the body temperature and because physical activity increases heat production, the most reliable temperature measurements are those made on just waking. Nevertheless, worry, illness, and irregular hours introduce variability into the temperature pattern and can make its interpretation difficult.

Intrauterine Devices (IUDs). Devices that are inserted into the uterine cavity are effective contraceptives. Unfortunately, as many as 30 percent of women fitted with an **intrauterine device** lose it from the uterus. Such loss is most common in those who have not borne children. To make matters worse, the woman is seldom aware her IUD is missing. Another disadvantage is that IUDs must be inserted by a physician or some other specially trained person.

Complications may include pelvic infections, especially during pregnancy that occurs while an IUD is in place. Severe bleeding may be another problem. Furthermore, an IUD occasionally penetrates the uterine wall; the repair constitutes major surgery.

Successful IUDs come in an amazing array of shapes. The mode of action remains uncertain. An IUD may act as a foreign body that stimulates uterine contractions, or it may attract phagocytic cells that attack sperm or the new embryo. IUDs wrapped with copper or infiltrated with progesterone may be more effective because of additional chemical action.

"The Pill." Oral contraceptives vary in their formulations, but they all contain synthetic compounds related to progesterone. These substances are synthesized from raw materials extracted from yams. Artificial progesterones suppress secretion of luteinizing hormone (LH) and prevent ovulation, just as natural progesterone does. Progesterones also alter the mucus of the cervix and of the uterine lining and thereby produce an environment inhospitable not only to sperm but to the implanting of embryos.

The standard contraceptive pills also contain estrogen, which inhibits the secretion of follicle-stimulating hormone (FSH) and thus the development of follicles. In addition, estrogen suppresses the irregular bleeding that sometimes occurs when only progesterones are used. Usually the pills are taken daily for three weeks and then skipped for a week. Withdrawal of the hormones permits bleeding, even as the natural decrease in hormones triggers menstruation. Some brands provide a pill for each day of the month; the pills for the fourth week contain only vitamins or some other harmless substance.

Not infrequently women experience side effects from oral contraceptives. Some side effects are favorable; they include reduction in premenstrual tension, less menstrual discomfort and blood loss, and fewer skin problems. Negative side effects include weight gain, tender breasts, and headaches. Blood clots occur with slightly increased frequency in women using oral contraceptives. Women over 30, especially those who smoke, have an increased risk of heart attacks if they take "the pill." Nevertheless, the danger of oral contraceptives is no greater than that of the childbirths that occur without effective contraception.

Other contraceptive methods, such as long-lasting progesterone injections and progesterone-impregnated vaginal rings, have proved effective when tested. It seems likely that these and other new contraceptive techniques will provide further options in the future.

Sterilization

The contraceptive practices we've described are temporary measures that usually have little effect on future fertility. In contrast, there is no assurance that surgical sterilization can be reversed. This accounts for the hesitancy with which both physicians and patients approach sterilization.

Vasectomy. Sterilization is simpler in the male than in the female. Only local anesthesia is needed, because the surgeon cuts the vasa deferentia just under the skin and ties or cauterizes (burns) the ends. After no more than a month, often much sooner, the man resumes normal sexual activities with no outward evidence of change. But now the sperm cannot traverse the vasa deferentia; instead, they are retained in the epididymides and are phagocytized there. Because most of the semen comes from the glands that join the vasa deferentia beyond the cuts, the ejaculate is normal in appearance. None of the nerves involved in sexual responses are harmed.

Complications of vasectomy are few. Occasionally a local inflammation occurs, apparently as the result of an allergic reaction to sperm that leak from the epididymis into tissue spaces. Because the sperm are not ordinarily in contact with the immune system, their components are not recognized as "self." It may be that vasectomized men risk rheumatoid arthritis or other autoimmune diseases.□ 216

If vasectomy is performed carefully, there is a chance of reversibility. Some physicians have achieved 70-percent reversibility as measured by sperm counts. Nevertheless, most men with reversed operations father no additional children. Although they produce motile sperm, their semen doesn't function normally.

Tubal Ligation. In the female, general anesthesia and abdominal surgery are required to sever and tie the Fallopian tubes. The technique has been perfected to such an extent that only a tiny incision is necessary. Although the risk of injury or death from tubal ligation is slight, it is somewhat greater than from vasectomy.

Abortion

For a long time, abortion during the first three months of pregnancy involved scraping the uterine lining to remove the newly implanted embryo. Now withdrawal of an early embryo is achieved by suction through a tube. Neither procedure requires general anesthesia, but there is always some risk of infection.

After three months of pregnancy, abortion may involve surgical removal of the **fetus.** Alternatively, injection of a salt solution into the uterus will kill the fetus and placenta. Death of the placenta cuts off the hormone supply that maintains a normal pregnancy. In the absence of placental hormones, the uterine muscle contracts and expels the dead fetus and placenta.

All these procedures carry some risk to the mother, but if done properly in the first three months of pregnancy, abortion is less dangerous than childbirth. Abortions performed after the first three months are only slightly more dangerous.

However, it isn't the inherent dangers of abortion that fuel pro-life campaigns. Opponents of abortion argue that to abort is to take human life. For others the question relates not to the ethics of taking life at this stage but to its desirability compared with the alternatives.

The Private Practice

Traditional morality has limited sexual expression to intercourse with the marriage partner. Under the influence of this teaching, self-gratification through **masturbation** became abhorrent. In Victorian times, frightening disabilities were attributed to self-stimulation. One of the motives for establishment of athletic clubs was to provide an opportunity for exercise, so that young men could expend their energies in acceptable ways.

Despite the concern about masturbation, there is no evidence that self-stimulation to orgasm is physically harmful. Although still vigorously condemned by some religious groups, masturbation is a common route to pleasure and to reduced sexual tensions. The incidence of masturbation varies with age and such social factors as the availability of a sexual partner. Nevertheless, surveys suggest that at least 95 percent of the men in the United States and more than 50 percent of the women masturbate at some time. If they sustain injury, it is mainly from guilt.

DIFFERENCES BETWEEN MEN AND WOMEN

Societies tend to prescribe specific social roles for each sex, but the nature of these roles varies so much among different societies that their biological basis is open to question. Although certain anatomical and functional differences between men and women are obvious, the biological components of other aspects, especially psychological ones, are unclear.

Development of Sexual Differences

Sexual differences are based on the distribution of chromosomes.□ Although the sex of an individual 269 is actually determined by the chromosomes received at conception, body differences appear only gradually. The external form of the early embryo is neither male nor female. As shown in Fig. 12.11, the external genitals of each sex arise from structures of an indifferent nature. In contrast, the early fetus possesses rudiments of the internal reproductive tracts of both males and females. The genetic sex determines which of these embryonic tracts will mature. Thus adult males have vestiges of the female tract, and vice versa.

Studies with laboratory animals indicate that secretions of the embryonic testis direct external structures into the male pattern, as well as supporting the growth of the male internal organs. In the absence of such secretions, the external genitals develop in the female pattern, and only female in-

FIGURE 12.11 Common Origin of the Male and Female External Organs.

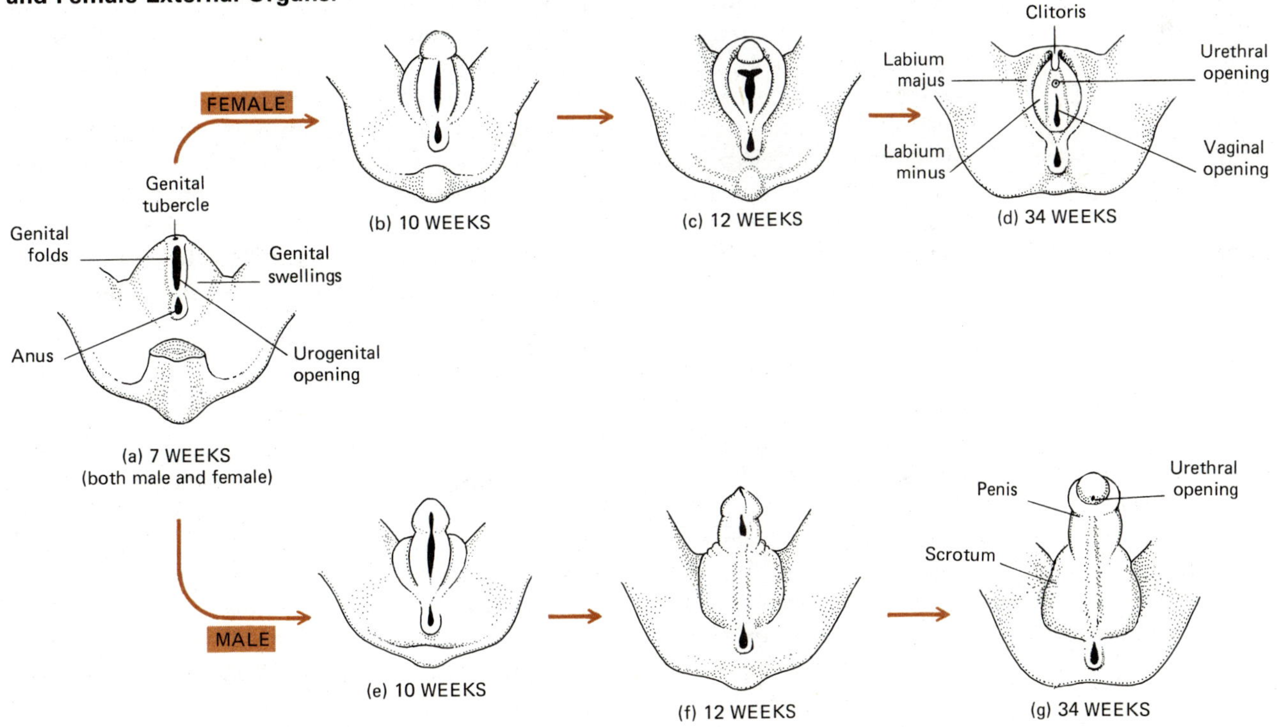

270 ternal structures mature. □ Thus mammals develop as females unless a particular genetic makeup triggers growth and secretion of testicular cells.

The Basis of Sexual Behavior

Just as the reproductive organs are initially neutral, so the embryonic brain is probably neither male nor female. Experiments with rats reveal that the presence of male hormone during a brief critical period a few days after birth patterns the brain for male sexual behavior. This is true, regardless of the genetic sex of the animal. Removal of either the testes or the ovaries from newborn rats, followed by testosterone treatments for a few days, results in adults that exhibit male behavior when given testosterone as adults. But if the ovaries or testes are removed at birth and no hormones are given before maturity, adults of either sex will show female behavior in response to hormone injections. Thus development of female behavior is independent of secretions from the embryonic gonads.

Whether similar mechanisms operate in humans remains to be established. It is certain that the development of human sexual identity involves genetic, hormonal, and environmental factors. In people, learning plays a large role. This fact is demonstrated by clinical studies of individuals whose reproductive structures are abnormal. The sexual identities of such individuals (as seen by themselves) correspond more often with the identities assigned by their parents than with their genetic or anatomical sex. The role of learning in human sexual behavior is emphasized by the effects of **castration** (removal of testes) in the male. Eunuchs who were castrated before puberty are incapable of performing the sex act. In contrast, mature men who were accidentally castrated after several years of sexual activity often remain potent for some time, even though their main source of testosterone is gone.

The Same Hormones in Both Sexes

This is a good time to point out that both males and females have hormones that are usually associated with the opposite sex. The adrenal cortex secretes testosterone as well as estrogen. When we speak of these as "male" and "female" hormones, we refer to the fact that males have more testosterone because of secretions from their testes. Similarly, females have more estrogen because of contributions from their ovaries. However, the ovary also secretes some testosterone and the testis some estrogen.

It is tempting to try to attribute what we interpret as characteristics of one sex to the presence of hormones normally associated with that sex. In fact, adrenal tumors that secrete testosterone can "masculinize" a woman. The most obvious symptoms are increased facial hair and depressed breast development. But in those rare individuals with atypical genitals, the adrenals are usually normal.

The hormonal similarities between the sexes extend to the pituitary. FSH and LH are secreted by the pituitary of the male, and they have functions in the male that are similar to those they have in the female. FSH stimulates development of the seminiferous tubules in the boy and maintains sperm formation in the man. LH is necessary for the development and health of the interstitial cells that secrete testosterone. For this reason LH in the male is known as **interstitial-cell-stimulating hormone** or ICSH. Just as LH is necessary for ovulation in the female, it is necessary for release of sperm from the testis.

Sexual Preference

Attempts to offer a biological explanation for the variable attraction humans experience toward individuals of their own or of the opposite sex have met with little success. In present-day Western societies some individuals seem to be rigidly heterosexual, and a number are heterosexual in most of their contacts but occasionally exhibit **homosexual behavior.** A small percentage are almost exclusively homosexual. However, differences in sexual preference vary ever so slightly from one individual to another instead of falling into distinct classes. Studies reveal that a large proportion of adults in the United States have had sexual encounters with individuals of both sexes. In many other societies homosexuality is taboo or even unknown. In some, however, it is widely tolerated or even prescribed under certain circumstances.

The innumerable variations in sexual preference suggest that many different factors may be involved. Although a genetic component has not been ruled out, there is no evidence that chromosomal abnormalities are involved in homosexuality. Furthermore, studies of hormone levels in homosexual and heterosexual individuals have shown no consistent differences.

BOX 12B

THE "PAP" SMEAR

Normal shed cervical epithelium

Cells found in cervical cancer

Sampling the loose cells on the cervical surface is a common part of routine health checkups for women. This sampling is the first step in a procedure designed to detect cancer. Swabs moist with cervical materials are smeared on glass slides, which are dipped into a mixture of alcohol and ether. This mixture fixes the smears (kills the cells and preserves them against decomposition). The slides are then shipped to a special laboratory, where the smears are stained by a method originated by George Papanicolaou. Hence they are called "Pap" smears.

If the cervical epithelium is normal, the cells will be uniformly large and will have small, densely stained nuclei. Cells such as these are continually shed from cervical and other surfaces, including the lining of the mouth. These cells originate in a lower layer of dividing cells. As younger cells push the older ones toward the surface, the older ones become thin sheets that protect deeper tissues. The dense nuclei of the shed cells are characteristic of inactive cells. In fact, the cells lost by a normal cervix are about to die and be replaced by others.

In contrast to the cells from a normal cervix, those shed from cancerous tissues are varied in size. Many exhibit the large nuclei seen in dividing cells. The multilobed nuclei of pus cells may also appear in smears from some tumors.

Techniques similar to the "Pap" smear are used to sample other internal body surfaces. Sputum coughed up from the lungs can be smeared, and the cells present can be stained to diagnose cancer of the respiratory tract. Urine or washings from the stomach may be filtered to obtain the cells present. When stained, the cells will reveal their normal or cancerous origins. All these various techniques are examples of exfoliative cytology, the study of cells shed like leaves from a tree. Healthy organs shed normal cells. Those with cancers of their surfaces will shed abnormal cells.

Nonreproductive Effects of Sex Hormones

Aside from overt sexual behavior, many psychological traits are often said to distinguish men and women. The biological basis of these traits remains an open question. Studies of sex-role learning demonstrate that parents have different behavioral expectations of boys and girls and therefore train them differently, both consciously and subconsciously. Boys are permitted and even encouraged to be aggressive outside the family. Boys are also more often reprimanded with physical punishment. Perhaps this accounts for the fact that males commit most of the crimes of violence.

However, there is reason to accept the premise that some of the aggressiveness of males has a biological basis. Consider the behavior of the males of other animal species. We recognize their aggressiveness when we use expressions such as "cocky" and "bully." On the other hand, attempts to correlate testosterone levels with social status or with aggressiveness are often unsuccessful. Socially dominant animals don't always have the highest testosterone levels. But testosterone sometimes increases with sexual activity. Animals may develop higher testosterone levels when they become dominant and have more sexual opportunities. Sometimes it appears that the amount of testosterone may reflect behavior rather than cause it.

Female hormones also have strong effects on the mind. Although testosterone injections increase libido (sex drive) in women, in most female mammals **estrus** ("heat" or willingness to mate) correlates with estrogen peaks. Marked alteration of sex hormone levels can have observable effects on the emotions of women. The severe drop in circulating estrogen and progesterone before menstruation appears responsible for the premenstrual tension that many women experience. Some women also notice a restlessness when estrogen levels dip after ovulation. At childbirth, loss of the tremendous progesterone and estrogen production of the placenta renders many new mothers psychologically vulnerable. Unusual stress at this time can precipitate severe depression, particularly in individuals with a history of emotional problems.

It is quite likely that reduced hormones are responsible for the emotional upsets that sometimes accompany menopause. Of course, there are other factors involved. It is only reasonable to be depressed by the involuntary loss of reproductive capacity and to be reminded that youth is past. The headaches, fatigue, and insomnia reported by some women may result from reduced estrogen. Ovarian secretion is irregular during menopause. At this time, fluctuation in estrogen is responsible for changes in the diameter of blood vessels near the surface of the body—the cause of "hot flashes." Apparently the nervous system adjusts to altered hormone levels since the symptoms of menopause gradually disappear. In general, changes in hormone levels, rather than absolute levels, seem to have the greatest effect on the nervous system.

Hormones and Vigor

Lowered estrogen levels appear to be responsible for some of the characteristic aging processes in women. Effects are most evident in the connective tissues. For example, thinning of the skin is one regularly observed change. With neither sufficient estrogen nor testosterone, the bones become increasingly brittle. The terminal tragedy for many women is a broken hip that never heals. Some physicians advocate replacement of the lost hormones through estrogen therapy; others fear meddling with natural hormone levels.

Sex hormones are responsible for many average physical differences between normal men and women. The importance of these differences varies, depending on the situation. Men are stronger than women, because testosterone causes muscle enlargement and makes muscle stronger per unit weight. This muscular strength combined with a larger skeleton and wider shoulders endows many men with a physique that can back up an aggressive personality. In primitive societies this combination was surely valuable in protecting the family and in hunting game. Similarly, it is useful in the many present-day roles that require physical strength.

On the other hand, a variety of traits, including larger adrenal glands and a circulatory system that can compensate rapidly for blood loss without risking shock, enable women to withstand physical damage much better than men do. Even the extensive fat layers that underlie the skin and give the typical feminine curves to the body come in handy when a woman is faced with cold or starvation. When relieved from the dangers of numerous ill-attended childbirths, women tend to outlive men in our own culture as well as in many others. Apparently females benefit from excellent homeostatic mechanisms that evolved as adaptations to the rigors of bearing and suckling the young.

A General View Again

Although sexual reproduction is the rule for vertebrates and the predominant method among all plants and animals, what we have said about human reproduction can't be applied in detail to other species. Taken together, our reproductive adaptations are unique to our species. They evolved as they contributed to reproductive success.

In looking at other animals, we find that most are periodic in their breeding. In many vertebrates the testes shrink after the breeding season and develop again only as the next breeding season approaches. Ovaries may also undergo cyclic growth and regression, especially in migratory birds for which a few grams of weight can be a burden.

Internal fertilization is also the exception rather than the rule. In general, it is practiced by terrestrial animals whose young develop inside the mother or in shelled eggs. For example, in reptiles and birds the eggs must be fertilized inside the female before the shell is deposited. On the other hand, aquatic animals, such as fish, amphibians, and many invertebrates, practice **ex-**

ternal fertilization. Often a courtship ensures that the male and female are ready to discharge sex cells at the same time. Then the male simply sheds sperm near or over the freshly laid eggs.

Much of the above also applies to plants, though in somewhat different ways. Like animals, plants have sexual reproduction and adaptive strategies that ensure that the sex cells come together. Internal fertilization has evolved in terrestrial plants as it has in terrestrial animals. You will find some of the details in later chapters. For now, remember that sexual reproduction is nearly universal.

Summary

1. In sexual reproduction, cells from two individuals fuse, producing a new organism with a different combination of characteristics. The varying traits of sexually produced individuals increase the probability of survival of the species in a changing environment. Asexual reproduction lacks this advantage, but it has another in that it requires only one parent.

2. Sperm are produced in the testes of the male. They are tiny, motile cells that contain only the structures necessary to carry genetic material to the egg. From the human testis the sperm pass through the epididymis, vas deferens, and urethra on their way out of the body. Along the way they are suspended in fluids from the seminal vesicles, prostate, and Cowper's glands.

3. Testosterone, the male hormone responsible for sex drive and secondary sex characteristics of males, is secreted by interstitial cells of the testes under control of the anterior pituitary.

4. Eggs originate in the ovaries of females. In humans they are most often fertilized in the Fallopian tubes, and from there the new embryo moves to the uterus.

5. Cyclic changes characterize the reproductive organs of human females. FSH from the pituitary stimulates development of ovarian follicles, which secrete estrogen as well as producing eggs. In response to estrogen acting on the hypothalamus, the pituitary reduces FSH production and increases secretion of LH. The next step is the release of an egg from a follicle and conversion of the empty follicle into a corpus luteum, which secretes progesterone. This hormone inhibits pituitary secretions and leads to death of the corpus luteum unless pregnancy occurs. Embryonic tissues secrete chorionic gonadotropin, another hormone that replaces LH in support of the corpus luteum.

6. Estrogen promotes growth of the uterine lining; later in the monthly cycle, progesterone increases the blood supply and development of glands in the lining. In the months in which pregnancy does not occur, withdrawal of estrogen and progesterone shrinks the lining and cuts off the blood supply to surface tissues. The deprived tissues die, and the menstrual flow is released.

7. In both sexes, arousal involves muscular tension and increased blood flow to specific tissues. In men, increased arterial blood to the penis engorges thin-walled vessels. Enlargement of the tissues puts pressure on the veins and traps enough blood to make the penis rigid and change it into an erect structure. Continued stimulation increases muscle tension and culminates in spasms that are responsible for the sensations of orgasm. In men, spasmotic contractions of smooth muscle in the reproductive tract and of skeletal muscle around these tubes ejaculate the semen. Variations in shapes and sizes of sexual organs do not limit sexual function. Humans retain sexual abilities into old age and despite many physical handicaps.

8. Contraceptive techniques and devices include timing of intercourse to avoid the presence of eggs; withdrawal by the male before ejaculation; condoms and diaphragms, which present physical barriers to sperm passage; sperm-killing chemicals; and intrauterine devices. Synthetic hormones in oral contraceptives inhibit pituitary function and prevent ovulation. The mode of function of IUDs is not well established.

9. Sterilization of men requires only severing the vasa deferentia where they lie under the skin. In contrast, sterilization of a woman by interrupting the Fallopian tubes requires surgical entrance into the abdominal cavity.

10. Chromosomal differences are at the base of differences between men and women. Both begin life with the same embryonic structures, and both secrete the same hormones, although the balance and time of secretions differ. Hormones from the embryonic testes mold development of reproductive organs into the male pattern and may also be responsible for effects on the brain that lead to male sexual patterns.

11. Testosterone increases libido in both men and women. It may account for some of the aggressiveness of males as well. Female hormones also have both psychological and physiological effects, which are most evident when hormone levels change. Homeostatic mechanisms enable women to tolerate hemorrhage and other physical stress better than men do.

Thought and Controversy

1. Traditionally, Western societies have treated women as the weaker sex and protected them from the rigors of warfare. How rational is this policy in the light of present knowledge and technology? In reaching an answer to this question, try to balance the following facts. Men have greater physical strength than women, but women have greater physiological resilience, which makes them less vulnerable to physical injury or exposure. Moreover, modern warfare relies heavily on mechanized weapons instead of brute force. Consider also that today's helicopter rescue teams can transport wounded soldiers to first-class hospitals only minutes after they are hurt.

2. Careful studies to determine any increased incidence of cervical cancer in women using oral contraceptives revealed a startling fact: a higher percentage of women choosing to use the pill than of those electing other methods of birth control showed precancerous changes *before taking the pill.* Evidence suggests that cervical cancer results from a virus infection transmitted through sexual contact. Apparently women who preferred the pill to other contraceptive techniques were sexually more experienced, and hence more of them had contracted the virus. Does this finding suggest possible pitfalls in other contraceptive studies?

3. Any irritation of the urethra can produce sexual arousal. For this reason a gonorrheal infection or even a very distended urinary bladder can cause an unexpected erection in men. In the past, a crude extract of certain beetles known as "Spanish fly" was taken orally as an **aphrodisiac** (sexual stimulant). The active ingredient is secreted into the urine, and it causes irritation of the urethra when urine is passed. Spanish fly also irritates other mucous membranes; side effects include vomiting, diarrhea, and sometimes serious kidney damage.

4. Pheromones, odorous secretions that alter social behavior, play major roles in animal reproduction. There is reason to think they may exist in humans. For example, it has been shown that girls living in a college dormitory tend to have their menstrual periods simultaneously. Although there may be other explanations of such occurrences, pheromone action offers an attractive hypothesis. It is also plausible that body odors are erotic. Vaginal secretions of female rhesus monkeys contain mixtures of short-chain fatty acids that, even when purified, stimulate sexual mounting in males. Perhaps bathing and using perfume masks the sexual effects of natural odors in humans. The belief that "cleanliness is next to godliness" may merely disguise sexual prudery.

Questions

1. Briefly characterize sexual reproduction. What is the biological advantage of sexual reproduction over asexual reproduction?

2. Trace the pathway of sperm from their origin into the female vagina. What are the sources of the fluids that suspend the sperm?

3. Compare the hypothalamic and pituitary hormones in men and women. Do both sexes exhibit negative-feedback control of sex-hormone production?

4. Describe the cyclic changes in the ovaries and uterus of a nonpregnant woman.

5. It is often said that there are endocrine organs within the ovaries. In what sense is this true? What are these "organs within organs"?

6. What is chorionic gonadotropin? Why is it necessary in pregnancy?

7. Compare the origin of the external reproductive organs of men and women. Based on this comparison, explain the similarities of function and sensation men and women experience during sexual intercourse.

8. Describe the standard sterilization procedures for men and women. Why is the male procedure simpler than the one for females?

9. What are the components of the usual oral contraceptives? Explain how they inhibit ovulation.

10. What are the nonreproductive differences between men and women? To what extent are these differences the result of sex hormones?

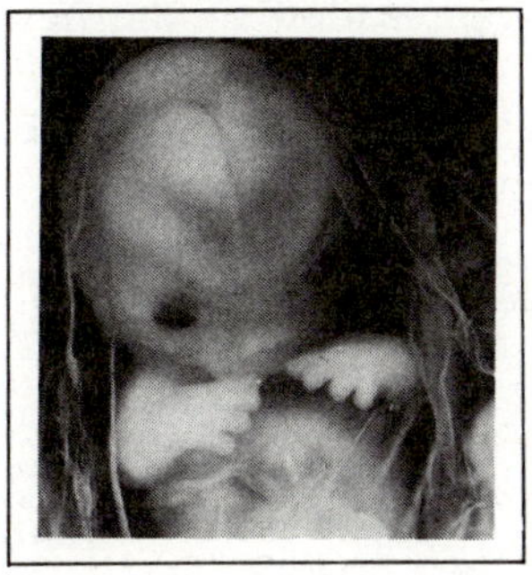

13

Development: From the Egg to Old Age

THE DEVELOPMENT OF ANY ORGANISM IS MARvelous to behold. How is it that a fertilized egg can become a frog or a puppy or a human baby? Much of what occurs involves molecular processes yet to be understood. But we do know that one of the first events is division of the fertilized egg into a mass of similar cells. This event is followed by a period of cell division, movement, and interaction that gives rise to distinct organs. Later divisions yield cells that become structurally and chemically specialized as they take on the characteristics of tissues such as muscle, nerve, and bone. After birth comes growth, maturation of reproductive structures, replacement of dying cells, and finally the degeneration of age. Although we are describing human development, similar processes occur across the animal kingdom.

FERTILIZATION

Initiation of development begins with fertilization of the egg by a sperm. Human sperm swim randomly, but contraction of the uterus propels the semen upward to the Fallopian tubes. The union of an egg with a particular sperm occurs by chance. But even though sperm approach an egg, fertilization cannot occur immediately (Fig. 13.1). First the sperm must penetrate the thick layer of follicle cells that surrounds the egg in the ovary and that stays with it after ovulation. Enzymes from sperm
279 acrosomes□ digest the intercellular cement that holds follicle cells together. It is quite likely that many different sperm contribute enzymes that separate

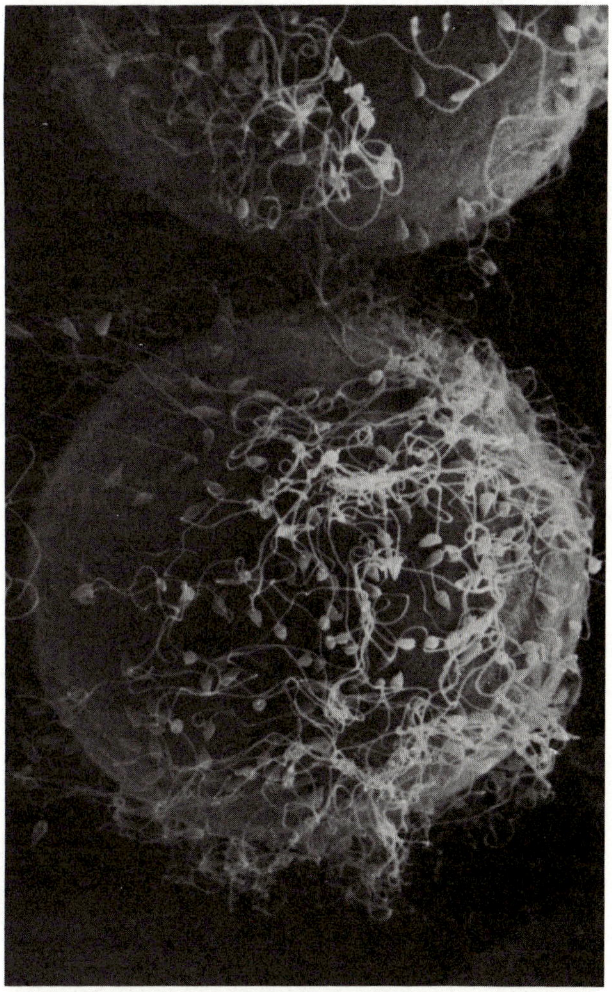

FIGURE 13.1 **Sperm on the Egg Surface.**

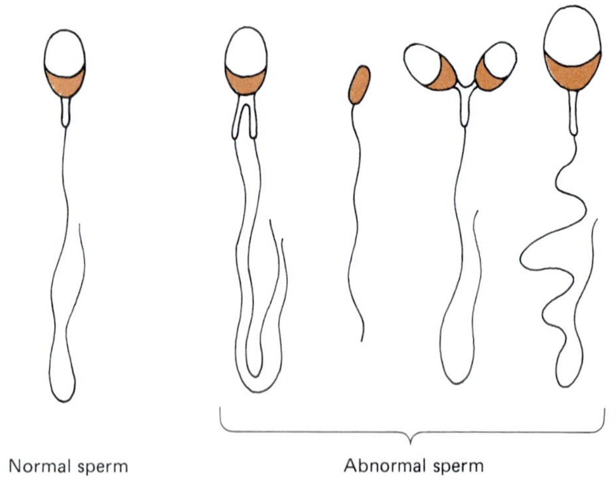

FIGURE 13.2 **Sperm Are Not All Normal.** One reason some men are unable to father children is that many of their sperm are deformed. Unusual sperm are also common in the semen of fully fertile men, however. How does each of the abnormal sperm pictured differ from the normal one?

the follicle cells about one egg. If so, this may explain why the number of sperm ejaculated and their concentration in the semen are so important to normal fertility. Although it may seem that production of any sperm at all should be sufficient to ensure fatherhood, many men are sterile if their semen contains fewer sperm than normal. A single ejaculate of a normal man may be a teaspoon of fluid containing about 400 million sperm. But infertility can be a problem if the ejaculate contains fewer than 50 million sperm per ml. Male infertility may also be caused by sperm abnormalities (Fig. 13.2).

Once enzymes from sperm acrosomes have loosened the barrier of follicle cells around the human egg, a single sperm can fertilize the egg by entering the cytoplasm, flagellum and all. Soon the nucleus of the sperm and that of the egg fuse. This union of the hereditary material from the mother with that of the father is but one aspect of fertilization. Equally important, fertilization results in **activation,** a series of changes within the egg cytoplasm. Our knowledge of this process in human eggs is scanty, so we rely on studies of other animals, such as sea urchins and frogs. In general, it has been found that a ripe egg is in a holding pattern, just waiting to be fertilized. Once fertilization occurs, the metabolic activity of the egg cytoplasm increases. Penetration by the sperm is also followed by cytoplasmic movements, especially in the surface layer of the egg. These movements mark the beginning of structural organization of the new animal.

It is important to note that the sperm contributes little cytoplasm to the **zygote** (fertilized egg). And the genetic material of the new individual doesn't function immediately. Instead, fertilization stimulates the egg cytoplasm to begin reorganization. That this organization is independent of fusion of the egg and sperm nuclei is evidenced by the fact that many physical and chemical stimuli can activate animal eggs in the absence of sperm. For example, exposure to cold or to salt solutions may be sufficient to initiate development. Such activation of an unfertilized egg is called **parthenogenesis.** It occurs naturally in some species, and it has been artificially induced in many others. Parthenogenesis is clear evidence that the sperm does not provide a pattern of development for the egg. Instead, fertilization initiates a process determined by the egg itself.

DEVELOPMENT OF THE NEW ORGANISM

Beyond the zygote stage the new organism is an **embryo.** Cell divisions, cell movements, growth, and the appearance of organ systems all characterize embryonic development. In the human, fertilization usually occurs within a Fallopian tube.□ 281 The zygote develops into an embryo as it passes along the tube into the uterus, where it embeds in the wall. By the time the embryo is two months old it has rudiments of all the usual organs and has thus become a **fetus.** During the remaining seven months, growth and differentiation produce the complete organs needed for independent function at birth.

Earliest Events

Immediately after fertilization the new zygote undertakes a series of mitotic divisions known as **cleavage.** By this process the zygote becomes two cells, which become four cells, which become eight, and so on. Although the nucleus is duplicated at each division, the cytoplasm doesn't increase in volume. The result is smaller and smaller cells.

At first thought, cleavage may seem so simple as to be trivial. The zygote is merely divided into a larger number of smaller cells. However, the egg cytoplasm is not uniform. Some regions of the egg

BOX 13A

DEVELOPMENTAL PATTERNS AND EVOLUTIONARY RELATIONSHIPS

Multicellular animals are all similar in many ways. Biologists recognize muscle, nerve, and epithelial cells in organisms as different as squid, spiders, and squirrels. Similarities extend to higher levels of organization. For example, each has a gut, a nervous system, and a specialized outer surface.

Resemblances among vertebrates are even closer. Not only are most tissues and organ systems similar in all vertebrates, but developmental patterns are strictly parallel. Consider the following facts.

1. The head end of vertebrate embryos always develops earlier and faster than more posterior regions.
2. The nervous system of vertebrates always forms from a tube on the dorsal side of the embryo.
3. The retina of the vertebrate eye always develops from the embryonic brain, and the lens develops from nearby surface epithelium.
4. Grooves develop on the sides of the pharynx of all vertebrate embryos. In some species these become functional gill slits used for gas exchange, but the embryos of reptiles, birds, and mammals that never have gills still have pharyngeal grooves and often slits. (Pharyngeal slits appear in humans, but they close long before birth.)
5. The vertebrate heart arises from two lateral regions that fuse into a single primitive tube-heart. (The left and right halves of the mammalian heart result from subdivision of the original single tube.)
6. The first kidney tissue always appears just behind the head, although in many vertebrates this kidney produces no urine.
7. At some time in their development, all vertebrate embryos have a tail—i.e., a body region that projects posterior to the hind limbs and anus.

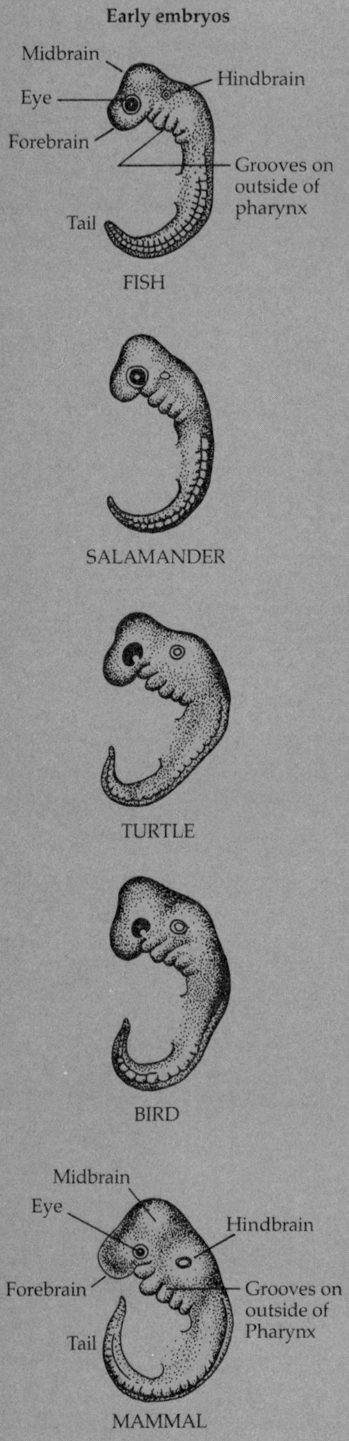

These facts constitute just a small sample of the ways in which vertebrate embryos are similar, but they are sufficient to raise the question of why the similarities exist.

At one time, embryonic similarities were explained by a "theory of recapitulation." The development of each individual was believed to retrace the steps in that individual's evolutionary history. Thus pharyngeal slits were present because ancestors had gill slits in that region of the body. And embryos had a simple tubular heart because their ancestors had such hearts. But close examination of embryos reveals that they are not identical to any adult organism. At most, modern vertebrate embryos are similar to the embryos of their ancestors in the ways that modern embryos are similar to one another.

One explanation for these similarities is that vertebrates are related to one another and that the historical pattern of development has been retained. For example, every vertebrate must have a heart that is essentially a muscular tube. It is the details of heart structure, which appear late in development, that make a difference in the suitability of the heart for life under specific conditions. Thus the later stages of development are subject to selection by the environment, but the early stages, which produce only

BOX 13A continued

a muscular tube, are insulated from such selective pressure.

Perhaps more important, some embryonic structures are retained because they have special roles that may not be evident in the final structure. The head kidney, which is found in all vertebrates, is a case in point. Although it never functions as a kidney in reptiles, birds, or mammals, this ancient kidney initiates the development of more posterior kidneys that do function. Without the initial formation of the head kidney, the animal can develop no kidney at all. We say that the head kidney organizes the remainder of the kidney tissue. Such organizational interactions are characteristic of development. These embryonic events may be so complexly timed and patterned that only certain deletions or shortcuts are possible. For these reasons, basic similarities are conserved, and we see in embryonic patterns the clear evidence of evolutionary relationships.

FIGURE 13.3 Fertilized Frog Eggs. Note that the upper surfaces of the eggs are rich in the black pigment known as melanin. Melanin absorbs ultraviolet light and thus screens the eggs from the ultraviolet radiation in sunlight, which might otherwise damage the hereditary material.

are richer in particular components than are other regions. The melanin of frog eggs (Fig. 13.3) is a highly visible example of the uneven distribution of cytoplasmic components in eggs. Because of the uneven distribution of substances in the cytoplasm, cleavage divisions result in cells with differing cytoplasmic properties. Even though the cleavage nuclei all contain the genetic potential to form an entire organism (Fig. 13.4), the cytoplasm varies from cell to cell. This segregation of cytoplasmic components is the first evidence of differentiation within the new individual.

Gastrulation and Induction

Cleavage forms a hollow ball of cells. In animals such as the frog, this embryonic stage is a **blastula** (Fig. 13.5), and descendants of all the cells will become part of the mature animal. In humans and related mammals, the equivalent stage is the **blastocyst** (Fig. 13.6). Only the **inner cell mass** of the blastocyst contributes to the fetus. The outer **trophoblast** becomes part of the placenta.

The next step in development is **gastrulation,** a process that produces a primitive digestive system. Gastrulation is best studied in amphibians, so again we look at the frog (Fig. 13.5c,d). Here gastrulation involves movements of cell sheets and masses, and results in a change in the relative positions of cells. At the end of cleavage the cells vary in their cytoplasmic composition, but similar cells are adjacent. At this time cytoplasmic differences consist of only gradual changes from cell to cell across the embryo. These smooth gradients are disrupted by the cell rearrangements that occur during

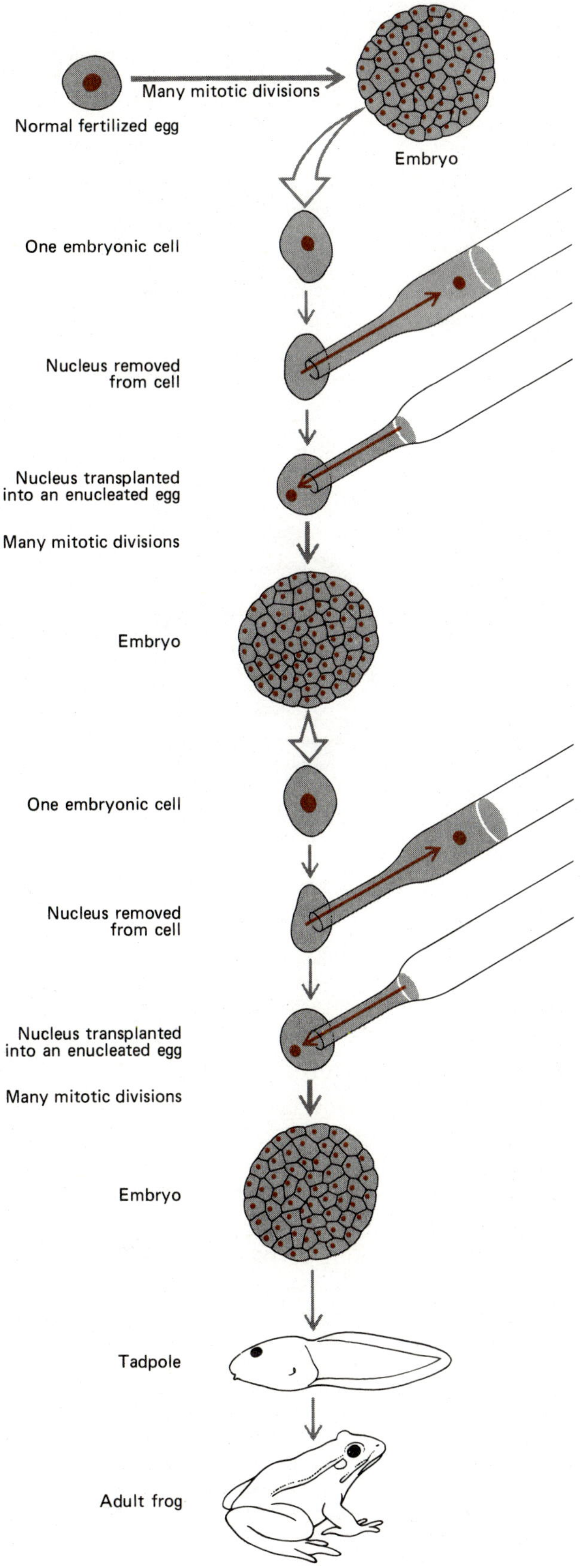

FIGURE 13.4 Proof that Cleavage Divisions Produce Genetically Identical Nuclei. When nuclei from embryonic cells are transplanted into eggs lacking nuclei, the eggs develop normally. In the preparatory steps of such experiments, the nucleus of the host egg is destroyed with ultraviolet radiation or physically withdrawn and discarded. Then the nucleus of an embryonic cell is transplanted into the egg cytoplasm. Development of such eggs indicates that each of the embryonic nuclei resulting from mitotic divisions contains all the hereditary information necessary for growth and function of the entire organism. Such experiments succeed even when the donor cells are gut lining cells from tadpoles or lymphocytes from older frogs.

gastrulation. As a result, cells with quite different cytoplasms come into contact.

This contact between different cells sets the stage for one cell type to influence the development of other cells. The first and most dramatic of these **inductions** involves the roof of the primitive gut. The cells here cause the overlying tissue layer to thicken and form a neural plate (Fig. 13.5d). This neural plate then rounds up and separates into the **neural tube** (Fig. 13.5f). The neural tube gives rise to the brain and spinal cord evident in Fig. 13.5g. While the roof of the primitive gut is inducing development of the neural tube, the roof itself is also directed to separate into the **notochord** and other basic embryonic organs. With this separation, the fundamental **embryonic tissue layers** become evident (Fig. 13.5f).

Control of Gene Action

It is important to recognize that the interactions between the primitive gut and the overlying tissue involve cells that differ only in their cytoplasm. As we pointed out earlier, all embryonic nuclei contain the full set of genes necessary to make a complete embryo. It is in their cytoplasm that cells differ. The clue to organization lies in the different kinds of cytoplasm brought into contact during gastrulation. Cells with particular cytoplasmic components are able to direct the development of adjacent cells that lack these cytoplasmic components. It is the environment of a cell, in this case the nature of the cytoplasm of adjacent cells, that determines which genes function in particular cells.

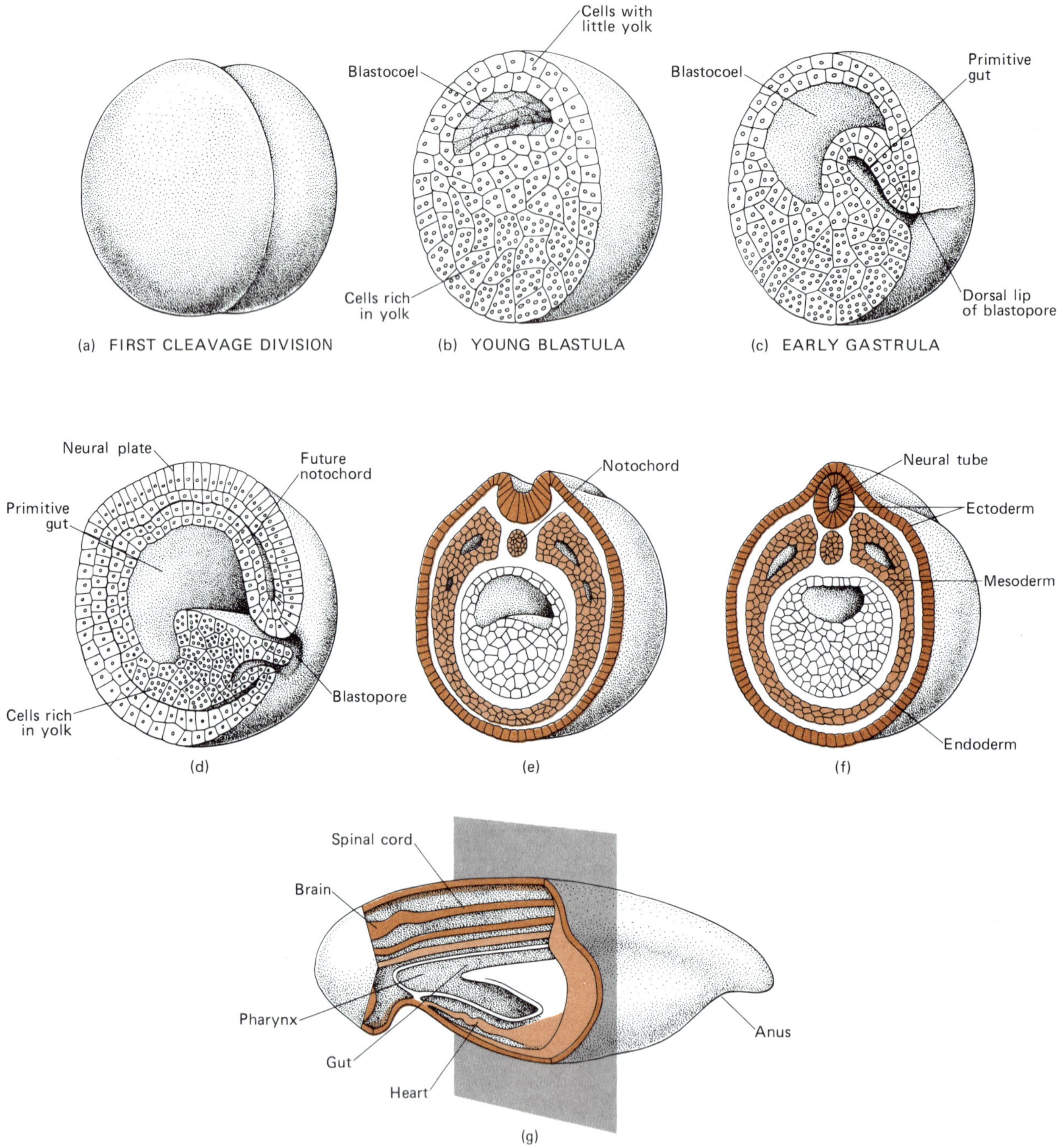

FIGURE 13.5 Early Development in Frogs. Early cleavages (a) divide the fertilized egg into two, four, and then many more cells. By the time cleavage is completed, the embryo consists of cells differing greatly in size and yolk content.

Organization of the frog embryo begins with an infolding of the blastopore at the posterior end of the embryo to form the primitive gut of the gastrula (c,d). This process, known as gastrulation, brings into contact cells with different cytoplasms. Contact between cytoplasmically diverse cells allow inductive interactions. For example, the roof of the primitive gut induces overlying tissue to thicken and form the neural tube from which the brain and spinal cord develop. At the same time, other cells are induced to become the notochord (a supporting rod), and other basic body structures (g).

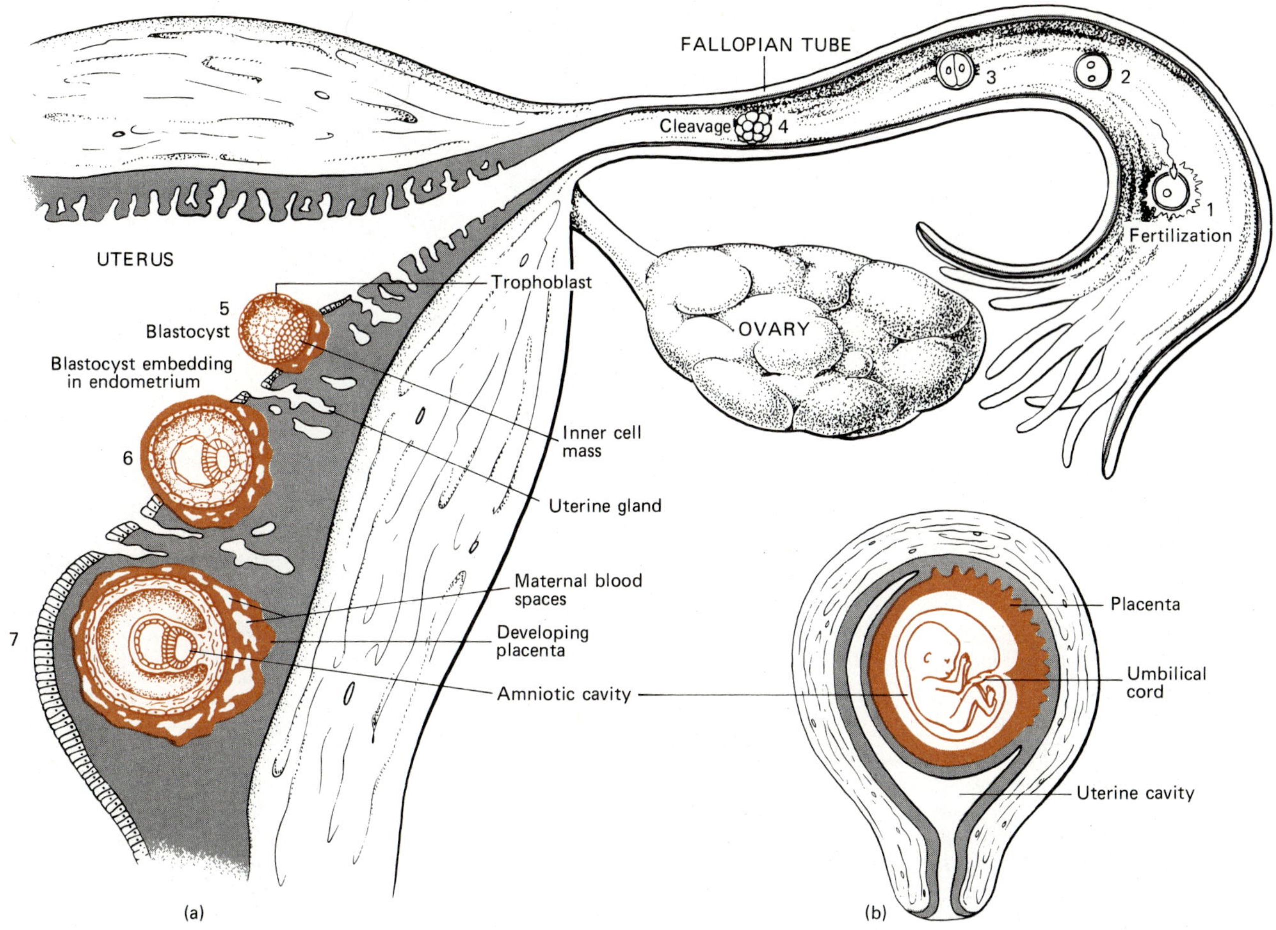

FIGURE 13.6 Human Development. Early development is shown in (a). After fertilization occurs in the Fallopian tube (1,2) the zygote undergoes cleavage divisions (3,4), forming the blastocyst (5) that begins to embed in the wall of the uterus. Note that the embryo develops from the inner cell mass and that the trophoblast forms part of the placenta (6,7). Because the embryo lies within the uterine wall, the placenta becomes extensive only on one side (b).

Early studies on the organization of the amphibian embryo established this importance of **cytoplasmic-nuclear interactions.** When the cells that normally form the roof of the primitive gut are transplanted into a host embryo, as shown in Fig. 13.7d, a second embryo is organized along with the original one. Note that the graft is made up of cells containing cytoplasm from a particular region of the egg. It is this region of the egg cytoplasm that has the properties to organize the embryo. When a host embryo contains two such organizing centers it develops two neural thickenings (Fig. 13.7e), and eventually the basic structures of two embryos (Fig. 13.7f,g).

Surprising as it may seem, considering the details of gene function presented in Chapter 11, there is but little specific information on control of gene action in development. The primary organization of the embryo involves large molecules that diffuse from one region to the other. The tissues that respond by forming the neural tube must first transcribe messenger RNA from nuclear DNA. The mechanism by which external substances trigger this mRNA synthesis is not established. One hy-

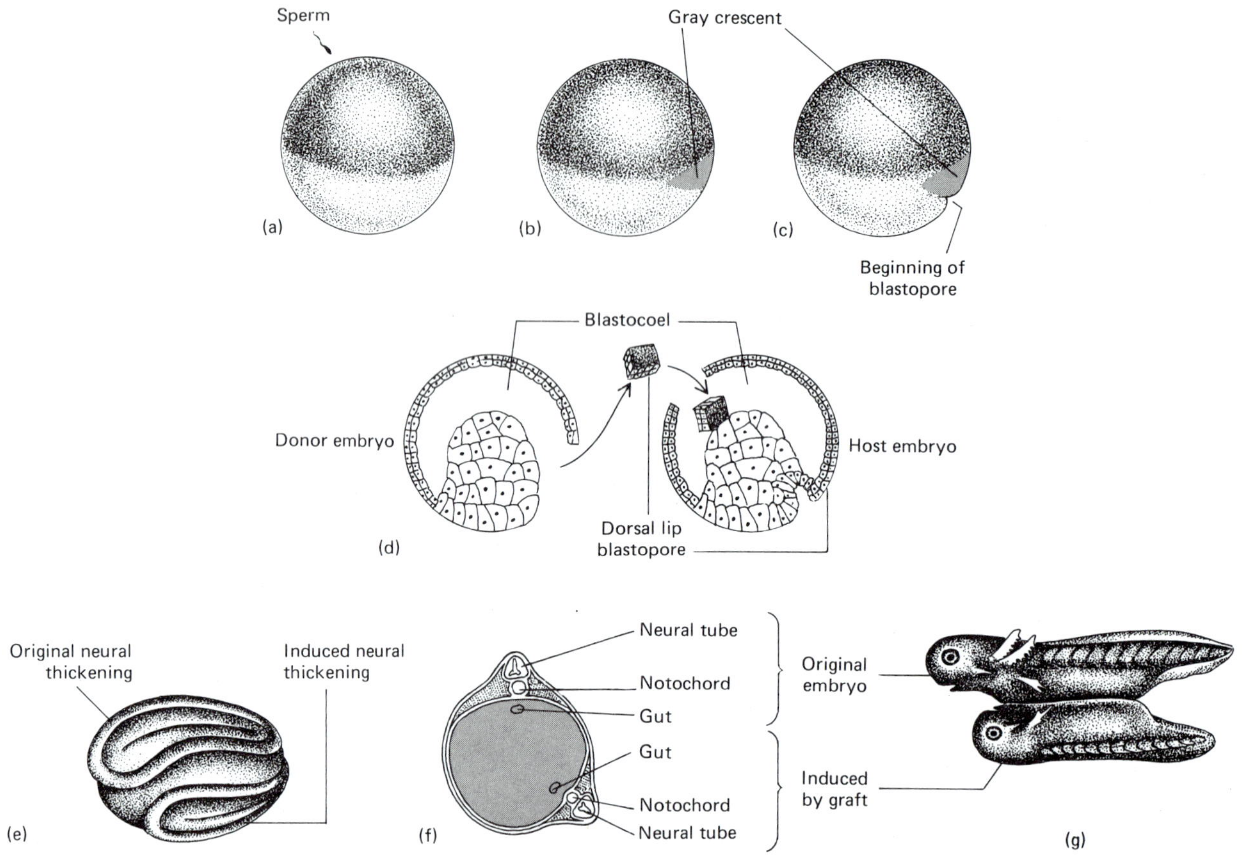

FIGURE 13.7 Organization of the Embryo Traces to a Region of the Egg Cytoplasm. In amphibians, fertilization (a) leads to a shift in the outermost layer of the egg cytoplasm. As a result of this shift, a gray crescent of unpigmented cytoplasm appears on the surface opposite the point of sperm entry (b). Cells in the gray crescent indent, giving rise to the blastopore (c). If the dorsal lip of the blastopore (containing cells with cytoplasm from the gray crescent) is cut from one embryo and transplanted to another embryo of the same age (d), the grafted material will start a second center of organization, so a double embryo results. First, two neural thickenings appear (e). Soon a section will reveal two embryos, one on each side (f). Although the secondary embryo contains grafted material, it is composed largely of host cells that have been induced to alter their fate. Thus cells with cytoplasm from the gray crescent can organize an entire animal (g).

pothesis is that cAMP is involved, as is so often true when cells respond to external messengers.

In the Uterus

The human embryo spends its first week traveling down the Fallopian tubes and finding a site in the uterus. During this time it survives on nutrients stored in the egg cytoplasm and materials absorbed from secretions of glands that dot the female tract. By the second week it is a blastocyst and is undertaking embryonic organization at the same time it is implanting in the uterine wall. Experimental studies with mice reveal that mammalian blastocysts develop into organized embryos by processes similar to those described for frogs and other amphibians.

Implantation is initiated by **trophoblast** cells, which secrete enzymes that digest the uterine lining and prepare this material to be absorbed by the embryo. The maternal tissue responds to this invasion, but not in a defensive manner. Rather, the mother's cells grow and increase their content of glycogen, an animal starch that nourishes blastocyst cells. While the embryo is digesting its way into the uterine wall, the wall is also growing over the embryo. Soon the overgrowth of maternal cells and invasion of the trophoblast have buried the embryo deep within the uterine wall (Fig. 13.6). This location necessitates rupture of the uterine lining before birth can occur. During the time when the human embryo is undergoing organization, the blastocyst is also giving rise to the embryonic membranes. One of these membranes, the **amnion** (Fig. 13.6), provides a fluid-filled sac within which the embryo is insulated from the outside world.

The Placenta. Once the embryo is embedded in the uterine wall, the trophoblast and surrounding maternal tissue begin to form the placenta. Blood vessels grow from the embryo into the trophoblast and become the **umbilical arteries** and **veins.** Soon blood circulates from the embryo, through the placenta, and back to the embryo. Digestion of the uterine lining by the trophoblast and growth of the mother's tissue over the embryo eventually place the fetal blood vessels within pools of blood from the mother's circulatory system (Fig. 13.6a). Contrary to a popular misconception, the baby's blood and the mother's blood do not mingle. Each has its own separate circulatory system. In the placenta the two circulations lie close together, separated only by delicate walls of tissue. Transfer of nutrients and oxygen into the embryo and removal of carbon dioxide and other wastes occur across a thin barrier.

Pregnancies Out of Place. Rarely, sperm reach and fertilize eggs that fall into the abdominal cavity. In a few instances in medical history this irregularity has led to the full development of a baby outside the female tract. Such development is possible because many tissues are capable of responding to the embryo and contributing to a placenta that will support a fetus. Children that come to term in the abdominal cavity must be delivered surgically.

If anything is to go wrong, the more likely possibility is that an embryo will settle down in a Fallopian tube rather than migrate to the uterus. These **tubal pregnancies** end abruptly and dangerously when the pressure of the expanding embryo causes muscles of the tube wall to contract and expel the embryo. The placental blood vessels are ruptured, and profuse bleeding results.

The First Trimester: How Quickly. By five weeks, a human embryo is about one centimeter (0.38 inches) long and C-shaped. Embryonic development proceeds rapidly. Growth and changes in proportion produce a characteristic human appearance by the end of the first trimester (the first three months after conception). See Fig. 13.8.

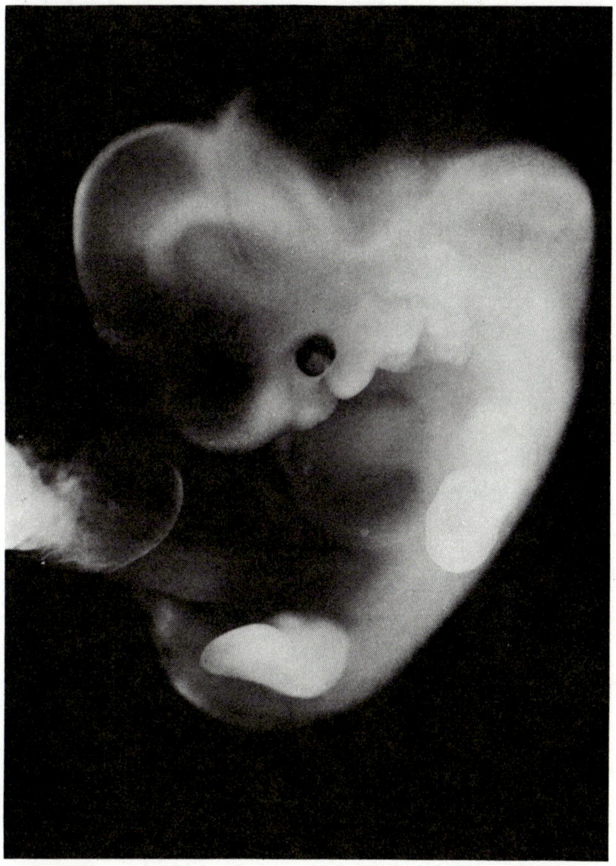

FIGURE 13.8 Human Embryo. By five weeks development is well underway.

The Second Trimester: Organ Development. With the second trimester the details of organ structure begin to appear. During the fourth month, hair develops on the head and in the eyebrow regions. The lips separate from the gums. The ears now protrude from the head. Friction ridges, which will later determine fingerprints, become established. Minerals are laid down in developing bones so that these show clearly on x-ray films of the fetus within its mother's uterus. While the head remains large in proportion to the trunk and limbs, these parts are beginning to catch up.

The fifth month brings basic reflexes such as the closing of the hand whenever the palm is stimulated. Many babies also begin to suck their thumbs about this time. Secretions of skin glands and shed skin cells form a cheese-like coating that protects the delicate skin. Fine body hair helps hold the cheesy coating in place.

By the end of the sixth month, the fetus is about 25 centimeters (10 inches) long. Its organs are sufficiently developed so that it has a fairly good chance of survival outside the mother, if it is provided with skilled care. The use of a respirator is virtually essential when birth occurs at this stage, because the lungs are not fully developed. However, the nervous system is able to control breathing.

The Last Trimester: Tremendous Growth and Perfection of Organs. During the final three months the fetus more than triples its weight. Along with this astounding growth, specialization of tissues continues in the various organs. The cerebral cortex takes on the convolutions and cell layers characteristic of humans. From the seventh month brain waves can be recorded through the mother's abdominal wall. Yet development of the nervous system will not be fully complete until the individual reaches puberty, perhaps a dozen years later. Other organs of the newborn also differ in detail from the adult pattern, but only the reproductive system is less complete than the nervous system.

By the time of birth, the fine body hair characteristic of the fetus has been shed. Although bone formation has progressed rapidly, much of the skeleton is still cartilage. The bones of the skull do not yet meet in certain places, often called "soft spots." The sutures between the skull bones are also flexible. Thus the skull can be deformed temporarily as it passes through the birth canal. Normally this does the brain no harm, and the skull resumes its familiar shape within a few days.

Twins

Fraternal twins result from the fertilization of two eggs by two sperm. Each fertilized egg forms a separate blastocyst, so each has its own placenta. Fraternal twins are no more alike than any other brothers or sisters, except that they are of the same age and therefore experience a more similar environment. Because fraternal twins result from two conceptions, one may be a boy and the other a girl, or both may be of the same sex.

Identical twins come from one fertilized egg that forms a single blastocyst. Either two inner cell masses develop, or—less commonly—two embryos organize within a single inner cell mass (Fig. 13.9). In either case the developing embryos lie within one trophoblast and come to share a common placenta. It is possible, but not documented, that identical twins can also arise from separation of the cleaving embryo into two parts before it forms a blastocyst. Such identical twins would have separate placentas. Except for this unsubstantiated possibility, the physician or midwife attending birth can determine whether twins are identical or fraternal merely by noting whether the afterbirth consists of one placenta or two.

Multiple births are not randomly distributed. The frequency of fraternal twins varies among races; the incidence is higher among Caucasians than among the Japanese. Studies of families also suggest that the tendency for women to ovulate two eggs in one cycle and thus to bear fraternal twins seems to be inherited. Births of identical twins are more common in older mothers. Recently developed treatments for a type of female sterility caused by a sluggish pituitary have led to numerous cases of three or more simultaneous births. This results from the fact that the drugs sometimes stimulate the release of several eggs at once.

Birth Defects

The dread of physical malformation is so great that almost all societies have pregnancy taboos designed to protect the unborn child. But despite magic and medicine, a large portion of conceptions produce defective embryos. Estimates range from 10 to 80 percent. These figures include pregnancies that terminate in spontaneous abortions and those that deliver babies with minor to severe handicaps. The large range in the estimates reflects disagreement

FIGURE 13.9 **How Twins Happen.** Each fraternal twin comes from a separate fertilized egg (a). It may be that identical twins can form by separation of cells prior to formation of the blastocyst. If so, each baby would have its own amnion and placenta (b), just as do fraternal twins. It is established that identical twins can result from the formation of two inner cell masses within one blastocyst (c). Because the inner cell mass forms the amnion, each twin has its own amnion. But because the trophoblast forms the placenta, two identical twins share one placenta. Sometimes identical twins develop from one partially divided inner cell mass. Such twins share a single amnion as well as one placenta.

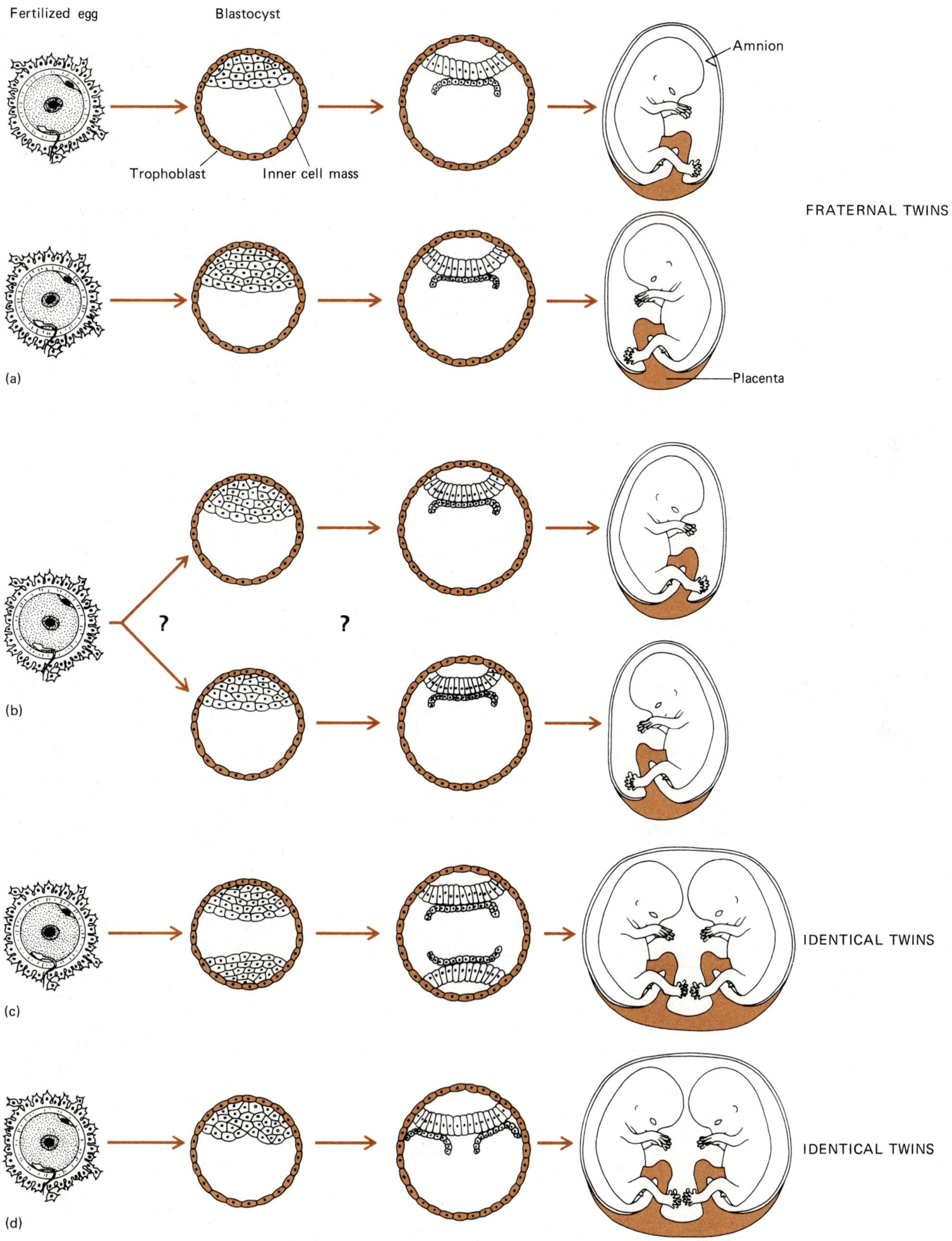
Fertilized egg
Blastocyst
Amnion
Trophoblast
Inner cell mass
FRATERNAL TWINS
(a)
Placenta
?
?
(b)
IDENTICAL TWINS
(c)
IDENTICAL TWINS
(d)

BOX 13B

TUMORS: ABNORMAL GROWTHS

Tumors develop from our own body tissues. Some tumors, such as common warts, are benign—that is, harmless. Other growths are malignant—cancers that are likely to cause death if they go untreated. Any tissue, even those of the embryo, can become malignant. Most cancers are solid masses, but some, such as leukemias and other cancers of the bone marrow, consist of free-floating cells. In leukemia the white blood cells proliferate and abnormal cells flood the circulatory system.

The harm done by malignant cells traces to their abnormal growth and organization and to the fact that they fail to differentiate properly. Because malignant cells grow more rapidly than normal cells, they use up nutrients and starve other cells. Growing tumors create pressure that can collapse blood vessels or otherwise interfere with important organs. For example, the accumulation of tumor cells replaces the alveolar cavities in cancerous lung tissue. The victim eventually loses the ability to exchange gases with the air and will literally suffocate.

But worst of all, malignant tumors are not contained by normal developmental patterns, and spread through the body. Tumor cells erode nearby organs and penetrate blood and lymphatic vessels; then they can spread through the body and establish new colonies of malignant cells.

Various types of radiation, components of plastics and cigarette smoke, asbestos fibers, and a long list of chemicals all cause cancer. Certain viruses are also carcinogenic (cancer-causing), and many cancers have a hereditary component. For example, people homozygous for a particular allele invariably develop xeroderma pigmentosum, a rare skin cancer, if they are exposed to excessive sunlight.

In some instances specific genes known as oncogenes are responsible for malignant growth. One oncogene isolated from a line of human-bladder cancer cells differs from the normal allele by a single nucleotide. Where the normal allele had a guanine, the oncogene carries a thymine. This single nucleotide change results in a protein differing from the normal protein by only a single amino acid substitution. Where the normal cell product contains glycine, a cell with the oncogene inserts valine. Other oncogenes do not alter the nature of the gene product but the amount. For example, the *ras* gene, responsible for a rat connective-tissue cancer, results in a dramatic increase of an otherwise normal cell product.

If some cancers have a clear genetic basis, those due to chemicals or radiation may involve mutations. Others may result from defects in the control of gene function. Consider that all body cells have the instructions for all body functions, but that a particular cell utilizes only a few of these genetic patterns. Furthermore, some instructions are used only at certain times, such as during embryonic development. Regulation of gene expression must involve complex mechanisms, most of which are yet to be discovered. It is not unlikely that

on the frequency and cause of very early spontaneous abortions. It is established that many embryos abort so early that the mother never knows of her pregnancy. But of how often this happens we are unsure. Although genetic defects are a major cause of abnormal embryonic development, nutritional deficiencies, infections, drugs, and maternal disease also contribute to the problem.

Viruses. **Rubella** (German measles), influenza, smallpox, and other viruses can penetrate the placenta and infect the fetus while it is in the uterus. Often the fetus dies as the result of infection, and the pregnancy comes to an early end. But in many cases only specific embryonic tissues die. For instance, rubella can damage cells that normally form
the cochlea□ of the ear or those that should form 195
the lens of the eye. As a result the child is deaf, or its vision is clouded by cataracts. Congenital malformations of the heart also appear in as many as 80 percent of those that survive **prenatal** (before birth) **rubella.** As a reflection of crucial steps in development, viral diseases are most serious at certain stages. For rubella, the most dangerous time is between the fourth and the twelfth week of pregnancy.

Susceptibility. Studies of palate development in two inbred strains of mice demonstrate the interaction of genetic and environmental influences on

cancer can involve defects in this regulatory mechanism.

The belief that cancer can result from failure of complex genetic controls is supported by simple breeding experiments with tropical fish. Platys are fish with black pigment spots in their dorsal fins. Rarely these pigment cells become malignant. Crosses between platys and swordtails (a related species that lacks black pigment) yield fish with much larger black fin spots. The increased pigment suggests decreased restraints on pigment cells. If the hybrids are crossed back to swordtails, most of the offspring develop massive pigmented tumors that invade other tissues and eventually kill the fish. Apparently multiplication and spread of the black pigment cells in the platy is controlled by numerous genes. As these controlling genes are diluted by crossing with the swordtails, the pigment cells escape restraint and become malignant.

Among the specific characteristics of malignant cells is the presence of unusual antigens on their surfaces. Many investigators believe that the body normally detects these antigens, recognizes them as foreign, and destroys tumor cells. If this is true, a cancer must develop only when the immune system fails. Several lines of evidence support this theory. First, drugs that suppress immune responses of people who receive kidney and other organ transplants seem to increase the incidence of malignancies. Some carcinogens are also immunosuppressants. Finally, the rare spontaneous regression of tumors may be related to sudden stimulation of the immune response.

The involvement of genes, viruses, and faulty immunity in cancer have recently been tied together with the discovery that a normal cellular gene (known as the *myc* gene) can cause cancer when it becomes incorporated in a virus. The hypothesis is that the virus inserts the *myc* gene into a key site between genes coding for antibody components. If the location of a gene can allow it to cause cancer by interfering with antibody production, it is easy to understand why so many cancers of B and T cells are associated with the exchange of arms between specific chromosomes. The chromosome breaks may also be located at sites where they interfere with antibody synthesis.

Most cancer treatments are only attempts to control multiplication of malignant cells. Of course, the most direct approach is to remove the growth surgically. Once malignant cells have infiltrated vital organs, surgical removal becomes impossible. The only alternative is to try to destroy the cancer cells with radiation or drugs that are more harmful to malignant tissue than to normal adult tissues. Destruction by such means is sometimes possible because the rapidly reproducing cancer cells are particularly sensitive to radiation and chemicals that interfere with mitosis. Unfortunately, no treatment is known that harms cancer cells while leaving normal cells unscathed. Only the seriousness of malignancy justifies the side effects risked with antitumor drugs or radiation therapy.

220 birth defects. Given at specific times, large doses of the adrenal hormone **cortisone**□ result in **cleft palate** in 100 percent of the offspring of one mouse strain known as A/J. The same doses given to C57BL mice at the same stage of pregnancy have no effect. As shown in Fig. 13.10, cleft palate results from failure of the two palatal shelves to fuse together. Formation of a continuous palate is possible only during a certain stage. After that time, growth of the head carries the palatal shelves apart faster than they can grow toward each other.

The growth of palatal shelves in A/J mice is always slower than in C57BL mice. Consequently, palatal fusion occurs later in the A/J strain. There is a high incidence of cleft palate in the A/J strain, even under the best conditions. When administration of cortisone further slows palatal growth, the shelves never fuse. In contrast, the palatal shelves of C57BL mice grow fast. In this strain, fusion occurs even in the presence of experimental doses of cortisone. Thus a physiological factor, cortisone, causes a birth defect in one strain but not in another. The inherited growth characteristics of A/J mice make them particularly susceptible to cortisone.

Sensitive Periods. Obviously cortisone can act on A/J mouse embryos only after certain developmental stages are reached and before the shelves have fused. Therefore A/J mouse embryos are sensitive to cortisone only during a particular period.

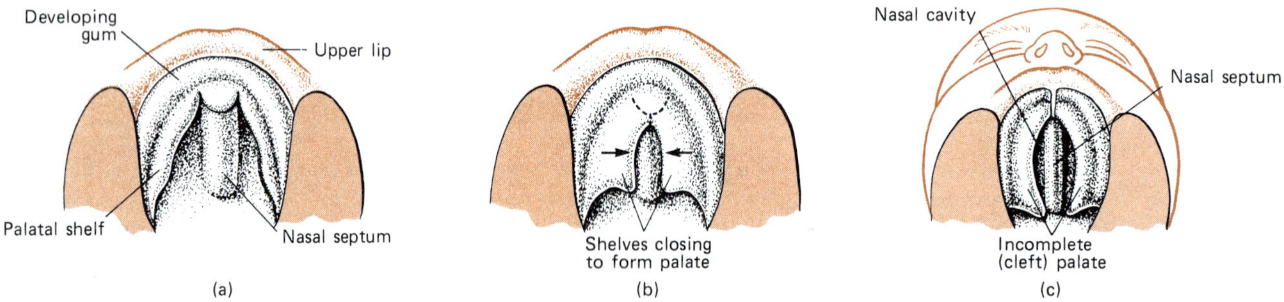

FIGURE 13.10 **Origin of Cleft Palate.** The palate begins to form by the sixth week (a). Three shelves grow out and fuse to make the roof of the mouth. As normal development continues (b), the median shelf first fuses with the two lateral shelves, which then proceed to merge with each other. Failure of the lateral shelves to grow together results in a cleft palate (c).

Such sensitive periods are characteristic of embryonic development. Because these periods reflect major organizational events, they are confined to early development.

The embryonic stages of human development most susceptible to deformity occur between two and six weeks of gestation. It is during this period that most major malformations originate (Fig. 13.11). The births of flipper-limbed babies to women who used the sedative thalidomide illustrate this problem (Fig. 13.12). It is tragic that the embryo reaches its most sensitive stages before the mother may be aware that she is pregnant. Thus the precautions expectant mothers take come too late to protect the baby from most environmental harm. The only answer to this problem is for women who may conceive to always take the same precautions that they would if they knew they were pregnant.

Neither premature birth nor **spontaneous abortion** (loss of fetus) is likely to result from exercise, travel, or sexual intercourse during pregnancy. In general, pregnant women are advised to continue an active life, to eat a balanced diet, and to get plenty of sleep. Avoidance of alcohol, cigarettes, caffeine-rich drinks, and other potentially harmful substances may be important. Spontaneous abortion and low birth weight are especially common when the mother smokes during pregnancy. Similarly, even moderate alcohol consumption during pregnancy may increase the likelihood of physical or mental defects in the child. It is also wise for expectant mothers to use no drugs or medicines not specifically prescribed for use during pregnancy.

Environmental factors are not the only ones that increase the likelihood of bearing a defective

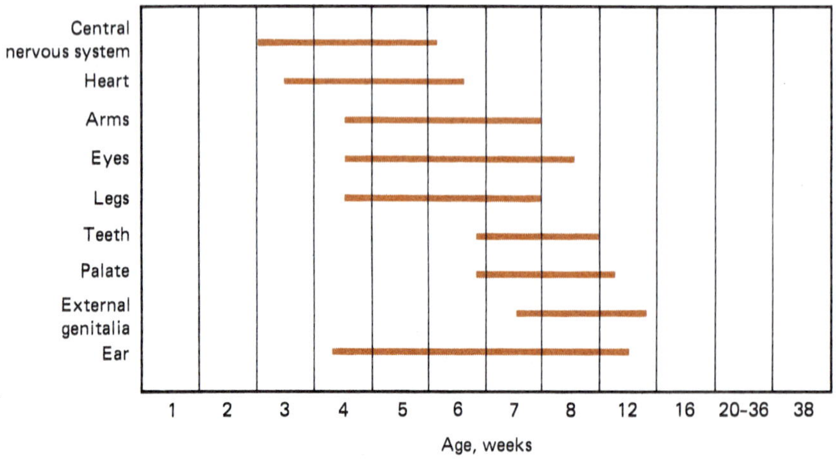

FIGURE 13.11 **Sensitive Periods in Development.** Drugs, irradiation, and other environmental factors induce malformation of specific embryonic structures. Note that until two weeks after conception, the embryo is apparently immune to damage. In fact, damage at this early stage kills the embryo and the mother is unaware that she has been pregnant.

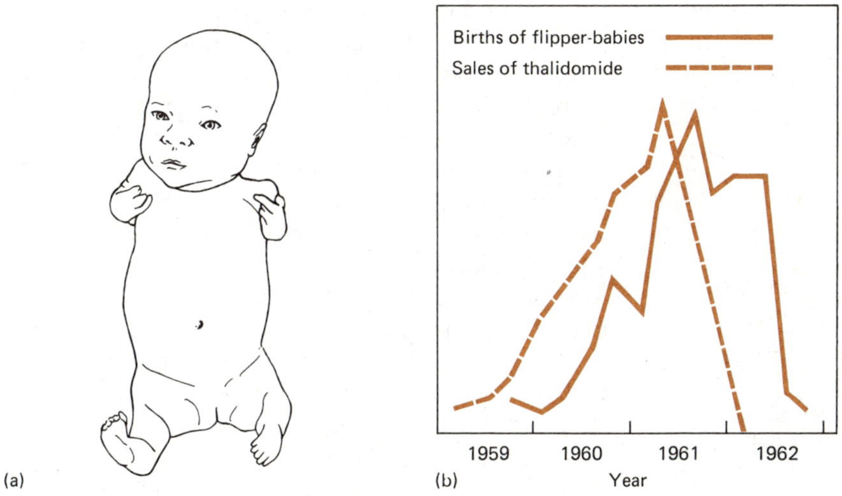

FIGURE 13.12 Sensitivity of Human Embryos to Thalidomide. Thalidomide was a new sedative introduced into European markets in the late 1950s. A high incidence of flipper-limbed babies (a) born to women using this drug led to its withdrawal from the market in 1962 (b).

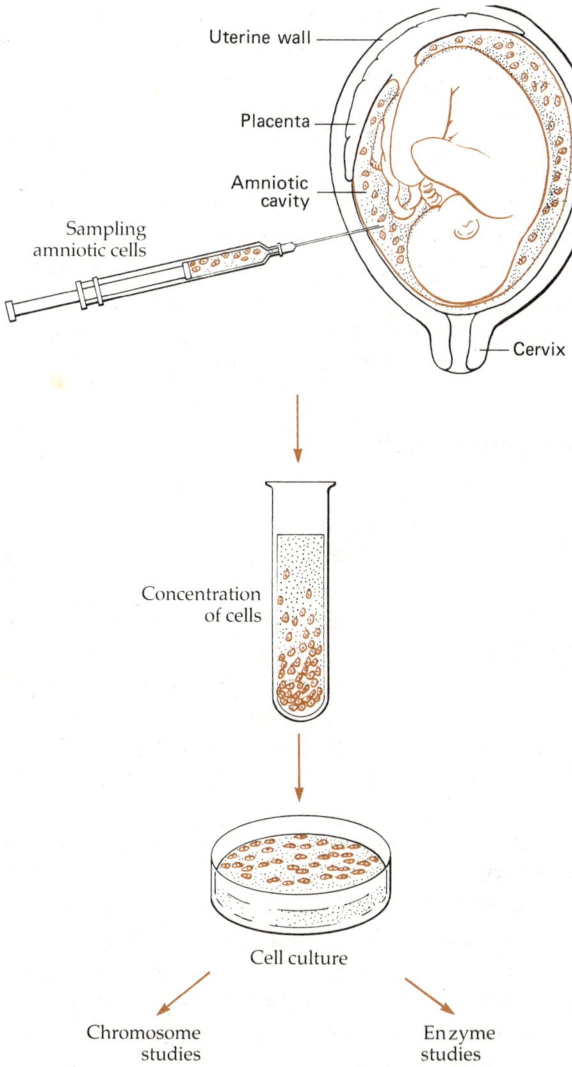

child. Women in their late thirties or older often produce eggs with chromosomal defects.□ The 268 presence of certain inherited diseases on either or both sides of the family also increases the risk of a defective baby. Thus some prospective parents are especially concerned about the fetus. Many choose to use **amniocentesis** (Fig. 13.13) to determine whether or not their baby will be normal. Amniocentesis can reveal genetic defects present in all the cells of the fetus but not malformations that have been induced by the action of environmental factors at a particular stage of development.

Since 96 percent of the fetuses checked by amniocentesis prove genetically normal, this procedure relieves a great deal of anxiety. It also can prevent the choice of abortion in high-risk cases, for more often than not the fetus proves healthy. The procedure of amniocentesis itself is usually harmless, but its use increases slightly the chance

FIGURE 13.13 Amniocentesis—Checking Out the Unborn. Amniocentesis is a procedure for sampling cells from the amnionic fluid that surrounds the fetus. Because both the fetus and the amnion arise from embryonic tissues, any cells that slough off into the amniotic fluid are representative of the fetus.

To carry out amniocentesis, the physician first determines the position of the fetus. A needle is inserted through the mother's abdominal wall and into her uterus. When the needle tip lies in the amniotic fluid around the fetus, the physician withdraws a small volume of the liquid. Cells separated from the fluid are grown in culture until there are enough for enzyme and chromosome studies.

of a spontaneous abortion. Reports that fetal cells regularly enter the mother's blood have led to suggestions for simpler methods to isolate fetal cells for laboratory study. Someday it may be necessary only to draw blood from the mother's arm.

BIRTH AND MOTHERHOOD

Childbearing is not a disease but a normal biological process. Nevertheless, medical supervision has become a pattern in the United States, and most babies are born in hospitals, often with the mother anesthetized. The desirability of anesthesia is contested by those who advocate "natural childbirth." Proponents of natural childbirth offer classes that teach prospective parents what to expect and provide the mother-to-be with exercises that improve muscle tone and with drills in respiratory patterns that may aid her during delivery. It isn't clear whether the reduced pain reported by women who have such training results from physical reasons or from lessened anxiety. But many parents trained in natural childbirth believe that it makes delivery a better experience, and that the less their child is exposed to anesthesia the better.

A parallel social movement would return childbirth to the home and to the hands of the midwife. Without doubt, the nurse-midwife can adequately attend to most deliveries. And there are advantages to home births, such as familiar surroundings and, sometimes, fewer infectious organisms. But a certain percentage of births inevitably require specialized medical personnel and equipment if the process is to be reasonably safe for both mother and child. The trade-offs between often impersonal hospital experiences and old-fashioned home births can make the choice difficult. But in every case the prospective mother should have periodic medical examinations during pregnancy and be advised of the risk attending home delivery.

Normally birth comes after about 266 days of **gestation** (development inside the mother). Four percent of births are late by three weeks or more, and more than seven percent yield babies classified as premature.

Giving Birth

The birth process (Fig. 13.14) begins with a prolonged period of **labor pains,** caused by uterine contractions that usually force the head of the baby against the cervix of the uterus. After a while this pressure dilates the passageway through the cervix. Dilation can take twelve hours, sometimes longer. During this time the amnion ruptures, and amniotic fluid is lost through the vagina. Eventually the baby is pushed out of the uterus by contractions of the uterine muscles, normally aided by voluntary contractions of muscles of the abdominal wall. Further contractions of the uterine walls squeeze blood from the placenta into the baby before the umbilical cord is ready to cut. (The cord eventually shrivels up, leaving only a scar known as the **navel.)** A few minutes later, the uterus expels the placenta and the amnion as the **afterbirth.** Because the embryo develops within the uterine wall, the uterine lining must be shed with the afterbirth. This accounts for the bleeding associated with childbirth.

The exact stimulus for birth remains uncertain. We do know that the placenta produces large quantities of both estrogen and progesterone. Estrogen causes the smooth muscle cells of the uterus to enlarge and multiply. It also increases the sensitivity of the muscle cells, causing them to contract in response to minor stimuli. Progesterone, on the other hand, inhibits uterine contractions. Indeed, this is one of its functions during pregnancy. Birth may be initiated at least in part by falling progesterone levels as the placenta ages late in pregnancy. **Oxytocin,** a hormone secreted by the posterior pituitary, also plays a role in birth. Physicians sometimes inject synthetic oxytocin to induce labor.

Birth Adjustments

The newborn must undertake for itself many functions that were previously performed by its mother. Whereas until now the baby has relied on its mother's lungs, now it must exchange gases directly with the air. The baby must now also regulate its water balance and excrete wastes through its kidneys, instead of depending on exchange with the mother's blood and regulation through her kidneys. And even though the mother provides the baby with food, it must now digest and absorb the food for itself.

Immediately after birth, the establishment of respiration has first priority. If the baby doesn't breathe spontaneously in about 30 seconds, the attendant tries mild mechanical stimulation, such as flicking the soles of the baby's feet. The gasp that usually results expands the delicate alveoli and transforms the lungs from solid masses into permanently frothy structures.

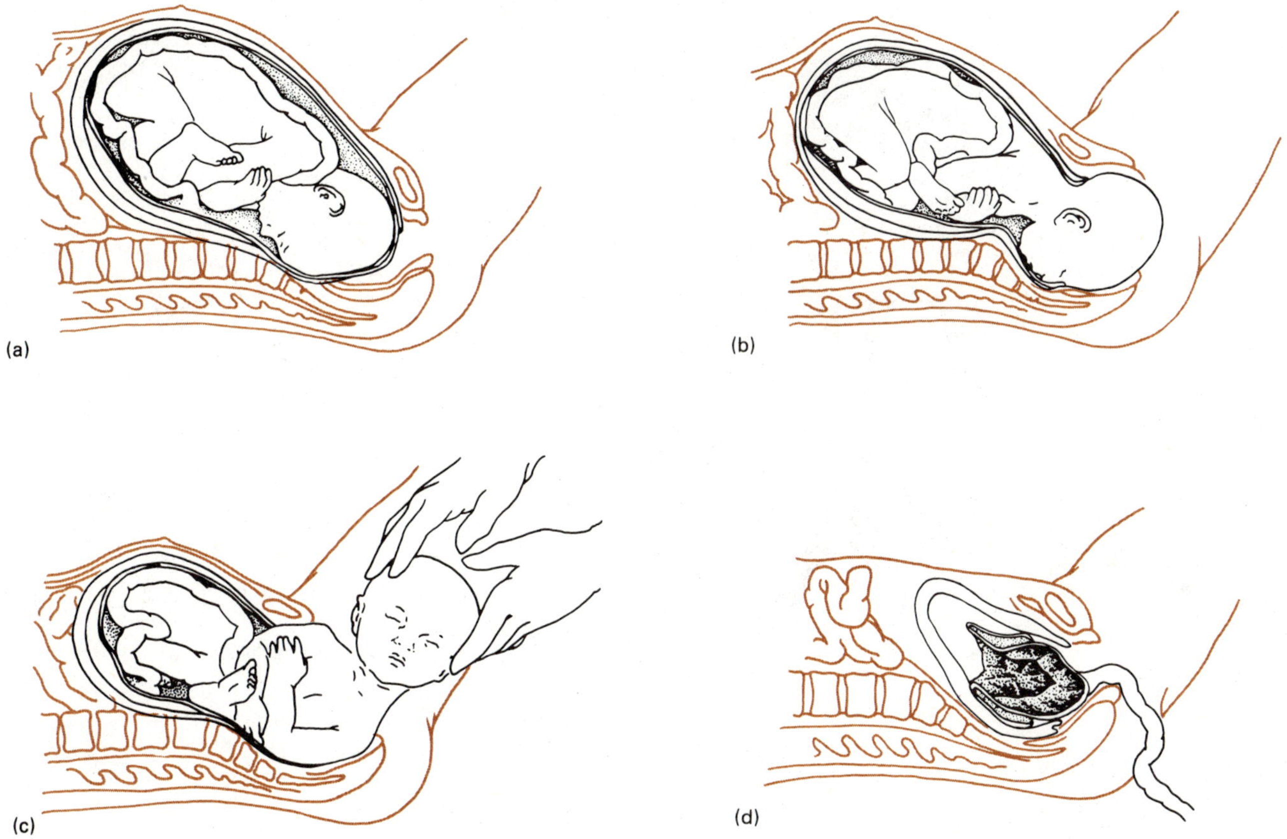

FIGURE 13.14 The Labor of Birth. Labor begins with widely spaced uterine contractions that force the baby against the cervix of the uterus. This pressure gradually dilates the cervix (a). As the cervix enlarges, the amniotic sac usually bursts and releases its watery fluid. (Sometimes this "loss of the water" occurs before labor begins.) In most births the crown of the head is the first part of the baby to become visible in the birth canal. This "crowning" marks the end of the first stage of labor, which may take a long time, often twelve hours or more (b).

Once the crown of the head, which is the largest part of the infant, passes through the cervix, birth can occur quickly. Now the frequent uterine contractions should be supplemented by conscious contraction of abdominal muscles by the mother to expel the baby (c). The final stage of labor separates the placenta from the uterine wall and pushes it out through the birth canal (d).

With the first breath, part of the fetal circulatory pattern becomes obsolete. During gestation, much of the fetal blood is shunted from the right side of the heart and the pulmonary aorta to the left side and the systemic aorta (Fig. 13.15). After all, the fetal lungs provide no gas exchange, so the flow through them needs to be sufficient only for development of the vessels themselves. With birth must come closure of these fetal circulatory bypasses. As soon as uterine contractions squeeze fetal blood from the placenta, the attendant ties and cuts the umbilical cord. Then the baby is on its own.

A change in the blood itself becomes evident a few days after birth, when most babies show **jaundice,**□ a yellow tinge to the sclera of the eyes 147
and, in some cases, to the skin. This unusual coloring is due to excess **bilirubin,** a pigment produced when hemoglobin is degraded. Abundance of bilirubin after birth results from a changeover in hemoglobin that accommodates the infant to new gas exchange conditions. The fetus has a special hemoglobin that can draw oxygen away from the mother's hemoglobin. After birth the fetal red cells with this fetal hemoglobin are destroyed and replaced with red blood cells containing adult-type hemoglobin suitable for taking oxygen from air.

Temperature regulation poses another new challenge to the newborn. The tiny infant has a much larger surface for its volume than do larger

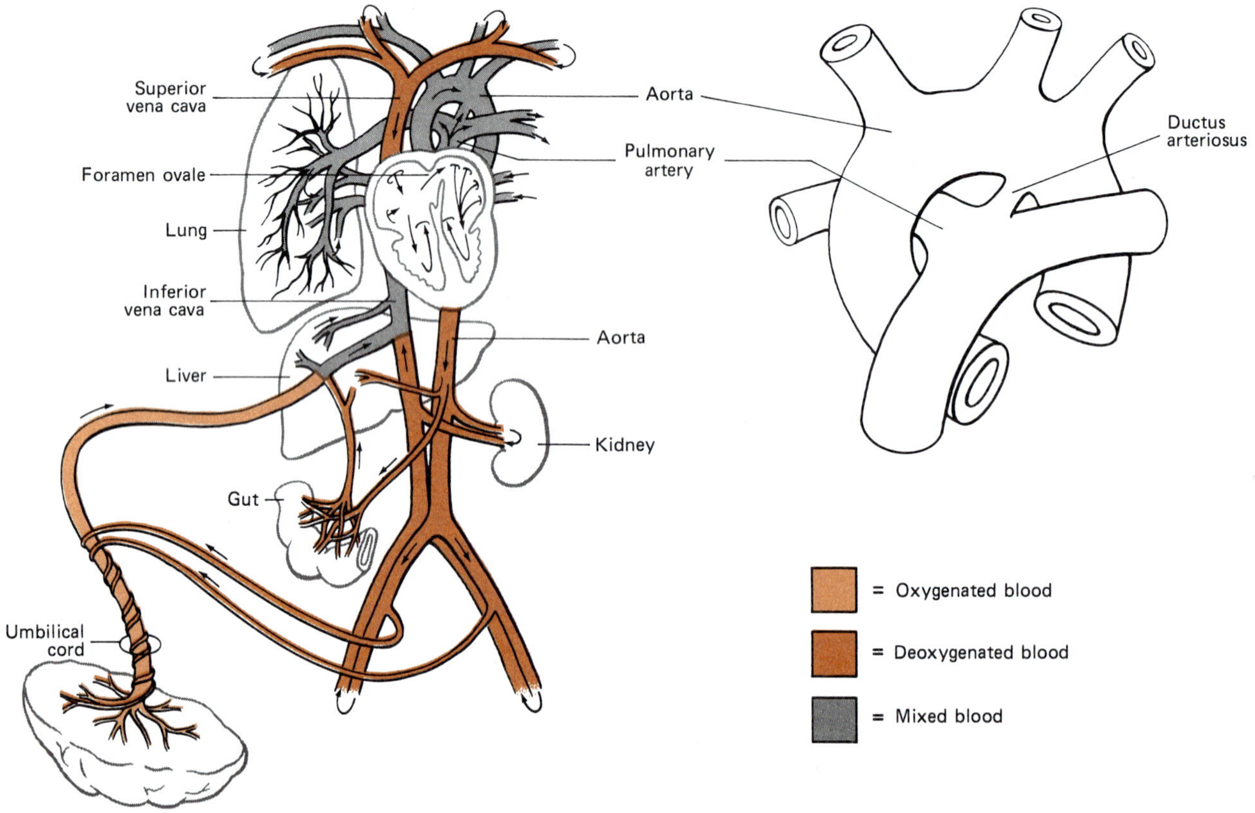

FIGURE 13.15 Circulatory Adaptations of the Fetus. The fetus relies on the placenta for both nutrients and gas exchange. Consequently, there is a special arterial supply to the placenta and a venous return from the placenta.

Because the lungs do not function before birth, the pulmonary circulation of the fetus serves only to develop the blood vessels of the lungs and to nourish the tissues there. The fetal lungs are so compact that passing all the blood through them would require excessive pressure. Consequently, there are special pathways that divert blood from the pulmonary circulation to the systemic circulation. One such shunt is the *ductus arteriosus.* After birth, the ductus arteriosus constricts and gradually turns into a cord of connective tissue.

Before birth, the high resistance to blood flow through the lungs causes the pressure in the right artrium to be higher than in the left atrium. The presence of the *foramen ovale,* an opening between the right and left atria, permits blood in the right atrium to flow into the left atrium. As soon as the baby breathes, blood can more easily pass through the lungs. Pressure in the left atrium is now higher than in the right atrium. This pressure pushes a flap of tissue over the foramen ovale, so it grows closed.

humans. This large surface area promotes heat loss. So does the fact that many new babies lack insulating fat layers under the skin. To compensate, deposits of special **brown fat** can provide heat to an inadequately clothed baby. Through an unusual metabolism, brown fat cells uncouple oxidation from
63 ATP production□ and release all available energy as heat.

Taken together, the adjustments of birth place a tremendous strain on the newborn. Many defective fetuses survive to term only to die in the next few hours or days. Even healthy babies lose weight for a time, but after a short period they begin to grow again.

Problems of the Premature

Infants born early but weighing at least 1 kg (2.2 lb) have adequate organs, so most survive. They need special care, including a uniformly warm environment, enriched in oxygen and free of disease microorganisms. Weight is used to predict survival, because length of gestation is difficult to establish. If both mother and fetus are healthy, a fetal weight of one kilogram reflects about seven months of gestation. Babies weighing less than 2.5 kg (5.5 lb) are considered premature. Premature infants that survive suffer disproportionately from brain damage, mental retardation, nearsightedness, and other defects. These conditions may result as much from the problems that caused premature birth as from meeting the world too soon. Frequently, prematurity is associated with multiple births or maternal illness.

Lactation and Nursing

When a baby is born, the **mammary** (milk) **glands** of the mother's breasts must be prepared to feed it. The breasts of nonpregnant women consist mostly of fat deposits. The glands themselves are rudimentary. During pregnancy, estrogen and progesterone from the placenta stimulate growth of the glands. Meanwhile, the same hormones suppress **lactation** (milk production) by inhibiting secretion of **prolactin** by the anterior pituitary. Loss of placental hormones at birth removes this inhibition and permits production of prolactin. This, in turn, helps stimulate secretion of milk.

Control of Milk Production after Birth. Milk produced by cells within the breast accumulates in the glands and in their ducts. Nursing initiates a reflex that releases the milk. Nerve impulses pass from receptors in the skin of the breast to the hypothalamus. Here there are cells that have processes extending into the posterior pituitary, where they secrete **oxytocin.** Once secreted into the blood of the posterior pituitary, oxytocin soon reaches the breasts. There it causes contraction of the glands, so milk is moved toward the nipples.
Adrenalin,□ the hormone associated with the sym- 175
pathetic fight-or-flight reaction, antagonizes the nursing-oxytocin reflex. Thus fright, anger, or other emotional upsets that cause adrenalin release also inhibit the flow of milk.

Antibodies in Milk. During the later part of pregnancy and for a few days after childbirth, the mammary glands secrete **colostrum.** This yellowish first
milk is rich in protein, especially antibodies,□ and 215
low in volume. Nursing immediately after birth protects the baby from infection through transfer of antibodies from the mother. True milk secretion begins on the fourth or fifth day after childbirth.

Importance of Neural Stimulus of Nursing. Regular stimulation of the breast is necessary for continued prolactin production. In the absence of nursing, the mother's milk supply soon dries up.

FIGURE 13.16 **Nursing Is Important.** Besides supplying the proper nutrients safely and conveniently, the experience of nursing helps build a secure relationship between mother and baby.

The neural stimulus of nursing also opposes release of luteinizing hormone (LH) and thus can prevent ovulation. Unfortunately this mechanism is not reliable enough to serve as a dependable birth-control measure. In primitive societies, however, prolonged nursing may have some function as a birth-spacing mechanism. Studies with the
40 !Kung San□ reveal that births in this group are widely spaced without any obvious contraceptive mechanism. In that culture babies are constantly with their mothers, and they feed at the breast every few minutes. Some infants nurse almost continuously throughout the night. It may be this continuous stimulus of the breast that accounts for birth spacing.

DEVELOPMENT AS A LIFELONG PROCESS

Development doesn't stop at birth. Characteristic changes occur throughout our life span. At least some of these changes reflect selection of traits that favor continuation of the species and are clearly inherited by us all.

Growth

A graph of the weight of an animal plotted against its age may yield an S-shaped curve (Fig. 13.17a). The slow increase at the beginning reflects initial organization of the embryo and adjustment to the environment. Once the basic structures are established, the embryo grows at an increasing rate until a maximum rate is reached. After a time, the growth rate begins to decrease, and eventually growth comes to an end. Of course, many animals deviate from this theoretical growth curve. For example, accumulation of fat and its loss during famine can distort the curve. So does the tendency for older organisms to contain less water per cell than younger animals do. In fact, growth curves are most meaningful if they reflect the number of cells in the organism. However, since it is impractical to count the cells in an animal, growth curves are often based on weight, length, or height.

For people, growth curves based on height vary from the general S-shaped curve in two ways. First, the newborn has already undergone the initial adjustments and entered a stage of rapid growth. This growth tapers off before birth but is later resumed. Second, the human growth curve shows a small hump known as the **adolescent growth spurt.** It appears at about the time the secondary sexual characteristics develop. In males the increase in height is accompanied by lengthening of the penis, enlargement of the testes, and appearance of the characteristic male pattern of pubic hair. Breast development occurs during the adolescent growth spurt of females. Menstruation begins near the end of the spurt.

Of course, different parts of the body grow at different rates. The brain gets its growth early (Fig. 13.17b), as shown by the fact that children have large heads in proportion to their bodies. Probably you have noted that cartoonists use this difference to distinguish the figures of children from those of adults. The early and rapid growth of the nervous system is necessary, because that system must be nearly complete before the child begins important learning tasks. In contrast, the reproductive system grows very slowly until the period just before sexual maturity.

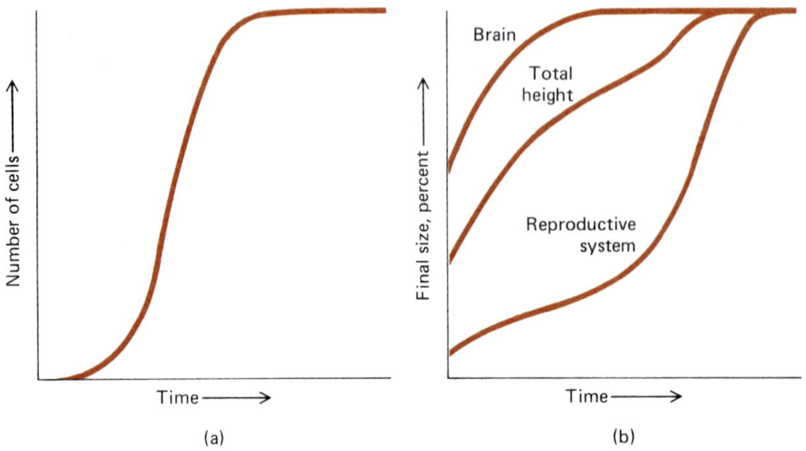

FIGURE 13.17 Growth Curves. Bacteria and isolated cells introduced into a culture medium divide slowly at first (a). After the cells have adapted to the environment, the growth rate increases to the maximum and then tapers off as conditions deteriorate. The generalized growth of animals plotted as the number of cells against age yields a similar curve. Actual growth measurements (b) differ from this general pattern.

In the sense that cell division continues, growth occurs throughout life. Although nerve and skeletal muscle cells cannot divide, perhaps because they are too specialized, most other tissues can replace old cells with new ones. In some tissues, such as the epithelium of the skin, division is confined to particular cells. In many organs, growth is limited to connective tissue that forms scars. This is true in the heart. Yet in other organs, most or all cells can divide. This is so for the liver, in that removal of a portion may be followed by appearance of new, properly organized lobes.

In considering growth, we must point out that addition of new cells is only one aspect of development. The new cells are useful only when they have **differentiated** (specialized) into characteristic tissues that function in cooperation with others in the body. Control of this process of differentiation is one of the intriguing problems facing biologists today.

Aging

Some biologists view aging as a part of development. In other words, aging may be programmed into the individual just as are other phases of development. There is good evidence that aging has some inherited basis. For example, the life spans of identical twins coincide more closely than do those of fraternal twins of the same sex. The life spans of children correlate well with those of their parents. Furthermore, there is an inherited disease, **progeria,** in which aging occurs prematurely. Individuals with progeria suffer degenerative changes, such as atherosclerosis, so early that death often comes in childhood.

To the degree that aging is genetically controlled, there may be little we can do to prevent its onset. The changes involved are too widespread to result from a single metabolic defect that could be cured as diabetes is "cured" by the regular injection of insulin.

According to another view, the degeneration of aging results from radiation or some other universally present environmental factors that act at random. Perhaps defects accumulate because of accidents during mitosis. But whatever the role of the environment in aging, it seems likely that our life-style may hurry or retard degeneration. Diet, smoking, alochol abuse, emotional stress, and physical exertion may all have a role in the aging process.

While biologists ponder the basic causes of aging, a desire for eternal youth lies deep within us. It supports a flourishing trade in popular literature that offers to tell us how to retain or regain youth. Some people submit to extreme procedures in the hope of being young again. During the 1930s, transplantation of monkey testes into old men was a fad. More recently people have sought restored youth through injections of cells from young animals, such as lambs.

Such farfetched schemes thrive because medical science has nothing to offer. Although control of infectious disease has increased the average human life span dramatically in this century, the maximum life span remains unchanged. People are becoming more aware of the infirmities of age as an ever-larger proportion of the population survives long enough to be affected.

Death

The more we learn about ourselves and other organisms, the harder it is to come up with an absolute definition of either life or death. A case in point concerns human cells that outlive the individual. Just like bacteria or yeast, many kinds of human cells can be grown in bottles and flasks if supplied with proper nutrients. The best-known human **cell line** was derived from the cervical cancer of a Baltimore woman who died in 1951. Biologists call these **HeLa cells** because, according to tradition, the woman's name was Henrietta Lacks.

HeLa cells (Fig. 13.18) are extremely easy to culture. If even a very small number of them contaminate other cultures, the HeLa cells may overgrow the rightful inhabitants of the container. Still, no one would deny that Henrietta Lacks is dead just because her cells multiply in laboratories around the world.

The Essence. Most people would agree that the essence of life in humans or other animals is centered in the brain and in the mind. But even severe brain damage may have little impact on such "vital" signs as breathing and heartbeat. And although the effort is often futile and wasteful, a heart-lung machine can support the body for some time after most of the brain has ceased to work.

No matter how many functions of the body are replaced with mechanical devices or transplants, no substitute nervous system can recreate a mind. If a brain could be transplanted, the identity of the

FIGURE 13.18 **Immortal Cells?** These HeLa cells are descendants of some cultured more than 30 years ago from cancerous tissue.

individual would very likely pass with the brain. For this reason, absence of electrical activity in the brain for some critical period may be the best criterion of death.

The End. Even though the brain, heart, and lungs no longer function, all the body cells do not die instantly. Just as it is possible to take a pint of blood from a healthy person and refrigerate it for weeks before using it in a transfusion, so it is possible to take healthy tissues, such as the cornea of the eye, from the body of someone who has recently died and use them as grafts in living people.

Once the person is dead, the body cools slowly. How slowly depends on weight, clothing, and the environment. Under ordinary conditions, about 24 hours pass before the body reaches room temperature. Within a few hours of death, blood begins to accumulate by gravity on the lower side of the body. Because deoxygenated hemoglobin is bluish-red, the lower surfaces take on a purplish hue.

As individual body cells die, their lysosomes disintegrate and release enzymes that destroy other cell components. Once the epithelial cells fall apart and phagocytes cease their work, the microorganisms of the normal flora invade unchecked. As our developmental cycle comes full turn, the chemical elements that compose our bodies move on in the biogeochemical cycles that make us one with 11
the biosphere.

Development: Challenge of Today

How a single cell becomes a human being is a puzzle that is far from solved. Much of what we know is in the "embryonic" stage. Our knowledge is mostly descriptive. We can observe the sequence of changes, but how it happens eludes us. In this chapter, we spoke of induction and of the interactions of cytoplasm and nucleus, but there are no clear explanations. We aren't even certain what triggers cells to divide. More perplexing is the question of how cells become as different as neurons and bone cells. The answer surely involves molecules and heredity, but exact pathways remain unknown.

Summary

1. In the process of fertilization, not only do the nuclei of the egg and sperm merge, but the egg cytoplasm is activated to develop. This development is a property of the egg cytoplasm, as shown by parthenogenesis, the activation of eggs without fertilization.

2. The zygote (fertilized egg) cleaves by mitosis. Although the resulting cells are identical in their genetic characteristics, the cytoplasms are different. The blastula, which results from cleavage, then undergoes gastrulation. This period of cell movements creates a multilayered embryo and brings into contact cells with different cytoplasmic characteristics. Interactions of the newly positioned cells induce the initial formation of organ systems.

3. The human equivalent of the blastula is the blastocyst. The inner cell mass of the blastula gives rise to the embryo. The human embryo follows the same basic steps of organ formation found in all vertebrate embryos. After about two months of gestation, the process of initiation of major organs is complete, and the embryo is then termed a fetus. During the remainder of gestation, the fetus grows rapidly, and organs continue their development.

4. The human blastocyst embeds in the wall of the uterus. The trophoblast of the blastocyst and tissues of the uterine lining together form a placenta. In this organ the fetal and maternal circulations exchange materials, although the blood of each remains separate.

5. Fraternal twins arise from two separately fertilized eggs, each of which produces a fetus with its own placenta. Identical twins result from either two inner cell masses within one blastocyst or from two embryos organizing within one inner cell mass. Thus both share one placenta and sometimes a single amnion.

6. Embryos are especially susceptible to damage by viruses, chemicals, or other factors during the time when organs are forming. Since particular organs develop at certain times, there are special sensitive periods. Most of these occur during the first two months of gestation.

7. Birth involves dilation of the cervix and expulsion of the fetus and the placenta. Expulsion is accomplished by contraction of uterine muscles, supplemented by voluntary contractions of muscles of the abdominal wall. Soon after birth the infant's circulatory system undergoes changes in the pattern of flow, resulting from interruption of the placental circulation and from the onset of breathing. Fetal red blood cells are also replaced with those containing adult-type hemoglobin. Heat released by metabolism of brown fat tissue aids the newborn in maintaining its body temperature.

8. The neural stimulus of nursing causes release of oxytocin from the posterior pituitary gland. This hormone promotes release of milk from the mammary glands, a process antagonized by adrenalin. Colostrum, the first milk, contains antibodies.

9. The growth of various organs occurs at different rates at different times. In some tissues all cells continue to divide throughout life, in others only particular cells divide, and in yet others division ceases.

10. It has been suggested that aging results from inherited characteristics. A second hypothesis is that it is due to the action of environmental factors.

Thought and Controversy

1. Readily repeatable experiments demonstrate that young rats that are fed balanced but short rations remain small and immature for as long as three years, a time equal to their normal life span. A full diet after this period permits such rats to complete their development and reach an age twice the maximum for those fed normally.

2. Manufacturers of baby formulas advertise throughout much of the world. Bottle-feeding is urged in Third World countries, as well as in industrialized nations. Not infrequently, mothers who can ill afford the money are tempted to bottle-feed their babies, either because doing so lends prestige or because they believe it is better for the baby. Open formulas should be refrigerated to prevent spoilage, but refrigerators are a luxury in underdeveloped countries. Worse still, many mothers don't understand the sanitation procedures that are necessary to keep baby bottles and nipples safe and clean. Intestinal upsets, poor growth, disease, and death too often result. What other undesirable influences may bottle-feeding have?

3. The Hydra of mythology was represented as a many-headed creature that regenerated two heads every time one was cut off. Indeed, the little freshwater *Hydra,* a relative of the jellyfish and corals, does grow new tentacles or other body parts. So can many other invertebrates, such as starfish and earthworms. Regeneration is such a common phenomenon that it is puzzling that the regenerative ability of vertebrates is so limited. It is true that fish and tadpoles can regenerate damaged fins, and that both larval and adult salamanders regenerate severed limbs. Lizards also show a little regeneration, such as replacing part of the tail. But attempts to demonstrate regeneration in higher vertebrates have been discouraging. It is known that continued irritation of the stump of a limb of an adult frog will stimulate regeneration that would not occur otherwise. However, nerves must be present for this regeneration, as well as for normal limb regeneration in salamanders. But it remains to be seen whether we will someday know how to stimulate regeneration of severed human limbs.

4. Cloning can be achieved by techniques illustrated in Fig. 13.4. If nuclei from the same donor are transplanted into many different eggs, it is possible to produce a number of genetically identical organisms. By definition, these individuals are a **clone.** Small clones of humans are well known—identical twins, identical triplets, and so on. It is possible that humans can be cloned artificially, too. But doing so on a scale that could alter human society would involve more than overcoming public opposition. There would be severe practical difficulties. For example, if some dictator decided to grow an army of ideal soldiers, would it be possible to find a donor with the perfect hereditary qualities to fill a wide range of military roles? Could any government predict the combination of physical and psychological traits that would be necessary in soldiers 20 years hence? (Would an army composed of millions of Douglas MacArthurs be useful today?) If a perfect donor could be found for such an experiment in human reproduction, where could one obtain egg cytoplasm identical to that which controlled the early development of this perfect soldier? Finally, given the necessary biological materials to clone donor cells and produce an army of babies, would it be possible to duplicate the environment that allowed development of desirable traits in the donor?

Questions

1. What is the role of the sperm in early development of the egg? How does parthenogenesis provide evidence that the sperm only activates a developmental pattern present in the egg cytoplasm?

2. Is the egg cytoplasm uniform? How are regional differences in the egg cytoplasm reflected in the cells produced by cleavage? How do the movements of gastrulation affect the distribution of cytoplasm substances within the embryo?

3. Compare the human blastocyst with the frog blastula. What are the fates of the inner cell mass and the trophoblast?

4. Describe the induction of the neural tube in amphibians. Relate induction to nuclear-cytoplasm interactions.

5. Describe implantation of the human blastocyst. Distinguish between the amnion and the placenta.

6. Describe the major events of each trimester of human gestation. Why are environmental effects, such as viral infections, more apt to be serious during the first trimester than later in pregnancy?

7. What are the methods by which identical twins are known to form? How can identical and fraternal twins be distinguished at birth?

8. What adjustments must the newborn make within the first few days of life? What adjustments occur in the mother's body?

9. Development continues after birth. How do the growth curves of various organ systems differ? Which cells continue to divide throughout life normally? Which cells divide to achieve repair?

10. Discuss two basic hypotheses used to explain aging. Give the evidence used in support of each hypothesis.

Further Reading for Part Three

Baconsfield, Peter, George Birdwood, and Rebecca Beaconsfield, 1980. The placenta. *Scientific American* 243(2):94–102. (August)

Beach, Frank (ed.), 1977. *Human Sexuality in Four Perspectives.* Johns Hopkins Press, Baltimore.

Chambon, Pierre, 1981. Split genes. *Scientific American* 244(5):60–71. (May)

Cohen, Stanley N., and James A. Shapiro, 1980. Transposable genetic elements. *Scientific American* 242(2):40–49. (February)

Crow, James F., 1979. Genes that violate Mendel's rules. *Scientific American* 240(2):134–146. (February)

Gold, Michael, 1981. The cells that would not die. *Science 81* 2(3):28–35.

Grabowski, Casimer T., 1983. *Human Reproduction and Development.* Saunders College Publishing, Philadelphia.

Grivell, L.A., 1983. Mitochondrial DNA. *Scientific American* 248(3):78–89.

Money, John, and Anke A. Ehrhardt, 1972. *Man & Woman: Boy & Girl.* Johns Hopkins Press, Baltimore.

Verny, Thomas, and John Kelly, 1981. *The Secret of the Unborn Child.* Summit Press, New York.

Warner, Robert, 1982. Metamorphosis: Among tropical fish, when the going gets tough, the tough change sex. *Science 82* 3(10):42–46.

Winchester, A.N., and T.R. Nertens, 1983. *Human Genetics* 4th ed. Merrill, Columbus, Ohio.

Youcha, Geraldine, 1982. Life before birth. *Science Digest* 90(12). (December)

SAILING

PART FOUR

Diverse Living

This text is intended to help the reader see the world through the eyes of biologists. So far we have focused inward, offering a mechanistic view of the processes that maintain the constant internal conditions necessary for life. We've shown you how the spark is passed to future generations. Now we are about to look at the world around us.

Endless numbers of species fill our world. This diversity results from countless evolutionary events that have molded organisms to take maximum advantage of their environment. Both the diversity and the adaptations of organisms provide constant reminders of the evolutionary process. Despite this diversity, life is not just a welter of species. Within the diversity we recognize similarities that are evidence of genetic relationships. Our classification schemes reflect our interpretation of these historical relationships.

Natural selection has left its stamp on every aspect of life. Some of the most interesting adaptations are to be found in the behavior of animals. The actions of our pets and dooryard birds make sense in terms of their adaptive values. Wherever biologists go, they find structure or behavior that they interpret as having special adaptive value. So it is that evolutionary mechanisms are the key to understanding life.

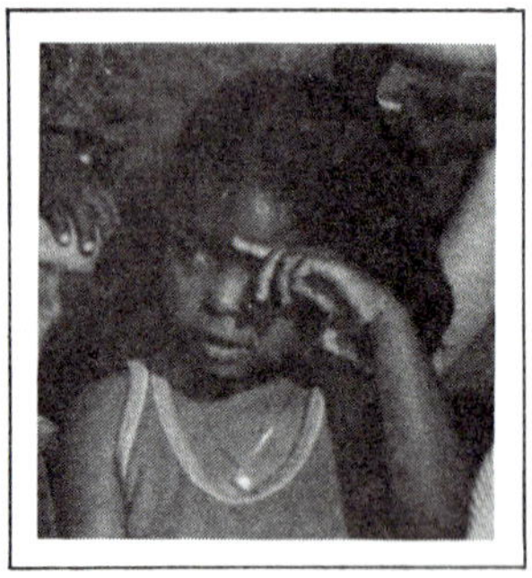

14

Genetics and Evolution: Past, Present, and Future

THE RESTLESS EARTH WAS BORN WITHOUT LIFE. Once life appeared, the ever-changing physical environment offered endless opportunities for the biological change we call evolution. As the crustal
24 plates grew and collided,□ and mountains rose only
26 to disappear in trickles of water,□ the earth changed. A dynamic earth demanded that organisms change, too. Populations evolved as well-adapted individuals were able to contribute more than their share of genes to the next generation. Some species were divided into two isolated populations in environments that favored different traits. Often one group came to be so unlike the other that interbreeding was no longer possible. Where once there had been a single species, now there were two. Over time, such processes have produced a million or more species.

This concept of **evolution** explains how each species has come to be so specifically adapted to its environment. Because it explains how species can be different and yet related, evolution also accounts for the unity of life, such as the fact that most organisms use the same enzyme pathways for energy metabolism. And all eucaryotes follow similar steps in cell division, both for mitosis and for meiosis. Furthermore, the theory of evolution accounts for the existence of fossils and the appearance and disappearance of major groups in the fossil record. Likewise, it explains the appearance and disappearance of numerous species. The idea of evolution fits into a coherent picture so many otherwise disconnected facts that almost all biologists accept it as a proven theory (Table 14.1).

NATURAL SELECTION

The history of life from the earliest simple forms to the present diversity can be summarized as change in the genetic makeup of **populations.** Populations, groups of organisms that have the opportunity for genetic exchange through interbreeding, are of fundamental importance in evolution, because genetic change occurs between generations, not within individuals. The only unit in which change occurs is the population to which the two generations belong. Natural selection is responsible for much of this change. The crux of natural

TABLE 14.1 **Some Evidences of Evolution**

Similiarities suggest relationship
Primate DNA, Fig. 2.10
Vertebrate development, Box 13A
Human and gorilla skeleton, Fig. 2.7
Vertebrate hearts, Fig. 6.17
Vertebrate brains, Fig. 8.11
Sense receptors, Fig. 9.10 and 9.11
Eucaryotic organelles basically the same
Uniform pattern of cell division (mitosis and meiosis)
Neuronal function, Fig. 8.14
Selection modifies species
Varieties of domestic plants and animals
Diversification within a group
Fossil record
Adaptive radiations, Box 14 D

selection is whether an individual survives long enough to reproduce successfully. Successful reproduction alone determines whether the individual's genes will be passed to the next generation and hence continue within the **gene pool** (a term applied to all the genes of a population).

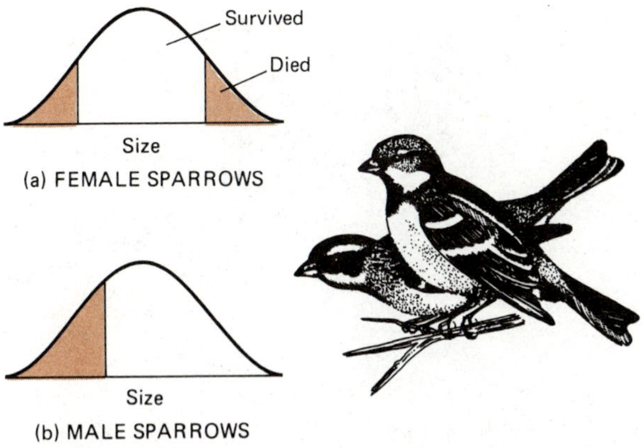

FIGURE 14.1. **It May Not Pay to Be Different.** A heavy storm of rain, snow, and ice in Providence, Rhode Island, during February 1898 provided H. C. Bumpus of Brown University with a unique opportunity to study the relationship of size to survival in house sparrows. Bumpus collected sparrows felled by the storm and compared those that revived with those that died. Neither large nor small female sparrows survived as well as those whose size was nearer the mean for the female population. The data on females (a) provide a typical graph of stabilizing selection. In contrast to the situation for female sparrows, selection removed the smaller males but not the larger ones (b). We can only speculate on why selection acted differently on males and females. Perhaps there was more competition among males, and the larger males were favored by their ability to command the most protected roosting sites.

Selection Can Change or Stabilize Populations

The effects of selective pressures vary with the environment. Natural selection always adapts organisms to their environments. It is only when the members of a population are ill-fitted to their environment that selection alters gene frequency.

Stabilizing Selection. When a species is in a stable environment in which it has long existed, it has adjusted to the conditions there. In such situations selection produces little change in gene frequencies. Instead, selection tends to stabilize the population by screening new generations and removing individuals that deviate from the best-adapted phenotypes. The selective pressures are so ever-present that we usually overlook them, but their existence is evident in the uniformity of members within a species. Surely you have noticed that it is difficult to distinguish a particular squirrel or sparrow from others of the same species, age, and sex. The reason is that unusual individuals are trimmed from natural populations by natural selection (Fig. 14.1). Thus under constant conditions, selective pressures keep the range of characteristics of a species within narrow limits.

If, for example, a female bird lays too many eggs in one clutch, she may be unable to feed the young that hatch. If most of the young starve, she will contribute fewer genes to the next generation than she would have if she had laid fewer eggs. On the other hand, if she lays too few eggs, she will contribute fewer genes to the next generation than will birds that lay a somewhat greater number of eggs. Thus selection favors birds that lay neither too many nor too few eggs, for these are the birds that will be best represented in the next generation.

Selection Can Favor Diversity. Although it is true that members of a species are often quite similar, there is diversity in the gene pool of every population. Strange though it may seem, natural selection often helps maintain this diversity. For example, a heterozygote can have a higher survival value than any homozygote. A well-known example involves the allele for sickle-cell anemia.

The red blood cells of individuals homozygous for the **sickle-cell anemia** trait contain an unusual hemoglobin. In blood that's well oxygenated, this sickle hemoglobin behaves almost normally. But in poorly oxygenated blood, such as exists in many capillary beds, sickle hemoglobin is insoluble. Here the sickle hemoglobin molecules stack themselves into long, stiff fibers that distort the cells into sickle, holly-leaf, or other bizarre shapes. These irregularly shaped cells (Fig. 14.2) catch on capillary walls, pile up, and plug the blood passages, depriving the tissue of oxygen. Pain and cell damage result. Frequently the rigid hemoglobin fibers destroy the blood cells by puncturing the plasma membrane. This loss of red blood cells causes anemia.

Fortunately, such severe effects appear only in people homozygous for the sickle-cell trait. Most heterozygotes are able to lead normal lives, because half their hemoglobin is normal and half is sickle

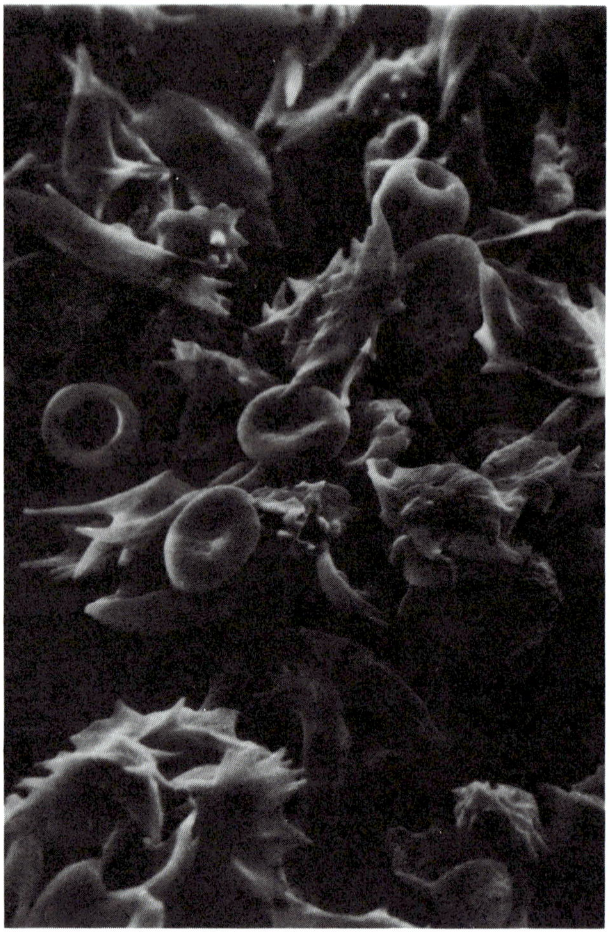

FIGURE 14.2. **Sickled Red Blood Cells.** People homozygous for the sickle-cell trait have a hemoglobin that distorts their blood cells into odd shapes.

hemoglobin. Nevertheless, red blood cells of heterozygotes are weakened by the presence of some sickle hemoglobin. Occasional blood cells collapse when the tissues are temporarily deprived of oxygen. This can occur at high altitudes or during strenuous exercise.

Despite the mild anemia it causes, the single sickle-cell gene of heterozygotes can be a blessing in disguise. Its presence confers immunity to a dangerous kind of malaria. Although the sickle-cell hemoglobin differs from normal hemoglobin in only two of its 600 amino acids, it creates an unacceptable environment for the malarial parasite. This is true whether all or only half of the hemoglobin is of the sickle type. But of course, early death of those with the sickle-cell disease makes resistance to malaria inconsequential. Only the heterozygotes benefit. Therefore in parts of West Africa, India, and some Mediterranean countries—areas where malaria is common—people are better off if they are heterozygous for the sickle-cell allele than if they have only normal hemoglobin. Because the sickle-cell allele and the normal hemoglobin allele are highly advantageous together, natural selection keeps both in populations exposed to malaria.

Selection Modifies Populations. In contrast to stabilizing selection that keeps a species closely adapted to a stable environment, **directional selection** drives populations to fit new or changing environments. Any alteration in an environment, whether due to natural processes, such as shifts in the climate, or to human intervention, modifies selective pressures. Under such circumstances, natural selection adjusts native populations to fit the new conditions. Likewise, a population entering a new environment will either be molded to fit that environment or go extinct. Thus a constant environment exerts stabilizing selection on populations, but a changing environment exerts pressures that change gene frequencies in particular directions. It is this directional selection that leads to evolution.

Small Changes Add Up to Big Differences

Whenever genetic variation is present, environmental pressures favor a particular genetic makeup that best suits the population to its conditions. Even the smallest differences in the value of alleles produce selective pressures that affect the abundance of alleles in the population. How common an allele is within a particular population is known as its **gene frequency**. See Box 14A for a further explanation of this key term and an explanation of how gene frequencies are calculated.

Selection Alters Gene Frequencies. The influence of selection on the genes of a population is expressed as a change in gene frequency. Although evolution may proceed at a snail's pace, the slightest disadvantage will inevitably lead to loss of one allele and the complete establishment of the more useful alternative. (The assumption is that there are only two alleles of that gene.) For example, if an allele increases successful reproduction by only one percent, such an allele can change from a frequency of 0.1 (1 in 10) to 0.999 (999 in 1000) in

BOX 14A

GENE FREQUENCY: A QUANTITATIVE MEASURE FOR STUDIES IN EVOLUTION

Among the alleles found in a population, some are more common than others. Just how common an allele is found to be is known as its frequency. The frequency of an allele is written as its decimal proportion of all the alleles of that gene within the populations. Obviously, the frequency of all alleles of a given gene must add up to 1.

As an example of how we express allele (gene) frequencies, we will consider the *MN* blood-type system in a population of 1000 people. Since humans are diploid, this population can be considered to have 2000 alleles for the *MN* system (2 chromosomes × 1000 people). Suppose that we blood-typed each person and totaled the number of *M* alleles and of *N* alleles in the population and determined that there were 600 *M* alleles and 1400 *N* alleles. If so, here is how we would calculate the gene frequencies. To determine the frequency of *M* in the population:

$$\frac{600\ M \text{ alleles}}{2000 \text{ alleles total}} = 0.3 \text{ (frequency of allele } M\text{)}.$$

Likewise:

$$\frac{1400\ N \text{ alleles}}{2000 \text{ alleles total}} = 0.7 \text{ (frequency of allele } N\text{)}.$$

Note that 0.3 + 0.7 = 1.0, and that frequencies can be expressed as percentages by multiplying by 100. Hence 30% + 70% = 100%. Or we could say that 30 of every 100 alleles will be *M* and 70 of every 100 alleles will be *N*.

If mating is random for the system under study, gene frequencies can be used to calculate the frequency of each genotype. In the example used, if mates are not selected for *MN* blood type, the gene frequencies readily give us the frequency of *MM, MN,* and *NN* people in the population. With fertilization random, we merely multiply the frequency of eggs of each kind by the frequency of sperm of each kind:

Allele frequency among eggs \ Allele frequency among sperm	0.3 *M*	0.7 *N*
0.3 *M*	0.09 *MM*	0.21 *MN*
0.7 *N*	0.21 *MN*	0.49 *NN*

Note that this box is much like a Punnett square, except that the numbers of *M* and *N* gametes differ. As with ordinary Punnett squares, the area of the box reflects the total population of offspring. Nine percent of the total (0.09) will be *MM.* Forty-nine percent (0.49) will be *NN.* Forty-two percent (0.21 + 0.21 = 0.42) will be *MN.*

A basic assumption of population genetics is that in the absence of mutation, natural selection, selective mating, and immigration, gene frequencies remain constant in large populations. The following example demonstrates this principle.

Assume that the allele for ability to taste PTC has a frequency in the population of 0.6, and that the allele for the inability to taste has a frequency of 0.4. These values may be used in a Punnett square in which the gametes of each type are assigned the known frequency.

Eggs \ Sperm	0.6 *T*	0.4 *t*
0.6 *T*	0.36 *TT*	0.24 *Tt*
0.4 *t*	0.24 *Tt*	0.16 *tt*

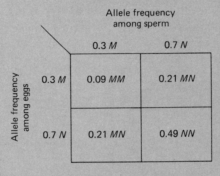

The frequency of the alleles in the new generation are:

From *TT* class
From *Tt* class 0.36

$$\frac{0.24 + 0.24}{2} = 0.24$$

0.60

From *tt* class 0.16
From *Tt* class

$$\frac{0.24 + 0.24}{2} = 0.24$$

0.40

Of course, environments change and bring adjustments in natural selection. Mutations occur; mating isn't always random; populations are often small; and organisms migrate in and out of the population. Each of these events changes the frequency of genes. Not all changes produce new species, but each change is a unit of evolution.

TABLE 14.2 How Selection Changes Gene Frequencies Over Time*

CHANGE IN FREQUENCY OF GENE *A*	NUMBER OF GENERATIONS REQUIRED FOR CHANGES	YEARS REQUIRED FOR THESE CHANGES IF GENERATION TIME IS:		
		20 MIN.	*1 YEAR*	*20 YEARS*
From 0.100 to 0.250	382	0.015	382	7,640
From 0.250 to 0.750	486	0.018	486	9,720
From 0.750 to 0.990	9,940	0.378	9,940	198,800
From 0.990 to 0.999	90,231	3.433	90,231	1,804,620

*This assumes that the fitness of *AA* = *Aa* = 1.0 and that the fitness of *aa* = 0.99. In other words, for every 100 *AA* or *Aa* that survive, 99 *aa* will survive. This example also assumes a large population in which chance has no effect on gene frequencies.

101,039 generations (Table 14.2). For humans, with a generation time of 20 years, such a change would require 2 million years. Slow as it seems, this change would be inevitable in a large population where chance has little effect on gene frequencies.

Such slow rates of genetic change may seem totally inadequate to explain the appearance of the many different species that have evolved. But remember, in the example we used the 20-year human generation time. In contrast, some bacteria can divide every twenty minutes, and most plants and animals have life cycles that require a year or less.

The discrimination of natural selection can be modest, but selective pressures are sometimes harsh. Those dominant alleles that lead to death prior to reproduction are completely removed from the population each generation. Such **dominant lethals** appear only as the result of new mutations.

Persistent Recessives. Dominant alleles are always affected by selection, but recessive alleles are exposed to selection only when they are homozygous. This permits harmful recessives to persist for long periods of time. Harmful rare alleles are difficult to eliminate from a population, simply because they are so rarely exposed to selection. As demonstrated above, the frequency of homozygotes is the product of the gene frequency ($MM = 0.3 \times 0.3 = 0.09$, and $NN = 0.7 \times 0.7 = 0.49$). Thus if a recessive allele has a frequency of 0.001, only one person in a million will exhibit the trait ($0.001 \times 0.001 = 0.000001$). This explains why lethal or severely handicapping genetic diseases continue to be fairly common. Even though no one afflicted with phenylketonuria (PKU) or similar diseases may manage to reproduce, a very low mutation rate can keep these alleles in the population, because most of these defective genes are in healthy, heterozygous people. If one person in ten thousand shows the trait, then two in a hundred also carry it and pass it on to half of their children.

The persistence of rare harmful-recessive alleles explains the common fallacy that recessives are harmful and dominant alleles are good. Dominant and recessive mutations are equally likely to be harmful, but damaging dominants are less common in the population because they tend to be removed as soon as they appear. In contrast, harmful recessives are discriminated against only when they appear in the homozygous state.

The **eugenics movement** (eugenics means "good breeding") has promoted legislation limiting reproduction by people with inherited defects. (Epileptics, whose condition sometimes comes from injuries, not always from genetic disease, have been a common target of such ill-conceived legislation.) The futility of this effort to improve public health is obvious when we consider the small portion of harmful genes contributed to the population by the afflicted. On the other hand, individuals with genetic disease should be counseled not only against marrying anyone with the same disease but against marrying cousins or other relatives. These nonrandom marriages are much more likely to produce genetically handicapped children than are random marriages. Even perfectly healthy relatives are more likely to carry the same recessive alleles. The irony of applying special rules to people handicapped by homozygous recessive genes lies in the fact that we all probably carry some harmful recessive alleles. Thus it is unwise for anyone to have children by a close relative.

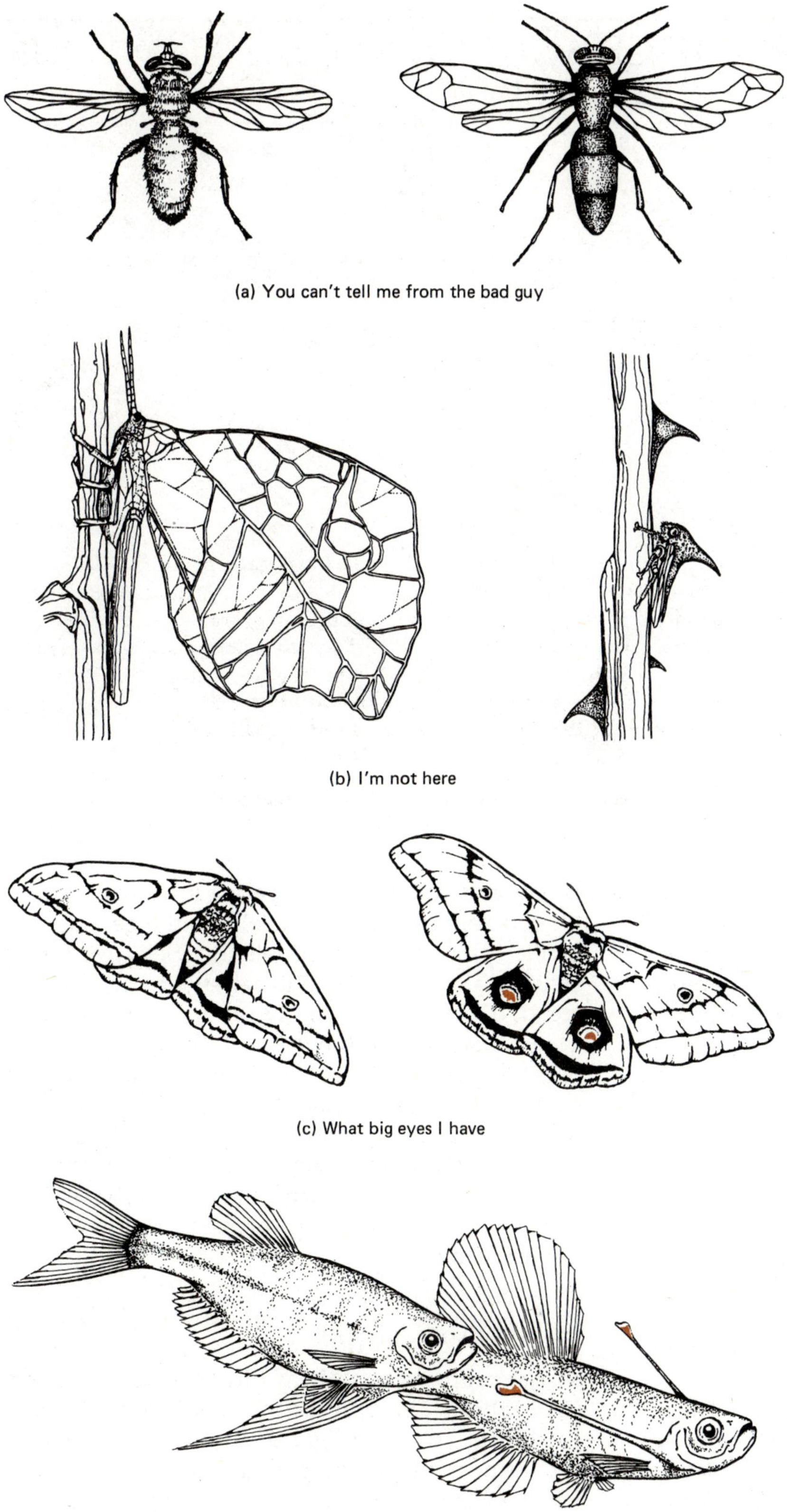

(a) You can't tell me from the bad guy

(b) I'm not here

(c) What big eyes I have

(d) Fishing for a mate

FIGURE 14.3. **Deceptive Adaptations Are Products of Evolution.** (a) *You can't tell me from the bad guy.* Here is a fly (distinguished by a single pair of wings) that resembles a stinging wasp living in the same area of Borneo. The fly has inconspicuous antennae, whereas those of the wasp are prominent. Note how the fly mimics the wasp's antennae. (b) *I'm not here.* These insects mimic plant parts and thus conceal themselves from predators or prey. (c) *What big eyes I have.* The flash of false eyespots when the polyphemus moth opens its wings can frighten away a predator or confuse the predator about the direction the moth may move. (d) *Fishing for a mate.* The swordtail characin courts his mate by offering her the tip of his gill cover which blushes to resemble a delicious tidbit. The gill cover tip is brightly colored only during mating.

BOX 14B

HOW TO CALCULATE THE CHANCE THAT YOU AND YOUR FIRST COUSIN SHARE A RARE ALLELE

According to the pedigree at right, the following statements are all true:

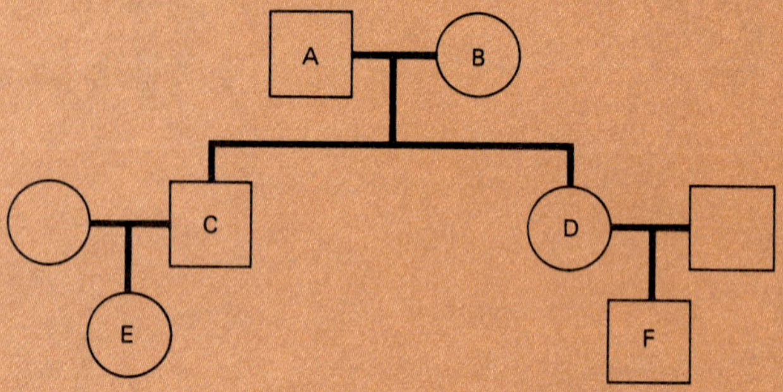

- **The chance is ½ that D will receive a given allele for which A is heterozygous.**
- **The chance is ½ that F will receive this allele from D.**
- **The chance is ½ that C will receive this same allele from A.**
- **The chance is ½ that E will receive this same allele from C.**

Therefore the chance that any allele in A goes to both E and F (i.e., that all the above events occur) is

$$\tfrac{1}{2} \times \tfrac{1}{2} \times \tfrac{1}{2} \times \tfrac{1}{2} = \tfrac{1}{16}.$$

Each of these occurrences is independent of the others. The likelihood that independent events will occur together is the product of the separate probabilities for all the events. The chance that any allele in B will be present in both E and F can be calculated the same way with the same result. Hence the likelihood that E and F have the same rare allele is $\tfrac{1}{16} + \tfrac{1}{16} = \tfrac{1}{8}$. What is the likelihood that a rare recessive allele for which A is homozygous will be present in both E and F? That any child of E and F will be homozygous for this rare recessive?

Selection and Population Growth. Selection can operate under a wide range of conditions. If a population has entered a new habitat with untapped resources, the population may be growing rapidly. Under such a circumstance some alleles will be better adapted than others. Individuals with the most useful alleles will, on the average, contribute the most genes to the next generation.

On the other hand, selection can operate equally efficiently in an adverse circumstance in which the population is shrinking. In this case, too, a favorable allele will increase the chance that the individual will contribute to the next generation.

SPECIES FORMATION

As important as natural selection is to evolution, it is only one factor among many. Gene frequencies can fluctuate dramatically in small populations. Here chance can play a role. Another factor is isolation. Although one species can change so drastically over time that it is recognized as a second species, only isolation can divide one species into two species. Of course, selection acts solely on the genetic variability present in the population. Selective forces cannot call up new genetic patterns as needed. Instead, new patterns—known as *mutations*—appear at random. Finally, the value of one gene depends on other genes, just as the value of a playing card depends on what else is in the hand. Through sexual reproduction, genes are tried out in different assortments. Most biologists agree that organisms lacking sexual reproduction are seriously handicapped and likely to find themselves at an evolutionary dead end.

Sex and Evolution

Sexual reproduction always involves meiosis and fertilization. The process of meiosis assorts chromosomes. Chance assigns one member of each pair of chromosomes to a particular daughter cell. Then, when fertilization occurs, fusion of eggs and sperm results in random combinations of chromosomes.

Together, meiosis and fertilization shuffle the genes and deal out new assortments. As a result, the young are genetically different from each other and from both parents.

Crossing-over Breaks Up the Old Gang. In ad-
243 dition to the assorting of chromosomes,[□] meiosis also contributes to genetic shuffling through chromosomal exchanges during the first division of meiosis. At this stage homologous chromosomes are synapsed and intertwined. Each consists of two chromatids, so the pair makes up four somewhat tangled strands. Frequently the chromatids break at points where two cross. These breaks usually heal, but the chromosomes often exchange parts of chromatids in the process. Such exchanges are known as **crossing-over.** Note that crossover can move alleles between homologous chromosomes. In this manner alleles that were at one time **linked** (inherited together) because they are on the same chromosome can later be separated and associated with other alleles (Fig. 14.4). Thus potentially useful alleles that might otherwise be suppressed can affect the phenotype and can be subject to natural selection. For example, an allele for long legs might never be favored by natural selection if it was always associated with a dominant allele for chondrodystrophic dwarfism (failure of cartilage formation necessary for growth of the long bones). But if this allele for longer legs were to separate from the chondrodystrophic gene and occur with those for normal bone growth, it might increase the chances that the individual would survive and reproduce. In this way, natural selection could increase the frequency of the "long-legs" allele.

Crossing-over, independent assortment, and fertilization together result in entirely new gene combinations. Indeed, no two individuals are ever identical except for identical twins, who can be traced to one fertilized egg. With every generation, the genes of a population are tried out in different combinations. Of course, environmental pressures act on genes not in a vacuum, but against the background of all the other genetic material of the individual. As a result, natural selection favors the gene combinations best suited to that particular environment.

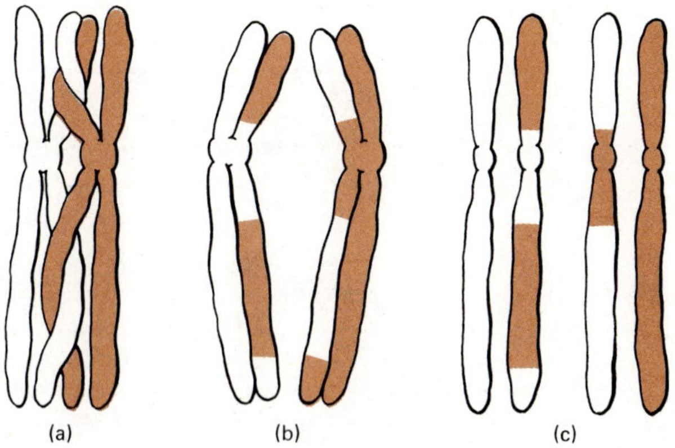

FIGURE 14.4. Crossing-Over When homologous chromosomes synapse during meiosis, the chromatids become tangled (a). Very often the chromatids break and exchange parts. These crossovers result in new assortments of alleles on the chromatids (b) and ultimately on the daughter chromosomes (c). Because genes on a chromosome often interact, crossovers can have a marked effect on gene expression. Of course, if there were no crossing-over, all the alleles on a given chromosome would be linked together permanently and inherited as a unit.

Sex Only Sometimes. The continual shuffling of genes may be of limited value in a stable environment, but it is absolutely essential if a population is to change with a changing environment. This explains why there are few species that reproduce only asexually. Most species capable of asexual reproduction also reproduce sexually, at least occasionally. For example, many aphids produce numerous asexual generations during the summer and then revert to sexual reproduction when conditions vary drastically in the fall. For aphids, sexual reproduction is necessary in the fall, because favorable summer weather can select gene combinations unsuited for over-wintering. Also, asexual reproduction may result in a population consisting of only a few genotypes. Shuffling the genes will create more genotypes, at least some of which are able to survive until spring. Occasional sexual reproduction may be essential if a species is to remain adapted to its environment.

Mutation: Raw Material for Evolution

In Chapter 11, we discussed how alteration in just a single nucleotide of DNA can make a difference in the structure of protein. Of course, any change in protein structure can alter enzyme function. But in addition to these small mutations, often termed **point mutations,** there are others that involve the gross structure of a chromosome.

BOX 14C

THE EVOLUTION OF EVOLUTIONARY THOUGHT

Until the last century, it was generally accepted that the earth had existed for only a brief time. On the basis of the number of known human generations and a literal interpretation of the Bible, religious historians had calculated that the world was created on October 23, 4004 B.C. But the world is far older than anyone then imagined. It is currently estimated that the earth is between four and five billion years old.

Clues to the antiquity of the earth have always abounded, but they were long unrecognized. For many years, people had observed that the earth's crust included many layers of rock. It was only near the end of the eighteenth century that scientists began to realize that many of these layers were compacted sediments that could have accumulated only over vast ages.

Although some ancients recognized fossils as the remains of organisms, others dismissed these remnants of life as curiously shaped stones. Usually people who understood the nature of fossils were at a loss to explain their origin. Some said they were the discarded mistakes of the Creator's endeavors. Others believed that fossils were the dead and hardened bodies of organisms drowned in the Great Flood described in the Bible.

Such theories were shattered by the work of two brilliant Frenchmen, George Cuvier (1769–1832) and Jean Lamarck (1744–1829). Working independently, they showed that the kinds of fossils changed from lower to higher strata. Moreover, it was apparent that deeper strata contained fossils less like modern species than did the more recent strata. The two men accounted for these observations in entirely different ways, however.

Cuvier imagined that the earth had undergone periodic catastrophes that had destroyed all existing life. He said that after each catastrophe, newly created organisms replaced those that had perished. The advantage of the theory of catastrophism was that it preserved the biblical story of the Great Flood, which, according to Cuvier, was the most recent catastrophe. Unlike his rival, Lamarck saw in the fossil record a history of the evolution of life.

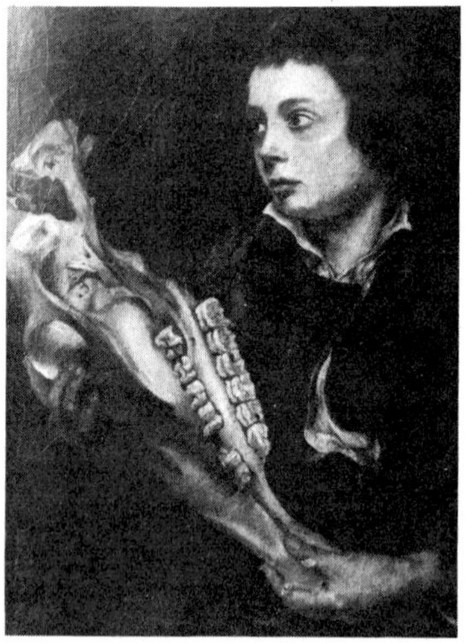

Georges Cuvier

Jean Baptiste Lamarck

Throughout his long career, Lamarck championed radical and unpopular scientific causes, not the least of which was his theory of evolution. Lamarck believed that the fossil record confirmed that the earth had witnessed a progressive development of organisms from simple to more complex. In 1809 he proposed a mechanism to explain how organisms might have evolved. It was Lamarck's contention that evolutionary modifications were initiated by an organism's response to environmental pressures. He was brought to this conviction by his observation that some body organs grew in size if they were constantly used, or became weakened through the lack of use. It seemed reasonable to Lamarck that new traits might be altered or new organs might develop. Similarly, disuse would cause an organ to shrink and disappear. In any case, Lamarck believed that changes, accumulated during the lifetime of an individual, could be inherited by its offspring. Using this approach, he concluded, for example, that giraffes acquired long necks from generations of stretching to reach the tender young leaves of tall trees.

The idea of the inheritance of acquired characteristics was not original with Lamarck. Although modern biologists may scoff at the notion, inheritance of acquired characteristics made sense to many earlier biologists. Lamarck's rival, Cuvier, an ardent antievolutionist and respected anatomist, was not among them. Cuvier saw no evidence that organisms could increase, develop, or lose organs—or, for that matter, change in any other way by their own desires. This fact prompted him to condemn the whole idea of evolution. Because Lamarck's mechanism for acquiring new characteristics could not be substantiated, the concept of evolution was shrugged off. But over the next century evidence against catastrophism accumulated, and the intellectual climate gradually changed.

By the middle of the nineteenth century many biologists probably believed in evolution by natural selection. At least two, Charles Darwin and Alfred Wallace, were putting their thoughts into writing. After years of travel and careful observation each had arrived at the same conclusion independently. Upon learning of each other's work, Darwin and Wallace joined forces and in 1858 published a paper "On the Tendency of Species to Form Varieties; and on the Perpetuation of Varieties and Species by Natural Selection." Neither man knew anything more about genetics (the word hadn't even been coined) than Lamarck had known. They weren't able to explain how evolutionary modifications came to be. But they recognized that the variations known to arise in natural populations were the units of evolution. On this basis, they argued that forces constantly at work in nature would "naturally" select those variations that were favorable. Accordingly, long-necked giraffes might have evolved because of the advantage long necks had for survival. Any long-necked individuals had an additional source of food and were therefore more likely to survive and produce offspring. Eventually the giraffe population consisted of longer-necked individuals.

Charles Darwin

Alfred Russel Wallace

In his famous book, *On the Origin of Species,* Darwin presented a mountain of evidence in support of the Darwin-Wallace theory. With its publication, a period of great public controversy about evolution began. The most serious scientific reservation was that the nature and origin of variation were not explained. It was almost the turn of the century before the Dutch botanist Hugo De Vries introduced the term mutation for the "sports"—entirely new types—he found in evening primroses. Although these different types of primroses are now known to arise from chromosomal abnormalities rather than changes in DNA structure, the concept of genetic change occurring in distinct jumps rather than gradually traces to De Vrie's work.

Even in the late nineteenth century, evolution satisfactorily explained an overwhelming body of data. Today the Darwin-Wallace theory is buttressed by an understanding of mutation and by mathematical analysis of populations. As a result, the theory of evolution by natural selection has remained fundamentally unchanged for more than a hundred years. It seems that the more biologists learn about the nature of life, whether it is biochemistry, genetics, physiology, anatomy, or behavior, the more certain the theory of evolution becomes.

Hugo De Vries

Chromosomal Alterations Are Mutations, Too. These large-scale mutations occur during crossing-over in the first division of meiosis. Ordinarily the breaks within synapsed chromosomes occur at exactly the same place on each chromatid (Fig. 14.4). Even if parts are exchanged, each chromatid will have one copy of each gene. Very occasionally these **crossovers** (exchanges) are uneven. The result is that one chromatid loses one or more genes, while another chromatid emerges with a segment duplicated (Fig. 14.5). The **duplication** of genetic information within a chromosome can affect the characteristics of the organism. This is illustrated in the bar-eyed fruit fly (Fig. 14.6).The loss of genetic material from the other chromosome can also constitute a mutation. Mutations resulting from loss of a chromosome section are known as **deletions.** Besides duplications and deletions, uneven crossovers may also produce **inversions,** which are changes in the order of genes along a chromosome. Sometimes pieces of one chromatid join to a nonhomologous chromosome. This movement of genetic material from one chromosome pair to another is called a **translocation.** Both inversions and translocations change the order of genes on the chromosome. The changed order alone can alter the characteristics of the organism.

FIGURE 14.5. Crossing-Over Mistakes Yield Chromosomal Changes that Qualify as Mutations.

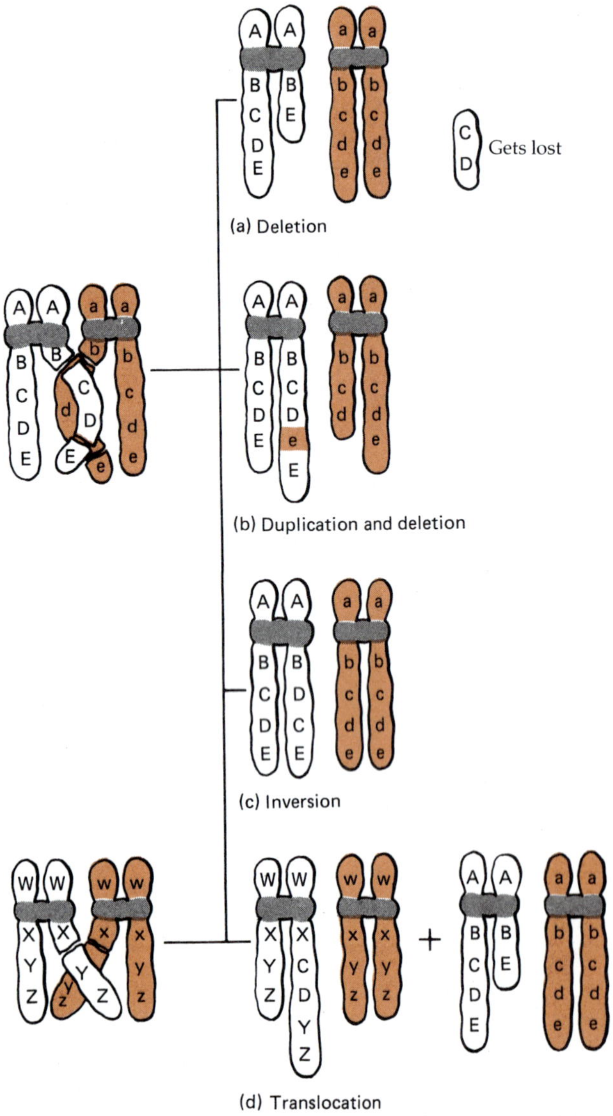

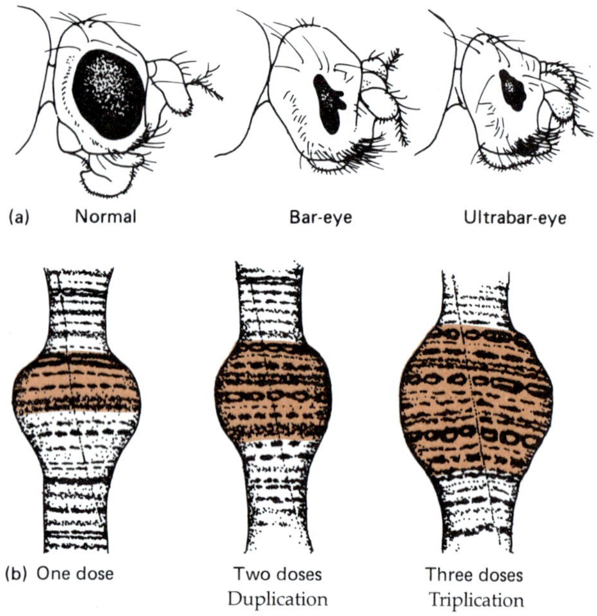

FIGURE 14.6. The Bar-Eye Duplication. Presence of giant chromosomes in fruit flies makes possible correlation of specific chromosome regions with the traits they control. In this example, duplication of one region narrows the eye and triplication reduces the eye to a tiny rod-shaped structure.

All of these alterations in chromosome structure are inherited changes in the genetic material and so are properly included as mutations. It may be that some recessive "alleles" are simply the absence of DNA lost in uneven exchanges. Long deletions frequently result in death early in development. Because translocations move material from one chromosome to another, the result can be much like a duplication and deletion. A chromosome that has been the source of a translocation is deficient, just as is one that has suffered a deletion. A cell with a chromosome that has received a translocation may have three doses of the translocated genes. These three doses are those of the normal chromosome pair (assuming neither is the source of the translocation) plus those of the translocated chromosomal region.

Additional sets of genes can be of special importance, because the duplicated DNA provides an opportunity for genetic experimentation without the risk that would be associated with changes in genetic material present in only one copy per chromosome. If there are extra copies, some can continue to produce the normal product, even if others undergo mutations that result in the synthesis of new products. In this way totally different genes (in contrast to alleles of existing genes) may arise. The result can be new variation that may promote evolution.

The Value of Mutations, Negative and Positive

The occurrence of mutations in a population constitutes both evolutionary insurance for the species and a threat to individuals. Most mutations are harmful, just as any random change is likely to harm an otherwise smoothly operating system. Imagine the result of a child's making a single change in the design or adjustment of an automobile engine—or someone dropping a brush on a wet oil painting. Similarly any unselected change in body chemistry, such as an alteration in the structure of a protein, is unlikely to be useful and quite probably will be harmful. We must stress that mutations are random events. There is no evidence that the environment or any other factor directs mutations to meet the needs of individuals or of the population.

Nevertheless, mutations are normal events. All species withstand mutation. Natural selection quickly weeds out some harmful mutations, especially dominant ones. If an organism is handicapped by a portion of its genetic material, it is less likely to survive to reproduce. Hence the genetic material responsible for the handicap may be lost to future generations. However, recessive genes are hidden more often than they are evident. For this reason, selection can seldom eliminate recessive mutations. Selection against harmful genes occurs continuously in natural populations. However, medical science tends to thwart this process among humans by treating people with genetic disease. Such treatment may reduce selective pressure against the defective alleles, but any increase in the frequency of such genes will be exceedingly slow, for it must result from mutation.

Despite the damage done by some mutations, alterations in genetic patterns can have a positive value. Sometimes a mutation results in an organism that is better suited to its environment, much as a chance alteration in auto design may occasionally result in a more efficient vehicle. Because environments are never stable indefinitely, variations in the genetic material are essential to allow the population to evolve with environmental change or to adapt to newly invaded habitats. Without mutation, it seems likely that all life would eventually come to an end. In essence, mutations are the units of evolution.

Isolation

Despite its importance, selection alone can never increase the number of living species. One species can be divided into two separate species only if there is some isolating mechanism that prevents the flow of genes between the two populations. The initial isolating mechanism is usually geographic. In one way or another a population becomes separated into two or more portions.

Barriers to **gene flow** can develop gradually, as, for example, when a river erodes its bed, forming either a canyon or a flood plain that is inhospitable to certain species. At other times, single dramatic episodes instantaneously isolate two por-

TABLE 14.3 **Barriers to Reproduction that Isolate Species**

Different breeding seasons
Courtship patterns
Species recognition (color markings, song patterns, pheromones)
Incompatibilities of male and female reproductive organs (prevent sperm transfer)
Female tract secretions inhibit or kill sperm
Genetic incompatibilities Embryos die because male and female chromosomes cannot function together Hybrid sterility because meiosis produces abnormal gametes (Fig. 14.7)

tions of a population. Numerous plants and animals have drifted or been blown to isolated islands. Only a few individuals—or even a single organism, such as a pregnant female mammal or the seed of a self-fertilizing plant—can sometimes found a new population.

Although it is easy to grasp how dramatic events such as individuals' drifting to far islands can completely isolate populations of a species, subtle changes can be equally effective in the interruption of gene flow. Slight increases in average rainfall can permit trees along small grassland streams to spread and form a forest. Within a century the grassland may be carved into isolated fragments. Gene flow will be interrupted in grassland species unable to cross the forest barrier.

However a population becomes divided, it is isolation that sets the stage for evolution of the separate populations into two species. No matter how different conditions are in two parts of a region with one continuous population, it is unlikely that this population will evolve into two species. As long as the population is continuous, there will be some exchange of genes among members in different areas. This gene flow will probably be sufficient to prevent development of the reproductive barriers that separate species.

Populations become transformed into new species when some barrier prevents successful interbreeding with other populations. Such **reproductive barriers** take many forms. For example, appropriate courtship patterns (see Box 15B) are necessary for many animals to mate. If these become sufficiently different in two populations, members of the populations cannot interbreed.

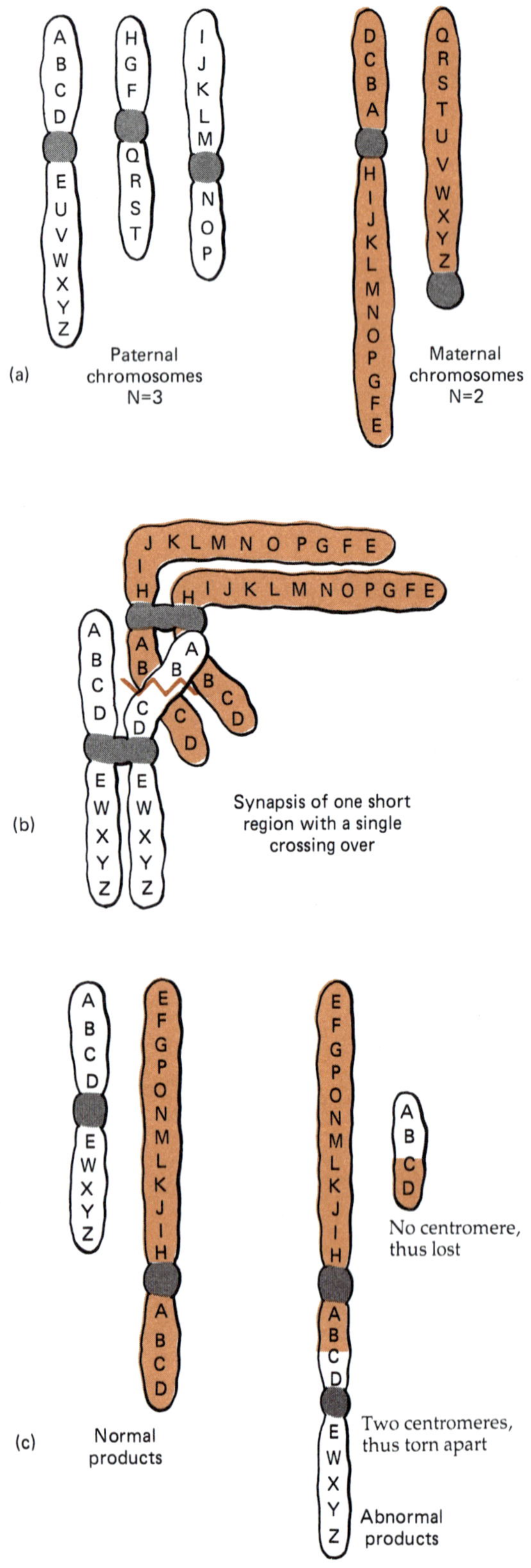

FIGURE 14.7. **Hybrid Sterility.** Hybrids between even closely related species are often sterile. One factor responsible for such sterility is the distribution of genes on different numbers of chromosomes and in different orders. Even with identical genes, the distribution on the maternal and paternal chromosomes can vary drastically (a). During meiosis in hybrids, portions of different chromosome pairs may synapse. In such cases crossovers such as one at the point marked by the wavy line will yield nonviable chromosome combinations (b). A chromosome with two centromeres is likely to be torn apart as the centromeres migrate to opposite poles. The portion lacking a centromere will not migrate and may be excluded from both cells (c).

Other prerequisites for matings include certain **pheromones** (odors that transmit information among members of a species). If the pheromones do not indicate the proper species or sex, the individual may not be accepted as a suitable mate.

When genetically different individuals do mate, there may be internal barriers to successful reproduction. For example, the vaginas of female fruit flies swell in response to foreign sperm. Such swelling blocks the passage of sperm, so fertilization cannot occur.

If young are produced in crosses between two species, these **hybrid** offspring are often defective. When eggs of one species of frog are fertilized with sperm from another species, development may begin, but the embryos often die. Death may occur because the genetic material in the egg and sperm nucleus is not compatible for regulation of developmental processes.

Even when the young of crosses between two species thrive, they may be sterile. This **hybrid sterility** occurs when the two species have compatible sets of genes but the genes are distributed differently on the chromosomes. As a result, meiosis produces defective gametes (Fig. 14.7). Mules are an example of this condition. Although mules, which result from a mating between a male donkey and a female horse, are exceedingly vigorous, they are sterile.

Genetic Drift

In small populations, chance can either speed the elimination or increase the frequency of any allele. Severely disadvantageous alleles that drift into abundance are subject to immediate heavy selective pressures that soon restore their previous status. Useful or only slightly disadvantageous alleles can benefit from random fluctuations, known as **genetic drift.**

Consider the effect of chance on the genes responsible for the inherited ability to taste phenylthiocarbamide (PTC), an apparently unimportant trait, among the twenty inhabitants of a small, hypothetical isle (Fig. 14.8). Although there is no known method of distinguishing homozygous tasters from heterozygous ones (other than by knowing their heritage), let us assume that at the time of the initial survey seventeen people are tasters, and of these ten are heterozygous. The other seven tasters are homozygous, and the remaining three people are nontasters. With these data we can calculate frequencies of the two alleles:

T = Taster of PTC

7 homozygous $TT = 2 \times 7 = 14$

10 heterozygous $= 1 \times 10 = 10$

24 T genes

$$\text{frequency of } T = \frac{24}{40} = 0.6$$

t = Nontaster of PTC

3 homozygous $tt = 2 \times 3 = 6$

10 heterozygous $= 1 \times 10 = 10$

16 t genes

$$\text{frequency of } t = \frac{16}{40} = 0.4$$

Suppose that by chance the three homozygous nontasters are all sons of two of the heterozygous tasters, and that these three young men leave the island to seek better financial opportunities. Two of the other heterozygotes are a couple who are unable to have children. Two more are married to homozygous tasters. These $TT \times Tt$ pairings produced the four remaining heterozygous individuals and the other five homozygous tasters. The year after the survey, two of the heterozygous children drown in a boating accident, and soon afterward another dies of acute appendicitis. The remaining heterozygote, a girl, marries a taster who settles on the island, and they have two children, both homozygous tasters. Unless another migrant brings the t gene to the island, it will soon disappear, for everyone carrying it has completed their family.

Chance has achieved in one generation what natural selection might have been unable to do in thousands. The reader may think it unlikely that chance would be so consistently "unfair" to any given allele. But remember, each population contains alleles of thousands of different genes. Only rarely does any small population pass through one generation without the frequency of one or more alleles being drastically altered by chance.

The Environment: Its Role in Evolution

Species must fit into their environment. When a new species is formed, its population is molded to take advantage of a particular environment in specific ways. Biologists term this role of a species its **ecological niche.** A species' ecological niche in-

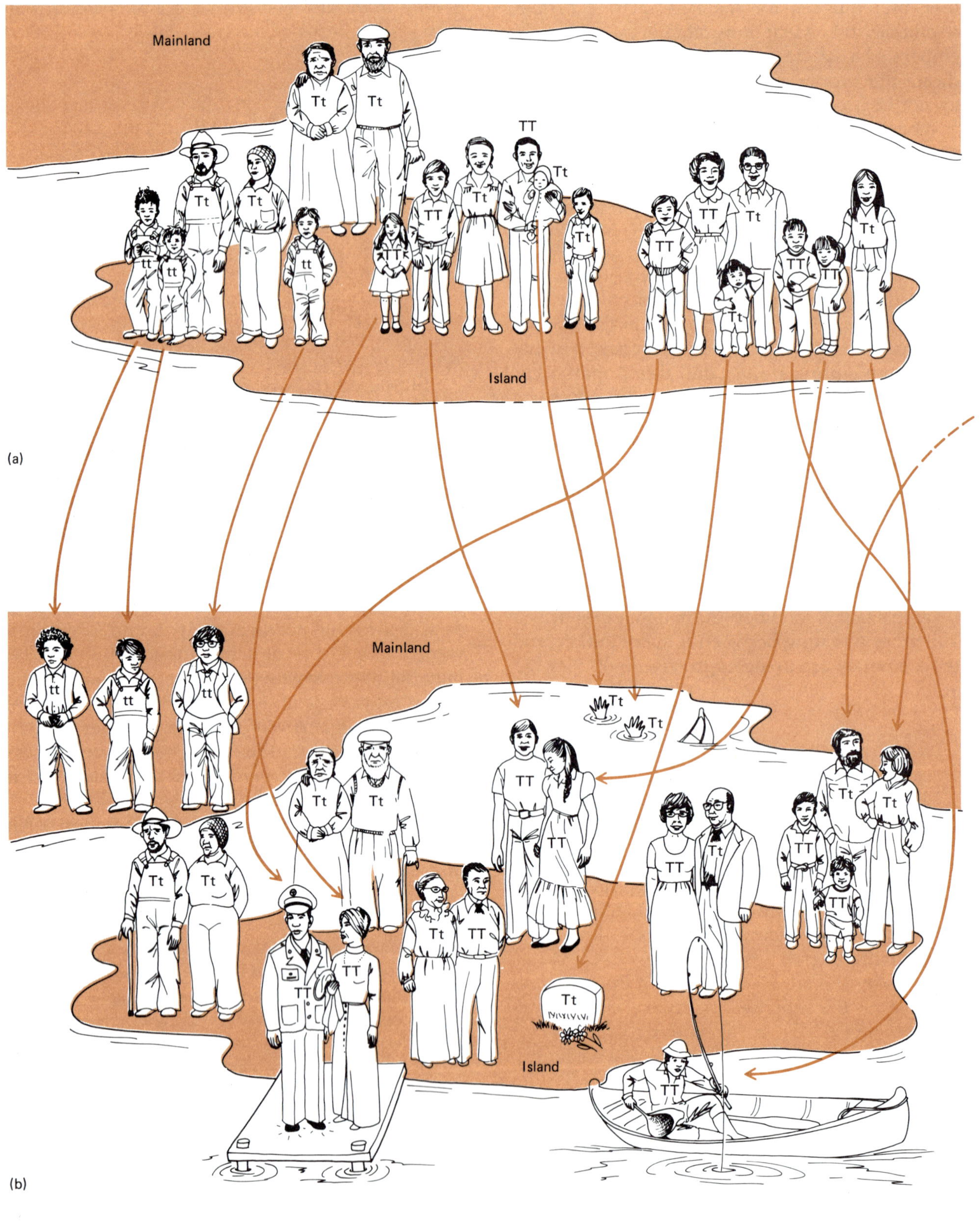
Mainland
Island
(a)
Mainland
Island
(b)

◀ FIGURE 14.8. **Genetic Drift.** Chance often changes gene frequencies faster than natural selection does. Consider the population of a small island in this hypothetical example. The genotypes of each person present on the island initially are shown in (a). The genotypes of everyone on the island one generation later are given in (b). Note that the drastic change in gene frequency was unrelated to any advantage conferred by the ability or inability to taste PTC.

cludes all its interactions with other organisms, as well as its requirements from—and contributions to—the nonliving world.

Ecological niche should not be confused with **habitat,** the physical location and normal surroundings. An analogy relating niche to occupation and habitat to address illustrates the difference. Just as a person's occupation—"dentist," for example—is not the same thing as his or her address—"1095 N.E. 3rd Street"—so the niche of a species (that is, its role) is not to be equated to its habitat (that is, the location where it occurs). Let's consider robins. The *habitat* of robins includes yards, gardens, orchards, meadows, open woodlands, forests, parks, and pasture land. In contrast, the robin's *ecological niche* includes consumption of insects, earthworms, and fruit; utilization of trees as nesting sites and roosts; dispersal of cherry and berry seeds in its droppings; and even fertilization of soil around these seeds. The robin's niche may also involve accumulation of DDT from poisoned caterpillars it eats and the transfer of this insecticide to the predator or scavenger that consumes the robin.

One Niche, One Species. The concept of ecological niche has implications for evolution. According to the **competitive exclusion principle,** two species cannot occupy identical niches. If they tried, one would inevitably prove superior and, in the resulting competition, would destroy the other. Thus each species has a unique niche. It may seem that we have merely said that different species are different. But it is important to recognize that differences extend to environmental requirements and interactions.

A classic demonstration that each species has its own niche resulted from an investigation of a complaint by British fishermen that two species of cormorants (Fig. 14.9) were depleting fish schools.

FIGURE 14.9. **Dividing Up Resources Reduces Competition.** Two species of European cormorants look much alike and even nest on the same cliffs in the British Isles. But the two species do not compete for either breeding space or food.

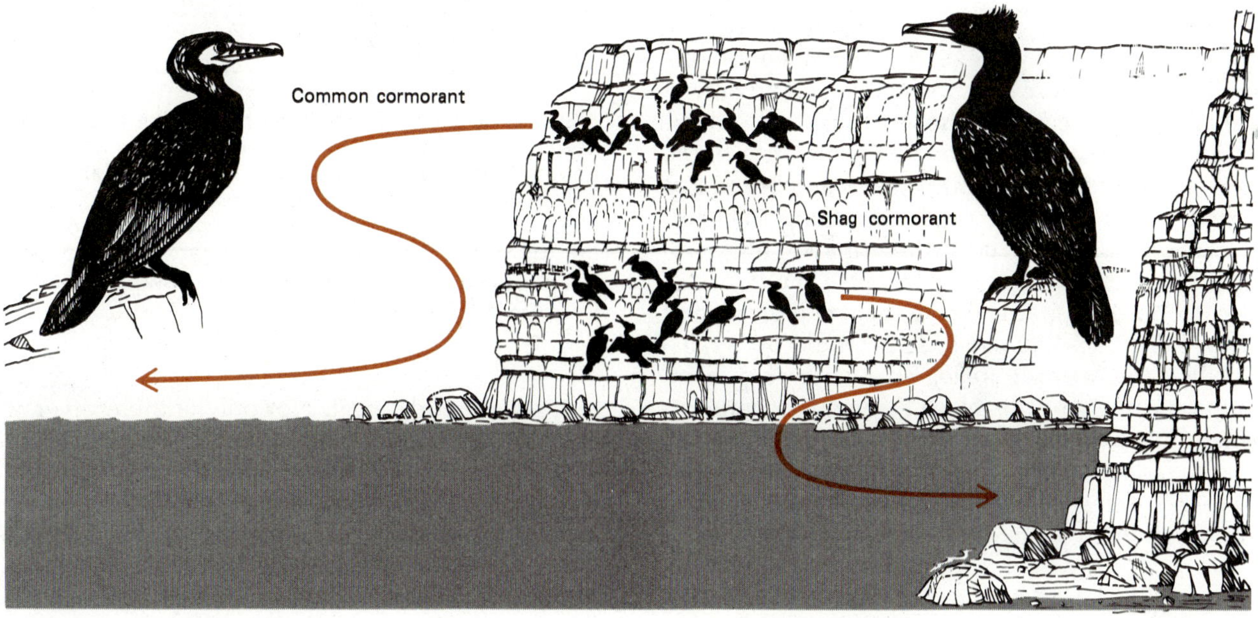

Although these birds look much alike, fish similarly, and are found together, careful observation reveals that each uses separate resources. The shag cormorant fishes mainly in shallow water and feeds on sand eels and sprats. The common cormorant works waters farther out to sea, where it takes shrimp and a few fish but no eels or sprats. Despite the fact that both kinds of cormorants nest on the same cliffs, they choose different elevations. As similar as these two species seem, they differ in how they live. (Incidentally, neither catches many fish of commercial value.)

Closely related pairs of species, such as the two British cormorants, surely evolve from common ancestors. Usually such evolution begins when the parent species is divided into geographically isolated populations. In the case of the cormorants, a violent storm may have carried a few birds to a distant shore. When the two groups were thus isolated from each other, the different environments could select particular traits and fit each population for a unique niche. Under these conditions reproduction isolation is likely to appear; even minor changes in behavior, physiology, or chromostructure can prevent interbreedings. If the ranges of the two new species later overlap, they may coexist and keep their separate identities. Of course, each species will use slightly different resources and thus they will evolve to become even less similar. Let us return to the cormorants to see how these two species might have responded to use of the same habitat.

Suppose, when one species of cormorant first invaded the range of the other, it happened that both preferred a single level at which to nest. Competition would have been inevitable. But any member of either species that chose a suitable site above or below the ledge preferred by the majority would have increased its opportunity to rear a brood and contribute to the gene pool. Assuming that nest site preference is genetically determined, minor reproductive advantages would cause the two species to diverge gradually in their choice of nest sites. Eventually the two species would prefer distinctly different nest areas. By such events, competition can alter or displace the genetic characteristics of a species. **Character displacement** contributes to differentiation of ecological niches. The niche of each species contracts or expands in specific response to changes in competition.

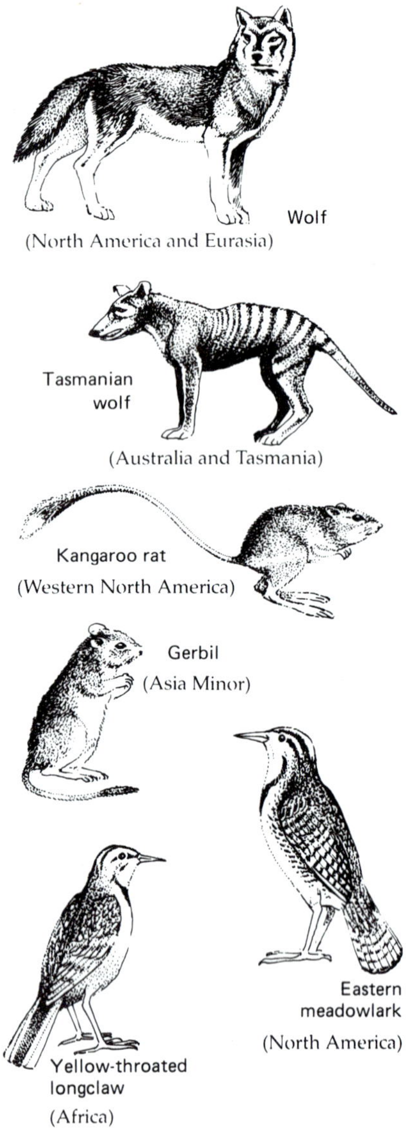

FIGURE 14.10. **Convergent Evolution.** The two members of each pair shown are only distantly related despite superficial similarities. The resemblances result from adaptations to ecological niches that share much in common. The two wolves are carnivores at the top of the food chain, the kangaroo rat and gerbil are desert rodents, and the longclaw and meadowlark are both grassland birds.

Geographical Variation. The fact that members of a species can interbreed successfully doesn't mean that they are identical. Not only is there diversity within local populations, but populations of one species will differ if they occupy dissimilar habitats. Some of this variation results directly from the environment. Everyone knows that a single packet of seeds will produce some short plants and some tall ones if they are watered unequally. But much of the variation within a species is genetic. A good

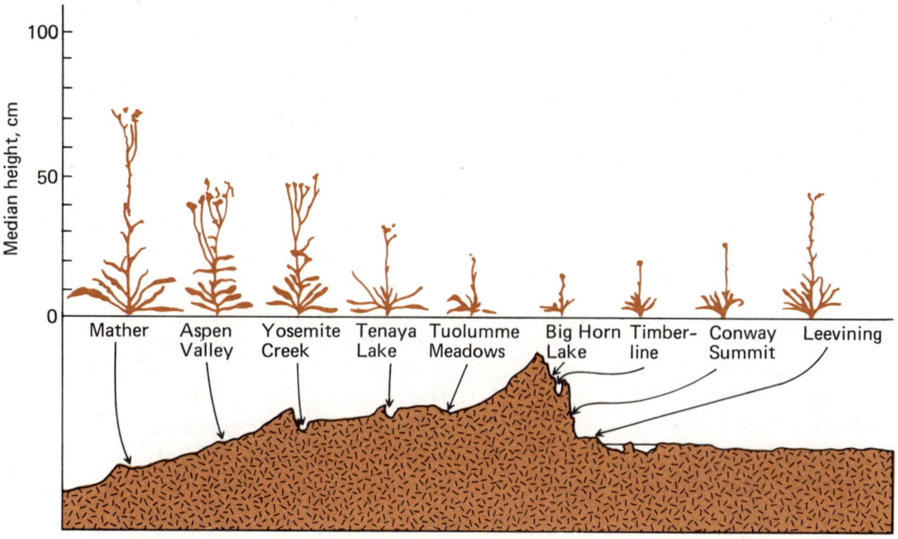

FIGURE 14.11. **Environmental Gradients Create Gradients in Inherited Traits.** Woolly yarrow seeds collected across central California and planted side-by-side in an experimental garden grew into plants of different heights.

example of this has been noted in woolly yarrow, a plant found across central California. Seeds collected at various locations in the Sierra Nevadas and sown side by side gave rise to readily distinguishable plant forms (Fig. 14.11). These recognizable forms are often termed **ecotypes.** In this example the various ecotypes are fitted to slightly different ecological niches although no barriers to gene flow have developed.

When populations differ in some clearly distinguishable way, they are considered to be **subspecies,** or sometimes labeled as races. Genetic drift contributes to population differences, especially when the population is small. Probably drift played an important role in the establishment of the so-called **human races.** But in thinking about human diversity, it is important to remember that races lie largely in the eye of the beholder. Our species has been divided into as few as three races or as many as hundreds, depending on the view of the individual. Some have based racial divisions on a handful of traits or even a single trait. The usefulness of such narrow distinctions is questionable.

How Fast Does Evolution Occur?

Time is a major factor in evolution. Nineteenth-century arguments about evolution involved as much dispute over the age of the earth as over the origin of species. The dating of rocks by radioisotope methods (Box 3A) settled this question. Dates of formation of sedimentary rocks containing fossils and on many fossil components have established the presence of organisms for billions of years.▫ Today there is no reason to doubt that life has existed long enough for small changes in gene frequency to add up to new species again and again. The record shows sufficient time to allow the evolution of all the diverse organisms on earth. But questions concerning the rate of evolution remain. 26

The Rate of Change: Slow or Jerky? How fast does evolution occur? The answer depends on the organism, the environment, and the trait. Evolution can be rapid when new ways of life become available, either because of a fundamental change in the organism or because the physical or biological environment has changed. Yet in some cases evolution can be slow to nonexistent.

Species such as the oyster, the horseshoe crab, and the opossum have shown no detectable change over millions of years. These so-called **living fossils** are well adjusted to their environments.

Certainly in the case of the horseshoe crab and the oyster a stable environment is at least partly responsible. Shallow waters of the necessary salt level appear to have existed for at least a billion years. In addition to this, the horseshoe crab and the oyster probably adapt easily to varying food sources. The horseshoe crab is a notorious scavenger, and the oyster filters a wide range of microorganisms from the water.

BOX 14D

THE GALÁPAGOS ISLANDS: INSIGHTS INTO EVOLUTION

The Galápagos are an isolated group of islands situated about 500 miles west of South America. Charles Darwin visited there in 1835 as part of his long voyage on the British naval vessel *Beagle.* Darwin's observations in the Galápagos greatly influenced his formulation of the theory of evolution by natural selection.

Darwin was struck by the small number of land animals on the Galápagos. Of land birds he found only 26 species, but of these at least 21 were not known elsewhere. Most important of all, these 21 species included 13 that belonged to a previously unknown group of finches. For Darwin and for many later biologists, the Galápagos and these finches have provided a natural laboratory of evolution.

The small numbers of organisms on the Galápagos can be explained by the isolation of the islands and by the fact that they were formed rather recently through volcanic eruptions. Apparently the islands have been populated by only a few animals that reached there from South America. Of course, of these migrants only those generally suited to conditions on the Galápagos survived for long. Probably natural selection quickly altered the early populations, so members were, after a few generations, better adapted to the new environment.

In the case of the finches, not only did the original population change, but geographical isolation and selection led to evolution of several more species. Not all species are present on each of the 14 major islands. Most islands support about ten species of finches, but some have as few as three.

In many ways all 13 species of the Galápagos finches look much alike. They all have short

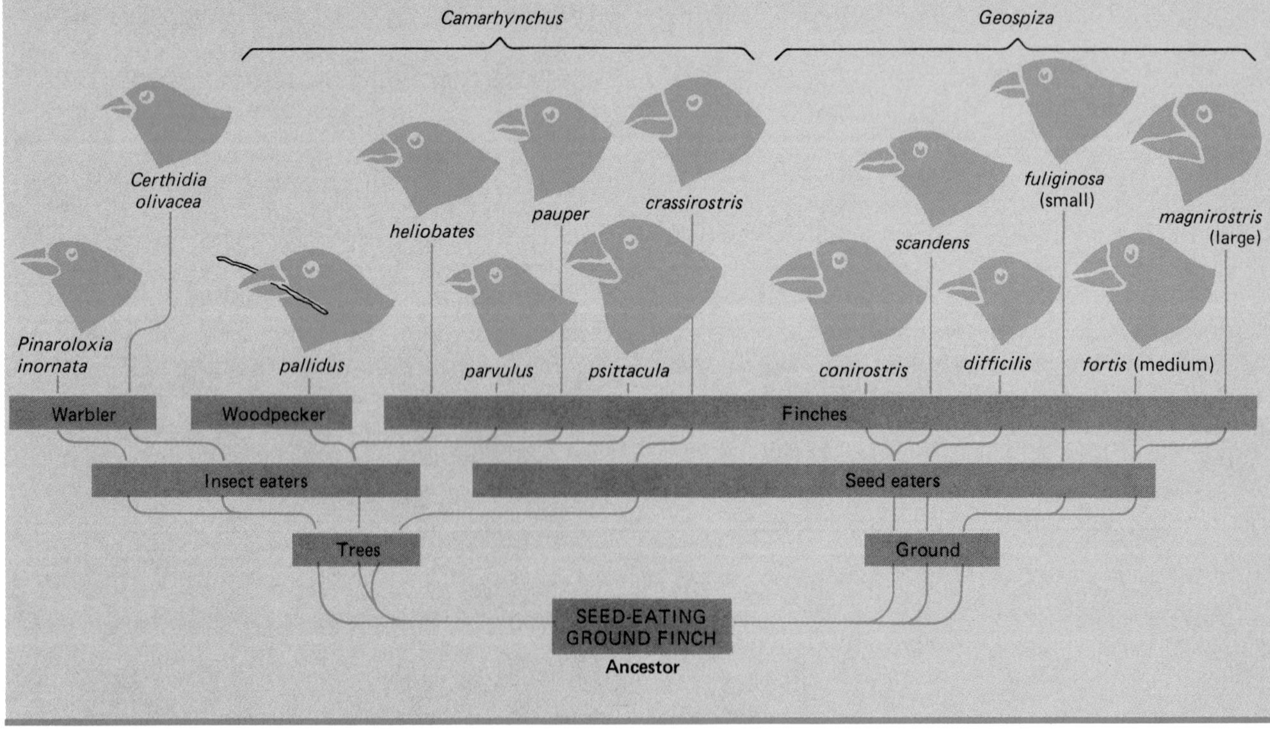

tails and dull plumage, and to the casual observer they may seem nearly indistinguishable. More careful examination reveals many differences. The most obvious are in their bills. These differences, in turn, reflect differences in diet and feeding habits.

One group, the *Geospiza,* feed on the ground or in cacti. These finches live in the harsh environment of the arid thorn thickets near sea level. Each has a short heavy bill, but the bill of each species is of unique shape and size. This fact suggests a diet of various types of seeds, although these finches eat other plant materials and, in some seasons, insects.

The genus *Camarhynchus* consists of tree finches found in the more humid forests of higher elevations. Most of the tree finches are mainly insect feeders, although one group eats buds, leaves and fruit. All tree finches have rather stout bills, but some are a little inflated and so look a bit parrot-like.

One finch is found on all the islands and in nearly every habitat. This finch is unusually distinctive. It feeds as warblers do, nervously probing about the vegetation looking for insects. This warbler finch differs from the other finches in that it has a long, thin bill, much as do warblers.

Perhaps most interesting of all is one of the tree finches, *Camarhynchus pallidus,* also known as the woodpecker finch. It uses its stout finch bill to chisel holes in tree trunks, as a woodpecker does. However, this finch lacks the long, barbed tongue with which woodpeckers spear grubs deep in the tree trunk. Instead, the woodpecker finch probes into its holes with a cactus spine it uses to fish out the deeply buried grubs.

Although no one witnessed the evolution of the woodpecker finch, it seems likely that the parent population contained in its gene pool the patterns that permitted it to locate grubs under tree bark and to dig into the wood. The finches on a particular island were selected for their ability to do this, perhaps by the abundance of grubs and a shortage of other foods. Difficulty in extracting the grubs may have favored a few finches with an inherited predisposition to pick up plant materials and probe with them. If this probing often resulted in retrieval of grubs that would have been missed otherwise, there would have been strong selective pressure that favored alleles for probing behavior. The increased food supply would have increased the reproductive success of finches with these alleles. Over time, the frequency of the alleles that determined probing would increase. Eventually these valuable alleles might replace all the other alleles of these genes in the populations. By changing the frequency of these alleles, selection would have changed the characteristics of the population.

Geographic isolation seems an important factor in evolution of the Galápagos finches. These birds are weak fliers. Once a storm carried a few to a new island, it might have been hundreds of years before more migrants arrived. But even though one island was surely colonized first and then another, each species did not necessarily arise on a separate island. Once natural selection and genetic drift had created reproductive barriers between two populations on separate islands, a few from island A might have reached island B. With no interbreeding between species A and species B, there would have been no gene flow, and the two would have remained separate. But competition between the A and B populations on the same island would produce new selective pressures that tended to make the two populations even less similar. This selection, combined with the chance effects of genetic drift, might have so altered the gene pool of the population of species A that they could no longer interbreed with their parent population. In this way a third species could have arisen.

Evolution has happened everywhere, but islands often have their own characteristic species because of the isolation of small populations. The Galápagos situation is special mainly in that the islands are recently formed. We do not know which birds colonized the Galápagos first, but it is likely that the early finch populations had little competition for a wide range of resources. This may explain both the many kinds of finches that evolved there and the very unfinchlike ways of some species. In the absence of woodpeckers there was no grub-eater on the Galápagos. If there had been, it is unlikely that the woodpecker finch would have evolved, for it is probably much less efficient at catching grubs than most woodpeckers are.

FIGURE 14.12. **A Living Fossil.** Opossums are identical, or nearly identical, to animals that lived millions of years ago. At least the bones of present-day opossums are indistinguishable from the fossil bones of their ancestors.

As for the opossum (Fig. 14.12), this animal has one of the most successful combinations of genes among mammals living today. Museum skeletal collections reveal opossums with healed fractures of nearly every bone in their body. Despite low intelligence, opossums have recently extended their range northward throughout most of the United States. Predation by cats and dogs and deaths under the tires of moving vehicles are offset by high reproduction. Ability to tolerate human disturbances has allowed opossums to take advantage of the extensive food supply created by gardens, orchards, and garbage cans.

But even if some species are stable over long periods, don't others change gradually? If change is going on, why can't we see it? The standard response to this question has been that change occurs so slowly we don't notice it. Undoubtedly this is part of the answer. But recently biologists examining the fossil record have suggested that evolution occurs at different rates in particular populations at various times. Populations may change little over long periods. Greatest change may occur in small, isolated populations that have invaded new habitats. Here, selection and drift can be powerful forces that quickly build barriers against gene flow. This view of evolution (Fig. 14.13) has been called **punctuated equilibrium** because it supposes that large populations are generally in equilibrium with their environment and change little. This interpretation is in accord with the fossil record, which shows that new species often seem to appear suddenly.

FIGURE 14.13. **Punctuated Equilibrium or Continuous Change?** Some biologists think most change in gene frequency occurs rapidly and under special conditions, as in (a). Other biologists believe change occurs continually (b).

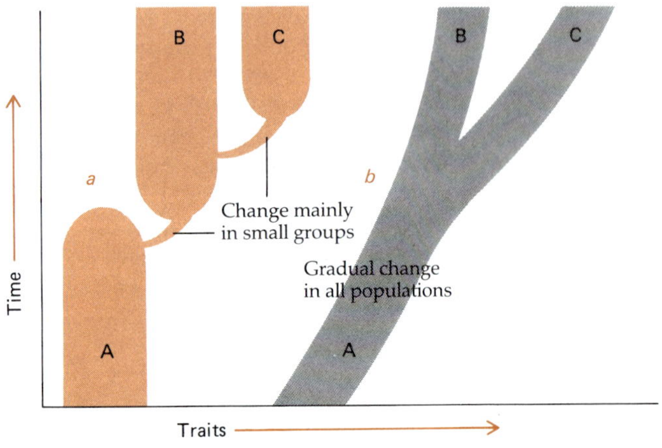

Instantaneous Speciation in Plants. Speciation can occur without natural selection or genetic drift. Any mechanism that doubles the chromosome number creates a barrier to gene flow. This barrier automatically produces a genetically isolated population that is a new species.

Any increase in the number of chromosome sets is known as **polyploidy.** The possession of three sets of chromosomes is known as **triploidy,** of four sets as **tetraploidy,** and so on. If a diploid cell doubles its chromosomes while failing to continue with cell division, it then becomes tetraploid. Such spontaneous doubling of the chromosome number is quite common in plants. In tetraploid cells, chromosomes pair regularly at meiosis and produce gametes with two full sets of chromosomes (diploid). Thus tetraploid flowers (arising through doubling of chromosomes in a single cell) may be self-fertile and may produce tetraploid seeds that grow into tetraploid plants.

Tetraploid plants are automatically new species, because such plants cannot produce fertile offspring in a mating with any but their own kind. Since tetraploids produce diploid gametes, if a tetraploid is crossed with its diploid parent, the resulting plants are triploid. (The diploid gamete of the tetraploid and the haploid gamete of the diploid fertilize to give three sets of chromosomes = triploidy). Such triploids have irregular chromosome pairing and separation at meiosis and are therefore sterile.

Usually tetraploid plants can be distinguished from their diploid ancestors, simply because the tetraploid grows larger. This is true of most plant polyploids and is due to the large size of polyploid cells. The large size of polyploids often makes them of special economic value. Commercial strawberries that are many times larger than their wild ancestors result from chromosomal manipulations. So do the giant snapdragons and tetraploid irises. Although humans have intentionally altered the chromosome number of many plants, some crop species result from natural polyploidy. Among these are oats and wheat.

There are many kinds of **wheat** planted or growing wild in the Old World. Among these are einkorn, with a chromosome number of 14, and emmer and durum wheats with chromosome numbers of 28. Although their chromosome numbers may lead you to expect that the emmer and durum are tetraploids of einkorn, the matter is more complex. Examination of the chromosomes suggests that emmer and durum have two sets of chromosomes, with fourteen in a set. In an ordinary tetraploid, we would expect four sets of chromosomes. The fact that emmer and durum have fourteen kinds of chromosomes instead of seven suggests a hybrid origin. Here is the hypothesis.

The fourteen kinds of chromosomes in emmer and durum are believed to trace to a hybrid between wild einkorn and one of the goat-faced grasses of the genus *Aegilops*. Both einkorn and *Aegilops* have seven kinds of chromosomes, and these have the appearance of the fourteen kinds in emmer and durum. A hybrid between einkorn and *Aegilops* would be sterile, but spontaneous doubling in this sterile hybrid would give a fertile tetraploid. As with all tetraploids, the chromosomes would be able to pair at meiosis and produce complete gametes. Because these gametes would be diploid, fertilization with either parent would yield sterile triploids. Thus the new hybrid tetraploid wheat would be reproductively isolated. Although this cross (Fig. 14.14) happened spontaneously, it was probably discovered by humans and then cultivated, because it produced high yields. The importance of polyploidy in plant evolution can't be overemphasized. According to one estimate, half the species of flowering plants may have arisen by this route.

LARGE-SCALE EVOLUTIONARY EVENTS

So far we have discussed the formation of species and the small changes in gene frequencies that fit a species to its environment. Such small adjustments can be defined as **special adaptations.** On the other hand, we have said nothing about the formation of new groups of organisms. Examination of the fossil record reveals the appearance of large numbers of related species at certain times. These groups of species share some **general adaptation** to a particular way of life. For birds, the ability to fly provided totally new opportunities. Likewise, evolution of an elongate body permitted snakes to live in underground burrows that afforded both protection and access to prey. Arboreal adaptations allowed primates to invade a habitat where there was little competition for resources. Each of these events led to the comparatively rapid appearance of numerous related species. Such an appearance is called an **adaptive radiation.**

Once a single species has achieved an evolutionary "breakthrough," diverse opportunities appear. Consider the ways of life open to winged, warm-blooded, vision-oriented animals (better known as birds). The ability to find dispersed re-

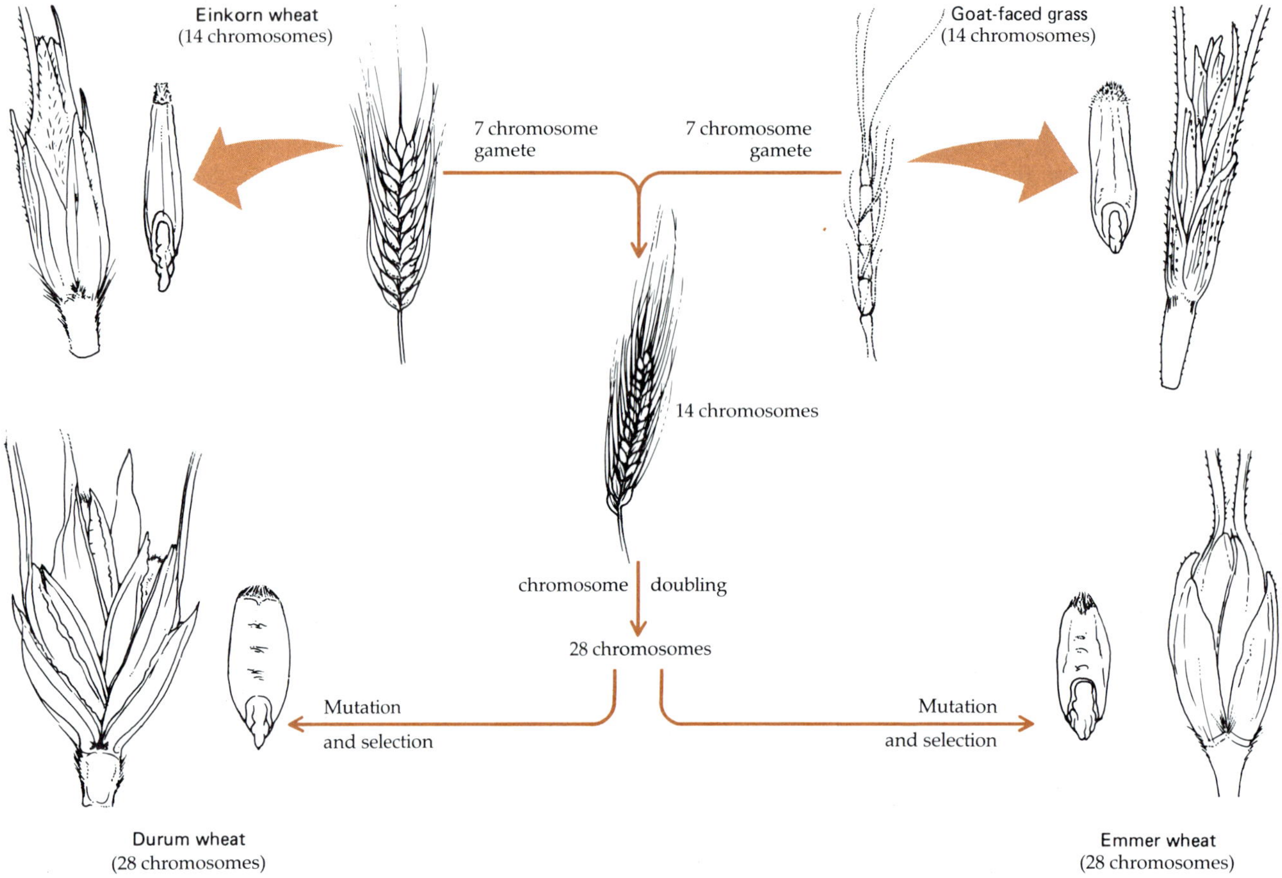

FIGURE 14.14. **Evolution of Wheat.** Most kinds of wheat are polyploids. Many of these polyploid varieties trace to a hybrid between einkorn (a wild wheat of the Near East) and one of the goat-faced grasses. One tetraploid derived from this hybrid is emmer, a major wheat recovered from villages at least 8000 years old. Another such tetraploid is durum, a wheat grown today for use in macaroni products. Most other present-day wheats are hexaploids (i.e., they have six sets of chromosomes).

sources, to escape into the air, and to gain security in high perches opened a multitude of ecological niches. Birds could fly or walk, swim, dabble in shallow water, hunt insects in any kind of vegetation or on the wing, feed on fruit, seeds, fish, frogs, small reptiles, mammals, other birds . . . the list is endless.

Some of the most fascinating biological puzzles are how organisms accumulate the assortment of genes necessary for basic innovations. The best explanation is that these genes are beneficial individually or in small groups. A key structure or ability may be functional and give some minor advantage in its least developed form. For example, the first land vertebrates were really air-breathing fish. Their primitive lungs allowed these fish to gasp air when water was too polluted to carry sufficient oxygen. But the very beginning of air breathing must have come much earlier, perhaps with a single mutation that increased the capillary bed in the lining of the mouth. This alone would have given an advantage to a fish in poorly oxygenated water. Later mutations that increased either surface area or blood supply provided additional advantages.

Traits that prove especially useful in new situations are termed **preadaptations.** Thus lungfish were preadapted for life on land. Use of this term does not imply some master plan or design that selects a trait for future use. Natural selection fits a population into its present niche. There is no way that selection can favor a trait except as it improves reproductive success in the present situation. Preadaptations are only established traits used in new ways.

Not all adaptive radiations are rooted in great innovations. Introduction of rather ordinary species into habitats with few competitors can result in adaptive radiations. This describes the origin of "Darwin's finches" in the Galápagos Islands. There was probably nothing special about the first finch species to reach these volcanic islands (see Box 14D), but in the absence of competition these little finches thrived. Repeated episodes of geographic isolation and reintroduction allow the original population to give rise to scores of species, each with its unique ecological niche.

Extinction

The fossil record shows that just as species appear, so they become extinct. The reasons for extinction are often unclear. Competition with new, more efficient species is probably a factor. In some cases loss of a number of related species in one group has been the prelude to an adaptive radiation in a second group that depended on similar resources.

Examination of the fossil record has caused some scientists to suggest that the incidence of extinction has been higher during particular periods. Environmental factors, especially climatic changes, may be responsible for unusually high rates of extinction. Some scientists relate times of extinction to cataclysms such as asteroids striking the earth and producing enough dust to cut off sunlight for days or weeks. But neither periods of excessive extinction nor cataclysms are certain events. The fossil record is not sufficiently studied that biologists can agree as to whether extinctions were more common at one time than another. It can be argued that extinction has occurred randomly at about the same rate as the appearance of new species. Of course, the situations of the past were quite different from those of the present; today's human cultural evolution is altering habitats and increasing competition for numerous species. It is likely that a great period of extinction is at hand.

Summary

1. Most biologists accept the theory of evolution, because it explains myriad observations.

2. Change in the frequency of genes constitutes the basic mechanism of evolution. This change occurs in the gene pool of a population over the generations. The adaptive value of an allele is determined solely by its influence on the organism's reproductive success.

3. Directional selection changes gene frequencies by increasing or decreasing the opportunity for genes to be passed to the next generation. Even the slightest differences in survival will eventually lead to marked changes. Selection can stabilize gene frequencies as well as alter them.

4. There is no necessary relationship between the dominant or recessive nature of an allele and its adaptive value. Likewise, selection can act in either a growing or a shrinking population.

5. Meiosis contributes to genetic assortment, not only by shuffling the chromosomes but also by crossing-over, a process that separates alleles previously linked together on one chromosome.

6. Natural selection must act not only on new assortments of genetic material, but also on new patterns known as mutations. Mutations can be due to gross rearrangements within chromosomes as well as to small alterations of DNA structure.

7. Formation of new species requires a barrier to gene flow. Usually this barrier begins as physical isolation, but a reproductive barrier must develop before a new species is established.

8. In small populations, chance events unrelated to the selective value of an allele may alter its frequency in the population.

9. The ecological niche of a species is the sum of its life requirements and its role in the ecosystem. Competition between two species can alter the ecological niche of each and permit them to share resources.

10. Populations of one species may differ somewhat as the result of selection in different environments. These different populations make up ecotypes, subspecies, and races.

11. Natural selection is stronger in some situations than in others; as a result, evolution occurs at variable rates. New plant species often arise instantaneously through doubling of the chromosomes. These polyploids are reproductively isolated because crosses with the diploid parents produce infertile triploids.

12. The fossil record reveals the formation of numerous related species over relatively brief periods of time. These adaptive radiations result from some fundamental new ability.

13. Over time, species become extinct. Extinction may be partly the result of chance and partly due to competition and large-scale environmental change.

Thought and Controversy

1. Richard Herrnstein, Professor of Psychology at Harvard University, believes that I.Q. tests are not culturally biased. He thinks that they reveal real differences and suggests that truly equal opportunities and an increasingly technical culture will encourage social stratification based on inherited intelligence. He goes so far as to say that "the tendency to be unemployed may run in the genes of a family about as certainly as bad teeth do now." According to Herrnstein, "If differences in mental abilities are inherited, and if success requires these abilities, and if earnings and prestige depend on success, then social standing will be based to some extent on inherited differences among people." Herrnstien's comments are based on data collected from whites, and he carefully states that "the overwhelming case is for believing that American blacks have been at an environmental disadvantage." Nevertheless, his suggestion that social success is a reflection of innate biological characteristics has resulted in charges of racism. Many of his students and colleagues seem to share the feelings of Richard Musgrave, a Harvard economist who wrote Herrnstein, "When dealing with propositions so monstrous and destructive to human relations and the cause of human dignity as that of hereditary racial inferiority, let this freedom [of inquiry] be tempered by the utmost caution and sense of responsibility."

Do you think it reasonable to assume that humans differ in the inherited biological capabilities that form the basis of intelligence? Is the difference in average I.Q. for any given race a proper subject for research?

2. Some geneticists argue that there are nonadaptive alleles. In other words, they believe that two or more alleles of any one gene can have exactly the same value, so natural selection will favor neither over the other. In earlier years the ABO blood types were often cited as resulting from nonadaptive alleles. Now it is known that the incidence of some diseases is greater among individuals of certain blood types. For example, stomach cancer is more frequent among type-A individuals, but the reason remains unknown. On the other hand, infants with type B or AB are more susceptible to infection by *Escherichia coli* and *Salmonella* (intestinal bacteria that vary from being harmless to producing typhoid fever) than are A or O babies. Also, the anti-A antibodies found in B and O people may cross-react with antigens of the smallpox virus and give a partial natural immunity to this disease.

3. Numerous studies on the relationship between an individual's I.Q. and the number of his or her brothers and sisters have revealed an inverse relationship—the higher the I.Q., the smaller the family. Recent studies of the United States and Sweden have compared, instead, the I.Q. of the individual and the number of children produced. Results indicate that many individuals of low intelligence fail to marry, and those that do often have few or no children. In fact, three recent studies of Caucasians in the United States show that people with I.Q.s of 130 or more have more children than those of lesser intelligence. Can you see any significance in the two kinds of comparisons?

Questions

1. List some of the evidences of evolution.

2. Explain how the sickle-cell trait is retained in some populations despite the fact that individuals homozygous for this allele suffer from a serious disease.

3. If the frequency of the *M* and *N* blood-group alleles in a population are 0.98 and 0.02 respectively, what will the frequencies be in another hundred years? What factors would affect your answer?

4. Explain how recessive alleles may be more common than dominant alleles. What determines the frequency of any allele?

5. Explain why it is unwise for anyone to have children by a close relative.

6. Describe two aspects of meiosis that contribute to the assortment of genes. How are these assortment processes important in evolution?

7. Explain why most mutations are harmful. How is it, then, that mutations are essential for the long-term survival of organisms?

8. How do small populations provide important opportunities for evolution? Why is it likely that human races trace to numerous small, isolated tribes?

9. It is often said that each species occupies a unique niche. Explain why two species can't share one niche.

10. Describe some of the barriers that prevent gene flow between species. Which one of these barriers can develop instantaneously in plants?

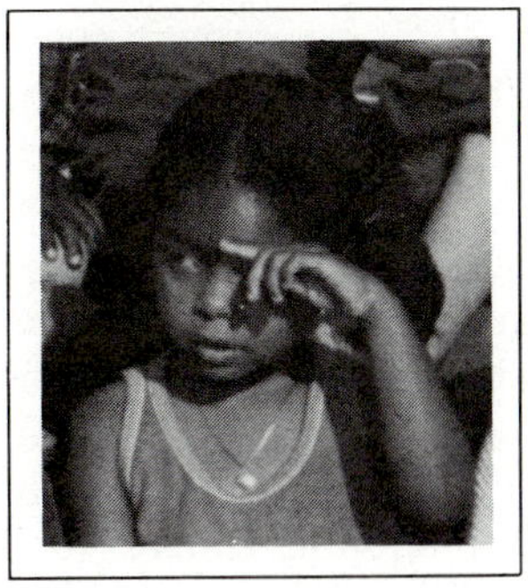

15

Behavior: Its Genetic Base and Adaptive Value

THE FROG THAT FALLS SILENT WHEN A SHADOW crosses his pond, the cow that bellows for her calf, and the fly drawn to a lighted windowpane are each behaving according to genetic instructions. Inheritance determines much, but certainly not all, animal behavior. Such inherited behavior patterns help organisms fit their ecological niches. In other words, behavior is adaptive and in many cases as much the result of natural selection as is the physical structure of the organism. In this chapter, we will show that particular behavior patterns benefit the individual and enhance survival and reproduction. The result is increased representation of that organism's genes in the next generation.

This emphasis on inherited behavior does not ignore the contribution of learning. Learned behaviors are important in many species. In a sense learned behavior has an inherited base because the capacity to learn is inherited. But much of the behavior of most animals is rooted directly in their genes. Learning serves largely to adapt inherited behavior to specific situations. Although it is tempting to suggest that animals choose their behavior with a clear view to the consequences, as humans are supposed to, the data seldom support such interpretations. Despite the emphasis on humans as animals, it is usually a mistake to attribute human motives to other animals. It is true that identification with the needs of an animal can provide insight into the adaptive value of behavior, and that biologists sometimes resort to **anthropomorphic language** to describe animals. However, any casting of animals into a human mold risks misunderstanding. Except in higher primates, animal behavior differs substantially from human behavior. Many of the components are the same, but different mechanisms dominate the mental process.

COMPONENTS OF BEHAVIOR

Classification of behavior into discrete units can promote understanding of the evolution of behavioral patterns. The classification units vary from species to species and with the types of behavior. We include only a few major examples.

Simple Behavior Units

Some behavioral patterns are exhibited by all members of a species under the same general conditions. Such patterns are **innate**—i.e., they are inborn characteristics. Many taxes, kineses, and releasing mechanisms are examples of inherited behavior. Some reflexes□ fall into this category, although others (such as pressing on the brake pedal in an automobile emergency) are learned, or conditioned, reflexes. 168

Taxes. All worker honeybees turn toward the pleasant odors emitted by certain nectar-bearing flowers. Sense receptors on the antennae of these bees respond to the concentration of odor in the air. If the concentration sensed by the two antennae differ, the bee turns toward the stronger stimulation until both antennae detect the same concentration of nectar. As the bee flies, it orients itself

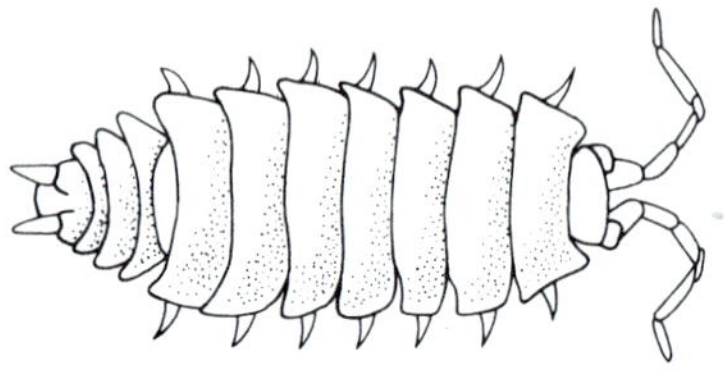

FIGURE 15.1 **Sow Bug.** This familiar creature is also known as a wood louse.

FIGURE 15.2 **Stickleback Releasing Factors.** The red belly of the breeding male is the releasing factor that causes a female to follow him to his nest. Females will respond to any of the models with red bellies but ignore a perfect replica of a male if it lacks red on the lower surface (a). The male shows his nest to the female who is following him (b). After the female enters the nest, the male's nudges (c) are the releasing factor necessary for her to lay eggs. Then she leaves (d) and he enters to fertilize the eggs.

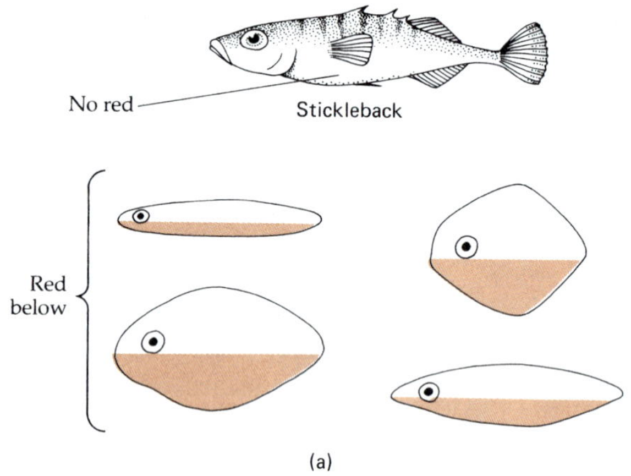

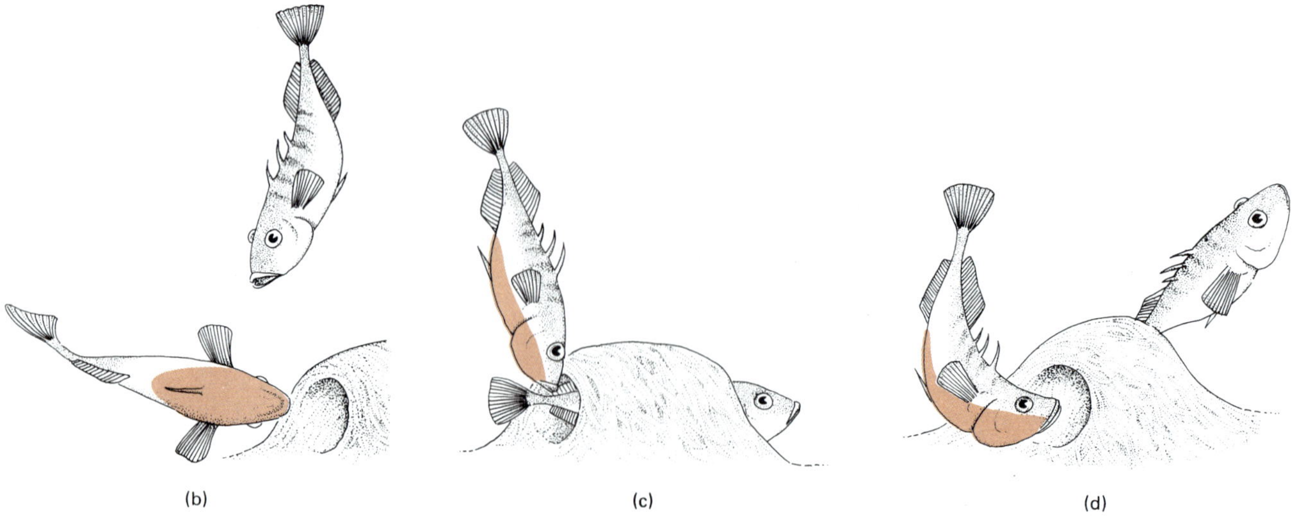

so that the concentration at the two antennae remain equal. Such characteristic movement toward or away from a particular stimulus constitutes a **taxis.** Worker honeybees show a positive taxis for many nectar components.

Kineses. Sowbugs, or wood lice as they are sometimes called (Fig. 15.1), often accumulate under rocks or boards. Each group of sowbugs is located in an area of optimal moisture concentration. Moisture is of special importance to sowbugs, for sowbugs breathe through gills like their aquatic relatives, the crabs and crayfish. To keep their gills moist so that oxygen will dissolve into body fluids, sowbugs must live in a humid environment. But though they cannot tolerate drying out, sowbugs are also susceptible to excessive dampness. When an environment is either too dry or too wet, sowbugs race about frantically. Their movements are random and eventually take them to a more favorable environment. Here the sowbugs slow down. When they reach an optimal humidity, they stop. This explains the aggregates of sowbugs found under flower pots and wood piles.

The humidity-related movement of sowbugs constitutes a **kinesis.** Kineses are behavioral patterns in which the rate of movement changes with suitability of the environment. In contrast to a taxis that determines the direction of movement, a kinesis involves random activity.

Releasing mechanisms. Some innate behavior will occur only when animals are subjected to specific stimuli while in a particular physiological state, such as a certain phase of the reproductive cycle. Consider the three-spined stickleback. The males of this species of small fish normally build nests on the bottoms of rivers and streams. After a male has completed his nest, he must entice a female to enter and lay her eggs. Then he spreads a milky sperm suspension over the eggs. Females tend to swim around in schools and ignore the males, even those that display before them in a zigzag "dance." But occasionally a female with a belly full of ripe eggs will leave the school and swim after a brightly colored, dancing male. Experiments with wood and paint models demonstrate that it is the red belly of the male that causes the female to follow him (Fig. 15.2a). The red belly serves as a releasing mechanism (environmental cue) that stimulates the female to exhibit a specific behavior appropriate to her reproductive state.

Once the female stickleback has entered the nest, the male noses her side and trembles (Fig. 15.2c). This nudging stimulates the female to shed eggs into the nest. Thus nudging is the stimulus that releases egg-laying behavior. Obviously, nudging a female will cause her to release eggs only if she is prepared to do so.

Stimulus-response behaviors that can be categorized as releasing mechanisms occur in animals as diverse as insects and mammals. Releasing mechanisms can involve two species as when a pattern in a flower attracts insect pollinators (Fig. 15.3). Releasing mechanisms lead predators to attack their prey. Often prey movements stimulate the attack. Sometimes "freezing" or "playing dead" will save an animal, even a human facing a grizzly bear.

Simple Behavior Patterns Can Have Varied Uses. Most animals have only a small number of basic behavior patterns. These simple units can be used in different combinations to serve more than one function. The display a male stickleback uses to drive other males from his nest territory involves the same digging motions he uses to build a nest.

Most birds feed their young, but many use the same feeding behavior as part of their courtship ritual. Often females solicit food just as young birds do. Male red-billed gulls mount their mates with food in their bill. Such **courtship feeding** strengthens the bond between the two gulls, makes the female more responsive to the male, and also increases the female's food supply at a time when her body is devoting resources to egg production.

FIGURE 15.3 **Honey Guides.** The dark lines on this hollyhock flower are releasers that draw insect pollinators toward glands in the center.

Just as other animals make many uses of a few actions, so do mammals. Wolves and dogs routinely sniff objects and mark them with urine. Odors in the urine identify individuals and signal their reproductive state. But when wolves visit locations where they have previously buried food and find their caches empty, they likewise emit squirts of urine. Marked caches are ignored in the future. The marking signals the absence of food and saves the effort of digging at an empty cache.

Social Organization and Interaction

Most animals live as members of social units. Males and females of some species form permanent or semipermanent pairs. In other species, individual males command harems. In still others, several individuals of each sex make up a band. Some species live in family groups. The variety of social organization and resulting relationships is endless. The

BOX 15A

LITTLE RED RIDING HOOD'S GRANDMOTHER AND MAN'S BEST FRIEND

Dominant male stands over subordinate male.

The responsiveness and faithfulness of dogs has won them a place in human societies around the world. Although these traits contrast vividly with the traditional view of the wolf as a vicious human enemy, the key dog traits can be traced to pack interactions of wolves. In essence, dogs are a population of highly selected and domesticated wolves. Dogs retain much of the behavior of wolves, but they include humans in their pack and see their owners as the dominant members of it.

The wolf pack is basically a large family group often including members of several different litters. But unrelated wolves sometimes join a pack, and family members sometimes leave. Dogs that have been abandoned and run wild also form packs; even pets allowed to roam the streets show elements of pack behavior. All dogs who are handled regularly by people during their first few months of life accept humans as members of their "pack." Pups isolated from other dogs soon after birth and raised by humans grow up to pay little attention to other dogs. Likewise, dogs who experience no human contact during their puppy and juvenile months never form strong ties to people.

The dominance and submission relationships of wolves are clearly related to dog–human interactions. When two wolves confront one another, the dominant animal holds its head high and walks with stiff legs as it holds its tail out straight. The submissive wolf keeps a low profile, with head and tail down. Dominance is sometimes contested; bickering can lead to bloody fights. The top-ranking male and female make up the alpha pair and are usually the only ones to reproduce. Among the younger wolves, dominance is influenced by age. But unlike somewhat older animals, pups are granted a great deal of social freedom. Pups approach dominant adults with an audacity forbidden to low-ranking adults.

Dogs exhibit wolf-like dominance and submission behavior. Sometimes, when two dogs meet, there is a fight. This is especially likely if the animals are strangers. As with wolves, fighting is more likely between members of the same sex. Very submissive animals roll on their backs and expose the vulnerable throat and belly even without a fight. Some dogs greet their owners this way, and all dogs give some sign of submission. The willingness of wolves to give visible signs of submission surely played a part in the ability of humans to tolerate certain wolves and tame them.

Unlike all dogs except the basenjis, wolves breed but once a year. Usually only the alpha female becomes pregnant. She aggressively dominates other females during the breeding season and suppresses their social activities; the result is that they seldom mate. Likewise, the alpha male does his best to prevent other males from mating. Members of the pack are together less regularly after the pups are born, perhaps because the breeding pair must stay near the den for several months. The female wolf attends her pups closely. After three weeks of nursing she begins to feed them warm, moist food that she has regurgitated, just as does the female dog. Unlike the male dog, the male wolf has a strong bond to his female; he brings food to the den and regurgitates it for the pups. Sometimes other members of the pack also feed the pups.

Although we cannot reconstruct with certainty the events that led to domestication of dogs, the usual suggestion is that wolf pups were stolen or orphaned and raised as pets. Only certain wolves would have had the temperament to accept human dominance. Anatomically some dogs are indistinguishable from wolves except that wolves have larger fangs. The tradition of large fangs indicating a wolf has come down to us in the story of Little Red Riding Hood. It is easy to understand that humans who were domesticating wolves would choose small-fanged ones.

It is possible that dogs were domesticated from some now-extinct species but there is no evidence that such a species existed. Besides the wolf, other possible dog ancestors are the coyote and the jackal. Differences in chromosome number isolate dogs from foxes and other related species. Fertile crosses occur not only between dogs and wolves, but also between dogs and coyotes, and dogs and jackals. Therefore the infusion of coyote or jackal genes into dog populations is a possibility. Behavior suggests, however, that few coyote or jackal genes are present in dogs. Neither jackals nor coyotes show the pack behavior characteristic of wolves and dogs. Instead, the basic social unit in these species is a mated pair. The young leave when they are sexually mature. Also, the posture of coyotes and jackals differs from that of dogs and wolves. For instance, coyotes arch their backs and lower their heads when challenging another animal. In dogs, this posture is not a sign of aggression, but rather an invitation to play. Also, coyotes and jackals usually urinate on strong-smelling substances, whereas dogs and wolves roll on such things. Altogether, the evidence suggests that dogs are highly selected, domesticated wolves.

Subordinate female slinks away from a dominant female.

social organization of a species may change with the season or depend on the environment. But at a minimum, all animals interact with others during reproduction, and even solitary individuals may defend their territories.

Experiences Bond Individuals Together. Members of a pair or group recognize one another, accept one another, and are often attracted to one another. This combination of recognition, acceptance, and attraction is the basis of social bonds. Such bonds are established and maintained by stimuli such as odors, appearances, or touch. The stimuli may be highly specific and are often effective only under special circumstances. Maternal or nest odors usually bond the young mammal to its mother. Likewise, odors allow the mother to recognize her young. The bonding may begin when the female licks her newborn and becomes accustomed to its odor. In many species cross-fostering of infants from one mother to another is successful only if the exchange occurs almost immediately after birth. Odors also allow litter mates to recognize one another and may decrease the likelihood of inbreeding. Deer fawns reared and bottle fed on inanimate "mother models" that were smeared with secretions from pronghorn antelopes later preferred pronghorns to their own species.

FIGURE 15.4 **Vervet Monkeys Fear the Python.**

Communication. Communication among animals maintains bonds and provides vital information. Particular channels of communication have special uses and limitations. For example, **sounds** can be used to draw the attention of otherwise occupied individuals. Animals need not be in view of one another to communicate by sound. Many vertebrates have a complex "vocabulary" of sounds, some with highly specific meanings. In Kenya adult vervet monkeys (Fig. 15.4) ignore more than 100 other species but give specific alarms for three important predators. "Leopard alarms" cause monkeys on the ground to climb into trees. At the sound of an "eagle alarm," monkeys look upward and often run for cover. "Python alarms" set off a careful search of the ground nearby.

Although each animal species communicates with its own specific sounds, certain sounds are recognized by other species. A number of bird species audibly scold crows, hawks, cats, and other predators as they dive toward these offenders. Usually one bird initiates the attack, and others join in. Frequently several species recognize the call and mob the predator simultaneously.

When individuals are in close proximity, **visual signals** are common. Many releasers, such as those described for sticklebacks, involve visual cues. Visual signals are important to the courtship displays of many species (Box 15C). Chimpanzees communicate a variety of messages through direction and intensity of gaze, enthusiasm of movement, pointing, and more subtle postural cues. Humans do, too. Consider the intimidating impression of an unblinking gaze and erect head-held-high posture. Not only other dominant primates, but also such animals as dogs use the same tactic on their subordinates.

As important as sight and sound are, animals in general probably rely more on **chemical communication.** The world is much richer in chemical messages than our poor human sense of smell would indicate. Many insects use pheromones as sex attractants, alarm messages, or to lay a trail(Fig. 15.5). Tomcats mark their territories by backing up to an object, extending the hind legs, raising the tail, and spraying urine from the backturned penis. Many lower primates rub urine on their feet or directly onto tree branches. Woodchucks and ground squirrels mark with secretions from cheek glands, whereas bears and camels mark with neck glands. Domestic rabbits and cats mark their mates with chin glands. A cat that rubs its chin on you is displaying part of its normal courtship behavior. The familiar musk that is used as a perfume base derives from sternal glands of the male musk deer. Musk hunters have driven this tiny oriental deer to the verge of extinction. Anal glands are another source of marking odors. Surely you have noticed dogs intently sniffing the feces of other dogs.

Despite their wide use, chemicals have serious limitations as modes of communication. Odors cling only where highly concentrated or protected from the wind. Just as some odors may disappear too soon, others linger so long that messages cannot be changed frequently. But whatever the method of communication, signals between individuals transmit vital information concerning both their own and other species.

Positive and Negative Interactions. Although the members of any social unit are dependent on one another, the self-interest of each is usually different. This conflict of interests gives rise to the **aggressive tactics** through which members of the unit compete. Because the members of a group usually benefit from group membership, it is to the advantage of each to promote social bonds and defuse excess aggression. One useful tactic in dealing with aggression is the acknowledged **dominance** of one animal over others. Dominance confers advantages depending on the species. Sometimes dominant animals have first access to food. In some cases only dominant animals are allowed to mate. Submissive animals usually step aside for dominant ones or defer to them in some other way. Dominance can be advantageous even to animals that must submit, for it reduces tensions within the group.

The importance of dominance varies among species. Only certain animals have the **linear dominance hierarchy** demonstrated by domestic chickens. Here we find the actual behavior that inspired the popular expression, **pecking order.** One hen dominates all others. A second hen dominates all but the "top hen." A third hen dominates all but those two, and so it goes on down the line. The

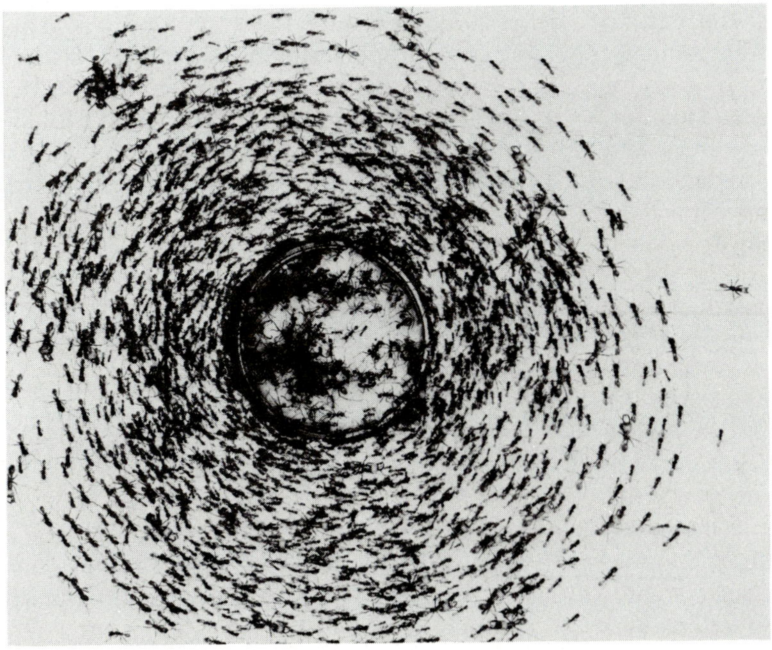

FIGURE 15.5 **An Army Tricked into Marching in Circles.** When army ants are on the march, the leaders lay down a pheromone that the others follow. The ants shown here have been led to marching in circles by an experimenter who made a circular pattern of pheromone and placed the ants on it.

lowest hen in the hierarchy is pecked by the entire flock and forbidden to feed about a crowded food dish. Such a bird may be pecked to death; however, it may survive to rise in the pecking order at a time when the flock is changed through loss or addition of other birds.

Contests for dominance often rely on threats rather than on outright fights. For example, two strange dogs may engage in shoulder pushing and thus manage to establish which is dominant without resorting to biting. Once established, dominance reduces future conflict. The dominance and submission displays among members of a stable wolf pack are little more than greeting formalities that strengthen bonds among pack members.

Positive interactions among the members of a social unit are important, especially between related individuals. Cows have definite preferences for **grazing companions.** Observations of large herds on the open range, where animals have a wide choice of companions, reveal that a cow will most often be found in the company of her mother, son, daughter, or sister. Grazing companions are also key grooming companions. **Grooming** behavior is widespread. Grooming not only cleans the skin and removes parasites, but touching and being touched contributes to the bond between two animals.

FIGURE 15.6 **Basenji Pups.**

INHERITANCE AND BEHAVIOR

Every animal breeder knows that certain aspects of behavior are inherited. For example, the natural trotting gait of horses results from an autosomally inherited dominant allele. Horses homozygous for the recessive allele normally pace instead of trot. It is widely recognized that laboratory mice and rats are more docile than the wild members of their species. The reason is obvious: animal-room personnel choose the tamest animals to keep and breed. Strains of animals maintained in various laboratories also differ. Selection may be involved, but 337 genetic drift□ can occur whenever a colony is started or maintained with a small number of animals.

Comparison of basenjis (Fig. 15.6), dogs used by the Pygmies of the Congo bush, with cocker spaniels illustrates breed differences. Basenjis are general-purpose hunting dogs. The pups are timid and wild, much like wolf pups. Basenjis tame easily, but they never fully accept the leash, and adults are highly aggressive. Although basenjis never bark, they raise a continual ruckus with their wailing and yodeling. By contrast, cocker spaniels behave well on the leash and seldom show fear or aggression. But though they are docile, cockers bark to excess—one dog is reported to have barked nonstop at the rate of 90 times a minute for ten minutes. Crosses between basenjis and cockers suggest that ease of barking is controlled by dominant alleles of two separate genes and that the duration of barking is determined by yet a third gene. Other behavioral characteristics such as wildness of pups, fighting the leash, and aggressiveness are also inherited according to Mendelian laws. These and other observations of domestic animals demonstrate that behavior is under genetic control.

The Advantage of Inherited Behavior Patterns

There is no doubt that inherited behavioral patterns are advantageous under natural conditions. For example, if young animals try to capture poisonous snakes they may not survive to learn from the experience. It isn't surprising that young motmots (snake-eating birds—Fig. 15.7) instinctively avoid objects with the bright red, yellow, and black bands that mark coral snakes.

Inherited behavior patterns not only avoid the risks and time necessary for learning, but also can be achieved with a small investment in living tissue. A relatively simple brain can handle a small number of stereotyped behaviors that are a direct result of the genetic program.

On the other hand, instinctive behavioral patterns represent gambles that a certain behavior is always best in a given situation. For example, toads normally benefit from snapping out their tongues and retrieving small moving objects. In nature such objects are usually insects, so this genetically programmed behavior is an efficient method for catching food. But in special situations, as when toads are around children who play with BBs, this inherited behavior works to the toad's disadvantage, for no toad benefits from a belly full of BBs. Thus we see that the value of inherited behavior depends on a predictable environment.

Genes and Learning

Natural selection can favor either inheritance of specific innate behavior patterns or inheritance of the ability to learn a certain type of behavior. Both abilities are inherited to a greater or lesser extent in all animals. Even though humans are distinguished by unusual learning ability, we do have some inherited behavior patterns, including inborn reflexes. Although learning capacity can prove surprisingly large, there are always limits. Some limits are set by ability to discriminate stimuli or by the nature of the effectors. People can learn to read the intentions of dogs as expressed in signals, for we see well. But we lack both the hearing ability and the neural capacity to learn to catch flying insects in a dark room, as bats do (Fig. 15.8). Brains are not just clean blackboards upon which anything can be written. Much learning is more similar to developing exposed film than to writing on a blackboard. Processing time and developing solutions affect the photographic image, but the shape of the image is determined in advance. For learning, the time and situation affect *what* is learned; but what *can be* learned is determined by the genetic pattern.

Learning as "development of exposed film" is illustrated by the song patterns of white-crowned sparrows. Males sing a species-characteristic song, but there are small differences in the songs of birds from various geographic regions. Birds from a given area sing a dialect, just as people in isolated areas speak in modifications of a common language. Individual birds can also be recognized by their song. Birds reared in isolation never learn to sing their species song accurately, nor do birds deafened before they begin to sing. To learn to sing properly, a white-crowned sparrow must hear the species song sung and also hear its own attempt to sing that song. Thus white-crowned sparrows learn to sing, but the song they learn is determined partly by inheritance. The adaptive value of a learned component in a species characteristic like song may lie in the resulting variability. Because no two birds learn to sing exactly the same, individuals can rec-

FIGURE 15.7 **Motmot.** The diet of this tropical bird includes lizards and snakes. Note the heavy bill.

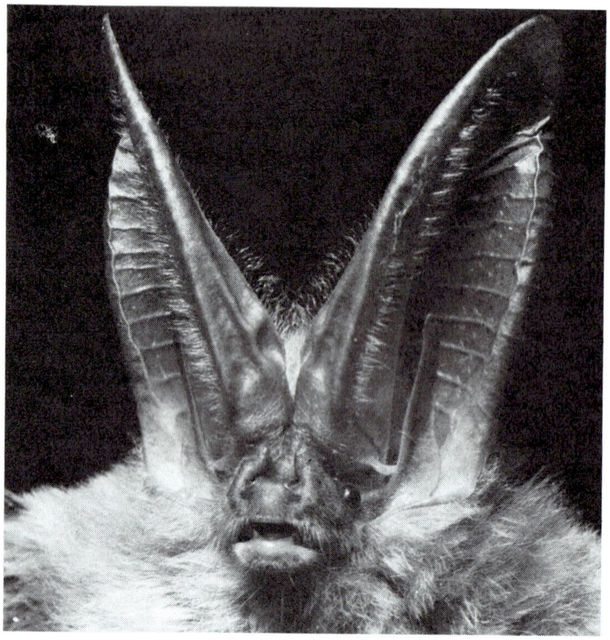

FIGURE 15.8 **Many Bats Use Ecolocation to Find Their Prey.** To do this, bats emit high-frequency squeaks and then listen for these sounds to be reflected back to them. The large external ears catch the faintest echos and funnel them to the sensory apparatus deep inside the head. This mechanism allows bats not only to catch flying insects on the wing, but also to maneuver effortlessly through a maze of delicate wires strung across a dark room.

ognize one another and newcomers can be identified readily.

Conditioning. Just as a reflex is an example of a simple behavior pattern, **conditioned reflexes** are examples of simple learning. The best-known early experiments in conditioning had to do with the salivation reflex of dogs. Dogs normally salivate at the sight of food, but if a bell is rung regularly before food is offered, a dog will learn to salivate at the sound of the bell alone. In other types of conditioning, animals learn to press levers to gain access to food. This ability to learn simple behavior patterns is advantageous, for it allows the animal to adjust to new circumstances with a minimal expenditure of energy.

Imprinting. Newly hatched Mallard ducklings kept in the dark for 15 hours and then exposed for 30 minutes to a moving model of a male duck will later run after any male duck and make the contentment call of ducklings. Such ducklings ignore female ducks but follow males just as ordinary ducklings follow their mother. On the other hand, ducklings first exposed to adults, or moving models of adults, when 30 hours old form no special attachments. Learning such as this, which can occur only at certain developmental stages, is known as **imprinting.** Imprinting has adaptive value; normally the first moving object that hatchlings see is their mother. She must search for food and the young must follow if they are to have food and protection. Imprinting occurs in the young of many precocial birds (those in which the young can walk as soon as they hatch). Experiments reveal that hatchlings of some species will imprint on a wider range of objects than other species. For example, chicks will imprint on a green box containing a ticking clock. So will the goslings of Canada geese, but Mallard ducklings will not. In other words, the specificity of the genetic program for the kind of learning we call imprinting differs in Mallards from that of the other two species.

Different Kinds of Intelligence. Comparison of intelligence among animal species can be meaningless, for each species is genetically adapted to learn a particular set of behavior patterns or to solve certain kinds of problems. For example, dogs usually approach the problem of getting food that's behind a fence by trying to reach through the fence, or dig under it, or climb over it. Most dogs have a great deal of difficulty turning away from the food and running some distance from it to get around the fence. Thus dogs usually use **trial and error** to solve such problems (Fig. 15.9). In contrast, many

FIGURE 15.9 **Trial-and-Error Behavior.** The more obvious the reward, the more attractive trial-and-error behavior becomes. The closer the food is to the fence, the harder it is for a dog to back away and go outside the enclosure to reach the food.

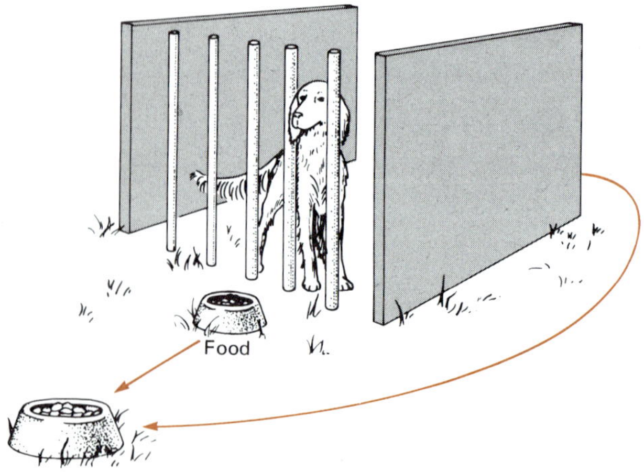

BOX 15B

SOME SHEEP DOGS HERD; OTHERS GUARD THE HERD

American sheep raisers lose over a million animals a year to predators. Most of the damage is done by coyotes or by dogs, some of which include neighbors' pets. The coyote problem alone is so great that the U.S. Department of Agriculture budgets several million dollars a year for sheep-predator control. Hunting, trapping, and poison baits are employed. The effect of poisons on coyotes and other species has fueled a long-term controversy between conservationists and sheep farmers.

In contrast to this situation, Old World sheep raisers report low losses, even in the mountains of southern and eastern Europe and Asia, where the wolf, bear, lynx, and jackal pose potential threats to sheep.

Guarding Dog and Its Flock. These sheep in the Shar Plania Mountains of Yugoslavia show no fear of the dog that guards them. Note the sheep-like appearance of the dog. The dog is shedding its winter coat and the sheep have recently been shorn of theirs.

A key difference between New World and Old World sheep raising lies in the behavior of the dogs kept on the ranches. U.S. ranchers use border collies and related breeds from the British Isles, where predators were long ago eradicated and pets are well controlled. These British herding dogs exhibit elements of wolf behavior, for they stalk sheep and even go for their necks in the classical wolf-kill behavior. When carefully supervised by humans, such dogs are effective for sheep herding. The sheep recognize the predator behavior of the dogs and flee, usually in the direction intended by the human shepherd. Herding keeps sheep from straying from the flock but does little to prevent predators from attacking the flock if a human isn't on the spot to frighten the predator away.

Eastern European sheep raisers rely on a very different type of sheep dogs; their animals guard sheep rather than herd them. These guarding dogs include the Italian Maremma, the Turkish Shepherd, the Hungarian Komodo, and the Yugoslavian Shar Planinetz. Guard dogs run with the sheep, and indeed look much like sheep themselves. Adults display pup-like behavior, soliciting play by bowing before the sheep, nuzzling their ears, and licking their faces in the manner that pups beg food from their mothers. Guard dogs even try to mount sheep that stand still before them. In fact, guard dogs have been described as exhibiting retarded social development, for they behave much like wolf pups. Herding dogs, on the other hand, show a fuller development of wolf-like behavior.

Guard dogs are larger than most other breeds. Neither coyotes nor smaller dogs are likely to approach a flock of sheep when a 100-pound guard dog is on duty. If potential predators do come near, guard dogs bark and move between the intruder and the flock. Interaction with the guard dog diverts the attention of would-be predators. Sometimes guard dogs do kill intruders, but often they do little more than play with them. Wherever guard dogs have been introduced in the United States, sheep losses have dropped dramatically. Levels of success depend somewhat on the sheep breed, too. Some breeds are more willing than others to accept the dogs and mingle with them freely.

Political pressure for coyote-eradication programs might be needless, and both wildlife and dollars might be saved, if all ranchers would examine the record and consider the guard-dog approach.

BOX 15C

COURTSHIP IS SERIOUS BUSINESS

Careful choice of a mate can increase the chances that the individual's traits will be passed on to later generations. Courtship usually provides an opportunity for the female to evaluate prospective mates. Males may be screened for vigor, for indication of how well they will care for young, or for physical resources they control.

Prairie-chicken roosters gather on communal mating grounds and attract hens with rolling calls that boom like thunder over the flat grasslands. Males strut and display before the hens that come to the mating ground. The hens are highly selective, and most prefer the same rooster. As a result, a tiny percentage of the males father almost all the chicks.

Each male sculpin has a territory, or "nest," under a flat rock. The female's selection of a mate is correlated with the male's ability to protect the eggs that the female glues to the roof of the nest. The larger the male, the greater the likelihood that the eggs will survive to hatch. Thus the larger the male, the more likely females are to deposit eggs for him to fertilize and guard. Males display before prospective mates by raising their fins and gill covers and opening their mouths. This display increases the appearance of their size.

Where food is abundant, some male redwing blackbirds have two mates simultaneously. The males are territorial, and only those with the best territories have more than one mate. Early-pairing females choose the males with the best territories. Late-pairing females must decide between single males with poor territories and paired males with good territories. Choice of the latter suggests that the female is picking a mate on the basis of his resources.

We often think of one individual as courting the other; in fact, both usually participate. Sometimes activities are mutual, as when the male and female great-crested grebes present each other with water weeds.

(a) Prairie chickens

(b) Sculpin

(c) Redwing blackbirds

(d) Grebes

primates will immediately size up such a situation and run around the end of the fence. In other words, they show **insight** into the problem. The ability to consider complex problems of how to get from here to there must be important in the arboreal habitat. The route to a tree on the left may lie through adjacent tree tops starting on the right. The wolves that were ancestral to dogs lived in a terrestrial environment. Their intelligence fitted them to trailing and killing large game. We must conclude that each species has its own peculiar kind of intelligence that suits it to a unique ecological niche.

NATURAL SELECTION AND BEHAVIOR STRATEGIES

Much of what we have written so far is designed to point out the importance of inheritance in behavior. Either behavior results directly from the action of genes, or genes define the behavior that is possible. This relationship between heredity and behavior means that behavior is subject to natural selection. Inheritance of behavior does not differ fundamentally from inheritance of body size, tooth shape, or hormone level. Nevertheless, a particular inherited behavioral pattern is often termed a *strategy*—or more specifically, an **evolutionary strategy.** The payoff of any successful evolutionary strategy is successful reproduction. The better the strategy for any given situation, the more likely the animal is to thrive and reproduce successfully. Please do not be misled by use of the term "strategy." These "strategies" are not planned in the usual sense of that word. Instead, they are the result of natural selection acting on the assortment of genetic material present in the population. This assortment may contain instructions for many specific behavior patterns as well as for the capacity to learn a variety of other patterns.

Reproductive Strategies: Investment versus Reward

Females have a large investment in each egg, and males only a minute investment in a single sperm. This difference explains many contrasts in reproductive behavior between the sexes. Males can increase their reproductive success by fertilizing as many eggs as possible. One way that females increase their reproductive success by selection of mates that offer the most resources for the young (Box 15C).

Low Investment and High Competition. Males not only compete in courtship,□ but even in species 360
with strong pair bonds one male will sometimes sneak a mating with another's female. This kind of competition explains why male starlings guard their mates during egg-laying season. Similar strategies are used by species lacking pair bonds. For example, many insects engage in prolonged mating that effectively guards the female against mating with a second male (Fig. 15.10). A male dragonfly clutches the female firmly and the two fly about in

FIGURE 15.10 Mate Guarding. The female damselfly (on the right) curls her abdomen forward to contact the sperm source located in the middle of the male's body. The male will continue to clasp the female's neck until she has laid her eggs. This prolonged embrace prevents a second male from mating with the female and leaving his sperm where they would be likely to fertilize the eggs.

BOX 15D

BABOON WATCHING

The highly social nature of baboon, their semiterrestrial habitat, and their varieties of social organizations have made baboons favorite subjects for studies in behavior. There are five kinds of baboons:

- **Chacma baboons**
- **Yellow (cynocephalus) baboons**
- **Olive (anubis) baboons**
- **Hamadryas baboons**
- **Gelada baboons**

All baboons live in groups of varying sizes but the organization varies greatly. The chacma, yellow, and olive baboon troops are multimale units. Male dominance affects access to females, but nevertheless females sometimes mate with subdominant males. This promiscuous behavior sets the stage for a variety of sexual strategies.

Among chacma, yellow, and olive baboons, males leave the troop of their birth and enter another troop. Such migrations reduce inbreeding but create social disturbance. Frequently infants are killed, presumably by new arrivals. Because nursing suppresses ovulation, loss of an infant soon results in the mother entering estrus. The new male benefits from his infanticide by having an opportunity to mate sooner, and his overall opportunities to leave offspring are increased. The promiscuous behavior of the females can be interpreted as a defense against the aggressive behavior of migrant males. Resident males tend to defend all infants, perhaps because they cannot be certain which are their own.

In contrast to this promiscuous mating system of chacma, yellow, and olive baboons, dominant male gelada and hamadryas baboons maintain harems. Here mating is polygamous. Among the hamadryas, the single-male

Adult male threatens infant.

tandem. In some species the male releases the female only after her eggs are fertilized and she has chosen a place to lay them. Certain bugs practice a form of homosexual "rape" in which one male forces his sperm into the reproductive tract of a competitor. If the raped male later mates, he will transmit the other's sperm to the female. Considered altogether, the strategies that promote fatherhood boggle the imagination.

High Investment. Although females usually provide the raw materials for their eggs, some male

Harems in a hamadryas troop.

units join together in bands and even large herds to sleep but separate in the morning to forage in their arid habitat. Since Hamadryas inhabit deserts, food is scarce; and without trees to climb, their only security is in numbers. Geladas, on the other hand, are found in the highlands. Here they find night-time security in single-male groups on small, isolated, rocky ledges. In the daytime numerous harems may forage together on lush alpine meadows.

Hamadryas males guard their harems jealously. Females are actually herded by the males. Should one stray a few feet too far, the harem master darts out and disciplines her with a nip on the neck. Despite this possessive behavior, males tolerate subadult males. These immature males are even permitted to copulate with females of the harem, but presumably do not impregnate them. The young male also kidnaps infants and fondles them for a few minutes at a time. As they mature, the males adopt and mother juvenile females to start their own harems. Through all this, the harem master and the young male maintain good relations. In the end, the harem master may be rewarded, for as his strength wanes, the younger male helps him retain harem members.

moths transfer nutrients to the female as part of
351 the semen. Courtship feeding□ is another example of a male making high energy investments in reproduction. Only in a few species, such as sea horses and phalaropes, do females court males and actively compete for matings. This reversal of courtship roles compensates for a reversal of investment roles, for in such species the males incubate the eggs and care for the young (Fig. 15.11).

Brood Parasitism: Letting Somebody Else Pay for Your Kids. Some birds lay their eggs in the nests

FIGURE 15.11 **Paternal Care.** This drab red phalarope male watches over his chick with the mother nowhere in sight. In phalaropes females are larger and more colorful than males who incubate the eggs and care for the young.

FIGURE 15.12 **Oropendola Nests.** These oropendola nests hang from branch tips where the young are protected from most predators but not from insect parasites.

of other species and let the foster parents raise the young. As you might expect, natural selection favors birds that can recognize the eggs of these **brood parasites.** Yet in certain situations the nest parasites pay their own way and are tolerated. Oropendolas, for instance (Fig. 15.12), are capable of recognizing and rejecting the young of the giant cowbirds that frequently parasitize oropendola nests. However, the young cowbirds groom oropendola nestlings and remove botfly larvae that would otherwise kill the baby oropendolas. Oropendolas eject cowbird eggs and chase female cowbirds away only where oropendola nests hang near colonies of wasps or bees that independently protect the area from the flesh-eating botflies.

Nepotism Wins

Although children's stories often portray one animal helping another, no organism can afford to do something for nothing. **Altruism,** the provision of goods or services at cost and without potential reward, may never occur. Natural selection discriminates against any animal that feeds or cares for another without genetic reward. Documented observations of one animal helping another probably involve the interactions of relatives. Obviously parents are genetically rewarded by the reproductive success of their young. Likewise, animals receive genetic rewards for actions that increase the repro-

FIGURE 15.13 **Termite Castes.** The giant worm-like queen lays all the eggs in this *Nasutitermes* colony and the male (the dark insect on her right) fertilizes all the eggs. The numerous smaller termites are workers and nasutes. The nasutes are distinguished by a dark, elongated head from which they eject a defensive chemical. Because all the members of the colony have many genes in common, the workers and nasutes assure the presence of their own genes in the next generation as they care for the reproductive caste and the young.

ductive success of less closely related individuals, because all related animals carry many genes in common. By helping a relative reproduce, you can increase the frequency of your own genes in the next generation.

The genetic rewards of assisting a close relative's reproduction help to explain the evolution of **social insects** such as honeybees, ants, and termites. In a **honeybee** society, thousands of sterile female workers devote their lives to providing food and care for the offspring of a single queen. But because the workers are daughters (or sisters) of the queen, helping her reproduction results in propagation of many of the worker's genes. Although honeybees are surely unaware of the results of their actions, the workers' behavior assures their genetic immortality. Similar factors are at work in termite colonies (Fig. 15.13).

Social Behavior and Evolution

As is true of other sciences, the study of animal behavior has moved from description and classification to a search for cause and effect. In biology such searches inevitably turn to genetics and evolution. In every case the inherited behavior of animals must be understood in terms of its selective value. That selective value is realized in the success of passing genes to the next generation.

The biological nature of humans dictates that these same rules apply to us. However, the impact of this fact depends on the role of inheritance in human behavior, a matter about which we have limited information. During the past decade attempts to apply **sociobiology** (theories on the biological basis of social behavior) to humans has created a furor. Part of this uproar results from sensational distortions. Many people reject attempts to define sex roles in sociobiological terms as ill-based speculation. Others find all aspects of human sociobiology offensive, for they view it as biological determinism. The suggestion that human behavior is the direct result of inheritance conflicts with their sense of human values.

Legitimate application of sociobiology to humans must await an improved understanding of the extent and details of inheritance of human behavior. In light of our extensive ability to learn, it is easy to argue that human behavior is far from determined. Nevertheless, we should not forget that we are the product of natural selection. It is this force that is responsible for our inherited ability to learn. We cannot hope to understand human behavior if we ignore its biological basis.

Summary

1. Behaviors adapt animals to their ecological niches. Natural selection is responsible for the characteristic behavior of a species, both learned and inborn.

2. Even within species with complex behavior patterns it is possible to recognize simple behavior units such as taxes, kineses, reflexes, and releasing mechanisms. Specific behavior patterns can serve different functions and are often used in a variety of situations.

3. Social bonds unite most animals into pairs, families, bands, or other groups. Specific visual, chemical, or other stimuli allow members of a unit to recognize and communicate with each other. Dominance/submission relationships and other established patterns of interaction between individuals are beneficial for they reduce stress experienced by members of the group.

4. Many specific behavioral patterns have a demonstrated genetic base. In some instances a single gene determines a characteristic behavior.

5. The neural basis of learned behavior is genetically determined and subject to natural selection. It is advantageous for an animal to learn simple as well as complex behavior. Examples of simple learned behavior include conditioned reflexes and the ability of young animals to imprint on a parentlike object.

6. The learning and problem-solving abilities of species differ both quantitatively and qualitatively. In each case natural selection has favored traits that fit individuals to their ecological niches.

7. Specific reproductive behaviors promote reproductive success of the individual. Usually male behavior increases the number of eggs fertilized. In contrast, female behavior favors the survival of offspring from a relatively small number of gametes.

8. Natural selection favors only behavior that promotes the contribution of genes to the next generation. Natural selection discriminates against any behavior that has no genetic reward. Animals that help others—for example, social insects that feed young other than their own—are indirectly promoting their own reproduction.

Thought and Controversy

1. Unlike many of their fellow mammals, the pig-like peccaries of the New World maintain uniformly friendly interactions with others of their band. Peccaries of both sexes and all ages associate freely. During most of their lives, the distance between adjacent animals averages only about 10 feet, but the peccaries seldom quarrel among themselves. Males exhibit no competition for mates, and adults are tolerant of all young animals even when the youngsters get in the way or crawl over their resting elders. Adults will yield food to young peccaries without disciplining them, and females nurse any suckling peccary that approaches. For peccaries, aggression and selfishness is restricted to predators and animals outside the band.

How can we understand this all-for-one and one-for-all behavior? The usual theories lead us to expect that natural selection will discriminate against inherited behavior patterns that do not favor the individual's offspring over all others. Any mutation for selfish behavior should be favored and should eventually swamp genes for altruistic behavior. Could the degree of inbreeding within a band affect the selective value of selfish behavior? Can you explain this?

2. If reproductive behaviors can be considered strategies to optimize transmission of genes to the next generation, one can't help wondering why some species have sexual reproduction. For species in which males make no investment that benefits either the young or the mother (in other words, they neither feed nor protect them), wouldn't females contribute more genes to the next generation if they were parthenogenic—that is, if they laid eggs that did not require fertilization? Parthenogenesis would allow females to double their contribution to the next generation, so why would natural selection favor those who contributed only half as much? What other advantages might sexual reproduction offer?

Questions

1. Compare and contrast taxes and kineses. Explain why these simple behavioral patterns are limited to lower animals, while reflexes occur even in humans.

2. Discuss the reasons dogs are thought to be domestic wolves.

3. Describe examples that support the hypothesis that learning is under genetic control. Considering that an animal depends on its environment, how can this hypothesis be true?

4. Explain why imprinting occurs only during a particular development phase of an animal's life.

5. Discuss why the reproductive strategies of males generally differ from those of females.

6. If natural selection discriminates against altruism, how is it that social insects such as ants, termites, and bees have evolved? Don't the workers of these species expend their energy feeding the young of other individuals? Explain.

7. If, when two strange dogs meet, one immediately rolls over onto its back, the other may sniff it but will seldom growl or bite. If neither dog shows submission, however, a fight may ensue. Classify the effect of one dog presenting its vulnerable belly and throat in terms of the kinds of simple behavior patterns described in this chapter.

8. Give an example of animals joined in a social bond. What factors promote the formation and maintenance of this bond? Discuss the value of social bonds in terms of their adaptive value.

9. Discuss the various modes of communication between animals, citing the advantages and disadvantages of each.

10. What is meant by an anthropomorphic argument? Why is such an argument apt to be misleading, especially in the area of animal behavior?

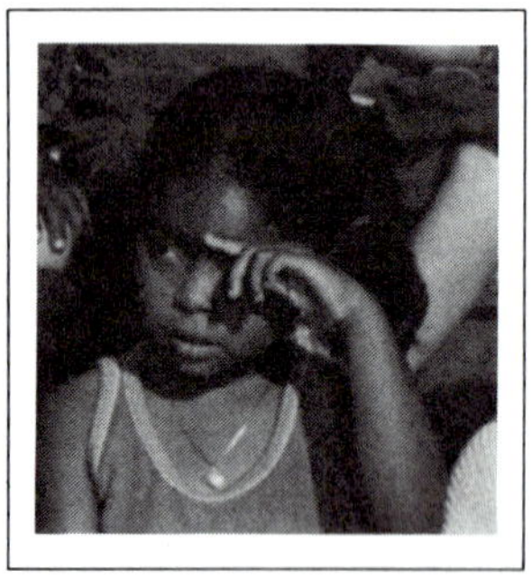

16

Diversity: The Product of Evolution

THE MILLION-PLUS SPECIES AROUND US ARE THE end products of billions of years of evolution. After a century of work by others, numerous biologists today devote their lives to the continued untangling of relationships among all these organisms. The conclusions biologists reach are expressed in the classification of organisms. But even with volumes of evidence, it remains impossible to establish relationships beyond doubt. If you examine various textbooks, you'll find that alternative classification schemes are common. As we explained earlier, only species have biological reality. The other categories are creations used by scientists to represent their understanding of the historic relationships of organisms. Both the number and level of these categories (kingdom, phylum, class, order,
16 family, genus, and so on) are arbitrary.□

FIVE KINGDOMS POINT UP THE GREAT DIVERSITY OF LIFE

Biologists often divide organisms into the following five great kingdoms to emphasize the drastic differences among the forms of life.

- □ Monera
- □ Protista
- □ Animalia
- □ Plantae
- □ Fungi

THE MONERA ARE PROCARYOTES

Monera include the bacteria and the cyanobacteria.□ These procaryotes are single-celled orga- 88
nisms that lack the mitochondria and the complex membrane systems found inside the cells of eucaryotes. As we observed in Chapter 10, the many kinds of bacteria include groups with highly diverse metabolic characteristics. Some are autotrophs that make their own organic molecules using either the energy of sunlight or energy from inorganic chemicals. Most are heterotrophs, but their chemical abilities are far from standard. It has been said with good reason that if anything is digestible, some bacterium can digest it.

Throughout all this metabolic diversity run threads of biochemical unity. Nonetheless, certain bacteria differ so remarkably from others in cell-wall components, transfer RNA structure, and metabolism, that it has been suggested that they represent another procaryotic kingdom. Some call this second procaryotic kingdom the **Archibacteria.**

PROTISTA: ONE-CELLED, YET COMPLEX

Grouped in the protista are the **protozoa** (Fig. 16.1), organisms that are animal-like but single celled, and other organisms that might reasonably be called one-celled plants. In fact, the diversity within the protista is so great that some might say the protista defy any general description. About all the protista have in common is

- small size in comparison with other eucaryotes,
- structural complexity in the absence of multicellularity, and
- (usually) the ability to move.

Collectively, the protista are the products of numerous adaptive radiations, perhaps each based on some special trait—a method of locomotion, for example. Certain protista, such as the amoeba, are deceptively simple and are often compared to white blood cells, for they feed by phagocytosis. Like white blood cells, amoebas and their relatives move by protoplasmic extensions known as **pseudopodia.** Nevertheless, these and all other protista

FIGURE 16.1 Protozoa, the Animal-like Protista.

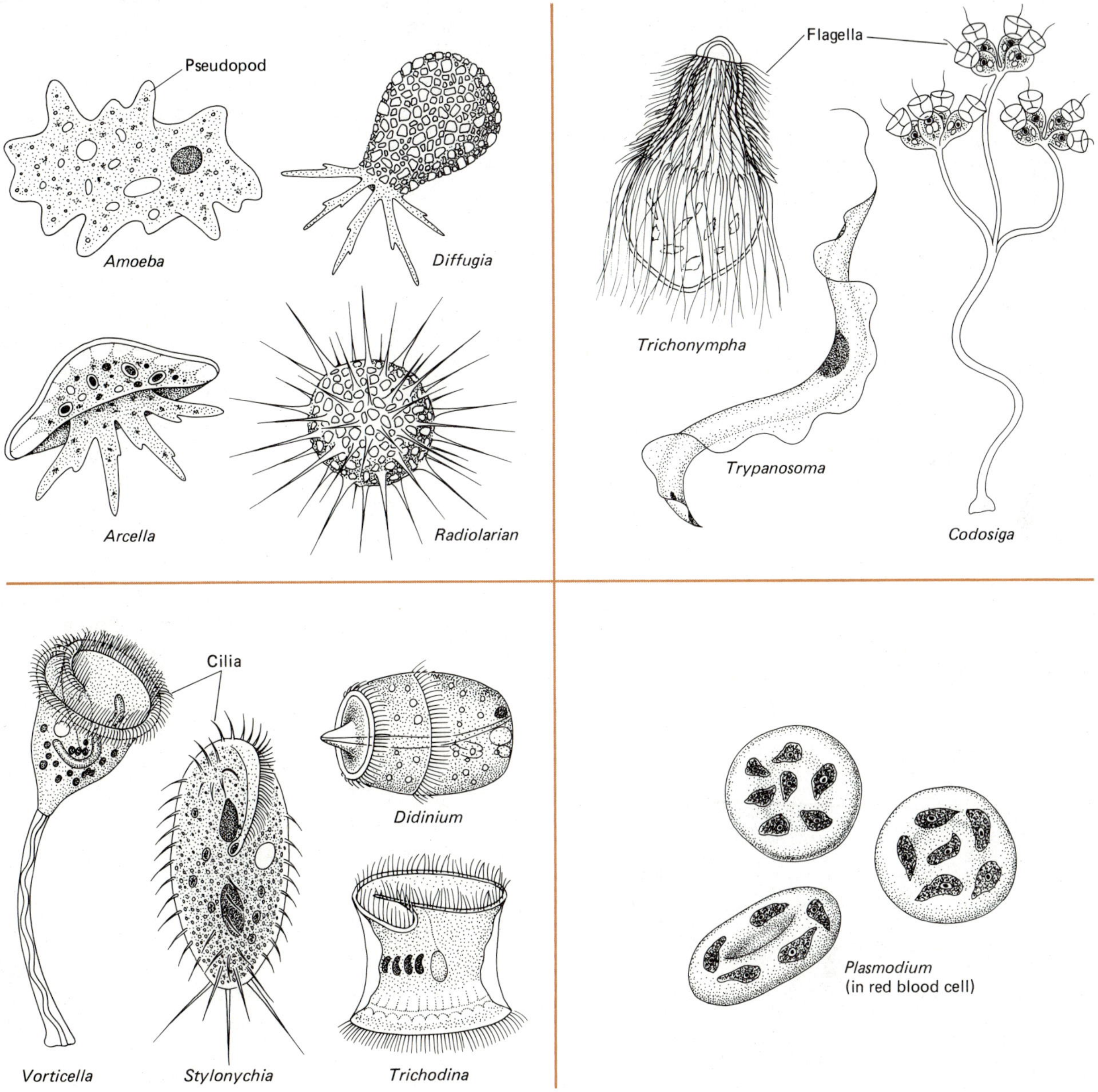

are whole organisms that maintain homeostasis and reproduce themselves. No single cell of the human body can approach this level of independence.

Cells with "Organs." Most protista exhibit marked structural specializations both internally and externally. In fact, parts of the cell can be compared fairly with the organs of multicellular animals. The body of **ciliates** is covered with cilia. Internally the cilia are connected by delicate fibrils that coordinate ciliary movements. Using its cilia, the protozoan swims and directs currents toward a permanent indentation that receives food. In paramecia food vacuoles formed at the base of this oral groove circulate about the cell. Later, indigestible remains are released at a particular point where food vacuoles always merge with the plasma membrane. Not only do ciliates have structures that can be thought of as a subcellular digestive system, but they also have more than one nuclei. And unlike nuclei of other eucaryotes, those of ciliates fall into two classes and have different functions. Such specialization on the subcellular level is characteristic of protista. Although most protista are motile and move by cilia, flagellae, or pseudopodia, a few are
232 not. For example, the **sporozoa** that cause malaria lack special organelles for movement. But these parasites have a highly complex reproductive cycle.

Many protista live in natural bodies of water where the physical support of a skeleton or some external coat is most useful. **Foraminifera,** relatives of the amoebas, are best known for the highly ornamented skeleton that lies just within their cell surfaces. Cytoplasmic projections extend through openings (foramina) in the skeleton. These projections phagocytize food particles and thus nuture the organism. Fossil foraminiferal skeletons (Fig. 16.2) form thick deposits on ocean bottoms. One famous bed of foraminiferal rock makes up the white cliffs of Dover on the English Channel.

FIGURE 16.2 **Foraminiferan Test.** This is really an internal skeleton of an amoeba-like organism.

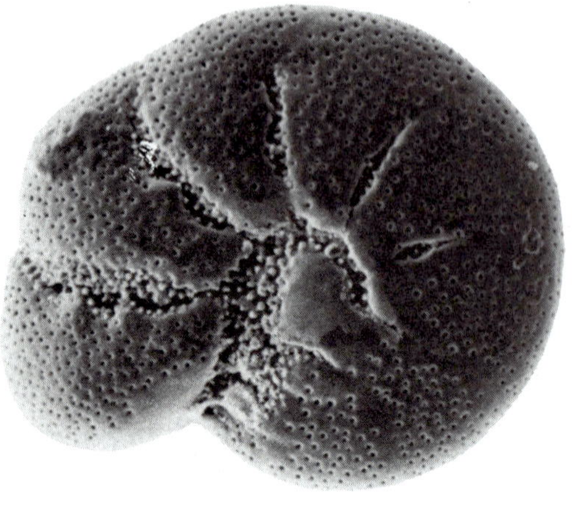

Photosynthetic Protista. Among the plant-like protista are the diatoms and dinoflagellates, which have key roles in aquatic ecosystems. The **dinoflagellates** (Fig. 16.3) are enclosed by a cellulose wall that often forms distinct plates. Due to the positions of their two flagellae, dinoflagellates swim about like slowly spinning tops. Some dinoflagellates produce toxins that are harmful to vertebrates. Many such species contain red pigments, which color the water when the dinoflagellates are abundant. The resulting "red tides" have become a signal that shellfish that feed on the dinoflagellates bear concentrated toxins dangerous to humans.

Unlike the cellulose armor of dinoflagellates, the enclosures of **diatoms** resemble delicately patterned glass boxes. The patterns and shapes of the boxes are species-specific and highly precise (Fig. 16.3). Growth is possible within the rigid boxes that make up the shells only because each box has an inner and an outer half. With cell division, each daughter cell makes a new half shell. One of the daughters makes a smaller half and thus must be a smaller cell (Fig. 16.4). Therefore half the diatoms diminish in size with each generation. This apparent dilemma is solved through sexual reproduction that involves fusion. The resulting larger cell makes an entirely new—and larger—shell. Although most diatoms are free in the water, many have stalks that cling to rocks, driftwood, or other surfaces. Due to the presence of a brownish pigment as well as chlorophylls, we see dense growths of diatoms on aquaria walls as yellow-brown scums.

Within the kingdom protista are organisms that could never fit comfortably into either the plant or the animal kingdom. One such misfit is *Euglena* and its relatives. The euglenids (Fig. 16.3) are photosynthetic, but also have a gullet that can be used to take in organic materials. These protista swim by a flagellum and use a light-sensitive "eye spot" to orient toward light. Euglena are easy to grow; they require only a dilute mineral solution and access to light.

If you cover a dish of euglena with a sheet of aluminum foil and make a tiny hole in the foil, the

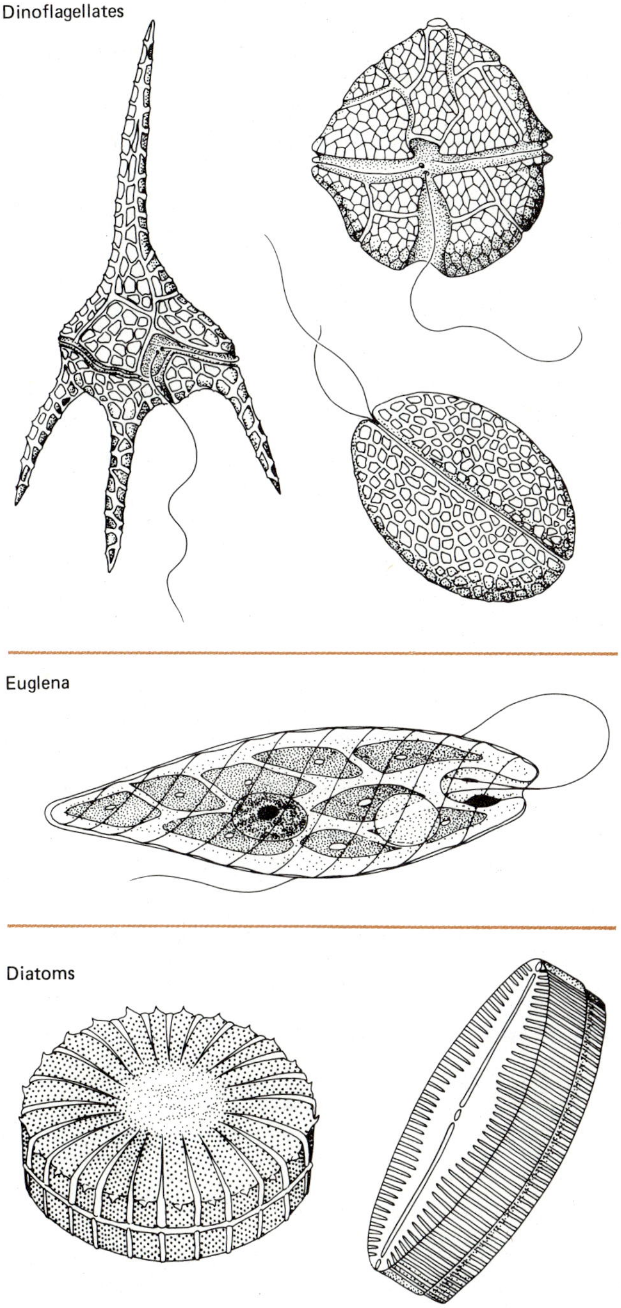

FIGURE 16.3 **Plant-like Protista.**

euglena will soon congregate in the spot of light under the hole. Yet if you keep the culture in the dark and add crushed seeds or other nutrients, the euglena thrive. Some strains may even lose their chlorophyll. One day they are autotrophs like plants, and the next day they are heterotrophs like animals.

A Symbiotic Origin for Eucaryotes? An interesting hypothesis traces eucaryotes to a mutually beneficial association between two or more procaryotes. One kind of procaryote was supposedly engulfed by another and, instead of being digested, survived to the benefit of both. The engulfed procaryote became a membranous organelle of its host. Repetition of this process accounts for several kinds of eucaryote organelles. Recounting some of the supporting facts may make this hypothesis seem more plausible.

Mitochondria□ are cellular dynamos bound by 87
two membrane layers. Without mitochondria, a cell can carry out only glycolysis, the first pathway in glucose metabolism and one that yields but a small percent of the total potential energy. A cell that was limited to glycolysis would gain much by harboring other cells that could complete the breakdown of glucose and share the proceeds. If mitochondria were once independent procaryotes, they must have been surrounded by a plasma membrane. Their outer membrane could belong to the host cell that phagocytized them into a membrane-

FIGURE 16.4 **Diatom Reproduction.** In asexual reproduction, diatoms get smaller with each generation. Sexual reproduction restores the larger size.

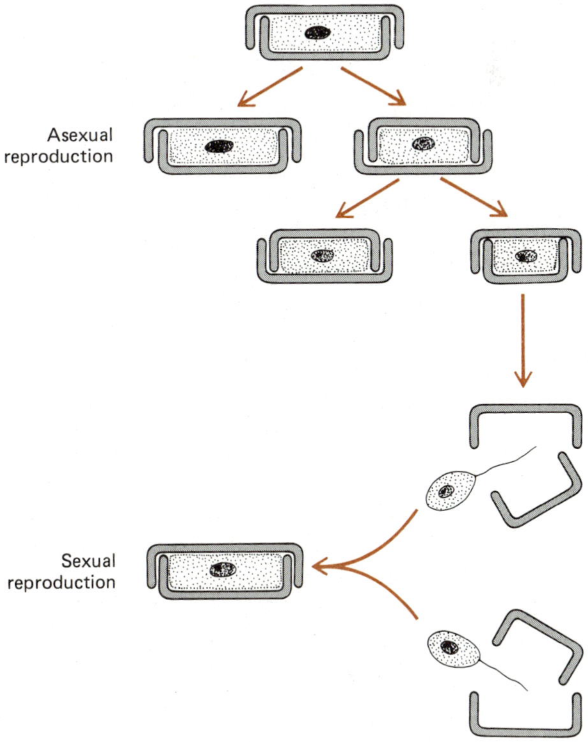

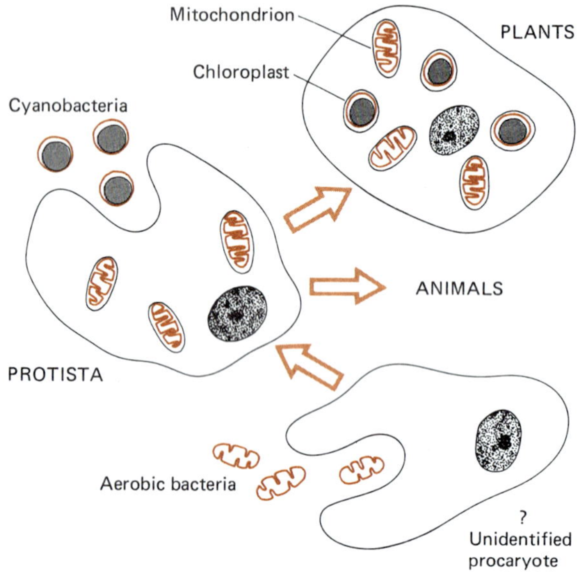

FIGURE 16.5 How Eucaryotes May Have Arisen. The facts behind this hypothesis suggest that one procaryote may have phagocytized others.

bound vacuole (Fig. 16.5). The argument that mitochondria were once independent is supported by the fact that they contain simple DNA strands much like those of bacteria. Ribosomes that resemble those of bacteria are also found in mitochondria. Furthermore, mitochondria reproduce themselves. Except for their intracellular location, mitochondria are much like procaryotes.

Chloroplasts, the photosynthetic organelles of green plants, are also double-membrane organelles containing their own DNA. Obviously any heterotroph that phagocytized and retained an autotrophic one could benefit from an internal source of glucose or other nutrients. The suggestion that one cell could live within another is not new. Hundreds of present-day eucaryotes harbor cells of other species inside their own cells. One example is the corals we'll describe in Chapter 20. Clearly, the evolution of eucaryotes as associations of procaryotic cells is not far-fetched. But neither is it proven.

THE ANIMAL KINGDOM

Although the earliest animals left no recognized fossils, it seems likely that they sorted out microscopic food from marine sediments. Among the several phyla present 650 million years ago, none give evidence of having jaws or any other method of engulfing large prey. Examination of animals showing the simplest organization supports the reasonable hypothesis that animals began by feeding on microorganisms. The opportunities open to motile, multicellular heterotrophs must have been tremendous, for within 150 million years all but one of the major phyla had appeared (Table 16.1).

TABLE 16.1 Geologic Time Scale

PERIODS	MYBP*	LIFE ON EARTH
Quaternary		Humans become dominant species; extinction of many large mammals.
	2.5	
Tertiary		Evolution of modern plant associations, including grasslands; also familiar families of mammals.
	63	
Cretaceous		Appearance of numerous kinds of flowering plants and insects. Last dinosaurs disappear.
	135	
Jurassic		Dinosaurs abundant; first birds. Worldwide gymnosperm forests.
	180	
Triassic		First mammals and first dinosaurs. Spread of gymnosperm forests.
	225	
Permian		Rise of conifers; decline of nonseed plants.
	270	
Pennsylvanian		Coal-producing swamp forests composed of nonseed plants. Earliest conifers. Appearance of reptiles. Giant insects.
	310	
Mississippian		Amphibians dominant land animals; earliest coal-producing swamp forests.
	350	
Devonian		Origin of amphibians from lobe-finned, air-breathing fish; extreme diversity of fish. Earliest insects.
	400	
Silurian		Earliest vascular plants. Reef-building corals common. Earliest land arthropods.
	430	
Ordovician		Early jawless fish; diverse invertebrates.
	500	
Cambrian		All major animal phyla present; many hard-shelled, all marine. Multicellular algae.
	570	
Ediacarian		Several soft-bodied animal phyla present.
	700	
Proterozoic		Origin of eucaryotes.
	3400	

*Million years before present

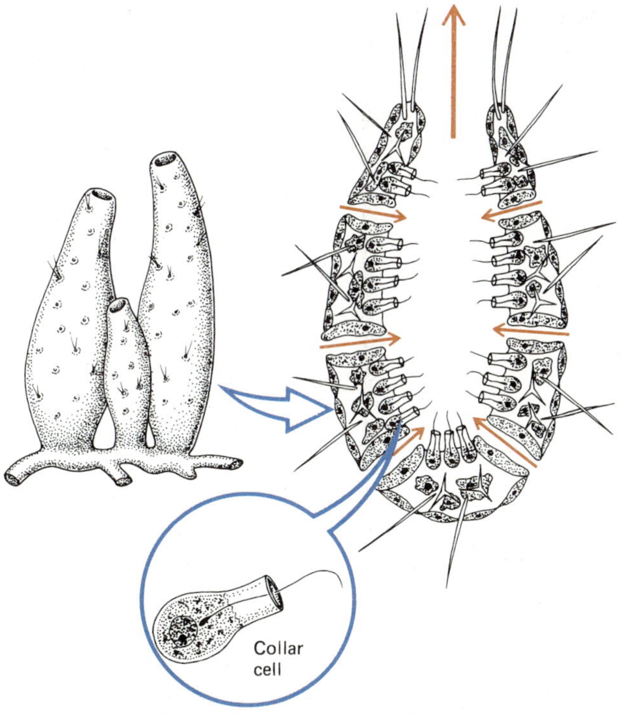

FIGURE 16.6 **Sponges Are Filters.** Flagellated collar cells create water currents that enter through large pores and exit through smaller pores. The collar cells phagocytize microscopic food particles from the water.

No other adaptive radiation□ can compare in scope with the establishment of the animal phyla. We will examine the major phyla briefly and look at their relationships. 345

Sponge Cells Resemble Cooperative Protozoa. It is mainly because of their skeletons that we hear about the simplest animals, the sponges. Some sponges have glassy skeletons, some limey, but those prized for scrubbing are of protein. All these sponge skeletons are cell products. The living sponge cells are arranged around the skeletal components so that they form a giant filter (Fig. 16.6). Within the sponge, flagellated **collar cells** create currents that draw in water through numerous fine pores and expel it through larger pores. As the water passes through the sponge, the collar cells phagocytize microscopic particles and pass nutrients to other cells. Although some sponge cells have special functions, there are no tissues or organs evident. The similarity between the collar cells of sponges and certain protista suggests that sponges originated from flagellated protista. The very simplicity of the filter-feeding sponges may be their greatest advantage. Sponges are so casual in their cellular association that after physical disaggregation the cells can reorganize themselves into irregular little sponges.

FIGURE 16.7 **Sponge.** Filtered water enters the sponge through the large pores.

TABLE 16.2 **Major Animal Phyla**

Sponges (Porifera)

Sac animals (Coelenterates or Cnidaria)
Jellyfish, sea anemones, corals, hydra

Flatworms (Platyhelminthes)
Planaria, flukes, tapeworms

Roundworms (Nematoda)

Wheel animals (Rotifera)

Segmented worms (Annelida)
Earthworms, clam worms, feather worms, leeches

Joint-legged animals (Arthropoda)
Crabs, sow bugs, insects, spiders

Mollusks (Mollusca)
Snails, slugs, oysters, squid

Spiny-skinned animals (Echinodermata)
Starfish, sea urchins, sea cucumbers, brittle stars, sea lilies

Chordates (Chordata)
Sea squirts, lancelets, fish, amphibians, reptiles, birds, mammals

Coelenterates Have a Radial Body Plan and a Sac Gut. Although the coelenterates include **sea anemones, jellyfish,** and other large animals that catch and eat fish, generally the coelenterate uses its tentacles to draw tiny organisms into its mouth. This mouth leads to a cavity where digestion occurs. Undigestible debris is spit back out the mouth. Other than gonads, organs are difficult to define in coelenterates. Nevertheless, coelenterates are highly diversified as a group; they include swimming animals (called **medusae**), as well as animals that adhere to the ocean bottom (**polyps**) (Fig. 16.8). Both forms occur in the life cycles of some species (Fig. 16.9). Note that coelenterate life cycles can be complex and involve asexual as well as sexual reproduction. The embryo of a coelenterate lacks a body cavity and resembles some giant multicellular ciliate. Thus this second relatively simple animal phylum may be traced to possible protistid ancestry.

FIGURE 16.8 **Coelenterates.** (a) This beautiful medusa was photographed using only light from the animal itself. Such bioluminescence involves breakdown of ATP and release of energy as light. (b) These sea anemones are typical polyps. (c–d) Some coelenterates are colonial. Note the numerous small polyps extending from the protective sheaths of these colonies.

(a)

(b)

(c)

(d)

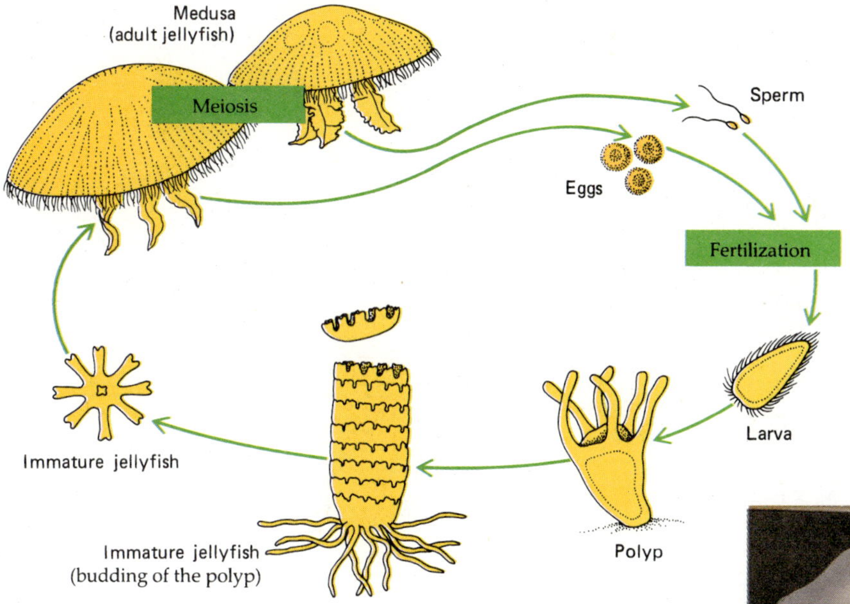

FIGURE 16.9 The Life Cycle of Jellyfish Involves Both Sexual and Asexual Reproduction.

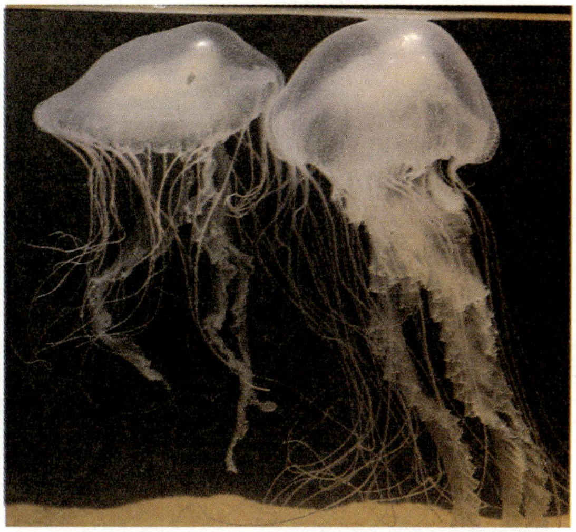

One special characteristic of all coelenterates is the presence of stinging cells (**cnidoblasts**), which they use to paralyze their prey. This single innovation allowed coelenterates to move from filtering out immobile organisms to stunning and engulfing animals. Coelenterates have a **radial symmetry;** that is, they can be divided into several similar pieces much like a pie (Fig. 16.10). Neither head nor tail has any meaning when applied to such animals. Although this is not the ideal organization for a predator, some coelenterates catch good-sized fish.

Flatworms Are the Simplest Bilateral Animals. The flatworms are the simplest animals that can be divided into right and left mirror images. Such **bilaterally symmetrical** animals (Fig. 16.10a.) have a head end that contains sense organs and a centralization of the nervous system known as the **brain.** Normally the head end leads as the animal moves. Flatworms not only exhibit the bilateral symmetry characteristic of higher animals, but also have well-developed organ systems. However, the digestive system is never more than a two-way sac with one opening serving as both mouth and anus. Although some flatworms engulf whole organisms, their digestive system seems best suited to organic debris. You can collect **planaria** (Fig. 16.11a), common freshwater flatworms, by placing pieces of liver in a stream. Check back the following day. If planaria are present, they will be sucking the rotting liver through the tube-like pharynx that enters the middle of their body.

FIGURE 16.10 Symmetry in Animals. Most animals can be divided into two mirror-image parts and thus are said to be bilaterally symmetrical. Radially symmetrical animals can be divided into several equal pie-shape

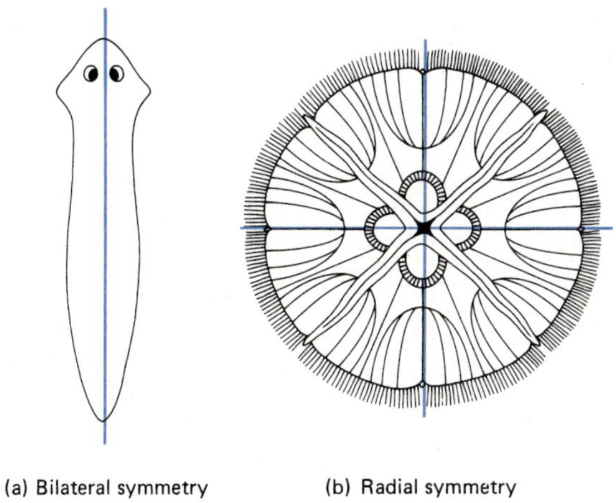

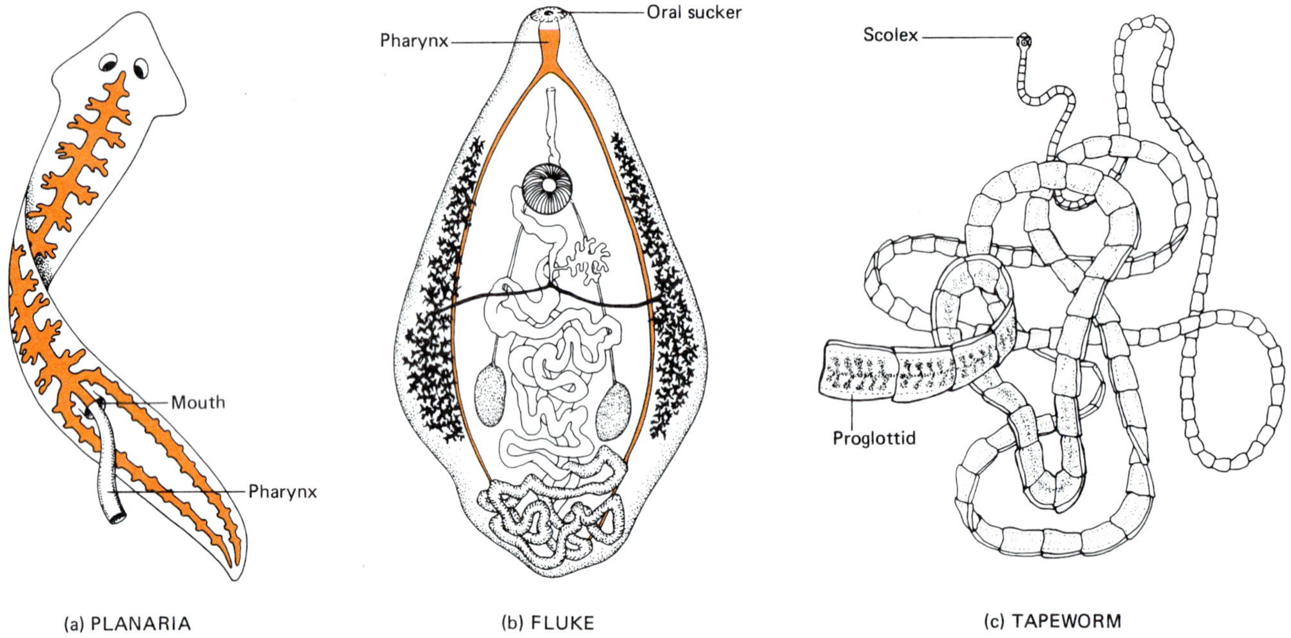

FIGURE 16.11 **Three Types of Flatworms.** The digestive systems are shown in color. The tapeworm has no digestive system. It merely absorbs nutrients through its body surface.

Planaria and many of their relatives use cilia for locomotion. Other than in its cellularity, such a small flatworm is much like a ciliated protistid. Bilateral symmetry and the presence of organ systems identify flatworms with the main line of animal evolution. But their two-way guts and absence of body cavities distinguishes flatworms from the major animal phyla. Considered together, their similarity to ciliates and their body organization has led biologists to place flatworms along the base of the main trunk of animal evolution. That such unimpressive animals are closely related to the ancestors of diverse higher animals is supported by the

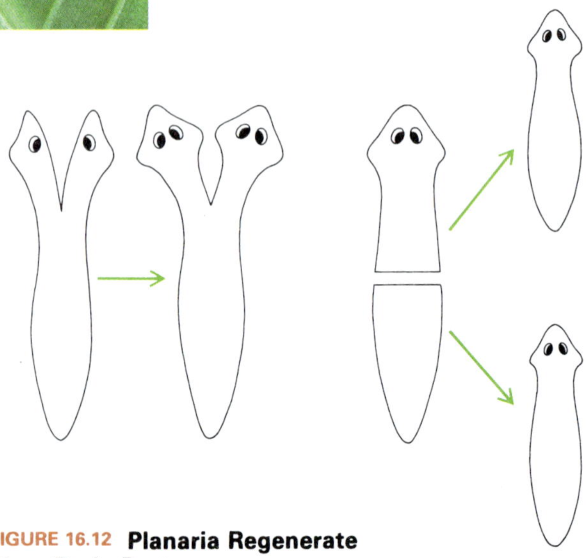

FIGURE 16.12 **Planaria Regenerate New Body Parts.**

FIGURE 16.13 **Nematode or Roundworm.**

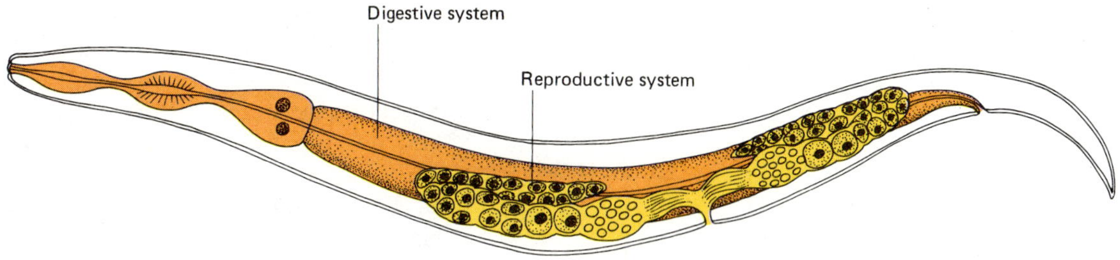

regenerative ability of flatworms. Mutilated flatworms immediately recoup (Fig. 16.12), revealing a fundamental flexibility of organization. The unusual characteristics of the parasitic flatworms known as **flukes** and **tapeworms** (Fig. 16.11 b and c) offer further evidence of flatworms' susceptibility to structural modification.

FIGURE 16.14 **Wheel-Animal.** Rotifers have a wheel organ that creates currents, bringing food to the mouth.

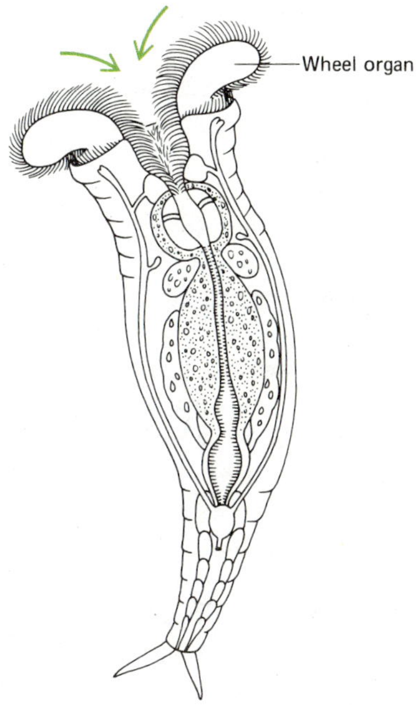

Roundworms and Rotifers Branched Off Early. The roundworms, or **nematodes** (Fig. 16.13) as they are often called, and the rotifers (Fig. 16.14) are highly successful but unusual animals. They share a distinctive characteristic, presence of a particular number of cells in each member of a species. Furthermore, individual cells are unusually large. Both rotifers and roundworms have well-defined organ systems including a complete gut with a mouth and an anus, but neither has the true body cavity characteristic of higher animals.

Rotifers are often known as **wheel animals** because of the constantly moving crown of cilia that collects food and directs it to the mouth. These filter-feeders are present in nearly every drop of pond water. Due to their small size and ciliary crown, beginners often mistake wheel animals for protozoa. Rotifers sometimes anchor themselves and at other times swim erratically. An acellular cuticle forms armor-like plates around the rotifer.

Do All Higher Animals Trace to Burrowing Ancestors?

The one unifying feature of all higher animals is a body cavity lined with connective tissue from the middle embryonic layer (mesoderm). The importance of this cavity has earned it a distinctive name, the **coelom** (Fig. 16.15). To relate this term to your own body, consider that the cavities in which your lungs expand and contract, the space in which your heart is free to beat, and the abdominal cavity in which your intestines move are all parts of your coelom. The coelom has multiple uses, but fundamentally it appears as a component of a hydrostatic skeleton. **Hydrostatic skeletons** derive support from the pressure of muscle contraction on

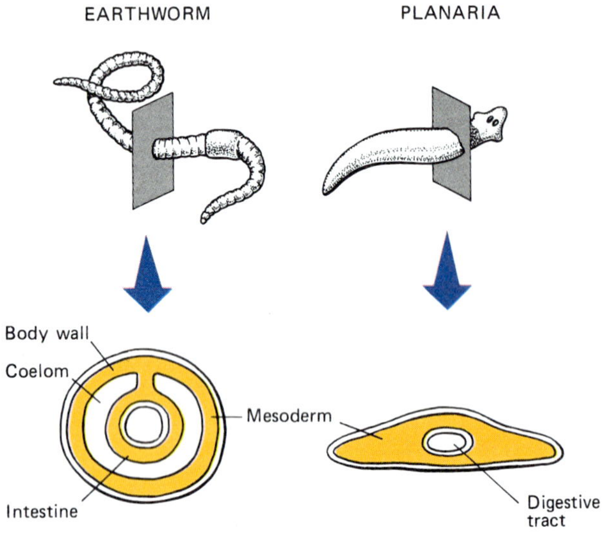

FIGURE 16.15 **The Coelom.** The internal organs of higher animals such as earthworms lie in a body cavity surrounded by mesoderm. Here the internal organs are unaffected by external pressures and can move freely.

fluids confined in the coelom. It is the hydrostatic skeleton that allows various kinds of worms to burrow through soil or soft sediments. In the **earthworm,** the body wall consists of an outer layer of circular muscle and an inner longitudinal muscle layer. Contraction of circular muscle against the coelomic fluid extends the animal in length. Similarly contraction of longitudinal muscle expands the diameter of the worm but shortens it. By using minute bristles to anchor particular body segments against the burrow wall, the earthworm can translate the alternate lengthening and shortening into linear motion.

Hydrostatic skeletons such as that of the earthworm can be used to support movement on surfaces, but they are most useful for burrowing where the entire outside of the body is in contact with solid surroundings. Since the primary function of the coelom is thought to be as part of such a skeleton, the presence of coeloms in all higher animals suggest burrowing-worm ancestors. These primitive worms, ancestral to most of the animal kingdom, may have lived in shifting marine sediments where they grubbed for buried nutrients. If these worms lacked hard parts, they could have left only fossil burrows. Structures interpreted as fossil worm burrows occur in the same rocks harboring the oldest identified animal fossils. It appears reasonable that segmented worms with hydrostatic skeletons were ancestral to most of the animals we know today.

Annelids: Segmented Worms. The segmentation 133 157
present in annelids such as earthworms involves not only compartmentation of the coelom, but also repeating sets of excretory tubules, blood vessels, and nerve ganglia. The basic simplicity of such a body plan makes regeneration of lost body regions a relatively simple matter. Some segmented worms also reproduce asexually by first fragmenting into pieces and then regenerating missing parts.

Although earthworms are important in gardens, bait shops, and biology laboratories, they are not the most representative annelids. For such an example we turn to the **polychaetes** (Fig. 16.16). **Paired lobes** on each segment bear numerous **bristles** (*chaeta;* hence *poly*chaeta). The lobes serve as primitive appendages, either for crawling or to draw water currents through the burrows. Diets vary from that of the **fan worm,** which filters microorganisms from the water to that of the carnivorous **bloodworm.** Neither the polychaetes, nor the earthworms and their relatives, nor the parasitic annelids we call **leeches** are primitive burrowing worms. But the annelid body plan suggests such an ancestor.

Armor for a Free-moving Existence. In places where the ocean bottom is solid, animals have many options other than that of burrowing beneath the surface. About a hundred million years after the first animals appeared, many new groups came on the scene. Perhaps the environment changed, for a number of the new phyla abandoned the protection of soft sediments in favor of lives on the surface or in the water above. Many did so with the evolution of armor. Yet these animals retained the coelom, and most show evidence of segmentation.

Closest to the annelids are nearly a million species of jointed-legged animals known as **arthropods.** A chitinous armour covers all external arthropod surfaces and folds inward, where it provides internal support and muscle attachment. A **waxy cuticle** covers the **chitinous external skeleton** of arthropods, reducing passage of water. Such a rigid external skeleton requires joints. These occur between body segments and at characteristic points in the limbs. From the **jointed appendages** comes
the phylum's name: *arthro-* (joint) *pod* (foot). 10 137 158 176 206

The diversity of arthropods defies any simple list. **Spiders, insects, millipedes, centipedes,** and **crustaceans** such as crabs and barnacles are a few

(a) (b)

FIGURE 16.16 **Polychaetes.** (a) Each segment of this worm bears a pair of fleshy, bristly appendages. The thread-like appendages on the anterior end are gills and feeding tentacles. Normally this worm lives in a tube with only its gills and tentacles extended. (b) Some tube-dwelling polychaetes bear fan-like structures they use to collect tiny floating plants and animals. This worm built its tube in a coral colony.

of the better-known arthropods. Although these are the product of a number of adaptive radiations, there is evidence that the phylum contains descendants of two quite different ancestral worms and should be divided. One stem of arthropod evolution produced the spiders, crustaceans, and the trilobites. **Trilobites** are long extinct but once numerous early arthropods whose legs were branched into two parts (Fig. 16.17). One branch was used for walking and the second served some other function, such as gas exchange. We see this pattern retained in present-day spiders and crustaceans, but centipedes, millipedes, and insects lack evidence of this primitive branched limb. Thus the evolution of an exoskeleton may have occurred independently in these two lines. Although the obvious advantage of an exoskeleton is protection against predators, it may have been more important to these animals as the basis for movement. Rigid appendages with well-formed joints can be adapted for swimming, feeding, and other activities that require precision and coordination.

Mollusks: A Shell and a Foot. Although not ob-
177 vious in either the squid□ or the octopus, shells and feet are primitive molluscan characteristics. The single molluscan **foot** first served to allow the animal to crawl like a snail over solid surfaces. The foot was later adapted to other uses (Fig. 16.18). The **shell,** a secretion of an epithelial **mantle** layer, protects the internal organs. These are set aside as a **visceral mass,** perhaps to allow more freedom for contraction of the muscular foot. Mollusks also have a small coelom and four pairs of ganglia that are possible evidence of segmentation.

Embryonic Patterns Provide the Key to Relationships. The relationship of mollusks to annelids is based on the nearly identical structure of their larvae. As we pointed out earlier,□ development pro- 299
vides strong clues to historical relationships. All coelomates that we've mentioned so far share certain similar embryonic patterns that link them closely to one another. As shown in Fig. 16.19, the blastopores of annelid and mollusk embryos develop into the mouth. Hence this group is known as the **protostomes:** *proto* (first) *stome* (mouth). In the second major coelomate line, the one to which vertebrates belong, the blastopore becomes the anus and the mouth forms later on the opposite end. These animals are called **deuterostomes:** *deutero* (second) *stome* (mouth).

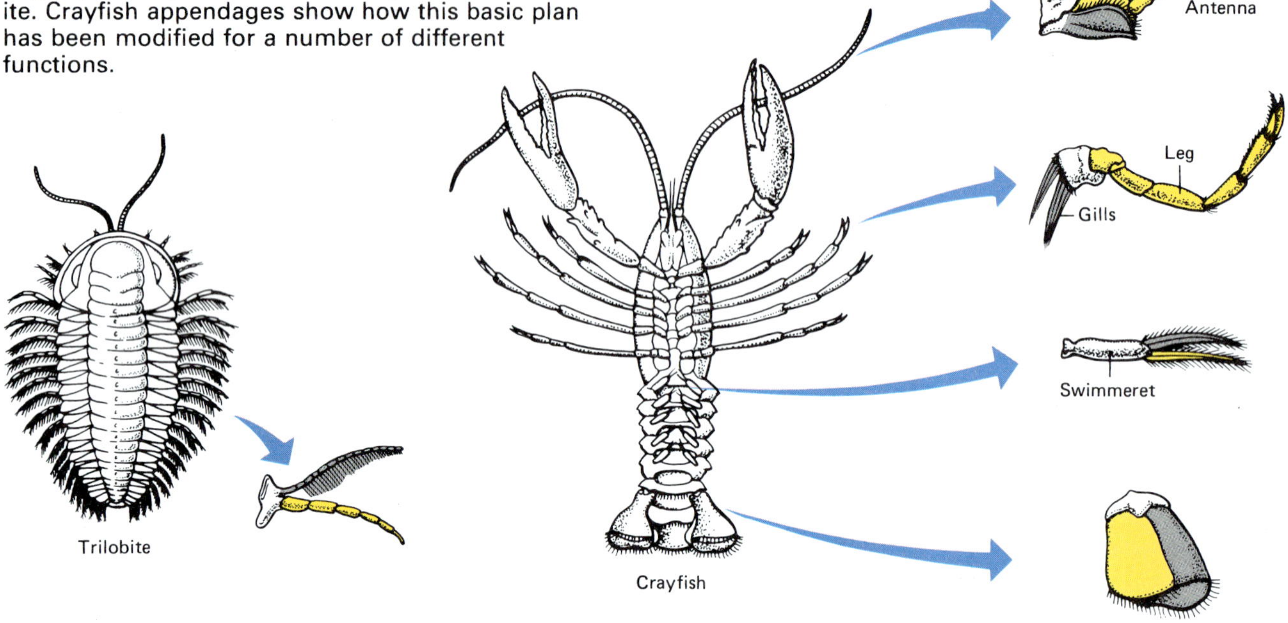

FIGURE 16.17 **Branched Appendages Are Good Raw Material for Specialization.** Primitive arthropod appendages probably had two branches, as in this trilobite. Crayfish appendages show how this basic plan has been modified for a number of different functions.

FIGURE 16.18 **Mollusk Forms.**

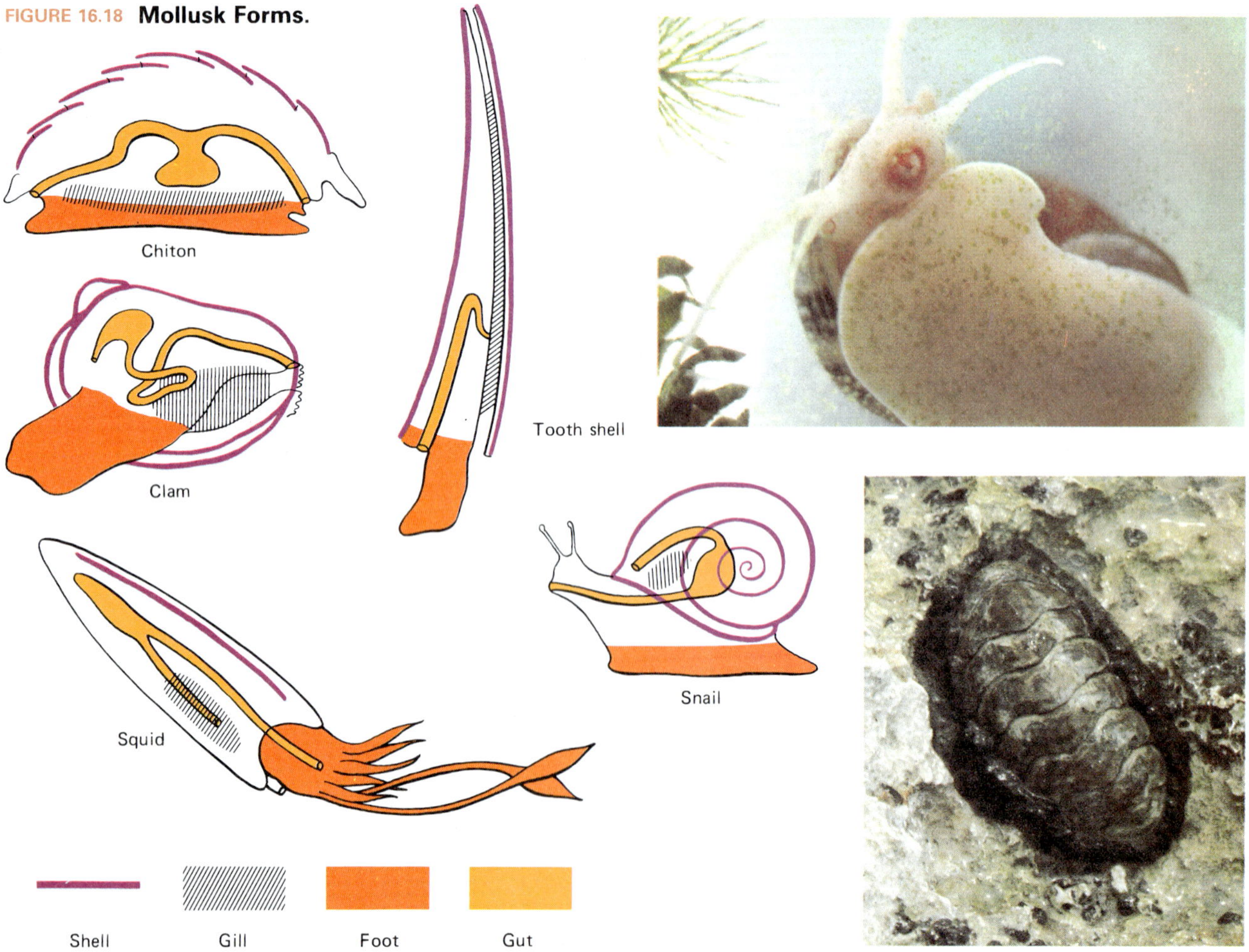

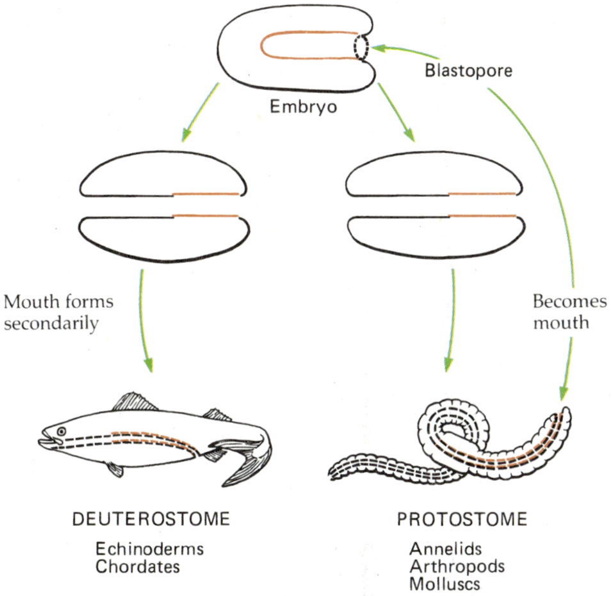

FIGURE 16.19 **Embryonic Patterns Divide Higher Animals.** The embryonic orientation differs in the two major animal groups. In one group the blastopore marks the front end of the animal; in the second group the blastopore marks the rear end.

Echinoderms: Protruding Skeletons Make Spiny Skins. Echinoderms (Fig. 16.20) make up the only major deuterostome phylum other than our own. The echinoderms are coelomates but give no evidence of segmentation. Like ourselves, echinoderms have a jointed calcareous internal skeleton. This skeleton lies so close to the surface that it forms spines on sea urchins and starfish and appears to make up the whole body of a brittle star. An even more bizarre characteristic is the **water vascular system** of echinoderms. This system ter-

FIGURE 16.20 **Echinoderms.** (a) The vermilion starfish preys on soft coelenterates that live on muddy bottoms. (b) Basketstars filter microscopic organisms from the water. (c) Sea cucumbers are also filter-feeders. This species occurs in densities of thousands of animals per square meter. In between the spines of the large purple sea urchin (d) are delicate red tube feet.

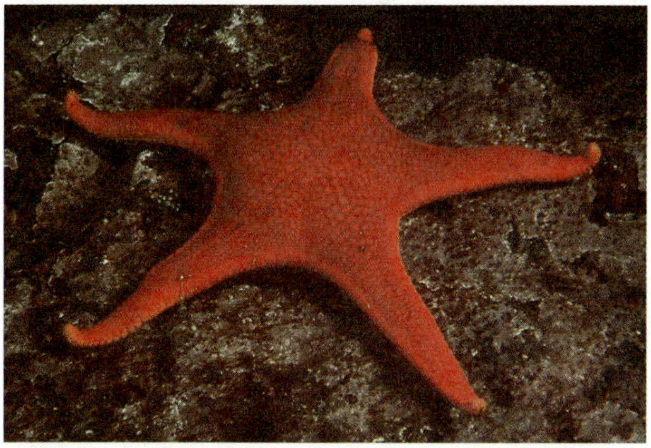
(a)

(b)

(c)

(d)

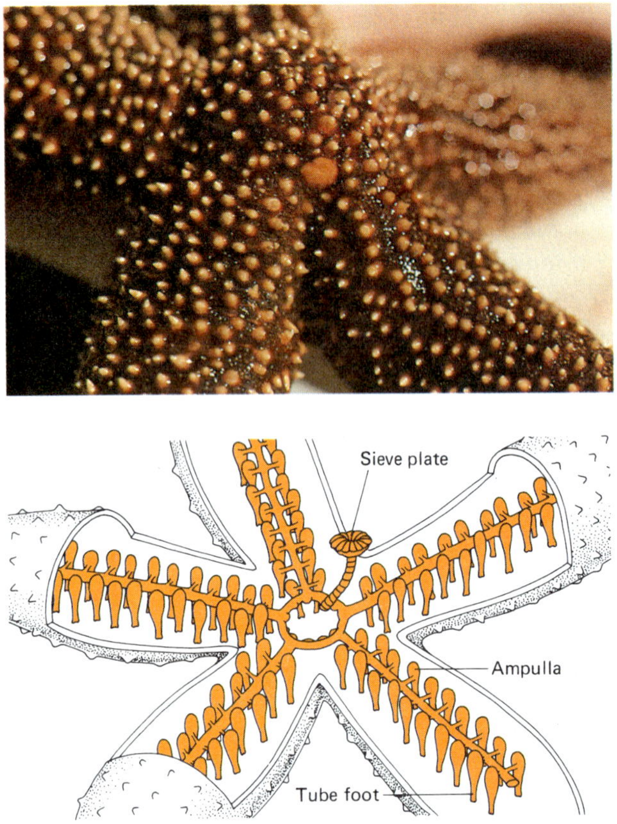

FIGURE 16.21 Water Vascular System of a Starfish. This special organ system of echinoderms is used for locomotion. Because this system is filled with water, contraction of the ampullae extends the tube feet. Then, when the ampullae relax, they draw fluid from the tube feet creating a suction cup on the bottom of each foot.

minates in **tube feet** (Fig. 16.21), which serve as a means of both locomotion and food collection. Sea lilies filter out small food particles with their tube feet, while starfish can open clam shells with theirs.

Chordates: Our Phylum. At last we arrive at the chordates, the phylum to which we and our many fellow **vertebrates** belong, only to find that we share it with two decidedly minor groups: the **sea squirts** and their relatives, and the **lancelets** (Fig. 16.22). The fact is that all three groups share evidence of

- □ a hollow nervous system located on the dorsal side of the body,□ 302
- 302 □ a notochord,□
- 299 □ pharyngeal slits□ whether or not there are gills.

Both sea squirts and lancelets are filter feeders and this is also thought to have been true of the earliest vertebrates. They were jawless fish that swam along the bottom sucking up food like vacuum cleaners. Jaws are derived from the skeletal elements that primitively supported a gill basket used for gas exchange and food collection (Fig. 16.22).

Vertebrates show not only the coelom of ancestral burrowing worms, but also extensive segmentation. The segments do not include divisions of the coelom, but repeating units of structure are evident in the **vertebrae** (backbones), in the paired spinal nerves,□ and in the arrangement of skeletal 170
muscle, especially in fish (Fig. 16.22). The flexibility that results from segmentation is so important to the swimming of fish that some biologists believe the first vertebrates must have appeared in streams or rivers where swimming was essential to fight the current. Fish are the most successful vertebrates in terms of both numbers of species and individuals. Biologists recognize seven different classes, of which the sharks and their relatives are only one example. Also characteristic of the vertebrates is a large and effective nervous system housed in a **skull.**

Terrestrial Adaptations

The major land animals are the insects and the vertebrates. Insects appeared about 300 million years ago, looking not unlike some of the forms present today. We know little about the evolutionary history of insects, but the presence of **tracheae**□ is an 137
obvious adaptation to breathing air. The arthropod exoskeleton is well adapted to support, and the outer waxy coat helps prevent evaporation.

In contrast to that of the insects, the history of vertebrates is known in detail. As mentioned earlier, the first land vertebrates were descendants of air-breathing fish.□ These early land-dwellers were 27
clumsy animals with limbs ill-suited for land. They resembled neither the frog, which so many people think of as a typical amphibian, nor the frog tadpole. Neither were they much like salamanders. But they did share with these surviving amphibians the habit of laying shell-less eggs in water. Because of this dependence on water, amphibians are not truly terrestrial.

Amniotes: Truly Terrestrial Vertebrates. From these early amphibians evolved the reptiles that finally conquered land. The internal fertilization

FIGURE 16.22 **Phylum Chordata.**

and shelled eggs of the early reptiles were only part of their key to success on dry land. Early in their development, reptilian embryos produce a series of embryonic membranes. One of these membranes, the **amnion** (Fig. 16.23), contains a fluid that continuously bathes the embryo. Such embryonic membranes are present not only around reptilian embryos, but also around those of birds and mammals. Amniotic fluid is one secret of our terrestrial success.

Bird eggs differ little from those of reptiles. Indeed it is often said that birds are only feathered reptiles. (But what a difference those feathers make!) Despite the anatomical similarity among birds, nearly 9000 separate species exist.

Whether or not **mammals** represent a single evolutionary line is open to argument. Although

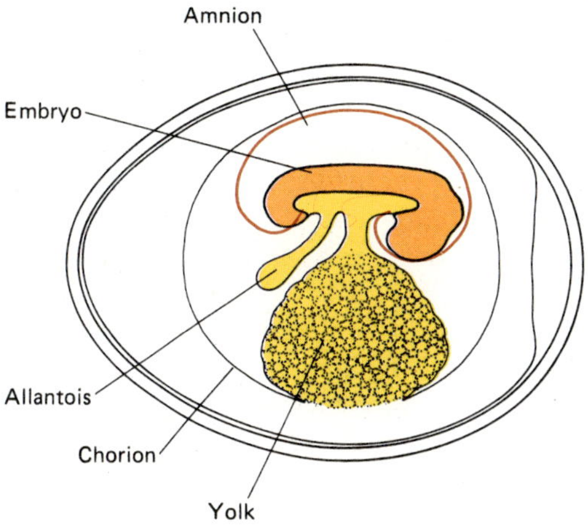

FIGURE 16.23 **The Embryonic Membranes of a Bird.**

all are hairy and warm-blooded, and all nurse their young, their reproductive patterns divide them into three distinct groups. Each of these may derive from a separate reptilian ancestor. The **monotremes** lay eggs much like bird eggs, yet after the young hatch they lick milk secreted by modified sweat glands on their mother's belly. Monotremes such as the **duckbilled platypus** are biological curiosities, rare and endangered. **Marsupial** mammals secrete no shells around their eggs, and the embryos remain for a few days in the uterus. Before nutrient demands become excessive, the young are born. They are so immature that they can barely crawl to the pouch (marsupium), where they attach to a teat and remain for a long time. People generally associate marsupials with Australia because most native Australian mammals are marsupials. However, marsupials are numerous in South America as well, and are represented in North America by the **opossum** (Fig. 14.12). In the third group of mammals the young develop in the uterus, where they are nurtured through a **placenta.** This group includes not only humans, but also the overwhelming majority of mammals. Nutrition through the placenta and protection in the uterus are highly successful reproductive adaptations.

THE PLANT KINGDOM

As you already know, plants (Table 16.3) are generally nonmotile, eucaryotic photosynthesizers with cell walls rich in cellulose. In addition to the familiar plants of our everyday environment, this definition includes the *algae.* Algae usually lack the cell differentiation found in the so-called "higher plants." Other than this, the algae have little in common with one another. Even the three major groups—the reds, the browns, and the greens (Fig. 16.24)—are so diverse that each may have evolved from a separate ancestor. The fossil record is of little help, but it seems likely that some algal groups are ancient, perhaps as old or older than the animals.

The **red algae** are mainly seaweeds that grow as flat sheets, branched filaments, or calcareous crusts resembling daubs of colored mortar. Their colors range from red to green to black, but all contain unusual reddish and bluish pigments otherwise found only in the cyanobacteria. These pigments have an auxiliary role in photosynthesis, for they absorb the light rays that penetrate water most deeply. Thus red algae can thrive at greater depths than can other algae. Because red algae share such pigments only with the cyanobacteria, it has been suggested that red algae trace to an independent symbiotic origin and have no direct relationship with other plants. The total absence of motility (even the sperm can only float passively) is further evidence of the unique nature of red algae. In addition to this, their polysaccharides are so unusual as to be nondigestible by the enzymes of terrestrial organisms.

TABLE 16.3 **Some Major Divisions of the Plant Kingdom**

Red algae (Rhodophyta)
Brown algae (Phaeophyta)
Green algae (Chlorophyta)
Mosses and liverworts (Bryophyta)
Vascular plants (Tracheophyta)
Clubmosses (Lycopsida)
Horsetails (Sphenopsida)
Ferns (Filicopsida)
Cycads and seed ferns (Cycadopsida)
Conifers and relatives (Coniferopsida)
Flowering plants (Angiospermopsida)
Monocots (Monocotyledonae)
Dicots (Dicotyledonae)

The **brown algae,** another seaweed group especially common along cool coasts, include a variety of species such as rockweed and the giant kelps. Some of the largest browns show considerable tissue differentiation; still, the level fails to approach that of higher plants. Like the red algae, the browns are distinguished by unusual pigments and polysaccharides. But the green algae are a different story.

Green Algae: The Ancestors of Land Plants

Green algae occur in a variety of forms ranging from single cells (Fig. 1.5a) to chains or colonies of cells, to complex sheets (Fig. 16.24a) and even tubes. Some kinds occur in fresh water, some are marine, and some form scums on damp soil or tree trunks. Despite their divergent ways, all green algae employ the same kinds of chlorophyll and all store carbohydrates as starch. They share these biochemical traits with all higher plants. For this reason it is believed that green algae are ancestors of the mosses, ferns, seed plants, and other lesser-known higher plants.

Just as algae have diverse forms, pigments, and environments, they likewise have diverse life cycles.

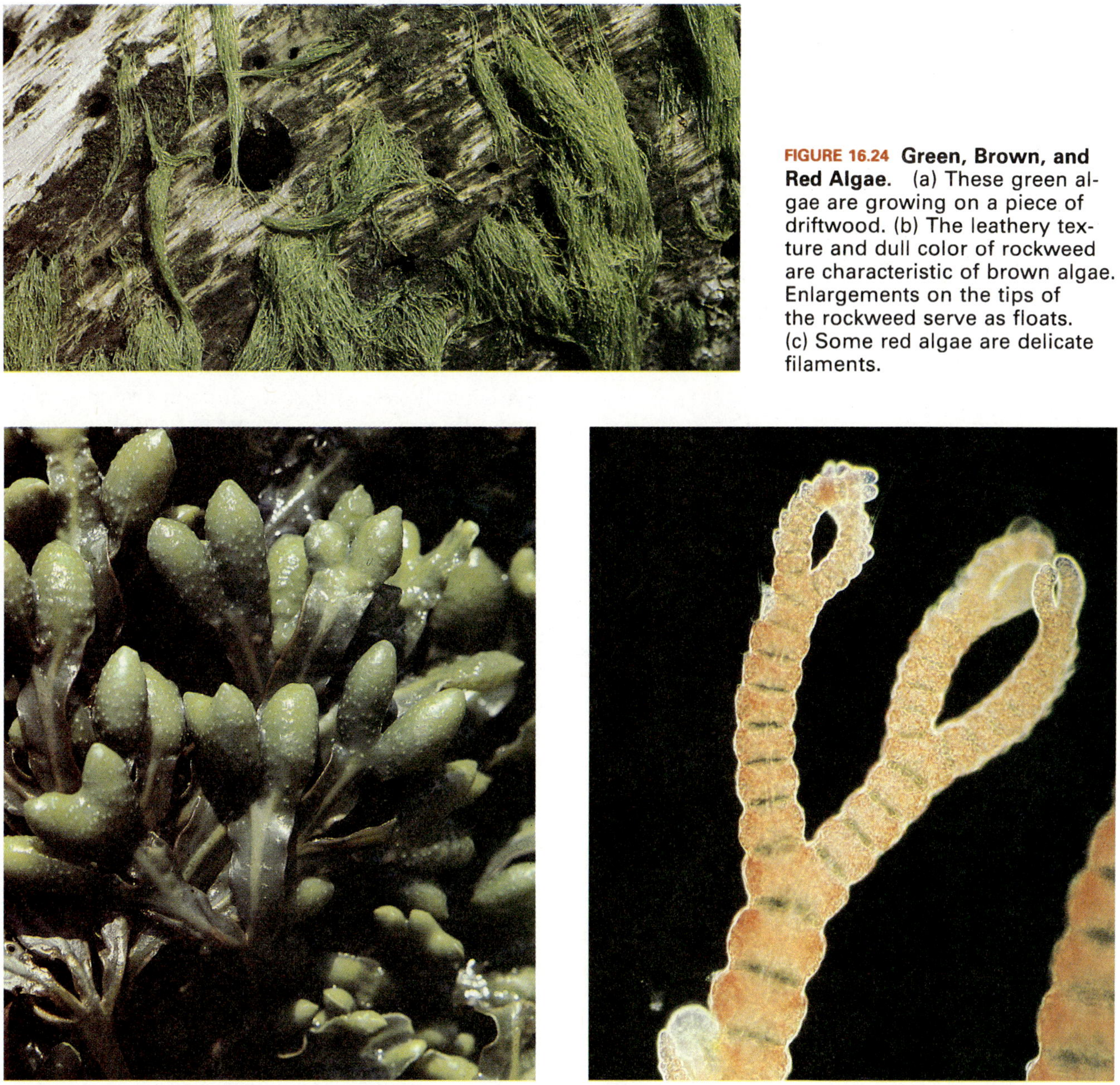

FIGURE 16.24 Green, Brown, and Red Algae. (a) These green algae are growing on a piece of driftwood. (b) The leathery texture and dull color of rockweed are characteristic of brown algae. Enlargements on the tips of the rockweed serve as floats. (c) Some red algae are delicate filaments.

This is true of red and brown algae, but the life cycles of the green algae are especially interesting because of their relationship to higher plants. The knowledge of reproductive cycles is so important to the understanding of higher plants that we will review the **life-cycle concept** before continuing our plant discussion.

As you saw in Chapter 11, most animals (including ourselves) are diploid throughout most of their life cycle. Diploid animal bodies contain cells that undergo meiosis producing haploid gametes that fuse into a diploid zygote. Beginning with the diploid zygote, mitosis and growth yield the diploid adult:

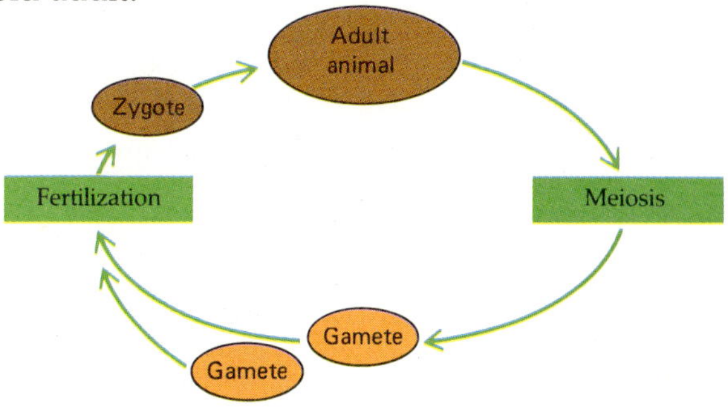

Even such animals as jellyfish, which have asexual stages in their life cycles, follow this pattern. All cells except gametes are diploid. In plants, this is not necessarily the case. Many plants have a multicellular haploid phase as well as a multicellular diploid phase. Such a plant life cycle may be diagrammed like this:

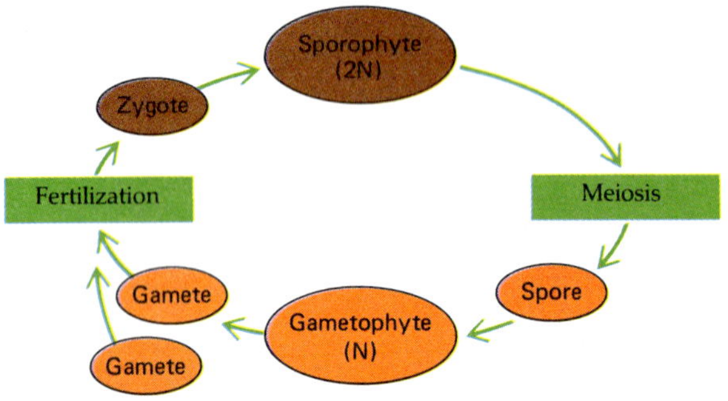

Because the multicellular haploid phase gives rise to gametes, it is known as the **gametophyte** (gamete plant). It follows that the multicellular, diploid **sporophyte** undergoes meiosis and produces spores.

Sea lettuce (*Ulva*) is a green alga of coastal waters that illustrates well the alternation of gametophyte and sporophyte generations. Some sea lettuce plants are diploid and others are haploid. Only microscopic study can distinguish the two plant types. Diploid plants undergo meiosis (Fig. 16.25), yielding haploid cells called spores. These spores germinate into cells that divide by mitosis to form haploid plants. Such haploid plants produce gametes by mitosis. The haploid gametes fuse into diploid zygotes that divide by mitosis and form diploid plants. The gametophyte and sporophyte are not of equal size in most plants. For example, Fig. 16.26 shows the life cycle of *Ulothrix,* a filamentous green alga. Note that the largest stage is the gametophyte (the haploid plant) and that the sporophyte is a single cell that undergoes meiosis.

The fossil record sheds not a bit of light on the origin of plant life cycles that involve an alternation of gamete-producing and spore-producing generations. Biologists speculate that the advantage of spore production lies in the possibility of selection for resistance to environmental factors. Gametes that must be capable of fertilization cannot have a particularly resistant coat. But since spores never fuse, they can have a waxy coat and become indigestible or resistant to dry conditions, or assume some other characteristic that enables them to survive for long periods in an inhospitable environment. Although spores are part of the sexual life cycle, their special function is to disperse the plant species far and wide. At least, this is the major function of spores in vascular plants such as ferns (Fig. 16.27). Before studying the vascular plants, review what you have learned about life cycles. Note that all life cycles, plant and animal, are fundamentally the same. The basic difference is that the following characteristics are peculiar to plants:

- Mitosis can occur in both haploid and diploid cells.
- Meiosis can produce not gametes, but haploid cells known as spores. These cells can

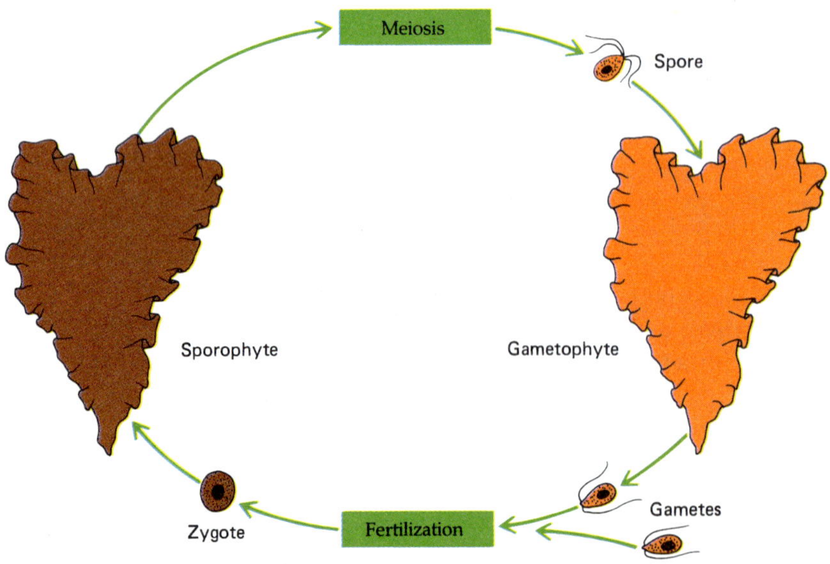

FIGURE 16.25 ***Ulva* Life Cycle.**

divide by mitosis and produce multicellular stages.

- Gametes can be the immediate product of mitosis in haploid cells.

Most Land Plants Are Vascular

Except for a few minor groups, land plants are distinguished by

- embryos (protected diploid tissue resulting from fertilization), and
- specialized supporting and conducting cells forming vascular tissue.

Although we know little about the transition of plants from water to land, **vascular tissue** was a crucial innovation. Much of the functional portion of vascular tissue consists of the walls of dead cells. These thick walls support the plant, obviously a much more difficult task in air than in water. Many of the thick cell walls are porous; stacks of such cells serve as pipes to carry water and minerals from the soil to the phytosynthetic tissue that lies above the surface in sunlight. Because not all tissues are exposed to light, nutrients must be distributed by the vascular tissue, as well.

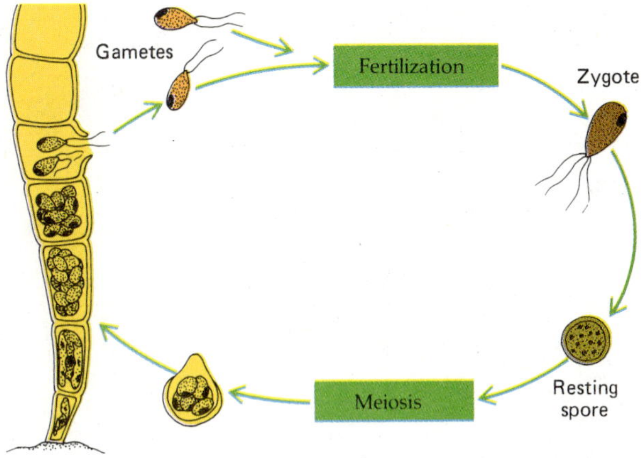

FIGURE 16.26 ***Ulothrix* Life Cycle.**

Drying out is the biggest threat to land organisms. As a general rule, the smaller the organism, the greater the threat. Single-celled stages, such as spores, are especially vulnerable. It isn't surprising that wax-coated spores occur among the oldest plant fossils.

The earliest land plants consisted only of branched stems, parts of which extended into the ground and parts into the air. But by the time ver-

FIGURE 16.27 **Fern Life Cycle.** In some ferns there are two separate kinds of gametophytes; male ones, which produce sperm, and female ones, which produce eggs.

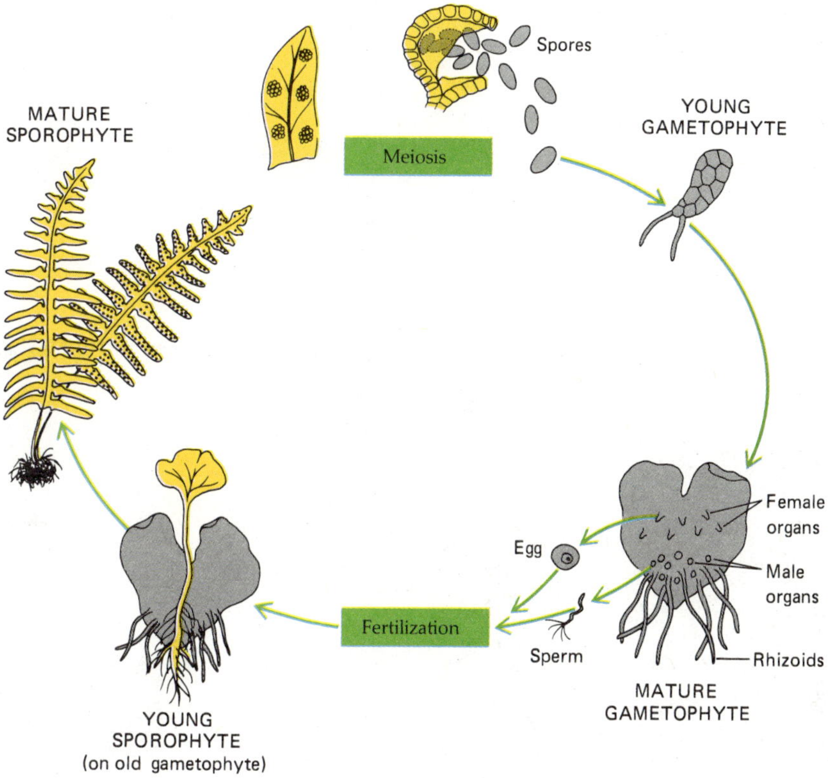

(a)

(b)

(c)

(a)

(b)

◀ FIGURE 16.28 **Primitive Vascular Plants.** Primitive vascular plants have free-living gametophytes and never produce seed. Horsetails (a) bear spores on strobili—cone-like structures at the tip of the stems. Clubmosses (b) also bear spores on strobili. Fern spores develop either on ordinary leaves in brown spots or masses (c), or on leaves so highly modified that they look like brown clubs.

tebrates invaded land, the support afforded by vascular tissue had permitted some land plants to achieve tree size. Among these early vascular plants were giant relatives of present-day **horsetails** (Fig. 16.28). Such plants have stems and tiny leaves but no true roots. Other early forest members belonged to the **clubmosses** (Fig. 16.28), the oldest plant group to have stems, roots, and leaves. The horsetails and clubmosses, like the **ferns,** have free-living gametophyte and sporophyte generations. Such life cycles involve external fertilization and hence require surface water. Primitive as they may seem, these plants were extremely successful; this is evident from the abundance of their fossil remains in **coal deposits.** And even during these early times, some plants reproduced by seeds just as most plants do today. We will discuss the advantage of seed life cycles shortly. But since we mentioned clubmosses, perhaps you are curious about where the true mosses fit into the picture.

Mosses, liverworts, and other **bryophytes** share many biochemical characteristics with green algae and vascular plants. However, bryophytes have no vascular tissue, and their cell walls lack **lignin,** the component that strengthens the cell walls of vascular plants. The weak bryophyte cell walls cannot provide the support necessary for large upright structures. As a result, all bryophytes are limited to a few inches in height. Like seed plants, bryophytes have embryos. In bryophytes these embryos remain attached to the gametophytes, where they grow into sporophytes (Fig. 16.29). Some moss sporophytes are as large—or larger—than the gametophytes that support them. Exactly how mosses fit in is unclear. They may represent an independent experiment in plant evolution tracing directly to the green algae.

◀ FIGURE 16.29 **Bryophytes.** This clump of leaf-like liverworts (a) is composed largely of gametophytes. The sporophytes are yet to develop. Each moss sporophyte capsule (b) contains a multitude of spores. The brown sporophytes are growing from gametophyte tissue not shown in the picture.

Seed Plants Dominate the Land Today

Seeds are one key to the exploitation of the myriad ecological niches filled by plants today. The dormant embryos within seeds are more or less resistant to heat, cold, and drying. Such embryos can nearly suspend life processes for months or years and then sprout immediately when conditions are right. Seed plants are always ready to take advantage of the opportunity to grow and reproduce.

Naked Seed Plants. Although seed plants have both gametophytes and sporophytes as do ferns, the gametophytes are even smaller and are difficult to find in the mass of the sporophyte tissue (Fig. 16.30). In **conifers,** such as cedar, spruce, fir, and pine (Fig. 16.31), the female gametophytes result from meiosis in tissue at the base of cone scales. One of the four cells is a megaspore that divides by mitosis and differentiates into a **female gametophyte,** which never leaves the cone. Certain cells of female gametophytes develop into eggs. Male gametophytes are pollen grains that trace to meiosis in other cones. Pollen is carried by the wind and widely scattered. When a pollen grain touches secretions of a female gametophyte, it grows an elongated pollen tube that penetrates the female gametophyte. A sperm nucleus of the male gametophyte fertilizes the egg of the female gametophyte. From this fusion arises a **diploid embryo,** the young **sporophyte.** The embryo, along with food stores from the female gametophyte and surrounding tissues from the parent sporophyte, forms the **seed.**

As is obvious from Fig. 16.30, the seeds of conifers are borne where they are exposed to insects and other seed-eaters. Conifers share this vulnerability with other more primitive seed plants, such as the now-extinct seed ferns, the cycads, and the ginkos. Because of their naked seeds, these four groups are known as **gymnosperms:** *gymno* (naked) *sperm* (seed). The fact that the seeds of gymnosperms are readily accessible to insects may explain why gymnosperms have been largely replaced by flowering plants that protect their seeds within fruit.

Flowering Plants Are Highly Successful. Flowering plants include all garden vegetables, fruit trees, and all lawn and forest trees except conifers and the ginko. Hay, cereal, and pasture crops are

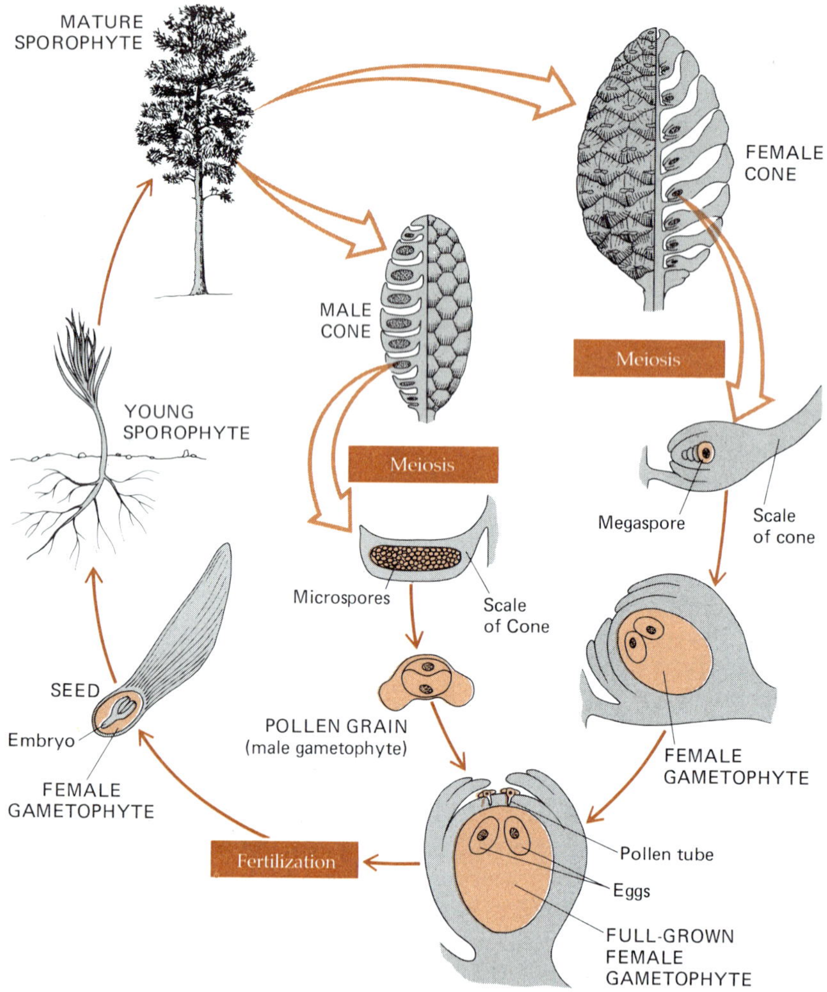

FIGURE 16.30 Life Cycle of a Pine Tree.

also flowering plants. So are most house plants, except for the ferns. If you are wondering where the flowers are on some of these examples, don't be concerned. They do flower, at least occasionally; but many, such as the grasses, bear inconspicuous flowers.

Collectively the flowering plants are known as the **angiosperms,** a name that emphasizes the **vessel elements** in their vascular tissue (*angion* = vessel; *sperma* = seed). Because of the importance of angiosperms, most of the next chapter is devoted to them. We will discuss only their life cycles here.

As in gymnosperms, the **pollen** grains of flowering plants are male gametophytes. But instead of arising in a cone, the pollen develops inside **anthers** of the flowers (Fig. 16.32). The female gametophytes lie buried in **ovaries** at the center of the flowers. Because the female gametophyte is hidden, the pollen attaches at the **stigma** and grows a great distance to reach a female gametophyte. Once the pollen tube reaches the female gametophyte, one male nucleus fertilizes an egg to form the new diploid organism. A second male nucleus usually joins with two other nuclei from the female gametophyte, producing a triploid **endosperm** tissue that nurtures the developing embryo. The seed itself consists of the embryo, the remains of the female gametophyte, the endosperm, and protective layers from the diploid flower tissue. The **ovary** in which the seed develops matures into the **fruit** that surrounds the seed.

Complex though the life cycle of a flowering plant may seem at first glance, it involves only minor modifications of the alternation of haploid gametophyte with the diploid sporophyte to which you were introduced in our discussion of sea lettuce (Fig. 16.25). In all seed plants the gametophytes are completely parasitic on the sporophyte.

(a)

(b)

(c)

FIGURE 16.31 **Gymnosperms.** Most gymnosperms are conifers such as the pine. Conifers bear separate male (a) and female cones (b). Yews (c) are conifers, but their cones are tiny and the seeds partially surrounded by a fleshy growth. This fleshy red structure is not a true fruit because it neither completely encloses the seed nor develops from an ovary.

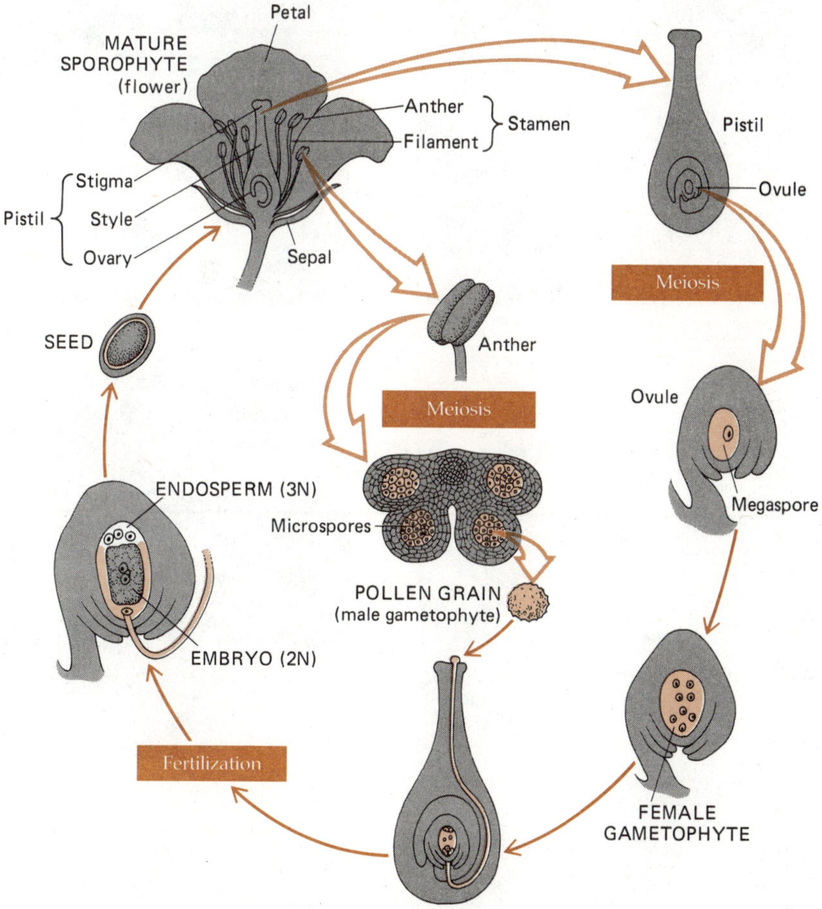

FIGURE 16.32 **Life Cycle of a Flowering Plant.**

FIGURE 16.33 **Angiosperms.** Try to identify stamens, pistils, petals, and sepals of the flowering plants shown here: (a) *Lilium superbum;* (b) banana; (c) *Commelina communis;* (d) a double buttercup; (e) the prickly pear cactus; (f) *Euphorbea obesa;* (g) the red maple; (h) *Lupinus perennis,* a legume; and (i) an aster, *Tragopogon dubius.* Aster flowers are really clusters of tiny individual flowers.

(h)

(i)

Flowering plants have gone one step further and hidden their gametophytes within the flower (Fig. 16.33) and their seeds within the fruit. But seeds must not be too well hidden. As we will see later, the next step is to advertise the presence of the fruit to attract animals that feed on the fruit and thereby spread the seed.

CHEMISTRY, STRUCTURE, AND REPRODUCTION DISTINGUISH FUNGI FROM PLANTS

Why not consider fungi as plants? After all, fungi have cell walls, and, like plants, they are generally stationary. Perhaps the most obvious difference is the absence of photosynthesis in fungi. But this is only one factor; fungi have other distinctive chemical characteristics. Chitin, the component of insect skeletons, is found in the cell walls of some fungi, for example. And while certain fungi, such as mushrooms, have a customary shape, all fungi are formed from simple strands of unspecialized cells. Although many (but not all) fungi are known to reproduce sexually, their life cycles are often unusual. In some, the fusion normally associated with fertilization produces a stage with two nuclei per cell. The actual union of nuclei occurs only later and only in cells that immediately undergo meiosis. The reproductive and chemical diversity of fungi are so great that we cannot discuss them further here. You will find some important groups described elsewhere: yeasts, molds, mushrooms in Chapter 18, and wheat rust in Chapter 21. 90

Each Species Is Unique

The diversity of life reflects millions of populations, each with an isolated gene pool and its own ecological niche. Together these species represent the end products of billions of years of evolutionary process. But if we are to understand the world of life, we must grasp more than its diversity. We must also begin to see how species interact in the biosphere. This will be our next topic.

Summary

1. Most biologists divide the world of life into five kingdoms: monera, protista, animals, plants, and fungi. All procaryotes, such as the bacteria, are placed in kingdom monera.

2. Protista are small, usually motile eucaryotes. These tiny organisms consist of only one cell, yet some exhibit amazing structural specialization on the subcellular level. The animal-like protista are protozoans such as amoebae, foraminifera, ciliates, and the parasite that causes malaria. Photosynthetic protista include dinoflagellates and diatoms. Some euglenoids are photosynthetic or autotrophic, depending on their environment.

3. Eucaryotes may have originated as associations of procaryotes. Mitochondria and chloroplasts are procaryote-like and may be the descendents of procaryotes that were phagocytized and retained within the cells of other procaryotes.

4. The earliest animals are believed to have fed by filtering microorganisms from the water. This is true of the sponges, the simplest of present-day animals. Sponges lack true tissue or organs; their collar cells resemble protozoa.

5. Coelenterate polyps and medusae exhibit radial symmetry around a two-way gut. Coelenterates have few characteristic organs and are otherwise quite unlike higher animals. Cnidoblasts allow coelenterates to paralyze their prey.

6. Flatworms are the simplest animals that have bilateral symmetry but, like coelenterates, lack the one-way gut of higher animals and have no body cavity. Some flatworms readily reorganize their body if mutilated and others, such as tapeworms, exhibit a bizarre body plan.

7. Despite distinct organ systems, absence of a true coelom in flatworms, nematodes, and rotifers distinguishes these phyla from the higher animals. The coelom is an integral part of the hydrostatic skeleton that is so useful for burrowing in soft mud. Perhaps all higher animals are derived from some burrowing, worm-like ancestor.

8. Annelids, including earthworms, polychaetes, and leeches, are characterized by a segmented body. To this segmented body arthropods add segmented appendages and a chitinized exoskeleton. Some authorities would divide the diverse arthropods into two separate phyla. Little is known about the origin of insects but their exoskeleton and tracheal system suit them for dwelling on land. Mollusks and annelids have protosome embryos and some molluscan structures hint of segmentation. Together, annelids, arthropods, and mollusks are thought to represent a major division of the animal kingdom.

9. Echinoderms are characterized by a water vascular system and by skeletal plates that lie just under the skin and often protrude as spines. Echinoderms are believed to be closely related to chordates because both have deuterostome larvae.

10. All chordates, including the vertebrates, have a hollow dorsal nervous system, a notochord, and pharyngeal slits. Vertebrates exhibit segmentation in their nervous system, muscles, and skeleton, and have a distinct brain in a skull.

11. The first terrestrial vertebrates, ancestral to present-day amphibians, derived from air-breathing fish. Reptiles trace to early amphibians but have an amnion and so need not return to water to reproduce.

12. Birds and mammals have amnions and share a reptilian ancestry. A few mammals lay shelled eggs, but in most the embryos develop in the uterus. Marsupial mammals never form a true placenta; their young are born early and nurtured on milk from glands in the mother's pouch.

13. Algae are photosynthetic, usually multicellular, organisms with cellulose walls but lacking the cellular specialization characteristic of higher plants. Red, brown, and green algae differ in chemical characteristics and may each have a separate origin. Similarities in pigments and storage products suggest that green algae are ancestral to vascular plants.

14. Plant life cycles may include a multicellular haploid generation known as the gametophyte. Meiosis in diploid plants (sporophytes) produces spores that germinate to form gametophytes. Gametophytes produce gametes by mitosis.

15. Higher plants have embryos, vascular tissue that supports the plant and conducts liquids, and resistant spores or male gametophytes. The horsetails, club-mosses, and ferns are primitive vascular plants that spread through spores rather than seed. True mosses and liverworts also spread by spores and are chemically related to vascular plants but lack vascular tissue.

16. The female gametophytes of seed plants remain within the sporophyte. Male gametophytes are pollen grains that grow tubes into the female gametophyte. Sperm nuclei move through these tubes and fertilize eggs that develop into embryos within the female gametophyte.

17. Seeds consist of embryos, remnants of the female gametophyte, and parent sporophyte tissue. In gymnosperms the seeds are exposed. In angiosperms they are enclosed in fruit that develop from the ovary of the flower.

18. Fungi have distinctive chemical and reproductive patterns. Their diverse forms are all composed of simple strands of cells.

Thought and Controversy

1. Why do birds have feathers? Probably the first answer that comes to mind is, "To fly, of course!" But was flying the *first* function of feathers, the selective advantage that promoted the evolution of feathers? Some biologists think not. *Archaeopteryx,* the oldest feathered fossil, had a long jointed tail—and teeth. In fact, *Archaeopteryx* was more like a feathered reptile than a bird. Furthermore, none of its feathers were anchored to bone as are the flight feathers of present-day birds. Feathers may have evolved as insulation and only later adapted to flight. *Archaeopteryx* is thought to have flapped its wings to gain speed as it chased its prey along the ground and perhaps used its outspread wings to herd or corner the small reptiles it fed upon.

2. Of what use are computers in the study of diversity? Beyond their obvious value in cataloging specimens and recording other data, computer models are giving insight into evolutionary history. One question currently under study is the origin of branching patterns in vascular plants. By programming the computer with data for the branching patterns observed in early fossil plants, and allowing the computer to generate the various possible combinations, researchers have obtained all present-day patterns. In other words, computer simulations suggest that what we see about us are random combinations of primitive patterns, not fundamental innovations. Of course, the retention of a particular pattern depends on its adaptive value. For example, a major problem of plants is how to take maximum advantage of sunlight for photosynthesis. Leaves are necessary for photosynthesis; but if one leaf shades another, additional leaves may bring little increase in photosynthesis. One solution to the problem is to grow one branch much longer than others. When this process is repeated many times it produces a layered-pagoda form. This is a shape common among tropical forest trees, and was one option suggested by the computer.

3. Thirty years ago, the history of life and the diverse groups of organisms formed the backbone of the discipline of biology. Most biology courses were organized largely as surveys of this diversity. Since then, remarkable advances in molecular and cellular biology have created whole new areas of biology. Often it seemed that the "new" biologists had little in common with their more traditional peers. Basic to this was the fact that scientists who used the tools of chemistry and physics often concentrated their study on a few species of common laboratory animals. But with time there grew up a new generation of biologists trained in a variety of techniques and interested in many kinds of organisms. Application of these new techniques led to repercussions throughout the field of biology. It has even affected our interpretation of the relationships among major groups of organisms. For example, chemical and microscopic studies of the water molds, long considered a group of fungi, indicate that these "molds" have little in common with other fungi and are probably green algae that have lost their photosynthetic ability.

Questions

1. List five major groups of protista and compare and contrast their characteristics.

2. Discuss the evidence for the symbiotic origin of eucaryotes.

3. Describe the ecological niches thought to be characteristic of the first animals.

4. Why are flatworms thought to be closely related to the ancestors of higher animals, whereas coelenterates and sponges are not considered to be so related?

5. Discuss the importance of coelom in primitive animals. Since the coelom is found in all higher animals, does this suggest that all such animals share a common ancestor?

6. What is the advantage of a segmented body plan? Describe an organism with such a body plan.

7. Echinoderms are thought to be more closely related to vertebrates than annelids are to vertebrates. Discuss the evidence used to support such an argument.

8. What is meant by "alternation of generations" in plants? Define gametophyte and sporophyte. Is mitosis limited to diploid cells?

9. Describe the plants that were the main source of the fossils that constitute our coal deposits. To what present-day plants are these most closely related?

10. Compare the life cycles of ferns, conifers, and flowering plants. Compared with ferns, what advantages do conifers and flowering plants have? What advantages do flowering plants have over conifers?

Further Reading for Part Four

Alcock, John, 1981. Seduction on the wing. *Natural History* 90(12):36–41. (December)

Archibald, J. David, and William A. Clemens, 1982. Late cretaceous extinctions. *American Scientist* 70:377–385.

Ayala, Francisco J., 1978. The mechanisms of evolution. *Scientific American* 239(3):56–69 (September)

Carlquist, Sherwin, 1965. *Island Life: A Natural History of the Islands of the World.* Natural History Press, Garden City, N.Y.

Cloud, Preston, and Martin F. Glaessner, 1982. The edicarian period and system: metazoa inherit the earth. *Science* 217:783–792.

Ligon, J. David, and Sandra H. Ligon, 1982. The cooperative breeding of the green woodhoopoe. *Scientific American* 247(1):126–134. (July)

Minkoff, Eli C., 1983. *Evolutionary Biology.* Addison-Wesley Publishing Co., Reading, Mass.

Mossman, David J., and William A.S. Sarjeant, 1983. The footprints of extinct animals. *Scientific American* 248(1):74–85. (January)

Rensberger, Boyce, 1982. To land, to seed, to flower. *Mosiac* 13(4):30–34.

Tinbergen, Niko, 1968. *Curious Naturalists.* Natural History Library, Doubleday & Co., Garden City, N.Y.

Wilson, Edward O., 1975. *Sociobiology.* The Belknap Press of Harvard University Press, Cambridge, Mass.

Woese, Carl R., 1981. Archaebacteria. *Scientific American* 244(6):98–120. (June)

PART FIVE

Living Ecosystems

Life characterizes all ecosystems. Every ecosystem involves a multitude of species, each with its own ecological niche. Within ecosystems the integration of plants, animals, and microorganisms with the physical environment creates an equilibrium reminiscent of homeostasis. Examination of individual ecosystems should help us understand the dynamic nature of life.

Our survey of ecosystems emphasizes those that people use. Studying these will help you understand the resources on which we rely. In addition, this section introduces the major forms of life and provides opportunities to become familiar with basic ecological principles.

Of course, plants are the producers in each ecosystem. They form the base of the food web and support all heterotrophic organisms, including humans. For this reason, we have introduced plant biology before examining specific ecosystems. As you will see, autotrophic plants have the same fundamental life needs that animals do, but they meet their needs in quite different ways.

17

Plants: The Producers

PLANTS AND PLANT PRODUCTS ARE IN A VERY real sense the basis of human life. Coal, oil, and natural gas, all from the long-dead bodies of plants, are the most important sources of energy we have available today. They heat our homes, run our automobiles and factories, and provide much of the electricity we use. Coal and oil are even used to synthesize rubber, plastics, and the miracle fibers that supposedly replace plant products! Plants are simply not replaceable. Our homes and furniture are made from timber. So is this book. Wood pulp is used to make rayon and cellulose acetate fabrics, in addition to paper. And certainly cotton clothing is common to most wardrobes.

Since time immemorial, humans have turned to plants for medicine. We still do. Nowadays, however, we often synthesize the medicines we once extracted from plants. The list of plant medicinals, which is extensive, includes aspirin, atropine, codeine, quinine, digitalis, and castor oil. Similarly, a variety of stimulants and narcotics are plant products—among them are caffeine, cola seed, tobacco, marijuana, cocaine, opium, heroin, and mescaline.

Most people would probably agree that plants are most important to humans as a source of food. Although food production is important, we are dependent on plants for another, related reason. Photosynthesis provides oxygen. Primeval plants produced—and modern plants renew—the oxy-
61 gen in the air we breathe. □

In this chapter, we will consider aspects of plant life that most plants have in common. What you will learn about photosynthesis, plant nutrition, and cell structure applies to all green plants. Other topics apply more specifically to the seed plants that dominate agriculture, forests, and the terrestrial landscape in general.

PHOTOSYNTHESIS AND PLANT NUTRITION

Although photosynthetic plants and heterotrophic animals share many fundamental features, their nutritional requirements are quite different. Most plants, in contrast to animals, are essentially complete biochemical factories. Animals must consume organic food in order to make up for their inability to synthesize required biological molecules, but plants have no real need for similar food. In general, most green plants cannot utilize organic food molecules that may be found in their environment. No mechanism exists for getting such molecules into the bodies of most plants.

Certain bog and marsh plants are exceptions to this rule. Venus's-flytraps (Fig. 17.2) and pitcher plants are *carnivorous plants* that have evolved the ability to trap and digest insects through the secretion of enzymes. These plants are basically photosynthetic but benefit from insect capture because they live in mineral-poor environments. But, as we have said, most green plants subsist on carbon dioxide, oxygen, water, and minerals. To turn these

FIGURE 17.1 **A Field of Sunflowers.** The crop is harvested primarily for oil.

FIGURE 17.2 **Venus's-Flytrap.** This insectivorous plant grows in mild, marshy environments. Its sticky traps snap shut when an insect contacts sensitive hairs.

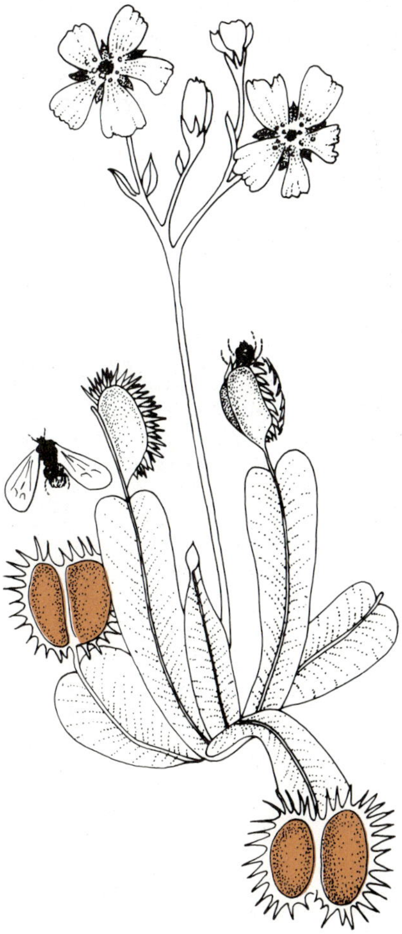

inorganic substances into plant material requires light energy.

The Light Reactions

The most obvious result of photosynthesis is **carbon-dioxide fixation,** so called because in this process green plants "fix" or incorporate gaseous carbon dioxide into organic compounds. The overall reaction for photosynthesis is:

$$\underset{\text{carbon dioxide}}{6\,CO_2} + \underset{\text{water}}{12\,H_2O} \xrightarrow{\text{sunlight}} \underset{\text{sugar}}{C_6H_{12}O_6} + \underset{\text{oxygen}}{6\,O_2} + \underset{\text{water}}{6\,H_2O}$$

One of the products of the reaction, sugar, has a much more complicated and orderly chemical structure than the raw materials used to make it. This high level of organization is created through an input of energy, just as the building of a house from a pile of lumber involves an input of energy. In photosynthesis, the energy used is the radiant energy of sunlight. All of us learn very early that light is energy. The sun warms and burns us. Little children use magnifying glasses to focus the sun's rays and burn holes in paper. It is sunlight that ultimately supplies energy for the entire biosphere.□ 10

Why Plants Are Green. Sunlight, which is white light, is actually a composite of the various colors we perceive. Physicists demonstrate the separation of the components of the light spectrum with a

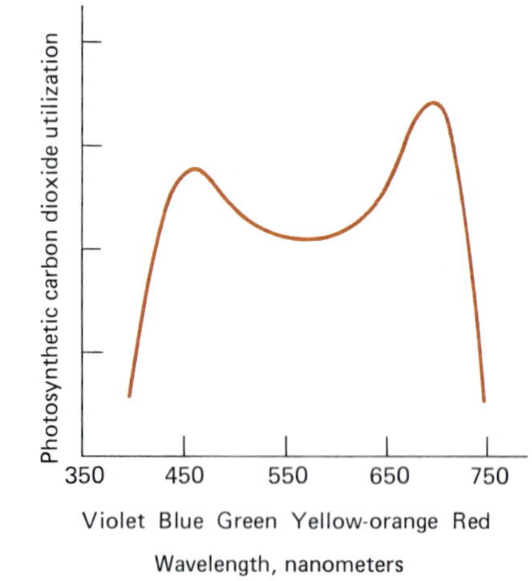

FIGURE 17.3 Photosynthetic Action Spectrum of Leaves. The peaks represent maximum carbon dioxide utilization and thus photosynthesis.

prism. Everyone sees a similar demonstration when raindrops act as prisms to produce a rainbow.

Each color of the spectrum has a characteristic wavelength and energy content.□ As indicated in 62
Fig. 17.3, not all wavelengths of light are equally useful for photosynthesis. Only light that is absorbed by a plant can be used to drive photosynthesis. Green plants contain a number of different **pigments** that absorb light energy. The reason most plants appear green is that the plant pigments absorb the other colors of the spectrum, leaving mostly green light, which is transmitted through the plant or reflected from the surface toward our eyes. The most important plant pigment is **chlorophyll** (Fig. 17.4).

Photosynthesis occurs only in those cells of a plant that contain chlorophyll. This pigment has a chemical structure that permits it to absorb the energy of red and blue light. Because green light is reflected (instead of absorbed), chlorophyll appears green in color.

Exciting Pigments. When pigments such as chlorophyll absorb light energy, they become "excited." As Fig. 17.5 shows, light energy excites pigments by causing electrons to jump to a higher energy level.

We are all familiar with everyday examples of the excitation of pigments by certain wavelengths of light. Some inks used to print posters contain pigments that are excited by certain almost invisible

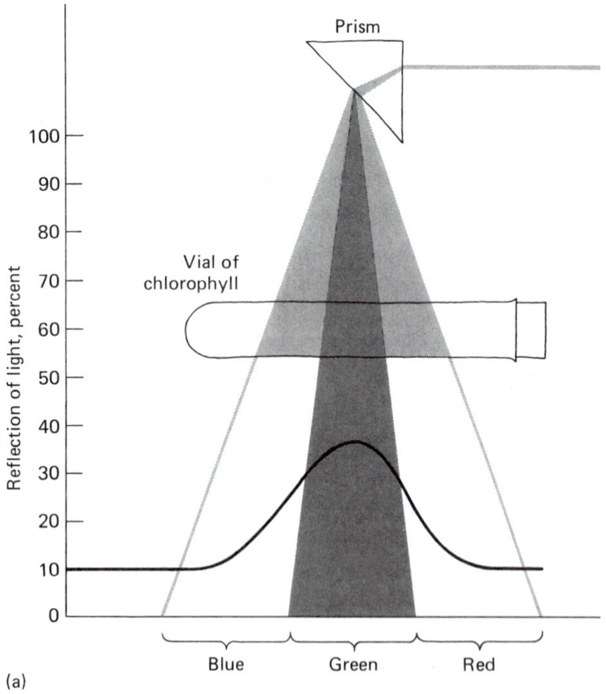

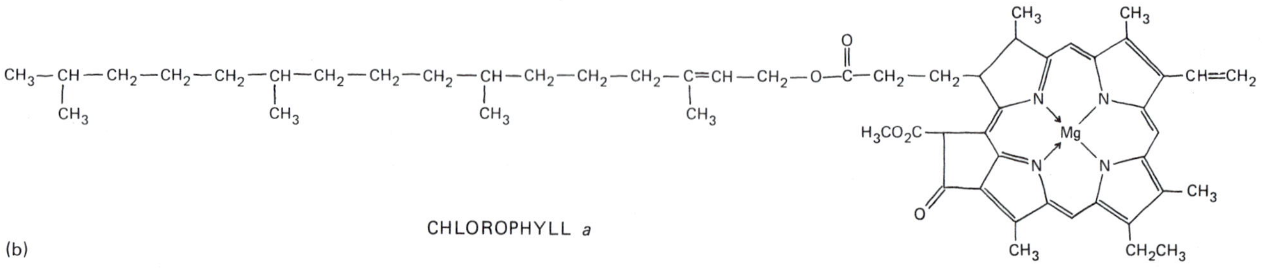

FIGURE 17.4 Absorption of Light by Chlorophyll. (a) The photosynthetic efficiency of blue and red light can be attributed to chlorophyll, because the pure pigment extracted from leaves reflects green light but absorbs all the others, especially red and blue light. (b) There is more than one kind of chlorophyll. They differ with respect to the wavelengths of light they absorb best, but they have very similar structures.

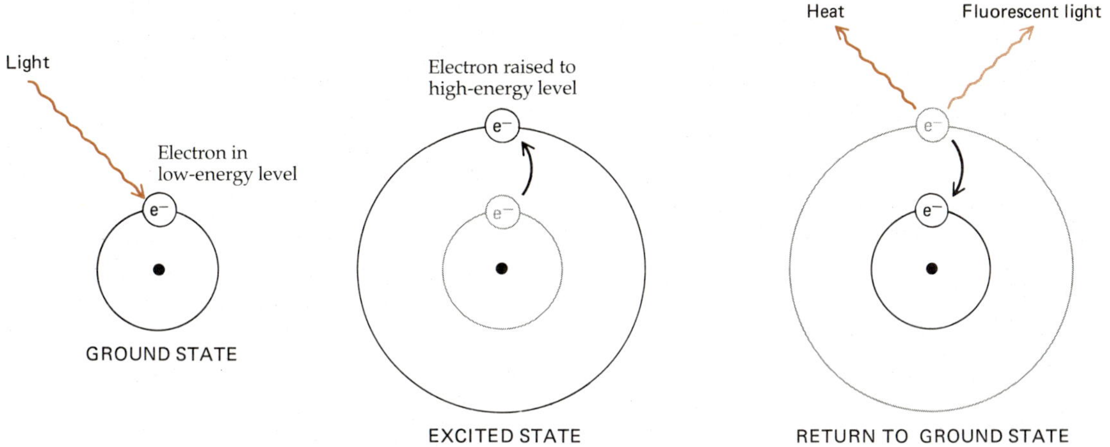

FIGURE 17.5 **Pigment Excitation.** Molecules such as chlorophyll become excited when they absorb light energy, and one or more electrons are raised to higher energy levels.

wavelengths of light. When illuminated by "blacklights," these pigments emit a fluorescent glow. This illustrates an important property of light-absorbing pigments. They can absorb only so much extra energy before they must give the energy away in order to remain stable. Sometimes the energy is released as heat or as light of a different wavelength from that originally absorbed. This is so when poster inks absorb blacklight and release fluorescent light. In the process, their excited electrons are returned to their normal, stable state.

When chlorophyll is chemically extracted from plant cells and then illuminated, it also releases the absorbed energy, giving out a fluorescent glow. As we all know, this does not happen in an intact plant. Here there are systems to trap the absorbed energy. The excited chlorophyll molecules still give up the extra energy, but it is caught by energy-acceptor molecules associated with the chlorophyll. Eventually this energy is used to propel the synthesis of ATP.

Chloroplasts. Although biologists can detect that ATP is produced from ADP and phosphate during photosynthesis, and even though they have been studying the process for many years, the precise mechanism is not clear. They do know, however, that the process occurs in the photochemical factories of the plant cell, the organelles called **chloroplasts.**

The chloroplast, like the mitochondrion, is a small body bound by membranes. Figure 17.6 illustrates that there are also extensive membranes

FIGURE 17.6 **The Chloroplast.**

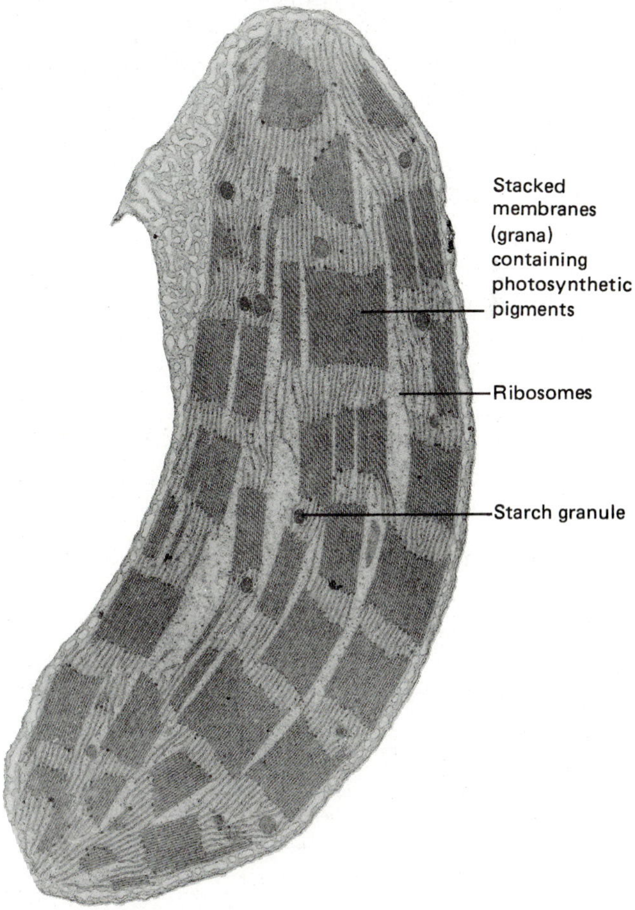

inside the organelle. Usually these membranes are layered, forming dense stacks. Within the chloroplast membranes, chlorophyll and **accessory pigments,** including yellow or orange **carotenoids,** are organized into light-gathering **photosystems.** As you might expect from the colors of the carotenoids, the accessory pigments absorb wavelengths of light not absorbed by chlorophyll. By collecting light not absorbed by chlorophyll, carotenoids and other accessory pigments enable plants to utilize more of the sun's energy than would otherwise be possible.

Photophosphorylation. Chloroplast photosystems are organized in such a way that light energy captured by the accessory pigments is funneled into chlorophyll. Certain chlorophyll electrons become so "excited" that they are driven away from the chlorophyll molecules altogether. These highly energetic electrons are captured by special acceptors that are bound to the choloroplast membranes. In a chain reaction reminiscent of those occurring
104 in mitochondria, □the electrons are then passed from one acceptor to another, losing a little energy with each passage. At some point along the way (no one is exactly sure where) ATP is formed from ADP and inorganic phosphate. Light-driven ATP synthesis is called **photophosphorylation.**

The light energy harnessed by chlorophyll does more than generate ATP. It may not be obvious from the general reaction for photosynthesis, but water is split apart in the process. The photosynthetic breakdown of water releases oxygen gas to the atmosphere. This splitting of water is also the source of the hydrogens that are necessary to the production of carbohydrates from carbon dioxide.

As pictured in Fig. 17.7, photophosphorylation involves two photosystems. The reactions we have just described occur in association with Photosystem II. The electrons driven away from the chlorophyll of Photosystem II are replaced by electrons obtained as water is split apart. The hydrogens that remain (remember that the oxygen is released as gas) are used in conjunction with Photosystem I.

In Photosystem I, excited electrons are trapped by a chain of electron carriers, which pass them to an electron acceptor called NADP to form $NADPH_2$. The hydrogens in the $NADPH_2$ come from water. One final point makes our story of photophosphorylation complete. The electrons driven away from the chlorophyll of Photosystem I are replaced by electrons from Photosystem II, which were drained of much of their energy during the synthesis of ATP.

As you can see, Photosystems I and II work together in carrying out the light reactions of pho-

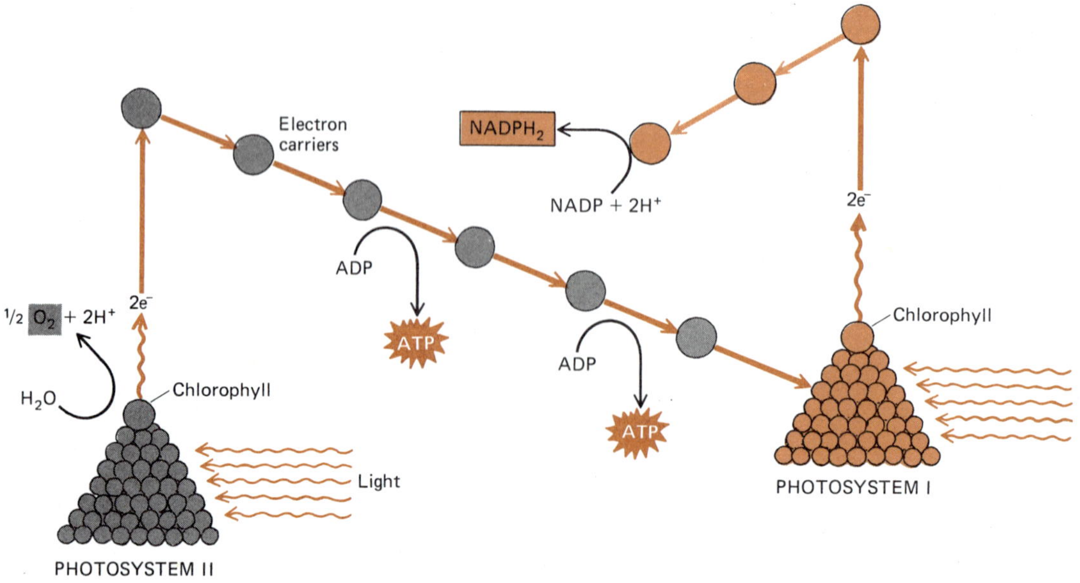

FIGURE 17.7 **Photophosphorylation.** Trace the flow of electrons from the chlorophyll of Photosystem II as they are excited by light energy and pass through a series of carriers to the chlorophyll of Photosystem I. The downward flow of the excited electrons is coupled to the formation of ATP. Photosystem I electrons are transferred through a system of carriers to NADP to form $NADPH_2$.

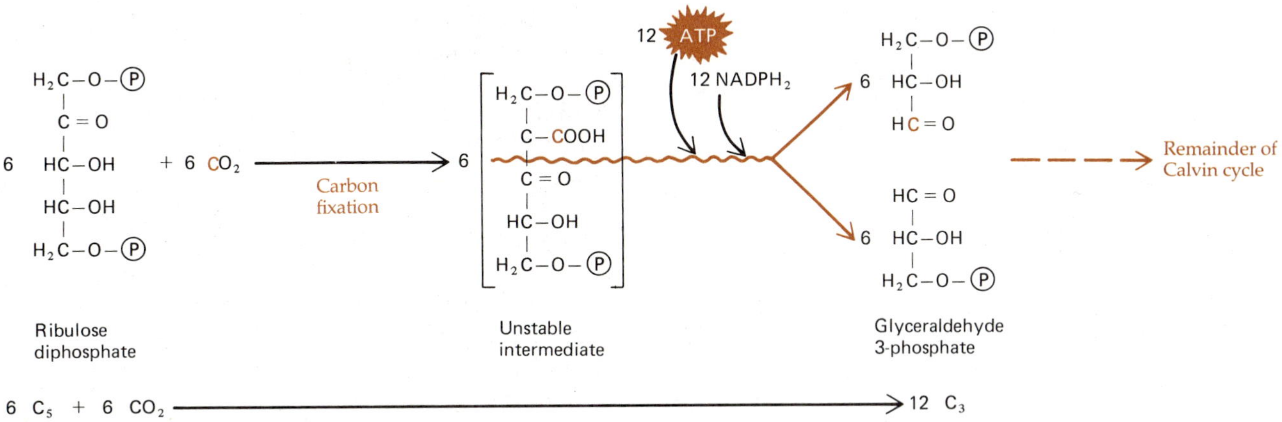

FIGURE 17.8 **Initial Steps of the Calvin Cycle.** Carbon dioxide is fixed by attachment to ribulose diphosphate. The unstable intermediate that results is split in half. Each half is then reduced in the presence of ATP and $NADPH_2$ provided by the light reactions. For every six carbon dioxide molecules that are fixed, twelve molecules of the glyceraldehyde-3-phosphate are formed.

tosynthesis. In the course of these reactions, light energy triggers a flow of electrons that eventually leads to the synthesis of ATP and $NADPH_2$.

The Dark Reactions

The dark reactions of photosynthesis are those involved in carbon fixation. They are designated dark reactions not because they necessarily occur in the dark, but because light is not directly involved. However, the dark reactions of photosynthesis require ATP and $NADPH_2$, the products of the light reactions. In addition, carbon dioxide, water, and minerals are needed.

Carbon dioxide, produced as a waste product of plant and animal respiration, is obtained from the air by the leaves of seed plants. Minerals dissolved in water enter through the roots. Hence the requirement for minerals is solved simultaneously with that for water.

The Calvin Cycle. Carbon fixation involves a complex series of reactions, the **Calvin cycle,** which begins with the incorporation of carbon dioxide into a five-carbon sugar called **ribulose diphosphate** (Fig. 17.8). It is called a *cycle* because the sugar is continuously regenerated. The overall reaction is:

$$\begin{aligned}&6 \text{ ribulose diphosphate} + 6\, CO_2 \\ &\qquad + 18 \text{ ATP} + 12\, NADPH_2 \rightarrow \\ &6 \text{ ribulose diphosphate} + \text{glucose} + 18 \text{ ADP} \\ &\qquad + 18 \text{ phosphate} + 12 \text{ NADP}\end{aligned}$$

Although the full story is complex, for every six carbon dioxides that enter the Calvin cycle, one glucose molecule is produced. The energy for this synthesis comes from ATP. The hydrogens are provided by $NADPH_2$ (Fig. 17.9).

The Calvin cycle reactions occur in the jellylike **stroma** that surrounds the internal chloroplast membranes. Chloroplasts, then, are perfect photosynthetic factories. They contain not only the necessary pigments but also the enzymes and other compounds to perform the complete photosynthetic process (Table 17.1).

Other Photosynthetic Products. Traditionally, sugar is considered to be the major product of photosynthesis, because many plants store this material as starch. At night when there is no light, or in the spring before seedlings have leaves, stored starch can be digested to provide raw materials and energy for plant growth and maintenance. The glucose obtained from starch is broken down by means of glycolysis and mitochondrial oxidations,□ just as 101
it is in animals. Thus all plant cells, and especially the nonphotosynthetic roots, need an adequate oxygen supply.

Although carbohydrates such as starch are the principal photosynthetic products, do not forget that plants are made up of proteins, lipids, and nucleic acids in addition to carbohydrates. These molecules and their amino acid, fatty acid, and nucleotide subunits can also be considered photosynthetic products. Many important building-block molecules are produced from sugar via the Krebs cycle□ in plant mitochondria, or they may be 108
produced directly from intermediates of the Calvin cycle. In fact, the need to manufacture noncarbo-

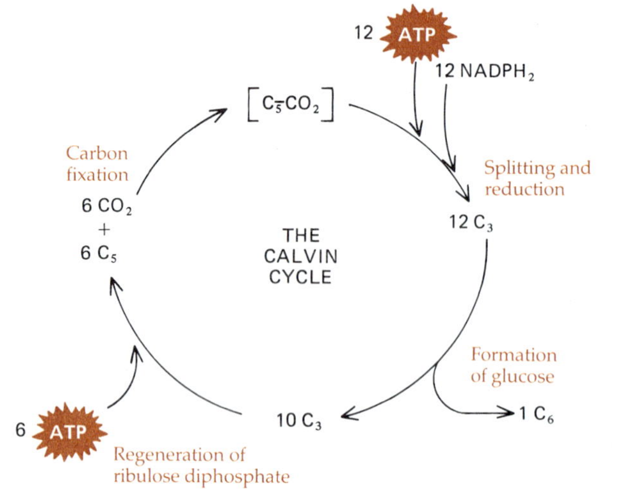

SUMMARY

Carbon fixation	6 C_5 + 6 CO_2	→	6C_5-CO_2
Splitting and reduction	6 C_5 – CO_2	→	12 C_3
Formation of sugar	12 C_3	→	10 C_3 + 1 C_6
Regeneration of ribulose diphosphate	10 C_3	→	6 C_5
	Net: 6 CO_2	→	1 C_6 (glucose)

FIGURE 17.9 **Summary of the Calvin Cycle.** Of the 12 three-carbon compounds produced following fixation of carbon dioxide, two are joined to form glucose. The ten remaining three-carbon compounds undergo a complex series of interactions to regenerate the six ribulose diphosphates required to continue the cycle.

hydrate cell components explains many of the mineral requirements of plants.

Mineral Needs. Plant growth is most commonly limited by the availability of the elements nitrogen, phosphorus, and potassium. **Nitrogen** is needed for the synthesis of proteins and chlorophyll. Although air has a high concentration of gaseous nitrogen (N_2), this form of nitrogen cannot be used by most plants. Instead, they require nitrate (NO_3) or ammonia (NH_3). The source of these compounds is explained in the discussion of the nitrogen cycle later in this chapter. Nitrogen-deficient plants grow poorly and are a pale green. On the other hand, excess nitrogen can be a problem, too. Farmers and nursery specialists know that an overabundance of nitrogen produces plants that grow vigorously but do not produce many flowers, fruits, or seeds.

Phosphorus is necessary for the synthesis of numerous biological compounds, including DNA, RNA, and ATP. Plants utilize phosphorus in the form of phosphate salts. It is easy to understand why many fertilizers are high in phosphate, which promotes root growth, hastens maturity, and improves fruit production.

In contrast to the clearly defined roles of nitrogen and phosphorus, the importance of potassium is still poorly understood. **Potassium** is required for protein synthesis, but it is involved in so many other cell processes that no single one seems to account for the dramatic effects of potassium deficiency. Without sufficient potassium, plants are

TABLE 17.1 **Summary of Photosynthesis**

Cell Structure Involved	*Requirements*	*Products*
Light Reactions Chloroplast membranes (grana)	Light Enzymes, electron carriers Chlorophyll, accessory pigments Water NADP ADP + phosphate	Oxygen NADPH$_2$ ATP
Dark Reactions Chloroplast stroma	Calvin cycle enzymes Ribulose diphosphate Carbon dioxide NADPH$_2$ ATP	Ribulose diphosphate Sugar NADP ADP + phosphate Water

spindly and their leaves often appear scorched around the edges.

Many other elements are essential in plant nutrition. **Calcium** serves as part of the cell cement that holds adjacent cells together. An atom of **magnesium** occupies the center of each chlorophyll molecule, just as an iron atom is part of every human hemoglobin molecule. **Sulfate** must be absorbed to supply the sulfur of some amino acids. Other minerals, such as **copper** and **zinc,** act as enzyme activators and are necessary in only trace amounts. **Manganese** and **iron** are important trace elements because of their roles in the biochemical reactions that lead to chlorophyll formation.

SPECIAL STRUCTURES OF PLANT CELLS

Plant cells contain mitochondria and most of the other organelles found in animal cells, but all plant cells have additional structures. Besides chloroplasts, plant cells may contain other membrane-bound organelles. Some of these contain only yellowish or reddish **carotenoids.** Such pigments attract animals that pollinate flowers or disperse seeds from fruits. It is not unlikely that carotenoid-containing organelles are derived from chloroplasts through the loss of chlorophyll. Also, plants often store starch in membranous organelles.

Plant cells usually contain water-filled, membrane-bound vacuoles. In higher plants, the large **central vacuole** is frequently the most prominent internal structure (Fig. 17.10). Within vacuoles the plant accumulates salts, sugars, pigments, waste products, and many other substances. **Calcium oxalate** is one of the most common wastes found in cell vacuoles. The original product is oxalic acid, the substance that makes rhubarb sour. Because of its acidity, this compound is poisonous in high concentrations. Within the vacuoles it precipitates with calcium to form dense, harmless crystals.

Anthocyanins, a group of water-soluble pigments, color the vacuoles of many plants. The red of beets, plums, and grapes and the blue and pink of hydrangeas all result from anthocyanins or related substances. In some cases the color of anthocyanins draws animals to fruit or flowers. This pigment also screens many plants against excessive radiation.

Cell Walls

Unlike animal cells, those of plants are surrounded by a thick, rigid, and protective cell wall. The plasma membrane of a plant cell is pressed closely to the inside surface of its cell wall.

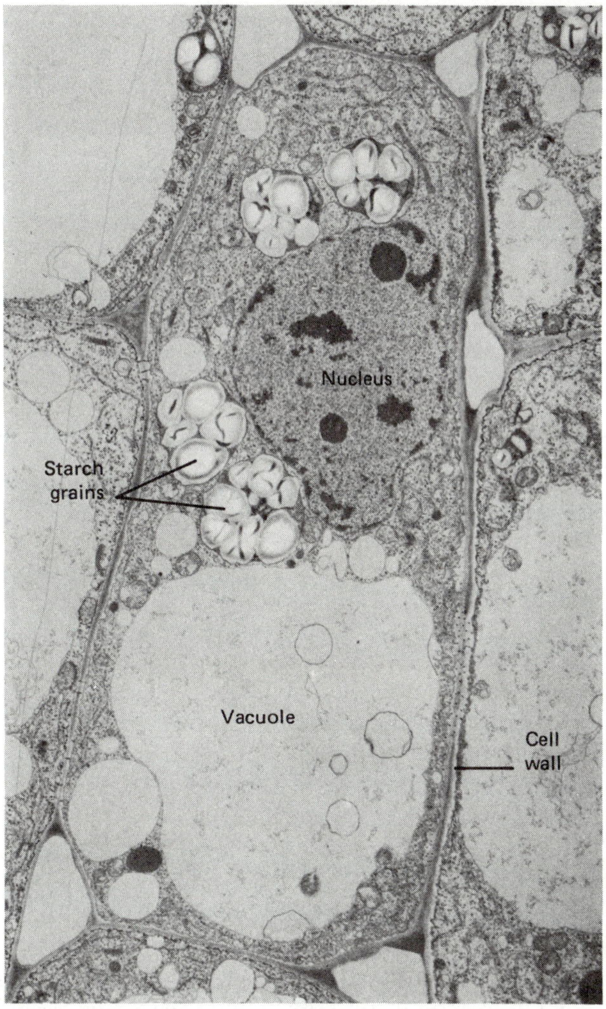

FIGURE 17.10 **A Plant Cell.**

The presence of a cell wall complicates cell division in plants. After a plant cell nucleus undergoes mitosis, a row of specialized vacuoles appears between the two new nuclei. These vacuoles soon coalesce to form the plasma membranes for the new cell surfaces. As the vacuoles merge, their contents are released and then used to make the **middle lamella.** This is a layer of calcium pectinate that will eventually lie between the walls of the two cells. Plant cell walls are perforated by plasma-membrane-lined channels called **plasmadesmata.** Thin strips of cytoplasm extend through the plasmadesmata and connect one plant cell to another.

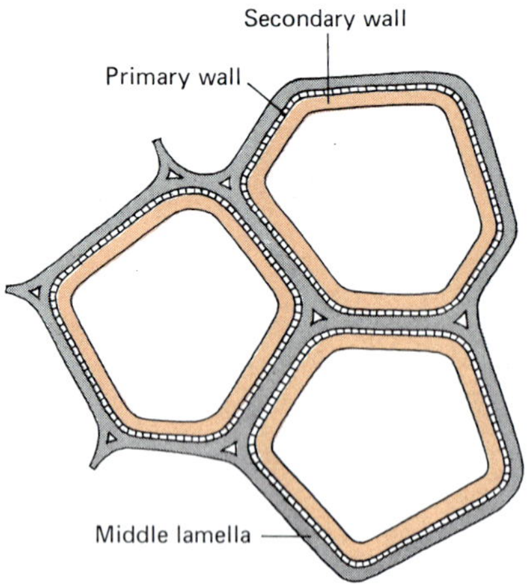

FIGURE 17.11 **Relationship of Primary Cell Wall, Secondary Cell Wall, and Middle Lamella.** Note that the secondary wall is internal to the primary wall.

Next, each cell secretes sugar molecules that become fused into **cellulose fibers.** Irregular "brush heaps" of these fibers fashion the **primary cell wall** adjacent to the middle lamella. The structure of the primary cell wall makes it somewhat pliable, so it can be stretched as new cells grow.

In many plants, cells may lay down a **secondary cell wall** (Fig. 17.11) consisting of precisely oriented layers of cellulose fibers, often infiltrated with an amorphous macromolecule, **lignin.** Perhaps because of the impenetrability of secondary walls, cells having them soon die. These dead cells act as fibrous supporting structures and, as we shall soon learn, form internal tubes for the movement of water and minerals.

Cellulose and lignin have different chemical properties. The long cellulose fibers are strong, but they retain flexibility. Cotton and linen fabrics consist of dead plant cells with thick secondary walls largely composed of cellulose. Paper and rayon are manufactured from similar cells in the wood of fast-growing trees.

Lignin, on the other hand, is stiff and rigid. Much of the hardness of wood results from its high lignin content. Because lignin is very resistant to decay, it is a troublesome waste to paper plants and other industries that process wood for its cellulose content. Together the properties of cellulose and lignin are complementary, just as are the col-
198 lagen and minerals in bone.□ Thick secondary cell walls provide the strength to hold trees hundreds of feet into the air.

Regulation by Plant Cells

Terrestrial (and freshwater) plants live in an environment that has a much lower concentration of dissolved minerals than is found inside the cells of the plants. That is to say, plant cells contain a concentrated solution of minerals, and the soil water is a much more dilute solution. Looking at it this way, we realize that the cells of healthy, growing plants have a lower concentration of water than is found in soil. This situation produces a high osmotic pressure□ that pulls water molecules into 130
plants.

Osmosis might be expected to continue until the concentration of water was the same in plant cells as in soil. But this does not happen. Because plant cells can expand only so much, they can take in only a limited amount of water. When their rigid cell walls reach the limit of elasticity, osmosis stops.

Normal, healthy plant cells are slightly swollen with water, a condition characterized as **turgidity** (Fig. 17.12). Expansion of the central vacuole presses the cell contents against the resistant cell wall. Turgor pressure is maintained so long as there is a continuous supply of water. If water becomes scarce, plant cells lose their turgidity as they use up their water supply through photosynthesis or evaporation. Accordingly, the cytoplasm shrivels up and shrinks away from the cell wall. If the walls are delicate, they collapse and the plant **wilts.** An ordinary household example illustrates the relationship between osmosis and turgidity. Lettuce leaves are subject to dehydration as soon as they are cut

FIGURE 17.12 **Plasmolysis.** Under dry conditions, or when the cell is placed in a concentrated sugar or salt solution, water moves out of the cell, and the cell becomes plasmolyzed.

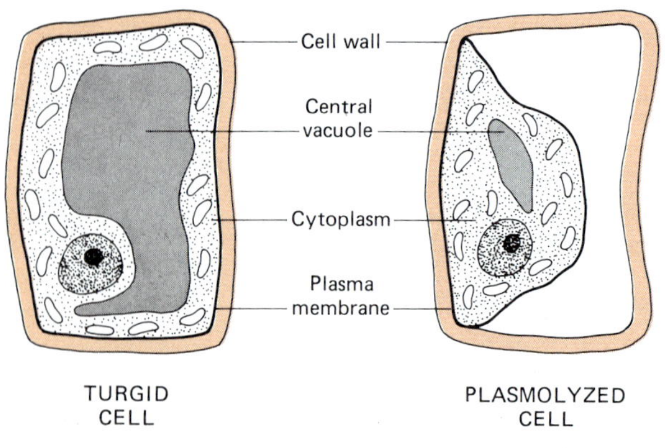

from the roots. Even refrigeration, which slows metabolism and therefore water use, cannot prevent wilting for long. However, if the cells remain alive, wilted lettuce leaves can be revived by soaking them in water.

LEAVES: DESIGN FOR PHOTOSYNTHESIS

Although photosynthesis occurs in all green tissues, even the outer parts of young stems, green fruits, and exposed roots, the **leaf** is the major photosynthetic organ of higher plants. Leaves provide a large surface to intercept a substantial amount of light and to carry out the gas exchange essential to photosynthesis (Fig. 17.13). Not only do photosynthetic cells need access to carbon dioxide, but the oxygen they produce must be dispersed, because high oxygen concentrations suppress photosynthesis. However, a good water supply is also necessary for photosynthesis. Therefore the same surfaces that permit gas exchange also allow water loss through evaporation. A certain amount of evaporation is essential, since it creates currents that carry minerals from the roots to the leaves, but excessive evaporation threatens the plant with dehydration. Hence leaf structure must be a compromise between several competing needs.

Typically, plants adapted to moderate climates have flat, thin leaves that permit them to take advantage of as much light as possible. The leaves of a tree may vary in structure, depending on their location. Those exposed to bright light are usually thicker and often smaller than leaves growing in deep shade. Even the position of individual leaves favors maximum light absorption. In some plants the leaves change position during the day as the sun moves across the sky.

Leaf Surfaces

The leaves of all plants except some adapted to an underwater existence are bound by a tightly cemented layer of **epidermal cells.** This layer stymies invader microorganisms and also helps to prevent evaporation. The waxy coat that covers the outside of the epidermis further reduces evaporation. There are openings in the waterproof epidermis to permit exchange of carbon dioxide and oxygen with the air. The **stomata** (mouths), as these openings are called (singular, **stoma**), are usually confined to the lower surface of the leaf. Because this shaded side is cooler, there is less evaporation from stomata there than would occur from openings on the upper surface.

FIGURE 17.13 **Leaf Venations, Types, and Arrangements.**

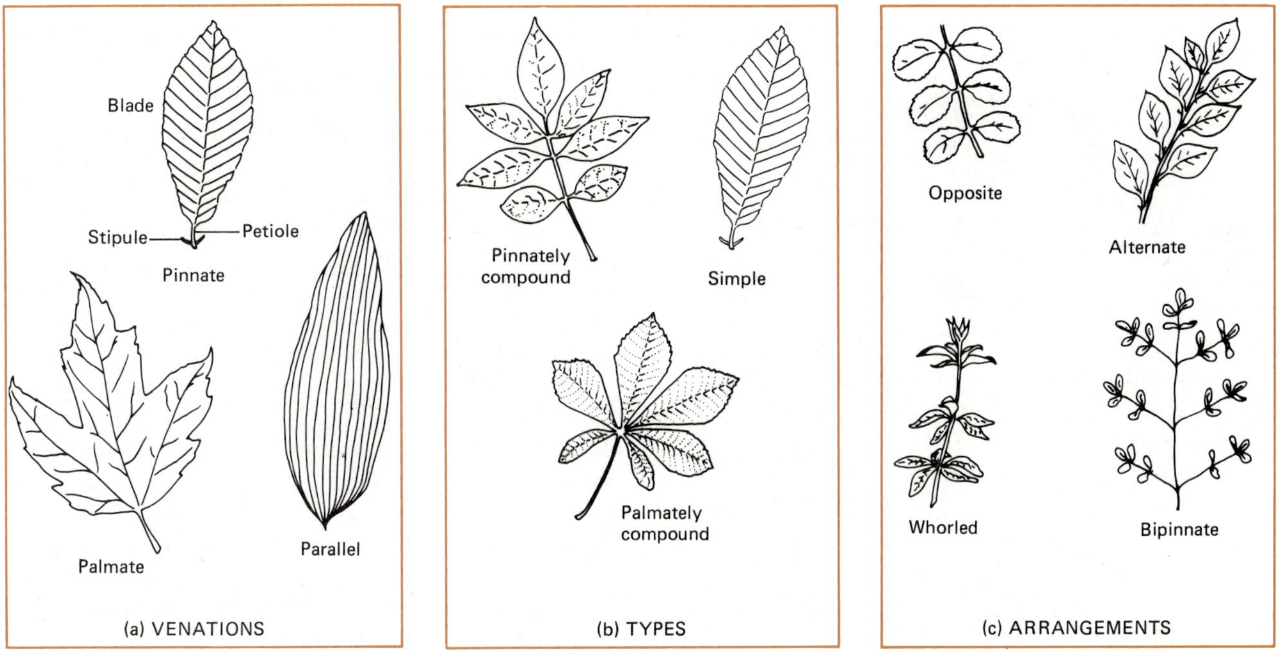

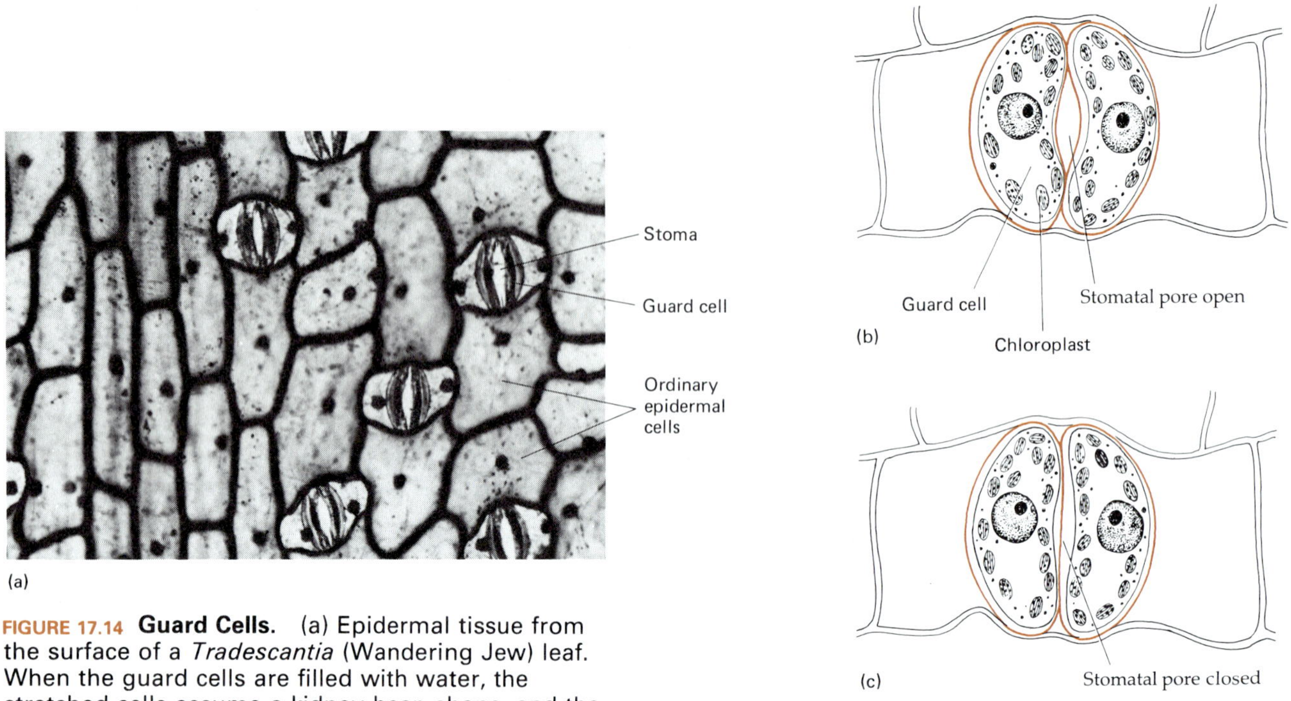

FIGURE 17.14 **Guard Cells.** (a) Epidermal tissue from the surface of a *Tradescantia* (Wandering Jew) leaf. When the guard cells are filled with water, the stretched cells assume a kidney-bean shape, and the stoma is open (b). But loss of turgor pressure—because of wilting, for example—causes the stoma to close (c).

FIGURE 17.15 **A Leaf Adaptation for Dry Environments.** Beach grass is adapted to a sunny, hot, and windy environment. The blade, seen here in cross section, is curled. The stomata are buried in deep pits protected by long hairs that inhibit air movements that would increase water loss by evaporation.

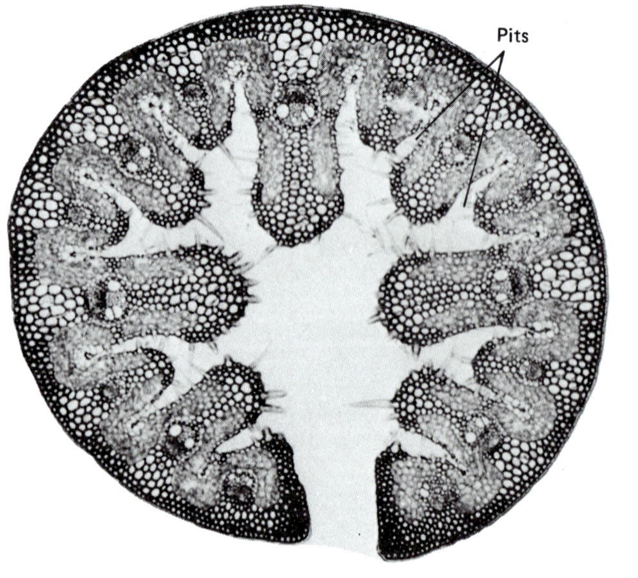

Two **guard cells** surround each stoma. Figure 17.14 shows that the inner wall of each guard cell (the wall toward the stoma) is thicker than are walls on the other sides. When water is abundant, the guard cells are turgid and the cells expand, stretching the thinner portion of their walls. This expansion forces the inner wall to curve much like a drawn bow, opening the stoma. Conversely, when evaporation threatens the plant, the guard cells lose water. The decreased pressure inside the cells permits the inner walls to straighten, and the stoma closes. This simple mechanism allows the plant to keep its stomata open for maximum gas exchange under moist conditions, but to close them automatically when moisture must be conserved. In many plants, increased carbon dioxide or decreased sunlight also causes the stomata to close. Exactly how either of these factors reduces the turgidity of the guard cell is not certain.

Not all leaves have exactly the same structure. Plants growing in different kinds of environments show structural adaptations that meet their special needs. Some adaptations are directed toward the reduction of excessive water loss (Fig. 17.15). For instance, leaves of plants growing in dry climates generally have a small number of stomata. Typically, the epidermis is modified to form hairs. The fuzzy leaf surface hinders air movements that would

FIGURE 17.16 The Prickly Pear Cactus Thrives in Dry Environments.

otherwise encourage evaporation. The cactus family has produced extreme adaptations to dry environments. They have lost their leaves to reduce water loss. The fleshy green stem of the plant carries out photosynthesis (Fig. 17.16).

Internal Structures

Sandwiched between the upper and lower epidermis of a leaf are the **mesophyll cells.** These middle-leaf cells are packed with chloroplasts. It is in the mesophyll that most photosynthesis takes place. In plants adapted to moderate climates, the upper mesophyll layer is regularly arranged, and that beneath it is spongy looking (Fig. 17.17). Large air spaces in the spongy mesophyll provide passageways for the movement of gases from the stomata into the interior of the leaf. These air spaces are only one part of an intercommunicating network that pervades almost all plant tissues, permitting gas exchange with the outside world.

Surely everyone has noticed that leaves have veins. These veins have branches throughout the mesophyll, and they are continuous with the transporting tissues of the stem. The leaf veins carry

FIGURE 17.17 A Leaf Is Like a Sandwich. The photosynthetic mesophyll cells lie between two layers of protective epidermal cells. Note that the layer of mesophyll next to the upper leaf surface consists of rather densely packed, elongated cells. Under this layer of palisade mesophyll is the spongy mesophyll. This name perfectly describes the loose, honeycombed organization of the cells. The many air spaces between the cells of the spongy mesophyll are interconnected, and they lead to the stomata through passages in the palisade mesophyll. Thus even the innermost mesophyll cells have access to fresh outside air.

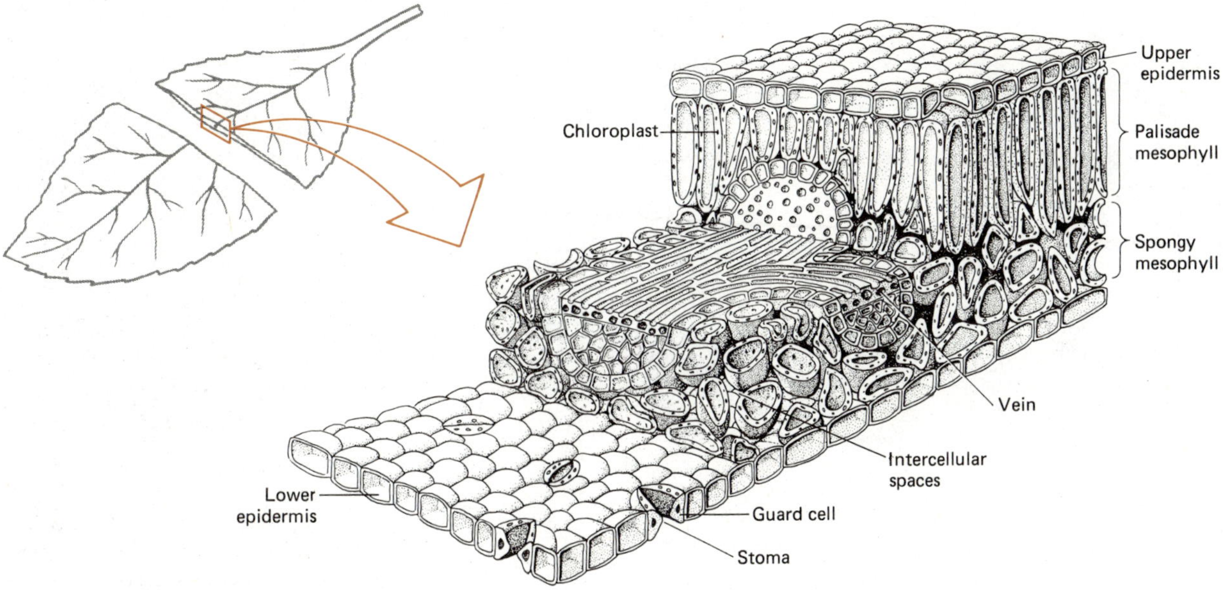

water and minerals to the mesophyll cells and collect the photosynthetic products for transport to other parts of the plant.

ROOTS AND STEMS: DUAL FUNCTIONS

Roots and stems serve for both transport and support. In a sense stems exist only to hold the leaves where they obtain sufficient sunlight for photosynthesis and to connect the leaves to the delicate root tips, where water and minerals are absorbed.

A cylinder of **vascular tissue** that provides for transport and support is present in stems and roots. The **vascular cylinder** consists of xylem and phloem. **Xylem** serves for support and to conduct water and minerals. It makes up the inner portion of the vascular cylinder. **Phloem** transports sugars and other organic compounds. It lies external to the xylem and is therefore closer to the periphery of the plant.

The structure of the vascular cylinder varies among plants and between roots and stems (Fig. 17.18). For example, in the stems of monocots, such as the grasses, the xylem and phloem occur in bundles. Young dicots also have vascular bundles in their stems, but in those that grow into trees, the bundles merge into a complete cylinder. Most roots contain solid cores of xylem that radiate outward in "arms." The phloem fills wedges between these arms.

A **cortex** composed of **parenchyma** (generalized cells) and **fiber cells** surrounds the vascular cylinder. In young plants an **epidermis** covers the outer surface. As the roots and stems of woody plants age, their epidermis is replaced by **cork.** Cork cells acquire a waxy coating and then die. Thus an outer layer of dead cells protects the living tissues of the stem and root. Cork is very resistant to physical damage; its waxy coat also minimizes water loss.

Bark consists of phloem, cortex, and either an epidermis or cork. What we call **wood** is, strictly speaking, the xylem. Bark and wood are separated by a thin ring of **cambium** cells. The cells of this layer divide to form additional vascular tissue as the plant grows in diameter. Cambium cells are so thin-walled that bark can be peeled from tree trunks, twigs, and roots.

Xylem and the Provision of Water and Minerals

Xylem contains several different kinds of cells, but the most important are tracheids and vessel elements (Fig. 17.19). The long, narrow, spindle-shaped **tracheids** are so arranged that their ends overlap. Even the **pits,** or gaps in the secondary walls of adjacent cells, match. At maturity the tracheids die. When the cytoplasm decays, only the empty walls remain. Then water and minerals can flow from

FIGURE 17.18 Tissue Organization of Stems and Roots.

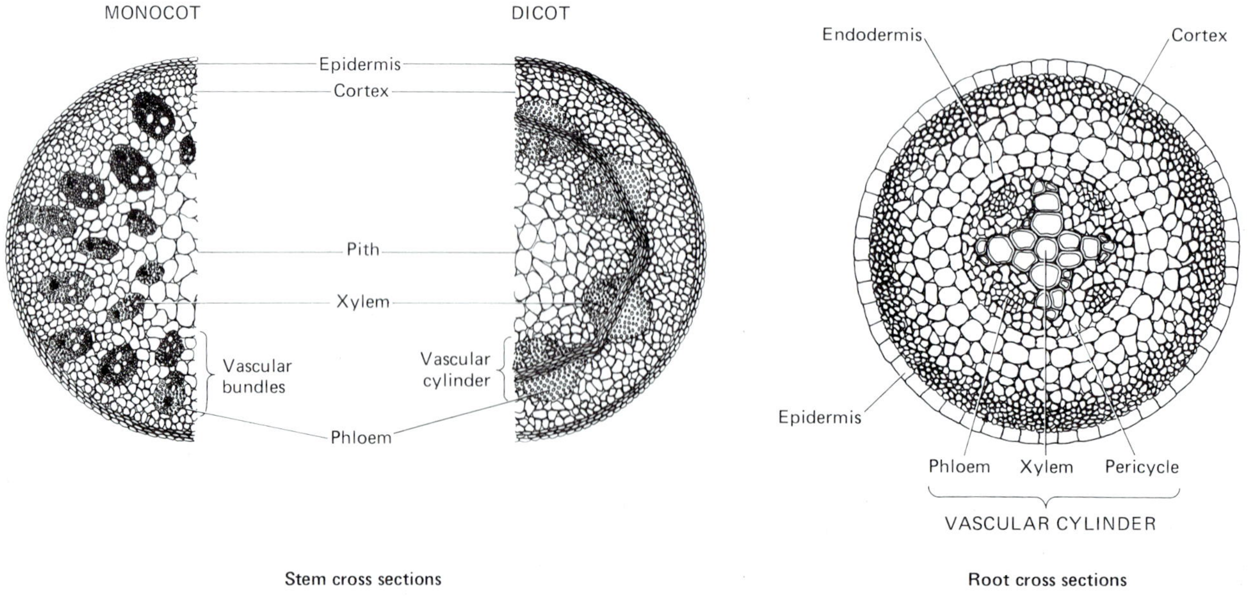

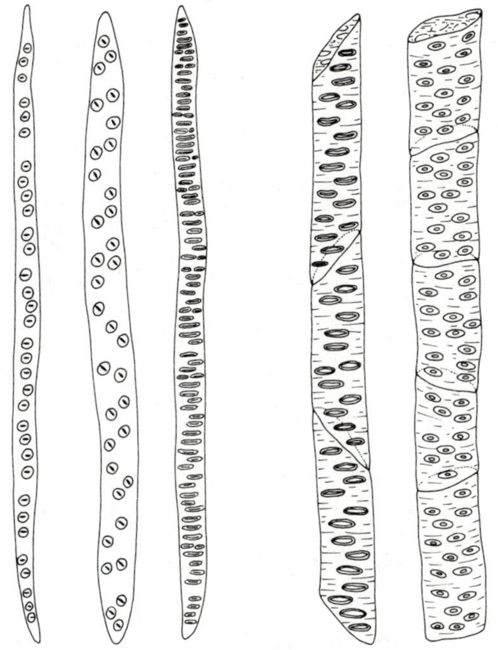

FIGURE 17.19 **Conducting Cells of Xylem.**

one tracheid to another, through the pits, up the root and stem, into the leaf.

Vessel elements are found only in flowering plants. Vessel elements are generally larger in diameter than tracheids are, and they have flattened ends. At maturity their cytoplasm and end walls disintegrate, so that individual cells fuse into continuous **vessels.**

Among the dead tracheids and vessel elements are fiber cells and living parenchymal cells. Many of the parenchymal cells are arranged in groups called **rays,** which extend through the xylem to the sides of the stem or root. The xylem rays provide lateral transport of water and other substances.

Obtaining Water. Near the tips of roots, the epidermal cells bear **root hairs** (Fig. 17.20) that greatly increase the root surface. The constantly growing root tips literally push their way through the soil. For a long time biologists assumed that water entered the root hairs and then passed from cell to cell to the xylem by osmosis. This seemed a reasonable explanation, since water is usually present in much higher concentration in soil than inside root cells. This explanation, however, may be much too simple.

Recent investigations indicate that osmosis may be supplemented by active transport, ▫in which root cells expend energy to pull in water. It is also likely that some water seeps along the walls of the cortex cells instead of from cell to cell through the cytoplasm. Once it was thought that water intake occurred only through the delicate young root tips. At least some water certainly enters older roots by absorption through the corky bark, either directly or through cracks. 78

Water Transport. Because the tracheids and vessel elements of xylem are dead, purely physical forces must move water through the vascular tissue. Continuous columns of water extend from the xylem of the root into the smallest leaf vein. Most of the water that gets to the leaves is lost by **transpiration.** In this process water evaporates from the surfaces of the mesophyll cells. Eventually the water vapor escapes from the leaves through the stomata. The amount of water lost from a plant through transpiration can be astonishing. For example, a single corn plant may transpire more than 50 gallons of water during a three-month growing season.

Although most of the water gathered by a plant evaporates into the atmosphere, this loss provides a method for moving water through the dead xylem vessels and tracheids. Transpiration from the mesophyll of the leaves causes these cells to draw

FIGURE 17.20 **Root Hairs Growing into Soil.** Root hairs provide a vast surface area for absorption of water and minerals.

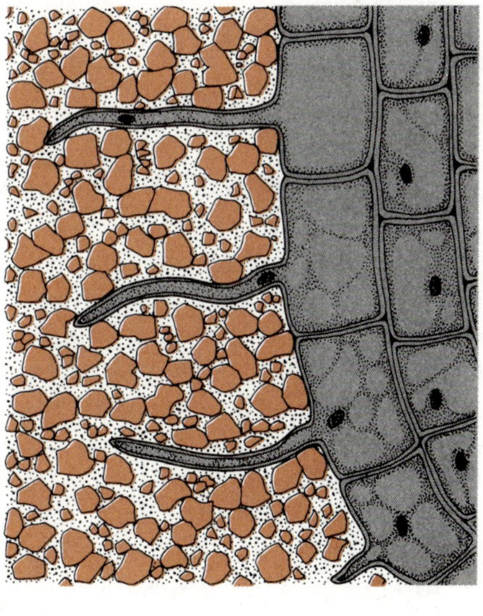

BOX 17A

WOOD

The wood used to manufacture lumber, furniture, and other objects of our everyday experience comes from the xylem of trees. Sawing tree stems in various planes reveals different wood patterns. These patterns arise from the arrangement of xylem rays, annual growth rings, and other structures.

Xylem cells formed in wet weather (usually spring in the temperate zone) are large. Consequently, there is relatively little cell wall material per unit area, and the wood formed at this time appears light in color. During drier seasons the cells formed are smaller; the wood laid down then is more dense with cell walls and appears darker. The relative widths of these portions of the annual growth rings not only add beauty to wood but also record the climate under which the wood was formed. Cores from living bristlecone pines in the southwestern United States reveal that some of these trees are more than 4000 years old. The rainfall patterns of prehistoric times are recorded in their xylem.

Because rainfall varies from year to year, so does xylem growth. The sequence of changes over several years forms nearly unique patterns of growth rings. Wood from ancient buildings or archeological "digs" can be dated if trees from that period are still living or if a series of wood pieces with overlapping ring patterns and hence overlapping ages can be extended to include living trees.

As trees age, the vessels and tracheids of the older xylem in the center of the trunk become

77 in more water by osmosis. This water comes from deeper cells that in turn replenish their supply by drawing water from yet deeper cells. Thus an **osmotic gradient** extends from outer mesophyll cells to those that take water from a xylem vessel or tracheid. In this way transpiration draws water from the roots and through the entire xylem system.

The upward movement of water depends on **cohesion**—that is, the attraction of water molecules to one another. The chemical basis for the cohesiveness of water is its hydrogen-bonding
55 capacity. Hydrogen bonding also explains why water molecules adhere so tightly to surfaces when they are confined in narrow spaces. The difficulty encountered when attempting to separate two pieces of glass held together by a film of water readily illustrates both the cohesive and adhesive properties of water.

Transpiration and cohesion together account for the movement of many gallons of water to heights of hundreds of feet in large trees, or just a few inches in a young plant. As a water molecule escapes from a leaf cell by transpiration, it is replaced by another. The replacement molecule drags its blocked with cell outgrowths or a variety of organic compounds. These deposits give the dry heartwood a darker color than the outer, functional sapwood. Some of the chemicals in heartwood may be only stored wastes. Others render the wood inhospitable to microorganisms that might otherwise destroy the heartwood and weaken the tree trunk. In the photograph on the facing page, 51 rings of xylem tell the age of the loblolly pine from which the section was cut. The distinction between dark heartwood and the lighter, functional sapwood is quite evident.

In the lumber trade, the gymnosperms such as firs, spruce, cedar, and pine are known as softwoods. The angiosperms, including basswood, cherry, willow, birch, beech, maple, walnut, and oak, are called hardwoods. On the average, angiosperm wood is probably harder than gymnosperm wood, but the range of hardness in each group is much greater than these common designations suggest. For example, basswood is softer than most gymnosperm woods, although some other angiosperms, including the hickories, have very hard wood. Also, southern yellow pine, a gymnosperm, produces a wood nearly as hard as any angiosperm wood.

Cross section showing that xylem cells of the summer wood of pine have smaller cavities and thicker walls than those of spring wood.

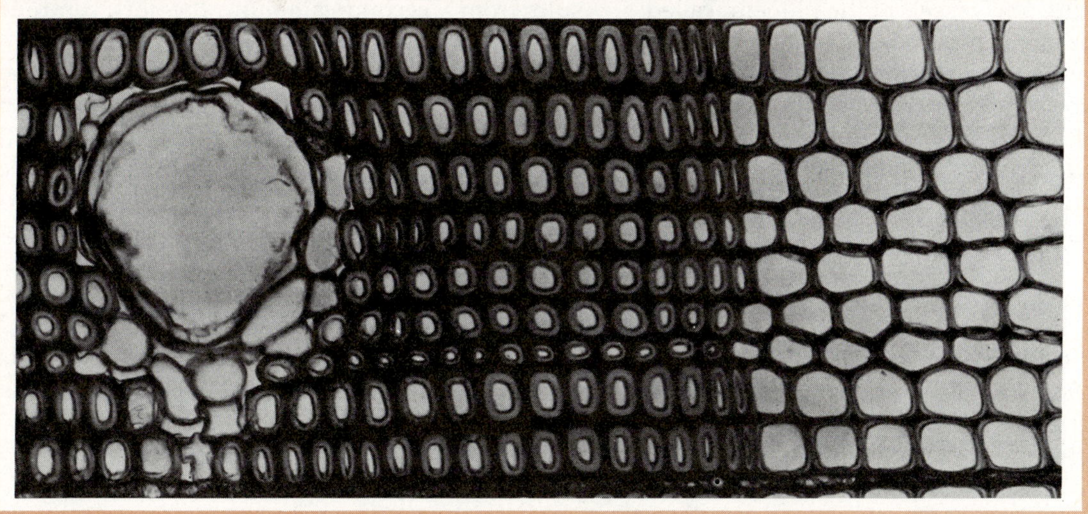

neighbor water molecule along behind it. In this manner a column of water continuously creeps upward through the long, narrow xylem channels.

Minerals. Numerous experiments have shown that root cells are highly selective in procuring mineral nutrients from the soil. Some of the essential elements are absorbed at higher rates than others, and the rates are not necessarily in accord with their relative abundance in the soil. For this reason biologists have concluded that mineral absorption cannot be explained by simple diffusion alone. The uptake of many minerals must be accomplished by specific, energy-consuming transport processes. On the other hand, dead xylem cells cannot carry out active transport, so minerals within the plant are carried passively along in the flow of water.

Phloem and the Transport of Organic Compounds

There is little doubt that the photosynthetic products and other organic compounds move principally in the phloem, but the mechanisms involved

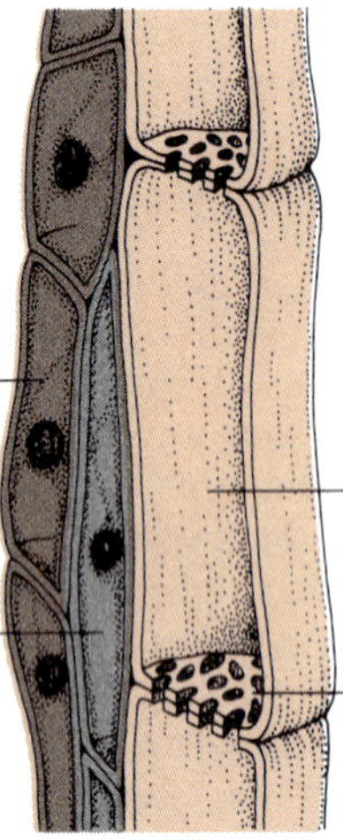

FIGURE 17.21 **Sieve Tube Cells and Their Companions.**

are poorly understood. In contrast to the tracheids and vessels of xylem, cells of phloem are very much alive. The conducting vessels of the phloem, called the **sieve tubes,** are composed of a number of sieve tube cells arranged end to end. As the name suggests, sieve tube cells have clusters of pores in their end walls that give the impression of a sieve (Fig. 17.21). The cytoplasm of adjacent sieve tube cells extend through the holes of the sieve plate from one cell to another.

Although a sieve tube cell is filled with living cytoplasm, it has no nucleus. In fact, many other organelles are missing. Some biologists claim that the sieve tube cell activities in flowering plants are regulated by the nuclei of the undistinguished **companion cells** that accompany them.

Most of the time, organic substances in the phloem move toward the roots; but substances stored in the lower parts of plants can also pass upward as needed. One example of this upward movement is the flow of sap that occurs when new leaves develop on trees in the spring.

Strength and Support

The thickened cell walls of tracheids and vessels provide the main support for most stems. Narrow **fiber cells** in xylem, phloem, and cortex give extra support. These slender dead cells are similar to tracheids but have far thicker walls and lack pits. Many plant fibers have economic value. For example, linen is made of the fiber cells of flax, and burlap comes from hemp fibers. These useful fibers can be isolated by allowing plant stems to rot. The unwanted weaker cells disintegrate, and the durable fibers are released and can be harvested.

PLANT GROWTH

In animals growth occurs throughout the body, but in plants growth is limited to localized tissues, called meristems. **Apical meristems,** found at the tips of stems and their branches and at the tips of roots (Fig. 17.22) and their branches, are responsible for growth in length. Division of apical meristem cells is accompanied by cell elongation and differentiation into characteristic plant tissues.

Growth in diameter does not involve apical meristems. Instead, a lateral meristem, the cambium we referred to earlier, produces new cell layers that thicken stems and roots. Growth in girth is most evident in trees and shrubs. A **vascular cambium** between xylem and phloem adds new xylem cells on the inside and new phloem cells on the outside every growing season (Fig. 17.23). Cork tissue results from a second cambium, the **cork cambium,** which forms in the cortex outside the phloem.

Grasses and most other monocots grow almost entirely from the tip. There is no cambium, so growth in any region ends when cells produced by the apical meristem reach maturity. Thus monocots usually show little growth in girth. However, monocot leaves are often wrapped almost entirely around the stem. This growth pattern not only strengthens the nonwoody stem, but also creates the impression of substantial girth. A corn plant (Fig. 17.24) illustrates this well. A few monocots such as palms can reach considerable size because of special growth tissues.

Growth of a Stem

A **terminal bud,** which contains the apical meristem and the rudiments (or **primordia)** of leaves, is located at the end of every stem (Fig. 17.25). When the growing season starts, the cells of the apical meristem begin to undergo rapid cell division and differentiation. Soon a young shoot emerges from the bud, along with a cluster or whorl of rudimentary leaves. Later, as the shoot continues to stretch outward, the leaves become more widely spaced along the stem.

Bits of meristematic tissue are left behind by the growing shoot tip. These become lateral buds. Although smaller, lateral buds are little different from terminal buds. Lateral buds may develop into branches, flowers, or other plant structures, or they

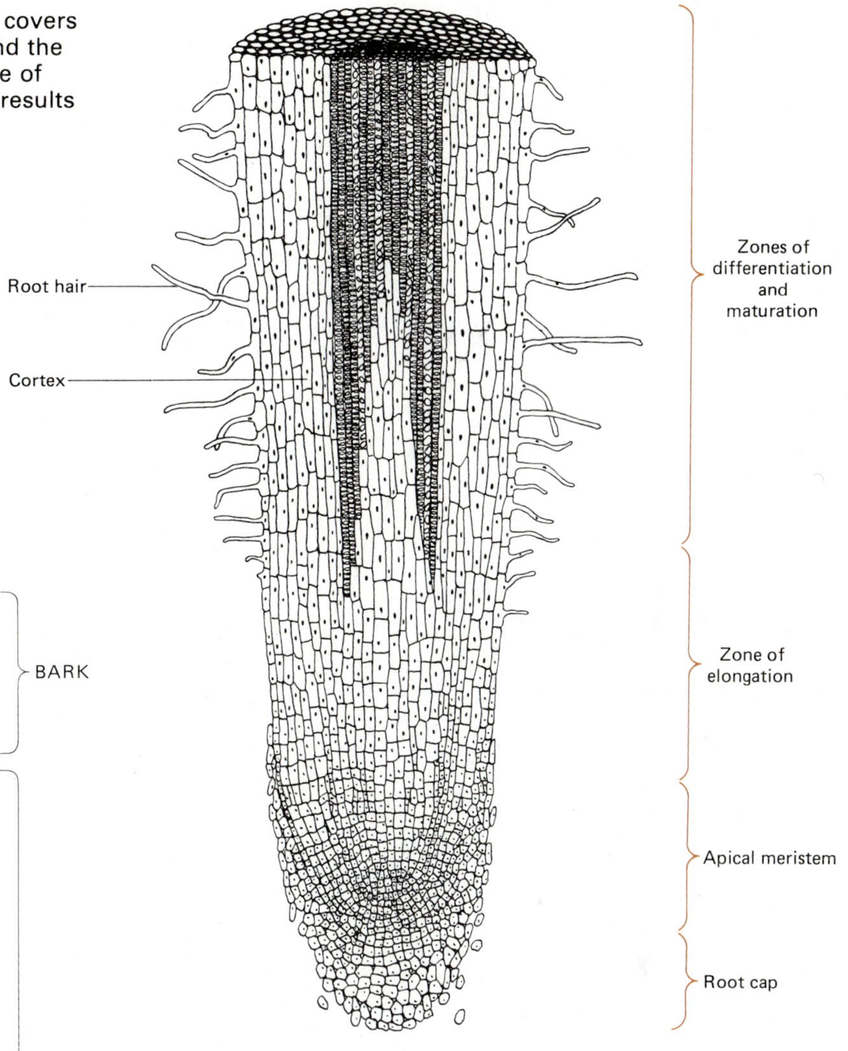

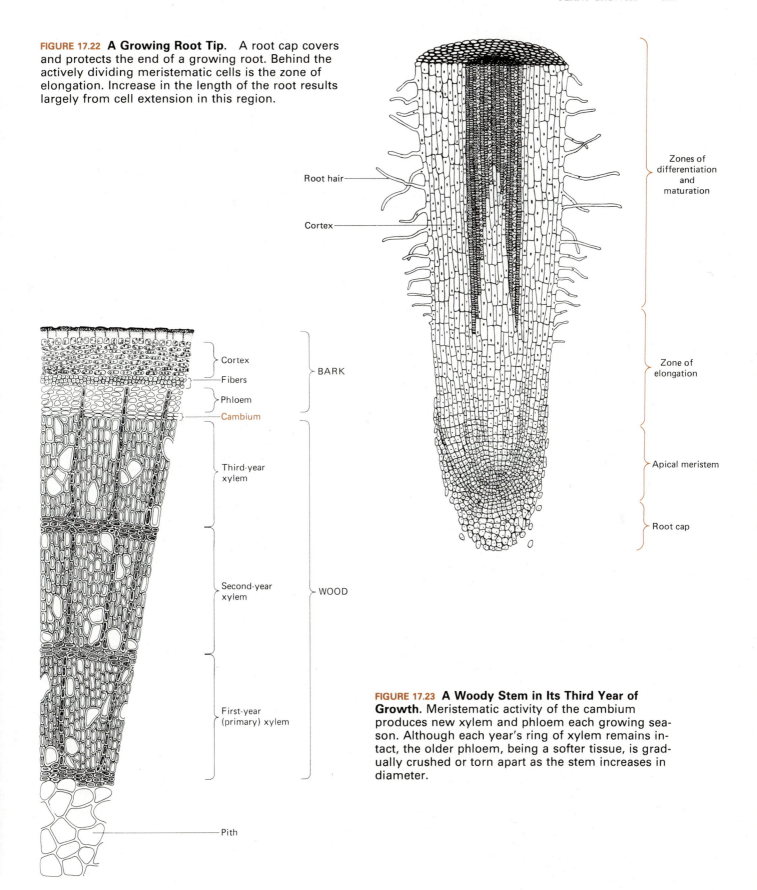

FIGURE 17.22 **A Growing Root Tip.** A root cap covers and protects the end of a growing root. Behind the actively dividing meristematic cells is the zone of elongation. Increase in the length of the root results largely from cell extension in this region.

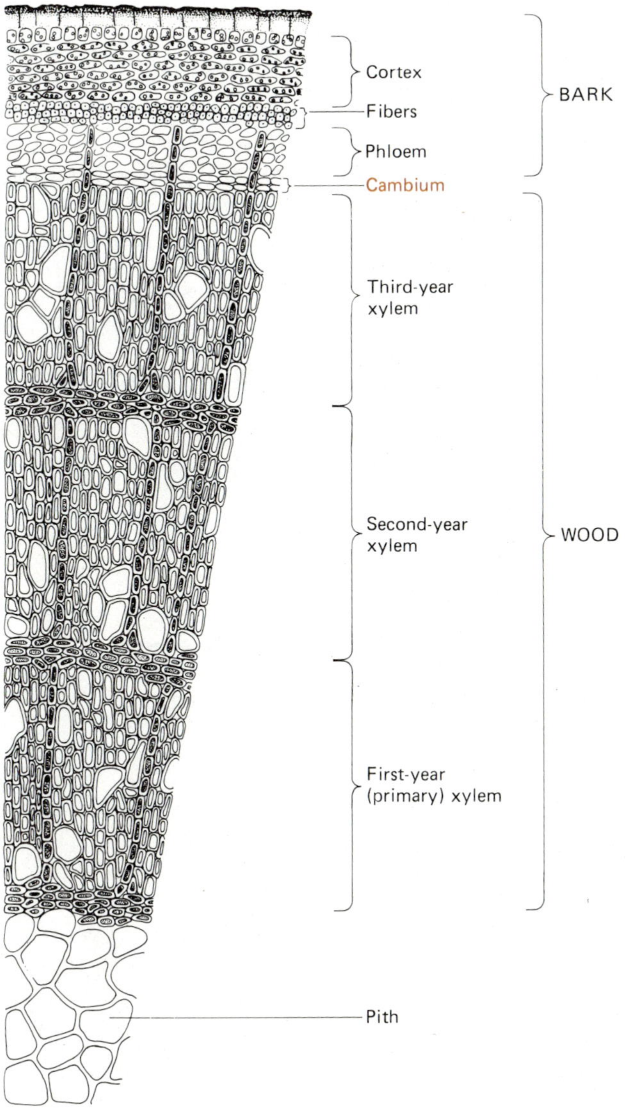

FIGURE 17.23 **A Woody Stem in Its Third Year of Growth.** Meristematic activity of the cambium produces new xylem and phloem each growing season. Although each year's ring of xylem remains intact, the older phloem, being a softer tissue, is gradually crushed or torn apart as the stem increases in diameter.

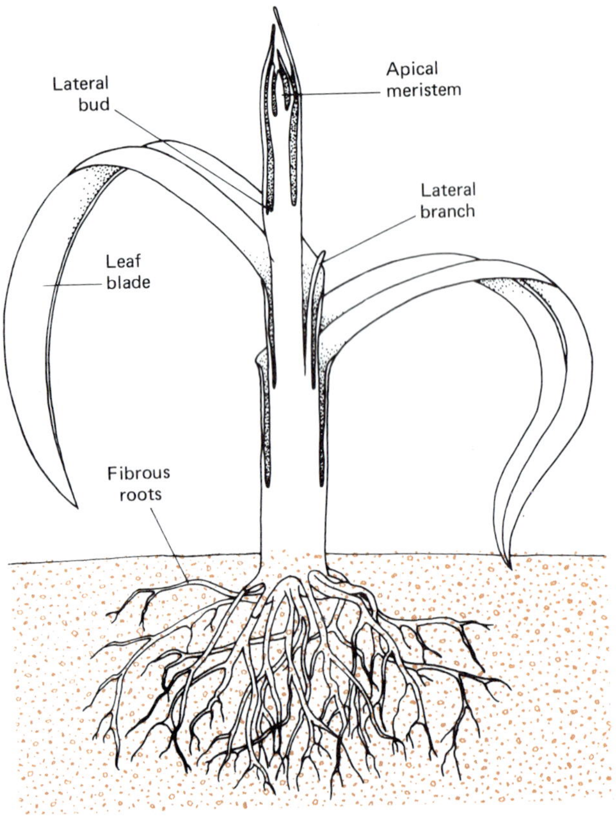

FIGURE 17.24 **Monocot Growth Points.**

may remain dormant. The buds of woody stems are protected from drying or winter injury by hard **bud scales.** When buds begin to grow, they swell and force the bud scales to peel away. This leaves a crinkled **bud scar** on the twig (Fig. 17.26). The span between the bud-scale scar and the terminal bud represents one season's growth. When leaves fall, **leaf scars** remain. On the surface of the leaf scar is an impression left by the severed vascular bundles. The buds of herbaceous (nonwoody) plants are unprotected. There is no need for such protection, even in the temperate zone, since herbaceous plants either die at the end of the growing season or overwinter underground.

The development of lateral buds depends on environmental factors and plant growth hormones, among them the **auxins.** In many species, auxin is secreted by terminal bud meristems and moves down through the stem to suppress the development of lateral buds (Fig. 17.27). Lateral buds closer to the terminal bud are more affected than are those farther away. This dominance of terminal buds over lateral buds permits plant resources to be devoted to lengthening the main stem, or **leader,** of a young plant. Branches are formed only after the plant has reached a certain size. However, if the terminal bud on a leader is destroyed, a lateral bud soon takes

FIGURE 17.25 **Dicot Growth Points.**

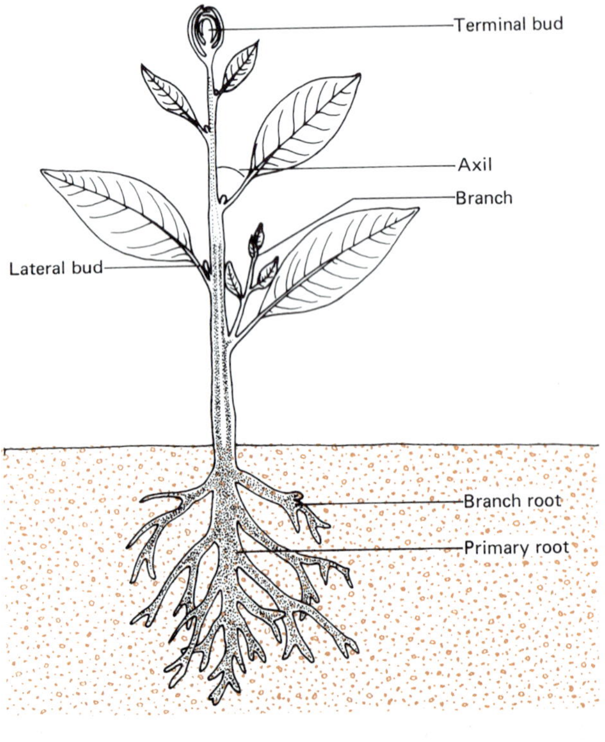

FIGURE 17.26 **A Dormant Woody Stem.**

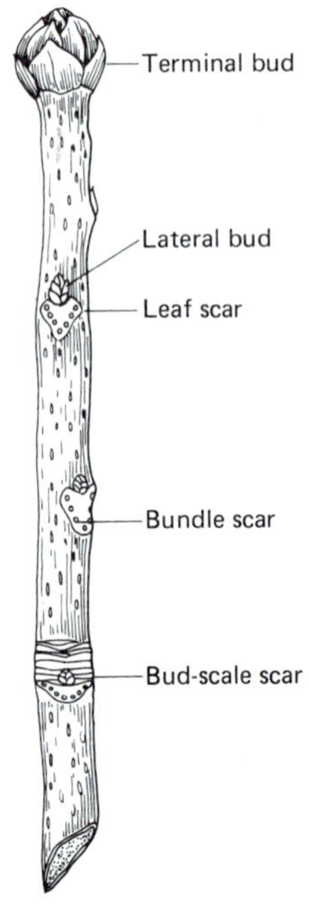

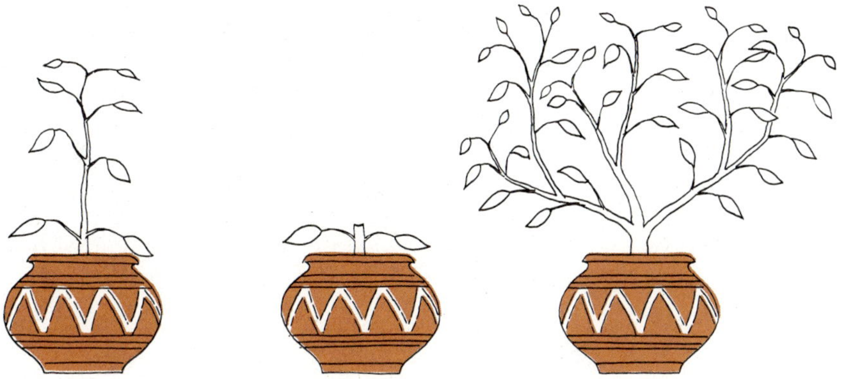

FIGURE 17.27 **Removal of the Terminal Bud Permits Lateral Buds to Grow.**

its place. By simply removing the terminal bud, gardeners can make plants with dominant terminal buds more bushy. With the growing tip gone, the source of auxin is eliminated, and the lateral buds begin to grow into major branches.

Auxins and Light

Auxins control many aspects of plant growth. Among their other effects, auxins promote stem growth by stimulating cell elongation, and they trigger cambial activities. However, at one concentration auxins may promote growth, and at other concentrations they may inhibit growth. A practical use of auxins is in rooting compounds. Low concentrations of the hormone initiate root formation by stem cuttings.

You have probably observed the bending of plants toward their source of light. This **positive phototropism** (light response) is often seen in houseplants placed near a window and not turned frequently (Fig. 17.28). It is due to different concentrations of auxin on the lighted and dark sides of the stem. As we mentioned, auxin migrates downward from the terminal bud. For some reason, less auxin moves down the lighted side of the stem than down the side that receives less light. Because cells on the darker side have more auxin, they elongate more than the cells on the other side, and the stem bends toward the light.

Branch Roots

Stem branches originate from buds, but roots have no buds. Root branches arise from a special layer of cells just under the root cortex. Thus secondary roots must grow through the cortex and epidermis before reaching the surrounding soil. The origins of both stem and root branches ensure that the vascular tissue of the branch is continuous with that of the parent structure.

FIGURE 17.28 **Positive Phototropism.**

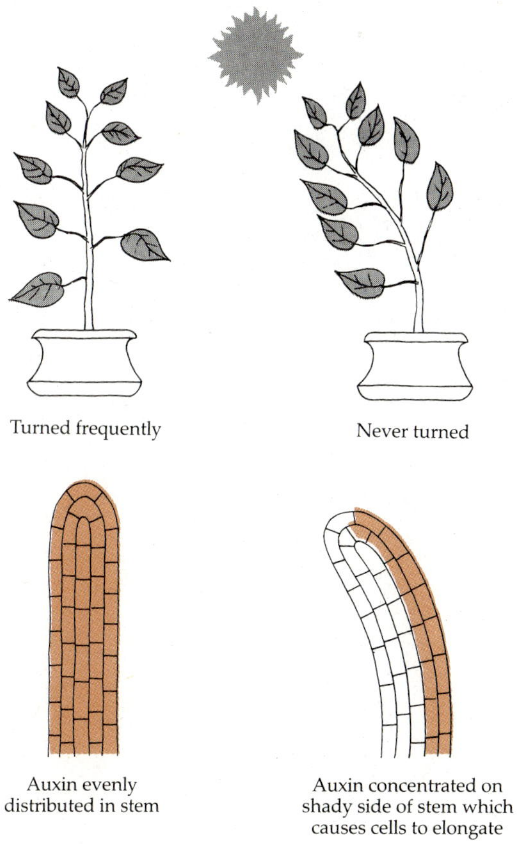

FLOWERS AND SEED PRODUCTION

We have already described how the sexual life cycle of plants alternates between a haploid gametophyte generation and a diploid sporophyte 386 generation.▫ But most plants can also reproduce asexually, or vegetatively. Gardeners recognize that new plants can often be produced from a root or stem cutting, or from a leaf (see Box 17B). Many weedy plants rapidly reproduce vegetatively by forming buds or **suckers** (shoots) on their roots. Tulip **bulbs,** grass **rhizomes,** and potato **tubers** are underground extensions of stems. Basically such devices serve for overwintering or to withstand drought (Fig. 17.29). But these structures also branch, giving rise to new individuals. Other plants produce above-ground reproductive structures. Strawberry plants, for instance, grow long **runners,** horizontal stems that sprout roots as they branch away from the parent (Fig. 17.30).

Plants that result from vegetative reproduction are **clones,** that is, genetic duplicates of their parents. Artificial cloning of economically important plants has been practiced for centuries. Plants that naturally carry out both asexual and sexual reproduction receive certain benefits. Vegetative reproduction perpetuates successful genetic combinations, while sexual reproduction provides the potential for genetic change.

Before we consider various aspects of flower diversity, recall that in flowering plants the microscopic gametophytes are parts of flowers and that fertilization occurs within protective female tissues. Remember, too, that fusion of gametes within the pistil produces a zygote that develops into an embryo protected by tough seed coats. Seeds are

FIGURE 17.29 **Some Kinds of Underground Stems.**

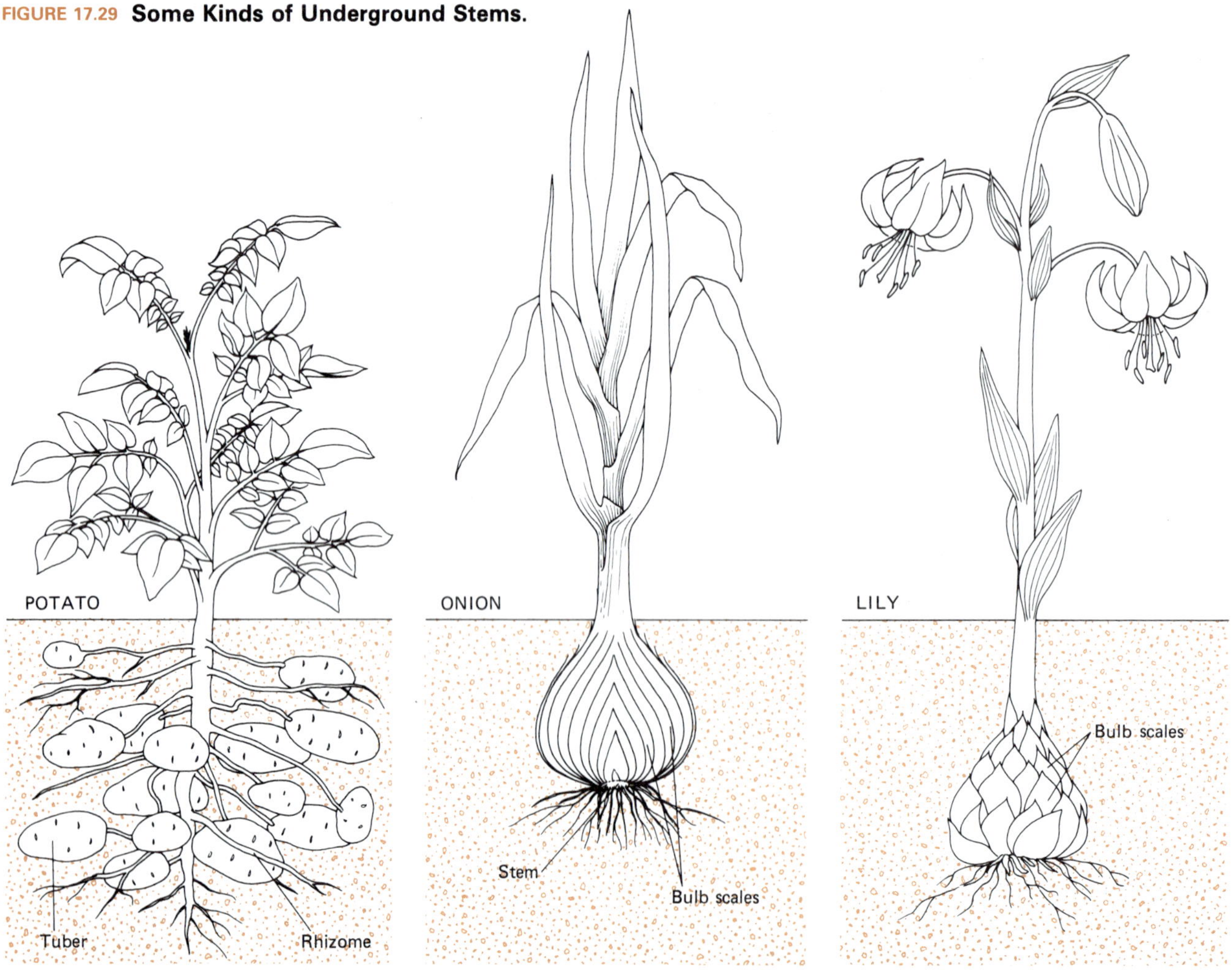

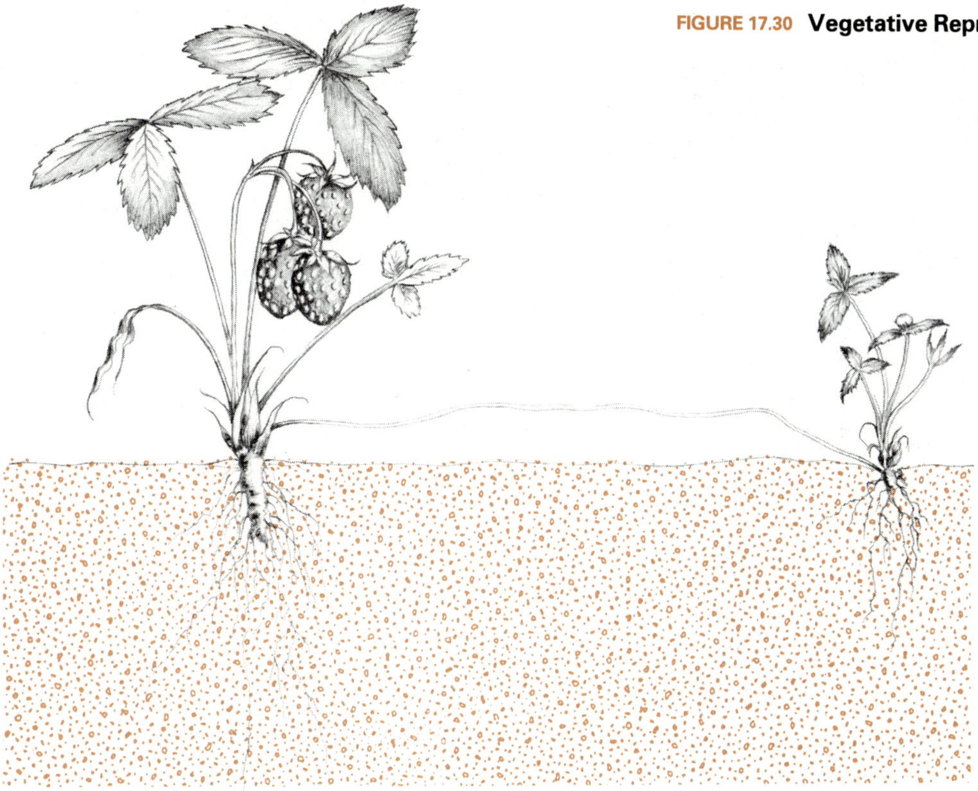

FIGURE 17.30 **Vegetative Reproduction in the Strawberry.**

389 found within the fruit that develops from the ovary at the base of the pistil.□

Floral Diversity

391 The reproductive parts of a flower, as we learned in the last chapter,□ are the male **stamens** and the female **pistil.** These structures are attached to the **receptacle** and are generally surrounded by bright-colored, showy **petals** and protective green **sepals.** The sepals serve their main function when a flower is still in bud (Fig. 17.31). Although many flowers are bisexual, others are unisexual, in which case a plant has separate male and female flowers.

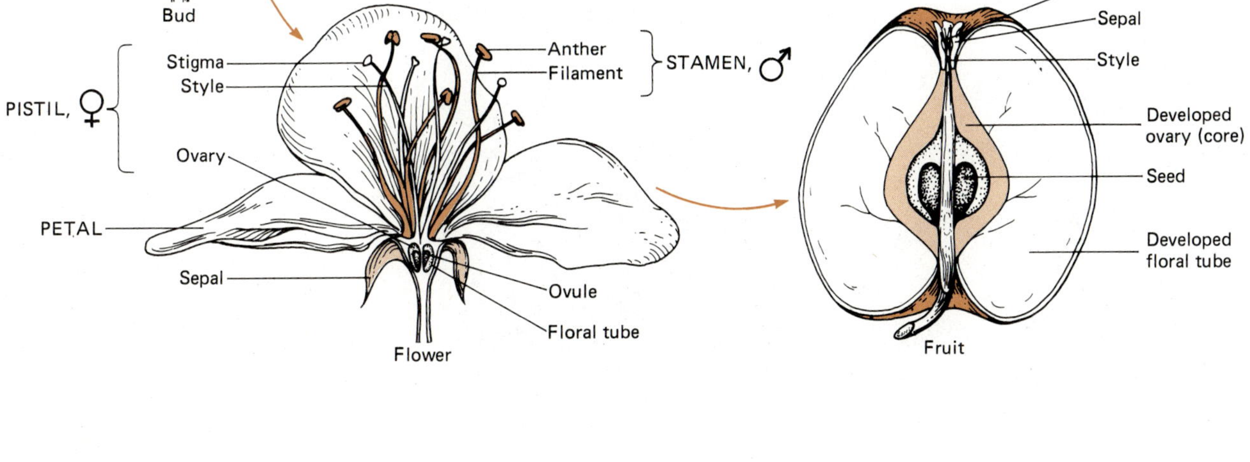

FIGURE 17.31 **From Apple Blossom to Fruit.**

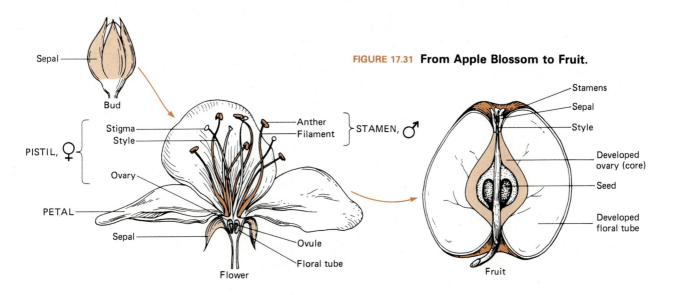

FIGURE 17.32 **Common Cowparsnip.** The cowparsnip inflorescence is an example of an umbel in which the flower stalks arise from the same point, just like the ribs of an umbrella. Carrot, dill, onion, and geranium flower clusters are also umbels.

Flowers may be produced individually or in a cluster called an **inflorescence** (Fig. 17.32). Lilac, dogwood, poinsettia and daisy flowers are examples of inflorescences. Surprisingly the large, attractive "petals" of dogwood and poinsettia flowers are in reality modified leaves or **bracts** (Fig. 17.33). In most inflorescences, however, bracts are very small compared with foliage leaves. The tassel-like **catkins** of aspen, birch, oak, and willow trees are examples of inflorescences that consist of clusters of pistils or clusters of stamens (Fig. 17.34). Daisy-type flowers are **composites.** What appear to be petals around the edge of the dense inflorescence are really individual female **ray flowers.** The pistils at the base of each ray flower form a ring around the central **disk flowers** in the "eye" of the daisy (Fig. 17.35). Each of the many disk flowers is complete, having both male and female parts.

Control of Flower Formation

A plant must reach a specific stage of development before flowering occurs. The required time is highly variable. Annuals usually reach flowering size in only a few weeks, while some trees may grow for 15 or 20 years before they can reproduce sexually. Although overall good health and vigor are necessary for flowering, light and temperature are

FIGURE 17.33 **Dogwood.** Four large white or pink bracts surround each inflorescence, which consists of several very small flowers.

FIGURE 17.34 **Staminate Catkins of the Burr Oak.**

thought to be the most critical environmental factors that control the flowering process.

Flowering of many tropical and subtropical plants depends on water availability; some plants bloom in the dry season and others in the wet season. Temperate plants are sometimes induced to flower only after a period of cold temperatures. Turnips, carrots, and other root crops are examples of **biennial** plants that normally flower in the second growing season, after accumulating storage reserves in the first year. For these plants, the cold of winter is necessary to induce flowering the next summer. Of course, farmers harvest root crops after the first season's growth.

Flowering may also be determined by day length. We can categorize plants according to the amount of daylight or **photoperiod** necessary to promote flowering. Fall-blooming chrysanthemums and ragweed are examples of **short-day plants,** while summer-blooming plants such as red clover and spinach are **long-day plants.** Tomatoes, roses, and corn are **day-neutral plants,** because they are apparently unaffected by photoperiod length.

Photoperiod perception by plants depends on the presence of photoreceptive pigments in plant tissues. These pigments, known as **phytochromes,** are located in the leaves. Although the mechanism is obscure, such pigments provide plants with a time-measuring device similar to the biological

FIGURE 17.35 **Arrowleaf Balsamroot, a Composite.**

BOX 17B

ASEXUAL PROPAGATION OF PLANTS

Pieces of stems bearing buds lack only roots to function as independent plants. Many species, including such common houseplants as geranium, coleus, *Dieffenbachia,* and begonia, can be multiplied by simply maintaining a stem cutting in damp but adequately aerated soil. After a root system develops, the plantlet is transferred to a container. The success of rooting depends on the season and the material selected and particularly on the species. Some are much easier to root than others. Much of horticulture is devoted to the propagation of plants through variations on this technique. With the discovery of auxins, preparations of "rooting hormones" became available commercially. These speed the initial appearance of roots and increase the percentage of success, but untreated cuttings soon catch up with those that are hormone-treated. Many difficult-to-root species do not respond at all to hormone treatments.

Single leaves of some plants, including African violets, *Sansevieria,* and hyacinths, can be rooted. The presence of a bud (containing a meristem) is necessary. Buds are almost always present in the angle between the leaf and the stem. Without a bud the leaf may root, but stem growth is impossible.

Tree saplings and many other plants can be propagated through layering. The stem or branch is shallowly buried at one or more points where there are buds. Soon the buds give rise to erect branches, and roots appear nearby. Then the original stem is severed to isolate the new plantlets. Many grapes, apples, philodendrons, rhododendrons, and berries are multiplied by this technique.

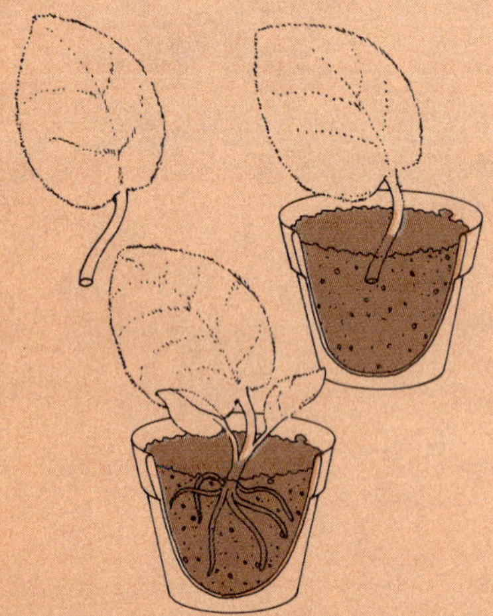

Rooting an African violet leaf

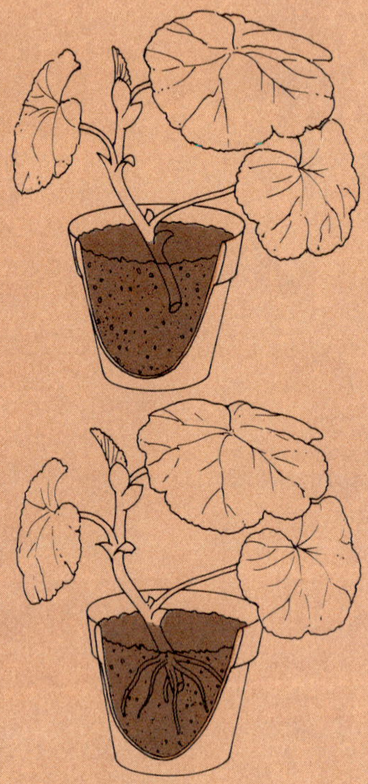

Rooting a geranium stem

189 clocks▫ recognized in animals. Exposure to light changes one form of phytochrome into another. The second phytochrome is converted back to the first at night. Time is apparently deduced from the proportion of the two forms at any given moment.

Pollination Mechanisms

Some plants pollinate themselves, but others require cross-pollination by another individual. Both types of pollination involve specific adaptations. Many plants, including important crops such as peas, beans, and tomatoes, are specialized for self-pollination. Such plants have small flowers in which the anthers and stigmas are always in close contact. In some self-pollinated species, the flowers never open.

The value of producing an embryo that is a hybrid of two different parents makes adaptations for cross-pollination understandable. In some flowers the location of anthers below the stigma discourages self-pollination. In other cases the sta-

Air-layering is much more dramatic. In this procedure the stem is damaged, and the injured area is packed with moist peat moss and wrapped in polyethylene. The plastic must be folded and tied at top and bottom so that the peat moss remains slightly damp but also so that water does not accumulate and stand. After roots become visible through the film, the stem is severed, pruned back, and transplanted. In grafting, a piece of one plant is made to grow as part of another or is moved from one place to another on the parent plant. Many different kinds of grafts are possible, but each involves only placing the grafted piece, or scion, so that its cambium directly contacts that of the host plant. Then the wound must be sealed to prevent drying and to keep disease organisms out.

Frequently grafting is used to transfer stems that produce high-quality fruit onto roots of special value. For example, most of the wine grapes of western Europe are produced by grafts onto rootstocks of native American grapes. Rootstocks of the American species are resistant to the grape phyloxera, an insect pest that once threatened the European wine industry.

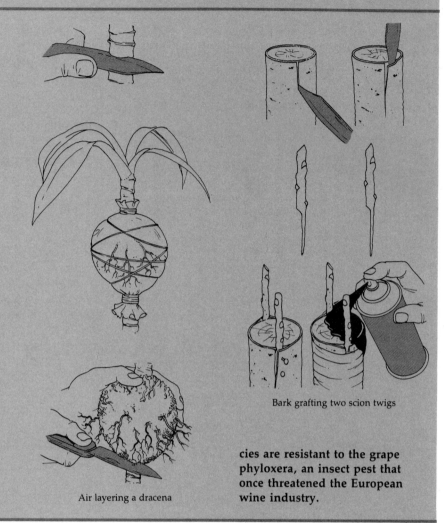

Air layering a dracena

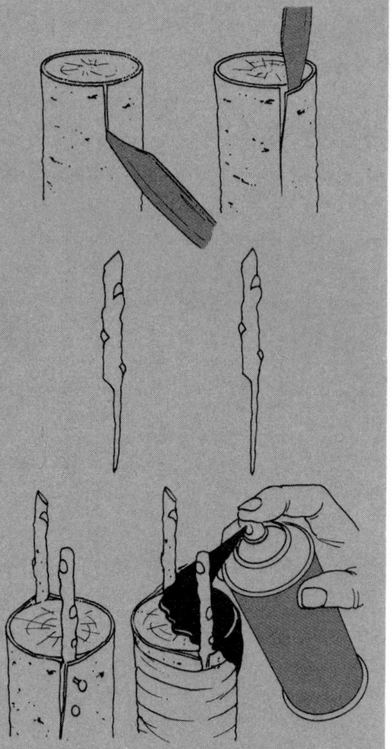

Bark grafting two scion twigs

mens and pistils mature at different times. Often the pollen and pistil tissues are incompatible, so self-pollination can never take place.

Adaptations by plants to attract animal pollinators are especially striking. Beetles, bees, wasps, flies, butterflies, moths, hummingbirds, and bats are among the animals drawn to flowers by their shape, color, fragrance, or nectar (Fig. 17.36). Bees are thought to be the most important pollinators. Fruit trees are among the many economically important crops they pollinate.

Pollen is an excellent sources of protein. As they forage for pollen, animals passively transfer the sticky, heavy pollen grains from plant to plant. So do animals that harvest nectar, a sugary secretion of the nectary glands, which are usually located deep within a flower. Often the arrangement of floral parts aids in the transfer of pollen to pollinators (Fig. 17.37).

Plants that lack bright-colored or fragrant flowers are generally wind pollinated. Grasses and most temperate-zone trees fall into this category. Male

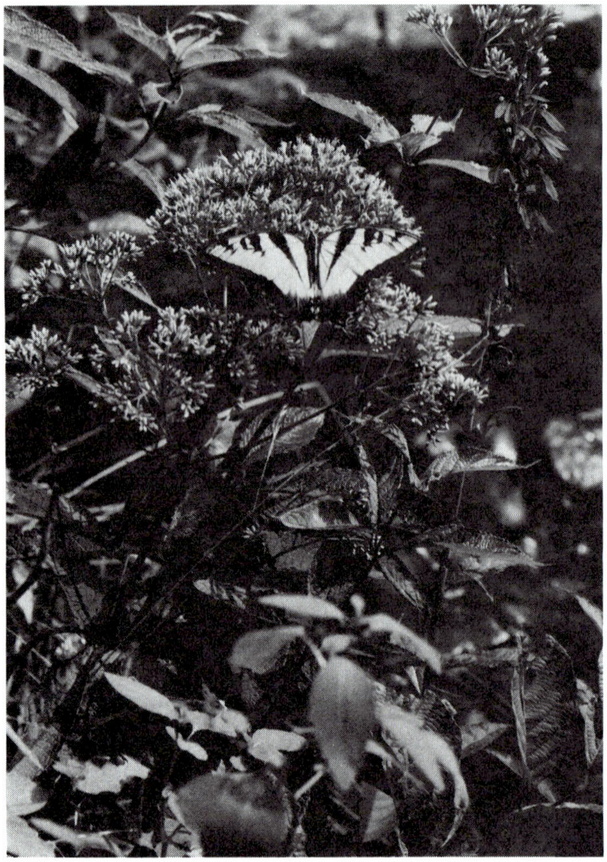

FIGURE 17.36 A Yellow Swallowtail Pollinating an Ironweed Plant.

catkins and dangling stamens of grasses spread pollen far and wide with every breeze (Fig. 17.38). Wind pollinated plants often have dry, lightweight pollen grains and unisexual flowers that make it difficult for the plants to pollinate themselves. As you may know, airborne pollen is responsible for hay-fever reactions. The source of the allergenic pollen varies from season to season. In spring, elms, oaks, and hickories are among the culprits; in midsummer, grasses are the likely offenders; and in late summer and autumn, often ragweed is to blame. Some people think the showy goldenrod causes fall hay fever, but that plant is insect pollinated, so its pollen grains are not often found in the air.

Fruits and Seed Dispersal

The ovary, often together with some surrounding tissue, matures into a fruit that encloses the seeds. Fruits such as peaches and acorns develop from the single ovary of a single pistil. In the flowers of other species, several pistils fuse to form one fruit. The partitions seen in a sliced tomato represent the fused walls of adjacent ovaries. In some species, such as the pineapple, a fruit results from the ovaries of several closely placed but separate flowers.

A fruit ripens when its seeds are ready for dispersal. In fleshy fruits this usually involves chlorophyll breakdown and substitution of pigments

FIGURE 17.37 Pollination of a Sage Flower. A foraging bee (a) gets dusted with pollen when it bumps into the swiveled ripe anther (b). Later the same bee transfers the pollen to another flower with a ripe pistil (c).

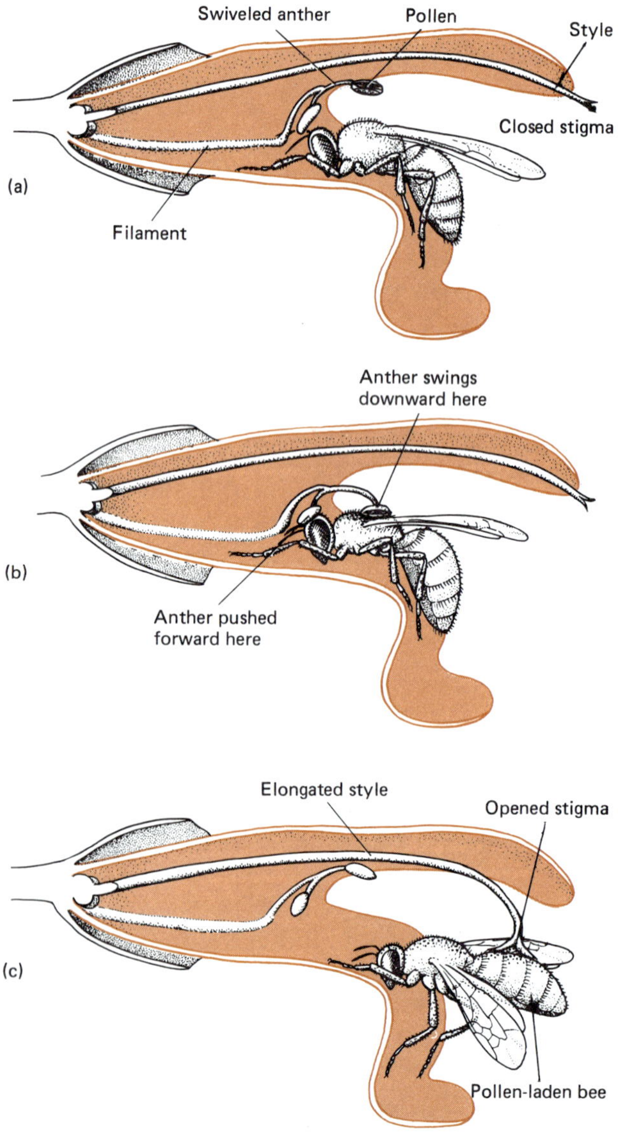

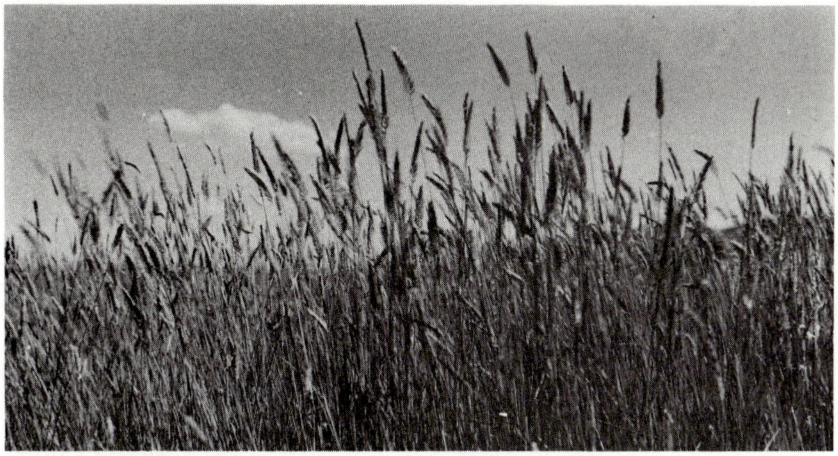

FIGURE 17.38 **Wheat and Other Grasses Are Wind Pollinated.**

of other colors, sugar accumulation, and softening of fruit tissues due to disintegration of cell walls. Dry fruits are different, however. Ripening of peas and beans, for example, involves drying out of tissues so that their pods split open to release seeds.

Although some fruits merely fall to the ground and decompose, most are highly specialized to ensure distribution of the seeds they contain (Fig. 17.39). Consider the fleshy fruits of tomatoes, apples, cherries, and melons. Their soft tissues attract

FIGURE 17.39 **Fruits and Seed Dispersal.** Some fruits (a, b, c, d, e, h) are good to eat; some (f, h) pop open; some (g) float; others (f) stick to passers-by and promote both seed dispersal and seed germination.

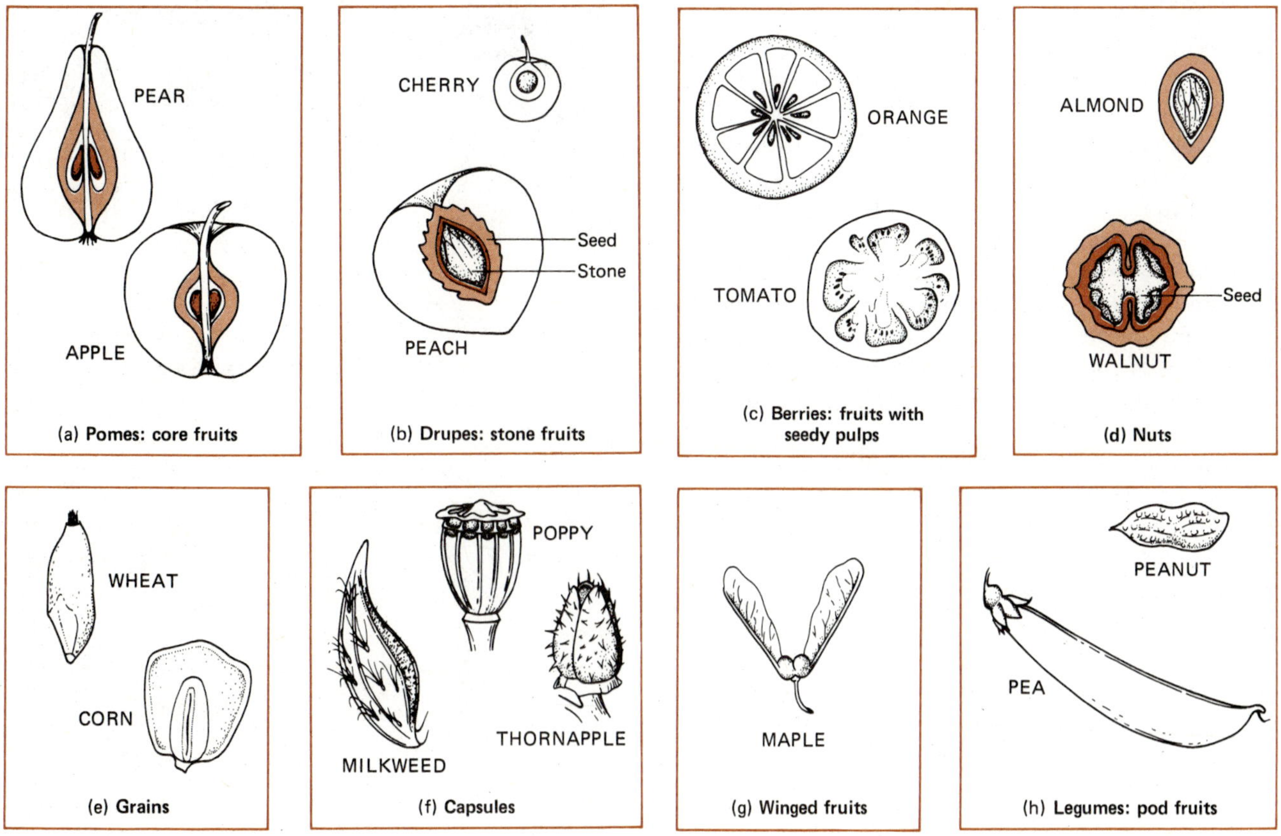

animals that feed on the fruit and spread the indigestible seeds with their feces. These seeds are thereby planted with their own fertilizer! Other fruit forms are pods or capsules, which explode open when ripe and scatter their seeds about. Still others (dandelions and maples come to mind) are borne away with the wind. "Tumbleweeds" are the broken-off tops of annual plants bearing attached fruits. Usually found in open, arid places, tumbleweeds scatter seeds far and wide as they are blown in the wind. Plants that grow along the shore are sometimes spread by water. This explains the worldwide distribution of coconut palms on tropical shores. Birds scatter seeds over wide areas. These include not only the seeds they eat and fail to digest, but also seeds that stick to the mud on the bottoms of their feet. Mice, chipmunks, and squirrels bury many kinds of fruits. Those they forget about often germinate in spring. Finally, anyone who has ever walked through brush knows about burdock and beggar ticks, two of the many kinds of plants whose fruits or seeds cling to animals and often are scratched or pulled off at some point far from their origin.

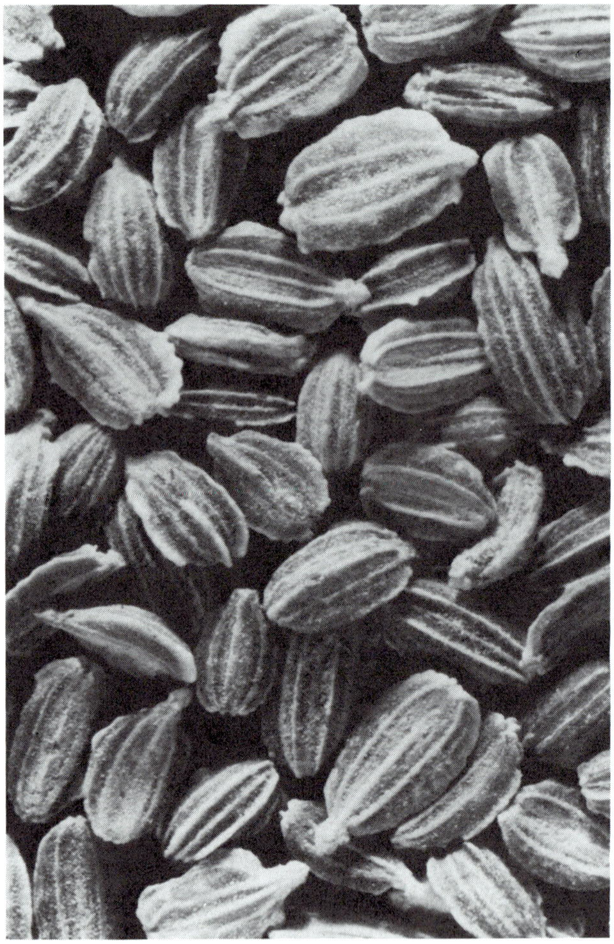

FIGURE 17.40 **Carrot Seeds, Close Up.** The tough outer seed coat protects the embryo within the seed. It forms no part of the plant that emerges during germination.

Germination

As we have already described, a seed consists of an embryo and stored nutrients surrounded by a
390 protective seed coat (Fig. 17.40). The embryo itself is a short slip of tissues. One end is the future stem and the other the future root. The seed leaves, or **cotyledons,** attach along the middle of the embryo. Cotyledons contain nutrients needed for future growth of the seedling. The material stored in the cotyledons is absorbed from the endosperm. In beans and many other plants this is accomplished as the seeds mature (Fig. 17.41). Some dicots, and all monocots, retain the endosperm until after germination begins (Fig. 17.42). After seeds mature, exposure to proper conditions will lead to sprouting, or **germination** (Fig. 17.43). If water can penetrate the seed coat, a warm, moist environment may be sufficient to stimulate germination. But in some species the seed coat must be scratched or otherwise damaged before water can enter and germination can begin.

The seeds of many temperate-zone plants will germinate only after exposure to a minimum period of cold. This prevents seedlings from developing during warm fall weather, only to die during the cold winter. Because the lower water content of

FIGURE 17.41 **A Bean, a Typical Dicot Seed.**

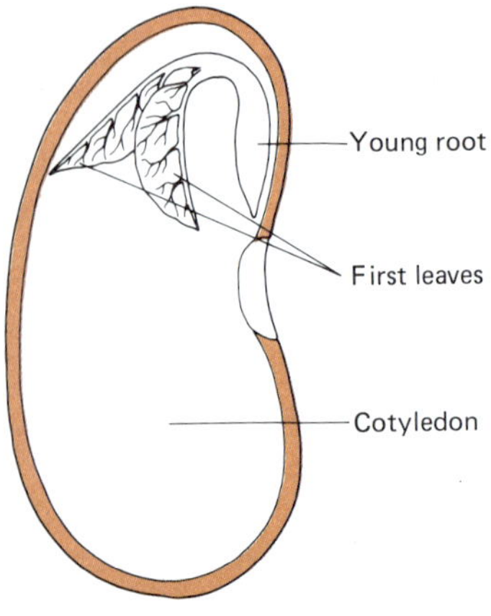

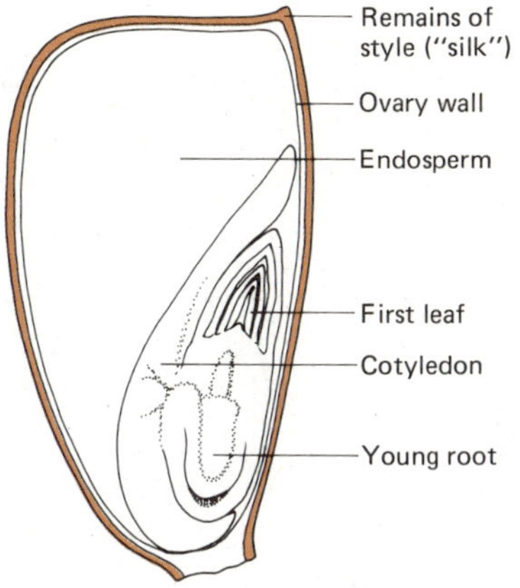

FIGURE 17.42 **A Corn Kernel.** Because its outermost coat is derived from an ovary, a corn kernel is really a fruit containing a seed.

seeds prevents formation of ice crystals, seeds are generally much more resistant to freezing than are seedlings.

Small seeds require light for germination and will not germinate if they are planted in any significant depth of soil. Even the shade of a large plant may inhibit their germination. Such a plant could outcompete the young seedling for water, nutrients, and light. The viability of seeds is extremely variable. Seeds of some tropical plants last only a few weeks, yet other types of seeds excavated from archeological sites have proven viable after a thousand years. Many seeds show a considerable increase in longevity if stored under cool and somewhat dry conditions. Light may help stimulate germination—it certainly helps orient the young root and stem, but photosynthesis is not necessary for germination because early growth of the seedling utilizes the energy obtained from endosperm and cotyledon food reserves. Water taken up during the early stages of germination activates digestive enzymes that degrade the starch, protein, or oil stored in the seed.

Once a seed has germinated, both the stem and the root start to grow, but usually the root becomes established first. This sequence ensures that the new leaves will have an immediate supply of water and minerals (Fig. 17.44).

Although most dormant seeds contain starch or other carbohydrates as an energy reserve, some are rich in oils and proteins. Germinating seeds and seedlings synthesize vitamins for their own use, and as a result, they are valuable foods. Enzymes produced during germination digest difficult-to-use carbohydrates, thus increasing the food value of seeds.

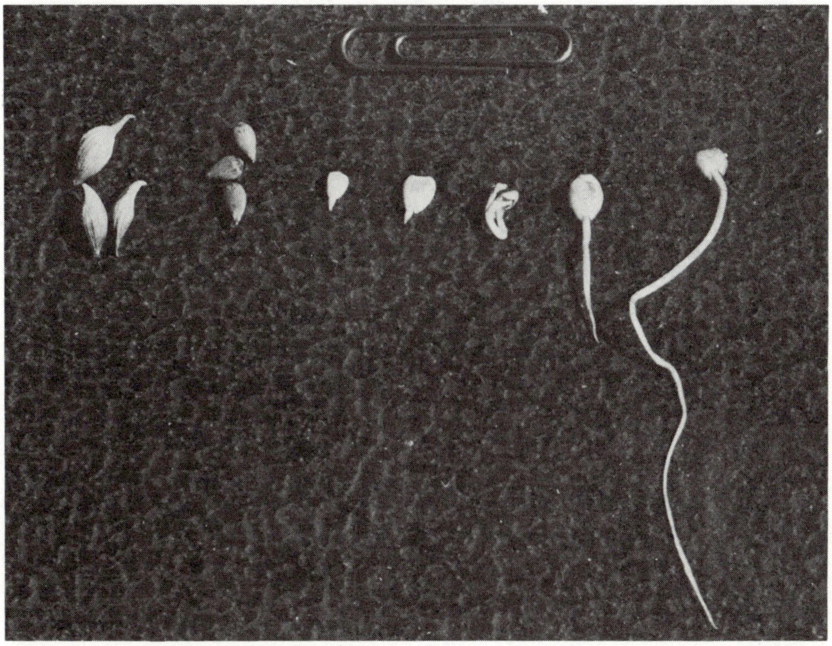

FIGURE 17.43 **Germination.** Fruits, seeds, an excised embryo, and four stages of development of a germinating embryo of bitterbrush.

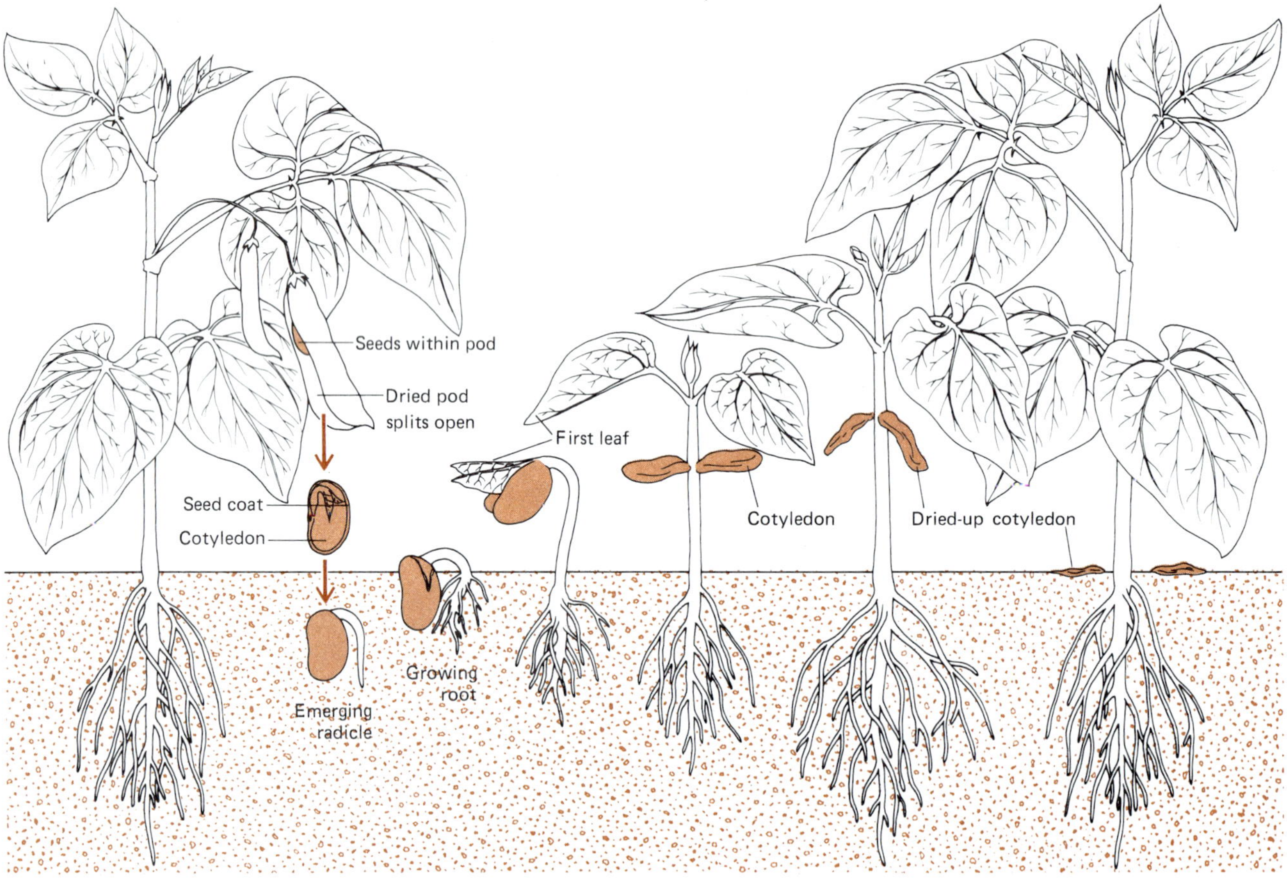

FIGURE 17.44 The Life History of a Garden Bean.

SOIL: SUBSTRATUM AND SOURCE

Soil is a complex mixture of rock particles and minerals, dead and decaying organic matter, water, air, and living organisms. Although soil may seem grubby and unimportant to us, it provides anchorage for plants, and is their source of water and minerals, as well as air to furnish oxygen for the respiration of root tissues.

How well suited any particular soil is for plant growth depends on its composition and organization. These characteristics are influenced by many factors: the climate, the nature of underlying rock, and the kinds of plants and animals in and on the soil. In fact, soil composition and organization are constantly changing because of the combined effects of physical forces and biological activities.

Rock as a Soil Source

Soil solids include both inorganic and organic materials. The inorganic portion of the soil consists of mineral particles of various sizes. These particles originate mostly from the weathering of rock. Over ages of time, rocks are slowly worn away by the abrasive action of wind and flowing water, or they are chipped and broken by the wedgelike force of water freezing within hairline cracks. Plant roots growing into cracks and crevices contribute to rock destruction (Fig. 17.45). Physical forces mix, move, grind, and sort particles, constantly modifying soil structure. Soil depth varies from place to place. The deep, rich soil of fertile river valleys results from erosion of nearby hills and mountains.

FIGURE 17.45 **Grass, Brush and Other Plants Growing in Crevices of Granite.**

In order of decreasing size, soil particles are classified as **sand, silt,** and **clay.** Farmers have long recognized that the size of particles has a definite effect on soil productivity. Sandy soils, containing large amounts of bigger particles, are porous and hold water poorly. Rainwater quickly sinks deep into the earth, out of the reach of plant roots. Furthermore, minerals are leached out of sandy soil as the water drains away. Fine clay soils present an opposite problem. They retain water too well, and the small particles become so compacted that roots actually drown for lack of oxygen! Silt particles are intermediate in size between sand and clay. Loam, an equal mixture of sand, silt, and clay, is good soil. A handful of moist loam holds its shape but crumbles easily. This type of soil retains an adequate supply of water, yet it is porous and therefore well aerated (Fig. 17.46).

FIGURE 17.46 **An Ideal Soil Is Easily Penetrated with the Hands.**

Modification of Soil by Organisms

In addition to distinctive amounts of sand, silt, or clay, soil contains organic matter derived from the decay of plant and animal tissues and animal wastes. These materials are collectively referred to as **humus.** Tremendous amounts of this organic matter are added to the soil each year. Most of it comes from plant remains, mainly leaf and stem litter on

FIGURE 17.47 **A Soil Profile.** Note the rich, dark humus layer of soil that surrounds the grass roots.

the surface and dying roots within the soil (Fig. 17.47). Humus modifies soil texture and increases capacity to hold air and water. It also supports vast numbers of decomposing organisms.

Every gram of soil teems with millions of microscopic bacteria and fungi. With the help of small scavengers such as millipedes and pillbugs, microorganisms decompose plant and animal remains to carbon dioxide, water, and minerals. Not only is this an essential aspect of the carbon cycle, but it helps ensure soil fertility by returning minerals to the soil. In one sense, humus is a reservoir of minerals. As it decays, minerals are released for plant growth. This decomposition takes place in the upper layers of the soil. For this reason, when topsoil is lost through erosion, soil fertility is greatly reduced.

Although all the biologically essential elements must be kept in circulation, nitrogen and phosphorus are of special importance. Plants take such quantities of these elements from the soil that their inavailability can be a major factor limiting plant growth. But whereas phosphorus has a slow and uncertain cycle, which we will discuss further in Chapter 21, nitrogen is continuously and actively circulated through every ecosystem.

The Nitrogen Cycle

Organic matter contains nitrogen mostly in the form of proteins and amino acids. Microorganisms convert the nitrogen in these compounds into ammonia (NH_3). Ammonia can be utilized directly by plants, or it can be converted to nitrate (NO_3) by certain groups of soil bacteria. Some plants prefer ammonia to nitrate as a source of nitrogen. However, most plants grow much better with nitrate.

A crucial aspect of the nitrogen cycle (Fig. 17.48) is that usable material tends to leak away. Certain soil bacteria convert nitrates to gaseous nitrogen, which then escapes into the atmosphere. This gas, which makes up almost 80 percent of the earth's atmosphere, is useless to most organisms. A little gaseous nitrogen is converted to nitrate by lightning, ultraviolet light, or cosmic radiation, but if it were not for **nitrogen-fixing microorganisms,** most of this nitrogen would be permanently unavailable to the biological world. Nitrogen fixers are able to incorporate gaseous nitrogen into organic com-

FIGURE 17.48 **The Nitrogen Cycle.**

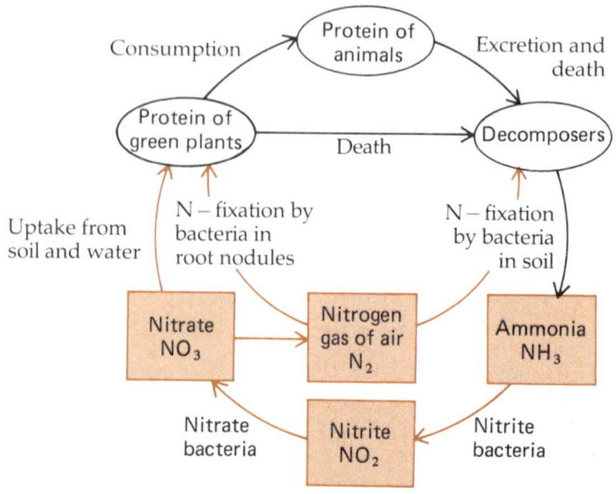

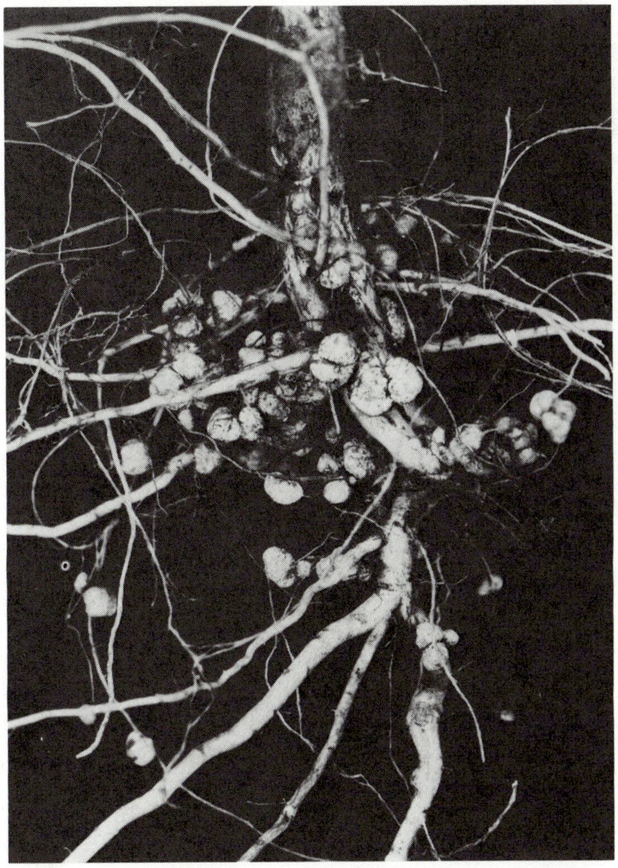

FIGURE 17.49 **Nitrogen-Fixing Nodules on Soybean Roots.**

pounds, thus providing for themselves and ensuring the cycling of nitrogen from the atmosphere back to the living world.

Root Symbionts. Although many microorganisms that fix nitrogen are free-living, the **rhizobia** are specialized soil bacteria that fix nitrogen inside other plants. These bacteria invade the roots of particular species, especially **legumes,** the important plant family that includes beans, peas, clovers, and peanuts. Once nitrogen-fixing bacteria gain entrance to the root cortex, they secrete hormone-like substances that stimulate root-cell division. The bacteria live in the resulting swellings, or nodules (Fig. 17.49).

Root nodules are able to convert gaseous nitrogen into organic nitrogen, a feat that cannot be performed by the bacteria or plant alone. The process of nitrogen fixation requires precise control of oxygen levels within the nodules. This control is accomplished by action of the oxygen-binding red pigment **leghemoglobin,** so named because it is similar to animal hemoglobin but produced by plants of the legume group. Leghemoglobin is found only in root nodules, its formation stimulated by the symbiosis with rhizobia.

Nitrogen-fixing bacteria growing in root nodules use atmospheric nitrogen to synthesize amino acids. A large portion of these amino acids are secreted by the bacteria and can be used by the host plant. Although both the bacteria and the plant can exist independently, in nature neither can fix nitrogen except when it grows with the other.

Many leguminous plants are important crops in themselves, but they assume additional importance because they carry out symbiotic nitrogen fixation and thus increase the fertility of the soil in which they grow. After harvest, the nitrogen-rich roots decay in the soil. A greater benefit is obtained when a leguminous crop is plowed under and allowed to rot. Some nonlegumes, including a few members of the rose family, the birch family, and some conifers, are also capable of symbiotic nitrogen fixation.

Soil Acidity and Nutrient Availability

Many of the elements that are essential for plant growth occur in the soil as positively charged ions (Ca^{++}, Mg^{++}, and K^{+}) bound to negatively charged clays or humic materials. Plant respiration, normal decay of organic matter, and agricultural practices produce acids in soil. Under acid conditions, positive ions are solubilized and thus made more available for use by plants. By the same token, acid soil tends to lose mineral nutrients because solubilized positive ions leach away with rainwater. Slightly acid soil is best for most plants because it strikes a balance between availability and loss of minerals. Some plants have become adapted to relatively high acid and others to alkaline conditions. **Lime** is an alkali that is commonly added to soil to reduce excess acidity and thereby increase fertility. As you might expect, alkaline soils tend to exist in arid regions where lack of rainfall and leaching causes the accumulation of positively charged mineral ions and alkaline conditions.

Fertilizers and Soil

Modern agriculture, with its intensive cultivation of the land, alters biogeochemical cycles. When plant material is harvested for human consumption, the

FIGURE 17.50 **Applying Fertilizer to a Corn Field.**

mineral content is not returned to the soil, which is therefore left less fertile. For this reason, fertilizers are added to the soil to restore minerals and maintain productivity (Fig. 17.50). Chemical fertilizers are desirable for this purpose for a number of reasons. Mined or chemically synthesized minerals can be conveniently packaged in mixtures according to specific ratios. It is simple to apply the right amount of the proper mix to ensure adequate minerals in a field. Because of the importance of nitrogen, phosphorus, and potassium, fertilizer labels commonly list the concentration of these ingredients in alphabetical order. For instance, "6–12–6" on a label indicates that the fertilizer contains enough of these elements to equal 6 percent nitrogen, 12 percent phosphorus (as phosphoric acid, P_2O_5), and 6 percent "potash," or potassium oxide.

Whereas commercial fertilizers contain minerals in the inorganic form required by plants, such "natural" fertilizers as manure and compost contain these substances chiefly in organic form. Mineralization of organic material occurs only by the decay process, which takes time. And of course, the mineral content of manure cannot be controlled. Manure and compost do have definite advantages, however. Gradual release of minerals is sometimes valuable. These natural fertilizers also add humus to the soil.

FIGURE 17.51 **You Can't Fool a Cow!** When allowed into a test field of fertilized and unfertilized plots, these cows went from one fertilized plot to the next without stopping in between.

Plants versus Animals: Different but Equal

It is sometimes a temptation to view plants as lowly organisms. To do so is a mistake. Although plants are at the base of each food chain and are the source of human food, fiber, and medicine, we should look at plants not as servants but as highly successful solutions to "the problems of life."

Studying plants provides another perspective on the relationship of form to function. The photosynthetic way of life makes it unnecessary to move, as animals must, in order to capture food. Plant cells, unlike animal cells, have a protective cell wall. The rigidity that cell walls give plants is clearly valuable to organisms that can't move to seek shelter. Nevertheless, cell walls are flexible and resilient. They permit the plant to "give a little" before the wind and other forces.

As we have seen, cell walls permit plants to tolerate dilute but variable soil waters. The same cell walls limit the possibilities for plant development, and they are probably responsible for the branching growth pattern of plants. Of course, branching roots and stems are useful adaptations that allow a stationary organism to take maximum advantage of its environment.

Finally, let us not overlook the fact that plants have homeostatic mechanisms, just as animals do. Plant hormones control growth and reproduction. Vascular tissues distribute materials in relation to need. Each plant species has specific adaptations to its environment. If we forget this point, our understanding of the biological world will be sadly deficient.

Summary

1. Light energy is absorbed by chlorophyll and accessory pigments that are located in chloroplast membranes of photosynthetic cells. The light reactions of photosynthesis use the energy of excited chlorophyll molecules to form ATP, $NADPH_2$, and oxygen from ADP, NAD, and water.

2. The dark reactions of photosynthesis, which occur in the chloroplast stroma, use the ATP and $NADPH_2$ produced by the light reactions to convert carbon dioxide to carbohydrate via the Calvin cycle.

3. In addition to having chloroplasts and the usual cell structures, plant cells are surrounded by a tough cellulose cell wall that provides support and protection.

4. The outside surface of a leaf consists of a waxy epidermis, which is punctuated by stomatal pores that are regulated by guard cells. Stomata are more common on the underside of a leaf. Sandwiched between the upper and lower epidermis are the photosynthetic mesophyll cells and veins that consist of xylem and phloem.

5. Xylem and phloem are arranged into a vascular cylinder that provides support for a plant, as well as a transport system to distribute water, minerals, and organic materials between leaves, stems, and roots. In many plants a layer of cambium separates the xylem and phloem of the vascular cylinder. The cambium produces new xylem and phloem.

6. Xylem functions to transport water and minerals absorbed by root hairs. Tracheids and vessel elements are hollow cells that form the conducting tubes of xylem tissue. Photosynthetic products are distributed via living sieve tube cells of phloem tissue.

7. Growth in length originates in apical meristems located in buds and root tips. Plant growth and development are controlled by the production of plant hormones such as the auxins, which regulate lateral bud growth as well as cell elongation.

8. Most plants reproduce asexually as well as sexually. Vegetative reproduction such as by cuttings or by bulbs, rhizomes, and runners produces offspring that are genetically identical to the parent.

9. Flowers can be bisexual—that is, they may contain both stamens and pistils—or they may be unisexual, having only male or female organs. Morphological variation in flower structure represents adaptations for self-pollination or cross-pollination.

10. As seeds develop, the ovary grows into a protective fruit. Fruits may be dry or fleshy, but they are specialized to disperse their own seeds. A seed contains an embryo, stored food reserves and embryonic leaves. Seeds are dormant, but under appropriate conditions germinate to produce a new plant.

11. Soil is a mixture of inorganic soil particles, organic debris, and living organisms. The size and nature of the soil particles and the amount and kind of organic debris determine the soil's fertility, as well as its ability to hold water and air. Soil fertility is also dependent on the biogeochemical activities of soil microorganisms that decay organic molecules and thus permit a constant recycling of nutrients.

Thought and Controversy

1. Can you offer a logical basis for each of the following practices?

a) Use of sprouted seeds such as cress, mustard, wheat, and mung bean.

b) Avoidance of foods grown with the aid of "chemical" fertilizers.

c) Fortifying garden plots with partially decomposed plant materials from "compost piles."

2. Wood chip "mulches" make very attractive gardens. Nevertheless, the ornamentals grown with such mulches often show the pale leaves characteristic of nitrogen deficiency. Can you relate this observation to the fact that the wood chips support large populations of cellulose-decomposing bacteria?

3. Knots in lumber represent branches. Can you reconcile this fact with the statement that branches arise on the outer surface of the vascular tissue of stems?

4. Earthworms abound in rich garden soil and actually increase its productivity. Can you account for this? *Hint:* Earthworms tunnel through the soil, feeding in one place and defecating in another.

Questions

1. What compound is the source of the oxygen atoms released as O_2 in photosynthesis? Are the light reactions or the dark reactions responsible for evolution of oxygen? Explain.

2. What products of the light reactions are required for the dark reactions to occur? Describe the function of each of the light-reaction products in carbon fixation.

3. Compare and contrast the roles of chlorophyll and accessory pigments in photosynthesis. How do these pigments relate to chloroplast photosystems?

4. Discuss the function of the cell wall, central vacuole, and mitochondria of plant cells.

5. Why is leaf structure said to resemble a sandwich? What role do guard cells have in leaf function?

7. How does the organization of vascular tissue differ in stems and roots? In monocots and dicots? Give the functions of the various tissues and cells that are found within vascular bundles and cylinders.

7. Name a plant hormone and list at least two of its functions.

8. Why do you think that most flowers are adapted for cross pollination? Describe some of the differences that distinguish animal-pollinated flowers from wind-pollinated ones.

9. Define the following terms:

germination	soil
endosperm	humus
cotyledon	

10. What is meant by nitrogen fixation? What organisms are involved in nitrogen fixation? How does nitrogen fixation affect the nitrogen cycle?

18

Ecosystems, Communities, and Populations: How the World Is Held Together

TO UNDERSTAND HOW THE LIVING WORLD IS held together, we must learn to recognize the various units and know how to interpret relationships among them. Up to now we have been concerned mainly with the inner workings of organisms. Soon we will look at major environments and examine how the components interact. But first we need to examine the organization of living things into populations, communities, and ecosystems. Learning now how biologists interpret their field observations and measurements will help you understand our later discussions of particular ecosystems and their management.

ECOSYSTEMS

Over the past several decades ecological theory has advanced with the application of physical sciences to the study of cells and organisms. We have learned that at the highest level of organization energy and matter serve as coinage for a commerce that binds organisms to one another and to the physical components of their environment. All components of an area are so intricately linked that fundamental understanding requires that they be considered as a whole. The basic ecological unit is not the living community but an ecosystem. **Ecosystems** include not only organisms, but also the physical environment, for these are all linked together by the passage of matter and energy.

Energy

The relationship between energy and order underlies life. Organisms are marvelously arranged molecular arrays. Directly and indirectly we expend energy to concentrate and precisely arrange atoms. Consider for a moment the lipids and proteins in cell membranes; the amino acids in enzymes; and the phosphates, nitrogenous bases, and sugars in chromosomes. These and many other molecules are synthesized in the body and harmonized as an interacting system. Each step requires energy. The apparent goal of each organism is to acquire more energy and matter to maintain its organized state and to produce more organisms like itself.

From one view, life involves a never-ending struggle for order. Organisms do not participate in this struggle consciously, but only those with the genetic patterns to maintain order have survived. The struggle for order is necessary for life, because the tendency of the universe is to disorder.□ 64 Organisms are maintained only by the constant work of synthesis and repair. And work takes energy. In supplying this energy, organisms engage in innumerable energy transfers.

Thermodynamics and Energy Flow. The physical laws of thermodynamics tell us that energy can neither be made nor destroyed. One exception to this rule is interconversion of matter and energy through nuclear reactions. Although such conversions are the source of sunlight and a possible source of energy for human societies (Fig. 18.1), they are of little consequence to the energy budgets of ecosystems. But in every ecosystem, photosynthetic organisms transform radiant energy of sunlight into

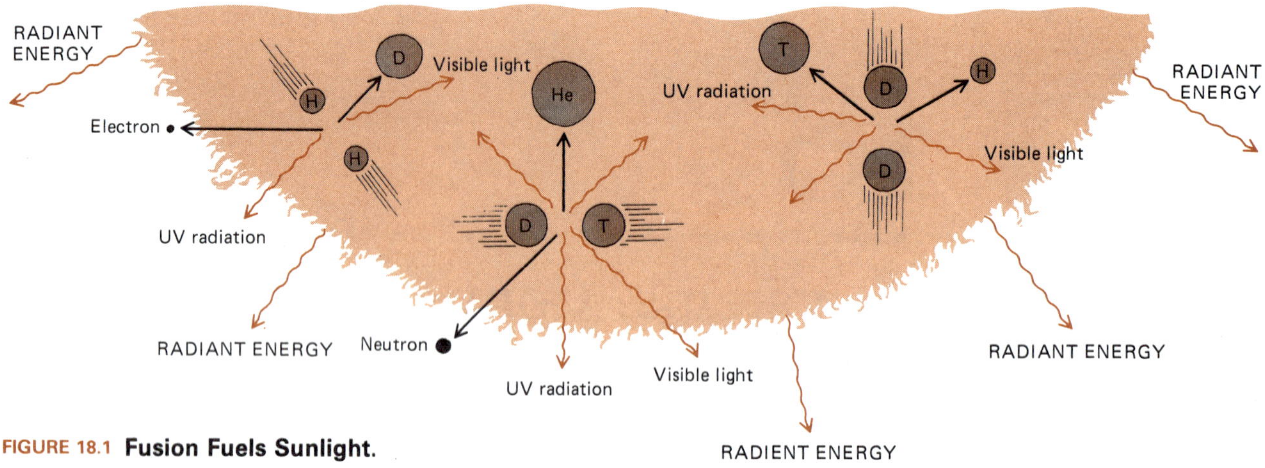

FIGURE 18.1 **Fusion Fuels Sunlight.**

chemical energy of glucose. Likewise, the chemical energy of glucose is cashed in for energy to synthesize molecules, create motion, or conduct nerve impulses. A full list of energy transfers would include every biochemical pathway in every organism on earth. In one sense, life is a series of energy conversions.

Each conversion is inefficient. Even though energy cannot be destroyed, every transformation decreases the energy available to do work. The "lost" energy is now heat energy. Heat consists of random molecular movements. The hotter the temperature, the faster molecules move, and such movements are forces of disorder. Nevertheless, heat can sometimes be used to do work. In a steam engine, for example, heat causes water to vaporize and expand as steam. Expansion of the steam moves a piston and turns a drive shaft. Such use of heat to do work is possible only when a portion of the world is hotter than its surroundings. Eventually the mechanical energy from a steam engine is expended and turned into heat energy. This heat

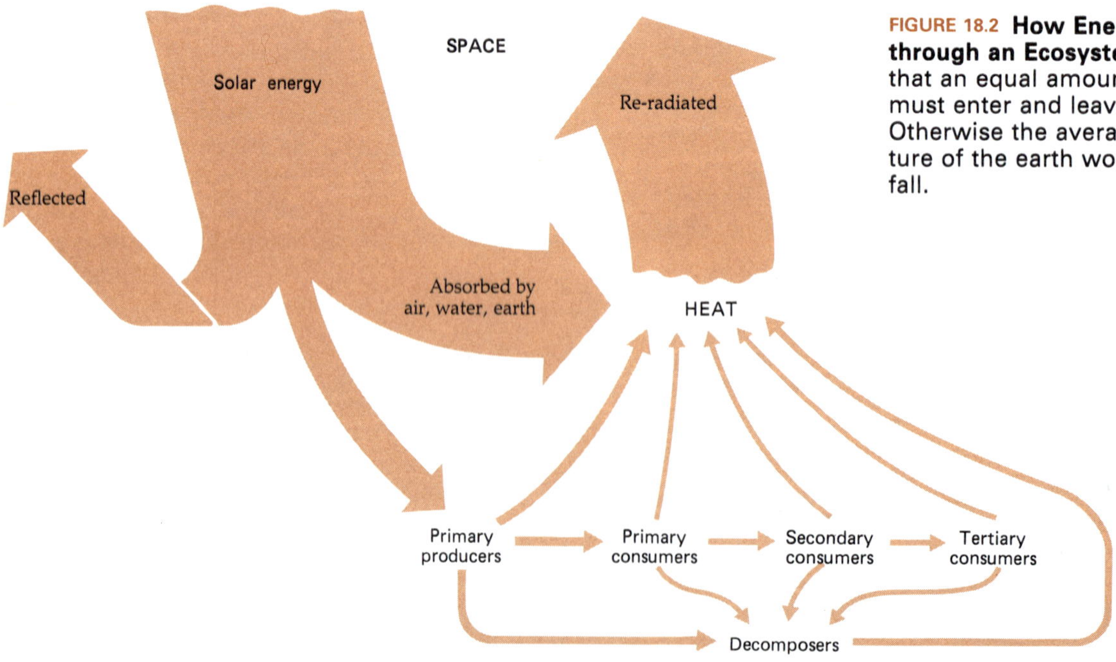

FIGURE 18.2 **How Energy Flows through an Ecosystem.** Note that an equal amount of energy must enter and leave the earth. Otherwise the average temperature of the earth would rise or fall.

gradually dissipates. The fate of all energy is to warm the universe ever so slightly and contribute to its randomness and disorder.

From the inefficient nature of energy conversions, it is apparent that usable energy disappears like water down the drain. To have a constant supply one must keep adding more. Such **energy flow** is characteristic of all ecosystems. Energy enters (usually as sunlight), moves through organisms, and eventually escapes to space as heat (Fig. 18.2).

Trophic Levels and Food Chains. The passage of energy through ecosystems occurs mainly within organic molecules. Radiant energy from the sun is converted by plants into organic molecules that are eventually eaten by animals or destroyed by microorganisms. The species that participate together in such conversions make up a **food chain** or **food web.** The **trophic** (food) **relationships** of real ecosystems are usually highly complex. The food web of an aspen forest is shown in Fig. 18.3. Although this diagram omits many details, it does serve to illustrate a number of trophic levels.

In the aspen forest the **primary producers** include aspen and dogwood trees, shrubs like the hazelnut, and many species of herbs, represented
389 387 here by sarsaparilla and wintergreen. Although not shown in this drawing, lichens, moss,□ ferns,□ and other lower plants are also important primary producers. All these photosynthetic organisms absorb radiant energy of sunlight and convert some of it to glucose and other organic molecules. **Primary consumers** feed on plants. In Fig. 18.3, primary consumers include aphids, ruffed grouse, various boring beetles, and snowshoe hares. A small portion of the energy trapped during photosynthesis is passed to such organisms. **Saprophytes,** which absorb organic material released during decay, can also be primary consumers. An example is the mushroom that is part of the decomposer food chain.

By definition, **secondary consumers** obtain their energy by eating primary consumers. According to Fig. 18.3, woodpeckers, pseudoscorpions, ground beetles, and lacewings qualify as secondary consumers. **Tertiary consumers,** such as the goshawk, eat secondary consumers, but the web of food relationships makes it difficult to assign some organisms to one specific **trophic level.** Chickadees and lacewings, for example, will both eat aphids; but the chickadees will also eat the lacewings. Thus chickadees are sometimes secondary consumers and sometimes tertiary consumers. To complicate matters further, there are parasites in or on every species. But examples such as these do not detract from the fact that energy in the form of food moves in a stepwise fashion from organism to organism. Each step is a trophic level. The significance of trophic levels lies in the inherent inefficiency of energy transformations. Hence there is less energy available to organisms at each higher level of the food chain. There is also less **biomass** (living matter).

Because each energy transformation is inefficient, only a small portion of the energy present at one level can be available to organisms at the next higher level. A surprisingly small portion of the energy of sunlight is converted into chemical energy by plants. Under ideal laboratory conditions, plants approach 25-percent efficiency, but in fields and natural ecosystems, the efficiency of plants on good land is nearer 2 percent.

Conversion of plant material into animal tissue is generally inefficient. For one thing, much plant material is never eaten. In most forests, less than 10 percent of the plant productivity is consumed by animals. Grazing animals do a little better; up to 30 percent of grassland productivity ends up in their stomachs. Aquatic animals get the highest marks in terms of overall consumption. In these ecosystems, as much as 95 percent of the primary production is eaten.

But merely eating plants isn't enough. Animals must digest and absorb nutrients before the plant energy becomes available, and in this process of assimilation we find further inefficiencies. The cellulose walls of plant cells must be broken open if cellular contents are to be digested. Much of the energy in leaves, stems, and roots is in the cellulose itself. Animals lack enzymes to attack this substance. Those animals that use cellulose (termites, for example) rely on cellulase-producing microorganisms in their digestive tracts. Altogether, a typical herbivore may absorb only 30 percent of the energy-rich compounds in its food. The remainder passes out of the body in the feces. However, insects that suck sap from the phloem may assimilate 90% of the food they consume. So may the various seed eaters.

The food of carnivores is quite similar in composition to that of their own bodies, yet energy conversion between primary consumers and secondary consumers remains inefficient. With every step of the food chain there is much less energy available. The energy lost can be accounted for only in terms of heat produced.

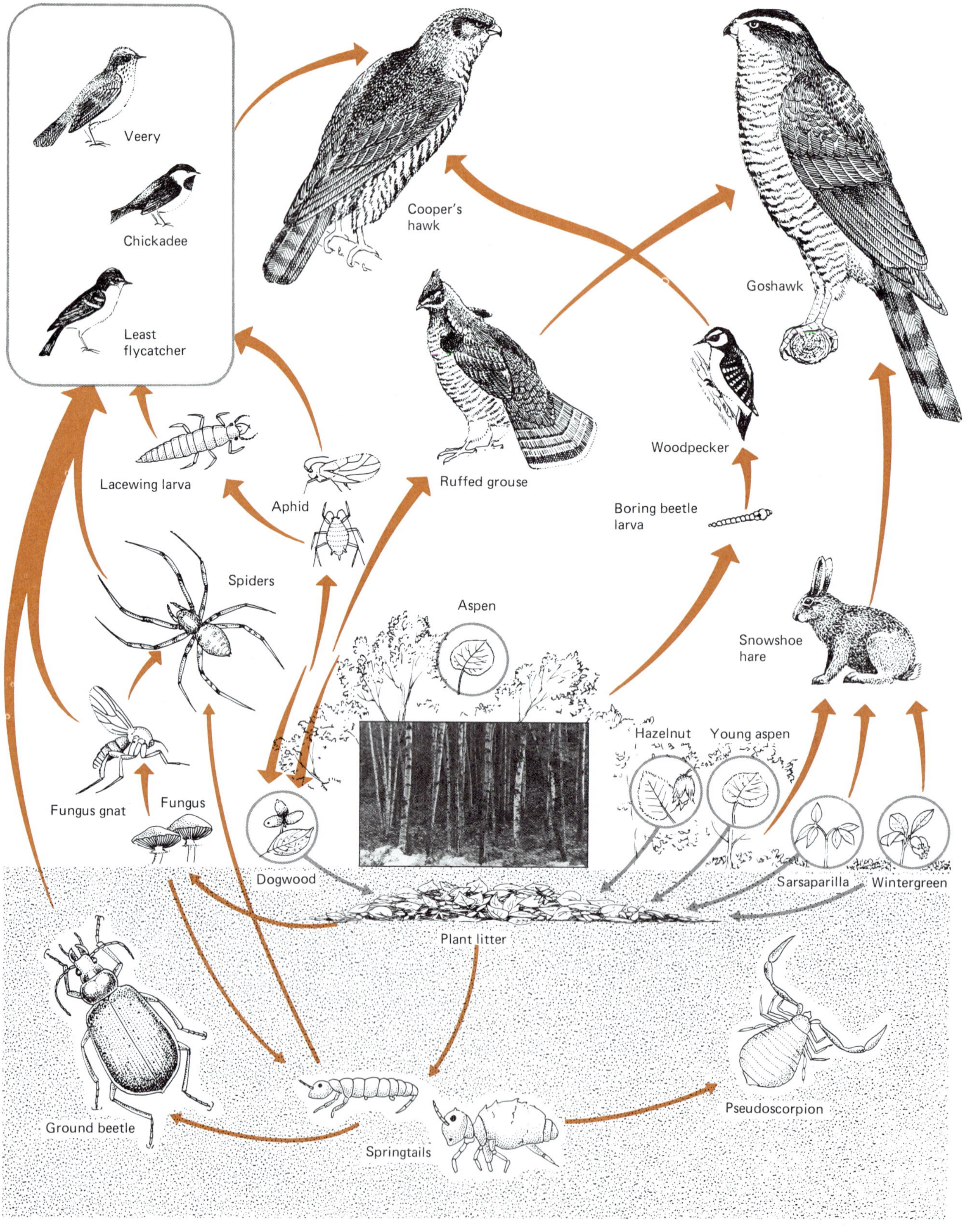
Veery
Chickadee
Least flycatcher
Cooper's hawk
Goshawk
Woodpecker
Ruffed grouse
Lacewing larva
Aphid
Boring beetle larva
Spiders
Aspen
Snowshoe hare
Hazelnut
Young aspen
Fungus gnat
Fungus
Dogwood
Sarsaparilla
Wintergreen
Plant litter
Pseudoscorpion
Ground beetle
Springtails

FIGURE 18.3 Food Web of an Aspen Forest. The arrows indicate the direction that nutrients move in the food web.

Heat energy is generally useless, but both plants and animals can benefit from heat production in cool climates. Birds and mammals conserve the "waste" heat from energy conversions inside their bodies. When temperatures fall, increased respiration consumes nutrients solely to produce enough heat to maintain the body temperature. We often ignore the heat production of lower animals and plants, but this production can be measured. All organisms subtly warm their environment. Since each trophic level has less energy than the one below it, when we diagram the energy present at the various trophic levels, we see a pyramidal shape (Fig. 18.4).

Cycles and Systems

Energy enters ecosystems, flows through them, and is lost to space, but elements can be completely confined to an ecosystem. In a stable ecosystem it is plausible that no chemical element will enter or leave over a long period of time. Nevertheless, no real ecosystem is completely closed. Even the **biosphere,** the master ecosystem that encompasses the entire world, is constantly losing gaseous molecules to space and always receiving bits of matter from the "great beyond."

Generally, the movement of elements within an ecosystem is broadly cyclic. However, these cycles are often complex and have numerous detours and way stations, as shown in the movement of
430 nitrogen. Many atoms move through food webs from one organism to another. But unlike energy, some atoms, such as those of oxygen, can enter at any level. Return of individual atoms to the same species or even to the same individual makes atomic movements truly cyclic. For example, an oxygen atom you just inhaled may be one you inhaled last year. Or it may at one time have entered King Tut or your own grandmother. A sodium atom in you could have been in the lattice of a rock crystal a few decades ago and in a clover leaf last year. As elements move from organism to organism and species to species, they bind the ecosystem together.

FIGURE 18.4 Less Room at the Top.

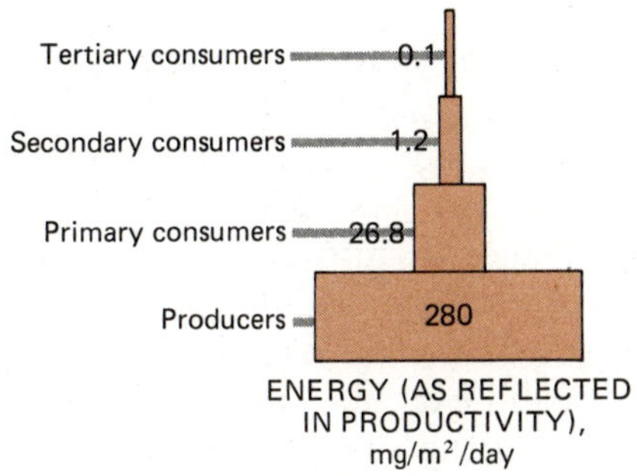

Carbon Cycle. As the term "cycle" implies, there is no beginning or end to the carbon cycle. Because of this there is no logical point at which to begin our discussion, so we will choose one. Let's start with terrestrial plants (Fig. 18.5). Carbon dioxide in the atmosphere is incorporated into organic compounds during **photosynthesis.** Some of the carbon withdrawn from the air is quickly returned by plant
respiration. Part of the carbon fixed into organic 403
molecules by plants is eaten by animals. A portion of this carbon passes along the food chain, but at each step some is released in carbon dioxide that is expired from the body. In most ecosystems the majority of plant carbon passes into plant litter as leaves fall or plants die.

Decomposers break down the carbon-rich matter of plant litter and also digest dead bodies of animals. As in other food chains, carbon atoms move through the decomposer chain and eventually escape in the form of carbon dioxide. Thus a great deal of carbon from the atmosphere enters plants and animals only to cycle directly back to the atmosphere.

Some plant carbon is buried and compressed
by geological forces to form peat or coal. Burning 498
these fossil fuels returns this carbon to circulation, often millions of years later. Forest fires, as well as the use of wood for fuel, cycle carbon back to the atmosphere in the form of carbon dioxide.

Carbon similarly cycles through the oceans of the earth. A tremendous amount of carbon dioxide can dissolve in seawater. In the oceans, microscopic floating plants known collectively as **phytoplankton** use dissolved carbon dioxide for photosynthesis. These tiny plants are consumed by small floating animals called **zooplankton.** Zooplankton are in turn eaten by other, larger animals. Thus the carbon fixed photosynthetically into organic compounds by phytoplankton is passed along

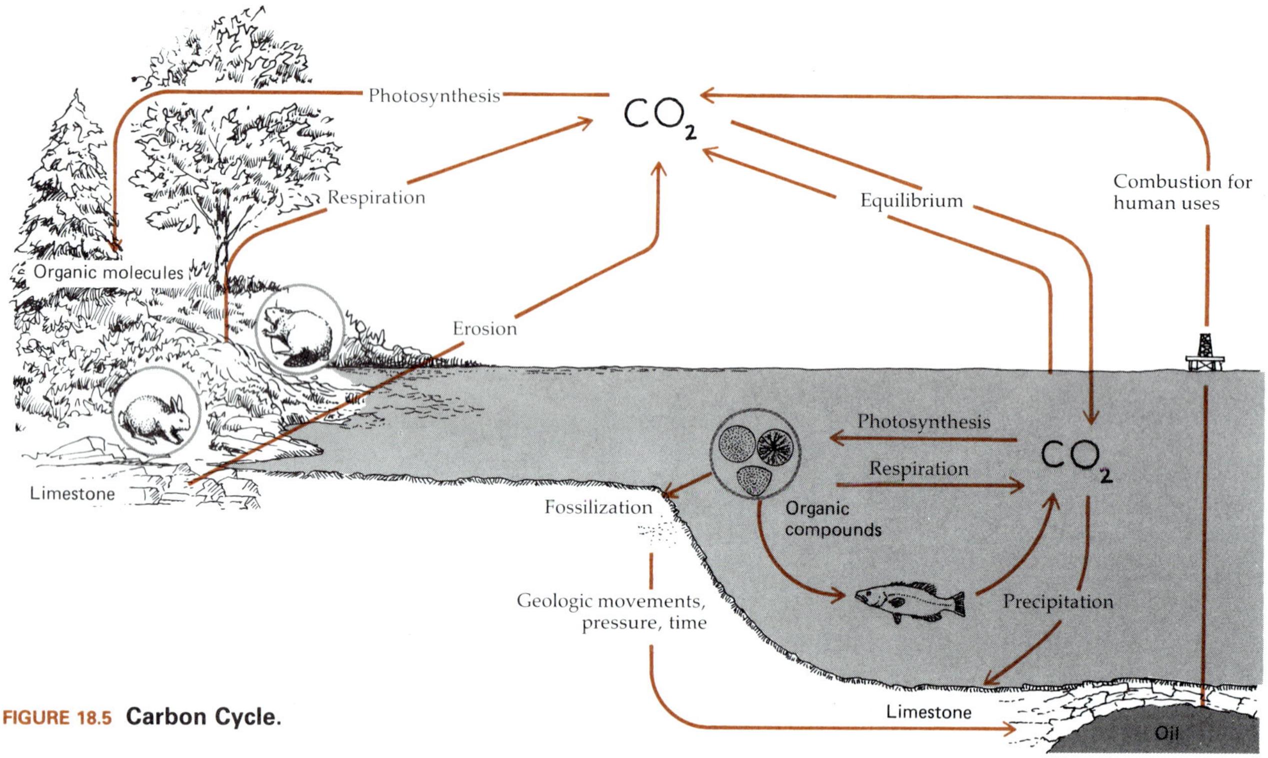

FIGURE 18.5 Carbon Cycle.

an oceanic food web. As on land, each link of the marine food chain releases some of the carbon as carbon dioxide.

Whenever the ocean becomes saturated with carbon dioxide, the excess precipitates and forms carbonate rocks, such as limestone. In a sense, marine rocks constitute a tremendous carbon "sink." Most carbon in such rocks is held for millions of years until movements of the earth's crust raise these rocks and make them part of a continent. Then erosion dissolves the rocks and releases carbon dioxide that can again enter organic molecules through the process of photosynthesis.

The carbon cycles of land and water are linked by more than carbonate rocks. The same atmosphere envelops the entire earth. Carbon dioxide from air can dissolve into water, and vice versa. In this way carbon dioxide from land organisms enters the ocean, and carbon dioxide from marine organisms may travel over continents. But because formation of limestone traps carbon, the usual direction of movement is from air into water. Probably **petroleum** also forms through marine fossilization. If so, combustion of gasoline and related substances provides another route for marine carbon to return to the atmosphere.

Unity through Cycles. Considering the carbon cycle alone, no one should doubt the interdependence of each part of the biosphere. Even certain rocks can owe their existence to organisms. And decay organisms, with all their stench, are essential to humans and every other species. Without decay, all the carbon in the world would eventually accumulate in dead organisms. But before that, the world would be knee-deep in plant litter and animal bodies. Sewage would be "indisposable," and potato peelings would be as permanent as aluminum cans. Inevitably, photosynthesis would halt, because plants would run out of carbon dioxide.

There are surely biogeochemical cycles for every element on earth. Of course, each cycle differs according to the element's chemical properties and its role in organisms. Some elements, such as oxygen and nitrogen, have great atmospheric reservoirs. As we will discuss in Chapter 22, the danger from radioactive isotopes depends largely on their natural cycles. So does limitation of plant growth due to shortages of nitrogen or phosphorus. Because certain cycles are of interest in particular contexts, we discussed the nitrogen cycle in Chapter 17, and we will examine the phosphorus cycle in Chapter 21 and the sulfur cycle in Chapter 22.

Resilience: The Ability to Withstand Abuse

Quite clearly, life—human life included—is possible only within the bounds of an ecosystem. As Western technology engulfs or at least nibbles at every natural ecosystem, thoughtful people are questioning the result. How will each ecosystem respond? Will it disintegrate, or will it withstand the changes? What will happen to the biosphere? Can it continue to support us? In reality there are two questions here. One concerns the ability of natural ecosystems to spring back and restore themselves. The other involves whether or not humans can convert natural ecosystems into permanently productive artificial ones.

Every ecosystem requires suitable temperatures, adequate energy input, continuous biogeochemical cycles, and a relative freedom from external disturbance. Because organisms maintain energy flow and biogeochemical cycles, the proper balance of species and certain numbers of each species are both important. Permanent productivity requires that an ecosystem be resilient. This means that the ecosystem must remain stable in the face of minor changes and able to restore itself quickly if it is badly abused. One of the ongoing controversies of biology concerns factors contributing to the stability of ecosystems.

The Role of Complexity. In a complex ecosystem, most animals have multiple food sources. Therefore loss or drastic reduction in certain species does not threaten the existence of others, because each has several alternative food supplies. If, as some biologists maintain, complexity contributes to stability, we can predict that simple ecosystems will be less stable than more complex ones will be. There is evidence that population numbers do fluctuate wildly in simple ecosystems. The greatest population explosions occur among insects and other pests that bedevil farmers. And, of course, farmers do their best to create the simplest ecosystems possible. They try to grow a crop of one species, and they work to harvest every bit of it for human use.

Among natural ecosystems, the most simple occur where the environment limits life to a few species with extreme tolerances. The evergreen forests and tundra of the far North are our best examples. Both are known for dramatic fluctuations in numbers. In some years and some places, the budworms that devour spruce trees across Canada are as numerous as bollworms in the most infested cotton patch. But at other times or places, budworms are absent from spruce forests.

Likewise, lemmings of the tundra are particularly known for their migrations. These migrations occur during years when the little rodents are unusually abundant. More direct evidence of lack of resilience by the tundra ecosystem is found in the inability of plants there to grow back after a disturbance. Any trail worn through the tundra remains visible decades after it is abandoned.

But if complexity encourages stability, why are tropical rain forests so susceptible to damage? Of all ecosystems, these harbor the largest number of species; yet such forests are easily damaged. It may be that these ecosystems are *too* complex to be stable. Damage to one or a few components may affect so many things that some fail to recover. This could explain why a relatively simple northern forest can restore itself within a few decades after trees are destroyed, but a tropical rain forest may require hundreds of years to recover from a similar tragedy.

BIOLOGICAL COMMUNITIES

The organisms of an ecosystem constitute a biological community. Thus a biological community is a group of interacting populations that share a common habitat. Definition of a particular community is largely arbitrary. Communities can be large or small. A scientist studying the tiny plants and animals on the surface of a single rock in a mountain stream may quite properly refer to these organisms as a community. Another researcher may just as easily consider the entire stream as a community.

Community Dominants

Communities are often named for plants, partly because plants are more obvious than animals. In many communities plants determine which animals thrive, although animals are equally essential to the survival of numerous plant species. In addition to the obvious role of plants as sources of animal food, plants modify the physical environment. You see this clearly in forests where trees create shelter from wind, rain, and sunlight. Most animals also rely on plants for cover that hides them from predators. In certain areas the members of a few plant species are so numerous that they have great impact on other community components. The number of these **ecological dominants**

BOX 18A

METAMORPHOSIS AND MIGRATION: HOW TO USE MORE THAN ONE HABITAT

Usually we think of each organism as having one particular habitat. But examination of grass frogs, Japanese beetles, salmon, whales, migratory birds, and numerous other species reveals use of different habitats within one lifetime.

Frogs, beetles, and many other animals rely on a change in form to take advantage of two habitats. Their eggs hatch into larvae, which later undergo a drastic change known as metamorphosis. In this process the larvae are transformed into adults. Frogs lay their eggs in ponds or streams. The larvae—or tadpoles, as they are called—feed on delicate aquatic plants. Small tadpoles are vulnerable to predators, but an abundant food supply permits large tadpole populations. Consequently some tadpoles survive to metamorphose. This transformation involves not only growth of legs and absorption of the tail, but also maturation of the reproductive organs and changes in the digestive system. The intestine shortens, reflecting the fact that the insect diet of frogs is more easily digested than the plant diet of tadpoles. The tongue becomes transformed into a long tube that can be extended almost instantaneously by means of increased lymphatic fluid pressure. Thus the sticky tip can be shot out to snap up insects. Not only are adult frogs adapted to a diet that is different from that of the tadpoles, but their legs allow them to hop to other ponds. Temporary pools, because they do not support fish that prey on tadpoles, are often the best sites for frog reproduction. But when a temporary pond dries up, migration becomes essential. Also, adult frogs of many species find most of their food on land. Thus, by allowing two different forms in the life cycle, metamorphosis permits animals such as frogs to make maximum use of two kinds of habitats.

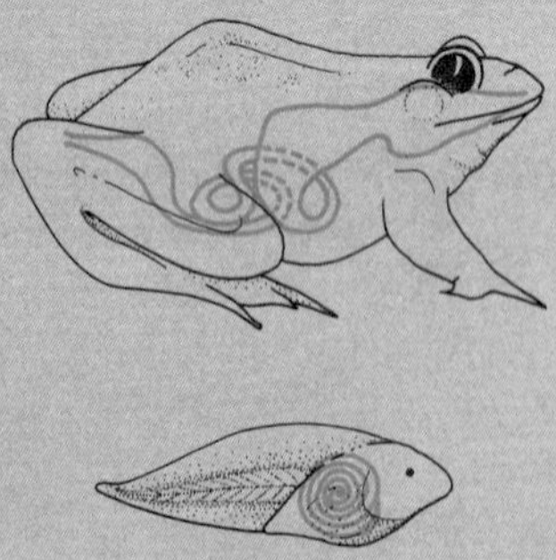

Bullfrog.

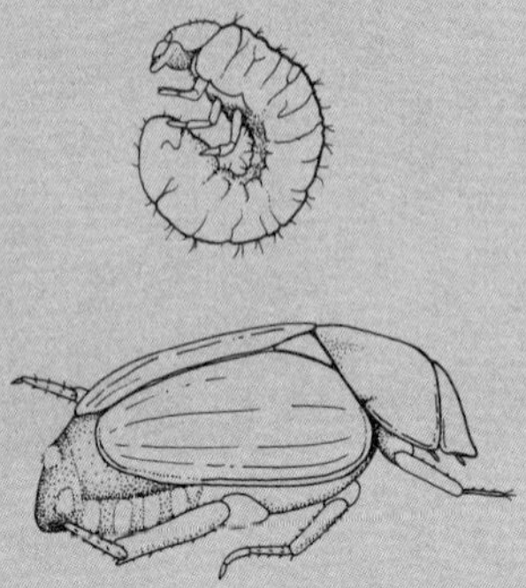

Japanese Beetle.

Compared with frogs, Japanese beetles undergo an even more drastic metamorphosis. The grubs (larvae) that feed on grass roots become pupae and then emerge as adults that eat leaves. As with frogs, metamorphosis allows the grub and the adult to take advantage of the resources of different habitats.

Migration is another strategy through which a species uses more than one habitat. For example, salmon lay their eggs in fresh water. After the young reach a certain size, they migrate downstream to the ocean and then swim northward. Salmon tagged in Scottish rivers have been caught off the coast of Greenland. Others tagged in streams on the West Coast of North America have been retrieved 2000 miles away in the Pacific. How long salmon stay at sea depends on their growth rates. But after several years they return to their

Salmon.

home river and eventually to the same small tributary where they hatched. There the females lay eggs in shallow depressions in the bottom, and the males shed sperm that fertilize the eggs. Over their lifetimes, salmon require food captured in streams, in rivers, and in the open ocean. The same animals that fatten on oceanic food chains must use clean, stony stream beds for reproduction.

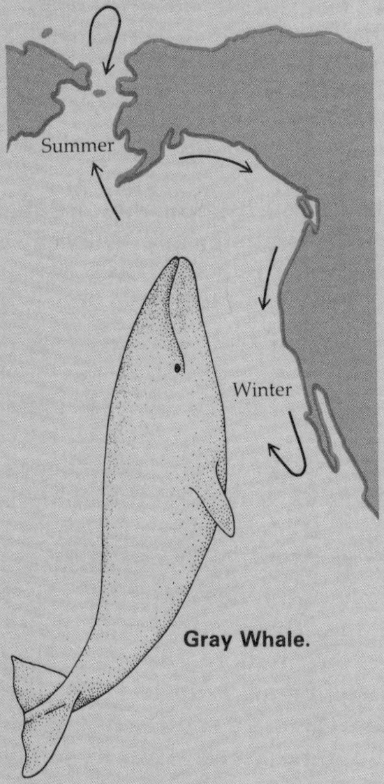

Gray Whale.

Marine mammals, such as seals and whales, commonly migrate, too. For example, the several species of large toothless whales spend six warm months feeding in Arctic or Antarctic waters. They eat at the top of short but rich food chains, for they strain tiny animals from the water and have no predators themselves. When the cold season comes, these whales migrate to tropical breeding grounds. There the young are born. The warm waters contain little food suitable for such whales, and some don't feed at all for months. Even the females that nurse the young survive off stored fat. But the infants thrive in the warm water, and they might be unable to maintain their body temperatures in polar waters.

Many species migrate through water, but other long-range migrants fly. Some bats are summer migrants to the temperate zone. Certain butterflies, such as the monarch, have regular migratory patterns. But to many people the most obvious migrants are birds.

Winter residents of temperate parts of the United States include northern shrikes, common redpolls, snow buntings, and many other birds that migrate north each summer and nest in the arctic. Although the cold winters of the Far North offer insufficient food or shelter for these species, summer resources are abundant. Mosquitoes and other insects that burst forth from the bogs and lakes provide plenty of high-protein food to support growth of the young birds. During the long summer days when these birds are feeding their nestlings, they are not in competition with species that nest in the temperate zone. Through migration, summer residents of the north find almost unlimited resources when their need is greatest but retreat to more moderate climates in winter after the young have matured and have reduced food demands.

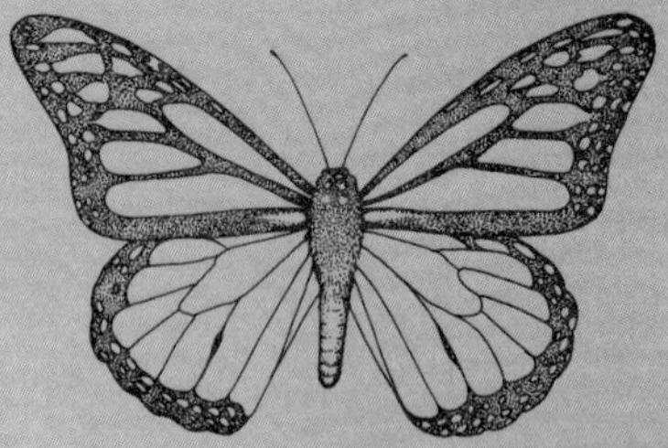
Monarch Butterfly.

Migration and metamorphosis are both evolved strategies that allow species to take maximum advantage of resources through use of different habitats. Of course, use of multiple habitats complicates the work of scientists who trace energy flow or biogeochemical cycles. But more important, these examples of migration and metamorphosis illustrate some of the factors that weave communities into the world ecosystem we call the biosphere.

FIGURE 18.6 Elephants as Community Dominants. The savannahs of Africa may owe their existence to the destructive habits of elephants. Savannah trees are widely scattered and grasses thrive in the areas between them. The balance between trees and grass is maintained by elephants that damage enough trees to prevent full forest development.

varies from a single species, as in a pure stand of Douglas fir, to hundreds of tree species in certain tropical rain forests.

In emphasizing the contribution of plants to the character of a community, we must not overlook the importance of animals and the drastic effects they can have on plants and on the community as a whole. Occasionally animals dominate an area, as when bison trample and wallow a grass-edged pond into a mudhole. In some places elephants are surely ecological dominants, since they can destroy woody vegetation and convert an area that would otherwise support a forest into an open savannah of grasses and scattered trees (Fig. 18.6).

One of the most important resources of terrestrial communities, the soil, results from interaction of plants and animals. Plants produce leaf litter, which reduces erosion, increases water-holding capacity, and changes soil texture. Through their ability to absorb minerals, plants retain elements that might otherwise leach (wash out) of the soil and be lost to the community. On the other hand, it is the action of innumerable tiny soil animals that initiates decomposition of litter. In most regions, earthworms aerate the soil by tunneling through it; they also work humus into the soil. The activity of the many species of termites and ants loosens soil. In many areas these insects greatly affect the distribution of organic matter.

Composition and Boundaries

The edges and characteristics of any particular community exist more in the human mind than in nature. Gradual changes in species composition occur on every scale from the largest to the smallest. This is true both among communities and from point to point within each one. At the same time, history is a factor in species distribution. The effect of previous events may be as simple as the fact that plants can grow only where there is a source of seed. The impact of past communities can also be exceedingly complex.

Succession. Previous interactions are so important that in some communities we recognize patterns of change known as **community succession.** When the vegetation in an area is destroyed, it is usually replaced. Often the new vegetation is different from what was destroyed. And in most cases, this new vegetation is gradually replaced with another and then another. The sequence for any particular area is usually the same. Eventually the vegetation becomes stabilized. This permanent, stable vegetation is said to be the **climax vegetation** for that particular region. The replacement of one vegetation and then another in a predictable sequence is known as succession. The fact that successional stages and climax vegetations differ from place to place results from differences both in the environment and in the history of the vegetation present. Obviously, a particular species can appear in a successional vegetation only if there is a seed source. The seed may be present in the ground or provided by patches of successional vegetation. Because climax vegetation is susceptible to destruction by fire, flood, or some other catastrophe, no area is long without successional growth. Succession occurs continuously on a smaller scale, too. For example, when a large tree dies, sunlight reaches a part of the forest floor that was formerly in shade, and successional growth begins. Most human societies continually disrupt natural vegetation. Consequently, the vegetation people see daily is successional rather than climax vegetation. Examples may be found in roadsides, fence rows, neglected yards and fields, and cut-over land.

When Europeans first visited American shores, a vast portion of the land supported climax vegetation. Because the forests seemed untouched by humans, they came to be known as **virgin forests.** Usually what the layperson calls a virgin forest the biologist recognizes as the local climax vegetation. The common term **second growth** most often refers to a successional forest.

The factors controlling successional patterns differ from place to place, and they are often poorly understood. Most studies have involved land that was cleared for agricultural use and then, later, abandoned. Whenever bare ground is left undisturbed, rapidly growing **annuals** (plants that set seed the first year and then die) may appear. Although there is a characteristic first-year vegetation in each plant community, in many places these plants are replaced by introduced annuals that everyone calls "weeds." This is one example of the fact that the history of an area affects the pattern of succession.

One of the best-studied successions is that of the deciduous forest biome that stretches southward through Pennsylvania and Virginia to the Carolinas and Tennessee (Fig. 18.7). When plowed land in this region is left uncultivated, not only annual weeds, but also **biennials** (two-year plants) and a few **perennials** (many-year plants) appear during the first year. By the second spring, the biennials draw on reserves stored in their roots and make such rapid growth that they crowd out the young annuals. Many biennial species have their early leaves in a whorl close against the ground. These leaves create dense shade around the base of the plant and contribute to suppression of nearby annuals.

Although the details vary for different reasons, one stage of succession leads to another. The growth habits of annuals and biennials may explain which are dominant the first and second year, but many other factors can be involved. Shade tolerance at various stages in the life cycle differs among tree species and may determine the pattern of forest succession. In much of the deciduous forest biome, pines precede the climax vegetation. Most pines are particularly vulnerable to shading. Lower limbs die as the pine forest grows dense, and pine seedlings never survive in deep forest shade. The oaks, maples, beeches, and other members of the climax forest are more shade-tolerant. Small trees become tall and thin in heavy shade but survive and eventually grow taller than the pines. Many pines die due to insufficient sunlight, but others live for years. However, there are no new pines because the seedlings cannot survive in the shade. The seedlings of the deciduous trees survive in the shade of larger ones, so there are always small trees in the understory. When a tree is blown over, others quickly replace it in the canopy. Thus shade tolerance helps explain why the deciduous trees replace the pines and also why the deciduous trees are the climax vegetation.

The series of vegetational stages that follow destruction of a climax vegetation, as we have just described, is often called **secondary succession.** Note that secondary succession begins when soil is available. **Primary succession** (Fig. 18.8) is a series of events whereby plants colonize an area that has never before supported vegetation. Such areas may have mineral soil formed by physical weathering of the rocks. Primary succession can begin on solid rock, even on fresh lava.

In our daily lives, we see the early stages of primary succession on rocky outcrops, brick walls, and tombstones. Often the original colonizing plants

FIGURE 18.7 Succession in Oak-Hickory Forests of Southeastern United States.

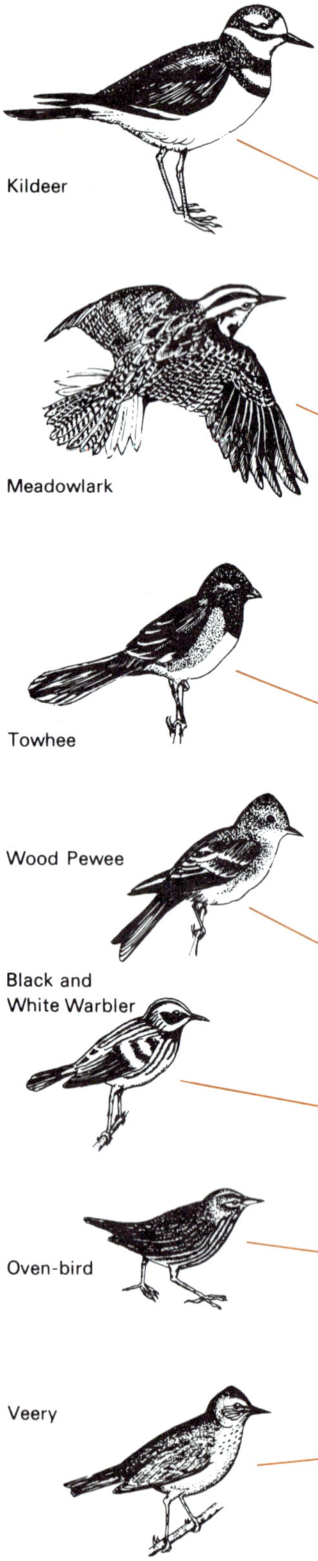

Years after plowing	Dominant vegetation
1	*Crabgrass and horseweed.* Horseweed germinates in the fall in which the land is plowed and does well in the absence of competition; grows to six feet. Crabgrass spreads rapidly on bare ground by rooting of stems at nodes.
2	*Biennials, such as wild asters and goldenrod.* Asters appear the first year but remain as small rosettes of leaves; develop large taproots that give them a head start on other vegetation the second spring.
3–15	*Broom sedge, pine seedlings, and miscellaneous weeds.* Aster seedlings require abundant light and water to become established, so a second crop does not usually appear. Broom sedge is present earlier but requires two years to seed, so it takes a while for sufficient seed to accumulate to develop a vigorous stand. Broom sedge growth is favored by decaying aster roots.
15–25	*Young pine forest.* Pines shade out most other vegetation, except for seedlings of certain deciduous trees.
25–50	*Pine forest with developing understory of dogwood, gum, and young oaks and hickories.*
50–150	*Pines intermixed with deciduous trees.* The oaks and hickories are shading out the pines. They kill both the large trees and the young seedlings.
150+	*Oak and hickory climax forest.* Deciduous trees of all ages. Although the shade-tolerant seedlings of these trees develop slowly, they are always available to replace larger trees that blow down.

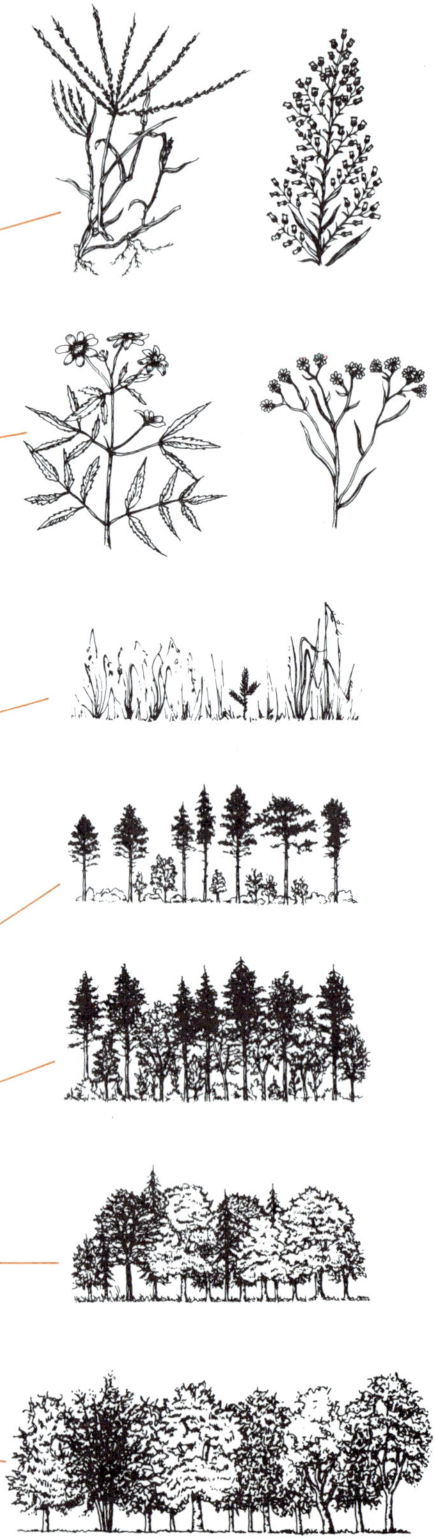

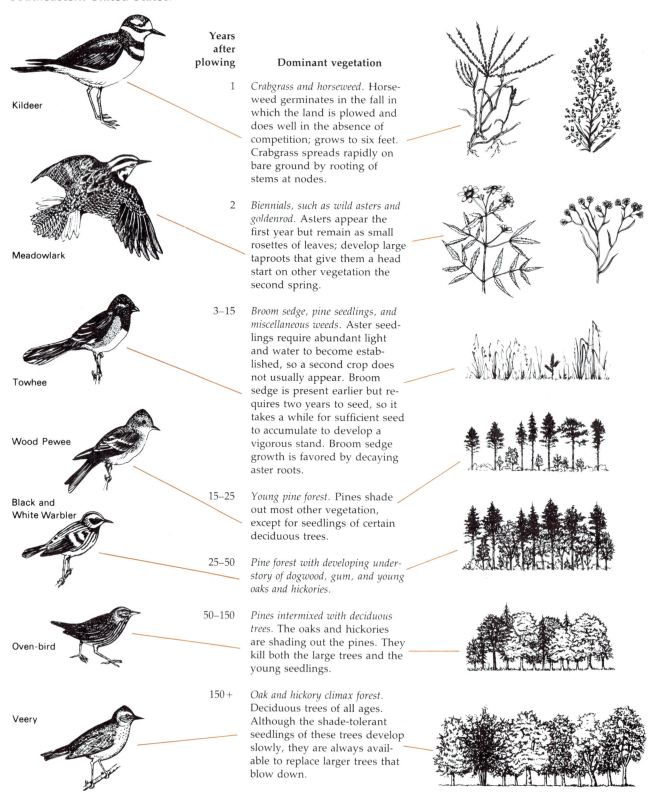

Each vegetational stage supports characteristic animal species. These birds are examples.

are **lichens** that produce acids. The acids dissolve certain minerals in the rocks. This process roughens the surface, so the lichens can attach better, and it also makes minerals available for lichen growth. Over the years, mineral grains released by the acids and decaying lichen components create a small amount of soil. Other plants, such as mosses, may grow in the lichen soil and become the second step in this primary succession. Lichens are not necessary for primary succession, however. Many trees and shrubs grow from seeds that have fallen into cracks in rocks where dust has collected.

Minimums and Tolerances. Environmental factors, including rainfall, drainage, mineral availability, and temperature extremes, affect various organisms differently. There are limits beyond which survival of a population becomes impossible. Dramatic **limits of tolerance** appear when temperatures are sufficiently high to denature☐ essential enzymes and kill members of a species (Fig. 18.9). But single factors seldom account for the distributional limits of any particular population. Instead, two or more factors usually interact, and their effects are compounded by competition, history, and chance. No one should be surprised when the range of a species proves unpredictable.

98

FIGURE 18.8 **Primary Succession.** A few seeds from nearby forests have found enough soil to germinate and grow on this thousand-year-old lava flow.

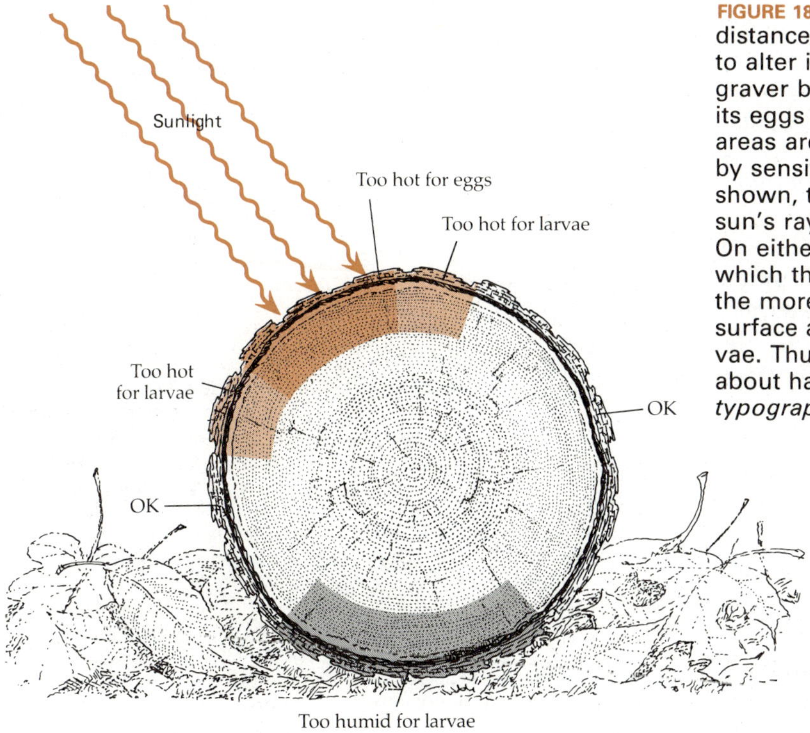

FIGURE 18.9 **Microhabitat and Microclimate.** Tiny distances can allow sufficient differences in habitat to alter its suitability for a particular species. The engraver beetle, *Ips typographicus,* digs chambers for its eggs under the bark of fallen trees. Not all bark areas are suitable, because of limitations imposed by sensitivity to heat and humidity. In the log shown, the surface most directly exposed to the sun's rays gets hot enough to kill the beetle eggs. On either side of this warmest region lies a band in which the eggs can hatch but that is too warm for the more sensitive larvae. On the other hand, the surface against the ground is too damp for the larvae. Thus the microclimate of the log leaves only about half of it suitable as a habitat for *Ips typographicus.*

Although the concepts of biomes and communities help us understand the world of life, all such units are human creations. To some extent, boundaries are arbitrary. Attempts to relate edges to individual environmental factors can be instructive, but simple explanations are seldom complete.

Edges. Beyond the fact that communities result from somewhat arbitrary definitions, and that the distribution of species is neither uniform nor wholly predictable, no community is completely independent of all others. Animals from one community inevitably make forays into those nearby to seek food, mates, or shelter. In fact, the combined resources of adjacent communities usually support larger numbers of species than are found in a uniform habitat far from a boundary. The characteristic diversity and abundance of life where differing environments meet has been recognized as the **edge effect.** The boundary areas are sometimes called **ecotones.** The junction of land and water almost always creates a zone unusually rich in life. The ecotone between a pond and a forest will contain frogs and salamanders and insects that hatch in the water but live part or all their adult life on land. Vegetation that falls into the water enriches the food supply there, supporting an abundance of organisms. Along the shore, reduced competition for water permits especially luxuriant plant growth. The pond-forest ecotone is a favored habitat for raccoons, which feed on the fruit of land plants and seek clams and crayfish in the muddy pond bottom. But in addition to the primarily terrestrial organisms that are favored by access to water, most other species from the land community are also present. Likewise, the outer few feet of water contain not only the decay organisms that use the rotting leaves and the animals that feed on these decay organisms, but also the fish and microscopic plants characteristic of water further from the edge. Altogether, ecotones provide more resources and support more species and more organisms than can similar-sized areas of either community alone.

Coevolution and Interactions between Species

The many populations that constitute a community have existed together for some time. Such populations have been subtly modified by natural selection so that they fit well into the community. In other words, the members of a community are attuned to one another. Every one can and does depend on others.

The interactions of organisms take many forms. Sometimes dependence *seems* only one-way, such as when one species uses another for food or shelter, but we may be overlooking the more subtle benefits. Some relationships are quite casual. For example, a pair of prothonotary warblers may choose to nest in a sycamore along a Maryland river, when they could just as well have selected a maple. In contrast to this are the instances where one species depends totally on another. The red-cockaded woodpecker is restricted to mature southern pine forests, because it can excavate nest holes only in tree trunks softened by "red-heart," a fungal disease. Since this fungus attacks only old pines, the tree-farm practice of removing all mature trees endangers the red-cockaded woodpecker.

Some organisms live together so closely that their interrelationships are obvious. Such close associations are sometimes said to be **symbiotic.** This term is derived from the word *symbiosis,* which

TABLE 18.1 Types of Interactions between Species*

	HOMO SAPIENS	SECOND SPECIES	
Competition	−	−	Insects compete with people for food resources.
Amensalism	0	−	Harmless bacteria in food are destroyed by stomach acids.
Parasitism	−	+	Tapeworm attached inside human intestine causes malnutrition while obtaining food for itself.
Predator–Prey	−	+	Humans collect and eat snails.
Commensalism	0	+	Mice nest in abandoned barns.
Mutualism	+	+	Some components of normal flora in human intestines synthesize vitamins while obtaining food and shelter.

*Any relationship between two species may be helpful (+), harmful (−) or of no effect (0) to either of the parties involved. Although humans were chosen as one member of each pair, interactions occur among all kinds of organisms.

FIGURE 18.10 Cleaner Symbiosis. Cleaners that feed on organisms attached to the body surfaces of other fish occupy an important ecological niche in ocean habitats. Cleaner fish maintain regular stations where larger species come to have encrustations of algae and fungi or animal parasites nibbled away. The larger fish are endlessly accommodating to their little cleaners, often permitting the cleaners to enter their mouths and leave unharmed or to work over the delicate gills or eyes. Some fish present a particular part of their bodies to the cleaner for attention. In a reef, each fish usually has its favorite cleaner and visits daily. On the other hand, injured fish move continuously from cleaner to cleaner.

means the interdependent living together of two dissimilar organisms. Unfortunately this term is sometimes used for only mutually beneficial associations and at other times stretched to include any predictable close association, even that of a parasite and its host. However they are defined, such close interrelationships must be the result of evolution. **Parasites** are able to survive only on or in their hosts because of the common evolutionary
224 history we discussed in Chapter 10.□ A parasite must be adapted not only to survive in its host, but to allow the host to survive as well. Likewise the host must evolve adaptations that moderate the harm done by its parasite. Table 18.1 lists some types of interactions between species. Interactions such as **commensalism,** wherein one organism benefits and the other is unaffected, are difficult to document in nature. Critics point out that minor influences can go undetected. A great many interactions are **mutualistic**—i.e., both species receive some benefit. One example is fish and their cleaners (Fig. 18.10).

Some mutualistic relationships are so close that the two species appear as one. This is true of the many kinds of **lichens** (Fig. 18.11), each of which

(a)

(b)

FIGURE 18.11 Lichens. (a) Encrusting lichen on rock. (b) Branching lichen growing on a tree. The algal and fungal partners within a lichen are so intimately combined that the two seem as one to the naked eye. Each symbiotic association of a specific alga and fungus has a characteristic appearance. The numerous associations differ greatly in color and growth forms.

consists of a photosynthetic partner held within a spongy fungal mass. In some lichens the photosynthetic member is a cyanobacterium, and in others it is a single-celled green alga. The photosynthetic partner in a lichen association provides energy, and the fungal partner absorbs water and minerals and attaches the association to some solid surface.

Many striking examples of coevolution involve insects and flowering plants. The frequency of these associations reflects the abundance of both types of organisms and the endless variability of their traits. However these insect-plant associations arise, they bind the community into an interdependent unit. Consider the mutual dependence of certain ants and the **bullhorn acacias** (Fig. 18.12), for example. At least some species of these thorny Central-American semidesert plants can't survive without their ants. From nests in the hollow spine of the acacia, the ants swarm out to attack any other animal that touches their plant. This defense is more than adequate to deter insects, birds, or mammals that would otherwise feed on the acacia leaves. The ants also destroy vines and other plants near their acacia, thus eliminating the threat of competition for light or water.

Plants often depend on insects for pollination; in turn, they provide the insects with essential resources. One striking example involves a yucca that is native to the western deserts and the pronuba moth. Female pronubas will lay their eggs only in yucca flowers. After a moth deposits her eggs into the flower ovaries, she stuffs pollen into the stigmas so that yucca seeds will develop (Fig. 18.13). Although the caterpillars that hatch from the eggs eat some of the developing seeds, enough seeds escape destruction to ensure successful reproduction of the yucca. The service of pollination is well worth the price the yucca plant pays in lost seed, for the moth is the only natural agent that can pollinate yucca flowers. The two species are totally dependent on each other for their continued existence.

Most plants that rely on animals for pollination are served by insects, but birds and bats are also regular plant pollinators, especially in the tropics 423
(Fig. 18.14). Birds and bats feed on nectar and pol-

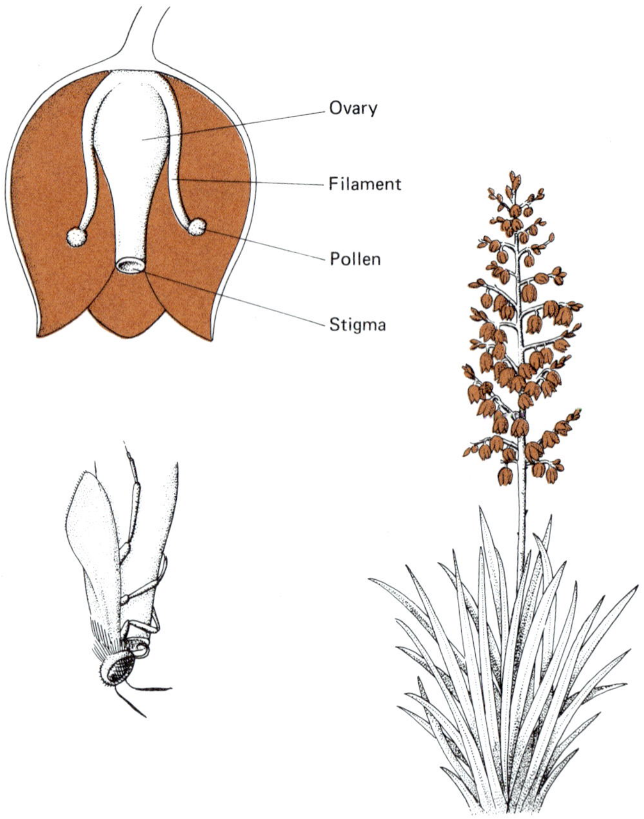

FIGURE 18.13 **Yucca and Its Pollinator.** The pronuba moth is the only pollinator of this yucca. After the moth lays her eggs in the ovary (a) she stuffs pollen in the stigma (b).

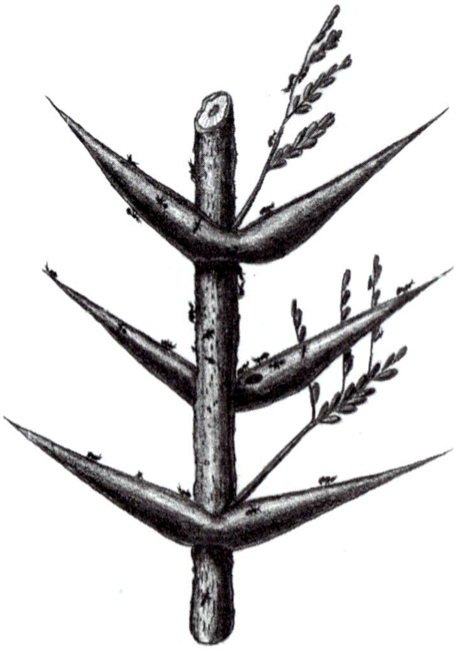

FIGURE 18.12 **Bullhorn Acacia.**

FIGURE 18.14 Pollinators. Some insects, such as bees, pollinate a wide range of plants. Other pollinators are more limited in their range of plant choices. Flower size and shape are two factors restricting pollinators.

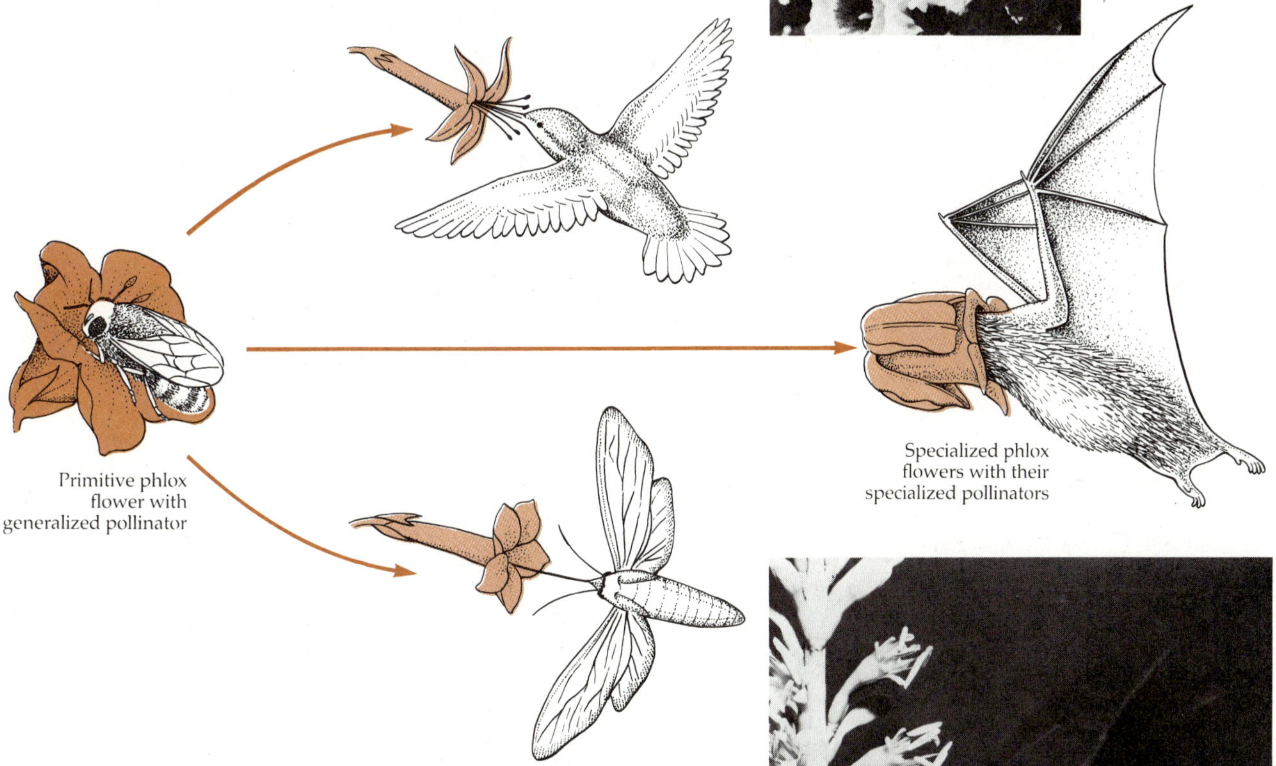

(a)

(b)

FIGURE 18.15 Predators and Prey. (a) Short-eared owl with vole. (b) Lioness with wildebeest. (c) European mantid with locust.

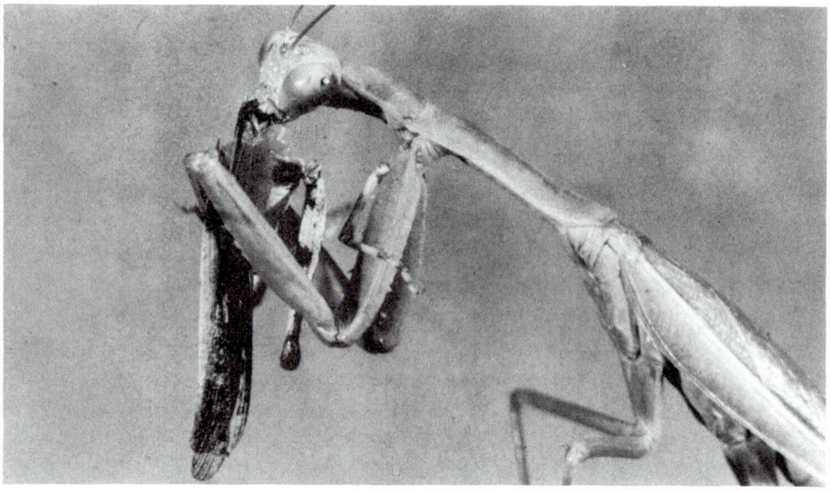

(c)

len much as insects do. If a plant species limits access to its pollen and has only specific animal pollinators, then the pollen is less likely to be wasted. Numerous adaptions increase the specificity of pollinator-plant interactions. For example, hummingbird-pollinated flowers are usually reddish and have long floral tubes accessible to long beaks but unreachable by many insects. Adaptations of the hummingbird include not only its needle-like beak, but also a long brush-tipped tongue useful in collecting pollen and minute insects from within the flower. Moths and bats are active at night. The flowers they pollinate release a heavy fragrance, which helps these nocturnal pollinators locate flowers in the dark. Obviously, all coevolved pollinators do not live closely together. Some organisms are highly interdependent without being symbiotic. As a matter of fact, some coevolved species do their best to avoid the species with which they have evolved. As we shall see, they have good reason.

Predators and their prey have evolved together. Both the behavior and the structure of predators suits them to catch certain sorts of prey. The acute hearing of owls (Fig. 18.15) and their relatively good night vision allow them to detect the movements of mice and other small animals that are active after dark. A startled mouse will dart into its hole or freeze motionless. Often such behavior allows it to escape notice by owls or other predators. Prey are so well adapted to their predators that when humans reduce the number of predators, the prey population can increase enough to alter the community.

Because prey are adapted to avoid their predators, attempts to introduce predators for pest control are often unsuccessful. A few overlooked prey can multiply to form large local populations before they are discovered. Perhaps you have noticed that aphids and other tiny garden pests occur in colonies here and there under plant leaves. The hide and seek nature of predator-prey relationships explains much of the patchy distribution of organisms in nature.

Just as animals have coevolved with their predators, plants have coevolved with herbivores (Fig. 18.16). Mammals that eat plants have grinding tooth surfaces. The size and strength of a bird's bill is

(a) (b) (c)

FIGURE 18.16 **Plants and Their Herbivores.** Harsh cell walls limit the range of animals that can feed on grasses. Broad, ridged teeth (a) allow horses, zebras, cattle, wildebeests (b), and related mammals to crush plant cell walls and release the nutrients within the cell. Potatoes are not toxic to the beetles in (c), perhaps because humans selected food plants that lacked the bitter (and poisonous) natural insecticides present in deadly nightshade and related members of the potato family.

related to the fruit, seeds, or other plant products it eats. Most plants synthesize chemicals that make them poisonous or at least unpalatable to animals. Of course, few plants escape completely. Most plants fall prey to just a few animal species that have evolved biochemical mechanisms to counter the plant's toxins. Humans who cultivate food plants choose the tastier varieties. As a result, our gardens and orchards are especially tempting to insects, birds, and mammals.

Numerous species **compete** with one another. When this occurs, natural selection favors individuals that specialize by using low-demand resources. 340 As the two species coevolve, competition is reduced.

Not a Superorganism

Despite all the interdependencies of each community, many associations and events are the result of chance. In well-studied associations, biologists can sometimes predict the general result—but not the specifics—of a particular disturbance. No community is so consistent that it can be treated as a superorganism with distinct boundaries, unalterable characteristics, and homeostatic mechanisms equivalent to those of an individual animal. At best, communities are associations that people find useful in ordering their thinking about the natural world.

POPULATIONS: THE FUNCTIONAL UNITS OF COMMUNITIES

Populations are groups of interbreeding organisms in some particular area. Communities have their reality only in the local populations of which they are composed. Whatever happens in a community happens on the population level. The regulation of population numbers ultimately determines the characteristics of a community.

All the interactions we've discussed so far affect population levels. Hosts and their parasites, predators and their prey, competitors, and mutualists all provide good examples. The effect of one population on another generally depends on population densities (the number of individuals per unit area). When a host species is numerous, parasites find it easy to move from host to host. More of the host population has parasites and the number of parasites per host is higher. When predators are numerous, there may not be enough prey to go around. Likewise, if herbivores are too numerous, there may not be enough plant food to go around. Quite casual interactions can affect a population. As you may recall from Bumpus's sparrows, 324 even the effect of weather can depend on the density of the population.

The negative effects of high population densities have favored evolution of numerous regulating mechanisms. Some species have evolved reproductive patterns that permit food supply to adjust population size with a minimum of wastage. Certain species of birds, such as parakeets (budgerigars) and many owls (Fig. 18.17) incubate their eggs from the day the first is laid. This practice contrasts with the more usual habit of incubating only after the entire clutch has been laid. When incubation commences with the first egg, the young hatch at intervals. If the food supply is adequate, the entire brood is likely to survive the nest period. If there is a shortage, the eldest nestling or the eldest two or three will live, but the younger birds may perish because they cannot compete at feeding time with their older siblings. But of course, the population is better off with a few healthy young than with nests of starving babies. Depressed reproduction is a common response to population highs (Table 18.2).

Emigration: One Way to Prevent Overpopulation

Intriguing patterns of population fluctuation occur among lemmings, voles, and many other small rodents. During population peaks many voles migrate from their colony. Studies suggest that the animals leaving are genetically different from those remaining behind. Emigrants have higher reproductive rates than stay-at-homes, and emigrants also have higher overall vigor. On the other hand, voles that remain at home are both more aggressive and more tolerant of crowding than are the emigrants. However, the stay-at-homes do not reproduce as rapidly as do emigrants, and the stay-at-homes also have higher mortality rates. Why they die, no one is certain. Infectious diseases aren't common, nor does outright starvation seem to occur. Perhaps one factor is increased dependency on toxic plants that increase in abundance as the more tasty and healthful ones are reduced by grazing.

Although rodent migrations are dramatic and often attract human attention, we should remember that they aren't catastrophes for the species.

FIGURE 18.17 **The Oldest Is the Largest.** The largest of these three Great Horned Owl nestlings hatched from the first egg laid. From the beginning it was the strongest and obtained an unfairly large share of food. Had prey been in short supply, the third and perhaps the second owlet would have starved.

TABLE 18.2 **Pregnancy Blocks Resulting from Contact with Strange Males**

SPECIES	EFFECTS
293 Sprague Dawley strain of laboratory rats *Rattus rattus*	Additional genital stimulation of female within 15 minutes of mating inhibits sperm transport to the uterus and thus inhibits pregnancy. Thus if several males have access to an estrus female, she may bear no young at all.
Prairie vole *Microtus ochrogaster*	Replacement of the original male with an unfamiliar male will induce estrus in an already pregnant female, even if the embryos are implanted. As a result, the litter will abort. With heavy populations, migrations, and population shifts, this may happen repeatedly. As a result, a female may bear no young.
House mouse *Mus musculus*	The odor (pheromone) of a strange male will cause a female carrying unimplanted embryos to abort her litter.

Instead, events common in natural populations are probably adaptive.

Breeding Territories: Another Way to Prevent Overpopulation

Many animals display territoriality, especially during the breeding season. Breeding territories are used as an undisturbed place to mate, as a secure place to raise young, as a source of food for the offspring, or for more than one of these purposes. These functions may justify the energy expended to establish and maintain the territories, but population regulation may be an equally important result.

Migratory songbirds provide classic examples of reproductive territoriality. Usually the males arrive a few days earlier than the females and establish the territories. Each territory includes suitable area for food collection, cover for a nesting site, and at least one high perch from which the male can sing to advertise himself and his territory. Although birds chirp the year around, their full songs are associated with nesting. Early in the spring, vigorous singing intimidates other males and at-

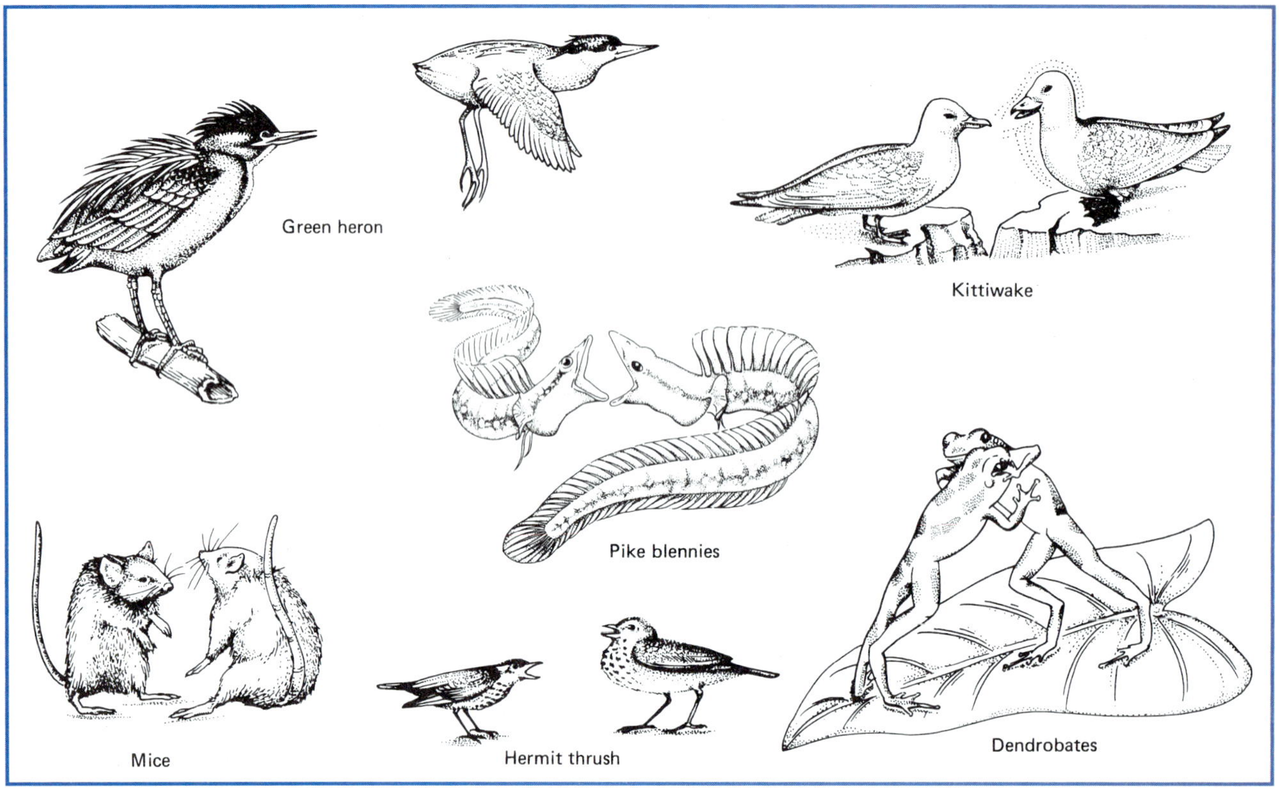

FIGURE 18.18 **Territorial Displays.**

tracts females to single males. So long as a territory is maintained, the male and often his mate defend it against intrusion by others of their species. In addition to song, defense may involve specific **display** activities (Fig. 18.18) that intimidate would-be trespassers. Frequently an intruder responds with a similar display, so the birds appear to be engaged in battle. However, these "fights" are largely symbolic. Usually neither bird is harmed.

As males arrive in spring, suitable habitats quickly become saturated. Boundary lines between territories fluctuate as the birds test themselves against one another. If the centers of two territories are so close that one bird cannot tolerate the aggressiveness of the other, the less tolerant will leave. Should the vanquished find no suitable habitat, it will remain unmated and thus leave no offspring.

It is easy to suggest how natural selection has favored territorial behavior. Displays have evolved along with a sensitivity to aggression that correlates with the minimum usable territory. The result is that each bird that nests has sufficient resources to support the young. Of course, these young tend to inherit the behavioral patterns of their parents. Birds without adequate territorial instincts may try to nest in crowded conditions, but with insufficient food or a poor nest site, they are unlikely to be successful. Thus territoriality promotes successful reproduction and at the same time keeps the population within the carrying capacity of its habitat.

Carrying Capacity

From a human viewpoint, the numbers of a particular species that a community can support can be extremely important. Although **carrying capacity** is a term originally coined to describe the number of cattle or sheep a particular range could support, ecologists define it as the number of one species that an area can maintain for a long period of time. In this definition, emphasis is placed on long-term support rather than on the maximum number that can be kept for a short while. One of the major questions facing humans today is how to keep our populations within the carrying capacity of the earth. This matter is so important that we devote an entire chapter to it. Thus you will find more about the biology of populations in Chapter 23.

The Bottom Line

Although many ecological principles seem merely common sense, these principles became recognized only after biologists began to stress quantification. How many are there of each species in this square meter? How many grams of carbon can this plant incorporate in one growing season? What proportion of the total phosphorus of this lake is present in living organisms? Today computers help with such calculations and can be used to simulate ecosystems and predict responses to disturbances.

It may take a mountain of data to explain even the simplest ecosystem. But the fundamental goal of ecological research is to understand the mechanisms of biological survival. After all, survival of the species is the bottom line—the mechanism and the reward of evolution.

In the final analysis, ecosystems are associations of components that have evolved together. Of course, it is only the organisms that have undergone the genetic changes of biological evolution. But the physical components have changed, too, and partly in response to living things. Interactions have occurred on every scale and in all directions. As a result, plants, animals, microorganisms, soil, water, rock, and air all fit together. Species are able to survive because they fit in.

Summary

1. For the sake of description and analysis, biologists divide the living world into biological communities and into ecosystems.

2. Organisms require energy because organisms characteristically consist of ordered arrangements, whereas the universe tends to disorder. Because all energy conversions are inefficient, all ecosystems require continuous additions of energy. Thus energy flows through ecosystems. The energy loss at each conversion is usually reflected in fewer organisms and less living matter at each higher trophic level.

3. Whereas energy flows through an ecosystem and is ultimately lost, chemical nutrients can cycle within the ecosystem. This is true for the biosphere, in which the path of carbon can be traced from land to water, as well as from rock to air and from plant to animal. Such biogeochemical cycles tend to bind the components of an ecosystem together, just as the flow of energy makes certain species dependent on others.

4. The carrying capacity of an ecosystem is the number of organisms the system can support. It is determined by density-dependent factors, such as food, for which individuals must compete.

5. Ecosystems contain communities of organisms that have evolved together within physical environments. A community consists of the organisms living together in some recognizably distinct area. An ecosystem includes both the organisms and all the other components of the physical environment.

6. The species of a community depend on others for food, shelter, and other essentials of life. The neat fit of the characteristics and needs of two species usually reflects a long association during which each has been selected for its adaptation to the other.

7. Destruction of the vegetation in any area is usually followed by a predictable pattern of new vegetational stages. However, this and other generalizations about community behavior have limited reliability, because communities are not superorganisms.

8. The edge where two communities meet supports more organisms and more species than either does alone.

9. Many of the interactions that bind communities together are the result of natural selection and coevolution.

10. Population regulation is at the core of a stable community. Regulation involves both interactions with other species and inherited characteristics, such as emigration patterns, interruption of pregnancies, and territoriality.

Thought and Controversy

1. Many biologists believe endangered species have reproductive strategies that differ in characteristic ways from those of animals that thrive despite human activities. English sparrows and similiarly common species are said to be *r*-adapted, whereas the endangered ones are said to be *K*-adapted.

The *r* species have a tremendous *reproduction potential,* a term used for the maximum theoretical reproductive capacity (*r*) of a species. These species have a diverse gene pool, too, and use a broad range of habitats. The *r* species survive easily in areas that humans disturb or manipulate.

The *K*-adapted species show traits opposite those of *r*-adapted ones. Often *K* species have evolved under conditions of extreme competition. This fact has favored evolution of extreme specialization. Some *K* species, such as the everglade kite that eats only snails, can use only one food source. Others (for example, the California condor) have rigid environmental requirements for breeding or for another phase of the life cycle. The habitat alterations worked by humans can be fatal to species with such narrow ecological niches.

Along with their extreme specialization, *K* species have evolved inherited strategies that protect them against predation. Many animals exhibit parental care of the young. A large number contain in their bodies chemicals that give them an unpalatable taste. Large adult size is another strategy. With predation kept low, a low reproductive potential is also advantageous. Each female can optimize the number of her offspring that will mature by spreading available resources among only a few young. Eggs may be large, or the young may be individually tended by the mother.

This low reproductive potential makes *K* species extremely vulnerable to increased predation. As humans have widened their ecological niche through cultural evolution, they have broadened their role as predators. In addition, they have introduced new predator species into many ecosystems. Other introduced species compete with *K*-adapted ones.

Populations of *K* species are naturally small because of the limited ecological niches. When habitat alteration or increased competition or heavier predation lowers population levels further, the low reproductive potential makes recovery a slow process. Predation may exceed births. If a species becomes rare, reproduction can be decreased further by lack of opportunity to breed. If deaths long exceed births, extinction is inevitable.

2. Hunters sometimes lobby their state game commissions to rear game, particularly birds, and release them into certain areas. Under what conditions are released game likely to survive and improve public hunting? Consider the question in terms of the ecological niche of the species and the carrying capacity of the ecosystem.

3. What is a species worth? The cost of keeping many endangered species will include large permanent reserves of undisturbed habitat. Many people in the United States think that India should preserve the tiger by setting aside large reserves. But what sacrifices are we willing to make to meet similar problems? Will we forgo dams that flood out endangered plants in the United States? Or those that ruin the habitat of stream fish? What guidelines can you suggest for these difficult decisions?

Questions

1. Explain why energy flows through ecosystems but matter cycles about an ecosystem.

2. Relate trophic levels and pyramids of energy and biomass.

3. Compare the carbon cycle on land and in the ocean. Are these related? Explain.

4. How are the complexity and the stability of an ecosystem related?

5. Why are communities named for plants rather than for animals?

6. Discuss the concept of community succession, using the deciduous forest biome as an example. Explain the mechanisms suggested to explain the various stages.

7. Discuss the reality of communities and ecosystems. What pitfalls are associated with these concepts?

8. What is the edge effect? How would you expect a region where two communities meet on a complex and meandering border to compare in species with an equal-sized area of either community?

9. Give some examples of the result of coevolution. Are all products of coevolution examples of mutualism? How are the numbers of a predator and its prey related? Are all predators carnivores?

10. What are some of the mechanisms that regulate animal populations?

19

Terrestrial Ecosystems: Life on the Surface of the Earth

TO UNDERSTAND THE BIOSPHERE, WE MUST EXamine the large terrestrial ecosystems known as **biomes** and ask not only how communities differ, but also why they do. Although no single factor defines an environment, environmental extremes may dramatically limit options. Consider, for example, the earth's poles. These ice-covered regions that the penguins and polar bears call home are the least hospitable areas of the earth. They are cold most of the year because of the pattern of sunlight, water currents, and wind. The brief summers are never warm enough to melt the accumulated ice packs. As a result, rooted plant life is impossible. In the north the food web is based on the producers of the Arctic Ocean. The continental land mass at the South Pole is an environment with little life. A well-developed food chain is present only at its edge.

In the Arctic north, the land of permanent ice is edged by a **tundra** that develops where more moderate day lengths and increased solar radiation leave the soil bare and soft for a few short months. Conditions permit terrestrial food chains to develop. Large, nomadic animals, such as reindeer and caribou, graze on the low, hardy vegetation (Fig. 19.1) but must range widely to find enough food. Predatory wolves and foxes follow the great herds or hunt lemmings and other small rodents that burrow in the ground. Although tundra soil is frozen much of the time, sunlight thaws the surface each spring. Suddenly plants burst into flower as the desolation of the dark, snowy winter is broken by the long, warm days of Arctic summer. Black flies, mosquitoes, and other insects emerge in great swarms. Migratory waterfowl, shorebirds, and songbirds arrive from thousands of miles away to nest and feed on hordes of insects from temporary ponds and thawing rivers.

Farther south, cold is not so pervading; here the land form and rainfall become important variables. As a result, the earth is blanketed with biomes like a giant patchwork quilt. Forests, grasslands, and deserts are scattered about. No two are alike, and of course, none remains untouched by human hands. Some we have only exploited. Others we have manipulated beyond all recognition. The story is at the same time fascinating, inspiring, and sad.

TEMPERATE DECIDUOUS FORESTS

European colonists found most of the eastern seaboard of North America covered with **deciduous** trees—trees that shed their broad leaves in the fall. Similar forests once blanketed most of Europe, the temperate coasts of Asia, and smaller areas of Australia and South America.

The Plant Community

Mature deciduous forests often contain dozens of tree species, but in any given area one or two kinds of oak, hickory, chestnut, maple, basswood, buckeye, or beech are common enough to give the forest a name. Big trees dominate the community by providing most of the food supply and by modifying the physical environment through shade and

(a)

(b)

FIGURE 19.1 **Tundra.** Perennial herbs and low shrubs form a scant layer of vegetation in the tundra. Insects breed in shallow ponds and provide food for birds that migrate northward to nest during the brief summer.

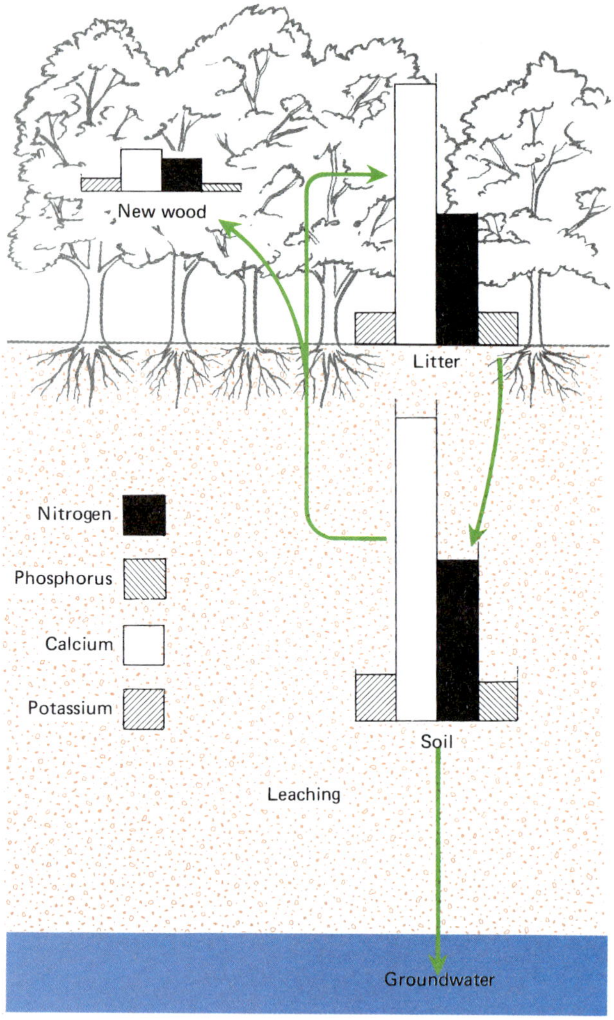

FIGURE 19.2 **Nutrient Cycling in a Beech Forest.**

windbreak action. The largest trees are widely spaced, but such a forest includes individuals of all ages and is a stable community that can maintain itself through continued reproduction.

Under the trees of a deciduous forest, shrubs and **herbaceous** (nonwoody) plants are scattered about, but few are abundant except in clearings. The density of the leafy canopy overhead and the time each year that the canopy is present regulate growth of **understory** (below the canopy) plants. Many of these are small herbs or "spring flowers" that grow rapidly as days first lengthen. They reproduce and carry out much of their photosynthesis before the tree leaves open and reduce the sunlight available on the forest floor.

Soils of some deciduous temperate forests are brown and rich-looking, but most of the available minerals cycle through the plants each year. As indicated in Fig. 19.2, only a small portion of the minerals absorbed are retained in the wood of the tree. The remainder returns to the ground as twig and leaf litter. Not all of the returned materials can be reused the following year, because decomposition takes a long time. Many plants grow directly in the remains of others (Fig. 19.3b). Of the min-

(a)

FIGURE 19.3 Temperate Deciduous Forests. In the fall, loss of chlorophyll from dying leaves allows carotenoids and xanthophylls to show their fiery colors (a). Young trees thrive if they grow from seeds that fall into a rotting log rich in minerals (b). The forest floor supports understory plants such as blueberries (c), especially at openings where sunlight is abundant. The rich vegetation supports many small rodents that in turn feed a diversity of animals. The snake in (d) has a visible lump in its abdomen because it has swallowed its furry prey whole.

(b)

(c)

(d)

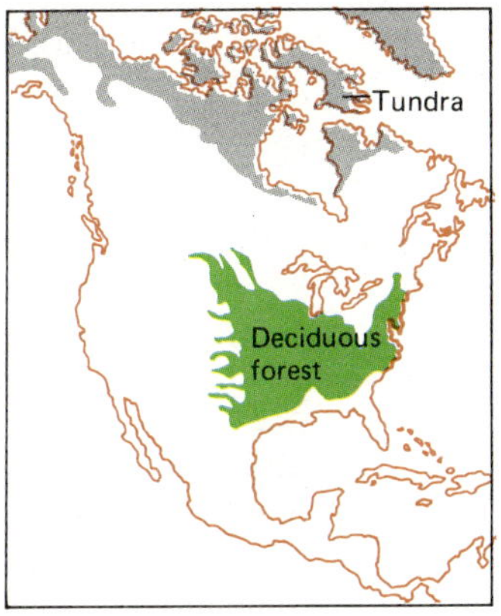

TABLE 19.1 Average Numbers of Organisms/2.6 km² (1 Square Mile) of Temperate North American Deciduous Forest During the Summer*

Plants	
Trees 7.5 cm (3 in.) or more in diameter	75,000
Tree seedlings	78,600
Shrubs	281,000
Soft-stemmed plants	345,000,000
Animals	
Invertebrates (insects, snails, centipedes, millipedes, earthworms, etc.)	2,688,000,000
Pairs of small nesting birds	768
Large predatory birds (owls and hawks)	2 to 5
Mice	240,000
Gray squirrels	1,500
Flying squirrels	1,500
White-tailed deer	40
Wild turkeys	20
Gray fox	3
Black bears	0.5
Mountain lions	0.2

*From estimates compiled by Victor E. Shelford in *The Ecology of North America,* University of Illinois Press, Urbana, 1963.

erals released from the litter, some invariably leach
431 away in rainwater. Humus from decomposing leaves and twigs helps hold both water and minerals.

Temperate deciduous forests are highly productive, and they support a large number of organisms (Table 19.1). Such forests are also quite diverse. An often overlooked part of the commu-
430 nity lives in the litter on the forest floor. Much of the biomass of the forest enters this decomposer food chain yearly. Litter decomposition involves the activity of multitudes of tiny animals and microorganisms. Insects such as springtails and other near-microscopic arthropods eat dead leaves. These primary consumers absorb less than 10 percent of the nutrients in the litter. However, as a result of their digestive processes, the remains that become feces are easily attacked by bacteria and fungi.

Animals not only consume and alter litter, but also mix it into the soil. Earthworms are among the most active litter mixers. The carnivores that eat the litter feeders also stir litter and mix it into the soil as they endlessly seek their prey.

Adaptation to Climate

Temperate deciduous forests have moderate temperatures and rainfall (about 70–100 cm or 28–40 in./yr) but are characteristically subject to frost. Shedding leaves in the fall protects the trees against cold damage. Otherwise the large leaf surface that favors transpiration and photosynthesis during the warm season would allow heavy evaporation and severe water loss during the winter. You will recall that the absorption of water by roots relies on diffusion, as well as on energy-consuming activities
of root cells. Both are slowed by cold, and of course, 411
frozen soil yields no water. Cold weather conditions cause greater plant dehydration than hot weather conditions do. This is especially true when cold weather is accompanied by strong winds. Furthermore, leaves are difficult to protect against freezing. Deciduous trees have evolved an effective strategy to prevent damage from winter cold. First they concentrate sugars and other organic compounds from their leaves into roots and stems. Here these large molecules lower the freezing point of cell fluids and prevent formation of ice crystals that could rupture cells. Then the trees simply shed their leaves.

The shedding of leaves is a preprogrammed process coded into the genetic structure of a plant and only slightly affected by the weather conditions of any particular year. In response to a decrease in auxins, an **abscission** (cutting-off) **layer** forms where the leaf stalk joins the stem (Fig. 19.4), and the cement between the cells in that area softens. In the absence of strong intercellular cements, the short cells of the abscission layer separate, permitting the leaf to drop off or blow away in a gentle breeze.

The color changes that foretell leaf drop in deciduous forests result from cessation of chlorophyll formation. Because chlorophyll breaks down spontaneously in light, leaves remain green only while they continue to synthesize chlorophyll. With the coming of fall, chlorophyll manufacture ceases, and this green pigment gradually bleaches in sunlight. In the absence of chlorophyll we see yellow or reddish pigments, mainly **carotenoids** that aid in light absorption for photosynthesis. Another source of red color results from interruption of phloem by

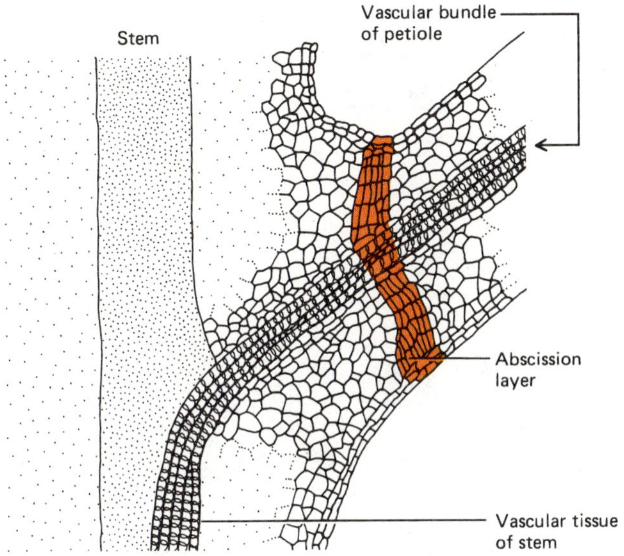

FIGURE 19.4 **Abscission Layer Aids Leaf Drop.** This band of specialized cells at the base of a leaf permits the leaf to break away cleanly. Before the leaf drops, the vascular tissue is plugged and other cells form a protective layer that prevents microorganisms from invading the tree.

the developing abscission layer. This causes sugars to accumulate in the leaves, where some are converted into reddish compounds.

What Humans Have Done with Deciduous Woodlands

Most of Europe was once covered with climax deciduous forests except at high elevations and in places where standing water created marshes. It has been said the forest canopy was so dense that a squirrel could travel from central Russia to the Atlantic coast without ever touching ground. On much of the continent the dominant species were oaks, but in some regions elms, beeches, and birches were prominent.

Fire and Axe. Many early forests succumbed to fire or flint axe. At first, people cut trees mainly to obtain building material or fuel, but sometimes trees were felled merely to clear the land. Initial clearings were often abandoned and re-covered by forest; scientists have determined this through studies of pollen buried in the mud of nearby lakes and bogs. The pollen profile in Fig.19.5 is that of a Danish bog typical of many in western Europe. Decreases in pollen of oak and ivy (a native understory vine) mark the first clearing of the forest. This stage is followed by high levels of weed pollen, which indicate a period of cultivation. Later peaks in hazel pollen show when these shrubby trees took over fields that must have been abandoned.

FIGURE 19.5 **Pollen from a Danish Bog Provides Evidence of Prehistoric Farming.** These graphs show the relative amounts of four kinds of pollen trapped in mud at different depths within a bog. Farming probably began around the time indicated by the vertical line *a*, for oaks declined then and plantain, a common weed, appeared. Later the land may have been abandoned. We can make this assumption because hazel, a forest succession shrub, peaked *b*, and oaks increased. Only fully mature ivy vines bear flowers, so the reappearance of ivy pollen was delayed *c*. Note that when the land was reclaimed by forest, plantain was crowded out *d*.

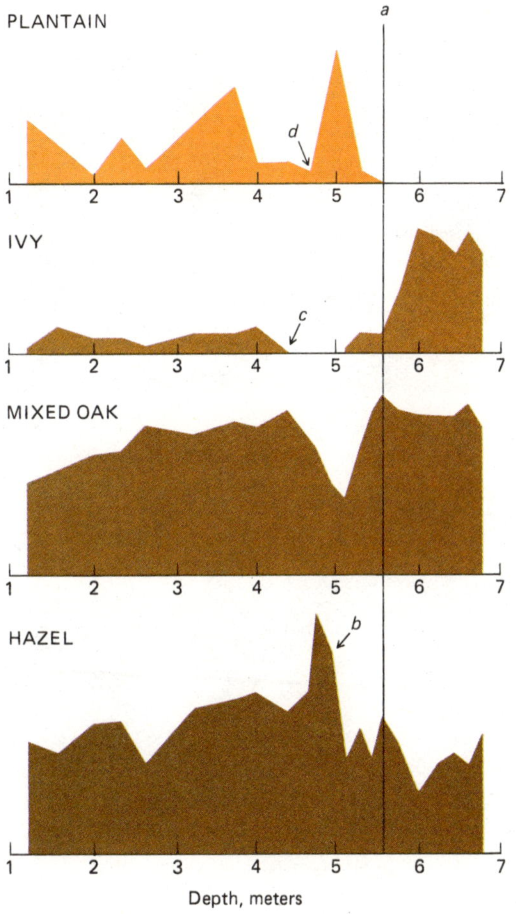

BOX 19A

FUNGI OF THE FOREST

The humus-rich soil of forests supports a large number of saprophytic plants. These non-green plants lack chlorophyll and therefore cannot trap energy from sunlight. Instead, they absorb organic compounds released from decaying plant and animal materials. Although a few of the saprophytes are seed-bearing plants, most are fungi. Many of these secrete enzymes into the area around them and thereby digest the dead matter into compounds they can absorb.

All fungi are composed of filaments of cells called hyphae. Soil fungi have most of their hyphae

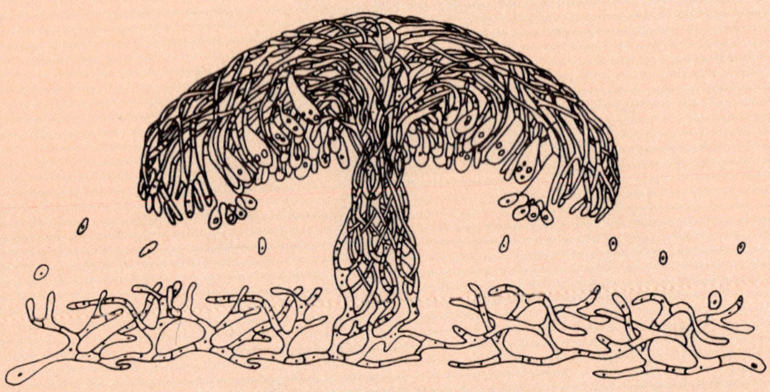

Poisonous Amanita.

Gill Mushroom.

Pore Mushroom.

arranged in a three-dimensional network, or mycelium. If you separate wet leaf litter or move a fallen branch, sometimes you will see white or yellowish fungal networks. These constitute the vegetative portion of the plant. Often the reproductive structures, or "fruiting bodies," are large and above-ground. The term mushroom refers to one type of reproductive structure. When you section a mushroom (especially an old one) with a sharp knife, you see the closely packed hyphae. If you place the cap on a sheet of paper and protect it from air currents for a few hours, you will find powdery spores on the paper. Each of these spores, which develop on the "gills" beneath the cap, has the potential to form a new mycelium.

Not only do fungi play important roles in maintaining the nutrient and carbon cycles of the forest by decomposing dead matter, but many also enter into complex, mutually beneficial relationships with the roots of other plants, including trees. The fungi form a mantle around the tips of the roots—hence the name mycorrhiza, or "fungus root." The fungi do not harm the plant, although some of the hyphae penetrate the outer layer of the root. The fungal hyphae are sometimes digested by the root enzymes—a process that supplies minerals to the plant. In many cases the hyphal layer absorbs water and supplies it to the root tissues. Often root cells exude small quantities of organic materials, particularly carbohydrates. It is not unlikely that these substances attract fungi and help establish the mycorrhizal relationship.

Bract Fungi.

Puff balls.

Mycelium.

Vast tracts of European climax forest still flourished in Roman times. Throughout that period the forest edge expanded and contracted with wars and other changes in human fortune. Eventually, the relentless demand for plowed land and forest products doomed the woodlands. As commerce and trade grew, more and more timber was needed for shipbuilding. Glass and soap manufacture required wood ash as a raw material. The smelting of tin, lead, copper, and iron depended on charcoal made from wood. By the eighteenth century, these industries had scalped the forests of England, and the British had turned to digging coal. The woodlands of western Europe disappeared a short time later.

Such drastic alteration of the landscape naturally had far-reaching effects. Rains began to wash the soil from the naked land. It is no coincidence that several British seaports filled with silt during the twelfth and thirteenth centuries and were abandoned when their waters were no longer deep enough to float seagoing vessels.

Erosion is still evident in parts of England. Some fields have been farmed with the same hedgerow boundaries ever since the land was cleared. In places where the hedges run across the middle of slopes, the soil is as deep as six feet on the upward side of the hedgerow but so thin on the lower side that rocks lie exposed. We have no idea how much more soil eroded away entirely and washed into the ocean.

Domestic animals prevented regeneration of most British woodlands. A great sheep industry thrived in England during the Middle Ages; grazing was so heavy that tree seedlings had no opportunity to grow out of reach of livestock. As sheep-rearing endeavors decreased, rabbits, introduced from the Continent, increased dramatically. The rabbits stripped bark from the young trees and did so much damage that few seedlings survived.

Conversion to Grassland and Moor. In many deforested areas of Britain the climate, soil, and grazing animals interacted to create a habitat favorable to coarse grasses. Manure from the sheep and rabbits returned minerals to the soil, established an efficient nutrient cycle, and permitted the formation of a crumbly soil that supported a heavy turf.

Not all the deforested British lands went to grass. On some soils the loss of trees raised the underground water level enough to create bogs. There is a simple explanation for this drastic change. Each day during the leafy season, large trees transpire tremendous volumes of water. Deforestation reduces this drain on the groundwater. Therefore cutting certain forests can lead to their replacement with bogs or wet, peaty moors that support low shrubs.

Fate of the Forests. Wherever civilization flourishes, forests are destroyed. The history of other forests differs little from that of European forests. The Chinese began clearing ground for crops at least 4000 years ago. The Mediterranean forests were already seriously damaged in Plato's time. As a rule, few forests remain where civilization has long thrived.

Although we must infer much of the history of Eurasian vegetation, we know a great deal about what happened in North America. Along the East Coast, the abundance of land and the need for a lightweight crop that could be traded in Europe promoted slash-and-burn tobacco farming. Not only did cutting and burning the trees clear the land, but it provided ashes that contained sufficient minerals to support a few crops of tobacco. However, these minerals were soon lost from American soil. The mineral-rich tobacco leaves were shipped to Europe and converted again to ashes, this time in foreign pipes. The broken nutrient cycles and rapid erosion quickly ruined the tobacco plantations. Whenever that happened, the owners merely moved westward and cut another area. In this way the forests around Chesapeake Bay were destroyed even before the American Revolution. So much soil washed into streams and rivers and settled into the bay that the shoreline we know is quite different from the one the early settlers found.

CONIFEROUS FORESTS

The conifers are **gymnosperms** that bear seeds in cones instead of within fruits as do the flowering plants.□ Familiar conifers include pines, spruces, 389
firs, cedars, and redwoods.

Boreal Forests

A wide band of conifers girdles Eurasia and North America north of the deciduous forests and grasslands. Most of these conifers retain their leaves the year around and shed one set only after the next is in place. Persistence of the leaves permits conifers to take immediate advantage of good weather, since they are able to begin photosynthesis without waiting to develop new leaves. This is a distinct advantage toward the poles, where the warm season is short.

These conifers also tolerate low temperatures. One reason is that they have stiff, wax-covered leaves known as "needles." When cold winds blow through the forests, the thick layer of wax retards water loss through evaporation. Of course, the leaves do dehydrate, and they would wilt if they were not rigid. Thus the stiffness of the needles, due to tissues with exceedingly thick cell walls, prevents damage that would otherwise be caused by wilting. The leaf structure of conifers clearly suits them to subarctic regions, where winter winds sweep across the landscape.

Coniferous communities have fewer species than do deciduous forests. One reason is that the ever-present shade of the year-round canopy restricts photosynthesis in understory plants. As a result, the ground is nearly bare except for a deep carpet of slowly decomposing needles. During dry weather the needles will support a fire hot enough to ignite the tree tops. Such a crown fire can destroy millions of acres of forest.

Acids from the slowly decomposing litter leach nutrients from the soil. Together the acids and the slow release of nutrients from the needles result in low soil fertility. Conifers generally have root fungi, known as **mycorrhiza,** which aid mineral accumulation (see Box 19A). Trees without such symbiotic partners are at a disadvantage.

Except in successional stages, boreal forests (Fig. 19.6) usually consist of one species of tree. Because

(a)

(b)

FIGURE 19.6 Boreal Forest. Northern forests are dense stands, usually of a single conifer species. Numerous lakes and ponds (a) provide additional resources for beaver, moose, and other mammals. Even in these forests succession creates diversity. Aspen springs up in disturbed areas in spruce forests but spruce seedlings appear (b) and eventually grow into trees that replace the aspen.

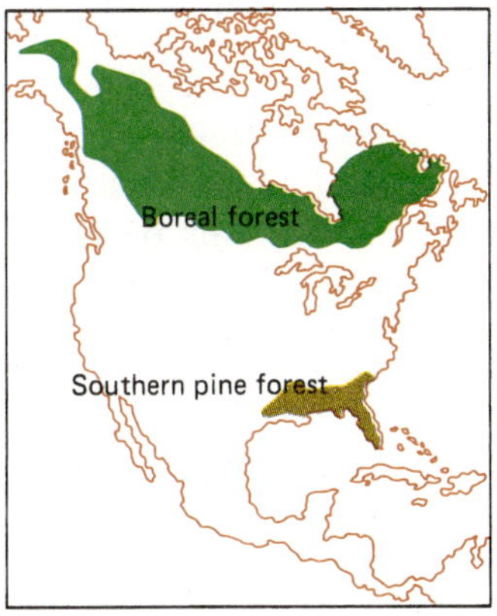

of their purity, these stands of timber invite exploitation for lumber. For the same reason, they sometimes support tremendous populations of herbivorous insects, such as the spruce
441 budworm. Single-species forests are vulnerable to epidemics of specific parasitic fungi, as well. White-pine blister rust is one example.

The boreal forests share the flatness of the tundra. Movement of Ice-Age glaciers ground these northern regions nearly level. Where the glaciers melted, mounds of sediments remain. The poor drainage has produced thousands of lakes and innumerable mossy bogs or **muskegs** (Fig. 19.6C). Moose frequent the lakes and bogs. Beavers build dams on the streams, and these dams produce new ponds every year.

Conifers of the Western Mountains

Southward extensions of the boreal communities lie along the Rocky Mountains, the Cascades, and the Sierra Nevada. Here high altitudes produce environments that are similar but not identical to those of high latitudes (Fig. 19.7). The major differences are in the length of the day and the intensity of sunlight. Where mountains are at temperate latitudes, organisms experience a day length typical of the temperate zone. But because mountains stand above much of the earth's atmosphere, the sun's radiation is more intense here than at lower altitudes. (This results from the fact that the atmosphere absorbs part of the radiation that reaches it.) Yet mountains cool quickly at night because radiant heat is lost through the thin atmosphere. This and exposure to winds make high altitudes colder than the adjacent lowlands. The cool weather of high altitudes creates environments resembling those toward the poles.

The habitats of mountainous regions differ greatly not only in temperature, but also in rainfall. Air masses approaching and passing over mountains rise and are cooled. The reduction in temperature reduces the ability of the air to hold water vapor. As a result, rain and snow are likely on the windward sides of mountain ranges. But as the air currents descend and warm, their water-vapor capacity increases; thus rain and snow decrease. This reduced precipitation produces a **rain shadow** on the leeward sides of mountains. The combination of water-laden ocean breezes and a number of mountain ranges accounts for the extremely diverse character of the Pacific Northwest.

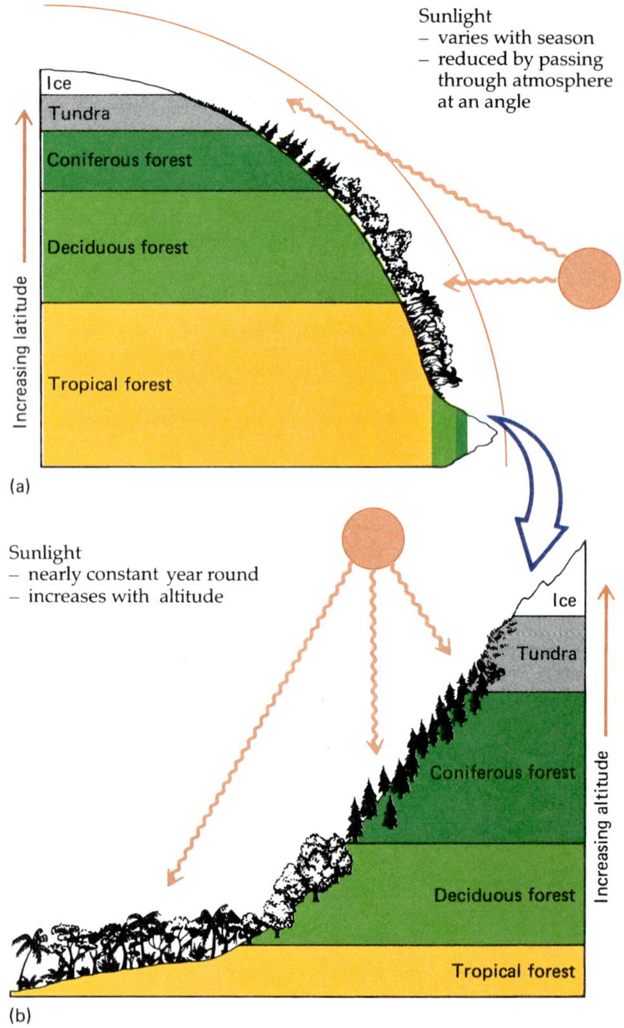

FIGURE 19.7 **Altitudinal and Latitudinal Zonation: Similar but Not Identical.** North–south zonation (latitudinal) is due largely to seasonal differences in sunlight, whereas mountain zonation (altitudinal) results from cooler temperatures associated with higher altitudes. The thin atmosphere exposes mountains to extreme sunlight in the daytime but provides little insulation against nighttime heat loss.

For example, the western side of the Olympic mountains supports a **temperate rain forest** with 450 cm (180 in.) of rain annually (Fig. 19.8a). Only fifty miles to the east, in the rain shadow, are areas with as little as 38 cm (15 in.) of rain annually. Similar—if less extreme—examples occur all along the coast. Air moving inland gradually picks up evaporated moisture, and the pattern is repeated at each mountain range: western slopes receive more rainfall than eastern slopes (Fig. 19.8b). Low levels of

(a)

(b)

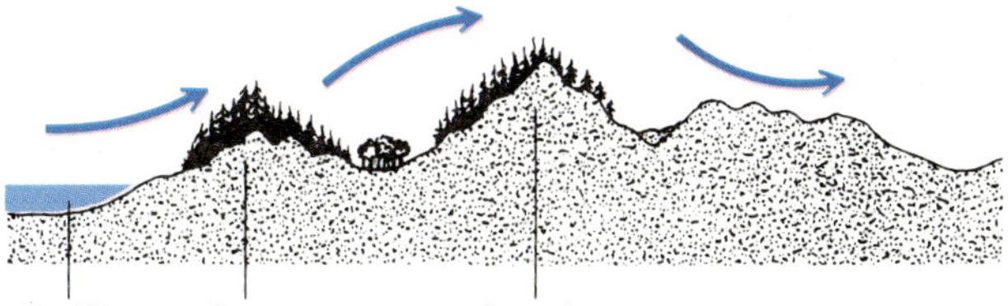

(c)

FIGURE 19.8 Conifers of the Mountainous Northwest. Heavy fog and rain produce a temperate rain forest on the coastal side of the Olympia Peninsula in Washington State (a). Clouds drop rain as they rise to pass over mountains (b); as they descend they release little moisture. Spacious stands of Ponderosa pine grow in the rain shadow on the eastern slopes of the Cascades (c).

rainfall combine with warm temperatures to convert some inland areas into grasslands or near-deserts.

Southern Conifers: A Fire Climax

The same adaptations that allow conifers to survive winter dryness in cold climates suit them also to hotter areas, especially where the soil is sandy and the water supply is unstable. In the southeastern United States, pines colonize abandoned fields and form major forests. Perhaps their initial success depends on mycorrhizae, since these soils are usually poor. Left undisturbed, many such pine forests are replaced by oak, hickory, or magnolia. Apparently fire set by lightning or by humans maintains these pine forests, since they tolerate fire, whereas the broad-leafed trees do not. The pines have a thin trunk bark through which new buds sprout if existing limbs are destroyed. A thick tuft of needles

(a) (b)

FIGURE 19.9 Southern Pine Forests. Typical pine stands (a) show the effects of ground fires. The growing tips of young pines (b) are protected from fire by dense tufts of needles. Small deciduous trees in the background would succumb to fire, whereas the pine would survive.

protects the terminal bud of the southern longleaf pine and makes it extremely resistant to fire (Fig. 19.9). As a matter of fact, longleaf pine seedlings seldom survive in the absence of fire, for they are sensitive to crowding and shading. Only when other vegetation is burned back can the little pines get enough light to grow.

If southern pine forests are burned every few years, the fires do little damage to wildlife, because the animals can escape by running through or flying over the low fire line. In fact, occasional burnings of patches of pine forest increase the population of bobwhite quail and wild turkeys. These birds find food and shelter in the successional stages that follow fire. We are not suggesting that fire is always beneficial, even in these forests. In contrast to the low, cool surface fires of frequently burned regions, fires in pine forests that have not burned recently will blaze up high and hot. Over many years without fire, a thick blanket of needles and fallen limbs accumulates on the ground. Once this litter is on fire, both the plant community and the wildlife are endangered.

GRASSLANDS

Most temperate grasslands have long since succumbed to the cow and the plow. Only a few retain the unmodified vegetation of the plains, prairies, steppes, velds, or pampas. But whether they bear native vegetation or support the highly selected grasses we know as grains, these grasslands supply the bulk of human food. Cattle and sheep graze on their grasses; cattle, hogs, and chickens fatten on corn grown on former grasslands; and most of our cereals, especially wheat and corn, are produced on soils that once supported native grasses.

Biology of Grasses

All the grasses belong to one large family and share distinctive characteristics that fit them to their environment and make them of particular use to humans. Many people are surprised to learn that
grasses are flowering plants.□ Open grasslands are 389
windy, and it is the wind that pollinates grass flowers. Natural selection has favored wind-pollinated

plants such as the grasses, which conserve their resources by producing small flowers that lack the showy petals necessary to attract animal pollinators.

A single head of oats or other grass contains numerous flowers (Fig. 19.10). Each tiny flower can form a single fruit called a **grain,** or kernel. The ovarian tissue of the fruit fuses with the single seed inside in such a way that they become one continuous structure.

Adapted to Withstand Grazing. As grasslands evolved, their abundant thin leaves offered a bonanza to herbivorous animals. As a result, there evolved a large group of grass-eating mammals, including the ancestors of today's cattle, sheep, and horses. The selective pressures of these grazers promoted evolution of traits that resist grazing damage. For one thing, grasses store nutrients in their roots. As a result, loss of stems does not substantially reduce their reserves. Another factor is the presence of silica, the substance we know as glass, in grass cell walls. Of course, grazers have evolved excellent grinding teeth. But grasses take their toll. Tooth wear is so severe that many old mammalian herbivores eventually starve to death.

FIGURE 19.10 **Structure of Grasses.**

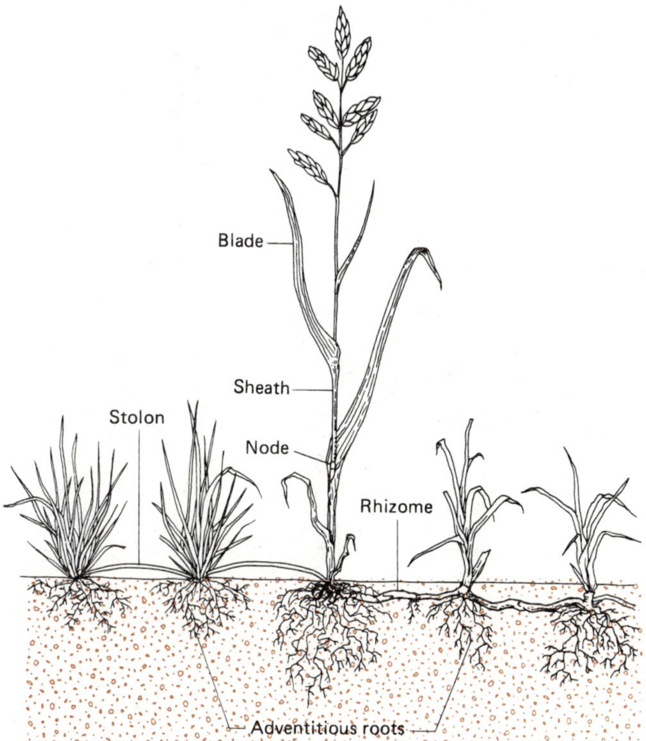

The growth pattern of grasses has several distinctive characteristics that may also adapt them to withstand grazing. The leaves retain a meristematic growth region at the base of the sheath and another at the base of the blade (Fig. 19.10). If the blade is cropped back, these meristems resume growth and lengthen the leaf to compensate for lost photosynthetic tissue. Thus grass leaves grow from the base rather than from the tip. You can see this growth pattern in any lawn.

Until time to flower, the grass stem remains short, and the leaves grow upward beyond the tip of the stem. Thus the stem tip is protected from damage as long as possible. Only when it is time to reproduce does the stem elongate between several nodes and the tip stretch skyward. Here the flowers develop where they are exposed to the winds that pollinate them.

Binding the Soil. Grasses bear abundant roots. Most are **adventitious roots,** which arise not from the primary root formed by the embryo but from the lower nodes of the stem (Fig. 19.10) The sod-forming perennial grasses have extensive stems lying just on top of the soil or in the upper soil layer; these serve both to hold the soil and to spread the plant. From **rhizomes** (underground stems) arise adventitious roots and occasional branches that penetrate to the surface, giving rise to what appear to be new plants.

Rhizomes and fibrous roots constitute over half the mass of a grass plant. Together they form a network penetrating throughout the soil and binding it into a nearly inseparable plant-soil complex known as **sod.** Neither wind nor water can erode a healthy sod. Growing roots and rhizomes break the soil repeatedly and contribute to the characteristic crumbly texture of grassland soils. Many of the roots of perennials die each year and are replaced by new roots. Decay of roots supplies humus□ and creates spaces that aerate the soil. Decay- 429
ing roots return minerals to the soil, where they are immediately reclaimed by other roots. This process is one of the reasons why grasslands have a rich and efficient nutrient cycle.

Dead stems and leaves provide an extensive ground cover in most grasslands. Unmowed grasses accumulate as much as 10,000 kg of humus per hectare (about 9000 lb/acre) each year. It takes three or four years for litter components to decompose. Hence the litter forms a deep layer that covers the ground and lessens evaporation due to wind. The litter also holds rainwater and aids its penetration

(a)

(b)

(c)

(d)

(e)

◀ FIGURE 19.11 **Grasslands.** In addition to grasses (a), prairies support many plants with showy flowers. The land is usually rolling, often with scattered trees. Although bison (b) prefer grasses, pronghorns (c) favor broad-leaved vegetation such as develops around prairie dog colonies (d). Efforts to eradicate prairie dogs have endangered their major predator, the black-footed ferret (e).

into the soil. Because the water soaks in, there is no surface runoff and therefore little erosion. Except in the most moist grasslands, the rainwater seldom soaks deep enough to join the groundwater. Instead the extensive root system picks up most rainfall while it lies in the upper layer of the soil. Then the xylem carries the water immediately to the leaves, where it is transpired back into the atmosphere. Because little water percolates down far into grassland soils, minerals are not leached
429 away;□ instead, they remain near the roots. Retention of minerals contributes to the richness of grassland soils. This and the crumbly texture produced by the roots make grassland soils excellent for agriculture.

Grassland Communities

The factors that limit forests and permit grasslands to develop are hard to determine. Some biologists maintain that grasslands develop only where there is insufficient rainfall to support trees that could shade out the grasses. On the other hand, there is both historical and experimental evidence that many grassland edges, such as those between the American prairies and the eastern deciduous forest, were maintained by fire. Where forests and grasslands meet, burning usually favors grasses over trees.

Contrary to popular belief, the American prairies were never a uniform sea of grass ranging from the deciduous forests of the East westward to the Rocky Mountains. Mixed in with the grasses there were other herbs, especially members of the aster family, and legumes, such as the lupines. Nitrogen
430 fixation□ by symbiotic bacteria in the nodules of the legume roots contributes to the fertility of the soil and the vigor of the community. The roots of various species extended to different levels and were best developed in specific regions of the soil. Concentration of roots of one species at a particular level reduces competition between species.

The grassland landscape is even more varied along the moist borders of streams, rivers, marshes, lakes, and ponds. Where inland waterways pass through grasslands, groves of trees and shrubs thrive, along with other organisms ordinarily associated with woodland communities.

Grassland Animals. A large and diverse animal community lives in every grassland. The deep soil that covers rocks and the absence of woody vegetation limit aboveground shelter. Thus most small animals depend on the soil for protection. Numerous little mammals burrow beneath the sod.

Prairie dogs (Fig. 19.11b), rodents related to squirrels, are symbolic of the short grasslands or Great Plains of North America. Ranchers exterminated most of the prairie dogs, believing that these animals competed with livestock for forage. Undoubtedly the selective grazing of prairie dogs on grasses favored the growth of other plants. Pronghorn antelopes, which were once almost as numerous as bison and are now few in numbers, relied heavily on the broad-leaved vegetation of prairie-dog "towns." Elimination of prairie dogs also resulted in near extinction of one of its predators, the black-footed ferret (Fig. 19.11d). Because vast numbers of prairie dogs are necessary to support even a tiny breeding population of ferrets, this species is now extremely rare.

The burrows of prairie dogs, gophers, pocket mice, kangaroo rats, and ground squirrels provide shelter for other animals, including grasshopper mice and snakes. At least one species of bird, the burrowing owl, relies on old rodent burrows for nesting sites. So do cottontail rabbits. Beetles and camel crickets also use burrows; the dung, fungi, and hoarded vegetation afford these insects a ready food supply. Ants are abundant in grassland soils; some species build huge mounds surrounded by a zone stripped clean of all visible life except for the ants themselves. Animals that dig underground benefit the grasses, because they aerate the soil and mix in dung and humus from the surface.

A number of medium-sized animals that live in the surface vegetation face danger from predators. Rapid movement through thick grasses is very difficult, and vision is limited; consequently, it is easy for predators to stalk their prey. Escape must be fast and sure; otherwise it comes too late. Consider how grasshoppers, jackrabbits, and jumping mice meet this challenge. Huge aerial leaps permit such animals to clear the top of the vegetation, get an unimpeded view for a moment, and then drop some distance away without leaving a trail.

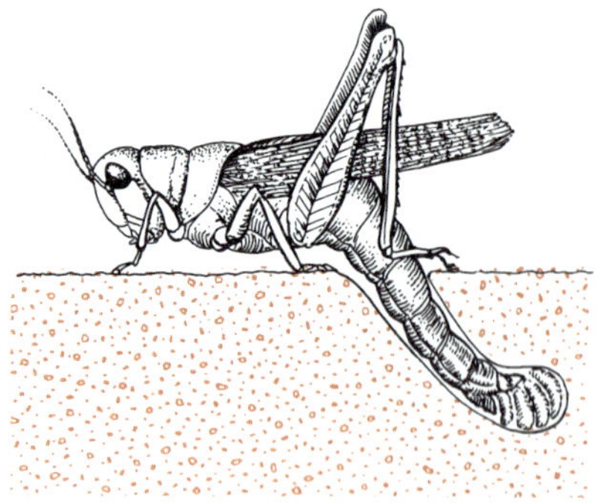

FIGURE 19.12 **A Female Grasshopper Buries Her Eggs.** Adult grasshoppers perish during the winter, but the species continues because the embryos of the next generation lie protected in the soil.

No Hiding Place. In wide-open habitats large animals find little or no shelter. Under these circumstances "predator control" becomes a group activity, and the animals aggregate together. The pronghorns, bison, and musk-oxen of North America, the kangaroos of Australia, the saga antelopes, wild horses, and asses of the steppes of Russia, the gnu and zebra and even the ostriches of Africa show herd instincts. In a group there are many eyes to watch for predators, and alarm spreads rapidly. Mixed herds, such as are common in Africa, cooperate in watching for danger. Ostriches are taller than most mammals they herd with and are usually the first to sound alarm.

Large grassland animals are exceedingly fleet; they have long legs that cover the ground quickly. The fastest runners in the world inhabit grasslands. The American pronghorn, our swiftest native animal, can do 60 miles an hour. At this rate the pronghorns leave a solitary predator or a pack of wolves so far behind that no wolf strategy or cunning can lead to another encounter until the pronghorns have had time to feed and recuperate from the original confrontation. Of course, natural selection has also promoted evolution of fast-running grassland predators. In Africa, the cheetah has been clocked at 65 miles an hour. It is known to accelerate from a stand-still to 45 miles an hour in a few seconds.

Grassland herbivores rely on the group not only for detection of predators but also for defense. When threatened, bison form protective head-outward circles. The young are secure in the center of the circle. Herding is a defensive measure in another sense. Predators are confused by large numbers of running animals. Thus if the individual under pursuit loses itself within the herd, the predator stops in confusion. For this reason, most predators kill only aged, diseased, deformed, and very young

FIGURE 19.13 **Native Grazers May Cooperate, Not Compete.** Movement of herds on the East African plains follows a pattern that promotes efficient use of the vegetation. When the grass is tall and beginning to head out, zebras (a) move in and crop the young heads. This stimulates further growth. With the coarse heads gone, the lower leaves are accessible to wildebeest herds (b) that follow the zebras. When the wildebeests have mowed back the grass, it is easy for gazelles (c) to reach the lower, broad-leaved plants.

animals that are unable to keep up with the herd. These same animals are especially vulnerable, because they are also weak.

Grazing and Overgrazing

Each grassland is a balanced ecosystem of producers and consumers. The native herbivores have evolved with the plants and are adapted to the vegetation and to one another (Fig. 19.13). However, natural grasslands are highly vulnerable to some of the animals that humans have introduced. Native grasses are not adapted to the grazing patterns of these non-native species. For example, sheep can graze more closely to the soil than can the native North American herbivores. North American grasses are vulnerable to the extensive loss of stems and leaves taken by sheep.

Overgrazing by these introduced animals is also common. The natural events that limit populations of wild grazers are carefully modified when humans manage herds. People do their best to protect their animals from severe weather and predators. When they select animals for slaughter, humans tend to choose young adults, particularly excess males and animals too old to breed. Females of good breeding age, especially pregnant females, are seldom killed. People exploit their understanding of animal reproduction to maximize the size of their herds.

Damage from Overgrazing. Repeated close cropping of grass blades reduces the photosynthetic potential of the plant and hence the energy that can be stored in the roots to support the following season's growth. In response to grazing, most grasses undertake a compensatory growth. Under excessive grazing some grasses continue to make new growth until their underground stores are exhausted.

Heavy grazing prevents the stems from growing out, blooming, and setting seed. Sometimes the supply of new plants is cut off completely. Close cropping of leaves and stems also inhibits normal growth of roots that must occur to replace old, dying roots. If all the leaves are gone, the grass **crown** (base of the stem) lies exposed to physical damage from freezing or trampling.

Reduced vegetation and surface litter increase evaporation and reduce water absorption. Much of the rain simply runs off along the surface, eroding the soil. Continuous trampling compacts barren soil and thereby destroys spaces between the particles. This reduces the soil's ability to hold air and water.

Range Management. Except for the constant pressure for short-term economic gains, range management is quite simple. Grasslands must be permitted to set seed. The manager can achieve this goal by dividing the land into plots and rotating the grazing so that every few seasons each plot remains ungrazed until after the seed has ripened and dispersed. If overgrazing on the other plots is to be prevented, more land must be available for a herd of a given size, or the total number of animals must be reduced. Another problem arises from the fact that grazing animals never use available forage uniformly. They always prefer some areas, especially those near water holes. Sometimes judicious placement of salt blocks can balance the distribution of grazing.

Drought, Dust, and Deserts

The moderately dry climate of grasslands carries the constant risk that fluctuation in rainfall will create drought. Twenty-three separate droughts have been recorded in the Russian steppes alone during the past century and a half. But the grassland community survives, because the plants are adapted to the ravages of drought. Overgrazing reduces the resistance of grasses to drought, and plowing the sod can lead to erosion that will nearly destroy the entire ecosystem.

The Dust Bowl. The late 1920s and early 1930s were marked with increased rainfall that permitted tall grasses to flourish on the American prairie. The seven-year drought that struck in 1933 drastically altered the species composition of the unplowed prairies, most of which had been subjected to heavy grazing. Dry-adapted grasses quickly replaced those requiring more moisture. The big bluestem grass that could grow nearly eight feet high almost disappeared; only a deep root system and underground food reserves permitted some plants to survive.

Even more drastic changes occurred in the normally drier Great Plains to the west. Grazed areas were badly damaged, but ranchers were reluctant to reduce their herds. One study in western Kansas showed less than half of the ground covered with vegetation in 1935 and only five percent in 1936. Great dust storms were both the cause and the

(a)

(b)

FIGURE 19.14 **Dust-Bowl Disasters.** During the 1930s, Midwestern fields became clouds of dust (a) and settled hundreds of miles away as a suffocating power (b) that destroyed crops.

result of the decreased vegetation. High temperatures and low rainfall prevented crop growth on plowed fields. Dry winds raised clouds of dust from these fields and from the poorly covered grasslands; when the dust fell from the air, it drifted like a horrible dark snow (Fig. 19.14). A deposit of only an inch was often sufficient to smother short grasses and produce another field of unstable soil.

Stressful as the great drought was, no species is known to have been completely eradicated. All survived in favorable habitats or as ungerminated seeds. But the rains that followed the drought fell on loose, naked soil that eroded into steep gullies. Even with sufficient water the crops grew poorly, because so much of the fertile topsoil was gone. We had lost in a decade much of the legacy of thousands of years of growth by native grasses.

Turning Grasslands into Deserts. Decades and even centuries of overgrazing have left their stamp on much of the American West. The latter part of the nineteenth century brought a tremendous increase in sheep and cattle raising. Thousands of these animals starved, and disastrous economic losses resulted, when drought struck during the 1890s. In many regions, weedy desert vegetation has replaced the natural grasses. Sagebrush now dominates places where cool, short grasslands once thrived. In warmer areas the creosote bush, cacti, and mesquite have replaced other grasses. Except on the highest peaks of the Sierra Nevada and the Rockies, the vegetation has been permanently altered. It is important to recognize that these "new" deserts are distressed ecosystems and lack the diversity and complexity of "true" deserts.

American ranchers have no monopoly on the conversion of grasslands to deserts. It has long been said that the Sahara Desert marches farther south each year. During the early 1970s drought coupled with high human and cattle populations led to loss of herds and massive starvation among the people of the sub-Saharan or Sahel grasslands. Some climatologists trace this disaster to major weather trends, but overgrazing has exaggerated the effects of drought.

DESERTS

The story of the desert has one theme—water. The distribution of water in time and space determines the nature of fragile desert ecosystems. An average rainfall of less than 25 cm (10 in.) a year will produce a desert; but each desert is unique, just as is each forest and grassland. Relative humidity, temperature extremes, the underlying rock and drainage—all contribute to the uniqueness of each desert.

Deserts are almost never totally dry; there is nearly always some water. Although dew can be of considerable importance in the water budget of certain organisms, most desert life relies largely on sporadic rainfall. Particles of desert soil hold surface layers of water, as do other soils. Any excess water flows downward to collect over impenetrable layers of rock. Groundwater lying near the surface produces springs and oases. Substantial layers of groundwater underlie many deserts; some are believed to represent the accumulations of thousands or even millions of years. Perhaps this "fossil water" can be traced to rainfall during periods when these lands that are now deserts had more humid climates. Or groundwater from regions with higher rainfall (such as adjacent mountains) may feed into the rock layers under deserts. In any case, water can be drawn from desert wells faster than it is replaced.

Only rarely does vegetation carpet the desert. Consequently, rains create flash floods that dig deep gullies and carve rugged landforms in the desert, as you saw in Fig. 2.4. Some desert soils developed where we find them; the wind has carried others hundreds of miles from their origin. Desert soils are surprisingly fertile; many support substantial vegetation after a good rain or when irrigated.

Desert Plants: Many Solutions to One Problem

Plants have evolved seemingly endless adaptations to desert conditions. Individuals divide the water supply so efficiently that they tap almost every drop. Most desert plants exhibit special modifications to gather and conserve water, but many merely become dormant during dry periods.

For example, lichen on desert rocks is active only intermittently. When dehydrated by hot desert days, these lichens suspend most life functions and for a time tolerate extremely high temperatures (to 80°C or 176°F). But after being dampened by night dews, these same plants revive and resume photosynthesis at dawn.

When the Rains Come. Although no higher plants withstand the severe dryness that lichens undergo, many live through drought as seeds, bulbs, or other low-moisture structures. Such plants usually have shallow roots that grow laterally through the top soil for considerable distance. This wide distribution of roots permits them to absorb substantial amounts of water from a light shower.

In the moister deserts, seeds of annuals germinate every year, and the plants bloom predictably, usually within a few weeks in early spring. But in many deserts, bloom is irregular. Certain species appear only at intervals of 10 or 20 years. They survive because their seeds remain alive but inactive in the soil. Seeds of some desert plants germinate any time there is sufficient moisture, but others rely on one or more additional cues, such as light and temperature.

Every Drop Counts. Root systems of perennial desert plants vary markedly. Some plants, especially those on hills far above groundwater, rely on extensive near-surface roots. Plants that grow near dry stream beds produce long taproots that reach far into the soil. Plants of stony deserts may send out a single root under each nearby rock; this allows them to absorb water that condenses during the cool desert nights.

The creosote bush, sagebrush, and a number of other desert shrubs secrete toxins that inhibit growth of other species. With no nearby neighbors there is less competition for moisture.

Many **succulent** (fleshy) desert plants, such as sedums and aloes of Africa and agaves of North America, store water in thick, permanent leaves. But whether the water-storage tissue is a modified leaf or a stem, as in cacti, it is usually green with photosynthetic pigments. In bright, unshaded deserts, sunlight penetrates to the deepest cells. Packing the photosynthetic tissue in stems or thick leaves permits sufficient photosynthesis and reduces the surface area from which water can evaporate.

Few desert perennials have large leaves. Some, like the gray sagebrush, grow bigger leaves in the moist season and progressively smaller ones with the coming of dry weather. The last leaves formed are mere scales. Other species, such as the crown of thorns of Africa, the ocotillo of the U. S. Southwest, and the boojum tree of Mexico (Fig. 19.15a), send out ordinary leaves during the moist season but drop them completely as soon as water is in short supply.

Special mechanisms doubtless regulate stomata in many desert plants. For example, cacti open their stomata only at night; during this time they absorb carbon dioxide and store it for use the following day. This is the reverse of the common pattern; plants of moist environments open their stomata during the day and close them at night.

Much dry-adapted vegetation bears spines or hairs. The adaptive value of these structures has been the subject of speculation. Obviously spines deter some animals from feeding on the water-rich tissues. Spines also shade and insulate the plant (Fig. 19.15b). When hairs are dense, they interfere with air movements near the surface. This reduces evaporation and holds an insulating layer of air that can slow the transfer of heat to the plant as the environment warms. Perhaps these spines and hairs also provide a surface on which water vapor condenses into dew.

Animal Adaptations to the Desert: A Tale of Water Conservation

Desert animals obtain their limited water rations from dew, occasionally from drinking water, but very largely from the water released during cellular respiration. In fact, this may provide the entire water supply of kangaroo rats. (You will recall that the respiration of glucose yields both carbon dioxide
and water.) Birds that eat insects may also obtain 96
sufficient water from their food. But those with a diet of dry seeds fly many miles daily to reach

(a)

(b)

(c)

FIGURE 19.15 **Deserts.** Many desert plants such as cacti and boojum trees (a) store water in fleshy stems. Among the functions of spines on desert plants is the provision of shade (b). Much of desert soil is barren of vegetation (c).

drinking water. Mammals, too, search for water. Some, such as the ibex and gazelle, will dig deep into the bottom of dry springs or temporary stream beds to reach groundwater.

Whatever their water source, desert animals have evolved strategies to conserve water. Many, including some reptiles and a multitude of small rodents, are nocturnal. They spend their days in cool underground burrows, where they waste little
192 water in evaporative cooling. Although desert birds are active during the day, they seek shelter in the shade of rocks, cliffs, or plants.

Camels, donkeys, sheep, and goats grow thick woolly coats that provide insulation from the desert sun. Both donkeys and sheep keep their body temperatures in check through evaporation associated with panting. Consequently, they must tolerate tremendous dehydration, because they use so much water in evaporative cooling. In fact, a well-dried-out donkey can guzzle a quarter of its body weight in water within only a few minutes. Instead of expending water through panting, goats and camels tolerate a rise of several degrees in their body temperatures. They accumulate heat during the day and dissipate the stored heat during the cool desert night.

Most desert rodents excrete as little water as possible with their wastes. Perhaps you have noticed the milky urine of a pet hamster. These natives of the Syrian deserts reabsorb so much water from their kidney tubules that the minerals precipitate and give hamster urine a milky appearance.

WARM-CLIMATE VEGETATION

Variations in terrestrial environments seem endless. Grasslands naturally merge into deserts, and a little abuse will make a desert out of a dry grassland. Similarly deserts grade into forests. Indeed, dry-adapted trees such as pistachios and acacias characterize certain deserts. Just as small differences in rainfall determine whether a region supports grasses or desert shrubs, patterns of temperature variation also affect which plants thrive. And with temperature as with rainfall, it is not only the average that affects organisms but also the fluctuations. In the United States, one has only to compare the maritime forests of the Southeast with the chaparral of the Southwest.

The **maritime forests** consist mainly of broad-leaved evergreen trees, especially live oaks. High rainfall permits the growth of trees that bear large leaves. The absence of severe frosts favors retention of leaves. In this humid environment smaller plants grow attached to the tree limbs. This **epiphytic** (upon-plant) life-style is common wherever plants are able to obtain sufficient water directly from the atmosphere. Thus epiphytes are found both in rain forests, such as the temperate ones on the Pacific coast of North America (Fig. 19.8a), and in cloud forests, where considerable moisture comes in the form of fog. Spanish moss (really a seed plant belonging to the bromeliad or pineapple family) is the major epiphyte of the maritime forest (Fig. 19.16). Epiphytes are not parasites, for they do not take

(a)

FIGURE 19.16 **Maritime Forest.** The live oaks (a) support epiphytic Spanish moss (b) that absorbs moisture from the humid air. Egrets nest in the dense vegetation where their young (c) find protection.

(b)

(c)

from their hosts. Epiphytes obtain water from rain, fog, or, in some cases, humid air. Dust, decaying leaves, and insects supply minerals to epiphytes.

Coastal areas of central and southern California have temperature patterns similar to those of the Georgia and Florida maritime forests. It's the moisture pattern that accounts for the differences. Unlike the humid East, this California region is dry during the hot months, while winter brings 50 cm (20 inches) of rain. In this Mediterranean-type climate, chamise, manzanita, and other shrubs bear leathery leaves 12 months a year. This plant community is identified as **chaparral.** Chaparral plants avoid severe dehydration during the dry season largely by closing their stomata. Extensive root systems penetrate as far as 8 meters (25 feet) into the soil, but the plants always suffer water shortages in summer.

The chaparral is a fire-climax community. Periodic summer fires sweep the chaparral, destroying all aboveground vegetation. After a fire, new sprouts rise from surviving roots and heat-activated seeds germinate. Fire converts most of the ecosystem's minerals to ashes. Of course, the winter rains tend to leach minerals out of the ashes and erode the barren soil. Chaparral plants compensate for mineral loss through nitrogen-fixing symbionants and mycorrhizal associates that gather minerals.

Farther south, in semitropical and tropical regions, rainfall is the major factor that determines vegetation growth forms. On dry parts of the Caribbean Islands, **thorn-shrub** communities thrive (Fig. 19.17a), while moss-laden trees grow in fog-forests on nearby mountains (Fig. 19.17b). On the mainland, **tropical deciduous forests** grow where dry

(a)

FIGURE 19.17 **Tropical Vegetation.** Compare the dry coastal vegetation (a) with the mossy elfin woodland (b). Differences in elevation and prevailing winds allow such different communities to exist as little as a hundred miles apart. Seasonal differences in rainfall account for leaf loss in this Costa Rican deciduous forest (c).

(b)

(c)

FIGURE 19.18 **Logging in a Tropical Rain Forest.**

and wet seasons alternate. During the dry season, tropical trees—like their temperate counterparts—drop their leaves until the rains come (Fig. 19.17c).

The wettest regions support epiphyte-laden **rain forests.** Here many of the trees are giants (Fig. 19.18), but there is a wide range of species with varied heights and growth forms. The canopy is multilayered (Fig. 19.19) partly because of the diverse species and partly because certain trees branch only near the top. Some trees have flattened plank-buttress roots that begin above ground and extend laterally. This shallow pattern of root growth may be related to the low mineral content of the soil. Litter decomposition in these hot, humid forests occurs rapidly. Minerals are either picked up immediately through surface roots aided by mycorrhizae, or they are leached away in rainwater.

FIGURE 19.19 **Multi-Storied Canopy of Tropical Rain Forests.**

Abundant rainfall favors epiphytes. Bromeliads, orchids, ferns, and mosses adorn every horizontal surface of rain-forest trees and some even attach on the vertical trunks. Some orchids soak up rainwater into the spongy outer layers of their roots. Bromeliads catch rain in cup-like leaf bases forming tiny pools that harbor numerous insects and even small frogs. Most rain-forest trees have simple oval leaves with a pointed **drip-tip** (Fig. 19.20). Water rains most rapidly off leaves of this shape and as a result, tiny epiphytes are less likely to coat the leaves and screen out sunlight.

FIGURE 19.20 **A Drip-Tip Leaf.**

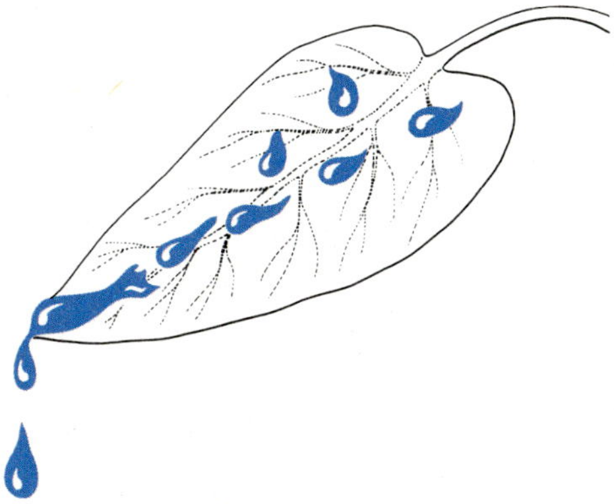

Seedlings of certain plants begin as epiphytes but later send roots to the ground. Some species, such as the **strangler** fig, eventually overgrow and kill the host that originally held it up to the sun-

FIGURE 19.21 **Leaf-Cutter Ants.** Ants carry pieces of leaves (a) to underground nests where the leaves are incorporated into fungal cultures (b). The ants feed the fungi to their young.

light. Giant vines are long enough not only to stretch from the ground to the canopy 100–200 feet above, but also to drape neighboring trees.

Despite the many trees and vines, most tropical forests are open enough for people to walk through easily. Impenetrable "jungles" occur only where there is substantial sunlight on the forest floor. When a large tree falls and opens the canopy, successional plants compete for a place in the sun. Of course, destruction of a forest by fire or logging results in dense successional vegetation. Abundant sunlight accounts for the thick understory vegetation along stream edges.

Just as the tropical forests include the greatest diversity of trees on earth, so they provide habitat for innumerable animals, especially insects. **Termites** are major decomposers throughout the tropics. The activity of bacteria and prozotoa in their intestines enables termites to utilize cellulose as a nutrient source. Altogether they play a major role in the carbon cycle. **Leaf-cutter ants** (Fig. 19.21) are major herbivores in tropical forests of the western hemisphere. They carry leaf pieces along established trails to their nests, where the leaves are used to support fungal growths. It is the fungi that the ants feed to their young.

A good example of plant-animal interdependence exists between certain species of fish and trees in the Amazon forests. The fish, some of them relatives of the fierce piranhas, invade the forest during times of flood and fatten on tree seeds that fall into temporary ponds. Many seeds pass undigested through the fish's intestines, resulting in distribution of the tree seeds.

The extreme diversity of tropical forests might suggest that these are old and stable ecosystems. Fossil pollen records, however, reveal that tropical forests have undergone continual change. This is consistent with the observation that the forest is easily damaged and slow to recover. A popular hypothesis holds that forest diversity results from speciation on "islands" of forest separated by arid regions during the Ice Ages. Whether or not this is true remains to be seen. Detailed studies of tropical forests are just getting under way; the forests may disappear before either their nature or their importance is thoroughly understood. Logging operations are in full swing in tropical forests. Because the world's demand for lumber has outstripped the production of temperate forests, many logging firms have transferred part of their activities to the tropics.

Where the Land Meets the Water

Throughout the continents, rivers and streams dissect the land and water accumulates in ponds and lakes. Ocean waves lap continuously at the continental edges. Few places on land are far from the ecotones where earth and water meet (Fig. 19.22). World nutrient cycles weave terrestrial and aquatic ecosystems into a single giant net. Energy flows from land to water by conduction, by the movement of organisms, and through numerous other methods. Just as terrestrial biomes are definitions of convenience, so is any division of the biosphere into aquatic and terrestrial ecosystems. As you move on to read about aquatic environments, remember that the world supports a single ecosystem—the biosphere.

FIGURE 19.22 **Land-Water Ecotones Can Be Stressful or Rich.** Tidal variations and storms are responsible for distinct beach zones (a). Plants vary in their tolerance of salt but few are able to live in spots where exposure to waves is frequent. Some grasses thrive in the wide, shallow river that defines the Florida Everglades (b). Although the grasses withstand drought that dries up the Everglades, many animals survive only in deep water holes. Most marshes are fairly stable and rich in nutrients from sediment and debris that washes in from the land. Wild rice is so abundant in some freshwater marshes (c) that it can be harvested commercially. In warm climates mangroves grow along waterways and their prop-like roots catch and hold sediments, gradually increasing the land (d).

(a)

(b)

(c)

(d)

Summary

1. Trees of temperate deciduous forests are adapted to moderate rainfall and to frost. As an adaptation to dehydration and protection against tissue damage in cold weather, these trees concentrate organic molecules from the leaves into permanent tissues and then shed the leaves. Color change in the leaves is due to loss of chlorophyll, which reveals other pigments.

2. Beneath the canopy of the temperate deciduous forests is an understory of shrubs and herbs. The decomposer food chain, which includes microarthropods, releases nutrients from the litter. These minerals reenter roots almost immediately; thus the soil is low in minerals, even though the biome is productive.

3. Whenever the vegetation of an area is destroyed and the area is then left undisturbed, a series of new vegetations will appear. Each replaces the former in a predictable sequence until a stable climax vegetation develops. This pattern of secondary succession is determined by climate, by physical characteristics of the environment, and by the properties of the species for which there are seed sources in the area. The virgin forests Europeans found in the Americas were climax vegetations. At present, most of the deciduous forest biome supports some stage of succession.

4. Most of western Europe was once covered with a deciduous forest, but that forest and others in centers of civilization were destroyed long ago. Grazing of deforested British land has led to establishment of grasslands and moors. In both Britain and America, silt from erosion of deforested areas has altered the waterways.

5. Waxy, rigid needle-like leaves permit conifers to withstand the dehydration of severely cold and windy weather. This capability and the year-round presence of needles that permits maximal opportunity for photosynthesis help explain the dominance of conifers in boreal forests. Tolerance to dehydration also favors other conifers, such as pines, that thrive in the hot summers and frequently dry sandy soils of the southeastern United States. Coniferous forest soils are poor, because the needles decompose slowly and release acids that leach away minerals. Under these conditions, mycorrhizae that aid mineral accumulation are valuable symbionts with the tree roots. Ever-present dense shade prevents development of an understory vegetation in coniferous forests. Presence of large numbers of trees of one species favors explosions of pest populations. Southern pine forests may exist because they are fire-tolerant.

6. Grasses are adapted to less rainfall than are forests; likewise they are adapted to the moderate grazing of native herbivores with which they have evolved. The sod of a healthy grassland is resistant to erosion. However, overgrazing weakens the plants and prevents reseeding. Combined with periodic drought, overgrazing results in replacement of grasslands with deserts.

7. Grassland soils are especially desirable for agriculture. The extensive root system of grasses captures all rainwater and prevents leaching. Growth of roots and underground stems produces a loose soil that holds water. Humus from decay of roots and other plant parts, coupled with mineral retention, makes these soils unusually rich.

8. Many small grassland animals move by leaping. Most find shelter in the soil. Larger herbivores must run from predators, and they have evolved herd behavior.

9. All desert organisms are adapted to a limited water budget. Because there is little vegetation to hold the soil, the occasional desert rains erode the landscape.

10. In warm climates, distribution of rainfall determines the variety of vegetation. Maritime forests of broad-leaved evergreens occur along the humid southeastern coast of the United States. The dry summers and rainy winters of California favor chaparral growth. Chaparral is a fire-climax community.

11. Vegetation in hot regions near the equator ranges from desert, to thorn-shrub, to tropical deciduous forest, or even to rain forest, depending on the precipitation. Despite the lushness of rain forests and their great diversity of species, vegetation there grows on poor soil and thrives because minerals released from decomposition are immediately picked up by roots. Epiphytes, stranglers, vines, and trees of various heights make up a complex and multilayered canopy; but the forest floor is open except where succession is occurring.

Thought and Controversy

1. Two schools of thought dominate the disagreement over desirable forest-management practices. One advocates selective cutting of mature trees; the other believes in clear-cutting. The U.S. Forest Service and most industry persons argue that clear-cutting is the most practical approach. With clear-cutting, all the timber is removed from a tract and used as fully as possible. Materials not suitable for lumber are scavenged for pulp mills. The land is then replanted with seeds or seedlings of a desirable species, often the dominant species of the forest that was recently removed. The goal is to either shortcut or avoid the normal succession and produce even-aged stands of good timber as quickly as possible.

Many conservationists complain about the ugliness of the fresh cuts left by clear-cutting, about the uniformity of the new forests and the accompanying reduction of ecological niches, about the increased opportunities for disease and pests in the simpler ecosystem, and about the fact that some species of wildlife are tremendously favored while habitat for others is reduced or eliminated. Clear-cutting advocates counter that this practice permits higher production, creates less erosion per board foot of lumber harvested, and leaves no damaged trees behind. They also point to the excellent yield of some game animals during early development of these new forests.

If these facts were true and if they were the only factors involved, the controversy might be considered only a conflict of value systems that could be settled by compromise. Unfortunately, studies of deforested lands suggest that the problem is more complex and more acute than many people realize. On the Hubbard Brook experimental tract in New Hampshire, scientists clear-cut 160,000 square meters (39 acres) of hardwoods by hand with almost no physical disturbance of the soil. They left the timber where it fell and treated the area with herbicides to prevent succession. Water draining from the plot was metered continuously, and the chemical constituents were measured.

In the absence of mechanical disturbance of the soil, no erosion was immediately evident, and the stream flow appeared clear. As was expected, the amount of run-off increased, as did the water temperature. The real surprise was the increased load of chemicals dissolved in the water. During the two years after cutting, the loss of calcium and magnesium quadrupled, potassium loss went up 15 times, and nitrate loss increased 56 times. In fact, nitrates in the stream reached twice the level that the U.S. Public Health Service permits in drinking water. Clearly, destruction of the forest broke the nutrient cycle and permitted the soil minerals to leach away immediately. Successional growth or reforestation would have reduced this loss, but not by much.

2. During the great Sahelian drought and starvation of the early 1970s, Norman H. MacLeod of American University noticed a peculiar pentagon of greenery on a NASA satellite photograph of the Sahel. A visit to the site revealed that it was simply a ranch fenced in with barbed wire and divided into five sections. Throughout the drought, cattle had been permitted to graze only a single sector each year. What relationship does this suggest between land use and drought effects?

3. Why were the prairies and plains the last major part of the United States to be settled, despite the fact that these former grasslands are some of the most productive agricultural lands in the world?

4. After a fire, chaparral soils are subject to heavy erosion. In fact, homes built in chaparral areas may escape destruction by fire only to be washed away in a sea of mud and water. Considering the danger of fire and mud slides, should construction of homes be permitted in the chaparral?

Questions

1. How does freezing affect plants? Explain the adaptations of deciduous trees to climates with severe frost.

2. It is generally thought that angiosperms have displaced conifers from much of their previous habitat. Nevertheless, conifers flourish in northern forests. What adaptations give conifers distinct advantages in this environment?

3. How are the effects of the boreal weather similar to those of the sandy soils in warmer climates? How are the dominant species of these biomes similar?

4. What factors may be responsible for the fire resistance of southern pine forests?

5. Discuss the roles of fungi in forest ecosystems.

6. Tundra is found on high mountains as well as in the Far North. How are these environments similar? In what ways are they different?

7. What is a rain shadow? Give an example.

8. Former grasslands are the "breadbaskets" where most agricultural activity centers. What are some of the reasons behind this fact?

9. How are grasses adapted to withstand grazing?

10. Discuss adaptations of animals to grassland habitats.

11. What are the problems in grassland (range) management? Explain.

12. How do desert animals manage in such dry environments? Discuss both their water sources and their water-conservation strategies.

13. What are the major adaptations of plants to desert environments?

14. Discuss the growth forms of major plant groups found in tropical rain forests.

15. Which of the biomes described in this chapter is most diverse? Least diverse? What factors may be responsible?

20

Aquatic Ecosystems: Waters of the World

ABOUT THREE-QUARTERS OF THE EARTH IS COVered by oceans, lakes, ponds, rivers, or streams. Not only is water all around us, but it is underground, too. When rain falls or ice and snow melt, part of the water runs off into streams, but much of it seeps into the soil. As it does, particles absorb and hold some water near the surface. Usually it is the **soil water** that plants use. Some of the water trickles down through subsoil until it is eventually stopped by an impenetrable barrier of rocks. Unable to drain further, **groundwater** accumulates atop the impervious rock.

The upper surface of groundwater is the **water table** (Fig. 20.1), which more or less parallels the surface of the land. Water fills every pore and crevice between the water table and the underlying

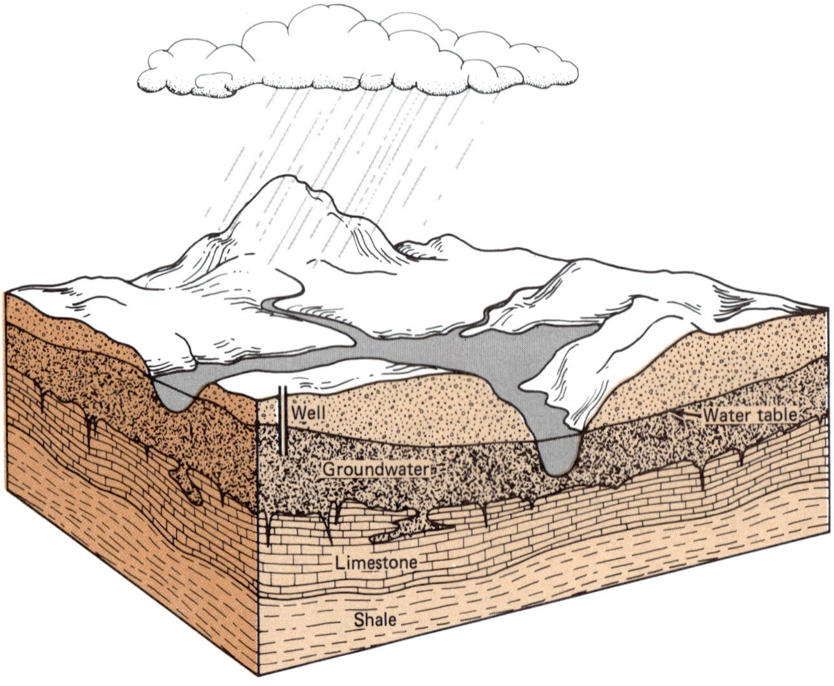

FIGURE 20.1 **Relationship of Surface Water to Subsurface Water.** Groundwater contributes to surface waters, such as the lake shown here, whenever the water table intersects the surface. Wells are dug by drilling down to the water table.

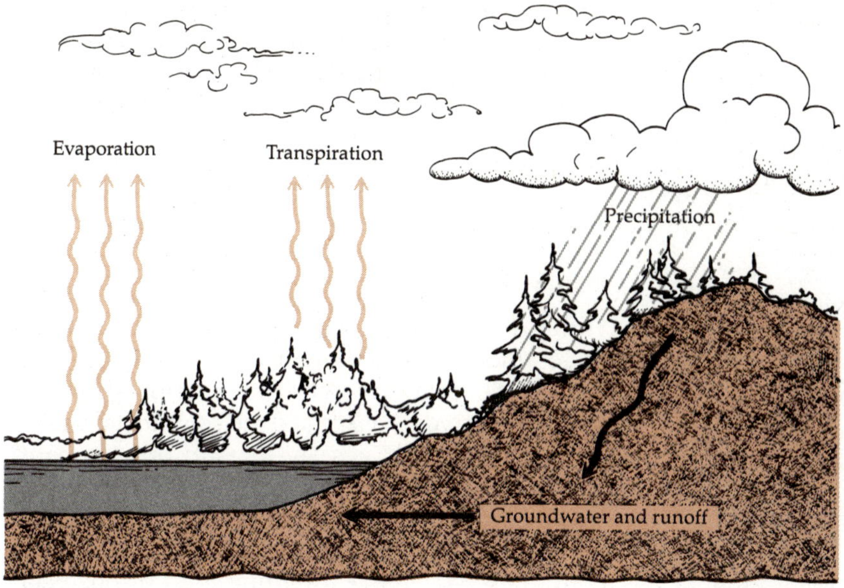

FIGURE 20.2 **The Water Cycle.**

rock. Swamps, springs, and other bodies of water develop wherever the water table is high enough to intersect the surface.

Groundwater, rainwater, and runoff water all participate in the **water cycle** (Fig. 20.2) driven by the sun. Solar energy evaporates tremendous amounts of water every day. This evaporation draws water from the soil, from plant leaves through
411 transpiration,□ and from each body of water, large or small. Drawn into the atmosphere in this way, the water falls again to earth as rain or snow. Thus there is continuous recycling of moisture between earth and atmosphere and back again.

Falling rain and snow are powerful erosive forces. Most landscapes, even those of arid countries, are carved by water action. Water that freezes in tiny crevices splits mighty boulders. Glaciers grind wide, smooth valleys between knife-sharp ridges (Fig. 20.3). Violent streams dig narrow canyons (Fig. 20.4) that in time become flat plains through which

FIGURE 20.3 **A Glacier Carves Its Way through a Mountain Range.**

FIGURE 20.4 The Grand Canyon Gorge of the Colorado River.

a much-tamed waterway meanders to the sea (Fig. 20.5). Without doubt the sun that powers the water cycle and the precipitation that condenses from water vapor are among the mightiest forces on earth. Oceans, lakes, and rivers are only a part of this great system.

THE OCEANS: THE BIGGEST PART OF THE WORLD

Water returning to the oceans from the land carries huge amounts of sediment. The buildup of these sediments, together with erosion of shores by pounding waves, has created the **continental shelves** that border the coasts. A sharp drop, the **continental slope,** marks the edge of the continental shelf and the boundary of the deep oceanic basins. The shelf, the slope, and in many places the ocean bottom are covered with a fine mud or ooze consisting of silt, minerals precipitated from sea water, and the microscopic shells of dead marine animals. Much of the ocean floor is a broad **abyssal plain,** interrupted by deep trenches and underwater mountains (Fig. 2.2). 24

Ocean Habitats

Salts are constantly added to the ocean through river water and rainwater runoff. Depending on

FIGURE 20.5 The Crooked River of Oregon.

drainage, currents, and temperature, the **salinity** (saltiness) of the oceans varies at different locations. The average salinity is about 3.5 percent, or (by weight) about 35 parts of salt to each 1000 parts of water. Most of the salt in seawater is ordinary table salt (sodium chloride), but sulfate, magnesium, calcium, and potassium salts are also abundant. In fact, seawater contains traces of just about every element.

These accumulated salts make seawater much denser than fresh water. This is the reason it is easier to swim or float in the ocean than in a river or a lake. It also means that salt water has a much lower freezing point than fresh water. In addition to salt, seawater also contains dissolved atmospheric gases. But seawater has less oxygen than fresh water, since salt decreases the solubility of oxygen in water.

Ocean Layers and Life. The sun heats and illuminates the ocean, although few of the sun's rays penetrate very far into the water. As a result, water temperature, illumination, and salinity (which is temperature dependent) are related to depth. Of course, all these characteristics influence the kinds of organisms found at a given location, but light is of special importance.

Because photosynthetic plants need light in order to live, they are found only in shallow water and in the surface layer of the open ocean. Almost all photosynthesis occurs in the upper 80 meters (260 feet) designated as the **euphotic** (good-light) zone. This includes most or all of the continental shelf. Here, sunlight and abundant nutrients that wash into the sea from nearby land provide for incredibly diverse communities. Most of the world's fishing grounds are located in the rich, relatively shallow continental-shelf waters.

Underneath the euphotic zone is a region of ever-deepening twilight. No sunlight penetrates below 600 meters (1967 feet). As a result, most of the ocean is in perpetual darkness and can be inhabited only by animals and decomposer bacteria
210 and fungi (Fig. 20.6.)□

Life at the Top. Microscopic floating algae, known collectively as **phytoplankton,** are the main producers in the oceans. **Diatoms** and **dinofla-**
371 **gellates**□ are the most prominent phytoplankton. Their collective biomass far outweighs that of the
385 more obvious seaweeds□ attached to rocks near the coast.

Phytoplankton are never evenly distributed. Not only are they limited to the top layer where there is light, but within that layer their density follows distribution of minerals. Organisms that die in deep water usually drift to the bottom. Similarly, feces settle out, and the valuable nutrients they contain are lost from surface waters. Currents and diffusion only slowly return precious nitrogen and phosphorus from the bottom to the euphotic zone. Shallow water over the continental shelves is usually fairly well mixed and contains more nutrients than does surface water over the open ocean. Here the deep water is quite undisturbed, and minerals are concentrated far below the euphotic zone.

During the winter, because sunlight striking temperate waters is less intense than at other seasons, photosynthesis is limited to the top few meters of water. With the coming of spring the phytoplankton multiply rapidly in response to increasing illumination. Exploding plankton populations are termed **plankton blooms,** because the masses of algae often color the water bright red, brown, or green. Although clearly visible, marine plankton blooms are never as dramatic as those of freshwater lakes. This difference in productivity may result from mineral deficiencies in illuminated marine waters.

Microscopic animals, often referred to as **zooplankton,** feed on phytoplankton. Copepods and krill, tiny relatives of crabs and shrimp, are among the most abundant zooplankton. Others are numbered among the unicellular protozoa and include
foraminifera and radiolarians.□ Typically, zoo- 370
plankton bear numerous projections that increase their surface area and help suspend them in the water. Most zooplankton both swim and float.

For the most part, relatively small fish, such as anchovies, herrings, and sardines, prey on zooplankton. There are exceptions, however. In the cold but fertile water around Antarctica, the penguins, squid, and even baleen whales feed directly on krill. The amount of zooplankton consumed by a large animal can be astounding. A single blue whale can eat three tons of krill a day.

The Briny Deep. Beneath the productive upper layer of the ocean lies as much as six miles of water. Throughout most of this space, life is sparse. Food from the top decomposes quite slowly.

Fish in deep, dark waters are mostly mouth. Good meals are rare here and few items are rejected as being too big. This is the province of the famous

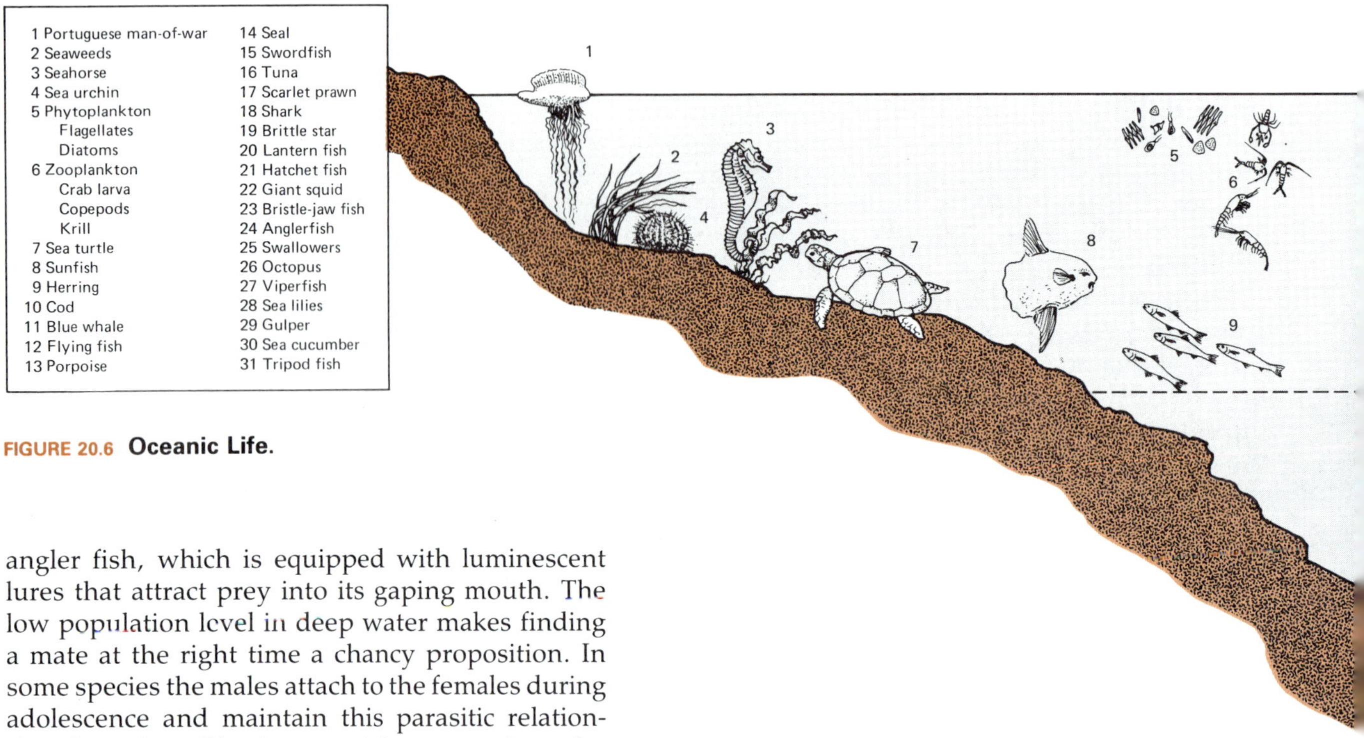

FIGURE 20.6 **Oceanic Life.**

angler fish, which is equipped with luminescent lures that attract prey into its gaping mouth. The low population level in deep water makes finding a mate at the right time a chancy proposition. In some species the males attach to the females during adolescence and maintain this parasitic relationship throughout life. As you might expect, the males of such species are tiny compared with their mates.

Rocks and Sand, Marsh and Muck

In contrast to the relatively uniform conditions of the open sea, a variety of habitats are found where water meets land. Each of these environments is unique, and each is intriguing in its own way. Perhaps rocky shores are the most interesting. Here we find a diverse community attuned to the rhythmically changing environment.

Living between the Tides. In the band that spans high and low tide, the priorities are to stay put, to keep wet, and to avoid being crushed. Waves pound the shores so vigorously that delicate organisms can be destroyed or carried away (Fig. 20.7). Alternately submerged and exposed, **intertidal species** (those that live between lowest low tide and highest high tide) must also withstand cold, heat, and a wide range of salinity. Summer sun can cook tissues, and evaporation of seawater deposits a crust of salt on every surface. Only a few months later,

FIGURE 20.7 **Algae Cover the Rocks of a Tidal Pool.**

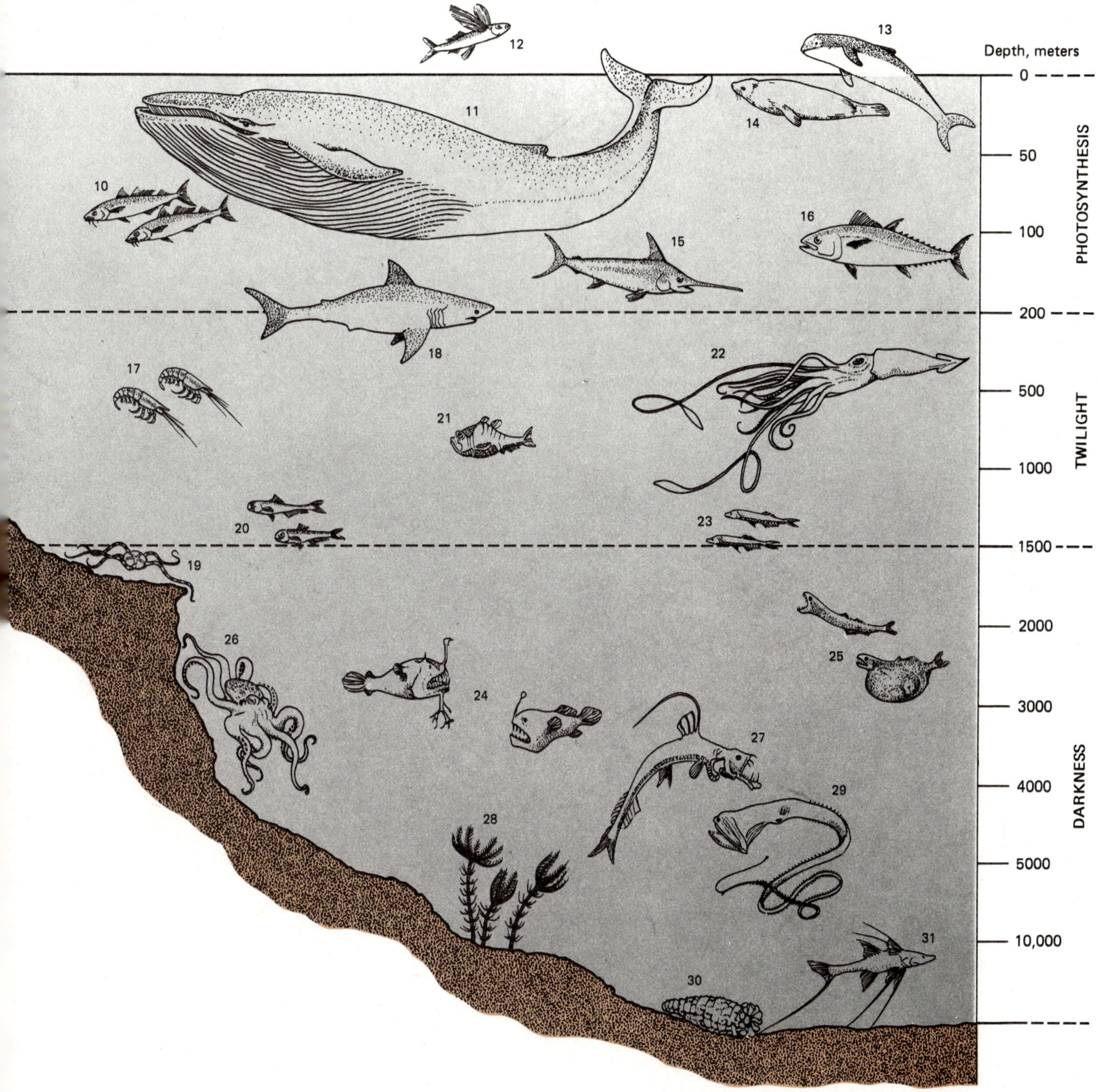

winter tides pull the protective layer of water away and leave organisms exposed to freezing cold or to torrents of fresh water. As adaptations to this extreme environment, intertidal organisms either cling tenaciously or dart about to find shelter. Their bodies are protected by shells, tough body walls, leathery surfaces, or mucus.

Since tidal exposure varies every day, there are distinct life zones along the shore (Fig. 20.8). The following description applies to the central California coast, but similar life zones exist on rocky shores from Mexico to Alaska and along the coast of Maine and the Maritime Provinces, as well as on other continents.

A dark band of cyanobacteria (blue-green algae) marks the highest zone where there is much marine life. Here numerous **periwinkles** scavenge. A distinct band of white **barnacles**□ grows below 378

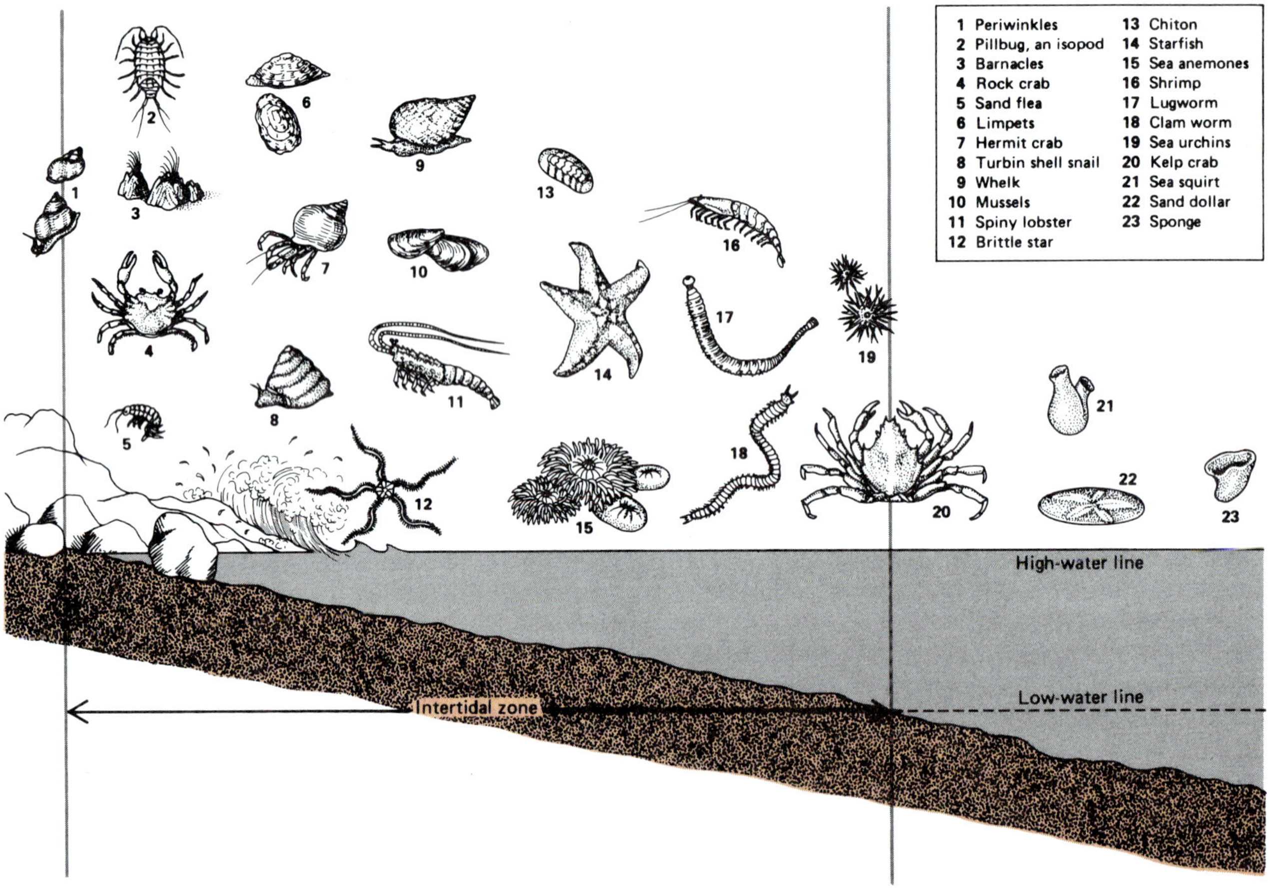

FIGURE 20.8 **Intertidal Animals.**

the black zone (Fig. 20.9). Barnacles lie on their backs, stuck to the rocks. When the tide goes out, barnacles close their limy shells to conserve water. When they are submerged, they open their shell plates and feed, using delicate, jointed appendages to kick food into their mouths.

Limpets are abundantly distributed among the barnacles. These marine snails use a tremendous suction foot to pull their shells tightly against the rock. This traps water under the shells and prevents dehydration at low tide.

A crowded strip of **mussels** stands just below the mean sea-level mark that coincides with the bottom of the barnacle region. The clam-like mussels spin proteinaceous fibers that attach their blue-black shells to the rocks.

Here too, we begin to find bushy **rockweeds,**
384 some green, but mostly brown algae,□ growing profusely. The gelatinous cell walls of these seaweeds protect them from dehydration and give them a slimy feel and appearance. Below this point, large brown algae known as **kelps** become more and more evident. Extensive, jungle-like kelp beds can be found in many shallow offshore waters. Some kelps reach a length of 100 yards and have gas-filled floats to buoy them in the water.

Tidal pools that provide a habitat for multicellular algae may also harbor rock crabs, hermit crabs, and large green sea anemones. Farther out, on the underside of large rocks and steep ledges hide sponges, sea cucumbers, sea squirts, chitons, and abalone. Shrimp and spiny lobsters lurk in the lowest tidal pools. No one has made a complete census of animals in the intertidal zone, but biologists familiar with the California coast estimate that there may be 3000 species there.

Without rocks to provide secure anchors, seaweeds and attached animals are generally absent from sandy seashores. But though the showy life of rocky shores is missing from **sandy beaches,**

FIGURE 20.9 Zonation along the Oregon Coast. A distinct ribbon of barnacles grows under the darker band of cyanobacteria.

organisms are present. It's just that most of them are hidden from view. Larger plants cannot attach to shifting sand, but diatoms that live between sand grains are plentiful. Burrowing, digging, and tunneling creatures, among them clams, mole crabs, tube worms, and olive shells, bury themselves in the sand (Fig. 20.10). Some animals survive (or hide) on surf-swept shores by digging into sand or mud deposits. A clam may sit half in and half out of its burrow so that it can feed by drawing water into its body through openings called siphons. Tube worms□ live inside elaborate structures that they secrete. Movements of the worm pull a constant stream of water and food particles into the tube. Some tube worms have long tentacles that wave above the surface. Other burrowing worms eat their way through the sand or mud and digest any organic material they consume along the way, much as earthworms do. Low tides expose some species periodically; others are permanently protected 379

FIGURE 20.10 Stick-in-the-Muds.

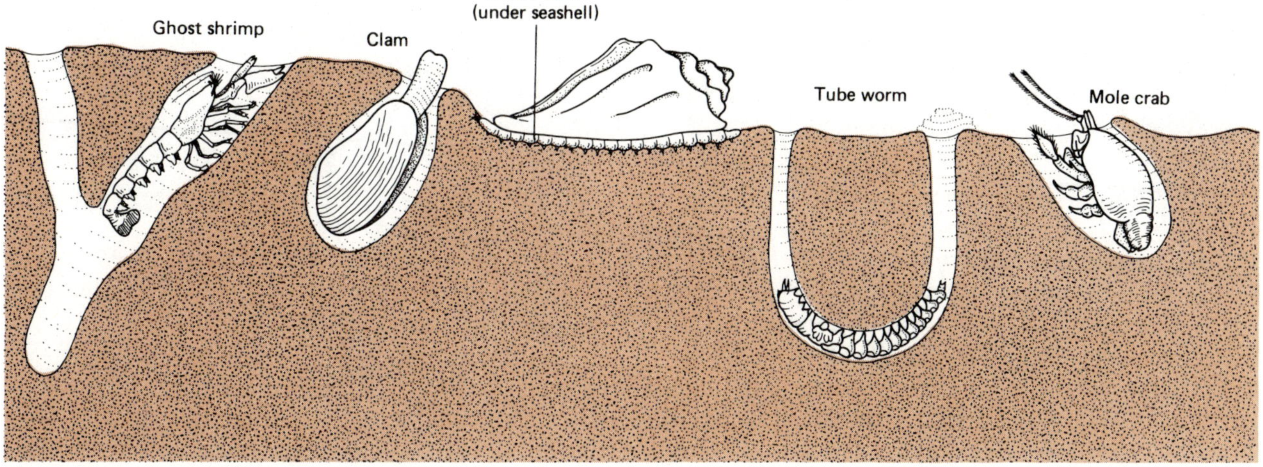

BOX 20A

REEFS

Plants and animals secreting limy walls or tubes build reefs in shallow marine waters. These calcareous formations catch and hold sand and shell fragments and provide hiding spots for other organisms. Although oyster beds can be considered reefs, this discussion is limited to the coral reefs of shallow tropical seas.

Present-day coral reefs tolerate only minor temperature fluctuations, and they are seldom found where the water temperature dips below 20°C (68°F). Corals themselves are a group of animals that secrete skeletons composed of calcium carbonate crystals. Growth patterns and thus skeletal configurations vary according to the species. Names such as staghorn, lettuce, brain, or cup coral indicate the diversity of these showy animals.

Often overlooked is the fact that algae are key components of coral reefs. Many red algae 384 secrete calcareous skeletons that may contribute more to the bulk of the reef than do the corals themselves. *Zooxanthellae* are algae that dwell inside tissue of corals. These unicellular plants use carbon dioxide and nitrogenous wastes from the coral and produce both carbohydrate and oxygen, which the corals use. Corals live only in shallow water because zooxanthellae require light for photosynthesis.

All in all, coral reefs are rich, low-stress communities. The warm tropical sea supplies a uniform temperature favorable to growth. Near the surface, wave action constantly stirs oxygen into the water, while the limy skeletons and the many nooks and crannies between them supply solid footholds and abundant shelter to reef animals. Finally, the filter-feeding corals and the abundant algae cycle nutrients efficiently.

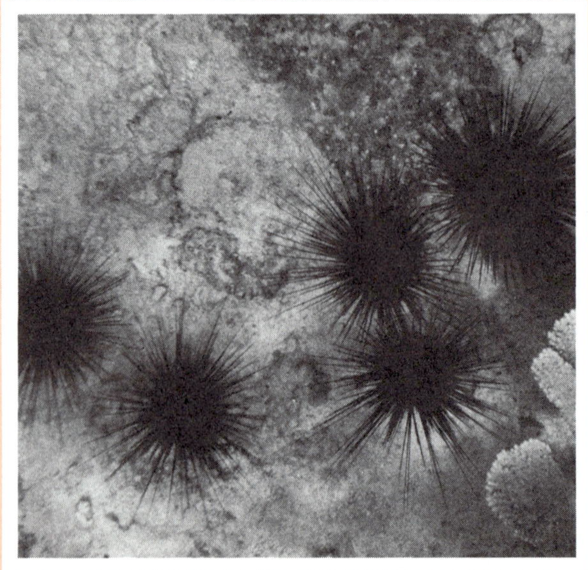

FIGURE 20.11 **A Salt Marsh.**

within their burrows. Typical residents below the low-tide line include whelks, swimming crabs, sand dollars, and hermit crabs.

Wetlands and Estuaries. Bays and river mouths where fresh and salt water meet are unusually fertile environments. The most valuable of such **estuaries** are broad, shallow basins created by silt deposits. Here **mud flats** and **tidal marshes** line channels of open water. Most of the silt and organic matter dumped from the river becomes trapped in its estuary. Slow currents, a large surface for evaporation, and presence of rooted vegetation all help make estuaries places where nutrients tarry.

Salt-marsh grasses, eel grasses, and other rooted plants take advantage of rich water and soft bottoms (Fig. 20.11). Algal scums cover mud flats, larger plants, and every solid surface, and dense phytoplankton blooms color the water. There is so much food that only a tiny part of the photosynthetic product finds its way directly into the mouths of herbivores. Instead, most plants die and, in the absence of swift currents, simply sink to the bottom and rot. The abundant organic matter supports a teeming broth of bacteria and fungi that use all available oxygen from the muddy bottom. As a result, other anaerobic microorganisms thrive there and release hydrogen sulfide. This noxious gas blackens marshland mucks and imparts a characteristic stench.

Their tremendous photosynthetic productivity and extensive decomposer food chain permit estuaries to literally teem with life. Microscopic decomposers are eaten by filter-feeding zooplankton, as well as by larger filter feeders such as worms, clams, and oysters. Estuaries serve as nurseries for numerous coastal fish. Menhaden, striped mullet, summer flounder, king whiting, croakers, striped bass, smelt, and sturgeon are all commercially important species that rely on estuaries sometime during their lives. The shrimp fisheries also depend on this resource, because young shrimp require the estuary habitat. Oysters, blue crabs, and several commercially valuable clam species are permanent estuarian residents. Furthermore, saltwater marshes are the natural home of most waterfowl.

As valuable as they are in their natural state, estuaries are often prized more for their land. Because protected harbors offer great advantage, most seaports have been built on estuaries. As early ports grew, the surrounding marshes and mud flats were usually drained, and regions of shallow water were dredged or filled to provide areas for docks, industries, airports, and even residences. In Washington, D.C., only the Tidal Basin remains to remind us that the Jefferson Memorial, Lincoln Memorial, and Washington Monument were built on land "reclaimed" from a marsh.

Leached free of their load of salt, drained tidal marshes become fertile farmland. Over the centuries, carefully engineered diking and pumping schemes created much of the Netherlands. But present generations seem little aware of the extent to which humans are responsible for our familiar shorelines and of how important estuaries are in the scheme of aquatic life. Today many of our least-modified estuaries are threatened with resort development.

LAKES: QUIET CHANGES

In many ways lakes resemble oceans. Of course, lakes are much smaller, and they usually contain
370 fresh water. **Diatoms** and **desmids** are the most abundant phytoplankton of lake environments. And though the shoreline vegetations and broad-leaved floating plants contribute much more to the productivity of fresh waters than marine seaweeds do to the oceans, zooplankton and fish are abundant in both habitats.

The most productive region of a lake or pond is near its edge, where flowering plants predominate. On or close to shore, grasses, cattails, rushes, and sedges stand above the water. In water just slightly deeper, water lilies and similar plants are rooted in the soil, but their flat leaves float on the surface. Other floating plants, such as the miniature duckweed, simply dangle their short roots in the nutrient-rich water. Below the surface grow bottom plants; *Elodea* (water weed) and water milfoil, for example, are familiar to most of us as aquarium plants.

Perhaps the most distinctive animal components of the freshwater food chain (Fig. 20.12) are the many insects, especially in their juvenile stages. Floating plants form mats over warm, shallow water and provide refuge and home for a diverse community of attached and crawling organisms. In this highly productive environment, hordes of protozoa and other small animals feed on phytoplankton and bits of organic matter. They may be grazed upon in turn by snails or consumed by filter-feeding clams.

Variations in climate, fertility, shape, and bottom characteristics cause lakes to be quite different from one another. But ultimately all these factors translate into nutrient availability. Unlike the oceans, temperate-zone lakes are stirred regularly. As a result, there is efficient nutrient cycling. This is what accounts for the much greater productivity of many lakes as compared with that of any ocean.

Seasonal Turnover

Swimmers know that lake water is warmer at the surface and colder at the depths. Thus in summer, lakes are stratified with lighter, warmer water at the top and colder, denser water toward the bottom.

As winter approaches, falling air temperatures and brisk winds slowly cool temperate-zone lakes. The fact that fresh water is most dense at 4°C (39°F) permits cooling lakes to be thoroughly stirred. When surface waters cool to 4°C, they sink to the bottom and displace the warmer, less dense water there (Fig. 20.13). This **turnover** brings nutrients from the bottom and spreads them throughout the lake. At some point the entire lake is at 4°C and lacks any density stratification. Absence of stratification allows the lake to be further stirred by the wind. Only after the whole lake reaches 4°C may the temperature of the surface dip lower. When this occurs, the colder, less dense water floats, and a layer of ice may eventually form.

In spring, the surface water gradually warms to 4°C. Then, as during the fall cooling, there is a period when all the water is 4°C and of uniform density. At this time winds blowing across the surface may set up currents that travel toward the shore, turn downward, and move across the bottom.

As you can see, there are two turnovers a year, one in spring and the other in fall. Both stir bottom sediments, and both also replenish the oxygen supply at the bottom. With available nutrients and increasing sunlight and warmth, plankton blooms color lake waters beginning in spring. Changes in temperature and nutrient levels cause one phytoplankton species to bloom and die, only to be followed by a population burst of another. The exact succession of blooms is determined by the requirements of the various species.

Nutrients, Pollution, and Aging

Lakes have a relatively short life span. It may take thousands or millions of years, but most lakes that we know are in the process of disappearing. At the time of formation, a young lake is usually low in nutrients and sparsely inhabited. As time goes by, the lake is enriched by accumulation of river sediments and nutrients leached by rainwater from the surrounding land. Further fertilization occurs as dead plants fall into the water and decay. This normal enrichment of a lake is known as **eutrophica-**

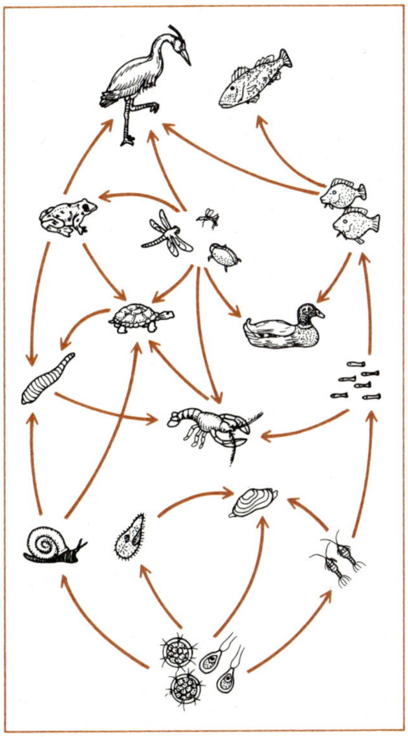

FIGURE 20.12 **A Freshwater Ecosystem.** A greatly simplified food web for this ecosystem is represented on the left.

tion (addition of good food). Eutrophication permits more and more organisms of increasingly different kinds to live in the lake. Clearly, the biological nature of a lake gradually changes as the lake ages.

The Fate of Lakes. Lakes undergo a process analogous to succession□ on land (Fig. 20.14). Bottom plants proliferate in the shallow, well-lighted water at a lake's edge. Their dead and decayed bodies accumulate and fill in the lake bottom with humus. As the water becomes more shallow, water plants, rooted in the mud, but with leaves and flowers floating on the surface, move into the area. These plants crowd out and shade the bottom-dwellers. Floating plants such as waterlilies and duckweed also contribute to the buildup of organic matter, so eventually a swamp develops in what was open water. Cattails and bullrushes replace water lilies and duckweed, further stabilizing the shore. With continued deposition, the soil becomes deeper and drier. Then grasses, sedges, and small shrubs begin to take hold. With time, trees invade the new land. In as few as 100 years a small lake may be replaced by a forest. 444

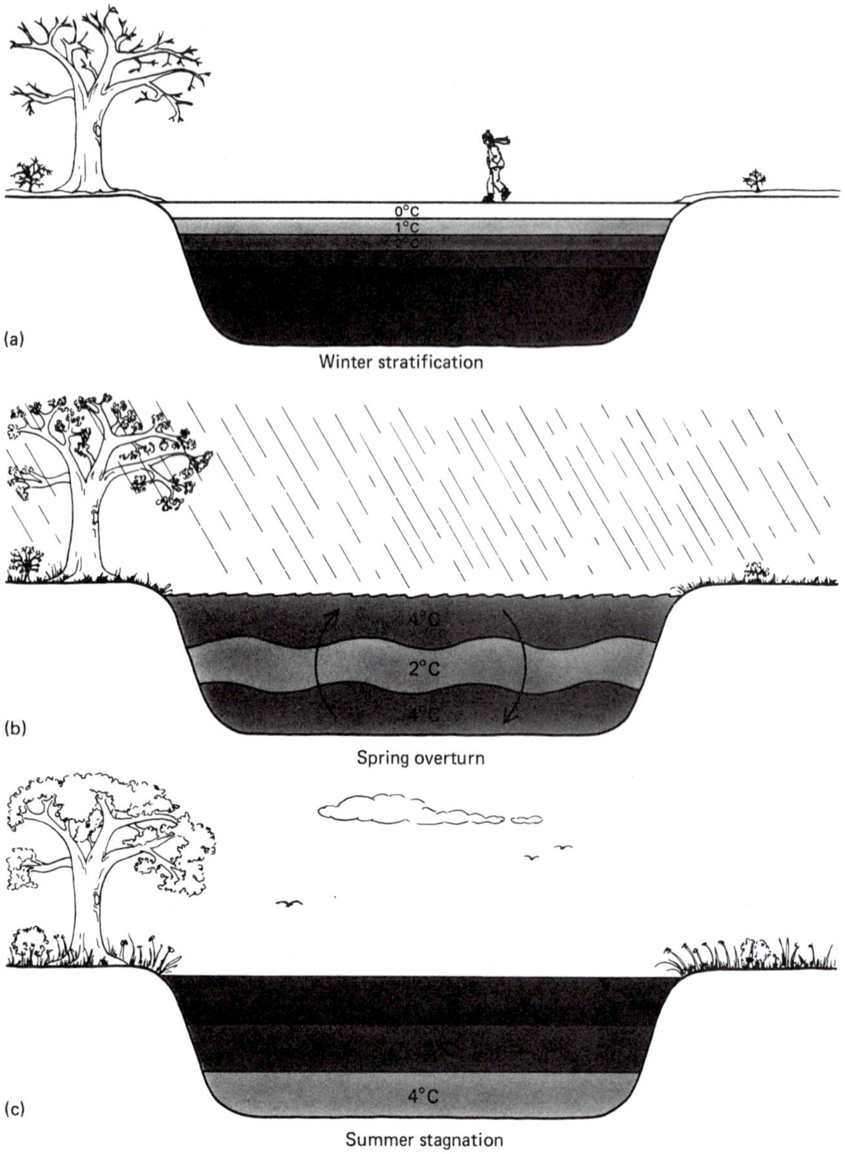

FIGURE 20.13 **Seasonal Temperature Changes in Lakes.** In winter (a) colder water and ice will be near the surface of a lake. When mild weather arrives in spring (b), the ice melts, and eventually the surface water warms to 4°C. As this denser water sinks, it creates currents that produce a "spring turnover." In the summer (c) three distinct temperature zones develop within the lake.

As sediments build up, filled-in lake margins develop into marshes or swamps. By definition, a **marsh** is a wet grassland and **swamps** are wet forests (Fig. 20.15). Like their saltwater counterparts, freshwater marshes support diverse communities adapted to slight variations in water levels. So do swamps. And like marine wetlands, those of fresh water are gradually disappearing. Conversion of the rich muck into farmland is the goal of many government-funded drainage and stream channelization projects.

In cold climates, lakes may eventually turn into spongy, wet **bogs.** Because of the cold, accumulated plant material decomposes poorly, and it is gradually transformed into **peat.** Humic acids derived from the peat further inhibit decomposition and give the water a characteristic brown tinge. Peat is often dug up, dried, and burned as fuel.

Excess Eutrophication. Although natural eutrophication is part of the aging process of every lake and tends to favor mineral accumulation, human activities accelerate the process, and excess eutrophication can lead to early death of a lake. Fertilizer washed into lakes from nearby farms and the addition of minerals in household or industrial sew-

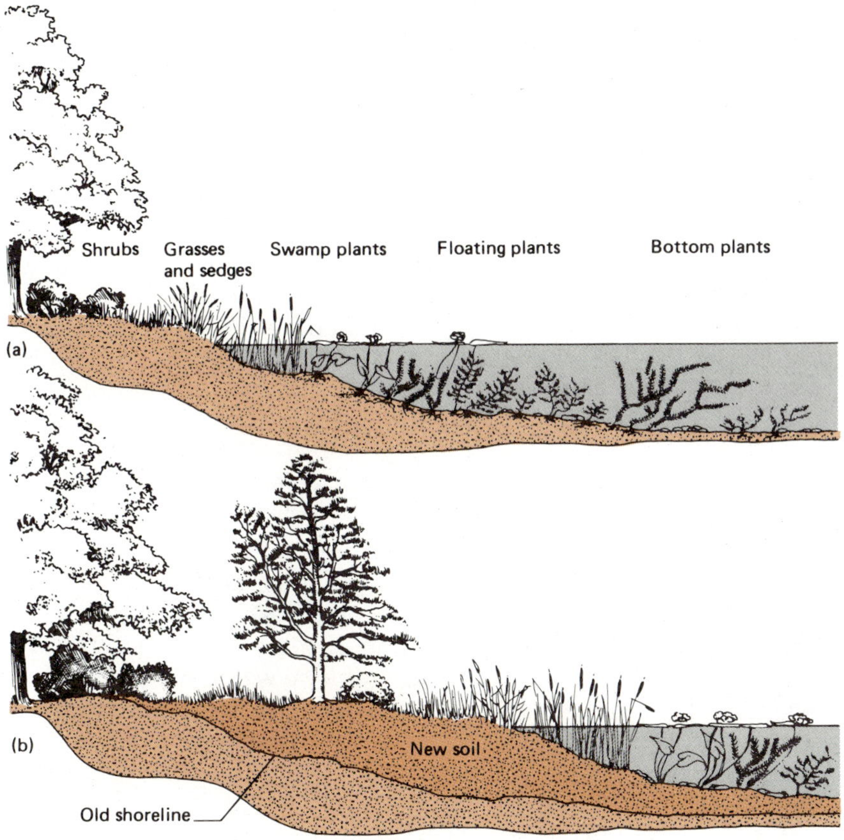

FIGURE 20.14 Succession Fills in a Lake.

FIGURE 20.15 Swamps and Succession. Dead tree trunks contribute to sediment buildup in this bald cypress swamp.

FIGURE 20.16 Excess Eutrophication. Dead and dying algae clog the shoreline of a lake polluted by sewage and agricultural runoff.

age can create an overabundance of nutrients in the water. Under these conditions algal blooms deplete oxygen in the water. Fish and other animals may simply choke to death. Increased turbidity of the water reduces light availability so that bottom plants also succumb (Fig. 20.16).

Studies of the Great Lakes trace their eutrophication to excess phosphorus. Experimental addition of phosphate to small lakes in the same region has produced conditions similar to the pollution found in the Great Lakes. Neither nitrogen nor carbon alone has a similar effect. Apparently the simple removal of phosphate from waste water, accomplished principally by banning phosphates in household detergents, would improve conditions markedly in many bodies of water.

RIVERS AND STREAMS: RUNNING WATERS

The continuous one-way flow of running waters distinguishes them from lakes. Indeed, many of the special characteristics of these waters are related to their turbulence. Because currents constantly bring new water into contact with a given organism, running water is effectively richer than still water, in which a static, "tired" layer surrounds each individual. And to be sure turbulence mixes air into running water and thus usually ensures a plentiful supply of oxygen (Fig. 20.17).

The Food Web of an Open System

Rivers and streams inevitably reflect the land they drain. Stream water arises mainly from groundwater, and surface runoff provides most of the remainder. Water from both sources carries mineral nutrients and human additives such as pesticides. But most of the organic matter that supports the food chains of running waters also washes in from the surrounding land—or simply falls in. Probably tree leaves supply more energy and more carbon than any other single source. Additional sources of carbon and energy are adult insects that flounder into the water, earthworms, and other small soil animals. Except in quiet streams that closely resemble lakes or ponds, there are few phytoplankton in rivers. Thus running waters are unusual ecosystems in that primary production accounts for but a small portion of the energy needed. Most

FIGURE 20.17 White Water of the Icicle River in Washington.

nutrients enter rivers and streams from the outside. Streams, therefore, are open ecosystems.

Most phytoplankton found in streams are diatoms. Although vascular plants are rare in rapidly running waters, filamentous algae and masses of water mosses populate many streams. Mayfly nymphs are among the herbivorous species to be found. Such animals burrow into the mud or find protection among the rocks. Caddis-fly larvae build cases to protect themselves from the strong currents. Others spin webs that also serve to catch food carried by the current. Although the adult blackfly is terrestrial, its larvae spin a silky thread that holds them to a rock. In most streams fish are the top carnivores; most eat water insects.

Adaptations to Current: Don't Get Carried Away!

Only careful strategies prevent the current from carrying stream organisms to different and less suitable habitats (Fig. 20.18). The familiar slickness of stones in streams is mostly due to the cementing substances secreted by attached diatoms. Larvae of blackflies and many other insects anchor themselves with holdfasts. Still others spin sticky threads about themselves or burrow into the mud. Many stream animals are streamlined. They have compact and flattened bodies and usually live under stones, where the current is reduced and where they are less visible to predators.

Fish can expend a great deal of energy swimming against the current—so they don't. Fish survive by finding shelter. As anyone who fishes knows, the best place to catch trout is in a deep bottom hole or along the downstream sides of large rocks or other obstacles. Generally, the larger the shelter, the larger the fish.

The adaptations of stream organisms truly illustrate the selective forces of this environment. Contrast the powerful streamlined bodies of trout and other fast-stream fish with fish of slower waters. Consider, for example, the corpulent carp and catfish that roam quiet river bottoms. Then, too, bass and other panfish that have compressed bodies are perfectly designed for weaving through the masses of pond-like vegetation that grow along the shores of slow streams.

FIGURE 20.18 A Lesson in Not Getting Carried Away.

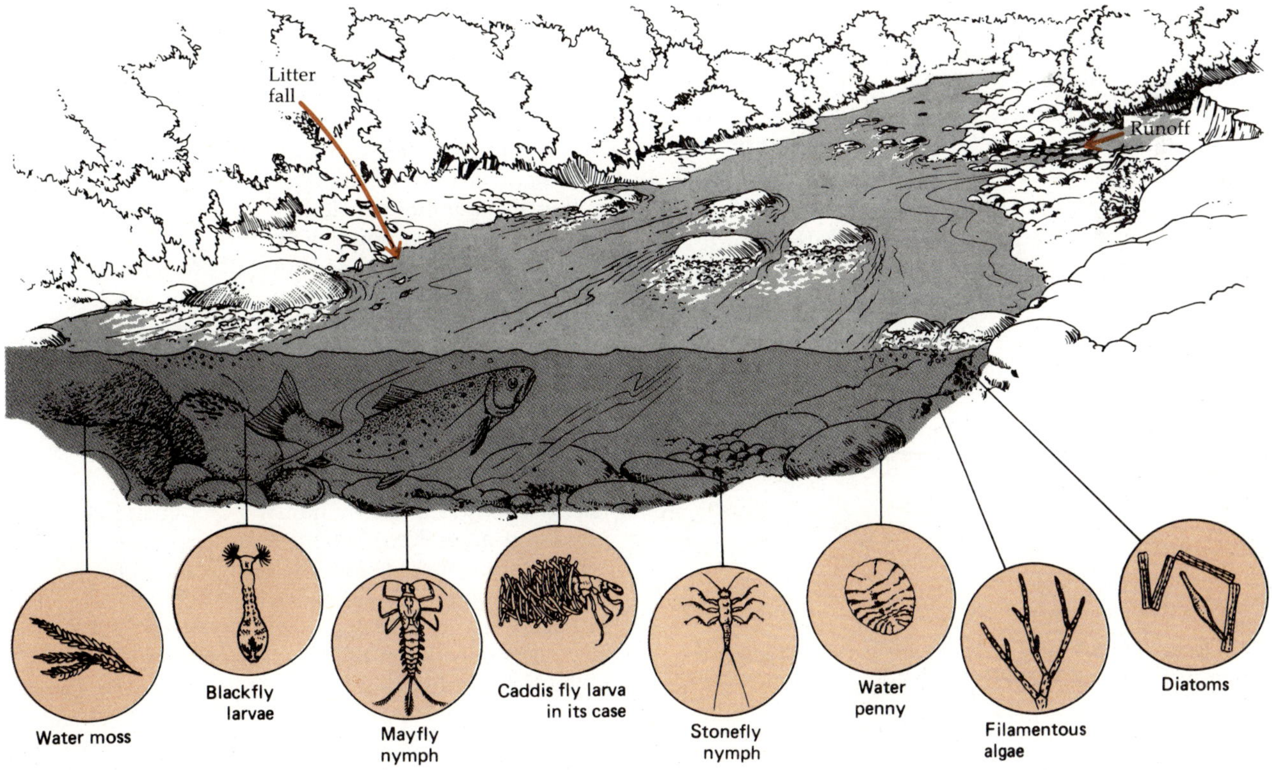

Living in Water: A Special Way of Life

To an animal, the fundamental difference between living on land and living in water is the availability of oxygen. Oxygen is so poorly soluble in water that it is hardly surprising no warm-blooded animals can live submerged for more than short periods. Aquatic mammals and birds, such as whales and penguins, all breathe air and thus obtain enough oxygen to sustain the high metabolic rate associated with a constantly warm
137 body. And surely the complexity of gills□ is related to the need for extensive surfaces for gas exchange with water. Gills are most often located where water can be readily pumped past them to maintain a constant supply of oxygen. As we will see in Chapter 22, the deadly effects of aquatic pollution can be traced to exhaustion of the oxygen supply.

Aquatic ecosystems are also unusual in that most producers are microscopic. Since so many people disregard anything they can't see, this may be why the structure of underwater communities escapes the understanding of many citizens. Microscopic producers dominate in water, because they have a large surface area compared with their volume. This ensures efficient absorp-
410 tion of nutrients. Furthermore, vascular tissue□ is unnecessary in this habitat, and large plants are subject to damage by waves or current.

Finally, the high specific heat of water gives aquatic environments a temperature stability unknown on land. Water is slow to warm and slow to cool. Large bodies of water, especially, fluctuate little in temperature. Not only are aquatic organisms freed from the usual problems of temperature regulation, but density changes associated with minor temperature shifts account for lake turnover and also affect ocean currents. Remembering these facts can help us maintain the integrity of aquatic ecosystems. This is an important step toward ensuring stability of the biosphere.

Summary

1. Oceans, lakes, and streams are perpetuated by the water cycle, which is driven by solar energy.

2. In addition to its vast size and diverse nature, one of the most obvious characteristics of the oceanic environment is its salt content. The main oceanic producers are microscopic phytoplankton that are limited to the euphotic zone. Because minerals sink to the bottom, productivity is richest where water is stirred. Animal life is limited except in the euphotic zone and at the ocean edge, since food is scarce elsewhere.

3. Coastal environments are far more variable than those of the open sea. Rocky shores provide habitats for organisms capable of surviving not only wave action, but also changing temperatures and osmotic conditions. Estuaries provide abundant nutrients for the growth of large and varied populations. Such environments are of tremendous economic and biological importance.

4. However similar freshwater lakes and oceans appear, there are differences. Seaweeds contribute little to ocean productivity, but shoreline vegetation and large floating plants are important in some lakes. Whereas animal life in the oceans is diverse, most large consumers in lakes are fish or insects. Seasonal turnover of temperate-zone lakes helps maintain the nutrient cycles. Lakes slowly disappear because of eutrophication.

5. Rivers and streams are frequently far more turbulent than lakes. As a result, fresh nutrients and oxygen are constantly made available to inhabitants. Photosynthesizers are rare in rivers and streams. Most organic nutrients enter the food chain from outside.

Thought and Controversy

1. The introduction of *Gambusi affinis,* the mosquito fish that feeds on rotifers, crustaceans, and insects, into artificial ponds resulted in dramatic changes in the phytoplankton populations. In fact, one cyanobacterium became so abundant that the water turned green. How may the introduction of this fish have caused changes in the phytoplankton populations? The eutrophication associated with increased plankton blooms is usually blamed on excess nitrogen or phosphorus. Does this experiment suggest another way that human intervention in the lake ecosystem can produce a similar effect?

2. Waterways made by humans can have dramatic effects on natural ecosystems, but decades or even centuries may pass before the brunt of the change is felt. For example, the Erie Canal was completed as far as Lake Ontario in 1819, but it was only in 1873 that alewives appeared in the lake; sea lampreys weren't noted there until the 1880s. From Lake Ontario these aliens spread to the other Great Lakes and together with the heavy fishing pressure of the last century contributed to the drastic reduction in native species. The sea lamprey attaches itself to large fish and sucks their blood through a wound it inflicts. Alewife populations sometimes reach dramatic peaks, and then the fish die by the millions, polluting the water.

Waterways built to connect two different marine environments have similar results. The construction of the Suez Canal permitted at least 24 kinds of fish and several species of crabs to invade the Mediterranean from the Red Sea. Although the canal opened in 1869, the effect on the Mediterranean remains uncertain. Some scientists believe that the Red Sea species are replacing the native Mediterranean forms. Can you suggest any reason why the migrations appear to be mainly one way? If so, which do you think is the older and hence the more stable ecosystem? Passage through the Suez is made difficult by the Bitter Lakes, where the water is about 4.5 percent salt.

3. Stream channelization is a process that involves straightening, widening, and deepening stream channels and removing debris and overhanging vegetation. This technique has been employed extensively, particularly in the southeastern United States. Proponents believe that channelization prevents flooding by hastening the passage of storm waters, promotes drainage of damp forest land so that it can be placed under cultivation, and increases access for sporting uses. How may channelization affect the fertility of the land drained? Channelization is often blamed for increased flooding downstream. Why?

4. Many fish of sluggish waters, including some species of carp and perch, attach their eggs to land plants only temporarily covered with flood waters. How will the construction of flood-control dams or stream-channelization efforts affect such fish?

Questions

1. How do groundwater, rainwater, and runoff water participate in the water cycle?

2. Define the following terms: continental shelf, continental slope, zooplankton, euphotic zone.

3. List the primary producers of (a) the open ocean, (b) rocky shores, (c) lakes and streams.

4. Are there any primary producers in the abyssal zone at the bottom of the ocean? Explain.

5. What is meant by a plankton bloom? Are plankton blooms equally likely to be found in marine and freshwater environments?

6. How does the greater density of 4°C water ensure the spring turnover of temperate lakes and ponds.

7. Describe in general terms the adaptations required for organisms to live in rocky, intertidal, and sandy shores.

8. How are estuaries, marshes, and swamps similar? Why are these important habitats disappearing?

9. Compare and contrast natural eutrophication and excess eutrophication.

10. Outline the food web of a rapid stream. How would a slow-stream food web differ? (Remember that slow streams are similar to lakes and ponds.)

Further Reading for Part Five

Ambroggi, Robert P., 1980. Water. *Scientific American* 243(3):101–116. (September)

Beddington, J.R., and Robert M. May, 1982. The harvesting of interacting species in a natural ecosystem. *Scientific American* 247(5):62–69. (November)

Cook, Robert E., 1983. Clonal plant populations. *American Scientist* 71(30):244–253.

Colinvaux, Paul, 1977. *Why Big Fierce Animals are Rare and Other Essays.* Princeton University Press, Princeton, N.J.

Holm, E., 1979. *The Biology of Flowers.* Penguin Books, New York.

Jordan, Carl F., 1982. Amazon rain forests. *American Scientist* 709:394–401.

Krebs, Charles J. 1978. *Ecology.* 2nd ed. Harper & Row, New York.

Leopold, Aldo, 1977. *A Sand Country Almanac.* Ballantine, New York.

Lewis, Walter H., and Memory P. F. Elvin-Lewis, 1977. *Medical Botany.* Wiley, New York.

McConnaughey, Bayard H., and Robert Zottoli, 1983. *Introduction to Marine Biology.* Mosby, St. Louis.

Merritt, Richard W., and J. Bruce Wallace, 1981. Filter-feeding insects. *Scientific American* 244(4):132–144. (June)

Miller, Kenneth R., 1979. The photosynthetic membrane. *Scientific American* 241(4):102–113. (October)

Pettit, John, Sophie Ducker, and Bruce Knox, 1981. Submarine pollination. *Scientific American* 244(3):134–143. (March)

Seeley, Thomas D. 1983. The ecology of temperate and tropical honeybee societies. *American Scientist* 71(30):264–272.

Smith, Robert Leo, 1980. *Ecology and Field Biology,* 3rd ed. Harper and Row, New York.

Saigo, R. H., and B. W. Saigo, 1983. *Botany: Principles and Applications.* Prentice-Hall, Englewood Cliffs, N.J.

Tuthill, Jo Ellen, 1983. The bugs of winter. *Science 83* 4(1):36–39. (January/February)

PART SIX

Living in the Biosphere

People are an integral part of the biosphere. As living organisms we are obliged to participate in an ecosystem that supplies food, water, and oxygen. To support human life for long periods, this ecosystem must be stable.

Human culture has given us an ability to manipulate our environment that dwarfs the impact of other species. We farm the fields, log the forests, mine the rocks, and fish the seas. The tremendous resources we have tapped and our ability to control infectious disease have permitted fantastic increases in human populations. But these populations must rely on the finite resources of the biosphere to meet their basic needs.

It is obvious that people now manage much of the earth. Unfortunately, this management is generally inept. We strip the land of its fertility, destroy wild species, add incomplete loops to natural cycles, and synthesize toxic chemicals with no thought as to their disposal. Our actions threaten the stability of many ecosystems. We cannot long afford such childish ways.

While some of us recklessly squeeze the biosphere to extract a higher standard of living, millions still starve. With no thought for tomorrow, we are unable to feed everyone today. How can we expect the earth to support billions of people for even a thousand years? The long-term existence of our species requires that we manage ecosystems more wisely.

Everyone has a lot to learn. We hope these closing chapters on agriculture, pollution, and population will help you contribute to the solution of pressing problems that face us today.

21

Agriculture: Managing Simplified Ecosystems

IN A PREAGRICULTURAL SOCIETY SUCH AS THAT
40 of the !Kung, people are but a minor part of a very complex food web. Only a small portion of the total photosynthetic product reaches humans. The basic strategy of agriculture is to increase the photosynthetic products available for human consumption. This goal is achieved by growing plants and animals that humans can use and by trying to exclude other consumers. At most, farmers permit one herbivorous animal in the food chain between photosynthetic plants and people. The result is an extremely simple and artificial ecosystem. Natural geochemical cycles are interrupted, and fertility can be maintained only with care and at considerable cost. Also, such artificial ecosystems lack natural population controls. Therefore pests that feed on the crops may grow to tremendous numbers.

STRATEGIES TO LIMIT COMPETITION

Agriculture is largely the management of simple artificial ecosystems. These differ from **natural ecosystems,** in which there are many different producers, as well as many animals and microorganisms. A large number of different species may feed on one plant, but most have several alternative food sources. Competition tends to limit populations of the various consumer species. Because most consumers use several species, any temporary increase or reduction in any particular species, either producer or consumer, has only muted effects on others. Thus a natural community has relatively few large fluctuations in population numbers. This is particularly true in moderate climates in which communities are composed of a great many species.

In contrast, agricultural ecosystems are simple, incomplete, and unstable. Farmers work to replace the complex food web of a wild ecosystem with a **monoculture** (one crop) (Fig. 21.1). If that crop is native to the region, it will have pests native to the region. If it is introduced, it is likely to be susceptible to native pests. And whether a crop is native or introduced, commerce inevitably introduces pests from elsewhere. When supplied with acre after acre of food, pest populations often multiply to tremendous levels. When the crop and the pest species have not evolved together, the damage may be particularly extensive, because the crop has not evolved resistance to the pest. To make matters worse, humans often unwittingly select varieties that lack the genes that give wild strains natural resistance to particular pests. The struggle to increase the human food supply is in large part one of competition with other consumers.

Insects and Their Control

Plant damage from competitors isn't limited to consumption of cells (Fig. 21.2). Many insects suck phloem juices and inject toxic saliva. Damage ranges from leaf spots with abnormally thick cells and degenerate chloroplasts to profound alterations of the entire plant. For example, mealy bugs that suck on pineapple leaves can cause the roots to stop grow-

FIGURE 21.1 **Typical Monoculture.** Herbicide use has destroyed all the weeds in this Illinois corn field.

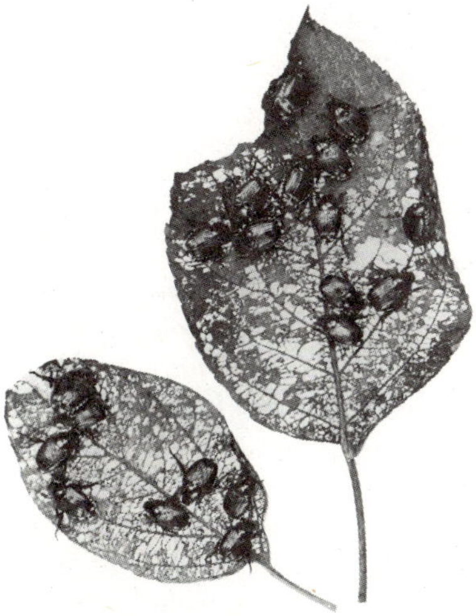

(a)

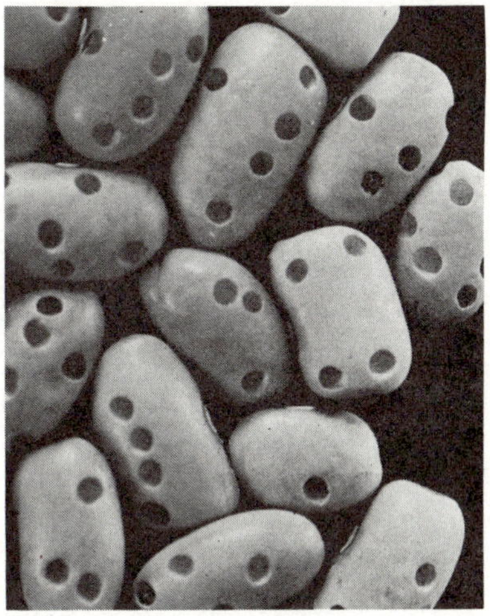

(b)

(c)

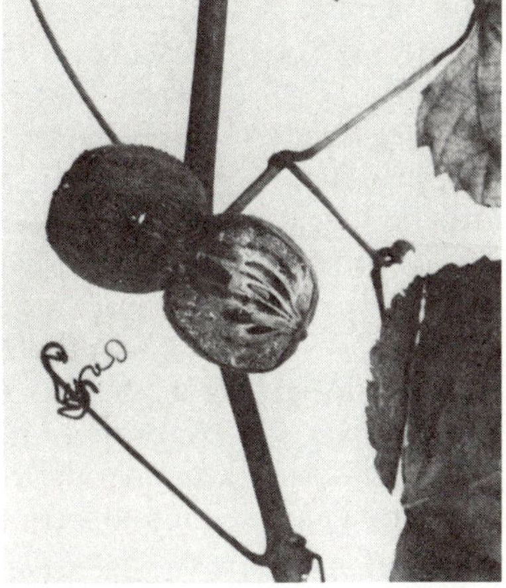

(d)

(e)

FIGURE 21.2 **Insect Damage to Plants.** Chewing insects such as Japanese beetles (a) skeletonize leaves and thereby reduce the plant's ability to carry on photosynthesis. Weevils destroy stored beans (b) and the corn earworm (c) damages the crop in the field. Characteristic growth responses of some plants to insect secretions result in distinctive galls (d). Sucking insects rob the plant of nutrition and often leave toxic salivary secretions that cause abnormal growth such as irregularities in xylem rings of wood (e).

ing and collapse. Soon the entire plant wilts. Even if the pineapple plant survives, it grows poorly and sets fruit prematurely.

Because insects inflict such heavy losses, any control measure can appear attractive. Even arsenic was used, before chemists began to synthesize organic pesticides. The history of modern insecticides began with the discovery of DDT and its use to control mosquitoes and lice during World War II. Early successes were so dramatic that insecticides promised to end the inroads not only of agricultural pests but also of malaria, yellow fever, typhus, and other insect-borne diseases. Of course, the real facts are more complex, and people have had many second thoughts on this extravagant promise.

One of the first difficulties recognized was that such **chlorinated hydrocarbons** as DDT, aldrin, and dieldrin are exceptionally stable or **persistent.** Neither the enzymes of living organisms nor spontaneous chemical reactions convert them rapidly into harmless substances. Most of the 300 million tons of DDT manufactured to date is probably still in existence as biologically active chemicals. Much lies buried at the bottom of lakes and oceans, where they are slowly released. Even if DDT applications ceased worldwide today, DDT residues would remain in the biosphere for centuries.

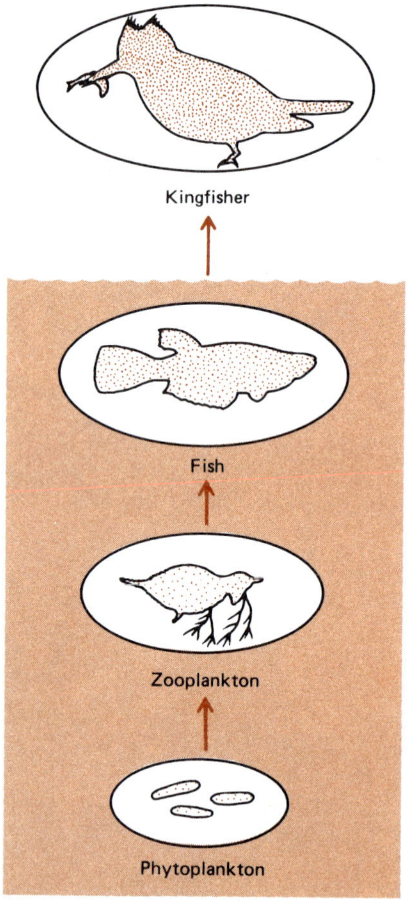

FIGURE 21.3 How DDT Is Concentrated in a Food Chain.

Biological Accumulation of Pesticides. Not only are chlorinated hydrocarbons persistent, but organisms lack efficient mechanisms to excrete these fat-soluble compounds. Once inside a plant or animal, such chemicals tend to stay for the organism's lifetime and to be passed on to the predator, scavenger, or decomposer that eventually consumes the body (Fig. 21.3). Animals hardest hit are those at the top of the food chain. They include pelicans, sea lions, bald eagles, and ospreys, all of which eat large fish. Another well-known victim, the peregrine falcon, preys on birds.

Because DDT is more soluble in lipids than in water, DDT accumulates in the fatty tissues. Acute poisoning usually occurs when animals expend their fat reserves for reproduction, migration, or other stressful activities.

Insecticides Can Increase Insect Populations. Despite early success, it was soon apparent that DDT was not controlling all the pests. One problem was that there were insect relatives, such as red mites, that were immune to DDT. And before long, even susceptible species showed resistance. Moreover, some previously minor pests became major problems. Overall, DDT had actually increased the pest problem.

This unexpected turn of events resulted from differences in characteristics between herbivorous insects and **entomophagous insects.** The latter are insects that eat other insects or, as in the case of ladybird beetles and larvae, suck their body fluids. Some entomophagous insects lay their eggs in the eggs, larvae, or pupae of host species (Fig. 21.4). The host provides a living food supply for the young parasitic insects.

Along with other top consumers, entomophagous insects accumulated DDT originally acquired by prey or host species. The heavy doses nearly wiped out the populations of some entomophagous insects that, like other top carnivores, naturally have relatively low population numbers. Furthermore, the small numbers of each species of entomophagous insects made evolution a slow process. While chance mutations that led to DDT resistance were rapidly accumulating in the large populations of herbivorous insects, comparable evolution in entomophagous insects moved at a snail's pace. Although resistance will give a large selective advantage to any insect species exposed to that insecticide, the chance that mutations for resistance will occur is much higher in a large population than in a small one. The few mutations in small populations of entomophagous insects, combined with their position high on the food chain where DDT accumulated, caused local disappearance of some species. Thus at the same time that DDT was selecting DDT-resistant pests, its use lifted natural controls on their population growth.

Resistance to DDT spurred efforts to develop other chemicals; it also led to heavier applications of DDT. Residues appeared in human milk and in polar bears hundreds of miles from the nearest site of application. Finally, in 1972, the Environmental Protection Agency banned agricultural application of DDT in the United States. Although DDT is still used in many places, continuing studies of several species (including oysters, certain birds, and eggs of some fish) show that DDT concentrations are falling. The breeding success of such threatened species as the brown pelican and the bald eagle seem to be improving.

Insecticide Toxicity. Excessive activity of the nervous system is the most obvious symptom of DDT

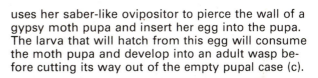

FIGURE 21.4 Parasitic Insects. A wasp (*Bathyplectus curculionia*) lays its eggs in an alfalfa weevil larva (a). When the egg hatches the young wasp larva will have a guaranteed food supply. Other wasps parasitize pupal stages. In (b), the wasp *Coccygomimus* uses her saber-like ovipositor to pierce the wall of a gypsy moth pupa and insert her egg into the pupa. The larva that will hatch from this egg will consume the moth pupa and develop into an adult wasp before cutting its way out of the empty pupal case (c).

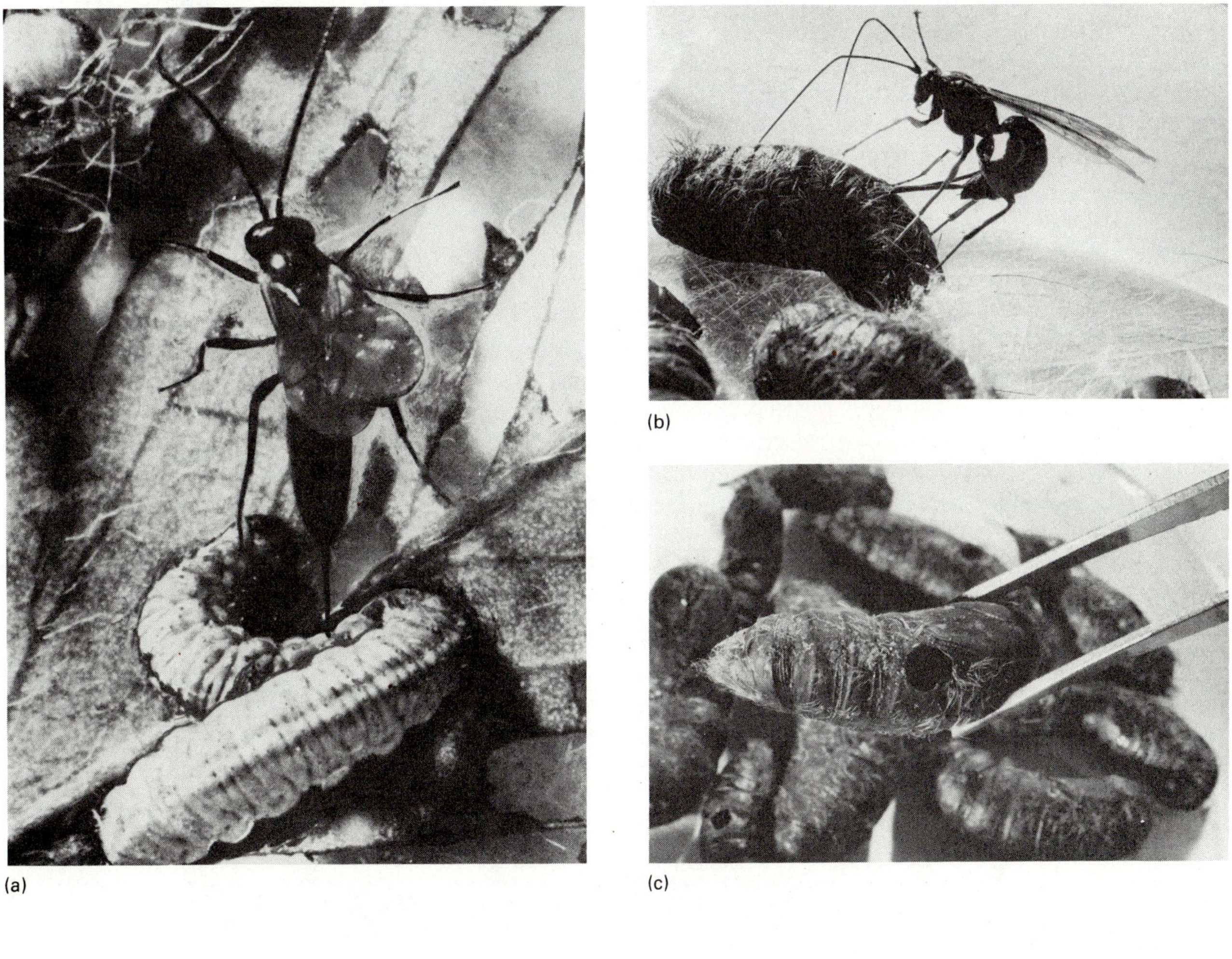

(a) (b) (c)

BOX 21A

FIGHTING THE SCREW WORM

The screw worm is the larva of a fly that lays its eggs in open sores of cattle and other animals. The umbilical scars of newborn calves are favorite targets; so are wounds resulting from dehorning or castration and even simple scratches or tick bites. Hundreds of worms can develop in a single sore and may kill their host within ten days. In warm climates, where the screw worm thrives, it inflicts millions of dollars of damage every year.

Screw-worm control has always been a problem. Application of insecticides to larvae inside range cattle is expensive and can be harmful. Thus the screw worm became an early target for biological control.

The initial test used the screw worm population on the Isle of Curaçao, in the West Indies. Here large numbers of laboratory-reared sterile male flies were released. The theory was that if there were more sterile males than fertile males, most of the females would mate with the sterile males. And since females of that species mate only once, most of the eggs would be infertile. Thus swamping generation after generation of the natural population with sterile males would eventually reduce the number of young produced to zero.

The 1958 project on Curaçao was a success. The flies were eliminated from the island. Since that time sterile-male release has been used to control the screw worm over a large region of the southwestern United States. But because screw worm habitat extends into Mexico, release of sterile males must be continued indefinitely along a buffer zone at the border. Local outbreaks still occur, perhaps in part because of genetic changes in laboratory-reared flies. Another factor is the existence of wild races that breed best among their own kind.

The sterile-male release principle is particularly suited to the control of small, isolated populations, such as those that result from accidental introduction. In recent years sterile-male release has wiped out potentially devastating populations of foreign fruit flies. (These are unrelated to the familiar *Drosophila* used in genetic research). Lapses in care may account for the 1981 California outbreak.

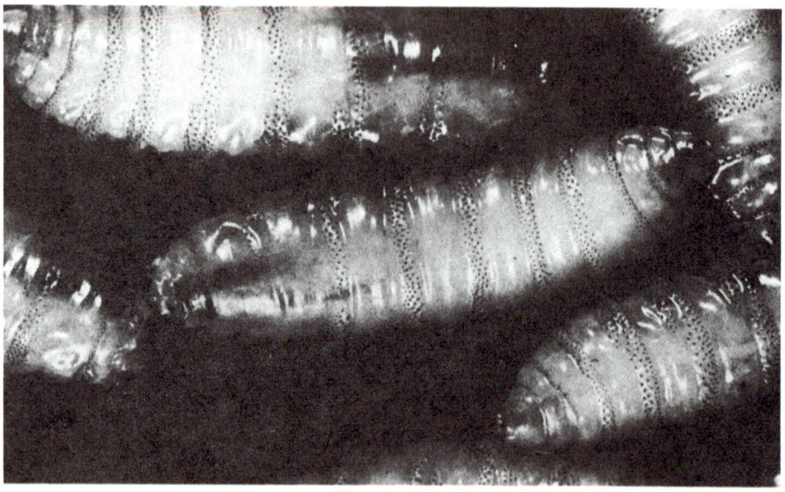

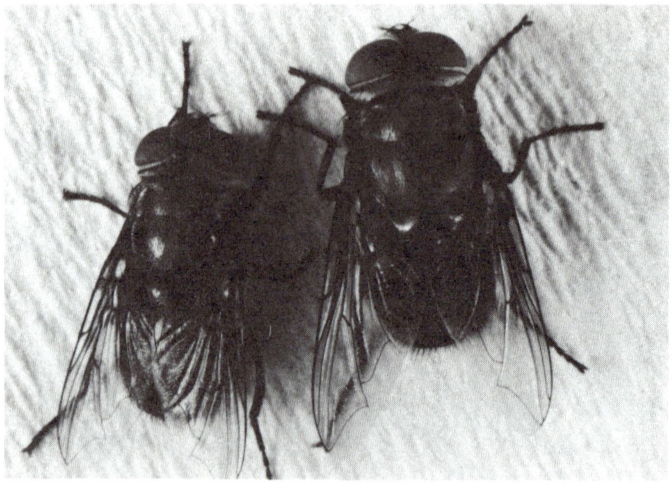

poisoning. However, even small quantities of DDT stimulate production of nonspecific **detoxification enzymes** within the liver. These enzymes, which protect the organism by destroying certain otherwise poisonous substances, also degrade reproductive hormones. Excess formation of detoxification enzymes may explain reproductive failures, including the production by birds of eggs so thin-shelled that they usually break before the young are ready to hatch. DDT also alters the ability of aquatic organisms to maintain a normal salt and water content. Both algae and fish are affected. But surely the most worrisome fact is that DDT produces tumors in laboratory animals.

The complex problems created by chlorinated hydrocarbons led to their replacement with **organophosphate insecticides** such as parathion and malathion, and with carbamates such as Sevin.® It has been accepted generally that organophosphates break down readily and so won't accumulate. However, recent studies suggest that anaerobic microorganisms bind organophosphates to the soil, where they are difficult to detect.

The **acute toxicity** (immediate poisoning effect) of organophosphates to vertebrates varies from high to low. In considering this statement, however, we should remember that DDT once seemed so harmless that it was used to delouse people.

Biological Control. The high cost of insecticide use, in terms of both money and ecosystem effects, promotes interest in biological control of insects. Because herbivore numbers are controlled by predators in natural ecosystems, it seems possible that such control might work in agriculture. Simple introduction of predators is sometimes effective. The earliest demonstration of biological control was the successful introduction of ladybird beetles to control the cottony cushion scale on citrus trees in California. Unfortunately there are few such examples. Most biological control involves sterile male release (see Box 21A), pathogenic microorganisms, synthetic biologic substances, or habitat manipulation.

The first practical control of an insect with a microorganism involved the Japanese beetle and **milky spore disease.** The bacterium that causes milky spore disease multiplies in the body cavity of the beetle larva until the blood turns milky with the bacteria. The bacteria are easy to grow, and they produce resistant spores that can be scattered on lawns or fields where they remain alive but dormant until eaten by a beetle grub. As you might expect, use of milky spore disease has resulted in the selection of genetically resistant beetles.

Nuclear polyhedrosis viruses (Fig. 21.5) form distinct masses found in the nuclei of insect cells. Many caterpillars and other insect pests are susceptible to a particular polyhedrosis virus. Since each kind of virus affects only one species, or at most a few closely related species, there is no danger to entomophagous insects. (These belong to groups distinctly different from the herbivorous ones.) There is also little potential for unexpected harm, since nuclear polyhedrosis viruses are already widespread at the end of each growing season. However, only a few virus particles survive the winter, so buildup of epidemics is slow. If the viruses could be propagated and sprayed on crops early in the spring, they would severely limit the target population. A few such viral insecticides are on the market, but since viruses multiply only in living cells,□ production is expensive. 93

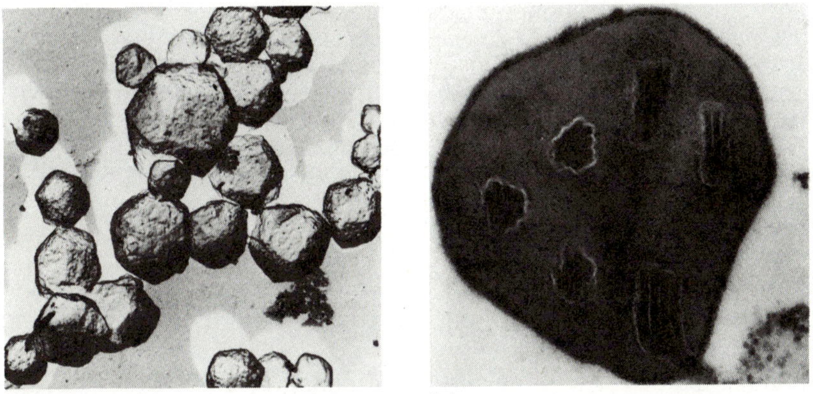

(a) (b)

FIGURE 21.5 Polyhedrosis Viruses. These insect pathogens form large crystal-like structures (a) inside insect cells. Sections of such polyhedral bodies (b) reveal virus rods inside. Viruses of this type are now used to control gypsy moth and corn earworm.

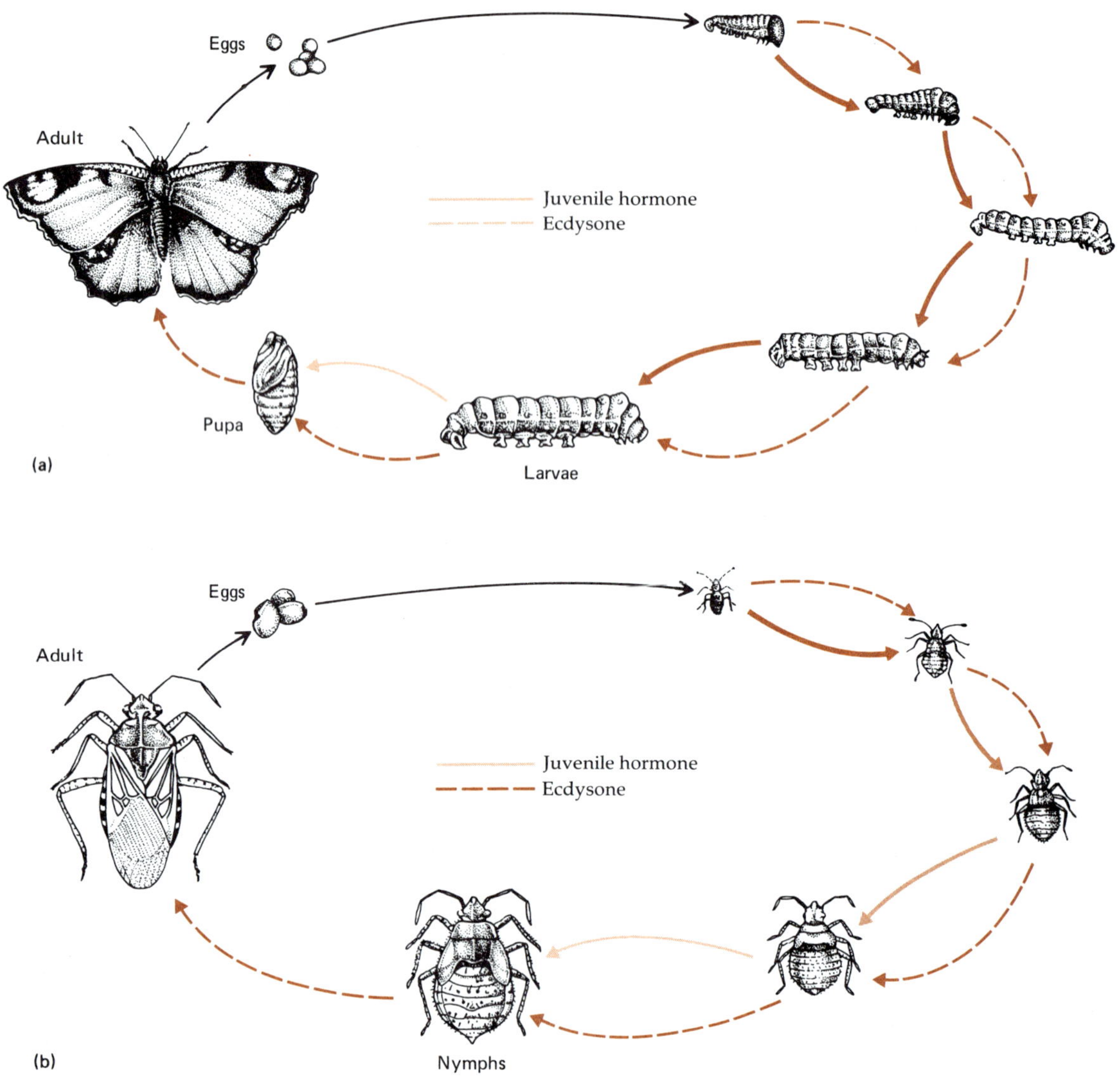

FIGURE 21.6 Hormones and Insect Development. Almost all insects undergo a distinctive change in appearance as they grow from young hatchling to sexually mature adult. Because body structure is determined largely by the rigid external skeleton, these changes, known as metamorphosis, occur only when the exoskeleton is molted. Acting alone, the molting hormone (ecdysone) stimulates the insect to form a new exoskeleton with adult structures, such as wings and genitals. Large amounts of juvenile hormone produced by young caterpillars (a) permit molting only to a larger larva. When the level of juvenile hormone is eventually reduced, the drastic change called complete metamorphosis occurs. In contrast, many insects, such as the true bugs (b), have a metamorphosis that occurs by gradual steps. Small decreases in juvenile hormone permit each immature stage to molt into another that resembles the adult just a bit more. During this gradual metamorphosis, structures of the adult grow slowly and are larger in each succeeding nymphal stage. However, these adult structures are fully developed only after the juvenile hormone is completely withdrawn prior to the adult molt. Note that complete metamorphosis requires a pupal stage during which the animal is quiet and secluded and does not feed at all.

Other ideas for insect control come from studies of behavior. Numerous female insects secrete
296 minute amounts of specific pheromones□ that attract males. Once the attractant of a particular species can be synthesized, it can be used to lure males into traps. Or large quantities can be distributed to mask the minute concentrations males follow to find mates.

Other potential biological insecticides include compounds that mimic insect hormones. Growth of insects requires a periodic molting in response to **ecdysone.** Although this hormone causes molting, the nature of the new structure formed after the molt is determined by a second hormone, **juvenile hormone.** Generally, the presence of juvenile hormone causes retention of larval or nymphal traits, and its absence permits adult structures to appear (Fig. 21.6). Application of compounds that are like juvenile hormone prevents insects from maturing and reproducing (Fig. 21.7). Some synthetic compounds affect only a few species and promise adequate selectivity to avoid harming beneficial insects. But caution seems advisable, because hormones are potent biological substances. And after all, any new insecticide will eventually select resistant pests. It seems likely that we will always share the product of our simple agricultural ecosystems with insects.

Integrated Control. Neither pesticides nor biological controls alone are particularly effective in the long-term management of insect pests, but sometimes the two approaches can be combined cheaply and safely. Recent studies suggest that grasshoppers (locusts) may be controlled by a bait containing tiny amounts of insecticide and the spores of a protozoan responsible for a grasshopper disease. Neither method is practical alone, but together they promise to be highly effective.

Frequently insecticides and biological methods are combined with simple cultural techniques such as the destruction of overwintering sites. This is a major factor in control of boll weevils, which once were the scourge of cotton fields. Insecticide application is limited to seasons when the weevils are most susceptible. New cold-tolerant strains of cotton are planted early and mature before the more numerous second-generation weevils emerge. Between 1964 and 1976 such integrated control allowed insecticide use to be cut by 90 percent in Texas cotton fields, while profits per acre increased significantly.

Microorganisms and Other Plant Pathogens

Just as medical science fights microbial disease, agricultural science struggles to control microorganisms that infect plants and animals. Among the microbial diseases of plant crops, the most important are caused by fungi, particularly **rusts, smuts,** and **mildews.** These microscopic fungi have, in some cases, determined the course of economic and political history. The Irish were so dependent on potatoes in 1845 that an epidemic of late blight of potatoes, a fungal disease, initiated a 15-year famine. More than a million people starved, and millions more emigrated, most to the United States.

In terms of present-day economic impact, **wheat rust** (Fig. 21.8) ranks as the number-one villain. Losses average more than 600 million bushels annually. Damage results from the ruptured epidermis that permits excessive water loss. The rust also robs nutrients from its host. The plants usually survive, but the grain that sets is ill nourished and often visibly shriveled.

Large-scale treatment of plant diseases is often impractical. The only effective control for wheat rust is selection of resistant wheat strains. But just as resistant wheat plants appear by mutation, so do new kinds of wheat rust. For the past 40 years geneticists have stayed one jump ahead of rust in the game of selection, but there have been some devastating outbreaks of the rust nevertheless.

(a) (b) (c)

FIGURE 21.7 **Synthetic Hormones Can Impede Insect Development.** Treatment with compounds related chemically to juvenile hormone prevents mealworm pupae from completing normal metamorphosis. Ordinarily, pupae (a) metamorphose into the adult form shown in (b). Exposure to substances that are like juvenile hormone results in a deformed beetle (c).

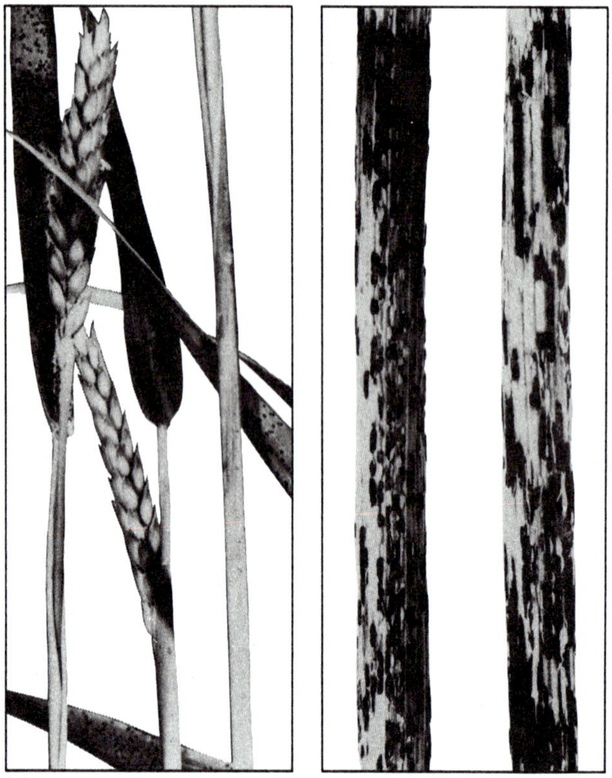

(a) (b)

FIGURE 21.8 **Wheat Rust.** Although this fungus has a complex sexual reproductive cycle, it is the blisters of reddish asexual spores (a) that give it its name. These asexual spores create airborne epidemics that sweep across a continent in a few weeks. A closeup of infected stems (b) shows them dried and shriveled.

Some fungal diseases can be controlled with chemicals, but these pose threats to ecosystems just as do insecticides and herbicides. One encouraging discovery is that certain soil bacteria can suppress fungal growths by colonizing the root surface. The bacteria compete with the fungi for iron and absorb so much that fungi do not thrive near the roots.

377 **Nematodes,** also known as roundworms, constitute another major group of agricultural pests. Nematodes abound in soil and water. Some are decomposers, and others eat bacteria or fungi. Still others attack plants or animals. Most nematodes that infest plants live part of their life free in the soil. Nematodes are particularly abundant immediately around roots. The concentration of nematodes may result from secretion of nutrients from roots into the soil. (The nutrients probably serve to attract microbial symbionts, including mycorrhizae.) 465

A roundworm enters a root after making an opening in the surface with a sharp stylet everted through its mouth. Most plant damage results from toxins released in the nematode saliva. The toxin may kill plant cells, produce abnormal growth, and provide entry routes for bacteria and fungi. Considerable effort has been devoted to controlling soil nematodes, but the results are discouraging. As with all agricultural pests, efforts to grow crops inevitably expand the habitat for some nematodes.

OTHER STRATEGIES TO PROMOTE PRODUCTION

Plant pests are only part of the problem in agricultural productivity. Few domestic plants can thrive in nature. The water and mineral supply are often inappropriate for plant crops; so are more subtle conditions, such as soil pH. Even temporary neglect of plant crops can result in their being overgrown by **weeds.**

Although the major objection to weeds is their competition for sunlight, water, and minerals, some weeds harbor destructive insects. For example, shepherd's purse, a highly tolerant and widespread little weed, supports leafhopper populations that transmit curly-top virus to sugar beets, beans, and tomatoes.

Tillage versus No-Tillage

Until recently, the expression "tilling the soil" has been almost synonymous with agriculture. Plowing turns weeds under and is the first step in creation of a soil layer easily penetrated by new plants. Early farmers worked the soil by hand; later they used cattle or horses to pull plows. Tractors were introduced early in the twentieth century, and have replaced animal power throughout much of the world. The cost of gasoline and diesel fuel has become a major item in the agricultural economy. But the hidden cost of soil loss through erosion may be more important. Whenever land is free of vegetation, it is vulnerable to erosion. Breaking the soil into small pieces increases the likelihood of erosion.

Sloped land is highly susceptible to water erosion. Individual raindrops can dislodge soil particles, which are then carried away in sheets of water. Winds blow dry soil away as dust. Soil loss exceeds

FIGURE 21.9 Contour Farming. This Wisconsin hillside is never barren, because strips are plowed and planted at different times. Some strips always support plants that catch and hold rainwater that would otherwise rush down the hillside carrying along the valuable soil. The furrows themselves also retard runoff, because they lie across the direction of flow.

the rate of soil formation on one-third of the land planted to corn or cotton and nearly one-half of the land planted to soybeans. Rolling fertile grasslands of eastern Washington lose 56 metric tons of soil per hectare (25 tons/acre) every year they are plowed and planted to wheat. Worldwide, this loss of soil is appalling. Contour farming (Fig. 21.9) is one strategy for reducing erosion on hilly ground. Another strategy is to not plow at all.

No-tillage agriculture relies on **herbicides** (chemicals that destroy plants) for weed control. Some techniques involve no tillage at all, but in others the land is worked lightly, or the seed is planted in narrow, cultivated strips. Often special machinery is required to plant the seeds and place fertilizer where it will be of benefit to the developing plants. Although such plantings may not produce as heavily as conventional ones, erosion may be reduced by as much as 80 percent. The savings in time and fuel may result in greater profits.

If weeds are controlled, uncultivated fields retain moisture better than tilled ones do. Disadvantages of no-tillage methods include poor germination and slow seedling growth. These conditions may result from toxins leached out of rotting crop remains (Fig. 21.10) or from the shade provided by this litter layer. The litter also harbors insects and disease organisms.

The biggest problem with the no-tillage strategy is the use of herbicides. There is danger that herbicides will wash off fields and destroy the remnants of native plant communities. Some herbi-

FIGURE 21.10 Planted without Plowing. Old wheat stubble is still visible between the soybean rows in this Kansas field.

cides are toxic to fish and other aquatic organisms. Common contaminants in herbicides have been demonstrated to cause embryonic abnormalities in mammals and there is concern that herbicides may be carcinogencic.

The Depleted Soil

The amount of minerals removed with each crop is sufficient to deplete the soil quickly (Table 21.1). If production is to continue season after season, these minerals must be replenished. Fertilizers that replace potassium, calcium, magnesium, and sulfur are easily manufactured from abundant raw materials or recycled chemical wastes. Nitrogen and phosphorus are another matter.

The commercial production of nitrogenous fertilizers involves a process of **nitrogen fixation** little different from that promoted by lightning or other natural energy sources. Molecular nitrogen is combined with hydrogen in a process that requires extreme temperatures. Present methods depend on petroleum products for an energy source.

The importance of biological nitrogen fixation becomes apparent when we compare the estimated 200 million tons produced by microorganisms annually with the industrial production of 30 million tons of nitrogen fertilizers. In rice paddies, biological fixation, 430 mainly by cyanobacteria, can yield as much as 63 kilograms of nitrogen per hectare (55 lb/acre) a year. Symbiotic microorganisms associated with legumes can yield up to 100 kilograms of nitrogen per hectare (90 lb/acre) annually.

Nitrogen fixation assures us a nitrogen supply so long as we can pay the energy costs, but artificial recycling of phosphorus may not be practical. The **phosphorus cycle** in nature moves very slowly (Fig. 21.11). Phosphate (PO_4) washes from the land into the sea, where it forms insoluble phosphate rocks. The phosphate returns to the soil only when the folding of the earth's crust transforms ocean sediments into mountain ranges, and rocks formed on the bottom of the ocean are finally eroded away.

Phosphate-rich rocks are the only major source of phosphorus fertilizers. The world supply of mineable phosphate rock is estimated at about 75,000 million metric tons. At present rates of use (100 million metric tons per year) this supply would last about 750 years. However, consumption of phos-

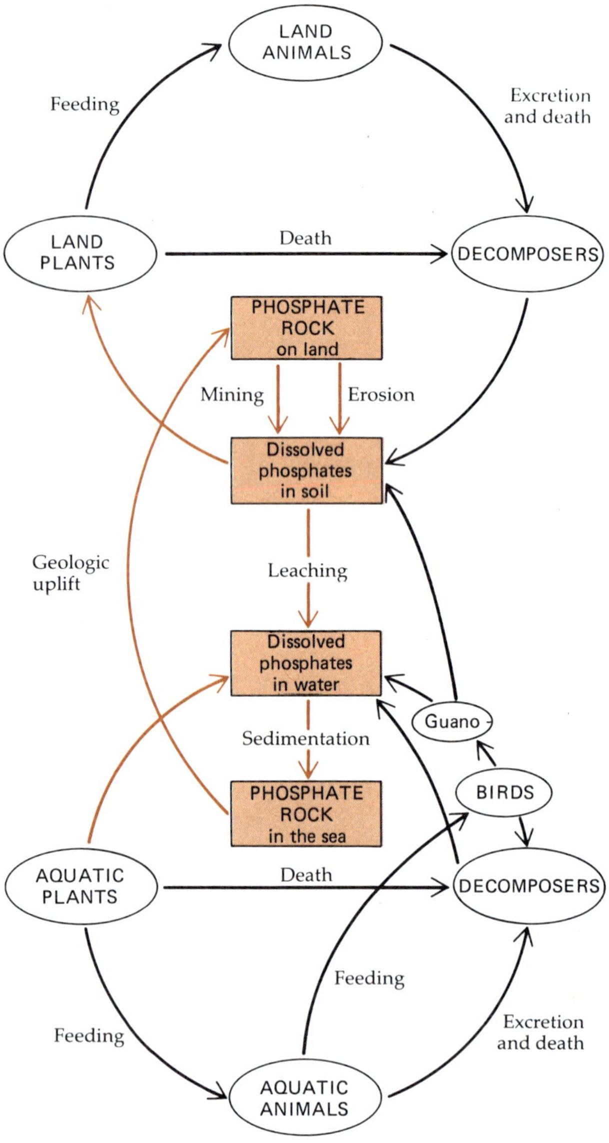

FIGURE 21.11 **Phosphorus Cycle.**

TABLE 21.1 **Minerals Needed to Grow an Acre of Corn***

	KILOGRAMS	POUNDS
Nitrogen	71	156
Phosphorus	12	26
Potassium	47	103
Calcium	13	29
Magnesium	11	24
Sulfur	8	18

*75 bushels (two tons) of grain.

phate fertilizers increases yearly as population increases and agricultural technology expands. Estimated annual world demand by the year 2000 is 390 million metric tons. When commercial phosphorus sources are exhausted, agricultural production may be reduced by half. The fact that there will be any substantial yield results from the fact that there is tightly bound (hence slowly available) phosphate in all soils.

Irrigation

Water shortages limit production of many crops in particular areas. Often the standard cure for this problem is irrigation. Water from wells, rivers, or lakes is carried to the field and distributed through canals, overhead sprinklers, or other systems (Fig. 21.12).

Of course, much of the water thrown into the air or dumped onto the soil surface evaporates. One-half or more of the water supplied through irrigation evaporates. This is not a trivial matter, for our freshwater supply is sorely limited. United States farmers presently use six times as much water for irrigation as is needed to meet the industrial and household needs of the entire nation. Irrigation has been responsible for reduction in river flow, which has altered the nature of natural waterways. So much water is pumped from the Colorado River that near its mouth this great river is little more than a muddy trickle. In other areas, such as parts of Texas and Oklahoma, irrigation has consumed enough groundwater that ranchers have had to cut back on irrigation plans.

Besides wasting water, surface evaporation can concentrate salt and other potentially harmful minerals in the plant-growth zone. When soil is thoroughly soaked, soluble minerals enter the water. As water is drawn toward the surface, minerals from deep in the soil move with the water and become concentrated in the upper soil regions. Thus irrigation can increase the salinity (saltiness) and the alkalinity of the soil. Many crops are highly sensitive to saline or alkaline soils. Whereas initial irrigation is valuable, continued irrigation may reduce the productivity of soil. Such changes are believed to have been the fundamental cause of the fall of early Middle-Eastern cultures, such as that along the Tigris-Euphrates River in Iraq. Archeological records reveal that wheat production in this irrigation-based culture declined, and that farmers switched to planting barley, a more salt-tolerant species. Eventually the barley failed, and there was no longer enough food production to support the human population necessary to maintain the extensive irrigation canals.

Water shortages and the threat of mineral accumulation has promoted more thoughtful water-management practices by some farmers. Rather than irrigating at any level that will increase production,

FIGURE 21.12 Irrigation. Shallow canals outline rows of young orange trees. To take advantage of the water-soaked soil, rows of lettuce will be grown between the rows of orange trees.

TABLE 21.2 **Key Food Crops (Approximate Annual World Production in Metric Tons)**

CROP	ORIGIN	PRODUCTION	CULTURE/FOOD VALUE/USES
GRASSES			
Rice *Oryza sativa*	Southeast Asia	320 million	Most varieties require intensive culture and carefully regulated flooding. Protein is concentrated in outer layers that are removed during polishing to produce white rice. 7% protein. Average U.S. yield: 2.3 tons/acre.
Wheat *Triticum* sp.	Near East	360 million	Does best in a cool climate with moderate rainfall and dry summers for harvest. Protein concentrated in outer layers that are removed as bran when wheat is milled to flour. 13% protein. Average U.S. yield: 0.9 ton/acre.
Corn *Zea mays*	New World	300 million	Needs long, moist growing season and warm weather. 9% protein. Lacks gluten, so can't be used alone to make raised bread. Average U.S. yield: 2 tons/acre.
Barley *Horedeum* sp.	Near East	170 million	Tolerates cool, short growing seasons and slightly saline soil. 13% protein. Low gluten content makes poor bread. Main uses are for animal feed and malt for beer.
Oats *Avena sativa*	Near East	50 million	Require moist temperate climate. 15% protein. Amino acid balance quite favorable for human food. No gluten. Average U.S. yield: 0.7 ton/acre.
Rye *Secale cereale*	Old World	30 million	Tolerates cold, dry climate; winter-hardy. Produces in poorer soils and colder climates than those required by other cereals. 13% protein. Some gluten; makes a coarse bread if used alone.
Sorghum *Sorghum bicolor*	Old World	50 million	A warm-climate, short-day species that does well in the tropics. Grain is 12% protein. Has no gluten so is eaten as mush or flatbread.
Millets (several species)	Old World	45 million	Fairly drought-resistant and tolerant of poor soil. Nutritionally equal to rice. No gluten; consumed as mush, flatbread, or beer.

good managers recognize the point of diminishing returns. They use a limited amount of water applied at crucial times. Under some conditions **dry-fallowing** is a better strategy than irrigation. In dry-fallowing, the land is cropped only every other year. The use of herbicides or cultivation prevents vegetation growth when there is no crop on the ground. With no loss through transpiration, water is accumulated one year for use during the next. This method is not entirely free of risk; obviously, leaving the land barren increases its vulnerability to erosion.

Domestic Plants and Animals

Most human food is produced by a handful of species that result from thousands of years of selection. Examination of the biological characteristics of these organisms reveals their important features and can provide insight into strategies that increase food production. The main food-producing plants are the grasses and legumes (Table 21.2).

Grasses. Corn, wheat, rice, oats, barley, millet, sorghum, and sugar cane are all grasses, just as are the plants you see in lawns. Although each of these crop species has been modified by human selection, they all retain the basic grass structure.□ 471

Production of a large crop that can be harvested efficiently underlies the usefulness of the specialized grasses grown for the fruits we commonly call **grains.** All grasses naturally grow densely and produce large numbers of one-seeded fruits (grains). In addition, the grain-laden heads protrude above the leaves at a height that is easily reached by hu-

CROP	ORIGIN	PRODUCTION	CULTURE/FOOD VALUE/USES
LEGUMES			
Broad beans or fava *Vicia fava*	Mediterranean	5 million	The only widely used bean in Europe and the Mediterranean countries before Columbus. 25% protein. Toxic to certain people.
Common beans *Phaseolus vulgaris*	New World	11 million (dry beans)	Large number of varieties, including kidney, pinto, navy, great northern. Immature pods are "green beans." Dried seeds 22% protein.
Mung beans *Phaseolus aureus*	Orient		Used mainly as bean sprouts.
Peas *Pisum sativum*	Old World	11 million (dry peas)	Dried peas widely used before Columbus. "Green" varieties appeared more recently.
Chick peas *Cicer* sp.	Old World	6 million	Also known as garbanzo. Use is concentrated in India, where the peas are ground into flour.
Cow peas *Vigna sinensis*	Africa	1 million (dry peas)	More closely related to *Phaseolus* than to *Pisum.*
Lentils *Lens esculenta*	Asia	1 million	25% protein.
Soybeans *Glycine max*	Southeast Asia	60 million	Require a warm, moist climate with a long growing season. 30–50% protein and 13–35% oil. Used extensively in margarine, as meat extender, as raw material for plastics, and for stock food.
Peanuts *Arachis hypogaea*	New World	17 million	Fertilized flower pushed underground, where the fruit in which nuts form develops; therefore must have a light, sandy soil. Seed is 30% protein and 48% oil. Used extensively for oil, peanut butter, and hog food.

mans. The grain itself is of low moisture content. Except in the most humid climates, it can be stored for long periods without rotting. Given these traits, wild grasses were logical candidates for domestication and improvement through selection.

Today the domesticated grasses we know as grains produce most of the calories that people consume. They have large fruits in comparison with most wild grasses, and they are capable of tremendous yields. However, starch constitutes the bulk of this calorie production. Only a few kinds of grain are more than 10 percent protein, and the amino acids present are not in the proportions that
109 humans need. □When used as a dietary staple, grains are usually mixed with a legume that is richer in protein and contains complementary amino acids.

Each grain and grain variety has its characteristic proteins. Some strains of wheat are high in **gluten,** a protein that is essential if bread is to rise. Gluten traps the bubbles of carbon dioxide produced when yeast metabolizes sugar, and it is these bubbles that raise bread dough. Rye has some gluten but not a sufficient amount for rye flour to be used alone to make a light bread. Most grains, including rice and corn, have almost no gluten. They are made into flatbreads, eaten as cereals, or consumed as beer. Corn is also refined to yield the gummy starch added to many manufactured foods. Corn and other grains are fed to animals that yield meat, milk, or eggs.

Corn: A Photosynthetic Factory. Despite its lack of gluten, corn is a mainstay of U.S. agriculture. It is an especially interesting crop, because there are so many kinds with such varied uses. The basic varieties (Fig. 21.13) were selected by American

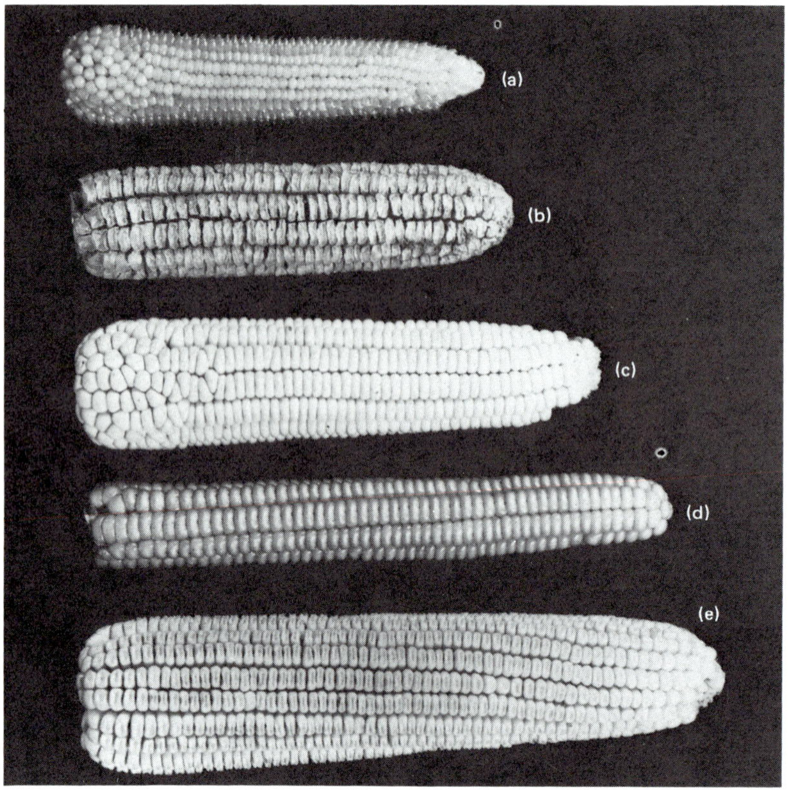

FIGURE 21.13 **A Corn for Every Purpose.** American Indians developed dozens of varieties of corn including popcorn (a), sweetcorn (b), floury corn (c), hard flint corn (d), and dent corn (e).

FIGURE 21.14 **Corn.** Corn has its male flowers in a tassel (t) at the top of the stalk. Female flowers, which consist only of pistils, lie in the ear (e) with the stigmas and styles protruding as the corn "silk."

Indians, who developed the species. The presence of two kinds of flower heads is an important characteristic of corn. One head is the **tassel** (Fig. 21.14), which consists of all-male flowers. The second is the **ear**, which contains female flowers that produce the grain.

C-4 Photosynthesis. Corn is a hot-weather crop. Its tremendous productivity results from special photosynthetic mechanisms it shares with sugar cane and certain other plants that are adapted to hot climates.

Experimental studies have explained this unusual productivity in hot weather. Radioactive carbon entering these species as labeled carbon dioxide is first detected in four-carbon compounds. Only later does this traceable carbon appear in the usual photosynthetic products (Fig. 21.15). Thus these plants, known as C-4 species, have different pathways for the fixation of carbon dioxide than do other species (referred to as C-3 plants). The enzyme that incorporates carbon dioxide into compounds of the C-4 pathway has been shown to be more efficient at low carbon-dioxide concentrations

FIGURE 21.15 **C-4 Photosynthesis.** The leaves of C-4 plants have a two-layered organization of photosynthetic cells. The outermost layer of mesophyllic cells is near the stomata and the intercellular air spaces. The function of the cells is to capture carbon dioxide and transfer it to the innermost layer, the bundle sheath cells that manufacture the photosynthetic product. Mesophyllic cells contain C-4 pathway enzymes that rapidly and efficiently fix carbon dioxide absorbed from the atmosphere. The process involves attachment of CO_2 to a three-carbon acceptor molecule (1). Carbon dioxide is carried to the underlying bundle sheath cells (2). Upon arriving inside the bundle sheath cells, the four-carbon intermediate is deprived of its carbon dioxide portion (3). This carbon dioxide is fed into the Calvin cycle (4). Eventually this carbon dioxide will appear in the photosynthetic product (5). As each four-carbon intermediate loses its carbon dioxide, the three-carbon acceptor is rejuvenated (6). It passes back into the mesophyllic cells (7) and is reused.

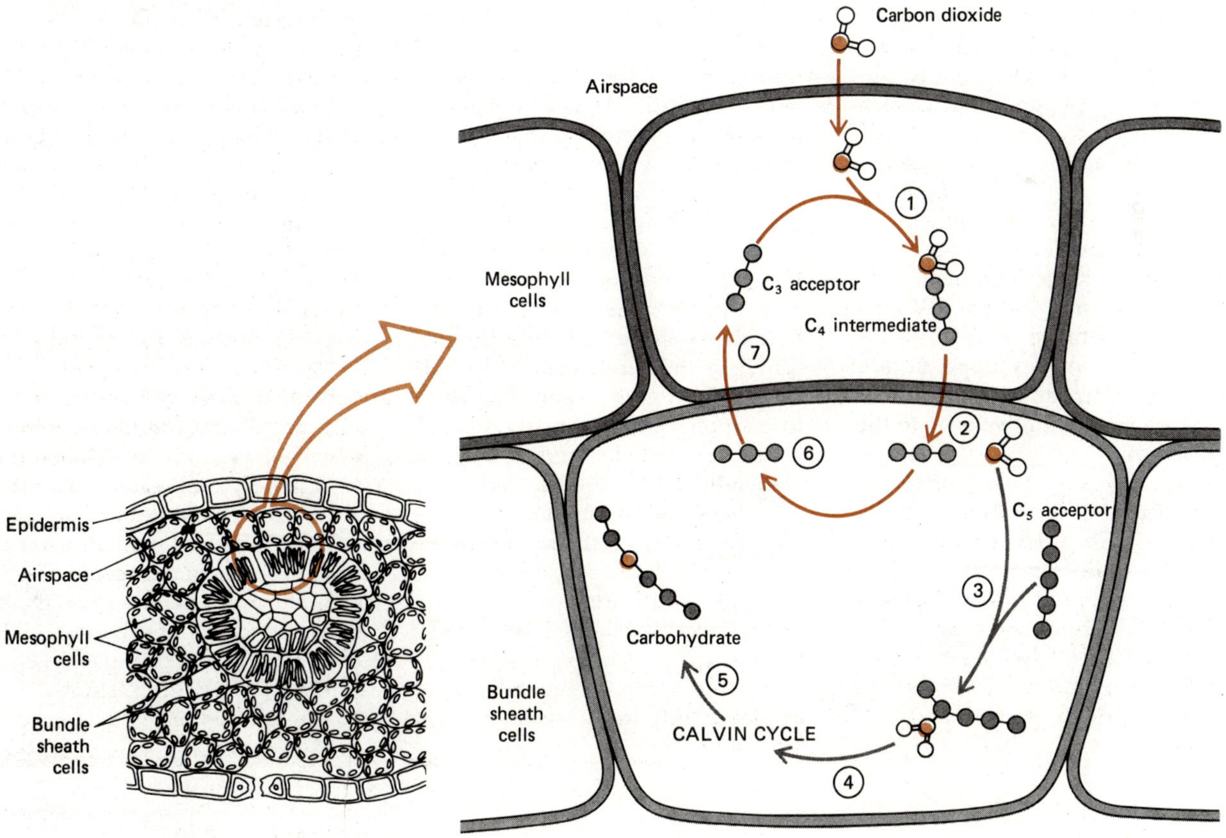

BOX 21B

HOW TECHNOLOGY HAS CHANGED WHAT WE EAT

Human diets have changed as much as any other aspect of our life. Most of our everyday foods are relatively new to Western diets. Consider what Europeans ate regularly 600 years ago.

In the cold, northern countries, where the main crops were rye and barley, rye bread was the staff of life. The barley was used to feed livestock and to make beer. Meals often consisted of only bread with a little butter or cheese, and they were washed down with an abundance of beer. Occasionally there was vegetable soup or a stew made with bits of salted meat.

Farther south, in the sunnier countries along the Mediterranean, the staples were wheat or barley bread, pasta (macaroni products made of flour and water), cheese (mostly from goats' milk), and grape wine. In large part, these diets were simply reflections of the foods that were available.

Before Columbus discovered the New World, tomatoes, peanuts, corn, chocolate, squash, white potatoes, red and green peppers, turkey, green beans, lima beans, navy beans, and all the other common table beans were unknown in Europe. Each of these familiar foods is the product of a species native only to the Americas.

Not only were New World crops missing from fourteenth-century Europe, but products of Africa and the Orient were unknown or at least rare and expensive. Until Dutch merchants established a worldwide sea trade, coffee, tea, cinnamon, cloves, nutmeg, ginger, pepper, and many other spices came to Europe by overland caravans or not at all.

Except for honey, there were no concentrated sweets. Sugar-cane plantations were developed only after the great sailing ships made world commerce a reality. Sugar beets became a second commercial source of sucrose (table sugar) in the nineteenth century.

Finally, many other products that we now take for granted were once available only seasonally or were generally scarce. In medieval Europe farm animals were used mainly to pull plows. Seldom was there sufficient hay and grain to grow cattle solely for meat. In some areas there was a thriving sheep industry, but sheep were kept primarily as a source of wool.

Although cows were used as draft animals, they were also milked as much as possible. But during the long winter months milk production waned. Often the cows were bred so that their calves would be born in the spring when the meadows turned green. Then, for a short period, there was an abundance of milk to be made into butter or cheese and stored for the year ahead. Although the butter was heavily salted, without refrigeration it inevitably turned rancid long before all of it was eaten.

Chickens, ducks, and geese were allowed to run free and were expected to pick up most of their food around the barnyard. Of course, predators got their share of these birds. The scarcity of fowl made each an asset to be sacrificed only for a special feast. Eggs were dear and generally available only in the spring, when the birds responded to increasing day length by building nests and laying eggs as wild birds do. At present, commercial egg production still peaks in the spring, but hens lay year-round, because they are kept under electric lights for 18 hours a day.

In Europe several centuries ago, consumption of fruits and vegetables was limited by storage problems, as well as by geography and climate. Some vegetables, such as carrots and turnips, nuts, and certain fruits, could be stored over winter in underground cellars that were cool and dry but protected from frost. Cucumbers or cabbage submerged in crocks of salt brine would support the growth of native bacteria. These microorganisms produced lactic acid that converted the produce into pickles or sauerkraut. In warm climates, dates and figs were dried, and grapes were dehydrated to make raisins. Except for the introduction of canning in the nineteenth century, these storage techniques were the only methods available until the development of refrigeration in the 1920s.

European diets in medieval times may sound dreary, but nineteenth-century fare was often worse. Although the well-to-do ate much as they do today, families of British industrial laborers lived largely on bread made with white flour, molasses or jam, and tea. The working men ate what little meat the family could afford. For many people the technological advances of the industrial revolution were accompanied by abominable nutrition, stunted growth, and poor health.

than is the carbon-dioxide-fixing enzyme of C-3 species. In hot weather, stomata must be closed to conserve water; this reduces the availability of carbon dioxide. Under these conditions C-3 species are handicapped by insufficient carbon dioxide. Thus C-4 plants have an advantage on bright, hot days. In addition to corn, crop species with C-4 metabolism include sugar cane, sorghum, and rice. The C-4 metabolism of crabgrass permits this lawn weed to overgrow the highly valued Kentucky bluegrass during hot weather. C-4 metabolism also occurs in plants other than grasses.

Hybrid Vigor. Corn naturally cross-fertilizes. Constant cross-pollination over the ages has favored genetic systems in which heterozygotes are more vigorous than homozygotes. This is known as **hybrid vigor.** Although the mechanisms underlying hybrid vigor remain unclear, its existence in corn is of great practical importance. Commercial corn crops are grown from hybrid seed that contain desirable genes in the heterozygous state. Because heterozygous plants produce offspring of several
259 types (don't breed true),□ seed to grow hybrid corn must be obtained from crosses of homozygous strains. This production of hybrid seed is a big business, based on careful planning and control of pollination.

Legumes. Legumes are cultivated almost everywhere. Their high protein content (usually 25 percent or more) makes them valuable despite a lower yield per acre than that obtained from grains. As mentioned previously, amino acids essential to the human diet are better represented in legumes than in grains.

The high protein content of legumes is asso-
431 ciated with their abundant nitrogen supply.□ Symbiotic bacteria in legume root nodules fix atmospheric nitrogen and make it available to the legume. This symbiotic relationship accounts not only for the high protein content of legumes, but also for the fact that they thrive in the poorest of soils. Thus legumes make proteins available to the people of regions where proteins are most needed.

Nitrogen-rich legumes also contribute to the human food supply indirectly. Clover and alfalfa are legumes that produce nutritious fodder for cattle. Traditionally, legumes are alternated with grains in a crop-rotation plan. A field in clover for a year or two will be greatly enriched with nitrogen. If wheat or corn is then planted in that field, it will produce heavily.

Legumes are also used as winter cover crops. Planted in fall in mild climates, they serve to reduce erosion on otherwise bare land. When plowed under in spring before the major crop is planted, these legumes provide humus as well as nitrogen enrichment.

Obviously, the nitrogen supply of legumes depends on presence of the proper bacteria. Although these bacteria may be present in the soil, many farmers dust their legume seed with a commercial mixture containing the bacteria.

Herbivores Depend on Microbial Digestion of Cellulose. Cattle, sheep, and goats are closely related. The ancestors of these and other hoofed mammals evolved at the time that grasses appeared. Cattle and sheep are especially adapted to graze on grasses. Goats can thrive by browsing on shrubs or low tree limbs. This ability to tolerate rough food makes goats especially destructive to natural vegetation.

All herbivorous mammals convert plant materials into meat, but some can use cellulose, the most abundant plant compound. This major component of plant cell walls is totally useless to humans as a foodstuff, because we lack the enzyme **cellulase,** which digests cellulose into glucose. Cattle, sheep, and goats provide access to the energy of cellulose through activity of the microbial symbionts in the **rumen,** one of their several stomach chambers (Fig. 21.16).

The rumen serves as a giant fermentation tank in which bacteria and protozoa digest cellulose. Neither the cow nor any other multicellular animal can secrete the cellulase necessary to carry out this digestion. Production of this enzyme is limited to protozoa, fungi, and bacteria. **Ruminants** (animals with a rumen), termites, and other animals that use cellulose do so through the activity of symbiotic microorganisms.

Within the rumen, bacterial fermentations produce many fatty acids that the cow or other host absorbs directly. Ruminants obtain additional nutrition through digestion of the tremendous numbers of microorganisms that grow in the rumen. These pass along with the food to be digested farther down the digestive tract.

Microorganisms in the rumen also increase their host's nitrogen utilization. Herbivores in general are unable to exploit all the amino acids in their diet, because plant amino acids occur in proportions that are different from those needed by animals. In the rumen, microorganisms use the plant

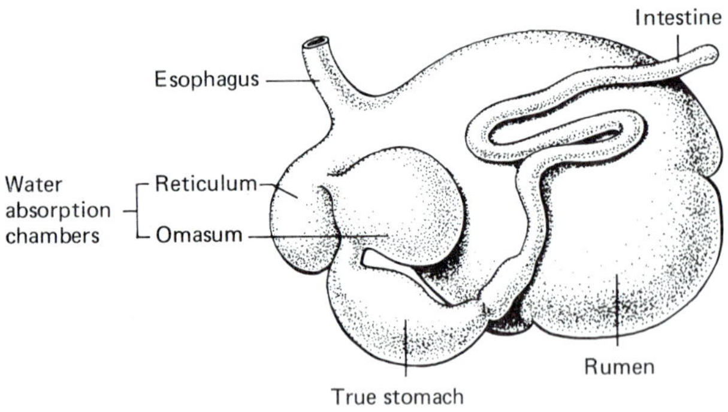

FIGURE 21.16 The Ruminant Stomach. The typical ruminant, such as a cow, eats a large volume of low-nutrient food, including grass or hay. Filling the stomach is a time-consuming process, and the animal chews the food only enough to permit it to be swallowed. From the esophagus the food initially enters the rumen, where it undergoes microbial digestion. Later, when the animal is at rest, it regurgitates food from the rumen in mouthfuls and chews this "cud" at its leisure. After the plant cell walls have been broken down by microorganisms and the food has been finely chewed, it is permitted to pass into the remaining chambers of the stomach. In the second and third chambers, water from the extensive salivary gland secretions is reabsorbed. The fourth chamber is the "true stomach," where digestive enzymes such as pepsin are secreted. Draw arrows on the diagram to show the passage of food through this highly specialized stomach.

amino acids as a nitrogen source to synthesize microbial amino acids, many of which are valuable to animals.

Urea recycling is another way that cattle manage their nitrogen supply. All animals oxidize excess amino acids for energy and incorporate the waste nitrogen into urea, which is largely excreted in the urine. Cattle secrete some urea in their saliva and thus recycle it to the rumen. There the urea provides an auxiliary nitrogen source for microorganisms and permits them to make even more amino acids. Although pigs are not ruminants, they, too, obtain energy from cellulose through the activity of symbionts. These symbionts occupy the **caecum,** a sac at the posterior end of the small intestine.

Cattle Management. Although beef is popular in many parts of the world, it is one of the most expensive meats. The high cost can be traced to the low efficiency of cattle in converting plant protein into meat protein (Table 21.3). Although rumen symbionts permit cattle to tap photosynthetic products that humans themselves can't use, this potential advantage is wasted when cattle are fed grains that people can eat.

According to standards set by the U.S. Department of Agriculture (USDA), the top grades of **beef** are marbled with fat. Fat adds flavor to meat, but its presence is also a reflection of the fact that the animals have been well fed but have had little opportunity for exercise. Lack of exercise retards development of tough connective tissues and keeps the muscles (meat) tender. Since most of the fat is trimmed off or melted away during cooking, almost all the calories used to fatten animals are ultimately wasted.

The active and aggressive nature of **bulls** (males) causes them to exercise more than females do. To prevent excessive activity and keep the meat tender, bull calves destined for the market are castrated. This removal of the testes makes them **steers.**

Like other female mammals, a cow secretes **milk** after giving birth. Although genetic factors certainly affect milk production, the continued stimulus of nursing prolongs milk secretion. In the 315 absence of a reflex initiated by the physical stimulus of nursing, the anterior pituitary ceases to secrete the hormone **prolactin,** and the mammary gland "goes dry." Continued regular milking maintains the reflex and increases the amount of milk from one pregnancy. Nevertheless, milk production gradually dwindles. Usually cows are bred about once a year and permitted to "go dry" some two months before they are to give birth. Thus each animal produces milk approximately ten months a year.

Bulls whose daughters are champion milk producers are in high demand to sire calves. So are those whose offspring grow rapidly and develop

TABLE 21.3 Efficiency of Conversion of Plant Protein into Animal Protein

PRODUCT	PERCENT EFFICIENCY
Milk (cows')	31–35
Eggs (chicken)	27
Chicken (young)	17
Rabbit (young)	17
Pork	9.4
Mutton	9
Lamb	6
Beef	6–6.5

(a)

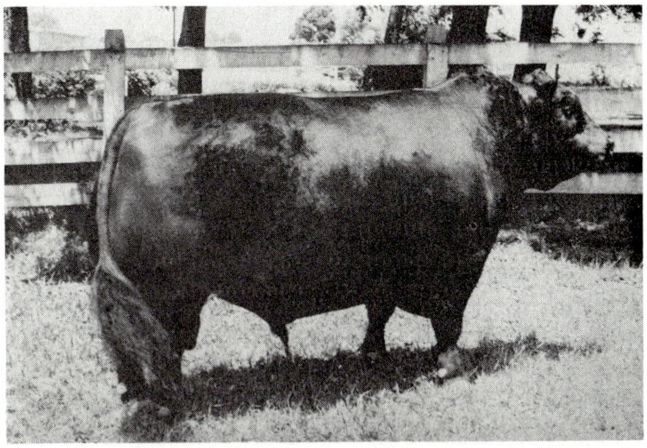

(b)

(c)

(d)

FIGURE 21.17 **Beef Breeds.** The Texas Longhorn (a) and the Black Angus (b) represent two extremes for selection of meat animals from the auroch, the original wild species that was domesticated to become the various types of European cattle. American Brahmans (c) are derived from the humped cattle of India. The Santa Gertruda (d) is a breed recently derived from crosses between Brahman and Shorthorn. The Shorthorn is a breed traceable to European stock.

into heavy beef animals. Through **artificial insemination** it is possible to increase the number of calves a single bull can father and to reduce expenses associated with breeding. The process requires only that semen be taken from the male and placed in the vagina of the cow.

For years bull sperm banks have served to multiply the offspring of bulls that carry genes for particularly desirable traits. Semen can be collected from individual bulls as often as twice a day (Fig. 21.18). A single bull ejaculate contains enough sperm to impregnate several hundred cows. Diluted semen can be stored for years in liquid nitrogen at − 196°C (− 321°F) and can be shipped without deterioration. Coupled with careful selection, artificial insemination provides an economical means of improving herd quality anywhere in the world.

FIGURE 21.18 **Collecting Bull Semen.** An artificial vagina is used here to obtain semen from a bull water buffalo. The ejaculated semen collects in the test tube hanging from the artificial vagina the attendant is holding.

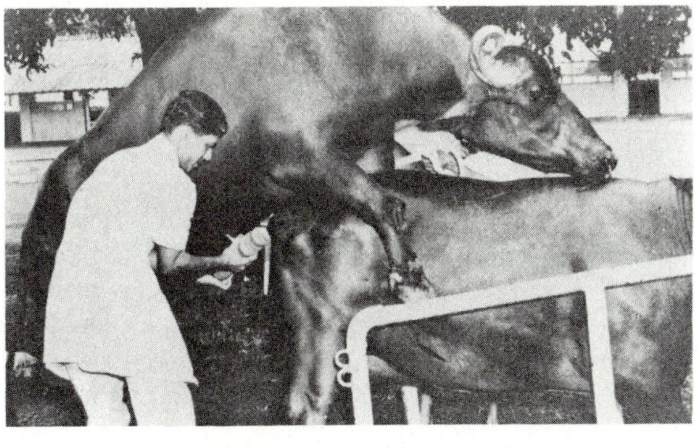

PROSPECTS FOR EXPANDED FOOD PRODUCTION

Increasing human populations create demands for greater and greater food production. While the United States had real surpluses during the 1970s, there was starvation in several parts of the world. This starvation could have been prevented, as many claimed, by establishing proper food-distribution networks and by feeding less grain to livestock and using it instead for human food. But even if we assume that political, economic, and social adjustments can achieve a more equal distribution of supplies, production must be enlarged if supplies are to keep up with population growth. Present production is insufficient to feed future world populations, even if population growth is limited according to the most optimistic estimates.

Genetic Improvements

Much of the hope for increased productivity lies in continued selection of new varieties of plants and new breeds of animals. The past record suggests this is an important strategy. During the 1960s, international efforts to develop new varieties of wheat were highly successful. This work was heralded as the beginning of a "green revolution." Much of the productivity of the new wheats depended on their stronger, stiffer, and often shorter stems, which can support the large heads of grain that result from generous fertilization and irrigation. Wheat yields increased in many countries, especially among large operations that invested heavily in fertilizers and water. Similar but less dramatic increases emerged from cooperative efforts to develop new varieties of rice, corn, and lentils.

Comparison of average yields with maximum yields shows that much remains to be done. Part of the problem lies in the fact that the new varieties are not well adapted to problem habitats. Recent development of a relatively salt-tolerant wheat illustrates the potential for varieties suited to special conditions. It may even be possible to select varieties that would thrive when irrigated with sea water.

Traditional methods introduce selected traits through hybridization. For successful fertilization and production of fertile hybrids, the two parent strains must be fairly closely related. Newer methods permit biologists to combine traits from very different species. One approach to producing fundamentally different plants combines techniques that fuse cells of different species and methods through which an entire sexually reproductive plant is grown from a single cell (Fig. 21.19). In this way, genes of widely separated species can be combined to obtain plants quite unlike either parent. For example, it might prove possible to develop a wheat strain capable of symbiotic nitrogen fixation. Alternatively, recombinant DNA techniques might be used to introduce nitrogen-fixing genes into a wide range of soil bacteria.

All the potential for selecting and combining traits depends on a source of variability. Biologists cannot make new genes to order; they can only recombine existing ones. In the past, whenever new mutants of old plant diseases threatened a crop, new disease-resistant varieties were introduced. Plant breeders regularly sent out professional collectors to find new stocks with resistant genes. Much of the huge grain production of the United States relies on disease-resistant genes obtained from abroad. But today collectors sent to foreign countries often return empty-handed. Most of the innumerable local varieties have been replaced with a few well-known kinds. One day, when mutations in pest microorganisms make present varieties obsolete, the only place to turn for new genes may be the random mutants produced by radiation. Sorting through these could be prohibitively expensive.

It is possible to preserve all still-existing varieties in **seed banks** to prevent further loss of variation. However, this is a costly undertaking, for the seeds must be planted and harvested regularly. The enormity of such a task is apparent when we consider that one international seed bank is attempting to maintain 60,000 different rice strains!

The hope for increased production through genetic manipulation is overshadowed by ultimate limits on available water, on minerals such as phosphorus, and even on energy resources (Fig. 21.20). But the most important limiting resource may be land.

There's Only So Much Land

Food production is limited as much by land as by any other factor. Only a small portion of the continents (24 percent of the ice-free area) is at all suitable for agriculture. Temperature, rainfall, soil type, and slope restrict use of much of this land. Obviously, some regions are more adaptable to intensive agriculture than others. To try to "stretch the

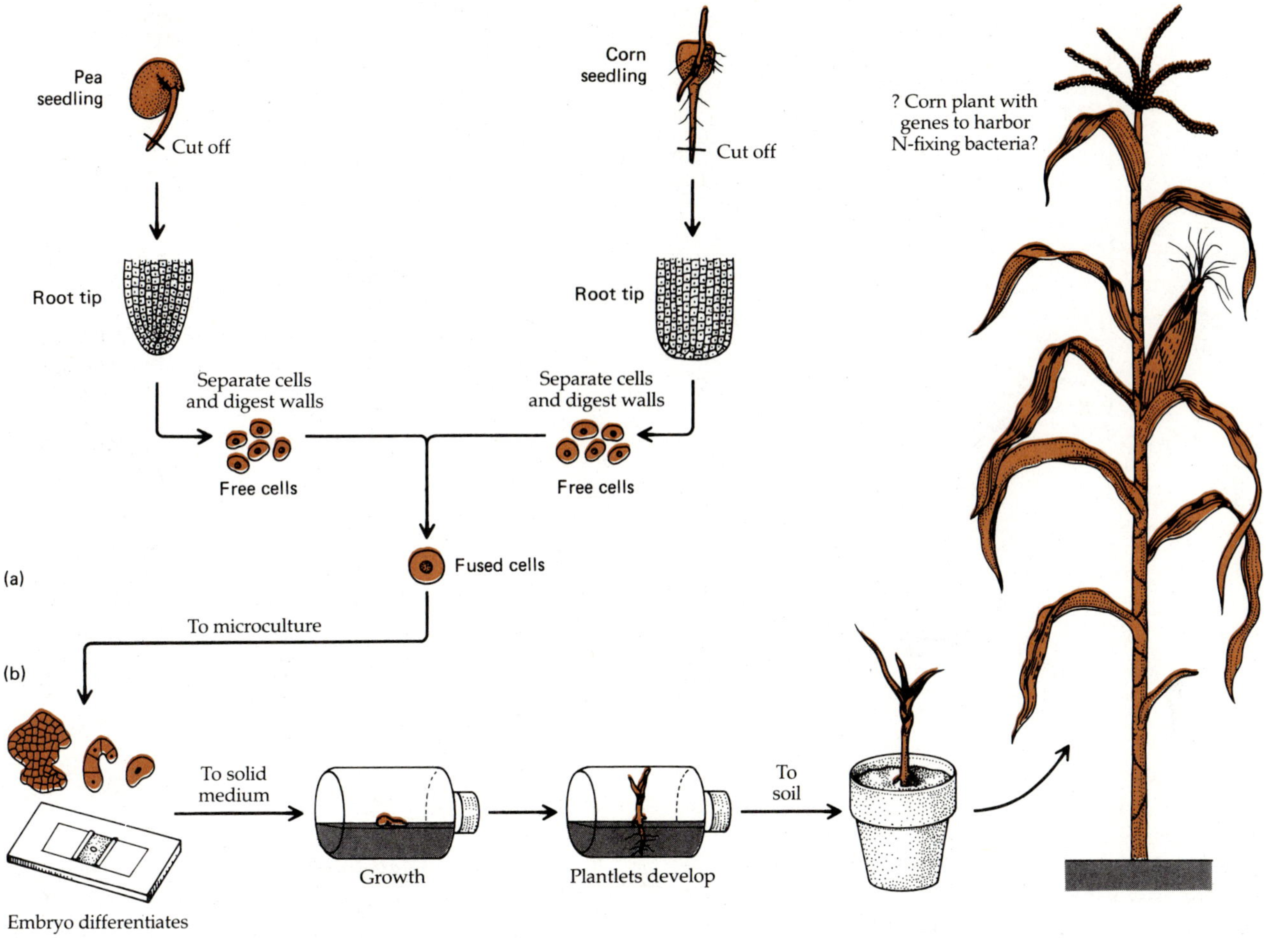

FIGURE 21.19 **Scheme for Development of Corn that Harbors Nitrogen-Fixing Bacteria.** At present it is possible to isolate plant cells from their cell walls and to cause two or more cells to fuse into a "supercell" (a). Fused cells generally lose many of their chromosomes, but a few attain a stable set with genes from both parents in a combination that permits long-term survival. By another technique, ordinary single plant cells can be grown into mature, sexually reproducing plants (b).

limits" and use land for purposes to which it is ill suited is to take serious risks. Wherever the environment is only marginally adequate for the crops attempted, production will be unpredictable. The fact that the U.S.S.R. has so many "crop failures" results in large part from attempts to grow wheat and other grains in near-deserts or where the average growing season is barely long enough for the crop to mature. Weather that is well within the range of normal for these regions can be totally unsuited for the crops planted.

Although expansion of the acreage under cultivation invites crop disasters, growing populations are gobbling up good agricultural lands for other purposes. In the United States thousands of acres are removed from farm use each year and "developed" for homes, schools, shopping centers, or factories. The problem is so serious that some areas have instituted rural zoning in an attempt to preserve agricultural land.

While we are facing the fact that most of the land suited to food production is already in use, we must also recognize that many countries have limited potential for food production. This is especially true of the tropical countries lush with rain forests. Visitors often view the tropics as a paradise; but the truth is that many of these lands are not particularly rich in agricultural resources.

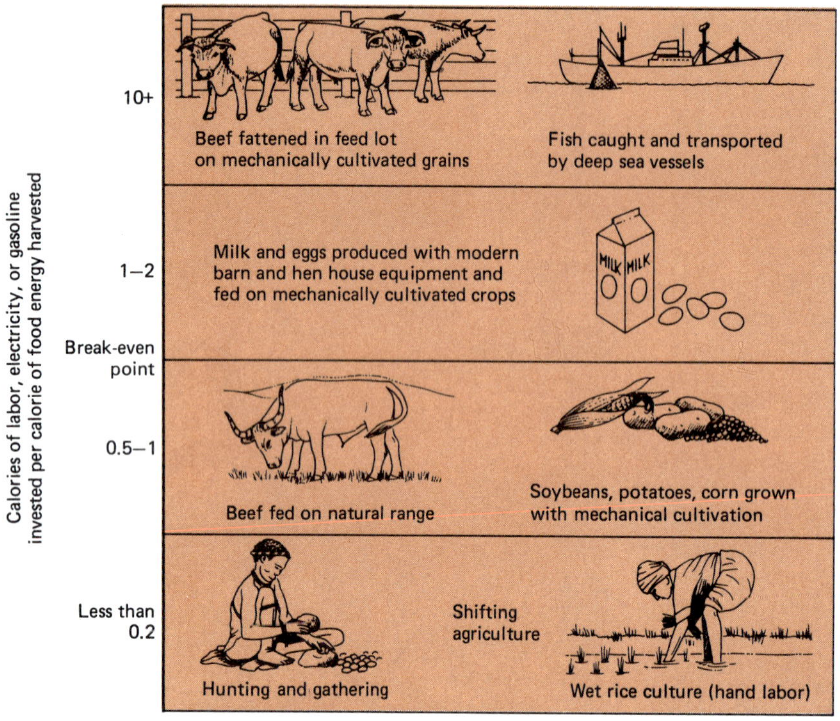

FIGURE 21.20 **It Takes Energy to Get Energy—but How Much?** Growing and harvesting any crop requires energy. Without the ability to tap other energy sources, this must be the energy of human muscles. Obviously, the human energy invested must be less than that obtained (from the diet as a whole). As shown above, primitive agricultural systems using hand labor require less than 0.2 calorie input for each calorie of food obtained. All modern mechanical food production systems require several times more energy than hand-labor techniques do.

Climate and Soil. Tropical rain forests (and the jungles that develop where such forests are destroyed) give a misleading impression of fertility. The great volume of plant material exists only because of a nearly closed nutrient cycle that conserves the limited mineral supply. When leaves fall or plants or animals die, the minerals released by decay are picked up immediately by plant roots.
431 Loss of nutrients through leaching▫ is minimal.

Although this tight nutrient cycle supports lush natural vegetation, agricultural productivity is modest. Bulldozing or burning of large tracts breaks the closed nutrient cycle and allows loss of minerals. This loss occurs because the newly planted crops fail to produce roots quickly enough to absorb minerals released from decaying vegetation or ashes. Now, with daily rain and warm temperatures, rapid leaching occurs. The minerals that once supported the forest simply wash away. When fertilizers are added to these soils, some components leach out; others, such as phosphorus, may be bound so tightly that they are unavailable to plants.

Climate and Pests. Large-scale agriculture almost always means a monoculture. Of course, monocultures invite competition from insects, fungi, and other organisms. But in tropical climates the situation is worse than in temperate areas. One problem is that insects reproduce the year around. In contrast, winter cold of temperate zones stops pest multiplication. Some species are able to complete only one generation before frost; others manage several generations each year, but the rigor of winter always curtails the number that survive. The next spring the population must rebuild from only a few individuals. This restraint on pests is missing in the tropics. As a consequence, plagues threaten fields of single crops.

Nevertheless, native vegetation largely escapes insect damage. How is this possible? First, like wild plants everywhere, tropical forest species synthesize chemicals that are repugnant or poisonous to most insects. Only a few kinds of insects have evolved biochemical mechanisms to tolerate the natural repellents of a particular plant species. Hence most plants of the tropical forest are immune to attack by most insects. But because humans also find these natural repellents unpleasant or even toxic, such natural safeguards have been reduced or eliminated in the selection of varieties used for food.

Native vegetation derives an additional advantage from its diversity. So many species are present in tropical rain forests that there is room for only a few individuals of each kind in any given area. For this reason, as well as because host toxins limit each pest to only a few species, no pest has a large food supply. Furthermore, two plants of the same kind are seldom sufficiently close together for pests to spread easily from one to another. When forests are converted into plantations, the scattered populations with natural repellents are replaced with solid stands of a single species. And that species usually lacks natural repellents and is thus palatable to many kinds of insect pests. It isn't surprising that tropical plantations have received massive doses of insecticides.

Often tropical agriculture is hampered not only by climate and soil properties, but also by the crops that are planted there. Domesticated plants, unlike the native plant community, are seldom adapted to this habitat. In tropical forests as many as 50 percent of trees have symbiotic nitrogen-fixing microorganisms. Other native plants harbor mycor-
465 rhizal fungi that scavenge minerals and supply them to the roots of their hosts. Except for the nitrogen-fixing symbionts of legumes, such built-in partners are lacking in domestic crops.

A Wet Breadbasket? There is a modern myth concerning food from the sea. Mention of impending famine can excite enthusiastic descriptions of "untapped fisheries," "marine agriculture," and "algal foods." Exactly how much food we can extract from the ocean no one knows. The amount of photosynthesis that occurs, the number of steps in the food chain, and the species we will eat all affect the answer. But the prospect for greatly expanded yields of human food from the ocean is, in fact, dim.

In the ocean, as elsewhere, there is less food at each succeeding level of the food chain. If people
489 could collect phytoplankton efficiently, and if they would eat it, we would have thousands of times more food than can ever be obtained from fish. But the cost of the harvest would be tremendous, and the food would surely be unacceptable. It seems likely that the only major food source we have in the sea is the fish.

Although a number of fishery biologists take issue with the figure, it has been estimated that sustained fish production for human consumption cannot far exceed 100 million tons a year. This figure is not much larger than present catches. The history of fisheries in the North Atlantic and adjacent seas supports the contention that we are nearly pushing the limit of ocean productivity. If we take the rule that a fishery is overexploited whenever increased effort in terms of vessels and quality of equipment fails to increase the catch, these waters are already overfished. The catch of one species after another has increased with increased fishing pressure, and then declined.

Some fishery experts argue that many fish stocks are underutilized at present. Undoubtedly this is true, but when the fishing pressure is switched to these stocks, they will collapse as well. We must remember that the question is: "Can the ocean be expected to yield significantly more fish permanently than it does at present?" The answer is "No."

Mariculture, as sea farming is known, has been touted as a way of using the sea to feed increasing human populations. Most of the techniques of mariculture are simple; some are thousands of years old. Oyster culture is a common example. By placing old oyster shells in healthy oyster beds, people provide places for the larval oysters to settle. Then the old shells with the attached baby oysters are moved to new beds that have been cleared of predators and fenced to keep predators out. Alternatively, shells bearing the young oysters are strung on strings and hung from rafts in plankton-rich waters.

The strategy underlying mariculture is simple. People collect the desired species, maintain them where natural food is abundant, and protect them from predators. Unfortunately, this is practical with only a few species and in a few localities, usually
estuaries that are used for many other purposes 495
and are often polluted.

The Answer Doesn't Lie in Agriculture

The answer to the prevention of famine does not lie in agriculture or, for that matter, in increased use of oceanic resources. The productivity of each is inherently limited. For agriculture, soil, minerals, and water are all factors. So are the pest problems created by attempts to simplify ecosystems. We may stretch present production here and there, at least for a while, but we cannot expect to produce ever-increasing quantities of food. In fact, food production may eventually decline. In any case, we should never doubt that there is a limit to the number of people the world can feed. Consideration of food requirements alone makes it clear that continued survival of our species requires that our population growth end.

Summary

1. Agriculture strives to increase the food supply for human use by simplifying the ecosystem so as to make humans the only consumers. This is inherently difficult, because wherever there is a food supply, other species compete for the product. Pests become numerous because of the abundance of one species that can serve as a food source, as well as lack of controls that regulate populations of more complex ecosystems. Insects, fungi, and nematodes cause most of the problems.

2. Attempts to control insects with chemicals have met with limited success. Many pest species have evolved resistance to various insecticides. Because of low populations, entomophagous insects have evolved little resistance. Destruction of these species, which normally control herbivorous insects, has permitted increases in some pest species. Because DDT is lipid-soluble, it is retained in most organisms for their lifetime and accumulated in the food chain. Such accumulation has threatened certain carnivorous species.

3. Biological control includes use of natural insect pathogens, sex attractants, synthetic hormones that inhibit development, and release of sterile males. A promising approach for many crops is to integrate limited pesticide use with biological controls and cultivation practices unfavorable to insect pests. Herbicides can replace plowing to destroy competing plants. This no-tillage method also reduces erosion.

4. Nitrogen fertilizers are readily manufactured but at a high cost in energy. Phosphorus is mined from high-phosphate rocks of marine origin, and the supply is limited. The phosphorus cycle moves extremely slowly, with phosphates leaching from the soil and being deposited in the ocean. Irrigation can result in water shortages and salt accumulation in top soil.

5. High productivity makes domesticated grasses, such as corn, rice, and wheat, major plant crops. The fruit of these grains is readily harvested, and it stores well. Corn is a C-4 plant; i.e., it has a special pathway for fixation of carbon dioxide that permits high efficiency in hot weather. Because heterozygotes have greater vigor than homozygotes, corn is raised from hybrid seed. The nitrogen-fixing root symbionts of legumes permit them to produce protein-rich food and fodder.

6. Any herbivorous mammal with a rumen is able to digest cellulose through an enzyme secreted by symbiotic microorganisms. This ability allows animals such as cattle, sheep, and goats access to an abundant energy supply that is unavailable to most other animals. The advantage is wasted, however, when the ruminants are fed grains that humans could eat. Cattle are often improved by means of artificial insemination of cows with semen from selected bulls.

7. Selection of favorable combinations of traits offers opportunities for continued improvement of domestic plants and animals. Cell fusion, tissue culture, and recombinant DNA methods permit genes from widely divergent species to be brought together.

8. Future production will be limited by energy, water, and fertilizer supplies, but especially by the available land. The prospects for use of tropical forest soils is discouraging. These soils can support lush growth only because tight nutrient cycles operate there and because many native trees have nitrogen-fixing symbionts. Most species also produce substances that inhibit local insects. Also, the diverse forest does not support the buildup of pest populations. Large-scale agriculture breaks the nutrient cycles by promoting leaching. Planting huge populations of one crop lacking insect inhibitors promotes the buildup of pest populations in an environment where climatic control is absent.

9. Prospects for greatly increased food from the ocean are poor. Use of phytoplankton is not practical; mariculture depends on unusual conditions; and fish are now exploited at or near the maximum level of production.

10. Sustained growth of the food supply at a rate sufficient to support significantly increasing human populations seems unlikely.

Thought and Controversy

1. Natives of tropical forests have long relied on small garden plots cut into the forest. The plots aren't completely freed of vegetation; they are simply cut and burned. Surviving trees in and around the plot provide litter that reduces surface erosion and roots that claim minerals that might otherwise leach away. The garden plots are planted to a variety of species, and weeds are not controlled closely. After a year or two, the plot is abandoned in favor of a new one. Switching plots gets away from growing insect populations and taps a new mineral supply. Of course, successional vegetation invades the abandoned plots, and minerals gradually accumulate again. This method of agriculture is often known as **slash-and-burn** agriculture or **swidden** agriculture.

Where human numbers are low, cultures relying on swidden techniques may use a piece of land only once every 40 or 50 years. Unfortunately, increasing populations are causing more frequent use in many areas, and the vegetation is no longer able to regenerate and recover nutrients. This fact, together with pressure for production of "cash crops" that can be exported in exchange for the amenities of Western life, may doom a stable agricultural system.

Too often, slash-and-burn agriculture has been criticized as being only "subsistence" agriculture, as opposed to "profit" agriculture—as if long-term subsistence were not the fundamental goal of all people. In fact, the low population density supported by classical swidden practices may reflect the level of human populations that these tropical lands can feed permanently.

2. The "green revolution" was much more successful in some localities than in others. Many small farmers in underdeveloped countries can't afford the fertilizer necessary to realize the potential productivity of the new varieties. Nor can they afford expensive new seed or the energy or water for irrigation. There is also reluctance to accept new varieties. Despite the reputation for high yields, the new varieties are genetically uniform. Resistance to weather and pests can vary with local conditions. Even under the worst of conditions, at least some of the numerous time-tested native varieties are likely to produce. Because a single crop failure can mean starvation for the poor, the security of a minimum harvest every year is more important to them than the possibility of high yields.

3. Traditionally, hybrid corn seed was obtained by planting the two parent varieties in adjacent rows. The tassels at the top of the plant, where the male flowers are borne, were removed from one parent before fertilization, and seed was later collected only from the detasseled variety. Detasseling is a labor-intensive chore. Discovery of an inherited characteristic that prevented pollen production permitted development of a less expensive method of growing hybrid corn seed. Pollenless plants were soon in use as the female parent for all hybrid seed crosses. The 1970 epidemic of southern corn leaf blight provided ample evidence of the dangers this change entailed. A new strain of fungus suddenly appeared and attacked hybrid corn across the country. It seems that other traits that were carried along with the male-sterile condition rendered the hybrid corn susceptible to the mutant fungus. Corn blight swept from the Gulf States through the Midwest and into Canada. Yields were reduced in some places; fields were devastated in others. This anecdote suggests why some scientists are skeptical of a "green revolution" based on genetic manipulation of seed stocks. Do you believe such skepticism is justified?

4. The staples of temperate areas are grains unsuited to the continuously wet tropical lands, for such crops require a dry period in which to set seed. Therefore some tropical regions rely largely on plants propagated by root or stem cuttings. Most of the calories of diets in these regions come from manioc, taro, sweet potatoes, various kinds of yams, or some of a great variety of plantains and bananas. Unfortunately, these roots and fruits are rich in carbohydrates but poor in protein.□ How may diets built around such products 116
affect child development?

Questions

1. Explain in theoretical terms why agriculture is beset with pest problems. Exactly what is meant by "monoculture"?

2. What is the practical importance of entomophagous insects? Why are such insects so susceptible to insecticides?

3. Describe some biological methods that are promising in insect control. In practice, such methods are often integrated with other methods. What is the advantage of such integrated control?

4. What kinds of microorganisms are present in soil? Give some examples of how these organisms affect crop production.

5. How may future energy shortages affect agricultural production? Explain in terms of the agricultural uses of energy.

6. Discuss the phosphorus cycle. Why are supplies of phosphate fertilizer effectively limited?

7. Discuss the opportunities for increased food production that would result from development of salt-tolerant plant varieties.

8. Discuss the unusual biological characteristics of the grass we call "corn."

9. How do herbivores obtain the glucose that makes up the abundant cellulose in plant cell walls? Explain.

10. Why are the soils of lush tropical forests poor prospects for expansion of agricultural acreage?

22

Pollution: Resources Out of Place

IDEALLY THERE IS NO WASTED MATTER IN A STABLE ecosystem. Every atom or molecule released by one organism enters another. Normally, substances cycle continuously through ecosystems; plants, animals, and microorganisms thrive therein with only modest changes in numbers. Unfortunately the balanced interrelations that develop as the members of an ecosystem evolve is disrupted wherever people are abundant or wherever people have advanced cultures. In general, humans produce wastes of such a nature or in such quantities as to disturb natural ecosystems. It is the accumulation of these materials and their effects that make them "dirty" and allow them to pollute the environment. Every substance has some use if it is in the proper form, the right amount, and the suitable place. Therefore pollutants are really nothing but resources out of place.

People are the cause of pollution. The two most important factors contributing to pollution are the total number of people and the nature of their wastes. Obviously, increasing human population can increase the amount of wastes produced. Furthermore, present-day people create wastes that differ in kind from those of the past. To the nutshells, cracked bones, baked hearths, and fecal matter of primitive people we now add plastic bottles, junk autos, synthetic organic molecules ranging from detergents to DDT, concrete fragments, sulfuric acid, rusty tin cans, and aluminum cans that won't rust. The list seems to grow every day. However, the objects that clutter our landscape are but a minor part of the problem. It is the molecules that enter soil, water, and air that most threaten stability of the biosphere.

AIR: INDUSTRY AND AUTOS

Air is of overwhelming importance to life. The very nature of air makes its pollution a matter for public concern. We all breathe from the one large sea of air we call the **atmosphere.** Pollutants released into the atmosphere are spread widely by the wind. There is no practical way we can individually control the air we breathe. And because the weather is largely an atmospheric phenomenon, modifying the air can change world climates.

Atmospheric components are links in many biogeochemical cycles. Frequently air pollutants modify these cycles. Perhaps there is no better evidence of the significance of air pollution than its effects on the sulfur cycle.

The Sulfur Cycle Today

Sulfur enters the atmosphere mainly as sulfur dioxide (SO_2), hydrogen sulfide (H_2S), and sulfates (SO_4). Burning high-sulfur fuels, smelting ores that contain sulfur compounds, and processing paper pulp introduce some 100 million tons of SO_2 into the atmosphere each year. Volcanic gases contribute additional SO_2 but probably much less than that generated by human activity.

Acid Rain. Although sulfur dioxide itself is not particularly toxic to animals, it reacts with oxy-

gen and water in the atmosphere to form **sulfuric acid.** Both ultraviolet light and fine dusts
97 with catalytic□ properties speed this reaction. Suspended droplets of highly corrosive sulfuric acid constitute one of the most harmful of all air pollutants. Sulfuric acid slowly destroys iron, steel, and other metals. It affects paper and paint and attacks fabrics. This strong acid erodes marble and limestone statues and eats away building stone, cement, and mortar (Fig. 22.1). People who breathe the insidious sulfuric acid vapor develop chronic
136 bronchitis, asthma, and emphysema.□

Not surprisingly, atmospheric sulfur dioxide results in harm to plants as well as animals. Some thin-leafed species, such as alfalfa and cotton, are sensitive indicators of sulfur dioxide. Their leaves begin to bleach and dry in the presence of less sulfur dioxide than produces visible effects on structural materials or animals.

Sulfuric acid in the air produces acidic rainwater and lowers the pH of lakes and streams. Any pH below 7 is acidic. The smaller the number, the greater the acidity. Also, each decrease of one pH
unit represents a tenfold increase in acidity.□ In 58
areas such as the Cascade Mountains of Oregon, where there is minimal industrial pollution, the pH of rain averaged between 5.7 and 6.3 a decade ago. In contrast, values as low as pH 2.8 have been recorded for rain in Sweden, where air from the Ruhr Valley and Britain carries heavy loads of sulfuric acid (Fig. 22.2). A raindrop in Sweden may contain 1000 times more acid than one falling from unpolluted air.

Acid rainwater can leach nutrients from the soil, reducing fertility of farmland and forests. When the acid water reaches streams and rivers, they will be affected. Salmon runs have disappeared from streams in southern Norway, probably because of effects of acid water on hatching of eggs and development of the young.

Increasingly acidic rain in forests of north-central New Hampshire during recent years has been traced to practices intended to reduce, not aggravate, air pollution. In an attempt to prevent local soot accumulation, industrial operations in the American Midwest and Canada have installed soot-

FIGURE 22.1 **Air Erosion.** In 1908 this beautiful sandstone carving (a) was more than 200 years old. Sixty years later, German industrial pollution had nearly destroyed the statue (b).

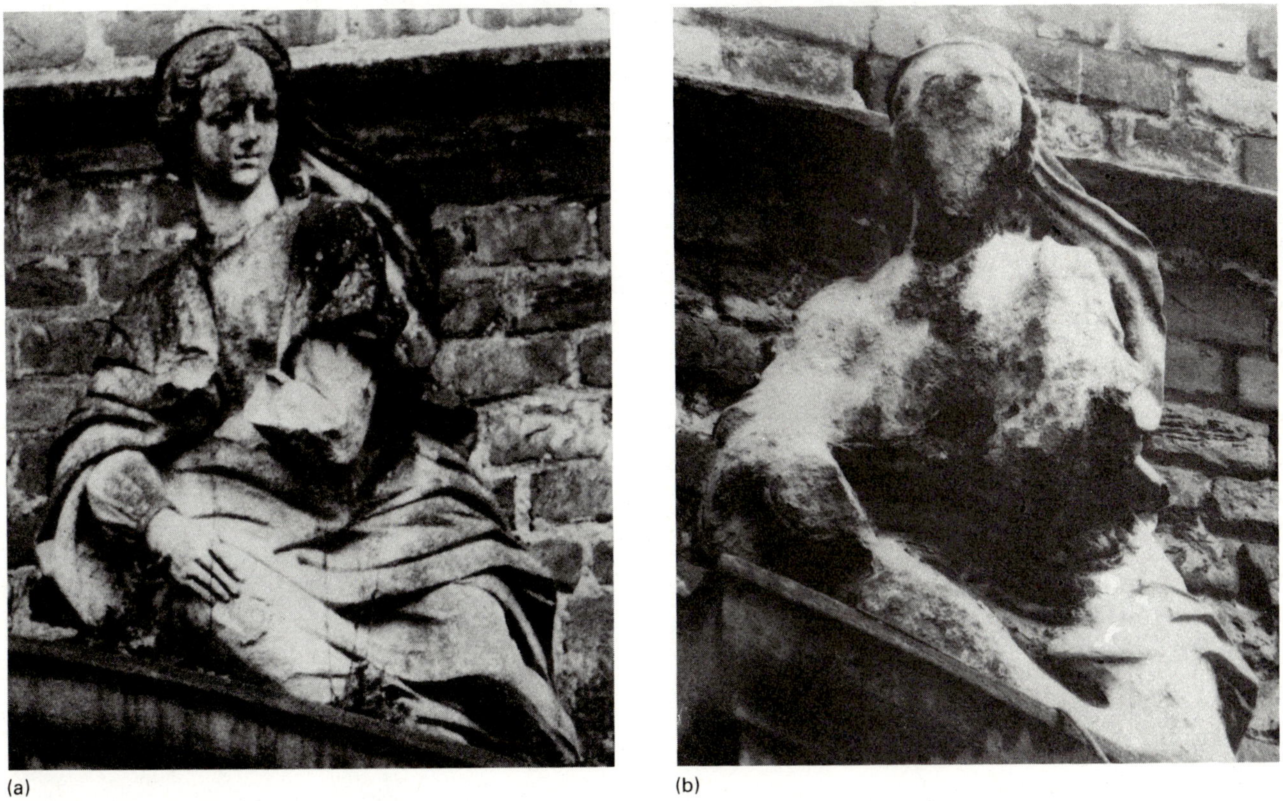

(a) (b)

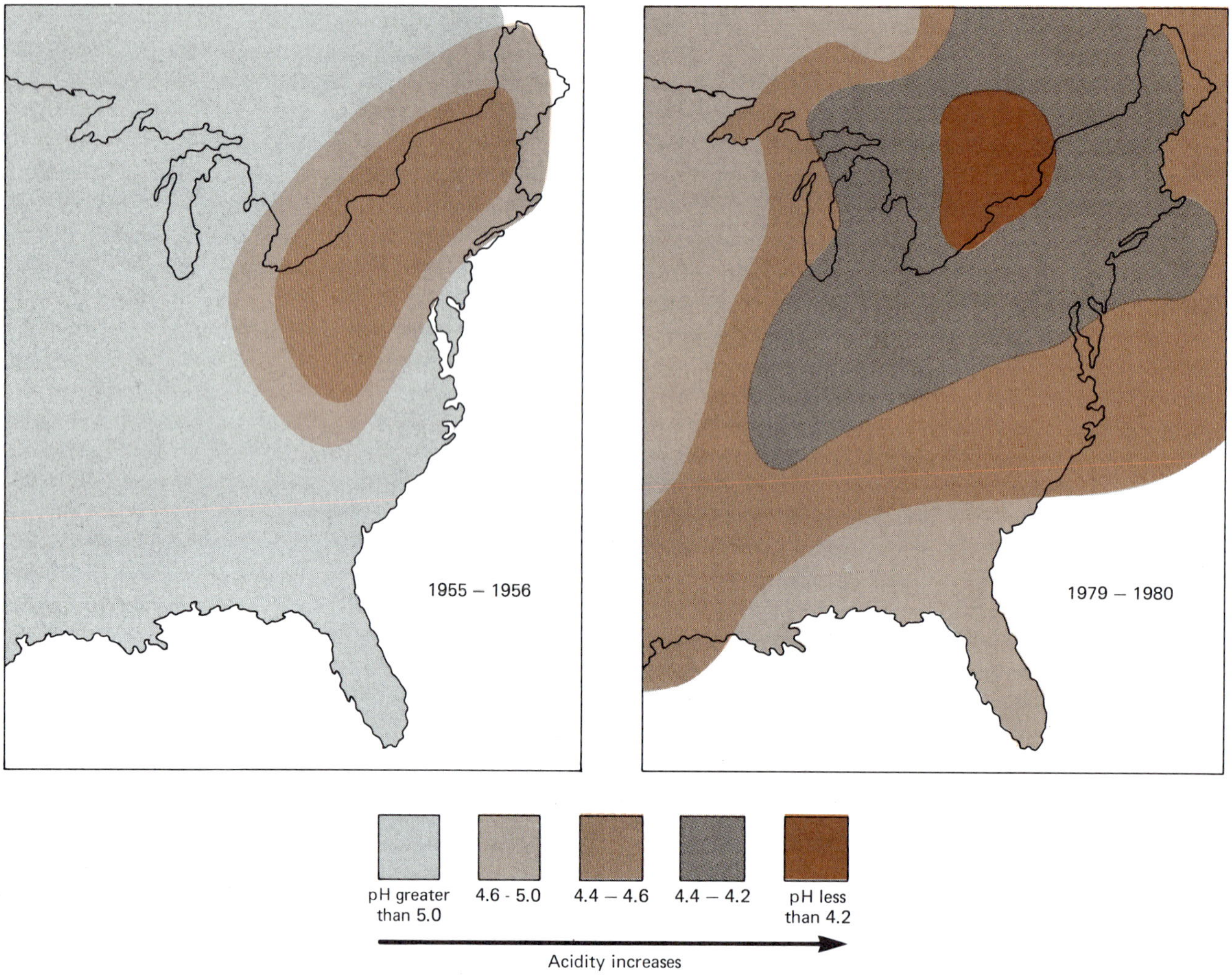

FIGURE 22.2 **Acid Rain in the Eastern United States.**

control devices in heightened smokestacks. Where once the soot catalyzed the conversion of SO_2 to sulfate, now, in its absence, the discharged SO_2 remains in the air to form sulfuric acid. The taller smoke stacks lead the SO_2 higher in the air, where currents carry it far from its source. The same industries that once produced local soot problems are now responsible for acid rain over a large region.

Sulfur dioxide and sulfuric acid eventually react with ammonia and other air contaminants to form ionic **sulfates** that fall to the earth as dust or dissolve in rainwater. Sulfates are quite harmless, and their distribution by the atmosphere is useful, because sulfur is an essential element for plant protein synthesis. Ocean spray also contributes sulfates to the atmosphere.

Because air pollutants such as sulfuric acid can be carried over long distances, states and nations tend to quarrel over the sources of pollution. There may be little local motivation to control sulfuric acid production when the damage is done elsewhere. Relationships between Canada and the United States have been strained over this issue. Present (1983) attempts to rewrite the Clean Air Act are stymied by controversy over whether the acid rain falling on the northeastern part of the United States originates in Canada or in the American Midwest.

Stench Can Be a Blessing. Anaerobic bacteria in soil and wetland muds reduce some of the sulfate from decaying organisms and release **hydrogen sulfide.** This gas is as poisonous as cyanide and

FIGURE 22.3 **The Sulfur Cycle Today.**

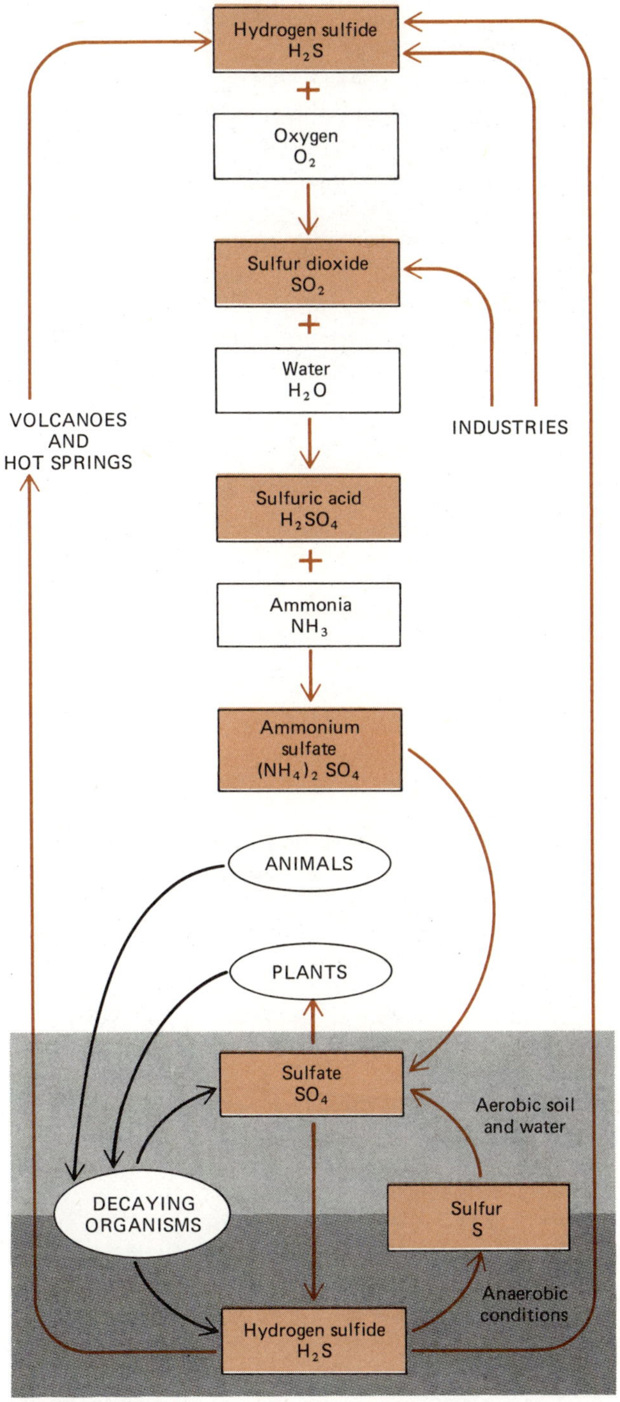

smells like rotten eggs. Refineries and petrochemical plants can also produce hydrogen sulfide, but fortunately the odor provides ample motivation for industries to keep atmospheric pollution well below toxic levels. Within soil, hydrogen sulfide may be oxidized by bacteria to sulfates, sulfur dioxide, or elemental sulfur. Hydrogen sulfide reaching the atmosphere reacts with oxygen to form sulfur dioxide. As summarized in Fig. 22.3, the sulfurous gases produced by human activities are added to those in the natural sulfur cycle and are eventually disposed of through the same processes.

Additions to the Carbon Cycle

Ideally, burning fossil fuel should release only carbon dioxide and water. Unfortunately, oxidation is sometimes incomplete, and much of the carbon appears as **carbon monoxide.** This colorless and odorless gas poisons animals by combining with hemoglobin and thus reducing the transport of oxygen by the blood.

Carbon monoxide combines with hemoglobin at the same site where oxygen normally does, but unlike oxygen, carbon monoxide clings tenaciously to hemoglobin for hours after exposure. Thus carbon-monoxide poisoning reduces the amount of hemoglobin▫ available to carry oxygen. 121

Probably people have breathed carbon monoxide since our ancestors first built open fires in caves or huts. At present, automobile exhausts account for most cases of carbon-monoxide poisoning. Air in stop-and-go traffic, highway tunnels, and underground parking and loading areas has as much as 70 parts per million (ppm) of carbon monoxide. Although this is only 0.007 percent, it is enough to reduce the oxygen-carrying capacity of the blood by 10 percent in those who spend a workday under these conditions. Carbon monoxide inhaled with cigarette smoke can further reduce the effectiveness of hemoglobin by 2–5 percent. Many people tolerate such losses just as they adapt to a moderate anemia▫ that also reduces the oxygen-carrying capacity of the blood. 121 Others are mentally dulled or suffer headache or dizziness. It is possible that some traffic accidents result from the mind-befuddling effects of low blood oxygen due to carbon-monoxide accumulation in the blood.

A thousand ppm of carbon monoxide is quickly lethal. The carbon-monoxide–hemoglobin complex is bright red. Hence individuals suffocated by carbon monoxide have a cherry-red complexion, in

BOX 22A

CLIMATE, ATMOSPHERE, AND CHANGE

Much of the energy that enters the biosphere as sunlight is converted into infrared radiation. Carbon dioxide absorbs infrared radiation and releases the energy as heat. Without atmospheric carbon dioxide, the energy of the infrared radiation would be lost to space. Thus the concentration of carbon dioxide in the atmosphere can affect the amount of heat retained in the atmosphere and contribute to modification of the climate.

In contrast to increases of carbon dioxide that tend to warm the biosphere, accumulations of dust cool the earth. When the sun's rays strike atmospheric dust particles, the light energy is reflected back into space. Therefore increased atmospheric dust results in the loss of more sunlight to the biosphere. With a reduction in sunlight that strikes the surface of the earth, there is less energy that can be converted into heat.

When Mt. Tambora on the isle of Sumbawa in Indonesia erupted heavily in 1815, the volcanic dust and gases that were forced into the higher atmosphere produced cool weather. Crop failures were widespread the following year. Snow fell in Boston during July and August of 1816, leading to that being remembered as the "year without a summer." Similar but less extensive effects followed the eruption of Mt. Katmai in the Aleutians during 1912, as well as other more recent eruptions.

Increases in atmospheric dust have been linked to the glacial episodes that marked the Pleistocene. Measurements of volcanic dust on the ocean floor indicate that Pleistocene times were marked by extensive volcanic eruptions. Some of this dust traces to vents of the major Cascade peaks, including Mt. St. Helens. Once large quantities of materials had been distributed in high air masses, they would surely have shaded the earth. With increased shade, less of the winter snowfall would have melted each summer, and the polar ice caps and mountain glaciers would have grown. The increased snow and ice may have further reduced temperatures, because the white surfaces reflect light rather than absorbing it and converting it to heat. Thus the cooling trend may have continued after the volcanic dusts settled, because the larger glaciers and polar caps reflected more light and reduced heat absorbed by the earth.

That volcanic activity initiated the Ice Ages is only a hypothesis—one among many. It seems likely that volcanic activity could initiate an ice age. Calculations show that a fourfold increase in suspended atmospheric particles would lower the average temperature by 3°C. This might be sufficient to initiate an "ice age." History substantiates the dramatic effect of atmospheric dust on general weather patterns.

The Pleistocene glaciations and their warmer interludes aren't the only puzzles often associated with climatic change. The extinction of many organisms, including the dinosaurs, toward the end of the Cretaceous is often attributed to climatic events. Whether volcanic activity or other weather-related events were involved remains unsettled. A recent explanation of the Cretaceous extinctions invokes collision of the earth with some extraterrestrial body.

contrast to the blue of people dying from simple lack of oxygen. Prolonged exposure to minute concentrations of carbon monoxide may also contribute to heart disease.

True Smog

Until recent years, the worst air pollution usually occurred in cold northern cities such as London, where a great deal of coal was burned. Smoke, sulfur dioxide, and carbon monoxide combine with cold fog to produce **smog.** Although air pollutants are produced continuously, true smog develops only when weather conditions prevent air movements or when there is no rain or snow to wash the air.

Unstable Air Columns. Ordinarily, air pollutants from cities and large industrial complexes are mixed into higher layers of the atmosphere. From here the pollutants are dispersed widely by the ever-present winds. This natural distribution of pollutants results from rising air currents. Generally, solar radiation warms the earth and adjacent surface air. Because heated air expands and becomes less dense, the warmed surface air rises. Heat pollution from factories and homes also helps lift air columns over cities. As the warm air rises, it expands further, because the force of gravity is reduced as the air recedes from the surface of the earth. The rising air creates a low-pressure area below it, and higher-pressure air from surrounding areas moves in to replace the warmed air. In this way columns of rising, expanding air are responsible for constant stirring of the atmosphere in many places (Fig. 22.4).

Stable Temperature Inversions. Under some conditions the usual temperature gradient of lighter, warmer air on the bottom and heavier, cooler air on top is reversed. Cold, dense air lies near the ground, with warmer, thinner air layered above. This is known as an **inversion.** Inversions may develop in rough country where hills lose heat faster at night than do pockets of air held over the valleys. The cooler and therefore denser air on the hillsides slides down to the valleys and forms a layer under the warm air. In a similar manner, cool ocean air can drift into protected bays and become trapped under warmer air masses that are displaced upward.

Cold, heavy air on the bottom and warmer, lighter air on top give a stable layering that resists mixing. The result is a stagnant air column. When such stable air layers lie over sources of air pollution, pollutants accumulate in the cold lower layer, because there are no air currents to carry them upward. Fog added to this dirty, stagnant air produces the kind of smog for which London was once famous. Fog arises from condensation in cooling air. Such condensation occurs because cold air can hold less water vapor than can warm air.

FIGURE 22.4 **Temperature Alters Air Circulation.** Cities are often warm, and they create heat islands (a). Here sunlight and heat pollution from homes and industries combine to warm surface air. This air expands, rises, and carries smoke and other pollutants upward, where high winds disperse them widely. On cold nights or during cold weather, certain cities lack sufficient heat to warm the surface air. If protected from wind, this cold dense air lies stagnant over the city and traps pollutants.

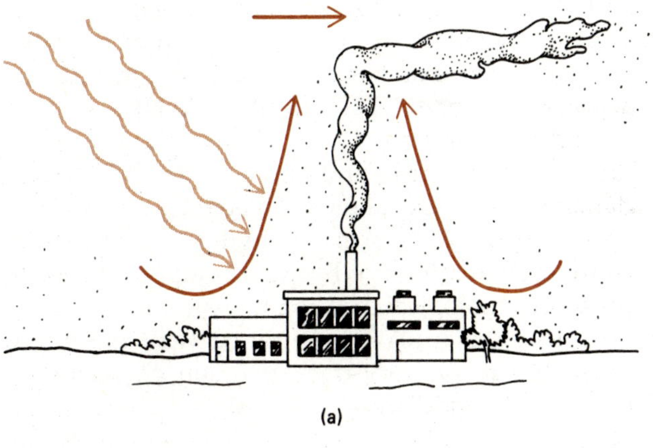

(a)

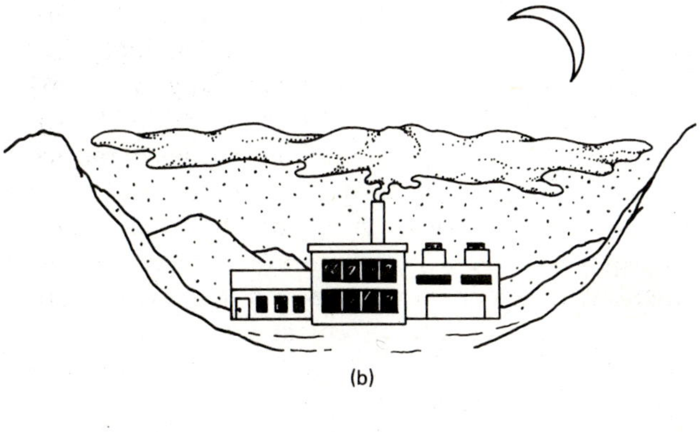

(b)

BOX 22B

DHANs AND NITROSAMINES: UNNATURAL CARCINOGENS IN NATURE

Human activities lead to the synthesis of many carcinogens within natural waters, in soil, and even in the food we eat. Attention centers on two groups of compounds formed by reactions of chemicals on naturally occurring substances.

- **Nitrosamines result when inorganic nitrogen compounds react with amines.**
- **DHANs are formed by the action of chlorine on amino acids or certain other organic molecules.**

Nitrogen oxides (NO and NO_2) in automobile exhausts; nitrate fertilizers; and the nitrates and nitrites used in preserving bacon can all supply the inorganic nitrogen necessary to form nitrosamines from amines. Decomposing proteins release amines in nature as do many industrial processes. Reactions that form nitrosamine occur spontaneously in the atmosphere and can also happen in our digestive systems.

Chlorine used to disinfect water supplies and treated sewage can convert innocent organic compounds into DHANs (dihaloacetonitriles). Waters of rivers such as the Mississippi that serve one city after another are cycled through water and sewage treatment plants again and again. There are numerous opportunities for organic substances to react with chlorine. DHANs aren't the only compounds formed. Chloroform, another carcinogen, was detected in the New Orleans water supply a few years ago.

It seems plausible that the increasing incidence of cancer results in large part from nitrosamines and DHANs. The fact that there are no documented cases of nitrosamine- or DHAN-induced cancer in people in no way invalidates this hypothesis. Only substances with very local distributions are easily associated with "epidemics" of malignancy. Carcinogens as widespread as nitrosamines and DHANs would cause an increase in malignancy throughout the entire population. Longstanding use of nitrates as food preservatives may account for some malignancies in preindustrial times.

Sunlight and Automobiles

With increased use of automobiles, an entirely different kind of smog has become a major problem in cities with warm climates. This **photochemical smog** is produced by irradiation of air pollutants, mainly pollutants from automobile exhausts. As a result, residents of once-sunny cities have become accustomed to living in an eye-smarting haze.

Exhaust Gases. Automobiles and other internal combustion engines burn fuel incompletely. Exhaust contains not only carbon dioxide and water, but also carbon monoxide and unburnt fuel. Operation of internal combustion engines at high temperatures also converts molecular nitrogen and oxygen from the air into nitrogen dioxide (NO_2). Attempts to redesign automobile engines to reduce emission of nitrogen dioxide are frustrated by the fact that the use of lower temperatures to reduce nitrogen dioxide production would increase production of carbon monoxide and loss of unburnt fuel. Nitrogen dioxide produces acute and chronic lung irritation, and it is as lethal as carbon monoxide. Just as sulfur dioxide can react with moisture to form sulfuric acid, so nitrogen dioxide and water form highly corrosive nitric acid.

Photochemical Smog. In addition to causing this direct harm, nitrogen dioxide is a crucial component of photochemical smog. The molecular structure of NO_2 causes it to absorb blue light and near-ultraviolet radiation. The energy of this radiation dissociates nitrogen dioxide into nitric oxide (NO) and atomic oxygen (O). As shown in Fig. 22.5, the atomic oxygen contributes to formation of ozone (O_3) and also oxidizes hydrocarbons. Further reactions yield **peroxyacyl nitrates (PAN).**

PAN damages both plants and animals. It inhibits photosynthesis and kills plant tissues. Leaves damaged by PAN take on a characteristic metallic appearance. PAN reacts with hydrocarbons to form **formaldehyde** (the eye-burning compound used to preserve zoological specimens) and many other noxious substances. These along with nitric acid cause the respiratory-tract irritation characteristic of photochemical smog.

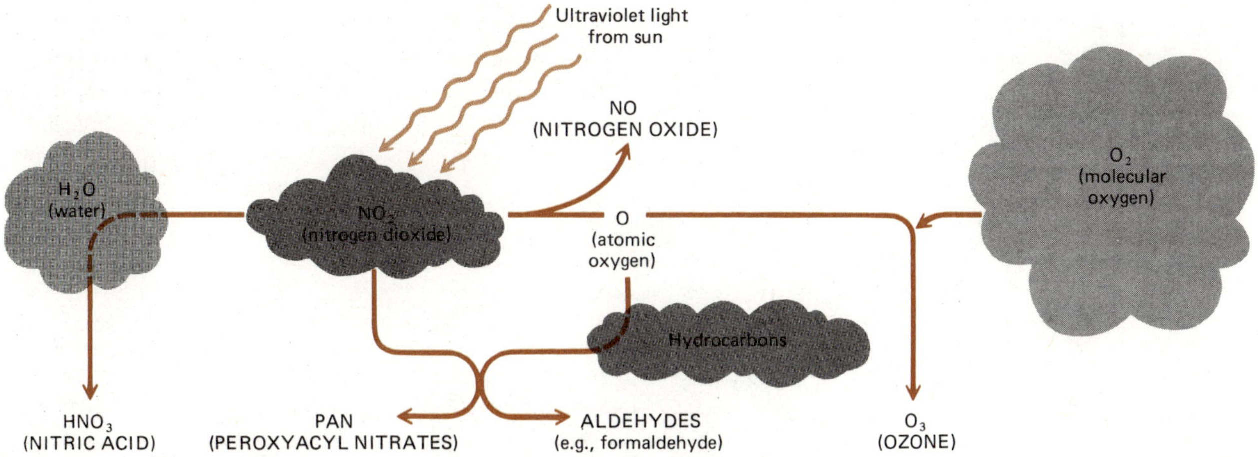

FIGURE 22.5 **Photochemical Reactions in Polluted Air.** Adding nitrogen dioxide and hydrocarbons to a normal sunny atmosphere yields PAN (peroxyacyl nitrates), aldehydes, ozone, nitrogen oxide, and nitric acid.

The brownish haze that makes the air look "smoggy" is due to two factors. Nitrogen dioxide absorbs the blue part of the visible spectrum and leaves the light somewhat brownish. Unburnt hydrocarbons from vehicle exhausts polymerize into larger molecules that scatter light sufficiently to produce a haze that reduces visibility.

WHEN WATER RECEIVES WASTES

Like air, water can be polluted a million ways. Some of these events, such as giant oil spills, are dramatic. Others, including acid drainage from chemical plants or mines, or the leaching of pesticides from farmlands, are less obvious but nonetheless have serious long-term consequences. However, the most common water pollution problem is addition of large quantities of naturally occurring organic substances (Fig. 22.6). This addition may be in the form of sewage from homes, animal wastes from slaughterhouses, or perhaps plant materials from food-processing factories.

Small amounts of organic matter can enter a lake or a river untreated and do little harm. Every body of water receives dead leaves and other organic litter from land. Aquatic plants and animals

FIGURE 22.6 **Sugar-Beet Wastes Dumped into a Stream Killed These Fish.**

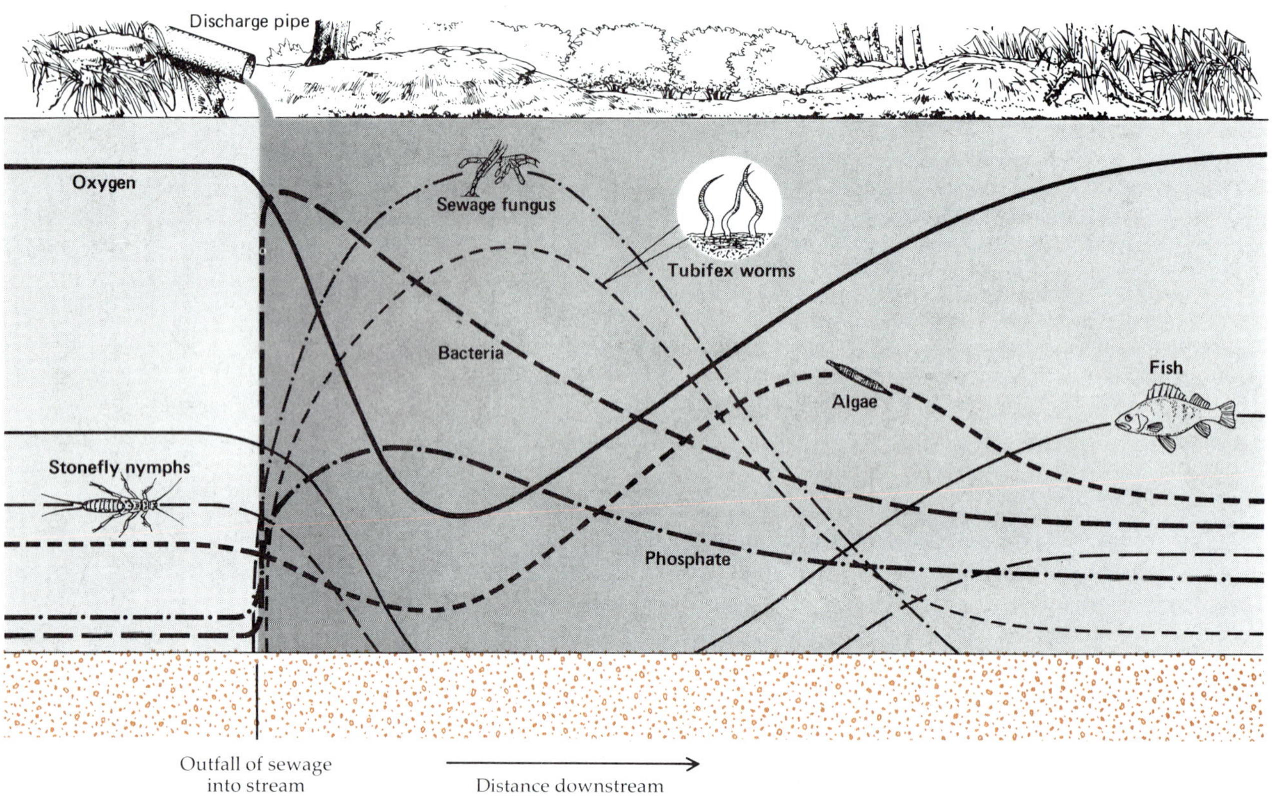

FIGURE 22.7 Where the Sewage Hits the Stream. Distinct biologic zones form downstream from the discharge of raw sewage. The length of each zone and its composition depend in part on the amount of sewage relative to the volume of water in the stream. There is always an abrupt change at the sewage outfall.

add their remains when they die. Bacteria, fungi, and protozoa in the water are part of a decomposer food chain that oxidizes this normal supply of organic matter to carbon dioxide and water.

Biological Oxygen Demand

Addition of a large quantity of sewage or other organic matter to water promotes rapid multiplication of decomposer microorganisms (Fig. 22.7). The metabolism of these organisms creates a high demand for oxygen that depletes the water of this essential gas. The resulting anaerobic conditions kill most members of the aquatic community, except for certain bacteria. These bacteria degrade the sewage very slowly and often yield foul-smelling sulfur compounds. Iron sulfide formed by such anaerobic bacteria turns the water and mud a grayish black.

Because the **biological oxygen demand** is related directly to the degree of pollution and is easily measured, it is a major water-pollution standard, often referred to simply as the **BOD.**

Sewage Treatment: A Less than Complete Solution

Sewage treatment plants permit microbial digestion of organic wastes before the water is returned to the natural ecosystem, as we observed in Fig. 10.3. But even though the carbon added to the water as organic matter is discharged as carbon dioxide that tends to enter the atmosphere, many other elements released through microbial decomposition of sewage remain in the discharge. Unless expensive chemical purification techniques are employed, the end product of sewage plants will be rich in nitrogen and phosphorus. Shortage of these elements normally limits growth of algae in most rivers and lakes. Enrichment with nitrogen and phosphorus permits growth of large populations of algae. Death of the short-lived algae adds organic matter to the water and, if it occurs on a large enough scale, stimulates growth of decomposer populations, just as would the addition of sewage. The result can be a high BOD and drastic alteration of the aquatic ecosystem.

In addition to organic matter, sewage contains other chemical wastes. Use of phosphate-rich detergent mixes in home laundries increases the phosphate load of the treated sewage. The increased phosphate alone may be sufficient to stimulate algal growths in some ecosystems. Industrial wastes are a problem, too. Because smaller volumes of water are cheaper to clean than larger ones, highly polluted industrial waste waters should be purified before they leave the factory.

In Hot Water

Frequently lakes and streams are used as sources of water to cool power plants, factories, or refineries. Such cooling is necessary, because all en-
64 ergy transformations are inefficient, □and they waste
55 energy as heat. The high heat capacity of water□
makes it an ideal medium for waste heat disposal.

Just as chemical pollutants favor one species while restricting another, so does excess heat. Slimeforming bacteria often grow so thick inside a cooling system that they reduce its heat-exchange capacity. To prevent such growth, the water is usually chlorinated as it is taken into the system. Together the chlorine and the abrupt heating doom most organisms sucked into cooling systems.

Use of a large part of a lake or stream for cooling can change the ecosystem drastically. Not only are organisms that are drawn into the cooling system killed, but the returned water also creates a warm zone at the outflow. This zone may be only a few degrees hotter than the remainder of the body of water, but that can be the difference between prime habitat and lethal environment. For example, brook trout eggs do best at 4°C (39°F) and die at 12°C (54°F). Heat also modifies the food chain by favoring the cyanobacteria while depressing growth of green algae and diatoms (Fig. 22.8).

The cyanobacteria do so well that there may be an actual increase in biomass. Of course, when these bacteria die, they support tremendous populations of heterotrophic microbes that require a great deal of oxygen. The reduced solubility of oxygen in the warmer water can make the availability of oxygen a critical matter whenever photosynthesis is curtailed.

Thus excess heat leads to chemical pollution of water as well as to intolerable temperatures for some species. And since the base of the food chain is altered, there are inevitable changes at other levels. In addition, excess heat affects the temperature stratification of lakes and may prevent the normal
seasonal turnover □ of the water. 496

Because the effects of thermal pollution from nuclear power plants can be great if the water is passed through the plant and returned to its source,

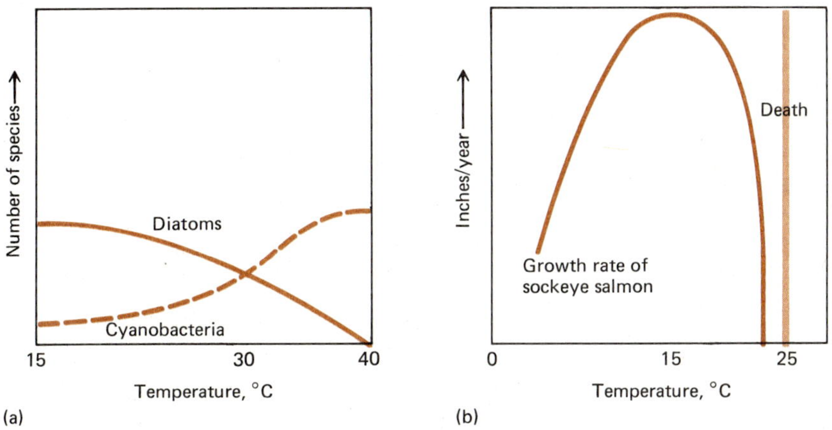

FIGURE 22.8 Effects of Heat Pollution on Aquatic Organisms. Warm water favors some groups of organisms and is disadvantageous to others. As shown in (a), cyanobacteria are more abundant in warmer waters, and diatoms are less abundant. Heat pollution has general effects on major groups of organisms, but it has very specific effects on individual species. For some, such as the sockeye salmon (b), the growth rate increases with temperature until it reaches an optimum. Beyond that optimum, growth is inhibited. Slightly higher temperatures can be lethal.

FIGURE 22.9 **Energy and Water Go Up in a Cloud.** Cooling towers are one way to cool the water used to remove excess heat from the nuclear power plant. Many cooling towers, such as the one shown here, are designed so that the hot water is sprayed into the top of the tower and cool air is drawn into the bottom of the tower. Evaporation cools the water and transfers the heat to the rising column of air. When the water vapor rises high enough to be cooled, it is transformed into tiny droplets of water that form a cloud over the cooling tower.

many are designed to recycle the water. These plants use giant cooling towers (Fig. 22.9) in which the heat is expended in evaporation of water. However, this process transfers the heat to the atmosphere and can alter the local climate.

RADIATION: MORE ENERGY POLLUTION

Just as heat out of place can be a pollutant, so too can increased radiant energy. The cause of the increase may be either human activity or unusual concentrations of naturally occurring radiation. There are many kinds of radiations (refer back to Box 3C), but those most often involved in radiation pollution arise from the decay of unstable isotopes. As shown in Table 22.1, **alpha, beta,** and **neutron radiations** have mass. **Gamma radiation,** which is part of the electromagnetic spectrum, does not. From the viewpoint of effect on organisms, the ability of radiation to penetrate is of great importance. Compare these and other properties of the four major kinds of nuclear radiations in Table 22.1.

Fission Reactions

All present-day nuclear power plants rely on nuclear fission, as did the original atomic bomb. The difference between natural fission and fission triggered by humans lies mainly in the concentration of fissionable materials. The energy released by splitting an atom can be greater than that used to initiate the fission. When an atom of uranium 235 splits, a single neutron is absorbed, but at least two more neutrons are released. The new neutrons can split two more uranium-235 atoms, yielding an average of four neutrons that may be used to split four more uranium atoms and cause their fission and release eight neutrons (Fig. 22.10). This **chain reaction** of increasing intensity will continue to expand so long as there is a concentration of uranium-

TABLE 22.1 **Types of Radiation and their Properties**

TYPE	NATURE	ENERGY (ELECTRON VOLTS)	MASS	PENETRANCE
Alpha	Nucleus of helium atom—positively charged	4–10 million	4	Cannot pass through outer dead layers of skin
Beta	Electrons—negatively charged	Up to 3 million	0.0005	Penetrates human skin
Neutron	Nuclear particles	1–12 million	1	Varies widely; some very high penetrance
Gamma	Electromagnetic waves (unit: photon)	1–2 million	None	Penetrates several cm of lead

235 atoms in the vicinity high enough for most of the neutrons to find their targets. By controlling the concentration and arrangement of susceptible atoms, engineers determine the proportion of neutrons that are used in nuclear reactions and thereby control the rate of these reactions. In this way they can achieve either a moderately fast reaction that is self-perpetuating and yields heat in usable amounts, or a rapidly accelerating reaction that produces an explosion.

The energy of the neutrons released during the fission of uranium 235 turns into heat when these neutrons strike other particles. It is this heat that uranium-powered nuclear energy plants use to make electricity. The heat of the reactions converts water to steam that drives turbines no different from those in power plants that burn coal or petroleum.

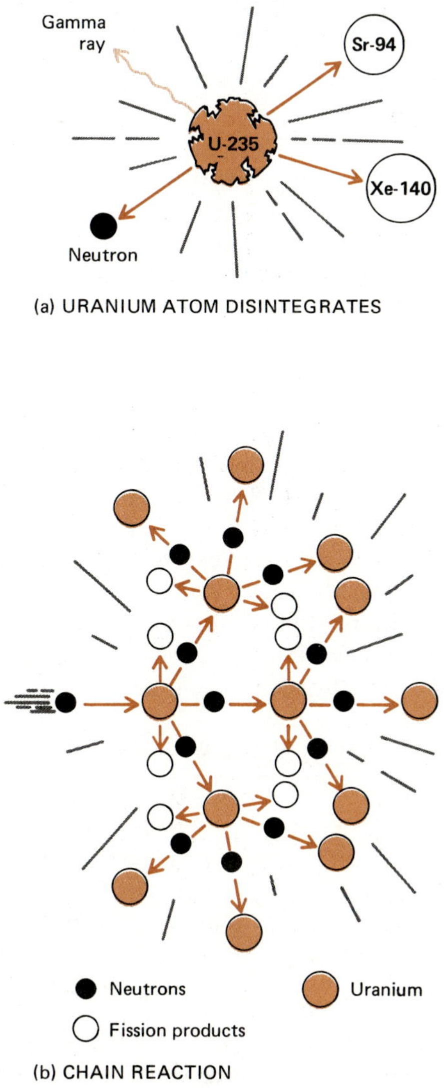

FIGURE 22.10 **Nuclear Fission.** Disintegration of uranium 235 releases other isotopes along with neutrons and gamma radiation. Part (a) shows formation of strontium 94 and xenon 140. In fact, any particular uranium-235 atom can break down into isotopes of several other elements.

When uranium 235 is concentrated, neutrons released by spontaneous decay of a few atoms will strike other uranium-235 atoms and initiate a chain reaction (b). If the uranium is not concentrated, most of the neutrons will fail to strike a uranium atom, and no chain reaction will develop. The chain reactions in nuclear power plants are controlled by inserting rods of cadmium or other substances that absorb neutrons readily and harmlessly.

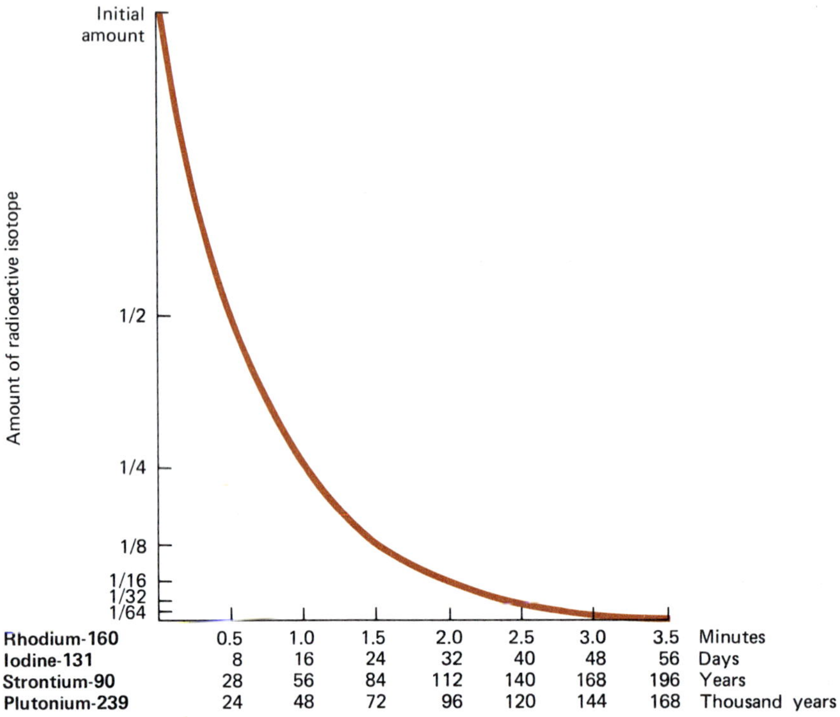

FIGURE 22.11 **How Much Radioactivity Remains?** By definition, the half-life of an isotope is the time required for one-half the initial amount to disintegrate. Half-lives of isotopes vary widely (Table 22.5). Thus the identity of the isotopes in the original wastes, their half-lives, and their concentrations all affect how long wastes must be stored before they can be released into the environment safely.

Radiation Pollution from Power Plants

All fission reactions inevitably increase radiation pollution. Careful design and maintenance of installations can limit release of radioactive wastes outside the plant, but higher levels of radiation pollution must accompany increased use of nuclear power. This pollution arises from unstable isotopes in nuclear fuels, fuel containers and reactor parts, and in the liquids and gases released during the reprocessing of spent fuel. Even the water used to cool the reactor accumulates radioactivity, partly through inevitable defects in the thin-walled fuel containers and partly because of irradiation of substances in the water. Some wastes, such as cooling and cleaning water, are only slightly contaminated but are produced in such large volumes that the only practical policy is to dump them almost immediately. The highly radioactive matter that accumulates in smaller amounts must be stored where it cannot enter natural biogeochemical cycles or come into contact with people before spontaneous decay has reduced radiation to a safe level. Depending on the concentration of isotopes and their identity, this decay can take thousands of years (Fig. 22.11). Not only does storage pose staggering technical problems, but the political ones seem overwhelming. It is inconceivable that any government will be stable enough to monitor stored wastes for thousands or hundreds of thousands of years.

Reactor accidents also contribute to radiation pollution. Although nuclear explosions in reactors are unlikely, other types of explosions can occur and may scatter radioactive materials into the surrounding area. In 1979 the threat of a hydrogen-bubble explosion (hydrogen will react explosively with oxygen to form water) in the malfunctioning Three Mile Island reactor in Pennsylvania caused nearby residents to flee their homes. Although the feared explosion never occurred, the release of contaminated substances inside the plant has pre-

TABLE 22.2 **Radiation Limits**

TISSUE	PERMISSIBLE DOSAGE (REMS*/YEAR)
Bone	3.0
Hands and forearms	7.5
Ovaries/testes	0.5
Red bone marrow	0.5
Skin	3.0
Thyroid	3.0
Other organs	1.5
Whole body	0.5

*The rem is defined in Table 22.3.

vented its repair. The cost of the cleanup will be staggering and will require many years.

Long-term disruption of a reactor cooling system could lead to temperatures high enough to melt the reactor core. Such a **meltdown** would release molten metals rich in radioactive fuel. The fiery liquid might be hot enough to melt the concrete floor of the reactor and work its way down through the soil. This seeping puddle would prob-
486 ably be hot enough to convert groundwater□ into steam instantly. Expansion of the steam could throw a geyser of radioactive mud into the atmosphere. Admittedly, this is a hypothetical scenario, because at this writing, a meltdown has yet to occur. But the prediction is consistent with physical principles, and it is worrisome. Like all other safety devices, cooling systems have the potential to fail. This may happen either because they are inherently faulty or because they are improperly used.

TABLE 22.3 Current Ordinary Exposure to Radiation

		UNITS (REMS*)/YEAR
NATURAL BACKGROUND RADIATION		
Body components	0.021	
Cosmic radiation	0.030	
Earth and building materials	0.050	
Inhaled atmosphere	0.050	
		0.106
EXPOSURE ADDED BY TECHNOLOGY		
Fallout	0.004	
Industry and its products	0.002	
Medical procedures	0.061	
		0.067
Average total exposure		0.173 units/year

*The rem is a measure of radiation that takes into consideration its biological effect. X-rays and gamma rays are arbitrarily assigned a biological effect of 1; neutrons and alpha radiation a biological effect of 10. Rems = rads × biological effect. A rad is defined as 100 ergs of absorbed energy/gram of tissue.

Radiation Damage to Organisms

Perhaps the greatest threat from increased radia-
265 tion is through increased mutations.□ The permissible dosage levels (Table 22.2) suggest that minute amounts of radiation are harmless. Whether or not this is true may be impossible to determine, because **natural background radiation** (Table 22.3) is always present. Some people maintain that there is a **threshold effect**—that is, a level below which radiation is harmless (Fig. 22.12). According to this
267 view, DNA repair mechanisms□ are so effective that low levels of radiation cause no mutations at all. But since it is nearly impossible to eliminate the low levels of background radiation, we do not know how much, if any, of the so-called spontaneous
266 mutation rate□ is due to this radiation.

Tremendous doses of high-energy radiation can cause instant death by denaturation of proteins in essential cells, such as those of the brain. The main factor in this denaturation□ is a flood of ions that 69
breaks the weak bonds that hold proteins in their three-dimensional shape and keep them in suspension in the watery cell fluids. Cells are highly susceptible to radiation damage of proteins in the plasma membrane. Not only are many processes endangered, but if the membrane is sufficiently weakened, the cell may burst.

The effects of exposure to moderately heavy radiation are not obvious immediately. Within a few days, however, an exposed person will experience nausea, vomiting, and diarrhea. Then the hair begins to fall out. Death frequently follows in days or weeks. A decrease in white blood cells and lowered resistance to infectious organisms are im-

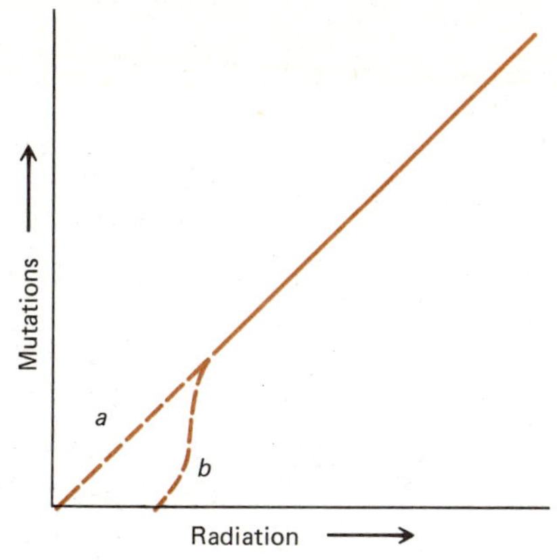

FIGURE 22.12 The Threshold Controversy. Whether tiny increases in low dosages cause small increases in the mutation rate is not established. If they do, the line in the graph should be extended along *a*. Some authorities argue that repair mechanisms are so effective at low dosages that there is a minimum, or threshold, level of radiation necessary to cause any mutation at all. They would draw the lower end of the graph as *b*. The matter remains unresolved because of the difficulty in detecting small changes in mutation rate.

TABLE 22.4 Effects of Massive Radiation

DOSAGE	RESULTS IN HUMANS
0–100 rem*	No immediate symptoms; increased incidence of cancer likely.
100–200	Radiation sickness, including vomiting, in three hours and reduced white blood cells for weeks.
200–600	Severe illness; many deaths.
600–1000	Most die from effects, usually within two months.
1000–5000	Death usually within two weeks.
5000+	Death within two days.

*See Table 22.3.

mediately responsible for death. The digestive problems, blood changes, and impaired immunity all trace to heavily irradiated cells that are unable to divide normally. Problems at cell division may result from breaks in the DNA strands that lead to loss of genetic material or to fusion between chromosomes. Impaired cell division interferes with cell replacement, a crucial need of all tissues directly involved in radiation sickness.

One tissue that requires a constant supply of new cells is the lining of the digestive tract. The single layer of epithelial cells that permits absorption of nutrients is constantly exposed to injury by the intestinal contents. These epithelial tissues must be continuously renewed by cell division. But after a large dose of whole-body irradiation, cell division ceases. As the old cells of the intestinal lining wear away, there are no new cells to replace them. Blood and tissue fluids seep out of the raw surface, and normal absorption of nutrients and water ceases. The nausea, vomiting, and diarrhea of radiation sickness result from this damage to the intestinal lining.

The absence of the normal protective cell layer over the intestinal surface permits bacteria to invade the intestinal walls. Meanwhile, white blood cells that are normally responsible for defense against foreign organisms have been depleted. This happens because blood cells, like intestinal lining cells, have a short life span and must be constantly replaced. After exposure to heavy radiation, blood-cell production ceases because of harm to developing blood cells in the bone marrow. It isn't surprising that the unchecked infections, dehydration, and starvation that accompany severe radiation sickness so often end in death.

The potential danger from radiation makes it prudent to carefully monitor human exposure. For this purpose radiation is usually reported in **rems.** A rem is a measure of the biological effect of radiation and takes into consideration the energy absorbed and the nature of the radiation. One calculation of average human exposure yields 0.173 rems/year (Table 22.3). Suggested permissible exposure for nonpregnant adults is 0.5 rems/year (Table 22.2).

Radiation Inside the Body

Because damage from radiation is limited by its penetration, radioactive isotopes that decay within body cells have greater potential for damage than do these same isotopes when they decay outside the body. Even low-energy alpha and beta radiation is dangerous if it originates inside body cells.

The method of entry of an isotope may determine the location of the radiation and the damage done. So may the chemical characteristics of the isotope. The lungs and digestive tract are the most common routes of entry for radioactive materials. Radioactive gases or dusts may be breathed in with the air and absorbed into lung tissue. Likewise, any radioactive dust suspended in the air may settle onto food or into the water supply and be taken in with food or drink. Foods may also be contaminated in the course of their growth.

Strontium 90. The travels of strontium 90 illustrate the indirect contamination of food by radioactive substances. Strontium behaves much like calcium, so biological processes that accumulate calcium concentrate strontium and promote its movement through the food chain. If soil becomes contaminated with strontium 90, this isotope will be absorbed by plants and, like calcium, be concentrated in the plant cell walls. Animals eating 405
strontium-rich plants pick up the strontium and

TABLE 22.5 Some Radioactive Nuclear Wastes

ISOTOPE	HALF-LIFE	RADIATION EMITTED
Rhodium 106	30 seconds	beta and gamma
Iodine 131	8 days	beta and gamma
Krypton 85	11 years	beta and gamma
Strontium 90	28 years	beta
Cesium 137	30 years	beta and gamma
Plutonium 239	24,000 years	alpha and gamma
Iodine 129	17 billion years	beta and gamma

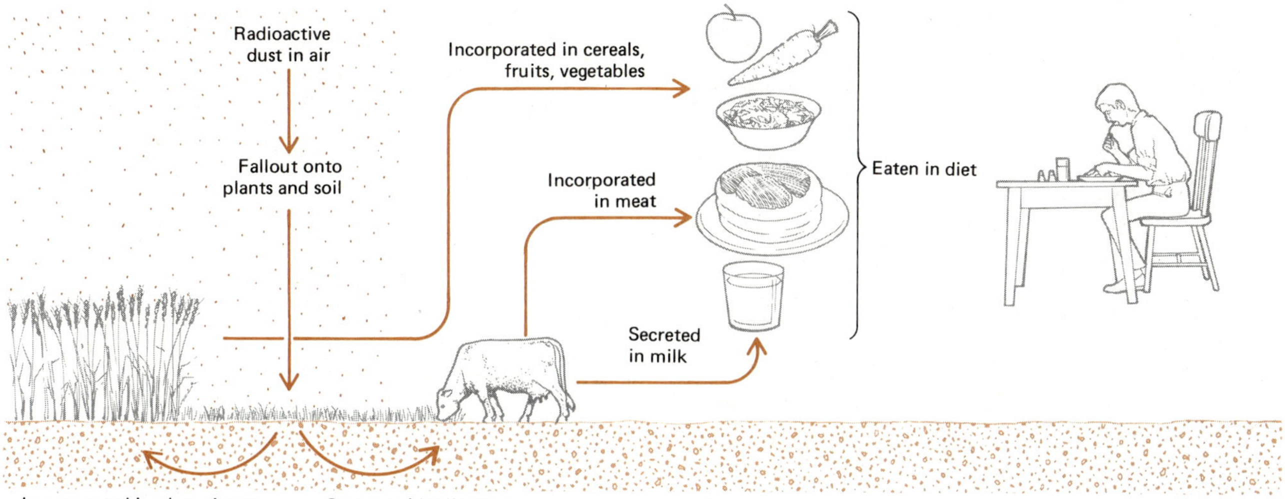

FIGURE 22.13 **The Pathway of Radioactive Cesium 137.** Because the properties of cesium are much like those of potassium, cesium is incorporated into living organisms and follows the same general pathways as potassium. Plants pick up cesium from the soil, and animals acquire it from the plants. In this way, cesium 137 enters a wide range of staple foods. Radioactive fallout can add to the biosphere a substantial amount of this otherwise rare isotope.

treat it as if it were calcium. Thus the strontium is deposited in the bones and secreted in milk. Children accumulate calcium in growing bones and teeth, and nursing mothers use a great deal to restore bone depleted of calcium during pregnancy and milk secretion. Consequently, strontium in the diet is retained in high concentrations by children and young mothers. Unfortunately, the dividing cells responsible for blood-cell production lie in the bone marrow, where they are irradiated by strontium 90 in the skeleton.

A moderately long half-life of 28 years (Table 22.5) also makes strontium 90 dangerous. It decays rapidly enough to yield considerable radiation in a short while, but half the original amount is still present 28 years later (Fig. 22.11). After 56 years, one-quarter of the original strontium will still exist. Therefore contamination of soil or water with strontium 90 creates a long-term threat of exposure to beta radiation.

Dangerous Reactor Products. Strontium 90 is an important radioactive waste from nuclear reactors. Others include iodine 131 and cesium 137. Iodine 131 is concentrated in the thyroid gland, just as is any iodine atom. However, radiation from iodine 131 can initiate cancer in sensitive thyroid cells. Although iodine 131 has a half-life of only 8 days and so disappears quickly, its rapid decay can yield a great deal of radiation within a short time. Iodine moves rapidly through the biosphere and shows up in human thyroids only a few days after introduction into the atmosphere. The first recorded nuclear reactor accident (at Windscale in Britain) was followed shortly by appearance of iodine 131 in milk produced by cows on nearby farms.

Cesium 137 mimics the properties of potassium, and so it is readily concentrated in the body (Fig. 22.13). This cesium isotope has a half-life of 30 years. Krypton 85 and tritium (hydrogen 3) are other radioactive isotopes produced in abundance by nuclear reactions. But since neither is concentrated in the body, both are less dangerous than strontium 90, iodine 131, or cesium 137.

METALS AND LIVING SYSTEMS

Metallic elements cycle through living organisms, just as do so many other elements. Even mercury and lead, which have no established value to most plants or animals, follow biogeochemical cycles and are normally found in some organisms. Apparently plants and animals are adjusted to substances ordinarily present in their ecological niches. On the other hand, newly introduced substances can be devastating. Because human activities alter the distribution of many elements, we create potentially dangerous situations.

Mercury

Our knowledge of the behavior of mercury in nature remains rudimentary. This element occurs at an average concentration of about 0.5 parts per million in the earth's crust. Pure mercury is a liquid at room temperature. Tiny amounts of this liquid vaporize into the atmosphere and enter natural waters.

Although industrial and agricultural use of mercury has led to serious pollution of water and soil in some areas, most of the distribution of mercury can be accounted for by vaporization, or "outgassing," from deposits present in the earth. A recent study of snowfields in Greenland revealed essentially uniform concentrations of mercury in the ice representing the snowfall of thousands of years. Only the most recent layers showed significant increases in mercury content. This additional mercury probably came from the smelting of ores, manufacture of cement, and combustion of fossil fuels. Each of these processes heats raw materials sufficiently to vaporize the mercury present.

Organic Mercurials. Mercury forms compounds with other inorganic elements and also enters organic compounds. An extensive array of organic mercurials are manufactured for use as fungicides and other purposes. Unfortunately the ability to make organic mercury compounds isn't limited to chemists. All organisms that can synthesize vitamin B_{12} have the enzymes to make **methyl mercury** from inorganic mercury. During the 1950s a number of cases of a peculiar neurological disease in people living around Minamata Bay in Japan gave the first indication of this natural entry of mercury into organic compounds.

The symptoms of **Minamata disease** ranged from lack of coordination and lameness to paralysis, from mental dulling and visual distortion to blindness. Young people proved more susceptible than adults. Eventually 46 people died. Cats fell ill, too, giving a hint that fish from the bay might be involved. Analyses showed that the fish and shellfish contained high concentrations of methyl mercury; so did the rich bay muds. The mercury was traced to wastes from a plastics plant. There mercuric chloride was used as a catalyst in the manufacture of vinyl chloride. Bay muds contained
210 abundant methane-producing bacteria that could convert inorganic mercury into the insidious methyl mercury. It was through these organisms that mercury entered the food chain of the bay.

Industrial or agricultural uses of mercury can easily contaminate soil and inland waters, even though the amount of mercury that humans release is small compared with the amount in the ocean or with that in the earth's crust. In 1969 and 1970 mercury escaping from chemical factories and paper plants had so contaminated lakes and streams that fishing was prohibited in many areas of the United States and Canada.

Concentration in Food Chains. Methyl mercury is concentrated in food chains, much as DDT is. 508
Both are sufficiently fat-soluble that they tend to be retained in organisms for some time, often until the animals die. Fish-eating birds such as the great blue heron and the common tern carry much heavier burdens of methyl mercury than do the fish they consume. After all, they have an opportunity to accumulate the mercury from thousands of fish. Similarly, fish bear greater concentrations than do planktonic organisms. In addition to absorbing methyl mercury from their food, pike and some other fish apparently concentrate mercury directly from the water into their gills.

The natural dissipation of mercury from mud or soil requires a very long time. Eventually mercury is washed into the ocean and widely distributed. One method of slowing the entry of mercury into aquatic food chains is to limit the bacteria that convert the inorganic mercury into organic forms. Because such bacteria are favored by nutrient-rich waters, standard water-pollution controls that lower the number of these bacteria will slow the production of methyl mercury.

The toxicity of methyl mercury results in large part from its long retention in the body. Methyl mercury forms stable complexes with body proteins of all kinds, including both enzymes and structural proteins. Combination with mercury compounds changes the shape of proteins and thus affects their roles in the body. Because the plasma membrane is the first cell structure to come into contact with such foreign chemicals, many symptoms of mercury poisoning result from impaired membrane function.

Lead

Just as mercury is naturally scattered about the biosphere, so is lead. And lead is also concentrated by human activities. Exhaust fumes from autos that burn leaded gasoline are the major source of human poisoning. Flaking lead house paint is also a threat to toddlers, who may try to eat anything they can put in their mouths, or to anyone who breathes the dust produced when lead-painted surfaces are sanded.

In contrast to the impression of inertness that "leaden" may imply, lead is readily absorbed, and once inside organisms, it interferes with many normal processes. Lead affects proteins, much as mercury does. Enzymes involved in hemoglobin synthesis are particularly susceptible. So are many others. Not surprisingly, the symptoms of lead poisoning include anemia, kidney damage, and enough destruction of nerve cells to produce irreversible loss of mental capacity. There are so many different symptoms that lead poisoning can be as difficult to diagnose as syphilis, long known as the great imitator of other diseases.

Because lead behaves somewhat like calcium, it tends to accumulate in calcareous tissues: the bones of vertebrates, the exoskeletons of lobsters and other crustaceans, and the cell walls of plants. Sometimes symptoms of lead poisoning occur only when bone calcium is heavily reabsorbed—during pregnancy, for example, or when an individual is suffering from rickets.

Metal poisoning isn't limited to mercury and lead. Even copper and zinc can be poisonous if consumed in soluble forms and sufficient quantities. Less common metals, such as beryllium, selenium, and arsenic, are even more harmful. Neither is mercury the only metal that can be methylated by microorganisms; Chesapeake Bay sediments contain microorganisms that incorporate tin into dangerous methylated compounds.

NEW CHEMICALS: DANGER IN NOVELTY

The chemical industry has given the world plastics with so many different properties and such a collection of other substances that no one remains unaffected by this "better life through chemistry." No part of the biosphere lies untouched by synthetic compounds.

However, the very fact that these substances are new to the world of life makes them potentially dangerous. Over the course of time, a species can evolve methods of detoxifying poisonous substances. Hence many organisms are immune to compounds that would otherwise be poisonous. But if the newly introduced material is particularly harmful, the evolution of resistance will involve the death of sensitive individuals. Species may disappear because too few members possess the mutant genes necessary to tolerate the poison. Without doubt, indiscriminate introduction of new chemicals can drastically affect the earth's biosphere.

Obviously, new chemicals should be carefully screened before being distributed. Unfortunately, this common sense precaution has been regularly ignored.

PCBs

The dangers of **PCBs** (*p*oly*c*hlorinated *b*iphenyl compounds) have been well publicized. Until recently these compounds were used in paints, refrigerants, lubricants, waxes, hydraulic fluids, printer's ink, carbonless copying paper, and insulators. They were also used as **plasticizers** (substances added to improve the properties of plastics). There are 210 different PCB compounds; the exhaustive list of all their uses would take up an entire chapter. It is sufficient to say that these compounds pervade our environment, that many of them are toxic, and that their long-range effects remain uncertain.

PCBs are concentrated in the food chain (Fig. 22.14), just as methyl mercury and DDT are. And, as is true of DDT, the acute toxicity of many PCBs is low; it is their chronic effects that are feared. But unlike pesticides, PCBs have never been spread throughout the environment intentionally. Their wide distribution results from leaching of compounds remaining in manufactured plastics, from evaporation of PCBs from paints and other fluids, and from accidental spills.

The contamination of food oil with a heat-exchange fluid containing PCBs poisoned more than 1000 people in Japan in 1968. Chronic eye discharges, dark skin discolorations, skin eruptions resembling acne, and liver damage resulted. Pregnant women consuming the oil gave birth to babies showing symptoms much like those of exposed adults. PCBs are also toxic to other animals, including birds, fish, and shrimp.

Although manufacture of PCBs in the United States is now curtailed, these compounds are widespread in the biosphere. And of course, other countries are unrestrained by U.S. decisions. Damage from these compounds will surely continue for some time.

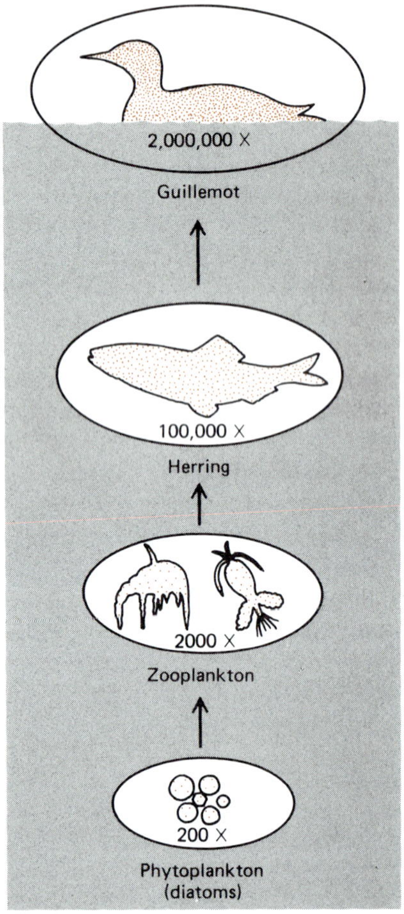

FIGURE 22.14 **Concentration of PCBs in a Marine Food Chain.**

Other Plasticizers

Phthalates are another group of synthetic organic compounds also widespread in the biosphere. These are used mainly to make **polyvinyl chloride (PVC)** plastics soft and flexible. PVC plastics may consist of up to 40 percent phthalates. Much of the phthalate is not part of the plastic macromolecules but floats freely within the molecular network from which it can escape into air or water. Not many years ago phthalate plasticizer from plastic interiors was responsible for a characteristic "new-car odor" and for the condensation of greasy substances on the inside of new car windows.

Experiences with PCBs and phthalates demonstrate that totally foreign substances can be readily incorporated into the biosphere. They move along pathways dictated by their physical properties and by the characteristics of living organisms and the nonliving environment. New substances have a way of appearing in unexpected places and causing unforeseen damage.

Pollution: Cause and Cure

Homo sapiens is part of nature. We evolved within a particular ecosystem, and today we are totally dependent on the biosphere. Nevertheless, we are far from living in harmony with the natural world. Our **cultural evolution** is the crux of the problem.

Over a mere ten generations, people have built great industrial societies that can harness energy sources never before available. In only a few generations, chemists have learned to make tens of thousands of new substances. But because organisms cannot evolve biologically as fast as human culture evolves, the biosphere cannot adapt to use the wastes we produce, nor can many species become immune to harmful wastes.

Since organisms cannot adapt biologically to the changes produced by human culture, we must restrain these changes. We should not release new materials into the biosphere before we determine whether they will do damage, and we must forego production of those that are harmful. We ought to restrain further exploitation of natural ecosystems as answers for disposal and find ways to recycle potential wastes.

As much as any other problem, the energy shortage requires response with restraint. For example, all mining exposes rocks from deep in the earth. These rocks contain sulfur and other compounds that leach out and make waste waters acid enough to kill vegetation. Strip mining, often the most efficient way to reach oil shales and coal deposits, literally puts a precious resource out of place (Fig. 22.15). The soil is

FIGURE 22.15 **Stripping the Earth.** Strip mining removes the overlying soil and rock instead of tunneling into the earth to reach the mineral deposit. The removed soil and rock must be piled somewhere. In this Montana mine we see row upon row of dumps. Some in the upper left have been contoured and graded and, perhaps, seeded in an attempt to reclaim the land. A great deal of time and energy are necessary to restore a strip-mined region to a condition approaching the original.

moved, the natural contours of land are destroyed, and the scene is set for erosion. Restoration is extremely expensive in time, energy, water, and fertilizer. We have already mentioned the effects of radiation and heat pollution from nuclear reactors. And as long as petroleum is available, its transportation is likely to involve tanker accidents that result in water pollution.

In short, all the traditional approaches to increasing the energy supply also increase pollution levels. Only solar power promises little pollution. Of course, the manufacture of solar collectors and of the photovoltaic cells that turn sunlight into electricity has a pollution price tag. But solar power produces no heat pollution, because most of the sun's rays that strike the earth are turned into heat anyway. Human use of the energy will not increase heat production.

Although we can develop low-pollution sources of energy, we need also to restrain our consumption, because all our resources are limited, and every action affects some ecosystem. Most important of all, we should limit population growth. Remember, each additional person requires food, clothing, shelter, and energy. Each strains the biosphere with additional pollution.

Summary

1. Pollution consists of matter and energy out of place. Natural ecosystems are adapted to cycle the elements in whatever forms those elements existed as the ecosystems evolved and to use the sources of energy that were present during that time. Through cultural evolution, humans have managed to alter the concentration, form, and location of the biosphere's matter and energy. Because organisms cannot adapt this rapidly, these changes have had widespread effects on the biosphere.

2. Sulfur dioxide from heating fuels and industrial operations forms sulfuric acid, which harms vegetation and animals and damages buildings. Eventually the sulfuric acid becomes sulfates, which enhance plant growth.

3. Cold smog results when temperature inversions trap pollutants in foggy air. Photochemical smog is produced when nitrogen dioxide and unburnt hydrocarbons from automobile exhausts react with atmospheric components and sunlight to form formaldehyde and other noxious substances. Carbon monoxide, another component of automobile exhaust, poisons the oxygen-carrying ability of hemoglobin.

4. A great deal of organic matter added to water will support enough microbial growth to use up the oxygen and kill most organisms present. Sewage treatment carries out this digestion before the waste water is released, but this treated water can still cause pollution because of the presence of excess nitrogen and phosphorus.

5. All increased energy use, except for solar radiation, adds heat to the biosphere. Acute effects are seen when power plants are cooled with water that is then returned to a river or lake.

6. Nuclear power plants employ fission reactions that produce radiation and radioactive isotopes. Included in the isotopes are strontium 90, iodine 131, and cesium 137. These follow biogeochemical cycles that cause them to be concentrated in the body, where radiation emitted from these isotopes is particularly damaging. For safety, these and other radioactive wastes must be stored for long periods; exactly how long depends on their concentration and half-lives. Some loss of radioactive isotopes to the environment is inevitable, even if there are no major reactor accidents.

7. Certain microorganisms incorporate mercury into organic compounds that readily enter food chains and become concentrated in fatty tissues. Lead enters organisms and is stored as if it were calcium. Both mercury and lead denature proteins.

8. Synthetic compounds are potentially dangerous, because organisms have not evolved with them and lack methods of dealing with those that disrupt biochemical pathways. Some, such as the PCBs, are concentrated in food chains.

9. Pollution problems require restraint in the use and distribution of materials and energy, as well as control of the number of humans present to pollute the environment.

Thought and Controversy

1. Electricity is often advertised as the "cleanest fuel." But there is more to using electricity than running wires into your house. The current must be generated at a hydroelectric plant, a nuclear power plant, or a plant that burns coal or petroleum products. Discuss the various kinds of pollutants that result from the use of electricity as an energy medium.

2. Did lead poisoning cause the fall of the ancient world? Lead was a favorite metal in ancient Greece and Rome. Elemental lead is soft and easy to work. Thus it was a favorite of ancient metal crafters. Also, unlike copper or bronze, lead gives no metallic flavor to wine or food. Consequently, the wealthy often stored their wine in lead-lined containers and used lead goblets and cookware. Weak acids, even those in wine, promote the solubility of lead, so people who used such vessels consumed large quantities of the metal. To make matters worse, lead compounds were sometimes added to wine intentionally. Lead salts are good preservatives (they kill microorganisms even more effectively than they do people), and some lead compounds are sweet. Not surprisingly, it was Hippocrates, the Greek father of medicine, who first described the colic of acute lead poisoning.

The Romans not only used lead containers and lead-salted wines but also constructed water distribution systems with lead pipes. In fact, the very word "plumbing" traces from the Latin *plumbum,* meaning lead. The Romans also colored their red and white paints with lead pigments. A high incidence of insanity and feeble-mindedness among the ruling classes, accompanied by low rates of reproduction, marked the fall of Rome. Was lead poisoning the root of the trouble? This hypothesis is consistent with the fact that the problems of the ruling classes were absent among the poor. Lead was expensive, and poor people used only pottery vessels.

3. Much of the controversy over development of nuclear energy turns on the amount of radiation that will be released if nuclear energy is exploited. Those who favor nuclear energy believe that the increased radiation will be minimal and the damage slight to nonexistent. They point to the fact that life has evolved in the presence of constant low levels of radiation from natural processes. The existence of DNA repair mechanisms is also cited in the argument that low levels of radiation may be harmless.

Some opponents of nuclear energy maintain that even miniscule increases in radiation are harmful. Merely because background radiation makes it impossible to determine the effects of small doses, we must not assume that such radiation is harmless. Instead, we should assume that small amounts of radiation cause small numbers of mutations, and that slight increases in radiation will increase the mutation rate somewhat. Since the evidence suggests that widespread use of nuclear energy will produce increases in nuclear radiation, it is only reasonable to believe that there will be a resulting increase in the incidence of genetic disease and cancer. As controversy builds over the issue of deploying nuclear weapons, it is important to remember these facts. If the slightest increase in radiation brings *some* harm, then the most limited nuclear warfare may have widespread negative effects. Considered in this light, even the careful manufacture of fuels for nuclear weapons becomes undesirable.

Questions

1. Describe the sulfur cycle. How do human activities affect the sulfur cycle?

2. Compare true smog and photochemical smog. Which is most often associated with a temperature inversion? Why?

3. List major air pollutants and discuss their effects on organisms.

4. Define biological oxygen demand. How is BOD a measure of water pollution?

5. Discuss the pollutants present in treated sewage when it is returned to natural bodies of water.

6. How is the aquatic ecosystem affected when water from a lake or river is used for cooling and then returned to its source at a slightly higher temperature?

7. Is it more dangerous to be near a radioisotope that's emitting alpha radiation or one that's emitting gamma radiation? Explain.

8. How does the chemical nature of radioactive isotopes affect their potential danger? Explain, using strontium 90 and iodine 131 as examples.

9. Discuss how mercury becomes incorporated into food chains and what effect it has on organisms.

10. Why are totally new substances often harmful compared with substances that were present as natural ecosystems evolved? Why are unusual concentrations of elements and radiation likewise harmful, even though small amounts have always been present?

23

Populations and People: A Problem in Regulation

IF BIRTHS EXCEED DEATHS, A POPULATION grows. When deaths predominate, the population shrinks. Inheritance and environment control the numbers. In many species there are built-in checks that prevent massive increases that could overburden the habitat and lead to death of the population. But in the course of evolution many populations die. And species become extinct.

By most accounts the human species is successful. We have spread to every part of the earth and conquered much of it. Neither predators nor parasites are the threats they once were, and we seem at a standoff with our serious competitors. But where do we go from here? Many signs indicate that the human population is approaching or has exceeded the limits of the earth to support it. How have we come to this state of affairs? What led to population levels that strain our resources? The fact is that humans, like other organisms, have an astonishing capacity for reproduction.

TABLE 23.1 **How Two Can Become a Hundred Thousand***

YEARS	POPULATION SIZE
0	2
1	4
2	8
3	16
4	32
5	64
6	128
7	256
8	512
9	1,024
10	2,048
11	4,096
12	8,192
13	16,384
14	32,768
15	65,536
16	131,072

*Assumes that a pair produces four young each year, the species matures in one year, all young survive to reproduce, and adults die after their first breeding season.

HOW POPULATIONS GROW

Almost everyone who has kept pet rabbits, mice, or hamsters has dealt with a population explosion. It doesn't take long for two to become twenty! Under favorable conditions a population may multiply itself by some factor each generation. Consider a hypothetical situation in which two adults produce four young each year. Assume the species matures in one year, that no adults survive to the second breeding season, and that there are no deaths among the young (Table 23.1). Since the population doubles each year, within 16 years the population would include 131,072 animals. Only rarely does a population swell so quickly. Young often die before they can reproduce. And of course, situations are seldom so simple. Adults have variable numbers of offspring, often spread over considerable time. Also, the life span of animals reaching maturity is never uniform. But whatever the pattern, any sustained growth will eventually double the population. And any population that doubles a number of times becomes extremely large.

Doubling time has come to be a common measure of potential for population growth. The length of time necessary for a population to double falls as the growth rate rises (Table 23.2). The drastic results of a 3-percent yearly growth rate or even of 0.5-percent growth in the human population are evident in Table 23.3. With 3-percent growth there will be 16 billion people on earth (four times the present number) when present-day college students are ready to retire. But at 0.5-percent growth it would take ten generations for us to reach the same point. Doubling time is about 40 years now. At this rate world population will reach 16 billion in the middle of the 21st century. Optimistically, let's assume that the growth rate will drop; still, so long as it remains positive, 16 billion people and more are inevitable someday. Unless, of course, something such as famine intervenes.

TABLE 23.2 The Compound Interest of Populations

ANNUAL GROWTH RATE (PERCENT)	DOUBLING TIME (YEARS)
0.2	347
0.4	173
0.6	116
0.8	87
1.0	69
1.2	58
1.4	50
1.6	43
1.8	38
2.0	35
2.2	32
2.4	29
2.6	27
2.8	25
3.0	23
3.2	22
3.4	20
4.0	17
7.0	10

Total Population

In simple terms, the size of a population is determined by the rate at which individuals are born and the rate at which they die. Each species has its own maximum rate of increase. However this **reproductive potential** is seldom, if ever, realized. The increase is always limited by crowding, food shortages, predation, disease, or other environmental factors. In other words, an environmental resistance opposes the reproductive potential of a population. Inherent in the concept of **environmental resistance** is the belief that members of a population compete for resources.□ 454 This is a commonsense assumption but one that is seldom documented in nature.

The reproductive potential of a human population is a reflection of the number of women of childbearing age, as well as physiological limits, such as how quickly after childbirth the mother's

TABLE 23.3 Doubling the Human Population: Population Levels that Would Result from Sustained Growth

		YEAR ATTAINED	
DOUBLINGS	WORLD POPULATION (BILLIONS)	*3% ANNUAL GROWTH (DOUBLE TIME: 23 YEARS)*	*0.5% ANNUAL GROWTH (DOUBLING TIME 139 YEARS)*
Initial level	4	1976	1976
1	8	1999	2115
2	16	2022	2254
3	32	2045	2393
4	64	2068	2523
5	128	2091	2671
6	256	2114	2810
7	512	2137	2949
8	1,024	2160	3088

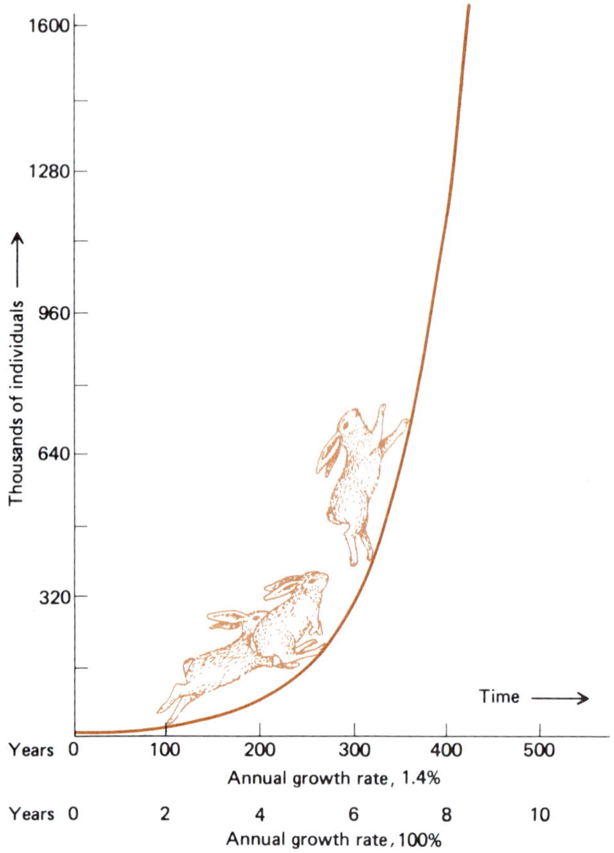

FIGURE 23.1 **J-Shaped Growth Curve.** Any constant growth rate, no matter how small, eventually produces a J-shaped curve.

ovulatory cycles return. Since annual birthrates higher than 50 babies per thousand people are not uncommon, the reproductive potential of many human populations must be at least that high. In the absence of environmental resistance, such populations might grow at the rate of 5 percent a year. The number of people would double in fewer than 14 years! But early deaths occur in all real populations, and the birthrate is usually less than 50 per thousand. Thanks to environmental resistance, human populations seldom grow faster than 3.5 percent a year. Even at that rate they double in 20 years.

From Fig. 23.1 it is evident that even with a constant growth rate, the size of a population doesn't increase in a linear manner. Instead, the total population rises only slowly at first. But after a while it is increasing rapidly, and eventually it grows almost instantaneously. This growth pattern occurs because the individuals added in one generation contribute to population growth in all later generations. Here is an example. A population of a million people that results from a steady growth rate of 3 percent will contain 1,030,000 individuals next year. Because of the growing number of people of reproductive age, the increase will then be 30,900 instead of 30,000. And the following year it will be 31,827. Readers with business backgrounds will recognize that populations grow like money invested with compound interest. Scientists call this **exponential growth,** because the total increases like numbers with increasing exponents (e.g., 2^2, 2^3, 2^4, 2^5, . . ., 2^n).

A graph of population growing at a constant rate inevitably produces a **J-shaped curve** (Fig. 23.1). This is a scale effect. The scale chosen for the population must be such that the initial population and its early growth are perceptible. But after the population has doubled a few times, the increases due to reproduction of the products of earlier growth dwarf the initial population. Graphed to the same

FIGURE 23.2 **S-Shaped Curves.** If a growing population adjusts gradually to its resources, it will produce an S-shaped population curve. Data for curves such as this come from studies of large populations of yeasts or other microorganisms in pure culture. For a constant number of organisms to be maintained, it is necessary to continuously replenish the medium.

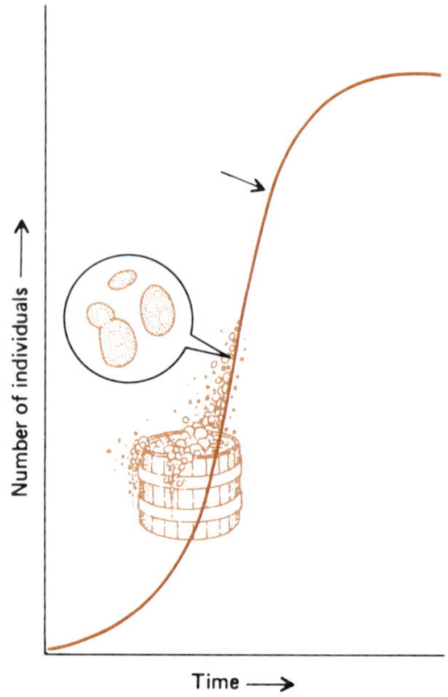

scale, the line representing population size soon becomes nearly vertical.

Eventually, environmental resistance dampens the growth of every population. Sometimes the rate of growth slows gradually as the impact of environmental resistance makes itself increasingly evident. This may convert a J-shaped curve into a sigmoid, or **S-shaped curve** (Fig. 23.2). If the top of the S is smooth, the highest point represents the carrying capacity of the habitat for that species. Real data seldom produce perfect S-shaped curves.

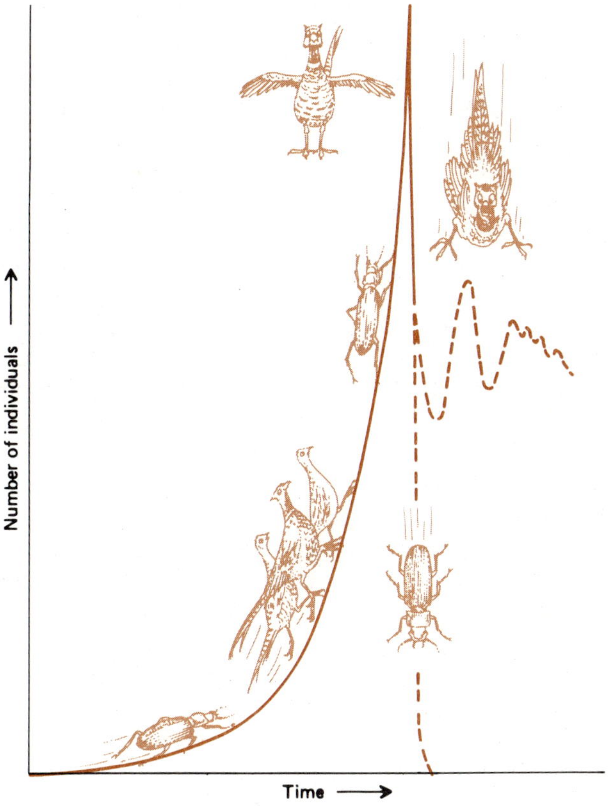

FIGURE 23.3 **J-with-a-Tail Curves.** Many populations in new, simple, or unstable environments grow to exceed the carrying capacity of resources and then crash abruptly. In some situations, such as beetles in a closed can of flour, the population may die out completely. In others, such as Chinese pheasants introduced into the United States, the population falls from an initial high and then fluctuates.

Overshooting Leads to a Crash. Under experimental conditions, populations often undergo exponential growth, level off briefly, and then crash. They have overshot their resources. As a result, the population must fall (Fig. 23.3). The environment may be damaged in such a way that its carrying capacity for that species is permanently reduced. If damage is extensive, the ecosystem may be unable to support the smallest population of that species. Examples of **J-with-a-tail growth curves** come from bacteria in test-tube cultures and beetles in closed cans of flour. In each there is no way to recycle or renew resources. Only an ecosystem with continued energy input and complete biogeochemical cycles can support any species forever. We should expect extremely simple artificial environments to wear out. But even in natural ecosystems population levels can fluctuate wildly (Fig. 23.4). As we discussed in Chapter 18, fluctuations are usually greater in simple ecosystems than in complex ones.

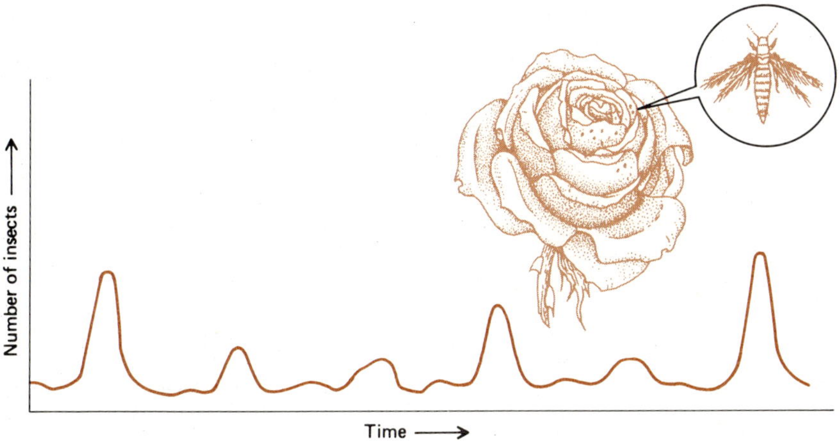

FIGURE 23.4 **Natural Populations Fluctuate.** Accurate data on total animal populations are difficult to obtain. H. G. Andrewartha, an Australian ecologist, made a simple but valuable contribution to knowledge of wild populations by regularly counting the number of thrips on twenty roses in a garden near his office. Although all the population peaks came during the southern summer, the average number of thrips per rose varied greatly from summer to summer, as well as at other times.

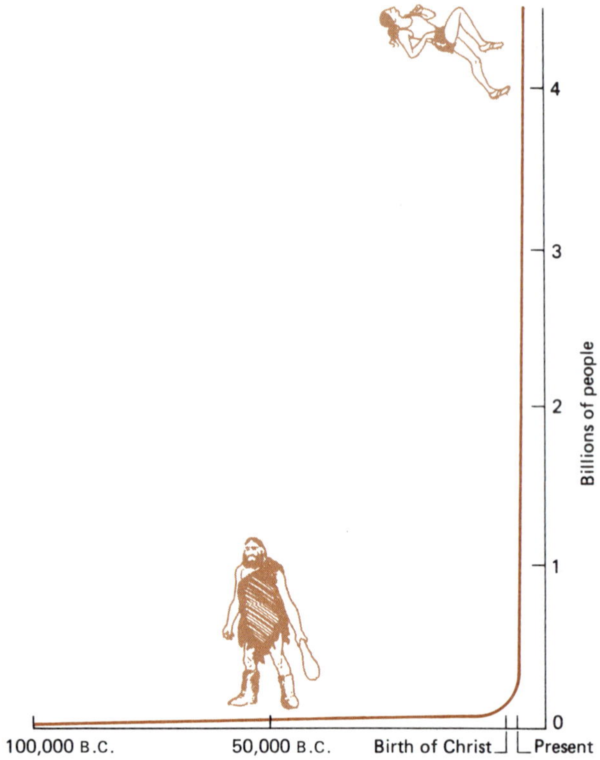

FIGURE 23.5 **The History of Human Population Growth.** This generalized curve represents an educated guess at the history of human population size.

The History of Human Populations. The processes outlined above apply to human populations as well as to any other. In any one area the number of people may be stable for some time. However, over most of history there has been a gradual rise in the total number of humans on earth (Fig. 23.5). This increase resulted from cultural evolution that improved the efficiency with which people used their habitat and the number of kinds of habitats they could exploit. In essence, people slowly altered their ecological niche so that any given area could support a larger population. The smoothness of the curve in Fig. 23.5 results partly from a shortage of data. Reasonably accurate population counts were seldom made until the twentieth century. Except for a few European countries, all earlier data rest on estimates. The fact that cultural advances happened at different times in various countries also blurs real changes in growth rate. Even allowing for these factors, an accurate graph of human populations would probably approximate a J-shaped curve.

Throughout prehistory, human populations may have grown no more than 0.0015 percent a year. The rate increased with the introduction of agriculture about 10,000 years ago. Surely an increased food supply relaxed environmental resistance, but the resource base grew slowly. A surge in population seems to have begun at about the time of Christ. But even this increase hardly foretold the meteoric rise in population that was to begin about 1750.

By the beginning of the eighteenth century, scientific and technical advances had greatly improved the efficiency of agriculture, of clothing manufacture, and of transportation. Continued innovations increased the carrying capacity; as a result, world population grew as it never had grown before. Finally, a chemical revolution during the 1940s introduced antibiotics and insecticides that drastically reduced mortality due to infection and insect-borne diseases. At about the same time, immunization against many infectious diseases became widely available, and food distribution improved. Pesticides also increased food production, as did increased use of chemical fertilizers. Soon world population was doubling every 35 years, and despite greater agricultural productivity, more and more countries faced chronic food shortages.

Mortality and Age

The impact of recent scientific advances on population levels traces largely to control of infectious diseases. Those who survive initial attacks of such diseases develop temporary or permanent immunity□ to the particular organism involved. Be- [215]
cause most microbial diseases appear frequently, it is usually only children who have not developed immunity and hence are susceptible. For this reason death due to infectious disease strikes mainly the young. In the past, a majority of children failed to survive to reproduce. But now immunization□ [217]
and antibiotics□ have changed all that. [226]

Infectious diseases are contained, if not conquered, and today most babies grow up to have children of their own. At present this is true even in underdeveloped countries. Simple graphs of life expectancy (Fig. 23.6) and age pyramids tell the story.

Age Pyramids. Age pyramids are bar graphs representing the portion of a population in each age category. Ordinarily these also reflect the sex ratio

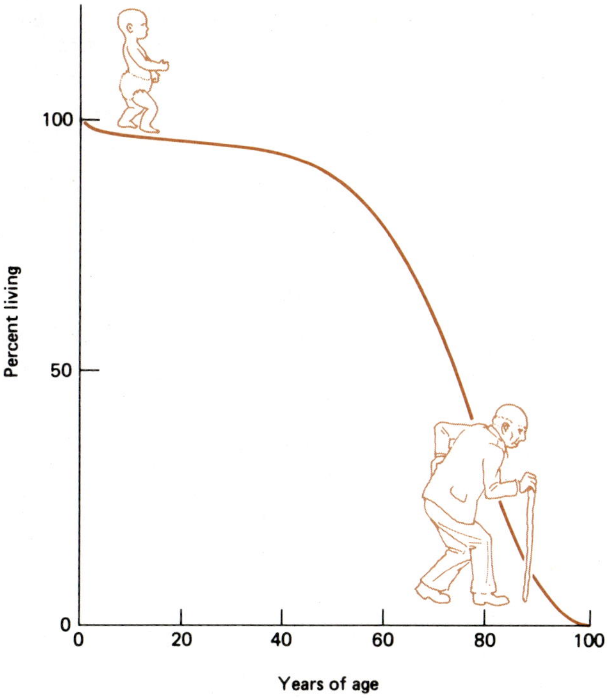

FIGURE 23.6 **Most People Live Long Enough to Reproduce.** Although this survivorship curve is based on U.S. data, the curve for other present-day human populations has a similar form.

FIGURE 23.7 **Age Structure of a Slowly Growing Population.** This age pyramid represents the United Kingdom in 1959.

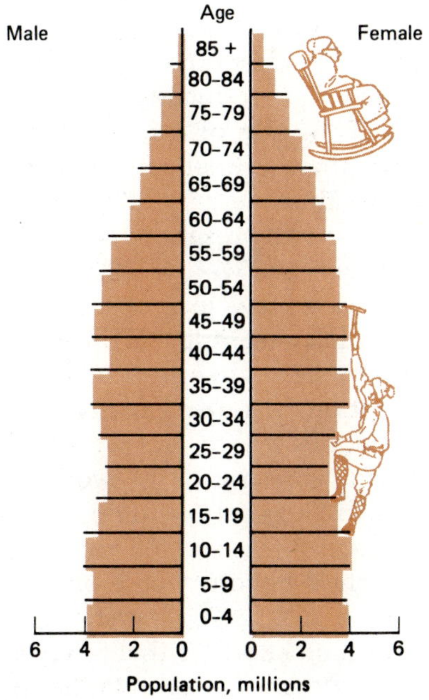

in each group. As you view the pyramids, males are on your left and females on your right. Figure 23.7 shows the structure of a population that is just replacing itself and has been doing so for several generations. In this population most mortality is confined to the postreproductive years. The number of children under the age of four is only very slightly larger than the number of adults between the ages of 25 and 29 years, the group that is most active in childbearing. If this population maintains the same structure, in 25 years there will be about the same number of 25–29-year-old women as there are today. Assuming that birth rates remain the same, we can expect that these young women will have just sufficient babies to replace themselves and their husbands. Contrast this with the pyramid drawn from 1980 data for Pakistan (Fig. 23.8).

Pakistan has a growth rate of 3 percent a year. Here we find a 0–4-year-old group that will be 25–29 years old in 2005. These people may produce a baby crop 15 times as numerous as the grandparents. Only catastrophic deaths in the meantime or marked reduction in family size can avert disastrous growth in an already overpopulated country. As we shall see shortly, marked reduction in fertility isn't likely to happen in an underdeveloped country such as Pakistan. Of course, famine may intervene, but to limit the population to present levels, half the children would have to starve. Other calamities are unlikely to make even a dent in the population. For example, the 300,000 lives lost in the catastrophic tidal wave that struck Bangladesh in 1970 were replaced by new births in only 40 days.

The Importance of Dying Young. To affect future reproduction, mortality must occur in age groups that haven't yet completed their reproductive lives. For practical purposes, these are women under 50 years. Deaths before 20 will clearly have a greater impact than deaths at 40, when family size is nearly complete. On the other hand, extended longevity has limited effect on population size. Of course, if more people live longer, there are more elderly people and a somewhat higher total human population. But once the life span stabilizes, there is no further contribution to population growth, for these older people no longer reproduce. Discussions of population size often are limited to females, because normally the number of females in a population sets the limit on reproduction. Of course, shortages of males can be important if the lack of men prevents women from conceiving.

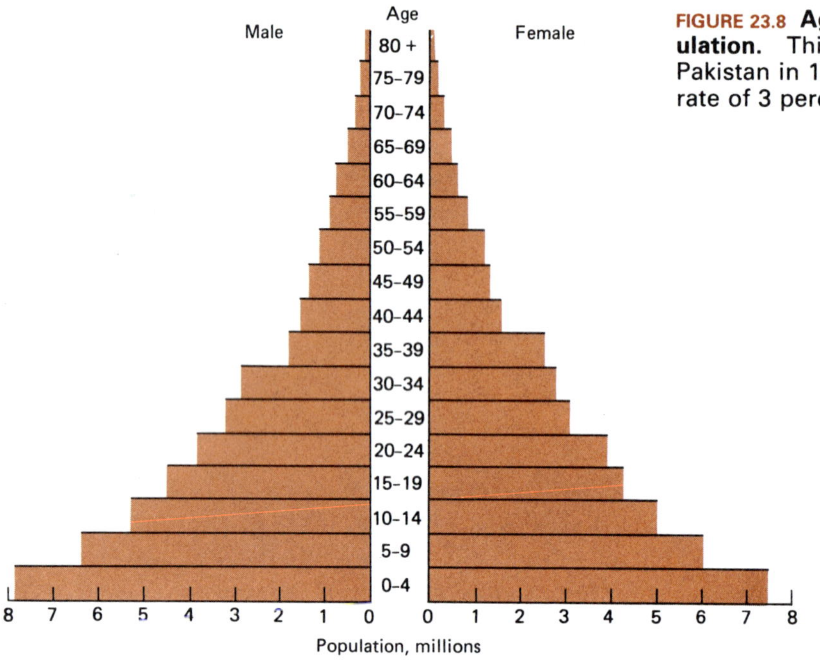

FIGURE 23.8 **Age Structure of a Rapidly Growing Population.** This age pyramid shows the population of Pakistan in 1980, a population that is growing at the rate of 3 percent a year.

ASSESSING THE SITUATION

How many people can the world support? Or expressed in ecological terms, what is the **carrying**
456 **capacity**□ of the earth for *Homo sapiens?* The answer to this question depends on a number of factors, each difficult to evaluate. One is the nature of future technological advances that can further alter our ecological niche and increase the number of people the earth can support. But the most important factor is the level of security we desire for our species. By further replacing our inherited biosphere with simple, artificial, and necessarily fragile ecosystems, we can have a larger population—but only at a high risk of partial or total loss. The slightest mismanagement could be catastrophic. Since we are gambling with the existence of our species, it would be prudent to seek a number that gives a margin of safety.

Too Many Now?

It seems likely that world population will soon exceed the number of people that the earth can safely support. Some authorities argue that we have already passed that point. Anyway, it would be foolhardy to try to exploit the full carrying capacity of the earth. We know too little about the biosphere and about our own species. To the powerful argument that security makes for limiting human populations immediately, we should add the normal desire for a "good life." This is highly subjective, but we know it includes a varied environment, a wide range of experiences, and a position high in the food web. None of these would be possible in a world supporting the maximum number of people.

In concrete terms, H. R. Hulett of Stanford University estimates that present food production would feed only 1.2 billion people by U.S. dietary standards. World energy production can serve only 600 million at the U.S. rate of consumption. And by U.S. standards there is adequate steel for 700 million people and aluminum for 500 million. (Only 6 percent of the world's present population reside in the United States, but we use 300 percent of the earth's resources.) How long resources and pollution will permit present levels of production remains uncertain. Of course, it can be argued that U.S. consumption is unnecessarily high, representing tremendous waste. But we should realize that the carrying capacity of the world may be as little as one-half billion people. If this figure or even a somewhat larger one is correct, we are in trouble. There are nearly 5 billion people on earth today, and estimates for A.D. 2000 range from 6–7 billion.

The **world food shortage** that receives periodic publicity is solid evidence of potential overpopulation. In the early 1970s minor weather fluctuations produced famine across arid sub-Saharan Africa from Senegal to Ethiopia. In desperation, starving rural people ate their breeding stock and seed grain. Many fled from the barren land to overcrowded refugee camps. Only international aid programs saved them. Now that the rain has returned, some of the people have gone back, but it may be impossible to restore the productivity of even a few years ago. Overgrazing at the time of the drought turned grasslands into desert. In plain fact, there are too many cattle and too many people on the land. This is only one example of a situation common throughout much of the world. Food problems ranging from minor shortages to near-famine conditions plague more than half of Africa, part of the Near East, India, Haiti, the Philippines, Indonesia, pockets of Central and South America, and perhaps part of China. Unless population growth is arrested quickly, widespread starvation seems inevitable.

TABLE 23.4 **Countries with Population Growth Rates over 3 Percent Yearly***

Kenya	3.9	Malawi	3.2
Syria	3.8	Morocco	3.2
Gaza	3.7	Nigeria	3.2
Honduras	3.5	Saudi Arabia	3.2
Libya	3.5	Sao Tom and Principe	3.2
Solomon Islands	3.5	Tanzania	3.2
Iraq	3.4	Uganda	3.2
Nicaragua	3.4	Bhana	3.1
Zimbabwe	3.4	Ecuador	3.1
Botswana	3.3	Iran	3.1
Algeria	3.2	Maladives	3.1
Guatemala	3.2		

*From *1982 World Population Data Sheet* of the Population Reference Bureau, Inc.

What Should We Do?

A glance at Table 23.4 reveals that most of the countries with high growth rates are those that are economically "underdeveloped." In many of these countries there is substantial resistance to using birth control. Large families are actively sought. This shouldn't be hard for people in the United States to understand, since so many people here, especially members of the older generation, cherish the large family as an ideal. And of course, for some there are religious incentives for having many children. But there can be economic motives, too.

Children as Social Security. The situation in Indian villages is typical of that in underdeveloped countries. Here families with many children have sufficient labor to take maximum advantage of the soil available. If they have more labor than is needed for the land they own, perhaps they can rent additional areas from families with few children, especially few sons. The extra labor may bring increased income that will eventually permit the large family to buy more land and increase its own security. Local social values also heap honor on parents of large families and place emphasis on leaving a male heir.

In a very real sense, children in these societies constitute social security, old-age assistance, and medical insurance for their parents. Living in a country where the government provides little, the members of a family must be highly interdependent. Old people without children often become destitute. Although everyone may agree that the country would be better off with fewer mouths, individuals who have few children make a sacrifice from which only others gain. There is no personal reward for population control. Instead, those who limit their offspring place themselves in jeopardy. It is quite apparent that one factor in regulation of the human population is the *need* for children. Remove that and we may reduce the number of births.

Some people argue that economic development is the main answer to the economic problems that promote large family size. Social scientists speak of a **demographic transition** that human populations undergo as a consequence of industrialization. Supposedly the death rate falls because of improved conditions, and then the birthrate follows. As an example, Japan underwent a nearly spontaneous revolution in childbearing not long ago. With 85 percent of their islands uninhabitable mountains, the Japanese have the highest population density for usable land for any nation on earth. But by the late 1940s, when a postwar baby boom was creating problems, Japan was a fully industrialized nation, and the old reasons for large families had nearly disappeared. Without any government action other than legislation permitting birth-control clinics, a change in thinking led to a 50-percent reduction in the birthrate. Probably a deluge of newspaper articles on the dangers of continued population growth was responsible in part for this social change.

The demographic transition seems to be a real phenomenon in all industrialized nations. Nevertheless, the reduced birthdate does not result in zero population growth. The United Kingdom has one of the lowest birthrates in the world, but the population there is still growing at an annual rate of 0.3 percent. This is enough to double the number of people in 231 years. And doubling anytime is dangerous.

Zero Population Growth

One way or another, human populations must be stabilized. This will require that the growth rate be reduced from an average of 1.9 percent worldwide to zero. Each generation in each country should just replace itself. To do this in the United States would mean that fertile couples would have an average of 2.3 children. (The 0.3 over and above the two necessary for direct replacement should compensate for childhood mortality and childless adults.)

Even reducing the birthrate to the replacement level will not stop population growth immediately. There is always a lag between reducing births to replacement level and the end of growth for the total population. This lag results from the fact that any excess children (those over the replacement number) already born will create further growth even if they have only 2.3 children per family. The increase happens because of the overlap of generations. Growth can stop immediately only if the excess young people of today have no children, or if their age group as a whole reduces its birthrate to achieve the same effect.

Some people believe that the risk from overpopulation is so great that we must strive for the "zero growth" now. To do this would require an average family size not far from one child per couple for many years. Other leaders, fearing the economic and social results of a birthrate well below replacement level, advocate working for "replacement only" in the immediate future. This policy will delay achievement of zero growth and will increase significantly the level at which world population will eventually stabilize (Fig. 23.9).

As imperative as it seems, limitation of the human population, either immediately or within a few years, has many opponents. Their arguments rest on a variety of assumptions. One of the most common is that continued population expansion is essential to continued economic growth and thereby to full employment and prosperity. Of course, there are other reasons, too. Some individuals equate growth with progress and find limitation on human population to be in conflict with what they see as our destiny. Others believe that God's will ordains people to "be fruitful and multiply and replenish the earth" (Genesis 1:28). The educational task of convincing everyone to cooperate in limiting our numbers is so great that even the most optimistic proponents recognize that progress will be slow. However, each delay increases the minimum stabilization level, stretches resources even more tightly, and reduces our options.

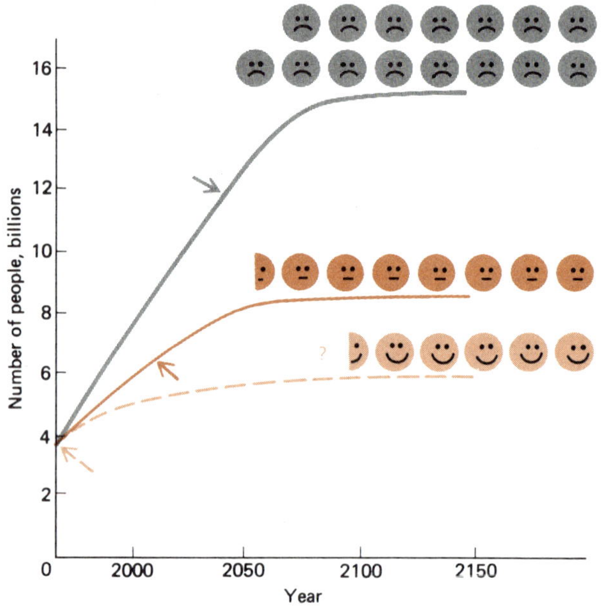

FIGURE 23.9 **How Soon? How Many?** The sooner the birthrate drops to replacement level (→) the lower total population we can achieve.

REGULATION OF POPULATION LEVELS

Although biological literature contains descriptions of numerous population explosions, each has passed without overwhelming the biosphere. Clearly there are inherent regulatory mechanisms that both pro-

454 mote and limit animal numbers. □Humans are surely subject to the same kinds of regulatory mechanisms as other animals are. Of course, cultural evolution may have rendered some of these mechanisms ineffective for our species.

We have seen that external factors, internal physiological mechanisms, and social behavior all serve to regulate animal populations. Do these same factors control human populations? There can be little doubt that starvation and disease take their toll of human lives. But the fact that long-established hunter-and-gatherer cultures exhibit limited population growth suggests other basic mechanisms that adjust human reproduction to fit the resources.

Nutrition and Ovulation

Studies of little-disturbed cultures such as the !Kung (see Box 2C) provide insight into the processes by which we once regulated our numbers. Among the !Kung there is an average of four years between births. This spacing is necessary, since the mothers nurse their children about three years, or until they are able to digest the available adult foods. The absence of contraceptive information and the rarity of infanticide suggest that some purely biological device is at work. One factor is the long nursing period; another is the fact that infants nurse at frequent intervals, day and night. This activity may suppress ovulation through hormonal means. The nutritional strain of long-continued nursing also may suppress ovulation.

Studies show a minimum of body fat to be necessary both for the onset of fertility in the young and for resumption of ovulation after childbirth. It seems possible that !Kung women, living an exceedingly active life on a low-calorie diet, do not restore their body fat to the critical level so long as they nurse a child. Observation on !Kung who have adopted a settled life support this notion. Women in these villages wean their babies early to a diet of grain meal and cow's milk. Among such settled !Kung the intervals between births have fallen, and the population is growing rapidly.

The effect of nutritional status on female fertility isn't limited to hunters and gatherers. It was demonstrated during World War II, when many European women lived in concentration camps or besieged cities such as Leningrad. Birthrates dropped to nearly zero among these populations. Only occasional women conceived; those who did had almost always received special dietary allotments.

Social and Economic Controls

The fact that nutritional status can limit reproduction among healthy women such as the !Kung doesn't mean that all hunters and gatherers rely on this mechanism. Many, including Eskimos and Australian aborigines, depend heavily on infanticide. Also, in many cultures, taboos regulate the resumption of sexual intercourse after childbirth.

Human population growth quickly recoups losses sustained in war or epidemics and takes advantage of political and technological developments that increase the carrying capacity. Such flexibility could hardly result from changes in mortality alone; there must also be alteration in the birthrate. It seems that for a long time most cultures have relied on contraception or on social means of regulating births. The interaction of social, economic, and biological factors is evident in preindustrial European populations.

Consider the French province of Beauvais between 1692 and 1695 (Fig. 23.10). Here the records of births, deaths, and marriages in three parishes reflect quite different responses to a series of unusually cold and rainy summers. Auneuil relied on mixed agriculture; people grew grain on plowed land and pastured animals in the meadows. The same summer rains that destroyed the wheat crop favored growth of grass and increased the supply of meat and milk. Breteuil, on the other hand, was an upland community where almost all the land was planted to wheat. Failure of that crop brought disaster. But it was in Mouy, a village that manufactured woolen goods, that people suffered the most. When the poor wheat crop caused flour prices to soar throughout the province, no one had money to buy clothes. In this simple economy the men and women of Mouy were caught between rising food costs and decreasing income.

There can be little doubt that the population of Beauvais hung poised near the carrying capacity of the land. The increased death rates may reflect the weakening effects of malnutrition that made people more susceptible to disease, even if no one died directly from starvation. Perhaps part of the dip in birthrates resulted from failure of ovulation in poorly nourished women. But there is evidence that the people also tried to control their repro-

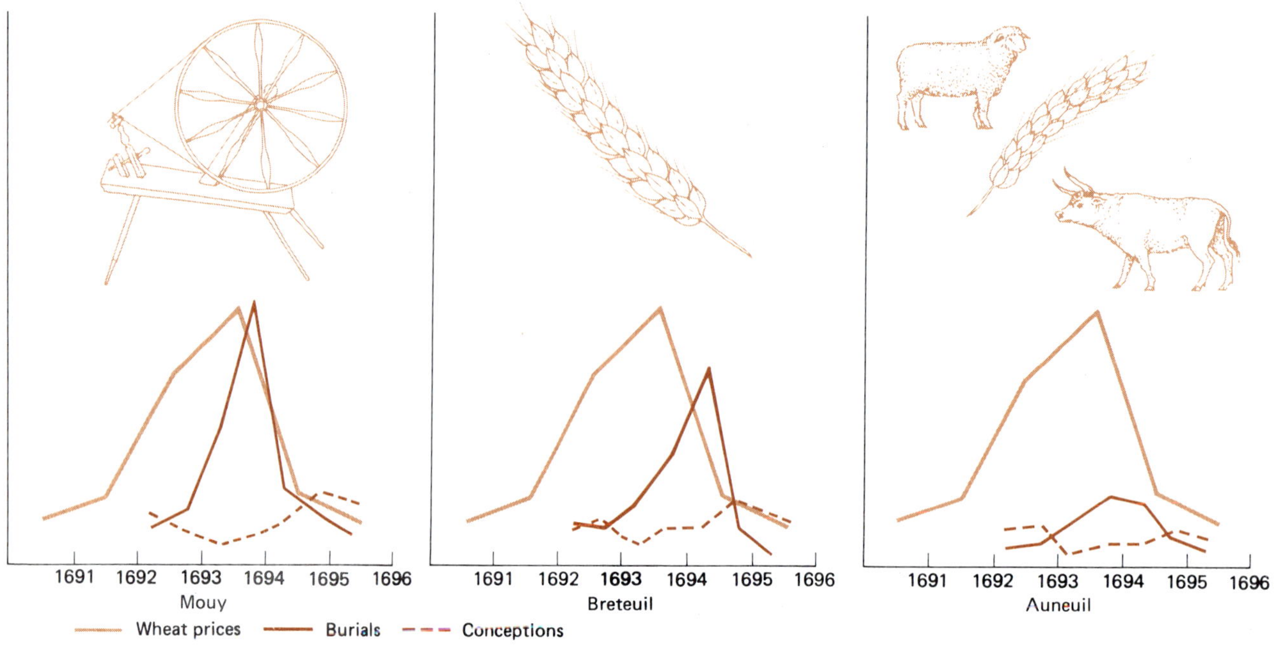

FIGURE 23.10 Famine in Seventeenth-Century France.

duction. Admonitions in midwives' oaths and charges in ecclesiastical courts show attempts by the authorities to suppress abortion, infanticide,
288 and contraception. Coitus interruptus□ and contraceptive douches were surely in use.

Marriages often increased immediately after a famine. There must have been a reservoir of unmarried adults. We can only speculate as to what prevented these people from marrying earlier, but the lack of vacant houses and the inability of men to secure sufficient acreage to support families seem likely factors. Direct social pressures were probably involved, too. At that time servants and tenants often needed the permission of landlords to marry. One family under one roof was generally the rule; couples were expected to establish their own home rather than move in with parents. In fact, in many European societies, only the eldest son inherited property and with that the right to marry. It is easy to see how such rules could limit population.

The Future: An Epilogue

What does the future hold for the human species? No one knows, but if we don't control our numbers quickly, surely we face intense competition for food and perhaps massive starvation. Thomas Malthus, the late eighteenth-century Anglican parson who first popularized the quandary we face, used the terms "misery and vice" to describe the alternatives to population control. Malthus recognized that populations grew exponentially but that the means of subsistence could never increase in that manner. In other words, the population increase of one generation contributes to increase in future generations. But success of one season's crops will not increase production in later years.

The nineteenth century mocked Malthus, partly because he was so unsympathetic to the poor and partly because he was a pessimist.

While industrial expansion and chemical and techological revolutions were expanding jobs, food, and shelter (at least for most people), Malthus was ignored. Despite devastating wars, widespread malnutrition, and numerous cases of starvation, people haven't often linked these causes of human misery to increasing population.

Now, as we approach the end of the twentieth century, many men and women recognize that Malthus was at least partly right. Populations do expand exponentially while resources are increasing linearly, if at all. But despite the need for population control, we know little more about this aspect of human biology than Malthus did. Until recently, prudishness and smugness made reproductive biology a poor stepchild to other disciplines. Coupled with our ignorance of population control mechanisms is the fact that public recognition of the risks of continued population growth is low in many groups. With the crisis upon us, too many people are unwilling to recognize it, much less to contribute to the solution.

There are over 100,000 more people on earth today than there were yesterday. There will be as many more tomorrow. It is foolish to look for technological "fixes" to feed these mouths, for that won't solve the problem. Every additional human is a potential parent. And we have seen that our manipulations often degrade the biosphere. Considering the interrelations of the biosphere, the only safe answer is to limit reproduction worldwide.

Summary

1. Environmental resistance prevents the reproductive potential of a population from being fully expressed. Again and again, technological advances have reduced the environmental resistance against human populations and permitted population increases. Human populations may now exceed the carrying capacity of the biosphere.

2. Any positive growth rate will eventually double a population. Such doubling will continue so long as growth occurs.

3. Growth of populations is exponential; i.e., growth of one generation causes an increased growth rate the next generation, even when the number of young per female remains constant.

4. Because death after the time of reproduction has no effect on the size of the next generation, lengthening this part of the life span is of little consequence to population growth. In contrast, childhood deaths and others that limit individuals' reproduction can alter population growth drastically.

5. Increases in the growth rate of humans during the twentieth century result largely from reduced infant and childhood mortality.

6. Because children today are more numerous than their parental generation, zero population growth could be achieved immediately only by restricting most families to one child.

7. Regulation of human populations often involves cultural factors, but there may be biological regulatory mechanisms as well. Prolonged nursing and poor nutritional status may depress ovulation.

Thought and Controversy

1. "Nobody ever dies of overpopulation."* Overpopulation never appears in reports of vital statistics as a cause of death. Instead, we find kwashiorkor,□ infec- 116
tious diseases to which the malnourished become susceptible, floods that wash away homes built on marginal lands, and emphysema caused by polluted air belching from factories essential to the support of large populations.

2. Opponents of population control sometimes argue that the United States is, in fact, woefully underpopulated, because it has a much lower average population density than some prosperous countries, such as the Netherlands. This "Netherlands fallacy" ignores the effect of patterns of concentration and dispersion of people in response to the quality of the land. The Netherlands is much like the state of New Jersey. Both are highly industrialized, both have some fine farmland, both rely heavily on ocean commerce, both are on the edge of continents with high agricultural productivity, and both have population densities near 900 people per square mile. And it is very likely that neither could survive if cut off from the remainder of the world. In fact, the people of the Netherlands and the people of New Jersey rely on food and fertilizer from around the world; in turn, they supply manufactured products and other services to distant people. How could anyone expect the Great Salt Lake Desert to

---

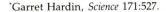

*Garret Hardin, *Science* 171:527.

support the same population that the Netherlands supports? Or if Iowa had as many people per acre as New Jersey has, who would feed either?

3. Population growth underlies almost every crisis or concern. Consider the question of food additives. Among the reasons for their use is the fact that increased population stimulates demand for food. Indeed, population growth has been possible partly because technical advances have permitted the transport of food from distant agricultural areas to large cities and allowed for storage long after harvest. Many food additives prevent spoilage in transport and storage and, in effect, increase the food supply. For example, fats turn rancid (oxidize) with time. The answer has been to use antioxidants such as BHA (butylated hydroxy anisole) and BHT (butylated hydroxytoluene). Other additives serve as cheap substitutes for scarce materials and, in one sense, stretch the food supply. For example, bakery products that normally contain eggs are yellow. Often yellow food coloring is used in eggless or nearly eggless recipes to create the illusion that the product is rich in eggs. Can you think of other examples?

4. Information on China, the most populous country in the world, is scant, both because records in that vast area are imperfectly kept, and because the government finds it advantageous to conceal information (a trait not limited to the Chinese). Since 1972, government representatives have claimed that the country is self-sufficient in food production, although fertilizer must be imported. There is evidence that the leaders understand the threat of continued population growth and willingly use economic coercion to limit births. When the Communists took over in the 1950s, a small amount of land in each community was set aside for private use. Crops grown on this land are for the sole use of the individual families working the plots. The remainder of the land is held and worked by the commune, and the produce is sold to the government. Although each worker shares in the receipts of the commune in accordance with his or her contribution in labor, the food grown on the private land contributes significantly to the individual diet. When the private land was initially assigned, each adult received a plot (1/150 of a hectare), and so did the two eldest children in each family. Additional children received no land. The plots are inherited, and now, a generation later, the shortage of land in some families provides strong motivation to limit the number of children. The government has also recognized that the aged traditionally depend on their children, and that fear of a hungry old age may compel peasants to have large families. Residences for the dependent elderly have been established and are supported by taxes on commune earnings. Whether such measures will curb population growth remains to be seen. If they do, can this success be used to justify the establishment of communistic governments in other developing countries? When pondering this question, remember the complexity and antiquity of Chinese culture.

Questions

1. What factors determine the reproductive potential of a human population? Is this full potential ever expressed?

2. Why do populations undergo exponential growth? Compare this exponential growth to the growth of resources.

3. Draw the three characteristic curves that describe population growth under various conditions. Explain each curve.

4. Draw one age pyramid for a country that has experienced rapid population growth over the past 50 years and another for a country that has grown slowly throughout this time.

5. Explain why reducing the birthrate to an average of two children per couple would result in continued population growth for many years.

6. What are some of the factors that maintain a high human birth rate?

7. Discuss the factors limiting human populations.

8. Compare the effects on population levels brought about by the following: (a) childhood mortality; (b) a high incidence of cancer and heart disease that causes many people to die early.

9. What evidence is there that the human population has approached or perhaps exceeded the carrying capacity of the earth?

10. Was Malthus basically right? What events prevented his predictions from being recognized as valid in the nineteenth century?

Further Reading for Part Six

Brill, Winston J., 1981. Agricultural microbiology. *Scientific American* 245(3):198–215. (October)

Brown, Lester R., 1979. Resource trends and population policy: A time for reassessment. *Worldwatch Papers.* Worldwatch Institute, Washington, D.C.

Burmaster, David E., 1982. The new pollution: Ground water contamination. *Environment* 24(2):6–26. (March)

Gwatkin, Davidson R., and Sarah K. Brandel, 1982. Life expectancy and population growth in the third world. *Scientific American* 246(5):57–65. (May)

Hayes, Denis, 1979. Pollution: The neglected dimensions. *Worldwatch Papers.* Worldwatch Institute, Washington, D.C.

Hiatt, Blanchard, 1982. To increase survival. *Mosaic:* 26–32. (May/June)

de Nevers, Noel, 1981. Measuring and managing pollutants. *Environment* 23(5):25–35 (June)

Revkin, Andrew C., 1983. Paraquat. *Science Digest* 91(6):36–104. (June)

Sheldon, Richard P., 1982. Phosphate rock. *Scientific American* 246(6):45–50. (June)

Shepard, James F., 1982. The regeneration of potato plants from leaf-cell protoplasts. *Scientific American* 246(5):154–166. (May)

Ware, Helen, 1978. The economic value of children in Asia and Africa: Comparative perspective. *Papers of the East-West Population Institute # 50.* East-West Population Institute, Honolulu. (April)

Glossary

Abortion Any premature termination of pregnancy. May occur spontaneously as the result of a defect in the embryo or placenta (a miscarriage) or be induced by outside intervention.
Abscission layer (ab-SCISS--shun) A region specialized for separation of a leaf from the stem.
Absorption Entrance of fluids or dissolved substances into cells or tissue.
Abyssal plain (a-BIS-al) The broad flat surface of the ocean floor.
Accommodation Adaptation; specifically adaptation of the eye to properly focus light from objects nearer or further away.
Acetylcholine (uh-SEET-ul-KO-leen) An organic compound secreted by the axons of many neurons; i.e., a neurotransmitter.
Acid (*L.* sour) A compound that yields hydrogen ions (protons) when added to water. Neutralized by bases, forming salts. Have a pH less than 7, the opposite of alkaline. (See **Base**.)
Actin (AK-tin) One of the proteins involved in muscle contraction; makes up the thin filaments.
Action potential The temporary reversal of the relative charge on the inner and outer surfaces of the plasma membrane. The action potential of a nerve cell is the physical basis of the nerve impulse.
Action spectrum A graphic representation of the effect of different wavelengths of light on some process or activity; for example, the rate of oxygen evolution by photosynthesizing plants.
Activation energy The minimum amount of energy needed to start a chemical reaction.
Active immunity Immunity that results from the stimulation of B-cell and/or T-cell activities by exposure to antigenic substances, such as that occurring from having a disease or by vaccination.
Active site That portion of an enzyme molecule that binds the substrate during catalysis.
Active transport An energy-requiring process by which materials move across the plasma membrane into or out of cells.
Adaptation A change in an organism that brings it into closer harmony with its environment. Individual organisms are capable of a variety of physiological adaptations that adjust body organs to changes in temperature, etc. This contrasts with evolutionary adaptations of species that arise by natural selection of individuals possessing hereditary traits best suited to the environment.
Adaptive radiation The formation of several new species from one possessing a characteristic or group of characteristics of special value.
Adenosine triphosphate (ATP) (uh-DEN-oh-seen try-FOSS-fate) A nucleotide that serves as the principal source of chemical energy in cell metabolism. On hydrolysis of ATP, energy is released with the formtion of inorganic phosphate and adenosine diphosphate (ADP).
Adhesion One substance sticking to another.
Adrenal (uh-DREEN-al) (*L.* upon + kidney) Glands that lie on the kidneys. Composed of an outer adrenal cortex that secretes steroid hormones such as aldosterone and an inner medulla that secretes epinephrin and norepinephrine.
Adrenal corticotropic hormone (ACTH) (CORE-tee-co-TROF-ik) Anterior pituitary secretion that promotes production by the adrenal cortex of hormones that stimulate glucose synthesis and inhibit inflammation.
Adrenalin (uh-DREN-uh-lun) (See **Epinephrine**.)
Adsorption Adhesion of a small molecule or particle to the surface; e.g., the attachment of a virus particle to the plasma membrane of its host cell.
Adventitious (ADD-ven-tis-us) (*L.* arrival) A root or other structure that originates in an unusual manner.

Aerobic (air-ROH-bik) (*Gk.* air + life) Requiring atmospheric oxygen.

Agglutination (uh-GLOOT-in-AY-shun) (*L.* to glue to a thing) The clumping of particles, cells, or molecules; the visible combination of an antibody and a particulate antigen.

Alcohol An easily vaporized organic compound containing one or several OH groups. (C_2H_5OH or methanol, CH_3OH).

Aldosterone (al-DOSS-tuh-rone) A steroid hormone produced by the adrenal cortex and involved in regulation of sodium and potassium in body fluids.

Algae Mostly aquatic photosynthetic eucaryotic organisms that lack vascular tissue and distinct organs. Some are unicellular; others, such as seaweeds, are multicellular.

Alkaline Pertaining to basic conditions; i.e., the opposite of acid; having a pH greater than 7. (See **Base**.)

Allele (uh-LEEL) (*Gk.* of one another) Alternative form of a gene. Alleles determine alternate expressions of the same trait and occupy similar sites on homologous chromosomes.

Allergy (AL-er-gee) A hypersensitivity to some substance in the environment. Involves inflammation due to reaction of antigens with antibodies attached to cell surfaces or the activities of activated T-cells.

All-or-none response An event occurring to its fullest extent or not at all. Describes the transmission of a nerve impulse.

Allosteric (al-o-STEHR-ik) (*Fr.* other + *Gk.* solid) Refers to regulatory enzymes with an active site for catalysis of a substrate and a different or allosteric site that reacts with another substance to alter the catalytic activity of the enzyme.

Alpha radiation Helium nuclei emitted from radioactive isotopes of elements.

Alternation of generations A plant life cycle in which the haploid gametophyte, or sexual phase, is followed by the diploid sporophyte, or asexual phase. Spores, produced from the sporophyte, give rise to new gametophytes.

Alveolus (al-VEE-uh-lus) (*L.* hollow) A tiny air sac in the lung. The site of gas exchange between the air and the capillaries.

Amino acid (am-EE-no) Organic acids that contain nitrogen in the form of an amino ($-NH_2$) group. The subunits of which proteins are composed.

Aminocentesis (AM-nee-oh-SEN-tee-sus) A method used to tap the amniotic fluid and obtain a sample of the cells present there.

Amino group A slightly basic chemical group ($-NH_2$), characteristic of nitrogenous bases and amino acids.

Amnion (AM-nee-on) (*Gk.* lamb) A membrane around the embryo of reptiles, birds, and mammals. Contains a fluid that bathes the embryo.

Amoeboid Resembling the protozoan *Amoeba* in the ability to change shape by alteration of the consistency of cytoplasm. Also used to describe a form of movement by cytoplasmic flow.

Amphibian (*Gk.* having a double life) Vertebrate animals that have characteristics between those of fish and repitiles and that live partly on land but usually reproduce in the water.

Amylase (AM-uh-lace)(*L.* starch) An enzyme that breaks down starch into sugar.

Anaerobic (an-uh-ROH-bik) (*Gk.* not + air + life) Without atmospheric oxygen.

Anamnestic response (an-am-NEHS-tihk) The rapid reappearance of an antibody in the blood of a previously immune individual after exposure to the antigen by infection or by a booster shot.

Anaphase (AN-uh-faze) (*Gk.* to carry back + phase) A stage of cell division characterized by movement of the chromosomes toward the poles of the spindle.

Anemia (uh-NEE-mee-uh) (*Gk.* no blood) A condition resulting from a decreased production or increased destruction of red blood cells; a lack of hemoglobin.

Angiosperm (AN-jee-uh-sperm) (*Gk.* vessel + seed) A flowering plant; a plant whose seeds are enclosed in fruits.

Annelid (ANN-uh-lid) A member of a major phylum of worms characterized by numerous similar body segments and the absence of jointed legs. Includes earthworms, tubeworms, clamworms, and leeches.

Annual plant A plant that normally reproduces and dies within a single year.

Anterior Located in or towards the front. In four-legged animals this refers to the head end. In humans it usually indicates in or toward the belly (ventral) surface.

Anther The pollen-bearing portion of a stamen of a flower.

Anthocyanins (anth-oh-SIan-ins) Water-soluble blue, purple, or red plant pigments found in vacuoles.

Anthropomorphic (AN-throw-po-MORE-fic) (*Gk.* human + form) Attributing human characteristics to nonhuman forms.

Antibiotic (an-tee-by-OTT-ik) (*Gk.* against + pertaining to life) A substance secreted by one microorganism that inhibits the growth of other microorganisms.

Antibody (*Gk.* against + body) A specific protein synthesized in response to the presence of a foreign substance. (See **Antigen**).

Anticodon (an-tee-KOH-don) (*L.* against + codon) The sequence of three nucleotides in transfer RNA that pairs complementarily with three nucleotide codons of messenger RNA.

Antidiuretic hormone (ADH) (an-tee-dy-yuh-RET-ik) A hormone produced in the hypothalamus and released from the posterior pituitary; promotes water resorption in the kidneys.

Antigen (AN-ti-jen) (*Gk.* against + produce) A foreign material that elicits the synthesis of a particular kind of molecule, the antibody, within an organism. (See **Antibody**.)

Antiserum (ANT-ih-sihr-uhm) Blood serum containing antibodies; injected to provide temporary immunity or as treatment for an illness.
Anus (*L.* annus, ring) The posterior opening of the digestive tract.
Aorta (a-ORE-ta) (*Gk.* airen = to lift) The major artery. It carries oxygenated blood away from the heart, and its branches distribute the blood throughout the body.
Ape A tailless primate with adaptations for brachiation and the same number of each tooth type as humans.
Apical Referring to the tip (apex) of a stem or root of a plant, as in apical meristem.
Apical meristem The plant tissue at the tip of a stem or root where continuing cell division causes growth in length; the growing tip.
Appendix The pencil-shaped sac on the colon near its junction with the small intestine. The lining is tonsil-like.
Arboreal (ar-BOR-e-al) (*L.* tree) Dwelling in trees.
Artery A vessel that carries blood away from the heart.
Arthropod (ARE-throw-pod) (*Gk.* joint + foot) A member of the largest animal phylum; characterized by an exoskeleton and jointed appendages. Includes crabs, krill, spiders, and insects.
Asexual reproduction Any method of reproduction not involving gametes.
Atherosclerosis (ATH-uh-roh-skloh-ROH-sis) Deposits of lipids and debris on the inside of arteries.
Atom (*Gk.* indivisible) The smallest unit of an element that has the properties of that element.
Atomic number The number of protons in the nucleus of an atom of a chemical element. In a neutral atom it is equal to the number of electrons.
Atomic weight The relative weight of an atom compared to a standard element, usually oxygen whose atomic weight is given as 16.
ATP See **Adenosine triphosphate**.
Atrium (A-tree-um) (pl. **Atria**) A chamber, especially a receiving chamber of the heart.
Autoimmune disease A disorder that results from an immune response to the body's own constituents.
Autonomic nervous system (ott-oh-NOM-ik) (*Gk.* independent) Neural centers and pathways that stimulate or inhibit action by internal organs without conscious decision. Involves nerves, ganglia, and parts of the brain and spinal cord. Divided into sympathetic and parasympathetic portions.
Autosome (OTT-oh-sohm) (*Gk.* self + body) Any chromosome that is not a sex chromosome; e.g., those human chromosomes other than the X- and Y-chromosomes.
Autotroph (OTT-oh-trohf) (*Gk.* self + to nourish) An organism capable of utilizing carbon dioxide as the sole source of carbon for the synthesis of organic compounds. Includes green plants, fungi, and some bacteria. (See **Heterotroph**.)
Auxin (OX-in) (*L.* increase) A plant-growth-regulating substance; e.g., indoleacetic acid (IAA).
Axon (AX-on) (*Gk.* = axis) A usually long and little-branched fiber of a neuron; carries impulses from the cell body toward the next neuron in the pathway.

Back cross In genetics, a test cross to determine whether an organism with a dominant phenotype is heterozygous or homozygous. The dominant is crossed with a homozygous recessive. If some progeny are recessive the dominant must have been heterozygous.
Bacteriophage (bak-TEE-ree-uh-fayj) (*L.* little rod + *Gk.* to eat) A virus that infects bacteria.
Bacterium (pl. **Bacteria**) Microscopic, unicellular procaryotic organisms.
Bark Tissues of a woody stem external to the cambium. Composed mainly of phloem and cork or epidermis.
Barr body (for M. L. Barr, an American geneticist) A dense nuclear region in the cells of female mammals. Represents a nonfunctional X-chromosome.
Basal body A centriole-like structure at the base of flagella and cilia of eucaryotic cells.
Base A substance that yields hydroxyl (OH^-) ions when added to water. Synonym of alkali. The opposite of an acid. (See **Acid**.)
Base pairing The hydrogen bonding of two nitrogenous bases—adenine with thymine (or uracil, in RNA) and cytosine with guanine—which stabilizes the DNA helix and specific DNA replication and RNA synthesis.
B Cells Lymphocytes that produce circulating antibodies or differentiate into plasma cells that produce such antibodies.
Benign (BEE-nine) Harmless; not malignant.
Benthic zone (BEN-thik) The ocean deeps, below the region of light penetration.
Beta radiation (BAY-tuh) Electrons emitted from radioactive isotopes of elements.
Biennial plant A plant that normally reproduces during its second year and then dies.
Bilateral symmetry The arrangement of parts so that the organism can be divided into mirror images by only one plane.
Bile Secretion of the liver, which is temporarily stored in the gall bladder; emulsifies fats in the small intestine.
Binary fission The splitting of an oganism into two parts. A form of asexual reproduction.
Binomial nomenclature The system of naming organisms by giving the genus name and the species name, in that order: e.g., *Homo sapiens*.
Biogeochemical cycle The circulation of the atoms of an element through the various living and nonliving components of the biosphere.
Biological oxygen demand (BOD) Oxygen necessary to support full activities of all organisms present. Used as a measure of water pollution.
Bioluminescence (by-oh-LOO-mi-NESS-ens) (*Gk.* life + *L.* light) The emission of light by living organisms; the direct conversion of chemical energy to light energy.

Biomass (BY-oh-MASS) The total weight of living matter in a particular category.
Biome (BY-ohm) A large biological community characterized by a general vegetation type.
Biosphere (BY-oh-SFEAR) The ecosystem encompassing all parts of the earth and its atmosphere that are inhabited by living things.
Biosynthesis Biological formation of complex organic molecules from simple building blocks.
Bird An endothermic vertebrate having feathers.
Blastocyst (BLAS-toh-sist) (*Gk.* germ + bag) The product of cleavage in mammals. This early stage is equivalent to the blastula of other vertebrates, but only the inner cell mass gives rise to the embryo proper.
Blastopore (blast-OH-pore) An embryonic opening into the digestive system.
Blastula (BLAS-chuh-luh) (*Gk.* germ) An early embryonic stage consisting of a hollow sphere of cells.
Bolus (BOH-luss) (*L.* morsel) A moistened, softened mass of food being passed through the digestive system.
Boreal (BORE-ee-ul) Northern, especially northern forests and tundra.
Bowman's capsule (after Sir William Bowman, nineteenth-century British physician) In a kidney, one of the microscopic cup-shaped structures at the end of a nephron; filters water and other substances from blood.
Brachiation (BRAK-ee-a-shon) (*L.* arm) Swinging from arm to arm along an overhead support.
Bract A small, specialized, leaflike structure.
Brainstem The stalk of the brain, relaying messages between the spinal cord and higher centers. It is divided into the medulla, pons, and midbrain.
Bronchus (BRONG-kus) (*Gk.* windpipe) One of the branches of the trachea serving as a passage for air in the lungs.
Bryophyte (bry-OH-fite) (*Gk.* moss + plant) One of many small, usually terestrial, plants biochemically related to vascular plants but lacking xylem and phloem.
Budding A form of asexual reproduction in which a new cell is formed as an outgrowth of the parent cell; common in yeasts.
Buffer A substance or mixture that tends to prevent a change in pH when acid or alkali are needed.
Bundle sheath A cellular layer around the veins of leaves.

Caecum (SEE-come) (*L.* blind) A sac on the small intestine near its junction with the large intestine; site of microbial digestion of cellulose in many mammals. In humans the caecum bears the appendix.
Calorie (*L.* to be warm) The amount of heat necessary to raise one gram of water one degree celsius.
Calvin cycle The process by which carbon dioxide is reduced to carbohydrates during photosynthesis.
Cambium (KAM-bee-um) (*L.* change) A thin layer of meristematic tissue whose cells, by repeated cell divisions, increase the diameter of stems and roots.
Camp See **Cyclic AMP**.
Cancer (*Gk.* crab) A malignant growth; a tumor that invades normal tissue and spreads.
Canopy The upper leafy layer of a forest.
Capillary (KAP-uh-layr-ee) (*L.* hair) A small, thin-walled vessel that permits exchange of nutrients and gases between the blood and tissues; the tiny connecting vessels between arteries and veins.
Capillary action The movement of water that results from the cohesion of water molecules as well as their adhesion to a surface such as the inside of a narrow tube.
Carbohydrates Organic compounds composed of carbon, hydrogen, and oxygen in the ratio 1:2:1. Serve as energy sources and storage substances in cell metabolism, more rarely as structural elements, e.g., sugars, starches, glycogen, cellulose.
Carbonates CO_3^- or compounds including such ions.
Carbon dioxide fixation The binding of gaseous carbon dioxide to an organic acceptor molecule such as in the Calvin cycle of photosynthesis.
Carbon monoxide (CO) A colorless, odorless gas; a product of incomplete oxidation of organic fuels, dangerous because it can displace oxygen in the red blood cells.
Carboxyl group A chemical group (–COOH) that confers weakly acidic properties to organic molecules.
Carcinogen Any agent that stimulates production of malignant tumors (cancer).
Cardiac (CAR-dee-ak) (*L.* heart) Pertaining to the heart.
Carnivore A flesh eater.
Carotenoid A class of fat-soluble pigments including carotenes and ranging in color from yellow to red.
Carpel (*Gk.* fruit) A leaflike structure that surrounds and supports the ovules.
Carrying capacity The population of a particular species that a given area can support permanently.
Cartilage A firm but not hard connective tissue found in the fetal skeleton and in joints. Consists largely of gelled cell products and lacks a direct blood supply.
Castration Removal of the gonads.
Catalyst (KAT-uh-list) (*Gk.* a throwing down) A substance that speeds up a chemical reaction without permanently entering into the reaction itself.
Catkin A scaly, generally drooping, unisexual inflorescence.
Cell (*L.* small room) The fundamental unit of organisms. Composed of a plasma membrane, cytoplasm and nuclear materials, and, often, organelles. Plant cells and bacteria have cell walls. (See **Procaryote** and **Eucaryote**.)
Cell body The region of a cell, usually a neuron, where the nucleus is located.
Cell cycle The life cycle of a cell, divided into phases; i.e., mitosis, pre-DNA synthesis, DNA synthesis, post-DNA synthesis.
Cell line Cells having a common origin; specifically cells that have multiplied from one tissue cultured at some particular time.
Cell membrane See **Plasma membrane.**

Cellular respiration See **Respiration.**
Cellulose (SELL-uh-lohs) A polysaccharide formed from glucose units; the main component of the cell wall in land plants.
Cell wall A more or less rigid cell structure located outside the plasma membrane in green plants, fungi, and bacteria. Its primary function is to provide support and protection.
Central dogma The belief that the genetic information of cells flows from DNA to RNA to protein.
Central nervous system (CNS) The brain and spinal cord.
Centriole (SEN-tree-ohl) (*L.* center) A self-replicating, cylindrical organelle composed of microtubules; located just outside the nucleus of animal and some plant cells. Centrioles occur in pairs, acting as focal points at opposite ends of the cell during nuclear division.
Centromere (SEN-troh-meer) (*Gk.* center + part) Region of a chromosome that attaches to the spindle during cell division.
Cerebellum (ser-uh-BELL-um) (*L.* brain) A large lobe of the hindbrain; contains centers for motor coordination.
Cerebral spinal fluid A watery liquid found in brain cavities and forming a cushion around the central nervous system. It is produced inside the brain and absorbed into blood vessels within the meninges.
Cerebrum (se-REE-brum) (*L.* brain) The largest region of the mammalian brain. This greatly enlarged portion of the forebrain consists of left and right hemispheres which, in humans, are highly convuluted and contain centers for locomotion and sensations; controls the higher functions.
Cervix (SER-viks) (*L.* neck) The constricted lower portion or "neck" of the uterus just above the vagina.
Chaparral (SHAP -uh-ral) (*Span.*) A vegetation of small trees and shrubs with small, leathery leaves.
Character displacement Alteration of the gene pool and hence the ecological niche of a species in response to competition.
Chemical bond An attractive force by which atoms are held in a close association.
Chemiosmotic theory The idea that energy for ATP synthesis can be obtained by the establishment of a proton gradient across the inner mitochondrial membrane.
Chemoreceptor (KEE-moh-ree-SEP-ter) Sense organ or cell that detects certain chemical substances.
Chemosynthesis A form of metabolism in which ATP can only be produced by the oxidation of chemical compounds.
Chemotherapy The treatment of disease by the administration of chemical agents.
Chiasma, pl. **chiasmata** (KYE-as-ma) The X-shaped junction of the chromatids of synapsed chromosomes; site where crossing-over occurs.
Chitin (KYE-tin) (*Gk.* tunic) An insoluble, tough, horny nitrogen-containing polysaccharide forming the cell wall of some fungi and the exoskeleton of the arthropods.
Chlorophyll (KLOR-oh-fill) (*Gk.* green + leaf) The green pigments of plant cells; absorb light energy during photosynthesis.
Chloroplast (KLOR-oh-plast) (*Gk.* green + formed) A chlorophyll-containing membraneous organelle of plant cells. Site of photosynthesis.
Cholesterol (Koh-LESS-tuh-role) A steroidal lipid important in the structure of many animal-cell plasma membranes. Also needed for the synthesis of bile and sex hormones.
Chordate (core-DATE) The animal phylum that includes sea squirts, lanclets, and vertebrates; characterized by a hollow dorsal nerve cord, a notochord, and pharyngeal slits.
Chorionic gonadotrophin (kohr-ee-ON-ok goh-nad-oh-TROH-fin) or **-tropin** (-TROH-pin) A hormone produced by the embryonic membranes that are incorporated into the placenta. Necessary to maintain the corpus luteum during pregnancy.
Chromatid (KRO-ma-tid) One of the two strands of a duplicated chromosome.
Chromatin (KRO-ma-tin) (*Gk.* color) The readily stainable material of the chromosomes; composed of DNA and proteins.
Chromosome (KROHM-uh-sohm) (*Gk.* color + body) Cell structure that contains hereditary units; i.e., genes. Visible only during cell division.
Chyme (KIME) A soupy slurry of partially digested food and enzymes.
Ciliate (SILLY-ate) A member of a group of protozoa that move by means of cilia.
Cilium (SILL-ee-um) pl. **Cilia** (*L.* eyelash) A short, hair-like locomotor structure on the surface of some cells. Generally found in large numbers.
Circadian rhythms (sir-KADE-de-un) (*L.* about + day) Patterns of activity about 24 hours in length.
Clay Extremely fine mineral particles, especially hydrated aluminum silicates. Forms a paste when wet and hardens when heated.
Cleavage The cell divisions that convert a fertilized egg into a blastula.
Climax vegetation The terminal stage of community succession. Maintains itself until disrupted by some external process.
Clitoris (KLIT-uh-riss) (*Gk.* small hill) A small female organ lying anterior to the urethral opening. Similar in sensory function and origin to the tip of the penis.
Cloaca (klo-A-ka) A common passageway out of the body for the products of the digestive, excretory, and reproductive systems in birds, reptiles, amphibians, and many fishes.
Clone (KLOHN) A group of genetically identical cells or organisms. Always arises asexually.
Cnidaria (NID-air-ea) See **Coelenterate.**
Cnidoblast (NID-oh-blast) Stinging cells of coelenterates and related animals of the phylum cnidaria.
Codon (KOH-don) A sequence of three nucleotides in

messenger RNA that specifies a single amino acid of a protein.

Coelenterate (see-lin-TER-ate) (*Gk.* cavity + intestine) A member of a phylum of animals including hydra, sea anemones, corals, and jelly fish. Body is a hollow sac with tentacles. Protected by stinging cells. Also known as Cnidaria.

Coelom (SEE-loam) (*Gk.* cavity) A body cavity completely lined with mesoderm.

Coenzyme (koh-EN-zime) (*L.* with + *Gk.* in + yeast) A compound generally derived from a vitamin; acts as an accessory in an enzyme-catalyzed reaction. Coenzymes often donate or accept substances involved in a reaction. *Example:* NAD, hydrogen carrier.

Coevolution The simultaneous evolution of two or more species in which each exerts selection on the other(s). Often coevolution produces mutual dependence.

Cohesion (co-HE-shun) The holding together of like molecules or substances.

Coitus (co-EE-tus) (*L.* meeting) Human copulation.

Collagen (*Gk.* glue) A tough fibrous protein that is an important component of cartilage, bone, and other connective tissues.

Colon (KOH-lun) The large intestine.

Colony A collection of microorganisms growing together on a surface.

Commensalism (come-MEN-sul-ism) (*L.* together + table) A relationship between individuals of different species that live in close association with one another; one individual benefits and the second is neither harmed nor benefited.

Community, biological The interacting organisms of a particular environmental unit.

Companion cell A slender, nucleated cell in the phloem of vascular plants.

Competitive exclusion principle The theory that each species has a unique ecological niche and that, where two species rely on the same resources, there is a division that reduces competition. Otherwise one species would prove better adapted than the other, which would be forced to extinction.

Complement A group of normal serum enzymes that combine with antigen-antibody complexes, thereby enhancing the immune response.

Complementary Adding to another to make a whole or more valuable result than either achieves alone.

Compound A substance whose molecules are composed of more than one kind of atom.

Concentration gradient See **Gradient.**

Congenital condition Present at birth.

Conifers Trees that reproduce by seeds borne in cones; e.g., pine, spruce, juniper, cedar.

Conjunctiva (con-JUNK-tie-vuh) A delicate, moist membrane that covers exposed eye surfaces and lines the underside of the eyelid.

Connective tissues Tissues that serve primarily to support the body and hold other tissues together. Characterized by a large proportion of cell products such as collagen.

Consumers, primary Organisms that obtain their nutrition from primary producers. Typically these are herbivores that obtain organic compounds by eating plants.

Consumers, secondary Organisms that obtain their nutrition from primary consumers. Typically these are carnivores that obtain organic components by eating herbivorous animals.

Continental shelf The gently sloping submarine plain that borders the continents.

Continental slope The steep incline that descends from the edge of the continental shelf to the ocean depths.

Contraceptive (con-TRA-sep-tive) (*L.* against + conception) A device, drug, or practice that prevents pregnancy; specifically one that reduces the likelihood of fertilization.

Contractile vacuole (kon-TRAK-tul VAK-yu-ohl) An intracellular organelle that acts as a reservoir of excess water in protozoa. The excess water is accumulated and then emptied to the outside.

Convergent evolution Selection of a given trait in distantly related organisms; occurs in species that occupy similar ecological niches.

Copulate (COP-you-late) (*L.* link) Sexual mating.

Cork Protective outer layer of woody plants; composed of dead cells.

Cornea (CORE-knee-uh) The clear curved surface of the eyeball covering the iris and pupil. Admits light and partially focuses it.

Coronary Pertaining to the heart.

Corpus luteum (KOHR-pus LOO-tee-um) A temporary endocrine gland that secretes estrogen and progesterone. It is formed in the ovary from the remnants of a follicle after release of an egg.

Cortex (KOHR-teks) (*L.* bark) The outer part of an organ; contrasts with the inner medulla. Storage tissue beneath the epidermis of stems and roots. (See **Medulla.**)

Cortisone A steroid hormone derived from secretions of the adrenal cortex; one of several glucocorticoids that reduce inflammation and promote synthesis of glucose.

Cotyledon (kot-uh-LEE-dun) (*Gk.* cup-shaped hollow) Seed leaf of the embryo of a plant.

Covalent bond (koh-VAY-lent) A chemical bond between atoms; formed by the sharing of one or more electrons.

Cowper's glands Small paired glands that secrete into the male urethra near the base of the penis. One source of fluids for the semen.

Creatine phosphate (KREE-uh-teen) A nitrogen-containing organic compound with a phosphate group attached by an energy-rich bond. Used as an energy source in muscle contraction.

Cristae (KRIS-tee) (*L.* cock's comb) The folded inner membranes of mitochondria which form in complete partitions; location of the mitochondrial electron-transport system.

Crop A storage segment in the digestive system from which food is released at controlled intervals. Found in various animals such as earthworms and birds.
Crossing over Exchange of regions between chromatids of two homologous chromosomes. Occurs during prophase I of meiosis.
Culture The act of growing organisms, especially microorganisms in the laboratory. A container with growing microorganisms.
Cuticle (KYOOT-i-kul) (*L.* skin) A waxy layer coating the outer surface of epidermal cells in plants. Prevents the loss of water.
Cyanobacteria Photosynthetic bacteria containing chlorophyll in membranous structures. Presence of bluish pigments have caused these procaryotes to be known as "blue-green bacteria" and "blue-green algae."
Cyclic AMP (cyclic adenosine monophosphate) A compound produced inside of cells in response to binding of hormones onto receptors on the plasma membrane; acts as a second messenger which promotes different biochemical reactions in specific cells.
Cyclic phosphorylation (SIK-lik FOSS-for-i-LAY-shun) That part of the light reactions of photosynthesis in some plants during which electrons are recycled and phosphorus is transferred; the only product is ATP.
Cytochrome (SIGH-toe-krohm) A carrier of electrons from oxidations during respiration in mitochondria and during photosynthesis in chloroplasts; an iron-containing protein.
Cytoplasm (SIGH-toe-plazm) That portion of a cell outside the nucleus but within the plasma membrane.

Deciduous (dee-SID-you-us) (*L.* to fall off) The characteristic of shedding; in plants, losing of leaves at a particular season.
Decomposers Bacteria, fungi, and other organisms that digest or decay the remains of organisms.
Demography The study of the characteristics of human populations.
Denaturation (dee-nay-chu-RAY-shun) Alteration of the three-dimensional organization of a protein with a consequent loss of its biological properties.
Dendrite (DEN-dryte) (*Gk.* tree) Treelike branches of a neuron that receive stimuli from axons of adjacent neurons.
Density dependent factor Any factor that changes with increase or decrease in the number of individuals per unit area.
Deoxyribonucleic acid (DNA) (dee-AHK-see-RYE-boe-new-KLAY-ik) The carrier of genetic information in cells. Composed of nucleotides arranged to form a double-stranded helix. Found in chromosomes.
Depolarization Loss of polarization; i.e., loss of a difference in electrical charge.
Desensitization Treatment that causes an organism to cease reacting immunologically to an allergen.
Desmid Microscopic, unicellular, fresh-water algae with cells deeply constricted into two mirror-image halves.
Desmosome (DES-moh-sohm) (*Gk.* binding + body) A specialized spot in the plasma membranes of adjacent cells. Causes the two cells to adhere together.
Detritus (deh-TRY-tus) (*L.* rubbing away) Finely divided organic matter in soil or water.
Deuterostome (due-ter-OH-stom) (*Gk.* second + mouth) Major division of the animal kingdom; during embryonic development the mouth forms on the end opposite the blastopore.
Dialysis (die-AL-uh-sis) A technique for removal of diffusible substances from a mixture by allowing the diffusible components to pass through a selectively permeable membrane.
Diaphragm (DIE-uh-fram) A muscular partition between the thoracic and abdominal cavities; contractions cause inspiration. Any separating partition.
Diastole (die-ASS-toe-lee) (*Gk.* expansion) Ventricular relaxation, when the ventricle of the heart receives blood from the contracting atrium.
Diatom Microscopic algae with double siliceous shells noted for their intricate patterns.
Dicot See **Dicotyledon.**
Dicotyledon (die-kot-uh-LEE-dun) (*Gk.* two + cotyledon) A flowering plant whose seeds have two embryonic leaves (cotyledons); e.g., beans, sunflowers, maples.
Differentiation The process of developmental change from an unspecialized cell to a specialized cell.
Diffusion (*L.* to pour out) The movement of molecules from a region of greater concentration toward a region of lesser concentration as a result of the random movement of the individual particles.
Digestion The process of breaking down large, complex, insoluble molecules of food into smaller, less complex, soluble molecules. May occur extracellularly or intracellularly.
Dihybrid cross (die-HY-brid) (*Gk.* two + *L.* mongrel) A genetic cross between individuals that differ in two inherited traits.
Dinoflagellate Unicellular marine and freshwater algae with a spinning motility due to two flagella; most have a bizarre armored appearance.
Diploid (DIP-loyd) (*Gk.* double) A cell having two full sets of chromosomes.
Dissacharide A double sugar; one composed of two monosaccharides; for example, sucrose, maltose, or lactose.
Dissociation The separation of a molecule into its constituent ions.
Disulfide bond A covalent bond between sulfur atoms of two parts of a molecule such as between two amino acids of a polypeptide chain (—S—S—).
Diurnal (die-UR-nal) Active during daylight hours.
DNA See **Deoxyribonucleic acid.**
Dominant Describes a gene that expresses itself to the exclusion of its recessive allele.

Dorsal (DOHR-sal) Toward the back surface. (See **Ventral.**)
Doubling time The time necessary for a population to double in number.
Duodenum (doo-oh-DEE-num) The portion of small intestine adjacent to the stomach.

Ecdysone (EK-die-sone) (*Gk.* stripping) A secretion of the insect brain; promotes molting of the exoskeleton.
Echolocation (EK-oh-loh-KAY-shun) Orientation to objects through emission of sounds and interpretation of their reflection.
Ecological niche (NITCH) The sum of the interactions of a species with other components of its ecosystem. Each species has characteristics that allow it to fill a unique niche.
Ecology (ee-KOL-uh-jee) (*Gk.* house + learning) The study of the interactions of organisms with their environment.
Ecosystem (EE-koh-sis-tum) All the organisms in a community together with the associated nonliving environment.
Ecotone (EE-koh-tohn) The species-rich border between two biological communities.
Ectoderm (EK-to-derm) (*Gk.* outer + skin) The outer of the three embryonic layers; origin of nervous system and epidermis.
Edema (uh-DEEM-uh) Swelling due to an abnormal accumulation of lymphatic fluids in the connective tissue or body cavities.
Effector system A collective term for the skeleton and skeletal muscles.
Ejaculation (ee-JAK-you-lay-shun) (*L.* to throw out) The forcible expulsion of semen from the male body during orgasm.
Electrode An electrical conductor used to collect or emit electrical charges.
Electromagnetic spectrum The series of radiant energies arranged according to their wavelengths and energy content.
Electron A subatomic particle having a negative charge of the same magnitude as the positive charge of a proton but having far less mass than a proton; normally orbits the atomic nucleus.
Electron acceptor A molecule which receives electrons in an oxidation-reduction reaction and is thereby reduced. Also called a hydrogen acceptor when a proton and an electron are accepted.
Electron carrier A molecule, such as a cytochrome, that can gain or lose electrons reversibly, passing the electrons to secondary carrier or to oxygen.
Electron donor A molecule that donates electrons in an oxidation-reduction reaction and is thereby oxidized. Also called a hydrogen donor if a proton accompanies the electron.
Electron shells The electrons in an atom are distributed in several different energy levels that are situated at different distances from the atomic nucleus. When an electron changes from one shell to another, it either releases or absorbs energy.
Electron transport system A group of closely associated enzymes on the inner membrane of mitochondria. Electrons move from one of the enzymes to the next, alternately reducing and oxidizing the enzyme and capturing energy by the synthesis of ATP.
Element A substance whose molecules consist of only one kind of atom.
Embryo The early developmental stages of sexually produced organisms that lead to the formation of the organs.
Emulsification The breakdown of fat droplets into smaller ones.
Endergonic (en-der-GAHN-ik) (*Gk.* within + work) Pertains to reactions that require energy.
Endocrine (EN-doh-krin) (*Gk.* in + separate) Pertaining to secretion of messenger substances (hormones) into body fluids, usually the blood. Endocrine glands lack the ducts associated with other glands that secrete onto internal or external surfaces.
Endocrine system A collective term for all glands and cells that secrete hormones.
Endoderm (IN-doe-derm) The inner of the three embryonic layers; origin of the lining of the digestive system and associated organs such as the liver and pancreas.
Endoplasmic reticulum (en-doe-PLAZ-mik reh-TIK-yu-lum) (*Gk.* within + *L.* net) An intricate network of double membranes in the cytoplasm of a cell; a system of channels through which materials move.
Endotherm An organism that maintains a relatively constant body temperature by regulating heat production and heat loss.
Endothermic (*Gk.* inside + heat) Pertains to reactions that require an input of energy; endergonic; the opposite of exothermic or exergonic.
Endosperm (EN-doh-spurm) (*Gk.* within + seed) A tissue that surrounds and nourishes the embryo in seeds of flowering plants.
Energy The capacity to do work.
Entomophagous (en-toe-moh-FAY-gus) Characterized by eating insects. Entomophagous insects are those that eat other insects.
Entropy A measure of the randomness or disorder of a system; the energy of a system unavailable to do work.
Environmental resistance All the aspects of the environment of a species that tend to limit the numbers of that species.
Enzyme (EN-zime) A protein that increases the rate of a chemical reaction without permanently entering into the reaction itself; an organic catalyst.
Epidermis (ep-i-DER-mis) The outer covering tissue. In plants it is an outer layer of living cells on leaves and young stems and roots. In vertebrates, the epidermis is many layers thick.
Epididymis (ep-i-DID-uh-muss) pl. **Epididymides** (*Gk.*

upon + testes) A coiled tube into which sperm pass upon leaving the vertebrate testis. Sperm are stored in the epididymis and, in the human, become mature there.

Epiglottis (ep-i-GLOT-is) (*Gk.* upon + tongue) A flap that prevents food from entering the respiratory tract during swallowing.

Epinephrin (ep-i-NEFF-rin) (*Gk.* upon + kidney) A hormone secreted by the adrenal medulla, especially during crises; adrenalin.

Epiphyte (ep-i-FITE) (*Gk.* upon + plant) A plant that uses another plant or other object for physical support but obtains water and minerals independently and hence is not a parasite.

Epithelium A type of highly cellular tissue covering all body surfaces and lining all passageways and cavities. Regulates movement of substances in and out of organisms.

Equilibrium A state of balance; a condition in which no further net change is occurring.

Erosion (ee-ROW-shun) The wearing away of rock or soil by chemical or physical processes.

Erythrocyte (ih-RITH-roh-site)(*Gk.* red + cell) See **Red blood cell**.

Esophagus (ih-SOFF-uh-guss) (*Gk.* I shall carry + to eat) A slender tube connecting the pharynx with the stomach.

Estrogen (ESS-troh-jen) (*L.* frenzy + *Gk.* birth A group of steroid hormones produced by the ovarian follicle, placenta, and adrenal cortex. Causes growth of uterine muscle and glands and is reponsible for female secondary sex characteristics.

Estrus (*L.* frenzy) Sexual receptivity of the female that is synchronized with ovulation; sexual "heat."

Estuary Broad, shallow basin at the mouths of a bay or river where fresh and salt water meet.

Ethology (ee-THOL-uh-jee) (*Gk.* custom + study) The study of animal behavior.

Ethylene (ETH-uh-leen) A plant growth hormone that hastens the ripening of fruits.

Eucaryote (you-CARRY-ote) (*Gk.* true + kernel) An organism in which the cells have a membrane-bound nucleus and possess mitochondria and other membraneous organelles. (See **Procaryote**.)

Euphotic zone (yu-FOTT-ik) (*Gk.* good + light) The upper layers of ocean or lake waters into which light penetrates.

Eustachian tube (yu-STAY-shun) Passageway between the middle ear and pharynx. Normally open to permit air pressure in the middle ear to rise or fall with changes in air pressure outside the ear drum.

Eutrophic (yu-TROH-fik) (*Gk.* good + food) Pertaining to a body of water containing an abundance of plant nutrients and therefore large populations of organisms, especially phytoplankton.

Eutrophication (YU-troh-fa-KAY-shun) Increased plant nutrients in water. Leads to increased phytoplankton and often to such high levels of aerobic decomposers that the oxygen levels are depleted and the fish die.

Evolution (*L.* an unrolling) A process of gradual change, especially the gradual change in a population of organisms over the generations.

Evolutionary strategy A genetically determined characteristic that is adaptive and hence has a positive selective value.

Excitation The act of absorbing or adding energy so that one or more electrons of an atom are ejected from their normal shells to ones farther from the atomic nucleus.

Excretion The process of removal of wastes and excess water and salts from the body.

Exergonic (ek-ser-GON-ik) (*L.* out + *Gk.* work) Pertaining to reactions that liberate energy.

Exoskeleton (*L.* outside + *Gk.* dried body) External coverings which provide protection and support.

Exothermic (ek-soh-THER-mik) (*L.* outside + *Gk.* heat) Pertaining to reactions that liberate heat or other forms of energy; exergonic.

Exponential growth Growth in which a population increases at intervals by some power (exponent); e.g., two cells divide into four (2^2) and the four divide into eight (2^3), etc.

Extensors Muscles which generally straighten joints. Work in opposition in flexors.

Extinction Death of all members of a species or group of species.

Facilitated diffusion (*L.* easy) The movement of molecules across a membrane from a region of high concentration to a region of lower concentration of the molecule by means of a carrier that "escorts" a molecule across; no energy is required.

Fallopian tube (fal-LO-pee-en) See **Oviduct**.

Fat A storage lipid composed of glycerol and three fatty acids; solid at room temperature. Triglyceride.

Fatty acids Weak organic acids containing long hydrocarbon chains; subunits of other lipids including fats, oils, and phospholipids.

Feces The unabsorbed material eliminated from the digestive tract; excrement.

Feedback control Arrangement in which the product of an action or process stimulates or depresses further activity. In negative feedback the product slows the action or process responsible for the product.

Feedback regulation See **Feedback control**.

Fermentation (*L.* leaven) The partial decomposition of organic molecules in the absence of free oxygen. End products may include gases, alcohols, and/or acids such as lactic acid.

Fertilization (*L.* to produce) Union of the egg and sperm to form a zygote.

Fetus (FEE-tuss) (*L.* offspring) The unborn young of a mammal; specifically the later stages devoted to growth and differentiation of the tissues.

Fiber Any small, elongate structure. The striated muscle fiber is a multinucleate, cellular unit. Collagen fibers are cell products. A nerve fiber is a portion of a neuron.

Fibril A threadlike structure, often a subunit of a fiber. Collagen fibrils are subunits of collagen fibers. (See **Myofibril**.)

First law of ecology "You can never do only one thing." An expression of the interaction of ecosystem components that causes one change to lead to another.

First law of thermodynamics Energy cannot be created or destroyed, although it can change form.

Flagellum (fluh-JELL-um) pl. **flagella** (*L.* whip) An elongate membrane-bound protrusion from a cell; used as a source of motion. In eucaryotes contains a circle of nine pair of microtubules and two central microtubules.

Flatworm A member of the phylum *Platyhelminthes*. Includes tapeworms, flukes, and many free-living forms. All are bilaterally symmetrical and lack a body cavity.

Flexors (FLEX-ores) Muscles that bend joints. Work in opposition to extensors.

Fluke A group of parasitic flatworms that suck nutrients from their hosts.

Fluorescence (flure-ESS-ens) Emission of light by a compound that is energized by photons or electrons.

Follicles, ovarian Spherical structures in the ovaries; secrete estrogen and nourish developing eggs. After release of the egg, the remnants of a follicle develop into a corpus luteum.

Follicle-stimulating hormone (FSH) A secretion of the anterior pituitary that promotes development of ovarian follicles.

Food chain A linear pattern of nutritional transfers among the organisms of an ecosystem.

Food web A complex pattern of nutritional transfers among the organisms of an ecosystem.

Foraminiferan (FOR-a-min-if-eran) (*L.* opening) A member of a large group of shelled protozoa that bear pseudopodia extending through numerous openings in the shell.

Forebrain The anterior part of the vertebrate brain. Includes the olfactory lobe, cerebrum, and hypothalamus.

Foreskin The fold of skin over the bulbous end of the human penis. Removed at circumcision.

Fossil (*L.* dug up) Any remains that preserve the structure of composition of an organism. May be little-altered tissue, mineral substances in the form of the organism or its parts, or some compound derived from the organism.

Fovea centralis (FOH-vee-ah SEN-tral-us) A small depression in the retina where objects in the center of the visual field are focused.

Fruit The mature or ripened ovary or ovaries of flowering plants. Contains the seeds.

Fungus Plantlike organisms considered members of a separate kingdom because their cell walls are usually chitin rather than cellulose, because they are heterotrophs rather than being photosynthetic, and because they have several unusual nuclear characteristics.

Gall bladder A bile-storage sac associated with the liver.

Gamete (GAM-meet) (*Gk.* to marry) A cell capable of participating in fertilization. An egg or sperm.

Gametophyte generation (guh-MEET-uh-fite) A gamete-producing haploid phase of plants.

Gamma globulin See **Immunoglobulin**.

Gamma radiation High-energy electromagnetic radiation (photons) emitted during nuclear reactions.

Ganglion (GANG-glee-un) (*Gk.* knot) A mass of neuronal cell bodies located outside the brain and spinal cord.

Gap junctions Regions of the plasma membranes of animal cells where the membranes of adjacent cells come into very close contact. Permit ion flow and exchange of substances between the cells.

Gastric Pertaining to the stomach.

Gastrulation (gas-truh-LAY-shun) (*Gk.* stomach) The phase of development during which movement of cell masses alters the position of some cells relative to others. The product is multilayered embryo usually with some organ rudiments such as a primitive digestive system.

Gene (JEEN) (*Gk.* to produce) A length of DNA that controls a specific cellular function; may code for a polypeptide, or regulate other genes.

Gene flow The movement of genes through a population or from one population to another.

Gene frequency The incidence of a given allele within a population in comparison with all the alleles of that gene.

Gene pool All the genes of all the individuals in a population.

General adaptation Acquisition of a characteristic(s) that opens a new way of life and permits the evolution of numerous species.

General adaptation syndrome A proposed mechanism of population regulation in mammals in which physical or psychological stress depresses reproductive hormones but stimulates the adrenal cortex to adjustments that are adaptive over a short term but that, if prolonged, can lead to death.

Generator potential Depolarization of the membrane of a sensory cell. A strong generator potential initiates an impulse in the sensory neuron.

Genetic (jen-ET-ik) Affected by the genes; inherited.

Genetic code The complete set of triplet nucleotide symbols that indicate specific amino acids. Described in terms of *m*RNA codons.

Genetic drift Changes in gene frequencies not due to selection. Result of chance in isolated small populations.

Genitals The external reproductive organs.

Genotype ((JEE-nuh-type) (*Gk.* to produce + type) The genetic makeup of an individual organism. (See **Phenotype**.)

Genus (JEAN-us) pl. **genera** A category of biological classifications smaller than a family. May include only one species or several closely related species.

Geology (GEE-ol-uh-jee) The study of the earth.

Germination (*L.* sprout) The beginning of growth by a spore, or of the embryo within a seed; sprouting of seeds.
Gestation (JESS-stay-shun) (*L.* to bear) The period during which the young develops within the mother.
Gill The gas-exchange organs of aquatic organisms.
Gland A cell or organ that discharges characteristic secretions to the outside of itself.
Glomerulus (glu-MARE-yu-luss) (*L.* a ball) A ball of capillaries intimately associated with the cup-shaped Bowman's capsule. Here blood plasma is filtered under pressure into the kidney nephron.
Glucagon (GLOO-kuh-gon) A pancreatic hormone that increases the blood-glucose level.
Glucose (*Gk.* sweet) A six-carbon sugar ($C_6H_{12}O_6$); the principal energy source of most cells.
Gluten (GLUE-ton) A viscous protein present in the seeds of certain cereals. Traps CO_2 bubbles in dough and thus is necessary for raised bread.
Glycerol A three-carbon alcohol derived from fats and some other lipids; glycerin.
Glycogen (GLY-koh-jen) A polysaccharide consisting of branched chains of glucose molecules; used for energy storage in animals; animal starch.
Glycolysis (gly-KOL-i-sis) (*Gk.* sweet + solution) The initial steps in the breakdown of glucose in energy metabolism. It is an anaerobic process that occurs in the cytoplasm and produces pyruvic acid.
Golgi body (GOAL-jee) (Camillo Golgi, nineteenth-century Italian biologist) A collection of membranes associated with endoplasmic reticulum; functions in the packaging of substances to be secreted. Also a likely source of lysosome formation.
Gonads (GO-nads) Organs that are the sources of gametes; testes and ovaries.
Gradient A gradual change in a quantity over distance.
Grain A single-seeded fruit characteristic of grasses. The ovary wall is fused to seed coat and nearly indistinguishable, so that such fruits are often referred to as seeds.
Grana (GRAY-nuh) (*L.* grain) Stacks of flattened, photosynthetic, membrane-bound vesicles (thykaloids) in a chloroplast.
Ground water Water that accumulates over impenetrable rock layers and is the source of water for wells and springs.
Growth An increase in the volume of living material. Can refer to an increase in an individual or a population.
Gymnosperm (JIM-nuh-sperm) (*Gk.* naked + seed) A plant whose seeds are not enclosed in fruits but are borne on the surface; e.g., in open cones.

Habitat (HAB-i-tat) (*L.* living place) The environment in which an organism occurs; the "address" of an organism.
Habituation (ha-bit-yu-AY-shun) A simple learning that leads to oft-repeated stimuli being ignored.
Hair cell A sensory cell that responds to stimuli which deform its microvilli. Basis of human detection of sound, acceleration, and gravity. Also known as a neuromast.
Half-life The time necessary for decay of half of the existing atoms of a radioactive isotope.
Haploid (HAP-loyd) (*Gk.* single) Having only one complete set of chromosomes.
Hardwood The wood of an angiosperm tree.
Heat of evaporation The amount of heat needed to convert a liquid at the boiling point to a gas at the boiling-point temperature. For water, 540 calories/gram.
Helix An object with a spiral shape.
Hemoglobin (HEE-moh-gloh-bin) (*Gk.* Blood + *L.* globe) The iron-containing protein pigment in the red blood cells. Transports oxygen and some carbon dioxide.
Hemolysis (he-MOL-a-sis) Breakdown of red blood cell structure with the release of hemoglobin.
Hepatic portal system (hugh-PAT-ik) A system of veins in which the blood coming from the intestine passes to capillaries in the liver before moving on to the heart.
Herbaceous (her-BAY-shus) Soft-stemmed; not woody.
Herbivore (*L.* grass + to devour) *Adj.* **herbivorous** An animal that eats plants.
Hermaphroditic (HER-maf-roh-DIT-ik) Producing both eggs and sperm.
Hernia A weakened region of the body wall into which some structure (such as a loop of the intestine) protrudes inappropriately. A rupture.
Heterotroph (HET-uh-ruh-trohf) (*Gk.* other + feeder) An organism that must consume organic food molecules because it is incapable of synthesizing organic molecules solely from inorganic nutrients, as can plants. (See **Autotroph**.)
Heterozygous (het-uh-ruh-ZY-gus) (*Gk.* other + yoke) Possessing two different alleles of a gene.
Hexaploid (HEX-uh-ployd) Having six sets of chromosomes.
Histamine A compound related to the amino acid histidine; causes enlargement of capillaries and other small blood vessels and promotes contraction of the muscle in the lung passages.
Histocompatability The compatability of tissues from different sources that results from the presence of similar cellular antigens; permits transplantation without rejection.
Histone (HISS-tone) A basic protein present in chromosomes of eucaryotes.
Homeostasis (hoe-mee-oh-STAY-sis) (*Gk.* unchanging + standing) The maintenance of a more or less constant internal environment in spite of external changes.
Hominid (*L.* homo = man) A humanlike creature; an organism classified in the same scientific family as humans (in contrast to apelike).
Homologous chromosomes (*Gk.* same) Chromosomes of a similar shape and size and containing the same genes (but not necessarily the same alleles) at the same locations.
Homo sapiens (HO-mo SAY-pee-ns) The scientific name of the human species.

Homozygous (*Gk.* same + yoke) Having two identical alleles at a given locus on homologous chromosomes.
Hormone (*Gk.* to arouse) A chemical compound secreted from an endocrine gland into body fluids, especially the blood. It affects specific "target" cells and in small quantities regulates their activities.
Host An organism that harbors a parasite or commensal.
Humor A fluid. The aqueous humor is a watery substance anterior to the lens of the eye. The vitreous humor is a gelled substance behind the lens.
Humus (HYU-mus) Partially decayed lignin-rich plant remains in the soil.
Hybrid (HY-brid) (*L.* mongrel) A union of unlike biological entities, as in species hybrids, genetic hybrids, or hybrid cells.
Hybrid sterility Inability of members of two species to interbreed and produce viable offspring.
Hydrocarbon Organic compounds composed only of carbon and hydrogen; e.g., methane (CH_4).
Hydrogen acceptor See **Electron acceptor**.
Hydrogen bond An extremely weak chemical bond formed by the attraction of a hydrogen bearing a slight positive charge to an oxygen or a nitrogen bearing a slight negative charge.
Hydrogen carrier See **Electron carrier**.
Hydrogen ion A free proton such as that released when an acid is dissolved in water; designated H^+ because it is identical to the nucleus of a hydrogen atom, which consists of one positively charged proton.
Hydrolysis (hy-DROL-uh-sis) (*Gk.* water + loosening) The splitting apart of a compound with the addition of a water molecule.
Hydrophilic (hy-druh-FILL-ik) (*Gk.* water + loving) Refers to molecules or portions of molecules that are attracted to water.
Hydrophobic (*L.* water + *Gk.* fearing) Having no affinity for water; not combining with water; applies to nonpolar substances such as fats and oils.
Hydrostatic skeleton Support based on the contraction of muscles against fluid confined in a body cavity.
Hydroxyl (1) the OH^- ion; (2) a chemical group ($-OH$) that confers alcoholic properties on an organic compound.
Hyperosmotic Having a concentration sufficiently high to draw water across a semipermeable membrane from another solution; having a high osmotic pressure.
Hypersensitivity See **Allergy**.
Hypha (HY-fa) (*Gk.* web) A threadlike filament of fungal cells of a fungus.
Hypoosmotic Having a concentration so low that water is lost across a semipermeable membrane to another solution; having a low osmotic pressure.
Hypothalamus (hy-poh-THAL-uh-mus) (*Gk.* under + inner room) A portion of the forebrain lying under the thalamus; source of posterior pituitary hormones and of releasing factors for anterior pituitary hormones. Controls many essential body functions and is the center of the autonomic nervous system.
Hypothesis (hy-POTH-uh-sus) (*Gk.* under + to put) An unsubstantiated explanation. To be of scientific value, an hypothesis should be testable.

Immunization Production of the immune state by injection of a vaccine containing antigens or antibodies or T-cells.
Immunoglobulin A protein having antibody activity; formerly called gamma globulin.
Implantation Sinking of the young embryo into the uterine lining.
Imprinting The rapid learning, during a limited developmental period and in response to a particular stimulus, of some highly specific behavior pattern.
Incomplete dominance The condition in which neither of the alleles that determine a characteristic is dominant to the other so that both are apparent in the phenotype.
Independent assortment, law of A generalization of Mendel. States that segregation of the two members of a pair of alleles in sexual reproduction is unaffected by the segregation of other pairs of alleles; i.e., genes assort independently of one another.
Induction, embyonic (*L.* to lead in) The influence of one embryonic region on the development of another region.
Inflammation Protective response to irritation characterized by increased blood flow and escape of plasma and white blood cells from small vessels into the tissues.
Inflorescence A solitary flow or a cluster of flowers.
Infrared radiation Long-wavelength electromagnetic radiation just outside the red portion of the visible spectrum but detectable as heat.
Inguinal (ING-gwu-null) Located in the groin.
Inorganic A chemical compound containing no carbon. An exception is carbon dioxide (CO_2).
Insect Member of a major division of the arthropods; characterized by a three-segmented thorax bearing three pairs of jointed walking legs, and a respiratory system consisting of tracheal tubes.
Inseminate (in-SEM-i-nate) To place semen in the female tract so that fertilization may occur.
Insulin (in-SUH-lin) A pancreatic hormone that facilitates entrance of glucose into cells and thus lowers the blood glucose level.
Interferon (in-ter-FEAR-on) A protein secreted by a virus-infected cell that inhibits viral multiplication in noninfected cells.
Intermediate inheritance See **Incomplete dominance.**
Interneuron (in-ter-NYU-ron) (*L.* between + *Gk.* nerve) A cell of the nervous system involved in associative activities; any neuron other than a motor neuron or a sensory neuron.
Interphase (INT-er-faze) (*L.* between + *Gk.* phase) The period between all divisions during which DNA duplicates.
Interstitial (EN-ter-stish-al) (*L.* between + to stand) Occurring between parts; between cells.

Interstitial cell-stimulating hormone (ICSH) An anterior pituitary secretion that stimulates testosterone production by the interstitial cells of the testis.
Intron See **Split gene.**
Invagination An ingrowth or infolding of a surface, as in gastrulation.
Inversion, atmospheric Stable layers of air with dense cold air near the ground and lighter, warmer air above. This is an inversion of the usual situation in which the air near the ground is warmed by heat from the earth and expands so that it becomes less dense and therefore rises, carrying air pollutants with it.
Invertebrate Any animal lacking the vertebral column and skull characteristic of the vertebrates; includes some chordates as well as all other animal phyla.
Ion (EYE-on) An electrically charged atom or group of atoms.
Ionic bond (eye-ON-ik) An attraction between two atoms due to the transfer of one or more electrons from one atom to the other.
Isomer (EYE-soh-mer) (*Gk.* equal + part) Compounds with identical components but different atomic arrangements in their molecules. The two sugars glucose ($C_6H_{12}O_6$) and fructose ($C_6H_{12}O_6$) are isomers.
Isoosmotic Having a concentration such that there is no net movement of water across a semipermeable membrane to or from another solution; having the same osmotic pressure.
Isotope (EYE-soh-tope) (*Gk.* equal + place) An atom of an element with the same number of protons and electrons as other atoms of the same element, but differing in the number of neutrons.

Jaundice (JON-dus) (*Fr.* yellow) An accumulation of bile pigments in the skin and the whites of the eyes giving them a yellow appearance.
Juvenile hormone A secretion of the insect corpora allata; high concentrations of this hormone inhibit development of adult structures.

k-adapted A reproductive strategy in which a species invests heavily in a few offspring.
Karyotype (CARRY-oh-type) (*Gk.* nucleus + type) The detailed appearance of a metaphase set of chromosomes.
Keratin A fibrous protein, rich in sulfur-containing amino acids; commonly found in epidermal structures including hair, nails, and feathers.
Kidney The organ that produces urine by filtration of water, salts, and nitrogenous waste from blood.
Kilocalorie (KEE-loh-cal-uh-ree) (*Gk.* thousand + *L.* heat) One thousand calories; abbreviated as Kcal or Calorie.
Kinesis (kin-EE-sis) (*Gk.* motion) Orientation method of simple organisms; rate of movement is dependent on strength of stimulus.
Kinetic energy The energy of motion.
Krebs cycle (tricarboxylic acid cycle; citric acid cycle; metabolic mill) (KREBZ) (Sir Hans Krebs, a British biochemist) The cyclic series of reactions in mitochondria that oxidize pyruvic acid and other metabolic intermediates to carbon dioxide and water. Under appropriate conditions, involved in the synthetic interconversion of carbohydrates, lipids, and proteins.

Labium majus (LAY-be-um MA-jus) pl. **labia majora** (LAY-be-uh ma-JOR-a) Folds of skin that form the outer lips of the female genitals.
Labium minus (LAY-be-um MI-nus) pl. **labia minora** (LAY-be-uh MY-nor-a) Narrow folds within the cleft between the labia majora.
Lactation Milk production.
Lactic acid A product of sugar fermentation by bacteria and muscle cells, among others. It is responsible for the normal souring of milk and, being slightly toxic, the oxygen debt of contracting muscle.
Lamella A thin layer or leaf.
Large intestine See **Colon.**
Larva pl. **larvae** (*L.* ghost) Immature stages of certain animals; the body form differs drastically from that of the adult.
Larynx (LAR-inks) (*Gk.* upper part of windpipe) The voice box; a cartilaginous structure at the top of the trachea. Contains the vocal chords.
Lateral Relating to or toward the side.
Leaching Removal of soluble components by water that soaks through the soil.
Legume (le-GUME) (*Fr.* vegetable) A member of the pea or bean family; the fruit of such plants.
Lesion Any abnormal change in an organ, tissue, or cell.
Leukocyte (LYU-koh-site) (*Gk.* white + cell) See **White blood cell.**
Libido (lah-BEA-doh) Sex drive.
Lichen (LIE-kun) A characteristic symbiotic association of a fungus and an alga or cyanobacterium.
Life cycle The life stages of an organism; in sexually reproducing organisms involves meiosis in diploid cells and fertilization of gametes.
Ligament A tough connective tissue band that holds bones together. Major component is the protein collagen.
Ligate (LIE-gate) To tie off. Especially to interrupt the passageway of a duct or vessel.
Lignin A polymer of complex alcohols; makes up 25 percent of wood and is responsible for much of wood's hardness and indigestibility.
Limbic system (*L.* border) A group of centers in the base of the forebrain; involved in emotions.
Linked genes Those genes that lie on the same chromosome and therefore are inherited together.
Lipid (LIP-id) An organic compound insoluble in water but soluble in ethers and alcohols and other lipids; e.g., fats, oils, steroids.
Litter Leaves, twigs, and other undecomposed plant debris.

Liver The largest gland. Processes substances absorbed from the digestive system and secretes bile. Also regulates the level of nutrients in the blood.
Luteinizing hormone (LH) (LEU-tee-un-eye-zing) A secretion of the anterior pituitary that, after ovulation, promotes development of an ovarian follicle into a corpus luteum.
Lymph (LIMF) A clear body fluid containing water, proteins, salts, and lymphocytes. Enters lymphatic vessels from the tissue spaces.
Lymphatic system (lim-FAT-ik) An auxiliary circulatory system made up of a network of thin-walled vessels and capillaries that carry lymph fluid. Lymph enters the blind ends of the capillaries and is carried to the veins where it joins the blood. Lymph nodes at junctions of lymphatic vessels filter the lymph.
Lymphatic tissue A connective tissue rich in lymphocytes and macrophages.
Lymph nodes Filtering organs located at junctions of lymph vessels. Here foreign cells and debris are phagocytized and antibodies produced.
Lymphocyte A kind of white blood cell found in blood and lymph and involved in immune response such as antibody formation.
Lysosome (LYE-soh-sohm) (*Gk.* loosening) A membrane-bound organelle containing enzymes that degrade cell components.
Lysozyme An antibacterial enzyme found in various body fluids.
Lytic (LIT-ik) (*Gk.* loosening) Capable of causing dissolution; used to describe the stage in which an infecting virus destroys a bacterial host cell.

Macromolecule (*Gk.* large) A very large molecule consisting of many repeating subunits linked together to form a chain; e.g., proteins, polysaccharides, and nucleic acids.
Macrophage (MAK-roh-fayj) (*Gk.* large + to eat) A scavenger cell found in the liver, bone marrow, or spleen. Derived from a blood monocyte.
Malignant tumor A tumor that spreads and threatens life.
Malpighian tubules Slender sacs attached to the arthropod hindgut; these tubules remove wastes from the body fluids and excrete them into the hindgut.
Mammal (*L.* breast) A class of vertebrates characterized by possession of hair, mammary glands, and ability to maintain a constant body temperature.
Mammary glands Milk-secreting glands, lying embedded in the fatty tissue of a woman's breasts.
Maritime forest A humid biome bordering the ocean.
Marsh A grassy wetland.
Matrix The background substance in which something is embedded. Used to describe intercellular substances and the semisolid material found in some cell organelles.
Mechanistic Explanations that involve only chemical or physical processes.
Medulla (muh-DULL-uh) (*L.* middle) The central region of an organ as opposed to surrounding cortex.
Medusa (mu-DUE-sa) A coelenterate that swims freely and reproduces sexually.
Meiosis (my-OH-sis) (*Gk.* diminution) The two nuclear divisions that result in the reduction of chromosome number from diploid to haploid. *Adj.* **meiotic.**
Melanin (MEL-uh-nin) (*Gk.* black) The brown or black pigment of hair, skin, and eyes.
Mendel's laws The basic rules of heredity. Mendel's first law recognizes that alleles segregate during meiosis so that each gamete carries only one of the two alleles present in other body cells. The second law recognizes the independent assortment of unlinked genes that produces gametes containing random combinations of genes.
Meninges (meh-NIN-jeez) (*Gk.* membrane) Three connective tissue layers that surround and protect the brain and spinal cord.
Menopause The normal termination of menstrual cycles with age.
Menstruation (MEN-strew-a-shun) The periodic sloughing of the uterine lining with release of stagnant blood. Occurs at the end of human ovarian cycles not resulting in fertilization.
Meristem (MARE-i-stem) Unspecialized plant tissue composed of potentially or actively dividing cells; growth region.
Mesoderm (mes-OH-derm) The middle of the three embryonic layers; origin of the muscles, skeleton, and most of the internal organs.
Mesophyll (MEZ-oh-fill) The major photosynthetic tissue of a leaf.
Messenger RNA (mRNA) A single-stranded nucleic acid that is transcribed from a DNA template; contains the "genetic message" to be translated into proteins.
Metabolism (ma-TAB-oh-lizm) (*Gk.* change) The totality of chemical reactions that occur in a cell or organism.
Metamorphosis (MET-uh-mor-fa-sus) (*L.*) A change in form.
Metamorphosis, complete A pattern of insect development in which the egg hatches as a larva that is drastically different from the adult. Each larval molt produces a larger larva, until the final larva molts into a resting pupal stage during which the body structure is reorganized. At the final molt the adult emerges.
Metamorphosis, gradual A pattern of insect development in which the newly hatched nymph resembles the adult but differs in proportions and the absence of wings and genitalia. With each molt the nymph becomes more similar to the adult.
Metaphase (MET-uh-faze) (*Gk.* change + phase) A stage of cell division during which the chromosomes are at the equator of the spindle and attached to the spindle fibers.
Microfilament An ultramicrosopic, threadlike, contractile structure; component of the cytoskeleton.
Micrometer (MY -cro-meet-her) One-millionth of a me-

ter; a unit used for measuring cells. Formerly called a *micron*.
Microorganism An organism so small that a microscope is required for observation; often unicellular; includes bacteria, many fungi and algae, and protozoa.
Microtubule (my-kro-TOO-byul) (*Gk.* small) A straight, thin, hollow cytoplasmic structure made of protein, associated with movement and cytoplasmic structure.
Microvillus (mike-row-VYL-lus) pl. **microvilli** Fingerlike projections of the plasma membrane of animal cells; they increase surface area.
Mimicry (MIM-ik-ree) (*Gk.* to imitate) Resemblance of an organism to another species or to an inanimate object, thereby increasing the organism's chances of survival.
Mineral A naturally occurring inorganic substance.
Mitochondrion (my-toe-KON-dree-on) (*Gk.* thread + granule) A cytoplasmic organelle that is the site of the metabolic mill (Krebs cycle) and the electron transport system. Most cellular ATP synthesis occurs here.
Mitosis (my-TOE-sis) (*Gk.* thread + state) *Adj.* **mitotic** Nuclear division producing two daughter nuclei each with chromosomes identical to those of the original cell. Usually, but not necessarily, accompanied by separation of the cytoplasm to form two new cells.
Mold Parasitic or decomposing fungi with a characteristic slimy, cottony, or filamentous growth pattern.
Molecule (MOLL-i-kyul) (*L.* little mass) The smallest unit into which a substance can be divided while still retaining the chemical properties of that substance.
Mollusc A member of a major phylem of soft-bodied animals that includes slugs, snails, oysters, and octopuses.
Monera (mo-NEAR-a) The kingdom to which all procaryotes are assigned.
Monocot See **Monocotyledon.**
Monocotyledon (MON-uh-kot-uh-LEE-dun) (*Gk.* single + cotyledon) A flowering plant with one seed leaf (cotyledon) in the embryo; e.g., corn, lilies, grass.
Monoculture The growth of a single species in an area.
Monocyte (MAAN-uh-syt) Large phagocytic white blood cells.
Monohybrid cross (*Gk.* one + mongrel) A cross between individuals differing in only one heritable trait, or in which only one trait is considered by an experimenter.
Mosaic Composed of distinct pieces or patches; mottled.
Motor Involved in production of movement.
Motor end plate The junction between an axon and a muscle fiber. Structure and function closely resembles a synapse between two neurons.
Motor unit The skeletal muscle fibers activated by a single motor neuron.
Mucus *Adj.* **mucous** A viscous secretion containing a polysaccharide-protein complex.
Multiple alleles (uh-LEELZ) Genes that are present in a population in more than two forms, although only two can be present in a single diploid organism; for example, the human ABO blood group.
Multiple copy DNA DNA sequences that are repeated many times in a cell; e.g. ribosomal genes.
Multiple genes Two or more different pairs of alleles at different loci on chromosomes, capable of adding quantitatively such traits as size and color.
Muscle fiber Spindle-shaped multinucleate cells of skeletal muscle.
Mutagen An agent that causes mutations.
Mutation (mew-TAY-shun) (*L.* change) An inheritable change in a gene; a change in nucleotide sequences in a DNA molecule.
Mycelium (my-SEE-lee-um) pl. **mycelia** (*Gk.* fungus) Fungus tissue; composed of hyphae.
Mycorrhiza (my-koh-RYE-zuh) pl. **mycorrhizae** (*Gk.* fungus + root) A symbiotic association of fungi with plant roots.
Myelin (my-UH-lin) (*Gk.* marrow) A covering found on many nerve fibers; consists of extremely thin extensions of sheathing cells wound many times around the fiber. The high membrane content makes myelin rich in lipids.
Myofibril (my-oh-FYBE-ril) (*Gk.* muscle + *L.* small fiber) The contractile fibers within muscle cells. Composed mainly of actin and myosin.
Myoglobin (my-oh-GLOW-bin) (*Gk.* muscle + ball, globe) An iron-containing protein of muscle that stores oxygen.
Myosin (MY-oh-sin) (*Gk.* muscle) One of the proteins involved in muscle contraction; makes up the thick filaments.

NAD See **Nicotinamide adenine dinucleotide**.
Nanometer (NAN-uh-mee-ter) One-billonth of a meter; used for measuring wavelengths of light and organelle structure.
Natural selection The process of the environment "selecting" for those individuals with traits that best suit them to their habitats. Such individuals are most apt to reproduce and pass inherited traits to offspring. The survival of the fittest.
Nematode One of a very large number of parasitic and free-living unsegmented worms characterized by movement by whiplike undulations and large cells; roundworms. Often assigned to the phylum *Aschelminthes*.
Nephridium (nuh-FRID-ee-um) (*Gk.* kidney) The excretory organ of the earthworm and other annelids.
Nephron (NEEF-ron)(*Gk.* kidney) The functional unit of excretion in the kidney; separates water, minerals, and nitrogenous waste from the blood, and makes urine.
Nerve (*L.* sinew) A bundle or bundles of neuronal fibers enclosed in a sheath of connective tissue.
Nerve impulse A wave of depolarization that passes along the membrane of an axon.
Neural (NYU-rul) Relating to the nervous system.
Neuron (NYU-ron) (*Gk.* nerve) A cell type of the nervous system. Neurons are characterized by the ability to respond to stimuli and transmit messages.

Neurotransmitter (NYU-row-TRANS-mitt-er) A compound secreted at the ends of axons; diffuses across the synaptic gap and depolarizes the membrane of the next neuron, thereby causing a nerve impulse in that neuron. Among the better known neurotransmitters are acetylcholine and noradrenalin.
Neutron (NEW-tron) (*L.* neither) An electrically neutral subatomic particle found in the nucleus.
Neutrophil (NOO-trah-fihl) A granular phagocytic white blood cell having a multilobed nucleus. The most numerous kind of white blood cell.
Nicotinamide adenine dinucleotide (NAD) A coenzyme that functions as a hydrogen acceptor in cellular oxidation. Derived from the vitamin niacin.
Nitrate NO_3^-; An ion formed by the dissolution of mineral nitrates such as potassium nitrate or by the oxidation of ammonia; the preferred source of nitrogen for most plants and thus required for soil fertility.
Nitrogen fixation The combination of atmospheric nitrogen with other elements to form nitrogen compounds that can be used by plants.
Nitrogenous base Any of a number of nitrogen-containing organic molecules (such as those found in nucleotides) that react with acids; purines and pyrimidines.
Nitrosamines Strongly carcinogenic compounds containing nitrogenous groups (—NNO) and readily derived from the breakdown products of amino acids.
Nocturnal (NOCK-tur-nal) Active at night; to be contrasted with diurnal.
Node (*L.* knot) The part of a stem bearing a leaf.
Nondisjunction Failure of homologous chromosomes to separate during meiosis.
Nonpolar molecules Molecules which have an even or equal distribution of electrical charges.
Norepinephrine (NOR-ep-i-NEFF-rin) Substance released as a neurotransmitter by sympathetic motor endings and by some neurons of the CNS. Also secreted by the adrenal medulla as a hormone. Chemically similar to epinephrin.
Normal flora The nonpathogenic microorganisms normally found on the skin and mucous membranes.
Notochord (NO-toe-cord) A supporting rod lying under the neural tube in the vetebrate embryo.
Nuclear fission The splitting of atoms yielding different kinds of atoms and releasing large amounts of energy.
Nuclear fusion The fusion of two atomic nuclei into one with the release of large quantities of energy.
Nucleic acids (new-KLAY-ik) Macromolecules that are polymers of nucleotides; DNA and RNAs.
Nucleolus (new-KLEE-uh-lus) A dense region of the nucleus where ribosomal RNA is produced.
Nucleosome A organizational component of chromosomes in which fibrous DNA molecules are wound about globular masses of proteins.
Nucleotide (NEW-klee-uh-tide) A molecule consisting of ribose or deoxyribose, a nitrogenous base, and a phosphate group; one of the units from which nucleic acids are synthesized.
Nucleus (NEW-klee-us) (*L.* kernel) (1) The control center of the cell containing the necessary information to direct the metabolism, replication, and heredity of cells. (2) The center of an atom.
Nutrient cycles The local geochemical cycles of minerals critical to plant growth.

Occipital (AWK-sip-puh-tul) Referring to the back of the skull.
Oils Compounds composed of glycerol and fatty acids. Identical with fats except liquid at room temperature.
Olfaction (ol-FACT-shun) The sense of smell.
Omnivorous (OM-ni-vore-us) (*L.* all + eat) Eating both plants and animals.
Operculum (oh-PER-kyu-lum) (*L.* cover, lid) (1) A tightly fitting, horny plate that covers the opening in the shells of some snails. (2) A bone-supported flap that covers the gill slits in fish. (3) The lidlike cover to the spore capsule of mosses.
Opportunist pathogen An organism that causes disease only when the host is especially vulnerable due to injury or other disease processes.
Orbital A specific space in the area about the atomic nucleus that is occupied by a pair of electrons.
Organ A body unit composed of characteristically arranged tissues with specific functions.
Organelle (or-guh-NELL) (*Gk.* bodily organ) A specialized subcellular structure, such as a mitochondrion, flagellum, lysosome, or Golgi apparatus.
Organic Chemically, pertaining to a compound, usually complex, containing carbon. Popularly, applied only to substances derived from living organisms.
Organ of Corti (CORE-tee) Inner-ear structure containing the hair cells that detect sound.
Orgasm (ORE-gass-um) A sexual climax.
Osmosis (OZ-MOE-sis) (*Gk.* impulsion) The diffusion of water through a selectively permeable membrane.
Osmotic pressure The pressure created by the osmosis of water, as it fills the space enclosed by a semipermeable membrane.
Ovary (OH-vuh-ree) (*L.* egg) An organ that produces eggs (ova).
Oviducts (OH-va-ducts) Tubes through which eggs pass after ovulation. In mammals these lead to the uterus and are known as Fallopian tubes.
Ovulation (awv-yu-LAY-shun) Release of an egg from the ovary.
Ovule The sporangium in the ovary of a flower that develops into a seed.
Ovum (OH-vum) pl. **ova** (*L.* egg) Egg; a female reproductive cell.
Oxidation (awk-si-DAY-shun) A chemical reaction in which electrons are removed from the substance being oxidized. (See **Reduction**.)

Oxidative phosphorylation Synthesis of ATP coupled to a flow of electrons in the respiratory chain.
Oxygen debt The accumulation of lactic acid when energy demands exceed the supply of oxygen necessary to convert glucose to carbon dioxide and water.
Oxytocin (awk-see-TOE-sin) A posterior pituitary hormone that stimulates uterine contractions at childbirth and promotes release of milk from the mammary glands.
Ozone (OH-zone) O_3; a highly reactive compound that tends to enter oxidative reactions.

Pacemaker A mass of cardiac tissue located at the junction of the *vena cava* and the right atrium; initiates the heartbeat. Also called the *sinoatrial node*.
Pancreas (PAN-kree-us) A gland located at the first bend of the small intestine. Secretes digestive enzymes that pass through ducts into the small intestine and also secretes the hormones insulin and glucogen into the blood.
Paradigm (pair-a-DIME) A model or pattern of interpretation.
Parasitism A symbiotic relationship in which one organism is totally dependent on another for nutrition and is of no benefit to this host.
Parasympathetic nervous system A portion of the autonomic nervous system that predominates when the organism is at rest.
Parathyroids (PAR-a-THIGH-roids) (*Gk.* beside + shield-shaped) Two pairs of small endocrine glands embedded in the thyroid; secrete parathormone which increases the calcium level in the blood.
Parenchyma A plant tissue composed of thin-walled, unspecialized cells; comprises the soft parts, including pith, cortex, leaf mesophyll, and the major part of most fruits.
Parietal (pah-RYE-i-tal) Forming the wall of a hollow structure, as the *parietal bones* of the skull.
Parthenogenesis (PAR-thin-o-JEN-uh-sis) (*Gk.* virgin + production) Development of an unfertilized egg.
Passive immunity Immunity achieved by injection of antibodies or by natural passage of antibodies from mother to young through the placenta or in milk.
Passive transport The movement of molecules across a membrane by diffusion.
Pathogen (PATH-uh-jen) (*L.* disease + cause) An agent that causes disease.
Pepsin (*Gk.* digestion) An enzyme secreted by stomach glands; converts proteins to polypeptides.
Peptide bond A covalent bond between the carboxyl group of one amino acid and the amino group of another; links amino acids in polypeptides and proteins.
Perennial (pah-RHEN-ee-ul) A plant that normally lives many years and reproduces more than once.
Pericycle (per-i-SY-kul) (*Gk.* around + circle) In roots and stems, a layer of parenchymal cells in the vascular cylinder. Gives rise to lateral roots.
Peripheral nervous system (PNS) The nerves and ganglia; includes both sensory and motor neurons.
Peristalsis (per-i-STOLL-sis) (*Gk.* around + contraction) A process that produces waves of muscular contractions along the digestive tract. Helps to propel food along.
Permeable (PER-mee-uh-bull) (*L.* through + to pass) The ability to allow passage of substances; said of a membrane.
Peroxyacyl nitrates (PAN) CH_3COONO_2 A noxious component of air pollution that damages plant and animal tissues. Formed from nitrogen oxides and hydrocarbons.
Petiole (PET-ee-ohl) A leaf stalk.
pH (potential of Hydrogen) A scale from 0 to 14 that measures the concentration of hydrogen ions free in water. The smaller the number below 7, the more acidic is the solution; the higher the number above 7, the more basic the solution. A pH of 7 is neutral.
Phage (FAYJ) (*Gk.* to eat) A virus that infects bacteria; a bacteriophage.
Phagocyte (FAG-oh-site) (*Gk.* to eat + cell) A cell that has the ability to engulf and digest foreign material.
Phagocytosis (FAG-oh-sy-TOE-sis) (*Gk.* to eat + hollow vessel + state, condition) Engulfing of bacteria or other particles by a cell; cell eating.
Pharynx (FAR-inks) (*Gk.* throat) An upper region of the throat shared by the digestive and respiratory tract.
Phenotype (FEE-nuh-type) (*Gk.* to show + type) The appearance or discernible character of an individual. Results from interaction of the genetic makeup and the environment. (See **Genotype**.)
Pheromone (FAIR-roh-moan) (*Gk.* carry + arouse) A secretion of one individual that modifies the behavior, development, or function of another of the same species.
Phloem (FLOH-em) (*Gk.* bark) The conducting tissue in vascular plants that carries dissolved nutrients. In trees, is present in the inner layer of the bark.
Phosphate (FOSS-fate) $PO_4^{=}$; a phosphorus-containing ion and compounds in which this ion occurs.
Phospholipids (fos-foh-LIP-idz) A group of fatty compounds that contain fatty acids, glycerol, and a phosphorylated alcohol.
Phosphorylation (fos-for-i-LAY-shun) (*Gk.* light + to carry) The addition of a phosphate group to an organic molecule.
Photon A unit of light energy; a quantum.
Photoperiodism (fot-toh-PEER-ee-ud-iz-um) The metabolic response of some organisms to variation in day length.
Photophosphorylation See **Cyclic** and **Noncyclic photophosphorylation**.
Photosynthesis (*Gk.* light + putting together) The synthesis of carbohydrate from water and carbon dioxide, using the energy of light captured by chlorophyll.
Phototropism A growth response triggered by light, as when a leaf turns toward a light source.
Phylum (FI-lum) (*Gk.* tribe) Category used in animal classification. A phylum is a major division of the animal kingdom.

Physiology (fizz-see-OL-uh-jee) Study of the internal function of organisms.
Phytochrome A plant pigment and photoreceptor responsible for time perception; involved in seed germination, flowering, and leaf formation.
Phytoplankton (FITE-oh-PLANK-tun) (*Gk.* plant + wanderer) Minute floating plants. Includes cyanobacteria, dinoflagellates, diatoms, and many other algae.
Pineal gland (PIE-neal) (*L.* pine cone) An endocrine structure in the roof of the midbrain. Involved in regulation of reproductive structures and response to light.
Pinocytosis (pin-uh-sy-TOE-sis) (*Gk.* to drink + cell + state) The engulfing of a droplet by a plasma membrane.
Pistil A female reproductive organ of a flower, consisting of the stigma, style, and ovary.
Pituitary (pi-TU-i-teh-ree) (*L.* secreting phlegm) An endocrine gland that lies in a depression in the floor of the skull, the hypophysis. The posterior portion is continuous with the brain and releases antidiuretic hormone and oxytocin from neurons that have their cell bodies in the hypothalamus. The anterior portion, which secretes hormones that regulate the adrenal, thyroid, and gonads, is itself regulated by hormones from the hypothalamus.
Placenta (pluh-SEN-tuh) (*L.* flat cake) In mammals, an organ for exchange of nutrients and wastes between the mother's blood and that of the young in her uterus. Derived from both maternal and embryonic tissues. Shed as the *afterbirth*.
Plankton (PLANK-tun) (*Gk.* wanderers) The microscopic, actively swimming or floating plants and animals of oceans and lakes.
Plankton bloom A sudden increase in a phytoplankton population. The heavy growth is evidenced by a colored area on the surface of the body of water.
Plaque (PLAK) (*Fr.* plate) An abnormal region on a surface.
Plasma (PLAZ-muh) The liquid portion of vertebrate blood; composed of water, dissolved solids including proteins, and dissolved gases.
Plasma cells See **B Cells**.
Plasmadesmata Thin strands of cytoplasm that extend through holes in plant cell walls and connect adjacent cells; function in cell-to-cell communication.
Plasma membrane The selectively permeable structure that bounds the cytoplasm of a cell; als called the cell membrane, composed primarily of phospholipids and protein.
Plasmid A small extrachromosomal genetic element found in bacteria; can be transmitted from one cell to another.
Plasmolysis (*Gk.* something formed + loosening) Shrinking of the plasma membrane away from the cell wall as the result of dehydration.
Platelets Membrane-bound cytoplasmic fragments normal to the mammalian blood. Source of substances that stimulate blood clotting.
Platyhelminthes (plat-EE-hel-men-thees) A phylum of lower invertebrates characterized by a flattened body, presence of distinct tissues, and absence of a coelom; includes free-living worms as well as the parasitic flukes and tapeworms.
Pleistocene (PLY-stuh-seen) The most recent geologic epoch; characterized by major climatic fluctuations; i.e., the Ice Ages. Began about 2.5 million years ago and ended only 10,000 years ago.
Pleura A thin membrane of mammals that lines the thoracic cavity and covers the lungs.
Point mutation A change in a single nucleotide of DNA.
Polar molecule A molecule one end of which is negative and the other positive.
Pollen The product of the anther in a flower. A tiny gametophyte in which sperm nuclei form.
Pollen tube A filament growing from a pollen grain and delivering the male nuclei to the ovule.
Pollination The movement of pollen from a male reproductive structure (anther) to a female reproductive structure, usually the stigma in a flower plant. Precedes fertilization.
Pollution The contamination of an area. Results from human interference in the biogeochemical cycles of ecosystems.
Polychaete (POLY-keet) (*Gk.* many + hairs) A class of annelids characterized by paired, lobelike appendages that bear numerous bristles.
Polychlorinated biophenyls (PCBs) A group of highly toxic industrial chemicals consisting of two six-membered organic rings (biphenyl) and various numbers of chlorine atoms.
Polygenic inheritance Concerns traits determined by the activity of several different genes each of which has an additive effect.
Polymer (*Gk.* many + parts) A chain of small repeating subunit molecules linked end to end; a macromolecule.
Polymerase An enzyme that catalyzes formation of large molecules (polymers) by combination of simpler subunits.
Polyp (pol-UP) A coelenterate that grows attached and bears tentacles on its free surface; may reproduce sexually or be an asexual stage of complex life cycle.
Polypeptide (pol-i-PEP-tide) A long chain of linked amino acids.
Polyploidy (POL-i-ployd-ee) (*Gk.* many + folds) Presence of more than two sets of chromosomes in the nucleus.
Polyribosome A string of several ribosomes linked together by a strand of *m*RNA during protein synthesis; a polysome.
Polysaccharide A complex carbohydrate, such as cellulose or starch, that is composed of numerous monosaccharide subunits.
Population A group of individuals of one species among whom genetic material is passed through interbreeding.
Posterior Located in or towards the rear. In four-legged animals, refers to the tail end. In humans it usually indicates in or toward the back (dorsal) surface.

Potency, sexual Ability to have an erection.
Potential (poh-TEN-shul) The difference in electrification of one point relative to another. Potential differences can be measured as an electric current.
Potential energy The energy of a position.
Preadaptation A genetically determined trait that was selected for its adaptive value in one ecological niche and that later proved adaptive in a different niche.
Prenatal (PRE-nay-tul) Prior to birth.
Primate (PRY-mate) (*L.* leader) The order of mammals that includes humans, apes, monkeys, baboons, lemurs, bushbabies, and similar animals.
Procaryote (pro-CARRY-ote) (*L.* before ± *Gk.* nucleus) A cell whose nucleus is not surrounded by a nuclear membrane and has no membrane-bound cytoplasmic organelles. Its single chromosome is composed almost solely of DNA, (See **Eucaryote**.)
Producers, primary Organisms that synthesize all their organic compounds; typically these are photosynthetic organisms that use light as an energy source.
Progesterone (proh-JES-tuh-rone) (*L.* before + to bear) A steroid hormone produced by the corpus luteum, placenta, and adrenal cortex.
Proglottid (proh-GLOT-id) (*L.* before + tongue) A body segment of a tapeworm.
Prolactin (proh-LAK-tin) (*Gk.* before + *L.* milk) An anterior pituitary hormone that promotes secretion of milk.
Prophase (*L.* before + *Gk.* phase) The first stage of cell division during which chromosomes appear and spindle fibers form.
Prophylactic (proh-fy-LACK-tik) Substance or device used to prevent disease. Because condoms were once sold to prevent transmission of venereal diseases, prophylactic is sometimes used as a synonym for contraceptive.
Prostaglandins (PROS-tuh-GLAN-dins) A group of organic acids widely distributed in body tissues. Originally discovered in the male reproductive system but now considered as modifiers of hormone action and stimulants of inflammation.
Prostate (PROS-tate) A glandular mass surrounding the male urethra at its union with the *vas deferentia*. One source of fluids for the semen.
Protein (*Gk.* first) Macromolecule composed of one or more chains of amino acids linked by peptide bonds.
Protista (pro-TEE-sta) A kingdom of eucaryotic unicellular organisms; some animallike and others plantlike.
Proton A positively charged subatomic particle found in the atomic nucleus. Its charge is equal to but opposite to that of an electron.
Protostome (PRO-toe-stom) (*Gk.* first + mouth) Major division of the animal kingdom; the mouth forms from the embryonic blastopore.
Protozoa Unicellular eucaryotic microorganisms. Heterotrophic and animallike in that they lack a cell wall and are capable of movement. Often considered an animal phylum.
Provirus The state of a virus when genetic material has become incorporated into the chromosome of a host cell.
Pseudopodium (soo-doh-POH-dee-um) (*Gk.* false + foot) A broad cytoplasmic extension of a cell. Often used for motion or to engulf food.
Puberty The stage when the individual becomes sufficiently mature to be capable of sexual reproduction.
Pulmonary Pertaining to the lungs.
Pulse The wave of systolic pressure that can be felt in an artery near the surface of the body.
Punctuated equilibrium A model of natural selection in which gene frequencies are generally stable and selective pressures act only sporadically.
Pure culture A culture of microorganisms derived from a single cell or from a number of identical cells; a culture containing only one type of organism.
Purine (PURE-een) A nitrogenous base composed of a double ring of carbon and nitrogen atoms; a constituent of DNA, RNA, ATP, NAD, etc.; e.g., adenine, guanine.
Pus The fluid that may accumulate at the site of inflammation. It contains serum, tissue debris, white blood cells, and microorganisms.
Pyrimidine (py-RIM-uh-deen) A nitrogenous base composed of a single ring of carbon and nitrogen atoms; a constituent of DNA and RNA; e.g., thymine, cytocine, uracil.
Pyruvic acid (py-ROO-vik) (*L.* pear.) A three-carbon organic acid which is the product of glycolysis; under aerobic conditions it is oxidized to carbon dioxide and water in the mitochondria.

Quantum See **Photon.**

RAD A measure of the energy of radiation. One rad is 100 ergs of absorbed energy per gram of tissue.
r-adapted A reproductive strategy in which a species has a large reproductive potential and invests little in individual offspring.
Radial As radii from a center, or having parts so arranged.
Radial symmetry The arrangement of parts so that the organism can be divided into mirror images by more than one plane.
Radioactive Capable of emitting rays or particles as the result of the decomposition of atomic nuclei.
Radioisotope An isotope that spontaneously decays with release of radiation.
Radula (RAJ-uh-luh) (*L.* scraper) A rasping mouth part in some molluscs.
Rainshadow A geographic region of low rainfall on the leeward side of a mountain; results when rising air drops most of its moisture on the windward side of the mountain.
Ray In plant anatomy, a radial strip of xylem cells.
Receptacle Portion of a flower stalk to which the floral organs are attached.

Receptor A structure capable of responding to changes in stimuli; transduces the energy of the stimulus into nerve impulses.

Recessive (ree-SESS-iv) Pertaining to a gene that is masked phenotypically in the presence of its dominant allele.

Recombinant DNA (ree-KOM-buh-nent) A segment of DNA enzymatically removed from one organism united with a strand of DNA from a second organism (frequently a virus), then inserted into a new host cell, sometimes into the host chromosome.

Rectum The terminal portion of the large intestine.

Red blood cells (erythrocytes) Biconcave cells that lack nuclei but contain hemoglobin and are thus responsible for the transport of oxygen and carbon dioxide.

Reduction A chemical reaction in which electrons are added to the substance being reduced. (See **Oxidation**.)

Reflex (*L.* to bend back) A behavioral pattern involving a predictable, stylized response to a specific stimulus; occurs without conscious thought. Reflex activity involves muscle contraction or gland secretion. Inborn reflexes are of obvious value to the organism but other reflexes can be learned.

Reflex arc The pathway of a reflex action. Always involves a sense organ, a sensory neuron, a motor neuron, and an effector.

Regeneration Regrowth of a lost or damaged part.

Releasing factor A hormone produced by the hypothalamus that stimulates secretion by the anterior pituitary. Also a behavioral stimulus. See also **releasing mechanism**.

Releasing mechanism A highly specific stimulus response mechanism. The stimulus may be termed a releasing factor.

Rem A measure of the biological effect of radiation. Rems = rads × biological effect. X-rays and gamma rays have a biological effect of 1; neutrons and alpha rays have a biological effect of 10.

Rennin (REN-in) An enzyme, secreted by stomach glands; curdles milk.

Replication Production of a copy; duplication.

Repressor The proteinaceous product of a control gene; prevents transcription when bound to a structural gene's start signal.

Reproductive potential Maximum ability of a species to produce young.

Reproductive strategy An evolutionary strategy involving reproduction.

Reptile A vertebrate having an amnion and lacking the characteristics of either birds or mammals.

Respiration (*L.* again + breath) (1) Breathing. (2) The cellular processes by which energy for biological use is released from glucose and other nutrient molecules.

Respiratory chain See **Electron transport system.**

Resting potential The small difference in electrical charge between the two sides of the plasma membrane of a muscle or nerve cell at rest. This difference is about 0.1 volts.

Reticular formation (rih-TIK-yu-lar) (*L.* net) A network of neurons in the base of the forebrain; determines which sensory information will be passed to higher centers such as the cerebrum.

Retina (RET-in-uh) (*L.* net) A complex layer of light-sensitive cells and neurons that lines the back of the eyeball.

Rhizoids Rootlike structures of fungi, mosses, and other lower plants but lacking the vascular tissue of true roots.

Rhizome An underground stem that grows laterally and gives rise to satellite plants.

Rhodopsin (roh-DOP-sin) (*Gk.* rose + sight) The light-sensitive pigment of rod cells in the eye, consisting of a colorless protein, opsin, and a colored carotenoid molecule, retinal (or retinene).

Ribonucleic acid (RNA) (rye-boe-new-KLAY-ik) A single-stranded nucleic acid containing the sugar ribose.

Ribosomal RNA (rRNA) (rye-boh-SOHM-ul) The ribonucleic acids that are constituents of ribosomes.

Ribosome (RYE-boh-sohm) Cytoplasmic structures composed of ribonucleic acid and protein; the site of protein synthesis.

RNA See **Ribonucleic acid.**

Root cap A thimble-shaped mass of loosely connected cells protecting the root tip.

Rotifer (ROW-ta-fer) Member of a group of microscopic, aquatic animals that collect food by means of cilia that make up a wheel organ.

Roundworm See **Nematode.**

Saline Salty; containing salt.

Salts Crystalline substances that form ions (other than hydrogen or hydroxyl ions) in solution.

Saprophyte (sap-row-FIGHT) (*Gk.* rotten) A plant that absorbs organic molecules from decaying organisms.

Saturated fat Fat with fatty acids whose carbon atoms have the maximum number of hydrogen atoms attached to them, i.e., there are no double bonds between adjacent carbon atoms.

Scrotum (SCROH-tum) The sac of skin in which the testes and epididymides lie.

Second law of thermodynamics States that whenever there is an energy conversion, some of the energy of the system is lost as heat.

Second-messenger concept A mechanism proposed for the action of some hormones based on the knowledge that in some cases a hormone, the "first messenger," causes the conversion of ATP to cyclic AMP inside a target cell. The cyclic AMT, the "second messenger," then diffuses throughout the cell and causes the cell to respond with its specific endocrine function.

Secretion The release of a cell product through the plasma membrane.

Sedimentary rock Rock formed from erosion products (e.g. gravel, sand, silt, clay) through the effects of pressure and heat.

Seed A mature ovule of seed plant, containing an embryo.
Segmentation Division of an organism into distinct repeating units.
Segregation, law of One of the principles of Mendelian genetics; states that contrasting characters in an individual separate when gametes are formed. Each gamete receives a gene for only one of each pair of alleles.
Selection, natural The influence of environmental factors that leads to differential survival of offspring. **Directional selection** occurs when the population is ill-adapted to its environment and results in a change in the gene pool. **Stabilizing selection** occurs in populations well-adapted to their environments and, by removing the more deviant members, maintains the gene pool constant.
Selective permeability Refers to the characteristic whereby a membrane permits the passage of some substances but not others.
Semen (SEE-men) (*L.* seed) Sperm and associated liquids released at male orgasm; seminal fluid.
Seminal vesicles (SEM-uh-nul VES-uh-kuls) Glands that secrete into the *vas deferentia* near their union with the urethra. One source of fluids for the semen.
Serum The straw-colored fluid that remains when blood clots.
Sex-linked Determined by a gene on a sex chromosome. Usually such genes are on the X-chromosome; in this case they are known as X-linked.
Sexual reproduction Production of new organisms through union of genetic material from two parents. In eucaryotes the union involves fusion of an egg and sperm. In the life cycle the fertilization alternates with meiosis.
Shock Drastically decreased blood pressure that can deprive vital organs of oxygen. May result from loss of blood from relaxation of muscle in the vessel walls, so that the capacity of the circulatory system increases.
Shoots The stems and leaves of a seed plant.
Sieve tube The transporting structure of phloem; consists of stacks of cells arranged end to end; in some plants, **sieve tube cells** are highly specialized and have perforated end walls.
Silica Silicon dioxide (SiO_2); a widely distributed insoluble mineral; found in many forms including sand, sandstone, quartz, onyx, and agate.
Silt Fine mineral particles larger than those of clay.
Sinoatrial (SA) node (sy-noh-AY-tree-ul) See **Pacemaker.**
Sinus A recess or cavity.
Skeletal muscle Flesh. Muscle tissue under conscious control. Consists of multinucleate fibers. See **Muscle fiber.**
Small intestine That part of the digestive tract between the stomach and large intestine, the site of most digestion and absorption of nutrients.
Smog Pollution that clouds the air. Originally a mixture of smoke and fog. Photochemical smog has no fog component and is due to the action of sunlight on pollutants from automobile exhausts.
Smooth muscle The muscle of internal organs other than the heart. Controlled by the autonomic nervous system.
Sociobiology The explanation of the behavior of humans or other animals in biological terms, especially in terms of its adaptive value.
Sod A complex of roots, undeground stems, and soil.
Sodium chloride Ordinary table salt; NaC1.
Softwood The wood of a coniferous tree.
Soil The loose surface matter of the earth; consists of disintegrated rock, minerals, humus, water, air, and living organisms.
Soil water Water in the loose surface matter of the earth where plants grow.
Solute (SOL-yute) Substance dissolved in a medium.
Solution A homogeneous mixture of dissolved substance(s) and a liquid.
Solvent The medium in which substances are dissolved.
Somatic mutation (SO-mat-ik) A mutation in any body cell not giving rise to eggs or sperm.
Spacer-DNA A segment of DNA found between genes.
Speciation (spee-shee-AY-shun) The formation of new species.
Species (SPEE-sheez) (*L.* kind) Any group of organisms capable of interbreeding and producing fertile offspring.
Specific heat The amount of heat required to raise one gram of a material one degree celsium; heat capacity.
Sperm (*Gk.* seed) The male gamete; spermatozoan. A haploid cell specialized to join with an egg in fertilization.
Sphincter A circular muscle that controls the passage of substances through a tubular organ.
Spindle The spindle-shaped arrangement of microtubles with which chromosomes are associated during cell division.
Spiracle (SPEER-uh-kul) (*L.* to breathe) A breathing hole along the sides of an insect abdomen, allowing for oxygen and carbon dioxide exchange.
Spleen An organ much like a large lymph node but capable of filtering blood.
Split gene A gene containing an **intron**, i.e. a segment that is transcribed but not translated.
Sponge A member of a phylum of simple animals, the *Porifera*. Water enters the body cavity through pores in the walls and leaves by larger openings. Individual cells are specialized but distinct organs are absent. Calcareous, glass, or protein skeleton supports the cells.
Spontaneous reactions Reactions that tend to proceed however slowly without outside assistance. When they occur energy is released.
Sporangium (spuh-RAN-jee-um) (*Gk.* seed vessel) Any plant part that produces spores.
Spore (*Gk.* seed) A nonsexual reproductive cell in plants; in bacteria a dormant, nonreproductive, resistant stage.
Sporophyte (SPOHR-uh-fite) The spore-producing, diploid phase of plants having alternation of generations.
Stamen (STAY-men) (*L.* thread) The pollen-producing organ in a flower, consisting of the anther and usually a supporting filament.
Sterilization To render free of life. Commonly, indi-

cates destruction of all microorganisms present. Also, destruction of the ability to reproduce sexually.

Steroid (STEER-oyd) One of a group of fat-soluble organic compounds with a characteristic ring structure. Includes cholesterol and the sex hormones.

Stolon (STOH-lun) (*L.* shoot) A horizontal stem that grows along the ground and forms adventitious roots and shoots, as in a strawberry plant and many grasses.

Stoma (STOW-muh) pl. **stomata** (*Gk.* mouth) A microscopic opening between epidermal cells on leaf surfaces, surrounded by a pair of guard cells.

Stomach In vertebrates, a saclike enlargement of the digestive canal where the early stages of digestion occur; located between the esophagus and the small intestine.

Stratum pl. **strata** A layer of rocks in the earth's crust.

Striated muscle See **Skeletal muscle.**

Striations (STRI-a-shons) Narrow parallel lines.

Stroma (STROH-muh) (*L.* bed covering) In chloroplasts, the jellylike material between the folded membranes. The region where the "dark reactions" of photosynthesis occur. In animals, the connective tissue of gland.

Structural gene A gene that produces messenger RNA and is therefore instrumental in the production of polypeptides that are components of enzymes. As opposed to control genes that regulate the activity of structural genes.

Substrate The molecule acted upon by an enzyme.

Substrate-level phosphorylation Synthesis of ATP directly coupled to the oxidation of an organic molecule rather than as the result of a flow of electrons in the respiratory chain.

Succession, community A predictable series of communities characteristic of a particular location. In **primary succession** the series begins with barren rock. The more common **secondary succession** is observed when an established community is destroyed.

Succulent (SUCK-yu-lent) Having thick, fleshy leaves or stems in which water is conserved.

Sucrose Table sugar, a disaccharide composed of glucose and fructose.

Sulfate A sulfur-containing ion ($SO_4^{=}$) and compounds in which this ion occurs.

Swamp A forest growing in wet, soggy, water-saturated soil.

Symbiosis (sim-bee-OH-sis) (*Gk.* together + life) The customary close physical association of one species with another, often such that one lives in or on the other.

Sympathetic nervous system A portion of the autonomic nervous system that predominates when the organism is stressed.

Synapse (SIN-aps) (*Gk.* union) The junction between two neurons. Usually involves a swollen axion and a dendrite separated by a narrow gap. (As a verb, refers to the process of **Synapsis.** See below.)

Synapsis A point-by-point paring of homologous chromosomes. Occurs during prophase I of meiosis and frequently leads to crossing over.

Synthesis The chemical or biochemical combination of simple substances to form more complex ones: formation of the various organic compounds.

Systole (SIS-toe-lee) (*Gk.* drawing together) Contraction of ventricles of the heart; forces blood into the arteries.

Tapeworm A flat-bodied worm parasitic in the intestine of humans and other animals.

Tap root A thick, tapering, primary root from which smaller branch roots arise.

Target cell A cell regulated by a particular hormone.

Taxis (TACK-sis) (*Gk.* arrangement) Movement toward or away from a stimulus such as heat, gravity, or light.

Taxonomy (tack-SON-uh-mee) (*Gk.* order + law) The study of classification, especially with the aim of arranging organisms to show their evolutionary relationships.

T-cells Lymphocytes that trace to the thymus and that attach to foreign cells or virus-infected cells and disrupt their plasma membranes; killer cells.

Tectonics The study of the movements of the earth's crust and the resulting formation of surface features (e.g., mountains).

Teleological (*Gk.* end) The result of foreplanning or design.

Telophase (TELL-uh-faze) (*Gk.* end + phase) The final stage of nuclear division in which the two daughter nuclei are formed.

Template A pattern used in the formation of a new structure or molecule.

Tendon (*Gk.* to stretch) Collagen-rich connective tissues that attach muscles to bones.

Test cross See **Backcross.**

Testis (TESS-tus) pl. **testes** The male gonads: the source of sperm and, in the vertebrates, of testosterone.

Testosterone (tess-TAHSS-tuh-rohn) The male hormone; a steroidal secretion of the testes necessary for sperm production and the male secondary sex characteristics.

Tetrad (TEH-trad) (*Gk.* four) In genetics, the complex of four chromatids during the pairing of homologous chromosomes during prophase I of meiosis.

Tetraploid (teh-TRA-ployd) Having four sets of chromosomes.

Theory A hypothesis that is widely accepted because it is supported by numerous observations and/or experiments.

Thermodynamics (THER-moh-dy-NAM-iks) (*Gk.* Heat + movement) The study of energy relations in biological, chemical, and physical processes.

Thorax In mammals, the chest. In insects, the part of the body bearing the wings and legs.

Three-dimensional configuration The shape or spatial organization of a polymer such as a twisted and folded polypeptide chain.

Threshold (THRESH-hold) A minimum level above which some action occurs.

Thrombosis Blockage of a blood vessel by an attached clot.

Thylakoid (THIGH-luh-koyd) (*Gk.* sack, pouch) A disk-like, membrane-bound vesicle in a chloroplast. Contains photosynthetic pigments.
Thymus (THIGH-mus) A lymphoid organ, located in the base of the throat. Its main function is development of T-cells. Regresses at puberty.
Thyroid (*Gk.* shield-shaped) An endocrine gland in the neck, source of thyroxine, which regulates energy metabolism, and calcitonin, which decreases the blood calcium level.
Thyroid-stimulating hormone (TSH) An anterior pituitary secretion that stimulates thyroxine production.
Thyroxine (thigh-ROCK-seen) A thyroid hormone that controls energy metabolism; consists of an amino acid that contains iodine.
Tissue (*L.* woven) Closely connected mass of cells and their products. The cells of a tissue are similar in structure and function.
Tissue culture The growth of cells or tissues in containers of liquid or solid nutrients. A container with such cells or tissues.
Tonoplast The vacuolar membrane of plant cell.
Tonsil An organ located in the lining of the respiratory or digestive tracts where lymphocytic tissue is exposed to foreign organisms and antibodies are produced.
Tonus (tone-US) A normal state of partial contraction of a muscle.
Toxin A poisonous substance produced by an organism.
Trachea (TRAY-kee-uh) (*Gk.* rough) In vertebrates, the windpipe. In insects and some other land-dwelling arthropods, one of the complex of air tubes in the body.
Tracheid (TRAY-kee-ud) (*Gk.* rough) A thickened and elongated water-conducting cell with closed tapered ends; a major xylem component.
Transcription (*L.* across + to write) Synthesis of messenger RNA from the DNA template.
Transducer A structure that converts one form of energy into another. Sense organs transduce the energy of the stimulus into the chemical energy of a nerve impulse.
Transfer RNA (tRNA) Forms of RNA that serve as adapter molecules in the synthesis of proteins. Each *t*RNA can combine with a particular amino acid and place it in its proper position in a growing polypeptide.
Transformation Genotypic changes in a bacterium caused by pure DNA extracted or released from donor bacteria.
Translation Synthesis of a protein from amino acids according to the specific nucleotide sequence of the *m*RNA molecule; occurs on ribosomes.
Transpiration The loss of water from a plant via evaporation from the stomata.
Transposable controlling element Movable genes; specifically control genes(s) bounded on either end by DNA sequences that permit detachment from one DNA site and insertion at another.
Trimester Three-month period; one-third the duration of human gestation.
Triploid (TRIP-loyd) Having three sets of chromosomes.
Trophic levels (TROH-fik) (*Gk.* food) The steps in a food chain.
Trophoblast (TROPH-fuh-blast) (*Gk.* food + bag) Outer portion of a blastocyst. Makes up the embryonic contribution to the placenta.
Tropism (TROH-piz-um) (*Gk.* a turning) A growth movement whose direction is determined by the direction from which the stimulus comes.
Tuber (*L.* swelling) An enlarged, fleshy underground stem having "eyes" or buds; for example, a potato.
Tumor (*L.* to swell) Any abnormal growth.
Tundra (ton-dra) A biome characterized by permanently frozen subsoil and low-growing perennial vegetation.
Turgor pressure The pressure against a plant-cell wall due to the expansion of the cytoplasm as water moves into the cell.

Ultraviolet radiation Short-wavelength electromagnetic radiation just outside the blue portion of the visible spectrum; the part of the sun's rays that causes sunburn.
Umbilicus (um-BILL-i-cuss) The navel.
Understory Forest vegetation shaded by the taller trees.
Unsaturated fat Fat whose constituent fatty acids contain some carbon atoms joined by double bonds.
Urea An organic waste found in urine; produced in the liver from CO_2 and excess ammonia that results when amino acids are oxidized.
Ureter (YUR-et-uh) (*Gk.* to urinate) A tube that carries urine from the kidney to the urinary bladder.
Urethra (yu-REE-thruh) (*Gk.* to urinate) The canal that conveys urine from the bladder to the outside of the body. In the male it also carries sperm from the vas deferens outside the body.
Uric acid A solid organic-waste material produced from excess ammonia that comes from oxidation of amino acids.
Urinary Pertaining to excretory system.
Urogenital (ur-OH-gen-it-al) Pertaining to a combination of urinary and reproductive characteristics.
Uterus (UY-tuh-rus) (*L.* womb) The muscular chamber of the female reproductive tract in which the fetus is nourished; the womb.

Vaccine Dead, weakened, or harmless microorganisms or viruses administered to stimulate antibody production.
Vacuole (VAK-you-ole) (*L.* empty) A membrane-bound sac in the cytoplasm. Contains water, but contents and functions vary with species and tissues. Fat vacuoles in animal tissues are not bound by a typical membrane.
Vagina (vuh-JINE-uh) The lower region of the female reproductive tract into which the male penis releases sperm during intercourse.
Vapor The gaseous state of a substance normally found as a solid or liquid.
Vascular cylinder The ring or core of xylem and phloem in stems and roots.

Vascular tissue (1) Transport or conducting tissue of plants, expecially xylem and phloem. (2) Less often, the tissues of animal circulatory systems.
Vas deferens (vass DEAF-er-ens) pl. **vas deferentia** (*L.* vessel + to carry away) Sperm ducts. In mammals, the tubular passage from the epididymis to the urethra.
Vector An organism that transmits pathogenic microorganisms.
Vegetative Referring to nonsexual activities of plants; e.g., growth of leaves.
Vein A vessel that carries blood toward the heart.
Venereal (vuh-NEER-ee-ul) (*L.* myth.: Venus, goddess of love) Relating to or resulting from sexual intercourse. Examples of venereal diseases are syphilis and gonorrhea.
Ventral Toward the belly surface. (See **Dorsal.**)
Ventricle (VEN-tri-kul) (*L.* stomach) A cavity in an organ, such as the major pumping chambers of the heart, or the cavities in the brain.
Vertebrates (*L.* jointed) The largest group of the phylum *Chordata;* characterized by possession of a skull surrounding the brain, a dorsally located vertebral column through which the spinal cord passes, and pharyngeal grooves and a notochord in the embryo. Includes all fish, amphibians, reptiles, birds, and mammals.
Vesicle A small membraneous sac found inside cells, or a larger sac whose walls are made up of many cells.
Vessel Any tubelike conducting structure including the blood and lymph conduits. The xylem of angiosperms contains vessels made up of numerous vessel elements arranged end to end; each vessel element consists of the remains of the cell wall from a large, cylindrical cell.
Villi (VILL-eye) (*L.* shaggy hair) Fingerlike projections of tissue such as those found in the lining of the small intestine or the chorionic membrane of the placenta. Provide increased surface area for the passage of materials.
Virulence (VIR-yoo-lence) Degree of pathogenicity of a microorganism as measured by fatality rates or invasiveness, etc.
Virus A noncellular particle consisting of a nucleic-acid core surrounded by a protein coat. Viruses are parasitic and can multiply only within their host cells.
Visceral (VIS-er-al) Pertaining to the internal organs, especially those in the body cavities.
Vitalism (*L.* life) Belief that biological phenomena cannot be explained solely in chemical and physical terms.
Vitamin An organic substance required in minute amounts in the diet; essential in supporting the work of enzymes, especially those involved in cellular respiration. (See **Coenzyme.**)

Water table The upper surface of the ground water.
Water vascular system An organ system unique to echinoderms; includes a water-filled cavity derived from the coelom and lying partly within the skeleton and partly within soft tissues such as the tube feet.
White blood cell (Leukocyte) Nucleated blood cells that function in resistance to disease. Unlike red blood cells, these lack hemoglobin and, when concentrated, appear white, as do all unpigmented tissues. Includes neutrophils, lymphocytes, and monocytes.
Wood The old xylem of plants that survive more than one year and produce new xylem each growing season.

X-linked See **Sex-linked.**
X-rays Short wavelength electromagnetic energy produced when high-speed electrons strike a metal target in a vacuum.
Xylem (ZYE-lem) (*Gk.* wood) The wood tissue through which most of the water and minerals of a plant are conducted.

Zooplankton (ZOH-plank-tun) Minute floating animals. Includes protozoa, microscopic adult arthropods such as water fleas, and the larvae of numerous fish and other animals.
Zygote (ZY-goat) (*Gk.* yoked together) A fertilized egg; product of the union of an egg and sperm.

Credits

Part One opener Ministry of Information and Tourism, Spain.

Chapter 1 Fig. 1.1: Barbara Miller. Fig. 1.2(a and b): Judith E. Skog; Fig. 1.2(c and d): Barbara Miller. Fig. 1.3(a and b): author photos; Fig. 1.3(c): Kenneth Sebens; Fig. 1.3(d): Barbara Miller. Fig. 1.5(a): R. Christian Jones; Fig. 1.5(b–h): Barbara Miller; Fig. 1.5(i): Animals Animals/David Fritts. Fig. 1.8: R. Christian Jones. Fig. 1.9: H. B. Kettlewell, Oxford University. Fig. 1.10(a–c): Barbara L. Thorne; Fig. 1.10(d–f): Barbara Miller. Fig. 1.12(top): Luther Brown; Fig. 1.12(bottom left): Barbara Miller; Fig. 1.12(bottom): NIH Photo Library.

Chapter 2 Fig. 2.4: Grant Heilman Photography. Fig. 2.5(a and b): © Zoological Society of San Diego. Box 2A(a): Barbara Miller; Box 2A(b): USDA; Box 2A(c): Barbara Miller; Box 2A(d): Harry B. Robinson, U.S. Park Service. Fig. 2.8: © National Geographic Society. Fig. 2.9: © Zoological Society of San Diego. Box 2B(top): Allan and Beatrice Gardner; Box 2B(bottom): Anthro Photo File. Box 2C: Anthro Photo File.

Part Two opener Elaine C. Joyce.

Chapter 3 Fig. 3.1: U.S. Forest Service. Fig. 3.2: Barbara Miller. Fig. 3.8: U.S. Soil Conservation Service. Fig. 3.15: USDA Photo. Fig. 3.17: U.S. Forest Service.

Chapter 4 Fig. 4.12(d): Paulette W. Royt. Fig. 4.17(b): Reproduced from *The Journal of Cell Biology*, 1982, *94*:613, by copyright permission of The Rockefeller University Press. Fig. 4.18(a and b): Mehdi Tavassoli, *J. Ultrastruct. Res.*, 1981, *75*:205. Reproduced with permission. Fig. 4.20: Reproduced from *The Journal of Cell Biology*, 1982, *94*:241, by copyright permission of The Rockefeller University Press. Fig. 4.22: Jan Endlich. Box 4B: Ellen Roter Dirksen. Fig. 4.23(a): E. de Harven, Sloan Kettering Institute for Cancer Research; from *The Nucleus*, Academic Press, New York/London, 1968. Fig. 4.24(a): Dr. Don Fawcett. Fig. 4.26(a): A. Barchi and G. B. Chapman, Department of Biology, Georgetown University. Fig. 4.27: E. A. Anderson and G. B. Chapman, Department of Biology, Georgetown University. Fig. 4.33(a): S. F. Zane and G. B. Chapman, Department of Biology, Georgetown University. Box 4C(a–d): author photos. Fig. 4.34(a and b): Reproduced from *The Journal of Cell Biology*, by copyright permission of the Rockefeller University Press; Fig. 4.34(c): NIH Photo Library; Fig. 4.34(e): H. Fernandez-Moran, University of Chicago.

Chapter 6 Fig. 6.2: NIH Photo Library. Fig. 6.3: Jan Endlich. Fig. 6.5: N. Rodman. Fig. 6.10: NIH Photo Library. Fig. 6.20(a and b): Patricia Delaney, American Lung Association.

Chapter 7 Fig. 7.5(a): Thomas H. Ermak, *J. Ultrastruct. Res.*, 1980, *70*:242. Reproduced by permission. Fig. 7.8: Robert J. Buschmann, *J. Ultrastruct. Res.*, 1981, *76*:1–26. Reproduced by permission.

Chapter 9 Fig. 9.12(a) Barbara Miller and Jan Endlich.

Chapter 10 Fig. 10.2(a): Schockman, "Autolytic mutants of *S. fascium*," *J. Bact.* *138*:601 (1979). Reproduced by permission; Fig. 10.2(b): Millipore Corporation; Fig. 10.2(c): Nyles Charon. Figs. 10.5 and 10.6: NIH Photo Library. Fig. 10.14: U.S. Forest Service. Fig. 10.15: Turtox/Cambosco. Fig. 10.16(a): NIH Photo Library; Fig. 10.16(b): Carolina Biological Supply. Box 10B: Carolina Biological Supply. Figs. 10.18 and 10.19: Centers for Disease Control. Fig. 10.21: NIH Photo Library.

Part Three opener By permission of Lennart Nilsson, from *A Child Is Born*. New York: Delacorte Press.

Chapter 11 Fig. 11.3: Donna F. Kubai, reproduced from *The Journal of Cell Biology*, 1982, *93*:655, by copyright permission of The Rockefeller University Press. Fig. 11.28: Barbara Miller.

Chapter 13 Fig. 13.1: Steven Rannels from Grant Heilman Photography. Fig. 13.8: By permission of Lennart Nilsson, from *A Child Is Born*. New York: Delacorte Press. Fig. 13.16: Photo © Richard Effitt, courtesy of La Leche League International. Fig. 13.18: Photograph supplied by Dr. Robert J. Hay, Cell Culture Department, American Type Culture Collection.

Part Four opener Stock, Boston.

Chapter 14 Fig. 14.2: Centers for Disease Control. Box 14C (page 332 and 333, middle and bottom): The Bettman Archive; Box 14C (page 333, top): Courtesy Burndy Library. Fig. 14.12: Grant Heilman Photography.

Chapter 15 Fig. 15.3: Barbara Miller. Box 15A: Rolf O. Peterson. Fig. 15.4: Anthro Photo. Fig. 15.5: Courtesy of the American Museum of Natural History. Fig. 15.6: A. Lewin. Fig. 15.7: Photographed for the Laboratory of Ornithology by John S. Dunning. Fig. 15.8: Andreas Feininger, LIFE Magazine. © 1953 Time Inc. Box 15B: Ray and Lorna Coppinger, Hampshire College. Fig. 15.10: Photograph by John Alcock. Box 15D: Anthro Photo. Fig. 15.11: Photo by Jim Erckmann. Fig. 15.12: O. S. Pettingill, Jr./VIREO. Fig. 15.13: Barbara Thorne.

Chapter 16 Fig. 16.2: Photograph courtesy of K. McDougall, U.S. Geographic Survey. Fig. 16.7: Ronald L. Shimek. Fig. 16.8(a and c): Ronald L. Shimek; Fig. 16.8(b): Kenneth Sebens; Fig. 16.8(d): Barbara Miller. Fig. 16.9: Grant Heilman Photography. Fig. 16.11: Animals Animals/Richard LaVal. Fig. 16.16(a): Runk Schoenberger, Grant Heilman Photography; Fig. 16.16(b): BPS. Fig. 16.18: Barbara Miller. Fig. 16.20(a–d): Ronald L. Shimek. Fig. 16.21: Barbara Miller. Fig. 16.22 (clockwise from top): Barbara Miller; Animals Animals/Oxford Scientific Films; Grant Heilman Photography. Fig. 16.24(a): Barbara Miller; Fig. 16.24(b): R. Christian Jones, George Mason University. Fig. 16.27: Barbara Miller. Fig. 16.28(a): BPS; Fig. 16.28(b and c): Barbara Miller. Figs. 16.29(a and b), 16.31(a–c), and 16.33(a–i): Barbara Miller.

Part Five opener USDA Photo.

Chapter 17 Fig. 17.1: USDA-SCS Photo by Gene Alexander. Fig. 17.6: Dr. Lewis K. Shumway, College of Eastern Utah—San Juan Center, Blanding, Utah. Fig. 17.10: William A. Jensen. Fig. 17.14(a): Turtox/Cambosco. Fig. 17.15: Carolina Biological Supply. Fig. 17.16: U.S. Forest Service. Box 17A (page 412): USDA Photo; Box 17A (page 413): U.S. Forest Service. Fig. 17.32: Forest Service, USDA. Fig. 17.33: Barbara Miller. Figs. 17.35, 17.36, and 17.38: U.S. Forest Service. Fig. 17.40: USDA Photo. Figs. 17.43, 17.45, and 17.46: U.S. Forest Service. Figs. 17.47 and 17.49: USDA Photos. Figs. 17.50 and 17.51: USDA—Soil Conservation Service.

Chapter 18 Fig. 18.3: U.S. Park Service. Figs. 18.8 and 18.11(a and b): Barbara Miller. Fig. 18.14(a–c): USDA Photos. Fig. 18.15(a): Brandenburg/Griffiths Photography; Fig. 18.15(b): Grant Heilman Photography; Fig. 18.15(c): Peter J. Bryant, BPS. Fig. 18.16(a and c): Barbara Miller; Fig. 18.16(b) Grant Heilman. Fig. 18.17: U.S. Forest Service.

Chapter 19 Fig. 19.1(a and b): Barbara Miller. Fig. 19.3(a): Dick Morton; Fig. 19.3(b and c): Barbara Miller; Fig. 19.3(d): R. Christian Jones, George Mason University. Box 19A: R. Christian Jones, George Mason University; Barbara Miller. Fig. 19.6(a): R. Christian Jones, George Mason University; Fig. 19.6(b): Barbara Miller. Fig. 19.8(a and b): Larry L. Rockwood; Fig. 19.8(c): Jay Shaffer. Fig. 19.9(a and b): Barbara Miller. Fig. 19.11(a): Jay Shaffer; Fig. 19.11(b): Brandenburg/Griffiths Photography; Fig. 19.11(c–e): USDA Photos. Fig. 19.14(a and b): USDA Photos. Fig. 19.15(a): Barbara Miller; Fig. 19.15(b): Alice M. Lindahl; Fig. 19.15(c): E. Egghart. Fig. 19.16(a–c): Barbara Miller. Fig. 19.17(a and b): Barbara Miller; Fig. 19.17(c): Kenneth E. Glander. Fig. 19.18: Larry L. Lockwood. Fig. 19.21: Barbara L. Thorne, Harvard University. Fig. 19.22(a and d): Barbara Miller; Fig. 19.22(b): Jay Shaffer; Fig. 19.22(c): U.S. Forest Service.

Chapter 20 Figs. 20.3 and 20.4: U.S. National Park Service. Figs. 20.5 and 20.7: U.S. Forest Service. Fig. 20.9: NOAA Photo. Box 20A(left): U.S. Department of the Interior, National Park Service; Box 20A(right): National Park Service Photo by M. Woodbridge Williams. Figs. 20.11 and 20.15: U.S. Forest Service. Fig. 20.16: EPA. Fig. 20.17: Forest Service, USDA.

Part Six opener EPA-Documerica, Bob. W. Smith, courtesy of U.S. Environmental Protection Agency.

Chapter 21 Fig. 21.1: Grant Heilman Photography. Fig. 21.2(a,c,d): USDA Photos; Fig. 21.2(b): Grant Heilman Photography; Fig. 21.2(e): U.S. Forest Service. Figs. 21.4(a–c), Box 21A, and Figs. 21.5(a and b), 21.7(a–c), and 21.8(a and b): USDA Photos. Figs. 21.9, 21.10, and 21.11: USDA—Soil Conservation Service. Figs. 21.13, 21.14(a), and 21.17(a–d): USDA Photos. Fig. 21.18: By permission of Enos J. Perry, Rutgers University Press.

Chapter 22 Fig. 22.1(a and b): Photos courtesy of Erhard M. Winkler, from *Stone: Properties, Durability in Man's Environment* (Springer-Verlag, New York, 1973). Photos used on the cover of *Science*, Vol. 181 (31 August 1973). Box 22A and Fig. 22.6: U.S. Forest Service. Fig. 22.9: Atomic Industrial Forum, Inc. Fig. 22.15: Bureau of Reclamation Photo by Lyle C. Axthelm.

Index